Crafting and Executing Strategy

THE QUEST FOR COMPETITIVE ADVANTAGE:

Concepts and Cases | TWENTY-FIRST EDITION

Arthur A. Thompson
The University of Alabama

Margaret A. Peteraf
Dartmouth College

John E. Gamble
Texas A&M University–Corpus Christi

A.J. Strickland III
The University of Alabama

CRAFTING AND EXECUTING STRATEGY

Published by McGraw-Hill Education, 2 Penn Plaza, New York, NY 10121.

This book is printed on acid-free paper.

3 4 5 6 7 8 9 LWI 21 20 19 18

ISBN 978-1-259-92199-5
MHID 1-259-92199-9

mheducation.com/highered

To our families and especially our spouses:
Hasseline, Paul, and Kitty.

ABOUT THE AUTHORS

Arthur A. Thompson, Jr., earned his B.S. and Ph.D. degrees in economics from The University of Tennessee, spent three years on the economics faculty at Virginia Tech, and served on the faculty of The University of Alabama's College of Commerce and Business Administration for 24 years. In 1974 and again in 1982, Dr. Thompson spent semester-long sabbaticals as a visiting scholar at the Harvard Business School.

His areas of specialization are business strategy, competition and market analysis, and the economics of business enterprises. In addition to publishing over 30 articles in some 25 different professional and trade publications, he has authored or co-authored five textbooks and six computer-based simulation exercises. His textbooks and strategy simulations have been used at well over 1,000 college and university campuses worldwide.

Dr. Thompson spends much of his off-campus time giving presentations, putting on management development programs, working with companies, and helping operate a business simulation enterprise in which he is a major partner.

Dr. Thompson and his wife of 56 years have two daughters, two grandchildren, and a Yorkshire Terrier.

Margaret A. Peteraf is the Leon E. Williams Professor of Management at the Tuck School of Business at Dartmouth College. She is an internationally recognized scholar of strategic management, with a long list of publications in top management journals. She has earned myriad honors and prizes for her contributions, including the 1999 Strategic Management Society Best Paper Award recognizing the deep influence of her work on the field of Strategic Management. Professor Peteraf is a fellow of the Strategic Management Society and the Academy of Management. She served previously as a member of the Board of Governors of both the Society and the Academy of Management and as Chair of the Business Policy and Strategy Division of the Academy. She has also served in various editorial roles and on numerous editorial boards, including the *Strategic Management Journal*, the *Academy of Management Review*, and *Organization Science*. She has taught in Executive Education programs in various programs around the world and has won teaching awards at the MBA and Executive level.

Professor Peteraf earned her Ph.D., M.A., and M.Phil. at Yale University and held previous faculty appointments at Northwestern University's Kellogg Graduate School of Management and at the University of Minnesota's Carlson School of Management.

John E. Gamble is a Professor of Management and Dean of the College of Business at Texas A&M University–Corpus Christi. His teaching and research for nearly 20 years has focused on strategic management at the undergraduate and graduate levels. He has conducted courses in strategic management in Germany since 2001, which have been sponsored by the University of Applied Sciences in Worms.

Dr. Gamble's research has been published in various scholarly journals and he is the author or co-author of more than 75 case studies published in an assortment of strategic management and strategic marketing texts. He has done consulting on industry and market analysis for clients in a diverse mix of industries.

Professor Gamble received his Ph.D., Master of Arts, and Bachelor of Science degrees from The University of Alabama and was a faculty member in the Mitchell College of Business at the University of South Alabama before his appointment to the faculty at Texas A&M University–Corpus Christi.

Dr. A. J. (Lonnie) Strickland is the Thomas R. Miller Professor of Strategic Management at the Culverhouse School of Business at The University of Alabama. He is a native of north Georgia, and attended the University of Georgia, where he received a Bachelor of Science degree in math and physics; Georgia Institute of Technology, where he received a Master of Science in industrial management; and Georgia State University, where he received his Ph.D. in business administration.

Lonnie's experience in consulting and executive development is in the strategic management arena, with a concentration in industry and competitive analysis. He has developed strategic planning systems for numerous firms all over the world. He served as Director of Marketing and Strategy at BellSouth, has taken two companies to the New York Stock Exchange, is one of the founders and directors of American Equity Investment Life Holding (AEL), and serves on numerous boards of directors. He is a very popular speaker in the area of strategic management.

Lonnie and his wife, Kitty, have been married for 49 years. They have two children and two grandchildren. Each summer, Lonnie and his wife live on their private game reserve in South Africa where they enjoy taking their friends on safaris.

PREFACE

By offering the most engaging, clearly articulated, and conceptually sound text on strategic management, *Crafting and Executing Strategy* has been able to maintain its position as the leading textbook in strategic management for over 30 years. With this latest edition, we build on this strong foundation, maintaining the attributes of the book that have long made it the most teachable text on the market, while updating the content, sharpening its presentation, and providing enlightening new illustrations and examples.

The distinguishing mark of the 21st edition is its enriched and enlivened presentation of the material in each of the 12 chapters, providing an as up-to-date and engrossing discussion of the core concepts and analytical tools as you will find anywhere. As with each of our new editions, there is an accompanying lineup of exciting new cases that bring the content to life and are sure to provoke interesting classroom discussions, deepening students' understanding of the material in the process.

While this 21st edition retains the 12-chapter structure of the prior edition, every chapter—indeed every paragraph and every line—has been reexamined, refined, and refreshed. New content has been added to keep the material in line with the latest developments in the theory and practice of strategic management. In other areas, coverage has been trimmed to keep the book at a more manageable size. Scores of new examples have been added, along with 17 new Illustration Capsules, to enrich understanding of the content and to provide students with a ringside view of strategy in action. The result is a text that cuts straight to the chase in terms of what students really need to know and gives instructors a leg up on teaching that material effectively. It remains, as always, solidly mainstream and balanced, mirroring *both* the penetrating insight of academic thought and the pragmatism of real-world strategic management.

A standout feature of this text has always been the tight linkage between the content of the chapters and the cases. The lineup of cases that accompany the 21st edition is outstanding in this respect—a truly appealing mix of strategically relevant and thoughtfully crafted cases, certain to engage students and sharpen their skills in applying the concepts and tools of strategic analysis. Many involve high-profile companies that the students will immediately recognize and relate to; all are framed around key strategic issues and serve to add depth and context to the topical content of the chapters. We are confident you will be impressed with how well these cases work in the classroom and the amount of student interest they will spark.

For some years now, growing numbers of strategy instructors at business schools worldwide have been transitioning from a purely text-case course structure to a more robust and energizing text-case-simulation course structure. Incorporating a competition-based strategy simulation has the strong appeal of providing class members with *an immediate and engaging opportunity to apply the concepts and analytical tools covered in the chapters and to become personally involved in crafting and executing a strategy for a virtual company that they have been assigned to manage and that competes head-to-head with companies run by other class members.* Two widely used and pedagogically effective online strategy simulations, *The Business Strategy Game* and *GLO-BUS,* are optional companions for this text. Both simulations were created by Arthur Thompson, one of the text authors, and, like the cases, are closely linked to the content of each chapter in the text. The Exercises for Simulation Participants, found at the end of each chapter, provide clear guidance to class members in applying the concepts and analytical tools covered in the chapters to the issues and decisions that they have to wrestle with in managing their simulation company.

To assist instructors in assessing student achievement of program learning objectives, in line with AACSB requirements, the 21st edition includes a set of Assurance of Learning Exercises at the end of each chapter that link to the specific learning objectives appearing at the beginning of each chapter and highlighted throughout the text. An important instructional feature of the 21st edition is its more closely *integrated* linkage of selected chapter-end Assurance of Learning Exercises and cases to the publisher's web-based assignment and assessment platform called Connect™. Your students will be able to use the online Connect™ supplement to (1) complete two of the Assurance of Learning Exercises appearing at the end of each of the 12 chapters, (2) complete chapter-end quizzes, and (3) enter their answers to a select number of the suggested assignment questions for 7 of the 31 cases in this edition. Many of the Connect™ exercises are automatically graded, thereby enabling you to easily assess the learning that has occurred.

In addition, both of the companion strategy simulations have a built-in Learning Assurance Report that quantifies how well each member of your class performed on nine skills/learning measures *versus tens of thousands of other students worldwide* who completed the simulation in the past 12 months. We believe the chapter-end Assurance of Learning Exercises, the all-new online and automatically graded Connect™ exercises, and the Learning Assurance Report generated at the conclusion of *The Business Strategy Game* and *GLO-BUS* simulations provide you with easy-to-use, empirical measures of student learning in your course. All can be used in conjunction with other instructor-developed or school-developed scoring rubrics and assessment tools to comprehensively evaluate course or program learning outcomes and measure compliance with AACSB accreditation standards.

Taken together, the various components of the 20th-edition package and the supporting set of instructor resources provide you with enormous course design flexibility and a powerful kit of teaching/learning tools. We've done our very best to ensure that the elements constituting the 20th edition will work well for you in the classroom, help you economize on the time needed to be well prepared for each class, and cause students to conclude that your course is one of the very best they have ever taken—from the standpoint of both enjoyment and learning.

DIFFERENTIATING FEATURES OF THE 21ST EDITION

Seven standout features strongly differentiate this text and the accompanying instructional package from others in the field:

1. *Our integrated coverage of the two most popular perspectives on strategic management—positioning theory and resource-based theory—is unsurpassed by any other leading strategy text.* Principles and concepts from both the positioning perspective and the resource-based perspective are prominently and comprehensively integrated into our coverage of crafting both single-business and multibusiness strategies. By highlighting the relationship between a firm's resources and capabilities to

the activities it conducts along its value chain, we show explicitly how these two perspectives relate to one another. Moreover, in Chapters 3 through 8 it is emphasized repeatedly that a company's strategy must be matched *not only* to its external market circumstances *but also* to its internal resources and competitive capabilities.

2. *Our coverage of cooperative strategies and the role that interorganizational activity can play in the pursuit of competitive advantage, is similarly distinguished.* The topics of the value net, ecosystems, strategic alliances, licensing, joint ventures, and other types of collaborative relationships are featured prominently in a number of chapters and are integrated into other material throughout the text. We show how strategies of this nature can contribute to the success of single-business companies as well as multibusiness enterprises, whether with respect to firms operating in domestic markets or those operating in the international realm.
3. The attention we give to international strategies, in all their dimensions, make this textbook an indispensable aid to understanding strategy formulation and execution in an increasingly connected, global world. Our treatment of this topic as one of the most critical elements of the *scope* of a company's activities brings home to students the connection between the topic of international strategy with other topics concerning firm scope, such as multibusiness (or corporate) strategy, outsourcing, insourcing, and vertical integration.
4. *With a stand-alone chapter devoted to this topic, our coverage of business ethics, corporate social responsibility, and environmental sustainability goes well beyond that offered by any other leading strategy text.* Chapter 9, "Ethics, Corporate Social Responsibility, Environmental Sustainability, and Strategy," fulfills the important functions of (1) alerting students to the role and importance of ethical and socially responsible decision making and (2) addressing the accreditation requirement of the AACSB International that business ethics be visibly and thoroughly embedded in the core curriculum. Moreover, discussions of the roles of values and ethics are integrated into portions of other chapters to further reinforce why and how considerations relating to ethics, values, social responsibility, and sustainability should figure prominently into the managerial task of crafting and executing company strategies.
5. *Long known as an important differentiator of this text, the case collection in the 21st edition is truly unrivaled* from the standpoints of student appeal, teachability, and suitability for drilling students in the use of the concepts and analytical treatments in Chapters 1 through 12. The 31 cases included in this edition are the very latest, the best, and the most on target that we could find. The ample information about the cases in the Instructor's Manual makes it effortless to select a set of cases each term that will capture the interest of students from start to finish.
6. *The text is now more tightly linked to the publisher's trailblazing web-based assignment and assessment platform called Connect*™. This will enable professors to gauge class members' prowess in accurately completing (a) selected chapter-end exercises, (b) chapter-end quizzes, and (c) the creative author-developed exercises for seven of the cases in this edition.
7. *Two cutting-edge and widely used strategy simulations—The Business Strategy Game and GLO-BUS—are optional companions to the 21st edition.* These give you an unmatched capability to employ a text-case-simulation model of course delivery.

ORGANIZATION, CONTENT, AND FEATURES OF THE 21ST-EDITION TEXT CHAPTERS

- Chapter 1 serves as a brief, general introduction to the topic of strategy, focusing on the central questions of *"What is strategy?"* and "Why *is it important?"* As such, it serves as the perfect accompaniment for your opening-day lecture on what the course is all about and why it matters. Using the newly added example of Starbucks to drive home the concepts in this chapter, we introduce students to what we mean by "competitive advantage" and the key features of business-level strategy. Describing strategy making as a process, we explain why a company's strategy is partly planned and partly reactive and why a strategy tends to co-evolve with its environment over time. We show that a viable business model must provide both an attractive value proposition for the company's customers and a formula for making profits for the company. A key feature of this chapter is a depiction of how the Value-Price-Cost Framework can be used to frame this discussion.We show how the mark of a winning strategy is its ability to pass three tests: (1) the *fit test* (for internal and external fit), (2) the *competitive advantage test,* and (3) the *performance test.* And we explain why good company performance depends not only upon a sound strategy but upon solid strategy execution as well.
- Chapter 2 presents a more complete overview of the strategic management process, covering topics ranging from the role of vision, mission, and values to what constitutes good corporate governance. It makes a great assignment for the second day of class and provides a smooth transition into the heart of the course. It introduces students to such core concepts as strategic versus financial objectives, the balanced scorecard, strategic intent, and business-level versus corporate-level strategies. It explains why *all managers are on a company's strategy-making, strategy-executing team* and why a company's strategic plan is a collection of strategies devised by different managers at different levels in the organizational hierarchy. The chapter concludes with a section on the role of the board of directors in the strategy-making, strategy-executing process and examines the conditions that led to recent high-profile corporate governance failures. A new illustration capsule on Volkswagen's emissions scandal brings this section to life.
- The next two chapters introduce students to the two most fundamental perspectives on strategy making: the positioning view, exemplified by Michael Porter's "five forces model of competition"; and the resource-based view. Chapter 3 provides *what has long been the clearest, most straightforward discussion of the five forces framework to be found in any text on strategic management.* It also offers a set of complementary analytical tools for conducting competitive analysis and demonstrates the importance of tailoring strategy to fit the circumstances of a company's industry and competitive environment. The chapter includes a discussion of the value net framework, which is useful for conducting analysis of how cooperative as well as competitive moves by various parties contribute to the creation and capture of value in an industry.
- Chapter 4 presents the resource-based view of the firm, showing why resource and capability analysis is such a powerful tool for sizing up a company's competitive assets. It offers a simple framework for identifying a company's resources and capabilities and explains how the VRIN framework can be used to determine

whether they can provide the company with a sustainable competitive advantage over its competitors. Other topics covered in this chapter include dynamic capabilities, SWOT analysis, value chain analysis, benchmarking, and competitive strength assessments, thus enabling a solid appraisal of a company's cost position and customer value proposition vis-á-vis its rivals. *An important feature of this chapter is a table showing how key financial and operating ratios are calculated and how to interpret them.* Students will find this table handy in doing the number crunching needed to evaluate whether a company's strategy is delivering good financial performance.

- Chapter 5 sets forth the basic approaches available for competing and winning in the marketplace in terms of the five generic competitive strategies—low-cost provider, broad differentiation, best-cost provider, focused differentiation, and focused low cost. It describes when each of these approaches works best and what pitfalls to avoid. It explains the role of *cost drivers* and *uniqueness drivers* in reducing a company's costs and enhancing its differentiation, respectively.
- Chapter 6 focuses on *other strategic actions* a company can take to complement its competitive approach and maximize the power of its overall strategy. These include a variety of offensive or defensive competitive moves, and their timing, such as blue-ocean strategies and first-mover advantages and disadvantages. It also includes choices concerning the breadth of a company's activities (or its *scope* of operations along an industry's entire value chain), ranging from horizontal mergers and acquisitions, to vertical integration, outsourcing, and strategic alliances. This material serves to segue into the scope issues covered in the next two chapters on international and diversification strategies.
- Chapter 7 takes up the topic of how to compete in international markets. It begins with a discussion of why differing market conditions across countries must necessarily influence a company's strategic choices about how to enter and compete in foreign markets. It presents five major strategic options for expanding a company's geographic scope and competing in foreign markets: export strategies, licensing, franchising, establishing a wholly owned subsidiary via acquisition or "greenfield" venture, and alliance strategies. It includes coverage of topics such as Porter's Diamond of National Competitive Advantage, profit sanctuaries, and the choice between multidomestic, global, and transnational strategies. This chapter explains the impetus for sharing, transferring, or accessing valuable resources and capabilities across national borders in the quest for competitive advantage, connecting the material to that on the resource-based view from Chapter 4. The chapter concludes with a discussion of the unique characteristics of competing in developing-country markets.
- Chapter 8 concerns strategy making in the multibusiness company, introducing the topic of corporate-level strategy with its special focus on diversification. The first portion of this chapter describes when and why diversification makes good strategic sense, the different means of diversifying a company's business lineup, and the pros and cons of related versus unrelated diversification strategies. The second part of the chapter looks at how to evaluate the attractiveness of a diversified company's business lineup, how to decide whether it has a good diversification strategy, and what strategic options are available for improving a diversified company's future performance. The evaluative technique integrates material concerning both industry analysis and the resource-based view, in that it considers the relative attractiveness of the various industries the company has diversified into,

the company's competitive strength in each of its lines of business, and the extent to which its different businesses exhibit both *strategic fit* and *resource fit.*

- Although the topic of ethics and values comes up at various points in this textbook, Chapter 9 brings more direct attention to such issues and may be used as a stand-alone assignment in either the early, middle, or late part of a course. It concerns the themes of ethical standards in business, approaches to ensuring consistent ethical standards for companies with international operations, corporate social responsibility, and environmental sustainability. The contents of this chapter are sure to give students some things to ponder, rouse lively discussion, and help to make students more *ethically aware* and conscious of *why all companies should conduct their business in a socially responsible and sustainable manner.*
- The next three chapters (Chapters 10, 11, and 12) comprise a module on strategy execution that is presented in terms of a 10-step framework. Chapter 10 provides an overview of this framework and then explores the first three of these tasks: (1) staffing the organization with people capable of executing the strategy well, (2) building the organizational capabilities needed for successful strategy execution, and (3) creating an organizational structure supportive of the strategy execution process.
- Chapter 11 discusses five additional managerial actions that advance the cause of good strategy execution: (1) *allocating resources* to enable the strategy execution process, (2) ensuring that *policies and procedures* facilitate rather than impede strategy execution, (3) using *process management tools* and *best practices* to drive continuous improvement in the performance of value chain activities, (4) installing *information and operating systems* that help company personnel carry out their strategic roles, and (5) using *rewards and incentives* to encourage good strategy execution and the achievement of performance targets.
- Chapter 12 completes the framework with a consideration of the roles of corporate culture and leadership in promoting good strategy execution. The recurring theme throughout the final three chapters is that executing strategy involves deciding on the specific actions, behaviors, and conditions needed for a smooth strategy-supportive operation and then following through to get things done and deliver results. The goal here is to ensure that students understand that the strategy-executing phase is a *make-things-happen and make-them-happen-right* kind of managerial exercise—one that is critical for achieving operating excellence and reaching the goal of strong company performance.

In this latest edition, we have put our utmost effort into ensuring that the 12 chapters are consistent with the latest and best thinking of academics and practitioners in the field of strategic management and provide the topical coverage required for both undergraduate and MBA-level strategy courses. The ultimate test of the text, of course, is the positive pedagogical impact it has in the classroom. If this edition sets a more effective stage for your lectures and does a better job of helping you persuade students that the discipline of strategy merits their rapt attention, then it will have fulfilled its purpose.

THE CASE COLLECTION

The 31-case lineup in this edition is flush with interesting companies and valuable lessons for students in the art and science of crafting and executing strategy. There's a good blend of cases from a length perspective—15 of the 31 cases are under 15 pages yet offer plenty for students to chew on; 11 are medium-length cases; and the remainder are detail-rich cases that call for more sweeping analysis.

At least 28 of the 31 cases involve companies, products, people, or activities that students will have heard of, know about from personal experience, or can easily identify with. The lineup includes at least 15 cases that will deepen student understanding of the special demands of competing in industry environments where product life cycles are short and competitive maneuvering among rivals is quite active. Twenty-three of the cases involve situations in which company resources and competitive capabilities play as large a role in the strategy-making, strategy executing scheme of things as industry and competitive conditions do. Scattered throughout the lineup are 16 cases concerning non-U.S. companies, globally competitive industries, and/or cross-cultural situations. These cases, in conjunction with the globalized content of the text chapters, provide abundant material for linking the study of strategic management tightly to the ongoing globalization of the world economy. You'll also find 11 cases dealing with the strategic problems of family-owned or relatively small entrepreneurial businesses and 21 cases involving public companies and situations where students can do further research on the Internet.

The "Guide to Case Analysis" follows the last case. It contains sections on what a case is, why cases are a standard part of courses in strategy, preparing a case for class discussion, doing a written case analysis, doing an oral presentation, and using financial ratio analysis to assess a company's financial condition. We suggest having students read this guide before the first class discussion of a case.

A number of cases have accompanying YouTube video segments which are listed in the Instructor's Manual.

THE TWO STRATEGY SIMULATION SUPPLEMENTS: *THE BUSINESS STRATEGY GAME* AND *GLO-BUS*

The Business Strategy Game and *GLO-BUS: Developing Winning Competitive Strategies*—two competition-based strategy simulations that are delivered online and that feature automated processing and grading of performance—are being marketed by the publisher as companion supplements for use with the 21st edition (and other texts in the field).

- *The Business Strategy Game* is the world's most popular strategy simulation, having been used by nearly 3,000 different instructors for courses involving some 800,000 students at 1,185+ university campuses in 72 countries. It features global competition in the athletic footwear industry, a product/market setting familiar to students everywhere and one whose managerial challenges are easily grasped.
- *GLO-BUS,* a newer and somewhat simpler strategy simulation first introduced in 2004 and freshly revamped in 2016 to center on competition in two exciting product categories--wearable miniature action cameras and unmanned camera-equipped drones suitable for multiple commercial purposes, has been used by 1,685+ different instructors for courses involving over 240,000 students at 730+ university campuses in 53 countries.

How the Strategy Simulations Work

In both *The Business Strategy Game (BSG)* and *GLO-BUS,* class members are divided into teams of one to five persons and assigned to run a company that competes head-to-head against companies run by other class members. In both simulations, companies compete in a global market arena, selling their products in four geographic regions—Europe-Africa, North America, Asia-Pacific, and Latin America. Each management team is called upon to craft a strategy for their company and make decisions relating to plant operations, workforce compensation, pricing and marketing, social responsibility/citizenship, and finance.

Company co-managers are held accountable for their decision making. Each company's performance is scored on the basis of earnings per share, return-on-equity investment, stock price, credit rating, and image rating. Rankings of company performance, along with a wealth of industry and company statistics, are available to company co-managers after each decision round to use in making strategy adjustments and operating decisions for the next competitive round. You can be certain that the market environment, strategic issues, and operating challenges that company co-managers must contend with are *very tightly linked* to what your class members will be reading about in the text chapters. The circumstances that co-managers face in running their simulation company embrace the very concepts, analytical tools, and strategy options they encounter in the text chapters (this is something you can quickly confirm by skimming through some of the Exercises for Simulation Participants that appear at the end of each chapter).

We suggest that you schedule 1 or 2 practice rounds and anywhere from 4 to 10 regular (scored) decision rounds (more rounds are better than fewer rounds). Each decision round represents a year of company operations and will entail roughly two hours of time for company co-managers to complete. In traditional 13-week, semester-long courses, there is merit in scheduling one decision round per week. In courses that run 5 to 10 weeks, it is wise to schedule two decision rounds per week for the last several weeks of the term (sample course schedules are provided for courses of varying length and varying numbers of class meetings).

When the instructor-specified deadline for a decision round arrives, the simulation server automatically accesses the saved decision entries of each company, determines the competitiveness and buyer appeal of each company's product offering relative to the other companies being run by students in your class, and then awards sales and market shares to the competing companies, geographic region by geographic region. The unit sales volumes awarded to each company *are totally governed by:*

- How its prices compare against the prices of rival brands.
- How its product quality compares against the quality of rival brands.
- How its product line breadth and selection compare.
- How its advertising effort compares.
- And so on, for a total of 11 competitive factors that determine unit sales and market shares.

The competitiveness and overall buyer appeal of each company's product offering *in comparison to the product offerings of rival companies* is all-decisive—this algorithmic feature is what makes *BSG* and *GLO-BUS* "competition-based" strategy simulations. Once each company's sales and market shares are awarded based on the competitiveness and buyer appeal of its respective overall product offering vis-à-vis those of rival companies, the various company and industry reports detailing the outcomes of the decision round are then generated. Company co-managers can access the results of the decision round 15 to 20 minutes after the decision deadline.

The Compelling Case for Incorporating Use of a Strategy Simulation

There are *three exceptionally important benefits* associated with using a competition-based simulation in strategy courses taken by seniors and MBA students:

- *A three-pronged text-case-simulation course model delivers significantly more teaching-learning power than the traditional text-case model.* Using *both* cases and a strategy simulation to drill students in thinking strategically and applying what they read in the text chapters is a stronger, more effective means of helping them connect theory with practice and develop better business judgment. What cases do that a simulation cannot is give class members broad exposure to a variety of companies and industry situations and insight into the kinds of strategy-related problems managers face. But what a competition-based strategy simulation does far better than case analysis is thrust class members squarely into *an active, hands-on managerial role* where they are totally responsible for assessing market conditions, determining how to respond to the actions of competitors, forging a long-term direction and strategy for their company, and making all kinds of operating decisions. Because they are held fully accountable for their decisions and their company's performance, *co-managers are strongly motivated* to dig deeply into company operations, probe for ways to be more cost-efficient and competitive, and ferret out strategic moves and decisions calculated to boost company performance. *Consequently, incorporating both case assignments and a strategy simulation to develop the skills of class members in thinking strategically and applying the concepts and tools of strategic analysis turns out to be more pedagogically powerful than relying solely on case assignments—there's stronger retention of the lessons learned and better achievement of course learning objectives.*

  To provide you with quantitative evidence of the learning that occurs with using *The Business Strategy Game* or *GLO-BUS,* there is a built-in Learning Assurance Report showing how well each class member performs on nine skills/learning measures versus tens of thousands of students worldwide who have completed the simulation in the past 12 months.
- *The competitive nature of a strategy simulation arouses positive energy and steps up the whole tempo of the course by a notch or two.* Nothing sparks class excitement quicker or better than the concerted efforts on the part of class members at each decision round to achieve a high industry ranking and avoid the perilous consequences of being outcompeted by other class members. Students really enjoy taking on the role of a manager, running their own company, crafting strategies, making all kinds of operating decisions, trying to outcompete rival companies, and getting immediate feedback on the resulting company performance. Lots of back-and-forth chatter occurs when the results of the latest simulation round become available and co-managers renew their quest for strategic moves and actions that will strengthen company performance. Co-managers become *emotionally invested* in running their company and figuring out what strategic moves to make to boost their company's performance. Interest levels climb. All this stimulates learning

and causes students to see the practical relevance of the subject matter and the benefits of taking your course.

As soon as your students start to say "Wow! Not only is this fun but I am learning a lot," *which they will,* you have won the battle of engaging students in the subject matter and moved the value of taking your course to a much higher plateau in the business school curriculum. This translates into *a livelier, richer learning experience from a student perspective and better instructor-course evaluations.*

- *Use of a fully automated online simulation reduces the time instructors spend on course preparation, course administration, and grading.* Since the simulation exercise involves a 20- to 30-hour workload for student teams (roughly 2 hours per decision round times 10 to 12 rounds, plus optional assignments), simulation adopters often compensate by trimming the number of assigned cases from, say, 10 to 12 to perhaps 4 to 6. This significantly reduces the time instructors spend reading cases, studying teaching notes, and otherwise getting ready to lead class discussion of a case or grade oral team presentations. Course preparation time is further cut because you can use several class days to have students meet in the computer lab to work on upcoming decision rounds or a three-year strategic plan (in lieu of lecturing on a chapter or covering an additional assigned case). Not only does use of a simulation permit assigning fewer cases, but it also permits you to eliminate at least one assignment that entails considerable grading on your part. Grading one less written case or essay exam or other written assignment saves enormous time. With *BSG* and *GLO-BUS,* grading is effortless and takes only minutes; once you enter percentage weights for each assignment in your online grade book, a suggested overall grade is calculated for you. You'll be pleasantly surprised—and quite pleased—at how little time it takes to gear up for and administer *The Business Strategy Game* or *GLO-BUS.*

In sum, incorporating use of a strategy simulation turns out to be *a win–win proposition for both students and instructors.* Moreover, a very convincing argument can be made that a competition-based strategy simulation is *the single most effective teaching/learning tool that instructors can employ to teach the discipline of business and competitive strategy, to make learning more enjoyable, and to promote better achievement of course learning objectives.*

A Bird's-Eye View of *The Business Strategy Game*

The setting for *The Business Strategy Game (BSG)* is the global athletic footwear industry (there can be little doubt in today's world that a globally competitive strategy simulation is *vastly superior* to a simulation with a domestic-only setting). Global market demand for footwear grows at the rate of 7 to 9 percent annually for the first five years and 5 to 7 percent annually for the second five years. However, market growth rates vary by geographic region—North America, Latin America, Europe-Africa, and Asia-Pacific.

Companies begin the simulation producing branded and private-label footwear in two plants, one in North America and one in Asia. They have the option to establish production facilities in Latin America and Europe-Africa, either by constructing new plants or by buying previously constructed plants that have been sold by competing companies. Company co-managers exercise control over production costs on the basis of the styling and quality they opt to manufacture, plant location (wages and incentive compensation vary from region to region), the use of best practices and Six Sigma programs to reduce the production of defective footwear and to boost worker productivity, and compensation practices.

All newly produced footwear is shipped in bulk containers to one of four geographic distribution centers. All sales in a geographic region are made from footwear inventories in that region's distribution center. Costs at the four regional distribution centers are a function of inventory storage costs, packing and shipping fees, import tariffs paid on incoming pairs shipped from foreign plants, and exchange rate impacts. At the start of the simulation, import tariffs average $4 per pair in Europe-Africa, $6 per pair in Latin America, and $8 in the Asia-Pacific region. However, the Free Trade Treaty of the Americas allows tariff-free movement of footwear between North America and Latin America. Instructors have the option to alter tariffs as the game progresses.

Companies market their brand of athletic footwear to footwear retailers worldwide and to individuals buying online at the company's website. Each company's sales and market share in the branded footwear segments hinge on its competitiveness on 11 factors: attractive pricing, footwear styling and quality, product line breadth, advertising, use of mail-in rebates, appeal of celebrities endorsing a company's brand, success in convincing footwear retailers to carry its brand, number of weeks it takes to fill retailer orders, effectiveness of a company's online sales effort at its website, and customer loyalty. Sales of private-label footwear hinge solely on being the low-price bidder.

All told, company co-managers make as many as 53 types of decisions each period that cut across production operations (up to 10 decisions per plant, with a maximum of four plants), plant capacity additions/sales/upgrades (up to 6 decisions per plant), worker compensation and training (3 decisions per plant), shipping (up to 8 decisions per plant), pricing and marketing (up to 10 decisions in four geographic regions), bids to sign celebrities (2 decision entries per bid), financing of company operations (up to 8 decisions), and corporate social responsibility and environmental sustainability (up to 6 decisions).

Each time company co-managers make a decision entry, an assortment of on-screen calculations instantly shows the projected effects on unit sales, revenues, market shares, unit costs, profit, earnings per share, ROE, and other operating statistics. The on-screen calculations help team members evaluate the relative merits of one decision entry versus another and put together a promising strategy.

Companies can employ any of the five generic competitive strategy options in selling branded footwear—low-cost leadership, differentiation, best-cost provider, focused low cost, and focused differentiation. They can pursue essentially the same strategy worldwide or craft slightly or very different strategies for the Europe-Africa, Asia-Pacific, Latin America, and North America markets. They can strive for competitive advantage based on more advertising, a wider selection of models, more appealing styling/quality, bigger rebates, and so on.

Any well-conceived, well-executed competitive approach is capable of succeeding, provided it is not overpowered by the strategies of competitors or defeated by the presence of too many copycat strategies that dilute its effectiveness. The challenge for each company's management team is to craft and execute a competitive strategy that produces good performance on five measures: earnings per share, return on equity investment, stock price appreciation, credit rating, and brand image.

All activity for *The Business Strategy Game* takes place at **www.bsg-online.com**.

A Bird's-Eye View of *GLO-BUS*

In *GLO-BUS,* class members run companies that are in a neck-and-neck race for global market leadership in two product categories: (1) wearable video cameras smaller than a teacup that deliver stunning video quality and have powerful photo capture capabilities (comparable to those designed and marketed by global industry leader GoPro and numerous others) and (2) sophisticated camera-equipped copter drones that incorporate a company designed and assembled action-capture camera and that are sold to commercial enterprises for prices in the $850 to $2,000+ range. Global market demand for action cameras grows at the rate of 6-8% annually for the first five years and 4-6% annually for the second five years. Global market demand for commercial drones grows briskly at rates averaging 20% for the first two years, then gradually slows over 8 years to a rate of 4-6%.

Companies assemble action cameras and drones of varying designs and performance capabilities at a Taiwan facility and ship finished goods directly to buyers in North America, Asia-Pacific, Europe-Africa, and Latin America. Both products are assembled usually within two weeks of being received and are then shipped to buyers no later than 2-3 days after assembly. Companies maintain no finished goods inventories and all parts and components are delivered by suppliers on a just-in-time basis (which eliminates the need to track inventories and simplifies the accounting for plant operations and costs).

Company co-managers determine the quality and performance features of the cameras and drones being assembled. They impact production costs by raising/lowering specifications for parts/components and expenditures for product R&D, adjusting work force compensation, spending more/less on worker training and productivity improvement, lengthening/shortening warranties offered (which affects warranty costs), and how cost-efficiently they manage assembly operations. They have options to manage/control selling and certain other costs as well.

Each decision round, company co-managers make some 50 types of decisions relating to the design and performance of the company's two products (21 decisions, 10 for cameras and 11 for drones), assembly operations and workforce compensation (up to 8 decision entries for each product), pricing and marketing (7 decisions for cameras and 5 for drones), corporate social responsibility and citizenship (up to 6 decisions), and the financing of company operations (up to 8 decisions). In addition, there are 10 entries for cameras and 7 entries for drones involving assumptions about the competitive actions of rivals; these entries help company co-managers to make more accurate forecasts of their company's unit sales (so they have a good idea of how many cameras and drones will need to be assembled each year to fill customer orders). Each time co-managers make a decision entry, an assortment of on-screen calculations instantly shows the projected effects on unit sales, revenues, market shares, total profit, earnings per share, ROE, costs, and other operating outcomes. All of these on-screen calculations help co-managers evaluate the relative merits of one decision entry versus another. Company managers can try out as many different decision combinations as they wish in stitching the separate decision entries into a cohesive whole that is projected to produce good company performance.

Competition in action cameras revolves around 11 factors that determine each company's unit sales/market share:

1. How each company's average wholesale price to retailers compares against the all-company average wholesale prices being charged in each geographic region.
2. How each company's camera performance and quality compares against industry-wide camera performance/quality.
3. How the number of week-long sales promotion campaigns a company has in each region compares against the regional average number of weekly promotions.

4. How the size of each company's discounts off the regular wholesale prices during sales promotion campaigns compares against the regional average promotional discount.
5. How each company's annual advertising expenditures compare against regional average advertising expenditures.
6. How the number of models in each company's camera line compares against the industry-wide average number of models.
7. The number of retailers stocking and merchandising a company's brand in each region.
8. Annual expenditures to support the merchandising efforts of retailers stocking a company's brand in each region.
9. The amount by which a company's expenditures for ongoing improvement and updating of its company's website in a region is above/below the all-company regional average expenditure.
10. How the length of each company's camera warranties compare against the warranty periods of rival companies.
11. How well a company's brand image/reputation compares against the brand images/ reputations of rival companies.

Competition among rival makers of commercial copter drones is more narrowly focused on just 9 sales-determining factors:

1. How a company's average retail price for drones at the company's website in each region compares against the all-company regional average website price.
2. How each company's drone performance and quality compares against the all-company average drone performance/quality.
3. How the number of models in each company's drone line compares against the industry-wide average number of models.
4. How each company's annual expenditures to recruit/support 3rd-party online electronics retailers in merchandising its brand of drones in each region compares against the regional average.
5. The amount by which a company's price discount to third-party online retailers is above/below the regional average discounted price.
6. How well a company's expenditures for search engine advertising in a region compares against the regional average.
7. How well a company's expenditures for ongoing improvement and updating of its website in a region compares against the regional average.
8. How the length of each company's drone warranties in a region compares against the regional average warranty period.
9. How well a company's brand image/reputation compares against the brand images/ reputations of rival companies.

Each company typically seeks to enhance its performance and build competitive advantage via its own custom-tailored competitive strategy based on more attractive pricing, greater advertising, a wider selection of models, more appealing performance/ quality, longer warranties, a better image/reputation, and so on. The greater the differences in the overall competitiveness of the product offerings of rival companies, the bigger the differences in their resulting sales volumes and market shares. Conversely, the smaller the overall competitive differences in the product offerings of rival companies, the smaller the differences in sales volumes and market shares. This algorithmic approach is what makes *GLO-BUS* a "competition-based" strategy simulation and accounts for why *the sales and market share outcomes for each decision round are always unique to the particular strategies and decision combinations employed by the competing companies.*

As with *BSG, all the various generic competitive strategy options*—low-cost leadership, differentiation, best-cost provider, focused low-cost, and focused differentiation—*are viable choices for pursuing competitive advantage and good company performance.* A company can have a strategy aimed at being the clear market leader in either action cameras or drones or both. It can focus its competitive efforts on one or two or three geographic regions or strive to build strong market positions in all four geographic regions. It can pursue essentially the same strategy worldwide or craft customized strategies for the Europe-Africa, Asia-Pacific, Latin America, and North America markets. Just as with *The Business Strategy Game, most any well-conceived, well-executed competitive approach is capable of succeeding, provided it is not overpowered by the strategies of competitors or defeated by the presence of too many copycat strategies that dilute its effectiveness.*

The challenge for each company's management team is to craft and execute a competitive strategy that produces good performance on five measures: earnings per share, return on equity investment, stock price appreciation, credit rating, and brand image.

All activity for *GLO-BUS* occurs at **www.glo-bus.com**.

Special Note: The time required of company co-managers to complete each decision round in *GLO-BUS* is typically about 15- to 30-minutes less than for *The Business Strategy Game* because

(a) there are only 8 market segments (versus 12 in *BSG*),

(b) co-managers have only one assembly site to operate (versus potentially as many as 4 plants in *BSG,* one in each geographic region), and

(c) newly-assembled cameras and drones are shipped directly to buyers, eliminating the need to manage finished goods inventories and operate distribution centers.

Administration and Operating Features of the Two Simulations

The Internet delivery and user-friendly designs of both *BSG* and *GLO-BUS* make them incredibly easy to administer, even for first-time users. And the menus and controls are so similar that you can readily switch between the two simulations or use one in your undergraduate class and the other in a graduate class. If you have not yet used either of the two simulations, you may find the following of particular interest:

- Setting up the simulation for your course is done online and takes about 10 to 15 minutes. Once setup is completed, no other administrative actions are required beyond those of moving participants to a different team (should the need arise) and monitoring the progress of the simulation (to whatever extent desired).
- Participant's Guides are delivered electronically to class members at the website—students can read the guide on their monitors or print out a copy, as they prefer.
- There are 2- to 4-minute Video Tutorials scattered throughout the software (including each decision screen and each page of each report) that provide on-demand guidance to class members who may be uncertain about how to proceed.

- Complementing the Video Tutorials are detailed and clearly written Help sections explaining "all there is to know" about (a) each decision entry and the relevant cause-effect relationships, (b) the information on each page of the Industry Reports, and (c) the numbers presented in the Company Reports. *The Video Tutorials and the Help screens allow company co-managers to figure things out for themselves, thereby curbing the need for students to ask the instructor "how things work."*
- Team members running the same company who are logged in simultaneously on different computers at different locations can click a button to enter Collaboration Mode, enabling them to work collaboratively from the same screen in viewing reports and making decision entries, and click a second button to enter Audio Mode, letting them talk to one another.
  - When in "Collaboration Mode," each team member sees the same screen at the same time as all other team members who are logged in and have joined Collaboration Mode. If one team member chooses to view a particular decision screen, that same screen appears on the monitors for all team members in Collaboration Mode.
  - Each team member controls their own color-coded mouse pointer (with their first-name appearing in a color-coded box linked to their mouse pointer) and can make a decision entry or move the mouse to point to particular on-screen items.
  - A decision entry change made by one team member is seen by all, in real time, and all team members can immediately view the on-screen calculations that result from the new decision entry.
  - If one team member wishes to view a report page and clicks on the menu link to the desired report, that same report page will immediately appear for the other team members engaged in collaboration.
  - Use of Audio Mode capability requires that each team member work from a computer with a built-in microphone (if they want to be heard by their team members) and speakers (so they may hear their teammates) or else have a headset with a microphone that they can plug into their desktop or laptop. A headset is recommended for best results, but most laptops now are equipped with a built-in microphone and speakers that will support use of our new voice chat feature.
  - Real-time VoIP audio chat capability among team members who have entered both the Audio Mode and the Collaboration Mode is a tremendous boost in functionality that enables team members to go online simultaneously on computers at different locations and conveniently and effectively collaborate in running their simulation company.
  - In addition, instructors have the capability to join the online session of any company and speak with team members, thus circumventing the need for team members to arrange for and attend a meeting in the instructor's office. Using the standard menu for administering a particular industry, instructors can connect with the company desirous of assistance. Instructors who wish not only to talk but also to enter Collaboration (highly recommended because all attendees are then viewing the same screen) have a red-colored mouse pointer linked to a red box labeled Instructor.

Without a doubt, the Collaboration and Voice-Chat capabilities are hugely valuable for students enrolled in online and distance-learning courses where meeting face-to-face is impractical or time-consuming. Likewise, the instructors of online and distance-learning courses will appreciate having the capability to join the online meetings of particular company teams when their advice or assistance is requested.

- Both simulations are quite suitable for use in distance-learning or online courses (and are currently being used in such courses on numerous campuses).
- Participants and instructors are notified via e-mail when the results are ready (usually about 15 to 20 minutes after the decision round deadline specified by the instructor/game administrator).
- Following each decision round, participants are provided with a complete set of reports—a six-page Industry Report, a one-page Competitive Intelligence report for each geographic region that includes strategic group maps and bulleted lists of competitive strengths and weaknesses, and a set of Company Reports (income statement, balance sheet, cash flow statement, and assorted production, marketing, and cost statistics).
- Two "open-book" multiple-choice tests of 20 questions are built into each simulation. The quizzes, which you can require or not as you see fit, are taken online and automatically graded, with scores reported instantaneously to participants and automatically recorded in the instructor's electronic grade book. Students are automatically provided with three sample questions for each test.
- Both simulations contain a three-year strategic plan option that you can assign. Scores on the plan are automatically recorded in the instructor's online grade book.
- At the end of the simulation, you can have students complete online peer evaluations (again, the scores are automatically recorded in your online grade book).
- Both simulations have a Company Presentation feature that enables each team of company co-managers to easily prepare PowerPoint slides for use in describing their strategy and summarizing their company's performance in a presentation to either the class, the instructor, or an "outside" board of directors.
- *A Learning Assurance Report provides you with hard data concerning how well your students performed vis-à-vis students playing the simulation worldwide over the past 12 months.* The report is based on nine measures of student proficiency, business know-how, and decision-making skill and can also be used in evaluating the extent to which your school's academic curriculum produces the desired degree of student learning insofar as accreditation standards are concerned.

For more details on either simulation, please consult Section 2 of the Instructor's Manual accompanying this text or register as an instructor at the simulation websites (**www.bsg-online.com** and **www.glo-bus.com**) to access even more comprehensive information. You should also consider signing up for one of the webinars that the simulation authors conduct several times each month (sometimes several times weekly) to demonstrate how the software works, walk you through the various features and menu options, and answer any questions. You have an open invitation to call the senior author of this text at (205) 722-9145 to arrange a personal demonstration or talk about how one of the simulations might work in one of your courses. We think you'll be quite impressed with the cutting-edge capabilities that have been programmed into *The Business Strategy Game* and *GLO-BUS,* the simplicity with which both simulations can be administered, and their exceptionally tight connection to the text chapters, core concepts, and standard analytical tools.

RESOURCES AND SUPPORT MATERIALS FOR THE 21ST EDITION

For Students

Key Points Summaries At the end of each chapter is a synopsis of the core concepts, analytical tools, and other key points discussed in the chapter. These chapter-end synopses, along with the core concept definitions and margin notes scattered throughout each chapter, help students focus on basic strategy principles, digest the messages of each chapter, and prepare for tests.

Two Sets of Chapter-End Exercises Each chapter concludes with two sets of exercises. The *Assurance of Learning Exercises* are useful for helping students prepare for class discussion and to gauge their understanding of the material. The *Exercises for Simulation Participants* are designed expressly for use in class which incorporate the use of a simulation. These exercises explicitly connect the chapter content to the simulation company the students are running. Even if they are not assigned by the instructor, they can provide helpful practice for students as a study aid.

The Connect™ Management Web-Based Assignment and Assessment Platform Beginning with the 18th edition, we began taking advantage of the publisher's innovative Connect™ assignment and assessment platform and created several features that simplify the task of assigning and grading three types of exercises for students:

- There are self-scoring chapter tests consisting of 20 to 25 multiple-choice questions that students can take to measure their grasp of the material presented in each of the 12 chapters.
- There are two author-developed Interactive Application exercises for each of the 12 chapters that drill students in the use and application of the concepts and tools of strategic analysis.
- The Connect™ platform also includes author-developed Interactive Application exercises for 12 of the 31 cases in this edition that require students to work through answers to a select number of the assignment questions for the case. These exercises have multiple components and can include calculating assorted financial ratios to assess a company's financial performance and balance sheet strength, identifying a company's strategy, doing five-forces and driving-forces analysis, doing a SWOT analysis, and recommending actions to improve company performance. The content of these case exercises is tailored to match the circumstances presented in each case, calling upon students to do whatever strategic thinking and strategic analysis are called for to arrive at pragmatic, analysis-based action recommendations for improving company performance.

All of the Connect™ exercises are automatically graded (with the exception of those exercise components that entail student entry of short-answer and/or essay answers), thereby simplifying the task of evaluating each class member's performance and monitoring the learning outcomes. The progress-tracking function built into the Connect™ Management system enables you to:

- View scored work immediately and track individual or group performance with assignment and grade reports.

- Access an instant view of student or class performance relative to learning objectives.
- Collect data and generate reports required by many accreditation organizations, such as AACSB International.

LearnSmart and SmartBook™ LearnSmart is an adaptive study tool proven to strengthen memory recall, increase class retention, and boost grades. Students are able to study more efficiently because they are made aware of what they know and don't know. Real-time reports quickly identify the concepts that require more attention from individual students—or the entire class. SmartBook is the first and only adaptive reading experience designed to change the way students read and learn. It creates a personalized reading experience by highlighting the most impactful concepts a student needs to learn at that moment in time. As a student engages with SmartBook, the reading experience continuously adapts by highlighting content based on what the student knows and doesn't know. This ensures that the focus is on the content he or she needs to learn, while simultaneously promoting long-term retention of material. Use SmartBook's real-time reports to quickly identify the concepts that require more attention from individual students–or the entire class. The end result? Students are more engaged with course content, can better prioritize their time, and come to class ready to participate.

For Instructors

Assurance of Learning Aids Each chapter begins with a set of Learning Objectives, which are tied directly to the material in the text meant to address these objectives with helpful signposts. At the conclusion of each chapter, there is a set of *Assurance of Learning Exercises* that can be used as the basis for class discussion, oral presentation assignments, short written reports, and substitutes for case assignments. Similarly, there is a set of *Exercises for Simulation Participants* that are designed expressly for use by adopters who have incorporated use of a simulation and want to go a step further in tightly and explicitly connecting the chapter content to the simulation company their students are running. The questions in both sets of exercises (along with those Illustration Capsules that qualify as "mini-cases") can be used to round out the rest of a 75-minute class period should your lecture on a chapter last for only 50 minutes.

Instructor Library The Connect Management Instructor Library is your repository for additional resources to improve student engagement in and out of class. You can select and use any asset that enhances your lecture.

Instructor's Manual The accompanying IM contains:

- A section on suggestions for organizing and structuring your course.
- Sample syllabi and course outlines.
- A set of lecture notes on each chapter.
- Answers to the chapter-end Assurance of Learning Exercises.
- A test bank for all 12 chapters.
- A comprehensive case teaching note for each of the 31 cases. These teaching notes are filled with suggestions for using the case effectively, have very thorough, analysis-based answers to the suggested assignment questions for the case, and contain an epilogue detailing any important developments since the case was written.

Test Bank The test bank contains over 900 multiple-choice questions and short-answer/essay questions. It has been tagged with AACSB and Bloom's Taxonomy criteria. All of the test bank questions are also accessible via **TestGen.** TestGen is a complete, state-of-the-art test generator and editing application software that allows instructors to quickly and easily select test items from McGraw Hill's TestGen test-bank content and to organize, edit, and customize the questions and answers to rapidly generate paper tests. Questions can include stylized text, symbols, graphics, and equations that are inserted directly into questions using built-in mathematical templates. TestGen's random generator provides the option to display different text or calculated number values each time questions are used. With both quick-and-simple test creation and flexible and robust editing tools, TestGen is a test generator system for today's educators.

PowerPoint Slides To facilitate delivery preparation of your lectures and to serve as chapter outlines, you'll have access to approximately 500 colorful and professional-looking slides displaying core concepts, analytical procedures, key points, and all the figures in the text chapters.

CREATE™ is McGraw-Hill's custom-publishing program where you can access full-length readings and cases that accompany *Crafting and Executing Strategy: The Quest for a Competitive Advantage* (**http://create.mheducation.com/thompson**). Through Create™, you will be able to select from 30 readings that go specifically with this textbook. These include cases and readings from Harvard, MIT, and much more! You can assemble your own course and select the chapters, cases, and readings that work best for you. Also, you can choose from several ready-to-go, author-recommended complete course solutions. Among the pre-loaded solutions, you'll find options for undergrad, MBA, accelerated, and other strategy courses.

The Business Strategy Game* and *GLO-BUS Online Simulations Using one of the two companion simulations is a powerful and constructive way of emotionally connecting students to the subject matter of the course. We know of no more effective way to arouse the competitive energy of students and prepare them for the challenges of real-world business decision making than to have them match strategic wits with classmates in running a company in head-to-head competition for global market leadership.

ACKNOWLEDGMENTS

We heartily acknowledge the contributions of the case researchers whose case-writing efforts appear herein and the companies whose cooperation made the cases possible. To each one goes a very special thank-you. We cannot overstate the importance of timely, carefully researched cases in contributing to a substantive study of strategic management issues and practices.

A great number of colleagues and students at various universities, business acquaintances, and people at McGraw-Hill provided inspiration, encouragement, and counsel during the course of this project. Like all text authors in the strategy field, we are intellectually indebted to the many academics whose research and writing have blazed new trails and advanced the discipline of strategic management. In addition, we'd like to thank the following reviewers who provided seasoned advice and splendid suggestions over the years for improving the chapters:

> Robert B. Baden, Edward Desmarais, Stephen F. Hallam, Joy Karriker, Wendell Seaborne, Joan H. Bailar, David Blair, Jane Boyland, William J. Donoher, Stephen A. Drew, Jo Anne Duffy, Alan Ellstrand, Susan Fox-Wolfgramm, Rebecca M. Guidice, Mark Hoelscher, Sean D. Jasso, Xin Liang, Paul Mallette, Dan Marlin, Raza Mir, Mansour Moussavi, James D. Spina, Monica A. Zimmerman, Dennis R. Balch, Jeffrey R. Bruehl, Edith C. Busija, Donald A. Drost, Randall Harris, Mark Lewis Hoelscher, Phyllis Holland, James W. Kroeger, Sal Kukalis, Brian W. Kulik, Paul Mallette, Anthony U. Martinez, Lee Pickler, Sabine Reddy, Thomas D. Schramko, V. Seshan, Charles Strain, Sabine Turnley, S. Stephen Vitucci, Andrew Ward, Sibin Wu, Lynne Patten, Nancy E. Landrum, Jim Goes, Jon Kalinowski, Rodney M. Walter, Judith D. Powell, Seyda Deligonul, David Flanagan, Esmerlda Garbi, Mohsin Habib, Kim Hester, Jeffrey E. McGee, Diana J. Wong, F. William Brown, Anthony F. Chelte, Gregory G. Dess, Alan B. Eisner, John George, Carle M. Hunt, Theresa Marron-Grodsky, Sarah Marsh, Joshua D. Martin, William L. Moore, Donald Neubaum, George M. Puia, Amit Shah, Lois M. Shelton, Mark Weber, Steve Barndt, J. Michael Geringer, Ming-Fang Li, Richard Stackman, Stephen Tallman, Gerardo R. Ungson, James Boulgarides, Betty Diener, Daniel F. Jennings, David Kuhn, Kathryn Martell, Wilbur Mouton, Bobby Vaught, Tuck Bounds, Lee Burk, Ralph Catalanello, William Crittenden, Vince Luchsinger, Stan Mendenhall, John Moore, Will Mulvaney, Sandra Richard, Ralph Roberts, Thomas Turk, Gordon Von Stroh, Fred Zimmerman, S. A. Billion, Charles Byles, Gerald L. Geisler, Rose Knotts, Joseph Rosenstein, James B. Thurman, Ivan Able, W. Harvey Hegarty, Roger Evered, Charles B. Saunders, Rhae M. Swisher, Claude I. Shell, R. Thomas Lenz, Michael C. White, Dennis Callahan, R. Duane Ireland, William E. Burr II, C. W. Millard, Richard Mann, Kurt Christensen, Neil W. Jacobs, Louis W. Fry, D. Robley Wood, George J. Gore, and William R. Soukup.

We owe a debt of gratitude to Professors Catherine A. Maritan, Jeffrey A. Martin, Richard S. Shreve, and Anant K. Sundaram for their helpful comments on various chapters. We'd also like to thank the following students of the Tuck School of Business for their assistance with the revisions: Sarah Boole, Katie Coster, Jacob Crandall, Robin Daley, Mike Gallagher, Danny Garver, Dennis L. Huggins, Peter Jacobson, Heather Levy, Ken Martin, Brian R. McKenzie, Kiera O'Brien, Sara Paccamonti, Byron Peyster, Jared Pomerance, Jeremy Reich, Christopher C. Sukenik, Frances Thunder, David Washer, Fan Zhou, and Nicholas J. Ziemba. And we'd like to acknowledge the help of Dartmouth students Mathieu A. Bertrand, Meghan L. Cooney, Margo Cox, Harold W. Greenstone, Maria Hart, Amy Li, Sara Peterson, Pallavi Saboo, Artie Santry, Isaac Takushi, as well as Tuck staff member Mary Biathrow.

As always, we value your recommendations and thoughts about the book. Your comments regarding coverage and contents will be taken to heart, and we always are grateful for the time you take to call our attention to printing errors, deficiencies, and other shortcomings. Please e-mail us at **athompso@cba.ua.edu**, **margaret.a.peteraf@tuck.dartmouth.edu**, **john.gamble@tamucc.edu**, or **astrickl@cba.ua.edu**.

Arthur A. Thompson

Margaret A. Peteraf

John E. Gamble

A. J. Strickland

The Business Strategy Game or *GLO-BUS* Simulation Exercises

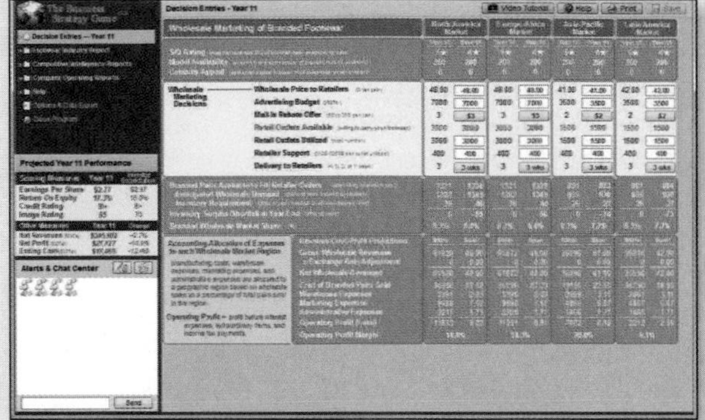

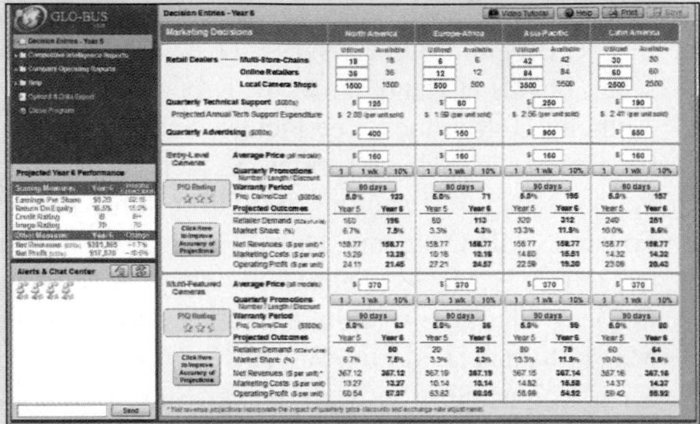

***The Business Strategy Game* or *GLO-BUS* Simulation Exercises**
Either one of these text supplements involves teams of students managing companies in a head-to-head contest for global market leadership. Company co-managers have to make decisions relating to product quality, production, workforce compensation and training, pricing and marketing, and financing of company operations. The challenge is to craft and execute a strategy that is powerful enough to deliver good financial performance despite the competitive efforts of rival companies. Each company competes in America, Latin America, Europe-Africa, and Asia-Pacific.

BRIEF CONTENTS

PART 1 Concepts and Techniques for Crafting and Executing Strategy

PART 2 Cases in Crafting and Executing Strategy

CONTENTS

Section C: Crafting a Strategy

PART 2 Cases in Crafting and Executing Strategy

Section A: Crafting Strategy in Single-Business Companies

PART 1

Concepts and Techniques for Crafting and Executing Strategy

CHAPTER 1

What Is Strategy and Why Is It Important?

© Fanatic Studio/Getty Images

Learning Objectives

THIS CHAPTER WILL HELP YOU UNDERSTAND:

LO 1 What we mean by a company's *strategy.*

LO 2 The concept of a *sustainable competitive advantage.*

LO 3 The five most basic strategic approaches for setting a company apart from rivals and winning a sustainable competitive advantage.

LO 4 That a company's strategy tends to evolve because of changing circumstances and ongoing efforts by management to improve the strategy.

LO 5 Why it is important for a company to have a viable business model that outlines the company's customer value proposition and its profit formula.

LO 6 The three tests of a winning strategy.

Strategy means making clear-cut choices about how to compete.

Jack Welch—*Former CEO of General Electric*

The underlying principles of strategy are enduring, regardless of technology or the pace of change.

Michael Porter—*Professor and consultant*

I believe that people make their own luck by great preparation and good strategy.

Jack Canfield—*Corporate trainer and entrepreneur*

According to *The Economist,* a leading publication on business, economics, and international affairs, "In business, strategy is king. Leadership and hard work are all very well and luck is mighty useful, but it is strategy that makes or breaks a firm."[1] Luck and circumstance can explain why some companies are blessed with initial, short-lived success. But only a well-crafted, well-executed, constantly evolving strategy can explain why an elite set of companies somehow manage to rise to the top and stay there, year after year, pleasing their customers, shareholders, and other stakeholders alike in the process. Companies such as Apple, Disney, Microsoft, Alphabet (parent company of Google), Berkshire Hathaway, General Electric, and Amazon come to mind—but long-lived success is not just the province of U.S. companies. Diverse kinds of companies, both large and small, from many different countries have been able to sustain strong performance records, including Korea's Samsung (in electronics), the United Kingdom's HSBC (in banking), Dubai's Emirates Airlines, Switzerland's Swatch Group (in watches and luxury jewelry), China Mobile (in telecommunications), and India's Tata Steel.

In this opening chapter, we define the concept of strategy and describe its many facets. We explain what is meant by a competitive advantage, discuss the relationship between a company's strategy and its business model, and introduce you to the kinds of competitive strategies that can give a company an advantage over rivals in attracting customers and earning above-average profits. We look at what sets a winning strategy apart from others and why the caliber of a company's strategy determines whether the company will enjoy a competitive advantage over other firms. By the end of this chapter, you will have a clear idea of why the tasks of crafting and executing strategy are core management functions and why excellent execution of an excellent strategy is the most reliable recipe for turning a company into a standout performer over the long term.

WHAT DO WE MEAN BY *STRATEGY*?

A company's **strategy** is the set of actions that its managers take to outperform the company's competitors and achieve superior profitability. The objective of a well-crafted strategy is not merely temporary competitive success and profits in the short run, but rather the sort of lasting success that can support growth and secure the

CORE CONCEPT

A company's **strategy** is the set of actions that its managers take to outperform the company's competitors and achieve superior profitability.

company's future over the long term. Achieving this entails making a managerial commitment to a coherent array of well-considered choices about how to compete.[2] These include:

- *How* to position the company in the marketplace.
- *How* to attract customers.
- *How* to compete against rivals.
- *How* to achieve the company's performance targets.
- *How* to capitalize on opportunities to grow the business.
- *How* to respond to changing economic and market conditions.

LO 1

What we mean by a company's *strategy*.

In most industries, companies have considerable freedom in choosing the *hows* of strategy.[3] Some companies strive to achieve lower costs than rivals, while others aim for product superiority or more personalized customer service dimensions that rivals cannot match. Some companies opt for wide product lines, while others concentrate their energies on a narrow product lineup. Some deliberately confine their operations to local or regional markets; others opt to compete nationally, internationally (several countries), or globally (all or most of the major country markets worldwide).

Strategy Is about Competing Differently

Mimicking the strategies of successful industry rivals—with either copycat product offerings or maneuvers to stake out the same market position—rarely works. Rather, every company's strategy needs to have some distinctive element that draws in customers and provides a competitive edge. Strategy, at its essence, is about competing differently—doing what rival firms *don't* do or what rival firms *can't* do.[4] This does not mean that the key elements of a company's strategy have to be 100 percent different, but rather that they must differ in at least *some important respects.* A strategy stands a better chance of succeeding when it is predicated on actions, business approaches, and competitive moves aimed at (1) appealing to buyers in ways that *set a company apart from its rivals* and (2) staking out a market position that is not crowded with strong competitors.

Strategy is about competing differently from rivals—doing what competitors don't do or, even better, doing what they can't do!

A company's strategy provides direction and guidance, in terms of not only what the company *should* do but also what it *should not* do. Knowing what not to do can be as important as knowing what to do, strategically. At best, making the wrong strategic moves will prove a distraction and a waste of company resources. At worst, it can bring about unintended long-term consequences that put the company's very survival at risk.

Figure 1.1 illustrates the broad types of actions and approaches that often characterize a company's strategy in a particular business or industry. For a more concrete example of the specific actions constituting a firm's strategy, see Illustration Capsule 1.1 describing Starbucks's strategy in the specialty coffee market.

LO 2

The concept of a *sustainable competitive advantage.*

Strategy and the Quest for Competitive Advantage

The heart and soul of any strategy are the actions in the marketplace that managers are taking to gain a competitive advantage over rivals. A company achieves a **competitive advantage** whenever it has some type of edge over rivals in attracting buyers and coping with competitive forces. There are many routes to competitive advantage, but they all involve either giving buyers what they perceive as superior value compared to the offerings of rival sellers or giving buyers the same value as others at a lower cost to the firm. Superior value can mean a good product at a lower price, a superior product that

FIGURE 1.1 Identifying a Company's Strategy—What to Look For

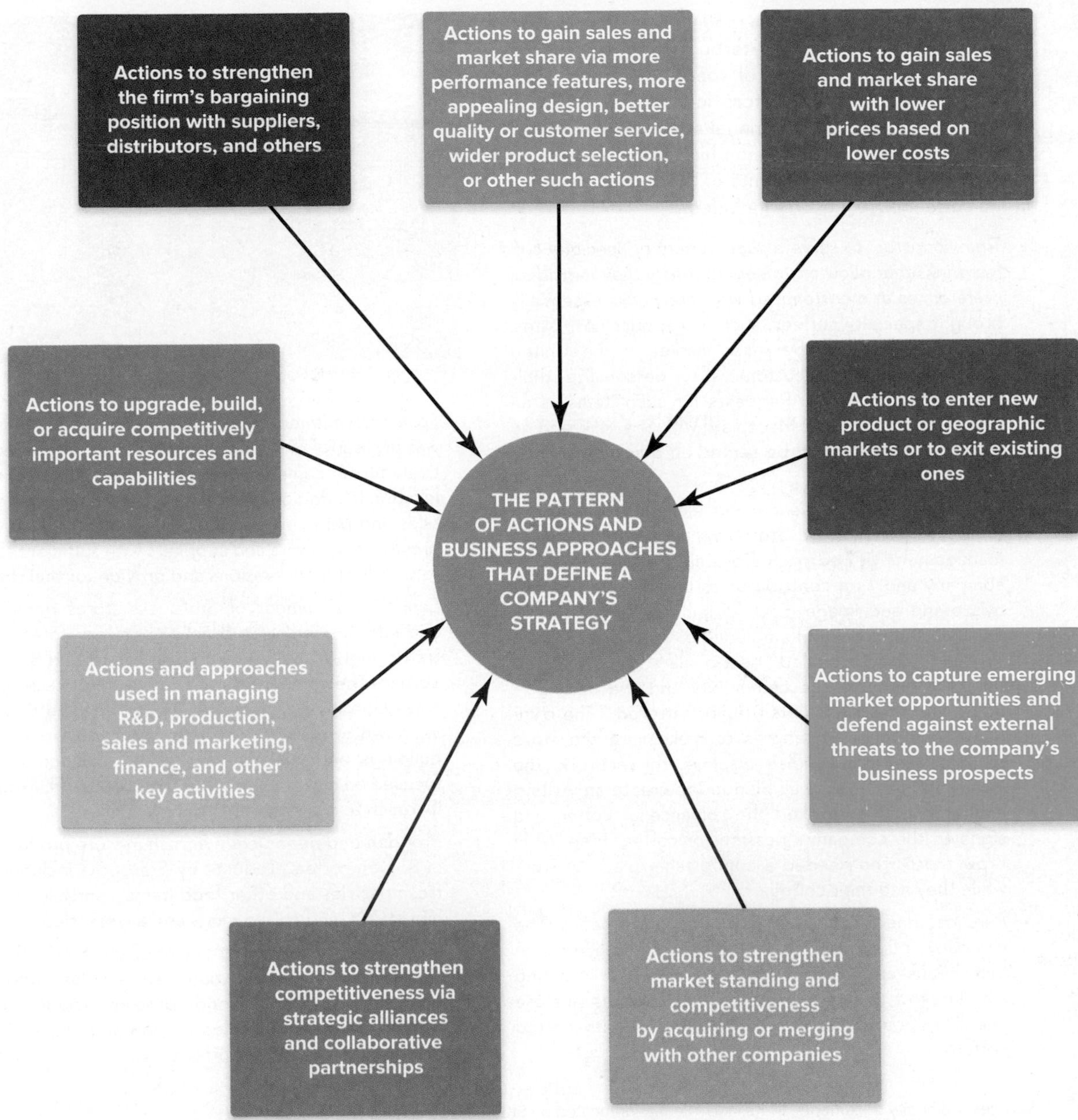

is worth paying more for, or a best-value offering that represents an attractive combination of price, features, quality, service, and other attributes. Delivering superior value or delivering value more efficiently—whatever form it takes—nearly always requires performing value chain activities differently than rivals and building capabilities that are not readily matched. In Illustration Capsule 1.1, it's evident that Starbucks has gained a competitive advantage over its rivals in the coffee shop industry through its efforts to create an upscale experience for coffee drinkers by catering to individualized tastes, enhancing the atmosphere and comfort of the shops, and delivering a premium product

ILLUSTRATION CAPSULE 1.1 Starbucks's Strategy in the Coffeehouse Market

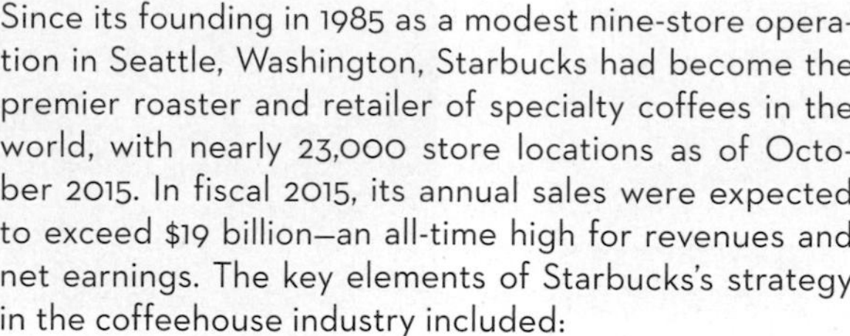

Since its founding in 1985 as a modest nine-store operation in Seattle, Washington, Starbucks had become the premier roaster and retailer of specialty coffees in the world, with nearly 23,000 store locations as of October 2015. In fiscal 2015, its annual sales were expected to exceed $19 billion—an all-time high for revenues and net earnings. The key elements of Starbucks's strategy in the coffeehouse industry included:

© Craig Warga/Bloomberg via Getty Images

- *Train "baristas" to serve a wide variety of specialty coffee drinks that allow customers to satisfy their individual preferences in a customized way.* Starbucks essentially brought specialty coffees, such as cappuccinos, lattes, and macchiatos, to the mass market in the United States, encouraging customers to personalize their coffee-drinking habits. Requests for such items as an "Iced Grande Hazelnut Macchiato with Soy Milk, and *no* Hazelnut Drizzle" could be served up quickly with consistent quality.
- *Emphasize store ambience and elevation of the customer experience at Starbucks stores.* Starbucks's management viewed each store as a billboard for the company and as a contributor to building the company's brand and image. Each detail was scrutinized to enhance the mood and ambience of the store to make sure everything signaled "best-of-class" and reflected the personality of the community and the neighborhood. The thesis was "everything mattered." The company went to great lengths to make sure the store fixtures, the merchandise displays, the artwork, the music, and the aromas all blended to create an inviting environment that evoked the romance of coffee and signaled the company's passion for coffee. Free Wi-Fi drew those who needed a comfortable place to work while they had their coffee.
- *Purchase and roast only top-quality coffee beans.* The company purchased only the highest-quality Arabica beans and carefully roasted coffee to exacting standards of quality and flavor. Starbucks did not use chemicals or artificial flavors when preparing its roasted coffees.
- *Foster commitment to corporate responsibility.* Starbucks was protective of the environment and contributed positively to the communities where Starbucks stores were located. In addition, Starbucks promoted fair trade practices and paid above-market prices for coffee beans to provide its growers and suppliers with sufficient funding to sustain their operations and provide for their families.
- *Expand the number of Starbucks stores domestically and internationally.* Starbucks operated stores in high-traffic, high-visibility locations in the United States and abroad. The company's ability to vary store size and format made it possible to locate stores in settings such as downtown and suburban shopping areas, office buildings, and university campuses. The company also focused on making Starbucks a global brand, expanding its reach to more than 65 countries in 2015.
- *Broaden and periodically refresh in-store product offerings.* Non-coffee products by Starbucks included teas, fresh pastries and other food items, candy, juice drinks, music CDs, and coffee mugs and accessories.
- *Fully exploit the growing power of the Starbucks name and brand image with out-of-store sales.* Starbucks's Consumer Packaged Goods division included domestic and international sales of Frappuccino, coffee ice creams, and Starbucks coffees.

Sources: Company documents, 10-Ks, and information posted on Starbucks's website.

---

produced under environmentally sound fair trade practices. By differentiating itself in this manner from other coffee purveyors, Starbucks has been able to charge prices for its coffee that are well above those of its rivals and far exceed the low cost of its inputs. Its expansion policies have allowed the company to make it easy for customers to find a Starbucks shop almost anywhere, further enhancing the brand and cementing customer loyalty. A creative *distinctive* strategy such as that used by Starbucks is a company's most reliable ticket for developing a competitive advantage over its rivals. If a strategy is not distinctive, then there can be no competitive advantage, since no firm would be meeting customer needs better or operating more efficiently than any other.

If a company's competitive edge holds promise for being *sustainable* (as opposed to just temporary), then so much the better for both the strategy and the company's future profitability. What makes a competitive advantage **sustainable** (or durable), as opposed to temporary, are elements of the strategy that give buyers lasting reasons to prefer a company's products or services over those of competitors—*reasons that competitors are unable to nullify or overcome despite their best efforts.* In the case of Starbucks, the company's unparalleled name recognition, its reputation for high-quality specialty coffees served in a comfortable, inviting atmosphere, and the accessibility of the shops make it difficult for competitors to weaken or overcome Starbucks's competitive advantage. Not only has Starbucks's strategy provided the company with a sustainable competitive advantage, but it has made Starbucks one of the most admired companies on the planet.

CORE CONCEPT

A company achieves a **competitive advantage** when it provides buyers with superior value compared to rival sellers or offers the same value at a lower cost to the firm. The advantage is **sustainable** if it persists despite the best efforts of competitors to match or surpass this advantage.

Five of the most frequently used and dependable strategic approaches to setting a company apart from rivals, building strong customer loyalty, and winning a competitive advantage are:

LO 3

The five most basic strategic approaches for setting a company apart from rivals and winning a sustainable competitive advantage.

1. *A low-cost provider strategy*—achieving a cost-based advantage over rivals. Walmart and Southwest Airlines have earned strong market positions because of the low-cost advantages they have achieved over their rivals. Low-cost provider strategies can produce a durable competitive edge when rivals find it hard to match the low-cost leader's approach to driving costs out of the business.
2. *A broad differentiation strategy*—seeking to differentiate the company's product or service from that of rivals in ways that will appeal to a broad spectrum of buyers. Successful adopters of differentiation strategies include Apple (innovative products), Johnson & Johnson in baby products (product reliability), LVMH (luxury and prestige), and BMW (engineering design and performance). One way to sustain this type of competitive advantage is to be sufficiently innovative to thwart the efforts of clever rivals to copy or closely imitate the product offering.
3. *A focused low-cost strategy*—concentrating on a narrow buyer segment (or market niche) and outcompeting rivals by having lower costs and thus being able to serve niche members at a lower price. Private-label manufacturers of food, health and beauty products, and nutritional supplements use their low-cost advantage to offer supermarket buyers lower prices than those demanded by producers of branded products.
4. *A focused differentiation strategy*—concentrating on a narrow buyer segment (or market niche) and outcompeting rivals by offering buyers customized attributes that meet their specialized needs and tastes better than rivals' products. Lululemon, for example, specializes in high-quality yoga clothing and the like, attracting a devoted set of buyers in the process. Jiffy Lube International in quick oil changes, McAfee in virus protection software, and The Weather Channel in cable TV provide some other examples of this strategy.
5. *A best-cost provider strategy*—giving customers more value for the money by satisfying their expectations on key quality features, performance, and/or service attributes while beating their price expectations. This approach is a hybrid strategy that blends elements of low-cost provider and differentiation strategies; the aim is to have lower costs than rivals while simultaneously offering better differentiating attributes. Target is an example of a company that is known for its hip product design (a reputation it built by featuring limited edition lines by designers

such as Jason Wu), as well as a more appealing shopping ambience for discount store shoppers. Its dual focus on low costs as well as differentiation shows how a best-cost provider strategy can offer customers great value for the money.

Winning a *sustainable* competitive edge over rivals with any of the preceding five strategies generally hinges as much on building competitively valuable expertise and capabilities that rivals cannot readily match as it does on having a distinctive product offering. Clever rivals can nearly always copy the attributes of a popular product or service, but for rivals to match the experience, know-how, and specialized capabilities that a company has developed and perfected over a long period of time is substantially harder to do and takes much longer. FedEx, for example, has superior capabilities in next-day delivery of small packages, while Apple has demonstrated impressive product innovation capabilities in digital music players, smartphones, and e-readers. Hyundai has become the world's fastest-growing automaker as a result of its advanced manufacturing processes and unparalleled quality control systems. Capabilities such as these have been hard for competitors to imitate or best.

LO 4

A company's strategy tends to evolve because of changing circumstances and ongoing efforts by management to improve the strategy.

Why a Company's Strategy Evolves over Time

The appeal of a strategy that yields a sustainable competitive advantage is that it offers the potential for an enduring edge over rivals. However, managers of every company must be willing and ready to modify the strategy in response to changing market conditions, advancing technology, unexpected moves by competitors, shifting buyer needs, emerging market opportunities, and new ideas for improving the strategy. Most of the time, a company's strategy evolves incrementally as management fine-tunes various pieces of the strategy and adjusts the strategy in response to unfolding events.[5] However, on occasion, major strategy shifts are called for, such as when the strategy is clearly failing or when industry conditions change in dramatic ways. Industry environments characterized by high-velocity change require companies to repeatedly adapt their strategies.[6] For example, companies in industries with rapid-fire advances in technology like medical equipment, shale fracking, and smartphones often find it essential to adjust key elements of their strategies several times a year, sometimes even finding it necessary to "reinvent" their approach to providing value to their customers.

Changing circumstances and ongoing management efforts to improve the strategy cause a company's strategy to evolve over time—a condition that makes the task of crafting strategy a *work in progress*, not a one-time event.

Regardless of whether a company's strategy changes gradually or swiftly, the important point is that the task of crafting strategy is not a one-time event but always a work in progress. Adapting to new conditions and constantly evaluating what is working well enough to continue and what needs to be improved are normal parts of the strategy-making process, resulting in an *evolving strategy*.[7]

A Company's Strategy Is Partly Proactive and Partly Reactive

A company's strategy is shaped partly by management analysis and choice and partly by the necessity of adapting and learning by doing.

The evolving nature of a company's strategy means that the typical company strategy is a blend of (1) *proactive,* planned initiatives to improve the company's financial performance and secure a competitive edge and (2) *reactive* responses to unanticipated developments and fresh market conditions. The biggest portion of a company's current strategy flows from previously initiated actions that have proven themselves in the marketplace and newly launched initiatives aimed at edging out rivals and boosting financial performance. This part of management's action plan for running the company is its **deliberate strategy,** consisting of proactive strategy elements that

FIGURE 1.2 A Company's Strategy Is a Blend of Proactive Initiatives and Reactive Adjustments

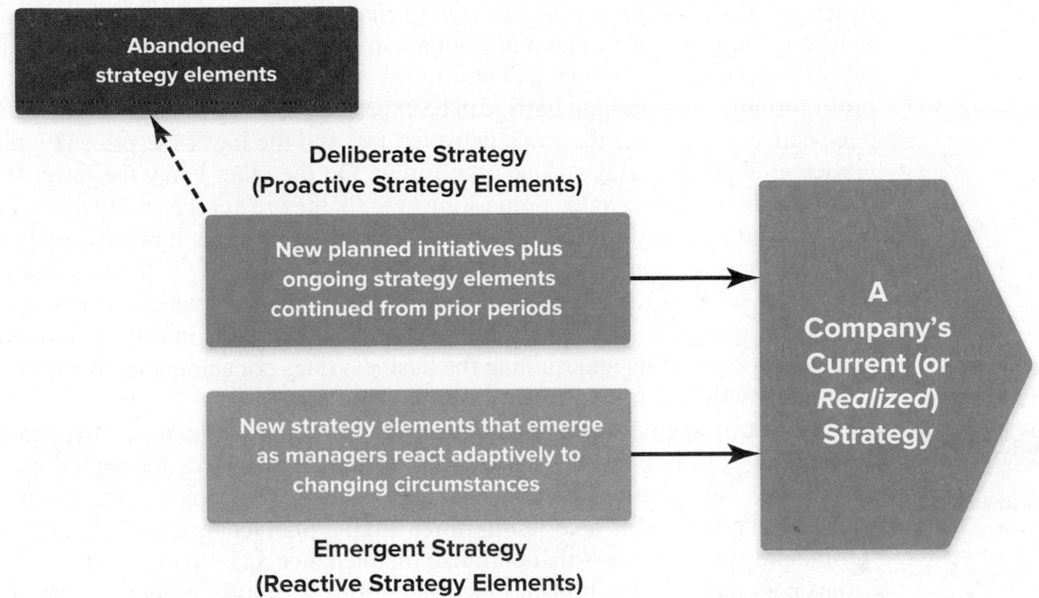

are both planned and realized as planned (while other planned strategy elements may not work out and are abandoned in consequence)—see Figure 1.2.[8]

But managers must always be willing to supplement or modify the proactive strategy elements with as-needed reactions to unanticipated conditions. Inevitably, there will be occasions when market and competitive conditions take an unexpected turn that calls for some kind of strategic reaction. Hence, *a portion of a company's strategy is always developed on the fly,* coming as a response to fresh strategic maneuvers on the part of rival firms, unexpected shifts in customer requirements, fast-changing technological developments, newly appearing market opportunities, a changing political or economic climate, or other unanticipated happenings in the surrounding environment. These adaptive strategy adjustments make up the firm's **emergent strategy.** A company's strategy *in toto* (its *realized strategy*) thus tends to be a *combination* of proactive and reactive elements, with certain strategy elements being *abandoned* because they have become obsolete or ineffective. A company's realized strategy can be observed in the pattern of its actions over time, which is a far better indicator than any of its strategic plans on paper or any public pronouncements about its strategy.

> **CORE CONCEPT**
>
> A company's **deliberate strategy** consists of *proactive* strategy elements that are planned; its **emergent strategy** consists of *reactive* strategy elements that emerge as changing conditions warrant.

A COMPANY'S STRATEGY AND ITS BUSINESS MODEL

At the core of every sound strategy is the company's **business model.** A business model is management's blueprint for delivering a valuable product or service to customers in a manner that will generate revenues sufficient to cover costs and yield an attractive profit.[9] The two elements of a company's business model are (1) its *customer value proposition* and (2) its *profit formula.* The customer value proposition lays out

LO 5

Why it is important for a company to have a viable business model that outlines the company's customer value proposition and its profit formula.

the company's approach to satisfying buyer wants and needs at a price customers will consider a good value. The profit formula describes the company's approach to determining a cost structure that will allow for acceptable profits, given the pricing tied to its customer value proposition. Figure 1.3 illustrates the elements of the business model in terms of what is known as the *value-price-cost framework*.[10] As the framework indicates, the customer value proposition can be expressed as $V - P$, which is essentially the customers' perception of how much value they are getting for the money. The profit formula, on a per-unit basis, can be expressed as $P - C$. Plainly, from a customer perspective, the greater the value delivered (V) and the lower the price (P), the more attractive is the company's value proposition. On the other hand, the lower the costs (C), given the customer value proposition ($V - P$), the greater the ability of the business model to be a moneymaker. Thus the profit formula reveals how efficiently a company can meet customer wants and needs and deliver on the value proposition. The nitty-gritty issue surrounding a company's business model is whether it can execute its customer value proposition profitably. Just because company managers have crafted a strategy for competing and running the business does not automatically mean that the strategy will lead to profitability—it may or it may not.

CORE CONCEPT

A company's **business model** sets forth the logic for how its strategy will create value for customers and at the same time generate revenues sufficient to cover costs and realize a profit.

Aircraft engine manufacturer Rolls-Royce employs an innovative "power-by-the-hour" business model that charges airlines leasing fees for engine use, maintenance, and repairs based on actual hours flown. The company retains ownership of the engines and is able to minimize engine maintenance costs through the use of sophisticated sensors that optimize maintenance and repair schedules. Gillette's business model in razor blades involves selling a "master product"—the razor—at an attractively low price and then making money on repeat purchases of razor blades that can be produced cheaply and sold at high profit margins. Printer manufacturers like Hewlett-Packard, Canon, and Epson pursue much the same business model as Gillette—selling printers at a low (virtually break-even) price and making large profit margins on the repeat purchases of ink cartridges and other printer supplies. McDonald's invented the business model for fast food—providing value to customers in the form of economical quick-service meals at clean, convenient locations. Its profit formula involves such elements as standardized cost-efficient store design, stringent specifications for ingredients, detailed operating procedures for each unit, sizable investment in human resources and training, and heavy reliance on advertising and in-store promotions to drive volume. Illustration Capsule 1.2 describes three contrasting business models in radio broadcasting.

FIGURE 1.3 The Business Model and the Value-Price-Cost Framework

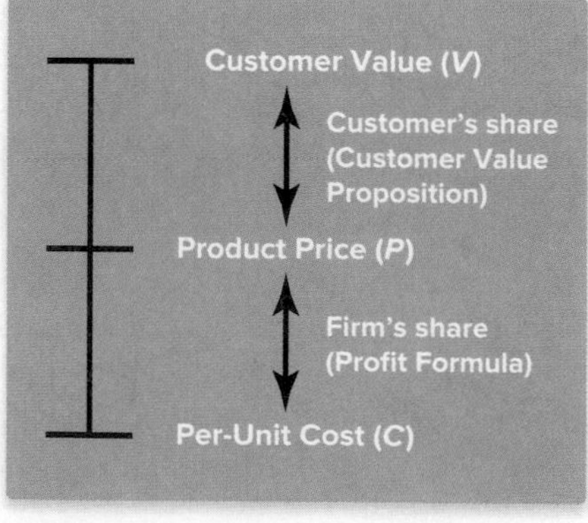

ILLUSTRATION CAPSULE 1.2

Pandora, SiriusXM, and Over-the-Air Broadcast Radio: Three Contrasting Business Models

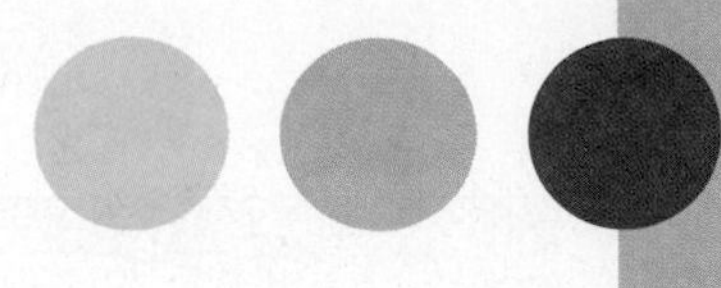

© Rob Kim/Getty Images

	Pandora	SiriusXM	Over-the-Air Radio Broadcasters
Customer value proposition	• Through free-of-charge Internet radio service, allowed PC, tablet computer, and smartphone users to create up to 100 personalized music and comedy stations. • Utilized algorithms to generate playlists based on users' predicted music preferences. • Offered programming interrupted by brief, occasional ads; eliminated advertising for Pandora One subscribers.	• For a monthly subscription fee, provided satellite-based music, news, sports, national and regional weather, traffic reports in limited areas, and talk radio programming. • Also offered subscribers streaming Internet channels and the ability to create personalized commercial-free stations for online and mobile listening. • Offered programming interrupted only by brief, occasional ads.	• Provided free-of-charge music, national and local news, local traffic reports, national and local weather, and talk radio programming. • Included frequent programming interruption for ads.
Profit formula	*Revenue generation:* Display, audio, and video ads targeted to different audiences and sold to local and national buyers; subscription revenues generated from an advertising-free option called Pandora One. *Cost structure:* Fixed costs associated with developing software for computers, tablets, and smartphones. Fixed and variable costs related to operating data centers to support streaming network, content royalties, marketing, and support activities.	*Revenue generation:* Monthly subscription fees, sales of satellite radio equipment, and advertising revenues. *Cost structure:* Fixed costs associated with operating a satellite-based music delivery service and streaming Internet service. Fixed and variable costs related to programming and content royalties, marketing, and support activities.	*Revenue generation:* Advertising sales to national and local businesses. *Cost structure:* Fixed costs associated with terrestrial broadcasting operations. Fixed and variable costs related to local news reporting, advertising sales operations, network affiliate fees, programming and content royalties, commercial production activities, and support activities.

Pandora	SiriusXM	Over-the-Air Radio Broadcasters
Profit margin: Profitability dependent on generating sufficient advertising revenues and subscription revenues to cover costs and provide attractive profits.	*Profit margin:* Profitability dependent on attracting a sufficiently large number of subscribers to cover costs and provide attractive profits.	*Profit margin:* Profitability dependent on generating sufficient advertising revenues to cover costs and provide attractive profits.

WHAT MAKES A STRATEGY A WINNER?

LO 6

The three tests of a winning strategy.

Three tests can be applied to determine whether a strategy is a *winning strategy:*

1. ***The Fit Test:*** *How well does the strategy fit the company's situation?* To qualify as a winner, a strategy has to be well matched to industry and competitive conditions, a company's best market opportunities, and other pertinent aspects of the business environment in which the company operates. No strategy can work well unless it exhibits good *external fit* with respect to prevailing market conditions. At the same time, a winning strategy must be tailored to the company's resources and competitive capabilities and be supported by a complementary set of functional activities (i.e., activities in the realms of supply chain management, operations, sales and marketing, and so on). That is, it must also exhibit *internal fit* and be compatible with a company's ability to execute the strategy in a competent manner. Unless a strategy exhibits good fit with both the external and internal aspects of a company's overall situation, it is likely to be an underperformer and fall short of producing winning results. Winning strategies also exhibit *dynamic fit* in the sense that they evolve over time in a manner that maintains close and effective alignment with the company's situation even as external and internal conditions change.[11]

To pass the *fit test,* a strategy must exhibit fit along three dimensions: (1) external, (2) internal, and (3) dynamic.

2. ***The Competitive Advantage Test:*** *Is the strategy helping the company achieve a sustainable competitive advantage?* Strategies that fail to achieve a persistent competitive advantage over rivals are unlikely to produce superior performance for more than a brief period of time. Winning strategies enable a company to achieve a competitive advantage over key rivals that is long-lasting. The bigger and more durable the competitive advantage, the more powerful it is.
3. ***The Performance Test:*** *Is the strategy producing superior company performance?* The mark of a winning strategy is strong company performance. Two kinds of performance indicators tell the most about the caliber of a company's strategy: (1) competitive strength and market standing and (2) profitability and financial strength. Above-average financial performance or gains in market share, competitive position, or profitability are signs of a winning strategy.

A **winning strategy** must pass three tests:

1. The fit test
2. The competitive advantage test
3. The performance test

Strategies—either existing or proposed—that come up short on one or more of the preceding tests are plainly less appealing than strategies passing all three tests with flying colors. New initiatives that don't seem to match the company's internal and external situations should be scrapped before they come to fruition, while existing strategies must be scrutinized on a regular basis to ensure they have good fit, offer a competitive advantage, and are contributing to above-average performance or performance improvements. Failure to pass one or more of the three tests should prompt managers to make immediate changes in an existing strategy.

WHY CRAFTING AND EXECUTING STRATEGY ARE IMPORTANT TASKS

Crafting and executing strategy are top-priority managerial tasks for two big reasons. First, a clear and reasoned strategy is management's prescription for doing business, its road map to competitive advantage, its game plan for pleasing customers, and its formula for improving performance. High-performing enterprises are nearly always the product of astute, creative, and proactive strategy making. Companies don't get to the top of the industry rankings or stay there with flawed strategies, copycat strategies, or timid attempts to try to do better. Only a handful of companies can boast of hitting home runs in the marketplace due to lucky breaks or the good fortune of having stumbled into the right market at the right time with the right product. Even if this is the case, success will not be lasting unless the companies subsequently craft a strategy that capitalizes on their luck, builds on what is working, and discards the rest. So there can be little argument that the process of crafting a company's strategy matters—and matters a lot.

Second, even the best-conceived strategies will result in performance shortfalls if they are not executed proficiently. The processes of crafting and executing strategies must go hand in hand if a company is to be successful in the long term. The chief executive officer of one successful company put it well when he said:

> In the main, our competitors are acquainted with the same fundamental concepts and techniques and approaches that we follow, and they are as free to pursue them as we are. More often than not, the difference between their level of success and ours lies in the relative thoroughness and self-discipline with which we and they develop and execute our strategies for the future.

Good Strategy + Good Strategy Execution = Good Management

Crafting and executing strategy are thus core management tasks. Among all the things managers do, nothing affects a company's ultimate success or failure more fundamentally than how well its management team charts the company's direction, develops competitively effective strategic moves, and pursues what needs to be done internally to produce good day-in, day-out strategy execution and operating excellence. Indeed, *good strategy and good strategy execution are the most telling and trustworthy signs of good management.* The rationale for using the twin standards of good strategy making and good strategy execution to determine whether a company is well managed is therefore compelling: *The better conceived a company's strategy and the more competently it is executed, the more likely the company will be a standout performer in the marketplace.* In stark contrast, a company that lacks clear-cut direction, has a flawed strategy, or can't execute its strategy competently is a company whose financial performance is probably suffering, whose business is at long-term risk, and whose management is sorely lacking.

THE ROAD AHEAD

How well a company performs is directly attributable to the caliber of its strategy and the proficiency with which the strategy is executed.

Throughout the chapters to come and in Part 2 of this text, the spotlight is on the foremost question in running a business enterprise: *What must managers do, and do well, to make a company a winner in the marketplace?* The answer that emerges is that doing a good job of managing inherently requires good strategic thinking and good management of the strategy-making, strategy-executing process.

The mission of this book is to provide a solid overview of what every business student and aspiring manager needs to know about crafting and executing strategy. We will explore what good strategic thinking entails, describe the core concepts and tools of strategic analysis, and examine the ins and outs of crafting and executing strategy. The accompanying cases will help build your skills in both diagnosing how well the strategy-making, strategy-executing task is being performed and prescribing actions for how the strategy in question or its execution can be improved. The strategic management course that you are enrolled in may also include a strategy simulation exercise in which you will run a company in head-to-head competition with companies run by your classmates. Your mastery of the strategic management concepts presented in the following chapters will put you in a strong position to craft a winning strategy for your company and figure out how to execute it in a cost-effective and profitable manner. As you progress through the chapters of the text and the activities assigned during the term, we hope to convince you that first-rate capabilities in crafting and executing strategy are essential to good management.

As you tackle the content and accompanying activities of this book, ponder the following observation by the essayist and poet Ralph Waldo Emerson: "Commerce is a game of skill which many people play, but which few play well." If your efforts help you become a savvy player and better equip you to succeed in business, the time and energy you spend here will indeed prove worthwhile.

KEY POINTS

1. A company's strategy is its game plan to attract customers, outperform its competitors, and achieve superior profitability.
2. The central thrust of a company's strategy is undertaking moves to build and strengthen the company's long-term competitive position and financial performance by *competing differently* from rivals and gaining a sustainable competitive advantage over them.
3. A company achieves a *competitive advantage* when it provides buyers with superior value compared to rival sellers or offers the same value at a lower cost to the firm. The advantage is *sustainable* if it persists despite the best efforts of competitors to match or surpass this advantage.
4. A company's strategy typically evolves over time, emerging from a blend of (1) proactive deliberate actions on the part of company managers to improve the strategy and (2) reactive emergent responses to unanticipated developments and fresh market conditions.
5. A company's business model sets forth the logic for how its strategy will create value for customers and at the same time generate revenues sufficient to cover costs and realize a profit. Thus, it contains two crucial elements: (1) the *customer value proposition*—a plan for satisfying customer wants and needs at a price

customers will consider good value, and (2) the *profit formula*—a plan for a cost structure that will enable the company to deliver the customer value proposition profitably. These elements are illustrated by the value-price-cost framework.

6. A winning strategy will pass three tests: (1) *fit* (external, internal, and dynamic consistency), (2) *competitive advantage* (durable competitive advantage), and (3) *performance* (outstanding financial and market performance).
7. Crafting and executing strategy are core management functions. How well a company performs and the degree of market success it enjoys are directly attributable to the caliber of its strategy and the proficiency with which the strategy is executed.

ASSURANCE OF LEARNING EXERCISES

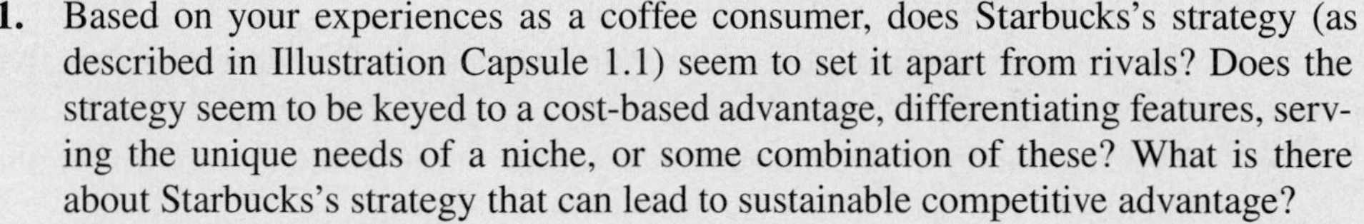

1. Based on your experiences as a coffee consumer, does Starbucks's strategy (as described in Illustration Capsule 1.1) seem to set it apart from rivals? Does the strategy seem to be keyed to a cost-based advantage, differentiating features, serving the unique needs of a niche, or some combination of these? What is there about Starbucks's strategy that can lead to sustainable competitive advantage? connect LO 1, LO 2, LO 3
2. Elements of the Hershey Company's strategy have evolved in meaningful ways since the company's founding as an American chocolate manufacturer in 1900. After reviewing the company's history at **www.thehersheycompany.com/about-hershey/our-story/hersheys-history.aspx** and the links at the company's investor relations site (**www.thehersheycompany.com/investors/company-profile.aspx**), prepare a one- to two-page report that discusses how its strategy has evolved. Your report should also assess how well Hershey's strategy passes the three tests of a winning strategy. LO 4, LO 6
3. Go to **investor.siriusxm.com** and check whether Sirius XM's recent financial reports indicate that its business model is working. Are its subscription fees increasing or declining? Are its revenue stream advertising and equipment sales growing or declining? Does its cost structure allow for acceptable profit margins? connect LO 5

EXERCISE FOR SIMULATION PARTICIPANTS

Three basic questions must be answered by managers of organizations of all sizes as they begin the process of crafting strategy:

- What is our present situation?
- Where do we want to go from here?
- How are we going to get there?

After you have read the Participant's Guide or Player's Manual for the strategy simulation exercise that you will participate in during this academic term, you and your co-managers should come up with brief one- or two-paragraph answers to these three questions *prior to* entering your first set of decisions. While your answer to the first of the three questions can be developed from your reading of the manual, the second and third questions will require a collaborative discussion among the members of your company's management team about how you intend to manage the company you have been assigned to run.

1. *What is our company's current situation?* A substantive answer to this question should cover the following issues:
   - Is your company in a good, average, or weak competitive position vis-à-vis rival companies?
   - Does your company appear to be in a sound financial condition?
   - Does it appear to have a competitive advantage, and is it likely to be sustainable?
   - What problems does your company have that need to be addressed?

LO 1, LO 2, LO 3

2. *Where do we want to take the company during the time we are in charge?* A complete answer to this question should say something about each of the following:
   - What goals or aspirations do you have for your company?
   - What do you want the company to be known for?
   - What market share would you like your company to have after the first five decision rounds?
   - By what amount or percentage would you like to increase total profits of the company by the end of the final decision round?
   - What kinds of performance outcomes will signal that you and your co-managers are managing the company in a successful manner?

LO 4, LO 6

3. *How are we going to get there?* Your answer should cover these issues:
   - Which one of the basic strategic and competitive approaches discussed in this chapter do you think makes the most sense to pursue?
   - What kind of competitive advantage over rivals will you try to achieve?
   - How would you describe the company's business model?
   - What kind of actions will support these objectives?

LO 4, LO 5

ENDNOTES

[1] B. R, "Strategy," *The Economist,* October 19, 2012, **www.economist.com/blogs/schumpeter/2012/10/z-business-quotations-1** (accessed January 4, 2014).
[2] Jan Rivkin, "An Alternative Approach to Making Strategic Choices," Harvard Business School case 9-702-433, 2001.
[3] Michael E. Porter, "What Is Strategy?" *Harvard Business Review* 74, no. 6 (November–December 1996), pp. 65–67.
[4] Ibid.
[5] Eric T. Anderson and Duncan Simester, "A Step-by-Step Guide to Smart Business Experiments," *Harvard Business Review* 89, no. 3 (March 2011).
[6] Shona L. Brown and Kathleen M. Eisenhardt, *Competing on the Edge: Strategy as Structured Chaos* (Boston, MA: Harvard Business School Press, 1998).
[7] Cynthia A. Montgomery, "Putting Leadership Back into Strategy," *Harvard Business Review* 86, no. 1 (January 2008).
[8] Henry Mintzberg and J. A. Waters, "Of Strategies, Deliberate and Emergent," *Strategic Management Journal* 6 (1985); Costas Markides, "Strategy as Balance: From 'Either-Or' to 'And,' " *Business Strategy Review* 12, no. 3 (September 2001).
[9] Mark W. Johnson, Clayton M. Christensen, and Henning Kagermann, "Reinventing Your Business Model," *Harvard Business Review* 86, no. 12 (December 2008); Joan Magretta, "Why Business Models Matter," *Harvard Business Review* 80, no. 5 (May 2002).
[10] A. Brandenburger and H. Stuart, "Value-Based Strategy," *Journal of Economics and Management Strategy* 5 (1996), pp. 5–24; D. Hoopes, T. Madsen, and G. Walker, "Guest Editors' Introduction to the Special Issue: Why Is There a Resource-Based View? Toward a Theory of Competitive Heterogeneity," *Strategic Management Journal* 24 (2003), pp. 889–992; M. Peteraf and J. Barney, "Unravelling the Resource-Based Tangle," *Managerial and Decision Economics* 24 (2003), pp. 309–323.
[11] Rivkin, "An Alternative Approach to Making Strategic Choices."

CHAPTER 2

Charting a Company's Direction

Its Vision, Mission, Objectives, and Strategy

© Fanatic Studio/Alamy Stock Photo

Learning Objectives

THIS CHAPTER WILL HELP YOU UNDERSTAND:

LO 1 Why it is critical for company managers to have a clear strategic vision of where a company needs to head.

LO 2 The importance of setting both strategic and financial objectives.

LO 3 Why the strategic initiatives taken at various organizational levels must be tightly coordinated to achieve companywide performance targets.

LO 4 What a company must do to achieve operating excellence and to execute its strategy proficiently.

LO 5 The role and responsibility of a company's board of directors in overseeing the strategic management process.

Sound strategy starts with having the right goal.

Michael Porter—*Professor and consultant*

Good business leaders create a vision, articulate the vision, passionately own the vision, and relentlessly drive it to completion.

Jack Welch—*Former CEO of General Electric*

Apple is so focused on its vision that it does things in a very careful, deliberate way.

John Sculley—*Former CEO of Apple*

Crafting and executing strategy are the heart and soul of managing a business enterprise. But exactly what is involved in developing a strategy and executing it proficiently? What goes into charting a company's strategic course and long-term direction? Is any analysis required? Does a company need a strategic plan? What are the various components of the strategy-making, strategy-executing process and to what extent are company personnel—aside from senior management—involved in the process?

This chapter presents an overview of the ins and outs of crafting and executing company strategies. The focus is on management's direction-setting responsibilities—charting a strategic course, setting performance targets, and choosing a strategy capable of producing the desired outcomes. There is coverage of why strategy making is a task for a company's entire management team and which kinds of strategic decisions tend to be made at which levels of management. The chapter concludes with a look at the roles and responsibilities of a company's board of directors and how good corporate governance protects shareholder interests and promotes good management.

WHAT DOES THE STRATEGY-MAKING, STRATEGY-EXECUTING PROCESS ENTAIL?

Crafting and executing a company's strategy is an ongoing process that consists of five interrelated stages:

1. *Developing a strategic vision* that charts the company's long-term direction, a *mission statement* that describes the company's purpose, and a set of *core values* to guide the pursuit of the vision and mission.
2. *Setting objectives* for measuring the company's performance and tracking its progress in moving in the intended long-term direction.
3. *Crafting a strategy* for advancing the company along the path management has charted and achieving its performance objectives.
4. *Executing the chosen strategy* efficiently and effectively.

FIGURE 2.1 The Strategy-Making, Strategy-Executing Process

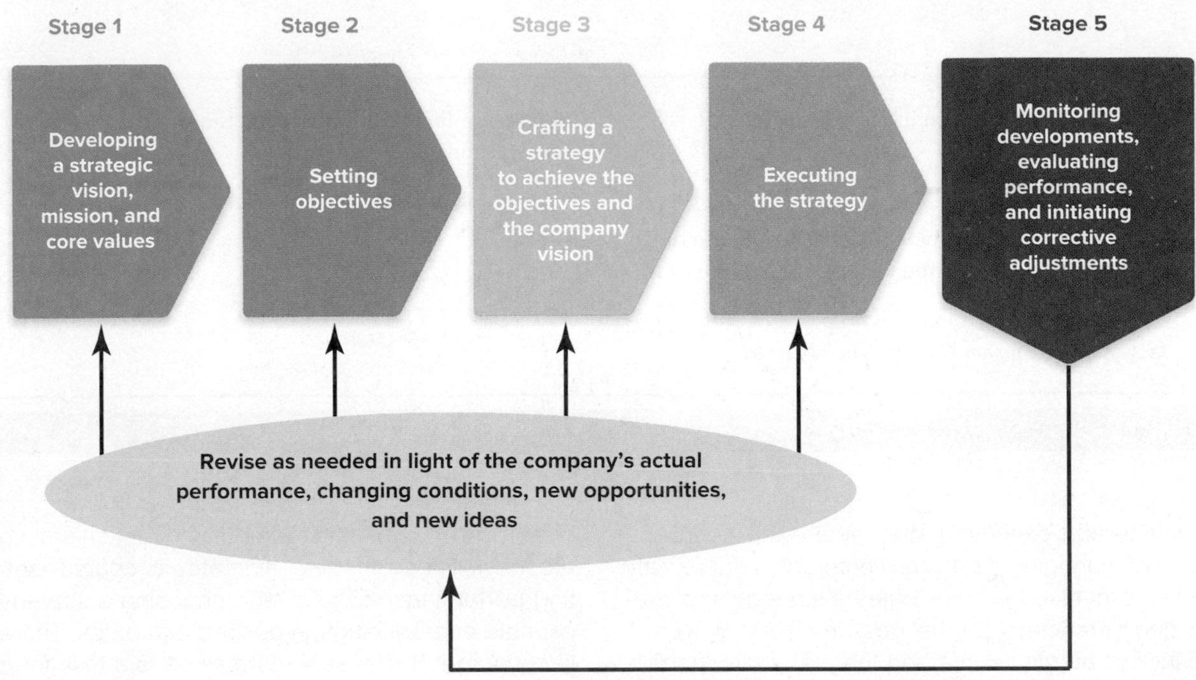

5. *Monitoring developments, evaluating performance, and initiating corrective adjustments* in the company's vision and mission statement, objectives, strategy, or approach to strategy execution in light of actual experience, changing conditions, new ideas, and new opportunities.

Figure 2.1 displays this five-stage process, which we examine next in some detail. The first three stages of the strategic management process involve making a strategic plan. A **strategic plan** maps out where a company is headed, establishes strategic and financial targets, and outlines the competitive moves and approaches to be used in achieving the desired business results.[1] We explain this more fully at the conclusion of our discussion of stage 3, later in this chapter.

STAGE 1: DEVELOPING A STRATEGIC VISION, MISSION STATEMENT, AND SET OF CORE VALUES

LO 1

Why it is critical for company managers to have a clear strategic vision of where a company needs to head.

Very early in the strategy-making process, a company's senior managers must wrestle with the issue of what directional path the company should take. Can the company's prospects be improved by changing its product offerings, or the markets in which it participates, or the customers it aims to serve? Deciding to commit the company to one path versus another pushes managers to draw some carefully reasoned conclusions about whether the company's present strategic course offers attractive opportunities for growth and profitability or whether changes of one kind or another in the company's strategy and long-term direction are needed.

Developing a Strategic Vision

Top management's views about the company's long-term direction and what product-market-customer business mix seems optimal for the road ahead constitute a **strategic vision** for the company. A strategic vision delineates management's aspirations for the company's future, providing a panoramic view of "where we are going" and a convincing rationale for why this makes good business sense. A strategic vision thus points an organization in a particular direction, charts a strategic path for it to follow, builds commitment to the future course of action, and molds organizational identity. A clearly articulated strategic vision communicates management's aspirations to stakeholders (customers, employees, stockholders, suppliers, etc.) and helps steer the energies of company personnel in a common direction. The vision of Google's cofounders Larry Page and Sergey Brin "to organize the world's information and make it universally accessible and useful" provides a good example. In serving as the company's guiding light, it has captured the imagination of stakeholders and the public at large, served as the basis for crafting the company's strategic actions, and aided internal efforts to mobilize and direct the company's resources.

CORE CONCEPT

A **strategic vision** describes management's aspirations for the company's future and the course and direction charted to achieve them.

Well-conceived visions are *distinctive* and *specific* to a particular organization; they avoid generic, feel-good statements like "We will become a global leader and the first choice of customers in every market we serve."[2] Likewise, a strategic vision proclaiming management's quest "to be the market leader" or "to be the most innovative" or "to be recognized as the best company in the industry" offers scant guidance about a company's long-term direction or the kind of company that management is striving to build.

A surprising number of the vision statements found on company websites and in annual reports are vague and unrevealing, saying very little about the company's future direction. Some could apply to almost any company in any industry. Many read like a public relations statement—high-sounding words that someone came up with because it is fashionable for companies to have an official vision statement.[3] An example is Hilton Hotel's vision "to fill the earth with light and the warmth of hospitality," which simply borders on the incredulous. The real purpose of a vision statement is to serve as a management tool for giving the organization a sense of direction.

For a strategic vision to function as a valuable management tool, it must convey what top executives want the business to look like and provide managers at all organizational levels with a reference point in making strategic decisions and preparing the company for the future. It must say something definitive about how the company's leaders intend to position the company beyond where it is today. Table 2.1 provides some dos and don'ts in composing an effectively worded vision statement. Illustration Capsule 2.1 provides a critique of the strategic visions of several prominent companies.

An effectively communicated vision is a valuable management tool for enlisting the commitment of company personnel to actions that move the company in the intended long-term direction.

Communicating the Strategic Vision

A strategic vision has little value to the organization unless it's effectively communicated down the line to lower-level managers and employees. A vision cannot provide direction for middle managers or inspire and energize employees unless everyone in the company is familiar with it and can observe senior management's commitment to the vision. It is particularly important for executives to provide a compelling rationale for a dramatically *new* strategic vision and company direction. When company personnel don't understand or accept the need for redirecting organizational efforts, they are prone to resist change. Hence, explaining the basis for the new direction,

TABLE 2.1 Wording a Vision Statement—the Dos and Don'ts

The Dos	The Don'ts
Be graphic. Paint a clear picture of where the company is headed and the market position(s) the company is striving to stake out.	**Don't be vague or incomplete.** Never skimp on specifics about where the company is headed or how the company intends to prepare for the future.
Be forward-looking and directional. Describe the strategic course that will help the company prepare for the future.	**Don't dwell on the present.** A vision is not about what a company once did or does now; it's about "where we are going."
Keep it focused. Focus on providing managers with guidance in making decisions and allocating resources.	**Don't use overly broad language.** Avoid all-inclusive language that gives the company license to pursue any opportunity.
Have some wiggle room. Language that allows some flexibility allows the directional course to be adjusted as market, customer, and technology circumstances change.	**Don't state the vision in bland or uninspiring terms.** The best vision statements have the power to motivate company personnel and inspire shareholder confidence about the company's future.
Be sure the journey is feasible. The path and direction should be within the realm of what the company can accomplish; over time, a company should be able to demonstrate measurable progress in achieving the vision.	**Don't be generic.** A vision statement that could apply to companies in any of several industries (or to any of several companies in the same industry) is not specific enough to provide any guidance.
Indicate why the directional path makes good business sense. The directional path should be in the long-term interests of stakeholders (especially shareholders, employees, and suppliers).	**Don't rely on superlatives.** Visions that claim the company's strategic course is the "best" or "most successful" usually lack specifics about the path the company is taking to get there.
Make it memorable. A well-stated vision is short, easily communicated, and memorable. Ideally, it should be reducible to a few choice lines or a one-phrase slogan.	**Don't run on and on.** A vision statement that is not concise and to the point will tend to lose its audience.

Sources: John P. Kotter, *Leading Change* (Boston: Harvard Business School Press, 1996); Hugh Davidson, *The Committed Enterprise* (Oxford: Butterworth Heinemann, 2002); Michel Robert, *Strategy Pure and Simple II* (New York: McGraw-Hill, 1992).

addressing employee concerns head-on, calming fears, lifting spirits, and providing updates and progress reports as events unfold all become part of the task in mobilizing support for the vision and winning commitment to needed actions.

Winning the support of organization members for the vision nearly always requires putting "where we are going and why" in writing, distributing the statement organizationwide, and having top executives personally explain the vision and its rationale to as many people as feasible. Ideally, executives should present their vision for the company in a manner that reaches out and grabs people. An engaging and convincing strategic vision has enormous motivational value—for the same reason that a stonemason is more inspired by the opportunity to build a great cathedral for the ages than a house. Thus, executive ability to paint a convincing and inspiring picture of a company's journey to a future destination is an important element of effective strategic leadership.

ILLUSTRATION CAPSULE 2.1

Examples of Strategic Visions—How Well Do They Measure Up?

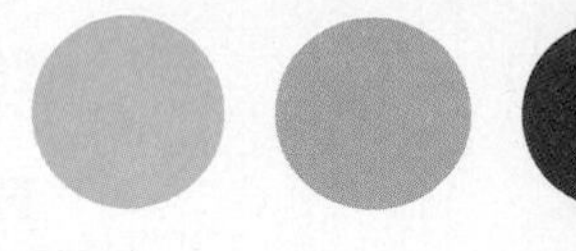

© Jeff Greenberg/UIG via Getty Images

Vision Statement	Effective Elements	Shortcomings
Whole Foods Whole Foods Market is a dynamic leader in the quality food business. We are a mission-driven company that aims to set the standards of excellence for food retailers. We are building a business in which high standards permeate all aspects of our company. Quality is a state of mind at Whole Foods Market. Our motto—Whole Foods, Whole People, Whole Planet—emphasizes that our vision reaches far beyond just being a food retailer. Our success in fulfilling our vision is measured by customer satisfaction, team member happiness and excellence, return on capital investment, improvement in the state of the environment and local and larger community support. Our ability to instill a clear sense of interdependence among our various stakeholders (the people who are interested and benefit from the success of our company) is contingent upon our efforts to communicate more often, more openly, and more compassionately. Better communication equals better understanding and more trust.	• Forward-looking • Graphic • Focused • Makes good business sense	• Long • Not memorable
Keurig Become the world's leading personal beverage systems company.	• Focused • Flexible • Makes good business sense	• Not graphic • Lacks specifics • Not forward-looking
Nike NIKE, Inc. fosters a culture of invention. We create products, services and experiences for today's athlete* while solving problems for the next generation. *If you have a body, you are an athlete.	• Forward-looking • Flexible	• Vague and lacks detail • Not focused • Generic • Not necessarily feasible

Note: Developed with Frances C. Thunder.

Source: Company websites (accessed online February 12, 2016).

Expressing the Essence of the Vision in a Slogan The task of effectively conveying the vision to company personnel is assisted when management can capture the vision of where to head in a catchy or easily remembered slogan. A number of organizations have summed up their vision in a brief phrase. Ben & Jerry's vision is "Making the best possible ice cream, in the nicest possible way," while Charles Schwab's is simply "Helping investors help themselves." Disney's overarching vision for its five business groups—theme parks, movie studios, television channels, consumer products, and interactive media entertainment—is to "create happiness by providing the finest in entertainment for people of all ages, everywhere." Even Scotland Yard has a catchy vision, which is to "make London the safest major city in the world." Creating a short slogan to illuminate an organization's direction and using it repeatedly as a reminder of "where we are headed and why" helps rally organization members to maintain their focus and hurdle whatever obstacles lie in the company's path.

Why a Sound, Well-Communicated Strategic Vision Matters A well-thought-out, forcefully communicated strategic vision pays off in several respects: (1) It crystallizes senior executives' own views about the firm's long-term direction; (2) it reduces the risk of rudderless decision making; (3) it is a tool for winning the support of organization members to help make the vision a reality; (4) it provides a beacon for lower-level managers in setting departmental objectives and crafting departmental strategies that are in sync with the company's overall strategy; and (5) it helps an organization prepare for the future. When top executives are able to demonstrate significant progress in achieving these five benefits, the first step in organizational direction setting has been successfully completed.

The distinction between a strategic vision and a mission statement is fairly clear-cut: A **strategic vision** portrays a company's aspirations for its *future* ("where we are going"), whereas a company's **mission** describes the scope and purpose of its *present* business ("who we are, what we do, and why we are here").

Developing a Company Mission Statement

The defining characteristic of a strategic vision is what it says about the company's *future strategic course*—"the direction we are headed and the shape of our business in the future." It is aspirational. In contrast, a **mission statement** describes the enterprise's *present business and purpose*—"who we are, what we do, and why we are here." It is purely descriptive. Ideally, a company mission statement (1) identifies the company's products and/or services, (2) specifies the buyer needs that the company seeks to satisfy and the customer groups or markets that it serves, and (3) gives the company its own identity. The mission statements that one finds in company annual reports or posted on company websites are typically quite brief; some do a better job than others of conveying what the enterprise's current business operations and purpose are all about.

Consider, for example, the mission statement of Singapore Airlines, which is consistently rated among the world's best in terms of passenger safety and comfort:

> Singapore Airlines is a global company dedicated to providing air transportation services of the highest quality and to maximizing returns for the benefit of its shareholders and employees.

Note that Singapore Airlines's mission statement does a good job of conveying "who we are, what we do, and why we are here," but it provides no sense of "where we are headed."

An example of a well-stated mission statement with ample specifics about what the organization does is that of St. Jude Children's Research Hospital: "to advance cures, and means of prevention, for pediatric catastrophic diseases through research and treatment. Consistent with the vision of our founder Danny Thomas, no child is denied treatment based on race, religion or a family's ability to pay." Facebook's mission statement, while short, still captures the essence of what the company is about: "to give people the power to share and make the world more open and connected." An example of a not-so-revealing mission statement is that of Microsoft: "To empower every person and every organization on the planet to achieve more." It says nothing about the company's products or business makeup and could apply to many companies in many different industries. A person unfamiliar with Microsoft could not discern from its mission statement that it is a globally known provider of PC software and a leading maker of video game consoles (the popular Xbox 360). Coca-Cola, which markets more than 500 beverage brands in over 200 countries, also has an uninformative mission statement: "to refresh the world; to inspire moments of optimism and happiness; to create value and make a difference." The usefulness of a mission statement that cannot convey the essence of a company's business activities and purpose is unclear.

Occasionally, companies couch their mission in terms of making a profit. This, too, is flawed. Profit is more correctly an *objective* and a *result* of what a company does. Moreover, earning a profit is the obvious intent of every commercial enterprise. Companies such as Gap Inc., Edward Jones, Honda, The Boston Consulting Group, Citigroup, DreamWorks Animation, and Intuit are all striving to earn a profit for shareholders; but plainly the fundamentals of their businesses are substantially different when it comes to "who we are and what we do." It is management's answer to "make a profit doing what and for whom?" that reveals the substance of a company's true mission and business purpose.

To be well worded, a company mission statement must employ language specific enough to distinguish its business makeup and purpose from those of other enterprises and give the company its own identity.

Linking the Vision and Mission with Company Values

Many companies have developed a set of values to guide the actions and behavior of company personnel in conducting the company's business and pursuing its strategic vision and mission. By **values** (or **core values,** as they are often called) we mean certain designated beliefs, traits, and behavioral norms that management has determined should guide the pursuit of its vision and mission. Values relate to such things as fair treatment, honor and integrity, ethical behavior, innovativeness, teamwork, a passion for top-notch quality or superior customer service, social responsibility, and community citizenship.

CORE CONCEPT

A company's **values** are the beliefs, traits, and behavioral norms that company personnel are expected to display in conducting the company's business and pursuing its strategic vision and mission.

Most companies have articulated four to eight core values that company personnel are expected to display and that are supposed to be mirrored in how the company conducts its business. At Samsung, five core values are linked to its desire to contribute to a better global society by creating superior products and services: (1) giving people opportunities to reach their full potential, (2) developing the best products and services on the market, (3) embracing change, (4) operating in an ethical way, and (5) being dedicated to social and environmental responsibility. American Express embraces seven core values: (1) respect for people, (2) commitment to customers, (3) integrity, (4) teamwork, (5) good citizenship, (6) a will to win, and (7) personal accountability.

Do companies practice what they preach when it comes to their professed values? Sometimes no, sometimes yes—it runs the gamut. At one extreme are companies with window-dressing values; the values are given lip service by top executives but have little discernible impact on either how company personnel behave or how the company operates. Such companies have value statements because they are in vogue and make the company look good. At the other extreme are companies whose executives are committed to grounding company operations on sound values and principled ways of doing business. Executives at these companies deliberately seek to ingrain the designated core values into the corporate culture—the core values thus become an integral part of the company's DNA and what makes the company tick. At such values-driven companies, executives "walk the talk" and company personnel are held accountable for embodying the stated values in their behavior.

At companies where the stated values are real rather than cosmetic, managers connect values to the pursuit of the strategic vision and mission in one of two ways. In companies with long-standing values that are deeply entrenched in the corporate culture, senior managers are careful to craft a vision, mission, strategy, and set of operating practices that match established values; moreover, they repeatedly emphasize how the value-based behavioral norms contribute to the company's business success. If the company changes to a different vision or strategy, executives make a point of explaining how and why the core values continue to be relevant. Few companies with sincere commitment to established core values ever undertake strategic moves that conflict with ingrained values. In new companies, top management has to consider what values and business conduct should characterize the company and then draft a value statement that is circulated among managers and employees for discussion and possible modification. A final value statement that incorporates the desired behaviors and that connects to the vision and mission is then officially adopted. Some companies combine their vision, mission, and values into a single statement or document, circulate it to all organization members, and in many instances post the vision, mission, and value statement on the company's website. Illustration Capsule 2.2 describes how core values underlie the company's mission at Patagonia, Inc., a widely known and quite successful outdoor clothing and gear company.

STAGE 2: SETTING OBJECTIVES

LO 2

The importance of setting both strategic and financial objectives.

The managerial purpose of setting **objectives** is to convert the vision and mission into specific performance targets. Objectives reflect management's aspirations for company performance in light of the industry's prevailing economic and competitive conditions and the company's internal capabilities. Well-stated objectives must be *specific, quantifiable* or *measurable,* and *challenging* and must contain a *deadline for achievement.* As Bill Hewlett, cofounder of Hewlett-Packard, shrewdly observed, "You cannot manage what you cannot measure. . . . And what gets measured gets done."[4] Concrete, measurable objectives are managerially valuable for three reasons: (1) They focus organizational attention and align actions throughout the organization, (2) they serve as *yardsticks* for tracking a company's performance and progress, and (3) they motivate employees to expend greater effort and perform at a high level.

CORE CONCEPT

Objectives are an organization's performance targets—the specific results management wants to achieve.

The Imperative of Setting Stretch Objectives

The experiences of countless companies teach that one of the best ways to promote outstanding company performance is for managers to set performance targets high enough to *stretch an organization to perform at its full potential and deliver the best possible results.* Challenging company personnel to go all out and deliver "stretch" gains in performance pushes an enterprise to be more inventive, to exhibit more urgency in improving both its financial performance and its business position,

ILLUSTRATION CAPSULE 2.2 Patagonia, Inc.: A Values-Driven Company

PATAGONIA'S MISSION STATEMENT

Build the best product, cause no unnecessary harm, use business to inspire and implement solutions to the environmental crisis.

PATAGONIA'S CORE VALUES

Quality: Pursuit of ever-greater quality in everything we do.

Integrity: Relationships built on integrity and respect.

Environmentalism: Serve as a catalyst for personal and corporate action.

Not Bound by Convention: Our success—and much of the fun—lies in developing innovative ways to do things.

© Robert Alexander/Getty Images

Patagonia, Inc. is an American outdoor clothing and gear company that clearly "walks the talk" with respect to its mission and values. While its mission is relatively vague about the types of products Patagonia offers, it clearly states the foundational "how" and "why" of the company. The four core values individually reinforce the mission in distinct ways, charting a defined path for employees to follow. At the same time, each value is reliant on the others for maximum effect. The values' combined impact on internal operations and public perception has made Patagonia a strong leader in the outdoor gear world.

While many companies espouse the pursuit of **quality** as part of their strategy, at Patagonia quality must come through honorable practices or not at all. Routinely, the company opts for more expensive materials and labor to maintain internal consistency with the mission. Patagonia learned early on that it could not make good products in bad factories, so it holds its manufacturers accountable through a variety of auditing partnerships and alliances. In this way, the company maintains relationships built on **integrity** and respect. In addition to keeping faith with those who make its products, Patagonia relentlessly pursues integrity in sourcing production inputs. Central to its **environmental** mission and core values, it targets for use sustainable and recyclable materials, ethically procured. Demonstrating leadership in environmentalism, Patagonia established foundations to support ecological causes, even **defying convention** by giving 1 percent of profits to conservation causes. These are but a few examples of the ways in which Patagonia's core values fortify each other and support the mission.

For Patagonia, quality would not be possible without integrity, unflinching environmentalism, and the company's unconventional approach. Since its founding in 1973 by rock climber Yvon Chouinard, Patagonia has remained remarkably consistent to the spirit of these values. This has endeared the company to legions of loyal customers while leading other businesses in protecting the environment. More than an apparel and gear company, Patagonia inspires everyone it touches to do their best for the planet and each other, in line with its mission and core values.

Note: Developed with Nicholas J. Ziemba.

Sources: Patagonia, Inc., "Corporate Social Responsibility," *The Footprint Chronicles,* 2007; "Becoming a Responsible Company," www.patagonia.com/us/patagonia.go?assetid=2329 (accessed February 28, 2014).

and to be more intentional and focused in its actions. Stretch objectives spur exceptional performance and help build a firewall against contentment with modest gains in organizational performance.

Manning Selvage & Lee (MS&L), a U.S. public relations firm, had originally set a goal of tripling its revenues to $100 million in five years, but managed to hit its target in just three years using ambitious stretch objectives. A company exhibits *strategic intent* when it relentlessly pursues an ambitious strategic objective, concentrating the full force of its resources and competitive actions on achieving that objective. MS&L's strategic intent was to become one of the leading global PR firms, which it achieved with the help of its stretch objectives. Both Google and Amazon have had the strategic intent of developing drones, Amazon's for delivery and Google's for both delivery of goods and access to high-speed Internet service from the skies. As of 2015, both companies had tested their systems and filed for Federal Aviation Administration registration of their drones. Elon Musk, CEO of both Tesla Motors and SpaceX, is well known for his ambitious stretch goals and strategic intent. In 2016, he said that his commercial flight program, SpaceX, should be ready to send people to Mars in 10 years.

CORE CONCEPT

Stretch objectives set performance targets high enough to *stretch* an organization to perform at its full potential and deliver the best possible results.

CORE CONCEPT

A company exhibits **strategic intent** when it relentlessly pursues an ambitious strategic objective, concentrating the full force of its resources and competitive actions on achieving that objective.

What Kinds of Objectives to Set

Two distinct types of performance targets are required: those relating to financial performance and those relating to strategic performance. **Financial objectives** communicate management's goals for financial performance. **Strategic objectives** are goals concerning a company's marketing standing and competitive position. A company's set of financial and strategic objectives should include both near-term and longer-term performance targets. Short-term (quarterly or annual) objectives focus attention on delivering performance improvements in the current period and satisfy shareholder expectations for near-term progress. Longer-term targets (three to five years off) force managers to consider what to do *now* to put the company in position to perform better later. Long-term objectives are critical for achieving optimal long-term performance and stand as a barrier to a near-sighted management philosophy and an undue focus on short-term results. When trade-offs have to be made between achieving long-term objectives and achieving short-term objectives, long-term objectives should take precedence (unless the achievement of one or more short-term performance targets has unique importance). Examples of commonly used financial and strategic objectives are listed in Table 2.2.

CORE CONCEPT

Financial objectives relate to the financial performance targets management has established for the organization to achieve. **Strategic objectives** relate to target outcomes that indicate a company is strengthening its market standing, competitive position, and future business prospects.

The Need for a Balanced Approach to Objective Setting

The importance of setting and attaining financial objectives is obvious. Without adequate profitability and financial strength, a company's long-term health and ultimate survival are jeopardized. Furthermore, subpar earnings and a weak balance sheet alarm shareholders and creditors and put the jobs of senior executives at risk. However, good financial performance, by itself, is not enough. Of equal or greater importance is a company's strategic performance—outcomes that indicate whether a company's market position and competitiveness are deteriorating, holding steady, or improving. *A stronger market standing and greater competitive vitality—especially when accompanied by competitive advantage—is what enables a company to improve its financial performance.*

Moreover, a company's financial performance measures are really *lagging indicators* that reflect the results of past decisions and organizational activities.[5] But a company's past or current financial performance is not a reliable indicator of its future prospects—poor financial performers often turn things around and do

CORE CONCEPT

The **Balanced Scorecard** is a widely used method for combining the use of both strategic and financial objectives, tracking their achievement, and giving management a more complete and balanced view of how well an organization is performing.

TABLE 2.2 Common Financial and Strategic Objectives

Financial Objectives	Strategic Objectives
• An *x* percent increase in annual revenues • Annual increases in after-tax profits of *x* percent • Annual increases in earnings per share of *x* percent • Annual dividend increases of *x* percent • Profit margins of *x* percent • An *x* percent return on capital employed (ROCE) or return on shareholders' equity (ROE) investment • Increased shareholder value in the form of an upward-trending stock price • Bond and credit ratings of *x* • Internal cash flows of *x* dollars to fund new capital investment	• Winning an *x* percent market share • Achieving lower overall costs than rivals • Overtaking key competitors on product performance, quality, or customer service • Deriving *x* percent of revenues from the sale of new products introduced within the past five years • Having broader or deeper technological capabilities than rivals • Having a wider product line than rivals • Having a better-known or more powerful brand name than rivals • Having stronger national or global sales and distribution capabilities than rivals • Consistently getting new or improved products to market ahead of rivals

better, while good financial performers can fall upon hard times. The best and most reliable *leading indicators* of a company's future financial performance and business prospects are strategic outcomes that indicate whether the company's competitiveness and market position are stronger or weaker. The accomplishment of strategic objectives signals that the company is well positioned to sustain or improve its performance. For instance, if a company is achieving ambitious strategic objectives such that its competitive strength and market position are on the rise, then there's reason to expect that its *future* financial performance will be better than its current or past performance. If a company is losing ground to competitors and its market position is slipping—outcomes that reflect weak strategic performance (and, very likely, failure to achieve its strategic objectives)—then its ability to maintain its present profitability is highly suspect.

Consequently, it is important to use a performance measurement system that strikes a *balance* between financial objectives and strategic objectives.[6] The most widely used framework of this sort is known as the **Balanced Scorecard**.[7] This is a method for linking financial performance objectives to specific strategic objectives that derive from a company's business model. It provides a company's employees with clear guidelines about how their jobs are linked to the overall objectives of the organization, so they can contribute most productively and collaboratively to the achievement of these goals. A 2013 survey by Bain & Company of 12,300 companies worldwide found that balanced scorecard methodology was one of the top-five management tools.[8] In 2015, nearly 50 percent of companies in the United States, Europe, and Asia employed a balanced scorecard approach to measuring strategic and financial performance.[9] Organizations that have adopted the balanced scorecard approach include 7-Eleven, Ann Taylor Stores, Allianz Italy, Wells Fargo Bank, Ford Motor Company, Verizon, ExxonMobil, Pfizer, DuPont, Royal Canadian Mounted Police, U.S. Army Medical Command, and over 30 colleges and universities.[10] Illustration Capsule 2.3 provides selected strategic and financial objectives of three prominent companies.

ILLUSTRATION CAPSULE 2.3 Examples of Company Objectives

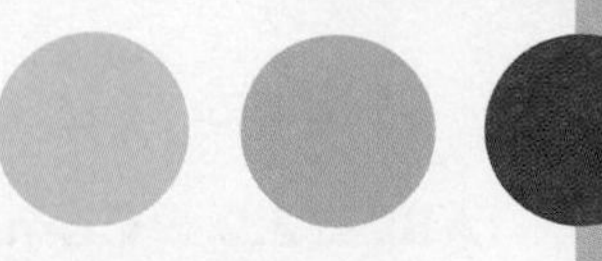

UPS

Increase the percentage of business-to-consumer package deliveries from 46 percent of domestic deliveries in 2014 to 51 percent of domestic deliveries in 2019; increase intraregional export shipments from 66 percent of exported packages in 2014 to 70 percent of exported packages in 2019; lower U.S. domestic average cost per package by 40 basis points between 2014 and 2019; increase total revenue from $58.2 billion in 2014 to $74.3–$81.6 billion in 2019; increase total operating profit from $4.95 billion in 2014 to $7.62–$9.12 billion by 2019; increase capital expenditures from 4 percent of revenues in 2014 to 5 percent of revenues in 2019.

© Luke Sharrett/Bloomberg via Getty Images

ALCOA

Increase revenues from higher margin aero/defense and transportation aluminum products from 31 percent of revenues in 2014 to 41 percent of revenues in 2016; increase automotive sheet shipments from $340 million in 2014 to $1.05 billion in 2016; increase alumina price index/spot pricing from 68 percent of third-party shipments in 2014 to 84 percent of third-party shipments in 2016; reduce product development to market cycle time from 52 weeks to 25 weeks.

YUM! BRANDS (KFC, PIZZA HUT, TACO BELL, WINGSTREET)

Add 1,000 new Taco Bell units in the United States by 2020; increase Taco Bell revenues from $7 billion in 2012 to $14 billion in 2022; achieve a number-two ranking in quick-service chicken in western Europe, the United Kingdom, and Australia; increase the percentage of franchised KFC units in China from 6 percent in 2013 to 10 percent in 2017; expand the number of Pizza Hut locations in China by 300 percent by 2020; increase the number of Pizza Hut Delivery stores in the United States from 235 in 2014 to 500 in 2016; expand the digital ordering options in all quick-service concepts; increase the number of restaurant locations in India from 705 in 2013 to 2,000 by 2020; increase the operating margin for KFC, Pizza Hut, and Taco Bell from 24 percent in 2014 to 30 percent in 2017; sustain double-digit EPS growth from 2015 through 2020.

Sources: Information posted on company websites.

Setting Objectives for Every Organizational Level

Objective setting should not stop with top management's establishing companywide performance targets. Company objectives need to be broken down into performance targets for each of the organization's separate businesses, product lines, functional departments, and individual work units. Employees within various functional areas and operating levels will be guided much better by specific objectives relating directly to their departmental activities than broad organizational-level goals. Objective setting is thus a *top-down process* that must extend to the lowest organizational levels. This means that each organizational unit must take care to set performance targets that support—rather than conflict with or negate—the achievement of companywide strategic and financial objectives.

The ideal situation is a team effort in which each organizational unit strives to produce results that contribute to the achievement of the company's performance targets and strategic vision. Such consistency signals that organizational units know their strategic role and are on board in helping the company move down the chosen strategic path and produce the desired results.

STAGE 3: CRAFTING A STRATEGY

LO 3

Why the strategic initiatives taken at various organizational levels must be tightly coordinated to achieve companywide performance targets.

As indicated in Chapter 1, the task of stitching a strategy together entails addressing a series of "hows": *how* to attract and please customers, *how* to compete against rivals, *how* to position the company in the marketplace, *how* to respond to changing market conditions, *how* to capitalize on attractive opportunities to grow the business, and *how* to achieve strategic and financial objectives. Astute entrepreneurship is called for in choosing among the various strategic alternatives and in proactively searching for opportunities to do new things or to do existing things in new or better ways.[11] The faster a company's business environment is changing, the more critical it becomes for its managers to be good entrepreneurs in diagnosing the direction and force of the changes under way and in responding with timely adjustments in strategy. Strategy makers have to pay attention to early warnings of future change and be willing to experiment with dare-to-be-different ways to establish a market position in that future. When obstacles appear unexpectedly in a company's path, it is up to management to adapt rapidly and innovatively. *Masterful strategies come from doing things differently from competitors where it counts—out-innovating them, being more efficient, being more imaginative, adapting faster—rather than running with the herd.* Good strategy making is therefore inseparable from good business entrepreneurship. One cannot exist without the other.

Strategy Making Involves Managers at All Organizational Levels

A company's senior executives obviously have lead strategy-making roles and responsibilities. The chief executive officer (CEO), as captain of the ship, carries the mantles of chief direction setter, chief objective setter, chief strategy maker, and chief strategy implementer for the total enterprise. Ultimate responsibility for *leading* the strategy-making, strategy-executing process rests with the CEO. And the CEO is always fully accountable for the results the strategy produces, whether good or bad. In some enterprises, the CEO or owner functions as chief architect of the strategy, personally deciding what the key elements of the company's strategy will be, although he or she may seek the advice of key subordinates and board members. A CEO-centered approach to strategy development is characteristic of small owner-managed companies and some large corporations that were founded by the present CEO or that have a CEO with strong strategic leadership skills. Elon Musk at Tesla Motors and SpaceX, Mark Zuckerberg at Facebook, Jeff Bezos at Amazon, Indra Nooyi at PepsiCo, Jack Ma of Alibaba, Warren Buffett at Berkshire Hathaway, and Irene Rosenfeld at Kraft Foods are examples of high-profile corporate CEOs who have wielded a heavy hand in shaping their company's strategy.

In most corporations, however, strategy is the product of more than just the CEO's handiwork. Typically, other senior executives—business unit heads, the chief financial officer, and vice presidents for production, marketing, and other functional departments—have influential strategy-making roles and help fashion the chief strategy components. Normally, a company's chief financial officer is in charge of devising and implementing an appropriate financial strategy; the production vice president takes the lead in developing the company's production strategy; the marketing vice president orchestrates sales and marketing strategy; a brand manager is in charge of the strategy for a particular brand in the company's product lineup; and so on. Moreover, the strategy-making efforts of top managers are complemented by advice and counsel from the company's board of directors; normally, all major strategic decisions are submitted to the board of directors for review, discussion, perhaps modification, and official approval.

In most companies, crafting and executing strategy is a *collaborative team effort* in which every manager has a role for the area he or she heads; it is rarely something that only high-level managers do.

But strategy making is by no means solely a *top* management function, the exclusive province of owner-entrepreneurs, CEOs, high-ranking executives, and board members. The more a company's operations cut across different products, industries, and geographic areas, the more that headquarters executives have little option but to delegate considerable strategy-making authority to down-the-line managers in charge of particular subsidiaries, divisions, product lines, geographic sales offices, distribution centers, and plants. On-the-scene managers who oversee specific operating units can be reliably counted on to have more detailed command of the strategic issues for the particular operating unit under their supervision since they have more intimate knowledge of the prevailing market and competitive conditions, customer requirements and expectations, and all the other relevant aspects affecting the several strategic options available. Managers with day-to-day familiarity of, and authority over, a specific operating unit thus have a big edge over headquarters executives in making wise strategic choices for their unit. The result is that, in most of today's companies, crafting and executing strategy is a *collaborative team effort* in which *every company manager plays a strategy-making role*—ranging from minor to major—for the area he or she heads.

The larger and more diverse the operations of an enterprise, the more points of strategic initiative it has and the more levels of management that have a significant strategy-making role.

Take, for example, a company like General Electric, a $150 billion global corporation with over 300,000 employees, operations in some 170 countries, and businesses that include jet engines, lighting, power generation, electric transmission and distribution equipment, oil and gas equipment, medical imaging and diagnostic equipment, locomotives, security devices, water treatment systems, and financial services. While top-level headquarters executives may well be personally involved in shaping GE's *overall* strategy and fashioning *important* strategic moves, they simply cannot know enough about the situation in every GE organizational unit to direct every strategic move made in GE's worldwide organization. Rather, it takes involvement on the part of GE's whole management team—top executives, business group heads, the heads of specific business units and product categories, and key managers in plants, sales offices, and distribution centers—to craft the thousands of strategic initiatives that end up composing the whole of GE's strategy.

A Company's Strategy-Making Hierarchy

In diversified companies like GE, where multiple and sometimes strikingly different businesses have to be managed, crafting a full-fledged strategy involves four distinct types of strategic actions and initiatives. Each of these involves different facets of the company's overall strategy and calls for the participation of different types of managers, as shown in Figure 2.2.

As shown in Figure 2.2, **corporate strategy** is orchestrated by the CEO and other senior executives and establishes an overall strategy for managing a *set of businesses*

FIGURE 2.2 A Company's Strategy-Making Hierarchy

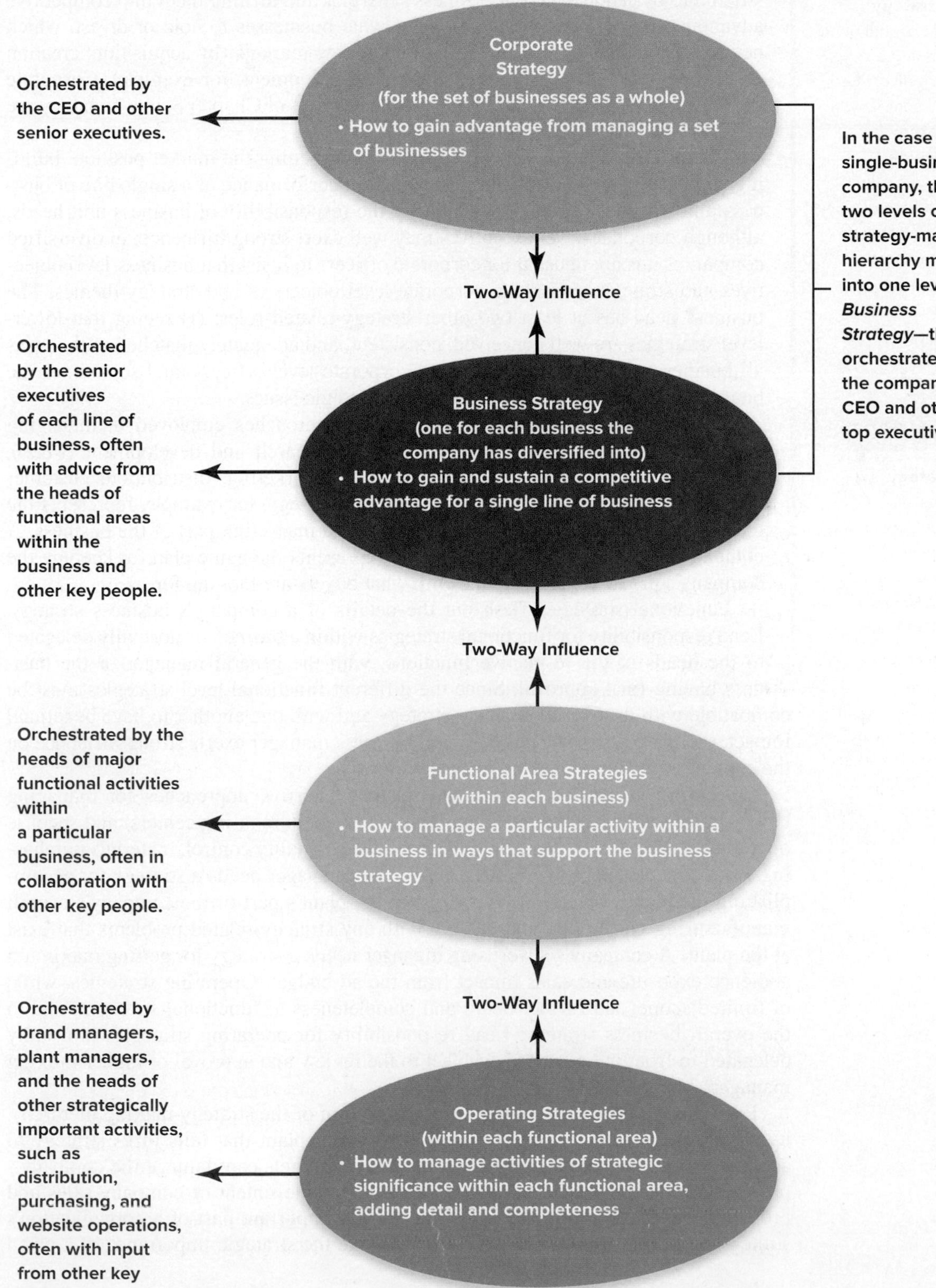

CORE CONCEPT

Corporate strategy establishes an overall game plan for managing a *set of businesses* in a diversified, multibusiness company.

Business strategy is primarily concerned with strengthening the company's market position and building competitive advantage in a *single-business company* or in a *single business unit* of a diversified multibusiness corporation.

CORE CONCEPT

Business strategy is strategy at the *single-business level,* concerning how to improve performance or gain a competitive advantage in a particular line of business.

in a diversified, multibusiness company. Corporate strategy concerns how to improve the combined performance of the set of businesses the company has diversified into by capturing cross-business synergies and turning them into competitive advantage. It addresses the questions of what businesses to hold or divest, which new markets to enter, and how to best enter new markets (by acquisition, creation of a strategic alliance, or through internal development, for example). Corporate strategy and business diversification are the subjects of Chapter 8, in which they are discussed in detail.

Business strategy is concerned with strengthening the market position, building competitive advantage, and improving the performance of a single line of business unit. Business strategy is primarily the responsibility of business unit heads, although corporate-level executives may well exert strong influence; in diversified companies it is not unusual for corporate officers to insist that business-level objectives and strategy conform to corporate-level objectives and strategy themes. The business head has at least two other strategy-related roles: (1) seeing that lower-level strategies are well conceived, consistent, and adequately matched to the overall business strategy; and (2) keeping corporate-level officers (and sometimes the board of directors) informed of emerging strategic issues.

Functional-area strategies concern the approaches employed in managing particular functions within a business—like research and development (R&D), production, procurement of inputs, sales and marketing, distribution, customer service, and finance. A company's marketing strategy, for example, represents the managerial game plan for running the sales and marketing part of the business. A company's product development strategy represents the game plan for keeping the company's product lineup in tune with what buyers are looking for.

Functional strategies flesh out the details of a company's business strategy. Lead responsibility for functional strategies within a business is normally delegated to the heads of the respective functions, with the general manager of the business having final approval. Since the different functional-level strategies must be compatible with the overall business strategy and with one another to have beneficial impact, there are times when the general business manager exerts strong influence on the content of the functional strategies.

Operating strategies concern the relatively narrow approaches for managing key operating units (e.g., plants, distribution centers, purchasing centers) and specific operating activities with strategic significance (e.g., quality control, materials purchasing, brand management, Internet sales). A plant manager needs a strategy for accomplishing the plant's objectives, carrying out the plant's part of the company's overall manufacturing game plan, and dealing with any strategy-related problems that exist at the plant. A company's advertising manager needs a strategy for getting maximum audience exposure and sales impact from the ad budget. Operating strategies, while of limited scope, add further detail and completeness to functional strategies and to the overall business strategy. Lead responsibility for operating strategies is usually delegated to frontline managers, subject to the review and approval of higher-ranking managers.

Even though operating strategy is at the bottom of the strategy-making hierarchy, its importance should not be downplayed. A major plant that fails in its strategy to achieve production volume, unit cost, and quality targets can damage the company's reputation for quality products and undercut the achievement of company sales and profit objectives. Frontline managers are thus an important part of an organization's strategy-making team. One cannot reliably judge the strategic importance of a given action simply by the strategy level or location within the managerial hierarchy where it is initiated.

A company's strategy is at full power only when its many pieces are united.

In single-business companies, the uppermost level of the strategy-making hierarchy is the business strategy, so a single-business company has three levels of strategy: business strategy, functional-area strategies, and operating strategies. Proprietorships, partnerships, and owner-managed enterprises may have only one or two strategy-making levels since it takes only a few key people to craft and oversee the firm's strategy. The larger and more diverse the operations of an enterprise, the more points of strategic initiative it has and the more levels of management that have a significant strategy-making role.

Uniting the Strategy-Making Hierarchy

Ideally, the pieces of a company's strategy up and down the strategy hierarchy should be cohesive and mutually reinforcing, fitting together like a jigsaw puzzle. *Anything less than a unified collection of strategies weakens the overall strategy and is likely to impair company performance.*[12] It is the responsibility of top executives to achieve this unity by clearly communicating the company's vision, objectives, and major strategy components to down-the-line managers and key personnel. Midlevel and frontline managers cannot craft unified strategic moves without first understanding the company's long-term direction and knowing the major components of the corporate and/or business strategies that their strategy-making efforts are supposed to support and enhance. Thus, as a general rule, strategy making must start at the top of the organization and then proceed downward from the corporate level to the business level and then from the business level to the associated functional and operating levels. Once strategies up and down the hierarchy have been created, lower-level strategies must be scrutinized for consistency with and support of higher-level strategies. Any strategy conflicts must be addressed and resolved, either by modifying the lower-level strategies with conflicting elements or by adapting the higher-level strategy to accommodate what may be more appealing strategy ideas and initiatives bubbling up from below.

A Strategic Vision + Mission + Objectives + Strategy = A Strategic Plan

Developing a strategic vision and mission, setting objectives, and crafting a strategy are basic direction-setting tasks. They map out where a company is headed, delineate its strategic and financial targets, articulate the basic business model, and outline the competitive moves and operating approaches to be used in achieving the desired business results. Together, these elements constitute a **strategic plan** for coping with industry conditions, competing against rivals, meeting objectives, and making progress along the chosen strategic course.[13] Typically, a strategic plan includes a commitment to allocate resources to carrying out the plan and specifies a time period for achieving goals.

CORE CONCEPT

A company's **strategic plan** lays out its future direction, business model, performance targets, and competitive strategy.

In companies that do regular strategy reviews and develop explicit strategic plans, the strategic plan usually ends up as a written document that is circulated to most managers. Near-term performance targets are the part of the strategic plan most often communicated to employees more generally and spelled out explicitly. A number of companies summarize key elements of their strategic plans in the company's annual report to shareholders, in postings on their websites, or in statements provided to the business media; others, perhaps for reasons of competitive sensitivity, make only vague, general statements about their strategic plans.[14] In small, privately owned companies it is rare for strategic plans to exist in written form. Small-company strategic plans tend to reside in the thinking and directives of owner-executives; aspects of the plan are revealed in conversations with company personnel about where to head, what to accomplish, and how to proceed.

STAGE 4: EXECUTING THE STRATEGY

LO 4

What a company must do to achieve operating excellence and to execute its strategy proficiently.

Managing the implementation of a strategy is easily the most demanding and time-consuming part of the strategy management process. Converting strategic plans into actions and results tests a manager's ability to direct organizational change, motivate company personnel, build and strengthen competitive capabilities, create and nurture a strategy-supportive work climate, and meet or beat performance targets. Initiatives to put the strategy in place and execute it proficiently must be launched and managed on many organizational fronts.

Management's action agenda for executing the chosen strategy emerges from assessing what the company will have to do to achieve the targeted financial and strategic performance. Each company manager has to think through the answer to the question "What needs to be done in my area to execute my piece of the strategic plan, and what actions should I take to get the process under way?" How much internal change is needed depends on how much of the strategy is new, how far internal practices and competencies deviate from what the strategy requires, and how well the present work culture supports good strategy execution. Depending on the amount of internal change involved, full implementation and proficient execution of the company strategy (or important new pieces thereof) can take several months to several years.

In most situations, managing the strategy execution process includes the following principal aspects:

- Creating a strategy-supporting structure.
- Staffing the organization to obtain needed skills and expertise.
- Developing and strengthening strategy-supporting resources and capabilities.
- Allocating ample resources to the activities critical to strategic success.
- Ensuring that policies and procedures facilitate effective strategy execution.
- Organizing the work effort along the lines of best practice.
- Installing information and operating systems that enable company personnel to perform essential activities.
- Motivating people and tying rewards directly to the achievement of performance objectives.
- Creating a company culture conducive to successful strategy execution.
- Exerting the internal leadership needed to propel implementation forward.

Good strategy execution requires diligent pursuit of operating excellence. It is a job for a company's whole management team. Success hinges on the skills and cooperation of operating managers who can push for needed changes in their organizational units and consistently deliver good results. Management's handling of the strategy implementation process can be considered successful if things go smoothly enough that the company meets or beats its strategic and financial performance targets and shows good progress in achieving management's strategic vision.

STAGE 5: EVALUATING PERFORMANCE AND INITIATING CORRECTIVE ADJUSTMENTS

The fifth component of the strategy management process—monitoring new external developments, evaluating the company's progress, and making corrective adjustments—is the trigger point for deciding whether to continue or change the company's vision and mission, objectives, strategy, and/or strategy execution methods.[15] As long as the company's strategy continues to pass the three tests of a winning strategy discussed in Chapter 1 (good fit, competitive advantage, strong performance), company executives may decide to stay the course. Simply fine-tuning the strategic plan and continuing with efforts to improve strategy execution are sufficient.

But whenever a company encounters disruptive changes in its environment, questions need to be raised about the appropriateness of its direction and strategy. If a company experiences a downturn in its market position or persistent shortfalls in performance, then company managers are obligated to ferret out the causes—do they relate to poor strategy, poor strategy execution, or both?—and take timely corrective action. A company's direction, objectives, and strategy have to be revisited anytime external or internal conditions warrant.

Likewise, managers are obligated to assess which of the company's operating methods and approaches to strategy execution merit continuation and which need improvement. Proficient strategy execution is always the product of much organizational learning. It is achieved unevenly—coming quickly in some areas and proving troublesome in others. Consequently, top-notch strategy execution entails vigilantly searching for ways to improve and then making corrective adjustments whenever and wherever it is useful to do so.

A company's vision, mission, objectives, strategy, and approach to strategy execution are never final; reviewing whether and when to make revisions is an ongoing process.

CORPORATE GOVERNANCE: THE ROLE OF THE BOARD OF DIRECTORS IN THE STRATEGY-CRAFTING, STRATEGY-EXECUTING PROCESS

LO 5

The role and responsibility of a company's board of directors in overseeing the strategic management process.

Although senior managers have the *lead responsibility* for crafting and executing a company's strategy, it is the duty of a company's board of directors to exercise strong oversight and see that management performs the various tasks involved in each of the five stages of the strategy-making, strategy-executing process in a manner that best serves the interests of shareholders and other stakeholders.[16] A company's board of directors has four important obligations to fulfill:

1. *Oversee the company's financial accounting and financial reporting practices.* While top executives, particularly the company's CEO and CFO (chief financial officer), are primarily responsible for seeing that the company's financial statements fairly and accurately report the results of the company's operations,

board members have a *legal obligation* to warrant the accuracy of the company's financial reports and protect shareholders. It is their job to ensure that generally accepted accounting principles (GAAP) are used properly in preparing the company's financial statements and that proper financial controls are in place to prevent fraud and misuse of funds. Virtually all boards of directors have an audit committee, always composed entirely of *outside directors* (*inside directors* hold management positions in the company and either directly or indirectly report to the CEO). The members of the audit committee have the lead responsibility for overseeing the decisions of the company's financial officers and consulting with both internal and external auditors to ensure accurate financial reporting and adequate financial controls.

2. *Critically appraise the company's direction, strategy, and business approaches.* Board members are also expected to guide management in choosing a strategic direction and to make independent judgments about the validity and wisdom of management's proposed strategic actions. This aspect of their duties takes on heightened importance when the company's strategy is failing or is plagued with faulty execution, and certainly when there is a precipitous collapse in profitability. But under more normal circumstances, many boards have found that meeting agendas become consumed by compliance matters with little time left to discuss matters of strategic importance. The board of directors and management at Philips Electronics hold annual two- to three-day retreats devoted exclusively to evaluating the company's long-term direction and various strategic proposals. The company's exit from the semiconductor business and its increased focus on medical technology and home health care resulted from management-board discussions during such retreats.[17]
3. *Evaluate the caliber of senior executives' strategic leadership skills.* The board is always responsible for determining whether the current CEO is doing a good job of strategic leadership (as a basis for awarding salary increases and bonuses and deciding on retention or removal).[18] Boards must also exercise due diligence in evaluating the strategic leadership skills of other senior executives in line to succeed the CEO. When the incumbent CEO steps down or leaves for a position elsewhere, the board must elect a successor, either going with an insider or deciding that an outsider is needed to perhaps radically change the company's strategic course. Often, the outside directors on a board visit company facilities and talk with company personnel personally to evaluate whether the strategy is on track, how well the strategy is being executed, and how well issues and problems are being addressed by various managers. For example, independent board members at GE visit operating executives at each major business unit once a year to assess the company's talent pool and stay abreast of emerging strategic and operating issues affecting the company's divisions. Home Depot board members visit a store once per quarter to determine the health of the company's operations.[19]
4. *Institute a compensation plan for top executives that rewards them for actions and results that serve stakeholder interests, and most especially those of shareholders.* A basic principle of corporate governance is that the owners of a corporation (the shareholders) delegate operating authority and managerial control to top management in return for compensation. In their role as *agents* of shareholders, top executives have a clear and unequivocal duty to make decisions and operate the company in accord with shareholder interests. (This does not mean disregarding

the interests of other stakeholders—employees, suppliers, the communities in which the company operates, and society at large.) Most boards of directors have a compensation committee, composed entirely of directors from *outside* the company, to develop a salary and incentive compensation plan that rewards senior executives for boosting the company's *long-term* performance on behalf of shareholders. The compensation committee's recommendations are presented to the full board for approval. But during the past 10 to 15 years, many boards of directors have done a poor job of ensuring that executive salary increases, bonuses, and stock option awards are tied tightly to performance measures that are truly in the long-term interests of shareholders. Rather, compensation packages at many companies have increasingly rewarded executives for short-term performance improvements—most notably, for achieving quarterly and annual earnings targets and boosting the stock price by specified percentages. This has had the perverse effect of causing company managers to become preoccupied with actions to improve a company's near-term performance, often motivating them to take unwise business risks to boost short-term earnings by amounts sufficient to qualify for multimillion-dollar compensation packages (that many see as obscenely large). The focus on short-term performance has proved damaging to long-term company performance and shareholder interests—witness the huge loss of shareholder wealth that occurred at many financial institutions in 2008–2009 because of executive risk taking in subprime loans, credit default swaps, and collateralized mortgage securities. As a consequence, the need to overhaul and reform executive compensation has become a hot topic in both public circles and corporate boardrooms. Illustration Capsule 2.4 discusses how weak governance at Volkswagen contributed to the 2015 emissions cheating scandal, which cost the company billions of dollars and the trust of its stakeholders.

Every corporation should have a strong independent board of directors that (1) is well informed about the company's performance, (2) guides and judges the CEO and other top executives, (3) has the courage to curb management actions the board believes are inappropriate or unduly risky, (4) certifies to shareholders that the CEO is doing what the board expects, (5) provides insight and advice to management, and (6) is intensely involved in debating the pros and cons of key decisions and actions.[20] Boards of directors that lack the backbone to challenge a strong-willed or "imperial" CEO or that rubber-stamp almost anything the CEO recommends without probing inquiry and debate abdicate their fiduciary duty to represent and protect shareholder interests.

Effective corporate governance requires the board of directors to oversee the company's strategic direction, evaluate its senior executives, handle executive compensation, and oversee financial reporting practices.

ILLUSTRATION CAPSULE 2.4 Corporate Governance Failures at Volkswagen

In 2015, Volkswagen admitted to installing "defeat devices" on at least 11 million vehicles with diesel engines. These devices enabled the cars to pass emission tests, even though the engines actually emitted pollutants up to 40 times above what is allowed in the United States. Current estimates are that it will cost the company at least €7 billion to cover the cost of repairs and lawsuits. Although management must have been involved in approving the use of cheating devices, the Volkswagen supervisory board has been unwilling to accept any responsibility. Some board members even questioned whether it was the board's responsibility to be aware of such problems, stating "matters of technical expertise were not for us" and "the scandal had nothing, not one iota, to do with the advisory board." Yet governing boards do have a responsibility to be well informed, to provide oversight, and to become involved in key decisions and actions. So what caused this corporate governance failure? Why is this the third time in the past 20 years that Volkswagen has been embroiled in scandal?

© Paul J. Richards/AFP/Getty Images

The key feature of Volkswagen's board that appears to have led to these issues is a lack of independent directors. However, before explaining this in more detail it is important to understand the German governance model. German corporations operate two-tier governance structures, with a management board, and a separate supervisory board that does not contain any current executives. In addition, German law requires large companies to have at least 50 percent supervisory board representation from workers. This structure is meant to provide more oversight by independent board members and greater involvement by a wider set of stakeholders.

In Volkswagen's case, these objectives have been effectively circumvented. Although Volkswagen's supervisory board does not include any current management, the chairmanship appears to be a revolving door of former senior executives. Ferdinand Piëch, the chair during the scandal, was CEO for 9 years prior to becoming chair in 2002. Martin Winterkorn, the recently ousted CEO, was expected to become supervisory board chair prior to the scandal. The company continues to elevate management to the supervisory board even though they have presided over past scandals. Hans Dieter Poetsch, the newly appointed chair, was part of the management team that did not inform the supervisory board of the EPA investigation for two weeks.

VW also has a unique ownership structure where a single family, Porsche, controls more than 50 percent of voting shares. Piëch, a family member and chair until 2015, forced out CEOs and installed unqualified family members on the board, such as his former nanny and current wife. He also pushed out independent-minded board members, such as Gerhard Cromme, author of Germany's corporate governance code. The company has lost numerous independent directors over the past 10 years, leaving it with only one non-shareholder, non-labor representative. Although Piëch has now been removed, it is unclear that Volkswagen's board has solved the underlying problem. Shareholders have seen billions of dollars wiped away and the Volkswagen brand tarnished. As long as the board continues to lack independent directors, change will likely be slow.

Note: Developed with Jacob M. Crandall.

Sources: "Piëch under Fire," *The Economist,* December 8, 2005; Chris Bryant and Richard Milne, "Boardroom Politics at Heart of VW Scandal," *Financial Times,* October 4, 2015; Andreas Cremer and Jan Schwartz, "Volkswagen Mired in Crisis as Board Members Criticize Piech," Reuters, April 24, 2015; Richard Milne, "Volkswagen: System Failure," *Financial Times,* November 4, 2015.

KEY POINTS

The strategic management process consists of five interrelated and integrated stages:

1. *Developing a strategic vision* of the company's future, a *mission statement* that defines the company's current purpose, and a set of *core values* to guide the pursuit of the vision and mission. This stage of strategy making provides direction for the company, motivates and inspires company personnel, aligns and guides actions throughout the organization, and communicates to stakeholders management's aspirations for the company's future.
2. *Setting objectives* to convert the vision and mission into performance targets that can be used as yardsticks for measuring the company's performance. Objectives need to spell out *how much* of *what kind* of performance *by when.* Two broad types of objectives are required: *financial objectives* and *strategic objectives.* A *balanced scorecard* approach for measuring company performance entails setting both financial objectives and strategic objectives. *Stretch objectives* spur exceptional performance and help build a firewall against complacency and mediocre performance. A company exhibits *strategic intent* when it relentlessly pursues an ambitious strategic objective, concentrating the full force of its resources and competitive actions on achieving that objective.
3. *Crafting a strategy* to achieve the objectives and move the company along the strategic course that management has charted. Masterful strategies come from doing things differently from competitors where it counts—out-innovating them, being more efficient, being more imaginative, adapting faster—rather than running with the herd. In large diversified companies, the strategy-making hierarchy consists of four levels, each of which involves a corresponding level of management: corporate strategy (multibusiness strategy), business strategy (strategy for individual businesses that compete in a single industry), functional-area strategies within each business (e.g., marketing, R&D, logistics), and operating strategies (for key operating units, such as manufacturing plants). Thus, strategy making is an inclusive collaborative activity involving not only senior company executives but also the heads of major business divisions, functional-area managers, and operating managers on the frontlines.
4. *Executing the chosen strategy* and converting the strategic plan into action. Management's agenda for executing the chosen strategy emerges from assessing what the company will have to do to achieve the targeted financial and strategic performance. Management's handling of the strategy implementation process can be considered successful if things go smoothly enough that the company meets or beats its strategic and financial performance targets and shows good progress in achieving management's strategic vision.
5. *Monitoring developments, evaluating performance, and initiating corrective adjustments* in light of actual experience, changing conditions, new ideas, and new opportunities. This stage of the strategy management process is the trigger point for deciding whether to continue or change the company's vision and mission, objectives, strategy, and/or strategy execution methods.

The sum of a company's strategic vision, mission, objectives, and strategy constitutes a *strategic plan* for coping with industry conditions, outcompeting rivals, meeting objectives, and making progress toward aspirational goals.

Boards of directors have a duty to shareholders to play a vigilant role in overseeing management's handling of a company's strategy-making, strategy-executing process.

This entails four important obligations: (1) Ensure that the company issues accurate financial reports and has adequate financial controls; (2) critically appraise the company's direction, strategy, and strategy execution; (3) evaluate the caliber of senior executives' strategic leadership skills; and (4) institute a compensation plan for top executives that rewards them for actions and results that serve stakeholder interests, most especially those of shareholders.

ASSURANCE OF LEARNING EXERCISES

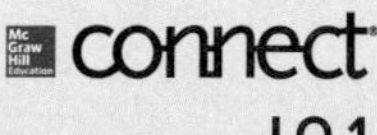

LO 1

1. Using the information in Table 2.1, critique the adequacy and merit of the following vision statements, listing effective elements and shortcomings. Rank the vision statements from best to worst once you complete your evaluation.

Vision Statement	Effective Elements	Shortcomings
American Express • We work hard every day to make American Express the world's most respected service brand.		
Hilton Hotels Corporation Our vision is to be the first choice of the world's travelers. Hilton intends to build on the rich heritage and strength of our brands by: • Consistently delighting our customers • Investing in our team members • Delivering innovative products and services • Continuously improving performance • Increasing shareholder value • Creating a culture of pride • Strengthening the loyalty of our constituents		
MasterCard • A world beyond cash.		
BASF We are "The Chemical Company" successfully operating in all major markets. • Our customers view BASF as their partner of choice. • Our innovative products, intelligent solutions and services make us the most competent worldwide supplier in the chemical industry. • We generate a high return on assets. • We strive for sustainable development. • We welcome change as an opportunity. • We, the employees of BASF, together ensure our success.		

Sources: Company websites and annual reports.

2. Go to the company investor relations websites for Starbucks (investor.starbucks.com), Pfizer (www.pfizer.com/investors), and Salesforce (investor.salesforce.com) to find examples of strategic and financial objectives. List four objectives for each company, and indicate which of these are strategic and which are financial. LO 2
3. American Airlines's Chapter 11 reorganization plan filed in 2012 involved the company reducing operating expenses by $2 billion while increasing revenues by $1 billion. The company's strategy to increase revenues included expanding the number of international flights and destinations and increasing daily departures for its five largest markets by 20 percent. The company also intended to upgrade its fleet by spending $2 billion to purchase new aircraft and refurbish the first-class cabins for planes not replaced. A final component of the restructuring plan included a merger with US Airways (completed in 2015) to create a global airline with more than 56,700 daily flights to 336 destinations in 56 countries. The merger was expected to produce cost savings from synergies of more than $1 billion and result in a stronger airline capable of paying creditors and rewarding employees and shareholders. Explain why the strategic initiatives at various organizational levels and functions require tight coordination to achieve the results desired by American Airlines. LO 3
4. Go to the investor relations website for Walmart (investors.walmartstores.com) and review past presentations Walmart has made during various investor conferences by clicking on the Events option in the navigation bar. Prepare a one- to two-page report that outlines what Walmart has said to investors about its approach to strategy execution. Specifically, what has management discussed concerning staffing, resource allocation, policies and procedures, information and operating systems, continuous improvement, rewards and incentives, corporate culture, and internal leadership at the company? LO 4
5. Based on the information provided in Illustration Capsule 2.4, describe the ways in which Volkswagen did not fulfill the requirements of effective corporate governance. In what ways did the board of directors sidestep its obligations to protect shareholder interests? How could Volkswagen better select its board of directors to avoid mistakes such as the emissions scandal in 2015? connect LO 5

EXERCISE FOR SIMULATION PARTICIPANTS

1. Meet with your co-managers and prepare a strategic vision statement for your company. It should be at least one sentence long and no longer than a brief paragraph. When you are finished, check to see if your vision statement meets the conditions for an effectively worded strategic vision set forth in Table 2.1. If not, then revise it accordingly. What would be a good slogan that captures the essence of your strategic vision and that could be used to help communicate the vision to company personnel, shareholders, and other stakeholders? LO 1
2. What are your company's financial objectives? What are your company's strategic objectives? LO 2
3. What are the three to four key elements of your company's strategy? LO 3

ENDNOTES

[1] Gordon Shaw, Robert Brown, and Philip Bromiley, "Strategic Stories: How 3M Is Rewriting Business Planning," *Harvard Business Review* 76, no. 3 (May–June 1998); David J. Collis and Michael G. Rukstad, "Can You Say What Your Strategy Is?" *Harvard Business Review* 86, no. 4 (April 2008) pp. 82–90.

[2] Hugh Davidson, *The Committed Enterprise: How to Make Vision and Values Work* (Oxford: Butterworth Heinemann, 2002); W. Chan Kim and Renée Mauborgne, "Charting Your Company's Future," *Harvard Business Review* 80, no. 6 (June 2002), pp. 77–83; James C. Collins and Jerry I. Porras, "Building Your Company's Vision," *Harvard Business Review* 74, no. 5 (September–October 1996), pp. 65–77; Jim Collins and Jerry Porras, *Built to Last: Successful Habits of Visionary Companies* (New York: HarperCollins, 1994); Michel Robert, *Strategy Pure and Simple II: How Winning Companies Dominate Their Competitors* (New York: McGraw-Hill, 1998).

[3] Davidson, *The Committed Enterprise,* pp. 20 and 54.

[4] As quoted in Charles H. House and Raymond L. Price, "The Return Map: Tracking Product Teams," *Harvard Business Review* 60, no. 1 (January–February 1991), p. 93.

[5] Robert S. Kaplan and David P. Norton, *The Strategy-Focused Organization* (Boston: Harvard Business School Press, 2001); Robert S. Kaplan and David P. Norton, *The Balanced Scorecard: Translating Strategy into Action* (Boston: Harvard Business School Press, 1996).

[6] Kaplan and Norton, *The Strategy-Focused Organization;* Kaplan and Norton, *The Balanced Scorecard;* Kevin B. Hendricks, Larry Menor, and Christine Wiedman, "The Balanced Scorecard: To Adopt or Not to Adopt," *Ivey Business Journal 69,* no. 2 (November–December 2004), pp. 1–7; Sandy Richardson, "The Key Elements of Balanced Scorecard Success," *Ivey Business Journal* 69, no. 2 (November–December 2004), pp. 7–9.

[7] Kaplan and Norton, *The Balanced Scorecard.*

[8] Ibid.

[9] Ibid.

[10] Information posted on the website of the Balanced Scorecard Institute, **balancedscorecard.org** (accessed October, 2015).

[11] Henry Mintzberg, Bruce Ahlstrand, and Joseph Lampel, *Strategy Safari: A Guided Tour through the Wilds of Strategic Management* (New York: Free Press, 1998); Bruce Barringer and Allen C. Bluedorn, "The Relationship between Corporate Entrepreneurship and Strategic Management," *Strategic Management Journal* 20 (1999), pp. 421–444; Jeffrey G. Covin and Morgan P. Miles, "Corporate Entrepreneurship and the Pursuit of Competitive Advantage," *Entrepreneurship: Theory and Practice* 23, no. 3 (Spring 1999), pp. 47–63; David A. Garvin and Lynne C. Levesque, "Meeting the Challenge of Corporate Entrepreneurship," *Harvard Business Review* 84, no. 10 (October 2006), pp. 102–112.

[12] Joseph L. Bower and Clark G. Gilbert, "How Managers' Everyday Decisions Create or Destroy Your Company's Strategy," *Harvard Business Review* 85, no. 2 (February 2007), pp. 72–79.

[13] Gordon Shaw, Robert Brown, and Philip Bromiley, "Strategic Stories: How 3M Is Rewriting Business Planning," *Harvard Business Review* 76, no. 3 (May–June 1998), pp. 41–50.

[14] Collis and, "Can You Say What Your Strategy Is?".

[15] Cynthia A. Montgomery, "Putting Leadership Back into Strategy," *Harvard Business Review* 86, no. 1 (January 2008), pp. 54–60.

[16] Jay W. Lorsch and Robert C. Clark, "Leading from the Boardroom," *Harvard Business Review* 86, no. 4 (April 2008), pp. 105–111.

[17] Ibid.

[18] Stephen P. Kaufman, "Evaluating the CEO," *Harvard Business Review* 86, no. 10 (October 2008), pp. 53–57.

[19] Ibid.

[20] David A. Nadler, "Building Better Boards," *Harvard Business Review* 82, no. 5 (May 2004), pp. 102–105; Cynthia A. Montgomery and Rhonda Kaufman, "The Board's Missing Link," *Harvard Business Review* 81, no. 3 (March 2003), pp. 86–93; John Carver, "What Continues to Be Wrong with Corporate Governance and How to Fix It," *Ivey Business Journal* 68, no. 1 (September–October 2003), pp. 1–5. See also Gordon Donaldson, "A New Tool for Boards: The Strategic Audit," *Harvard Business Review* 73, no. 4 (July–August 1995), pp. 99–107.

CHAPTER 3

Evaluating a Company's External Environment

© Bull's Eye/Image Zoo/Getty Images

Learning Objectives

THIS CHAPTER WILL HELP YOU UNDERSTAND:

LO 1 How to recognize the factors in a company's broad macro-environment that may have strategic significance.

LO 2 How to use analytic tools to diagnose the competitive conditions in a company's industry.

LO 3 How to map the market positions of key groups of industry rivals.

LO 4 How to determine whether an industry's outlook presents a company with sufficiently attractive opportunities for growth and profitability.

No matter what it takes, the goal of *strategy* is to beat the competition.

Kenichi Ohmae—*Consultant and author*

There is no such thing as weak competition; it grows all the time.

Nabil N. Jamal—*Consultant and author*

Sometimes by losing a battle you find a new way to win the war.

Donald Trump—*President of the United States and founder of Trump Entertainment Resorts*

In order to chart a company's strategic course wisely, managers must first develop a deep understanding of the company's present situation. Two facets of a company's situation are especially pertinent: (1) its external environment—most notably, the competitive conditions of the industry in which the company operates; and (2) its internal environment—particularly the company's resources and organizational capabilities.

Insightful diagnosis of a company's external and internal environments is a prerequisite for managers to succeed in crafting a strategy that is an excellent *fit* with the company's situation—the first test of a winning strategy. As depicted in Figure 3.1, strategic thinking begins with an appraisal of the company's external and internal environments (as a basis for deciding on a long-term direction and developing a strategic vision), moves toward an evaluation of the most promising alternative strategies and business models, and culminates in choosing a specific strategy.

This chapter presents the concepts and analytic tools for zeroing in on those aspects of a company's external environment that should be considered in making strategic choices. Attention centers on the broad environmental context, the specific market arena in which a company operates, the drivers of change, the positions and likely actions of rival companies, and the factors that determine competitive success. In Chapter 4, we explore the methods of evaluating a company's internal circumstances and competitive capabilities.

THE STRATEGICALLY RELEVANT FACTORS IN THE COMPANY'S MACRO-ENVIRONMENT

LO 1

How to recognize the factors in a company's broad macro-environment that may have strategic significance.

Every company operates in a broad **"macro-environment"** that comprises six principal components: political factors; economic conditions in the firm's general environment (local, country, regional, worldwide); sociocultural forces; technological factors; environmental factors (concerning the natural environment); and legal/regulatory conditions. Each of these components has the potential to affect the firm's more immediate industry and competitive environment, although some are likely to have a more important effect than others (see Figure 3.2). An analysis of the impact of these factors is often referred to as **PESTEL analysis,** an acronym that serves as a reminder of the six components involved (political, economic, sociocultural, technological, environmental, legal/regulatory).

FIGURE 3.1 From Thinking Strategically about the Company's Situation to Choosing a Strategy

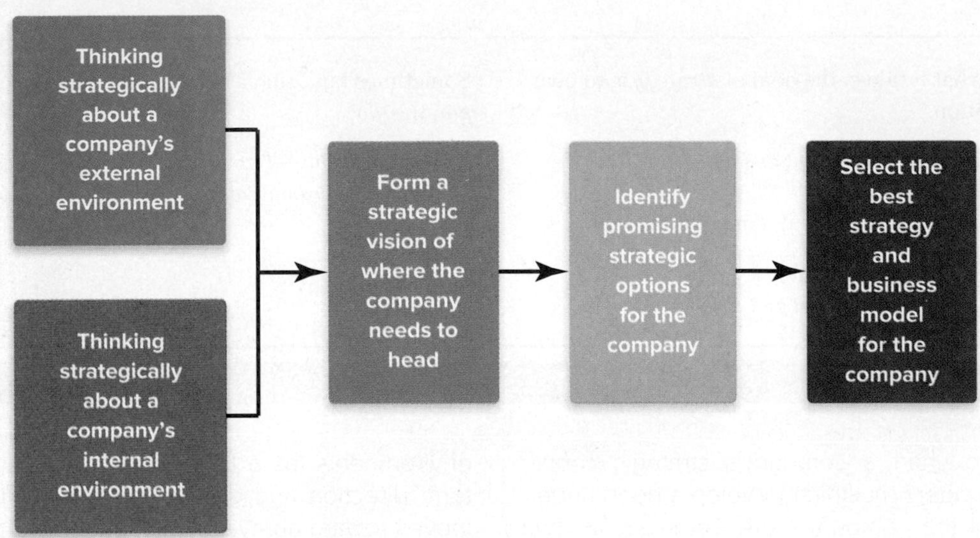

CORE CONCEPT

The **macro-environment** encompasses the broad environmental context in which a company's industry is situated.

CORE CONCEPT

PESTEL analysis can be used to assess the strategic relevance of the six principal components of the macro-environment: **P**olitical, **E**conomic, **S**ocial, **T**echnological, **E**nvironmental, and **L**egal/Regulatory forces.

Since macro-economic factors affect different industries in different ways and to different degrees, it is important for managers to determine which of these represent the most *strategically relevant factors* outside the firm's industry boundaries. By *strategically relevant,* we mean important enough to have a bearing on the decisions the company ultimately makes about its long-term direction, objectives, strategy, and business model. The impact of the outer-ring factors depicted in Figure 3.2 on a company's choice of strategy can range from big to small. But even if those factors change slowly or are likely to have a low impact on the company's business situation, they still merit a watchful eye.

For example, the strategic opportunities of cigarette producers to grow their businesses are greatly reduced by antismoking ordinances, the decisions of governments to impose higher cigarette taxes, and the growing cultural stigma attached to smoking. Motor vehicle companies must adapt their strategies to customer concerns about high gasoline prices and to environmental concerns about carbon emissions. Companies in the food processing, restaurant, sports, and fitness industries have to pay special attention to changes in lifestyles, eating habits, leisure-time preferences, and attitudes toward nutrition and fitness in fashioning their strategies. Table 3.1 provides a brief description of the components of the macro-environment and some examples of the industries or business situations that they might affect.

As company managers scan the external environment, they must be alert for potentially important outer-ring developments, assess their impact and influence, and adapt the company's direction and strategy as needed. However, the factors in a company's environment having the *biggest* strategy-shaping impact typically pertain to the company's immediate industry and competitive environment. Consequently, it is on a company's industry and competitive environment that we concentrate the bulk of our attention in this chapter.

FIGURE 3.2 The Components of a Company's Macro-Environment

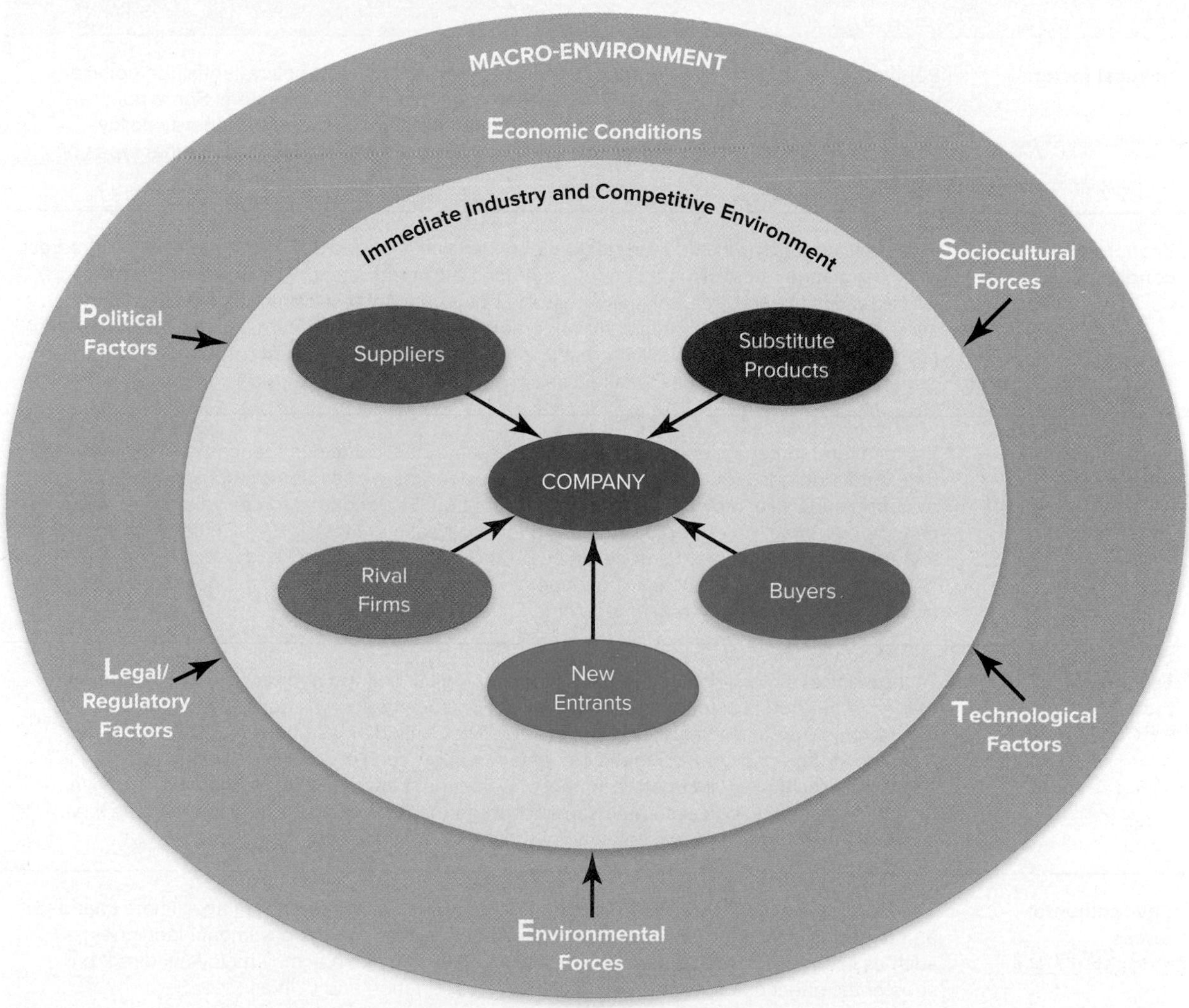

ASSESSING THE COMPANY'S INDUSTRY AND COMPETITIVE ENVIRONMENT

LO 2

How to use analytic tools to diagnose the competitive conditions in a company's industry.

Thinking strategically about a company's industry and competitive environment entails using some well-validated concepts and analytic tools. These include the five forces framework, the value net, driving forces, strategic groups, competitor analysis, and key success factors. Proper use of these analytic tools can provide managers with the understanding needed to craft a strategy that fits the company's situation within their industry environment. The remainder of this chapter is devoted to describing how managers can use these tools to inform and improve their strategic choices.

TABLE 3.1 The Six Components of the Macro-Environment

Component	Description
Political factors	Pertinent political factors include matters such as tax policy, fiscal policy, tariffs, the political climate, and the strength of institutions such as the federal banking system. Some political policies affect certain types of industries more than others. An example is energy policy, which clearly affects energy producers and heavy users of energy more than other types of businesses.
Economic conditions	Economic conditions include the general economic climate and specific factors such as interest rates, exchange rates, the inflation rate, the unemployment rate, the rate of economic growth, trade deficits or surpluses, savings rates, and per-capita domestic product. Some industries, such as construction, are particularly vulnerable to economic downturns but are positively affected by factors such as low interest rates. Others, such as discount retailing, benefit when general economic conditions weaken, as consumers become more price-conscious.
Sociocultural forces	Sociocultural forces include the societal values, attitudes, cultural influences, and lifestyles that impact demand for particular goods and services, as well as demographic factors such as the population size, growth rate, and age distribution. Sociocultural forces vary by locale and change over time. An example is the trend toward healthier lifestyles, which can shift spending toward exercise equipment and health clubs and away from alcohol and snack foods. The demographic effect of people living longer is having a huge impact on the health care, nursing homes, travel, hospitality, and entertainment industries.
Technological factors	Technological factors include the pace of technological change and technical developments that have the potential for wide-ranging effects on society, such as genetic engineering, nanotechnology, and solar energy technology. They include institutions involved in creating new knowledge and controlling the use of technology, such as R&D consortia, university-sponsored technology incubators, patent and copyright laws, and government control over the Internet. Technological change can encourage the birth of new industries, such as the connected wearable devices, and disrupt others, such as the recording industry.
Environmental forces	These include ecological and environmental forces such as weather, climate, climate change, and associated factors like water shortages. These factors can directly impact industries such as insurance, farming, energy production, and tourism. They may have an indirect but substantial effect on other industries such as transportation and utilities.
Legal and regulatory factors	These factors include the regulations and laws with which companies must comply, such as consumer laws, labor laws, antitrust laws, and occupational health and safety regulation. Some factors, such as financial services regulation, are industry-specific. Others, such as minimum wage legislation, affect certain types of industries (low-wage, labor-intensive industries) more than others.

THE FIVE FORCES FRAMEWORK

The character and strength of the competitive forces operating in an industry are never the same from one industry to another. The most powerful and widely used tool for diagnosing the principal competitive pressures in a market is the *five forces framework*.[1] This framework, depicted in Figure 3.3, holds that competitive pressures on

FIGURE 3.3 The Five Forces Model of Competition: A Key Analytic Tool

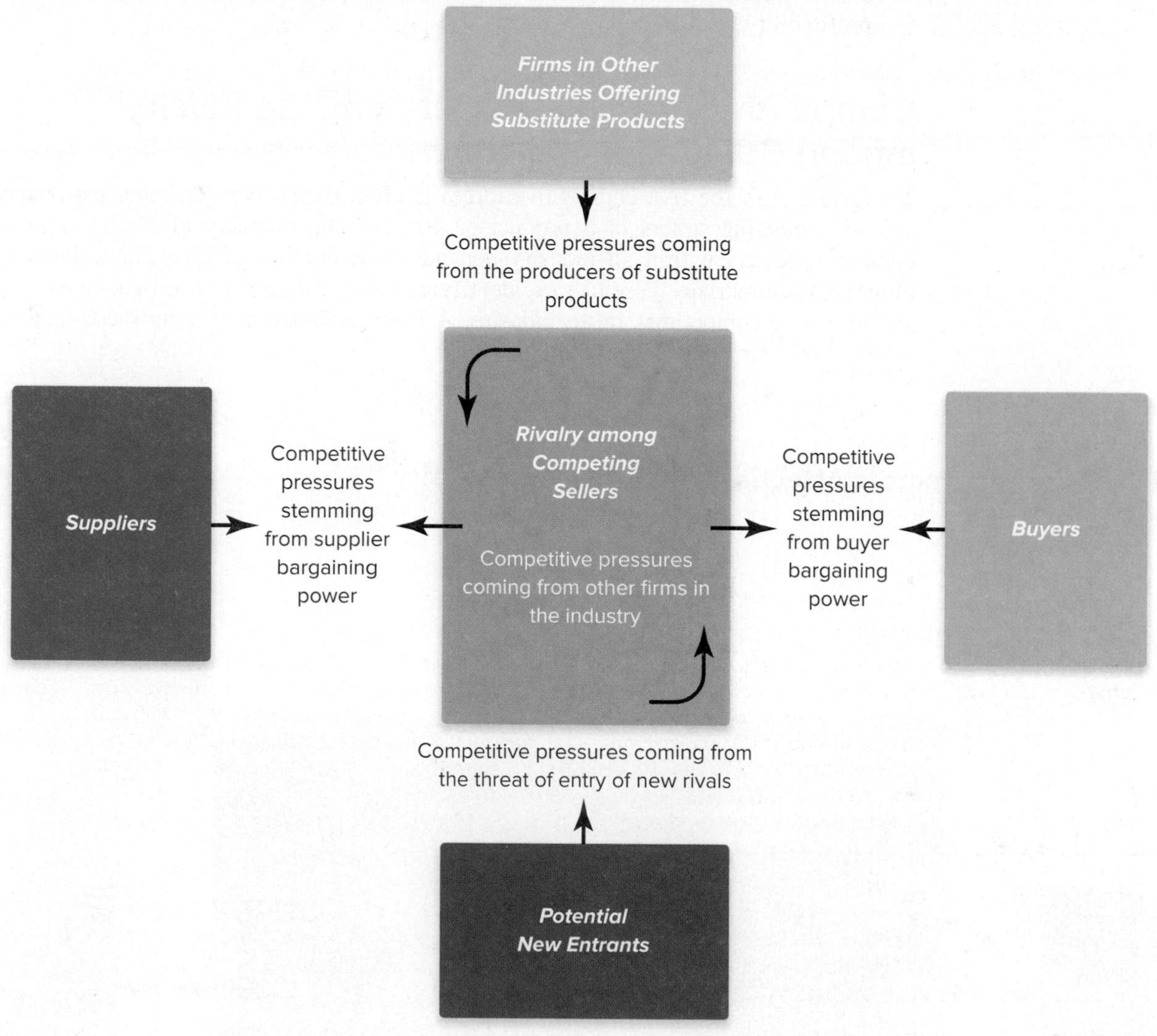

Sources: Adapted from M. E. Porter, "How Competitive Forces Shape Strategy," *Harvard Business Review* 57, no. 2 (1979), pp. 137–145; M. E. Porter, "The Five Competitive Forces That Shape Strategy," *Harvard Business Review* 86, no. 1 (2008), pp. 80–86.

companies within an industry come from five sources. These include (1) competition from *rival sellers,* (2) competition from *potential new entrants* to the industry, (3) competition from producers of *substitute products,* (4) *supplier* bargaining power, and (5) *customer* bargaining power.

Using the five forces model to determine the nature and strength of competitive pressures in a given industry involves three steps:

- *Step 1:* For each of the five forces, identify the different parties involved, along with the specific factors that bring about competitive pressures.

- *Step 2:* Evaluate how strong the pressures stemming from each of the five forces are (strong, moderate, or weak).
- *Step 3:* Determine whether the five forces, overall, are supportive of high industry profitability.

Competitive Pressures Created by the Rivalry among Competing Sellers

The strongest of the five competitive forces is often the rivalry for buyer patronage among competing sellers of a product or service. The intensity of rivalry among competing sellers within an industry depends on a number of identifiable factors. Figure 3.4 summarizes these factors, identifying those that intensify or weaken rivalry among direct competitors in an industry. A brief explanation of why these factors affect the degree of rivalry is in order:

FIGURE 3.4 Factors Affecting the Strength of Rivalry

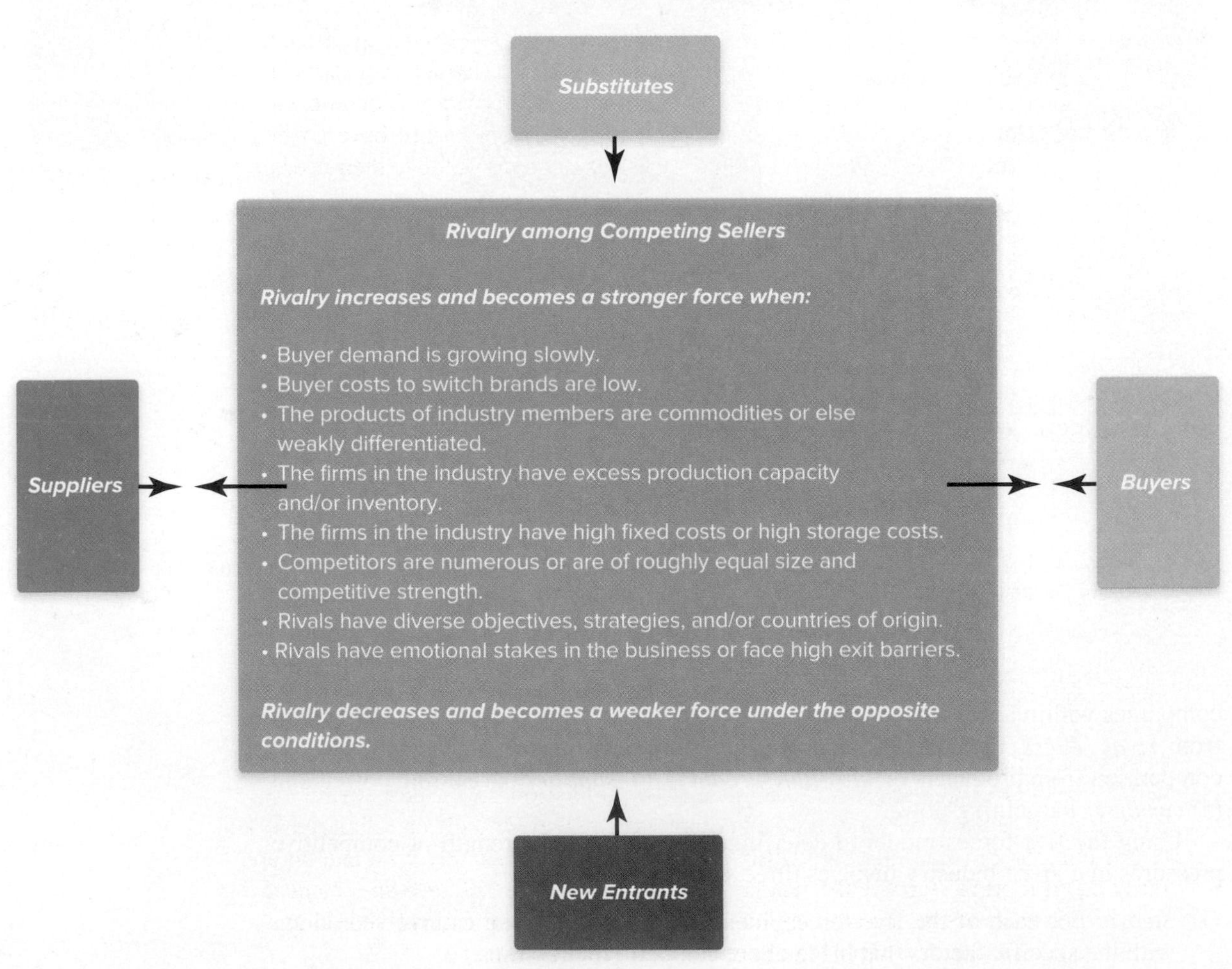

- *Rivalry increases when buyer demand is growing slowly or declining.* Rapidly expanding buyer demand produces enough new business for all industry members to grow without having to draw customers away from rival enterprises. But in markets where buyer demand is slow-growing or shrinking, companies eager to gain more business are likely to engage in aggressive price discounting, sales promotions, and other tactics to increase their sales volumes at the expense of rivals, sometimes to the point of igniting a fierce battle for market share.
- *Rivalry increases as it becomes less costly for buyers to switch brands.* The less costly it is for buyers to switch their purchases from one seller to another, the easier it is for sellers to steal customers away from rivals. When the cost of switching brands is higher, buyers are less prone to brand switching and sellers have protection from rivalrous moves. Switching costs include not only monetary costs but also the time, inconvenience, and psychological costs involved in switching brands. For example, retailers may not switch to the brands of rival manufacturers because they are hesitant to sever long-standing supplier relationships or incur the additional expense of retraining employees, accessing technical support, or testing the quality and reliability of the new brand.
- *Rivalry increases as the products of rival sellers become less strongly differentiated.* When the offerings of rivals are identical or weakly differentiated, buyers have less reason to be brand-loyal—a condition that makes it easier for rivals to convince buyers to switch to their offerings. Moreover, when the products of different sellers are virtually identical, shoppers will choose on the basis of price, which can result in fierce price competition among sellers. On the other hand, strongly differentiated product offerings among rivals breed high brand loyalty on the part of buyers who view the attributes of certain brands as more appealing or better suited to their needs.
- *Rivalry is more intense when industry members have too much inventory or significant amounts of idle production capacity, especially if the industry's product entails high fixed costs or high storage costs.* Whenever a market has excess supply (overproduction relative to demand), rivalry intensifies as sellers cut prices in a desperate effort to cope with the unsold inventory. A similar effect occurs when a product is perishable or seasonal, since firms often engage in aggressive price cutting to ensure that everything is sold. Likewise, whenever fixed costs account for a large fraction of total cost so that unit costs are significantly lower at full capacity, firms come under significant pressure to cut prices whenever they are operating below full capacity. Unused capacity imposes a significant cost-increasing penalty because there are fewer units over which to spread fixed costs. The pressure of high fixed or high storage costs can push rival firms into offering price concessions, special discounts, and rebates and employing other volume-boosting competitive tactics.
- *Rivalry intensifies as the number of competitors increases and they become more equal in size and capability.* When there are many competitors in a market, companies eager to increase their meager market share often engage in price-cutting activities to drive sales, leading to intense rivalry. When there are only a few competitors, companies are more wary of how their rivals may react to their attempts to take market share away from them. Fear of retaliation and a descent into a damaging price war leads to restrained competitive moves. Moreover, when rivals are of comparable size and competitive strength, they can usually compete on a fairly equal footing—an evenly matched contest tends to be fiercer than a contest in which one or more industry members have commanding market shares and substantially greater resources than their much smaller rivals.

- *Rivalry becomes more intense as the diversity of competitors increases in terms of long-term directions, objectives, strategies, and countries of origin.* A diverse group of sellers often contains one or more mavericks willing to try novel or rule-breaking market approaches, thus generating a more volatile and less predictable competitive environment. Globally competitive markets are often more rivalrous, especially when aggressors have lower costs and are intent on gaining a strong foothold in new country markets.
- *Rivalry is stronger when high exit barriers keep unprofitable firms from leaving the industry.* In industries where the assets cannot easily be sold or transferred to other uses, where workers are entitled to job protection, or where owners are committed to remaining in business for personal reasons, failing firms tend to hold on longer than they might otherwise—even when they are bleeding red ink. Deep price discounting of this sort can destabilize an otherwise attractive industry.

The previous factors, taken as whole, determine whether the rivalry in an industry is relatively strong, moderate, or weak. When rivalry is *strong,* the battle for market share is generally so vigorous that the profit margins of most industry members are squeezed to bare-bones levels. When rivalry is *moderate,* a more normal state, the maneuvering among industry members, while lively and healthy, still allows most industry members to earn acceptable profits. When rivalry is *weak,* most companies in the industry are relatively well satisfied with their sales growth and market shares and rarely undertake offensives to steal customers away from one another. Weak rivalry means that there is no downward pressure on industry profitability due to this particular competitive force.

The Choice of Competitive Weapons

Competitive battles among rival sellers can assume many forms that extend well beyond lively price competition. For example, competitors may resort to such marketing tactics as special sales promotions, heavy advertising, rebates, or low-interest-rate financing to drum up additional sales. Rivals may race one another to differentiate their products by offering better performance features or higher quality or improved customer service or a wider product selection. They may also compete through the rapid introduction of next-generation products, the frequent introduction of new or improved products, and efforts to build stronger dealer networks, establish positions in foreign markets, or otherwise expand distribution capabilities and market presence. Table 3.2 displays the competitive weapons that firms often employ in battling rivals, along with their primary effects with respect to price (*P*), cost (*C*), and value (*V*)—the elements of an effective business model and the value-price-cost framework, discussed in Chapter 1.

Competitive Pressures Associated with the Threat of New Entrants

New entrants into an industry threaten the position of rival firms since they will compete fiercely for market share, add to the number of industry rivals, and add to the industry's production capacity in the process. But even the *threat* of new entry puts added competitive pressure on current industry members and thus functions as an important competitive force. This is because credible threat of entry often prompts industry members to lower their prices and initiate defensive actions in an attempt

TABLE 3.2 Common "Weapons" for Competing with Rivals

Types of Competitive Weapons	Primary Effects
Discounting prices, holding clearance sales	Lowers price (*P*), increases total sales volume and market share, lowers profits if price cuts are not offset by large increases in sales volume
Offering coupons, advertising items on sale	Increases sales volume and total revenues, lowers price (*P*), increases unit costs (*C*), may lower profit margins per unit sold (*P* – *C*)
Advertising product or service characteristics, using ads to enhance a company's image	Boosts buyer demand, increases product differentiation and perceived value (*V*), increases total sales volume and market share, but may increase unit costs (*C*) and lower profit margins per unit sold
Innovating to improve product performance and quality	Increases product differentiation and value (*V*), boosts buyer demand, boosts total sales volume, likely to increase unit costs (*C*)
Introducing new or improved features, increasing the number of styles to provide greater product selection	Increases product differentiation and value (*V*), strengthens buyer demand, boosts total sales volume and market share, likely to increase unit costs (*C*)
Increasing customization of product or service	Increases product differentiation and value (*V*), increases buyer switching costs, boosts total sales volume, often increases unit costs (*C*)
Building a bigger, better dealer network	Broadens access to buyers, boosts total sales volume and market share, may increase unit costs (*C*)
Improving warranties, offering low-interest financing	Increases product differentiation and value (*V*), increases unit costs (*C*), increases buyer switching costs, boosts total sales volume and market share

to deter new entrants. Just how serious the threat of entry is in a particular market depends on two classes of factors: (1) the *expected reaction of incumbent firms to new entry* and (2) what are known as *barriers to entry.* The threat of entry is low in industries where incumbent firms are likely to retaliate against new entrants with sharp price discounting and other moves designed to make entry unprofitable (due to the expectation of such retaliation). The threat of entry is also low when entry barriers are high (due to such barriers). Entry barriers are high under the following conditions:[2]

- *There are sizable economies of scale in production, distribution, advertising, or other activities.* When incumbent companies enjoy cost advantages associated with large-scale operations, outsiders must either enter on a large scale (a costly and perhaps risky move) or accept a cost disadvantage and consequently lower profitability.
- *Incumbents have other hard to replicate cost advantages over new entrants.* Aside from enjoying economies of scale, industry incumbents can have cost advantages that stem from the possession of patents or proprietary technology,

exclusive partnerships with the best and cheapest suppliers, favorable locations, and low fixed costs (because they have older facilities that have been mostly depreciated). Learning-based cost savings can also accrue from experience in performing certain activities such as manufacturing or new product development or inventory management. The extent of such savings can be measured with learning/experience curves. The steeper the learning/experience curve, the bigger the cost advantage of the company with the largest *cumulative* production volume. The microprocessor industry provides an excellent example of this:

> *Manufacturing unit costs for microprocessors tend to decline about 20 percent each time cumulative production volume doubles. With a 20 percent experience curve effect, if the first 1 million chips cost $100 each, once production volume reaches 2 million, the unit cost would fall to $80 (80 percent of $100), and by a production volume of 4 million, the unit cost would be $64 (80 percent of $80).*[3]

- *Customers have strong brand preferences and high degrees of loyalty to seller.* The stronger the attachment of buyers to established brands, the harder it is for a newcomer to break into the marketplace. In such cases, a new entrant must have the financial resources to spend enough on advertising and sales promotion to overcome customer loyalties and build its own clientele. Establishing brand recognition and building customer loyalty can be a slow and costly process. In addition, if it is difficult or costly for a customer to switch to a new brand, a new entrant may have to offer a discounted price or otherwise persuade buyers that its brand is worth the switching costs. Such barriers discourage new entry because they act to boost financial requirements and lower expected profit margins for new entrants.
- *Patents and other forms of intellectual property protection are in place.* In a number of industries, entry is prevented due to the existence of intellectual property protection laws that remain in place for a given number of years. Often, companies have a "wall of patents" in place to prevent other companies from entering with a "me too" strategy that replicates a key piece of technology.
- *There are strong "network effects" in customer demand.* In industries where buyers are more attracted to a product when there are many other users of the product, there are said to be "network effects," since demand is higher the larger the network of users. Video game systems are an example because users prefer to have the same systems as their friends so that they can play together on systems they all know and can share games. When incumbents have a large existing base of users, new entrants with otherwise comparable products face a serious disadvantage in attracting buyers.
- *Capital requirements are high.* The larger the total dollar investment needed to enter the market successfully, the more limited the pool of potential entrants. The most obvious capital requirements for new entrants relate to manufacturing facilities and equipment, introductory advertising and sales promotion campaigns, working capital to finance inventories and customer credit, and sufficient cash to cover startup costs.
- *There are difficulties in building a network of distributors/dealers or in securing adequate space on retailers' shelves.* A potential entrant can face numerous distribution-channel challenges. Wholesale distributors may be reluctant to take on a product that lacks buyer recognition. Retailers must be recruited and

convinced to give a new brand ample display space and an adequate trial period. When existing sellers have strong, well-functioning distributor–dealer networks, a newcomer has an uphill struggle in squeezing its way into existing distribution channels. Potential entrants sometimes have to "buy" their way into wholesale or retail channels by cutting their prices to provide dealers and distributors with higher markups and profit margins or by giving them big advertising and promotional allowances. As a consequence, a potential entrant's own profits may be squeezed unless and until its product gains enough consumer acceptance that distributors and retailers are willing to carry it.

- *There are restrictive regulatory policies.* Regulated industries like cable TV, telecommunications, electric and gas utilities, radio and television broadcasting, liquor retailing, nuclear power, and railroads entail government-controlled entry. Government agencies can also limit or even bar entry by requiring licenses and permits, such as the medallion required to drive a taxicab in New York City. Government-mandated safety regulations and environmental pollution standards also create entry barriers because they raise entry costs. Recently enacted banking regulations in many countries have made entry particularly difficult for small new bank startups—complying with all the new regulations along with the rigors of competing against existing banks requires very deep pockets.
- *There are restrictive trade policies.* In international markets, host governments commonly limit foreign entry and must approve all foreign investment applications. National governments commonly use tariffs and trade restrictions (antidumping rules, local content requirements, quotas, etc.) to raise entry barriers for foreign firms and protect domestic producers from outside competition.

Figure 3.5 summarizes the factors that cause the overall competitive pressure from potential entrants to be strong or weak. An analysis of these factors can help managers determine whether the threat of entry into their industry is high or low, *in general*. But certain kinds of companies—those with sizable financial resources, proven competitive capabilities, and a respected brand name—may be able to hurdle an industry's entry barriers even when they are high.[4] For example, when Honda opted to enter the U.S. lawn-mower market in competition against Toro, Snapper, Craftsman, John Deere, and others, it was easily able to hurdle entry barriers that would have been formidable to other newcomers because it had long-standing expertise in gasoline engines and a reputation for quality and durability in automobiles that gave it instant credibility with homeowners. As a result, Honda had to spend relatively little on inducing dealers to handle the Honda lawn-mower line or attracting customers. Similarly, Samsung's brand reputation in televisions, DVD players, and other electronics products gave it strong credibility in entering the market for smartphones—Samsung's Galaxy smartphones are now a formidable rival of Apple's iPhone.

Whether an industry's entry barriers ought to be considered high or low depends on the resources and capabilities possessed by the pool of potential entrants.

It is also important to recognize that the barriers to entering an industry can become stronger or weaker over time. For example, key patents that had prevented new entry in the market for functional 3-D printers expired in February 2014, opening the way for new competition in this industry. Use of the Internet for shopping has made it much easier for e-tailers to enter into competition against some of the best-known retail chains. On the other hand, new strategic actions by incumbent firms to increase advertising, strengthen distributor–dealer relations, step up R&D, or improve product quality can erect higher roadblocks to entry.

High entry barriers and weak entry threats today do not always translate into high entry barriers and weak entry threats tomorrow.

FIGURE 3.5 Factors Affecting the Threat of Entry

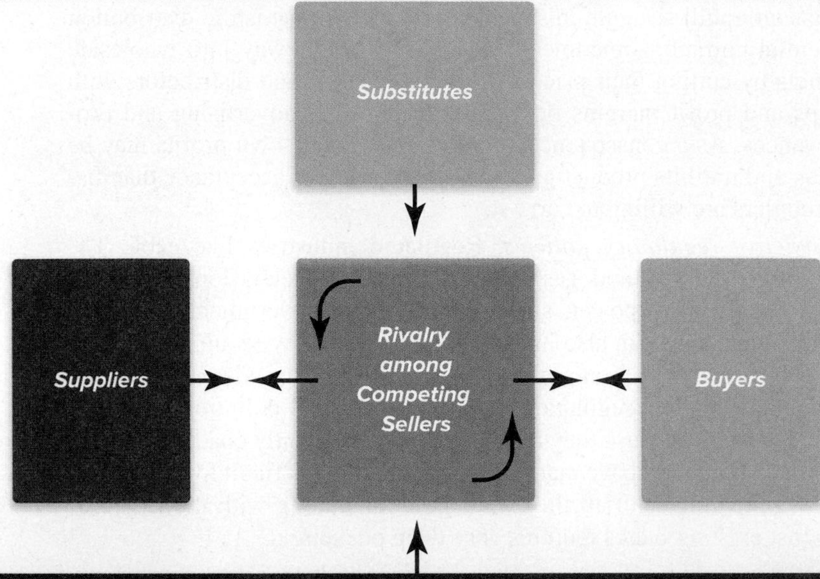

Competitive Pressures from Potential Entrants

Threat of entry is a stronger force when incumbents are unlikely to make retaliatory moves against new entrants and entry barriers are low. Entry barriers are high (and threat of entry is low) when:

- Incumbents have large cost advantages over potential entrants due to:
  - High economies of scale
  - Significant experience-based cost advantages or learning curve effects
  - Other cost advantages (e.g., favorable access to inputs, technology, location, or low fixed costs)
- Customers have strong brand preferences and/or loyalty to incumbent sellers.
- Patents and other forms of intellectual property protection are in place.
- There are strong network effects.
- Capital requirements are high.
- There is limited new access to distribution channels and shelf space.
- Government policies are restrictive.
- There are restrictive trade policies.

Competitive Pressures from the Sellers of Substitute Products

Companies in one industry are vulnerable to competitive pressure from the actions of companies in a closely adjoining industry whenever buyers view the products of the two industries as good substitutes. For instance, the producers of eyeglasses and contact lens face competitive pressures from the doctors who do corrective laser surgery. Similarly, the producers of sugar experience competitive pressures from the producers of sugar substitutes (high-fructose corn syrup, agave syrup, and artificial sweeteners). Internet providers of news-related information have put brutal competitive pressure on the publishers of newspapers.

As depicted in Figure 3.6, three factors determine whether the competitive pressures from substitute products are strong or weak. Competitive pressures are stronger when:

1. *Good substitutes are readily available and attractively priced.* The presence of readily available and attractively priced substitutes creates competitive pressure by placing a ceiling on the prices industry members can charge without risking sales erosion. This price ceiling, at the same time, puts a lid on the profits that industry members can earn unless they find ways to cut costs.
2. *Buyers view the substitutes as comparable or better in terms of quality, performance, and other relevant attributes.* The availability of substitutes inevitably invites customers to compare performance, features, ease of use, and other attributes besides price. The users of paper cartons constantly weigh the

FIGURE 3.6 Factors Affecting Competition from Substitute Products

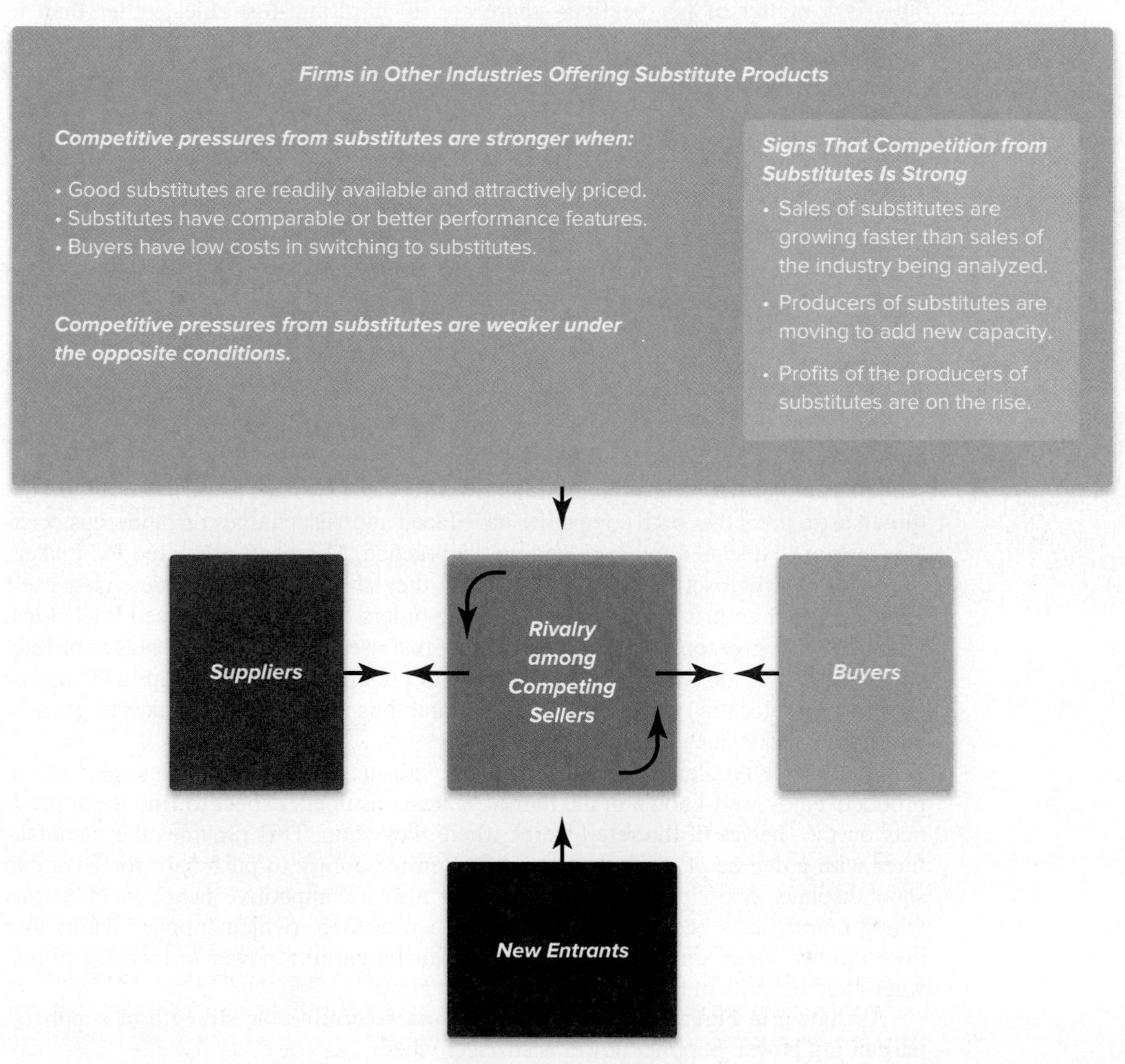

price-performance trade-offs with plastic containers and metal cans, for example. Movie enthusiasts are increasingly weighing whether to go to movie theaters to watch newly released movies or wait until they can watch the same movies streamed to their home TV by Netflix, Amazon Prime, cable providers, and other on demand sources.

3. *The costs that buyers incur in switching to the substitutes are low.* Low switching costs make it easier for the sellers of attractive substitutes to lure buyers to their offerings; high switching costs deter buyers from purchasing substitute products.

Before assessing the competitive pressures coming from substitutes, company managers must identify the substitutes, which is less easy than it sounds since it involves (1) determining where the industry boundaries lie and (2) figuring out which other products or services can address the same basic customer needs as those produced by industry members. Deciding on the industry boundaries is necessary for determining which firms are direct rivals and which produce substitutes. This is a matter of perspective—there are no hard-and-fast rules, other than to say that other brands of the same basic product constitute rival products and not substitutes.

Competitive Pressures Stemming from Supplier Bargaining Power

Whether the suppliers of industry members represent a weak or strong competitive force depends on the degree to which suppliers have sufficient *bargaining power* to influence the terms and conditions of supply in their favor. Suppliers with strong bargaining power are a source of competitive pressure because of their ability to charge industry members higher prices, pass costs on to them, and limit their opportunities to find better deals. For instance, Microsoft and Intel, both of which supply PC makers with essential components, have been known to use their dominant market status not only to charge PC makers premium prices but also to leverage their power over PC makers in other ways. The bargaining power of these two companies over their customers is so great that both companies have faced antitrust charges on numerous occasions. Prior to a legal agreement ending the practice, Microsoft pressured PC makers to load only Microsoft products on the PCs they shipped. Intel has defended itself against similar antitrust charges, but in filling orders for newly introduced Intel chips, it continues to give top priority to PC makers that use the biggest percentages of Intel chips in their PC models. Being on Intel's list of preferred customers helps a PC maker get an early allocation of Intel's latest chips and thus allows the PC maker to get new models to market ahead of rivals.

Small-scale retailers often must contend with the power of manufacturers whose products enjoy well-known brand names, since consumers expect to find these products on the shelves of the retail stores where they shop. This provides the manufacturer with a degree of pricing power and often the ability to push hard for favorable shelf displays. Supplier bargaining power is also a competitive factor in industries where unions have been able to organize the workforce (which supplies labor). Air pilot unions, for example, have employed their bargaining power to increase pilots' wages and benefits in the air transport industry.

As shown in Figure 3.7, a variety of factors determine the strength of suppliers' bargaining power. Supplier power is stronger when:

FIGURE 3.7 Factors Affecting the Bargaining Power of Suppliers

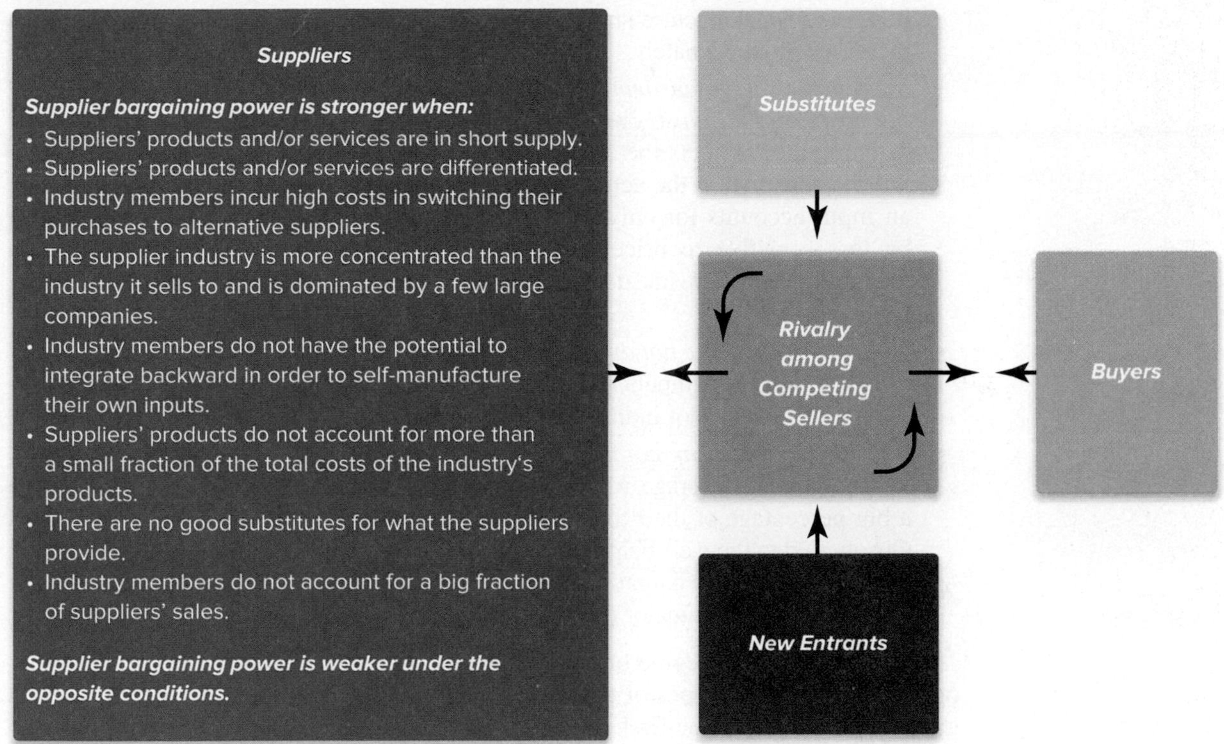

- *Demand for suppliers' products is high and the products are in short supply.* A surge in the demand for particular items shifts the bargaining power to the suppliers of those products; suppliers of items in short supply have pricing power.
- *Suppliers provide differentiated inputs that enhance the performance of the industry's product.* The more valuable a particular input is in terms of enhancing the performance or quality of the products of industry members, the more bargaining leverage suppliers have. In contrast, the suppliers of commodities are in a weak bargaining position, since industry members have no reason other than price to prefer one supplier over another.
- *It is difficult or costly for industry members to switch their purchases from one supplier to another.* Low switching costs limit supplier bargaining power by enabling industry members to change suppliers if any one supplier attempts to raise prices by more than the costs of switching. Thus, the higher the switching costs of industry members, the stronger the bargaining power of their suppliers.
- *The supplier industry is dominated by a few large companies and it is more concentrated than the industry it sells to.* Suppliers with sizable market shares and strong demand for the items they supply generally have sufficient bargaining power to charge high prices and deny requests from industry members for lower prices or other concessions.
- *Industry members are incapable of integrating backward to self-manufacture items they have been buying from suppliers.* As a rule, suppliers are safe from the

threat of self-manufacture by their customers until the volume of parts a customer needs becomes large enough for the customer to justify backward integration into self-manufacture of the component. When industry members can threaten credibly to self-manufacture suppliers' goods, their bargaining power over suppliers increases proportionately.

- *Suppliers provide an item that accounts for no more than a small fraction of the costs of the industry's product.* The more that the cost of a particular part or component affects the final product's cost, the more that industry members will be sensitive to the actions of suppliers to raise or lower their prices. When an input accounts for only a small proportion of total input costs, buyers will be less sensitive to price increases. Thus, suppliers' power increases when the inputs they provide do *not* make up a large proportion of the cost of the final product.
- *Good substitutes are not available for the suppliers' products.* The lack of readily available substitute inputs increases the bargaining power of suppliers by increasing the dependence of industry members on the suppliers.
- *Industry members are not major customers of suppliers.* As a rule, suppliers have less bargaining leverage when their sales to members of the industry constitute a big percentage of their total sales. In such cases, the well-being of suppliers is closely tied to the well-being of their major customers, and their dependence upon them increases. The bargaining power of suppliers is stronger, then, when they are *not* bargaining with major customers.

In identifying the degree of supplier power in an industry, it is important to recognize that different types of suppliers are likely to have different amounts of bargaining power. Thus, the first step is for managers to identify the different types of suppliers, paying particular attention to those that provide the industry with important inputs. The next step is to assess the bargaining power of each type of supplier separately.

Competitive Pressures Stemming from Buyer Bargaining Power and Price Sensitivity

Whether buyers are able to exert strong competitive pressures on industry members depends on (1) the degree to which buyers have bargaining power and (2) the extent to which buyers are price-sensitive. Buyers with strong bargaining power can limit industry profitability by demanding price concessions, better payment terms, or additional features and services that increase industry members' costs. Buyer price sensitivity limits the profit potential of industry members by restricting the ability of sellers to raise prices without losing revenue due to lost sales.

As with suppliers, the leverage that buyers have in negotiating favorable terms of sale can range from weak to strong. Individual consumers seldom have much bargaining power in negotiating price concessions or other favorable terms with sellers. However, their price sensitivity varies by individual and by the type of product they are buying (whether it's a necessity or a discretionary purchase, for example). Similarly, small businesses usually have weak bargaining power because of the small-size orders they place with sellers. Many relatively small wholesalers and retailers join buying groups to pool their purchasing power and approach manufacturers for better terms than could be gotten individually. Large business buyers, in contrast, can have considerable bargaining power. For example, large retail chains like

Walmart, Best Buy, Staples, and Home Depot typically have considerable bargaining power in purchasing products from manufacturers, not only because they buy in large quantities, but also because of manufacturers' need for access to their broad base of customers. Major supermarket chains like Kroger, Albertsons, Hannaford, and Aldi have sufficient bargaining power to demand promotional allowances and lump-sum payments (called *slotting fees*) from food products manufacturers in return for stocking certain brands or putting them in the best shelf locations. Motor vehicle manufacturers have strong bargaining power in negotiating to buy original-equipment tires from tire makers such as Goodyear, Michelin, and Pirelli, partly because they buy in large quantities and partly because consumers are more likely to buy replacement tires that match the tire brand on their vehicle at the time of its purchase.

Figure 3.8 summarizes the factors determining the strength of buyer power in an industry. Note that the first five factors are the mirror image of those determining the bargaining power of suppliers, as described next.

Buyer bargaining power is stronger when:

- *Buyer demand is weak in relation to the available supply.* Weak or declining demand and the resulting excess supply create a "buyers' market," in which bargain-hunting buyers have leverage in pressing industry members for better deals and special treatment. Conversely, strong or rapidly growing market demand creates a "sellers'

FIGURE 3.8 Factors Affecting the Bargaining Power of Buyers

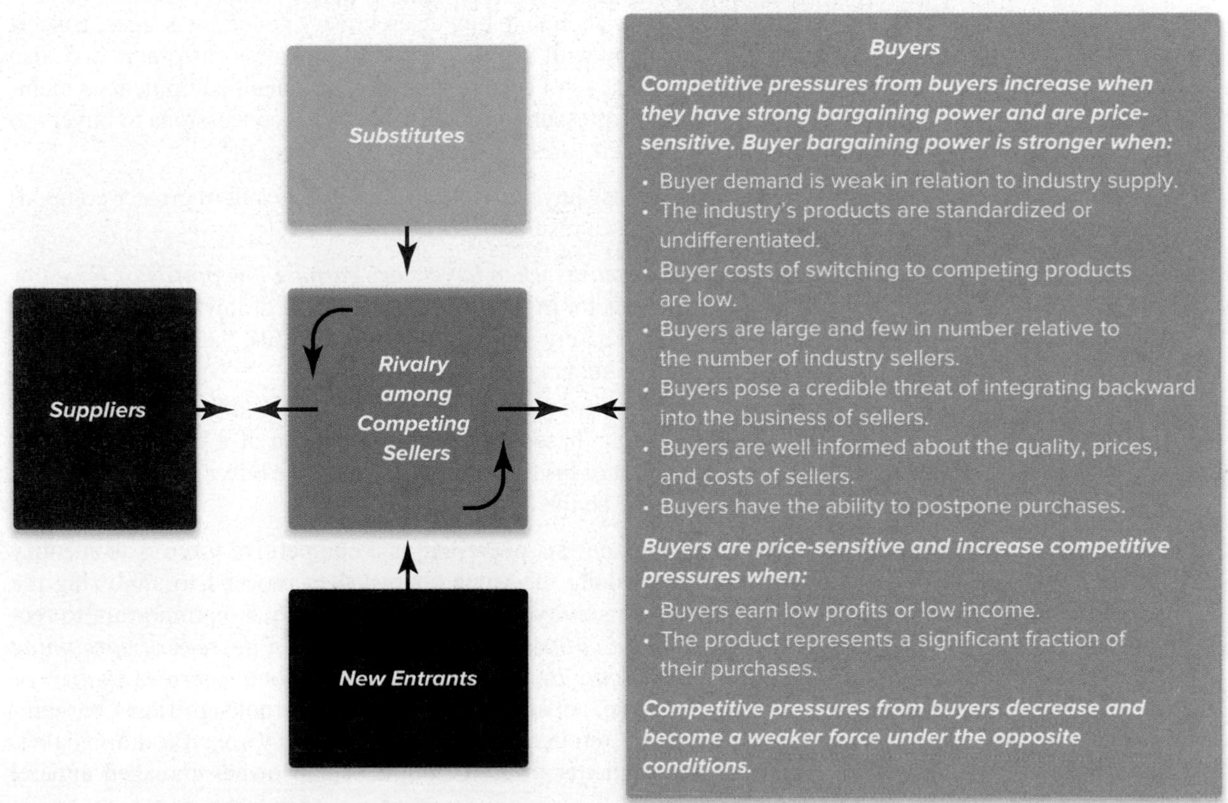

market" characterized by tight supplies or shortages—conditions that put buyers in a weak position to wring concessions from industry members.

- *Industry goods are standardized or differentiation is weak.* In such circumstances, buyers make their selections on the basis of price, which increases price competition among vendors.
- *Buyers' costs of switching to competing brands or substitutes are relatively low.* Switching costs put a cap on how much industry producers can raise prices or reduce quality before they will lose the buyer's business.
- *Buyers are large and few in number relative to the number of sellers.* The larger the buyers, the more important their business is to the seller and the more sellers will be willing to grant concessions.
- *Buyers pose a credible threat of integrating backward into the business of sellers.* Companies like Anheuser-Busch, Coors, and Heinz have partially integrated backward into metal-can manufacturing to gain bargaining power in obtaining the balance of their can requirements from otherwise powerful metal-can manufacturers.
- *Buyers are well informed about the product offerings of sellers (product features and quality, prices, buyer reviews) and the cost of production (an indicator of markup).* The more information buyers have, the better bargaining position they are in. The mushrooming availability of product information on the Internet (and its ready access on smartphones) is giving added bargaining power to consumers, since they can use this to find or negotiate better deals.
- *Buyers have discretion to delay their purchases or perhaps even not make a purchase at all.* Consumers often have the option to delay purchases of durable goods (cars, major appliances), or decline to buy discretionary goods (massages, concert tickets) if they are not happy with the prices offered. Business customers may also be able to defer their purchases of certain items, such as plant equipment or maintenance services. This puts pressure on sellers to provide concessions to buyers so that the sellers can keep their sales numbers from dropping off.

The following factors increase buyer price sensitivity and result in greater competitive pressures on the industry as a result:

- *Buyer price sensitivity increases when buyers are earning low profits or have low income.* Price is a critical factor in the purchase decisions of low-income consumers and companies that are barely scraping by. In such cases, their high price sensitivity limits the ability of sellers to charge high prices.
- *Buyers are more price-sensitive if the product represents a large fraction of their total purchases.* When a purchase eats up a large portion of a buyer's budget or represents a significant part of his or her cost structure, the buyer cares more about price than might otherwise be the case.

The starting point for the analysis of buyers as a competitive force is to identify the different types of buyers along the value chain—then proceed to analyzing the bargaining power and price sensitivity of each type separately. It is important to recognize that *not all buyers of an industry's product have equal degrees of bargaining power with sellers, and some may be less sensitive than others to price, quality, or service differences.* For example, apparel manufacturers confront significant bargaining power when selling to big retailers like Nordstrom, Macy's, or Bloomingdale's, but they can command much better prices selling to small owner-managed apparel boutiques.

Is the Collective Strength of the Five Competitive Forces Conducive to Good Profitability?

Assessing whether each of the five competitive forces gives rise to strong, moderate, or weak competitive pressures sets the stage for evaluating whether, overall, the strength of the five forces is conducive to good profitability. Is any of the competitive forces sufficiently powerful to undermine industry profitability? Can companies in this industry reasonably expect to earn decent profits in light of the prevailing competitive forces?

The most extreme case of a "competitively unattractive" industry occurs when all five forces are producing strong competitive pressures: Rivalry among sellers is vigorous, low entry barriers allow new rivals to gain a market foothold, competition from substitutes is intense, and both suppliers and buyers are able to exercise considerable leverage. Strong competitive pressures coming from all five directions drive industry profitability to unacceptably low levels, frequently producing losses for many industry members and forcing some out of business. But an industry can be competitively unattractive without all five competitive forces being strong. In fact, *intense competitive pressures from just one of the five forces may suffice to destroy the conditions for good profitability and prompt some companies to exit the business.*

As a rule, *the strongest competitive forces determine the extent of the competitive pressure on industry profitability.* Thus, in evaluating the strength of the five forces overall and their effect on industry profitability, managers should look to the strongest forces. Having more than one strong force will not worsen the effect on industry profitability, but it does mean that the industry has multiple competitive challenges with which to cope. In that sense, an industry with three to five strong forces is even more "unattractive" as a place to compete. Especially intense competitive conditions seem to be the norm in tire manufacturing, apparel, and commercial airlines, three industries where profit margins have historically been thin.

CORE CONCEPT

The strongest of the five forces determines the extent of the downward pressure on an industry's profitability.

In contrast, when the overall impact of the five competitive forces is moderate to weak, an industry is "attractive" in the sense that the *average* industry member can reasonably expect to earn good profits and a nice return on investment. The ideal competitive environment for earning superior profits is one in which both suppliers and customers are in weak bargaining positions, there are no good substitutes, high barriers block further entry, and rivalry among present sellers is muted. Weak competition is the best of all possible worlds for also-ran companies because even they can usually eke out a decent profit—if a company can't make a decent profit when competition is weak, then its business outlook is indeed grim.

Matching Company Strategy to Competitive Conditions

Working through the five forces model step by step not only aids strategy makers in assessing whether the intensity of competition allows good profitability but also promotes sound strategic thinking about how to better match company strategy to the specific competitive character of the marketplace. Effectively matching a company's business strategy to prevailing competitive conditions has two aspects:

1. Pursuing avenues that shield the firm from as many of the different competitive pressures as possible.
2. Initiating actions calculated to shift the competitive forces in the company's favor by altering the underlying factors driving the five forces.

A company's strategy is increasingly effective the more it provides some insulation from competitive pressures, shifts the competitive battle in the company's favor, and positions the firm to take advantage of attractive growth opportunities.

But making headway on these two fronts first requires identifying competitive pressures, gauging the relative strength of each of the five competitive forces, and gaining a deep enough understanding of the state of competition in the industry to know which strategy buttons to push.

COMPLEMENTORS AND THE VALUE NET

Not all interactions among industry participants are necessarily competitive in nature. Some have the potential to be cooperative, as the value net framework demonstrates. Like the five forces framework, the value net includes an analysis of buyers, suppliers, and substitutors (see Figure 3.9). But it differs from the five forces framework in several important ways.

CORE CONCEPT

Complementors are the producers of complementary products, which are products that enhance the value of the focal firm's products when they are used together.

First, the analysis focuses on the interactions of industry participants with a particular company. Thus it places that firm in the center of the framework, as Figure 3.9 shows. Second, the category of "competitors" is defined to include not only the focal firm's direct competitors or industry rivals but also the sellers of substitute products and potential entrants. Third, the value net framework introduces a new category of industry participant that is not found in the five forces framework—that of "complementors." **Complementors** are the producers of complementary products, which are products that enhance the value of the focal firm's products when they are used together. Some examples include snorkels and swim fins or shoes and shoelaces.

The inclusion of complementors draws particular attention to the fact that success in the marketplace need not come at the expense of other industry participants.

FIGURE 3.9 The Value Net

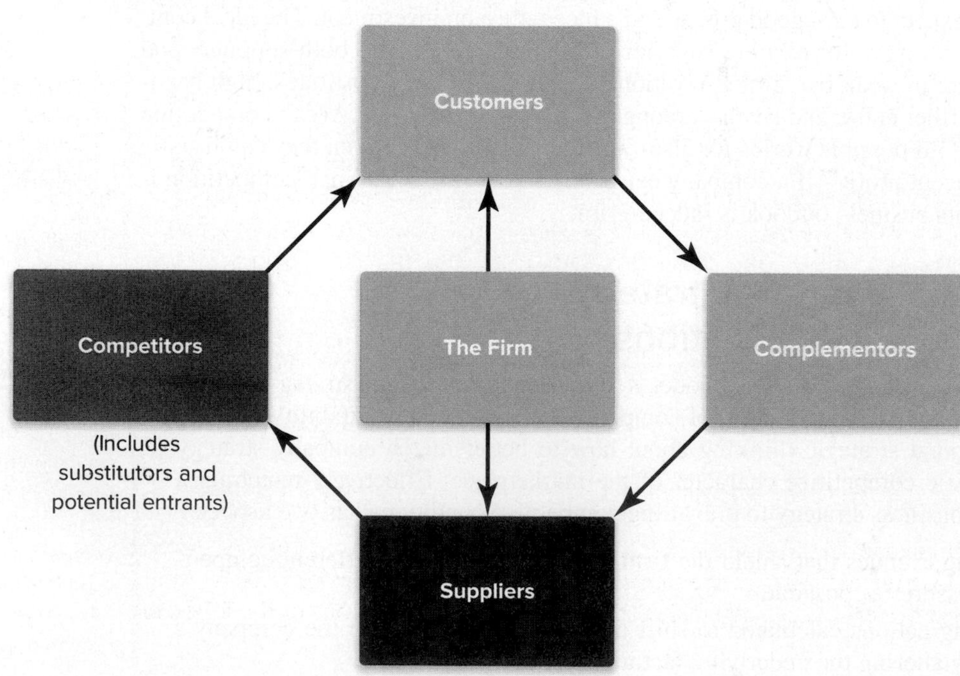

Interactions among industry participants may be cooperative in nature rather than competitive. In the case of complementors, an increase in sales for them is likely to increase the sales of the focal firm as well. But the value net framework also encourages managers to consider other forms of cooperative interactions and realize that value is created jointly by all industry participants. For example, a company's success in the marketplace depends on establishing a reliable supply chain for its inputs, which implies the need for cooperative relations with its suppliers. Often a firm works hand in hand with its suppliers to ensure a smoother, more efficient operation for both parties. Newell-Rubbermaid, for example, works cooperatively as a supplier to companies such as Kmart and Kohl's. Even direct rivals may work cooperatively if they participate in industry trade associations or engage in joint lobbying efforts. Value net analysis can help managers discover the potential to improve their position through cooperative as well as competitive interactions.

INDUSTRY DYNAMICS AND THE FORCES DRIVING CHANGE

While it is critical to understand the nature and intensity of competitive and cooperative forces in an industry, it is equally critical to understand that the intensity of these forces is fluid and subject to change. All industries are affected by new developments and ongoing trends that alter industry conditions, some more speedily than others. The popular hypothesis that industries go through a life cycle of takeoff, rapid growth, maturity, market saturation and slowing growth, followed by stagnation or decline is but one aspect of industry change—many other new developments and emerging trends cause industry change.[5] Any strategies devised by management will therefore play out in a dynamic industry environment, so it's imperative that managers consider the factors driving industry change and how they might affect the industry environment. Moreover, with early notice, managers may be able to influence the direction or scope of environmental change and improve the outlook.

Industry and competitive conditions change because forces are enticing or pressuring certain industry participants (competitors, customers, suppliers, complementors) to alter their actions in important ways. The most powerful of the change agents are called **driving forces** because they have the biggest influences in reshaping the industry landscape and altering competitive conditions. Some driving forces originate in the outer ring of the company's macro-environment (see Figure 3.2), but most originate in the company's more immediate industry and competitive environment.

CORE CONCEPT

Driving forces are the major underlying causes of change in industry and competitive conditions.

Driving-forces analysis has three steps: (1) identifying what the driving forces are; (2) assessing whether the drivers of change are, on the whole, acting to make the industry more or less attractive; and (3) determining what strategy changes are needed to prepare for the impact of the driving forces. All three steps merit further discussion.

Identifying the Forces Driving Industry Change

Many developments can affect an industry powerfully enough to qualify as driving forces. Some drivers of change are unique and specific to a particular industry situation, but most drivers of industry and competitive change fall into one of the following categories:

- *Changes in an industry's long-term growth rate.* Shifts in industry growth up or down have the potential to affect the balance between industry supply and buyer demand, entry and exit, and the character and strength of competition. Whether demand is growing or declining is one of the key factors influencing the intensity of rivalry in an industry, as explained earlier. But the strength of this effect will depend on how changes in the industry growth rate affect entry and exit in the industry. If entry barriers are low, then growth in demand will attract new entrants, increasing the number of industry rivals and changing the competitive landscape.
- *Increasing globalization.* Globalization can be precipitated by such factors as the blossoming of consumer demand in developing countries, the availability of lower-cost foreign inputs, and the reduction of trade barriers, as has occurred recently in many parts of Latin America and Asia. The forces of globalization are sometimes such a strong driver that companies find it highly advantageous, if not necessary, to spread their operating reach into more and more country markets.
- *Emerging new Internet capabilities and applications.* The Internet of the future will feature faster speeds, dazzling applications, and over a billion connected gadgets performing an array of functions, thus driving a host of industry and competitive changes. But Internet-related impacts vary from industry to industry. The challenges are to assess precisely how emerging Internet developments are altering a particular industry's landscape and to factor these impacts into the strategy-making equation.
- *Shifts in who buys the products and how the products are used.* Shifts in buyer demographics and the ways products are used can greatly alter competitive conditions. Longer life expectancies and growing percentages of relatively well-to-do retirees, for example, are driving demand growth in such industries as cosmetic surgery, assisted living residences, and vacation travel. The burgeoning popularity of streaming video has affected broadband providers, wireless phone carriers, and television broadcasters, and created opportunities for such new entertainment businesses as Hulu and Netflix.
- *Technological change and manufacturing process innovation.* Advances in technology can cause disruptive change in an industry by introducing substitutes or can alter the industry landscape by opening up whole new industry frontiers. For instance, revolutionary change in self-driving technology has enabled even companies such as Google to enter the motor vehicle market.
- *Product innovation.* An ongoing stream of product innovations tends to alter the pattern of competition in an industry by attracting more first-time buyers, rejuvenating industry growth, and/or increasing product differentiation, with concomitant effects on rivalry, entry threat, and buyer power. Product innovation has been a key driving force in the smartphone industry, which in an ever more connected world is driving change in other industries. Phillips Company, for example, has introduced a new wireless lighting system (Hue) that allows homeowners to use a smartphone app to remotely turn lights on and off and program them to blink if an intruder is detected. Wearable action-capture cameras and unmanned aerial view drones are rapidly becoming a disruptive force in the digital camera industry by enabling photography shots and videos not feasible with handheld digital cameras.

- *Entry or exit of major firms.* Entry by a major firm thus often produces a new ball game, not only with new key players but also with new rules for competing. Similarly, exit of a major firm changes the competitive structure by reducing the number of market leaders and increasing the dominance of the leaders who remain.
- *Diffusion of technical know-how across companies and countries.* As knowledge about how to perform a particular activity or execute a particular manufacturing technology spreads, products tend to become more commodity-like. Knowledge diffusion can occur through scientific journals, trade publications, onsite plant tours, word of mouth among suppliers and customers, employee migration, and Internet sources.
- *Changes in cost and efficiency.* Widening or shrinking differences in the costs among key competitors tend to dramatically alter the state of competition. Declining costs of producing tablets have enabled price cuts and spurred tablet sales (especially lower-priced models) by making them more affordable to lower-income households worldwide. Lower-cost e-books are cutting into sales of costlier hardcover books as increasing numbers of consumers have laptops, iPads, Kindles, and other brands of tablets.
- *Reductions in uncertainty and business risk.* Many companies are hesitant to enter industries with uncertain futures or high levels of business risk because it is unclear how much time and money it will take to overcome various technological hurdles and achieve acceptable production costs (as is the case in the solar power industry). Over time, however, diminishing risk levels and uncertainty tend to stimulate new entry and capital investments on the part of growth-minded companies seeking new opportunities, thus dramatically altering industry and competitive conditions.
- *Regulatory influences and government policy changes.* Government regulatory actions can often mandate significant changes in industry practices and strategic approaches—as has recently occurred in the world's banking industry. New rules and regulations pertaining to government-sponsored health insurance programs are driving changes in the health care industry. In international markets, host governments can drive competitive changes by opening their domestic markets to foreign participation or closing them to protect domestic companies.
- *Changing societal concerns, attitudes, and lifestyles.* Emerging social issues as well as changing attitudes and lifestyles can be powerful instigators of industry change. Growing concern about the effects of climate change has emerged as a major driver of change in the energy industry. Concerns about the use of chemical additives and the nutritional content of food products have been driving changes in the restaurant and food industries. Shifting societal concerns, attitudes, and lifestyles alter the pattern of competition, favoring those players that respond with products targeted to the new trends and conditions.

While many forces of change may be at work in a given industry, *no more than three or four* are likely to be true driving forces powerful enough to qualify as the *major determinants* of why and how the industry is changing. Thus, company strategists must resist the temptation to label every change they see as a driving force. Table 3.3 lists the most common driving forces.

The most important part of driving-forces analysis is to determine whether the collective impact of the driving forces will increase or decrease market demand, make competition more or less intense, and lead to higher or lower industry profitability.

TABLE 3.3 The Most Common Drivers of Industry Change

- Changes in the long-term industry growth rate
- Increasing globalization
- Emerging new Internet capabilities and applications
- Shifts in buyer demographics
- Technological change and manufacturing process innovation
- Product and marketing innovation
- Entry or exit of major firms
- Diffusion of technical know-how across companies and countries
- Changes in cost and efficiency
- Reductions in uncertainty and business risk
- Regulatory influences and government policy changes
- Changing societal concerns, attitudes, and lifestyles

Assessing the Impact of the Forces Driving Industry Change

The second step in driving-forces analysis is to determine whether the prevailing change drivers, on the whole, are acting to make the industry environment more or less attractive. Three questions need to be answered:

The real payoff of driving-forces analysis is to help managers understand what strategy changes are needed to prepare for the impacts of the driving forces.

1. Are the driving forces, on balance, acting to cause demand for the industry's product to increase or decrease?
2. Is the collective impact of the driving forces making competition more or less intense?
3. Will the combined impacts of the driving forces lead to higher or lower industry profitability?

Getting a handle on the collective impact of the driving forces requires looking at the likely effects of each factor separately, since the driving forces may not all be pushing change in the same direction. For example, one driving force may be acting to spur demand for the industry's product while another is working to curtail demand. Whether the net effect on industry demand is up or down hinges on which change driver is the most powerful.

Adjusting the Strategy to Prepare for the Impacts of Driving Forces

The third step in the strategic analysis of industry dynamics—where the real payoff for strategy making comes—is for managers to draw some conclusions about *what strategy adjustments will be needed to deal with the impacts of the driving forces.* But taking the "right" kinds of actions to prepare for the industry and competitive changes being wrought by the driving forces first requires accurate diagnosis of the forces driving industry change and the impacts these forces will have on both the industry environment and the company's business. To the extent that managers are unclear about the drivers of industry change and their impacts, or if their views are off-base, the chances of making astute and timely strategy adjustments are slim. So driving-forces analysis is not something to take lightly; it has practical value and is basic to the task of thinking strategically about where the industry is headed and how to prepare for the changes ahead.

STRATEGIC GROUP ANALYSIS

LO 3

How to map the market positions of key groups of industry rivals.

Within an industry, companies commonly sell in different price/quality ranges, appeal to different types of buyers, have different geographic coverage, and so on. Some are more attractively positioned than others. Understanding which companies are strongly positioned and which are weakly positioned is an integral part of analyzing an industry's competitive structure. The best technique for revealing the market positions of industry competitors is **strategic group mapping.**

Using Strategic Group Maps to Assess the Market Positions of Key Competitors

CORE CONCEPT

Strategic group mapping is a technique for displaying the different market or competitive positions that rival firms occupy in the industry.

A **strategic group** consists of those industry members with similar competitive approaches and positions in the market. Companies in the same strategic group can resemble one another in a variety of ways. They may have comparable product-line breadth, sell in the same price/quality range, employ the same distribution channels, depend on identical technological approaches, compete in much the same geographic areas, or offer buyers essentially the same product attributes or similar services and technical assistance.[6] Evaluating strategy options entails examining what strategic groups exist, identifying the companies within each group, and determining if a competitive "white space" exists where industry competitors are able to create and capture altogether new demand. As part of this process, the number of strategic groups in an industry and their respective market positions can be displayed on a strategic group map.

The procedure for constructing a *strategic group map* is straightforward:

CORE CONCEPT

A **strategic group** is a cluster of industry rivals that have similar competitive approaches and market positions.

- Identify the competitive characteristics that delineate strategic approaches used in the industry. Typical variables used in creating strategic group maps are price/quality range (high, medium, low), geographic coverage (local, regional, national, global), product-line breadth (wide, narrow), degree of service offered (no frills, limited, full), use of distribution channels (retail, wholesale, Internet, multiple), degree of vertical integration (none, partial, full), and degree of diversification into other industries (none, some, considerable).
- Plot the firms on a two-variable map using pairs of these variables.
- Assign firms occupying about the same map location to the same strategic group.
- Draw circles around each strategic group, making the circles proportional to the size of the group's share of total industry sales revenues.

This produces a two-dimensional diagram like the one for the U.S. casual dining industry in Illustration Capsule 3.1.

Several guidelines need to be observed in creating strategic group maps. First, the two variables selected as axes for the map should *not* be highly correlated; if they are, the circles on the map will fall along a diagonal and reveal nothing more about the relative positions of competitors than would be revealed by comparing the rivals

ILLUSTRATION CAPSULE 3.1

Comparative Market Positions of Selected Companies in the Casual Dining Industry: A Strategic Group Map Example

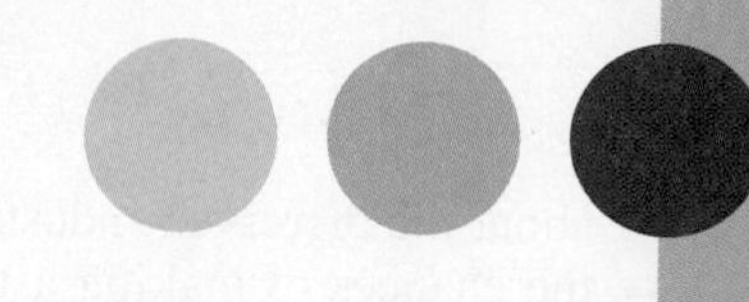

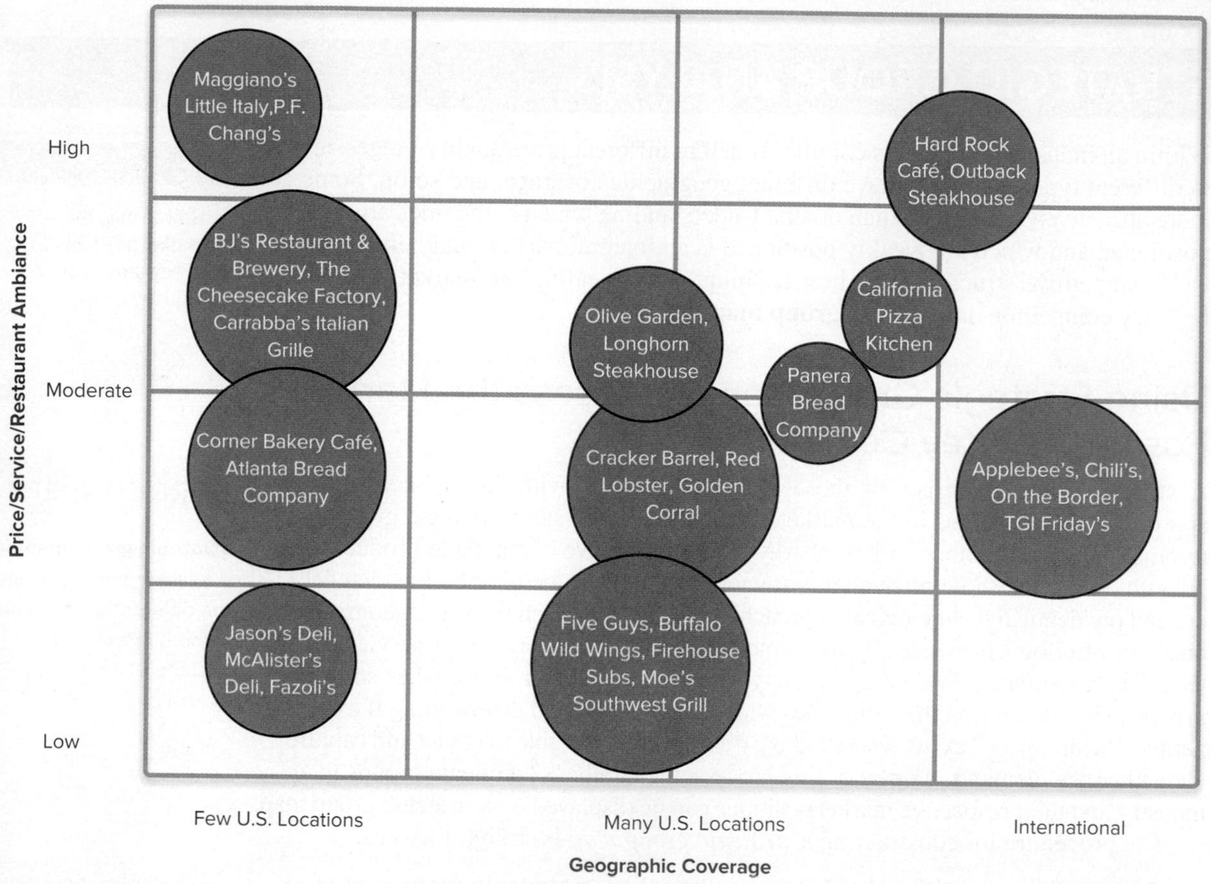

Note: Circles are drawn roughly proportional to the sizes of the chains, based on revenues.

on just one of the variables. For instance, if companies with broad product lines use multiple distribution channels while companies with narrow lines use a single distribution channel, then looking at the differences in distribution-channel approaches adds no new information about positioning.

Second, the variables chosen as axes for the map should reflect important differences among rival approaches—when rivals differ on both variables, the locations of the rivals will be scattered, thus showing how they are positioned differently. Third, the variables used as axes don't have to be either quantitative or continuous; rather, they can be discrete variables, defined in terms of distinct classes and combinations. Fourth, drawing the sizes of the circles on the map proportional to the combined sales of the firms in each strategic group allows the map to reflect the relative sizes of each strategic group. Fifth, if more than two good variables can be used as axes for the map, then it is wise to draw several maps to give different exposures to the competitive positioning relationships present in the industry's structure—there is not necessarily one best map for portraying how competing firms are positioned.

The Value of Strategic Group Maps

Strategic group maps are revealing in several respects. The most important has to do with identifying which industry members are close rivals and which are distant rivals. Firms in the same strategic group are the closest rivals; the next closest rivals are in the immediately adjacent groups. Often, firms in strategic groups that are far apart on the map hardly compete at all. For instance, Walmart's clientele, merchandise selection, and pricing points are much too different to justify calling Walmart a close competitor of Neiman Marcus or Saks Fifth Avenue. For the same reason, the beers produced by Yuengling are really not in competition with the beers produced by Pabst.

Strategic group maps reveal which companies are close competitors and which are distant competitors.

The second thing to be gleaned from strategic group mapping is that *not all positions on the map are equally attractive.*[7] Two reasons account for why some positions can be more attractive than others:

1. *Prevailing competitive pressures from the industry's five forces may cause the profit potential of different strategic groups to vary.* The profit prospects of firms in different strategic groups can vary from good to poor because of differing degrees of competitive rivalry within strategic groups, differing pressures from potential entrants to each group, differing degrees of exposure to competition from substitute products outside the industry, and differing degrees of supplier or customer bargaining power from group to group. For instance, in the ready-to-eat cereal industry, there are significantly higher entry barriers (capital requirements, brand loyalty, etc.) for the strategic group comprising the large branded-cereal makers than for the group of generic-cereal makers or the group of small natural-cereal producers. Differences among the branded rivals versus the generic cereal makers make rivalry stronger within the generic strategic group. In the retail chain industry, the competitive battle between Walmart and Target is more intense (with consequently smaller profit margins) than the rivalry among Prada, Versace, Gucci, Armani, and other high-end fashion retailers.
2. *Industry driving forces may favor some strategic groups and hurt others.* Likewise, industry driving forces can boost the business outlook for some strategic groups and adversely impact the business prospects of others. In the news industry, for example, Internet news services and cable news networks are gaining ground at the expense of newspapers and networks due to changes in technology and changing social lifestyles. Firms in strategic groups that are being adversely impacted by driving forces may try to shift to a more favorably situated position. If certain firms are known to be trying to change their competitive positions on the map, then attaching arrows to the circles showing the targeted direction helps clarify the picture of competitive maneuvering among rivals.

Some strategic groups are more favorably positioned than others because they confront weaker competitive forces and/or because they are more favorably impacted by industry driving forces.

Thus, part of strategic group map analysis always entails drawing conclusions about where on the map is the "best" place to be and why. Which companies/strategic groups are destined to prosper because of their positions? Which companies/strategic groups seem destined to struggle? What accounts for why some parts of the map are better than others?

COMPETITOR ANALYSIS

Studying competitors' past behavior and preferences provides a valuable assist in anticipating what moves rivals are likely to make next and outmaneuvering them in the marketplace.

Unless a company pays attention to the strategies and situations of competitors and has some inkling of what moves they will be making, it ends up flying blind into competitive battle. As in sports, scouting the opposition is an essential part of game plan development. Gathering competitive intelligence about the strategic direction and likely moves of key competitors allows a company to prepare defensive countermoves, to craft its own strategic moves with some confidence about what market maneuvers to expect from rivals in response, and to exploit any openings that arise from competitors' missteps. The question is where to look for such information, since rivals rarely reveal their strategic intentions openly. If information is not directly available, what are the best indicators?

Michael Porter's **Framework for Competitor Analysis** points to four indicators of a rival's likely strategic moves and countermoves. These include a rival's *current strategy, objectives, resources and capabilities,* and *assumptions* about itself and the industry, as shown in Figure 3.10. A strategic profile of a rival that provides good clues to its behavioral proclivities can be constructed by characterizing the rival along these four dimensions.

Current Strategy To succeed in predicting a competitor's next moves, company strategists need to have a good understanding of each rival's current strategy, as an indicator of its pattern of behavior and best strategic options. Questions to consider include: How is the competitor positioned in the market? What is the basis for

FIGURE 3.10 A Framework for Competitor Analysis

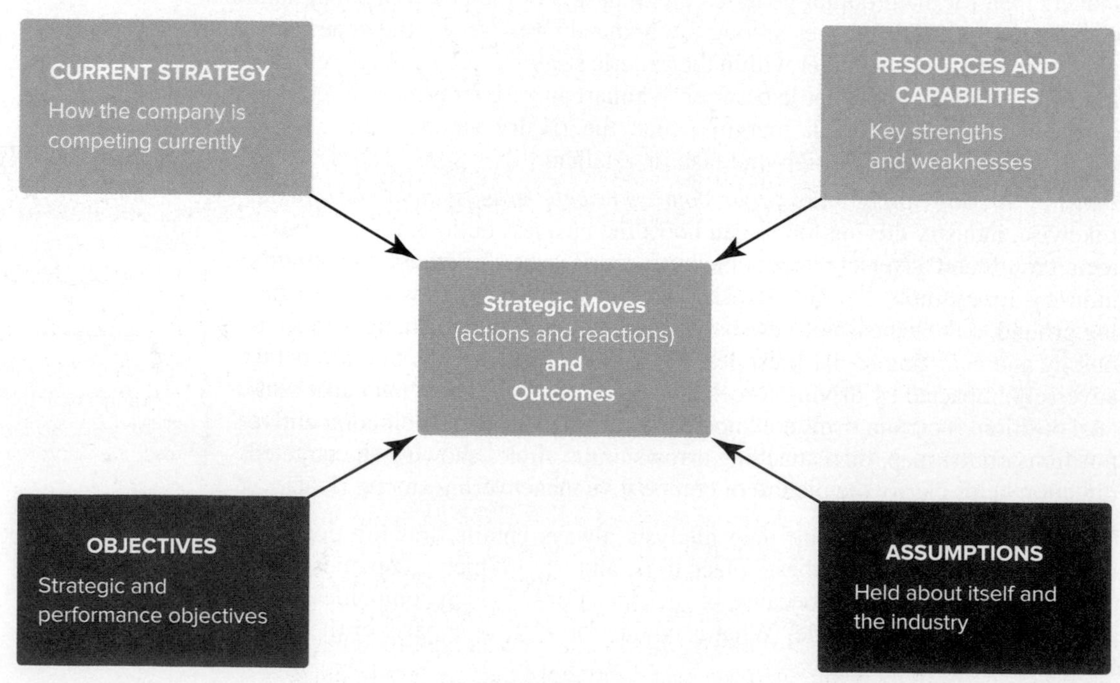

its competitive advantage (if any)? What kinds of investments is it making (as an indicator of its growth trajectory)?

Objectives An appraisal of a rival's objectives should include not only its financial performance objectives but strategic ones as well (such as those concerning market share). What is even more important is to consider the extent to which the rival is meeting these objectives and whether it is under pressure to improve. Rivals with good financial performance are likely to continue their present strategy with only minor fine-tuning. Poorly performing rivals are virtually certain to make fresh strategic moves.

Resources and Capabilities A rival's strategic moves and countermoves are both enabled and constrained by the set of resources and capabilities the rival has at hand. Thus a rival's resources and capabilities (and efforts to acquire new resources and capabilities) serve as a strong signal of future strategic actions (and reactions to your company's moves). Assessing a rival's resources and capabilities involves sizing up not only its strengths in this respect but its weaknesses as well.

Assumptions How a rival's top managers think about their strategic situation can have a big impact on how the rival behaves. Banks that believe they are "too big to fail," for example, may take on more risk than is financially prudent. Assessing a rival's assumptions entails considering its assumptions about itself as well as about the industry it participates in.

Information regarding these four analytic components can often be gleaned from company press releases, information posted on the company's website (especially the presentations management has recently made to securities analysts), and such public documents as annual reports and 10-K filings. Many companies also have a competitive intelligence unit that sifts through the available information to construct up-to-date strategic profiles of rivals. Doing the necessary detective work can be time-consuming, but scouting competitors well enough to anticipate their next moves allows managers to prepare effective countermoves (perhaps even beat a rival to the punch) and to take rivals' probable actions into account in crafting their own best course of action.

KEY SUCCESS FACTORS

An industry's **key success factors (KSFs)** are those competitive factors that most affect industry members' ability to survive and prosper in the marketplace: the particular strategy elements, product attributes, operational approaches, resources, and competitive capabilities that spell the difference between being a strong competitor and a weak competitor—and between profit and loss. KSFs by their very nature are so important to competitive success that *all firms* in the industry must pay close attention to them or risk becoming an industry laggard or failure. To indicate the significance of KSFs another way, how well the elements of a company's strategy measure up against an industry's KSFs determines whether the company can meet the basic criteria for surviving and thriving in the industry. Identifying KSFs, in light of the prevailing and anticipated industry and competitive conditions, is therefore always a top priority in analytic and strategy-making considerations. Company strategists need to understand the industry landscape well enough to separate the factors most important to competitive success from those that are less important.

CORE CONCEPT

Key success factors are the strategy elements, product and service attributes, operational approaches, resources, and competitive capabilities that are essential to surviving and thriving in the industry.

Key success factors vary from industry to industry, and even from time to time within the same industry, as change drivers and competitive conditions change. But regardless of the circumstances, an industry's key success factors can always be deduced by asking the same three questions:

1. On what basis do buyers of the industry's product choose between the competing brands of sellers? That is, what product attributes and service characteristics are crucial?
2. Given the nature of competitive rivalry prevailing in the marketplace, what resources and competitive capabilities must a company have to be competitively successful?
3. What shortcomings are almost certain to put a company at a significant competitive disadvantage?

Only rarely are there more than five key factors for competitive success. And even among these, two or three usually outrank the others in importance. Managers should therefore bear in mind the purpose of identifying key success factors—to determine which factors are most important to competitive success—and resist the temptation to label a factor that has only minor importance as a KSF.

In the beer industry, for example, although there are many types of buyers (wholesale, retail, end consumer), it is most important to understand the preferences and buying behavior of the beer drinkers. Their purchase decisions are driven by price, taste, convenient access, and marketing. Thus the KSFs include a *strong network of wholesale distributors* (to get the company's brand stocked and favorably displayed in retail outlets, bars, restaurants, and stadiums, where beer is sold) and *clever advertising* (to induce beer drinkers to buy the company's brand and thereby pull beer sales through the established wholesale and retail channels). Because there is a potential for strong buyer power on the part of large distributors and retail chains, competitive success depends on some mechanism to offset that power, of which advertising (to create demand pull) is one. Thus the KSFs also include *superior product differentiation* (as in microbrews) or *superior firm size and branding capabilities* (as in national brands). The KSFs also include *full utilization of brewing capacity* (to keep manufacturing costs low and offset the high costs of advertising, branding, and product differentiation).

Correctly diagnosing an industry's KSFs also raises a company's chances of crafting a sound strategy. The key success factors of an industry point to those things that every firm in the industry needs to attend to in order to retain customers and weather the competition. If the company's strategy cannot deliver on the key success factors of its industry, it is unlikely to earn enough profits to remain a viable business.

THE INDUSTRY OUTLOOK FOR PROFITABILITY

Each of the frameworks presented in this chapter—PESTEL, five forces analysis, driving forces, strategy groups, competitor analysis, and key success factors—provides a useful perspective on an industry's outlook for future profitability. Putting them all together provides an even richer and more nuanced picture. Thus, the final step in evaluating the industry and competitive environment is to use the results of each of the analyses performed to determine whether the industry presents the company with strong prospects for competitive success and attractive profits. The important factors on which to base a conclusion include:

LO 4

How to determine whether an industry's outlook presents a company with sufficiently attractive opportunities for growth and profitability.

- How the company is being impacted by the state of the macro-environment.
- Whether strong competitive forces are squeezing industry profitability to subpar levels.
- Whether the presence of complementors and the possibility of cooperative actions improve the company's prospects.
- Whether industry profitability will be favorably or unfavorably affected by the prevailing driving forces.
- Whether the company occupies a stronger market position than rivals.
- Whether this is likely to change in the course of competitive interactions.
- How well the company's strategy delivers on the industry key success factors.

As a general proposition, *the anticipated industry environment is fundamentally attractive if it presents a company with good opportunity for above-average profitability; the industry outlook is fundamentally unattractive if a company's profit prospects are unappealingly low.*

However, it is a mistake to think of a particular industry as being equally attractive or unattractive to all industry participants and all potential entrants.[8] Attractiveness is relative, not absolute, and conclusions one way or the other have to be drawn from the perspective of a particular company. For instance, a favorably positioned competitor may see ample opportunity to capitalize on the vulnerabilities of weaker rivals even though industry conditions are otherwise somewhat dismal. At the same time, industries attractive to insiders may be unattractive to outsiders because of the difficulty of challenging current market leaders or because they have more attractive opportunities elsewhere.

The degree to which an industry is attractive or unattractive is not the same for all industry participants and all potential entrants.

When a company decides an industry is fundamentally attractive and presents good opportunities, a strong case can be made that it should invest aggressively to capture the opportunities it sees and to improve its long-term competitive position in the business. When a strong competitor concludes an industry is becoming less attractive, it may elect to simply protect its present position, investing cautiously—if at all—and looking for opportunities in other industries. A competitively weak company in an unattractive industry may see its best option as finding a buyer, perhaps a rival, to acquire its business.

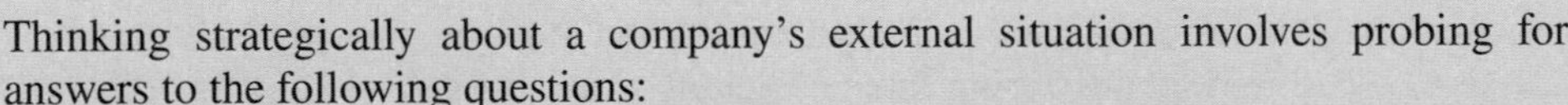

KEY POINTS

Thinking strategically about a company's external situation involves probing for answers to the following questions:

1. *What are the strategically relevant factors in the macro-environment, and how do they impact an industry and its members?* Industries differ significantly as to how they are affected by conditions and developments in the broad macro-environment. Using PESTEL analysis to identify which of these factors is strategically relevant is the first step to understanding how a company is situated in its external environment.

2. *What kinds of competitive forces are industry members facing, and how strong is each force?* The strength of competition is a composite of five forces: (1) rivalry within the industry, (2) the threat of new entry into the market, (3) inroads being made by the sellers of substitutes, (4) supplier bargaining power, and (5) buyer bargaining power. All five must be examined force by force, and their collective strength evaluated. One strong force, however, can be sufficient to keep average industry profitability low. Working through the five forces model aids strategy makers in assessing how to insulate the company from the strongest forces, identify attractive arenas for expansion, or alter the competitive conditions so that they offer more favorable prospects for profitability.
3. *What cooperative forces are present in the industry, and how can a company harness them to its advantage?* Interactions among industry participants are not only competitive in nature but cooperative as well. This is particularly the case when complements to the products or services of an industry are important. The value net framework assists managers in sizing up the impact of cooperative as well as competitive interactions on their firm.
4. *What factors are driving changes in the industry, and what impact will they have on competitive intensity and industry profitability?* Industry and competitive conditions change because certain forces are acting to create incentives or pressures for change. The first step is to identify the three or four most important drivers of change affecting the industry being analyzed (out of a much longer list of potential drivers). Once an industry's change drivers have been identified, the analytic task becomes one of determining whether they are acting, individually and collectively, to make the industry environment more or less attractive.
5. *What market positions do industry rivals occupy—who is strongly positioned and who is not?* Strategic group mapping is a valuable tool for understanding the similarities, differences, strengths, and weaknesses inherent in the market positions of rival companies. Rivals in the same or nearby strategic groups are close competitors, whereas companies in distant strategic groups usually pose little or no immediate threat. The lesson of strategic group mapping is that some positions on the map are more favorable than others. The profit potential of different strategic groups may not be the same because industry driving forces and competitive forces likely have varying effects on the industry's distinct strategic groups.
6. *What strategic moves are rivals likely to make next?* Anticipating the actions of rivals can help a company prepare effective countermoves. Using the Framework for Competitor Analysis is helpful in this regard.
7. *What are the key factors for competitive success?* An industry's key success factors (KSFs) are the particular strategy elements, product attributes, operational approaches, resources, and competitive capabilities that all industry members must have in order to survive and prosper in the industry. For any industry, they can be deduced by answering three basic questions: (1) On what basis do buyers of the industry's product choose between the competing brands of sellers, (2) what resources and competitive capabilities must a company have to be competitively successful, and (3) what shortcomings are almost certain to put a company at a significant competitive disadvantage?
8. *Is the industry outlook conducive to good profitability?* The last step in industry analysis is summing up the results from applying each of the frameworks employed

in answering questions 1 to 6: PESTEL, five forces analysis, driving forces, strategic group mapping, competitor analysis, and key success factors. Applying multiple lenses to the question of what the industry outlook looks like offers a more robust and nuanced answer. If the answers from each framework, seen as a whole, reveal that a company's profit prospects in that industry are above-average, then the industry environment is basically attractive *for that company*. What may look like an attractive environment for one company may appear to be unattractive from the perspective of a different company.

Clear, insightful diagnosis of a company's external situation is an essential first step in crafting strategies that are well matched to industry and competitive conditions. To do cutting-edge strategic thinking about the external environment, managers must know what questions to pose and what analytic tools to use in answering these questions. This is why this chapter has concentrated on suggesting the right questions to ask, explaining concepts and analytic approaches, and indicating the kinds of things to look for.

ASSURANCE OF LEARNING EXERCISES

1. Prepare a brief analysis of the organic food industry using the information provided by the Organic Trade Association at **www.ota.com** and the ***Organic Report*** magazine at **theorganicreport.com**. That is, based on the information provided on these websites, draw a five forces diagram for the organic food industry and briefly discuss the nature and strength of each of the five competitive forces. connect **LO 2**
2. Based on the strategic group map in Illustration Capsule 3.1, which casual dining chains are Applebee's closest competitors? With which strategic group does California Pizza Kitchen compete the least, according to this map? Why do you think no casual dining chains are positioned in the area above the Olive Garden's group? connect **LO 3**
3. The National Restaurant Association publishes an annual industry fact book that can be found at **imis.restaurant.org/store/detail.aspx?id=FOR2016FB**. Based on information in the latest report, does it appear that macro-environmental factors and the economic characteristics of the industry will present industry participants with attractive opportunities for growth and profitability? Explain. **LO 1, LO 4**

EXERCISE FOR SIMULATION PARTICIPANTS

LO 1, LO 2, LO 3, LO 4

1. Which of the factors listed in Table 3.1 might have the most strategic relevance for your industry?
2. Which of the five competitive forces is creating the strongest competitive pressures for your company?
3. What are the "weapons of competition" that rival companies in your industry can use to gain sales and market share? See Table 3.2 to help you identify the various competitive factors.

4. What are the factors affecting the intensity of rivalry in the industry in which your company is competing? Use Figure 3.4 and the accompanying discussion to help you in pinpointing the specific factors most affecting competitive intensity. Would you characterize the rivalry and jockeying for better market position, increased sales, and market share among the companies in your industry as fierce, very strong, strong, moderate, or relatively weak? Why?
5. Are there any driving forces in the industry in which your company is competing? If so, what impact will these driving forces have? Will they cause competition to be more or less intense? Will they act to boost or squeeze profit margins? List at least two actions your company should consider taking in order to combat any negative impacts of the driving forces.
6. Draw a strategic group map showing the market positions of the companies in your industry. Which companies do you believe are in the most attractive position on the map? Which companies are the most weakly positioned? Which companies do you believe are likely to try to move to a different position on the strategic group map?
7. What do you see as the key factors for being a successful competitor in your industry? List at least three.
8. Does your overall assessment of the industry suggest that industry rivals have sufficiently attractive opportunities for growth and profitability? Explain.

ENDNOTES

[1] Michael E. Porter, *Competitive Strategy* (New York: Free Press, 1980); Michael E. Porter, "The Five Competitive Forces That Shape Strategy," *Harvard Business Review* 86, no. 1 (January 2008), pp. 78–93.
[2] J. S. Bain, *Barriers to New Competition* (Cambridge, MA: Harvard University Press, 1956); F. M. Scherer, *Industrial Market Structure and Economic Performance* (Chicago: Rand McNally, 1971).
[3] Ibid.
[4] C. A. Montgomery and S. Hariharan, "Diversified Expansion by Large Established Firms," *Journal of Economic Behavior & Organization* 15, no. 1 (January 1991).
[5] For a more extended discussion of the problems with the life-cycle hypothesis, see Porter, *Competitive Strategy*, pp. 157–162.
[6] Mary Ellen Gordon and George R. Milne, "Selecting the Dimensions That Define Strategic Groups: A Novel Market-Driven Approach," *Journal of Managerial Issues* 11, no. 2 (Summer 1999), pp. 213–233.
[7] Avi Fiegenbaum and Howard Thomas, "Strategic Groups as Reference Groups: Theory, Modeling and Empirical Examination of Industry and Competitive Strategy," *Strategic Management Journal* 16 (1995), pp. 461–476; S. Ade Olusoga, Michael P. Mokwa, and Charles H. Noble, "Strategic Groups, Mobility Barriers, and Competitive Advantage," *Journal of Business Research* 33 (1995), pp. 153–164.
[8] B. Wernerfelt and C. Montgomery, "What Is an Attractive Industry?" *Management Science* 32, no. 10 (October 1986), pp. 1223–1230.

CHAPTER 4

Evaluating a Company's Resources, Capabilities, and Competitiveness

© Ikon Images/Alamy Stock Photo

Learning Objectives

THIS CHAPTER WILL HELP YOU UNDERSTAND:

LO 1 How to take stock of how well a company's strategy is working.

LO 2 Why a company's resources and capabilities are centrally important in giving the company a competitive edge over rivals.

LO 3 How to assess the company's strengths and weaknesses in light of market opportunities and external threats.

LO 4 How a company's value chain activities can affect the company's cost structure and customer value proposition.

LO 5 How a comprehensive evaluation of a company's competitive situation can assist managers in making critical decisions about their next strategic moves.

Crucial, of course, is having a difference that matters in the industry.

Cynthia Montgomery—*Professor and author*

If you don't have a competitive advantage, don't compete

Jack Welch—*Former CEO of General Electric*

Organizations succeed in a competitive marketplace over the long run because they can do certain things their customers value better than can their competitors.

Robert Hayes, Gary Pisano, and David Upton—*Professors and consultants*

Chapter 3 described how to use the tools of industry and competitor analysis to assess a company's external environment and lay the groundwork for matching a company's strategy to its external situation. This chapter discusses techniques for evaluating a company's internal situation, including its collection of resources and capabilities and the activities it performs along its value chain. Internal analysis enables managers to determine whether their strategy is likely to give the company a significant competitive edge over rival firms. Combined with external analysis, it facilitates an understanding of how to reposition a firm to take advantage of new opportunities and to cope with emerging competitive threats. The analytic spotlight will be trained on six questions:

1. How well is the company's present strategy working?
2. What are the company's most important resources and capabilities, and will they give the company a lasting competitive advantage over rival companies?
3. What are the company's strengths and weaknesses in relation to the market opportunities and external threats?
4. How do a company's value chain activities impact its cost structure and customer value proposition?
5. Is the company competitively stronger or weaker than key rivals?
6. What strategic issues and problems merit front-burner managerial attention?

In probing for answers to these questions, five analytic tools—resource and capability analysis, SWOT analysis, value chain analysis, benchmarking, and competitive strength assessment—will be used. All five are valuable techniques for revealing a company's competitiveness and for helping company managers match their strategy to the company's particular circumstances.

QUESTION 1: HOW WELL IS THE COMPANY'S PRESENT STRATEGY WORKING?

LO 1

How to take stock of how well a company's strategy is working.

In evaluating how well a company's present strategy is working, the best way to start is with a clear view of what the strategy entails. Figure 4.1 shows the key components of a single-business company's strategy. The first thing to examine is the company's competitive approach. What moves has the company made recently to attract customers and improve its market position—for instance, has it cut prices, improved the design of its product, added new features, stepped up advertising, entered a new geographic market, or merged with a competitor? Is it striving for a competitive advantage based on low costs or a better product offering? Is it concentrating on serving a broad spectrum of customers or a narrow market niche? The company's functional strategies in R&D, production, marketing, finance, human resources, information technology, and so on further characterize company strategy, as do any efforts to establish alliances with other enterprises.

The three best indicators of how well a company's strategy is working are (1) whether the company is achieving its stated financial and strategic objectives, (2) whether its financial performance is above the industry average, and (3) whether it is gaining customers and gaining market share. Persistent shortfalls in meeting company performance targets and weak marketplace performance relative to rivals are reliable warning signs that the company has a weak strategy, suffers from poor strategy execution, or both. Specific indicators of how well a company's strategy is working include:

- Trends in the company's sales and earnings growth.
- Trends in the company's stock price.
- The company's overall financial strength.
- The company's customer retention rate.

FIGURE 4.1 Identifying the Components of a Single-Business Company's Strategy

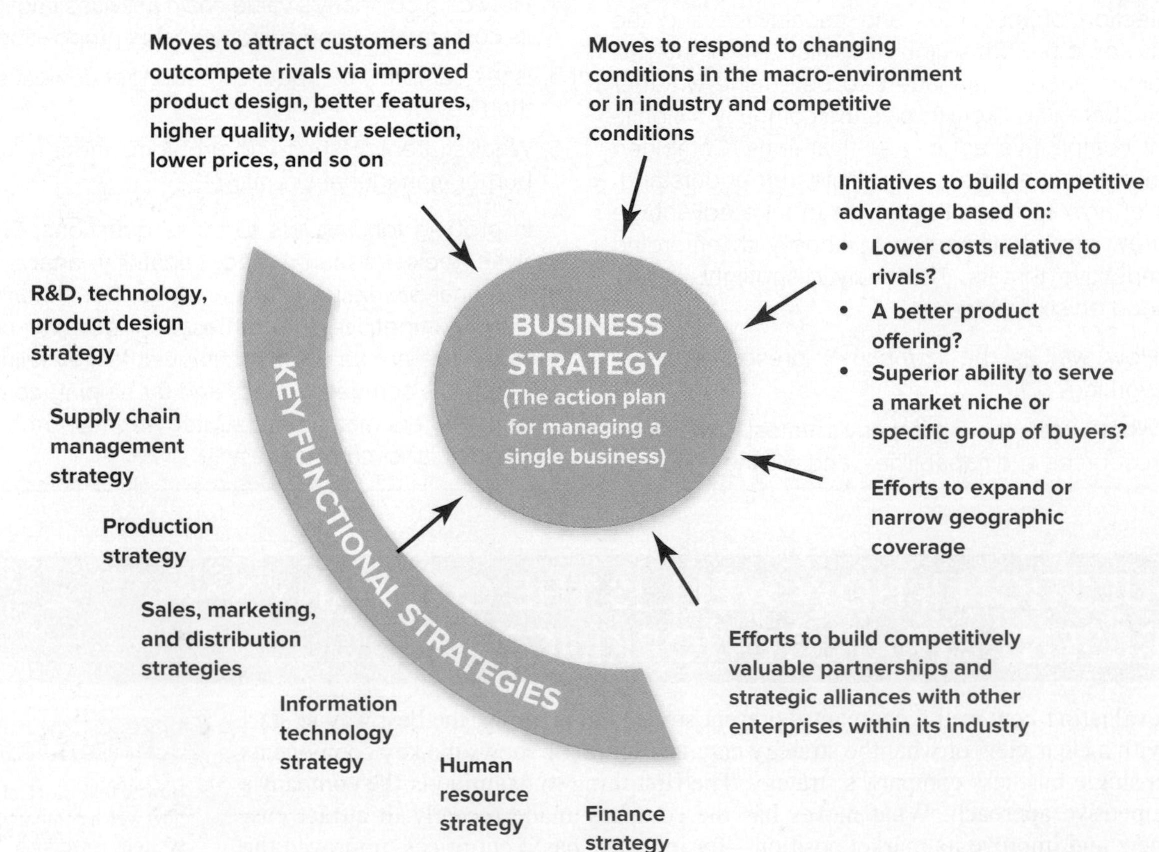

- The rate at which new customers are acquired.
- Evidence of improvement in internal processes such as defect rate, order fulfillment, delivery times, days of inventory, and employee productivity.

The stronger a company's current overall performance, the more likely it has a well-conceived, well-executed strategy. The weaker a company's financial performance and market standing, the more its current strategy must be questioned and the more likely the need for radical changes. Table 4.1 provides a compilation of the financial ratios most commonly used to evaluate a company's financial performance and balance sheet strength.

Sluggish financial performance and second-rate market accomplishments almost always signal weak strategy, weak execution, or both.

TABLE 4.1 Key Financial Ratios: How to Calculate Them and What They Mean

Ratio	How Calculated	What It Shows
Profitability ratios		
1. Gross profit margin	$\frac{\text{Sales revenues} - \text{Cost of goods sold}}{\text{Sales revenues}}$	Shows the percentage of revenues available to cover operating expenses and yield a profit.
2. Operating profit margin (or return on sales)	$\frac{\text{Sales revenues} - \text{Operating expenses}}{\text{Sales revenues}}$ *or* $\frac{\text{Operating income}}{\text{Sales revenues}}$	Shows the profitability of current operations without regard to interest charges and income taxes. Earnings before interest and taxes is known as *EBIT* in financial and business accounting.
3. Net profit margin (or net return on sales)	$\frac{\text{Profits after taxes}}{\text{Sales revenues}}$	Shows after-tax profits per dollar of sales.
4. Total return on assets	$\frac{\text{Profits after taxes} + \text{Interest}}{\text{Total assets}}$	A measure of the return on total investment in the enterprise. Interest is added to after-tax profits to form the numerator, since total assets are financed by creditors as well as by stockholders.
5. Net return on total assets (ROA)	$\frac{\text{Profits after taxes}}{\text{Total assets}}$	A measure of the return earned by stockholders on the firm's total assets.
6. Return on stockholders' equity (ROE)	$\frac{\text{Profits after taxes}}{\text{Total stockholders' equity}}$	The return stockholders are earning on their capital investment in the enterprise. A return in the 12%–15% range is average.
7. Return on invested capital (ROIC)—sometimes referred to as return on capital employed (ROCE)	$\frac{\text{Profits after taxes}}{\text{Long-term debt} + \text{Total stockholders' equity}}$	A measure of the return that shareholders are earning on the monetary capital invested in the enterprise. A higher return reflects greater bottom-line effectiveness in the use of long-term capital.
Liquidity ratios		
1. Current ratio	$\frac{\text{Current assets}}{\text{Current liabilities}}$	Shows a firm's ability to pay current liabilities using assets that can be converted to cash in the near term. Ratio should be higher than 1.0.

(continued)

TABLE 4.1 *(continued)*

Ratio	How Calculated	What It Shows
2. Working capital	Current assets − Current liabilities	The cash available for a firm's day-to-day operations. Larger amounts mean the company has more internal funds to (1) pay its current liabilities on a timely basis and (2) finance inventory expansion, additional accounts receivable, and a larger base of operations without resorting to borrowing or raising more equity capital.
Leverage ratios		
1. Total debt-to-assets ratio	$\frac{\text{Total debt}}{\text{Total assets}}$	Measures the extent to which borrowed funds (both short-term loans and long-term debt) have been used to finance the firm's operations. A low ratio is better—a high fraction indicates overuse of debt and greater risk of bankruptcy.
2. Long-term debt-to-capital ratio	$\frac{\text{Long-term debt}}{\text{Long-term debt + Total stockholders' equity}}$	A measure of creditworthiness and balance sheet strength. It indicates the percentage of capital investment that has been financed by both long-term lenders and stockholders. A ratio below 0.25 is preferable since the lower the ratio, the greater the capacity to borrow additional funds. Debt-to-capital ratios above 0.50 indicate an excessive reliance on long-term borrowing, lower creditworthiness, and weak balance sheet strength.
3. Debt-to-equity ratio	$\frac{\text{Total debt}}{\text{Total stockholders' equity}}$	Shows the balance between debt (funds borrowed both short term and long term) and the amount that stockholders have invested in the enterprise. The further the ratio is below 1.0, the greater the firm's ability to borrow additional funds. Ratios above 1.0 put creditors at greater risk, signal weaker balance sheet strength, and often result in lower credit ratings.
4. Long-term debt-to-equity ratio	$\frac{\text{Long-term debt}}{\text{Total stockholders' equity}}$	Shows the balance between long-term debt and stockholders' equity in the firm's *long-term* capital structure. Low ratios indicate a greater capacity to borrow additional funds if needed.
5. Times-interest-earned (or coverage) ratio	$\frac{\text{Operating income}}{\text{Interest expenses}}$	Measures the ability to pay annual interest charges. Lenders usually insist on a minimum ratio of 2.0, but ratios above 3.0 signal progressively better creditworthiness.
Activity ratios		
1. Days of inventory	$\frac{\text{Inventory}}{\text{Cost of goods sold} \div 365}$	Measures inventory management efficiency. Fewer days of inventory are better.
2. Inventory turnover	$\frac{\text{Cost of goods sold}}{\text{Inventory}}$	Measures the number of inventory turns per year. Higher is better.
3. Average collection period	$\frac{\text{Accounts receivable}}{\text{Total sales} \div 365}$ *or* $\frac{\text{Accounts receivable}}{\text{Average daily sales}}$	Indicates the average length of time the firm must wait after making a sale to receive cash payment. A shorter collection time is better.

(continued)

TABLE 4.1 *(continued)*

Ratio	How Calculated	What It Shows
Other important measures of financial performance		
1. Dividend yield on common stock	$\frac{\text{Annual dividends per share}}{\text{Current market price per share}}$	A measure of the return that shareholders receive in the form of dividends. A "typical" dividend yield is 2%–3%. The dividend yield for fast-growth companies is often below 1%; the dividend yield for slow-growth companies can run 4%–5%.
2. Price-to-earnings (P/E) ratio	$\frac{\text{Current market price per share}}{\text{Earnings per share}}$	P/E ratios above 20 indicate strong investor confidence in a firm's outlook and earnings growth; firms whose future earnings are at risk or likely to grow slowly typically have ratios below 12.
3. Dividend payout ratio	$\frac{\text{Annual dividends per share}}{\text{Earnings per share}}$	Indicates the percentage of after-tax profits paid out as dividends.
4. Internal cash flow	After-tax profits + Depreciation	A rough estimate of the cash a company's business is generating after payment of operating expenses, interest, and taxes. Such amounts can be used for dividend payments or funding capital expenditures.
5. Free cash flow	After-tax profits + Depreciation – Capital expenditures – Dividends	A rough estimate of the cash a company's business is generating after payment of operating expenses, interest, taxes, dividends, and desirable reinvestments in the business. The larger a company's free cash flow, the greater its ability to internally fund new strategic initiatives, repay debt, make new acquisitions, repurchase shares of stock, or increase dividend payments.

QUESTION 2: WHAT ARE THE COMPANY'S MOST IMPORTANT RESOURCES AND CAPABILITIES, AND WILL THEY GIVE THE COMPANY A LASTING COMPETITIVE ADVANTAGE OVER RIVAL COMPANIES?

An essential element of deciding whether a company's overall situation is fundamentally healthy or unhealthy entails examining the attractiveness of its resources and capabilities. A company's resources and capabilities are its **competitive assets** and determine whether its competitive power in the marketplace will be impressively strong or disappointingly weak. Companies with second-rate competitive assets nearly always are relegated to a trailing position in the industry.

CORE CONCEPT

A company's resources and capabilities represent its **competitive assets** and are determinants of its competitiveness and ability to succeed in the marketplace.

Resource and capability analysis provides managers with a powerful tool for sizing up the company's competitive assets and determining whether they can provide the foundation necessary for competitive success in the marketplace. This is a two-step process. The first step is to identify the company's resources and

Resource and capability analysis is a powerful tool for sizing up a company's competitive assets and determining whether the assets can support a sustainable competitive advantage over market rivals.

capabilities. The second step is to examine them more closely to ascertain which are the most competitively important and whether they can support a sustainable competitive advantage over rival firms.[1] This second step involves applying the *four tests of a resource's competitive power.*

Identifying the Company's Resources and Capabilities

LO 2

Why a company's resources and capabilities are centrally important in giving the company a competitive edge over rivals.

A firm's resources and capabilities are the fundamental building blocks of its competitive strategy. In crafting strategy, it is essential for managers to know how to take stock of the company's full complement of resources and capabilities. But before they can do so, managers and strategists need a more precise definition of these terms.

In brief, a **resource** is a productive input or competitive asset that is owned or controlled by the firm. Firms have many different types of resources at their disposal that vary not only in kind but in quality as well. Some are of a higher quality than others, and some are more competitively valuable, having greater potential to give a firm a competitive advantage over its rivals. For example, a company's brand is a resource, as is an R&D team—yet some brands such as Coca-Cola and Xerox are well known, with enduring value, while others have little more name recognition than generic products. In similar fashion, some R&D teams are far more innovative and productive than others due to the outstanding talents of the individual team members, the team's composition, its experience, and its chemistry.

A **capability (**or **competence)** is the capacity of a firm to perform some internal activity competently. Capabilities or competences also vary in form, quality, and competitive importance, with some being more competitively valuable than others. American Express displays superior capabilities in brand management and marketing; Starbucks's employee management, training, and real estate capabilities are the drivers behind its rapid growth; LinkedIn relies on superior software innovation capabilities to increase new user memberships. *Organizational capabilities are developed and enabled through the deployment of a company's resources.*[2] For example, Nestlé's brand management capabilities for its 2,000+ food, beverage, and pet care brands draw on the knowledge of the company's brand managers, the expertise of its marketing department, and the company's relationships with retailers in nearly 200 countries. W. L. Gore's product innovation capabilities in its fabrics and medical and industrial product businesses result from the personal initiative, creative talents, and technological expertise of its associates and the company's culture that encourages accountability and creative thinking.

CORE CONCEPT

A **resource** is a competitive asset that is owned or controlled by a company; a **capability** (or **competence**) is the capacity of a firm to perform some internal activity competently. Capabilities are developed and enabled through the deployment of a company's resources.

Types of Company Resources A useful way to identify a company's resources is to look for them within categories, as shown in Table 4.2. Broadly speaking, resources can be divided into two main categories: **tangible** and **intangible** resources. Although *human resources* make up one of the most important parts of a company's resource base, we include them in the intangible category to emphasize the role played by the skills, talents, and knowledge of a company's human resources.

Tangible resources are the most easily identified, since tangible resources are those that can be *touched* or *quantified* readily. Obviously, they include various types of *physical resources* such as manufacturing facilities and mineral resources, but they also include a company's *financial resources, technological resources,* and *organizational resources* such as the company's communication and control systems. Note

TABLE 4.2 Types of Company Resources

Tangible resources
• *Physical resources:* land and real estate; manufacturing plants, equipment, and/or distribution facilities; the locations of stores, plants, or distribution centers, including the overall pattern of their physical locations; ownership of or access rights to natural resources (such as mineral deposits)
• *Financial resources:* cash and cash equivalents; marketable securities; other financial assets such as a company's credit rating and borrowing capacity
• *Technological assets:* patents, copyrights, production technology, innovation technologies, technological processes
• *Organizational resources:* IT and communication systems (satellites, servers, workstations, etc.); other planning, coordination, and control systems; the company's organizational design and reporting structure
Intangible resources
• *Human assets and intellectual capital:* the education, experience, knowledge, and talent of the workforce, cumulative learning, and tacit knowledge of employees; collective learning embedded in the organization, the intellectual capital and know-how of specialized teams and work groups; the knowledge of key personnel concerning important business functions; managerial talent and leadership skill; the creativity and innovativeness of certain personnel
• *Brands, company image, and reputational assets:* brand names, trademarks, product or company image, buyer loyalty and goodwill; company reputation for quality, service, and reliability; reputation with suppliers and partners for fair dealing
• *Relationships:* alliances, joint ventures, or partnerships that provide access to technologies, specialized know-how, or geographic markets; networks of dealers or distributors; the trust established with various partners
• *Company culture and incentive system:* the norms of behavior, business principles, and ingrained beliefs within the company; the attachment of personnel to the company's ideals; the compensation system and the motivation level of company personnel

that technological resources are included among tangible resources, *by convention,* even though some types, such as copyrights and trade secrets, might be more logically categorized as intangible.

Intangible resources are harder to discern, but they are often among the most important of a firm's competitive assets. They include various sorts of *human assets and intellectual capital,* as well as a company's *brands, image, and reputational assets.* While intangible resources have no material existence on their own, they are often embodied in something material. Thus, the skills and knowledge resources of a firm are embodied in its managers and employees; a company's brand name is embodied in the company logo or product labels. Other important kinds of intangible resources include a company's *relationships* with suppliers, buyers, or partners of various sorts, and the *company's culture and incentive system.* A more detailed listing of the various types of tangible and intangible resources is provided in Table 4.2.

Listing a company's resources category by category can prevent managers from inadvertently overlooking some company resources that might be competitively important. At times, it can be difficult to decide exactly how to categorize certain types of resources. For example, resources such as a work group's specialized expertise in developing innovative products can be considered to be technological assets or human assets or intellectual capital and knowledge assets; the work ethic and drive of a company's workforce could be included under the company's human assets or its culture and incentive system. In this regard, it is important to remember that *it is not exactly how a resource is categorized that matters but, rather, that all of the company's different types of resources are included in the inventory.* The real purpose of using categories in identifying a company's resources is *to ensure that none of a company's resources go unnoticed when sizing up the company's competitive assets.*

Identifying Capabilities Organizational capabilities are more complex entities than resources; indeed, they are built up through the use of resources and draw on some combination of the firm's resources as they are exercised. Virtually all organizational capabilities are *knowledge-based, residing in people and in a company's intellectual capital, or in organizational processes and systems, which embody tacit knowledge.* For example, Amazon's speedy delivery capabilities rely on the knowledge of its fulfillment center managers, its relationship with the United Postal Service, and the experience of its merchandisers to correctly predict inventory flow. Bose's capabilities in auditory system design arise from the talented engineers that form the R&D team as well as the company's strong culture, which celebrates innovation and beautiful design.

Because of their complexity, capabilities are harder to categorize than resources and more challenging to search for as a result. There are, however, two approaches that can make the process of uncovering and identifying a firm's capabilities more systematic. The first method takes the completed listing of a firm's resources as its starting point. Since capabilities are built from resources and utilize resources as they are exercised, a firm's resources can provide a strong set of clues about the types of capabilities the firm is likely to have accumulated. This approach simply involves looking over the firm's resources and considering whether (and to what extent) the firm has built up any related capabilities. So, for example, a fleet of trucks, the latest RFID tracking technology, and a set of large automated distribution centers may be indicative of sophisticated capabilities in logistics and distribution. R&D teams composed of top scientists with expertise in genomics may suggest organizational capabilities in developing new gene therapies or in biotechnology more generally.

The second method of identifying a firm's capabilities takes a functional approach. Many capabilities relate to fairly specific functions; these draw on a limited set of resources and typically involve a single department or organizational unit. Capabilities in injection molding or continuous casting or metal stamping are manufacturing-related; capabilities in direct selling, promotional pricing, or database marketing all connect to the sales and marketing functions; capabilities in basic research, strategic innovation, or new product development link to a company's R&D function. This approach requires managers to survey the various functions a firm performs to find the different capabilities associated with each function.

A problem with this second method is that many of the most important capabilities of firms are inherently *cross-functional.* Cross-functional capabilities draw on a number of different kinds of resources and are multidimensional in nature—they spring from the effective collaboration among people with different types of expertise working in different organizational units. Warby Parker draws from its cross-functional design process to create its popular eyewear. Its design capabilities are not just due to its creative designers, but are the product of their capabilities in market research and engineering as well as their relations with suppliers and manufacturing companies. Cross-functional capabilities and other complex capabilities involving numerous linked and closely integrated competitive assets are sometimes referred to as **resource bundles.**

It is important not to miss identifying a company's resource bundles, since they can be the most competitively important of a firm's competitive assets. Resource bundles can sometimes pass the four tests of a resource's competitive power (described below) even when the individual components of the resource bundle cannot. Although PetSmart's supply chain and marketing capabilities are matched well by rival Petco, the company has and continues to outperform competitors through its customer service capabilities (including animal grooming and veterinary and day care services). Nike's bundle of styling expertise, marketing research skills, professional endorsements, brand name, and managerial know-how has allowed it to remain number one in the athletic footwear and apparel industry for more than 20 years.

CORE CONCEPT

A **resource bundle** is a linked and closely integrated set of competitive assets centered around one or more cross-functional capabilities.

Assessing the Competitive Power of a Company's Resources and Capabilities

To assess a company's competitive power, one must go beyond merely identifying its resources and capabilities to probe its *caliber*.[3] Thus, the second step in resource and capability analysis is designed to ascertain which of a company's resources and capabilities are competitively superior and to what extent they can support a company's quest for a sustainable competitive advantage over market rivals. When a company has competitive assets that are central to its strategy and superior to those of rival firms, they can support a competitive advantage, as defined in Chapter 1. If this advantage proves durable despite the best efforts of competitors to overcome it, then the company is said to have a *sustainable* **competitive advantage.** While it may be difficult for a company to achieve a sustainable competitive advantage, it is an important strategic objective because it imparts a potential for attractive and long-lived profitability.

The Four Tests of a Resource's Competitive Power The competitive power of a resource or capability is measured by how many of four specific tests it can pass.[4] These tests are referred to as the **VRIN tests for sustainable competitive advantage**—*VRIN* is a shorthand reminder standing for *Valuable, Rare, Inimitable,* and *Nonsubstitutable.* The first two tests determine whether a resource or capability can support a competitive advantage. The last two determine whether the competitive advantage can be sustained.

CORE CONCEPT

The **VRIN tests for sustainable competitive advantage** ask whether a resource is valuable, rare, inimitable, and nonsubstitutable.

1. *Is the resource or capability competitively* ***Valuable?*** To be competitively valuable, a resource or capability must be directly relevant to the company's strategy, making the company a more effective competitor. Unless the resource or capability contributes to the effectiveness of the company's strategy, it cannot pass this first test. An indicator of its effectiveness is whether the resource enables the company to strengthen its business model by improving its customer value proposition and/or profit formula (see Chapter 1). Companies have to guard against contending that something they do well is necessarily competitively valuable. Apple's OS X operating system for its personal computers by some accounts is superior to Microsoft's Windows 10, but Apple has failed in converting its resources devoted to operating system design into anything more than moderate competitive success in the global PC market.
2. *Is the resource or capability* ***Rare****—is it something rivals lack?* Resources and capabilities that are common among firms and widely available cannot be a source of competitive advantage. All makers of branded cereals have valuable marketing

capabilities and brands, since the key success factors in the ready-to-eat cereal industry demand this. They are not rare. However, the brand strength of Oreo cookies is uncommon and has provided Kraft Foods with greater market share as well as the opportunity to benefit from brand extensions such as Double Stuf Oreos and Mini Oreos. A resource or capability is considered rare if it is held by only a small number of firms in an industry or specific competitive domain. Thus, while general management capabilities are not rare in an absolute sense, they are relatively rare in some of the less developed regions of the world and in some business domains.

3. *Is the resource or capability* ***Inimitable****—is it hard to copy?* The more difficult and more costly it is for competitors to imitate a company's resource or capability, the more likely that it can also provide a *sustainable* competitive advantage. Resources and capabilities tend to be difficult to copy when they are unique (a fantastic real estate location, patent-protected technology, an unusually talented and motivated labor force), when they must be built over time in ways that are difficult to imitate (a well-known brand name, mastery of a complex process technology, years of cumulative experience and learning), and when they entail financial outlays or large-scale operations that few industry members can undertake (a global network of dealers and distributors). Imitation is also difficult for resources and capabilities that reflect a high level of *social complexity* (company culture, interpersonal relationships among the managers or R&D teams, trust-based relations with customers or suppliers) and *causal ambiguity,* a term that signifies the hard-to-disentangle nature of the complex resources, such as a web of intricate processes enabling new drug discovery. Hard-to-copy resources and capabilities are important competitive assets, contributing to the longevity of a company's market position and offering the potential for sustained profitability.

CORE CONCEPT

Social complexity and *causal ambiguity* are two factors that inhibit the ability of rivals to imitate a firm's most valuable resources and capabilities. Causal ambiguity makes it very hard to figure out how a complex resource contributes to competitive advantage and therefore exactly what to imitate.

4. *Is the resource or capability* **Nonsubstitutable***—is it invulnerable to the threat of substitution from different types of resources and capabilities?* Even resources that are competitively valuable, rare, and costly to imitate may lose much of their ability to offer competitive advantage if rivals possess equivalent substitute resources. For example, manufacturers relying on automation to gain a cost-based advantage in production activities may find their technology-based advantage nullified by rivals' use of low-wage offshore manufacturing. Resources can contribute to a sustainable competitive advantage only when resource substitutes aren't on the horizon.

The vast majority of companies are not well endowed with standout resources or capabilities, capable of passing all four tests with high marks. Most firms have a mixed bag of resources—one or two quite valuable, some good, many satisfactory to mediocre. Resources and capabilities that are valuable pass the first of the four tests. As key contributors to the effectiveness of the strategy, they are relevant to the firm's competitiveness but are no guarantee of competitive advantage. They may offer no more than competitive parity with competing firms.

Passing both of the first two tests requires more—it requires resources and capabilities that are not only valuable but also rare. This is a much higher hurdle that can be cleared only by resources and capabilities that are *competitively superior.* Resources and capabilities that are competitively superior are the company's true strategic assets. They provide the company with a competitive advantage over its competitors, if only in the short run.

To pass the last two tests, a resource must be able to maintain its competitive superiority in the face of competition. It must be resistant to imitative attempts and efforts by competitors to find equally valuable substitute resources. Assessing the availability of substitutes is the most difficult of all the tests since substitutes are harder to recognize, but the key is to look for resources or capabilities held by other firms or being developed that *can serve the same function* as the company's core resources and capabilities.[5]

Very few firms have resources and capabilities that can pass all four tests, but those that do enjoy a sustainable competitive advantage with far greater profit potential. Costco is a notable example, with strong employee incentive programs and capabilities in supply chain management that have surpassed those of its warehouse club rivals for over 35 years. Lincoln Electric Company, less well known but no less notable in its achievements, has been the world leader in welding products for over 100 years as a result of its unique piecework incentive system for compensating production workers and the unsurpassed worker productivity and product quality that this system has fostered.

A Company's Resources and Capabilities Must Be Managed Dynamically Even companies like Costco and Lincoln Electric cannot afford to rest on their laurels. Rivals that are initially unable to replicate a key resource may develop better and better substitutes over time. Resources and capabilities can depreciate like other assets if they are managed with benign neglect. Disruptive changes in technology, customer preferences, distribution channels, or other competitive factors can also destroy the value of key strategic assets, turning resources and capabilities "from diamonds to rust."[6]

Resources and capabilities must be continually strengthened and nurtured to sustain their competitive power and, at times, may need to be broadened and deepened to allow the company to position itself to pursue emerging market opportunities.[7] Organizational resources and capabilities that grow stale can impair competitiveness unless they are refreshed, modified, or even phased out and replaced in response to ongoing market changes and shifts in company strategy. Management's challenge in managing the firm's resources and capabilities dynamically has two elements: (1) attending to the ongoing modification of existing competitive assets, and (2) casting a watchful eye for opportunities to develop totally new kinds of capabilities.

A company requires a dynamically evolving portfolio of resources and capabilities to sustain its competitiveness and help drive improvements in its performance.

The Role of Dynamic Capabilities Companies that know the importance of recalibrating and upgrading their most valuable resources and capabilities ensure that these activities are done on a continual basis. By incorporating these activities into their routine managerial functions, they gain the experience necessary to be able to do them consistently well. At that point, their ability to freshen and renew their competitive assets becomes a capability in itself—a **dynamic capability.** A dynamic capability is the ability to modify, deepen, or augment the company's existing resources and capabilities.[8] This includes the capacity to improve existing resources and capabilities incrementally, in the way that Toyota aggressively upgrades the company's capabilities in fuel-efficient hybrid engine technology and constantly fine-tunes its famed Toyota production system. Likewise, management at BMW developed new organizational capabilities in hybrid engine design that allowed the company to launch its highly touted i3 and i8 plug-in hybrids.

CORE CONCEPT

A **dynamic capability** is an ongoing capacity of a company to modify its existing resources and capabilities or create new ones.

A dynamic capability also includes the capacity to add new resources and capabilities to the company's competitive asset portfolio. One way to do this is through alliances and acquisitions. An example is Bristol-Meyers Squibb's famed "string of pearls" acquisition capabilities, which have enabled it to replace degraded resources such as expiring patents with new patents and newly acquired capabilities in drug discovery for new disease domains.

QUESTION 3: WHAT ARE THE COMPANY'S STRENGTHS AND WEAKNESSES IN RELATION TO THE MARKET OPPORTUNITIES AND EXTERNAL THREATS?

LO 3

How to assess the company's strengths and weaknesses in light of market opportunities and external threats.

In evaluating a company's overall situation, a key question is whether the company is in a position to pursue attractive market opportunities and defend against external threats to its future well-being. The simplest and most easily applied tool for conducting this examination is widely known as **SWOT analysis**, so named because it zeros in on a company's internal **S**trengths and **W**eaknesses, market **O**pportunities, and external **T**hreats. A first-rate SWOT analysis provides the basis for crafting a strategy that capitalizes on the company's strengths, overcomes its weaknesses, aims squarely at capturing the company's best opportunities, and defends against competitive and macro-environmental threats.

SWOT analysis is a simple but powerful tool for sizing up a company's strengths and weaknesses, its market opportunities, and the external threats to its future well-being.

Identifying a Company's Internal Strengths

A **strength** is something a company is good at doing or an attribute that enhances its competitiveness in the marketplace. A company's strengths depend on the quality of its resources and capabilities. Resource and capability analysis provides a way for managers to assess the quality objectively. While resources and capabilities that pass the VRIN tests of sustainable competitive advantage are among the company's greatest strengths, other types can be counted among the company's strengths as well. A capability that is not potent enough to produce a sustainable advantage over rivals may yet enable a series of temporary advantages if used as a basis for entry into a new market or market segment. A resource bundle that fails to match those of top-tier competitors may still allow a company to compete successfully against the second tier.

Basing a company's strategy on its most competitively valuable strengths gives the company its best chance for market success.

Assessing a Company's Competencies—What Activities Does It Perform Well? One way to appraise the degree of a company's strengths has to do with the company's skill level in performing key pieces of its business—such as supply chain management, R&D, production, distribution, sales and marketing, and customer service. A company's skill or proficiency in performing different facets of its operations can range from the extreme of having minimal ability to perform an activity (perhaps having just struggled to do it the first time) to the other extreme of being able to perform the activity better than any other company in the industry.

When a company's proficiency rises from that of mere ability to perform an activity to the point of being able to perform it consistently well and at acceptable cost, it is said to have a **competence**—a true *capability,* in other words. If a company's competence level in some activity domain is superior to that of its rivals it is known as a **distinctive competence.** A **core competence** is a proficiently performed internal activity that is *central* to a company's strategy and is typically distinctive as well. A core competence is a more competitively valuable strength than a competence because of the activity's key role in the company's strategy and the contribution it makes to the company's market success and profitability. Often, core competencies can be leveraged to create new markets or new product demand, as the engine behind a company's growth. Procter and Gamble has a core competence in brand management, which has led to an ever increasing portfolio of market-leading consumer products, including Charmin, Tide, Crest, Tampax, Olay, Febreze, Luvs, Pampers, and Swiffer. Nike has a core competence in designing and marketing innovative athletic footwear and sports apparel. Kellogg has a core competence in developing, producing, and marketing breakfast cereals.

CORE CONCEPT

A **competence** is an activity that a company has learned to perform with proficiency.

A **distinctive competence** is a capability that enables a company to perform a particular set of activities better than its rivals.

CORE CONCEPT

A **core competence** is an activity that a company performs proficiently and that is also central to its strategy and competitive success.

Identifying Company Weaknesses and Competitive Deficiencies

A **weakness,** or *competitive deficiency,* is something a company lacks or does poorly (in comparison to others) or a condition that puts it at a disadvantage in the marketplace. A company's internal weaknesses can relate to (1) inferior or unproven skills, expertise, or intellectual capital in competitively important areas of the business; (2) deficiencies in competitively important physical, organizational, or intangible assets; or (3) missing or competitively inferior capabilities in key areas. *Company weaknesses are thus internal shortcomings that constitute competitive liabilities.* Nearly all companies have competitive liabilities of one kind or another. Whether a company's internal weaknesses make it competitively vulnerable depends on how much they matter in the marketplace and whether they are offset by the company's strengths.

CORE CONCEPT

A company's **strengths** represent its competitive assets; its **weaknesses** are shortcomings that constitute competitive liabilities.

Table 4.3 lists many of the things to consider in compiling a company's strengths and weaknesses. Sizing up a company's complement of strengths and deficiencies is akin to constructing a *strategic balance sheet,* where strengths represent *competitive assets* and weaknesses represent *competitive liabilities.* Obviously, the ideal condition is for the company's competitive assets to outweigh its competitive liabilities by an ample margin—a 50–50 balance is definitely not the desired condition!

Identifying a Company's Market Opportunities

Market opportunity is a big factor in shaping a company's strategy. Indeed, managers can't properly tailor strategy to the company's situation without first identifying its market opportunities and appraising the growth and profit potential each one holds. Depending on the prevailing circumstances, a company's opportunities can be plentiful or scarce, fleeting or lasting, and can range from wildly attractive to marginally interesting to unsuitable. Table 4.3 displays a sampling of potential market opportunities.

Newly emerging and fast-changing markets sometimes present stunningly big or "golden" opportunities, but it is typically hard for managers at one company to peer into "the fog of the future" and spot them far ahead of managers at other companies.[9]

TABLE 4.3 What to Look for in Identifying a Company's Strengths, Weaknesses, Opportunities, and Threats

Potential Strengths and Competitive Assets	Potential Weaknesses and Competitive Deficiencies
• Competencies that are well matched to industry key success factors • Ample financial resources to grow the business • Strong brand-name image and/or company reputation • Economies of scale and/or learning- and experience-curve advantages over rivals • Other cost advantages over rivals • Attractive customer base • Proprietary technology, superior technological skills, important patents • Strong bargaining power over suppliers or buyers • Resources and capabilities that are valuable and rare • Resources and capabilities that are hard to copy and for which there are no good substitutes • Superior product quality • Wide geographic coverage and/or strong global distribution capability • Alliances and/or joint ventures that provide access to valuable technology, competencies, and/or attractive geographic markets	• No clear strategic vision • No well-developed or proven core competencies • No distinctive competencies or competitively superior resources • Lack of attention to customer needs • A product or service with features and attributes that are inferior to those of rivals • Weak balance sheet, insufficient financial resources to grow the firm • Too much debt • Higher overall unit costs relative to those of key competitors • Too narrow a product line relative to rivals • Weak brand image or reputation • Weaker dealer network than key rivals and/or lack of adequate distribution capability • Lack of management depth • A plague of internal operating problems or obsolete facilities • Too much underutilized plant capacity • Resources that are readily copied or for which there are good substitutes
Potential Market Opportunities	**Potential External Threats to a Company's Future Profitability**
• Meeting sharply rising buyer demand for the industry's product • Serving additional customer groups or market segments • Expanding into new geographic markets • Expanding the company's product line to meet a broader range of customer needs • Utilizing existing company skills or technological know-how to enter new product lines or new businesses • Taking advantage of falling trade barriers in attractive foreign markets • Taking advantage of an adverse change in the fortunes of rival firms • Acquiring rival firms or companies with attractive technological expertise or capabilities • Taking advantage of emerging technological developments to innovate • Entering into alliances or joint ventures to expand the firm's market coverage or boost its competitive capability	• Increased intensity of competition among industry rivals—may squeeze profit margins • Slowdowns in market growth • Likely entry of potent new competitors • Growing bargaining power of customers or suppliers • A shift in buyer needs and tastes away from the industry's product • Adverse demographic changes that threaten to curtail demand for the industry's product • Adverse economic conditions that threaten critical suppliers or distributors • Changes in technology—particularly disruptive technology that can undermine the company's distinctive competencies • Restrictive foreign trade policies • Costly new regulatory requirements • Tight credit conditions • Rising prices on energy or other key inputs

But as the fog begins to clear, golden opportunities are nearly always seized rapidly—and the companies that seize them are usually those that have been actively waiting, staying alert with diligent market reconnaissance, and preparing themselves to capitalize on shifting market conditions by patiently assembling an arsenal of resources to enable aggressive action when the time comes. In mature markets, unusually attractive market opportunities emerge sporadically, often after long periods of relative calm—but future market conditions may be more predictable, making emerging opportunities easier for industry members to detect.

In evaluating a company's market opportunities and ranking their attractiveness, managers have to guard against viewing every *industry* opportunity as a *company* opportunity. Rarely does a company have the resource depth to pursue all available market opportunities simultaneously without spreading itself too thin. Some companies have resources and capabilities better-suited for pursuing some opportunities, and a few companies may be hopelessly outclassed in competing for any of an industry's attractive opportunities. *The market opportunities most relevant to a company are those that match up well with the company's competitive assets, offer the best prospects for growth and profitability, and present the most potential for competitive advantage.*

A company is well advised to pass on a particular market opportunity unless it has or can acquire the resources and capabilities needed to capture it.

Identifying the Threats to a Company's Future Profitability

Often, certain factors in a company's external environment pose *threats* to its profitability and competitive well-being. Threats can stem from such factors as the emergence of cheaper or better technologies, the entry of lower-cost foreign competitors into a company's market stronghold, new regulations that are more burdensome to a company than to its competitors, unfavorable demographic shifts, and political upheaval in a foreign country where the company has facilities. Table 4.3 shows a representative list of potential threats.

External threats may pose no more than a moderate degree of adversity (all companies confront some threatening elements in the course of doing business), or they may be imposing enough to make a company's situation look tenuous. On rare occasions, market shocks can give birth to a *sudden-death* threat that throws a company into an immediate crisis and a battle to survive. Many of the world's major financial institutions were plunged into unprecedented crisis in 2008–2009 by the aftereffects of high-risk mortgage lending, inflated credit ratings on subprime mortgage securities, the collapse of housing prices, and a market flooded with mortgage-related investments (collateralized debt obligations) whose values suddenly evaporated. It is management's job to identify the threats to the company's future prospects and to evaluate what strategic actions can be taken to neutralize or lessen their impact.

Simply making lists of a company's strengths, weaknesses, opportunities, and threats is not enough; the payoff from SWOT analysis comes from the conclusions about a company's situation and the implications for strategy improvement that flow from the four lists.

What Do the SWOT Listings Reveal?

SWOT analysis involves more than making four lists. The two most important parts of SWOT analysis are *drawing conclusions* from the SWOT listings about the company's overall situation and *translating these conclusions into strategic actions* to better match the company's strategy to its internal strengths and market opportunities, to correct important weaknesses, and to defend against external threats. Figure 4.2 shows the steps involved in gleaning insights from SWOT analysis.

FIGURE 4.2 The Steps Involved in SWOT Analysis: Identify the Four Components of SWOT, Draw Conclusions, Translate Implications into Strategic Actions

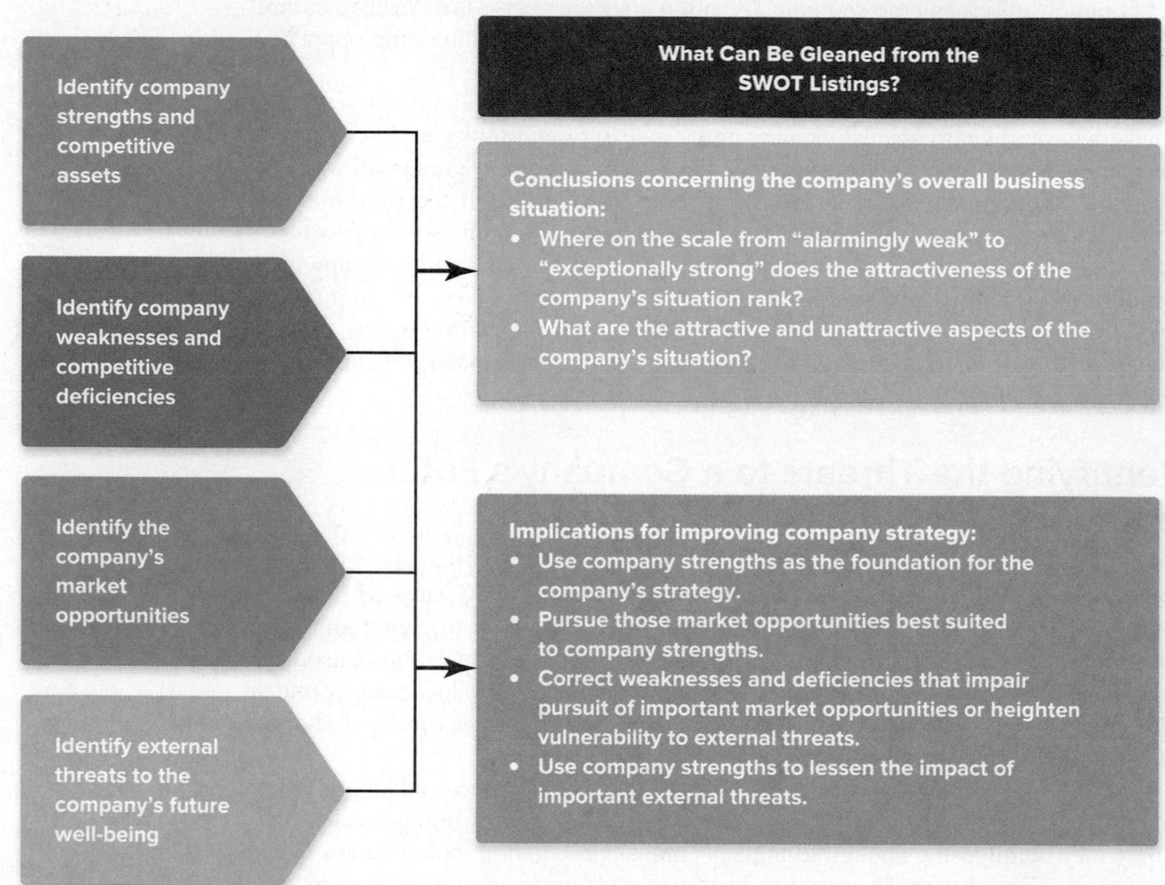

The final piece of SWOT analysis is to translate the diagnosis of the company's situation into actions for improving the company's strategy and business prospects. *A company's internal strengths should always serve as the basis of its strategy—placing heavy reliance on a company's best competitive assets is the soundest route to attracting customers and competing successfully against rivals.*[10] As a rule, strategies that place heavy demands on areas where the company is weakest or has unproven competencies should be avoided. Plainly, managers must look toward correcting competitive weaknesses that make the company vulnerable, hold down profitability, or disqualify it from pursuing an attractive opportunity. Furthermore, a company's strategy should be aimed squarely at capturing attractive market opportunities that are suited to the company's collection of capabilities. How much attention to devote to defending against external threats to the company's future performance hinges on how vulnerable the company is, whether defensive moves can be taken to lessen their impact, and whether the costs of undertaking such moves represent the best use of company resources.

QUESTION 4: HOW DO A COMPANY'S VALUE CHAIN ACTIVITIES IMPACT ITS COST STRUCTURE AND CUSTOMER VALUE PROPOSITION?

Company managers are often stunned when a competitor cuts its prices to "unbelievably low" levels or when a new market entrant introduces a great new product at a surprisingly low price. While less common, new entrants can also storm the market with a product that ratchets the quality level up so high that customers will abandon competing sellers even if they have to pay more for the new product. This is what seems to have happened with Apple's iPhone 6 and iMac computers; it is what Apple is betting on with the Apple Watch.

LO 4

How a company's value chain activities can affect the company's cost structure and customer value proposition.

Regardless of where on the quality spectrum a company competes, it must remain competitive in terms of its customer value proposition in order to stay in the game. Patagonia's value proposition, for example, remains attractive to customers who value quality, wide selection, and corporate environmental responsibility over cheaper outerwear alternatives. Since its inception in 1925, the *New Yorker*'s customer value proposition has withstood the test of time by providing readers with an amalgam of well-crafted, rigorously fact-checked, and topical writing.

The value provided to the customer depends on how well a customer's needs are met for the price paid. How well customer needs are met depends on the perceived quality of a product or service as well as on other, more tangible attributes. The greater the amount of customer value that the company can offer profitably compared to its rivals, the less vulnerable it will be to competitive attack. For managers, the key is to keep close track of how *cost-effectively* the company can deliver value to customers relative to its competitors. If it can deliver the same amount of value with lower expenditures (or more value at the same cost), it will maintain a competitive edge.

The higher a company's costs are above those of close rivals, the more competitively vulnerable the company becomes.

The greater the amount of customer value that a company can offer profitably relative to close rivals, the less competitively vulnerable the company becomes.

Two analytic tools are particularly useful in determining whether a company's costs and customer value proposition are competitive: value chain analysis and benchmarking.

The Concept of a Company Value Chain

Every company's business consists of a collection of activities undertaken in the course of producing, marketing, delivering, and supporting its product or service. All the various activities that a company performs internally combine to form a **value chain**—so called because the underlying intent of a company's activities is ultimately to *create value for buyers.*

CORE CONCEPT

A company's **value chain** identifies the primary activities and related support activities that create customer value.

As shown in Figure 4.3, a company's value chain consists of two broad categories of activities: the *primary activities* foremost in creating value for customers and the requisite *support activities* that facilitate and enhance the performance of the primary activities.[11] The kinds of primary and secondary activities that constitute a company's value chain vary according to the specifics of a company's business; hence, the listing of the primary and support activities in Figure 4.3 is illustrative rather than definitive. For example, the primary activities at a hotel operator like Starwood Hotels and Resorts mainly consist of site selection and construction, reservations, and hotel operations (check-in and check-out, maintenance and housekeeping, dining and room service, and conventions and meetings); principal support

FIGURE 4.3 A Representative Company Value Chain

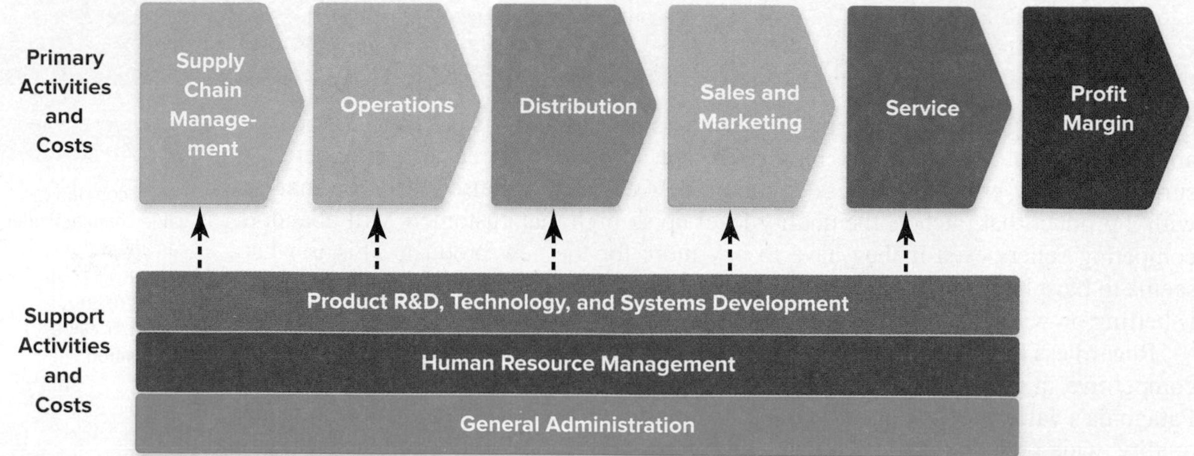

PRIMARY ACTIVITIES

- **Supply Chain Management**—Activities, costs, and assets associated with purchasing fuel, energy, raw materials, parts and components, merchandise, and consumable items from vendors; receiving, storing, and disseminating inputs from suppliers; inspection; and inventory management.
- **Operations**—Activities, costs, and assets associated with converting inputs into final product form (production, assembly, packaging, equipment maintenance, facilities, operations, quality assurance, environmental protection).
- **Distribution**—Activities, costs, and assets dealing with physically distributing the product to buyers (finished goods warehousing, order processing, order picking and packing, shipping, delivery vehicle operations, establishing and maintaining a network of dealers and distributors).
- **Sales and Marketing**—Activities, costs, and assets related to sales force efforts, advertising and promotion, market research and planning, and dealer/distributor support.
- **Service**—Activities, costs, and assets associated with providing assistance to buyers, such as installation, spare parts delivery, maintenance and repair, technical assistance, buyer inquiries, and complaints.

SUPPORT ACTIVITIES

- **Product R&D, Technology, and Systems Development**—Activities, costs, and assets relating to product R&D, process R&D, process design improvement, equipment design, computer software development, telecommunications systems, computer-assisted design and engineering, database capabilities, and development of computerized support systems.
- **Human Resource Management**—Activities, costs, and assets associated with the recruitment, hiring, training, development, and compensation of all types of personnel; labor relations activities; and development of knowledge-based skills and core competencies.
- **General Administration**—Activities, costs, and assets relating to general management, accounting and finance, legal and regulatory affairs, safety and security, management information systems, forming strategic alliances and collaborating with strategic partners, and other "overhead" functions.

Source: Based on the discussion in Michael E. Porter, *Competitive Advantage* (New York: Free Press, 1985), pp. 37–43.

activities that drive costs and impact customer value include hiring and training hotel staff and handling general administration. Supply chain management is a crucial activity for J.Crew and Boeing but is not a value chain component at Facebook, LinkedIn, or Goldman Sachs. Sales and marketing are dominant activities at GAP and Match.com but have only minor roles at oil-drilling companies and natural gas pipeline companies. Customer delivery is a crucial activity at Domino's Pizza but insignificant at Starbucks.

With its focus on value-creating activities, the value chain is an ideal tool for examining the workings of a company's customer value proposition and business model. It permits a deep look at the company's cost structure and ability to offer low prices. It reveals the emphasis that a company places on activities that enhance differentiation and support higher prices, such as service and marketing. It also includes a profit margin component, since profits are necessary to compensate the company's owners and investors, who bear risks and provide capital. Tracking the profit margin along with the value-creating activities is critical because unless an enterprise succeeds in delivering customer value profitably (with a sufficient return on invested capital), it can't survive for long. Attention to a company's profit formula in addition to its customer value proposition is the essence of a sound business model, as described in Chapter 1.

Illustration Capsule 4.1 shows representative costs for various value chain activities performed by Boll & Branch, a maker of luxury linens and bedding sold directly to consumers online.

Comparing the Value Chains of Rival Companies Value chain analysis facilitates a comparison of how rivals, activity by activity, deliver value to customers. Even rivals in the same industry may differ significantly in terms of the activities they perform. For instance, the "operations" component of the value chain for a manufacturer that makes all of its own parts and components and assembles them into a finished product differs from the "operations" of a rival producer that buys the needed parts and components from outside suppliers and performs only assembly operations. How each activity is performed may affect a company's relative cost position as well as its capacity for differentiation. Thus, even a simple comparison of how the activities of rivals' value chains differ can reveal competitive differences.

A Company's Primary and Secondary Activities Identify the Major Components of Its Internal Cost Structure The combined costs of all the various primary and support activities constituting a company's value chain define its internal cost structure. Further, the cost of each activity contributes to whether the company's overall cost position relative to rivals is favorable or unfavorable. The roles of value chain analysis and benchmarking are to develop the data for comparing a company's costs activity by activity against the costs of key rivals and to learn which internal activities are a source of cost advantage or disadvantage.

A company's cost-competitiveness depends not only on the costs of internally performed activities (its own value chain) but also on costs in the value chains of its suppliers and distribution-channel allies.

Evaluating a company's cost-competitiveness involves using what accountants call *activity-based costing* to determine the costs of performing each value chain activity.[12] The degree to which a company's total costs should be broken down into costs for specific activities depends on how valuable it is to know the costs of specific activities versus broadly defined activities. At the very least, cost estimates are needed for each broad category of primary and support activities, but

ILLUSTRATION CAPSULE 4.1

The Value Chain for Boll & Branch

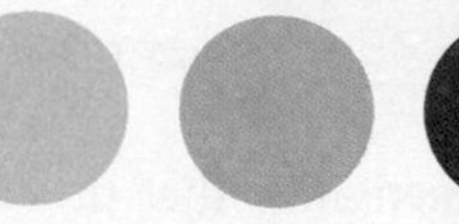

© belchonock/iStock/Getty Images

A king-size set of sheets from Boll & Branch is made from 6 meters of fabric, requiring 11 kilograms of raw cotton.

Raw Cotton	$ 28.16	
Spinning/Weaving/Dyeing	12.00	
Cutting/Sewing/Finishing	9.50	
Material Transportation	3.00	
Factory Fee	15.80	
Cost of Goods		**$ 68.46**
Inspection Fees	5.48	
Ocean Freight/Insurance	4.55	
Import Duties	8.22	
Warehouse/Packing	8.50	
Packaging	15.15	
Customer Shipping	14.00	
Promotions/Donations*	30.00	
Total Cost		**$154.38**
Boll & Brand Markup	About 60%	
Boll & Brand Retail Price		**$250.00**
Gross Margin**	**$ 95.62**	

Source: Adapted from Christina Brinkley, "What Goes into the Price of Luxury Sheets?" *The Wall Street Journal,* March 29, 2014, www.wsj.com/articles/SB10001424052702303725404579461953672838672 (accessed February 16, 2016).

cost estimates for more specific activities within each broad category may be needed if a company discovers that it has a cost disadvantage vis-à-vis rivals and wants to pin down the exact source or activity causing the cost disadvantage. However, a company's own *internal costs* may be insufficient to assess whether its product offering and customer value proposition are competitive with those of rivals. Cost and price differences among competing companies can have their origins in activities performed by suppliers or by distribution allies involved in getting the product to the final customers or end users of the product, in which case the company's entire *value chain system* becomes relevant.

The Value Chain System

A company's value chain is embedded in a larger system of activities that includes the value chains of its suppliers and the value chains of whatever wholesale distributors and retailers it utilizes in getting its product or service to end users. This *value chain system* (sometimes called a vertical chain) has implications that extend far beyond the company's costs. It can affect attributes like product quality that enhance differentiation and have importance for the company's customer value proposition, as well as its profitability.[13] Suppliers' value chains are relevant because suppliers perform activities and incur costs in creating and delivering the purchased inputs utilized in a company's own value-creating activities. The costs, performance features, and quality of these inputs influence a company's own costs and product differentiation capabilities. Anything a company can do to help its suppliers drive down the costs of their value chain activities or improve the quality and performance of the items being supplied can enhance its own competitiveness—a powerful reason for working collaboratively with suppliers in managing supply chain activities.[14] For example, automakers have encouraged their automotive parts suppliers to build plants near the auto assembly plants to facilitate just-in-time deliveries, reduce warehousing and shipping costs, and promote close collaboration on parts design and production scheduling.

Similarly, the value chains of a company's distribution-channel partners are relevant because (1) the costs and margins of a company's distributors and retail dealers are part of the price the ultimate consumer pays and (2) the activities that distribution allies perform affect sales volumes and customer satisfaction. For these reasons, companies normally work closely with their distribution allies (who are their direct customers) to perform value chain activities in mutually beneficial ways. For instance, motor vehicle manufacturers have a competitive interest in working closely with their automobile dealers to promote higher sales volumes and better customer satisfaction with dealers' repair and maintenance services. Producers of kitchen cabinets are heavily dependent on the sales and promotional activities of their distributors and building supply retailers and on whether distributors and retailers operate cost-effectively enough to be able to sell at prices that lead to attractive sales volumes.

As a consequence, *accurately assessing a company's competitiveness entails scrutinizing the nature and costs of value chain activities throughout the entire value chain system for delivering its products or services to end-use customers.* A typical value chain system that incorporates the value chains of suppliers and forward-channel allies (if any) is shown in Figure 4.4. As was the case with company value chains, the specific activities constituting value chain systems vary significantly from industry to industry. The primary value chain system activities in the pulp and paper industry (timber farming, logging, pulp mills, and papermaking) differ from the primary value

FIGURE 4.4 A Representative Value Chain System

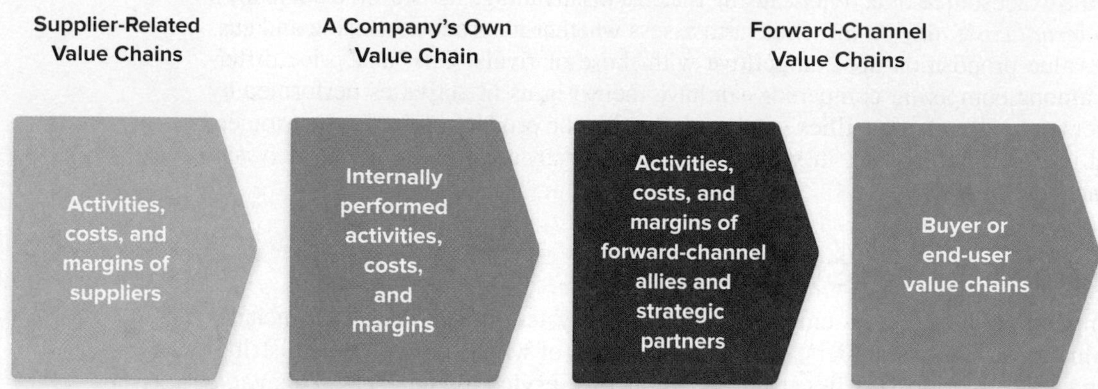

Source: Based in part on the single-industry value chain displayed in Michael E. Porter, *Competitive Advantage* (New York: Free Press, 1985), p. 35.

chain system activities in the home appliance industry (parts and components manufacture, assembly, wholesale distribution, retail sales) and yet again from the computer software industry (programming, disk loading, marketing, distribution).

Benchmarking: A Tool for Assessing Whether the Costs and Effectiveness of a Company's Value Chain Activities Are in Line

CORE CONCEPT

Benchmarking is a potent tool for improving a company's own internal activities that is based on learning how other companies perform them and borrowing their "best practices."

CORE CONCEPT

A **best practice** is a method of performing an activity that consistently delivers superior results compared to other approaches.

Benchmarking entails comparing how different companies (both inside and outside the industry) perform various value chain activities—how materials are purchased, how inventories are managed, how products are assembled, how fast the company can get new products to market, how customer orders are filled and shipped—and then making cross-company comparisons of the costs and effectiveness of these activities.[15] The objectives of benchmarking are to identify the best means of performing an activity and to emulate those best practices.

A **best practice** is a method of performing an activity or business process that consistently delivers superior results compared to other approaches.[16] To qualify as a legitimate best practice, the method must have been employed by at least one enterprise and shown to be *consistently more effective* in lowering costs, improving quality or performance, shortening time requirements, enhancing safety, or achieving some other highly positive operating outcome. Best practices thus identify a path to operating excellence with respect to value chain activities.

Xerox pioneered the use of benchmarking to become more cost-competitive, quickly deciding not to restrict its benchmarking efforts to its office equipment rivals but to extend them to *any company regarded as "world class"* in performing *any activity* relevant to Xerox's business. Other companies quickly picked up on Xerox's approach. Toyota managers got their idea for just-in-time inventory deliveries by studying how U.S. supermarkets replenished their shelves. Southwest Airlines reduced the turnaround time of its aircraft at each scheduled stop by studying pit crews on the auto racing circuit. More than 80 percent of Fortune 500 companies reportedly use benchmarking for comparing themselves against rivals on cost and other competitively important measures.

The tough part of benchmarking is not whether to do it but, rather, how to gain access to information about other companies' practices and costs. Sometimes benchmarking can be accomplished by collecting information from published reports, trade groups, and industry research firms or by talking to knowledgeable industry analysts, customers, and suppliers. Sometimes field trips to the facilities of competing or noncompeting companies can be arranged to observe how things are done, compare practices and processes, and perhaps exchange data on productivity and other cost components. However, such companies, even if they agree to host facilities tours and answer questions, are unlikely to share competitively sensitive cost information. Furthermore, comparing two companies' costs may not involve comparing apples to apples if the two companies employ different cost accounting principles to calculate the costs of particular activities.

However, a third and fairly reliable source of benchmarking information has emerged. The explosive interest of companies in benchmarking costs and identifying best practices has prompted consulting organizations (e.g., Accenture, A. T. Kearney, Benchnet—The Benchmarking Exchange, and Best Practices, LLC) and several associations (e.g., the QualServe Benchmarking Clearinghouse, and the Strategic Planning Institute's Council on Benchmarking) to gather benchmarking data, distribute information about best practices, and provide comparative cost data without identifying the names of particular companies. Having an independent group gather the information and report it in a manner that disguises the names of individual companies protects competitively sensitive data and lessens the potential for unethical behavior on the part of company personnel in gathering their own data about competitors. Illustration Capsule 4.2 describes benchmarking practices in the cement industry.

Benchmarking the costs of company activities against those of rivals provides hard evidence of whether a company is cost-competitive.

Strategic Options for Remedying a Cost or Value Disadvantage

The results of value chain analysis and benchmarking may disclose cost or value disadvantages relative to key rivals. Such information is vital in crafting strategic actions to eliminate any such disadvantages and improve profitability. Information of this nature can also help a company find new avenues for enhancing its competitiveness through lower costs or a more attractive customer value proposition. There are three main areas in a company's total value chain system where company managers can try to improve its efficiency and effectiveness in delivering customer value: (1) a company's own internal activities, (2) suppliers' part of the value chain system, and (3) the forward-channel portion of the value chain system.

Improving Internally Performed Value Chain Activities Managers can pursue any of several strategic approaches to reduce the costs of internally performed value chain activities and improve a company's cost-competitiveness. They can *implement best practices* throughout the company, particularly for high-cost activities. They can *redesign the product and/or some of its components* to eliminate high-cost components or facilitate speedier and more economical manufacture or assembly. They can *relocate high-cost activities* (such as manufacturing) to geographic areas where they can be performed more cheaply or *outsource activities* to lower-cost vendors or contractors.

ILLUSTRATION CAPSULE 4.2

Delivered-Cost Benchmarking in the Cement Industry

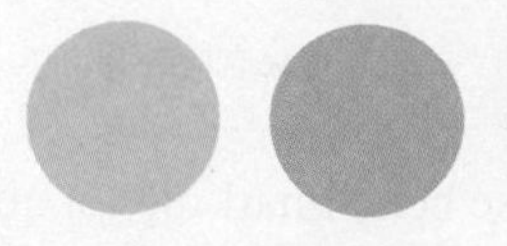

Cement is a dry powder that creates concrete when mixed with water and sand. People interact with concrete every day. It is often the building material of choice for sidewalks, curbs, basements, bridges, and municipal pipes. Cement is manufactured at billion-dollar continuous-process plants by mining limestone, crushing it, scorching it in a kiln, and then milling it again.

About 24 companies (CEMEX, Holcim, and Lafarge are some of the biggest) manufacture cement at 90 U.S. plants with the capacity to produce 110 million tons per year. Plants serve tens of markets distributed across multiple states. Companies regularly benchmark "delivered costs" to understand whether their plants are cost leaders or laggards.

© Ulrich Doering/Alamy Stock Photo

Delivered-cost benchmarking studies typically subdivide manufacturing and logistics costs into five parts: fixed-bin, variable-bin, freight-to-terminal, terminal operating, and freight-to-customer costs. These cost components are estimated using different sources.

Fixed- and variable-bin costs represent the cost of making a ton of cement and moving it to the plant's storage silos. They are the hardest to estimate. Fortunately, the Portland Cement Association, or PCA (the cement industry's association), publishes key data for every plant that features plant location, age, capacity, technology, and fuel. Companies combine the industry data, satellite imagery revealing quarry characteristics, and news reports with the company's proprietary plant-level financial data to develop their estimates of competitors' costs. The basic assumption is that plants of similar size utilizing similar technologies and raw-material inputs will have similar cost performance.

Logistics costs (including freight-to-terminal, terminal operating, and freight-to-customer costs) are much easier to accurately estimate. Cement companies use common carriers to move their product by barge, train, and truck transit modes. Freight pricing is competitive on a per-mile basis by mode, meaning that the company's per-ton-mile barge cost applies to the competition. By combining the per-ton-mile cost with origin-destination distances, freight costs are easily calculated. Terminal operating costs, the costs of operating barge or rail terminals that store cement and transfer it to trucks for local delivery, represent the smallest fraction of total supply chain cost and typically vary little within mode type. For example, most barge terminals cost $10 per ton to run, whereas rail terminals are less expensive and cost $5 per ton.

By combining all five estimated cost elements, the company benchmarks its estimated relative cost position by market. Using these data, strategists can identify which of the company's plants are most exposed to volume fluctuations, which are in greatest need of investment or closure, which markets the company should enter or exit, and which competitors are the most likely candidates for product or asset swaps.

Note: Developed with Peter Jacobson.

Source: www.cement.org (accessed January 25, 2014).

To improve the effectiveness of the company's customer value proposition and enhance differentiation, managers can take several approaches. They can *adopt best practices for quality, marketing, and customer service*. They can *reallocate resources to activities that address buyers' most important purchase criteria*, which will have the biggest impact on the value delivered to the customer. They can *adopt new technologies that spur innovation, improve design, and enhance creativity*. Additional approaches to managing value chain activities to lower costs and/or enhance customer value are discussed in Chapter 5.

Improving Supplier-Related Value Chain Activities Supplier-related cost disadvantages can be attacked by pressuring suppliers for lower prices, switching to lower-priced substitute inputs, and collaborating closely with suppliers to identify mutual cost-saving opportunities.[17] For example, just-in-time deliveries from suppliers can lower a company's inventory and internal logistics costs and may also allow suppliers to economize on their warehousing, shipping, and production scheduling costs—a win–win outcome for both. In a few instances, companies may find that it is cheaper to integrate backward into the business of high-cost suppliers and make the item in-house instead of buying it from outsiders.

Similarly, a company can enhance its customer value proposition through its supplier relationships. Some approaches include selecting and retaining suppliers that meet higher-quality standards, providing quality-based incentives to suppliers, and integrating suppliers into the design process. Fewer defects in parts from suppliers not only improve quality throughout the value chain system but can lower costs as well since less waste and disruption occur in the production processes.

Improving Value Chain Activities of Distribution Partners Any of three means can be used to achieve better cost-competitiveness in the forward portion of the industry value chain:

1. Pressure distributors, dealers, and other forward-channel allies to reduce their costs and markups.
2. Collaborate with them to identify win–win opportunities to reduce costs—for example, a chocolate manufacturer learned that by shipping its bulk chocolate in liquid form in tank cars instead of as 10-pound molded bars, it could not only save its candy bar manufacturing customers the costs associated with unpacking and melting but also eliminate its own costs of molding bars and packing them.
3. Change to a more economical distribution strategy, including switching to cheaper distribution channels (selling direct via the Internet) or integrating forward into company-owned retail outlets.

The means to enhancing differentiation through activities at the forward end of the value chain system include (1) engaging in cooperative advertising and promotions with forward allies (dealers, distributors, retailers, etc.), (2) creating exclusive arrangements with downstream sellers or utilizing other mechanisms that increase their incentives to enhance delivered customer value, and (3) creating and enforcing standards for downstream activities and assisting in training channel partners in business practices. Harley-Davidson, for example, enhances the shopping experience and perceptions of buyers by selling through retailers that sell Harley-Davidson motorcycles exclusively and meet Harley-Davidson standards.

Translating Proficient Performance of Value Chain Activities into Competitive Advantage

A company that does a *first-rate job* of managing its value chain activities *relative to competitors* stands a good chance of profiting from its competitive advantage. A company's value-creating activities can offer a competitive advantage in one of two ways (or both):

1. They can contribute to greater efficiency and lower costs relative to competitors.
2. They can provide a basis for differentiation, so customers are willing to pay relatively more for the company's goods and services.

Achieving a cost-based competitive advantage requires determined management efforts to be cost-efficient in performing value chain activities. Such efforts have to be ongoing and persistent, and they have to involve each and every value chain activity. The goal must be continuous cost reduction, not a one-time or on-again–off-again effort. Companies like Dollar General, Nucor Steel, Irish airline Ryanair, T.J.Maxx, and French discount retailer Carrefour have been highly successful in managing their value chains in a low-cost manner.

Ongoing and persistent efforts are also required for a competitive advantage based on differentiation. Superior reputations and brands are built up slowly over time, through continuous investment and activities that deliver consistent, reinforcing messages. Differentiation based on quality requires vigilant management of activities for quality assurance throughout the value chain. While the basis for differentiation (e.g., status, design, innovation, customer service, reliability, image) may vary widely among companies pursuing a differentiation advantage, companies that succeed do so on the basis of a commitment to coordinated value chain activities aimed purposefully at this objective. Examples include Cartier (status), Room and Board (craftsmanship), American Express (customer service), Dropbox (innovation), and FedEx (reliability).

How Value Chain Activities Relate to Resources and Capabilities

There is a close relationship between the value-creating activities that a company performs and its resources and capabilities. An organizational capability or competence implies a *capacity* for action; in contrast, a value-creating activity *initiates* the action. With respect to resources and capabilities, activities are "where the rubber hits the road." When companies engage in a value-creating activity, they do so by drawing on specific company resources and capabilities that underlie and enable the activity. For example, brand-building activities depend on human resources, such as experienced brand managers (including their knowledge and expertise in this arena), as well as organizational capabilities in advertising and marketing. Cost-cutting activities may derive from organizational capabilities in inventory management, for example, and resources such as inventory tracking systems.

Because of this correspondence between activities and supporting resources and capabilities, value chain analysis can complement resource and capability analysis as another tool for assessing a company's competitive advantage. Resources and capabilities that are *both valuable and rare* provide a company with *what it takes* for competitive advantage. For a company with competitive assets of this sort, the potential is there. When these assets are deployed in the form of a value-creating activity, that potential is realized due to their competitive superiority. Resource analysis is one tool for identifying competitively superior resources and capabilities. But their value and the competitive superiority of that value can be assessed objectively only *after* they are deployed. Value chain analysis and benchmarking provide the type of data needed to make that objective assessment.

There is also a dynamic relationship between a company's activities and its resources and capabilities. Value-creating activities are more than just the embodiment of a resource's or capability's potential. They also contribute to the formation and development of capabilities. The road to competitive advantage begins with management efforts to build organizational expertise in performing certain competitively important value chain activities. With consistent practice and continuous investment of company resources, these activities rise to the level of a reliable organizational capability or a competence. To the extent that top management makes the growing capability a cornerstone of the company's strategy, this capability becomes a core competence for the company. Later, with further organizational

Performing value chain activities with capabilities that permit the company to either outmatch rivals on differentiation or beat them on costs will give the company a competitive advantage.

learning and gains in proficiency, the core competence may evolve into a distinctive competence, giving the company superiority over rivals in performing an important value chain activity. Such superiority, if it gives the company significant competitive clout in the marketplace, can produce an attractive competitive edge over rivals. Whether the resulting competitive advantage is on the cost side or on the differentiation side (or both) will depend on the company's choice of which types of competence-building activities to engage in over this time period.

QUESTION 5: IS THE COMPANY COMPETITIVELY STRONGER OR WEAKER THAN KEY RIVALS?

LO 5

How a comprehensive evaluation of a company's competitive situation can assist managers in making critical decisions about their next strategic moves.

Using resource analysis, value chain analysis, and benchmarking to determine a company's competitiveness on value and cost is necessary but not sufficient. A more comprehensive assessment needs to be made of the company's *overall* competitive strength. The answers to two questions are of particular interest: First, how does the company rank relative to competitors on each of the important factors that determine market success? Second, all things considered, does the company have a *net* competitive advantage or disadvantage versus major competitors?

An easy-to-use method for answering these two questions involves developing quantitative strength ratings for the company and its key competitors on each industry key success factor and each competitively pivotal resource, capability, and value chain activity. Much of the information needed for doing a competitive strength assessment comes from previous analyses. Industry and competitive analyses reveal the key success factors and competitive forces that separate industry winners from losers. Benchmarking data and scouting key competitors provide a basis for judging the competitive strength of rivals on such factors as cost, key product attributes, customer service, image and reputation, financial strength, technological skills, distribution capability, and other factors. Resource and capability analysis reveals which of these are competitively important, given the external situation, and whether the company's competitive advantages are sustainable. SWOT analysis provides a more comprehensive and forward-looking picture of the company's overall situation.

Step 1 in doing a competitive strength assessment is to make a list of the industry's key success factors and other telling measures of competitive strength or weakness (6 to 10 measures usually suffice). Step 2 is to assign weights to each of the measures of competitive strength based on their perceived importance. (The sum of the weights for each measure must add up to 1.) Step 3 is to calculate weighted strength ratings by scoring each competitor on each strength measure (using a 1-to-10 rating scale, where 1 is very weak and 10 is very strong) and multiplying the assigned rating by the assigned weight. Step 4 is to sum the weighted strength ratings on each factor to get an overall measure of competitive strength for each company being rated. Step 5 is to use the overall strength ratings to draw conclusions about the size and extent of the company's net competitive advantage or disadvantage and to take specific note of areas of strength and weakness.

Table 4.4 provides an example of competitive strength assessment in which a hypothetical company (ABC Company) competes against two rivals. In the example, relative cost is the most telling measure of competitive strength, and the other strength measures are of lesser importance. The company with the highest rating on a given measure has an implied competitive edge on that measure, with the size of its edge reflected in the difference between its weighted rating and rivals' weighted ratings.

TABLE 4.4 A Representative Weighted Competitive Strength Assessment

		Competitive Strength Assessment (rating scale: 1 = very weak, 10 = very strong)					
		ABC Co.		Rival 1		Rival 2	
Key Success Factor/Strength Measure	Importance Weight	Strength Rating	Weighted Score	Strength Rating	Weighted Score	Strength Rating	Weighted Score
Quality/product performance	0.10	8	0.80	5	0.50	1	0.10
Reputation/image	0.10	8	0.80	7	0.70	1	0.10
Manufacturing capability	0.10	2	0.20	10	1.00	5	0.50
Technological skills	0.05	10	0.50	1	0.05	3	0.15
Dealer network/ distribution capability	0.05	9	0.45	4	0.20	5	0.25
New product innovation capability	0.05	9	0.45	4	0.20	5	0.25
Financial resources	0.10	5	0.50	10	1.00	3	0.30
Relative cost position	0.30	5	1.50	10	3.00	1	0.30
Customer service capabilities	0.15	5	0.75	7	1.05	1	0.15
Sum of importance weights	**1.00**						
Overall weighted competitive strength rating			**5.95**		**7.70**		**2.10**

For instance, Rival 1's 3.00 weighted strength rating on relative cost signals a considerable cost advantage over ABC Company (with a 1.50 weighted score on relative cost) and an even bigger cost advantage over Rival 2 (with a weighted score of 0.30). The measure-by-measure ratings reveal the competitive areas in which a company is strongest and weakest, and against whom.

The overall competitive strength scores indicate how all the different strength measures add up—whether the company is at a net overall competitive advantage or disadvantage against each rival. The higher a company's *overall weighted strength rating,* the stronger its *overall competitiveness* versus rivals. The bigger the difference between a company's overall weighted rating and the scores of *lower-rated* rivals, the greater is its implied *net competitive advantage*. Thus, Rival 1's overall weighted score of 7.70 indicates a greater net competitive advantage over Rival 2 (with a score of 2.10) than over ABC Company (with a score of 5.95). Conversely, the bigger the difference between a company's overall rating and the scores of *higher-rated* rivals, the greater its implied *net competitive disadvantage*. Rival 2's score of 2.10 gives it a smaller net competitive disadvantage against ABC Company (with an overall score of 5.95) than against Rival 1 (with an overall score of 7.70).

High-weighted competitive strength ratings signal a strong competitive position and possession of competitive advantage; low ratings signal a weak position and competitive disadvantage.

Strategic Implications of Competitive Strength Assessments

In addition to showing how competitively strong or weak a company is relative to rivals, the strength ratings provide guidelines for designing wise offensive and defensive strategies. For example, if ABC Company wants to go on the offensive to win additional sales and market share, such an offensive probably needs to be aimed directly at winning customers away from Rival 2 (which has a lower overall strength score) rather than Rival 1 (which has a higher overall strength score). Moreover, while ABC has high ratings for technological skills (a 10 rating), dealer network/distribution capability (a 9 rating), new product innovation capability (a 9 rating), quality/product performance (an 8 rating), and reputation/image (an 8 rating), these strength measures have low importance weights—meaning that ABC has strengths in areas that don't translate into much competitive clout in the marketplace. Even so, it outclasses Rival 2 in all five areas, plus it enjoys substantially lower costs than Rival 2 (ABC has a 5 rating on relative cost position versus a 1 rating for Rival 2)—and relative cost position carries the highest importance weight of all the strength measures. ABC also has greater competitive strength than Rival 3 regarding customer service capabilities (which carries the second-highest importance weight). Hence, because ABC's strengths are in the very areas where Rival 2 is weak, ABC is in a good position to attack Rival 2. Indeed, ABC may well be able to persuade a number of Rival 2's customers to switch their purchases over to its product.

A company's competitive strength scores pinpoint its strengths and weaknesses against rivals and point directly to the kinds of offensive and defensive actions it can use to exploit its competitive strengths and reduce its competitive vulnerabilities.

But ABC should be cautious about cutting price aggressively to win customers away from Rival 2, because Rival 1 could interpret that as an attack by ABC to win away Rival 1's customers as well. And Rival 1 is in far and away the best position to compete on the basis of low price, given its high rating on relative cost in an industry where low costs are competitively important (relative cost carries an importance weight of 0.30). Rival 1's strong relative cost position vis-à-vis both ABC and Rival 2 arms it with the ability to use its lower-cost advantage to thwart any price cutting on ABC's part. Clearly ABC is vulnerable to any retaliatory price cuts by Rival 1—Rival 1 can easily defeat both ABC and Rival 2 in a price-based battle for sales and market share. If ABC wants to defend against its vulnerability to potential price cutting by Rival 1, then it needs to aim a portion of its strategy at lowering its costs.

The point here is that a competitively astute company should utilize the strength scores in deciding what strategic moves to make. When a company has important competitive strengths in areas where one or more rivals are weak, it makes sense to consider offensive moves to exploit rivals' competitive weaknesses. When a company has important competitive weaknesses in areas where one or more rivals are strong, it makes sense to consider defensive moves to curtail its vulnerability.

QUESTION 6: WHAT STRATEGIC ISSUES AND PROBLEMS MERIT FRONT-BURNER MANAGERIAL ATTENTION?

The final and most important analytic step is to zero in on exactly what strategic issues company managers need to address—and resolve—for the company to be more financially and competitively successful in the years ahead. This step involves drawing on the results of both industry analysis and the evaluations of the company's internal situation. The task here is to get a clear fix on exactly what strategic and competitive challenges confront the company, which of the company's competitive shortcomings need fixing, and what specific problems merit company managers' front-burner attention. *Pinpointing the specific issues that management needs to address sets the agenda for deciding what actions to take next to improve the company's performance and business outlook.*

Compiling a "priority list" of problems creates an agenda of strategic issues that merit prompt managerial attention.

A good strategy must contain ways to deal with all the strategic issues and obstacles that stand in the way of the company's financial and competitive success in the years ahead.

The "priority list" of issues and problems that have to be wrestled with can include such things as *how* to stave off market challenges from new foreign competitors, *how* to combat the price discounting of rivals, *how* to reduce the company's high costs, *how* to sustain the company's present rate of growth in light of slowing buyer demand, *whether* to correct the company's competitive deficiencies by acquiring a rival company with the missing strengths, *whether* to expand into foreign markets, *whether* to reposition the company and move to a different strategic group, *what to do* about growing buyer interest in substitute products, and *what to do* to combat the aging demographics of the company's customer base. The priority list thus always centers on such concerns as "how to . . . ," "what to do about . . . ," and "whether to . . ." The purpose of the priority list is to identify the specific issues and problems that management needs to address, not to figure out what specific actions to take. Deciding what to do—which strategic actions to take and which strategic moves to make—comes later (when it is time to craft the strategy and choose among the various strategic alternatives).

If the items on the priority list are relatively minor—which suggests that the company's strategy is mostly on track and reasonably well matched to the company's overall situation—company managers seldom need to go much beyond fine-tuning the present strategy. If, however, the problems confronting the company are serious and indicate the present strategy is not well suited for the road ahead, the task of crafting a better strategy needs to be at the top of management's action agenda.

KEY POINTS

There are six key questions to consider in evaluating a company's ability to compete successfully against market rivals:

1. *How well is the present strategy working?* This involves evaluating the strategy in terms of the company's financial performance and market standing. The stronger a company's current overall performance, the less likely the need for radical strategy changes. The weaker a company's performance and/or the faster the

changes in its external situation (which can be gleaned from PESTEL and industry analysis), the more its current strategy must be questioned.

2. *What are the company's most important resources and capabilities and can they give the company a sustainable advantage over competitors?* A company's resources can be identified using the tangible/intangible typology presented in this chapter. Its capabilities can be identified either by starting with its resources to look for related capabilities or looking for them within the company's different functional domains.

   The answer to the second part of the question comes from conducting the four tests of a resource's competitive power—the VRIN tests. If a company has resources and capabilities that are competitively *valuable* and *rare,* the firm will have a competitive advantage over market rivals. If its resources and capabilities are also hard to copy *(inimitable),* with no good substitutes *(nonsubstitutable),* then the firm may be able to sustain this advantage even in the face of active efforts by rivals to overcome it.

3. *Is the company able to seize market opportunities and overcome external threats to its future well-being?* The answer to this question comes from performing a SWOT analysis. The two most important parts of SWOT analysis are (1) drawing conclusions about what strengths, weaknesses, opportunities, and threats tell about the company's overall situation; and (2) acting on the conclusions to better match the company's strategy to its internal strengths and market opportunities, to correct the important internal weaknesses, and to defend against external threats. A company's strengths and competitive assets are strategically relevant because they are the most logical and appealing building blocks for strategy; internal weaknesses are important because they may represent vulnerabilities that need correction. External opportunities and threats come into play because a good strategy necessarily aims at capturing a company's most attractive opportunities and at defending against threats to its well-being.

4. *Are the company's cost structure and value proposition competitive?* One telling sign of whether a company's situation is strong or precarious is whether its costs are competitive with those of industry rivals. Another sign is how the company compares with rivals in terms of differentiation—how effectively it delivers on its customer value proposition. Value chain analysis and benchmarking are essential tools in determining whether the company is performing particular functions and activities well, whether its costs are in line with those of competitors, whether it is differentiating in ways that really enhance customer value, and whether particular internal activities and business processes need improvement. They complement resource and capability analysis by providing data at the level of individual activities that provide more objective evidence of whether individual resources and capabilities, or bundles of resources and linked activity sets, are competitively superior.

5. *On an overall basis, is the company competitively stronger or weaker than key rivals?* The key appraisals here involve how the company matches up against key rivals on industry key success factors and other chief determinants of competitive success and whether and why the company has a *net* competitive advantage or disadvantage. Quantitative competitive strength assessments, using the method

presented in Table 4.4, indicate where a company is competitively strong and weak and provide insight into the company's ability to defend or enhance its market position. As a rule, a company's competitive strategy should be built around its competitive strengths and should aim at shoring up areas where it is competitively vulnerable. When a company has important competitive strengths in areas where one or more rivals are weak, it makes sense to consider offensive moves to exploit rivals' competitive weaknesses. When a company has important competitive weaknesses in areas where one or more rivals are strong, it makes sense to consider defensive moves to curtail its vulnerability.

6. *What strategic issues and problems merit front-burner managerial attention?* This analytic step zeros in on the strategic issues and problems that stand in the way of the company's success. It involves using the results of industry analysis as well as resource and value chain analysis of the company's competitive situation to identify a "priority list" of issues to be resolved for the company to be financially and competitively successful in the years ahead. Actually deciding on a strategy and what specific actions to take is what comes after developing the list of strategic issues and problems that merit front-burner management attention.

Like good industry analysis, solid analysis of the company's competitive situation vis-à-vis its key rivals is a valuable precondition for good strategy making.

ASSURANCE OF LEARNING EXERCISES

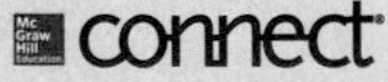

LO 1

1. Using the financial ratios provided in Table 4.1 and the financial statement information presented below for Costco Wholesale Corporation, calculate the following ratios for Costco for both 2013 and 2014:
   a. Gross profit margin
   b. Operating profit margin
   c. Net profit margin
   d. Times-interest-earned (or coverage) ratio
   e. Return on stockholders' equity
   f. Return on assets
   g. Debt-to-equity ratio
   h. Days of inventory
   i. Inventory turnover ratio
   j. Average collection period

   Based on these ratios, did Costco's financial performance improve, weaken, or remain about the same from 2013 to 2014?

Consolidated Income Statements for Costco Wholesale Corporation, 2013–2014 (in millions, except per share data)

	2014	2013
Net sales	$110,212	$102,870
Membership fees	2,428	2,286
Total revenue	112,640	105,156
Merchandise costs	98,458	$ 91,948
Selling, general, and administrative	10,899	10,155
Operating income	3,220	3,053
Other income (expense)		
Interest expense	(113)	(99)
Interest income and other, net	90	97
Income before income taxes	3,197	3,051
Provision for income taxes	1,109	990
Net income including noncontrolling interests	2,088	2,061
Net income attributable to noncontrolling interests	(30)	(22)
Net income	$ 2,058	$ 2,039
Basic earnings per share	$ 4.69	$ 4.68
Diluted earnings per share	$ 4.65	$ 4.63

Source: Costco Wholesale Corporation 2014 10-K.

Consolidated Balance Sheets for Costco Wholesale Corporation, 2013–2014 (in millions, except per share data)

	August 31, 2014	September 1, 2013
Assets		
Current Assets		
Cash and cash equivalents	$ 5,738	$ 4,644
Short-term investments	1,577	1,480
Receivables, net	1,148	1,026
Merchandise inventories	8,456	7,894

(continued)

	August 31, 2014	September 1, 2013
Deferred income taxes and other current assets	669	621
Total current assets	17,588	$15,840
Property and Equipment		
Land	$ 4,716	$ 4,409
Buildings and improvements	12,522	11,556
Equipment and fixtures	4,845	4,472
Construction in progress	592	585
	22,675	21,022
Less accumulated depreciation and amortization	(7,845)	(7,141)
Net property and equipment	14,830	13,881
Other assets	606	562
Total assets	$33,024	$30,283
Liabilities and Equity		
Current Liabilities		
Accounts payable	$ 8,491	$ 7,872
Accrued salaries and benefits	2,231	2,037
Accrued member rewards	773	710
Accrued sales and other taxes	442	382
Deferred membership fees	1,254	1,167
Other current liabilities	1,221	1,089
Total current liabilities	14,412	13,257
Long-term debt, excluding current portion	5,093	4,998
Deferred income taxes and other liabilities	1,004	1,016
Total liabilities	20,509	$19,271
Commitments and Contingencies		
Equity		
Preferred stock $0.005 par value; 100,000,000 shares authorized; no shares issued and outstanding	0	0
Common stock $0.005 par value; 900,000,000 shares authorized; 436,839,000 and 432,350,000 shares issued and outstanding	2	2
Additional paid-in capital	$ 4,919	$ 4,670
Accumulated other comprehensive (loss) income	(76)	(122)

(continued)

	August 31, 2014	September 1, 2013
Retained earnings	7,458	6,283
Total Costco stockholders' equity	12,303	10,833
Noncontrolling interests	212	179
Total equity	12,515	11,012
Total Liabilities and Equity	$33,024	$30,283

Source: Costco Wholesale Corporation 2014 10-K.

2. Panera Bread operates more than 1,900 bakery-cafés in more than 45 states and Canada. How many of the four tests of the competitive power of a resource does the store network pass? Using your general knowledge of this industry, perform a SWOT analysis. Explain your answers. **LO 2, LO 3**
3. Review the information in Illustration Capsule 4.1 concerning Boll & Branch's average costs of producing and selling a king-size sheet set, and compare this with the representative value chain depicted in Figure 4.3. Then answer the following questions: connect **LO 4**
   a. Which of the company's costs correspond to the primary value chain activities depicted in Figure 4.3?
   b. Which of the company's costs correspond to the support activities described in Figure 4.3?
   c. What value chain activities might be important in securing or maintaining Boll & Branch's competitive advantage? Explain your answer.
4. Using the methodology illustrated in Table 4.3 and your knowledge as an automobile owner, prepare a competitive strength assessment for General Motors and its rivals Ford, Chrysler, Toyota, and Honda. Each of the five automobile manufacturers should be evaluated on the key success factors and strength measures of cost-competitiveness, product-line breadth, product quality and reliability, financial resources and profitability, and customer service. What does your competitive strength assessment disclose about the overall competitiveness of each automobile manufacturer? What factors account most for Toyota's competitive success? Does Toyota have competitive weaknesses that were disclosed by your analysis? Explain. **LO 5**

EXERCISE FOR SIMULATION PARTICIPANTS

1. Using the formulas in Table 4.1 and the data in your company's latest financial statements, calculate the following measures of financial performance for your company: **LO 1**
   a. Operating profit margin
   b. Total return on total assets

c. Current ratio
d. Working capital
e. Long-term debt-to-capital ratio
f. Price-to-earnings ratio

LO 1 2. On the basis of your company's latest financial statements and all the other available data regarding your company's performance that appear in the industry report, list the three measures of financial performance on which your company did best and the three measures on which your company's financial performance was worst.

LO 1 3. What hard evidence can you cite that indicates your company's strategy is working fairly well (or perhaps not working so well, if your company's performance is lagging that of rival companies)?

LO 2, LO 3 4. What internal strengths and weaknesses does your company have? What external market opportunities for growth and increased profitability exist for your company? What external threats to your company's future well-being and profitability do you and your co-managers see? What does the preceding SWOT analysis indicate about your company's present situation and future prospects—where on the scale from "exceptionally strong" to "alarmingly weak" does the attractiveness of your company's situation rank?

LO 2, LO 3 5. Does your company have any core competencies? If so, what are they?

LO 4 6. What are the key elements of your company's value chain? Refer to Figure 4.3 in developing your answer.

LO 5 7. Using the methodology presented in Table 4.4, do a weighted competitive strength assessment for your company and two other companies that you and your co-managers consider to be very close competitors.

ENDNOTES

[1] Birger Wernerfelt, "A Resource-Based View of the Firm," *Strategic Management Journal* 5, no. 5 (September–October 1984), pp. 171–180; Jay Barney, "Firm Resources and Sustained Competitive Advantage," *Journal of Management* 17, no. 1 (1991), pp. 99–120.

[2] R. Amit and P. Schoemaker, "Strategic Assets and Organizational Rent," *Strategic Management Journal* 14 (1993).

[3] Jay B. Barney, "Looking Inside for Competitive Advantage," *Academy of Management Executive* 9, no. 4 (November 1995), pp. 49–61; Christopher A. Bartlett and Sumantra Ghoshal, "Building Competitive Advantage through People," *MIT Sloan Management Review* 43, no. 2 (Winter 2002), pp. 34–41; Danny Miller, Russell Eisenstat, and Nathaniel Foote, "Strategy from the Inside Out: Building Capability-Creating Organizations," *California Management Review* 44, no. 3 (Spring 2002), pp. 37–54.

[4] M. Peteraf and J. Barney, "Unraveling the Resource-Based Tangle," *Managerial and Decision Economics* 24, no. 4 (June–July 2003), pp. 309–323.

[5] Margaret A. Peteraf and Mark E. Bergen, "Scanning Dynamic Competitive Landscapes: A Market-Based and Resource-Based Framework," *Strategic Management Journal* 24 (2003), pp. 1027–1042.

[6] C. Montgomery, "Of Diamonds and Rust: A New Look at Resources," in C. Montgomery (ed.), *Resource-Based and Evolutionary Theories of the Firm* (Boston: Kluwer Academic, 1995), pp. 251–268.

[7] Constance E. Helfat and Margaret A. Peteraf, "The Dynamic Resource-Based View: Capability Lifecycles," *Strategic Management Journal* 24, no. 10 (2003).

[8] D. Teece, G. Pisano, and A. Shuen, "Dynamic Capabilities and Strategic Management," *Strategic Management Journal* 18, no. 7 (1997), pp. 509–533; K. Eisenhardt and J. Martin, "Dynamic Capabilities: What Are They?" *Strategic Management Journal* 21, no. 10–11 (2000), pp. 1105–1121; M. Zollo and S. Winter, "Deliberate Learning and the Evolution of Dynamic Capabilities," *Organization Science* 13 (2002), pp. 339–351; C. Helfat et al., *Dynamic Capabilities: Understanding Strategic Change in Organizations* (Malden, MA: Blackwell, 2007).

[9] Donald Sull, "Strategy as Active Waiting," *Harvard Business Review* 83, no. 9 (September 2005), pp. 121–126.

[10] M. Peteraf, "The Cornerstones of Competitive Advantage: A Resource-Based View," *Strategic Management Journal,* March 1993, pp. 179–191.
[11] Michael Porter in his 1985 best seller *Competitive Advantage* (New York: Free Press).
[12] John K. Shank and Vijay Govindarajan, *Strategic Cost Management* (New York: Free Press, 1993), especially chaps. 2–6, 10, and 11; Robin Cooper and Robert S. Kaplan, "Measure Costs Right: Make the Right Decisions," *Harvard Business Review* 66, no. 5 (September–October, 1988), pp. 96–103; Joseph A. Ness and Thomas G. Cucuzza, "Tapping the Full Potential of ABC," *Harvard Business Review* 73, no. 4 (July–August 1995), pp. 130–138.
[13] Porter, *Competitive Advantage,* p. 34.
[14] Hau L. Lee, "The Triple-A Supply Chain," *Harvard Business Review* 82, no. 10 (October 2004), pp. 102–112.
[15] Gregory H. Watson, *Strategic Benchmarking: How to Rate Your Company's Performance against the World's Best* (New York: Wiley, 1993); Robert C. Camp, *Benchmarking: The Search for Industry Best Practices That Lead to Superior Performance* (Milwaukee: ASQC Quality Press, 1989); Dawn Iacobucci and Christie Nordhielm, "Creative Benchmarking," *Harvard Business Review* 78 no. 6 (November–December 2000), pp. 24–25.
[16] **www.businessdictionary.com/definition/best-practice.html** (accessed December 2, 2009).
[17] Reuben E. Stone, "Leading a Supply Chain Turnaround," *Harvard Business Review* 82, no. 10 (October 2004), pp. 114–121.

CHAPTER 5

The Five Generic Competitive Strategies

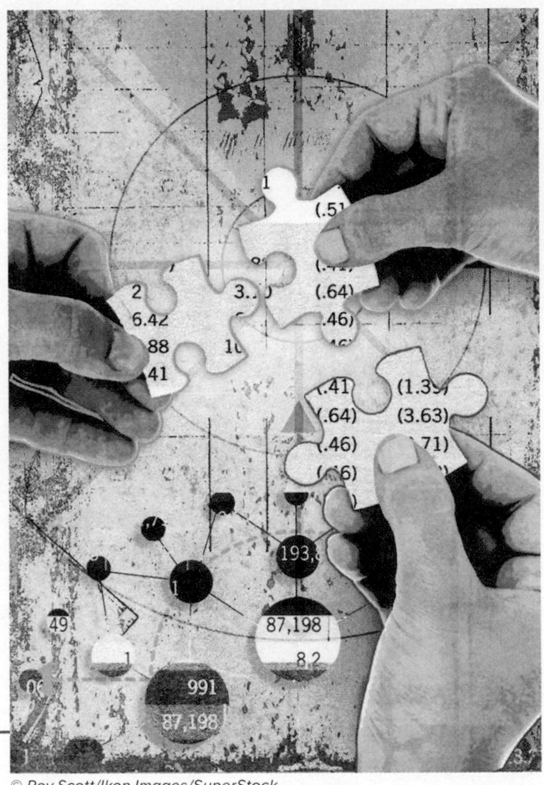

© Roy Scott/Ikon Images/SuperStock

Learning Objectives

THIS CHAPTER WILL HELP YOU UNDERSTAND:

LO 1 What distinguishes each of the five generic strategies and why some of these strategies work better in certain kinds of competitive conditions than in others.

LO 2 The major avenues for achieving a competitive advantage based on lower costs.

LO 3 The major avenues to a competitive advantage based on differentiating a company's product or service offering from the offerings of rivals.

LO 4 The attributes of a best-cost provider strategy—a hybrid of low-cost provider and differentiation strategies.

Strategy 101 is about choices: You can't be all things to all people.

Michael E. Porter—*Professor, author, and cofounder of Monitor Consulting*

Strategy is all about combining choices of what to do and what not to do into a system that creates the requisite fit between what the environment needs and what the company does.

Costas Markides—*Professor and consultant*

I learnt the hard way about positioning in business, about catering to the right segments.

Shaffi Mather—*Social entrepreneur*

A company can employ any of several basic approaches to competing successfully and gaining a competitive advantage over rivals, but they all involve *delivering more value* to customers than rivals or *delivering value more efficiently* than rivals (or both). More value for customers can mean a good product at a lower price, a superior product worth paying more for, or a best-value offering that represents an attractive combination of price, features, service, and other appealing attributes. Greater efficiency means delivering a given level of value to customers at a lower cost to the company. But whatever approach to delivering value the company takes, it nearly always requires performing value chain activities differently than rivals and building competitively valuable resources and capabilities that rivals cannot readily match or trump.

This chapter describes the five *generic competitive strategy options.* Which of the five to employ is a company's first and foremost choice in crafting an overall strategy and beginning its quest for competitive advantage.

TYPES OF GENERIC COMPETITIVE STRATEGIES

LO 1

What distinguishes each of the five generic strategies and why some of these strategies work better in certain kinds of competitive conditions than in others.

A company's competitive strategy *deals exclusively with the specifics of management's game plan for competing successfully*—its specific efforts to position itself in the marketplace, please customers, ward off competitive threats, and achieve a particular kind of competitive advantage. The chances are remote that any two companies—even companies in the same industry—will employ competitive strategies that are exactly alike in every detail. However, when one strips away the details to get at the real substance, the two biggest factors that distinguish one competitive strategy from another boil down to (1) whether a company's market target is broad or narrow and (2) whether the company is pursuing a competitive advantage linked to lower costs or differentiation. These two factors give rise to five competitive strategy options, as shown in Figure 5.1 and listed next.[1]

1. *A low-cost provider strategy*—striving to achieve lower overall costs than rivals on comparable products that attract a broad spectrum of buyers, usually by underpricing rivals.

FIGURE 5.1 The Five Generic Competitive Strategies

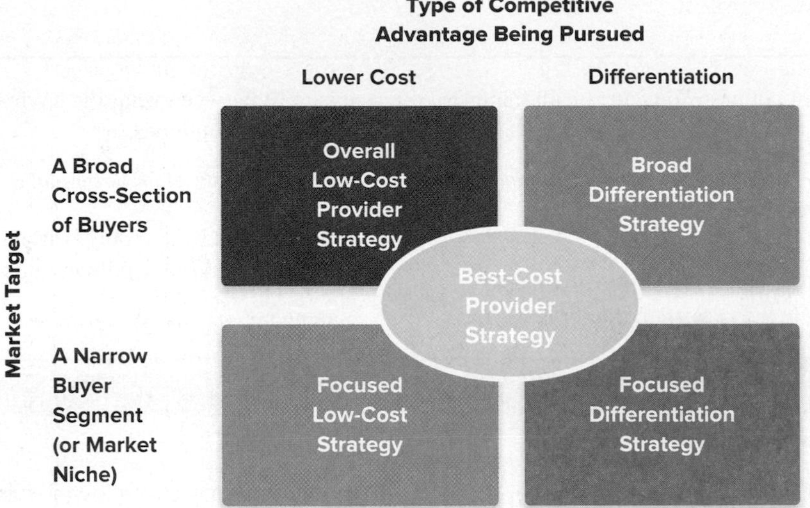

Source: This is an expanded version of a three-strategy classification discussed in Michael E. Porter, *Competitive Strategy* (New York: Free Press, 1980).

2. *A broad differentiation strategy*—seeking to differentiate the company's product offering from rivals' with attributes that will appeal to a broad spectrum of buyers.
3. *A focused low-cost strategy*—concentrating on the needs and requirements of a narrow buyer segment (or market niche) and striving to meet these needs at lower costs than rivals (thereby being able to serve niche members at a lower price).
4. *A focused differentiation strategy*—concentrating on a narrow buyer segment (or market niche) and outcompeting rivals by offering niche members customized attributes that meet their tastes and requirements better than rivals' products.
5. *A best-cost provider strategy*—striving to incorporate upscale product attributes at a lower cost than rivals. Being the "best-cost" producer of an upscale, multifeatured product allows a company to *give customers more value for their money* by underpricing rivals whose products have similar upscale, multifeatured attributes. This competitive approach is a *hybrid* strategy that *blends elements of the previous four options* in a unique and often effective way.

The remainder of this chapter explores the ins and outs of these five generic competitive strategies and how they differ.

LOW-COST PROVIDER STRATEGIES

Striving to achieve lower overall costs than rivals is an especially potent competitive approach in markets with many price-sensitive buyers. A company achieves **low-cost leadership** when it becomes the industry's lowest-cost provider rather than just being one of perhaps several competitors with comparatively low costs. A low-cost provider's foremost strategic objective is meaningfully lower costs than rivals—*but not* *necessarily the absolutely lowest possible cost.* In striving for a cost advantage over rivals, company managers must incorporate features and services that buyers consider essential. A product offering that is too frills-free can be viewed by consumers as offering little value regardless of its pricing.

LO 2

The major avenues for achieving a competitive advantage based on lower costs.

A company has two options for translating a low-cost advantage over rivals into attractive profit performance. Option 1 is to use the lower-cost edge to underprice competitors and attract price-sensitive buyers in great enough numbers to increase total profits. Option 2 is to maintain the present price, be content with the present market share, and use the lower-cost edge to earn a higher profit margin on each unit sold, thereby raising the firm's total profits and overall return on investment.

CORE CONCEPT

A **low-cost provider's** basis for competitive advantage is lower overall costs than competitors. Successful **low-cost leaders,** who have the lowest industry costs, are exceptionally good at finding ways to drive costs out of their businesses and still provide a product or service that buyers find acceptable.

While many companies are inclined to exploit a low-cost advantage by using option 1 (attacking rivals with lower prices), this strategy can backfire if rivals respond with retaliatory price cuts (in order to protect their customer base and defend against a loss of sales). A rush to cut prices can often trigger a price war that lowers the profits of all price discounters. The bigger the risk that rivals will respond with matching price cuts, the more appealing it becomes to employ the second option for using a low-cost advantage to achieve higher profitability.

The Two Major Avenues for Achieving a Cost Advantage

To achieve a low-cost edge over rivals, a firm's cumulative costs across its overall value chain must be lower than competitors' cumulative costs. There are two major avenues for accomplishing this:[2]

A low-cost advantage over rivals can translate into better profitability than rivals attain.

1. Perform value chain activities more cost-effectively than rivals.
2. Revamp the firm's overall value chain to eliminate or bypass some cost-producing activities.

CORE CONCEPT

A **cost driver** is a factor that has a strong influence on a company's costs.

Cost-Efficient Management of Value Chain Activities For a company to do a more cost-efficient job of managing its value chain than rivals, managers must diligently search out cost-saving opportunities in every part of the value chain. No activity can escape cost-saving scrutiny, and all company personnel must be expected to use their talents and ingenuity to come up with innovative and effective ways to keep down costs. Particular attention must be paid to a set of factors known as **cost drivers** that have a strong effect on a company's costs and can be used as levers to lower costs. Figure 5.2 shows the most important cost drivers. Cost-cutting approaches that demonstrate an effective use of the cost drivers include:

1. *Capturing all available economies of scale.* Economies of scale stem from an ability to lower unit costs by increasing the scale of operation. Economies of scale may be available at different points along the value chain. Often a large plant is more economical to operate than a small one, particularly if it can be operated round the clock robotically. Economies of scale may be available due to a large warehouse operation on the input side or a large distribution center on the output side. In global industries, selling a mostly standard product worldwide tends to lower unit costs as opposed to making separate products for each country market, an approach in which costs are typically higher due to an inability to reach the most economic scale of production for each country. There are economies of scale in advertising as well. For example, Anheuser-Busch could

FIGURE 5.2 Cost Drivers: The Keys to Driving Down Company Costs

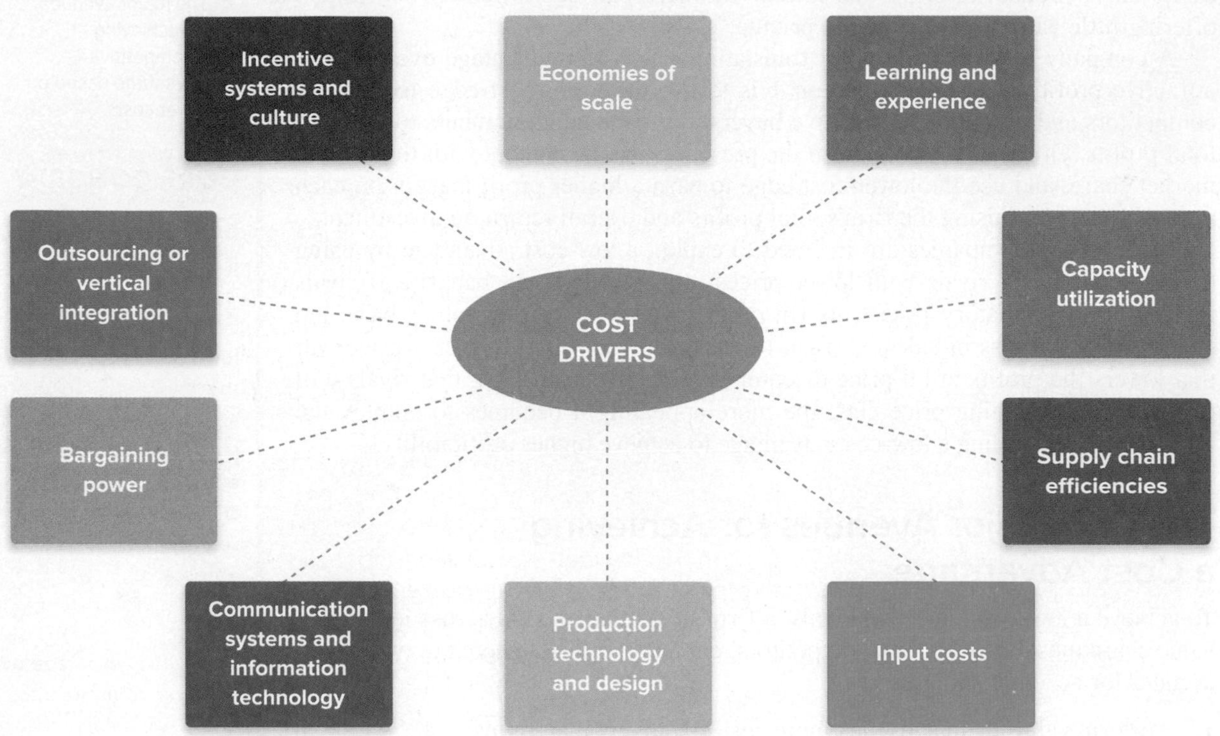

Source: Adapted from Michael E. Porter, *Competitive Advantage: Creating and Sustaining Superior Performance* (New York: Free Press, 1985).

afford to pay the $5 million cost of a 30-second Super Bowl ad in 2016 because the cost could be spread out over the hundreds of millions of units of Budweiser that the company sells.

2. *Taking full advantage of experience and learning-curve effects.* The cost of performing an activity can decline over time as the learning and experience of company personnel build. Learning and experience economies can stem from debugging and mastering newly introduced technologies, using the experiences and suggestions of workers to install more efficient plant layouts and assembly procedures, and the added speed and effectiveness that accrues from repeatedly picking sites for and building new plants, distribution centers, or retail outlets.
3. *Operating facilities at full capacity.* Whether a company is able to operate at or near full capacity has a big impact on unit costs when its value chain contains activities associated with substantial fixed costs. Higher rates of capacity utilization allow depreciation and other fixed costs to be spread over a larger unit volume, thereby lowering fixed costs per unit. The more capital-intensive the business and the higher the fixed costs as a percentage of total costs, the greater the unit-cost penalty for operating at less than full capacity.
4. *Improving supply chain efficiency.* Partnering with suppliers to streamline the ordering and purchasing process, to reduce inventory carrying costs via just-in-time inventory practices, to economize on shipping and materials handling, and to

ferret out other cost-saving opportunities is a much-used approach to cost reduction. A company with a distinctive competence in cost-efficient supply chain management, such as BASF (the world's leading chemical company), can sometimes achieve a sizable cost advantage over less adept rivals.

5. *Substituting lower-cost inputs wherever there is little or no sacrifice in product quality or performance.* If the costs of certain raw materials and parts are "too high," a company can switch to using lower-cost items or maybe even design the high-cost components out of the product altogether.
6. *Using the company's bargaining power vis-à-vis suppliers or others in the value chain system to gain concessions.* Home Depot, for example, has sufficient bargaining clout with suppliers to win price discounts on large-volume purchases.
7. *Using online systems and sophisticated software to achieve operating efficiencies.* For example, sharing data and production schedules with suppliers, coupled with the use of enterprise resource planning (ERP) and manufacturing execution system (MES) software, can reduce parts inventories, trim production times, and lower labor requirements.
8. *Improving process design and employing advanced production technology.* Often production costs can be cut by (1) using design for manufacture (DFM) procedures and computer-assisted design (CAD) techniques that enable more integrated and efficient production methods, (2) investing in highly automated robotic production technology, and (3) shifting to a mass-customization production process. Dell's highly automated PC assembly plant in Austin, Texas, is a prime example of the use of advanced product and process technologies. Many companies are ardent users of total quality management (TQM) systems, business process reengineering, Six Sigma methodology, and other business process management techniques that aim at boosting efficiency and reducing costs.
9. *Being alert to the cost advantages of outsourcing or vertical integration.* Outsourcing the performance of certain value chain activities can be more economical than performing them in-house if outside specialists, by virtue of their expertise and volume, can perform the activities at lower cost. On the other hand, there can be times when integrating into the activities of either suppliers or distribution-channel allies can lower costs through greater production efficiencies, reduced transaction costs, or a better bargaining position.
10. *Motivating employees through incentives and company culture.* A company's incentive system can encourage not only greater worker productivity but also cost-saving innovations that come from worker suggestions. The culture of a company can also spur worker pride in productivity and continuous improvement. Companies that are well known for their cost-reducing incentive systems and culture include Nucor Steel, which characterizes itself as a company of "20,000 teammates," Southwest Airlines, and Walmart.

Revamping of the Value Chain System to Lower Costs Dramatic cost advantages can often emerge from redesigning the company's value chain system in ways that eliminate costly work steps and entirely bypass certain cost-producing value chain activities. Such value chain revamping can include:

- *Selling direct to consumers and bypassing the activities and costs of distributors and dealers.* To circumvent the need for distributors and dealers, a company can (1) create its own direct sales force (which adds the costs of maintaining and supporting a sales force but which may well be cheaper than using independent distributors and dealers to access buyers) and/or (2) conduct sales operations at the company's website (incurring costs for website operations and shipping may be a substantially cheaper way to make sales than going through distributor–dealer channels). Costs in the wholesale and retail portions of the value chain frequently represent 35 to 50 percent of the final price consumers pay, so establishing a direct sales force or selling online may offer big cost savings.

- *Streamlining operations by eliminating low-value-added or unnecessary work steps and activities.* At Walmart, some items supplied by manufacturers are delivered directly to retail stores rather than being routed through Walmart's distribution centers and delivered by Walmart trucks. In other instances, Walmart unloads incoming shipments from manufacturers' trucks arriving at its distribution centers and loads them directly onto outgoing Walmart trucks headed to particular stores without ever moving the goods into the distribution center. Many supermarket chains have greatly reduced in-store meat butchering and cutting activities by shifting to meats that are cut and packaged at the meatpacking plant and then delivered to their stores in ready-to-sell form.
- *Reducing materials handling and shipping costs by having suppliers locate their plants or warehouses close to the company's own facilities.* Having suppliers locate their plants or warehouses close to a company's own plant facilitates just-in-time deliveries of parts and components to the exact workstation where they will be used in assembling the company's product. This not only lowers incoming shipping costs but also curbs or eliminates the company's need to build and operate storerooms for incoming parts and components and to have plant personnel move the inventories to the workstations as needed for assembly.

Illustration Capsule 5.1 describes the path that Amazon.com, Inc. has followed on the way to becoming not only the largest online retailer (as measured by revenues) but also the lowest-cost provider in the industry.

Examples of Companies That Revamped Their Value Chains to Reduce Costs Nucor Corporation, the most profitable steel producer in the United States and one of the largest steel producers worldwide, drastically revamped the value chain process for manufacturing steel products by using relatively inexpensive electric arc furnaces and continuous casting processes. Using electric arc furnaces to melt recycled scrap steel eliminated many of the steps used by traditional steel mills that made their steel products from iron ore, coke, limestone, and other ingredients using costly coke ovens, basic oxygen blast furnaces, ingot casters, and multiple types of finishing facilities—plus Nucor's value chain system required far fewer employees. As a consequence, Nucor produces steel with a far lower capital investment, a far smaller workforce, and far lower operating costs than traditional steel mills. Nucor's strategy to replace the traditional steelmaking value chain with its simpler, quicker value chain approach has made it one of the world's lowest-cost producers of steel, allowing it to take a huge amount of market share away from traditional steel companies and earn attractive profits. (Nucor reported a profit in 188 out of 192 quarters during 1966–2014—a remarkable feat in a mature and cyclical industry notorious for roller-coaster bottom-line performance.)

Southwest Airlines has achieved considerable cost savings by reconfiguring the traditional value chain of commercial airlines, thereby permitting it to offer travelers dramatically lower fares. Its mastery of fast turnarounds at the gates (about 25 minutes

ILLUSTRATION CAPSULE 5.1

Amazon's Path to Becoming the Low-Cost Provider in E-commerce

In 1996, shortly after founding Amazon.com, CEO Jeff Bezos told his employees, *"When you are small, someone else that is bigger can always come along and take away what you have."* Since then, the company has relentlessly pursued growth, aiming to become the global cost leader in "customer-centric E-commerce" across nearly all consumer merchandise lines. Amazon.com now offers over 230 million items for sale in America—approximately 30 times more than Walmart—and its annual sales are greater than the next five largest e-retailers combined.

In scaling up, Amazon has achieved lower costs not only through economies of scale, but also by increasing its bargaining power over its supplies and distribution partners. With thousands of suppliers, Amazon.com is not reliant on any one relationship. Suppliers, however, have few other alternative e-retailers that can match Amazon's reach and popularity. This gives Amazon bargaining power when negotiating revenue sharing and payment schedules. Amazon has even been able to negotiate for space inside suppliers' warehouses, reducing their own inventory costs.

On the distribution side, Amazon has been developing its own capabilities to reduce reliance on third-party delivery services. Unlike most mega retailers, Amazon's distribution operation was designed to send small orders to residential customers. Amazon.com attained proximity to its customers by building a substantial network of warehousing facilities and processing capability—249 fulfillment and delivery stations globally. This wide footprint decreases the marginal cost of quick delivery, as well as Amazon's reliance on cross-country delivery services. In addition, Amazon has adopted innovative delivery services to further lower costs and extend its reach. In India and the UK, for example, through Easy

© Sean Gallup/Getty Images

Ship Amazon's crew picks up orders directly from sellers, eliminating the time and cost of sending goods to a warehouse and the need for more space.

Amazon's size has also enabled it to spread the fixed costs of its massive up-front investment in automation across many units. Amazon.com was a pioneer of algorithms generating customized recommendations for customers. While developing these algorithms was resource-intensive, the costs of employing them are low. The more Amazon uses its automated sales tools to drive revenue, the more the up-front development cost is spread thin across total revenue. As a result, the company has lower capital intensity for each dollar of sales than other large retailers (like Walmart and Target). Other proprietary tools that increase the volume and speed of sales—without increasing variable costs—include Amazon.com's patented One Click Buy feature. All in all, these moves have been helping secure Amazon's position as the low-cost provider in this industry.

Note: Developed with Danielle G. Garver.

Sources: Company websites; seekingalpha.com/article/2247493-amazons-competitive-advantage-quantified; Brad Stone, *The Everything Store* (New York: Back Bay Books, 2013); www.reuters.com/article/us-amazon-com-india-logistics-idUSKCN0T12PL20151112 (accessed February 16, 2016).

---

versus 45 minutes for rivals) allows its planes to fly more hours per day. This translates into being able to schedule more flights per day with fewer aircraft, allowing Southwest to generate more revenue per plane on average than rivals. Southwest does not offer assigned seating, baggage transfer to connecting airlines, or first-class seating and service, thereby eliminating all the cost-producing activities associated with these features. The company's fast and user-friendly online reservation system facilitates e-ticketing and reduces staffing requirements

Success in achieving a low-cost edge over rivals comes from out-managing rivals in finding ways to perform value chain activities faster, more accurately, and more cost-effectively.

at telephone reservation centers and airport counters. Its use of automated check-in equipment reduces staffing requirements for terminal check-in. The company's carefully designed point-to-point route system minimizes connections, delays, and total trip time for passengers, allowing about 75 percent of Southwest passengers to fly nonstop to their destinations and at the same time reducing Southwest's costs for flight operations.

The Keys to Being a Successful Low-Cost Provider

While low-cost providers are champions of frugality, they seldom hesitate to spend aggressively on resources and capabilities *that promise to drive costs out of the business.* Indeed, having competitive assets of this type and ensuring that they remain competitively superior is essential for achieving competitive advantage as a low-cost provider. Walmart, for example, has been an early adopter of state-of-the-art technology throughout its operations; however, the company *carefully estimates the cost savings of new technologies before it rushes to invest in them.* By continuously investing in complex, cost-saving technologies that are hard for rivals to match, Walmart has sustained its low-cost advantage for over 30 years.

Other companies noted for their successful use of low-cost provider strategies include Vizio in big-screen TVs, EasyJet and Ryanair in airlines, Huawei in networking and telecommunications equipment, Bic in ballpoint pens, Stride Rite in footwear, and Poulan in chain saws.

When a Low-Cost Provider Strategy Works Best

A low-cost provider strategy becomes increasingly appealing and competitively powerful when:

1. *Price competition among rival sellers is vigorous.* Low-cost providers are in the best position to compete offensively on the basis of price, to gain market share at the expense of rivals, to win the business of price-sensitive buyers, to remain profitable despite strong price competition, and to survive price wars.
2. *The products of rival sellers are essentially identical and readily available from many eager sellers.* Look-alike products and/or overabundant product supply set the stage for lively price competition; in such markets, it is the less efficient, higher-cost companies whose profits get squeezed the most.
3. *It is difficult to achieve product differentiation in ways that have value to buyers.* When the differences between product attributes or brands do not matter much to buyers, buyers are nearly always sensitive to price differences, and industry-leading companies tend to be those with the lowest-priced brands.
4. *Most buyers use the product in the same ways.* With common user requirements, a standardized product can satisfy the needs of buyers, in which case low price, not features or quality, becomes the dominant factor in causing buyers to choose one seller's product over another's.
5. *Buyers incur low costs in switching their purchases from one seller to another.* Low switching costs give buyers the flexibility to shift purchases to lower-priced sellers having equally good products or to attractively priced substitute products. A low-cost leader is well positioned to use low price to induce potential customers to switch to its brand.

Pitfalls to Avoid in Pursuing a Low-Cost Provider Strategy

Perhaps the biggest mistake a low-cost provider can make is getting carried away with overly aggressive price cutting. *Higher unit sales and market shares do not automatically translate into higher profits.* Reducing price results in earning a lower profit margin on each unit sold. Thus reducing price improves profitability *only if* the lower price increases unit sales enough to offset the loss in revenues due to the lower per unit profit margin. A simple numerical example tells the story: Suppose a firm selling 1,000 units at a price of $10, a cost of $9, and a profit margin of $1 opts to cut price 5 percent to $9.50—which reduces the firm's profit margin to $0.50 per unit sold. If unit costs remain at $9, then it takes a 100 percent sales increase to 2,000 units just to offset the narrower profit margin and get back to total profits of $1,000. Hence, whether a price cut will result in higher or lower profitability depends on how big the resulting sales gains will be and how much, if any, unit costs will fall as sales volumes increase.

A low-cost provider is in the best position to win the business of price-sensitive buyers, set the floor on market price, and still earn a profit.

A second pitfall is *relying on cost reduction approaches that can be easily copied by rivals.* If rivals find it relatively easy or inexpensive to imitate the leader's low-cost methods, then the leader's advantage will be too short-lived to yield a valuable edge in the marketplace.

Reducing price does not lead to higher total profits unless the added gains in unit sales are large enough to offset the loss in revenues due to lower margins per unit sold.

A third pitfall is *becoming too fixated on cost reduction.* Low costs cannot be pursued so zealously that a firm's offering ends up being too feature-poor to generate buyer appeal. Furthermore, a company driving hard to push down its costs has to guard against ignoring declining buyer sensitivity to price, increased buyer interest in added features or service, or new developments that alter how buyers use the product. Otherwise, it risks losing market ground if buyers start opting for more upscale or feature-rich products.

A low-cost provider's product offering must always contain enough attributes to be attractive to prospective buyers—low price, by itself, is not always appealing to buyers.

Even if these mistakes are avoided, a low-cost provider strategy still entails risk. An innovative rival may discover an even lower-cost value chain approach. Important cost-saving technological breakthroughs may suddenly emerge. And if a low-cost provider has heavy investments in its present means of operating, then it can prove costly to quickly shift to the new value chain approach or a new technology.

BROAD DIFFERENTIATION STRATEGIES

LO 3

The major avenues to a competitive advantage based on differentiating a company's product or service offering from the offerings of rivals.

Differentiation strategies are attractive whenever buyers' needs and preferences are too diverse to be fully satisfied by a standardized product offering. Successful product differentiation requires careful study to determine what attributes buyers will find appealing, valuable, and worth paying for.[3] Then the company must incorporate a combination of these desirable features into its product or service that will be different enough to stand apart from the product or service offerings of rivals. A broad differentiation strategy achieves its aim when a wide range of buyers find the company's offering more appealing than that of rivals and worth a somewhat higher price.

Successful differentiation allows a firm to do one or more of the following:

- Command a premium price for its product.
- Increase unit sales (because additional buyers are won over by the differentiating features).

CORE CONCEPT

The essence of a **broad differentiation strategy** is to offer unique product attributes that a wide range of buyers find appealing and worth paying more for.

- Gain buyer loyalty to its brand (because buyers are strongly attracted to the differentiating features and bond with the company and its products).

Differentiation enhances profitability whenever a company's product can command a sufficiently higher price or generate sufficiently bigger unit sales *to more than cover the added costs of achieving the differentiation.* Company differentiation strategies fail when buyers don't place much value on the brand's uniqueness and/or when a company's differentiating features are easily matched by its rivals.

Companies can pursue differentiation from many angles: a unique taste (Red Bull, Listerine); multiple features (Microsoft Office, Apple Watch); wide selection and one-stop shopping (Home Depot, Alibaba.com); superior service (Ritz-Carlton, Nordstrom); spare parts availability (John Deere; Morgan Motors); engineering design and performance (Mercedes, BMW); high fashion design (Prada, Gucci); product reliability (Whirlpool and Bosch in large home appliances); quality manufacture (Michelin); technological leadership (3M Corporation in bonding and coating products); a full range of services (Charles Schwab in stock brokerage); and wide product selection (Campbell's soups).

Managing the Value Chain to Create the Differentiating Attributes

Differentiation is not something hatched in marketing and advertising departments, nor is it limited to the catchalls of quality and service. Differentiation opportunities can exist in activities all along an industry's value chain. The most systematic approach that managers can take, however, involves focusing on the **value drivers,** a set of factors—analogous to cost drivers—that are particularly effective in creating differentiation. Figure 5.3 contains a list of important value drivers. Ways that managers can enhance differentiation based on value drivers include the following:

CORE CONCEPT

A **value driver** is a factor that can have a strong differentiating effect.

1. *Create product features and performance attributes that appeal to a wide range of buyers.* The physical and functional features of a product have a big influence on differentiation, including features such as added user safety or enhanced environmental protection. Styling and appearance are big differentiating factors in the apparel and motor vehicle industries. Size and weight matter in binoculars and mobile devices. Most companies employing broad differentiation strategies make a point of incorporating innovative and novel features in their product or service offering, especially those that improve performance and functionality.
2. *Improve customer service or add extra services.* Better customer services, in areas such as delivery, returns, and repair, can be as important in creating differentiation as superior product features. Examples include superior technical assistance to buyers, higher-quality maintenance services, more and better product information provided to customers, more and better training materials for end users, better credit terms, quicker order processing, and greater customer convenience.
3. *Invest in production-related R&D activities.* Engaging in production R&D may permit custom-order manufacture at an efficient cost, provide wider product variety and selection through product "versioning," or improve product quality. Many manufacturers have developed flexible manufacturing systems that allow different models and product versions to be made on the same assembly line. Being able to provide buyers with made-to-order products can be a potent differentiating capability.

FIGURE 5.3 Value Drivers: The Keys to Creating a Differentiation Advantage

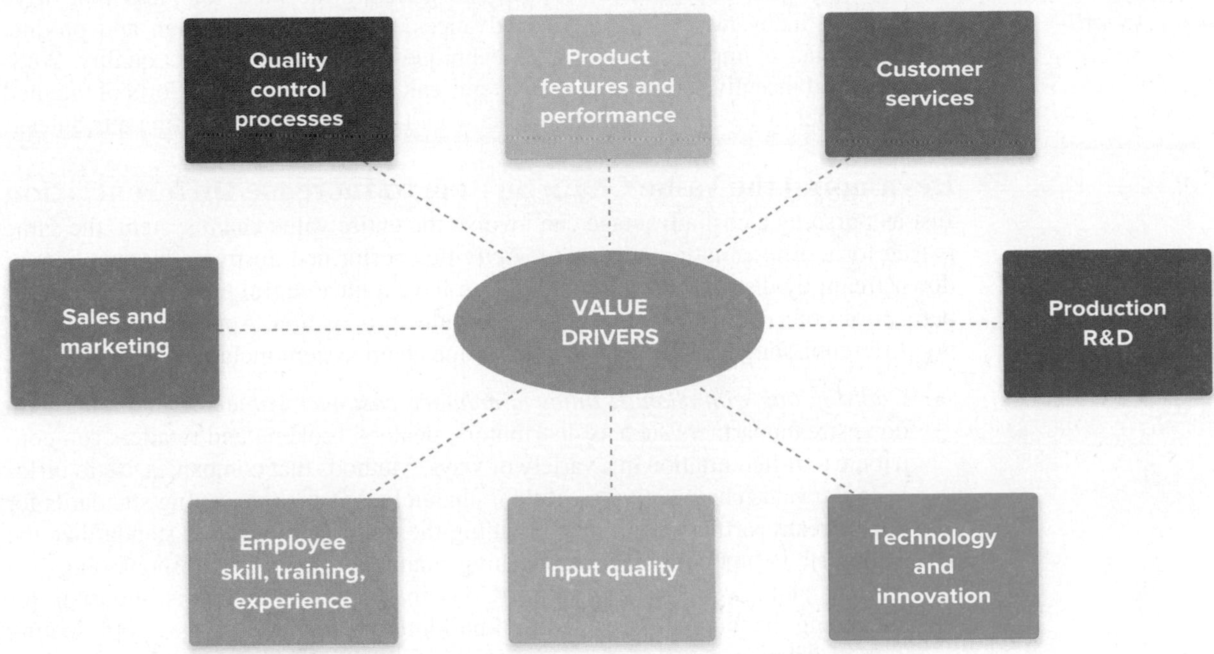

Source: Adapted from Michael E. Porter, *Competitive Advantage: Creating and Sustaining Superior Performance* (New York: Free Press, 1985).

4. *Strive for innovation and technological advances.* Successful innovation is the route to more frequent first-on-the-market victories and is a powerful differentiator. If the innovation proves hard to replicate, through patent protection or other means, it can provide a company with a first-mover advantage that is sustainable.
5. *Pursue continuous quality improvement.* Quality control processes reduce product defects, prevent premature product failure, extend product life, make it economical to offer longer warranty coverage, improve economy of use, result in more end-user convenience, or enhance product appearance. Companies whose quality management systems meet certification standards, such as the ISO 9001 standards, can enhance their reputation for quality with customers.
6. *Increase marketing and brand-building activities.* Marketing and advertising can have a tremendous effect on the value perceived by buyers and therefore their willingness to pay more for the company's offerings. They can create differentiation even when little tangible differentiation exists otherwise. For example, blind taste tests show that even the most loyal Pepsi or Coke drinkers have trouble telling one cola drink from another.[4] Brands create customer loyalty, which increases the perceived "cost" of switching to another product.
7. *Seek out high-quality inputs.* Input quality can ultimately spill over to affect the performance or quality of the company's end product. Starbucks, for example, gets high ratings on its coffees partly because it has very strict specifications on the coffee beans purchased from suppliers.

8. *Emphasize human resource management activities that improve the skills, expertise, and knowledge of company personnel.* A company with high-caliber intellectual capital often has the capacity to generate the kinds of ideas that drive product innovation, technological advances, better product design and product performance, improved production techniques, and higher product quality. Well-designed incentive compensation systems can often unleash the efforts of talented personnel to develop and implement new and effective differentiating attributes.

Revamping the Value Chain System to Increase Differentiation

Just as pursuing a cost advantage can involve the entire value chain system, the same is true for a differentiation advantage. Activities performed upstream by suppliers or downstream by distributors and retailers can have a meaningful effect on customers' perceptions of a company's offerings and its value proposition. Approaches to enhancing differentiation through changes in the value chain system include:

- *Coordinating with channel allies to enhance customer value.* Coordinating with downstream partners such as distributors, dealers, brokers, and retailers can contribute to differentiation in a variety of ways. Methods that companies use to influence the value chain activities of their channel allies include setting standards for downstream partners to follow, providing them with templates to standardize the selling environment or practices, training channel personnel, or cosponsoring promotions and advertising campaigns. Coordinating with retailers is important for enhancing the buying experience and building a company's image. Coordinating with distributors or shippers can mean quicker delivery to customers, more accurate order filling, and/or lower shipping costs. The Coca-Cola Company considers coordination with its bottler-distributors so important that it has at times taken over a troubled bottler to improve its management and upgrade its plant and equipment before releasing it again.[5]
- *Coordinating with suppliers to better address customer needs.* Collaborating with suppliers can also be a powerful route to a more effective differentiation strategy. Coordinating and collaborating with suppliers can improve many dimensions affecting product features and quality. This is particularly true for companies that engage only in assembly operations, such as Dell in PCs and Ducati in motorcycles. Close coordination with suppliers can also enhance differentiation by speeding up new product development cycles or speeding delivery to end customers. Strong relationships with suppliers can also mean that the company's supply requirements are prioritized when industry supply is insufficient to meet overall demand.

Delivering Superior Value via a Broad Differentiation Strategy

Differentiation strategies depend on meeting customer needs in unique ways or creating new needs through activities such as innovation or persuasive advertising. The objective is to offer customers something that rivals can't—at least in terms of the level of satisfaction. There are four basic routes to achieving this aim.

The first route is to incorporate product attributes and user features that *lower the buyer's overall costs* of using the company's product. This is the least obvious and most overlooked route to a differentiation advantage. It is a differentiating factor since it can help business buyers be more competitive in their markets and more profitable. Producers of materials and components often win orders for their products by reducing a buyer's raw-material waste (providing cut-to-size components), reducing a buyer's inventory requirements (providing just-in-time deliveries), using online systems to reduce a buyer's procurement and order processing costs, and providing free technical support. This route to differentiation can also appeal to individual consumers who are looking to economize on their overall costs of consumption. Making a company's product more economical for a buyer to use can be done by incorporating energy-efficient features (energy-saving appliances and lightbulbs help cut buyers' utility bills; fuel-efficient vehicles cut buyer costs for gasoline) and/or by increasing maintenance intervals and product reliability to lower buyer costs for maintenance and repairs.

A second route is to incorporate *tangible* features that increase customer satisfaction with the product, such as product specifications, functions, and styling. This can be accomplished by including attributes that add functionality; enhance the design; save time for the user; are more reliable; or make the product cleaner, safer, quieter, simpler to use, more portable, more convenient, or longer-lasting than rival brands. Smartphone manufacturers are in a race to introduce next-generation devices capable of being used for more purposes and having simpler menu functionality.

Differentiation can be based on *tangible* or *intangible* attributes.

A third route to a differentiation-based competitive advantage is to incorporate *intangible* features that enhance buyer satisfaction in noneconomic ways. Toyota's Prius appeals to environmentally conscious motorists not only because these drivers want to help reduce global carbon dioxide emissions but also because they identify with the image conveyed. Bentley, Ralph Lauren, Louis Vuitton, Burberry, Cartier, and Coach have differentiation-based competitive advantages linked to buyer desires for status, image, prestige, upscale fashion, superior craftsmanship, and the finer things in life. Intangibles that contribute to differentiation can extend beyond product attributes to the reputation of the company and to customer relations or trust.

The fourth route is to *signal the value* of the company's product offering to buyers. Typical signals of value include a high price (in instances where high price implies high quality and performance), more appealing or fancier packaging than competing products, ad content that emphasizes a product's standout attributes, the quality of brochures and sales presentations, and the luxuriousness and ambience of a seller's facilities (important for high-end retailers and for offices or other facilities frequented by customers). They make potential buyers aware of the professionalism, appearance, and personalities of the seller's employees and/or make potential buyers realize that a company has prestigious customers. Signaling value is particularly important (1) when the nature of differentiation is based on intangible features and is therefore subjective or hard to quantify, (2) when buyers are making a first-time purchase and are unsure what their experience with the product will be, (3) when repurchase is infrequent, and (4) when buyers are unsophisticated.

Regardless of the approach taken, achieving a successful differentiation strategy requires, first, that the company have capabilities in areas such as customer service, marketing, brand management, and technology that can create and support differentiation. That is, the resources, competencies, and value chain activities of the company must be well matched to the requirements of the strategy. For the strategy to result in competitive advantage, the company's competencies must also be sufficiently unique in delivering value to buyers that they help set its product offering apart from those of rivals. They must be competitively superior. There are numerous examples of companies that have differentiated themselves on the basis of distinctive capabilities. Health care facilities like M.D. Anderson, Mayo Clinic, and Cleveland Clinic have specialized expertise and equipment for treating certain diseases that most hospitals and health care providers cannot afford to emulate. When a major news event occurs, many people turn to Fox News and CNN because they have the capabilities to get reporters on the scene quickly, break away from their regular programming (without suffering a loss of advertising revenues associated with regular programming), and devote extensive air time to newsworthy stories.

Easy-to-copy differentiating features cannot produce sustainable competitive advantage.

The most successful approaches to differentiation are those that are difficult for rivals to duplicate. Indeed, this is the route to a sustainable differentiation advantage. While resourceful competitors can, in time, clone almost any tangible product attribute, socially complex intangible attributes such as company reputation, long-standing relationships with buyers, and image are much harder to imitate. Differentiation that creates switching costs that lock in buyers also provides a route to sustainable advantage. For example, if a buyer makes a substantial investment in learning to use one type of system, that buyer is less likely to switch to a competitor's system. (This has kept many users from switching away from Microsoft Office products, despite the fact that there are other applications with superior features.) As a rule, differentiation yields a longer-lasting and more profitable competitive edge when it is based on a well-established brand image, patent-protected product innovation, complex technical superiority, a reputation for superior product quality and reliability, relationship-based customer service, and unique competitive capabilities.

When a Differentiation Strategy Works Best

Differentiation strategies tend to work best in market circumstances where:

- *Buyer needs and uses of the product are diverse.* Diverse buyer preferences allow industry rivals to set themselves apart with product attributes that appeal to particular buyers. For instance, the diversity of consumer preferences for menu selection, ambience, pricing, and customer service gives restaurants exceptionally wide latitude in creating a differentiated product offering. Other industries with diverse buyer needs include magazine publishing, automobile manufacturing, footwear, and kitchen appliances.
- *There are many ways to differentiate the product or service that have value to buyers.* Industries in which competitors have opportunities to add features to products and services are well suited to differentiation strategies. For example, hotel chains can differentiate on such features as location, size of room, range of guest services, in-hotel dining, and the quality and luxuriousness of bedding and furnishings. Similarly, cosmetics producers are able to differentiate based on prestige and image, formulations that fight the signs of aging, UV light protection, exclusivity of retail locations, the inclusion of antioxidants and natural ingredients, or prohibitions against animal testing. Basic commodities, such as chemicals, mineral deposits, and agricultural products, provide few opportunities for differentiation.
- *Few rival firms are following a similar differentiation approach.* The best differentiation approaches involve trying to appeal to buyers on the basis of attributes that rivals are not emphasizing. A differentiator encounters less head-to-head rivalry when it goes its own separate way in creating value and does not try to out-differentiate rivals on the very same attributes. When many rivals base their differentiation efforts on the same attributes, the most likely result is weak brand differentiation and "strategy overcrowding"—competitors end up chasing much the same buyers with much the same product offerings.
- *Technological change is fast-paced and competition revolves around rapidly evolving product features.* Rapid product innovation and frequent introductions of next-version products heighten buyer interest and provide space for companies

to pursue distinct differentiating paths. In smartphones and wearable Internet devices, drones for hobbyists and commercial use, automobile lane detection sensors, and battery-powered cars, rivals are locked into an ongoing battle to set themselves apart by introducing the best next-generation products. Companies that fail to come up with new and improved products and distinctive performance features quickly lose out in the marketplace.

Pitfalls to Avoid in Pursuing a Differentiation Strategy

Differentiation strategies can fail for any of several reasons. *A differentiation strategy keyed to product or service attributes that are easily and quickly copied is always suspect.* Rapid imitation means that no rival achieves differentiation, since whenever one firm introduces some value-creating aspect that strikes the fancy of buyers, fast-following copycats quickly reestablish parity. This is why a firm must seek out sources of value creation that are time-consuming or burdensome for rivals to match if it hopes to use differentiation to win a sustainable competitive edge.

Any differentiating feature that works well is a magnet for imitators.

Differentiation strategies can also falter when buyers see little value in the unique attributes of a company's product. Thus, even if a company succeeds in setting its product apart from those of rivals, its strategy can result in disappointing sales and profits if the product does not deliver adequate value to buyers. Anytime many potential buyers look at a company's differentiated product offering with indifference, the company's differentiation strategy is in deep trouble.

The third big pitfall is overspending on efforts to differentiate the company's product offering, thus eroding profitability. Company efforts to achieve differentiation nearly always raise costs—often substantially, since marketing and R&D are expensive undertakings. The key to profitable differentiation is either to keep the unit cost of achieving differentiation below the price premium that the differentiating attributes can command (thus increasing the profit margin per unit sold) or to offset thinner profit margins per unit by selling enough additional units to increase total profits. If a company goes overboard in pursuing costly differentiation, it could be saddled with unacceptably low profits or even losses.

Other common mistakes in crafting a differentiation strategy include:

- *Offering only trivial improvements in quality, service, or performance features vis-à-vis rivals' products.* Trivial differences between rivals' product offerings may not be visible or important to buyers. If a company wants to generate the fiercely loyal customer following needed to earn superior profits and open up a differentiation-based competitive advantage over rivals, then its strategy must result in *strong rather than weak product differentiation.* In markets where differentiators do no better than achieve weak product differentiation, customer loyalty is weak, the costs of brand switching are low, and no one company has enough of a differentiation edge to command a price premium over rival brands.
- *Over-differentiating so that product quality, features, or service levels exceed the needs of most buyers.* A dazzling array of features and options not only drives up product price but also runs the risk that many buyers will conclude that a less deluxe and lower-priced brand is a better value since they have little occasion to use the deluxe attributes.
- *Charging too high a price premium.* While buyers may be intrigued by a product's deluxe features, they may nonetheless see it as being overpriced relative to the value delivered by the differentiating attributes. A company must guard against

Over-differentiating and overcharging are fatal differentiation strategy mistakes.

A low-cost provider strategy can defeat a differentiation strategy when buyers are satisfied with a basic product and don't think "extra" attributes are worth a higher price.

turning off would-be buyers with what is perceived as "price gouging." Normally, the bigger the price premium for the differentiating extras, the harder it is to keep buyers from switching to the lower-priced offerings of competitors.

FOCUSED (OR MARKET NICHE) STRATEGIES

What sets focused strategies apart from low-cost provider and broad differentiation strategies is concentrated attention on a narrow piece of the total market. The target segment, or niche, can be in the form of a geographic segment (such as New England), or a customer segment (such as urban hipsters), or a product segment (such as a class of models or some version of the overall product type). Community Coffee, the largest family-owned specialty coffee retailer in the United States, has a geographic focus on the state of Louisiana and communities across the Gulf of Mexico. Community holds only a small share of the national coffee market but has recorded sales in excess of $100 million and has won a strong following in the 20-state region where its coffee is distributed. Examples of firms that concentrate on a well-defined market niche keyed to a particular product or buyer segment include Zipcar (car rental in urban areas), Airbnb and VRBO (by-owner lodging rental), Comedy Central (cable TV), Blue Nile (online jewelry), Tesla Motors (electric cars), and CGA, Inc. (a specialist in providing insurance to cover the cost of lucrative hole-in-one prizes at golf tournaments). Microbreweries, local bakeries, bed-and-breakfast inns, and retail boutiques have also scaled their operations to serve narrow or local customer segments.

A Focused Low-Cost Strategy

A focused low-cost strategy aims at securing a competitive advantage by serving buyers in the target market niche at a lower cost and lower price than those of rival competitors. This strategy has considerable attraction when a firm can lower costs significantly by limiting its customer base to a well-defined buyer segment. The avenues to achieving a cost advantage over rivals also serving the target market niche are the same as those for low-cost leadership—use the cost drivers to perform value chain activities more efficiently than rivals and search for innovative ways to bypass nonessential value chain activities. The only real difference between a low-cost provider strategy and a focused low-cost strategy is the size of the buyer group to which a company is appealing—the former involves a product offering that appeals broadly to almost all buyer groups and market segments, whereas the latter aims at just meeting the needs of buyers in a narrow market segment.

Focused low-cost strategies are fairly common. Producers of private-label goods are able to achieve low costs in product development, marketing, distribution, and advertising by concentrating on making generic items imitative of name-brand merchandise and selling directly to retail chains wanting a low-priced store brand. The Perrigo Company has become a leading manufacturer of over-the-counter health care products, with 2014 sales of over $4 billion, by focusing on producing private-label brands for retailers such as Walmart, CVS, Walgreens, Rite Aid, and Safeway. Budget motel chains, like Motel 6, Sleep Inn, and Super 8, cater to price-conscious travelers who just want to pay for a clean, no-frills place to spend the night. Illustration Capsule 5.2 describes how Clinícas del Azúcar's focus on lowering the costs of diabetes care is allowing it to address a major health issue in Mexico.

ILLUSTRATION CAPSULE 5.2 Clinícas del Azúcar's Focused Low-Cost Strategy

Though diabetes is a manageable condition, it is the leading cause of death in Mexico. Over 14 million adults (14 percent of all adults) suffer from diabetes, 3.5 million cases remain undiagnosed, and more than 80,000 die due to related complications each year. The key driver behind this public health crisis is limited access to affordable, high-quality care. Approximately 90 percent of the population cannot access diabetes care due to financial and time constraints; private care can cost upwards of $1,000 USD per year (approximately 45 percent of Mexico's population has an annual income less than $2,000 USD) while average wait times alone at public clinics surpass five hours. Clinícas del Azúcar (CDA), however, is quickly scaling a solution that uses a *focused low-cost strategy* to provide affordable and convenient care to low-income patients.

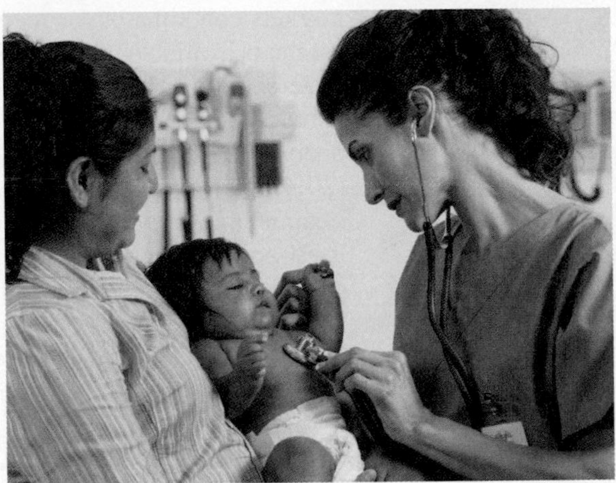

© Ariel Skelley/Blend Images/Getty Images

By relentlessly focusing only on the needs of its target population, CDA has reduced the cost of diabetes care by more than 70 percent and clinic visit times by over 80 percent. The key has been the use of proprietary technology and a streamlined care system. First, CDA leverages evidence-based algorithms to diagnose patients for a fraction of the costs of traditional diagnostic tests. Similarly, its mobile outreach significantly reduces the costs of supporting patients in managing their diabetes after leaving CDA facilities. Second, CDA has redesigned the care process to implement a streamlined "patient process flow" that eliminates the need for multiple referrals to other care providers and brings together the necessary professionals and equipment into one facility. Consequently, CDA has become a one-stop shop for diabetes care, providing every aspect of diabetes treatment under one roof.

The bottom line: CDA's cost structure allows it to keep its prices for diabetes treatment very low, saving patients both time and money. Patients choose from three different care packages, ranging from preventive to comprehensive care, paying an annual fee that runs between approximately $70 and $200 USD. Given this increase in affordability and convenience, CDA estimates that it has saved its patients over $2 million USD in medical costs and will soon increase access to affordable, high-quality care for 10 to 80 percent of the population. These results have attracted investment from major funders including Endeavor, Echoing Green, and the Clinton Global Initiative. As a result, CDA and others expect CDA to grow from 5 clinics serving approximately 5,000 patients to more than 50 clinics serving over 100,000 patients throughout Mexico by 2020.

Note: Developed with David B. Washer.

Sources: www.clinicasdelazucar.com; "Funding Social Enterprises Report," *Echoing Green,* June 2014; Jude Webber, "Mexico Sees Poverty Climb Despite Rise in Incomes," *Financial Times* online, July 2015, www.ft.com/intl/cms/s/3/98460bbc-31e1-11e5-8873-775ba7c2ea3d.html#axzz3zz8grtec; "Javier Lozano," Schwab Foundation for Social Entrepreneurship online, 2016, www.schwabfound.org/content/javier-lozano.

A Focused Differentiation Strategy

Focused differentiation strategies involve offering superior products or services tailored to the unique preferences and needs of a narrow, well-defined group of buyers. Successful use of a focused differentiation strategy depends on (1) the existence of a buyer segment that is looking for special product attributes or seller capabilities and (2) a firm's ability to create a product or service offering that stands apart from that of rivals competing in the same target market niche.

Companies like L.A. Burdick (gourmet chocolates), Rolls-Royce, and Ritz-Carlton Hotel Company employ successful differentiation-based focused strategies targeted at upscale buyers wanting products and services with world-class attributes. Indeed, most markets contain a buyer segment willing to pay a big price premium for the very finest items available, thus opening the strategic window for some competitors to pursue differentiation-based focused strategies aimed at the very top of the market pyramid. Whole Foods Market, which bills itself as "America's Healthiest Grocery Store," has become the largest organic and natural foods supermarket chain in the United States (2014 sales of $14.2 billion) by catering to health-conscious consumers who prefer organic, natural, minimally processed, and locally grown foods. Whole Foods prides itself on stocking the highest-quality organic and natural foods it can find; the company defines quality by evaluating the ingredients, freshness, taste, nutritive value, appearance, and safety of the products it carries. Illustration Capsule 5.3 describes how Canada Goose has been gaining attention with a focused differentiation strategy.

When a Focused Low-Cost or Focused Differentiation Strategy Is Attractive

A focused strategy aimed at securing a competitive edge based on either low costs or differentiation becomes increasingly attractive as more of the following conditions are met:

- The target market niche is big enough to be profitable and offers good growth potential.
- Industry leaders have chosen not to compete in the niche—in which case focusers can avoid battling head to head against the industry's biggest and strongest competitors.
- It is costly or difficult for multisegment competitors to meet the specialized needs of niche buyers and at the same time satisfy the expectations of their mainstream customers.
- The industry has many different niches and segments, thereby allowing a focuser to pick the niche best suited to its resources and capabilities. Also, with more niches there is room for focusers to concentrate on different market segments and avoid competing in the same niche for the same customers.
- Few if any rivals are attempting to specialize in the same target segment—a condition that reduces the risk of segment overcrowding.

The advantages of focusing a company's entire competitive effort on a single market niche are considerable, especially for smaller and medium-sized companies that may lack the breadth and depth of resources to tackle going after a broader customer base with a more complex set of needs. YouTube has become a household name by concentrating on short video clips posted online. Papa John's and Domino's Pizza have created impressive businesses by focusing on the home delivery segment.

The Risks of a Focused Low-Cost or Focused Differentiation Strategy

Focusing carries several risks. One is the chance that competitors outside the niche will find effective ways to match the focused firm's capabilities in serving the target niche—perhaps by coming up with products or brands specifically designed to

ILLUSTRATION CAPSULE 5.3 Canada Goose's Focused Differentiation Strategy

Open up a winter edition of *People* and you will probably see photos of a celebrity sporting a Canada Goose parka. Recognizable by a distinctive red, white, and blue arm patch, the brand's parkas have been spotted on movie stars like Emma Stone and Bradley Cooper, on New York City streets, and on the cover of *Sports Illustrated*. Lately, Canada Goose has become extremely successful thanks to a focused differentiation strategy that enables it to thrive within its niche in the $1.2 trillion fashion industry. By targeting upscale buyers and providing a uniquely functional and stylish jacket, Canada Goose can charge nearly $1,000 per jacket and never need to put its products on sale.

© Richard Lautens/Toronto Star via Getty Images

While Canada Goose was founded in 1957, its recent transition to a focused differentiation strategy allowed it to rise to the top of the luxury parka market. In 2001, CEO Dani Reiss took control of the company and made two key decisions. First, he cut private-label and non-outerwear production in order to focus on the branded outerwear portion of Canada Goose's business. Second, Reiss decided to remain in Canada despite many North American competitors moving production to Asia to increase profit margins. Fortunately for him, these two strategy decisions have led directly to the company's current success. While other luxury brands, like Moncler, are priced similarly, no competitor's products fulfill the promise of handling harsh winter weather quite like a Canada Goose "Made in Canada" parka. The Canadian heritage, use of down sourced from rural Canada, real coyote fur (humanely trapped), and promise to provide warmth in sub-25°F temperatures have let Canada Goose break away from the pack when it comes to selling parkas. The company's distinctly Canadian product has made it a hit among buyers, which is reflected in the willingness to pay a steep premium for extremely high-quality and warm winter outerwear.

Since Canada Goose's shift to a focused differentiation strategy, the company has seen a boom in revenue and appeal across the globe. Prior to Reiss's strategic decisions in 2001, Canada Goose had annual revenue of about $3 million. Within a decade, the company had experienced over 4,000 percent growth in annual revenue; by the end of 2015, sales were expected to exceed $300 million in more than 50 countries. At this pace, it looks like Canada Goose will remain a hot commodity as long as winter temperatures remain cold.

Note: Developed with Arthur J. Santry.

Sources: Drake Bennett, "How Canada Goose Parkas Migrated South," *Bloomberg Businessweek*, March 13, 2015, www.bloomberg.com; Hollie Shaw, "Canada Goose's Made-in-Canada Marketing Strategy Translates into Success," *Financial Post*, May 18, 2012, www.financialpost.com; "The Economic Impact of the Fashion Industry," *The Economist*, June 13, 2015, www.maloney.house.gov; and company website (accessed February 21, 2016).

appeal to buyers in the target niche or by developing expertise and capabilities that offset the focuser's strengths. In the lodging business, large chains like Marriott and Hilton have launched multibrand strategies that allow them to compete effectively in several lodging segments simultaneously. Marriott has flagship JW Marriott and Ritz-Carlton hotels with deluxe accommodations for business travelers and resort vacationers. Its Courtyard by Marriott and SpringHill Suites brands cater to business travelers looking for moderately priced lodging, whereas Marriott Residence Inns and TownePlace Suites are designed as a "home away from home" for travelers staying five or more nights. Its Fairfield Inn & Suites is intended to appeal to travelers looking for quality lodging at an "affordable" price. Marriott has also added Edition, AC Hotels by Marriott, and Autograph Collection hotels that offer stylish, distinctive decors and personalized services that appeal to young professionals seeking distinctive lodging alternatives. Multibrand strategies are attractive to large companies like Marriott, Procter & Gamble, and Nestlé precisely because they enable entry into smaller market segments and siphon away business from companies that employ a focused strategy.

A second risk of employing a focused strategy is the potential for the preferences and needs of niche members to shift over time toward the product attributes desired by buyers in the mainstream portion of the market. An erosion of the differences across buyer segments lowers entry barriers into a focuser's market niche and provides an open invitation for rivals in adjacent segments to begin competing for the focuser's customers. A third risk is that the segment may become so attractive that it is soon inundated with competitors, intensifying rivalry and splintering segment profits. And there is always the risk for segment growth to slow to such a small rate that a focuser's prospects for future sales and profit gains become unacceptably dim.

BEST-COST PROVIDER STRATEGIES

As Figure 5.1 indicates, **best-cost provider strategies** stake out a middle ground between pursuing a low-cost advantage and a differentiation advantage and between appealing to the broad market as a whole and a narrow market niche. This permits companies to aim squarely at the sometimes great mass of value-conscious buyers looking for a better product or service at an economical price. Value-conscious buyers frequently shy away from both cheap low-end products and expensive high-end products, but they are quite willing to pay a "fair" price for extra features and functionality they find appealing and useful. The essence of a best-cost provider strategy is giving customers *more value for the money* by satisfying buyer desires for appealing features and charging a lower price for these attributes compared to rivals with similar-caliber product offerings.[6] From a competitive-positioning standpoint, best-cost strategies are thus a *hybrid,* balancing a strategic emphasis on low cost against a strategic emphasis on differentiation (desirable features delivered at a relatively low price).

CORE CONCEPT

Best-cost provider strategies are a *hybrid* of low-cost provider and differentiation strategies that aim at providing more desirable attributes (quality, features, performance, service) while beating rivals on price.

To profitably employ a best-cost provider strategy, a company *must have the capability to incorporate upscale attributes into its product offering at a lower cost than rivals.* When a company can incorporate more appealing features, good to excellent product performance or quality, or more satisfying customer service into its product offering *at a lower cost than rivals,* then it enjoys "best-cost" status—it is the low-cost provider of a product or service with *upscale attributes.* A best-cost provider can use its low-cost advantage to underprice rivals whose products or services have similarly upscale attributes and it still earns attractive profits.

Being a best-cost provider is different from being a low-cost provider because the additional attractive attributes entail additional costs (which a low-cost provider can avoid by offering buyers a basic product with few frills). Moreover, the two strategies aim at a distinguishably different market target. *The target market for a best-cost provider is value-conscious buyers*—buyers who are looking for appealing extras and functionality at a comparatively low price. Value-hunting buyers (as distinct from *price-conscious buyers* looking for a basic product at a bargain-basement price) often constitute a very sizable part of the overall market for a product or service.

Toyota has employed a classic best-cost provider strategy for its Lexus line of motor vehicles. It has designed an array of high-performance characteristics and upscale features into its Lexus models to make them comparable in performance and luxury to Mercedes, BMW, Audi, Jaguar, Cadillac, and Lincoln models. To further draw buyer attention, Toyota established a network of Lexus dealers, separate from Toyota dealers, dedicated to providing exceptional customer service. Most important, though, Toyota has drawn on its considerable know-how in making high-quality vehicles at low cost to produce its high-tech upscale-quality Lexus models at substantially lower costs than other luxury vehicle makers have been able to achieve in producing their models. To capitalize on its lower manufacturing costs, Toyota prices its Lexus models below those of comparable Mercedes, BMW, Audi, and Jaguar models to induce value-conscious luxury car buyers to purchase a Lexus instead. The price differential has typically been quite significant. For example, in 2015 the Lexus RX 350, a mid-sized SUV, had a sticker price of $43,395 for the all-wheel-drive model with standard equipment, whereas the base price of a comparable Mercedes M-class SUV was $51,725 and the base price of a comparable BMW X5 SUV was $57,150.

When a Best-Cost Provider Strategy Works Best

LO 4

The attributes of a best-cost provider strategy—a hybrid of low-cost provider and differentiation strategies.

A best-cost provider strategy works best in markets where product differentiation is the norm and an attractively large number of value-conscious buyers can be induced to purchase midrange products rather than cheap, basic products or expensive, top-of-the-line products. A best-cost provider needs to position itself *near the middle of the market* with either a medium-quality product at a below-average price or a high-quality product at an average or slightly higher price. Best-cost provider strategies also work well in recessionary times, when masses of buyers become value-conscious and are attracted to economically priced products and services with more appealing attributes. But unless a company has the resources, know-how, and capabilities to incorporate upscale product or service attributes at a lower cost than rivals, adopting a best-cost strategy is ill-advised. Illustration Capsule 5.4 describes how American Giant has applied the principles of the best-cost provider strategy in producing and marketing its hoodie sweatshirts.

The Risk of a Best-Cost Provider Strategy

A company's biggest vulnerability in employing a best-cost provider strategy is getting squeezed between the strategies of firms using low-cost and high-end differentiation strategies. Low-cost providers may be able to siphon customers away with the appeal of a lower price (despite less appealing product attributes). High-end differentiators may be able to steal customers away with the appeal of better product attributes (even though their products carry a higher price tag). Thus, to be successful, a best-cost provider must achieve significantly lower costs in providing upscale features so that it can outcompete high-end differentiators on the basis of a *significantly* lower price. Likewise, it must offer buyers *significantly* better product attributes to justify a price above what low-cost leaders are charging. In other words, it must offer buyers a more attractive customer value proposition.

ILLUSTRATION CAPSULE 5.4

American Giant's Best-Cost Provider Strategy

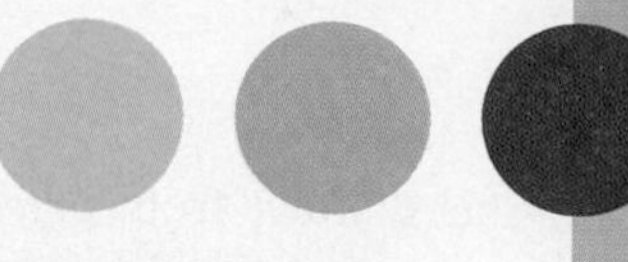

Bayard Winthrop, founder and owner of American Giant, set out to make a hoodie like the soft, ultra-thick Navy sweatshirts his dad used to wear in the 1950s. But he also had two other aims: He wanted it to have a more updated look with a tailored fit, and he wanted it produced cost-effectively so that it could be sold at a great price. To accomplish these aims, he designed the sweatshirt with the help of a former industrial engineer from Apple and an internationally renowned pattern maker, rethinking every aspect of sweatshirt design and production along the way. The result was a hoodie differentiated from others on the basis of extreme attention to fabric, fit, construction, and durability. The hoodie is made from heavy-duty cotton that is run through a machine that carefully picks loops of thread out of the fabric to create a thick, combed, ring-spun fleece fabric that feels three times thicker than most sweatshirts. A small amount of spandex paneling along the shoulders and sides creates the fitted look and maintains the shape, keeping the sweatshirt from looking slouchy or sloppy. It has double stitching with strong thread on critical seams to avoid deterioration and boost durability. The zippers and draw cord are customized to match the sweatshirt's color—an uncommon practice in the business.

American Giant sources yarn from Parkdale, South Carolina, and turns it into cloth at the nearby Carolina Cotton Works. This reduces transport costs, creates a more dependable, durable product that American Giant can easily quality-check, and shortens product turnaround to about a month, lowering inventory costs. This process also enables the company to use a genuine "Made in the U.S.A." label, a perceived quality driver.

American Giant disrupts the traditional, expensive distribution models by having no stores or resellers.

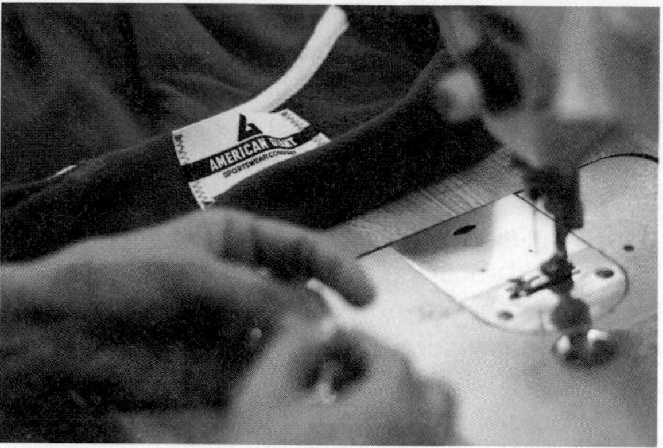

© David Paul Morris/Getty Images

Instead, it sells directly to customers from its website, with free two-day shipping and returns. Much of the company's growth comes from word of mouth and a strong public relations effort that promotes the brand in magazines, newspapers, and key business-oriented television programs. American Giant has a robust refer-a-friend program that offers a discount to friends of, and a credit to, current owners. Articles in popular media proclaiming its product "the greatest hoodie ever made" have made demand for its sweatshirts skyrocket.

At $89 for the original men's hoodie, American Giant is not cheap but offers customers value in terms of both price and quality. The price is higher than what one would pay at The Gap or American Apparel and comparable to Levi's, J.Crew, or Banana Republic. But its quality is more on par with high-priced designer brands, while its price is far more affordable.

Note: Developed with Sarah Boole.

Sources: www.nytimes.com/2013/09/20/business/us-textile-factories-return.html?emc=eta1&_r=0; www.american-giant.com; www.slate.com/articles/technology/technology/2012/12/american_giant_hoodie_this_is_the_greatest_sweatshirt_known_to_man.html; www.businessinsider.com/this-hoodie-is-so-insanely-popular-you-have-to-wait-months-to-get-it-2013-12.

THE CONTRASTING FEATURES OF THE FIVE GENERIC COMPETITIVE STRATEGIES: A SUMMARY

Deciding which generic competitive strategy should serve as the framework on which to hang the rest of the company's strategy is not a trivial matter. Each of the five generic competitive strategies *positions* the company differently in its market and competitive environment. Each establishes a *central theme* for how the company will endeavor to outcompete rivals. Each creates some boundaries or guidelines for maneuvering as market circumstances unfold and as ideas for improving the strategy are debated. Each entails differences in terms of product line, production emphasis, marketing emphasis, and means of maintaining the strategy, as shown in Table 5.1

A company's competitive strategy should be well matched to its internal situation and predicated on leveraging its collection of competitively valuable resources and capabilities.

Thus a choice of which generic strategy to employ spills over to affect many aspects of how the business will be operated and the manner in which value chain activities must be managed. Deciding which generic strategy to employ is perhaps the most important strategic commitment a company makes—it tends to drive the rest of the strategic actions a company decides to undertake.

Successful Competitive Strategies Are Resource-Based

For a company's competitive strategy to succeed in delivering good performance and gain a competitive edge over rivals, it has to be well matched to a company's internal situation and underpinned by an appropriate set of resources, know-how, and competitive capabilities. To succeed in employing a low-cost provider strategy, a company must have the resources and capabilities to keep its costs below those of its competitors. This means having the expertise to cost-effectively manage value chain activities better than rivals by leveraging the cost drivers more effectively, and/or having the innovative capability to bypass certain value chain activities being performed by rivals. To succeed in a differentiation strategy, a company must have the resources and capabilities to leverage value drivers more effectively than rivals and incorporate attributes into its product offering that a broad range of buyers will find appealing. Successful focus strategies (both low cost and differentiation) require the capability to do an outstanding job of satisfying the needs and expectations of niche buyers. Success in employing a best-cost strategy requires the resources and capabilities to incorporate upscale product or service attributes at a lower cost than rivals. *For all types of generic strategies, success in sustaining the competitive edge depends on having resources and capabilities that rivals have trouble duplicating and for which there are no good substitutes.*

TABLE 5.1 Distinguishing Features of the Five Generic Competitive Strategies

	Low-Cost Provider	Broad Differentiation	Focused Low-Cost Provider	Focused Differentiation	Best-Cost Provider
Strategic target	• A broad cross-section of the market.	• A broad cross-section of the market.	• A narrow market niche where buyer needs and preferences are distinctively different.	• A narrow market niche where buyer needs and preferences are distinctively different.	• Value-conscious buyers. • A middle-market range.
Basis of competitive strategy	• Lower overall costs than competitors.	• Ability to offer buyers something attractively different from competitors' offerings.	• Lower overall cost than rivals in serving niche members.	• Attributes that appeal specifically to niche members.	• Ability to offer better goods at attractive prices.
Product line	• A good basic product with few frills (acceptable quality and limited selection).	• Many product variations, wide selection; emphasis on differentiating features.	• Features and attributes tailored to the tastes and requirements of niche members.	• Features and attributes tailored to the tastes and requirements of niche members.	• Items with appealing attributes and assorted features; better quality, not best.
Production emphasis	• A continuous search for cost reduction without sacrificing acceptable quality and essential features.	• Build in whatever differentiating features buyers are willing to pay for; strive for product superiority.	• A continuous search for cost reduction for products that meet basic needs of niche members.	• Small-scale production or custom-made products that match the tastes and requirements of niche members.	• Build in appealing features and better quality at lower cost than rivals.
Marketing emphasis	• Low prices, good value. • Try to make a virtue out of product features that lead to low cost.	• Tout differentiating features. • Charge a premium price to cover the extra costs of differentiating features.	• Communicate attractive features of a budget-priced product offering that fits niche buyers' expectations.	• Communicate how product offering does the best job of meeting niche buyers' expectations.	• Emphasize delivery of best value for the money.
Keys to maintaining the strategy	• Economical prices, good value. • Strive to manage costs down, year after year, in every area of the business.	• Stress constant innovation to stay ahead of imitative competitors. • Concentrate on a few key differentiating features.	• Stay committed to serving the niche at the lowest overall cost; don't blur the firm's image by entering other market segments or adding other products to widen market appeal.	• Stay committed to serving the niche better than rivals; don't blur the firm's image by entering other market segments or adding other products to widen market appeal.	• Unique expertise in simultaneously managing costs down while incorporating upscale features and attributes.
Resources and capabilities required	• Capabilities for driving costs out of the value chain system. • *Examples:* large-scale automated plants, an efficiency-oriented culture, bargaining power.	• Capabilities concerning quality, design, intangibles, and innovation. • *Examples:* marketing capabilities, R&D teams, technology.	• Capabilities to lower costs on niche goods. • *Examples:* lower input costs for the specific product desired by the niche, batch production capabilities.	• Capabilities to meet the highly specific needs of niche members. • *Examples:* custom production, close customer relations.	• Capabilities to simultaneously deliver lower cost and higher-quality/differentiated features. • *Examples:* TQM practices, mass customization.

KEY POINTS

1. Deciding which of the five generic competitive strategies to employ—overall low cost, broad differentiation, focused low cost, focused differentiation, or best cost—is perhaps the most important strategic commitment a company makes. It tends to drive the remaining strategic actions a company undertakes and sets the whole tone for pursuing a competitive advantage over rivals.
2. In employing a low-cost provider strategy and trying to achieve a low-cost advantage over rivals, a company must do a better job than rivals of cost-effectively managing value chain activities and/or it must find innovative ways to eliminate cost-producing activities. An effective use of cost drivers is key. Low-cost provider strategies work particularly well when price competition is strong and the products of rival sellers are virtually identical, when there are not many ways to differentiate, when buyers are price-sensitive or have the power to bargain down prices, when buyer switching costs are low, and when industry newcomers are likely to use a low introductory price to build market share.
3. Broad differentiation strategies seek to produce a competitive edge by incorporating attributes that set a company's product or service offering apart from rivals in ways that buyers consider valuable and worth paying for. This depends on the appropriate use of value drivers. Successful differentiation allows a firm to (1) command a premium price for its product, (2) increase unit sales (if additional buyers are won over by the differentiating features), and/or (3) gain buyer loyalty to its brand (because some buyers are strongly attracted to the differentiating features and bond with the company and its products). Differentiation strategies work best when buyers have diverse product preferences, when few other rivals are pursuing a similar differentiation approach, and when technological change is fast-paced and competition centers on rapidly evolving product features. A differentiation strategy is doomed when competitors are able to quickly copy the appealing product attributes, when a company's differentiation efforts fail to interest many buyers, and when a company overspends on efforts to differentiate its product offering or tries to overcharge for its differentiating extras.
4. A focused strategy delivers competitive advantage either by achieving lower costs than rivals in serving buyers constituting the target market niche or by developing a specialized ability to offer niche buyers an appealingly differentiated offering that meets their needs better than rival brands do. A focused strategy based on either low cost or differentiation becomes increasingly attractive when the target market niche is big enough to be profitable and offers good growth potential, when it is costly or difficult for multisegment competitors to meet the specialized needs of the target market niche and at the same time satisfy the expectations of their mainstream customers, when there are one or more niches that present a good match for a focuser's resources and capabilities, and when few other rivals are attempting to specialize in the same target segment.
5. Best-cost strategies create competitive advantage by giving buyers *more value for the money*—delivering superior quality, features, performance, and/or service attributes while also beating customer expectations on price. To profitably employ a best-cost provider strategy, a company *must have the capability to incorporate*

attractive or upscale attributes at a lower cost than rivals. A best-cost provider strategy works best in markets with large numbers of value-conscious buyers desirous of purchasing better products and services for less money.

6. In all cases, competitive advantage depends on having competitively superior resources and capabilities that are a good fit for the chosen generic strategy. A sustainable advantage depends on maintaining that competitive superiority with resources, capabilities, and value chain activities that rivals have trouble matching and for which there are no good substitutes.

ASSURANCE OF LEARNING EXERCISES

LO 1, LO 2, LO 3, LO 4

1. Best Buy is the largest consumer electronics retailer in the United States, with 2015 sales of over $50 billion. The company competes aggressively on price with such rivals as Costco, Sam's Club, Walmart, and Target, but it is also known by consumers for its first-rate customer service. Best Buy customers have commented that the retailer's sales staff is exceptionally knowledgeable about the company's products and can direct them to the exact location of difficult-to-find items. Best Buy customers also appreciate that demonstration models of PC monitors, digital media players, and other electronics are fully powered and ready for in-store use. Best Buy's Geek Squad tech support and installation services are additional customer service features that are valued by many customers.

   How would you characterize Best Buy's competitive strategy? Should it be classified as a low-cost provider strategy? A differentiation strategy? A best-cost strategy? Explain your answer.

connect

LO 2

2. Illustration Capsule 5.1 discusses Amazon's low-cost position in the electronic commerce industry. Based on information provided in the capsule, explain how Amazon has built its low-cost advantage in the industry and why a low-cost provider strategy is well suited to the industry.

LO 1, LO 2, LO 3, LO 4

3. USAA is a Fortune 500 insurance and financial services company with 2014 annual sales exceeding $24 billion. The company was founded in 1922 by 25 Army officers who decided to insure each other's vehicles and continues to limit its membership to active-duty and retired military members, officer candidates, and adult children and spouses of military-affiliated USAA members. The company has received countless awards, including being listed among *Fortune*'s World's Most Admired Companies in 2014 and 2015 and 100 Best Companies to Work For in 2010 through 2015. USAA was also ranked as the number-one Bank, Credit Card, and Insurance Company by Forrester Research from 2013 to 2015. You can read more about the company's history and strategy at **www.usaa.com**.

   How would you characterize USAA's competitive strategy? Should it be classified as a low-cost provider strategy? A differentiation strategy? A best-cost strategy? Also, has the company chosen to focus on a narrow piece of the market, or does it appear to pursue a broad market approach? Explain your answer.

4. Explore lululemon athletica's website at **info.lululemon.com** and see if you can identify at least three ways in which the company seeks to differentiate itself from rival athletic apparel firms. Is there reason to believe that lululemon's differentiation strategy has been successful in producing a competitive advantage? Why or why not?

connect

LO 3

EXERCISE FOR SIMULATION PARTICIPANTS

LO 1, LO 2, LO 3, LO 4

1. Which one of the five generic competitive strategies best characterizes your company's strategic approach to competing successfully?
2. Which rival companies appear to be employing a low-cost provider strategy?
3. Which rival companies appear to be employing a broad differentiation strategy?
4. Which rival companies appear to be employing a best-cost provider strategy?
5. Which rival companies appear to be employing some type of focused strategy?
6. What is your company's action plan to achieve a sustainable competitive advantage over rival companies? List at least three (preferably more than three) specific kinds of decision entries on specific decision screens that your company has made or intends to make to win this kind of competitive edge over rivals.

ENDNOTES

[1] Michael E. Porter, *Competitive Strategy: Techniques for Analyzing Industries and Competitors* (New York: Free Press, 1980), chap. 2; Michael E. Porter, "What Is Strategy?" *Harvard Business Review* 74, no. 6 (November–December 1996).

[2] Michael E. Porter, *Competitive Advantage: Creating and Sustaining Superior Performance* (New York: Free Press, 1985).

[3] Richard L. Priem, "A Consumer Perspective on Value Creation," *Academy of Management Review* 32, no. 1 (2007), pp. 219–235.

[4] **jrscience.wcp.muohio.edu/nsfall01/FinalArticles/Final-IsitWorthitBrandsan.html.**

[5] D. Yoffie, "Cola Wars Continue: Coke and Pepsi in 2006," Harvard Business School case 9-706-447.

[6] Peter J. Williamson and Ming Zeng, "Value-for-Money Strategies for Recessionary Times," *Harvard Business Review* 87, no. 3 (March 2009), pp. 66–74.

CHAPTER 6

Strengthening a Company's Competitive Position

Strategic Moves, Timing, and Scope of Operations

© Fanatic Studio/Getty Images

Learning Objectives

THIS CHAPTER WILL HELP YOU UNDERSTAND:

LO 1 Whether and when to pursue offensive or defensive strategic moves to improve a company's market position.

LO 2 When being a first mover or a fast follower or a late mover is most advantageous.

LO 3 The strategic benefits and risks of expanding a company's horizontal scope through mergers and acquisitions.

LO 4 The advantages and disadvantages of extending the company's scope of operations via vertical integration.

LO 5 The conditions that favor farming out certain value chain activities to outside parties.

LO 6 When and how strategic alliances can substitute for horizontal mergers and acquisitions or vertical integration and how they can facilitate outsourcing.

Whenever you look at any potential merger or acquisition, you look at the potential to create value for your shareholders.

Dilip Shanghvi—*Founder and managing director of Sun Pharmaceuticals*

In the virtual economy, collaboration is a new competitive imperative.

Michael Dell—*Founder and CEO of Dell Inc.*

Alliances and partnerships produce stability when they reflect realities and interests.

Stephen Kinzer—*Author, journalist, and academic*

Once a company has settled on which of the five generic competitive strategies to employ, attention turns to what *other strategic actions* it can take to complement its competitive approach and maximize the power of its overall strategy. The first set of decisions concerns whether to undertake offensive or defensive competitive moves, and the timing of such moves. The second set concerns the breadth of a company's activities (or its *scope* of operations along an industry's entire value chain). All in all, the following measures to strengthen a company's competitive position must be considered:

- Whether to go on the offensive and initiate aggressive strategic moves to improve the company's market position.
- Whether to employ defensive strategies to protect the company's market position.
- When to undertake strategic moves—whether advantage or disadvantage lies in being a first mover, a fast follower, or a late mover.
- Whether to bolster the company's market position by merging with or acquiring another company in the same industry.
- Whether to integrate backward or forward into more stages of the industry value chain system.
- Which value chain activities, if any, should be outsourced.
- Whether to enter into strategic alliances or partnership arrangements with other enterprises.

This chapter presents the pros and cons of each of these strategy-enhancing measures.

LAUNCHING STRATEGIC OFFENSIVES TO IMPROVE A COMPANY'S MARKET POSITION

No matter which of the five generic competitive strategies a firm employs, there are times when a company should *go on the offensive* to improve its market position and performance. **Strategic offensives** are called for when a company spots opportunities to gain profitable market share at its rivals' expense or when a company has no choice

LO 1

Whether and when to pursue offensive or defensive strategic moves to improve a company's market position.

but to try to whittle away at a strong rival's competitive advantage. Companies like AutoNation, Amazon, Apple, and Google play hardball, aggressively pursuing competitive advantage and trying to reap the benefits a competitive edge offers—a leading market share, excellent profit margins, and rapid growth.[1] The best offensives tend to incorporate several principles: (1) focusing relentlessly on building competitive advantage and then striving to convert it into a sustainable advantage, (2) applying resources where rivals are least able to defend themselves, (3) employing the element of surprise as opposed to doing what rivals expect and are prepared for, and (4) displaying a capacity for swift and decisive actions to overwhelm rivals.[2]

Sometimes a company's best strategic option is to seize the initiative, go on the attack, and launch a strategic offensive to improve its market position.

Choosing the Basis for Competitive Attack

As a rule, challenging rivals on competitive grounds where they are strong is an uphill struggle.[3] Offensive initiatives that exploit competitor weaknesses stand a better chance of succeeding than do those that challenge competitor strengths, especially if the weaknesses represent important vulnerabilities and weak rivals can be caught by surprise with no ready defense.

The best offensives use a company's most powerful resources and capabilities to attack rivals in the areas where they are competitively weakest.

Strategic offensives should exploit the power of a company's strongest competitive assets—its most valuable resources and capabilities such as a better-known brand name, a more efficient production or distribution system, greater technological capability, or a superior reputation for quality. But a consideration of the company's strengths should not be made without also considering the rival's strengths and weaknesses. A strategic offensive should be based on those areas of strength where the company has its greatest competitive advantage over the targeted rivals. If a company has especially good customer service capabilities, it can make special sales pitches to the customers of those rivals that provide subpar customer service. Likewise, it may be beneficial to pay special attention to buyer segments that a rival is neglecting or is weakly equipped to serve. The best offensives use a company's most powerful resources and capabilities to attack rivals in the areas where they are weakest.

Ignoring the need to tie a strategic offensive to a company's competitive strengths and what it does best is like going to war with a popgun—the prospects for success are dim. For instance, it is foolish for a company with relatively high costs to employ a price-cutting offensive. Likewise, it is ill-advised to pursue a product innovation offensive without having proven expertise in R&D and new product development.

The principal offensive strategy options include the following:

1. *Offering an equally good or better product at a lower price.* Lower prices can produce market share gains if competitors don't respond with price cuts of their own and if the challenger convinces buyers that its product is just as good or better. However, such a strategy increases total profits only if the gains in additional unit sales are enough to offset the impact of thinner margins per unit sold. Price-cutting offensives should be initiated only by companies that have *first achieved a cost advantage.*[4] British airline EasyJet used this strategy successfully against rivals such as British Air, Alitalia, and Air France by first cutting costs to the bone and then targeting leisure passengers who care more about low price than in-flight amenities and service.[5]
2. *Leapfrogging competitors by being first to market with next-generation products.* In technology-based industries, the opportune time to overtake an entrenched competitor is when there is a shift to the next generation of the technology. Microsoft

got its next-generation Xbox 360 to market a full 12 months ahead of Sony's PlayStation 3 and Nintendo's Wii, helping it build a sizable market share on the basis of cutting-edge innovation in the video game industry. Sony was careful to avoid a repeat, releasing its PlayStation 4 in November 2013 just as Microsoft released its Xbox One. With better graphical performance than Xbox One, along with some other advantages, the PS4 was able to boost Sony back into the lead position.

3. *Pursuing continuous product innovation to draw sales and market share away from less innovative rivals.* Ongoing introductions of new and improved products can put rivals under tremendous competitive pressure, especially when rivals' new product development capabilities are weak. But such offensives can be sustained only if a company can keep its pipeline full with new product offerings that spark buyer enthusiasm.
4. *Pursuing disruptive product innovations to create new markets.* While this strategy can be riskier and more costly than a strategy of continuous innovation, it can be a game changer if successful. Disruptive innovation involves perfecting a new product with a few trial users and then quickly rolling it out to the whole market in an attempt to get many buyers to embrace an altogether new and better value proposition quickly. Examples include online universities, Bumble (dating site), Venmo (digital wallet), Apple Music, CampusBookRentals, and Amazon's Kindle.
5. *Adopting and improving on the good ideas of other companies (rivals or otherwise).* The idea of warehouse-type home improvement centers did not originate with Home Depot cofounders Arthur Blank and Bernie Marcus; they got the "big-box" concept from their former employer, Handy Dan Home Improvement. But they were quick to improve on Handy Dan's business model and take Home Depot to the next plateau in terms of product-line breadth and customer service. Offensive-minded companies are often quick to adopt any good idea (not nailed down by a patent or other legal protection) and build on it to create competitive advantage for themselves.
6. *Using hit-and-run or guerrilla warfare tactics to grab market share from complacent or distracted rivals.* Options for "guerrilla offensives" include occasionally lowballing on price (to win a big order or steal a key account from a rival), surprising rivals with sporadic but intense bursts of promotional activity (offering a discounted trial offer to draw customers away from rival brands), or undertaking special campaigns to attract the customers of rivals plagued with a strike or problems in meeting buyer demand.[6] Guerrilla offensives are particularly well suited to small challengers that have neither the resources nor the market visibility to mount a full-fledged attack on industry leaders.
7. *Launching a preemptive strike to secure an industry's limited resources or capture a rare opportunity.*[7] What makes a move preemptive is its one-of-a-kind nature—whoever strikes first stands to acquire competitive assets that rivals can't readily match. Examples of preemptive moves include (1) securing the best distributors in a particular geographic region or country; (2) obtaining the most favorable site at a new interchange or intersection, in a new shopping mall, and so on; (3) tying up the most reliable, high-quality suppliers via exclusive partnerships, long-term contracts, or acquisition; and (4) moving swiftly to acquire the assets of distressed rivals at bargain prices. To be successful, a preemptive move doesn't have to totally block rivals from following; it merely needs to give a firm a prime position that is not easily circumvented.

How long it takes for an offensive to yield good results varies with the competitive circumstances.[8] It can be short if buyers respond immediately (as can occur with a dramatic cost-based price cut, an imaginative ad campaign, or a disruptive innovation). Securing a competitive edge can take much longer if winning consumer acceptance of the company's product will take some time or if the firm may need several years to debug a new technology or put a new production capacity in place. But how long it takes for an offensive move to improve a company's market standing—and whether the move will prove successful—depends in part on whether market rivals recognize the threat and begin a counterresponse. Whether rivals will respond depends on whether they are capable of making an effective response and if they believe that a counterattack is worth the expense and the distraction.[9]

Choosing Which Rivals to Attack

Offensive-minded firms need to analyze which of their rivals to challenge as well as how to mount the challenge. The following are the best targets for offensive attacks:[10]

- *Market leaders that are vulnerable.* Offensive attacks make good sense when a company that leads in terms of market share is not a true leader in terms of serving the market well. Signs of leader vulnerability include unhappy buyers, an inferior product line, aging technology or outdated plants and equipment, a preoccupation with diversification into other industries, and financial problems. Caution is well advised in challenging strong market leaders—there's a significant risk of squandering valuable resources in a futile effort or precipitating a fierce and profitless industrywide battle for market share.
- *Runner-up firms with weaknesses in areas where the challenger is strong.* Runner-up firms are an especially attractive target when a challenger's resources and capabilities are well suited to exploiting their weaknesses.
- *Struggling enterprises that are on the verge of going under.* Challenging a hard-pressed rival in ways that further sap its financial strength and competitive position can weaken its resolve and hasten its exit from the market. In this type of situation, it makes sense to attack the rival in the market segments where it makes the most profits, since this will threaten its survival the most.
- *Small local and regional firms with limited capabilities.* Because small firms typically have limited expertise and resources, a challenger with broader and/or deeper capabilities is well positioned to raid their biggest and best customers—particularly those that are growing rapidly, have increasingly sophisticated requirements, and may already be thinking about switching to a supplier with a more full-service capability.

Blue-Ocean Strategy—a Special Kind of Offensive

CORE CONCEPT

A **blue-ocean strategy** offers growth in revenues and profits by discovering or inventing new industry segments that create altogether new demand.

A **blue-ocean strategy** seeks to gain a dramatic and durable competitive advantage by abandoning efforts to beat out competitors in existing markets and, instead, *inventing a new market segment that renders existing competitors irrelevant and allows a company to create and capture altogether new demand.*[11] This strategy views the business universe as consisting of two distinct types of market space. One is where industry boundaries are well defined, the competitive rules of the game are understood, and companies try to outperform rivals by capturing a bigger share of existing demand. In such markets, intense competition constrains a company's prospects for rapid growth and superior profitability since rivals move quickly to either imitate or counter the successes of competitors. The second type of market space is a "blue ocean," where the industry does not really exist yet, is untainted by competition, and offers wide-open opportunity for profitable and rapid growth if a company can create new demand with a new type of product offering.

A terrific example of such blue-ocean market space is the online auction industry that eBay created and now dominates. Other companies that have created blue-ocean market spaces include NetJets in fractional jet ownership, Drybar in hair blowouts, Tune Hotels in limited service "backpacker" hotels, and Cirque du Soleil in live entertainment. Cirque du Soleil "reinvented the circus" by pulling in a whole new group of customers—adults and corporate clients—who not only were noncustomers of traditional circuses (like Ringling Brothers) but also were willing to pay several times more than the price of a conventional circus ticket to have a "sophisticated entertainment experience" featuring stunning visuals and star-quality acrobatic acts. Zipcar Inc. has been using a blue-ocean strategy to compete against entrenched rivals in the rental-car industry. It rents cars by the hour or day (rather than by the week) to members who pay a yearly fee for access to cars parked in designated spaces located conveniently throughout large cities. By allowing drivers under 25 years of age to rent cars and by targeting city dwellers who need to supplement their use of public transportation with short-term car rentals, Zipcar entered uncharted waters in the rental-car industry, growing rapidly in the process. Illustration Capsule 6.1 provides another example of a company that has thrived by seeking uncharted blue waters.

Blue-ocean strategies provide a company with a great opportunity in the short run. But they don't guarantee a company's long-term success, which depends more on whether a company can protect the market position it opened up and sustain its early advantage. Gilt Groupe serves as an example of a company that opened up new competitive space in online luxury retailing only to see its blue-ocean waters ultimately turn red. Its competitive success early on prompted an influx of fast followers into the luxury flash-sale industry, including HauteLook, RueLaLa, Lot18, and MyHabit.com. The new rivals not only competed for online customers, who could switch costlessly from site to site (since memberships were free), but also competed for unsold designer inventory. In recent years, Gilt Groupe has been forced to downsize and still has yet to go public, contrary to early expectations.

DEFENSIVE STRATEGIES—PROTECTING MARKET POSITION AND COMPETITIVE ADVANTAGE

In a competitive market, all firms are subject to offensive challenges from rivals. The purposes of defensive strategies are to lower the risk of being attacked, weaken the impact of any attack that occurs, and induce challengers to aim their efforts at other rivals. While defensive strategies usually don't enhance a firm's competitive advantage, they can definitely help fortify the firm's competitive position, protect its most valuable resources and capabilities from imitation, and defend whatever competitive advantage it might have. Defensive strategies can take either of two forms: actions to block challengers or actions to signal the likelihood of strong retaliation.

ILLUSTRATION CAPSULE 6.1

Bonobos's Blue-Ocean Strategy in the U.S. Men's Fashion Retail Industry

It was not too long ago that young, athletic men struggled to find clothing that adequately fit their athletic frames. It was this issue that led two male Stanford MBA students, in 2007, to create Bonobos, a men's clothing brand that initially focused on selling well-fitting men's pants via the Internet. At the time, this concept occupied relatively blue waters as most other clothing brands and retailers in reasonable price ranges had largely focused on innovating in women's clothing, as opposed to men's. In the years since, Bonobos has expanded its product portfolio to include a full line of men's clothing, while growing its revenue from $4 million in 2009 to over $100 million in 2016.

This success has not gone unnoticed by both established players as well as other entrepreneurs. Numerous startups have jumped on the custom men's clothing bandwagon ranging from the low-cost Combatant Gentlemen, to the many bespoke suit tailors that exist in major cities around the United States. In addition, more mainstream clothing retailers have also identified this new type of male customer, with the CEO of Men's Wearhouse, Doug Ewert, stating that he views custom clothing as a "big growth opportunity." That company recently acquired Joseph Abboud to focus more on millennial customers, and plans to begin offering more types of customized clothing in the future.

In response, Bonobos has focused on a new area of development to move to bluer waters in the brick-and-mortar space. The company's innovation is the Guideshop—a store where you can't actually buy anything to take home. Instead, the Guideshop allows men to have

© Patti McConville/Alamy Stock Photo

a personalized shopping experience, where they can try on clothing in any size or color, and then have it delivered the next day to their home or office. This model was based on the insight that most men want an efficient shopping experience, with someone to help them identify the right product and proper fit, so that they could order with ease in the future. As Bonobos CEO Andy Dunn stated more simply, the idea was to provide a different experience from existing retail, which had become "a job about keeping clothes folded [rather] than delivering service." Since opening its first Guideshop in 2011, the company has now expanded to 20 Guideshops nationwide and plans to continue this growth moving forward. This strategy has been fueling the company's success, but how long Bonobos has before retail clothing copycats turn these blue waters red remains to be seen.

Note: Developed with Jacob M. Crandall.

Sources: Richard Feloni, "After 8 Years and $128 Million Raised, the Clock Is Ticking for Men's Retailer Bonobos," BusinessInsider.com, October 6, 2015; Vikram Alexei Kansara, "Andy Dunn of Bonobos on Building the Armani of the E-commerce Era," Businessoffashion.com, July 19, 2013; Hadley Malcolm, "Men's Wearhouse Wants to Suit Up Millennials," *USA Today,* June 8, 2015.

Blocking the Avenues Open to Challengers

Good defensive strategies can help protect a competitive advantage but rarely are the basis for creating one.

The most frequently employed approach to defending a company's present position involves actions that restrict a challenger's options for initiating a competitive attack. There are any number of obstacles that can be put in the path of would-be challengers. A defender can introduce new features, add new models, or broaden its product line to close off gaps and vacant niches to opportunity-seeking challengers. It can thwart rivals' efforts to attack with a lower price by maintaining its own lineup of economy-priced options. It can discourage buyers from trying competitors' brands by lengthening warranties, making early announcements about impending new products or price changes, offering free training and support services, or providing coupons and sample giveaways to buyers most prone to experiment. It can induce potential buyers to reconsider switching. It can challenge the quality or safety of rivals' products. Finally, a defender can grant volume discounts or better financing terms to dealers and distributors to discourage them from experimenting with other suppliers, or it can convince them to handle its product line *exclusively* and force competitors to use other distribution outlets.

Signaling Challengers That Retaliation Is Likely

The goal of signaling challengers that strong retaliation is likely in the event of an attack is either to dissuade challengers from attacking at all or to divert them to less threatening options. Either goal can be achieved by letting challengers know the battle will cost more than it is worth. Signals to would-be challengers can be given by:

There are many ways to throw obstacles in the path of would-be challengers.

- Publicly announcing management's commitment to maintaining the firm's present market share.
- Publicly committing the company to a policy of matching competitors' terms or prices.
- Maintaining a war chest of cash and marketable securities.
- Making an occasional strong counterresponse to the moves of weak competitors to enhance the firm's image as a tough defender.

To be an effective defensive strategy, however, signaling needs to be accompanied by a *credible commitment* to follow through.

TIMING A COMPANY'S STRATEGIC MOVES

When to make a strategic move is often as crucial as *what* move to make. Timing is especially important when **first-mover advantages and disadvantages** exist. Under certain conditions, being first to initiate a strategic move can have a high payoff in the form of a competitive advantage that later movers can't dislodge. Moving first is no guarantee of success, however, since first movers also face some significant disadvantages. Indeed, there are circumstances in which it is more advantageous to be a fast follower or even a late mover. Because the timing of strategic moves can be consequential, it is important for company strategists to be aware of the nature of first-mover advantages and disadvantages and the conditions favoring each type of move.[12]

CORE CONCEPT

Because of **first-mover advantages and disadvantages,** competitive advantage can spring from when a move is made as well as from what move is made.

The Potential for First-Mover Advantages

LO 2

When being a first mover or a fast follower or a late mover is most advantageous.

Market pioneers and other types of first movers typically bear greater risks and greater development costs than firms that move later. If the market responds well to its initial move, the pioneer will benefit from a monopoly position (by virtue of being first to market) that enables it to recover its investment costs and make an attractive profit. If the firm's pioneering move gives it a competitive advantage that can be sustained even after other firms enter the market space, its first-mover advantage will be greater still. The extent of this type of advantage, however, will depend on whether and how fast follower firms can piggyback on the pioneer's success and either imitate or improve on its move.

There are five such conditions in which first-mover advantages are most likely to arise:

1. *When pioneering helps build a firm's reputation and creates strong brand loyalty.* Customer loyalty to an early mover's brand can create a tie that binds, limiting the

success of later entrants' attempts to poach from the early mover's customer base and steal market share.

2. *When a first mover's customers will thereafter face significant switching costs.* Switching costs can protect first movers when consumers make large investments in learning how to use a specific company's product or in purchasing complementary products that are also brand-specific. Switching costs can also arise from loyalty programs or long-term contracts that give customers incentives to remain with an initial provider.
3. *When property rights protections thwart rapid imitation of the initial move.* In certain types of industries, property rights protections in the form of patents, copyrights, and trademarks prevent the ready imitation of an early mover's initial moves. First-mover advantages in pharmaceuticals, for example, are heavily dependent on patent protections, and patent races in this industry are common. In other industries, however, patents provide limited protection and can frequently be circumvented. Property rights protections also vary among nations, since they are dependent on a country's legal institutions and enforcement mechanisms.
4. *When an early lead enables the first mover to move down the learning curve ahead of rivals.* When there is a steep learning curve and when learning can be kept *proprietary,* a first mover can benefit from volume-based cost advantages that grow ever larger as its experience accumulates and its scale of operations increases. This type of first-mover advantage is self-reinforcing and, as such, can preserve a first mover's competitive advantage over long periods of time. Honda's advantage in small multiuse motorcycles has been attributed to such an effect.
5. *When a first mover can set the technical standard for the industry.* In many technology-based industries, the market will converge around a single technical standard. By establishing the industry standard, a first mover can gain a powerful advantage that, like experience-based advantages, builds over time. The lure of such an advantage, however, can result in standard wars among early movers, as each strives to set the industry standard. The key to winning such wars is to enter early on the basis of strong fast-cycle product development capabilities, gain the support of key customers and suppliers, employ penetration pricing, and make allies of the producers of complementary products.

Illustration Capsule 6.2 describes how Uber achieved a first-mover advantage in ride-hailing services.

The Potential for Late-Mover Advantages or First-Mover Disadvantages

In some instances there are advantages *to being an adept follower* rather than a first mover. Late-mover advantages (or *first-mover disadvantages*) arise in four instances:

- When the costs of pioneering are high relative to the benefits accrued and imitative followers can achieve similar benefits with far lower costs. This is often the case when second movers can learn from a pioneer's experience and avoid making the same costly mistakes as the pioneer.
- When an innovator's products are somewhat primitive and do not live up to buyer expectations, thus allowing a follower with better-performing products to win disenchanted buyers away from the leader.

ILLUSTRATION CAPSULE 6.2 Uber's First-Mover Advantage in Mobile Ride-Hailing Services

In February 2008, Travis Kalanick and Garrett Camp stood on a Paris street struggling to hail a cab when an idea hit them: get a ride by using an app on your smartphone. The result of this brainstorm was the ride-sharing company Uber. The company's mobile app pairs individuals looking for a car with the nearest available driver. Within minutes of summoning a car with Uber, a rider can be on her way. The Uber app takes care of everything: giving the driver directions, charging the ride to the customer's credit card, and tipping the driver. There is no need to carry cash or scan streets for an open cab. Uber has been extremely successful with customers looking for an on-demand cab and individuals looking to make money driving. After its founding in March 2009, Uber became one of the fastest-growing companies in history, faster than Facebook or Twitter, and dominated the on-demand transportation market, leaving competitors like Lyft, Taxify, and Sidecar in the dust.

© Mark Ralston/AFP/Getty Images

Uber's rapid rise had much to do with the advantages of being the first mover in the on-demand transportation market. Upon introducing its car service to new cities, Uber aggressively established itself, offering monetary bonuses for drivers who signed up and providing free first rides to encourage new customers to download the Uber app. When competitors entered a city after Uber, they found that the market was largely saturated; many potential customers and drivers were already using Uber. Once the app was downloaded, Uber customers had little reason to try a new ride-sharing service. With more drivers working for them, Uber could provide customers with shorter wait times, on average. Similarly, with more customers using Uber's app, drivers had little incentive to work a competitor since Uber could provide steadier work.

In 2015, Uber served over 300 cities worldwide, dwarfing Lyft's availability in just 65 cities. The company expanded its product offering, with low-cost UberX and UberPool, to capture new customer segments before competitors could; both times, Lyft launched similar services later but had already missed out on most of the market. With rapid growth and a large customer base, Uber earned a $50 billion valuation and expected revenue of $2 billion in 2015. However, future success depends on whether Uber continues to stay a step ahead of its competition. In China, where Uber lacks the recognition and reputational advantage that it has in the United States, a similar service called Didi Kuaidi has been beating Uber at its own game, by being the first to enter many Chinese cities.

Note: Developed with Arthur J. Santry.

Sources: D. MacMillan and T. Demos, "Uber Valued at More Than $50 Billion," *Wall Street Journal* Online, July 15, 2015, www.wsj.com; Edmund Ingham, "Start-ups Take Note," *Forbes,* December 5, 2014, www.forbes.com; Heather Kelly, "Lyft Battles Uber for Drivers with New Perks," CNN, October 8, 2015, www.cnn.com; "Uber: Driving Hard," *The Economist,* June 13, 2015, www.economist.com; company website (accessed November 30, 2015).

- When rapid market evolution (due to fast-paced changes in either technology or buyer needs) gives second movers the opening to leapfrog a first mover's products with more attractive next-version products.
- When market uncertainties make it difficult to ascertain what will eventually succeed, allowing late movers to wait until these needs are clarified.
- When customer loyalty to the pioneer is low and a first mover's skills, know-how, and actions are easily copied or even surpassed

To Be a First Mover or Not

In weighing the pros and cons of being a first mover versus a fast follower versus a late mover, it matters whether the race to market leadership in a particular industry is a 10-year marathon or a 2-year sprint. In marathons, a slow mover is not unduly penalized—first-mover advantages can be fleeting, and there's ample time for fast followers and sometimes even late movers to catch up.[13] Thus the speed at which the pioneering innovation is likely to catch on matters considerably as companies struggle with whether to pursue an emerging market opportunity aggressively (as a first mover) or cautiously (as a late mover). For instance, it took 5.5 years for worldwide mobile phone use to grow from 10 million to 100 million, and it took close to 10 years for the number of at-home broadband subscribers to grow to 100 million worldwide. The lesson here is that there is a market penetration curve for every emerging opportunity. Typically, the curve has an inflection point at which all the pieces of the business model fall into place, buyer demand explodes, and the market takes off. The inflection point can come early on a fast-rising curve (like the use of e-mail and watching movies streamed over the Internet) or farther up on a slow-rising curve (as with battery-powered motor vehicles, solar and wind power, and digital textbooks for college students). Any company that seeks competitive advantage by being a first mover thus needs to ask some hard questions:

- Does market takeoff depend on the development of complementary products or services that currently are not available?
- Is new infrastructure required before buyer demand can surge?
- Will buyers need to learn new skills or adopt new behaviors?
- Will buyers encounter high switching costs in moving to the newly introduced product or service?
- Are there influential competitors in a position to delay or derail the efforts of a first mover?

When the answers to any of these questions are yes, then a company must be careful not to pour too many resources into getting ahead of the market opportunity—the race is likely going to be closer to a 10-year marathon than a 2-year sprint.[14] On the other hand, if the market is a winner-take-all type of market, where powerful first-mover advantages insulate early entrants from competition and prevent later movers from making any headway, then it may be best to move quickly despite the risks.

STRENGTHENING A COMPANY'S MARKET POSITION VIA ITS SCOPE OF OPERATIONS

Apart from considerations of competitive moves and their timing, there is another set of managerial decisions that can affect the strength of a company's market position. These decisions concern the scope of a company's operations—the breadth of its activities and the extent of its market reach. Decisions regarding the **scope of the firm** focus on which activities a firm will perform internally and which it will not.

Consider, for example, Ralph Lauren Corporation. In contrast to Rare Essentials, a boutique clothing store that sells apparel at a single retail store, Ralph Lauren designs, markets, and distributes fashionable apparel and other merchandise to approximately

13,000 major department stores and specialty retailers throughout the world. In addition, it operates over 400 Ralph Lauren retail stores, more than 250 factory stores, and 10 e-commerce sites. Scope decisions also concern which segments of the market to serve—decisions that can include geographic market segments as well as product and service segments. Almost 40 percent of Ralph Lauren's sales are made outside the United States, and its product line includes apparel, fragrances, home furnishings, eyewear, watches and jewelry, and handbags and other leather goods. The company has also expanded its brand lineup through the acquisitions of Chaps menswear and casual retailer Club Monaco.

CORE CONCEPT

The **scope of the firm** refers to the range of activities that the firm performs internally, the breadth of its product and service offerings, the extent of its geographic market presence, and its mix of businesses.

Decisions such as these, in essence, determine where the boundaries of a firm lie and the degree to which the operations within those boundaries cohere. They also have much to do with the direction and extent of a business's growth. In this chapter, we introduce the topic of company scope and discuss different types of scope decisions in relation to a company's business-level strategy. In the next two chapters, we develop two additional dimensions of a firm's scope. Chapter 7 focuses on international expansion—a matter of extending the company's geographic scope into foreign markets. Chapter 8 takes up the topic of corporate strategy, which concerns diversifying into a mix of different businesses. *Scope issues are at the very heart of corporate-level strategy.*

CORE CONCEPT

Horizontal scope is the range of product and service segments that a firm serves within its focal market.

Several dimensions of firm scope have relevance for business-level strategy in terms of their capacity to strengthen a company's position in a given market. These include the firm's **horizontal scope,** which is the range of product and service segments that the firm serves within its product or service market. Mergers and acquisitions involving other market participants provide a means for a company to expand its horizontal scope. Expanding the firm's vertical scope by means of vertical integration can also affect the success of its market strategy. **Vertical scope** is the extent to which the firm engages in the various activities that make up the industry's entire value chain system, from initial activities such as raw-material production all the way to retailing and after-sale service activities. *Outsourcing decisions* concern another dimension of scope since they involve narrowing the firm's boundaries with respect to its participation in value chain activities. We discuss the pros and cons of each of these options in the sections that follow. Because *strategic alliances and partnerships* provide an alternative to vertical integration and acquisition strategies and are sometimes used to facilitate outsourcing, we conclude this chapter with a discussion of the benefits and challenges associated with *cooperative arrangements* of this nature.

CORE CONCEPT

Vertical scope is the extent to which a firm's internal activities encompass the range of activities that make up an industry's entire value chain system, from raw-material production to final sales and service activities.

HORIZONTAL MERGER AND ACQUISITION STRATEGIES

LO 3

The strategic benefits and risks of expanding a company's horizontal scope through mergers and acquisitions.

Mergers and acquisitions are much-used strategic options to strengthen a company's market position. A *merger* is the combining of two or more companies into a single corporate entity, with the newly created company often taking on a new name. An *acquisition* is a combination in which one company, the acquirer, purchases and absorbs the operations of another, the acquired. The difference between a merger and an acquisition relates more to the details of ownership, management control, and financial arrangements than to strategy and competitive advantage. The resources and competitive capabilities of the newly created enterprise end up much the same whether the combination is the result of an acquisition or a merger.

Horizontal mergers and acquisitions, which involve combining the operations of firms *within the same product or service market,* provide an effective means for firms to rapidly increase the scale and horizontal scope of their core business. For example, the merger of AMR Corporation (parent of American Airlines) with US Airways has increased the airlines' scale of operations and extended their reach geographically to create the world's largest airline.

Merger and acquisition strategies typically set sights on achieving any of five objectives:[15]

1. *Creating a more cost-efficient operation out of the combined companies.* When a company acquires another company in the same industry, there's usually enough overlap in operations that less efficient plants can be closed or distribution and sales activities partly combined and downsized. Likewise, it is usually feasible to squeeze out cost savings in administrative activities, again by combining and downsizing such administrative activities as finance and accounting, information technology, human resources, and so on. The combined companies may also be able to reduce supply chain costs because of greater bargaining power over common suppliers and closer collaboration with supply chain partners. By helping consolidate the industry and remove excess capacity, such combinations can also reduce industry rivalry and improve industry profitability.
2. *Expanding a company's geographic coverage.* One of the best and quickest ways to expand a company's geographic coverage is to acquire rivals with operations in the desired locations. Since a company's size increases with its geographic scope, another benefit is increased bargaining power with the company's suppliers or buyers. Greater geographic coverage can also contribute to product differentiation by enhancing a company's name recognition and brand awareness. Banks like JPMorgan Chase, Wells Fargo, and Bank of America have used acquisition strategies to establish a market presence and gain name recognition in an ever-growing number of states and localities. Food products companies like Nestlé, Kraft, Unilever, and Procter & Gamble have made acquisitions an integral part of their strategies to expand internationally.
3. *Extending the company's business into new product categories.* Many times a company has gaps in its product line that need to be filled in order to offer customers a more effective product bundle or the benefits of one-stop shopping. For example, customers might prefer to acquire a suite of software applications from a single vendor that can offer more integrated solutions to the company's problems. Acquisition can be a quicker and more potent way to broaden a company's product line than going through the exercise of introducing a company's own new product to fill the gap. Coca-Cola has increased the effectiveness of the product bundle it provides to retailers by acquiring beverage makers Minute Maid, Odwalla, Hi-C, and Glacéau Vitaminwater.
4. *Gaining quick access to new technologies or other resources and capabilities.* Making acquisitions to bolster a company's technological know-how or to expand its skills and capabilities allows a company to bypass a time-consuming and expensive internal effort to build desirable new resources and capabilities. From 2000 through December 2015, Cisco Systems purchased 128 companies to give it

more technological reach and product breadth, thereby enhancing its standing as the world's largest provider of hardware, software, and services for creating and operating Internet networks.

5. *Leading the convergence of industries whose boundaries are being blurred by changing technologies and new market opportunities.* In fast-cycle industries or industries whose boundaries are changing, companies can use acquisition strategies to hedge their bets about the direction that an industry will take, to increase their capacity to meet changing demands, and to respond flexibly to changing buyer needs and technological demands. News Corporation has prepared for the convergence of media services with the purchase of satellite TV companies to complement its media holdings in TV broadcasting (the Fox network and TV stations in various countries), cable TV (Fox News, Fox Sports, and FX), filmed entertainment (Twentieth Century Fox and Fox studios), newspapers, magazines, and book publishing.

Horizontal mergers and acquisitions can strengthen a firm's competitiveness in five ways: (1) by improving the efficiency of its operations, (2) by heightening its product differentiation, (3) by reducing market rivalry, (4) by increasing the company's bargaining power over suppliers and buyers, and (5) by enhancing its flexibility and dynamic capabilities.

Illustration Capsule 6.3 describes how Bristol-Myers Squibb developed its "string-of-pearls" horizontal acquisition strategy to fill in its pharmaceutical product development gaps.

Why Mergers and Acquisitions Sometimes Fail to Produce Anticipated Results

Despite many successes, mergers and acquisitions do not always produce the hoped-for outcomes.[16] Cost savings may prove smaller than expected. Gains in competitive capabilities may take substantially longer to realize or, worse, may never materialize at all. Efforts to mesh the corporate cultures can stall due to formidable resistance from organization members. Key employees at the acquired company can quickly become disenchanted and leave; the morale of company personnel who remain can drop to disturbingly low levels because they disagree with newly instituted changes. Differences in management styles and operating procedures can prove hard to resolve. In addition, the managers appointed to oversee the integration of a newly acquired company can make mistakes in deciding which activities to leave alone and which activities to meld into their own operations and systems.

A number of mergers and acquisitions have been notably unsuccessful. Google's \$12.5 billion acquisition of struggling smartphone manufacturer Motorola Mobility in 2012 turned out to be minimally beneficial in helping to "supercharge Google's Android ecosystem" (Google's stated reason for making the acquisition). When Google's attempts to rejuvenate Motorola's smartphone business by spending over \$1.3 billion on new product R&D and revamping Motorola's product line resulted in disappointing sales and huge operating losses, Google sold Motorola Mobility to China-based PC maker Lenovo for \$2.9 billion in 2014 (however, Google retained ownership of Motorola's extensive patent portfolio). The jury is still out on whether Lenovo's acquisition of Motorola will prove to be a moneymaker.

ILLUSTRATION CAPSULE 6.3 Bristol-Myers Squibb's "String-of-Pearls" Horizontal Acquisition Strategy

Back in 2007, the pharmaceutical company Bristol-Myers Squibb had a problem: Its top-selling drugs, Plavix and Abilify, would go off patent by 2012 and its drug pipeline was nearly empty. Together these drugs (the first for heart attacks, the second for depression) accounted for nearly half of the company's sales. Not surprisingly, the company's stock price had stagnated and was underperforming that of its peers.

Developing new drugs is difficult: New drugs must be identified, tested in increasingly sophisticated trials, and approved by the Food and Drug Administration. On average, this process takes 13 years and costs $2 billion. The success rate is low: Only one drug in eight manages to pass through clinical testing. In 2007, Bristol-Myers Squibb had only six new drugs at the clinical testing stage.

© John Greim/LightRocket via Getty Images

At the time, many drug companies were diversifying into new markets like over-the-counter drugs to better manage drug development risk. Bristol-Myers Squibb's management pursued a different strategy: product diversification through horizontal acquisitions. Bristol-Myers Squibb targeted small companies in new treatment areas, with the objective of reducing new product development risk by betting on pre-identified drugs. The small companies it targeted, with one or two drugs in development, needed cash; Bristol-Myers Squibb needed new drugs. The firm's management called this its "string-of-pearls" strategy.

To implement its approach and obtain the cash it needed, Bristol-Myers Squibb sold its stake in Mead Johnson, a nutritional supplement manufacturer. Then it went on a shopping spree. Starting in 2007, the company spent over $8 billion on 18 transactions, including 12 horizontal acquisitions. In the process, the company acquired many promising new drug candidates for common diseases such as cancer, cardiovascular disease, rheumatoid arthritis, and hepatitis C.

By early 2012, the company's string-of-pearls acquisitions were estimated to have added over $4 billion of new revenue to the company's coffers. Despite management changes over the subsequent year leading to the loss of two of the visionaries of the string-of-pearls concept, the new R&D chief remained committed to continuing the strategy. Analysts reported that Bristol-Myers Squibb had one of the best pipelines among drug makers. Investors agreed: The company's stock price has climbed consistently since 2007, outperforming its competitors and experiencing annual growth of over 20 percent.

Note: Developed with Dennis L. Huggins.

Sources: D. Armstrong and M. Tirrell, "Bristol's Buy of Inhibitex for Hepatitis Drug Won't Be Last," *Bloomberg Businessweek,* January 2012, **www.bloomberg.com** (accessed January 30, 2012); S. M. Paul et al., "How to Improve R&D Productivity: The Pharmaceutical Industry's Grand Challenge," *Nature Reviews,* March 2010, pp. 203–214; Bristol-Myers Squibb 2007 and 2011 annual reports; D. Armstrong, "Bristol-Myers New R&D Chief Plans to Keep Focus on Cancer," *Bloomberg* Online, April 8, 2013.

VERTICAL INTEGRATION STRATEGIES

Expanding the firm's vertical scope by means of a vertical integration strategy provides another possible way to strengthen the company's position in its core market. A **vertically integrated firm** is one that participates in multiple stages of an industry's value chain system. Thus, if a manufacturer invests in facilities to produce component parts that it had formerly purchased from suppliers, or if it opens its own chain of retail stores to bypass its former distributors, it is engaging in vertical integration. A good example of a vertically integrated firm is Maple Leaf Foods, a major Canadian producer of fresh and processed meats whose best-selling brands include Maple Leaf and Schneiders. Maple Leaf Foods participates in hog and poultry production, with company-owned hog and poultry farms; it has its own meat-processing and rendering facilities; it packages its products and distributes them from company-owned distribution centers; and it conducts marketing, sales, and customer service activities for its wholesale and retail buyers but does not otherwise participate in the final stage of the meat-processing vertical chain—the retailing stage.

LO 4

The advantages and disadvantages of extending the company's scope of operations via vertical integration.

CORE CONCEPT

A **vertically integrated firm** is one that performs value chain activities along more than one stage of an industry's value chain system.

A vertical integration strategy can expand the firm's range of activities *backward* into sources of supply and/or *forward* toward end users. When Tiffany & Co., a manufacturer and retailer of fine jewelry, began sourcing, cutting, and polishing its own diamonds, it integrated backward along the diamond supply chain. Mining giant De Beers Group and Canadian miner Aber Diamond integrated forward when they entered the diamond retailing business.

A firm can pursue vertical integration by starting its own operations in other stages of the vertical activity chain or by acquiring a company already performing the activities it wants to bring in-house. Vertical integration strategies can aim at *full integration* (participating in all stages of the vertical chain) or *partial integration* (building positions in selected stages of the vertical chain). Firms can also engage in *tapered integration* strategies, which involve a mix of in-house and outsourced activity in any given stage of the vertical chain. Oil companies, for instance, supply their refineries with oil from their own wells as well as with oil that they purchase from other producers—they engage in tapered backward integration. Coach, Inc., the maker of Coach handbags and accessories, engages in tapered forward integration since it operates full-price and factory outlet stores but also sells its products through third-party department store outlets.

The Advantages of a Vertical Integration Strategy

Under the right conditions, a vertical integration strategy can add materially to a company's technological capabilities, strengthen the firm's competitive position, and boost its profitability.[17] But it is important to keep in mind that vertical integration has no real payoff strategy-wise or profit-wise unless the extra investment can be justified by compensating improvements in company costs, differentiation, or competitive strength.

Integrating Backward to Achieve Greater Competitiveness It is harder than one might think to generate cost savings or improve profitability by integrating backward into activities such as the manufacture of parts and components (which could otherwise be purchased from suppliers with specialized expertise in making the parts and components). For **backward integration** to be a cost-saving and profitable strategy, a company must be able to (1) achieve the same scale economies as outside suppliers and (2) match or beat suppliers' production efficiency with no drop-off in quality. Neither outcome is easily achieved. To begin with, a company's in-house requirements are often too small to reach the optimum size for low-cost operation. For instance, if it takes a minimum production volume of 1 million units to achieve scale economies and a company's in-house requirements are just 250,000 units, then it falls far short of being able to match the costs

CORE CONCEPT

Backward integration involves entry into activities previously performed by suppliers or other enterprises positioned along earlier stages of the industry value chain system; **forward integration** involves entry into value chain system activities closer to the end user.

of outside suppliers (which may readily find buyers for 1 million or more units). Furthermore, matching the production efficiency of suppliers is fraught with problems when suppliers have considerable production experience, when the technology they employ has elements that are hard to master, and/or when substantial R&D expertise is required to develop next-version components or keep pace with advancing technology in components production.

That said, occasions still arise when a company can improve its cost position and competitiveness by performing a broader range of industry value chain activities internally rather than having such activities performed by outside suppliers. When there are few suppliers and when the item being supplied is a major component, vertical integration can lower costs by limiting supplier power. Vertical integration can also lower costs by facilitating the coordination of production flows and avoiding bottlenecks and delays that disrupt production schedules. Furthermore, when a company has proprietary know-how that it wants to keep from rivals, then in-house performance of value-adding activities related to this know-how is beneficial even if such activities could otherwise be performed by outsiders.

Apple decided to integrate backward into producing its own chips for iPhones, chiefly because chips are a major cost component, suppliers have bargaining power, and in-house production would help coordinate design tasks and protect Apple's proprietary iPhone technology. International Paper Company backward integrates into pulp mills that it sets up near its paper mills and reaps the benefits of coordinated production flows, energy savings, and transportation economies. It does this, in part, because outside suppliers are generally unwilling to make a site-specific investment for a buyer.

Backward vertical integration can produce a differentiation-based competitive advantage when performing activities internally contributes to a better-quality product or service offering, improves the caliber of customer service, or in other ways enhances the performance of the final product. On occasion, integrating into more stages along the industry value chain system can add to a company's differentiation capabilities by allowing it to strengthen its core competencies, better master key skills or strategy-critical technologies, or add features that deliver greater customer value. Spanish clothing maker Inditex has backward integrated into fabric making, as well as garment design and manufacture, for its successful Zara brand. By tightly controlling the process and postponing dyeing until later stages, Zara can respond quickly to changes in fashion trends and supply its customers with the hottest items. News Corp backward integrated into film studios (Twentieth Century Fox) and TV program production to ensure access to high-quality content for its TV stations (and to limit supplier power).

Integrating Forward to Enhance Competitiveness Like backward integration, **forward integration** can lower costs by increasing efficiency and bargaining power. In addition, it can allow manufacturers to gain better access to end users, improve market visibility, and enhance brand name awareness. For example, Harley's company-owned retail stores are essentially little museums, filled with iconography, that provide an environment conducive to selling not only motorcycles and gear but also memorabilia, clothing, and other items featuring the brand. Insurance companies and brokerages like Allstate and Edward Jones have the ability to make consumers' interactions with local agents and office personnel a differentiating feature by focusing on building relationships.

In many industries, independent sales agents, wholesalers, and retailers handle competing brands of the same product and have no allegiance to any one company's brand—they tend to push whatever offers the biggest profits. To avoid dependence on distributors and dealers with divided loyalties, Goodyear has integrated forward into company-owned and franchised retail tire stores. Consumer-goods companies like Coach, Under Armour, Pepperidge Farm, Bath & Body Works, Nike, Tommy Hilfiger, and Ann Taylor have integrated forward into retailing and operate their own branded stores in factory outlet malls, enabling them to move overstocked items, slow-selling items, and seconds.

Some producers have opted to integrate forward by selling directly to customers at the company's website. Bypassing regular wholesale and retail channels in favor of direct sales and Internet retailing can have appeal if it reinforces the brand and enhances consumer satisfaction or if it lowers distribution costs, produces a relative cost advantage over certain rivals, and results in lower selling prices to end users. In addition, sellers are compelled to include the Internet as a retail channel when a sufficiently large number of buyers in an industry prefer to make purchases online. However, a company that is vigorously pursuing online sales to consumers at the same time that it is also heavily promoting sales to consumers through its network of wholesalers and retailers is *competing directly against its distribution allies.* Such actions constitute *channel conflict* and create a tricky route to negotiate. A company that is actively trying to expand online sales to consumers is signaling a weak strategic commitment to its dealers *and* a willingness to cannibalize dealers' sales and growth potential. The likely result is angry dealers and loss of dealer goodwill. Quite possibly, a company may stand to lose more sales by offending its dealers than it gains from its own online sales effort. Consequently, in industries where the strong support and goodwill of dealer networks is essential, companies may conclude that it is important to avoid channel conflict and that *their websites should be designed to partner with dealers rather than compete against them.*

The Disadvantages of a Vertical Integration Strategy

Vertical integration has some substantial drawbacks beyond the potential for channel conflict.[18] The most serious drawbacks to vertical integration include the following concerns:

- Vertical integration raises a firm's capital investment in the industry, thereby *increasing business risk* (what if industry growth and profitability unexpectedly go sour?).
- Vertically integrated companies are often *slow to adopt technological advances or more efficient production methods* when they are saddled with older technology or facilities. A company that obtains parts and components from outside suppliers can always shop the market for the newest, best, and cheapest parts, whereas a vertically integrated firm with older plants and technology may choose to continue making suboptimal parts rather than face the high costs of writing off undepreciated assets.
- Vertical integration can result in *less flexibility in accommodating shifting buyer preferences.* It is one thing to eliminate use of a component made by a supplier and another to stop using a component being made in-house (which can mean laying off employees and writing off the associated investment in equipment and facilities). Integrating forward or backward locks a firm into relying on its own in-house activities and sources of supply. Most of the world's automakers,

despite their manufacturing expertise, have concluded that purchasing a majority of their parts and components from best-in-class suppliers results in greater design flexibility, higher quality, and lower costs than producing parts or components in-house.

- Vertical integration *may not enable a company to realize economies of scale* if its production levels are below the minimum efficient scale. Small companies in particular are likely to suffer a cost disadvantage by producing in-house.
- Vertical integration poses all kinds of *capacity-matching problems*. In motor vehicle manufacturing, for example, the most efficient scale of operation for making axles is different from the most economic volume for radiators, and different yet again for both engines and transmissions. Building the capacity to produce just the right number of axles, radiators, engines, and transmissions in-house—and doing so at the lowest unit costs for each—poses significant challenges and operating complications.
- Integration forward or backward typically *calls for developing new types of resources and capabilities*. Parts and components manufacturing, assembly operations, wholesale distribution and retailing, and direct sales via the Internet represent different kinds of businesses, operating in different types of industries, with different key success factors. Many manufacturers learn the hard way that company-owned wholesale and retail networks require skills that they lack, fit poorly with what they do best, and detract from their overall profit performance. Similarly, a company that tries to produce many components in-house is likely to find itself very hard-pressed to keep up with technological advances and cutting-edge production practices for each component used in making its product.

In today's world of close working relationships with suppliers and efficient supply chain management systems, relatively few companies can make a strong economic case for integrating backward into the business of suppliers. The best materials and components suppliers stay abreast of advancing technology and best practices and are adept in making good quality items, delivering them on time, and keeping their costs and prices as low as possible.

Weighing the Pros and Cons of Vertical Integration

All in all, therefore, a strategy of vertical integration can have both strengths and weaknesses. The tip of the scales depends on (1) whether vertical integration can enhance the performance of strategy-critical activities in ways that lower cost, build expertise, protect proprietary know-how, or increase differentiation; (2) what impact vertical integration will have on investment costs, flexibility, and response times; (3) what administrative costs will be incurred by coordinating operations across more vertical chain activities; and (4) how difficult it will be for the company to acquire the set of skills and capabilities needed to operate in another stage of the vertical chain. *Vertical integration strategies have merit according to which capabilities and value-adding activities truly need to be performed in-house and which can be performed better or cheaper by outsiders.* Absent solid benefits, integrating forward or backward is not likely to be an attractive strategy option.

Kaiser Permanente, the largest managed care organization in the United States, has made vertical integration a central part of its strategy, as described in Illustration Capsule 6.4.

ILLUSTRATION CAPSULE 6.4 Kaiser Permanente's Vertical Integration Strategy

Kaiser Permanente's unique business model features a vertical integration strategy that enables it to deliver higher-quality care to patients at a lower cost. Kaiser Permanente is the largest vertically integrated health care delivery system in the United States, with $56.4 billion in revenues and $3.1 billion in net income in 2014. It functions as a health insurance company with over 10 million members and a provider of health care services with 28 hospitals, 619 medical offices, and nearly 18,000 physicians. As a result of its vertical integration, Kaiser Permanente is better able to efficiently match demand for services by health plan members to capacity of its delivery infrastructure, including physicians and hospitals. Moreover, its prepaid financial model helps incentivize the appropriate delivery of health care services.

Unlike Kaiser Permanente, the majority of physicians and hospitals in the United States provide care on a fee-for-service revenue model or per-procedure basis. Consequently, most physicians and hospitals earn higher revenues by providing more services, which limits investments in preventive care. In contrast, Kaiser Permanente providers are incentivized to focus on health promotion, disease prevention, and chronic disease management. Kaiser Permanente pays primary care physicians more than local averages to attract top talent, and surgeons are salaried rather than paid by procedure to encourage the optimal level of care. Physicians from multiple specialties work collaboratively to coordinate care and treat the overall health of patients rather than individual health issues.

© Bryan Chan/Los Angeles Times via Getty

One result of this strategy is enhanced efficiency, enabling Kaiser Permanente to provide health insurance that is, on average, 10 percent cheaper than that of its competitors. Further, the care provided is of higher quality based on national standards of care. For the seventh year in a row, Kaiser Permanente health plans received the highest overall quality-of-care rating of any health plan in California, which accounts for almost 8 million of its 10 million members. Kaiser Permanente is also consistently praised for member satisfaction. Four of Kaiser's health plan regions, accounting for 90 percent of its membership, were ranked highest in member satisfaction by J.D. Power and Associates. The success of Kaiser Permanente's vertical integration strategy is the primary reason why many health care organizations are seeking to replicate its model as they transition from a fee-for-service revenue model to an accountable care model.

Note: Developed with Christopher C. Sukenik.

Sources: "Kaiser Foundation Hospitals and Health Plan Report Fiscal Year 2013 and Fourth Quarter Financial Results," *PR Newswire*, February 14, 2014, **www.prnewswire.com**; Kaiser Permanente website and 2012 annual report; J. O'Donnell, "Kaiser Permanente CEO on Saving Lives, Money," *USA Today*, October 23, 2012.

OUTSOURCING STRATEGIES: NARROWING THE SCOPE OF OPERATIONS

LO 5

The conditions that favor farming out certain value chain activities to outside parties.

In contrast to vertical integration strategies, outsourcing strategies narrow the scope of a business's operations, in terms of what activities are performed internally. **Outsourcing** involves contracting out certain value chain activities that are normally performed in-house to outside vendors.[19] Many PC makers, for example, have shifted from assembling units in-house to outsourcing the entire assembly process to manufacturing specialists, which can operate more efficiently due to their greater scale, experience, and bargaining power over components makers. Nearly all name-brand apparel firms have in-house capability to design, market, and distribute their products but they outsource all fabric manufacture and garment-making activities. Starbucks finds purchasing coffee beans from independent growers far more advantageous than having its own coffee-growing operation, with locations scattered across most of the world's coffee-growing regions.

CORE CONCEPT

Outsourcing involves contracting out certain value chain activities that are normally performed in-house to outside vendors.

Outsourcing certain value chain activities makes strategic sense whenever:

- *An activity can be performed better or more cheaply by outside specialists.* A company should generally *not* perform any value chain activity internally that can be performed more efficiently or effectively by outsiders—the chief exception occurs when a particular activity is strategically crucial and internal control over that activity is deemed essential. Dolce & Gabbana, for example, outsources the manufacture of its brand of sunglasses to Luxottica—a company considered to be the world's best sunglass manufacturing company, known for its Oakley, Oliver Peoples, and Ray-Ban brands.
- *The activity is not crucial to the firm's ability to achieve sustainable competitive advantage.* Outsourcing of support activities such as maintenance services, data processing, data storage, fringe-benefit management, and website operations has become commonplace. Colgate-Palmolive, for instance, has reduced its information technology operational costs by more than 10 percent annually through an outsourcing agreement with IBM.
- *The outsourcing improves organizational flexibility and speeds time to market.* Outsourcing gives a company the flexibility to switch suppliers in the event that its present supplier falls behind competing suppliers. Moreover, seeking out new suppliers with the needed capabilities already in place is frequently quicker, easier, less risky, and cheaper than hurriedly retooling internal operations to replace obsolete capabilities or trying to install and master new technologies.
- *It reduces the company's risk exposure to changing technology and buyer preferences.* When a company outsources certain parts, components, and services, its suppliers must bear the burden of incorporating state-of-the-art technologies and/or undertaking redesigns and upgrades to accommodate a company's plans to introduce next-generation products. If what a supplier provides falls out of favor with buyers, or is rendered unnecessary by technological change, it is the supplier's business that suffers rather than the company's.
- *It allows a company to concentrate on its core business, leverage its key resources, and do even better what it already does best.* A company is better able to enhance its own capabilities when it concentrates its full resources and energies on performing only those activities. United Colors of Benetton and Sisley, for example, outsource the production of handbags and other leather goods while devoting their energies to the clothing lines for which they are known. Apple outsources production of its iPod, iPhone, and iPad models to Chinese contract manufacturer Foxconn and concentrates in-house on design, marketing, and innovation. Hewlett-Packard and IBM have sold some of their manufacturing plants to outsiders and contracted to repurchase the output instead from the new owners.

The Risk of Outsourcing Value Chain Activities

The biggest danger of outsourcing is that a company will farm out the wrong types of activities and thereby hollow out its own capabilities.[20] For example, in recent years companies eager to reduce operating costs have opted to outsource such strategically important activities as product development, engineering design, and sophisticated manufacturing tasks—the very capabilities that underpin a company's ability to lead sustained product innovation. While these companies have apparently been able to lower their operating costs by outsourcing these functions to outsiders, *their ability to lead the development of innovative new products is weakened because so many of the cutting-edge ideas and technologies for next-generation products come from outsiders.*

A company must guard against outsourcing activities that hollow out the resources and capabilities that it needs to be a master of its own destiny.

Another risk of outsourcing comes from the lack of direct control. It may be difficult to monitor, control, and coordinate the activities of outside parties via contracts and arm's-length transactions alone. Unanticipated problems may arise that cause delays or cost overruns and become hard to resolve amicably. Moreover, contract-based outsourcing can be problematic because outside parties lack incentives to make investments specific to the needs of the outsourcing company's internal value chain.

Companies like Cisco Systems are alert to these dangers. Cisco guards against loss of control and protects its manufacturing expertise by designing the production methods that its contract manufacturers must use. Cisco keeps the source code for its designs proprietary, thereby controlling the initiation of all improvements and safeguarding its innovations from imitation. Further, Cisco has developed online systems to monitor the factory operations of contract manufacturers around the clock so that it knows immediately when problems arise and can decide whether to get involved.

STRATEGIC ALLIANCES AND PARTNERSHIPS

LO 6

When and how strategic alliances can substitute for horizontal mergers and acquisitions or vertical integration and how they can facilitate outsourcing.

Strategic alliances and cooperative partnerships provide one way to gain some of the benefits offered by vertical integration, outsourcing, and horizontal mergers and acquisitions while minimizing the associated problems. Companies frequently engage in cooperative strategies as an alternative to vertical integration or horizontal mergers and acquisitions. Increasingly, companies are also employing strategic alliances and partnerships to extend their scope of operations via international expansion and diversification strategies, as we describe in Chapters 7 and 8. Strategic alliances and cooperative arrangements are now a common means of narrowing a company's scope of operations as well, serving as a useful way to manage outsourcing (in lieu of traditional, purely price-oriented contracts).

For example, oil and gas companies engage in considerable vertical integration—but Shell Oil Company and Pemex (Mexico's state-owned petroleum company) have found that joint ownership of their Deer Park Refinery in Texas lowers their investment costs and risks in comparison to going it alone. The colossal failure of the Daimler–Chrysler merger formed an expensive lesson for Daimler AG about what can go wrong with horizontal mergers and acquisitions; its 2010 strategic alliance with Renault–Nissan is allowing the two companies to achieve jointly the global scale required for cost-competitiveness in cars and trucks while avoiding the type of problems that so plagued DaimlerChrysler. Ford Motor Company joined Daimler AG and Renault–Nissan more recently in an effort to develop affordable, mass-market hydrogen fuel cell vehicles by 2017.

Many companies employ strategic alliances to manage the problems that might otherwise occur with outsourcing—Cisco's system of alliances guards against loss of control, protects its proprietary manufacturing expertise, and enables the company to monitor closely the assembly operations of its partners while devoting its energy to designing new generations of the switches, routers, and other Internet-related equipment for which it is known.

CORE CONCEPT

A **strategic alliance** is a formal agreement between two or more separate companies in which they agree to work cooperatively toward some common objective.

CORE CONCEPT

A **joint venture** is a partnership involving the establishment of an independent corporate entity that the partners own and control jointly, sharing in its revenues and expenses.

A **strategic alliance** is a formal agreement between two or more separate companies in which they agree to work collaboratively toward some strategically relevant objective. Typically, they involve shared financial responsibility, joint contribution of resources and capabilities, shared risk, shared control, and mutual dependence. They may be characterized by cooperative marketing, sales, or distribution; joint production; design collaboration; or projects to jointly develop new technologies or products. They can vary in terms of their duration and the extent of the collaboration; some are intended as long-term arrangements, involving an extensive set of cooperative activities, while others are designed to accomplish more limited, short-term objectives.

Collaborative arrangements may entail a contractual agreement, but they commonly stop short of formal ownership ties between the partners (although sometimes an alliance member will secure minority ownership of another member).

A special type of strategic alliance involving ownership ties is the **joint venture.** A joint venture entails forming a *new corporate entity that is jointly owned* by two or more companies that agree to share in the revenues, expenses, and control of the newly formed entity. Since joint ventures involve setting up a mutually owned business, they tend to be more durable but also riskier than other arrangements. In other types of strategic alliances, the collaboration between the partners involves a much less rigid structure in which the partners retain their independence from one another. If a strategic alliance is not working out, a partner can choose to simply walk away or reduce its commitment to collaborating at any time.

An alliance becomes "strategic," as opposed to just a convenient business arrangement, when it serves any of the following purposes:[21]

1. It facilitates achievement of an important business objective (like lowering costs or delivering more value to customers in the form of better quality, added features, and greater durability).
2. It helps build, strengthen, or sustain a core competence or competitive advantage.
3. It helps remedy an important resource deficiency or competitive weakness.
4. It helps defend against a competitive threat, or mitigates a significant risk to a company's business.
5. It increases bargaining power over suppliers or buyers.
6. It helps open up important new market opportunities.
7. It speeds the development of new technologies and/or product innovations.

Strategic cooperation is a much-favored approach in industries where new technological developments are occurring at a furious pace along many different paths and where advances in one technology spill over to affect others (often blurring industry boundaries). Whenever industries are experiencing high-velocity technological advances in many areas simultaneously, firms find it virtually essential to have cooperative relationships with other enterprises to stay on the leading edge of technology, even in their own area of specialization. In industries like these, alliances are all about fast cycles of learning, gaining quick access to the latest round of technological know-how, and developing dynamic capabilities. In bringing together firms with different skills and knowledge bases, alliances open up learning opportunities that help partner firms better leverage their own resources and capabilities.[22]

It took a $3.2 billion joint venture involving the likes of Sprint-Nextel, Clearwire, Intel, Time Warner Cable, Google, Comcast, and Bright House Networks to roll out next-generation 4G wireless services based on Sprint's and Clearwire's WiMax mobile networks. WiMax was an advanced Wi-Fi technology that allowed people to browse the Internet at speeds as great as 10 times faster than other cellular Wi-Fi technologies. The venture was a necessity for Sprint-Nextel and Clearwire since they lacked the financial resources to handle the rollout on their own. The appeal of the partnership for Time Warner, Comcast, and Bright House was the ability to bundle the sale of wireless services to their cable customers, while Intel had the chip sets for WiMax and hoped that WiMax would become the dominant wireless Internet format. Google's interest in the alliance was its desire to strengthen its lead in desktop searches on wireless devices.

iHeartMedia (formerly Clear Channel Communications) entered into a series of early partnerships to provide a multiplatform launchpad for artists like Taylor Swift, Phoenix, and Sara Bareilles. More recently, they formed a partnership with Microsoft involving Windows 10. iHeartMedia benefits because people who buy Windows 10 automatically have access to its content, and Microsoft benefits because there are iHeartMedia features that are exclusive to Windows 10, thus potentially drawing in customers.

Companies that have formed a host of alliances need to manage their alliances like a portfolio.

Because of the varied benefits of strategic alliances, many large corporations have become involved in 30 to 50 alliances, and a number have formed hundreds of alliances. Genentech, a leader in biotechnology and human genetics, has formed R&D alliances with over 30 companies to boost its prospects for developing new cures for various diseases and ailments. Companies that have formed a host of alliances need to manage their alliances like a portfolio—terminating those that no longer serve a useful purpose or that have produced meager results, forming promising new alliances, and restructuring existing alliances to correct performance problems and/or redirect the collaborative effort.

The best alliances are highly selective, focusing on particular value chain activities and on obtaining a specific competitive benefit. They enable a firm to build on its strengths and to learn.

Capturing the Benefits of Strategic Alliances

The extent to which companies benefit from entering into alliances and partnerships seems to be a function of six factors:[23]

1. *Picking a good partner.* A good partner must bring complementary strengths to the relationship. To the extent that alliance members have nonoverlapping strengths, there is greater potential for synergy and less potential for coordination problems and conflict. In addition, a good partner needs to share the company's vision about the overall purpose of the alliance and to have specific goals that either match or complement those of the company. Strong partnerships also depend on good chemistry among key personnel and compatible views about how the alliance should be structured and managed.
2. *Being sensitive to cultural differences.* Cultural differences among companies can make it difficult for their personnel to work together effectively. Cultural differences can be problematic among companies from the same country, but when the partners have different national origins, the problems are often magnified. Unless there is respect among all the parties for cultural differences, including those stemming from different local cultures and local business practices, productive working relationships are unlikely to emerge.
3. *Recognizing that the alliance must benefit both sides.* Information must be shared as well as gained, and the relationship must remain forthright and trustful. If either

partner plays games with information or tries to take advantage of the other, the resulting friction can quickly erode the value of further collaboration. Open, trustworthy behavior on both sides is essential for fruitful collaboration.

4. *Ensuring that both parties live up to their commitments.* Both parties have to deliver on their commitments for the alliance to produce the intended benefits. The division of work has to be perceived as fairly apportioned, and the caliber of the benefits received on both sides has to be perceived as adequate.
5. *Structuring the decision-making process so that actions can be taken swiftly when needed.* In many instances, the fast pace of technological and competitive changes dictates an equally fast decision-making process. If the parties get bogged down in discussions or in gaining internal approval from higher-ups, the alliance can turn into an anchor of delay and inaction.
6. *Managing the learning process and then adjusting the alliance agreement over time to fit new circumstances.* One of the keys to long-lasting success is adapting the nature and structure of the alliance to be responsive to shifting market conditions, emerging technologies, and changing customer requirements. Wise allies are quick to recognize the merit of an evolving collaborative arrangement, where adjustments are made to accommodate changing conditions and to overcome whatever problems arise in establishing an effective working relationship.

Most alliances that aim at sharing technology or providing market access turn out to be temporary, lasting only a few years. This is not necessarily an indicator of failure, however. Strategic alliances can be terminated after a few years simply because they have fulfilled their purpose; indeed, many alliances are intended to be of limited duration, set up to accomplish specific short-term objectives. Longer-lasting collaborative arrangements, however, may provide even greater strategic benefits. Alliances are more likely to be long-lasting when (1) they involve collaboration with partners that do not compete directly, such as suppliers or distribution allies; (2) a trusting relationship has been established; and (3) both parties conclude that continued collaboration is in their mutual interest, perhaps because new opportunities for learning are emerging.

The Drawbacks of Strategic Alliances and Partnerships

While strategic alliances provide a way of obtaining the benefits of vertical integration, mergers and acquisitions, and outsourcing, they also suffer from some of the same drawbacks. Anticipated gains may fail to materialize due to an overly optimistic view of the synergies or a poor fit in terms of the combination of resources and capabilities. When outsourcing is conducted via alliances, there is no less risk of becoming dependent on other companies for essential expertise and capabilities—indeed, this may be the Achilles' heel of such alliances. Moreover, there are additional pitfalls to collaborative arrangements. The greatest danger is that a partner will gain access to a company's proprietary knowledge base, technologies, or trade secrets, enabling the partner to match the company's core strengths and costing the company its hard-won competitive advantage. This risk is greatest when the alliance is among industry rivals or when the alliance is for the purpose of collaborative R&D, since this type of partnership requires an extensive exchange of closely held information.

The question for managers is when to engage in a strategic alliance and when to choose an alternative means of meeting their objectives. The answer to this question depends on the relative advantages of each method and the circumstances under which each type of organizational arrangement is favored.

The principal advantages of strategic alliances over vertical integration or horizontal mergers and acquisitions are threefold:

1. They lower investment costs and risks for each partner by facilitating resource pooling and risk sharing. This can be particularly important when investment needs and uncertainty are high, such as when a dominant technology standard has not yet emerged.
2. They are more flexible organizational forms and allow for a more adaptive response to changing conditions. Flexibility is essential when environmental conditions or technologies are changing rapidly. Moreover, strategic alliances under such circumstances may enable the development of each partner's dynamic capabilities.
3. They are more rapidly deployed—a critical factor when speed is of the essence. Speed is of the essence when there is a winner-take-all type of competitive situation, such as the race for a dominant technological design or a race down a steep experience curve, where there is a large first-mover advantage.

The key advantages of using strategic alliances rather than arm's-length transactions to manage outsourcing are (1) the increased ability to exercise control over the partners' activities and (2) a greater willingness for the partners to make relationship-specific investments. Arm's-length transactions discourage such investments since they imply less commitment and do not build trust.

On the other hand, there are circumstances when other organizational mechanisms are preferable to alliances and partnering. Mergers and acquisitions are especially suited for situations in which strategic alliances or partnerships do not go far enough in providing a company with access to needed resources and capabilities. Ownership ties are more permanent than partnership ties, allowing the operations of the merger or acquisition participants to be tightly integrated and creating more in-house control and autonomy. Other organizational mechanisms are also preferable to alliances when there is limited property rights protection for valuable know-how and when companies fear being taken advantage of by opportunistic partners.

While it is important for managers to understand when strategic alliances and partnerships are most likely (and least likely) to prove useful, it is also important to know how to manage them.

How to Make Strategic Alliances Work

A surprisingly large number of alliances never live up to expectations. Even though the number of strategic alliances increases by about 25 percent annually, about 60 to 70 percent of alliances continue to fail each year.[24] The success of an alliance depends on how well the partners work together, their capacity to respond and adapt to changing internal and external conditions, and their willingness to renegotiate the bargain if circumstances so warrant. A successful alliance requires real in-the-trenches collaboration, not merely an arm's-length exchange of ideas. Unless partners place a high value on the contribution each brings to the alliance and the cooperative arrangement results in valuable win–win outcomes, it is doomed to fail.

While the track record for strategic alliances is poor on average, many companies have learned how to manage strategic alliances successfully and routinely defy this average. Samsung Group, which includes Samsung Electronics, successfully manages an ecosystem of over 1,300 partnerships that enable productive activities from global procurement to local marketing to collaborative R&D. Companies that have greater success in managing their strategic alliances and partnerships often credit the following factors:

- *They create a system for managing their alliances.* Companies need to manage their alliances in a systematic fashion, just as they manage other functions. This means setting up a process for managing the different aspects of alliance management from partner selection to alliance termination procedures. To ensure that the system is followed on a routine basis by all company managers, many companies create a set of explicit procedures, process templates, manuals, or the like.
- *They build relationships with their partners and establish trust.* Establishing strong interpersonal relationships is a critical factor in making strategic alliances work since such relationships facilitate opening up channels of communication, coordinating activity, aligning interests, and building trust.
- *They protect themselves from the threat of opportunism by setting up safeguards.* There are a number of means for preventing a company from being taken advantage of by an untrustworthy partner or unwittingly losing control over key assets. Contractual safeguards, including noncompete clauses, can provide other forms of protection.
- *They make commitments to their partners and see that their partners do the same.* When partners make credible commitments to a joint enterprise, they have stronger incentives for making it work and are less likely to "free-ride" on the efforts of other partners. Because of this, equity-based alliances tend to be more successful than nonequity alliances.[25]
- *They make learning a routine part of the management process.* There are always opportunities for learning from a partner, but organizational learning does not take place automatically. Whatever learning occurs cannot add to a company's knowledge base unless the learning is incorporated systematically into the company's routines and practices.

Finally, managers should realize that alliance management is an organizational capability, much like any other. It develops over time, out of effort, experience, and learning. For this reason, it is wise to begin slowly, with simple alliances designed to meet limited, short-term objectives. Short-term partnerships that are successful often become the basis for much more extensive collaborative arrangements. Even when strategic alliances are set up with the hope that they will become long-term engagements, they have a better chance of succeeding if they are phased in so that the partners can learn how they can work together most fruitfully.

KEY POINTS

1. Once a company has settled on which of the five generic competitive strategies to employ, attention turns to how strategic choices regarding (1) competitive actions, (2) timing of those actions, and (3) scope of operations can complement its competitive approach and maximize the power of its overall strategy.
2. Strategic offensives should, as a general rule, be grounded in a company's strategic assets and employ a company's strengths to attack rivals in the competitive areas where they are weakest.

3. Companies have a number of offensive strategy options for improving their market positions: using a cost-based advantage to attack competitors on the basis of price or value, leapfrogging competitors with next-generation technologies, pursuing continuous product innovation, adopting and improving the best ideas of others, using hit-and-run tactics to steal sales away from unsuspecting rivals, and launching preemptive strikes. A blue-ocean type of offensive strategy seeks to gain a dramatic new competitive advantage by inventing a new industry or distinctive market segment that renders existing competitors largely irrelevant and allows a company to create and capture altogether new demand.
4. The purposes of defensive strategies are to lower the risk of being attacked, weaken the impact of any attack that occurs, and influence challengers to aim their efforts at other rivals. Defensive strategies to protect a company's position usually take one of two forms: (1) actions to block challengers or (2) actions to signal the likelihood of strong retaliation.
5. The timing of strategic moves also has relevance in the quest for competitive advantage. Company managers are obligated to carefully consider the advantages or disadvantages that attach to being a first mover versus a fast follower versus a late mover.
6. Decisions concerning the scope of a company's operations—which activities a firm will perform internally and which it will not—can also affect the strength of a company's market position. The *scope of the firm* refers to the range of its activities, the breadth of its product and service offerings, the extent of its geographic market presence, and its mix of businesses. Companies can expand their scope horizontally (more broadly within their focal market) or vertically (up or down the industry value chain system that starts with raw-material production and ends with sales and service to the end consumer). Horizontal mergers and acquisitions (combinations of market rivals) provide a means for a company to expand its horizontal scope. Vertical integration expands a firm's vertical scope.
7. Horizontal mergers and acquisitions typically have any of five objectives: lowering costs, expanding geographic coverage, adding product categories, gaining new technologies or other resources and capabilities, and preparing for the convergence of industries. They can strengthen a firm's competitiveness in five ways: (1) by improving the efficiency of its operations, (2) by heightening its product differentiation, (3) by reducing market rivalry, (4) by increasing the company's bargaining power over suppliers and buyers, and (5) by enhancing its flexibility and dynamic capabilities.
8. Vertical integration, forward or backward, makes most strategic sense if it strengthens a company's position via either cost reduction or creation of a differentiation-based advantage. Otherwise, the drawbacks of vertical integration (increased investment, greater business risk, increased vulnerability to technological changes, less flexibility in making product changes, and the potential for channel conflict) are likely to outweigh any advantages.
9. Outsourcing involves contracting out pieces of the value chain formerly performed in-house to outside vendors, thereby narrowing the scope of the firm. Outsourcing can enhance a company's competitiveness whenever (1) an activity can be performed better or more cheaply by outside specialists; (2) the activity is not crucial to the firm's ability to achieve sustainable competitive advantage; (3) the

outsourcing improves organizational flexibility, speeds decision making, and cuts cycle time; (4) it reduces the company's risk exposure; and (5) it permits a company to concentrate on its core business and focus on what it does best.

10. Strategic alliances and cooperative partnerships provide one way to gain some of the benefits offered by vertical integration, outsourcing, and horizontal mergers and acquisitions while minimizing the associated problems. They serve as an alternative to vertical integration and mergers and acquisitions, and as a supplement to outsourcing, allowing more control relative to outsourcing via arm's-length transactions.
11. Companies that manage their alliances well generally (1) create a system for managing their alliances, (2) build relationships with their partners and establish trust, (3) protect themselves from the threat of opportunism by setting up safeguards, (4) make commitments to their partners and see that their partners do the same, and (5) make learning a routine part of the management process.

ASSURANCE OF LEARNING EXERCISES

connect
LO 1, LO 2, LO 3

1. Live Nation operates music venues, provides management services to music artists, and promotes more than 22,000 live music events annually. The company merged with Ticketmaster and acquired concert and festival promoters in the United States, Australia, and Great Britain. How has the company used horizontal mergers and acquisitions to strengthen its competitive position? Are these moves primarily offensive or defensive? Has either Live Nation or Ticketmaster achieved any type of advantage based on the timing of its strategic moves?

connect
LO 4

2. Kaiser Permanente, a standout among managed health care systems, has become a model of how to deliver good health care cost-effectively. Illustration Capsule 6.4 describes how Kaiser Permanente has made vertical integration a central part of its strategy. What value chain segments has Kaiser Permanente chosen to enter and perform internally? How has vertical integration aided the organization in building competitive advantage? Has vertical integration strengthened its market position? Explain why or why not.

LO 5

3. Perform an Internet search to identify at least two companies in different industries that have entered into outsourcing agreements with firms with specialized services. In addition, describe what value chain activities the companies have chosen to outsource. Do any of these outsourcing agreements seem likely to threaten any of the companies' competitive capabilities?

LO 6

4. Perform a thought experiment whereby two popular specialty food stores, Trader Joe's and Whole Foods, join forces in a strategic alliance in the near future. Conduct some research on the market niches that these food stores operate in to determine whether there might be an opportunity for some kind of fruitful partnership. Explain the nature of the proposed partnership, along with its potential advantages and disadvantages and what hurdles the two companies might need to overcome in order to benefit from the strategic alliance.

EXERCISE FOR SIMULATION PARTICIPANTS

1. Has your company relied more on offensive or defensive strategies to achieve your rank in the industry? What options for being a first mover does your company have? Do any of these first-mover options hold competitive advantage potential? **LO 1, LO 2**
2. Does your company have the option to merge with or acquire other companies? If so, which rival companies would you like to acquire or merge with? **LO 3**
3. Is your company vertically integrated? Explain. **LO 4**
4. Is your company able to engage in outsourcing? If so, what do you see as the pros and cons of outsourcing? Are strategic alliances involved? Explain. **LO 5, LO 6**

ENDNOTES

[1] George Stalk, Jr., and Rob Lachenauer, "Hardball: Five Killer Strategies for Trouncing the Competition," *Harvard Business Review* 82, no. 4 (April 2004); Richard D'Aveni, "The Empire Strikes Back: Counterrevolutionary Strategies for Industry Leaders," *Harvard Business Review* 80, no. 11 (November 2002); David J. Bryce and Jeffrey H. Dyer, "Strategies to Crack Well-Guarded Markets," *Harvard Business Review* 85, no. 5 (May 2007).

[2] George Stalk, "Playing Hardball: Why Strategy Still Matters," *Ivey Business Journal* 69, no.2 (November–December 2004), pp. 1–2; W. J. Ferrier, K. G. Smith, and C. M. Grimm, "The Role of Competitive Action in Market Share Erosion and Industry Dethronement: A Study of Industry Leaders and Challengers," *Academy of Management Journal* 42, no. 4 (August 1999), pp. 372–388.

[3] David B. Yoffie and Mary Kwak, "Mastering Balance: How to Meet and Beat a Stronger Opponent," *California Management Review* 44, no. 2 (Winter 2002), pp. 8–24.

[4] Ian C. MacMillan, Alexander B. van Putten, and Rita Gunther McGrath, "Global Gamesmanship," *Harvard Business Review* 81, no. 5 (May 2003); Ashkay R. Rao, Mark E. Bergen, and Scott Davis, "How to Fight a Price War," *Harvard Business Review* 78, no. 2 (March–April 2000).

[5] D. B. Yoffie and M. A. Cusumano, "Judo Strategy–the Competitive Dynamics of Internet Time," *Harvard Business Review* 77, no. 1 (January–February 1999), pp. 70–81.

[6] Ming-Jer Chen and Donald C. Hambrick, "Speed, Stealth, and Selective Attack: How Small Firms Differ from Large Firms in Competitive Behavior," *Academy of Management Journal* 38, no. 2 (April 1995), pp. 453–482; William E. Rothschild, "Surprise and the Competitive Advantage," *Journal of Business Strategy* 4, no. 3 (Winter 1984), pp. 10–18.

[7] Ian MacMillan, "Preemptive Strategies," *Journal of Business Strategy* 14, no. 2 (Fall 1983), pp. 16–26.

[8] Ian C. MacMillan, "How Long Can You Sustain a Competitive Advantage?" in Liam Fahey (ed.), *The Strategic Planning Management Reader* (Englewood Cliffs, NJ: Prentice Hall, 1989), pp. 23–24.

[9] Kevin P. Coyne and John Horn, "Predicting Your Competitor's Reactions," *Harvard Business Review* 87, no. 4 (April 2009), pp. 90–97.

[10] Philip Kotler, *Marketing Management*, 5th ed. (Englewood Cliffs, NJ: Prentice Hall, 1984).

[11] W. Chan Kim and Renée Mauborgne, "Blue Ocean Strategy," *Harvard Business Review* 82, no. 10 (October 2004), pp. 76–84.

[12] Jeffrey G. Covin, Dennis P. Slevin, and Michael B. Heeley, "Pioneers and Followers: Competitive Tactics, Environment, and Growth," *Journal of Business Venturing* 15, no. 2 (March 1999), pp. 175–210; Christopher A. Bartlett and Sumantra Ghoshal, "Going Global: Lessons from Late-Movers," *Harvard Business Review* 78, no. 2 (March-April 2000), pp. 132–145.

[13] Costas Markides and Paul A. Geroski, "Racing to Be 2nd: Conquering the Industries of the Future," *Business Strategy Review* 15, no. 4 (Winter 2004), pp. 25–31.

[14] Fernando Suarez and Gianvito Lanzolla, "The Half-Truth of First-Mover Advantage," *Harvard Business Review* 83, no. 4 (April 2005), pp. 121–127.

[15] Joseph L. Bower, "Not All M&As Are Alike–and That Matters," *Harvard Business Review* 79, no. 3 (March 2001); O. Chatain and P. Zemsky, "The Horizontal Scope of the Firm: Organizational Tradeoffs vs. Buyer-Supplier Relationships," *Management Science* 53, no.4 (April 2007), pp. 550–565.

[16] Jeffrey H. Dyer, Prashant Kale, and Harbir Singh, "When to Ally and When to Acquire," *Harvard Business Review* 82, no. 4 (July–August 2004), pp. 109–110.

[17] John Stuckey and David White, "When and When Not to Vertically Integrate," *Sloan Management Review* (Spring 1993), pp. 71–83.

[18] Thomas Osegowitsch and Anoop Madhok, "Vertical Integration Is Dead, or Is It?" *Business Horizons* 46, no. 2 (March–April 2003), pp. 25–35.

[19] Ronan McIvor, "What Is the Right Outsourcing Strategy for Your Process?" *European Management Journal* 26, no. 1 (February 2008), pp. 24–34.

[20] Gary P. Pisano and Willy C. Shih, "Restoring American Competitiveness," *Harvard Business Review* 87, no. 7-8 (July–August 2009), pp. 114–125; Jérôme Barthélemy, "The Seven Deadly Sins of Outsourcing," *Academy of Management Executive* 17, no. 2 (May 2003), pp. 87–100.

[21] Jason Wakeam, "The Five Factors of a Strategic Alliance," *Ivey Business Journal* 68, no. 3 (May–June 2003), pp. 1–4.

[22] A. Inkpen, "Learning, Knowledge Acquisition, and Strategic Alliances," *European Management Journal* 16, no. 2 (April 1998), pp. 223–229.

[23] *Advertising Age*, May 24, 2010, p. 14.

[24] Patricia Anslinger and Justin Jenk, "Creating Successful Alliances," *Journal of Business Strategy* 25, no. 2 (2004), pp. 18–23; Rosabeth Moss Kanter, "Collaborative Advantage: The Art of the Alliance," *Harvard Business Review* 72, no. 4 (July–August 1994), pp. 96-108; Gary Hamel, Yves L. Doz, and C. K. Prahalad, "Collaborate with Your Competitors–and Win," *Harvard Business Review* 67, no. 1 (January–February 1989), pp. 133–139.

[25] Y. G. Pan and D. K. Tse, "The Hierarchical Model of Market Entry Modes," *Journal of International Business Studies* 31, no. 4 (2000), pp. 535–554.

CHAPTER 7

Strategies for Competing in International Markets

© Kenneth Batelman/Ikon Images/SuperStock

Learning Objectives

THIS CHAPTER WILL HELP YOU UNDERSTAND:

LO 1 The primary reasons companies choose to compete in international markets.

LO 2 How and why differing market conditions across countries influence a company's strategy choices in international markets.

LO 3 The five major strategic options for entering foreign markets.

LO 4 The three main strategic approaches for competing internationally.

LO 5 How companies are able to use international operations to improve overall competitiveness.

LO 6 The unique characteristics of competing in developing-country markets.

Our key words now are globalization, new products and businesses, and speed.

Tsutomu Kanai—*Former chair and president of Hitachi*

You have no choice but to operate in a world shaped by globalization and the information revolution. There are two options: Adapt or die.

Andy Grove—*Former chair and CEO of Intel*

A sharing of control with local partners will lead to a greater contribution from them, which can assist in coping with circumstances that are unfamiliar to the foreign partner.

Yanni Yan—*Business author and academic*

Any company that aspires to industry leadership in the 21st century must think in terms of global, not domestic, market leadership. The world economy is globalizing at an accelerating pace as ambitious, growth-minded companies race to build stronger competitive positions in the markets of more and more countries, as countries previously closed to foreign companies open up their markets, and as information technology shrinks the importance of geographic distance. The forces of globalization are changing the competitive landscape in many industries, offering companies attractive new opportunities and at the same time introducing new competitive threats. Companies in industries where these forces are greatest are therefore under considerable pressure to come up with a strategy for competing successfully in international markets.

This chapter focuses on strategy options for expanding beyond domestic boundaries and competing in the markets of either a few or a great many countries. In the process of exploring these options, we introduce such concepts as multidomestic, transnational, and global strategies; the Porter diamond of national competitive advantage; and profit sanctuaries. The chapter also includes sections on cross-country differences in cultural, demographic, and market conditions; strategy options for entering foreign markets; the importance of locating value chain operations in the most advantageous countries; and the special circumstances of competing in developing markets such as those in China, India, Brazil, Russia, and eastern Europe.

WHY COMPANIES DECIDE TO ENTER FOREIGN MARKETS

LO 1

The primary reasons companies choose to compete in international markets.

A company may opt to expand outside its domestic market for any of five major reasons:

1. *To gain access to new customers.* Expanding into foreign markets offers potential for increased revenues, profits, and long-term growth; it becomes an especially attractive option when a company encounters dwindling growth opportunities in its home market. Companies often expand internationally to extend the life cycle

of their products, as Honda has done with its classic 50-cc motorcycle, the Honda Cub (which is still selling well in developing markets, more than 50 years after it was first introduced in Japan). A larger target market also offers companies the opportunity to earn a return on large investments more rapidly. This can be particularly important in R&D-intensive industries, where development is fast-paced or competitors imitate innovations rapidly.

2. *To achieve lower costs through economies of scale, experience, and increased purchasing power.* Many companies are driven to sell in more than one country because domestic sales volume alone is not large enough to capture fully economies of scale in product development, manufacturing, or marketing. Similarly, firms expand internationally to increase the rate at which they accumulate experience and move down the learning curve. International expansion can also lower a company's input costs through greater pooled purchasing power. The relatively small size of country markets in Europe and limited domestic volume explains why companies like Michelin, BMW, and Nestlé long ago began selling their products all across Europe and then moved into markets in North America and Latin America.
3. *To gain access to low-cost inputs of production.* Companies in industries based on natural resources (e.g., oil and gas, minerals, rubber, and lumber) often find it necessary to operate in the international arena since raw-material supplies are located in different parts of the world and can be accessed more cost-effectively at the source. Other companies enter foreign markets to access low-cost human resources; this is particularly true of industries in which labor costs make up a high proportion of total production costs.
4. *To further exploit its core competencies.* A company may be able to extend a market-leading position in its domestic market into a position of regional or global market leadership by leveraging its core competencies further. H&M is capitalizing on its considerable expertise in online retailing to expand its reach internationally. By bringing its easy-to-use and mobile-friendly online shopping to 23 different countries, the company hopes to pave the way for setting up physical stores in these countries. Companies can often leverage their resources internationally by replicating a successful business model, using it as a basic blueprint for international operations, as Starbucks and McDonald's have done.[1]
5. *To gain access to resources and capabilities located in foreign markets.* An increasingly important motive for entering foreign markets is to acquire resources and capabilities that may be unavailable in a company's home market. Companies often make acquisitions abroad or enter into cross-border alliances to gain access to capabilities that complement their own or to learn from their partners.[2] In other cases, companies choose to establish operations in other countries to utilize local distribution networks, gain local managerial or marketing expertise, or acquire technical knowledge.

In addition, companies that are the suppliers of other companies often expand internationally when their major customers do so, to meet their customers' needs abroad and retain their position as a key supply chain partner. For example, when motor vehicle companies have opened new plants in foreign locations, big automotive parts suppliers have frequently opened new facilities nearby to permit timely delivery of their parts and components to the plant. Similarly, Newell-Rubbermaid, one of Walmart's biggest suppliers of household products, has followed Walmart into foreign markets.

WHY COMPETING ACROSS NATIONAL BORDERS MAKES STRATEGY MAKING MORE COMPLEX

Crafting a strategy to compete in one or more countries of the world is inherently more complex for five reasons. First, different countries have different home-country advantages in different industries; competing effectively requires an understanding of these differences. Second, there are location-based advantages to conducting particular value chain activities in different parts of the world. Third, different political and economic conditions make the general business climate more favorable in some countries than in others. Fourth, companies face risk due to adverse shifts in currency exchange rates when operating in foreign markets. And fifth, differences in buyer tastes and preferences present a challenge for companies concerning customizing versus standardizing their products and services.

LO 2

How and why differing market conditions across countries influence a company's strategy choices in international markets.

Home-Country Industry Advantages and the Diamond Model

Certain countries are known for their strengths in particular industries. For example, Chile has competitive strengths in industries such as copper, fruit, fish products, paper and pulp, chemicals, and wine. Japan is known for competitive strength in consumer electronics, automobiles, semiconductors, steel products, and specialty steel. Where industries are more likely to develop competitive strength depends on a set of factors that describe the nature of each country's business environment and vary from country to country. Because strong industries are made up of strong firms, the strategies of firms that expand internationally are usually grounded in one or more of these factors. The four major factors are summarized in a framework developed by Michael Porter and known as the *Diamond of National Competitive Advantage* (see Figure 7.1).[3]

Demand Conditions The demand conditions in an industry's home market include the relative size of the market, its growth potential, and the nature of domestic buyers' needs and wants. Differing population sizes, income levels, and other demographic factors give rise to considerable differences in market size and growth rates from country to country. Industry sectors that are larger and more important in their home market tend to attract more resources and grow faster than others. For example, owing to widely differing population demographics and income levels, there is a far bigger market for luxury automobiles in the United States and Germany than in Argentina, India, Mexico, and China. At the same time, in developing markets like India, China, Brazil, and Malaysia, market growth potential is far higher than it is in the more mature economies of Britain, Denmark, Canada, and Japan. The potential for market growth in automobiles is explosive in China, where 2015 sales of new vehicles amounted to 26.4 million, surpassing U.S. sales of 17.2 million and making China the world's largest market for the sixth year in a row.[4] Demanding domestic buyers for an industry's products spur greater innovativeness and improvements in quality. Such conditions foster the development of stronger industries, with firms that are capable of translating a home-market advantage into a competitive advantage in the international arena.

FIGURE 7.1 The Diamond of National Competitive Advantage

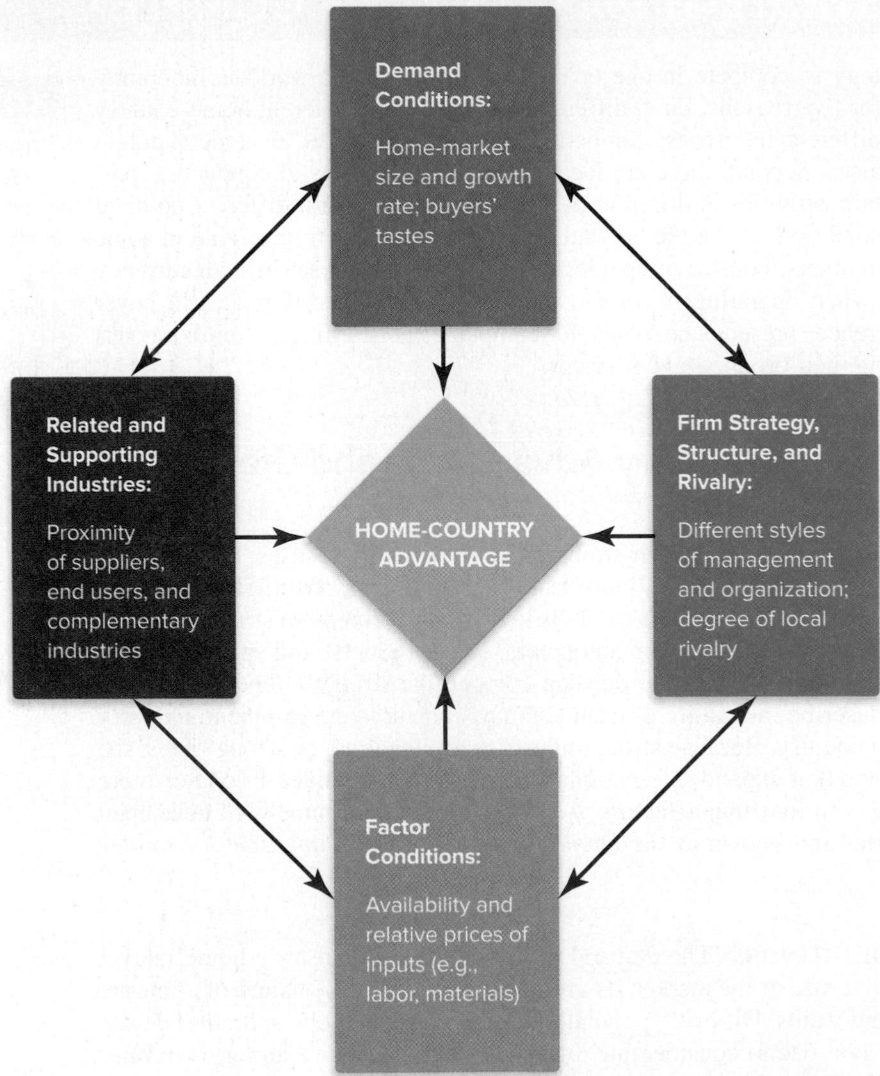

Source: Adapted from Michael E. Porter, "The Competitive Advantage of Nations," *Harvard Business Review,* March–April 1990, pp. 73–93.

Factor Conditions Factor conditions describe the availability, quality, and cost of raw materials and other inputs (called *factors of production*) that firms in an industry require for producing their products and services. The relevant factors of production vary from industry to industry but can include different types of labor, technical or managerial knowledge, land, financial capital, and natural resources. Elements of a country's infrastructure may be included as well, such as its transportation, communication, and banking systems. For instance, in India there are efficient, well-developed national channels for distributing groceries, personal care items, and other packaged products to the country's 3 million retailers, whereas in China distribution is primarily local and there is a limited national network for distributing most products. Competitively strong industries and firms develop where relevant factor conditions are favorable.

Related and Supporting Industries Robust industries often develop in locales where there is a cluster of related industries, including others within the same value chain system (e.g., suppliers of components and equipment, distributors) and the makers of complementary products or those that are technologically related. The sports car makers Ferrari and Maserati, for example, are located in an area of Italy known as the "engine technological district," which includes other firms involved in racing, such as Ducati Motorcycles, along with hundreds of small suppliers. The advantage to firms that develop as part of a related-industry cluster comes from the close collaboration with key suppliers and the greater knowledge sharing throughout the cluster, resulting in greater efficiency and innovativeness.

Firm Strategy, Structure, and Rivalry Different country environments foster the development of different styles of management, organization, and strategy. For example, strategic alliances are a more common strategy for firms from Asian or Latin American countries, which emphasize trust and cooperation in their organizations, than for firms from North America, where individualism is more influential. In addition, countries vary in terms of the competitive rivalry of their industries. Fierce rivalry in home markets tends to hone domestic firms' competitive capabilities and ready them for competing internationally.

For an industry in a particular country to become competitively strong, all four factors must be favorable for that industry. When they are, the industry is likely to contain firms that are capable of competing successfully in the international arena. Thus the diamond framework can be used to reveal the answers to several questions that are important for competing on an international basis. First, it can help predict *where foreign entrants into an industry are most likely to come from.* This can help managers prepare to cope with new foreign competitors, since the framework also reveals something about the basis of the new rivals' strengths. Second, it can reveal the countries in which foreign rivals are likely to be weakest and thus can help managers decide *which foreign markets to enter first.* And third, because it focuses on the attributes of a country's business environment that allow firms to flourish, it reveals something about the advantages of conducting particular business activities in that country. Thus the diamond framework is an aid to deciding *where to locate different value chain activities most beneficially*—a topic that we address next.

Opportunities for Location-Based Advantages

Increasingly, companies are locating different value chain activities in different parts of the world to exploit location-based advantages that vary from country to country. This is particularly evident with respect to the location of manufacturing activities. Differences in wage rates, worker productivity, energy costs, and the like create sizable variations in manufacturing costs from country to country. By locating its plants in certain countries, firms in some industries can reap major manufacturing cost advantages because of lower input costs (especially labor), relaxed government regulations, the proximity of suppliers and technologically related industries, or unique natural resources. In such cases, the low-cost countries become principal production sites, with most of the output being exported to markets in other parts of the world. Companies that build production facilities in low-cost countries (or that source their products from contract manufacturers in these countries) gain a competitive advantage over rivals with plants in countries where costs are higher. The competitive role of low manufacturing costs is most evident in low-wage countries like China, India,

Pakistan, Cambodia, Vietnam, Mexico, Brazil, Guatemala, the Philippines, and several countries in Africa and eastern Europe that have become production havens for manufactured goods with high labor content (especially textiles and apparel). Hourly compensation for manufacturing workers in 2013 averaged about $1.46 in India, $2.12 in the Philippines, $3.07 in China, $6.82 in Mexico, $9.37 in Taiwan, $9.44 in Hungary, $10.69 in Brazil, $12.90 in Portugal, $21.96 in South Korea, $25.85 in New Zealand, $29.13 in Japan, $36.33 in Canada, $36.34 in the United States, $48.98 in Germany, and $65.86 in Norway.[5] China emerged as the manufacturing capital of the world in large part because of its low wages—virtually all of the world's major manufacturing companies now have facilities in China. This in turn has driven up their wages to nearly double the average wage offered in 2012.

For other types of value chain activities, input quality or availability are more important considerations. Tiffany & Co. entered the mining industry in Canada to access diamonds that could be certified as "conflict free" and not associated with either the funding of African wars or unethical mining conditions. Many U.S. companies locate call centers in countries such as India and Ireland, where English is spoken and the workforce is well educated. Other companies locate R&D activities in countries where there are prestigious research institutions and well-trained scientists and engineers. Likewise, concerns about short delivery times and low shipping costs make some countries better locations than others for establishing distribution centers.

The Impact of Government Policies and Economic Conditions in Host Countries

Cross-country variations in government policies and economic conditions affect both the opportunities available to a foreign entrant and the risks of operating within the host country. The governments of some countries are eager to attract foreign investments, and thus they go all out to create a business climate that outsiders will view as favorable. Governments eager to spur economic growth, create more jobs, and raise living standards for their citizens usually enact policies aimed at stimulating business innovation and capital investment; Ireland is a good example. They may provide such incentives as reduced taxes, low-cost loans, site location and site development assistance, and government-sponsored training for workers to encourage companies to construct production and distribution facilities. When new business-related issues or developments arise, "pro-business" governments make a practice of seeking advice and counsel from business leaders. When tougher business-related regulations are deemed appropriate, they endeavor to make the transition to more costly and stringent regulations somewhat business-friendly rather than adversarial.

On the other hand, governments sometimes enact policies that, from a business perspective, make locating facilities within a country's borders less attractive. For example, the nature of a company's operations may make it particularly costly to achieve compliance with a country's environmental regulations. Some governments provide subsidies and low-interest loans to domestic companies to enable them to better compete against foreign companies. To discourage foreign imports, governments may enact deliberately burdensome procedures and requirements regarding customs inspection for foreign goods and may impose tariffs or quotas on imports. Additionally, they may specify that a certain percentage of the parts and components used in manufacturing a product be obtained from local suppliers, require prior approval of capital spending projects, limit withdrawal of funds from the country, and require partial ownership of foreign company operations by local companies or investors. There are times when a government may place restrictions on exports to ensure adequate local supplies and regulate the prices of imported and locally produced goods. Such government actions make a country's business climate less attractive and in some cases may be sufficiently onerous as to discourage a company from locating facilities in that country or even selling its products there.

A country's business climate is also a function of the political and economic risks associated with operating within its borders. **Political risks** have to do with the instability of weak governments, growing possibilities that a country's citizenry will revolt against dictatorial government leaders, the likelihood of new onerous legislation or regulations on foreign-owned businesses, and the potential for future elections to produce corrupt or tyrannical government leaders. In industries that a government deems critical to the national welfare, there is sometimes a risk that the government will nationalize the industry and expropriate the assets of foreign companies. In 2012, for example, Argentina nationalized the country's top oil producer, YPF, which was owned by Spanish oil major Repsol. Other political risks include the loss of investments due to war or political unrest, regulatory changes that create operating uncertainties, security risks due to terrorism, and corruption. **Economic risks** have to do with instability of a country's economy and monetary system—whether inflation rates might skyrocket or whether uncontrolled deficit spending on the part of government or risky bank lending practices could lead to a breakdown of the country's monetary system and prolonged economic distress. In some countries, the threat of piracy and lack of protection for intellectual property are also sources of economic risk. Another is fluctuations in the value of different currencies—a factor that we discuss in more detail next.

CORE CONCEPT

Political risks stem from instability or weakness in national governments and hostility to foreign business. **Economic risks** stem from instability in a country's monetary system, economic and regulatory policies, and the lack of property rights protections.

The Risks of Adverse Exchange Rate Shifts

When companies produce and market their products and services in many different countries, they are subject to the impacts of sometimes favorable and sometimes unfavorable changes in currency exchange rates. The rates of exchange between different currencies can vary by as much as 20 to 40 percent annually, with the changes occurring sometimes gradually and sometimes swiftly. *Sizable shifts in exchange rates pose significant risks for two reasons:*

1. They are hard to predict because of the variety of factors involved and the uncertainties surrounding when and by how much these factors will change.
2. They create uncertainty regarding which countries represent the low-cost manufacturing locations and which rivals have the upper hand in the marketplace.

To illustrate the economic and competitive risks associated with fluctuating exchange rates, consider the case of a U.S. company that has located manufacturing facilities in Brazil (where the currency is *reals*—pronounced "ray-alls") and that exports most of the Brazilian-made goods to markets in the European Union (where the currency is euros). To keep the numbers simple, assume that the exchange rate is 4 Brazilian reals for 1 euro and that the product being made in Brazil has a manufacturing cost of 4 Brazilian reals (or 1 euro). Now suppose that the exchange rate shifts from 4 reals per euro to 5 reals per euro (meaning that the real has declined in value and that the euro is stronger). Making the product in Brazil is now more cost-competitive because a Brazilian good costing 4 reals to produce has fallen to only 0.8 euro at the new exchange rate (4 reals divided by 5 reals per euro = 0.8 euro). This clearly puts the producer of the Brazilian-made good *in a better position to compete* against the European makers of the same good. On the other hand, should the value of the Brazilian real grow stronger in relation to the euro—resulting in an exchange rate of 3 reals to 1 euro—the same Brazilian-made good formerly costing 4 reals (or 1 euro) to produce now has a cost of 1.33 euros (4 reals divided by 3 reals per euro = 1.33 euros), putting the producer of the Brazilian-made good in a weaker competitive position vis-à-vis the European producers. Plainly, the attraction of manufacturing a good in Brazil and selling it in Europe is far greater when the euro is strong (an exchange rate of 1 euro for 5 Brazilian reals) than when the euro is weak and exchanges for only 3 Brazilian reals.

But there is one more piece to the story. When the exchange rate changes from 4 reals per euro to 5 reals per euro, not only is the cost-competitiveness of the Brazilian manufacturer stronger relative to European manufacturers of the same item but the Brazilian-made good that formerly cost 1 euro and now costs only 0.8 euro can also be sold to consumers in the European Union for a lower euro price than before. In other words, the combination of a stronger euro and a weaker real acts to *lower the price of Brazilian-made goods* in all the countries that are members of the European Union, which is likely to *spur sales of the Brazilian-made good in Europe and boost Brazilian exports to Europe.* Conversely, should the exchange rate shift from 4 reals per euro to 3 reals per euro—which makes the Brazilian manufacturer less cost-competitive with European manufacturers of the same item—the Brazilian-made good that formerly cost 1 euro and now costs 1.33 euros will sell for a higher price in euros than before, thus weakening the demand of European consumers for Brazilian-made goods and acting to reduce Brazilian exports to Europe. Brazilian exporters are likely to experience (1) rising demand for their goods in Europe whenever the Brazilian real grows weaker relative to the euro and (2) falling demand for their goods in Europe whenever the real grows stronger relative to the euro. Consequently, from the standpoint of a company with Brazilian manufacturing plants, *a weaker Brazilian real is a favorable exchange rate shift* and *a stronger Brazilian real is an unfavorable exchange rate shift.*

It follows from the previous discussion that shifting exchange rates have a big impact on the ability of domestic manufacturers to compete with foreign rivals. For example, U.S.-based manufacturers locked in a fierce competitive battle with low-cost foreign imports benefit from a *weaker* U.S. dollar. There are several reasons why this is so:

- Declines in the value of the U.S. dollar against foreign currencies raise the U.S. dollar costs of goods manufactured by foreign rivals at plants located in the countries whose currencies have grown stronger relative to the U.S. dollar. A *weaker* dollar acts to reduce or eliminate whatever cost advantage foreign manufacturers may have had over U.S. manufacturers (and helps protect the manufacturing jobs of U.S. workers).
- A *weaker* dollar makes foreign-made goods more expensive in dollar terms to U.S. consumers—this curtails U.S. buyer demand for foreign-made goods, stimulates greater demand on the part of U.S. consumers for U.S.-made goods, and reduces U.S. imports of foreign-made goods.
- A *weaker* U.S. dollar enables the U.S.-made goods to be sold at lower prices to consumers in countries whose currencies have grown stronger relative to the U.S. dollar—such lower prices boost foreign buyer demand for the now relatively cheaper U.S.-made goods, thereby stimulating exports of U.S.-made goods to foreign countries and creating more jobs in U.S.-based manufacturing plants.

- A *weaker* dollar has the effect of increasing the dollar value of profits a company earns in foreign-country markets where the local currency is stronger relative to the dollar. For example, if a U.S.-based manufacturer earns a profit of €10 million on its sales in Europe, those €10 million convert to a larger number of dollars when the dollar grows weaker against the euro.

Fluctuating exchange rates pose significant economic risks to a company's competitiveness in foreign markets. Exporters are disadvantaged when the currency of the country where goods are being manufactured grows stronger relative to the currency of the importing country.

A weaker U.S. dollar is therefore an economically favorable exchange rate shift for manufacturing plants based in the United States. A decline in the value of the U.S. dollar strengthens the cost-competitiveness of U.S.-based manufacturing plants and boosts buyer demand for U.S.-made goods. When the value of the U.S. dollar is expected to remain weak for some time to come, foreign companies have an incentive to build manufacturing facilities in the United States to make goods for U.S. consumers rather than export the same goods to the United States from foreign plants where production costs in dollar terms have been driven up by the decline in the value of the dollar. Conversely, a *stronger* U.S. dollar is an *unfavorable exchange rate shift* for U.S.-based manufacturing plants because it makes such plants less cost-competitive with foreign plants and weakens foreign demand for U.S.-made goods. A strong dollar also weakens the incentive of foreign companies to locate manufacturing facilities in the United States to make goods for U.S. consumers. The same reasoning applies to companies that have plants in countries in the European Union where euros are the local currency. A weak euro versus other currencies enhances the cost-competitiveness of companies manufacturing goods in Europe vis-à-vis foreign rivals with plants in countries whose currencies have grown stronger relative to the euro; a strong euro versus other currencies weakens the cost-competitiveness of companies with plants in the European Union.

Domestic companies facing competitive pressure from lower-cost imports benefit when their government's currency grows *weaker* in relation to the currencies of the countries where the lower-cost imports are being made.

Cross-Country Differences in Demographic, Cultural, and Market Conditions

Buyer tastes for a particular product or service sometimes differ substantially from country to country. In France, consumers prefer top-loading washing machines, whereas in most other European countries consumers prefer front-loading machines. People in Hong Kong prefer compact appliances, but in Taiwan large appliances are more popular. Novelty ice cream flavors like eel, shark fin, and dried shrimp have more appeal to East Asian customers than they have for customers in the United States and in Europe. Sometimes, product designs suitable in one country are inappropriate in another because of differing local standards—for example, in the United States electrical devices run on 110-volt electric systems, but in some European countries the standard is a 240-volt electric system, necessitating the use of different electrical designs and components. Cultural influences can also affect consumer demand for a product. For instance, in South Korea many parents are reluctant to purchase PCs even when they can afford them because of concerns that their children will be distracted from their schoolwork by surfing the Web, playing PC-based video games, and becoming Internet "addicts."[6]

Consequently, companies operating in an international marketplace have to wrestle with *whether and how much to customize their offerings in each country market to match local buyers' tastes and preferences or whether to pursue a strategy of offering a mostly standardized product worldwide.* While making products that are closely matched to local tastes makes them more appealing to local buyers, customizing a company's products country by country may raise production and distribution costs due to the greater variety of designs and components, shorter production runs, and the complications of added inventory handling and distribution logistics. Greater standardization of a global company's product offering, on the other hand, can lead to scale economies and learning-curve effects, thus reducing per-unit production costs and contributing to the achievement of a low-cost advantage. *The tension between the market pressures to localize a company's product offerings country by country and the competitive pressures to lower costs is one of the big strategic issues that participants in foreign markets have to resolve.*

STRATEGIC OPTIONS FOR ENTERING INTERNATIONAL MARKETS

LO 3

The five major strategic options for entering foreign markets.

Once a company decides to expand beyond its domestic borders, it must consider the question of how to enter foreign markets. There are five primary strategic options for doing so:

1. Maintain a home-country production base and *export* goods to foreign markets.
2. *License* foreign firms to produce and distribute the company's products abroad.
3. Employ a *franchising* strategy in foreign markets.
4. Establish a *subsidiary* in a foreign market via acquisition or internal development.
5. Rely on *strategic alliances* or joint ventures with foreign companies.

Which option to employ depends on a variety of factors, including the nature of the firm's strategic objectives, the firm's position in terms of whether it has the full range of resources and capabilities needed to operate abroad, country-specific factors such as trade barriers, and the transaction costs involved (the costs of contracting with a partner and monitoring its compliance with the terms of the contract, for example). The options vary considerably regarding the level of investment required and the associated risks—but higher levels of investment and risk generally provide the firm with the benefits of greater ownership and control.

Export Strategies

Using domestic plants as a production base for exporting goods to foreign markets is an excellent initial strategy for pursuing international sales. It is a conservative way to test the international waters. The amount of capital needed to begin exporting is often minimal; existing production capacity may well be sufficient to make goods for export. With an export-based entry strategy, a manufacturer can limit its involvement in foreign markets by contracting with foreign wholesalers experienced in importing to handle the entire distribution and marketing function in their countries or regions of the world. If it is more advantageous to maintain control over these functions, however, a manufacturer can establish its own distribution and sales organizations in some or all of the target foreign markets. Either way, a home-based production and export strategy helps the firm minimize its direct investments in foreign countries. Such strategies are commonly favored by Chinese, Korean, and Italian companies—products are designed and manufactured at home and then distributed through local channels in the importing countries. The primary functions performed abroad relate chiefly to establishing a network of distributors and perhaps conducting sales promotion and brand-awareness activities.

Whether an export strategy can be pursued successfully over the long run depends on the relative cost-competitiveness of the home-country production base. In some industries, firms gain additional scale economies and learning-curve benefits from centralizing production in plants whose output capability exceeds demand in any one country market; exporting enables a firm to capture such economies. However, an export strategy is vulnerable when (1) manufacturing costs in the home country are substantially higher than in foreign countries where rivals have plants, (2) the costs of shipping the product to distant foreign markets are relatively high, (3) adverse shifts occur in currency exchange rates, and (4) importing countries impose tariffs or erect other trade barriers. Unless an exporter can keep its production and shipping costs competitive with rivals' costs, secure adequate local distribution and marketing support of its products, and effectively hedge against unfavorable changes in currency exchange rates, its success will be limited.

Licensing Strategies

Licensing as an entry strategy makes sense when a firm with valuable technical know-how, an appealing brand, or a unique patented product has neither the internal organizational capability nor the resources to enter foreign markets. Licensing also has the advantage of avoiding the risks of committing resources to country markets that are unfamiliar, politically volatile, economically unstable, or otherwise risky. By licensing the technology, trademark, or production rights to foreign-based firms, a company can generate income from royalties while shifting the costs and risks of entering foreign markets to the licensee. The big disadvantage of licensing is the risk of providing valuable technological know-how to foreign companies and thereby losing some degree of control over its use; monitoring licensees and safeguarding the company's proprietary know-how can prove quite difficult in some circumstances. But if the royalty potential is considerable and the companies to which the licenses are being granted are trustworthy and reputable, then licensing can be a very attractive option. Many software and pharmaceutical companies use licensing strategies to participate in foreign markets.

Franchising Strategies

While licensing works well for manufacturers and owners of proprietary technology, franchising is often better suited to the international expansion efforts of service and retailing enterprises. McDonald's, Yum! Brands (the parent of Pizza Hut, KFC, Taco Bell, and WingStreet), the UPS Store, Roto-Rooter, 7-Eleven, and Hilton Hotels have all used franchising to build a presence in foreign markets. Franchising has many of the same advantages as licensing. The franchisee bears most of the costs and risks of establishing foreign locations; a franchisor has to expend only the resources to recruit, train, support, and monitor franchisees. The problem a franchisor faces is maintaining quality control; foreign franchisees do not always exhibit strong commitment to consistency and standardization, especially when the local culture does not stress the same kinds of quality concerns. A question that can arise is whether to allow foreign franchisees to make modifications in the franchisor's product offering so as to better satisfy the tastes and expectations of local buyers. Should McDonald's give franchisees in each nation some leeway in what products they put on their menus?

Should franchised KFC units in China be permitted to substitute spices that appeal to Chinese consumers? Or should the same menu offerings be rigorously and unvaryingly required of all franchisees worldwide?

CORE CONCEPT

A **greenfield venture** (or internal startup) is a subsidiary business that is established by setting up the entire operation from the ground up.

Foreign Subsidiary Strategies

Very often companies electing to compete internationally or globally prefer to have direct control over all aspects of operating in a foreign market. Companies that want to direct performance of all essential value chain activities typically establish a wholly owned subsidiary, either by acquiring a local company or by establishing its own new operating organization from the ground up. A subsidiary business that is established internally from scratch is called an *internal startup* or a **greenfield venture.**

Acquiring a local business is the quicker of the two options; it may be the least risky and most cost-efficient means of hurdling such entry barriers as gaining access to local distribution channels, building supplier relationships, and establishing working relationships with government officials and other key constituencies. Buying an ongoing operation allows the acquirer to move directly to the task of transferring resources and personnel to the newly acquired business, redirecting and integrating the activities of the acquired business into its own operation, putting its own strategy into place, and accelerating efforts to build a strong market position.

One thing an acquisition-minded firm must consider is whether to pay a premium price for a successful local company or to buy a struggling competitor at a bargain price. If the buying firm has little knowledge of the local market but ample capital, it is often better off purchasing a capable, strongly positioned firm. However, when the acquirer sees promising ways to transform a weak firm into a strong one and has the resources and managerial know-how to do so, a struggling company can be the better long-term investment.

Entering a new foreign country via a greenfield venture makes sense when a company already operates in a number of countries, has experience in establishing new subsidiaries and overseeing their operations, and has a sufficiently large pool of resources and capabilities to rapidly equip a new subsidiary with the personnel and competencies it needs to compete successfully and profitably. Four other conditions make a greenfield venture strategy appealing:

- When creating an internal startup is cheaper than making an acquisition.
- When adding new production capacity will not adversely impact the supply–demand balance in the local market.
- When a startup subsidiary has the ability to gain good distribution access (perhaps because of the company's recognized brand name).
- When a startup subsidiary will have the size, cost structure, and capabilities to compete head-to-head against local rivals.

Greenfield ventures in foreign markets can also pose problems, just as other entry strategies do. They represent a costly capital investment, subject to a high level of risk. They require numerous other company resources as well, diverting them from other uses. They do not work well in countries without strong, well-functioning markets and institutions that protect the rights of foreign investors and provide other legal protections. Moreover, an important disadvantage of greenfield ventures relative to other means of international expansion is that they are the slowest entry route—particularly if the objective is to achieve a sizable market share. On the other hand, successful greenfield ventures may offer higher returns to compensate for their high risk and slower path.

Alliance and Joint Venture Strategies

Collaborative strategies involving alliances or joint ventures with foreign partners are a popular way for companies to edge their way into the markets of foreign countries.

Strategic alliances, joint ventures, and other cooperative agreements with foreign companies are a widely used means of entering foreign markets.[7] A company can benefit immensely from a foreign partner's familiarity with local government regulations, its knowledge of the buying habits and product preferences of consumers, its distribution-channel relationships, and so on.[8] Both Japanese and American companies are actively forming alliances with European companies to better compete in the 27-nation European Union (and the five countries that are candidates to become EU members). Many U.S. and European companies are allying with Asian companies in their efforts to enter markets in China, India, Thailand, Indonesia, and other Asian countries.

Cross-border alliances enable a growth-minded company to widen its geographic coverage and strengthen its competitiveness in foreign markets; at the same time, they offer flexibility and allow a company to retain some degree of autonomy and operating control.

Another reason for cross-border alliances is to capture economies of scale in production and/or marketing. By joining forces in producing components, assembling models, and marketing their products, companies can realize cost savings not achievable with their own small volumes. A third reason to employ a collaborative strategy is to share distribution facilities and dealer networks, thus mutually strengthening each partner's access to buyers. A fourth benefit of a collaborative strategy is the learning and added expertise that comes from performing joint research, sharing technological know-how, studying one another's manufacturing methods, and understanding how to tailor sales and marketing approaches to fit local cultures and traditions. A fifth benefit is that cross-border allies can direct their competitive energies more toward mutual rivals and less toward one another; teaming up may help them close the gap on leading companies. And, finally, alliances can be a particularly useful way for companies across the world to gain agreement on important technical standards—they have been used to arrive at standards for assorted PC devices, Internet-related technologies, high-definition televisions, and mobile phones.

Cross-border alliances are an attractive means of gaining the aforementioned types of benefits (as compared to merging with or acquiring foreign-based companies) because they allow a company to preserve its independence (which is not the case with a merger) and avoid using scarce financial resources to fund acquisitions. Furthermore, an alliance offers the flexibility to readily disengage once its purpose has been served or if the benefits prove elusive, whereas mergers and acquisitions are more permanent arrangements.[9]

Alliances may also be used to pave the way for an intended merger; they offer a way to test the value and viability of a cooperative arrangement with a foreign partner before making a more permanent commitment. Illustration Capsule 7.1 shows how Walgreens pursued this strategy with Alliance Boots in order to facilitate its expansion abroad.

The Risks of Strategic Alliances with Foreign Partners Alliances and joint ventures with foreign partners have their pitfalls, however. Sometimes a local partner's knowledge and expertise turns out to be less valuable than expected (because its knowledge is rendered obsolete by fast-changing market conditions or because its operating practices are archaic). Cross-border allies typically must overcome language and cultural barriers and figure out how to deal with diverse (or conflicting) operating practices. The transaction costs of working out a mutually agreeable

ILLUSTRATION CAPSULE 7.1

Walgreens Boots Alliance, Inc.: Entering Foreign Markets via Alliance Followed by Merger

Walgreens pharmacy began in 1901 as a single store on the South Side of Chicago, and grew to become the largest chain of pharmacy retailers in America. Walgreens was an early pioneer of the "self-service" pharmacy and found success by moving quickly to build a vast domestic network of stores after the Second World War. This growth-focused strategy served Walgreens well up until the beginning of the 21st century, by which time it had nearly saturated the U.S. market. By 2014, 75 percent of Americans lived within five miles of a Walgreens. The company was also facing threats to its core business model. Walgreens relies heavily on pharmacy sales, which generally are paid for by someone other than the patient, usually the government or an insurance company. As the government and insurers started to make a more sustained effort to cut costs, Walgreens's core profit center was at risk. To mitigate these threats, Walgreens looked to enter foreign markets.

© Michael Nagle/Bloomberg via Getty Images

Walgreens found an ideal international partner in Alliance Boots. Based in the UK, Alliance Boots had a global footprint with 3,300 stores across 10 countries. A partnership with Alliance Boots had several strategic advantages, allowing Walgreens to gain swift entry into foreign markets as well as complementary assets and expertise. First, it gave Walgreens access to new markets beyond the saturated United States for its retail pharmacies. Second, it provided Walgreens with a new revenue stream in wholesale drugs. Alliance Boots held a vast European distribution network for wholesale drug sales; Walgreens could leverage that network and expertise to build a similar model in the United States. Finally, a merger with Alliance Boots would strengthen Walgreens's existing business by increasing the company's market position and therefore bargaining power with drug companies. In light of these advantages, Walgreens moved quickly to partner with and later acquire Alliance Boots and merged both companies in 2014 to become Walgreens Boots Alliance. Walgreens Boots Alliance, Inc. is now one of the world's largest drug purchasers, able to negotiate from a strong position with drug companies and other suppliers to realize economies of scale in its current businesses.

The market has thus far responded favorably to the merger. Walgreens Boots Alliance's stock has more than doubled in value since the first news of the partnership in 2012. However, the company is still struggling to integrate and faces new risks such as currency fluctuation in its new combined position. Yet as the pharmaceutical industry continues to consolidate, Walgreens is in an undoubtedly stronger position to continue to grow in the future thanks to its strategic international acquisition.

Note: Developed with Katherine Coster.

Sources: Company 10-K Form, 2015, **investor.walgreensbootsalliance.com/secfiling.cfm?filingID=1140361-15-38791&CIK=1618921**; L. Capron and W. Mitchell, "When to Change a Winning Strategy," *Harvard Business Review*, July 25, 2012, **hbr.org/2012/07/when-to-change-a-winning-strat**; T. Martin and R. Dezember, "Walgreen Spends $6.7 Billion on Alliance Boots Stake," *The Wall Street Journal*, June 20, 2012.

arrangement and monitoring partner compliance with the terms of the arrangement can be high. The communication, trust building, and coordination costs are not trivial in terms of management time.[10] Often, partners soon discover they have conflicting objectives and strategies, deep differences of opinion about how to proceed, or important differences in corporate values and ethical standards. Tensions build, working relationships cool, and the hoped-for benefits never materialize.[11] It is not unusual for there to be little personal chemistry among some of the key people on whom the success or failure of the alliance depends—the rapport such personnel need to work well together may never emerge. And even if allies are able to develop productive personal relationships, they can still have trouble reaching mutually agreeable ways to deal with key issues or launching new initiatives fast enough to stay abreast of rapid advances in technology or shifting market conditions.

One worrisome problem with alliances or joint ventures is that a firm may risk losing some of its competitive advantage if an alliance partner is given full access to its proprietary technological expertise or other competitively valuable capabilities. There is a natural tendency for allies to struggle to collaborate effectively in competitively sensitive areas, thus spawning suspicions on both sides about forthright exchanges of information and expertise. It requires many meetings of many people working in good faith over a period of time to iron out what is to be shared, what is to remain proprietary, and how the cooperative arrangements will work.

Even if the alliance proves to be a win–win proposition for both parties, there is the danger of becoming overly dependent on foreign partners for essential expertise and competitive capabilities. Companies aiming for global market leadership need to develop their own resource capabilities in order to be masters of their destiny. Frequently, experienced international companies operating in 50 or more countries across the world find less need for entering into cross-border alliances than do companies in the early stages of globalizing their operations.[12] Companies with global operations make it a point to develop senior managers who understand how "the system" works in different countries, plus they can avail themselves of local managerial talent and know-how by simply hiring experienced local managers and thereby detouring the hazards of collaborative alliances with local companies. One of the lessons about cross-border partnerships is that they are more effective in helping a company establish a beachhead of new opportunity in world markets than they are in enabling a company to achieve and sustain global market leadership.

INTERNATIONAL STRATEGY: THE THREE MAIN APPROACHES

LO 4

The three main strategic approaches for competing internationally.

Broadly speaking, a firm's **international strategy** is simply its strategy for competing in two or more countries simultaneously. Typically, a company will start to compete internationally by entering one or perhaps a select few foreign markets—selling its products or services in countries where there is a ready market for them. But as it expands further internationally, it will have to confront head-on two conflicting pressures: the demand for responsiveness to local needs versus the prospect of efficiency gains from offering a standardized product globally. Deciding on the degree to vary its competitive approach to fit the specific market conditions and buyer preferences in each host country is perhaps the foremost strategic issue that must be addressed when a company is operating in two or more foreign markets.[13] Figure 7.2 shows a company's three options for resolving this issue: choosing a *multidomestic, global,* or *transnational* strategy.

CORE CONCEPT

An **international strategy** is a strategy for competing in two or more countries simultaneously.

FIGURE 7.2 Three Approaches for Competing Internationally

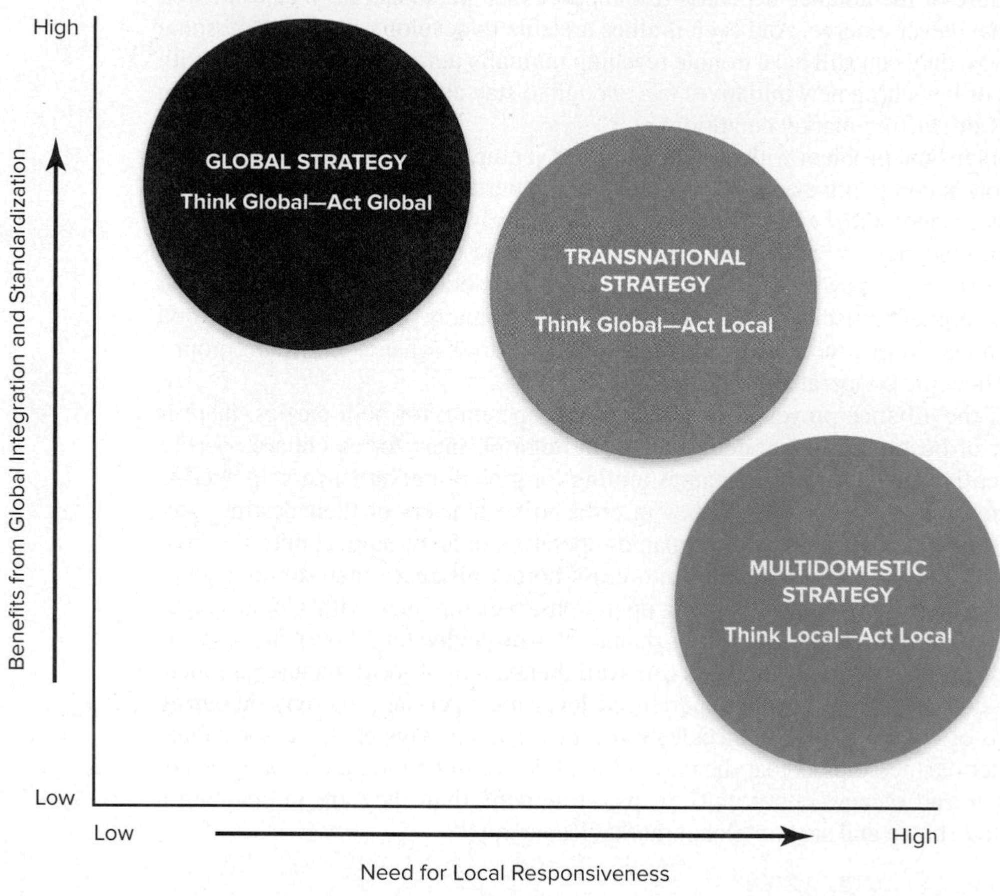

Multidomestic Strategies—a "Think-Local, Act-Local" Approach

> **CORE CONCEPT**
>
> A **multidomestic strategy** is one in which a company varies its product offering and competitive approach from country to country in an effort to be responsive to differing buyer preferences and market conditions. It is a **think-local, act-local** type of international strategy, facilitated by decision making decentralized to the local level.

A **multidomestic strategy** is one in which a company varies its product offering and competitive approach from country to country in an effort to meet differing buyer needs and to address divergent local-market conditions. It involves having plants produce different product versions for different local markets and adapting marketing and distribution to fit local customs, cultures, regulations, and market requirements. Castrol, a specialist in oil lubricants, produces over 3,000 different formulas of lubricants to meet the requirements of different climates, vehicle types and uses, and equipment applications that characterize different country markets. In the food products industry, it is common for companies to vary the ingredients in their products and sell the localized versions under local brand names to cater to country-specific tastes and eating preferences. Government requirements for gasoline additives that help reduce carbon monoxide, smog, and other emissions are almost never the same from country to country. BP utilizes localized strategies in its gasoline and service station business segment because of these cross-country formulation differences and because of customer familiarity with local brand names. For example, the company markets gasoline in the United States under its BP and Arco brands, but markets gasoline in Germany, Belgium, Poland, Hungary, and the Czech Republic under the Aral brand.

In essence, a multidomestic strategy represents a **think-local, act-local** approach to international strategy. A think-local, act-local approach to strategy making is most appropriate when the need for local responsiveness is high due to significant cross-country differences in demographic, cultural, and market conditions and when the potential for efficiency gains from standardization is limited, as depicted in Figure 7.2. A think-local, act-local approach is possible only when decision making is decentralized, giving local managers considerable latitude for crafting and executing strategies for the country markets they are responsible for. Giving local managers decision-making authority allows them to address specific market needs and respond swiftly to local changes in demand. It also enables them to focus their competitive efforts, stake out attractive market positions vis-à-vis local competitors, react to rivals' moves in a timely fashion, and target new opportunities as they emerge.[14]

Despite their obvious benefits, think-local, act-local strategies have three big drawbacks:

1. They hinder transfer of a company's capabilities, knowledge, and other resources across country boundaries, since the company's efforts are not integrated or coordinated across country boundaries. This can make the company less innovative overall.
2. They raise production and distribution costs due to the greater variety of designs and components, shorter production runs for each product version, and complications of added inventory handling and distribution logistics.
3. They are not conducive to building a single, worldwide competitive advantage. When a company's competitive approach and product offering vary from country to country, the nature and size of any resulting competitive edge also tends to vary. At the most, multidomestic strategies are capable of producing a group of local competitive advantages of varying types and degrees of strength.

Global Strategies—a "Think-Global, Act-Global" Approach

A **global strategy** contrasts sharply with a multidomestic strategy in that it takes a standardized, globally integrated approach to producing, packaging, selling, and delivering the company's products and services worldwide. Companies employing a global strategy sell the same products under the same brand names everywhere, utilize much the same distribution channels in all countries, and compete on the basis of the same capabilities and marketing approaches worldwide. Although the company's strategy or product offering may be adapted in minor ways to accommodate specific situations in a few host countries, the company's fundamental competitive approach (low cost, differentiation, best cost, or focused) remains very much intact worldwide and local managers stick close to the global strategy.

A **think-global, act-global** approach prompts company managers to integrate and coordinate the company's strategic moves worldwide and to expand into most, if not all, nations where there is significant buyer demand. It puts considerable strategic emphasis on building a *global* brand name and aggressively pursuing opportunities to transfer ideas, new products, and capabilities from one country to another. Global strategies are characterized by relatively centralized value chain activities, such as production and distribution. While there may be more than one manufacturing plant and distribution center to minimize transportation costs, for example, they tend to be few in number. Achieving the efficiency potential of a global strategy requires that resources and best practices be shared, value chain

CORE CONCEPT

A **global strategy** is one in which a company employs the same basic competitive approach in all countries where it operates, sells standardized products globally, strives to build global brands, and coordinates its actions worldwide with strong headquarters control. It represents a **think-global, act-global** approach.

activities be integrated, and capabilities be transferred from one location to another as they are developed. These objectives are best facilitated through centralized decision making and strong headquarters control.

Because a global strategy cannot accommodate varying local needs, it is an appropriate strategic choice when there are pronounced efficiency benefits from standardization and when buyer needs are relatively homogeneous across countries and regions. A globally standardized and integrated approach is especially beneficial when high volumes significantly lower costs due to economies of scale or added experience (moving the company further down a learning curve). It can also be advantageous if it allows the firm to replicate a successful business model on a global basis efficiently or engage in higher levels of R&D by spreading the fixed costs and risks over a higher-volume output. It is a fitting response to industry conditions marked by global competition.

Ford's global design strategy is a move toward a think-global, act-global strategy, involving the development and production of standardized models with country-specific modifications limited to what is required to meet local country emission and safety standards. The 2010 Ford Fiesta and 2011 Ford Focus were the company's first global design models to be marketed in Europe, North America, Asia, and Australia. Whenever country-to-country differences are small enough to be accommodated within the framework of a global strategy, a global strategy is preferable because a company can more readily unify its operations and focus on establishing a brand image and reputation that are uniform from country to country. Moreover, with a global strategy a company is better able to focus its full resources on securing a sustainable low-cost or differentiation-based competitive advantage over both domestic rivals and global rivals.

There are, however, several drawbacks to global strategies: (1) They do not enable firms to address local needs as precisely as locally based rivals can; (2) they are less responsive to changes in local market conditions, in the form of either new opportunities or competitive threats; (3) they raise transportation costs and may involve higher tariffs; and (4) they involve higher coordination costs due to the more complex task of managing a globally integrated enterprise.

Transnational Strategies—a "Think-Global, Act-Local" Approach

CORE CONCEPT

A **transnational strategy** is a **think-global, act-local** approach that incorporates elements of both multidomestic and global strategies.

A **transnational strategy** (sometimes called *glocalization*) incorporates elements of both a globalized and a localized approach to strategy making. This type of middle-ground strategy is called for when there are relatively high needs for local responsiveness as well as appreciable benefits to be realized from standardization, as Figure 7.2 suggests. A transnational strategy encourages a company to use a **think-global, act-local** approach to balance these competing objectives.

Often, companies implement a transnational strategy with mass-customization techniques that enable them to address local preferences in an efficient, semi-standardized manner. McDonald's, KFC, and Starbucks have discovered ways to customize their menu offerings in various countries without compromising costs, product quality, and operating effectiveness. Unilever is responsive to local market needs regarding its consumer products, while realizing global economies of scale in certain functions. Otis Elevator found that a transnational strategy delivers better results than a global strategy when it is competing in countries like China, where local needs are highly differentiated. By switching from its customary single-brand approach to a multi-brand strategy aimed at serving different segments of the market, Otis was able to double its market share in China and increased its revenues sixfold over a nine-year period.[15]

As a rule, most companies that operate internationally endeavor to employ as global a strategy as customer needs and market conditions permit. Electronic Arts (EA) has two major design studios—one in Vancouver, British Columbia, and one in Los Angeles—and smaller design studios in locations including San Francisco, Orlando, London, and Tokyo. This dispersion of design studios helps EA design games that are specific to different cultures—for example, the London studio took the lead in designing the popular FIFA Soccer game to suit European tastes and to replicate the stadiums, signage, and team rosters; the U.S. studio took the lead in designing games involving NFL football, NBA basketball, and NASCAR racing.

A transnational strategy is far more conducive than other strategies to transferring and leveraging subsidiary skills and capabilities. But, like other approaches to competing internationally, transnational strategies also have significant drawbacks:

1. They are the most difficult of all international strategies to implement due to the added complexity of varying the elements of the strategy to situational conditions.
2. They place large demands on the organization due to the need to pursue conflicting objectives simultaneously.
3. Implementing the strategy is likely to be a costly and time-consuming enterprise, with an uncertain outcome.

Illustration Capsule 7.2 explains how Four Seasons Hotels has been able to compete successfully on the basis of a transnational strategy.

Table 7.1 provides a summary of the pluses and minuses of the three approaches to competing internationally.

TABLE 7.1 Advantages and Disadvantages of Multidomestic, Global, and Transnational Strategies

	Advantages	Disadvantages
Multidomestic (think local, act local)	• Can meet the specific needs of each market more precisely • Can respond more swiftly to localized changes in demand • Can target reactions to the moves of local rivals • Can respond more quickly to local opportunities and threats	• Hinders resource and capability sharing or cross-market transfers • Has higher production and distribution costs • Is not conducive to a worldwide competitive advantage
Global (think global, act global)	• Has lower costs due to scale and scope economies • Can lead to greater efficiencies due to the ability to transfer best practices across markets • Increases innovation from knowledge sharing and capability transfer • Offers the benefit of a global brand and reputation	• Cannot address local needs precisely • Is less responsive to changes in local market conditions • Involves higher transportation costs and tariffs • Has higher coordination and integration costs
Transnational (think global, act local)	• Offers the benefits of both local responsiveness and global integration • Enables the transfer and sharing of resources and capabilities across borders • Provides the benefits of flexible coordination	• Is more complex and harder to implement • Entails conflicting goals, which may be difficult to reconcile and require trade-offs • Involves more costly and time-consuming implementation

ILLUSTRATION CAPSULE 7.2

Four Seasons Hotels: Local Character, Global Service

© Stephen Hilger/Bloomberg via Getty Images

Four Seasons Hotels is a Toronto, Canada-based manager of luxury hotel properties. With 98 properties located in many of the world's most popular tourist destinations and business centers, Four Seasons commands a following of many of the world's most discerning travelers. In contrast to its key competitor, Ritz-Carlton, which strives to create one uniform experience globally, Four Seasons Hotels has gained market share by deftly combining local architectural and cultural experiences with globally consistent luxury service.

When moving into a new market, Four Seasons always seeks out a local capital partner. The understanding of local custom and business relationships this financier brings is critical to the process of developing a new Four Seasons hotel. Four Seasons also insists on hiring a local architect and design consultant for each property, as opposed to using architects or designers it's worked with in other locations. While this can be a challenge, particularly in emerging markets, Four Seasons has found it is worth it in the long run to have a truly local team.

The specific layout and programming of each hotel is also unique. For instance, when Four Seasons opened its hotel in Mumbai, India, it prioritized space for large banquet halls to target the Indian wedding market. In India, weddings often draw guests numbering in the thousands. When moving into the Middle East, Four Seasons designed its hotels with separate prayer rooms for men and women. In Bali, where destination weddings are common, the hotel employs a "weather shaman" who, for some guests, provides reassurance that the weather will cooperate for their special day. In all cases, the objective is to provide a truly local experience.

When staffing its hotels, Four Seasons seeks to strike a fine balance between employing locals who have an innate understanding of the local culture alongside expatriate staff or "culture carriers" who understand the DNA of Four Seasons. It also uses global systems to track customer preferences and employs globally consistent service standards. Four Seasons claims that its guests experience the same high level of service globally but that no two experiences are the same.

While it is much more expensive and time-consuming to design unique architectural and programming experiences, doing so is a strategic trade-off Four Seasons has made to achieve the local experience demanded by its high-level clientele. Likewise, it has recognized that maintaining globally consistent operation processes and service standards is important too. Four Seasons has struck the right balance between thinking globally and acting locally—the marker of a truly transnational strategy. As a result, the company has been rewarded with an international reputation for superior service and a leading market share in the luxury hospitality segment.

Note: Developed with Brian R. McKenzie.

Sources: Four Seasons annual report and corporate website; interview with Scott Woroch, executive vice president of development, Four Seasons Hotels, February 22, 2014.

INTERNATIONAL OPERATIONS AND THE QUEST FOR COMPETITIVE ADVANTAGE

There are three important ways in which a firm can gain competitive advantage (or offset domestic disadvantages) by expanding outside its domestic market. First, it can use location to lower costs or achieve greater product differentiation. Second, it can transfer competitively valuable resources and capabilities from one country to another or share them across international borders to extend its competitive advantages. And third, it can benefit from cross-border coordination opportunities that are not open to domestic-only competitors.

LO 5

How companies are able to use international operations to improve overall competitiveness.

Using Location to Build Competitive Advantage

To use location to build competitive advantage, a company must consider two issues: (1) whether to concentrate each activity it performs in a few select countries or to disperse performance of the activity to many nations, and (2) in which countries to locate particular activities.

Companies that compete internationally can pursue competitive advantage in world markets by locating their value chain activities in whatever nations prove most advantageous.

When to Concentrate Activities in a Few Locations It is advantageous for a company to concentrate its activities in a limited number of locations when:

- *The costs of manufacturing or other activities are significantly lower in some geographic locations than in others.* For example, much of the world's athletic footwear is manufactured in Asia (China and Korea) because of low labor costs; much of the production of circuit boards for PCs is located in Taiwan because of both low costs and the high-caliber technical skills of the Taiwanese labor force.
- *Significant scale economies exist in production or distribution.* The presence of significant economies of scale in components production or final assembly means that a company can gain major cost savings from operating a few super-efficient plants as opposed to a host of small plants scattered across the world. Makers of digital cameras and LED TVs located in Japan, South Korea, and Taiwan have used their scale economies to establish a low-cost advantage in this way. Achieving low-cost provider status often requires a company to have the largest worldwide manufacturing share (as distinct from brand share or market share), with production centralized in one or a few giant plants. Some companies even use such plants to manufacture units sold under the brand names of rivals to further boost production-related scale economies. Likewise, a company may be able to reduce its distribution costs by establishing large-scale distribution centers to serve major geographic regions of the world market (e.g., North America, Latin America, Europe and the Middle East, and the Asia-Pacific region).
- *Sizable learning and experience benefits are associated with performing an activity.* In some industries, learning-curve effects can allow a manufacturer to lower unit costs, boost quality, or master a new technology *more quickly* by concentrating production in a few locations. The key to riding down the learning curve is to concentrate production in a few locations to increase the cumulative volume at a plant (and thus the experience of the plant's workforce) as rapidly as possible.
- *Certain locations have superior resources, allow better coordination of related activities, or offer other valuable advantages.* Companies often locate a research unit or a sophisticated production facility in a particular country to take advantage of its pool of technically trained personnel. Samsung became a leader in memory chip technology by establishing a major R&D facility in Silicon Valley and

transferring the know-how it gained back to its operations in South Korea. Where just-in-time inventory practices yield big cost savings and/or where an assembly firm has long-term partnering arrangements with its key suppliers, parts manufacturing plants may be clustered around final-assembly plants. A customer service center or sales office may be opened in a particular country to help cultivate strong relationships with pivotal customers located nearby.

When to Disperse Activities across Many Locations In some instances, dispersing activities across locations is more advantageous than concentrating them. Buyer-related activities—such as distribution, marketing, and after-sale service—usually must take place close to buyers. This makes it necessary to physically locate the capability to perform such activities in every country or region where a firm has major customers. For example, firms that make mining and oil-drilling equipment maintain operations in many locations around the world to support customers' needs for speedy equipment repair and technical assistance. Large public accounting firms have offices in numerous countries to serve the foreign operations of their international corporate clients. Dispersing activities to many locations is also competitively important when high transportation costs, diseconomies of large size, and trade barriers make it too expensive to operate from a central location. Many companies distribute their products from multiple locations to shorten delivery times to customers. In addition, dispersing activities helps hedge against the risks of fluctuating exchange rates, supply interruptions (due to strikes, natural disasters, or transportation delays), and adverse political developments. Such risks are usually greater when activities are concentrated in a single location.

Even though global firms have strong reason to disperse buyer-related activities to many international locations, such activities as materials procurement, parts manufacture, finished-goods assembly, technology research, and new product development can frequently be decoupled from buyer locations and performed wherever advantage lies. Components can be made in Mexico; technology research done in Frankfurt; new products developed and tested in Phoenix; and assembly plants located in Spain, Brazil, Taiwan, or South Carolina, for example. Capital can be raised wherever it is available on the best terms.

Sharing and Transferring Resources and Capabilities across Borders to Build Competitive Advantage

When a company has competitively valuable resources and capabilities, it may be able to leverage them further by expanding internationally. If its resources retain their value in foreign contexts, then entering new foreign markets can extend the company's resource-based competitive advantage over a broader domain. For example, companies like Hermes, Prada, and Gucci have utilized their powerful brand names to extend their differentiation-based competitive advantages into markets far beyond their home-country origins. In each of these cases, the luxury brand name represents a valuable competitive asset that can readily be *shared* by all of the company's international stores, enabling them to attract buyers and gain a higher degree of market penetration over a wider geographic area than would otherwise be possible.

Another way for a company to extend its competitive advantage internationally is to *transfer* technological know-how or other important resources and capabilities from its operations in one country to its operations in other countries. For instance, if a company discovers ways to assemble a product faster and more cost-effectively at one plant, then that know-how can be transferred to its assembly plants in other countries. Whirlpool, the leading global manufacturer of home appliances, with 70 manufacturing and technology research centers around the world, uses an online global information technology platform to quickly and effectively transfer key product innovations and improved production techniques both across national borders and across various appliance brands. Walmart is expanding its international operations with a strategy that involves transferring its considerable resource capabilities in distribution and discount retailing to its retail units in 28 foreign countries.

Cross-border sharing or transferring resources and capabilities provides a cost-effective way for a company to leverage its core competencies more fully and extend its competitive advantages into a wider array of geographic markets. The cost of sharing or transferring already developed resources and capabilities across country borders is low in comparison to the time and considerable expense it takes to create them. Moreover, deploying them abroad spreads the fixed development costs over a greater volume of unit sales, thus contributing to low unit costs and a potential cost-based competitive advantage in recently entered geographic markets. Even if the shared or transferred resources or capabilities have to be adapted to local-market conditions, this can usually be done at low additional cost.

Consider the case of Walt Disney's theme parks as an example. The success of the theme parks in the United States derives in part from core resources such as the Disney brand name and characters like Mickey Mouse that have universal appeal and worldwide recognition. These resources can be freely shared with new theme parks as Disney expands internationally. Disney can also replicate its theme parks in new countries cost-effectively since it has already borne the costs of developing its core resources, park attractions, basic park design, and operating capabilities. The cost of replicating its theme parks abroad should be relatively low, even if the parks need to be adapted to a variety of local country conditions. By expanding internationally, Disney is able to enhance its competitive advantage over local theme park rivals. It does so by leveraging the differentiation advantage conferred by resources such as the Disney name and the park attractions. And by moving into new foreign markets, it augments its competitive advantage worldwide through the efficiency gains that come from cross-border resource sharing and low-cost capability transfer and business model replication.

Sharing and transferring resources and capabilities across country borders may also contribute to the development of broader or deeper competencies and capabilities—helping a company achieve *dominating depth* in some competitively valuable area. For example, the reputation for quality that Honda established worldwide began in motorcycles but enabled the company to command a position in both automobiles and outdoor power equipment in multiple-country markets. A one-country customer base is often too small to support the resource buildup needed to achieve such depth; this is particularly true in a developing or protected market, where competitively powerful resources are not required. By deploying capabilities across a larger international domain, a company can gain the experience needed to upgrade them to a higher performance standard. And by facing a more challenging set of international competitors, a company may be spurred to develop a stronger set of competitive capabilities. Moreover, by entering international markets, firms may be able to augment their capability set by learning from international rivals, cooperative partners, or acquisition targets.

However, cross-border resource sharing and transfers of capabilities are not guaranteed recipes for competitive success. For example, whether a resource or capability can confer a competitive advantage abroad depends on the conditions of rivalry in each particular market. If the rivals in a foreign-country market have superior resources and capabilities, then an entering firm may find itself at a competitive disadvantage even if it has a resource-based advantage domestically and can transfer the resources at low cost. In addition, since lifestyles and buying habits differ internationally, resources and capabilities that are valuable in one country may not have value in another. Sometimes a popular or well-regarded brand in one country turns out to have little competitive clout against local brands in other countries.

To illustrate, Netherlands-based Royal Philips Electronics, with 2012 sales of about €25 billion in more than 60 countries, is a leading seller of electric shavers, lighting products, small appliances, televisions, DVD players, and health care products. It has proven competitive capabilities in a number of businesses and countries and has been consistently profitable on a global basis. But the company's Philips and Magnavox brand names and the resources it has invested in its North American organization have proved inadequate in changing its image as a provider of low-end TVs and DVD players, recruiting retailers that can effectively merchandise its Magnavox and Philips products, and exciting consumers with the quality and features of its products. It has lost money in North America every year since 1988.

Benefiting from Cross-Border Coordination

Companies that compete on an international basis have another source of competitive advantage relative to their purely domestic rivals: They are able to benefit from coordinating activities across different countries' domains.[16] For example, an international manufacturer can shift production from a plant in one country to a plant in another to take advantage of exchange rate fluctuations, to cope with components shortages, or to profit from changing wage rates or energy costs. Production schedules can be coordinated worldwide; shipments can be diverted from one distribution center to another if sales rise unexpectedly in one place and fall in another. By coordinating their activities, international companies may also be able to enhance their leverage with host-country governments or respond adaptively to changes in tariffs and quotas. Efficiencies can also be achieved by shifting workloads from where they are unusually heavy to locations where personnel are underutilized.

CROSS-BORDER STRATEGIC MOVES

While international competitors can employ any of the offensive and defensive moves discussed in Chapter 6, there are two types of strategic moves that are particularly suited for companies competing internationally. Both involve the use of "profit sanctuaries."

Profit sanctuaries are country markets (or geographic regions) in which a company derives substantial profits because of a strong or protected market position. In most cases, a company's biggest and most strategically crucial profit sanctuary is its home market, but international and global companies may also enjoy profit sanctuary status in other nations where they have a strong position based on some type of competitive advantage. Companies that compete globally are likely to have more profit sanctuaries than companies that compete in just a few country markets; a domestic-only competitor, of course, can have only one profit sanctuary. Nike, which markets its products in 190 countries, has two major profit sanctuaries: North America and Greater China (where it earned $13.7 billion and $3.1 billion, respectively, in revenues in 2015).

Using Profit Sanctuaries to Wage a Strategic Offensive

Profit sanctuaries are valuable competitive assets, providing the financial strength to support strategic offensives in selected country markets and fuel a company's race for world-market leadership. The added financial capability afforded by multiple profit sanctuaries gives an international competitor the financial strength to wage a market offensive against a domestic competitor whose only profit sanctuary is its home market. The international company has the flexibility of lowballing its prices or launching high-cost marketing campaigns in the domestic company's home market and grabbing market share at the domestic company's expense. Razor-thin margins or even losses in these markets can be subsidized with the healthy profits earned in its profit sanctuaries—a practice called **cross-market subsidization.** The international company can adjust the depth of its price cutting to move in and capture market share quickly, or it can shave prices slightly to make gradual market inroads (perhaps over a decade or more) so as not to threaten domestic firms precipitously and trigger protectionist government actions. If the domestic company retaliates with matching price cuts or increased marketing expenses, it thereby exposes its entire revenue stream and profit base to erosion; its profits can be squeezed substantially and its competitive strength sapped, even if it is the domestic market leader.

CORE CONCEPT

Cross-market subsidization—supporting competitive offensives in one market with resources and profits diverted from operations in another market—can be a powerful competitive weapon.

When taken to the extreme, cut-rate pricing attacks by international competitors may draw charges of unfair "dumping." A company is said to be *dumping* when it sells its goods in foreign markets at prices that are (1) well below the prices at which it normally sells them in its home market or (2) well below its full costs per unit. Almost all governments can be expected to retaliate against perceived dumping practices by imposing special tariffs on goods being imported from the countries of the guilty companies. Indeed, as the trade among nations has mushroomed over the past 10 years, most governments have joined the World Trade Organization (WTO), which promotes fair trade practices among nations and actively polices dumping. Companies deemed guilty of dumping frequently come under pressure from their own government to cease and desist, especially if the tariffs adversely affect innocent companies based in the same country or if the advent of special tariffs raises the specter of an international trade war.

Using Profit Sanctuaries to Defend against International Rivals

Cross-border tactics involving profit sanctuaries can also be used as a means of defending against the strategic moves of rivals with multiple profit sanctuaries of their own. If a company finds itself under competitive attack by an international rival in one country market, one way to respond is to conduct a counterattack against the rival in one of its key markets in a different country—preferably where the rival is least protected and has the most to lose. This is a possible option when rivals compete against one another in much the same markets around the world.

For companies with at least one profit sanctuary, having a presence in a rival's key markets can be enough to deter the rival from making aggressive attacks. The reason for this is that the combination of market presence in the rival's key markets and a profit sanctuary elsewhere can send a signal to the rival that the company could quickly ramp up production (funded by the profit sanctuary) to mount a competitive counterattack if the rival attacks one of the company's key markets.

CORE CONCEPT

When the same companies compete against one another in multiple geographic markets, the threat of cross-border counterattacks may be enough to deter aggressive competitive moves and encourage **mutual restraint** among international rivals.

When international rivals compete against one another in multiple-country markets, this type of deterrence effect can restrain them from taking aggressive action against one another, due to the fear of a retaliatory response that might escalate the battle into a cross-border competitive war. **Mutual restraint** of this sort tends to stabilize the competitive position of multimarket rivals against one another. And while it may prevent each firm from making any major market share gains at the expense of its rival, it also protects against costly competitive battles that would be likely to erode the profitability of both companies without any compensating gain.

STRATEGIES FOR COMPETING IN THE MARKETS OF DEVELOPING COUNTRIES

LO 6

The unique characteristics of competing in developing-country markets.

Companies racing for global leadership have to consider competing in developing-economy markets like China, India, Brazil, Indonesia, Thailand, Poland, Mexico, and Russia—countries where the business risks are considerable but where the opportunities for growth are huge, especially as their economies develop and living standards climb toward levels in the industrialized world.[17] In today's world, a company that aspires to international market leadership (or to sustained rapid growth) cannot ignore the market opportunities or the base of technical and managerial talent such countries offer. For example, in 2015 China was the world's second-largest economy (behind the United States), based on purchasing power and its population of over 1.6 billion people. China's growth in demand for consumer goods has made it the fifth largest market for luxury goods, with sales greater than those in developed markets such as Germany, Spain, and the United Kingdom. Thus, no company that aspires to global market leadership can afford to ignore the strategic importance of establishing competitive market positions in the so-called BRIC countries (Brazil, Russia, India, and China), as well as in other parts of the Asia-Pacific region, Latin America, and eastern Europe.

Tailoring products to fit market conditions in developing countries, however, often involves more than making minor product changes and becoming more familiar with local cultures. McDonald's has had to offer vegetable burgers in parts of Asia and to rethink its prices, which are often high by local standards and affordable only by the well-to-do. Kellogg has struggled to introduce its cereals successfully because consumers in many less developed countries do not eat cereal for breakfast. Single-serving packages of detergents, shampoos, pickles, cough syrup, and cooking oils are very popular in India because they allow buyers to conserve cash by purchasing only what they need immediately. Thus, many companies find that trying to employ a strategy akin to that used in the markets of developed countries is hazardous.[18] Experimenting with some, perhaps many, local twists is usually necessary to find a strategy combination that works.

Strategy Options for Competing in Developing-Country Markets

There are several options for tailoring a company's strategy to fit the sometimes unusual or challenging circumstances presented in developing-country markets:

- *Prepare to compete on the basis of low price.* Consumers in developing markets are often highly focused on price, which can give low-cost local competitors the edge unless a company can find ways to attract buyers with bargain prices as well as better products. For example, in order to enter the market for laundry detergents in India, Unilever had to develop a low-cost detergent (named Wheel), construct new low-cost production facilities, package the detergent in single-use amounts so that it could be sold at a very low unit price, distribute the product to local merchants by handcarts, and craft an economical marketing campaign that included painted signs on buildings and demonstrations near stores. The new brand quickly captured $100 million in sales and by 2014 was the top detergent brand in India based dollar sales. Unilever replicated the strategy in India with low-priced packets of shampoos and deodorants and in South America with a detergent brand-named Ala.

- *Modify aspects of the company's business model to accommodate the unique local circumstances of developing countries.* For instance, Honeywell had sold industrial products and services for more than 100 years outside the United States and Europe using a foreign subsidiary model that focused international activities on sales only. When Honeywell entered China, it discovered that industrial customers in that country considered how many key jobs foreign companies created in China, in addition to the quality and price of the product or service when making purchasing decisions. Honeywell added about 150 engineers, strategists, and marketers in China to demonstrate its commitment to bolstering the Chinese economy. Honeywell replicated its "East for East" strategy when it entered the market for industrial products and services in India. Within 10 years of Honeywell establishing operations in China and three years of expanding into India, the two emerging markets accounted for 30 percent of the firm's worldwide growth.
- *Try to change the local market to better match the way the company does business elsewhere.* An international company often has enough market clout to drive major changes in the way a local country market operates. When Japan's Suzuki entered India, it triggered a quality revolution among Indian auto parts manufacturers. Local component suppliers teamed up with Suzuki's vendors in Japan and worked with Japanese experts to produce higher-quality products. Over the next two decades, Indian companies became proficient in making top-notch components for vehicles, won more prizes for quality than companies in any country other than Japan, and broke into the global market as suppliers to many automakers in Asia and other parts of the world. Mahindra and Mahindra, one of India's premier automobile manufacturers, has been recognized by a number of organizations for its product quality. Among its most noteworthy awards was its number-one ranking by J.D. Power Asia Pacific for new-vehicle overall quality.
- *Stay away from developing markets where it is impractical or uneconomical to modify the company's business model to accommodate local circumstances.* Home Depot's executive vice president and CFO, Carol Tomé, argues that there are few developing countries where Home Depot can operate successfully.[19] The company expanded successfully into Mexico, but it has avoided entry into other developing countries because its value proposition of good quality, low prices, and attentive customer service relies on (1) good highways and logistical systems to minimize store inventory costs, (2) employee stock ownership to help motivate store personnel to provide good customer service, and (3) high labor costs for housing construction and home repairs that encourage homeowners to engage in do-it-yourself projects. Relying on these factors in North American markets has worked spectacularly for Home Depot, but the company found that it could not count on these factors in China, from which it withdrew in 2012.

Profitability in developing markets rarely comes quickly or easily—new entrants have to adapt their business models to local conditions, which may not always be possible.

Company experiences in entering developing markets like Argentina, Vietnam, Malaysia, and Brazil indicate that profitability seldom comes quickly or easily. Building a market for the company's products can often turn into a long-term process that involves reeducation of consumers, sizable investments in advertising to alter tastes and buying habits, and upgrades of the local infrastructure (transportation systems, distribution channels, etc.). In such cases, a company must be patient, work within the system to improve the infrastructure, and lay the foundation for generating sizable revenues and profits once conditions are ripe for market takeoff.

DEFENDING AGAINST GLOBAL GIANTS: STRATEGIES FOR LOCAL COMPANIES IN DEVELOPING COUNTRIES

If opportunity-seeking, resource-rich international companies are looking to enter developing-country markets, what strategy options can local companies use to survive? As it turns out, the prospects for local companies facing global giants are by no means grim. Studies of local companies in developing markets have disclosed five strategies that have proved themselves in defending against globally competitive companies.[20]

1. *Develop business models that exploit shortcomings in local distribution networks or infrastructure.* In many instances, the extensive collection of resources possessed by the global giants is of little help in building a presence in developing markets. The lack of well-established local wholesaler and distributor networks, telecommunication systems, consumer banking, or media necessary for advertising makes it difficult for large internationals to migrate business models proved in developed markets to emerging markets. Emerging markets sometimes favor local companies whose managers are familiar with the local language and culture and are skilled in selecting large numbers of conscientious employees to carry out labor-intensive tasks. Shanda, a Chinese producer of massively multiplayer online role-playing games (MMORPGs), overcame China's lack of an established credit card network by selling prepaid access cards through local merchants. The company's focus on online games also protects it from shortcomings in China's software piracy laws. An India-based electronics company carved out a market niche for itself by developing an all-in-one business machine, designed especially for India's millions of small shopkeepers, that tolerates the country's frequent power outages.
2. *Utilize keen understanding of local customer needs and preferences to create customized products or services.* When developing-country markets are largely made up of customers with strong local needs, a good strategy option is to concentrate on customers who prefer a local touch and to accept the loss of the customers attracted to global brands.[21] A local company may be able to astutely exploit its local orientation—its familiarity with local preferences, its expertise in traditional products, its long-standing customer relationships. A small Middle Eastern cell phone manufacturer competes successfully against industry giants Samsung, Apple, Nokia, and Motorola by selling a model designed especially for Muslims—it is loaded with the Koran, alerts people at prayer times, and is equipped with a compass that points them toward Mecca. Shenzhen-based Tencent has become the leader in instant messaging in China through its unique understanding of Chinese behavior and culture.
3. *Take advantage of aspects of the local workforce with which large international companies may be unfamiliar.* Local companies that lack the technological capabilities of foreign entrants may be able to rely on their better understanding of the local labor force to offset any disadvantage. Focus Media is China's largest outdoor advertising firm and has relied on low-cost labor to update its more than 170,000 LCD displays and billboards in over 90 cities in a low-tech manner, while

international companies operating in China use electronically networked screens that allow messages to be changed remotely. Focus uses an army of employees who ride to each display by bicycle to change advertisements with programming contained on a USB flash drive or DVD. Indian information technology firms such as Infosys Technologies and Satyam Computer Services have been able to keep their personnel costs lower than those of international competitors EDS and Accenture because of their familiarity with local labor markets. While the large internationals have focused recruiting efforts in urban centers like Bangalore and Delhi, driving up engineering and computer science salaries in such cities, local companies have shifted recruiting efforts to second-tier cities that are unfamiliar to foreign firms.

4. *Use acquisition and rapid-growth strategies to better defend against expansion-minded internationals.* With the growth potential of developing markets such as China, Indonesia, and Brazil obvious to the world, local companies must attempt to develop scale and upgrade their competitive capabilities as quickly as possible to defend against the stronger international's arsenal of resources. Most successful companies in developing markets have pursued mergers and acquisitions at a rapid-fire pace to build first a nationwide and then an international presence. Hindalco, India's largest aluminum producer, has followed just such a path to achieve its ambitions for global dominance. By acquiring companies in India first, it gained enough experience and confidence to eventually acquire much larger foreign companies with world-class capabilities.[22] When China began to liberalize its foreign trade policies, Lenovo (the Chinese PC maker) realized that its long-held position of market dominance in China could not withstand the onslaught of new international entrants such as Dell and HP. Its acquisition of IBM's PC business allowed Lenovo to gain rapid access to IBM's globally recognized PC brand, its R&D capability, and its existing distribution in developed countries. This has allowed Lenovo not only to hold its own against the incursion of global giants into its home market but also to expand into new markets around the world.[23]

5. *Transfer company expertise to cross-border markets and initiate actions to contend on an international level.* When a company from a developing country has resources and capabilities suitable for competing in other country markets, launching initiatives to transfer its expertise to foreign markets becomes a viable strategic option. Televisa, Mexico's largest media company, used its expertise in Spanish culture and linguistics to become the world's most prolific producer of Spanish-language soap operas. By continuing to upgrade its capabilities and learn from its experience in foreign markets, a company can sometimes transform itself into one capable of competing on a worldwide basis, as an emerging global giant. Sundaram Fasteners of India began its foray into foreign markets as a supplier of radiator caps to General Motors—an opportunity it pursued when GM first decided to outsource the production of this part. As a participant in GM's supplier network, the company learned about emerging technical standards, built its capabilities, and became one of the first Indian companies to achieve QS 9000 quality certification. With the expertise it gained and its recognition for meeting quality standards, Sundaram was then able to pursue opportunities to supply automotive parts in Japan and Europe.

Illustration Capsule 7.3 discusses how a travel agency in China used a combination of these strategies to become that country's largest travel consolidator and online travel agent.

ILLUSTRATION CAPSULE 7.3

How Ctrip Successfully Defended against International Rivals to Become China's Largest Online Travel Agency

© Nelson Ching/Bloomberg via Getty Images

Ctrip has utilized a business model tailored to the Chinese travel market, its access to low-cost labor, and its unique understanding of customer preferences and buying habits to build scale rapidly and defeat foreign rivals such as Expedia and Travelocity in becoming the largest travel agency in China. The company was founded in 1999 with a focus on business travelers, since corporate travel accounts for the majority of China's travel bookings. The company initially placed little emphasis on online transactions because at the time there was no national ticketing system in China, most hotels did not belong to a national or international chain, and most consumers preferred paper tickets to electronic tickets. To overcome this infrastructure shortcoming and enter the online market, the company established its own central database of 5,600 hotels located throughout China and flight information for all major airlines operating in China. Ctrip set up a call center of 3,000 representatives that could use its proprietary database to provide travel information for up to 100,000 customers per day. Because most of its transactions were not done over the Internet at the start, the company hired couriers in all major cities in China to ride by bicycle or scooter to collect payments and deliver tickets to Ctrip's corporate customers. Ctrip also initiated a loyalty program that provided gifts and incentives to the administrative personnel who arranged travel for business executives, who were more likely to use online services. By 2011, Ctrip.com held 60 percent of China's online travel market, having grown 40 percent every year since 1999, leading to a market cap coming close to those of some major U.S. online travel agencies.

However, the phenomenal growth of the Chinese market for such travel agency services, along with changing technological ability and preferences, has led to a new type of competition: online, and more pivotally, mobile travel booking. Dominance in the mobile space drove a competitor, Qunar, to experience a huge surge in growth. While this competition was a negative in the traditional financial sense for Ctrip, analysts believe that new technology has ended up benefiting the entire industry. Additionally, this has provided the two companies with the opportunity to utilize another important local strategy to grow and remain competitive against global firms—a partnership, which Ctrip and Qunar undertook in 2013, combining their unique advantages to cross-sell travel products. The solidity of this partnership was furthered in late 2015, when the two companies agreed to an alliance through the exchange of shares in one another's companies. Together, the two companies control more than 80 percent of China's hotel and air ticket markets. The long-term effects of the new agreement still have yet to be seen, but the success of Ctrip has demonstrated the potential benefits of an effective local-market strategy.

Note: Developed with Harold W. Greenstone.

Sources: Arindam K. Bhattacharya and David C. Michael, "How Local Companies Keep Multinationals at Bay," *Harvard Business Review* 86, no. 3 (March 2008), pp. 85–95; B. Perez, "Ctrip Likely to Gain More Business from Stronger Qunar Platform," *South China Morning Press* online, October 2, 2013 (accessed April 3, 2014); B. Cao, "Qunar Jumps on Mobile User Growth as Ctrip Tumbles," *Bloomberg* online, January 5, 2014 (accessed April 3, 2014); **www.thatsmags.com/shanghai/article/detail/480/a-journey-with-ctrip; money.cnn.com/quote/quote.html?symb5EXPE** (accessed March 28, 2012).

KEY POINTS

1. Competing in international markets allows a company to (1) gain access to new customers; (2) achieve lower costs through greater economies of scale, learning, and increased purchasing power; (3) gain access to low-cost inputs of production; (4) further exploit its core competencies; and (5) gain access to resources and capabilities located outside the company's domestic market.
2. Strategy making is more complex for five reasons: (1) Different countries have *home-country advantages* in different industries; (2) there are location-based advantages to performing different value chain activities in different parts of the world; (3) varying political and economic risks make the business climate of some countries more favorable than others; (4) companies face the risk of adverse shifts in exchange rates when operating in foreign countries; and (5) differences in buyer tastes and preferences present a conundrum concerning the trade-off between customizing and standardizing products and services.
3. The strategies of firms that expand internationally are usually grounded in home-country advantages concerning demand conditions; factor conditions; related and supporting industries; and firm strategy, structure, and rivalry, as described by the Diamond of National Competitive Advantage framework.
4. There are five strategic options for entering foreign markets. These include maintaining a home-country production base and *exporting* goods to foreign markets, *licensing* foreign firms to produce and distribute the company's products abroad, employing a *franchising* strategy, establishing a foreign *subsidiary via an acquisition or greenfield venture,* and using *strategic alliances or other collaborative partnerships.*
5. A company must choose among three alternative approaches for competing internationally: (1) a *multidomestic strategy*—a *think-local, act-local* approach to crafting international strategy; (2) a *global strategy*—a *think-global, act-global* approach; and (3) a combination *think-global, act-local* approach, known as a *transnational strategy.* A multidomestic strategy (think local, act local) is appropriate for companies that must vary their product offerings and competitive approaches from country to country in order to accommodate different buyer preferences and market conditions. The global strategy (think global, act global) works best when there are substantial cost benefits to be gained from taking a standardized, globally integrated approach and there is little need for local responsiveness. A transnational strategy (think global, act local) is called for when there is a high need for local responsiveness as well as substantial benefits from taking a globally integrated approach. In this approach, a company strives to employ the same basic competitive strategy in all markets but still customizes its product offering and some aspect of its operations to fit local market circumstances.
6. There are three general ways in which a firm can gain competitive advantage (or offset domestic disadvantages) in international markets. One way involves locating various value chain activities among nations in a manner that lowers costs or achieves greater product differentiation. A second way draws on an international competitor's ability to extend its competitive advantage by cost-effectively sharing, replicating, or transferring its most valuable resources and capabilities across borders. A third looks for benefits from cross-border coordination that are unavailable to domestic-only competitors.

7. Two types of strategic moves are particularly suited for companies competing internationally. Both involve the use of profit sanctuaries—country markets where a company derives substantial profits because of its strong or protected market position. Profit sanctuaries are useful in waging strategic offenses in international markets through *cross-subsidization*—a practice of supporting competitive offensives in one market with resources and profits diverted from operations in another market (the profit sanctuary). They may be used defensively to encourage *mutual restraint* among competitors when there is international *multimarket competition* by signaling that each company has the financial capability for mounting a strong counterattack if threatened. For companies with at least one profit sanctuary, having a presence in a rival's key markets can be enough to deter the rival from making aggressive attacks.
8. Companies racing for global leadership have to consider competing in developing markets like the BRIC countries—Brazil, Russia, India, and China—where the business risks are considerable but the opportunities for growth are huge. To succeed in these markets, companies often have to (1) compete on the basis of low price, (2) modify aspects of the company's business model to accommodate local circumstances, and/or (3) try to change the local market to better match the way the company does business elsewhere. Profitability is unlikely to come quickly or easily in developing markets, typically because of the investments needed to alter buying habits and tastes, the increased political and economic risk, and/or the need for infrastructure upgrades. And there may be times when a company should simply stay away from certain developing markets until conditions for entry are better suited to its business model and strategy.
9. Local companies in developing-country markets can seek to compete against large international companies by (1) developing business models that exploit shortcomings in local distribution networks or infrastructure, (2) utilizing a superior understanding of local customer needs and preferences or local relationships, (3) taking advantage of competitively important qualities of the local workforce with which large international companies may be unfamiliar, (4) using acquisition strategies and rapid-growth strategies to better defend against expansion-minded international companies, or (5) transferring company expertise to cross-border markets and initiating actions to compete on an international level.

ASSURANCE OF LEARNING EXERCISES

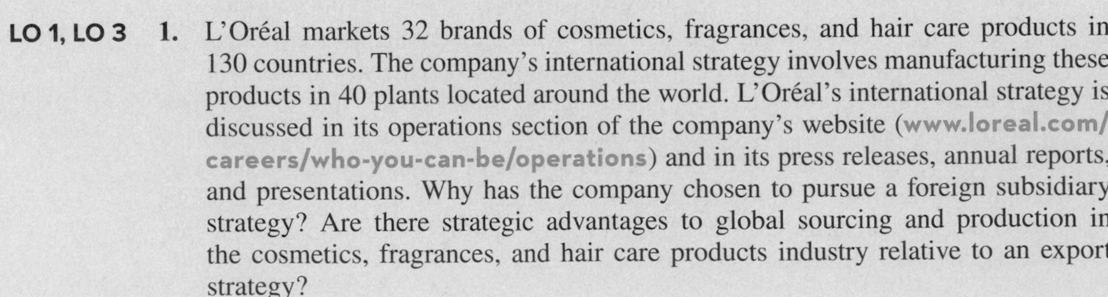

LO 1, LO 3 1. L'Oréal markets 32 brands of cosmetics, fragrances, and hair care products in 130 countries. The company's international strategy involves manufacturing these products in 40 plants located around the world. L'Oréal's international strategy is discussed in its operations section of the company's website (**www.loreal.com/careers/who-you-can-be/operations**) and in its press releases, annual reports, and presentations. Why has the company chosen to pursue a foreign subsidiary strategy? Are there strategic advantages to global sourcing and production in the cosmetics, fragrances, and hair care products industry relative to an export strategy?

2. Alliances, joint ventures, and mergers with foreign companies are widely used as a means of entering foreign markets. Such arrangements have many purposes, including learning about unfamiliar environments, and the opportunity to access the complementary resources and capabilities of a foreign partner. Illustration Capsule 7.1 provides an example of how Walgreens used a strategy of entering foreign markets via alliance, followed by a merger with the same entity. What was this entry strategy designed to achieve, and why would this make sense for a company like Walgreens? connect LO 1, LO 3

3. Assume you are in charge of developing the strategy for an international company selling products in some 50 different countries around the world. One of the issues you face is whether to employ a multidomestic strategy, a global strategy, or a transnational strategy. connect LO 2, LO 4
   a. If your company's product is mobile phones, which of these strategies do you think it would make better strategic sense to employ? Why?
   b. If your company's product is dry soup mixes and canned soups, would a multidomestic strategy seem to be more advisable than a global strategy or a transnational strategy? Why or why not?
   c. If your company's product is large home appliances such as washing machines, ranges, ovens, and refrigerators, would it seem to make more sense to pursue a multidomestic strategy, a global strategy, or a transnational strategy? Why?

4. Using your university library's subscription to LexisNexis, EBSCO, or a similar database, identify and discuss three key strategies that Volkswagen is using to compete in China. LO 5, LO 6

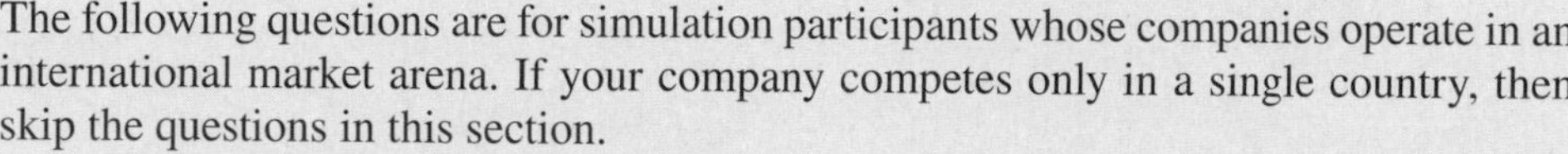

EXERCISE FOR SIMULATION PARTICIPANTS

The following questions are for simulation participants whose companies operate in an international market arena. If your company competes only in a single country, then skip the questions in this section.

1. To what extent, if any, have you and your co-managers adapted your company's strategy to take shifting exchange rates into account? In other words, have you undertaken any actions to try to minimize the impact of adverse shifts in exchange rates? LO 2
2. To what extent, if any, have you and your co-managers adapted your company's strategy to take geographic differences in import tariffs or import duties into account? LO 2
3. Which one of the following best describes the strategic approach your company is taking in trying to compete successfully on an international basis? LO 4
   - Multidomestic or think-local, act-local approach.
   - Global or think-global, act-global approach.
   - Transnational or think-global, act-local approach.

   Explain your answer and indicate two or three chief elements of your company's strategy for competing in two or more different geographic regions.

ENDNOTES

[1] Sidney G. Winter and Gabriel Szulanski, "Getting It Right the Second Time," *Harvard Business Review* 80, no. 1 (January 2002), pp. 62–69.

[2] P. Dussauge, B. Garrette, and W. Mitchell, "Learning from Competing Partners: Outcomes and Durations of Scale and Link Alliances in Europe, North America and Asia," *Strategic Management Journal* 21, no. 2 (February 2000), pp. 99–126; K. W. Glaister and P. J. Buckley, "Strategic Motives for International Alliance Formation," *Journal of Management Studies* 33, no. 3 (May 1996), pp. 301–332.

[3] Michael E. Porter, "The Competitive Advantage of Nations," *Harvard Business Review*, March–April 1990, pp. 73–93.

[4] Tom Mitchell and Avantika Chilkoti, "China Car Sales Accelerate Away from US and Brazil in 2013," *Financial Times*, January 9, 2014, www.ft.com/cms/s/0/8c649078-78f8-11e3-b381-00144feabdc0.html#axzz2rpEqjkZO.

[5] U.S. Department of Labor, Bureau of Labor Statistics, "International Comparisons of Hourly Compensation Costs in Manufacturing 2012," August 9, 2013. (The numbers for India and China are estimates.)

[6] Sangwon Yoon, "South Korea Targets Internet Addicts; 2 Million Hooked," *Valley News*, April 25, 2010, p. C2.

[7] Joel Bleeke and David Ernst, "The Way to Win in Cross-Border Alliances," *Harvard Business Review* 69, no. 6 (November–December 1991), pp. 127-133; Gary Hamel, Yves L. Doz, and C. K. Prahalad, "Collaborate with Your Competitors–and Win," *Harvard Business Review* 67, no. 1 (January–February 1989), pp. 134–135.

[8] K. W. Glaister and P. J. Buckley, "Strategic Motives for International Alliance Formation," *Journal of Management Studies* 33, no. 3 (May 1996), pp. 301–332.

[9] Jeffrey H. Dyer, Prashant Kale, and Harbir Singh, "When to Ally and When to Acquire," *Harvard Business Review* 82, no. 7–8 (July–August 2004).

[10] Yves Doz and Gary Hamel, Alliance Advantage: *The Art of Creating Value through Partnering* (Harvard Business School Press, 1998); Rosabeth Moss Kanter, "Collaborative Advantage: The Art of the Alliance," *Harvard Business Review* 72, no. 4 (July–August 1994), pp. 96–108.

[11] Jeremy Main, "Making Global Alliances Work," *Fortune*, December 19, 1990, p. 125.

[12] C. K. Prahalad and Kenneth Lieberthal, "The End of Corporate Imperialism," *Harvard Business Review* 81, no. 8 (August 2003), pp. 109–117.

[13] Pankaj Ghemawat, "Managing Differences: The Central Challenge of Global Strategy," *Harvard Business Review* 85, no. 3 (March 2007).

[14] C. A. Bartlett and S. Ghoshal, *Managing across Borders: The Transnational Solution*, 2nd ed. (Boston: Harvard Business School Press, 1998).

[15] Lynn S. Paine, "The China Rules," *Harvard Business Review* 88, no. 6 (June 2010), pp. 103–108.

[16] C. K. Prahalad and Yves L. Doz, *The Multinational Mission: Balancing Local Demands and Global Vision* (New York: Free Press, 1987).

[17] David J. Arnold and John A. Quelch, "New Strategies in Emerging Markets," *Sloan Management Review* 40, no. 1 (Fall 1998), pp. 7–20.

[18] Tarun Khanna, Krishna G. Palepu, and Jayant Sinha, "Strategies That Fit Emerging Markets," *Harvard Business Review* 83, no. 6 (June 2005), p. 63; Arindam K. Bhattacharya and David C. Michael, "How Local Companies Keep Multinationals at Bay," *Harvard Business Review* 86, no. 3 (March 2008), pp. 94–95.

[19] www.ajc.com/news/business/home-depot-eschews-large-scale-international-expan/nSQBh/ (accessed February 2, 2014).

[20] Tarun Khanna and Krishna G. Palepu, "Emerging Giants: Building World-Class Companies in Developing Countries," *Harvard Business Review* 84, no. 10 (October 2006), pp. 60–69.

[21] Niroj Dawar and Tony Frost, "Competing with Giants: Survival Strategies for Local Companies in Emerging Markets," *Harvard Business Review* 77, no. 1 (January-February 1999), p. 122; Guitz Ger, "Localizing in the Global Village: Local Firms Competing in Global Markets," *California Management Review* 41, no. 4 (Summer 1999), pp. 64–84.

[22] N. Kumar, "How Emerging Giants Are Rewriting the Rules of M&A," *Harvard Business Review*, May 2009, pp. 115–121.

[23] H. Rui and G. Yip, "Foreign Acquisitions by Chinese Firms: A Strategic Intent Perspective," *Journal of World Business* 43 (2008), pp. 213–226.

CHAPTER 8

Corporate Strategy

Diversification and the Multibusiness Company

© Roy Scott/Ikon Images/age fotostock

Learning Objectives

THIS CHAPTER WILL HELP YOU UNDERSTAND:

LO 1 When and how business diversification can enhance shareholder value.

LO 2 How related diversification strategies can produce cross-business strategic fit capable of delivering competitive advantage.

LO 3 The merits and risks of unrelated diversification strategies.

LO 4 The analytic tools for evaluating a company's diversification strategy.

LO 5 What four main corporate strategy options a diversified company can employ for solidifying its strategy and improving company performance.

The roll of takeovers is to improve unsatisfactory companies and to allow healthy companies to grow strategically by acquisitions.

Sir James Goldsmith—*Billionaire financier*

Make winners out of every business in your company. Don't carry losers.

Jack Welch—*Legendary CEO of General Electric*

Fit between a parent and its businesses is a two-edged sword: A good fit can create value; a bad one can destroy it.

Andrew Campbell, Michael Goold, and Marcus Alexander—*Academics, authors, and consultants*

This chapter moves up one level in the strategy-making hierarchy, from strategy making in a single-business enterprise to strategy making in a diversified enterprise. Because a diversified company is a collection of individual businesses, the strategy-making task is more complicated. In a one-business company, managers have to come up with a plan for competing successfully in only a single industry environment—the result is what Chapter 2 labeled as *business strategy* (or *business-level strategy*). But in a diversified company, the strategy-making challenge involves assessing multiple industry environments and developing a *set of business strategies,* one for each industry arena in which the diversified company operates. And top executives at a diversified company must still go one step further and devise a companywide (or *corporate*) strategy for improving the performance of the company's overall business lineup and for making a rational whole out of its diversified collection of individual businesses.

In the first portion of this chapter, we describe what crafting a diversification strategy entails, when and why diversification makes good strategic sense, the various approaches to diversifying a company's business lineup, and the pros and cons of related versus unrelated diversification strategies. The second part of the chapter looks at how to evaluate the attractiveness of a diversified company's business lineup, how to decide whether it has a good diversification strategy, and the strategic options for improving a diversified company's future performance.

WHAT DOES CRAFTING A DIVERSIFICATION STRATEGY ENTAIL?

The task of crafting a diversified company's overall *corporate strategy* falls squarely in the lap of top-level executives and involves three distinct facets:

1. *Picking new industries to enter and deciding on the means of entry.* Pursuing a diversification strategy requires that management decide which new industries to enter and then, for each new industry, whether to enter by starting a new business

from the ground up, by acquiring a company already in the target industry, or by forming a joint venture or strategic alliance with another company.

2. *Pursuing opportunities to leverage cross-business value chain relationships, where there is strategic fit, into competitive advantage.* The task here is to determine whether there are opportunities to strengthen a diversified company's businesses by such means as transferring competitively valuable resources and capabilities from one business to another, combining the related value chain activities of different businesses to achieve lower costs, sharing the use of a powerful and well-respected brand name across multiple businesses, and encouraging knowledge sharing and collaborative activity among the businesses.
3. *Initiating actions to boost the combined performance of the corporation's collection of businesses.* Strategic options for improving the corporation's overall performance include (1) sticking closely with the existing business lineup and pursuing opportunities presented by these businesses, (2) broadening the scope of diversification by entering additional industries, (3) retrenching to a narrower scope of diversification by divesting either poorly performing businesses or those that no longer fit into management's long-range plans, and (4) broadly restructuring the entire company by divesting some businesses, acquiring others, and reorganizing, to put a whole new face on the company's business lineup.

The demanding and time-consuming nature of these four tasks explains why corporate executives generally refrain from becoming immersed in the details of crafting and executing business-level strategies. Rather, the normal procedure is to delegate lead responsibility for business strategy to the heads of each business, giving them the latitude to develop strategies suited to the particular industry environment in which their business operates and holding them accountable for producing good financial and strategic results.

WHEN TO CONSIDER DIVERSIFYING

As long as a company has plentiful opportunities for profitable growth in its present industry, there is no urgency to pursue diversification. But growth opportunities are often limited in mature industries and markets where buyer demand is flat or declining. In addition, changing industry conditions—new technologies, inroads being made by substitute products, fast-shifting buyer preferences, or intensifying competition—can undermine a company's ability to deliver ongoing gains in revenues and profits. Consider, for example, what the growing use of debit cards and online bill payment has done to the check-printing business and what mobile phone companies and marketers of Voice over Internet Protocol (VoIP) have done to the revenues of long-distance providers such as AT&T, British Telecommunications, and NTT in Japan. Thus, diversifying into new industries always merits strong consideration whenever a single-business company encounters diminishing market opportunities and stagnating sales in its principal business.

The decision to diversify presents wide-ranging possibilities. A company can diversify into closely related businesses or into totally unrelated businesses. It can diversify its present revenue and earnings base to a small or major extent. It can move into one or two large new businesses or a greater number of small ones. It can achieve diversification by acquiring an existing company, starting up a new business from scratch, or forming a joint venture with one or more companies to enter new businesses. In every case, however, the decision to diversify must start with a strong economic justification for doing so.

BUILDING SHAREHOLDER VALUE: THE ULTIMATE JUSTIFICATION FOR DIVERSIFYING

Diversification must do more for a company than simply spread its business risk across various industries. In principle, diversification cannot be considered wise or justifiable unless it results in *added long-term economic value for shareholders*—value that shareholders cannot capture on their own by purchasing stock in companies in different industries or investing in mutual funds to spread their investments across several industries. A move to diversify into a new business stands little chance of building shareholder value without passing the following three **Tests of Corporate Advantage.**[1]

LO 1

When and how business diversification can enhance shareholder value.

1. *The industry attractiveness test.* The industry to be entered through diversification must be structurally attractive (in terms of the five forces), have resource requirements that match those of the parent company, and offer good prospects for growth, profitability, and return on investment.
2. *The cost of entry test.* The cost of entering the target industry must not be so high as to exceed the potential for good profitability. A catch-22 can prevail here, however. The more attractive an industry's prospects are for growth and good long-term profitability, the more expensive it can be to enter. Entry barriers for startup companies are likely to be high in attractive industries—if barriers were low, a rush of new entrants would soon erode the potential for high profitability. And buying a well-positioned company in an appealing industry often entails a high acquisition cost that makes passing the cost of entry test less likely. Since the owners of a successful and growing company usually demand a price that reflects their business's profit prospects, it's easy for such an acquisition to fail the cost of entry test.
3. *The better-off test.* Diversifying into a new business must offer potential for the company's existing businesses and the new business to perform better together under a single corporate umbrella than they would perform operating as independent, stand-alone businesses—an effect known as **synergy.** For example, let's say that company A diversifies by purchasing company B in another industry. If A and B's consolidated profits in the years to come prove no greater than what each could have earned on its own, then A's diversification won't provide its shareholders with any added value. Company A's shareholders could have achieved the same 1 + 1 = 2 result by merely purchasing stock in company B. Diversification does not result in added long-term value for shareholders unless it produces a 1 + 1 = 3 effect, whereby the businesses *perform better together as part of the same firm than they could have performed as independent companies.*

CORE CONCEPT

To add shareholder value, a move to diversify into a new business must pass the three **Tests of Corporate Advantage:**

1. The industry attractiveness test
2. The cost of entry test
3. The better-off test

CORE CONCEPT

Creating added value for shareholders via diversification requires building a multibusiness company in which the whole is greater than the sum of its parts; such 1 + 1 = 3 effects are called **synergy.**

Diversification moves must satisfy all three tests to grow shareholder value over the long term. Diversification moves that can pass only one or two tests are suspect.

APPROACHES TO DIVERSIFYING THE BUSINESS LINEUP

The means of entering new businesses can take any of three forms: acquisition, internal startup, or joint ventures with other companies.

Diversifying by Acquisition of an Existing Business

Acquisition is a popular means of diversifying into another industry. Not only is it quicker than trying to launch a new operation, but it also offers an effective way to hurdle such entry barriers as acquiring technological know-how, establishing supplier relationships, achieving scale economies, building brand awareness, and securing adequate distribution. Acquisitions are also commonly employed to access resources and capabilities that are complementary to those of the acquiring firm and that cannot be developed readily internally. Buying an ongoing operation allows the acquirer to move directly to the task of building a strong market position in the target industry, rather than getting bogged down in trying to develop the knowledge, experience, scale of operation, and market reputation necessary for a startup entrant to become an effective competitor.

CORE CONCEPT

An **acquisition premium,** or control premium, is the amount by which the price offered exceeds the preacquisition market value of the target company.

However, acquiring an existing business can prove quite expensive. The costs of acquiring another business include not only the acquisition price but also the costs of performing the due diligence to ascertain the worth of the other company, the costs of negotiating the purchase transaction, and the costs of integrating the business into the diversified company's portfolio. If the company to be acquired is a successful company, the acquisition price will include a hefty *premium* over the preacquisition value of the company for the right to control the company. For example, the $28 billion that Berkshire Hathaway and 3G Capital agreed to pay for H. J. Heinz Company in 2014 included a 30 percent premium over its one-year average share price.[2] Premiums are paid in order to convince the shareholders and managers of the target company that it is in their financial interests to approve the deal. The average premium paid by U.S. companies was 19 percent in 2013, but it was more often in the 20 to 25 percent range over the last 10 years.[3]

While acquisitions offer an enticing means for entering a new business, many fail to deliver on their promise.[4] Realizing the potential gains from an acquisition requires a successful integration of the acquired company into the culture, systems, and structure of the acquiring firm. This can be a costly and time-consuming operation. Acquisitions can also fail to deliver long-term shareholder value if the acquirer overestimates the potential gains and pays a premium in excess of the realized gains. High integration costs and excessive price premiums are two reasons that an acquisition might fail the cost of entry test. Firms with significant experience in making acquisitions are better able to avoid these types of problems.[5]

CORE CONCEPT

Corporate venturing (or *new venture development*) is the process of developing new businesses as an outgrowth of a company's established business operations. It is also referred to as *corporate entrepreneurship* or *intrapreneurship* since it requires entrepreneurial-like qualities within a larger enterprise.

Entering a New Line of Business through Internal Development

Achieving diversification through *internal development* involves starting a new business subsidiary from scratch. Internal development has become an increasingly important way for companies to diversify and is often referred to as **corporate venturing** or *new venture development.* Although building a new business from the ground up is generally a time-consuming and uncertain process, it avoids the pitfalls associated with entry via acquisition and may allow the firm to realize greater profits in the end. It may offer a viable means of entering a new or emerging industry where there are no good acquisition candidates.

Entering a new business via internal development, however, poses some significant hurdles. An internal new venture not only has to overcome industry entry barriers but also must invest in new production capacity, develop sources of supply, hire and train employees, build channels of distribution, grow a customer base, and so on, unless the new business is quite similar to the company's existing business. The risks associated with internal startups can be substantial, and the likelihood of failure is often high. Moreover, the culture, structures, and organizational systems of some companies may impede innovation and make it difficult for corporate entrepreneurship to flourish.

Generally, internal development of a new business has appeal only when (1) the parent company already has in-house most of the resources and capabilities it needs to piece together a new business and compete effectively; (2) there is ample time to launch the business; (3) the internal cost of entry is lower than the cost of entry via acquisition; (4) adding new production capacity will not adversely impact the supply–demand balance in the industry; and (5) incumbent firms are likely to be slow or ineffective in responding to a new entrant's efforts to crack the market.

Using Joint Ventures to Achieve Diversification

Entering a new business via a joint venture can be useful in at least three types of situations.[6] First, a joint venture is a good vehicle for pursuing an opportunity that is too complex, uneconomical, or risky for one company to pursue alone. Second, joint ventures make sense when the opportunities in a new industry require a broader range of competencies and know-how than a company can marshal on its own. Many of the opportunities in satellite-based telecommunications, biotechnology, and network-based systems that blend hardware, software, and services call for the coordinated development of complementary innovations and the tackling of an intricate web of financial, technical, political, and regulatory factors simultaneously. In such cases, pooling the resources and competencies of two or more companies is a wiser and less risky way to proceed. Third, companies sometimes use joint ventures to diversify into a new industry when the diversification move entails having operations in a foreign country. However, as discussed in Chapters 6 and 7, partnering with another company has significant drawbacks due to the potential for conflicting objectives, disagreements over how to best operate the venture, culture clashes, and so on. Joint ventures are generally the least durable of the entry options, usually lasting only until the partners decide to go their own ways.

Choosing a Mode of Entry

The choice of how best to enter a new business—whether through internal development, acquisition, or joint venture—depends on the answers to four important questions:

- Does the company have all of the resources and capabilities it requires to enter the business through internal development, or is it lacking some critical resources?
- Are there entry barriers to overcome?
- Is speed an important factor in the firm's chances for successful entry?
- Which is the least costly mode of entry, given the company's objectives?

The Question of Critical Resources and Capabilities If a firm has all the resources it needs to start up a new business or will be able to easily purchase or lease any missing resources, it may choose to enter the business via internal development. However, if missing critical resources cannot be easily purchased or leased, a firm wishing to enter a new business must obtain these missing resources through either acquisition or joint venture. Bank of America acquired Merrill Lynch to obtain critical investment banking resources and capabilities that it lacked. The acquisition of these additional capabilities complemented Bank of America's strengths in corporate banking and opened up new business opportunities for the company. Firms often acquire other companies as a way to enter foreign markets where they lack local marketing knowledge, distribution capabilities, and relationships with local suppliers or customers. McDonald's acquisition of Burghy, Italy's only national hamburger chain, offers an example.[7] If there are no good acquisition opportunities or if the firm wants to avoid the high cost of acquiring and integrating another firm, it may choose to enter via joint venture. This type of entry mode has the added advantage of spreading the risk of entering a new business, an advantage that is particularly attractive when uncertainty is high. De Beers's joint venture with the luxury goods company LVMH provided De Beers not only with the complementary marketing capabilities it needed to enter the diamond retailing business but also with a partner to share the risk.

The Question of Entry Barriers The second question to ask is whether entry barriers would prevent a new entrant from gaining a foothold and succeeding in the industry. If entry barriers are low and the industry is populated by small firms, internal development may be the preferred mode of entry. If entry barriers are high, the company may still be able to enter with ease if it has the requisite resources and capabilities for overcoming high barriers. For example, entry barriers due to reputational advantages may be surmounted by a diversified company with a widely known and trusted corporate name. But if the entry barriers cannot be overcome readily, then the only feasible entry route may be through acquisition of a well-established company. While entry barriers may also be overcome with a strong complementary joint venture, this mode is the more uncertain choice due to the lack of industry experience.

The Question of Speed Speed is another determining factor in deciding how to go about entering a new business. Acquisition is a favored mode of entry when speed is of the essence, as is the case in rapidly changing industries where fast movers can secure long-term positioning advantages. Speed is important in industries where early movers gain experience-based advantages that grow ever larger over time as they move down the learning curve. It is also important in technology-based industries where there is a race to establish an industry standard or leading technological platform. But in other cases it can be better to enter a market after the uncertainties about technology or consumer preferences have been resolved and learn from the missteps of early entrants. In these cases, joint venture or internal development may be preferred.

CORE CONCEPT

Transaction costs are the costs of completing a business agreement or deal, over and above the price of the deal. They can include the costs of searching for an attractive target, the costs of evaluating its worth, bargaining costs, and the costs of completing the transaction.

The Question of Comparative Cost The question of which mode of entry is most cost-effective is a critical one, given the need for a diversification strategy to pass the cost of entry test. Acquisition can be a high-cost mode of entry due to the need to pay a premium over the share price of the target company. When the premium is high, the price of the deal will exceed the worth of the acquired company as a stand-alone business by a substantial amount. Whether it is worth it to pay that high a price will depend on how much extra value will be created by the new combination of companies in the form of synergies. Moreover, the true cost of an acquisition must include the **transaction costs** of identifying and evaluating potential targets, negotiating a price, and completing other aspects of deal making. In addition, the true cost must take into account the costs of integrating the acquired company into the parent company's portfolio of businesses.

Joint ventures may provide a way to conserve on such entry costs. But even here, there are organizational coordination costs and transaction costs that must be considered, including settling on the terms of the arrangement. If the partnership doesn't proceed smoothly and is not founded on trust, these costs may be significant.

CHOOSING THE DIVERSIFICATION PATH: RELATED VERSUS UNRELATED BUSINESSES

Once a company decides to diversify, it faces the choice of whether to diversify into **related businesses, unrelated businesses,** or some mix of both. Businesses are said to be *related* when their value chains exhibit competitively important cross-business commonalities. By this, we mean that there is a close correspondence between the businesses in terms of *how they perform* key value chain activities and *the resources and capabilities each needs* to perform those activities. The big appeal of related diversification is the opportunity to build shareholder value by leveraging these cross-business commonalities into competitive advantages, thus allowing the company as a whole to perform better than just the sum of its individual businesses. Businesses are said to be *unrelated* when the resource requirements and key value chain activities are so dissimilar that no competitively important cross-business commonalities exist.

The next two sections explore the ins and outs of related and unrelated diversification.

CORE CONCEPT

Related businesses possess competitively valuable cross-business value chain and resource commonalities; **unrelated businesses** have dissimilar value chains and resource requirements, with no competitively important cross-business commonalities at the value chain level.

DIVERSIFICATION INTO RELATED BUSINESSES

A related diversification strategy involves building the company around businesses where there is good *strategic fit across corresponding value chain activities.* **Strategic fit** exists whenever one or more activities constituting the value chains of different businesses are sufficiently similar to present opportunities for cross-business sharing or transferring of the resources and capabilities that enable these activities.[8] Prime examples of such opportunities include:

LO 2

How related diversification strategies can produce cross-business strategic fit capable of delivering competitive advantage.

- *Transferring specialized expertise, technological know-how, or other competitively valuable strategic assets from one business's value chain to another's.* Google's ability to transfer software developers and other information technology specialists from other business applications to the development of its Android mobile operating system and Chrome operating system for PCs aided considerably in the success of these new internal ventures.
- *Sharing costs between businesses by combining their related value chain activities into a single operation.* For instance, it is often feasible to manufacture the

CORE CONCEPT

Strategic fit exists whenever one or more activities constituting the value chains of different businesses are sufficiently similar to present opportunities for cross-business sharing or transferring of the resources and capabilities that enable these activities.

products of different businesses in a single plant, use the same warehouses for shipping and distribution, or have a single sales force for the products of different businesses if they are marketed to the same types of customers.

- *Exploiting the common use of a well-known brand name.* For example, Yamaha's name in motorcycles gave the company instant credibility and recognition in entering the personal-watercraft business, allowing it to achieve a significant market share without spending large sums on advertising to establish a brand identity for the WaveRunner. Likewise, Apple's reputation for producing easy-to-operate computers was a competitive asset that facilitated the company's diversification into digital music players, smartphones, and connected watches.
- *Sharing other resources (besides brands) that support corresponding value chain activities across businesses.* When Disney acquired Marvel Comics, management saw to it that Marvel's iconic characters, such as Spiderman, Iron Man, and the Black Widow, were shared with many of the other Disney businesses, including its theme parks, retail stores, motion picture division, and video game business. (Disney's characters, starting with Mickey Mouse, have always been among the most valuable of its resources.) Automobile companies like Ford share resources such as their relationships with suppliers and dealer networks across their lines of business.
- *Engaging in cross-business collaboration and knowledge sharing to create new competitively valuable resources and capabilities.* Businesses performing closely related value chain activities may seize opportunities to join forces, share knowledge and talents, and collaborate to create altogether new capabilities (such as virtually defect-free assembly methods or increased ability to speed new products to market) that will be mutually beneficial in improving their competitiveness and business performance.

Related diversification is based on value chain matchups with respect to *key* value chain activities—those that play a central role in each business's strategy and that link to its industry's key success factors. Such matchups facilitate the sharing or transfer of the resources and capabilities that enable the performance of these activities and underlie each business's quest for competitive advantage. By facilitating the sharing or transferring of such important competitive assets, related diversification can elevate each business's prospects for competitive success.

CORE CONCEPT

Related diversification involves sharing or transferring *specialized* resources and capabilities. **Specialized resources and capabilities** have very specific applications and their use is limited to a restricted range of industry and business types, in contrast to **general resources and capabilities,** which can be widely applied and can be deployed across a broad range of industry and business types.

The resources and capabilities that are leveraged in related diversification are **specialized resources and capabilities.** By this we mean that they have very *specific* applications; their use is restricted to a limited range of business contexts in which these applications are competitively relevant. Because they are adapted for particular applications, specialized resources and capabilities must be utilized by particular types of businesses operating in specific kinds of industries to have value; they have limited utility outside this designated range of industry and business applications. This is in contrast to **general resources and capabilities** (such as general management capabilities, human resource management capabilities, and general accounting services), which can be applied usefully across a wide range of industry and business types.

L'Oréal is the world's largest beauty products company, with more than $30 billion in revenues and a successful strategy of related diversification built on leveraging a highly specialized set of resources and capabilities. These include 23 dermatologic and cosmetic research centers, R&D capabilities and scientific knowledge concerning skin and hair care, patents and secret formulas for hair and skin care products, and robotic applications developed specifically for testing the safety of hair and skin care products. These resources and capabilities are highly valuable for businesses focused on products for human skin and hair—they are *specialized* to such applications, and, in consequence, they are of little or no value beyond this restricted range of applications. To leverage these resources in a way that maximizes their potential value, L'Oréal has diversified into cosmetics, hair care products, skin care products, and fragrances (but not food, transportation, industrial services, or any application area far from the narrow domain in which its specialized resources are competitively relevant). L'Oréal's businesses are related to one another on the basis of its value-generating specialized resources and capabilities and the cross-business linkages among the value chain activities that they enable.

Corning's most competitively valuable resources and capabilities are specialized to applications concerning fiber optics and specialty glass and ceramics. Over the course of its 150-year history, it has developed an unmatched understanding of fundamental glass science and related technologies in the field of optics. Its capabilities now span a variety of sophisticated technologies and include expertise in domains such as custom glass composition, specialty glass melting and forming, precision optics, high-end transmissive coatings, and optomechanical materials. Corning has leveraged these specialized capabilities into a position of global leadership in five related market segments: display technologies based on glass substrates, environmental technologies using ceramic substrates and filters, optical fibers and cables for telecommunications, optical biosensors for drug discovery, and specialty materials employing advanced optics and specialty glass solutions. The market segments into which Corning has diversified are all related by their reliance on Corning's specialized capability set and by the many value chain activities that they have in common as a result.

General Mills has diversified into a closely related set of food businesses on the basis of its capabilities in the realm of "kitchen chemistry" and food production technologies. Its five U.S. retail divisions—meals, cereal, snacks, baking, and yogurt—include brands such as Old El Paso, Green Giant, Lucky Charms and General Mills brand cereals, Nature Valley, Annie's Organic, Pillsbury and Betty Crocker, and Yoplait yogurt. Earlier it had diversified into restaurant businesses on the mistaken notion that all food businesses were related. By exiting these businesses in the mid-1990s, the company was able to improve its overall profitability and strengthen its position in its remaining businesses. The lesson from its experience—and a takeaway for the managers of any diversified company—is that *it is not product relatedness that defines a well-crafted related diversification strategy.* Rather, *the businesses must be related in terms of their key value chain activities and the specialized resources and capabilities that enable these activities.*[9] An example is Citizen Holdings Company, whose products appear to be different (watches, miniature card calculators, handheld televisions) but are related in terms of their common reliance on miniaturization know-how and advanced precision technologies.

While companies pursuing related diversification strategies may also have opportunities to share or transfer their *general* resources and capabilities (e.g., information systems; human resource management practices; accounting and tax services; budgeting, planning, and financial reporting systems; expertise in legal and regulatory affairs; and fringe-benefit management systems), *the most competitively valuable opportunities for resource sharing or transfer always come from leveraging their specialized resources and capabilities.* The reason for this is that specialized resources and capabilities drive the key value-creating activities that both connect the businesses (at points along their value chains where there is strategic fit) and link to the

FIGURE 8.1 Related Businesses Provide Opportunities to Benefit from Competitively Valuable Strategic Fit

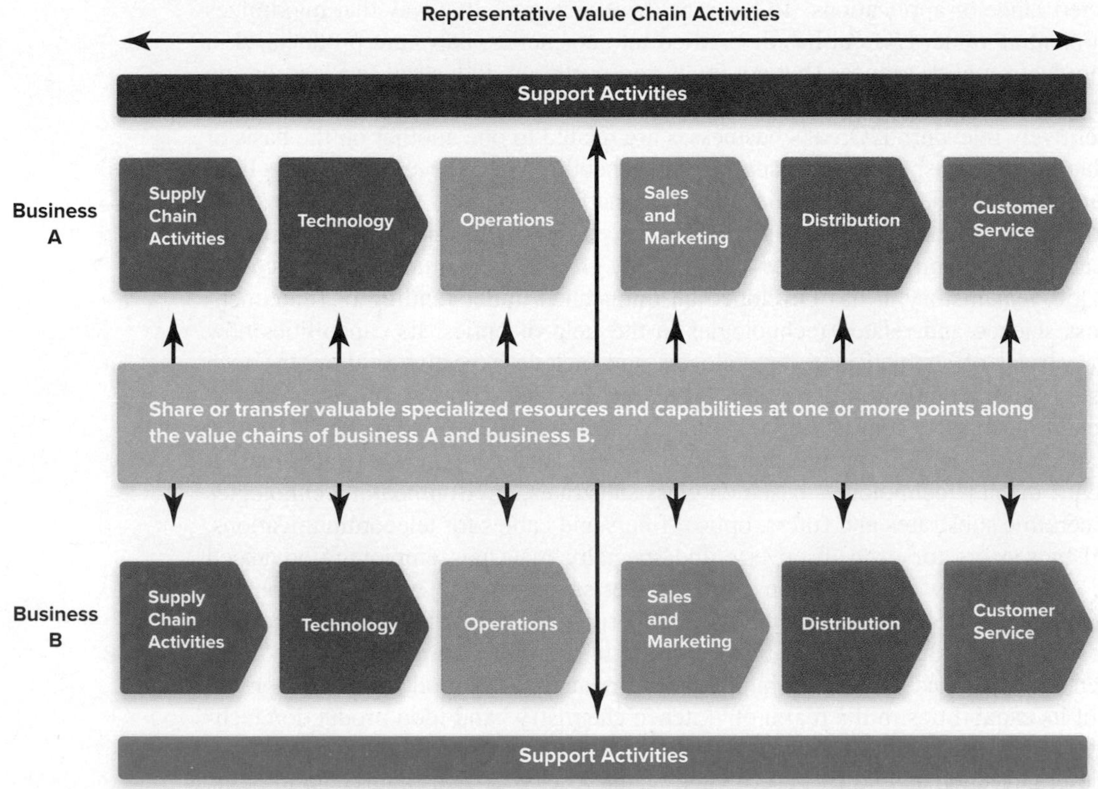

key success factors in the markets where they are competitively relevant. Figure 8.1 illustrates the range of opportunities to share and/or transfer specialized resources and capabilities among the value chain activities of related businesses. It is important to recognize that *even though general resources and capabilities may be shared by multiple business units, such resource sharing alone cannot form the backbone of a strategy keyed to related diversification.*

Identifying Cross-Business Strategic Fit along the Value Chain

Cross-business strategic fit can exist anywhere along the value chain—in R&D and technology activities, in supply chain activities and relationships with suppliers, in manufacturing, in sales and marketing, in distribution activities, or in customer service activities.[10]

Strategic Fit in Supply Chain Activities Businesses with strategic fit with respect to their supply chain activities can perform better together because of the potential for transferring skills in procuring materials, sharing resources and capabilities in logistics, collaborating with common supply chain partners, and/or increasing leverage with shippers in securing volume discounts on incoming parts and components. Dell Computer's strategic partnerships with leading suppliers of microprocessors, circuit boards, disk drives, memory chips, flat-panel displays, wireless capabilities, long-life batteries, and other PC-related components have been an important element of the company's strategy to diversify into servers, data storage devices, networking components, and LED TVs—products that include many components common to PCs and that can be sourced from the same strategic partners that provide Dell with PC components.

Strategic Fit in R&D and Technology Activities Businesses with strategic fit in R&D or technology development perform better together than apart because of potential cost savings in R&D, shorter times in getting new products to market, and more innovative products or processes. Moreover, technological advances in one business can lead to increased sales for both. Technological innovations have been the driver behind the efforts of cable TV companies to diversify into high-speed Internet access (via the use of cable modems) and, further, to explore providing local and long-distance telephone service to residential and commercial customers either through a single wire or by means of Voice over Internet Protocol (VoIP) technology. These diversification efforts have resulted in companies such as DISH, XFINITY, and Comcast now offering TV, Internet, and phone bundles.

Manufacturing-Related Strategic Fit Cross-business strategic fit in manufacturing-related activities can be exploited when a diversifier's expertise in quality control and cost-efficient production methods can be transferred to another business. When Emerson Electric diversified into the chain-saw business, it transferred its expertise in low-cost manufacture to its newly acquired Beaird-Poulan business division. The transfer drove Beaird-Poulan's new strategy—to be the low-cost provider of chain-saw products—and fundamentally changed the way Beaird-Poulan chain saws were designed and manufactured. Another benefit of production-related value chain commonalities is the ability to consolidate production into a smaller number of plants and significantly reduce overall production costs. When snowmobile maker Bombardier diversified into motorcycles, it was able to set up motorcycle assembly lines in the manufacturing facility where it was assembling snowmobiles. When Smucker's acquired Procter & Gamble's Jif peanut butter business, it was able to combine the manufacture of the two brands of peanut butter products while gaining greater leverage with vendors in purchasing its peanut supplies.

Strategic Fit in Sales and Marketing Activities Various cost-saving opportunities spring from diversifying into businesses with closely related sales and marketing activities. When the products are sold directly to the same customers, sales costs can often be reduced by using a single sales force instead of having two different salespeople call on the same customer. The products of related businesses can be promoted at the same website and included in the same media ads and sales brochures. There may be opportunities to reduce costs by consolidating order processing and billing and by using common promotional tie-ins. When global power toolmaker Black & Decker acquired Vector Products, it was able to use its own global sales force to sell the newly acquired Vector power inverters, vehicle battery chargers, and rechargeable spotlights because the types of customers that carried its power tools (discounters like Kmart, home centers, and hardware stores) also stocked the types of products produced by Vector.

A second category of benefits arises when different businesses use similar sales and marketing approaches. In such cases, there may be competitively valuable opportunities to transfer selling, merchandising, advertising, and product differentiation skills from one business to another. Procter & Gamble's product lineup includes Pampers diapers, Olay beauty products, Tide laundry detergent, Crest toothpaste, Charmin toilet tissue, Gillette razors and blades, Swiffer cleaning products, Oral-B toothbrushes, and Head & Shoulders shampoo. All of these have different competitors and different supply chain and production requirements, but they all move through the same wholesale distribution systems, are sold in common retail settings to the same shoppers, and require the same marketing and merchandising skills.

Distribution-Related Strategic Fit Businesses with closely related distribution activities can perform better together than apart because of potential cost savings in sharing the same distribution facilities or using many of the same wholesale distributors and retail dealers. When Conair Corporation acquired Allegro Manufacturing's travel bag and travel accessory business, it was able to consolidate its own distribution centers for hair dryers and curling irons with those of Allegro, thereby generating cost savings for both businesses. Likewise, since Conair products and Allegro's neck rests, ear plugs, luggage tags, and toiletry kits were sold by the same types of retailers (discount stores, supermarket chains, and drugstore chains), Conair was able to convince many of the retailers not carrying Allegro products to take on the line.

Strategic Fit in Customer Service Activities Strategic fit with respect to customer service activities can enable cost savings or differentiation advantages, just as it does along other points of the value chain. For example, cost savings may come from consolidating after-sale service and repair organizations for the products of closely related businesses into a single operation. Likewise, different businesses can often use the same customer service infrastructure. For instance, an electric utility that diversifies into natural gas, water, appliance repair services, and home security services can use the same customer data network, the same call centers and local offices, the same billing and accounting systems, and the same customer service infrastructure to support all of its products and services. Through the transfer of best practices in customer service across a set of related businesses or through the sharing of resources such as proprietary information about customer preferences, a multibusiness company can also create a differentiation advantage through higher-quality customer service.

Strategic Fit, Economies of Scope, and Competitive Advantage

What makes related diversification an attractive strategy is the opportunity to convert cross-business strategic fit into a competitive advantage over business rivals whose operations do not offer comparable strategic-fit benefits. The greater the relatedness among a diversified company's businesses, the bigger a company's window for converting strategic fit into competitive advantage via (1) transferring skills or knowledge, (2) combining related value chain activities to achieve lower costs, (3) leveraging the use of a well-respected brand name, (4) sharing other valuable resources, and (5) using cross-business collaboration and knowledge sharing to create new resources and capabilities and drive innovation.

Strategic Fit and Economies of Scope Strategic fit in the value chain activities of a diversified corporation's different businesses opens up opportunities for **economies of scope**—a concept distinct from *economies of scale*. Economies of *scale* are cost savings that accrue directly from a larger-sized operation—for example, unit costs may be lower in a large plant than in a small plant. Economies of *scope,* however, *stem directly from strategic fit along the value chains of related businesses,* which in turn enables the businesses to share resources or to transfer them from business to business at low cost. Such economies are open only to firms engaged in related diversification, since they are the result of related businesses performing R&D together, transferring managers from one business to another, using common manufacturing or distribution facilities, sharing a common sales force or dealer network, using the same established brand name, and the like. *The greater the cross-business economies associated with resource sharing and transfer, the greater the potential for a related diversification strategy to give a multibusiness enterprise a cost advantage over rivals.*

CORE CONCEPT

Economies of scope are cost reductions that flow from operating in multiple businesses (a larger scope of operation). This is in contrast to economies of scale, which accrue from a larger-sized operation.

From Strategic Fit to Competitive Advantage, Added Profitability, and Gains in Shareholder Value The cost advantage from economies of scope is due to the fact that resource sharing allows a multibusiness firm to spread resource costs across its businesses and to avoid the expense of having to acquire and maintain duplicate sets of resources—one for each business. But related diversified companies can benefit from strategic fit in other ways as well.

Sharing or transferring valuable specialized assets among the company's businesses can help each business perform its value chain activities more proficiently. This translates into competitive advantage for the businesses in one or two basic ways: (1) The businesses can contribute to greater efficiency and lower costs relative to their competitors, and/or (2) they can provide a basis for differentiation so that customers are willing to pay relatively more for the businesses' goods and services. In either or both of these ways, a firm with a well-executed related diversification strategy can boost the chances of its businesses attaining a competitive advantage.

The competitive advantage potential that flows from the capture of strategic-fit benefits is what enables a company pursuing related diversification to achieve 1 + 1 = 3 financial performance and the hoped-for gains in shareholder value. The greater the relatedness among a diversified company's businesses, the bigger a company's window for converting strategic fit into competitive advantage. The strategic and business logic is compelling: Capturing the benefits of strategic fit along the value chains of its related businesses gives a diversified company a clear path to achieving competitive advantage over undiversified competitors and competitors whose own diversification efforts don't offer equivalent strategic-fit benefits.[11] Such competitive advantage potential provides a company with a dependable basis for earning profits and a return on investment that exceeds what the company's businesses could earn as stand-alone enterprises. Converting the competitive advantage potential into greater profitability is what fuels 1 + 1 = 3 gains in shareholder value—the necessary outcome for satisfying the *better-off test* and proving the business merit of a company's diversification effort.

Diversifying into related businesses where competitively valuable strategic-fit benefits can be captured puts a company's businesses in position to perform better financially as part of the company than they could have performed as independent enterprises, thus providing a clear avenue for increasing shareholder value and satisfying the better-off test.

There are five things to bear in mind here:

1. Capturing cross-business strategic-fit benefits via a strategy of related diversification builds shareholder value in ways that shareholders cannot undertake by simply owning a portfolio of stocks of companies in different industries.

2. The capture of cross-business strategic-fit benefits is possible only via a strategy of related diversification.
3. The greater the relatedness among a diversified company's businesses, the bigger the company's window for converting strategic fit into competitive advantage.
4. The benefits of cross-business strategic fit come from the transferring or sharing of competitively valuable resources and capabilities among the businesses—resources and capabilities that are *specialized* to certain applications and have value only in specific types of industries and businesses.
5. The benefits of cross-business strategic fit are not automatically realized when a company diversifies into related businesses; *the benefits materialize only after management has successfully pursued internal actions to capture them.*

Illustration Capsule 8.1 describes the merger of Kraft Foods Group, Inc. with the H. J. Heinz Holding Corporation, in pursuit of the strategic-fit benefits of a related diversification strategy.

DIVERSIFICATION INTO UNRELATED BUSINESSES

LO 3

The merits and risks of unrelated diversification strategies.

Achieving cross-business strategic fit is not a motivation for unrelated diversification. Companies that pursue a strategy of unrelated diversification generally exhibit a willingness to diversify into *any business in any industry* where senior managers see an opportunity to realize consistently good financial results. Such companies are frequently labeled *conglomerates* because their business interests range broadly across diverse industries. Companies engaged in unrelated diversification nearly always enter new businesses by acquiring an established company rather than by forming a startup subsidiary within their own corporate structures or participating in joint ventures.

With a strategy of unrelated diversification, an acquisition is deemed to have potential if it passes the industry-attractiveness and cost of entry tests and if it has good prospects for attractive financial performance. Thus, with an unrelated diversification strategy, company managers spend much time and effort screening acquisition candidates and evaluating the pros and cons of keeping or divesting existing businesses, using such criteria as:

- Whether the business can meet corporate targets for profitability and return on investment.
- Whether the business is in an industry with attractive growth potential.
- Whether the business is big enough to contribute *significantly* to the parent firm's bottom line.

But the key to successful unrelated diversification is to go beyond these considerations and *ensure that the strategy passes the better-off test as well.* This test requires more than just growth in revenues; it requires *growth in profits*—beyond what could be achieved by a mutual fund or a holding company that owns shares of the businesses without adding any value. Unless the combination of businesses is more profitable together under the corporate umbrella than they are apart as independent businesses, *the strategy cannot create economic value for shareholders.* And unless it does so, there is *no real justification for unrelated diversification,* since top executives have a fiduciary responsibility to maximize long-term shareholder value for the company's owners (its shareholders).

ILLUSTRATION CAPSULE 8.1

The Kraft–Heinz Merger: Pursuing the Benefits of Cross-Business Strategic Fit

The $62.6 billion merger between Kraft and Heinz that was finalized in the summer of 2015 created the third largest food and beverage company in North America and the fifth largest in the world. It was a merger predicated on the idea that the strategic fit between these two companies was such that they could create more value as a combined enterprise than they could as two separate companies. As a combined enterprise, Kraft Heinz would be able to exploit its cross-business value chain activities and resource similarities to more efficiently produce, distribute, and sell profitable processed food products.

© Scott Olson/Getty Images

Kraft and Heinz products share many of the same raw materials (milk, sugar, salt, wheat, etc.), which allows the new company to leverage its increased bargaining power as a larger business to get better deals with suppliers, using strategic fit in supply chain activities to achieve lower input costs and greater inbound efficiencies. Moreover, because both of these brands specialized in prepackaged foods, there is ample manufacturing-related strategic fit in production processes and packaging technologies that allow the new company to trim and streamline manufacturing operations.

Their distribution-related strategic fit will allow for the complete integration of distribution channels and transportation networks, resulting in greater outbound efficiencies and a reduction in travel time for products moving from factories to stores. The Kraft Heinz Company is currently looking to leverage Heinz's global platform to expand Kraft's products internationally. By utilizing Heinz's already highly developed global distribution network and brand familiarity (key specialized resources), Kraft can more easily expand into the global market of prepackaged and processed food. Because these two brands are sold at similar types of retail stores (supermarket chains, wholesale retailers, and local grocery stores), they are now able to claim even more shelf space with the increased bargaining power of the combined company.

Strategic fit in sales and marketing activities will allow the company to develop coordinated and more effective advertising campaigns. Toward this aim, the Kraft Heinz Company is moving to consolidate its marketing capabilities under one marketing firm. Also, by combining R&D teams, the Kraft Heinz Company could come out with innovative products that may appeal more to the growing number of on-the-go and health-conscious buyers in the market. Many of these potential and predicted synergies for the Kraft Heinz Company have yet to be realized, since merger integration activities always take time.

Note: Developed with Maria Hart.

Sources: www.forbes.com/sites/paulmartyn/2015/03/31/heinz-and-kraft-merger-makes-supply-management-sense/; fortune.com/2015/03/25/kraft-mess-how-heinz-deal-helps/; www.nytimes.com/2015/03/26/business/dealbook/kraft-and-heinz-to-merge.html?_r=2; company websites (accessed December 3, 2015).

Building Shareholder Value via Unrelated Diversification

Given the absence of cross-business strategic fit with which to create competitive advantages, building shareholder value via unrelated diversification ultimately hinges on the ability of the parent company to improve its businesses (and make the combination *better off*) via other means. Critical to this endeavor is the role that the parent company plays as a *corporate parent*.[12] To the extent that a company has strong *parenting capabilities*—capabilities that involve nurturing, guiding, grooming, and governing constituent businesses—a corporate parent can propel its businesses forward and help them gain ground over their market rivals. Corporate parents also contribute to the competitiveness of their unrelated businesses by sharing or transferring *general resources and capabilities* across the businesses—competitive assets that have utility in *any type* of industry and that can be leveraged across a wide range of business types as a result. Examples of the kinds of general resources that a corporate parent leverages in unrelated diversification include the corporation's reputation, credit rating, and access to financial markets; governance mechanisms; management training programs; a corporate ethics program; a central data and communications center; shared administrative resources such as public relations and legal services; and common systems for functions such as budgeting, financial reporting, and quality control.

The Benefits of Astute Corporate Parenting One of the most important ways that corporate parents contribute to the success of their businesses is by offering high-level oversight and guidance.[13] The top executives of a large diversified corporation have among them many years of accumulated experience in a variety of business settings and can often contribute expert problem-solving skills, creative strategy suggestions, and first-rate advice and guidance on how to improve competitiveness and financial performance to the heads of the company's various business subsidiaries. This is especially true in the case of newly acquired, smaller businesses. Particularly astute high-level guidance from corporate executives can help the subsidiaries perform better than they would otherwise be able to do through the efforts of the business unit heads alone. The outstanding leadership of Royal Little, the founder of Textron, was a major reason that the company became an exemplar of the unrelated diversification strategy while he was CEO. Little's bold moves transformed the company from its origins as a small textile manufacturer into a global powerhouse known for its Bell helicopters, Cessna aircraft, and a host of other strong brands in a wide array of industries. Norm Wesley, a former CEO of the conglomerate Fortune Brands, is similarly credited with driving the sharp rise in the company's stock price while he was at the helm. Under his leadership, Fortune Brands became the $7 billion maker of products ranging from spirits (e.g., Jim Beam bourbon and rye, Gilbey's gin and vodka, Courvoisier cognac) to golf products (e.g., Titleist golf balls and clubs, FootJoy golf shoes and apparel, Scotty Cameron putters) to hardware (e.g., Moen faucets, American Lock security devices). (Fortune Brands has since been converted into two separate entities, Beam Inc. and Fortune Brands Home & Security.)

CORE CONCEPT

Corporate parenting refers to the role that a diversified corporation plays in nurturing its component businesses through the provision of top management expertise, disciplined control, financial resources, and other types of general resources and capabilities such as long-term planning systems, business development skills, management development processes, and incentive systems. The parenting activities of corporate executives often include recruiting and hiring talented managers to run individual businesses.

Corporate parents can also create added value for their businesses by providing them with other types of general resources that lower the operating costs of the individual businesses or that enhance their operating effectiveness. The administrative resources located at a company's corporate headquarters are a prime example. They typically include legal services, accounting expertise and tax services, and other elements of the administrative infrastructure, such as risk management capabilities, information technology resources, and public relations capabilities. Providing individual businesses with general support resources such as these creates value by *lowering companywide overhead costs,* since each business would otherwise have to duplicate the centralized activities.

Corporate brands that do not connote any specific type of product are another type of general corporate resource that can be shared among unrelated businesses. General Electric, for example, has successfully applied its GE brand to such unrelated products and businesses as appliances (GE refrigerators, ovens, and washer-dryers), medical products and health care (GE Healthcare), jet engines (GE Aviation), and power and water optimization technologies (GE Power and Water). Corporate brands that are applied in this fashion are sometimes called **umbrella brands.** Utilizing a well-known corporate name (GE) in a diversified company's individual businesses has the potential not only to lower costs (by spreading the fixed cost of developing and maintaining the brand over many businesses) but also to enhance each business's customer value proposition by linking its products to a name that consumers trust. In similar fashion, a corporation's reputation for well-crafted products, for product reliability, or for trustworthiness can lead to greater customer willingness to purchase the products of a wider range of a diversified company's businesses. Incentive systems, financial control systems, and a company's culture are other types of general corporate resources that may prove useful in enhancing the daily operations of a diverse set of businesses.

An **umbrella brand** is a corporate brand name that can be applied to a wide assortment of business types. As such, it is a type of general resource that can be leveraged in unrelated diversification.

We discuss two other commonly employed ways for corporate parents to add value to their unrelated businesses next.

Judicious Cross-Business Allocation of Financial Resources

By reallocating surplus cash flows from some businesses to fund the capital requirements of other businesses—in essence, having the company serve as an *internal capital market*—corporate parents may also be able to create value. Such actions can be particularly important in times when credit is unusually tight (such as in the wake of the worldwide banking crisis that began in 2008) or in economies with less well developed capital markets. Under these conditions, with strong financial resources a corporate parent can add value by shifting funds from business units generating excess cash (more than they need to fund their own operating requirements and new capital investment opportunities) to other, cash-short businesses with appealing growth prospects. A parent company's ability to function as its own internal capital market enhances overall corporate performance and increases shareholder value to the extent that (1) its top managers have better access to information about investment opportunities internal to the firm than do external financiers or (2) it can provide funds that would otherwise be unavailable due to poor financial market conditions.

Acquiring and Restructuring Undervalued Companies

Another way for parent companies to add value to unrelated businesses is by acquiring weakly performing companies at a bargain price and then *restructuring* their operations in ways that produce sometimes dramatic increases in profitability. **Restructuring** refers to overhauling and streamlining the operations of a business—combining plants with excess capacity, selling off underutilized assets, reducing unnecessary expenses, revamping its product offerings, consolidating administrative functions to reduce overhead costs, and otherwise improving the operating efficiency and profitability of a company. Restructuring generally involves transferring seasoned managers to the newly acquired business, either to replace the top layers of management or to step in temporarily until the business is returned to profitability or is well on its way to becoming a major market contender.

CORE CONCEPT

Restructuring refers to overhauling and streamlining the activities of a business—combining plants with excess capacity, selling off underutilized assets, reducing unnecessary expenses, and otherwise improving the productivity and profitability of a company.

Restructuring is often undertaken when a diversified company acquires a new business that is performing well below levels that the corporate parent believes are achievable. Diversified companies that have proven *turnaround capabilities* in rejuvenating weakly performing companies can often apply these capabilities in a relatively wide range of unrelated industries. Newell Rubbermaid (whose diverse product line includes Sharpie pens, Levolor window treatments, Goody hair accessories, Calphalon cookware, and Lenox power and hand tools—all businesses with different value chain activities) developed such a strong set of turnaround capabilities that the company was said to "Newellize" the businesses it acquired.

Successful unrelated diversification strategies based on restructuring require the parent company to have considerable expertise in identifying underperforming target companies and in negotiating attractive acquisition prices so that each acquisition passes the cost of entry test. The capabilities in this regard of Lord James Hanson and Lord Gordon White, who headed up the storied British conglomerate Hanson Trust, played a large part in Hanson Trust's impressive record of profitability.

The Path to Greater Shareholder Value through Unrelated Diversification

For a strategy of unrelated diversification to produce companywide financial results above and beyond what the businesses could generate operating as stand-alone entities, corporate executives must do three things to pass the three tests of corporate advantage:

1. Diversify into industries where the businesses can produce consistently good earnings and returns on investment (to satisfy the industry-attractiveness test).
2. Negotiate favorable acquisition prices (to satisfy the cost of entry test).
3. Do a superior job of corporate parenting via high-level managerial oversight and resource sharing, financial resource allocation and portfolio management, and/or the restructuring of underperforming businesses (to satisfy the better-off test).

CORE CONCEPT

A diversified company has a **parenting advantage** when it is more able than other companies to boost the combined performance of its individual businesses through high-level guidance, general oversight, and other corporate-level contributions.

The best corporate parents understand the nature and value of the kinds of resources at their command and know how to leverage them effectively across their businesses. Those that are able to create more value in their businesses than other diversified companies have what is called a **parenting advantage.** When a corporation has a parenting advantage, its top executives have the best chance of being able to craft and execute an unrelated diversification strategy that can satisfy all three tests of corporate advantage and truly enhance long-term economic shareholder value.

The Drawbacks of Unrelated Diversification

Unrelated diversification strategies have two important negatives that undercut the pluses: very demanding managerial requirements and limited competitive advantage potential.

Demanding Managerial Requirements Successfully managing a set of fundamentally different businesses operating in fundamentally different industry and competitive environments is a challenging and exceptionally difficult proposition.[14] Consider, for example, that corporations like General Electric, ITT, Mitsubishi, and Bharti Enterprises have dozens of business subsidiaries making hundreds and sometimes thousands of products. While headquarters executives can glean information about an industry from third-party sources, ask lots of questions when making occasional visits to the operations of the different businesses, and do their best to learn about the company's different businesses, they still remain heavily dependent on briefings from business unit heads and on "managing by the numbers"—that is, keeping a close track on the financial and operating results of each subsidiary. Managing by the numbers works well enough when business conditions are normal and the heads of the various business units are capable of consistently meeting their numbers. But problems arise if things start to go awry in a business and corporate management has to get deeply involved in the problems of a business it does not know much about. Because every business tends to encounter rough sledding at some juncture, unrelated diversification is thus a somewhat risky strategy from a managerial perspective.[15] Just one or two unforeseen problems or big strategic mistakes—which are much more likely without close corporate oversight—can cause a precipitous drop in corporate earnings and crash the parent company's stock price.

Hence, competently overseeing a set of widely diverse businesses can turn out to be much harder than it sounds. In practice, comparatively few companies have proved that they have top-management capabilities that are up to the task. There are far more companies whose corporate executives have failed at delivering consistently good financial results with an unrelated diversification strategy than there are companies with corporate executives who have been successful.[16] Unless a company truly has a parenting advantage, the odds are that the result of unrelated diversification will be 1 + 1 = 2 or even less.

Relying solely on leveraging general resources and the expertise of corporate executives to wisely manage a set of unrelated businesses is a much weaker foundation for enhancing shareholder value than is a strategy of related diversification.

Limited Competitive Advantage Potential The second big negative is that *unrelated diversification offers only a limited potential for competitive advantage beyond what each individual business can generate on its own.* Unlike a related diversification strategy, unrelated diversification provides no cross-business strategic-fit benefits that allow each business to perform its key value chain activities in a more efficient and effective manner. A cash-rich corporate parent pursuing unrelated diversification can provide its subsidiaries with much-needed capital, may achieve economies of scope in activities relying on general corporate resources, and may even offer some managerial know-how to help resolve problems in particular business units, but otherwise it has little to offer in the way of enhancing the competitive strength of its individual business units. In comparison to the highly specialized resources that facilitate related diversification, the general resources that support unrelated diversification tend to be relatively low value, for the simple reason that they are more common. Unless they are of exceptionally high quality (such as GE's world-renowned general management capabilities or Newell Rubbermaid's turnaround capabilities), resources and capabilities that are general in nature are less likely to provide a source of competitive advantage for diversified companies. Without the competitive advantage potential of strategic fit in competitively important value chain activities, consolidated performance of an unrelated group of businesses stands to be little more than the sum of what the individual business units could achieve if they were independent, in most circumstances.

Misguided Reasons for Pursuing Unrelated Diversification

Companies sometimes pursue unrelated diversification for reasons that are misguided. These include the following:

- *Risk reduction.* Spreading the company's investments over a set of diverse industries to spread risk cannot create long-term shareholder value since the company's shareholders can more flexibly (and more efficiently) reduce their exposure to risk by investing in a diversified portfolio of stocks and bonds.

- *Growth.* While unrelated diversification may enable a company to achieve rapid or continuous growth, firms that pursue growth for growth's sake are unlikely to maximize shareholder value. Only *profitable growth*—the kind that comes from creating added value for shareholders—can justify a strategy of unrelated diversification.
- *Stabilization.* Managers sometimes pursue broad diversification in the hope that market downtrends in some of the company's businesses will be partially offset by cyclical upswings in its other businesses, thus producing somewhat less earnings volatility. In actual practice, however, there's no convincing evidence that the consolidated profits of firms with unrelated diversification strategies are more stable or less subject to reversal in periods of recession and economic stress than the profits of firms with related diversification strategies.
- *Managerial motives.* Unrelated diversification can provide benefits to managers such as higher compensation (which tends to increase with firm size and degree of diversification) and reduced unemployment risk. Pursuing diversification for these reasons will likely reduce shareholder value and violate managers' fiduciary responsibilities.

Only profitable growth–the kind that comes from creating added value for shareholders–can justify a strategy of unrelated diversification.

Because unrelated diversification strategies *at their best* have only a limited potential for creating long-term economic value for shareholders, it is essential that managers not compound this problem by taking a misguided approach toward unrelated diversification, in pursuit of objectives that are more likely to destroy shareholder value than create it.

COMBINATION RELATED–UNRELATED DIVERSIFICATION STRATEGIES

There's nothing to preclude a company from diversifying into both related and unrelated businesses. Indeed, in actual practice the business makeup of diversified companies varies considerably. Some diversified companies are really *dominant-business enterprises*—one major "core" business accounts for 50 to 80 percent of total revenues and a collection of small related or unrelated businesses accounts for the remainder. Some diversified companies are *narrowly diversified* around a few (two to five) related or unrelated businesses. Others are *broadly diversified* around a wide-ranging collection of related businesses, unrelated businesses, or a mixture of both. A number of multibusiness enterprises have diversified into unrelated areas but have a collection of related businesses within each area—thus giving them a business portfolio consisting of *several unrelated groups of related businesses*. There's ample room for companies to customize their diversification strategies to incorporate elements of both related and unrelated diversification, as may suit their own competitive asset profile and strategic vision. *Combination related–unrelated diversification strategies have particular appeal for companies with a mix of valuable competitive assets, covering the spectrum from general to specialized resources and capabilities.*

Figure 8.2 shows the range of alternatives for companies pursuing diversification.

FIGURE 8.2 Three Strategy Options for Pursuing Diversification

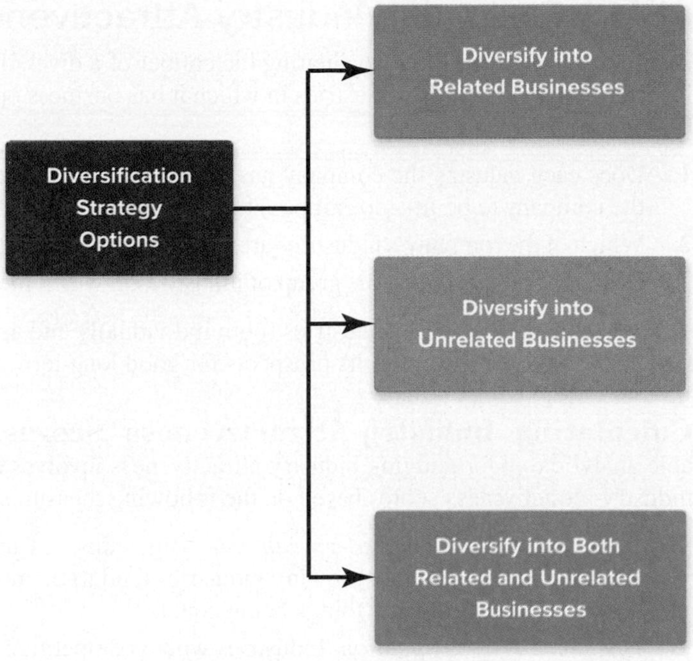

EVALUATING THE STRATEGY OF A DIVERSIFIED COMPANY

LO 4

The analytic tools for evaluating a company's diversification strategy.

Strategic analysis of diversified companies builds on the concepts and methods used for single-business companies. But there are some additional aspects to consider and a couple of new analytic tools to master. The procedure for evaluating the pluses and minuses of a diversified company's strategy and deciding what actions to take to improve the company's performance involves six steps:

1. Assessing the attractiveness of the industries the company has diversified into, both individually and as a group.
2. Assessing the competitive strength of the company's business units and drawing a nine-cell matrix to simultaneously portray industry attractiveness and business unit competitive strength.
3. Evaluating the extent of cross-business strategic fit along the value chains of the company's various business units.
4. Checking whether the firm's resources fit the requirements of its present business lineup.
5. Ranking the performance prospects of the businesses from best to worst and determining what the corporate parent's priorities should be in allocating resources to its various businesses.
6. Crafting new strategic moves to improve overall corporate performance.

The core concepts and analytic techniques underlying each of these steps merit further discussion.

Step 1: Evaluating Industry Attractiveness

A principal consideration in evaluating the caliber of a diversified company's strategy is the attractiveness of the industries in which it has business operations. Several questions arise:

1. Does each industry the company has diversified into represent a good market for the company to be in—does it pass the industry-attractiveness test?
2. Which of the company's industries are most attractive, and which are least attractive?
3. How appealing is the whole group of industries in which the company has invested?

The more attractive the industries (both individually and as a group) that a diversified company is in, the better its prospects for good long-term performance.

Calculating Industry-Attractiveness Scores A simple and reliable analytic tool for gauging industry attractiveness involves calculating quantitative industry-attractiveness scores based on the following measures:

- *Market size and projected growth rate.* Big industries are more attractive than small industries, and fast-growing industries tend to be more attractive than slow-growing industries, other things being equal.
- *The intensity of competition.* Industries where competitive pressures are relatively weak are more attractive than industries where competitive pressures are strong.
- *Emerging opportunities and threats.* Industries with promising opportunities and minimal threats on the near horizon are more attractive than industries with modest opportunities and imposing threats.
- *The presence of cross-industry strategic fit.* The more one industry's value chain and resource requirements match up well with the value chain activities of other industries in which the company has operations, the more attractive the industry is to a firm pursuing related diversification. However, cross-industry strategic fit is not something that a company committed to a strategy of unrelated diversification considers when it is evaluating industry attractiveness.
- *Resource requirements.* Industries in which resource requirements are within the company's reach are more attractive than industries in which capital and other resource requirements could strain corporate financial resources and organizational capabilities.
- *Social, political, regulatory, and environmental factors.* Industries that have significant problems in such areas as consumer health, safety, or environmental pollution or those subject to intense regulation are less attractive than industries that do not have such problems.
- *Industry profitability.* Industries with healthy profit margins and high rates of return on investment are generally more attractive than industries with historically low or unstable profits.

Each attractiveness measure is then assigned a weight reflecting its relative importance in determining an industry's attractiveness, since not all attractiveness measures are equally important. The intensity of competition in an industry should nearly always carry a high weight (say, 0.20 to 0.30). Strategic-fit considerations should be assigned a high weight in the case of companies with related diversification strategies; but for companies with an unrelated diversification strategy, strategic fit with other industries may be dropped from the list of attractiveness measures altogether. The importance weights must add up to 1.

Finally, each industry is rated on each of the chosen industry-attractiveness measures, using a rating scale of 1 to 10 (where a *high* rating signifies *high* attractiveness, and a *low* rating signifies *low* attractiveness). *Keep in mind here that the more intensely competitive an industry is, the lower the attractiveness rating for that industry.* Likewise, the more the resource requirements associated with being in a particular industry are beyond the parent company's reach, the lower the attractiveness rating. On the other hand, the presence of good cross-industry strategic fit should be given a very high attractiveness rating, since there is good potential for competitive advantage and added shareholder value. Weighted attractiveness scores are then calculated by multiplying the industry's rating on each measure by the corresponding weight. For example, a rating of 8 times a weight of 0.25 gives a weighted attractiveness score of 2. The sum of the weighted scores for all the attractiveness measures provides an overall industry-attractiveness score. This procedure is illustrated in Table 8.1.

Interpreting the Industry-Attractiveness Scores Industries with a score much below 5 probably do not pass the attractiveness test. If a company's industry-attractiveness scores are all above 5, it is probably fair to conclude that the group of industries the company operates in is attractive as a whole. But the group of industries takes on a decidedly lower degree of attractiveness as the number of industries with scores below 5 increases, especially if industries with low scores account for a sizable fraction of the company's revenues.

For a diversified company to be a strong performer, a substantial portion of its revenues and profits must come from business units with relatively high attractiveness scores. It is particularly important that a diversified company's principal businesses be in industries with a good outlook for growth and above-average profitability. Having a big fraction of the company's revenues and profits come from industries with slow growth, low profitability, intense competition, or other troubling conditions tends to drag overall company performance down. Business units in the least attractive industries are potential candidates for divestiture, unless they are positioned strongly enough to overcome the unattractive aspects of their industry environments or they are a strategically important component of the company's business makeup.

Step 2: Evaluating Business Unit Competitive Strength

The second step in evaluating a diversified company is to appraise the competitive strength of each business unit in its respective industry. Doing an appraisal of each business unit's strength and competitive position in its industry not only reveals its chances for success in its industry but also provides a basis for ranking the units from competitively strongest to competitively weakest and sizing up the competitive strength of all the business units as a group.

TABLE 8.1 Calculating Weighted Industry-Attractiveness Scores

		Industry-Attractiveness Assessments					
		Industry A		Industry B		Industry C	
Industry-Attractiveness Measure	Importance Weight	Attractiveness Rating*	Weighted Score	Attractiveness Rating*	Weighted Score	Attractiveness Rating*	Weighted Score
Market size and projected growth rate	0.10	8	0.80	3	0.30	5	0.50
Intensity of competition	0.25	8	2.00	2	0.50	5	1.25
Emerging opportunities and threats	0.10	6	0.60	5	0.50	4	0.40
Cross-industry strategic fit	0.30	8	2.40	2	0.60	3	0.90
Resource requirements	0.10	5	0.50	5	0.50	4	0.40
Social, political, regulatory, and environmental factors	0.05	8	0.40	3	0.15	7	1.05
Industry profitability	0.10	5	0.50	4	0.40	6	0.60
Sum of importance weights	**1.00**						
Weighted overall industry-attractiveness scores			**7.20**		**2.95**		**5.10**

Rating scale: 1 = very unattractive to company; 10 = very attractive to company.

Calculating Competitive-Strength Scores for Each Business Unit Quantitative measures of each business unit's competitive strength can be calculated using a procedure similar to that for measuring industry attractiveness. The following factors are used in quantifying the competitive strengths of a diversified company's business subsidiaries:

- *Relative market share.* A business unit's *relative market share* is defined as the ratio of its market share to the market share held by the largest rival firm in the industry, with market share measured in unit volume, not dollars. For instance, if business A has a market-leading share of 40 percent and its largest rival has 30 percent, A's relative market share is 1.33. (Note that only business units that are market share leaders in their respective industries can have relative market shares greater than 1.) If business B has a 15 percent market share and B's largest rival has 30 percent, B's relative market share is 0.5. *The further below 1 a business unit's relative market share is, the weaker its competitive strength and market position vis-à-vis rivals.*

- *Costs relative to competitors' costs.* Business units that have low costs relative to those of key competitors tend to be more strongly positioned in their industries than business units struggling to maintain cost parity with major rivals. The only time a business unit's competitive strength may not be undermined by having higher costs than rivals is when it has incurred the higher costs to strongly differentiate its product offering and its customers are willing to pay premium prices for the differentiating features.
- *Ability to match or beat rivals on key product attributes.* A company's competitiveness depends in part on being able to satisfy buyer expectations with regard to features, product performance, reliability, service, and other important attributes.
- *Brand image and reputation.* A widely known and respected brand name is a valuable competitive asset in most industries.
- *Other competitively valuable resources and capabilities.* Valuable resources and capabilities, including those accessed through collaborative partnerships, enhance a company's ability to compete successfully and perhaps contend for industry leadership.
- *Ability to benefit from strategic fit with other business units.* Strategic fit with other businesses within the company enhances a business unit's competitive strength and may provide a competitive edge.
- *Ability to exercise bargaining leverage with key suppliers or customers.* Having bargaining leverage signals competitive strength and can be a source of competitive advantage.
- *Profitability relative to competitors.* Above-average profitability on a consistent basis is a signal of competitive advantage, whereas consistently below-average profitability usually denotes competitive disadvantage.

After settling on a set of competitive-strength measures that are well matched to the circumstances of the various business units, the company needs to assign weights indicating each measure's importance. As in the assignment of weights to industry-attractiveness measures, the importance weights must add up to 1. Each business unit is then rated on each of the chosen strength measures, using a rating scale of 1 to 10 (where a *high* rating signifies competitive *strength,* and a *low* rating signifies competitive *weakness*). In the event that the available information is too limited to confidently assign a rating value to a business unit on a particular strength measure, it is usually best to use a score of 5—this avoids biasing the overall score either up or down. Weighted strength ratings are calculated by multiplying the business unit's rating on each strength measure by the assigned weight. For example, a strength score of 6 times a weight of 0.15 gives a weighted strength rating of 0.90. The sum of the weighted ratings across all the strength measures provides a quantitative measure of a business unit's overall competitive strength. Table 8.2 provides sample calculations of competitive-strength ratings for three businesses.

Interpreting the Competitive-Strength Scores Business units with competitive-strength ratings above 6.7 (on a scale of 1 to 10) are strong market contenders in their industries. Businesses with ratings in the 3.3-to-6.7 range have

TABLE 8.2 Calculating Weighted Competitive-Strength Scores for a Diversified Company's Business Units

		Competitive-Strength Assessments					
		Business A in Industry A		Business B in Industry B		Business C in Industry C	
Competitive-Strength Measures	Importance Weight	Strength Rating*	Weighted Score	Strength Rating*	Weighted Score	Strength Rating*	Weighted Score
Relative market share	0.15	10	1.50	2	0.30	6	0.90
Costs relative to competitors' costs	0.20	7	1.40	4	0.80	5	1.00
Ability to match or beat rivals on key product attributes	0.05	9	0.45	5	0.25	8	0.40
Ability to benefit from strategic fit with sister businesses	0.20	8	1.60	4	0.80	8	0.80
Bargaining leverage with suppliers/customers	0.05	9	0.45	2	0.10	6	0.30
Brand image and reputation	0.10	9	0.90	4	0.40	7	0.70
Other valuable resources/ capabilities	0.15	7	1.05	2	0.30	5	0.75
Profitability relative to competitors	0.10	5	0.50	2	0.20	4	0.40
Sum of importance weights	**1.00**						
Weighted overall competitive strength scores			**7.85**		**3.15**		**5.25**

**Rating scale:* 1 = very weak; 10 = very strong.

moderate competitive strength vis-à-vis rivals. Businesses with ratings below 3.3 have a competitively weak standing in the marketplace. If a diversified company's business units all have competitive-strength scores above 5, it is fair to conclude that its business units are all fairly strong market contenders in their respective industries. But as the number of business units with scores below 5 increases, there's reason to question whether the company can perform well with so many businesses in relatively weak competitive positions. This concern takes on even more importance when business units with low scores account for a sizable fraction of the company's revenues.

Using a Nine-Cell Matrix to Simultaneously Portray Industry Attractiveness and Competitive Strength The industry-attractiveness and business-strength scores can be used to portray the strategic positions of each business in a diversified company. Industry attractiveness is plotted on the vertical axis and competitive strength on the horizontal axis. A nine-cell grid emerges from dividing the vertical axis into three regions (high, medium, and low attractiveness) and the horizontal axis into three regions (strong, average, and weak competitive strength). As shown in Figure 8.3, scores of 6.7 or greater on a rating scale of 1 to 10 denote high industry attractiveness, scores of 3.3 to 6.7 denote medium attractiveness, and scores below 3.3 signal low attractiveness. Likewise, high competitive strength is defined as scores greater than 6.7, average strength as scores of 3.3 to 6.7, and low strength as scores below 3.3. *Each business unit is plotted on the nine-cell matrix according to its*

FIGURE 8.3 A Nine-Cell Industry-Attractiveness–Competitive-Strength Matrix

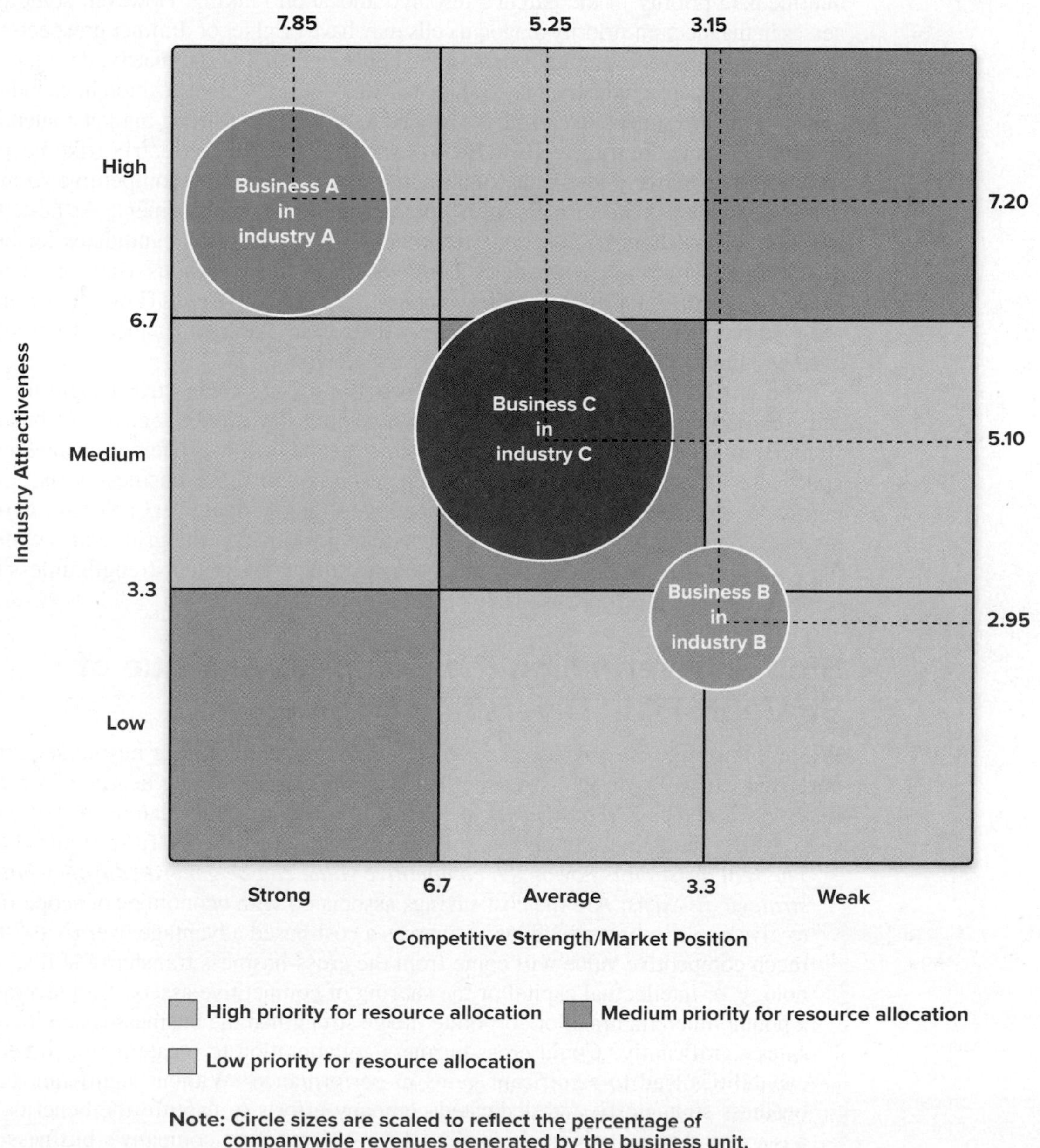

overall attractiveness score and strength score, and then it is shown as a "bubble." The size of each bubble is scaled to the percentage of revenues the business generates relative to total corporate revenues. The bubbles in Figure 8.3 were located on the grid using the three industry-attractiveness scores from Table 8.1 and the strength scores for the three business units in Table 8.2.

The locations of the business units on the attractiveness–strength matrix provide valuable guidance in deploying corporate resources. Businesses positioned in the three cells in the upper left portion of the attractiveness–strength matrix (like business A) have both favorable industry attractiveness and competitive strength.

Next in priority come businesses positioned in the three diagonal cells stretching from the lower left to the upper right (like business C). Such businesses usually merit intermediate priority in the parent's resource allocation ranking. However, some businesses in the medium-priority diagonal cells may have brighter or dimmer prospects than others. For example, a small business in the upper right cell of the matrix, despite being in a highly attractive industry, may occupy too weak a competitive position in its industry to justify the investment and resources needed to turn it into a strong market contender.

Businesses in the three cells in the lower right corner of the matrix (like business B) have comparatively low industry attractiveness and minimal competitive strength, making them weak performers with little potential for improvement. At best, they have the lowest claim on corporate resources and may be good candidates for being divested (sold to other companies). However, there are occasions when a business located in the three lower-right cells generates sizable positive cash flows. It may make sense to retain such businesses and divert their cash flows to finance expansion of business units with greater potential for profit growth.

The nine-cell attractiveness–strength matrix provides clear, strong logic for why a diversified company needs to consider both industry attractiveness and business strength in allocating resources and investment capital to its different businesses. A good case can be made for concentrating resources in those businesses that enjoy higher degrees of attractiveness and competitive strength, being very selective in making investments in businesses with intermediate positions on the grid, and withdrawing resources from businesses that are lower in attractiveness and strength unless they offer exceptional profit or cash flow potential.

Step 3: Determining the Competitive Value of Strategic Fit in Diversified Companies

While this step can be bypassed for diversified companies whose businesses are all unrelated (since, by design, strategic fit is lacking), assessing the degree of strategic fit across a company's businesses is central to evaluating its related diversification strategy. But more than just checking for the presence of strategic fit is required here.

The real question is how much competitive value can be generated from whatever strategic fit exists. Are the cost savings associated with economies of scope likely to give one or more individual businesses a cost-based advantage over rivals? How much competitive value will come from the cross-business transfer of skills, technology, or intellectual capital or the sharing of competitive assets? Can leveraging a potent umbrella brand or corporate image strengthen the businesses and increase sales significantly? Could cross-business collaboration to create new competitive capabilities lead to significant gains in performance? Without significant cross-business strategic fit and dedicated company efforts to capture the benefits, one has to be skeptical about the potential for a diversified company's businesses to perform better together than apart.

The greater the value of cross-business strategic fit in enhancing the performance of a diversified company's businesses, the more competitively powerful is the company's related diversification strategy.

FIGURE 8.4 Identifying the Competitive Advantage Potential of Cross-Business Strategic Fit

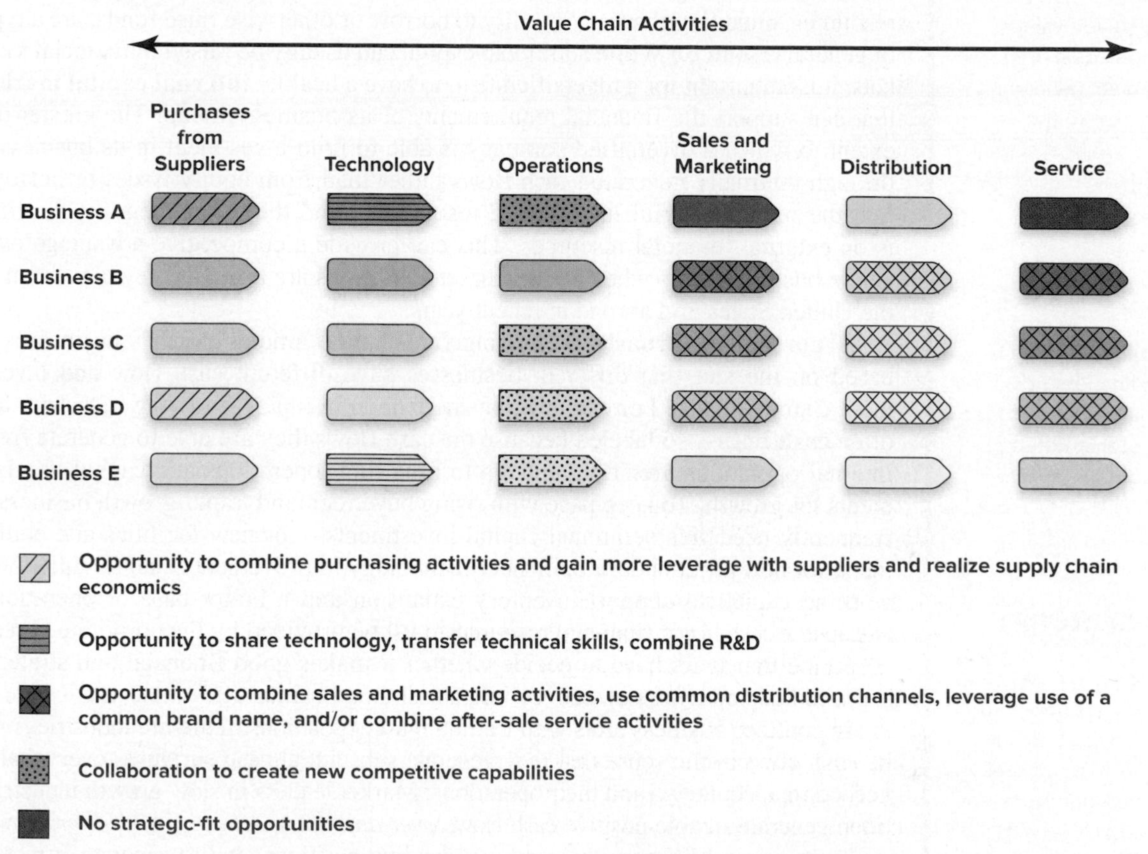

Figure 8.4 illustrates the process of comparing the value chains of a company's businesses and identifying opportunities to exploit competitively valuable cross-business strategic fit.

Step 4: Checking for Good Resource Fit

The businesses in a diversified company's lineup need to exhibit good **resource fit.** In firms with a related diversification strategy, good resource fit exists *when the firm's businesses have well-matched specialized resource requirements at points along their value chains* that are critical for the businesses' market success. Matching resource requirements are important in related diversification because they facilitate resource sharing and low-cost resource transfer. In companies pursuing unrelated diversification, resource fit exists when the company has solid *parenting capabilities or resources of a general nature that it can share or transfer to its component businesses.* Firms pursuing related diversification and firms with combination related–unrelated diversification strategies can also benefit from leveraging corporate parenting capabilities and other general resources. Another dimension of resource fit that concerns all types of multibusiness firms is whether they have resources sufficient to support their group of businesses without being spread too thin.

CORE CONCEPT

A company pursuing related diversification exhibits **resource fit** when its businesses have matching specialized resource requirements along their value chains; a company pursuing unrelated diversification has resource fit when the parent company has adequate corporate resources (parenting and general resources) to support its businesses' needs and add value.

CORE CONCEPT

A strong **internal capital market** allows a diversified company to add value by shifting capital from business units generating free cash flow to those needing additional capital to expand and realize their growth potential.

CORE CONCEPT

A **portfolio approach** to ensuring financial fit among a firm's businesses is based on the fact that different businesses have different cash flow and investment characteristics.

CORE CONCEPT

A **cash hog** business generates cash flows that are too small to fully fund its growth; it thereby requires cash infusions to provide additional working capital and finance new capital investment.

CORE CONCEPT

A **cash cow** business generates cash flows over and above its internal requirements, thus providing a corporate parent with funds for investing in cash hog businesses, financing new acquisitions, or paying dividends.

Financial Resource Fit The most important dimension of financial resource fit concerns whether a diversified company can generate the internal cash flows sufficient to fund the capital requirements of its businesses, pay its dividends, meet its debt obligations, and otherwise remain financially healthy. (Financial resources, including the firm's ability to borrow or otherwise raise funds, are a type of general resource.) While additional capital can usually be raised in financial markets, it is important for a diversified firm to have a healthy **internal capital market** that can support the financial requirements of its business lineup. The greater the extent to which a diversified company is able to fund investment in its businesses through internally generated cash flows rather than from equity issues or borrowing, the more powerful its financial resource fit and the less dependent the firm is on external financial resources. This can provide a competitive advantage over single business rivals when credit market conditions are tight, as they have been in the United States and abroad in recent years.

A **portfolio approach** to ensuring financial fit among a firm's businesses is based on the fact that different businesses have different cash flow and investment characteristics. For example, business units in rapidly growing industries are often **cash hogs**—so labeled because the cash flows they are able to generate from internal operations aren't big enough to fund their operations and capital requirements for growth. To keep pace with rising buyer demand, rapid-growth businesses frequently need sizable annual capital investments—for new facilities and equipment, for new product development or technology improvements, and for additional working capital to support inventory expansion and a larger base of operations. Because a cash hog's financial resources must be provided by the corporate parent, corporate managers have to decide whether it makes good financial and strategic sense to keep pouring new money into a cash hog business.

In contrast, business units with leading market positions in mature industries may be **cash cows** in the sense that they generate substantial cash surpluses over what is needed to adequately fund their operations. Market leaders in slow-growth industries often generate sizable positive cash flows *over and above what is needed for growth and reinvestment* because their industry-leading positions tend to generate attractive earnings and because the slow-growth nature of their industry often entails relatively modest annual investment requirements. Cash cows, although not attractive from a growth standpoint, are valuable businesses from a financial resource perspective. The surplus cash flows they generate can be used to pay corporate dividends, finance acquisitions, and provide funds for investing in the company's promising cash hogs. It makes good financial and strategic sense for diversified companies to keep cash cows in a healthy condition, fortifying and defending their market position so as to preserve their cash-generating capability and have an ongoing source of financial resources to deploy elsewhere. General Electric considers its advanced materials, equipment services, and appliance and lighting businesses to be cash cow businesses.

Viewing a diversified group of businesses as a collection of cash flows and cash requirements (present and future flows) can be helpful in understanding what the financial ramifications of diversification are and why having businesses with good financial resource fit can be important. For instance, *a diversified company's businesses exhibit good financial resource fit when the excess cash generated by its cash cow businesses is sufficient to fund the investment requirements of promising cash hog businesses.* Ideally, investing in promising cash hog businesses over time results in growing the hogs into self-supporting *star businesses* that have strong or market-leading competitive positions in attractive, high-growth markets and high levels of profitability. Star businesses are often the cash cows of the future. When the markets of star businesses begin to mature and their growth slows, their competitive strength should produce self-generated cash flows that are more than sufficient to cover their investment needs. The "success sequence" is thus cash hog to young star (but perhaps still a cash hog) to self-supporting star to cash cow. While the practice of viewing a diversified company in terms of cash cows and cash hogs has declined in popularity, it illustrates one approach to analyzing financial resource fit and allocating financial resources across a portfolio of different businesses.

Aside from cash flow considerations, there are two other factors to consider in assessing whether a diversified company's businesses exhibit good financial fit:

- *Do any of the company's individual businesses present financial challenges with respect to contributing adequately to achieving companywide performance targets?* A business exhibits poor financial fit if it soaks up a disproportionate share of the company's financial resources, while making subpar or insignificant contributions to the bottom line. Too many underperforming businesses reduce the company's overall performance and ultimately limit growth in shareholder value.
- *Does the corporation have adequate financial strength to fund its different businesses and maintain a healthy credit rating?* A diversified company's strategy fails the resource-fit test when the resource needs of its portfolio unduly stretch the company's financial health and threaten to impair its credit rating. Many of the world's largest banks, including Royal Bank of Scotland, Citigroup, and HSBC, recently found themselves so undercapitalized and financially overextended that they were forced to sell off some of their business assets to meet regulatory requirements and restore public confidence in their solvency.

Nonfinancial Resource Fit Just as a diversified company must have adequate financial resources to support its various individual businesses, it must also have a big enough and deep enough pool of managerial, administrative, and other parenting capabilities to support all of its different businesses. The following two questions help reveal whether a diversified company has sufficient nonfinancial resources:

- *Does the parent company have (or can it develop) the specific resources and capabilities needed to be successful in each of its businesses?* Sometimes the resources a company has accumulated in its core business prove to be a poor match with the competitive capabilities needed to succeed in the businesses into which it has diversified. For instance, BTR, a multibusiness company in Great Britain, discovered that the company's resources and managerial skills were quite well suited for parenting its industrial manufacturing businesses but not for parenting its distribution businesses (National Tyre Services and Texas-based Summers Group). As a result, BTR decided to divest its distribution businesses and focus exclusively on diversifying around small industrial manufacturing. For companies pursuing related diversification strategies, a mismatch between the company's competitive assets and the key success factors of an industry can be serious enough to warrant divesting businesses in that industry or not acquiring a new business. In contrast, when a company's resources and capabilities are a good match with the key success factors of industries it is not presently in, it makes sense to take a hard look at acquiring companies in these industries and expanding the company's business lineup.
- *Are the parent company's resources being stretched too thinly by the resource requirements of one or more of its businesses?* A diversified company must guard

against overtaxing its resources and capabilities, a condition that can arise when (1) it goes on an acquisition spree and management is called on to assimilate and oversee many new businesses very quickly or (2) it lacks sufficient resource depth to do a creditable job of transferring skills and competencies from one of its businesses to another. The broader the diversification, the greater the concern about whether corporate executives are overburdened by the demands of competently parenting so many different businesses. Plus, the more a company's diversification strategy is tied to transferring know-how or technologies from existing businesses to newly acquired businesses, the more time and money that has to be put into developing a deep-enough resource pool to supply these businesses with the resources and capabilities they need to be successful.[17] Otherwise, its resource pool ends up being spread too thinly across many businesses, and the opportunity for achieving 1 + 1 = 3 outcomes slips through the cracks.

Step 5: Ranking Business Units and Assigning a Priority for Resource Allocation

Once a diversified company's strategy has been evaluated from the perspective of industry attractiveness, competitive strength, strategic fit, and resource fit, the next step is to use this information to rank the performance prospects of the businesses from best to worst. Such ranking helps top-level executives assign each business a priority for resource support and capital investment.

The locations of the different businesses in the nine-cell industry-attractiveness–competitive-strength matrix provide a solid basis for identifying high-opportunity businesses and low-opportunity businesses. Normally, competitively strong businesses in attractive industries have significantly better performance prospects than competitively weak businesses in unattractive industries. Also, the revenue and earnings outlook for businesses in fast-growing industries is normally better than for businesses in slow-growing industries. As a rule, *business subsidiaries with the brightest profit and growth prospects, attractive positions in the nine-cell matrix, and solid strategic and resource fit should receive top priority for allocation of corporate resources.* However, in ranking the prospects of the different businesses from best to worst, it is usually wise to also take into account each business's past performance in regard to sales growth, profit growth, contribution to company earnings, return on capital invested in the business, and cash flow from operations. While past performance is not always a reliable predictor of future performance, it does signal whether a business is already performing well or has problems to overcome.

Allocating Financial Resources Figure 8.5 shows the chief strategic and financial options for allocating a diversified company's financial resources. Divesting businesses with the weakest future prospects and businesses that lack adequate strategic fit and/or resource fit is one of the best ways of generating additional funds for redeployment to businesses with better opportunities and better strategic and resource fit. Free cash flows from cash cow businesses also add to the pool of funds that can be usefully redeployed. *Ideally,* a diversified company will have sufficient financial resources to strengthen or grow its existing businesses, make any new acquisitions that are desirable, fund other promising business opportunities, pay off existing debt, and periodically increase dividend payments to shareholders and/or repurchase shares of stock. But, as a practical matter, a company's financial resources are limited. Thus, to make the best use of the available funds, top executives must steer resources to those businesses with the best prospects and either divest or allocate minimal resources to businesses with marginal prospects—this is why ranking the performance prospects of the various businesses from best to worst is so crucial. *Strategic* uses of corporate financial resources should usually take precedence over strictly financial considerations (see Figure 8.5) unless there is a compelling reason to strengthen the firm's balance sheet or better reward shareholders.

Step 6: Crafting New Strategic Moves to Improve Overall Corporate Performance

LO 5

What four main corporate strategy options a diversified company can employ for solidifying its strategy and improving company performance.

The conclusions flowing from the five preceding analytic steps set the agenda for crafting strategic moves to improve a diversified company's overall performance. The strategic options boil down to four broad categories of actions (see Figure 8.6):

1. Sticking closely with the existing business lineup and pursuing the opportunities these businesses present.
2. Broadening the company's business scope by making new acquisitions in new industries.
3. Divesting certain businesses and retrenching to a narrower base of business operations.
4. Restructuring the company's business lineup and putting a whole new face on the company's business makeup.

FIGURE 8.5 The Chief Strategic and Financial Options for Allocating a Diversified Company's Financial Resources

FIGURE 8.6 A Company's Four Main Strategic Alternatives after It Diversifies

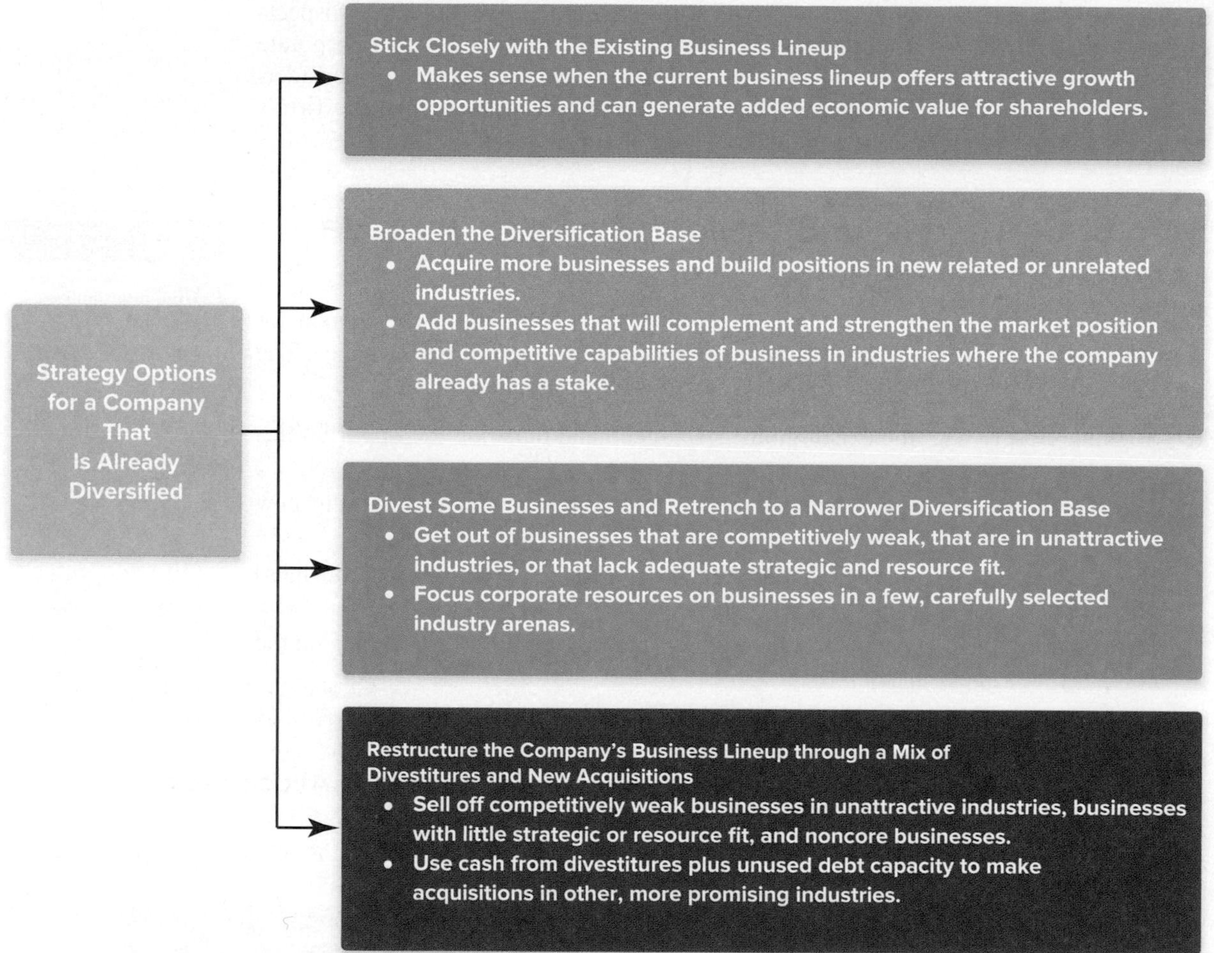

Sticking Closely with the Present Business Lineup The option of sticking with the current business lineup makes sense when the company's existing businesses offer attractive growth opportunities and can be counted on to create economic value for shareholders. As long as the company's set of existing businesses have good prospects and are in alignment with the company's diversification strategy, then major changes in the company's business mix are unnecessary. Corporate executives can concentrate their attention on getting the best performance from each of the businesses, steering corporate resources into the areas of greatest potential and profitability. The specifics of "what to do" to wring better performance from the present business lineup have to be dictated by each business's circumstances and the preceding analysis of the corporate parent's diversification strategy.

Broadening a Diversified Company's Business Base Diversified companies sometimes find it desirable to build positions in new industries, whether related or unrelated. Several motivating factors are in play. One is sluggish growth that makes the potential revenue and profit boost of a newly acquired business look attractive. A second is the potential for transferring resources and capabilities to other related or complementary businesses. A third is rapidly changing conditions in one or more of a company's core businesses, brought on by technological, legislative, or demographic changes. For instance, the passage of legislation in the United States allowing banks, insurance companies, and stock brokerages to enter each other's businesses spurred a raft of acquisitions and mergers to create full-service financial enterprises capable of meeting the multiple financial needs of customers. A fourth, and very important, motivating factor for adding new businesses is to complement and strengthen the market position and competitive capabilities of one or more of the company's present businesses. Procter & Gamble's acquisition of Gillette strengthened and extended P&G's reach into personal care and household products—Gillette's businesses included Oral-B toothbrushes, Gillette razors and razor blades, Duracell batteries, Braun shavers, small appliances (coffeemakers, mixers, hair dryers, and electric toothbrushes), and toiletries.

Another important avenue for expanding the scope of a diversified company is to grow by extending the operations of existing businesses into additional country markets, as discussed in Chapter 7. Expanding a company's geographic scope may offer an exceptional competitive advantage potential by facilitating the full capture of economies of scale and learning- and experience-curve effects. In some businesses, the volume of sales needed to realize full economies of scale and/or benefit fully from experience-curve effects exceeds the volume that can be achieved by operating within the boundaries of just one or several country markets, especially small ones.

Retrenching to a Narrower Diversification Base A number of diversified firms have had difficulty managing a diverse group of businesses and have elected to exit some of them. Selling a business outright to another company is far and away the most frequently used option for divesting a business. In 2012, Sara Lee Corporation sold its International Coffee and Tea business to J.M. Smucker, while Nike sold its Umbro and Cole Haan brands to focus on brands like Jordan and Converse that are more complementary to the Nike brand. But sometimes a business selected for divestiture has ample resources and capabilities to compete successfully on its own. In such cases, a corporate parent may elect to spin the unwanted business off as a financially and managerially independent company, either by selling shares to the public via an initial public offering or by distributing shares in the new company to shareholders of the corporate parent. In 2015, health care company Baxter International spun off its biotech arm into a new company, Baxalta, leaving its parent company to focus on medical products and equipment. eBay spun off PayPal in 2015 at a valuation of $45 billion—a value 30 times more than what eBay paid for the company in a 2002 acquisition.

Retrenching to a narrower diversification base is usually undertaken when top management concludes that its diversification has ranged too far afield and that the company can improve long-term performance by concentrating on a smaller number of businesses. But there are other important reasons for divesting one or more of a company's present businesses. Sometimes divesting a business has to be considered because market conditions in a once-attractive industry have badly deteriorated. A business can become a prime candidate for divestiture because it lacks adequate strategic or resource fit, because it is a cash hog with questionable long-term potential, or because remedying its competitive weaknesses is too expensive relative to the likely gains in profitability. Sometimes a company

A **spin-off** is an independent company created when a corporate parent divests a business either by selling shares to the public via an initial public offering or by distributing shares in the new company to shareholders of the corporate parent.

acquires businesses that, down the road, just do not work out as expected even though management has tried its best. Subpar performance by some business units is bound to occur, thereby raising questions of whether to divest them or keep them and attempt a turnaround. Other business units, despite adequate financial performance, may not mesh as well with the rest of the firm as was originally thought. For instance, PepsiCo divested its group of fast-food restaurant businesses to focus on its core soft-drink and snack-food businesses, where their specialized resources and capabilities could add more value.

On occasion, a diversification move that seems sensible from a strategic-fit standpoint turns out to be a poor *cultural fit*.[18] When several pharmaceutical companies diversified into cosmetics and perfume, they discovered their personnel had little respect for the "frivolous" nature of such products compared to the far nobler task of developing miracle drugs to cure the ill. The absence of shared values and cultural compatibility between the medical research and chemical-compounding expertise of the pharmaceutical companies and the fashion and marketing orientation of the cosmetics business was the undoing of what otherwise was diversification into businesses with technology-sharing potential, product development fit, and some overlap in distribution channels.

Diversified companies need to divest low-performing businesses or businesses that don't fit in order to concentrate on expanding existing businesses and entering new ones where opportunities are more promising.

A useful guide to determine whether or when to divest a business subsidiary is to ask, "If we were not in this business today, would we want to get into it now?" When the answer is no or probably not, divestiture should be considered. Another signal that a business should be divested occurs when it is worth more to another company than to the present parent; in such cases, shareholders would be well served if the company sells the business and collects a premium price from the buyer for whom the business is a valuable fit.

Restructuring a Diversified Company's Business Lineup

Restructuring a diversified company on a companywide basis *(corporate restructuring)* involves divesting some businesses and/or acquiring others, so as to put a whole new face on the company's business lineup.[19] Performing radical surgery on a company's business lineup is appealing when its financial performance is being squeezed or eroded by:

CORE CONCEPT

Companywide restructuring *(corporate restructuring)* involves making major changes in a diversified company by divesting some businesses and/or acquiring others, so as to put a whole new face on the company's business lineup.

- A serious mismatch between the company's resources and capabilities and the type of diversification that it has pursued.
- Too many businesses in slow-growth, declining, low-margin, or otherwise unattractive industries.
- Too many competitively weak businesses.
- The emergence of new technologies that threaten the survival of one or more important businesses.
- Ongoing declines in the market shares of one or more major business units that are falling prey to more market-savvy competitors.
- An excessive debt burden with interest costs that eat deeply into profitability.
- Ill-chosen acquisitions that haven't lived up to expectations.

On occasion, corporate restructuring can be prompted by special circumstances—such as when a firm has a unique opportunity to make an acquisition so big and important that it has to sell several existing business units to finance the new acquisition or when a company needs to sell off some businesses in order to raise the cash for entering a potentially big industry with wave-of-the-future technologies or products. As businesses are divested, corporate restructuring generally involves aligning the remaining business units into groups with the best strategic fit and then redeploying the cash flows from the divested businesses to either pay down debt or make new acquisitions to strengthen the parent company's business position in the industries it has chosen to emphasize.

Over the past decade, corporate restructuring has become a popular strategy at many diversified companies, especially those that had diversified broadly into many different industries and lines of business. VF Corporation, maker of North Face and other popular "lifestyle" apparel brands, has used a restructuring strategy to provide its shareholders with returns that are more than five times greater than shareholder returns for competing apparel makers. Since its acquisition and turnaround of North Face in 2000, VF has spent nearly $5 billion to acquire 19 additional businesses, including about $2 billion in 2011 for Timberland. New apparel brands acquired by VF Corporation include 7 For All Mankind sportswear, Vans skateboard shoes, Nautica, John Varvatos, Reef surf wear, and Lucy athletic wear. By 2015, VF Corporation had become a $12 billion powerhouse—one of the largest and most profitable apparel and footwear companies in the world. It was listed as number 248 on *Fortune*'s 2015 list of the 500 largest U.S. companies.

Illustration Capsule 8.2 discusses how Hewlett-Packard (HP) has been restructuring its operations to address internal problems and improve its profitability.

ILLUSTRATION CAPSULE 8.2

Restructuring for Better Performance at Hewlett-Packard (HP)

© Angel Navarrete/Bloomberg via Getty Images

Since its misguided acquisition of PC maker Compaq (under former CEO Carly Fiorina), Hewlett-Packard has been struggling. In the past few years, it has faced declining demand, rapid technological change, and fierce new competitors, such as Google and Apple, in its core markets. To address these problems, CEO Meg Whitman announced a restructuring of the company that was approved by the company's board of directors in October 2015. In addition to trimming operations, the plan was to split the company into two independent entities: HP Inc. and HP Enterprise. The former would primarily house the company's legacy PC and printer businesses, while the latter would retain the company's technology infrastructure, services, and cloud computing businesses.

A variety of benefits were anticipated as a result of this fundamental reshaping of the company. First, the split would enable the faster-growing enterprise business to pursue opportunities that are less relevant to the concerns of its more staid sister business. As several have observed, "it is hard to be good at both consumer and enterprise computing," which suggests an absence of strategic fit along the value chains of the two newly separated businesses. Second, in creating smaller, more nimble entities, the new companies would be better positioned to respond to competitive moves and anticipate the evolving needs of customers. This is primarily because management teams would be responsible for a smaller, more focused set of products, which would leave them better equipped to innovate in the fast-moving world of technology. Third, the more streamlined organizations would better align incentives for managers, since they would be more likely to see their individual efforts hit the bottom line under a more focused operation.

By cutting back operations to match areas of declining demand and moving some operations overseas, the company anticipates a reduction in costs of more than $2 billion. And while this will be offset by the costs of restructuring (including the need for duplicate administrative functions), the hope is that, overall, these moves will soon return the company to profitability.

Note: Developed with Ken Martin, CFA.

Sources: CNBC Online, "Former HP Chair: Spinoff Not a Defensive Play," October 6, 2015, **www.cnbc.com/2014/10/06/hairman-spin-off-not-a-defensive-play.html**; S. Mukherjee and E. Chan, Reuters Online, "Hewlett-Packard to Split into Two Public Companies, Lay Off 5,000," October 6, 2015, **www.reuters.com/article/us-hp-restructuring-idUSKCN0HV0U720141006**; J. Vanian, *Fortune* Online, "How Hewlett-Packard Plans to Split in Two," July 1, 2015, **fortune.com/2015/07/01/hewlett-packard-filing-split/**; company website (accessed March 3, 2016).

KEY POINTS

1. A "good" diversification strategy must produce increases in long-term shareholder value—increases that shareholders cannot otherwise obtain on their own. For a move to diversify into a new business to have a reasonable prospect of adding shareholder value, it must be capable of passing the industry attractiveness test, the cost-of-entry test, and the better-off test.

2. Entry into new businesses can take any of three forms: acquisition, internal startup, or joint venture. The choice of which is best depends on the firm's resources and capabilities, the industry's entry barriers, the importance of speed, and relative costs.
3. There are two fundamental approaches to diversification—into related businesses and into unrelated businesses. The rationale for *related* diversification is to benefit from *strategic fit:* Diversify into businesses with commonalities across their respective value chains, and then capitalize on the strategic fit by sharing or transferring the resources and capabilities across matching value chain activities to gain competitive advantages.
4. *Unrelated* diversification strategies surrender the competitive advantage potential of strategic fit at the value chain level in return for the potential that can be realized from superior corporate parenting or the sharing and transfer of general resources and capabilities. An outstanding corporate parent can benefit its businesses through (1) providing high-level oversight and making available other corporate resources, (2) allocating financial resources across the business portfolio, and (3) restructuring underperforming acquisitions.
5. Related diversification provides a stronger foundation for creating shareholder value than does unrelated diversification, since the *specialized resources and capabilities* that are leveraged in related diversification tend to be more valuable competitive assets than the *general resources and capabilities* underlying unrelated diversification, which in most cases are relatively common and easier to imitate.
6. Analyzing how good a company's diversification strategy is consists of a six-step process:

   Step 1: *Evaluate the long-term attractiveness of the industries into which the firm has diversified.* Determining industry attractiveness involves developing a list of industry-attractiveness measures, each of which might have a different importance weight.

   Step 2: *Evaluate the relative competitive strength of each of the company's business units.* The purpose of rating the competitive strength of each business is to gain a clear understanding of which businesses are strong contenders in their industries, which are weak contenders, and what the underlying reasons are for their strength or weakness. The conclusions about industry attractiveness can be joined with the conclusions about competitive strength by drawing a nine-cell industry-attractiveness–competitive-strength matrix that helps identify the prospects of each business and the level of priority each business should be given in allocating corporate resources and investment capital.

   Step 3: *Check for the competitive value of cross-business strategic fit.* A business is more attractive strategically when it has value chain relationships with the other business units that offer the potential to (1) combine operations to realize economies of scope, (2) transfer technology, skills, know-how, or other resource capabilities from one business to another, (3) leverage the use of a trusted brand name or other resources that enhance differentiation, (4) share other competitively valuable resources among the company's businesses, and (5) build new resources and competitive capabilities via cross-business collaboration. Cross-business strategic fit represents a significant avenue for producing competitive advantage beyond what any one business can achieve on its own.

Step 4: *Check whether the firm's resources fit the resource requirements of its present business lineup.* In firms with a related diversification strategy, resource fit exists when the firm's businesses have matching resource requirements at points along their value chains that are critical for the businesses' market success. In companies pursuing unrelated diversification, resource fit exists when the company has solid parenting capabilities or resources of a general nature that it can share or transfer to its component businesses. When there is financial resource fit among the businesses of any type of diversified company, the company can generate internal cash flows sufficient to fund the capital requirements of its businesses, pay its dividends, meet its debt obligations, and otherwise remain financially healthy.

Step 5: *Rank the performance prospects of the businesses from best to worst, and determine what the corporate parent's priority should be in allocating resources to its various businesses.* The most important considerations in judging business unit performance are sales growth, profit growth, contribution to company earnings, and the return on capital invested in the business. Normally, strong business units in attractive industries should head the list for corporate resource support.

Step 6: *Craft new strategic moves to improve overall corporate performance.* This step draws on the results of the preceding steps as the basis for selecting one of four different strategic paths for improving a diversified company's performance: (1) Stick closely with the existing business lineup and pursue opportunities presented by these businesses, (2) broaden the scope of diversification by entering additional industries, (3) retrench to a narrower scope of diversification by divesting poorly performing businesses, or (4) broadly restructure the business lineup with multiple divestitures and/or acquisitions.

ASSURANCE OF LEARNING EXERCISES

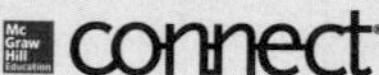

LO 1, LO 2, LO 3, LO 4

1. See if you can identify the value chain relationships that make the businesses of the following companies related in competitively relevant ways. In particular, you should consider whether there are cross-business opportunities for (1) transferring skills and technology, (2) combining related value chain activities to achieve economies of scope, and/or (3) leveraging the use of a well-respected brand name or other resources that enhance differentiation.

   Bloomin' Brands

   - Outback Steakhouse
   - Carrabba's Italian Grill
   - Roy's Restaurant (Hawaiian fusion cuisine)
   - Bonefish Grill (market-fresh fine seafood)
   - Fleming's Prime Steakhouse & Wine Bar

L'Oréal

- Maybelline, Lancôme, essie, and Shu Uemura cosmetics
- Redken, Matrix, L'Oréal Professional, Garnier, Kiehl's, and Kérastase hair care and skin care products
- Ralph Lauren, Yves Saint Laurent, and Giorgio Armani fragrances
- La Roche-Posay, Vichy Laboratories, and SkinCeuticals dermocosmetics

Johnson & Johnson

- Baby products (powder, shampoo, oil, lotion)
- Band-Aids and other first-aid products
- Women's health and personal care products (Stayfree, Carefree, Sure & Natural)
- Neutrogena, Lubriderm, and Aveeno skin care products
- Nonprescription drugs (Tylenol, Motrin, Pepcid AC, Mylanta, Monistat)
- Prescription drugs
- Prosthetic and other medical devices
- Surgical and hospital products
- Acuvue contact lenses

2. Peruse the business group listings for Ingersoll Rand shown below and listed at its website (**company.ingersollrand.com/ircorp/en/discover-us/our-global-brands.html**). How would you characterize the company's corporate strategy—related diversification, unrelated diversification, or a combination related–unrelated diversification strategy? Explain your answer. **LO 1, LO 2, LO 3, LO 4**

   - Club car—golf carts and other zero-emissions electric vehicles
   - Thermo King—transportation temperature control systems for truck, trailer, transit, marine, and rail applications
   - Ingersoll Rand—compressed air systems, tools and pumps, and fluid handling systems
   - Trane—heating, ventilating, and air conditioning systems
   - American Standard—home heating and air conditioning systems
   - ARO—fluid handling equipment for chemical, manufacturing, energy, pharmaceutical, and mining industries

3. ITT is a technology-oriented engineering and manufacturing company with the following business divisions and products: Mc Graw Hill Education connect

   LO 1, LO 2, LO 3, LO 4, LO 5

   - Industrial Process Division—industrial pumps, valves, and monitoring and control systems; aftermarket services for the chemical, oil and gas, mining, pulp and paper, power, and biopharmaceutical markets
   - Motion Technologies Division—durable brake pads, shock absorbers, and damping technologies for the automotive and rail markets
   - Interconnect Solutions—connectors and fittings for the production of automobiles, aircraft, railcars and locomotives, oil field equipment, medical equipment, and industrial equipment

- Control Technologies—energy absorption and vibration dampening equipment, transducers and regulators, and motion controls used in the production of robotics, medical equipment, automobiles, subsea equipment, industrial equipment, aircraft, and military vehicles

Based on the previous listing, would you say that ITT's business lineup reflects a strategy of related diversification, unrelated diversification, or a combination of related and unrelated diversification? What benefits are generated from any strategic fit existing between ITT's businesses? Also, what types of companies should ITT consider acquiring that might improve shareholder value? Justify your answer.

EXERCISE FOR SIMULATION PARTICIPANTS

LO 1, LO 2, LO 3

1. In the event that your company has the opportunity to diversify into other products or businesses of your choosing, would you opt to pursue related diversification, unrelated diversification, or a combination of both? Explain why.

LO 1, LO 2

2. What specific resources and capabilities does your company possess that would make diversifying into related businesses attractive? Indicate what kinds of strategic-fit benefits could be captured by transferring these resources and competitive capabilities to newly acquired related businesses.

LO 1, LO 2

3. If your company opted to pursue a strategy of related diversification, what industries or product categories could it diversify into that would allow it to achieve economies of scope? Name at least two or three such industries or product categories, and indicate the specific kinds of cost savings that might accrue from entry into each.

LO 1, LO 3

4. If your company opted to pursue a strategy of unrelated diversification, what industries or product categories could it diversify into that would allow it to capitalize on using its present brand name and corporate image to good advantage in the newly entered businesses or product categories? Name at least two or three such industries or product categories, and indicate the *specific benefits* that might be captured by transferring your company's umbrella brand name to each.

ENDNOTES

[1] Michael E. Porter, "From Competitive Advantage to Corporate Strategy," *Harvard Business Review* 45, no. 3 (May–June 1987), pp. 46–49.

[2] www.zerohedge.com/news/2013-02-14/heinz-confirms-it-will-be-acquired-buffett-28-billion-transaction-7250share (accessed February 2, 2014).

[3] finance.fortune.cnn.com/2012/07/31/-companies-are-paying-up-for-deals/; blogs.wsj.com/cfo/2013/11/26/why-are-takeover-prices-plummeting/ (accessed February 2, 2014).

[4] A. Shleifer and R. Vishny, "Takeovers in the 60s and the 80s—Evidence and Implications," *Strategic Management Journal* 12 (Winter 1991), pp. 51–59; T. Brush, "Predicted Change in Operational Synergy and Post-Acquisition Performance of Acquired Businesses," *Strategic Management Journal* 17, no. 1 (1996), pp. 1–24; J. P. Walsh, "Top Management Turnover Following Mergers and Acquisitions," *Strategic Management Journal* 9, no. 2 (1988), pp. 173–183; A. Cannella and D. Hambrick, "Effects of Executive Departures on the Performance of Acquired Firms," *Strategic Management Journal* 14 (Summer 1993), pp. 137–152; R. Roll, "The Hubris Hypothesis of Corporate Takeovers," *Journal of Business* 59, no. 2 (1986), pp. 197–216; P. Haspeslagh and D. Jemison, *Managing Acquisitions* (New York: Free Press, 1991).

[5] M.L.A. Hayward, "When Do Firms Learn from Their Acquisition Experience? Evidence from 1990–1995," *Strategic Management Journal* 23, no. 1 (2002), pp. 21–29; G. Ahuja and R. Katila, "Technological Acquisitions and the Innovation Performance of Acquiring Firms:

A Longitudinal Study," *Strategic Management Journal* 22, no. 3 (2001), pp. 197–220; H. Barkema and F. Vermeulen, "International Expansion through Start-Up or Acquisition: A Learning Perspective," *Academy of Management Journal* 41, no. 1 (1998), pp. 7–26.

[6] Yves L. Doz and Gary Hamel, *Alliance Advantage: The Art of Creating Value through Partnering* (Boston: Harvard Business School Press, 1998), chaps. 1 and 2.

[7] J. Glover, "The Guardian," March 23, 1996, **www.mcspotlight.org/media/press/guardpizza_23mar96.html**.

[8] Michael E. Porter, *Competitive Advantage* (New York: Free Press, 1985), pp. 318–319, 337–353; Porter, "From Competitive Advantage to Corporate Strategy," pp. 53–57; Constantinos C. Markides and Peter J. Williamson, "Corporate Diversification and Organization Structure: A Resource-Based View," *Academy of Management Journal* 39, no. 2 (April 1996), pp. 340–367.

[9] David J. Collis and Cynthia A. Montgomery, "Creating Corporate Advantage," *Harvard Business Review* 76, no. 3 (May–June 1998), pp. 72–80; Markides and Williamson, "Corporate Diversification and Organization Structure."

[10] Jeanne M. Liedtka, "Collaboration across Lines of Business for Competitive Advantage," *Academy of Management Executive* 10, no. 2 (May 1996), pp. 20–34.

[11] Kathleen M. Eisenhardt and D. Charles Galunic, "Coevolving: At Last, a Way to Make Synergies Work," *Harvard Business Review* 78, no. 1 (January–February 2000), pp. 91–101; Constantinos C. Markides and Peter J. Williamson, "Related Diversification, Core Competences and Corporate Performance," *Strategic Management Journal* 15 (Summer 1994), pp. 149–165.

[12] A. Campbell, M. Goold, and M. Alexander, "Corporate Strategy: The Quest for Parenting Advantage," *Harvard Business Review* 73, no. 2 (March–April 1995), pp. 120–132.

[13] Cynthia A. Montgomery and B. Wernerfelt, "Diversification, Ricardian Rents, and Tobin-Q," *RAND Journal of Economics* 19, no. 4 (1988), pp. 623–632.

[14] Patricia L. Anslinger and Thomas E. Copeland, "Growth through Acquisitions: A Fresh Look," *Harvard Business Review* 74, no. 1 (January–February 1996), pp. 126–135.

[15] M. Lubatkin and S. Chatterjee, "Extending Modern Portfolio Theory," *Academy of Management Journal* 37, no.1 (February 1994), pp. 109–136.

[16] Lawrence G. Franko, "The Death of Diversification? The Focusing of the World's Industrial Firms, 1980–2000," *Business Horizons* 47, no. 4 (July–August 2004), pp. 41–50.

[17] David J. Collis and Cynthia A. Montgomery, "Competing on Resources: Strategy in the 90s," *Harvard Business Review* 73, no. 4 (July–August 1995), pp. 118–128.

[18] Peter F. Drucker, *Management: Tasks, Responsibilities, Practices* (New York: Harper & Row, 1974), p. 709.

[19] Lee Dranikoff, Tim Koller, and Anton Schneider, "Divestiture: Strategy's Missing Link," *Harvard Business Review* 80, no. 5 (May 2002), pp. 74–83.

CHAPTER 9

Ethics, Corporate Social Responsibility, Environmental Sustainability, and Strategy

© Boris Lyubner/age fotostock

Learning Objectives

THIS CHAPTER WILL HELP YOU UNDERSTAND:

LO 1 How the standards of ethical behavior in business are no different from the ethical standards and norms of the larger society and culture in which a company operates.

LO 2 What drives unethical business strategies and behavior.

LO 3 The costs of business ethics failures.

LO 4 The concepts of corporate social responsibility and environmental sustainability and how companies balance these duties with economic responsibilities to shareholders.

We don't think of ourselves as do-gooders or altruists. It's just that somehow we're trying our best to be run with some sense of moral compass even in a business environment that is growing.

Craig Newmark—*Founder of Craigslist*

Sustainability, ensuring the future of life on Earth, is an infinite game, the endless expression of generosity on behalf of all.

Paul Hawken—*Founder of Erewhon Trading Co.; cofounder of Smith & Hawken*

The time is always right to do what is right.

Martin Luther King, Jr.—*Civil rights activist and humanitarian*

Clearly, in capitalistic or market economies, a company has a responsibility to make a profit and grow the business. Managers of public companies have a fiduciary duty to operate the enterprise in a manner that creates value for the company's shareholders. Just as clearly, a company and its personnel are duty-bound to obey the law and comply with governmental regulations. But does a company also have a duty to go beyond legal requirements and hold all company personnel responsible for conforming to high ethical standards? Does it have an obligation to contribute to the betterment of society, independent of the needs and preferences of the customers it serves? Should a company display a social conscience by devoting a portion of its resources to bettering society? Should its strategic initiatives be screened for possible negative effects on future generations of the world's population?

This chapter focuses on whether a company, in the course of trying to craft and execute a strategy that delivers value to both customers and shareholders, also has a duty to (1) act in an ethical manner; (2) be a committed corporate citizen and allocate some of its resources to improving the well-being of employees, the communities in which it operates, and society as a whole; and (3) adopt business practices that conserve natural resources, protect the interests of future generations, and preserve the well-being of the planet.

WHAT DO WE MEAN BY *BUSINESS ETHICS*?

Ethics concerns principles of right or wrong conduct. **Business ethics** is the application of ethical principles and standards to the actions and decisions of business organizations and the conduct of their personnel.[1] *Ethical principles in business are not materially different from ethical principles in general.* Why? Because business actions have to be judged in the context of society's standards of right and wrong, not with respect to a special set of ethical standards applicable only to business situations. If dishonesty is considered unethical and immoral, then dishonest behavior in business—whether it relates to customers, suppliers, employees, shareholders,

CORE CONCEPT

Business ethics deals with the application of general ethical principles to the actions and decisions of businesses and the conduct of their personnel.

LO 1

How the standards of ethical behavior in business are no different from the ethical standards and norms of the larger society and culture in which a company operates.

competitors, or government—qualifies as equally unethical and immoral. If being ethical entails not deliberately harming others, then businesses are ethically obliged to recall a defective or unsafe product swiftly, regardless of the cost. If society deems bribery unethical, then it is unethical for company personnel to make payoffs to government officials to win government contracts or bestow favors to customers to win or retain their business. In short, ethical behavior in business situations requires adhering to generally accepted norms about right or wrong conduct. As a consequence, company managers have an obligation—indeed, a duty—to observe ethical norms when crafting and executing strategy.

WHERE DO ETHICAL STANDARDS COME FROM—ARE THEY UNIVERSAL OR DEPENDENT ON LOCAL NORMS?

Notions of right and wrong, fair and unfair, moral and immoral are present in all societies and cultures. But there are three distinct schools of thought about the extent to which ethical standards travel across cultures and whether multinational companies can apply the same set of ethical standards in any and all locations where they operate.

The School of Ethical Universalism

CORE CONCEPT

The school of **ethical universalism** holds that the most fundamental conceptions of right and wrong are *universal* and apply to members of all societies, all companies, and all businesspeople.

According to the school of **ethical universalism,** the most fundamental conceptions of right and wrong are *universal* and transcend culture, society, and religion.[2] For instance, being truthful (not lying and not being deliberately deceitful) strikes a chord of what's right in the peoples of all nations. Likewise, demonstrating integrity of character, not cheating or harming people, and treating others with decency are concepts that resonate with people of virtually all cultures and religions.

Common moral agreement about right and wrong actions and behaviors across multiple cultures and countries gives rise to universal ethical standards that apply to members of all societies, all companies, and all businesspeople. These universal ethical principles set forth the traits and behaviors that are considered virtuous and that a good person is supposed to believe in and to display. Thus, adherents of the school of ethical universalism maintain that it is entirely appropriate to expect all members of society (including all personnel of all companies worldwide) to conform to these universal ethical standards.[3] For example, people in most societies would concur that it is unethical for companies to knowingly expose workers to toxic chemicals and hazardous materials or to sell products known to be unsafe or harmful to the users.

The strength of ethical universalism is that it draws on the collective views of multiple societies and cultures to put some clear boundaries on what constitutes ethical and unethical business behavior, regardless of the country or culture in which a company's personnel are conducting activities. This means that with respect to basic moral standards that do not vary significantly according to local cultural beliefs, traditions, or religious convictions, a multinational company can develop a code of ethics that it applies more or less evenly across its worldwide operations. It can avoid the slippery slope that comes from having different ethical standards for different company personnel depending on where in the world they are working.

The School of Ethical Relativism

While undoubtedly there are some universal moral prescriptions (like being truthful and trustworthy), there are also observable variations from one society to another as to what constitutes ethical or unethical behavior. Indeed, differing religious beliefs, social customs, traditions, core values, and behavioral norms frequently give rise to different standards about what is fair or unfair, moral or immoral, and ethically right or wrong. For instance, European and American managers often establish standards of business conduct that protect human rights such as freedom of movement and residence, freedom of speech and political opinion, and the right to privacy. In China, where societal commitment to basic human rights is weak, human rights considerations play a small role in determining what is ethically right or wrong in conducting business activities. In Japan, managers believe that showing respect for the collective good of society is a more important ethical consideration. In Muslim countries, managers typically apply ethical standards compatible with the teachings of Muhammad. Consequently, the school of **ethical relativism** holds that a "one-size-fits-all" template for judging the ethical appropriateness of business actions and the behaviors of company personnel is totally inappropriate. Rather, the underlying thesis of ethical relativism is that whether certain actions or behaviors are ethically right or wrong depends on the ethical norms of the country or culture in which they take place. For businesses, this implies that when there are cross-country or cross-cultural differences in ethical standards, it is appropriate for *local ethical standards to take precedence over what the ethical standards may be in a company's home market.*[4] In a world of ethical relativism, there are few absolutes when it comes to business ethics, and thus few ethical absolutes for consistently judging the ethical correctness of a company's conduct in various countries and markets.

CORE CONCEPT

The school of **ethical relativism** holds that differing religious beliefs, customs, and behavioral norms across countries and cultures give rise to *multiple sets of standards concerning what is ethically right or wrong.* These differing standards mean that whether business-related actions are right or wrong depends on the prevailing local ethical standards.

This need to contour local ethical standards to fit local customs, local notions of fair and proper individual treatment, and local business practices gives rise to multiple sets of ethical standards. It also poses some challenging ethical dilemmas. Consider the following two examples.

Under ethical relativism, there can be no one-size-fits-all set of authentic ethical norms against which to gauge the conduct of company personnel.

The Use of Underage Labor

In industrialized nations, the use of underage workers is considered taboo. Social activists are adamant that child labor is unethical and that companies should neither employ children under the age of 18 as full-time employees nor source any products from foreign suppliers that employ underage workers. Many countries have passed legislation forbidding the use of underage labor or, at a minimum, regulating the employment of people under the age of 18. However, in Eretria, Uzbekistan, Myanmar, Somalia, Zimbabwe, Afghanistan, Sudan, North Korea, Yemen, and more than 50 other countries, it is customary to view children as potential, even necessary, workers. In other countries, like China, India, Russia, and Brazil, child labor laws are often poorly enforced.[5] As of 2013, the International Labor Organization estimated that there were about 168 million child laborers age 5 to 17 and that some 85 million of them were engaged in hazardous work.[6]

While exposing children to hazardous work and long work hours is unquestionably deplorable, the fact remains that poverty-stricken families in many poor countries cannot subsist without the work efforts of young family members; sending their children to school instead of having them work is not a realistic option. If such children are not permitted to work (especially those in the 12-to-17 age group)—due to pressures imposed by activist groups in industrialized nations—they may be forced to go out on the streets begging or to seek work in parts of the "underground" economy such as drug trafficking and prostitution.[7] So, if all businesses in countries where employing underage workers is common succumb to the pressures to stop employing underage labor, then have they served the best interests of the underage workers, their families, and society in general? Illustration Capsule 9.1 describes IKEA's approach to dealing with this issue regarding its global supplier network.

The Payment of Bribes and Kickbacks

A particularly thorny area facing multinational companies is the degree of cross-country variability in paying bribes.[8] In many countries in eastern Europe, Africa, Latin America, and Asia, it is customary to pay bribes to government officials in order to win a government contract, obtain a license or permit, or facilitate an administrative ruling.[9] In some developing nations, it is difficult for any company, foreign or domestic, to move goods through customs without paying off low-level officials. Senior managers in China and Russia often use their power to obtain kickbacks when they purchase materials or other products for their companies.[10] Likewise, in many countries it is normal to make payments to prospective customers in order to win or retain their business. Some people stretch to justify the payment of bribes and kickbacks on grounds that bribing government officials to get goods through customs or giving kickbacks to customers to retain their business or win new orders is simply a payment for services rendered, in the same way that people tip for service at restaurants.[11] But while this is a clever rationalization, it rests on moral quicksand.

Companies that forbid the payment of bribes and kickbacks in their codes of ethical conduct and that are serious about enforcing this prohibition face a particularly vexing problem in countries where bribery and kickback payments are an entrenched local custom. Complying with the company's code of ethical conduct in these countries is very often tantamount to losing business to competitors that have no such scruples—an outcome that penalizes ethical companies and ethical company personnel (who may suffer lost sales commissions or bonuses). On the other hand, the payment of bribes or kickbacks not only undercuts the company's code of ethics but also risks breaking the law. The Foreign Corrupt Practices Act (FCPA) prohibits U.S. companies from paying bribes to government officials, political parties, political candidates, or others in all countries where they do business. The Organization for Economic Cooperation and Development (OECD) has antibribery standards that criminalize the bribery of foreign public officials in international business transactions—all 35 OECD member countries and 7 nonmember countries have adopted these standards.

Despite laws forbidding bribery to secure sales and contracts, the practice persists. As of June 2014, 263 individuals and 164 entities were sanctioned under criminal proceedings for foreign bribery by the OECD. At least 80 of the sanctioned individuals were sentenced to prison. In 2014, Alcoa agreed to pay $384 million to settle charges brought by the Justice Department and the Securities and Exchange Commission (SEC) that it used bribes to lock in lucrative contracts in Bahrain. French oil giant Total settled criminal charges for $398 million the prior year for similar behavior in Iran. Other well-known companies caught up in recent or ongoing bribery cases include Archer Daniels Midland, the global agribusiness trader; Swiss oil-field services firm Weatherford; Avon; and Walmart. In 2013, the Ralph Lauren Corporation struck a non-prosecution agreement with the SEC to forfeit illicit profits made due to bribes paid by a subsidiary in Argentina. When the parent company found the problem, it immediately reported it to the SEC and provided substantial assistance with the investigation. The company paid only $882,000 in penalties (above the forfeited profits) as a result.

ILLUSTRATION CAPSULE 9.1

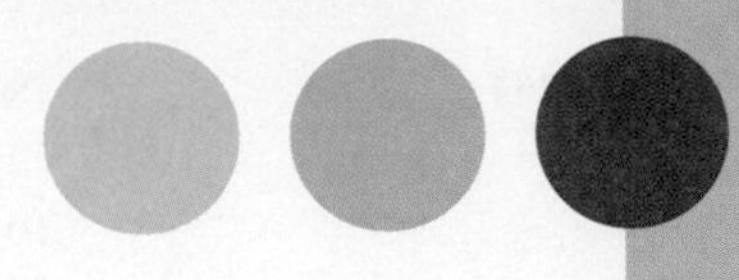

IKEA's Global Supplier Standards: Maintaining Low Costs While Fighting the Root Causes of Child Labor

© Holly Hildreth/Moment/Getty Images

Known for its stylish ready-to-assemble home furnishings, IKEA has long relied on an extensive supplier network to manufacture its products and support its rapid global expansion. It has worked hard to develop a successful approach to encourage high ethical standards among its suppliers, including standards concerning the notoriously difficult issue of child labor.

IKEA's initial plan to combat the use of child labor by its suppliers involved (1) contracts that threatened immediate cancellation and (2) random audits by a third-party partner. Despite these safeguards, the company discovered that some of its Indian suppliers were still employing children. IKEA realized that this issue would crop up again and again if it continued to use low-cost suppliers in developing countries—a critical element in its cost-containment strategy.

To address this problem, IKEA developed and introduced its new code for suppliers, IWAY, which addresses social, safety, and environmental issues across its purchasing model. When faced with a supplier slip-up, IKEA works with the company to figure out and tackle the root cause of violations. Using child labor, for example, can signal bigger problems: production inefficiencies that require the lowest-cost labor, lack of alternative options for children like school or supervised community centers, family health or income challenges that mean children need to become breadwinners, and so on. IKEA takes action to provide technical expertise to improve working conditions and processes, offer financing help at reasonable rates, run training programs onsite, and help develop resources and infrastructure in areas where its suppliers are based. The IKEA foundation also began focusing on these issues through partnerships with UNICEF and Save the Children aimed at funding long-term community programs that support access to education, health care, and sustainable family incomes. As of 2016, their efforts have improved the education opportunities of more than 12 million children in 46 different countries.

IKEA's proactive approach has reduced some of the risks involved in relying on suppliers in developing countries. Through its approach, IKEA has been able to maintain its core strategic principles even when they seem to be at odds: low costs, great design, adherence to its ethical principles, and a commitment to a better world.

Note: Developed with Kiera O'Brien.

Sources: IKEA, "About the Company: This Is IKEA," **www.ikea.com/ms/en_US/this-is-ikea/people-and-planet/people-and-communities/**; Elain Cohen, "Banning Child Labor: The Symptom or the Cause?" *CSR Newswire*, **www.csrwire.com/blog/posts/547-banning-child-labor-the-symptom-or-the-cause**; UNICEF Press Center, Joint Press Release, **www.unicef.org/media/media_89819.html** (accessed February 2, 2016).

Using the Principle of Ethical Relativism to Create Ethical Standards Is Problematic for Multinational Companies Relying on the principle of ethical relativism to determine what is right or wrong poses major problems for multinational companies trying to decide which ethical standards to enforce companywide. It is a slippery slope indeed to resolve conflicting ethical standards for operating in different countries without any kind of higher-order moral compass. Consider, for example, the ethical inconsistency of a multinational company that, in the name of ethical relativism, declares it impermissible

Codes of conduct based on ethical relativism can be *ethically problematic* for multinational companies by creating a maze of conflicting ethical standards.

to engage in kickbacks unless such payments are customary and generally overlooked by legal authorities. It is likewise problematic for a multinational company to declare it ethically acceptable to use underage labor at its plants in those countries where child labor is allowed but ethically inappropriate to employ underage labor at its plants elsewhere. If a country's culture is accepting of environmental degradation or practices that expose workers to dangerous conditions (toxic chemicals or bodily harm), should a multinational company lower its ethical bar in that country but rule the very same actions to be ethically wrong in other countries?

Business leaders who rely on the principle of ethical relativism to justify conflicting ethical standards for operating in different countries have little moral basis for establishing or enforcing ethical standards companywide. Rather, when a company's ethical standards vary from country to country, the clear message being sent to employees is that the company has no ethical standards or convictions of its own and prefers to let its standards of ethical right and wrong be governed by the customs and practices of the countries in which it operates. Applying multiple sets of ethical standards without some kind of higher-order moral compass is scarcely a basis for holding company personnel to high standards of ethical behavior. And it can lead to prosecutions of both companies and individuals alike when there are conflicting sets of laws.

Ethics and Integrative Social Contracts Theory

CORE CONCEPT

According to **integrated social contracts theory,** universal ethical principles based on the collective views of multiple societies form a "social contract" that all individuals and organizations have a duty to observe in all situations. *Within the boundaries of this social contract,* local cultures or groups can specify what *additional* actions may or may not be ethically permissible.

Integrative social contracts theory provides a middle position between the opposing views of ethical universalism and ethical relativism.[12] According to this theory, the ethical standards a company should try to uphold are governed by both (1) a limited number of universal ethical principles that are widely recognized as putting legitimate ethical boundaries on behaviors in *all* situations and (2) the circumstances of local cultures, traditions, and values that further prescribe what constitutes ethically permissible behavior. The universal ethical principles are based on the collective views of multiple cultures and societies and combine to form a "social contract" that all individuals, groups, organizations, and businesses in all situations have a duty to observe. *Within the boundaries of this social contract,* local cultures or groups can specify what *other* actions may or may not be ethically permissible. While this system leaves some "moral free space" for the people in a particular country (or local culture, or profession, or even a company) to make specific interpretations of what other actions may or may not be permissible, *universal ethical norms always take precedence.* Thus, local ethical standards can be *more* stringent than the universal ethical standards but *never less so.* For example, both the legal and medical professions have standards regarding what kinds of advertising are ethically permissible that extend beyond the universal norm that advertising not be false or misleading.

According to integrated social contracts theory, adherence to universal or "first-order" ethical norms should always take precedence over local or "second-order" norms.

The strength of integrated social contracts theory is that it accommodates the best parts of ethical universalism and ethical relativism. Moreover, integrative social contracts theory offers managers in multinational companies clear guidance in resolving cross-country ethical differences: Those parts of the company's code of ethics that involve universal ethical norms must be enforced worldwide, but within these boundaries there is room for ethical diversity and the opportunity for host-country cultures to exert *some* influence over the moral and ethical standards of business units operating in that country.

A good example of the application of integrative social contracts theory to business involves the payment of bribes and kickbacks. Yes, bribes and kickbacks are common in some countries. But the fact that bribery flourishes in a country does not mean it is an authentic or legitimate ethical norm. Virtually all of the world's major religions (e.g., Buddhism, Christianity, Confucianism, Hinduism, Islam, Judaism, Sikhism, and Taoism) and all moral schools of thought condemn bribery and corruption. Therefore, a multinational company might reasonably conclude that there is a universal ethical principle to be observed here—one of refusing to condone bribery and kickbacks on the part of company personnel no matter what the local custom is and no matter what the sales consequences are.

In instances involving *universally applicable* ethical norms (like paying bribes), there can be *no compromise* on what is ethically permissible and what is not.

HOW AND WHY ETHICAL STANDARDS IMPACT THE TASKS OF CRAFTING AND EXECUTING STRATEGY

Many companies have acknowledged their ethical obligations in official codes of ethical conduct. In the United States, for example, the Sarbanes–Oxley Act, passed in 2002, requires that companies whose stock is publicly traded have a code of ethics or else explain in writing to the SEC why they do not. But the senior executives of ethically principled companies understand that there's a big difference between having a code of ethics because it is mandated and having ethical standards that truly provide guidance for a company's strategy and business conduct.[13] They know that *the litmus test of whether a company's code of ethics is cosmetic is the extent to which it is embraced in crafting strategy and in operating the business day to day.* Executives committed to high standards make a point of considering three sets of questions whenever a new strategic initiative or policy or operating practice is under review:

- Is what we are proposing to do fully compliant with our code of ethical conduct? Are there any areas of ambiguity that may be of concern?
- Is there any aspect of the strategy (or policy or operating practice) that gives the appearance of being ethically questionable?
- Is there anything in the proposed action that customers, employees, suppliers, stockholders, competitors, community activists, regulators, or the media might consider ethically objectionable?

Unless questions of this nature are posed—either in open discussion or by force of habit in the minds of company managers—there's a risk that strategic initiatives and/or the way daily operations are conducted will become disconnected from the company's code of ethics. If a company's executives believe strongly in living up to the company's ethical standards, they will unhesitatingly reject strategic initiatives and operating approaches that don't measure up. However, in companies with a cosmetic approach to ethics, any linkage of the professed standards to its strategy and operating practices stems mainly from a desire to avoid the risk of embarrassment and possible disciplinary action for approving actions that are later deemed unethical and perhaps illegal.

While most company managers are careful to ensure that a company's strategy is within the bounds of what is *legal,* evidence indicates they are not always so careful to ensure that all elements of their strategies and operating activities are within the bounds of what is considered *ethical.* In recent years, there have been revelations of ethical misconduct on the part of managers at such companies as Koch Industries, Las Vegas Sands, BP, Halliburton, Hewlett-Packard, GlaxoSmithKline, Marathon Oil

LO 2

What drives unethical business strategies and behavior.

Corporation, Kraft Foods Inc., Motorola Solutions, Pfizer, several leading investment banking firms, and a host of mortgage lenders. The consequences of crafting strategies that cannot pass the test of moral scrutiny are manifested in sizable fines, devastating public relations hits, sharp drops in stock prices that cost shareholders billions of dollars, criminal indictments, and convictions of company executives. The fallout from all these scandals has resulted in heightened management attention to legal and ethical considerations in crafting strategy.

DRIVERS OF UNETHICAL BUSINESS STRATEGIES AND BEHAVIOR

Apart from the "business of business is business, not ethics" kind of thinking apparent in recent high-profile business scandals, three other main drivers of unethical business behavior also stand out:[14]

- Faulty oversight, enabling the unscrupulous pursuit of personal gain and self-interest.
- Heavy pressures on company managers to meet or beat short-term performance targets.
- A company culture that puts profitability and business performance ahead of ethical behavior.

Faulty Oversight, Enabling the Unscrupulous Pursuit of Personal Gain and Self-Interest People who are obsessed with wealth accumulation, power, status, and their own self-interest often push aside ethical principles in their quest for personal gain. Driven by greed and ambition, they exhibit few qualms in skirting the rules or doing whatever is necessary to achieve their goals. A general disregard for business ethics can prompt all kinds of unethical strategic maneuvers and behaviors at companies.

The U.S. government has been conducting a multiyear investigation of insider trading, the illegal practice of exchanging confidential information to gain an advantage in the stock market. Focusing on the hedge fund industry and nicknamed "Operation Perfect Hedge," the investigation has brought to light scores of violations. The six-year crackdown on insider trading yielded 87 convictions, although 14 were dismissed by prosecutors or lost on appeal by 2015. Among the most prominent of those convicted was Raj Rajaratnam, the former head of Galleon Group, who was sentenced to 11 years in prison and fined $10 million. At SAC Capital, a $14 billion hedge fund, eight hedge fund managers were convicted of insider trading, in what has been called the most lucrative insider trading scheme in U.S. history. The company agreed to pay $1.8 billion in penalties and has been forced to stop managing money for outside investors.[15] Since Operation Perfect Hedge began, abnormal jumps in the stock price of target firms (a sign of insider trading) have fallen 45 percent.

CORE CONCEPT

Self-dealing occurs when managers take advantage of their position to further their own private interests rather than those of the firm.

Responsible corporate governance and oversight by the company's corporate board is necessary to guard against self-dealing and the manipulation of information to disguise such actions by a company's managers. **Self-dealing** occurs when managers take advantage of their position to further their own private interests rather than those of the firm. As discussed in Chapter 2, the duty of the corporate board (and its compensation and audit committees in particular) is to guard against such actions. A strong, independent board is necessary to have proper oversight of the company's financial practices and to hold top managers accountable for their actions.

A particularly egregious example of the lack of proper oversight is the scandal over mortgage lending and banking practices that resulted in a crisis for the U.S. residential real estate market and heartrending consequences for many home buyers. This scandal stemmed from consciously unethical strategies at many banks and mortgage companies to boost the fees they earned on home mortgages by deliberately lowering lending standards to approve so-called subprime loans for home buyers whose incomes were insufficient to make their monthly mortgage payments. Once these lenders earned their fees on these loans, they repackaged the loans to hide their true nature and auctioned them off to unsuspecting investors, who later suffered huge losses when the high-risk borrowers began to default on their loan payments. (Government authorities later forced some of the firms that auctioned off these packaged loans to repurchase them at the auction price and bear the losses themselves.) A lawsuit by the attorneys general of 49 states charging widespread and systematic fraud ultimately resulted in a $26 billion settlement by the five largest U.S. banks (Bank of America, Citigroup, JPMorgan Chase, Wells Fargo, and Ally Financial). Included in the settlement were new rules designed to increase oversight and reform policies and practices among the mortgage companies. The settlement includes what are believed to be a set of robust monitoring and enforcement mechanisms that should help prevent such abuses in the future.[16]

Heavy Pressures on Company Managers to Meet Short-Term Performance Targets When key personnel find themselves scrambling to meet the quarterly and annual sales and profit expectations of investors and financial analysts, they often feel enormous pressure to *do whatever it takes* to protect their reputation for delivering good results. Executives at high-performing companies know that investors will see the slightest sign of a slowdown in earnings growth as a red flag and drive down the company's stock price. In addition, slowing growth or declining profits could lead to a downgrade of the company's credit rating if it has used lots of debt to finance its growth. The pressure to "never miss a quarter"—to not upset the expectations of analysts, investors, and creditors—prompts nearsighted managers to engage in short-term maneuvers to make the numbers, regardless of whether these moves are really in the best long-term interests of the company. Sometimes the pressure induces company personnel to continue to stretch the rules until the limits of ethical conduct are overlooked.[17] Once ethical boundaries are crossed in efforts to "meet or beat their numbers," the threshold for making more extreme ethical compromises becomes lower.

In 2014, the SEC charged Diamond Foods (maker of Pop Secret and Emerald Nuts) with accounting fraud, alleging that the company falsified costs in order to boost earnings and stock prices. The company paid $5 million to the SEC to settle fraud charges, while its (now ousted) CEO paid $125,000 to settle a separate charge of negligence and returned $4 million in bonuses to the company. The company's now-former CFO initially fought the charges, but eventually settled by paying a $125,000 fine. The real blow for the company was that its pending acquisition of potato chip giant Pringles fell apart as a result of the scandal, thwarting the company's dreams of becoming the second-largest snack company in the world.[18]

Company executives often feel pressured to hit financial performance targets because their compensation depends heavily on the company's performance. Over the last two decades, it has become fashionable for boards of directors to grant lavish

CORE CONCEPT

Short-termism is the tendency for managers to focus excessively on short-term performance objectives at the expense of longer-term strategic objectives. It has negative implications for the likelihood of ethical lapses as well as company performance in the longer run.

bonuses, stock option awards, and other compensation benefits to executives for meeting specified performance targets. So outlandishly large were these rewards that executives had strong personal incentives to bend the rules and engage in behaviors that allowed the targets to be met. Much of the accounting manipulation at the root of recent corporate scandals has entailed situations in which executives benefited enormously from misleading accounting or other shady activities that allowed them to hit the numbers and receive incentive awards ranging from $10 million to more than $1 billion for hedge fund managers.

The fundamental problem with **short-termism**—the tendency for managers to focus excessive attention on short-term performance objectives—is that it doesn't create value for customers or improve the firm's competitiveness in the marketplace; that is, it sacrifices the activities that are the most reliable drivers of higher profits and added shareholder value in the long run. Cutting ethical corners in the name of profits carries exceptionally high risk for shareholders—the steep stock price decline and tarnished brand image that accompany the discovery of scurrilous behavior leave shareholders with a company worth much less than before—and the rebuilding task can be arduous, taking both considerable time and resources.

A Company Culture That Puts Profitability and Business Performance Ahead of Ethical Behavior When a company's culture spawns an ethically corrupt or amoral work climate, people have a company-approved license to ignore "what's right" and engage in any behavior or strategy they think they can get away with. Such cultural norms as "Everyone else does it" and "It is okay to bend the rules to get the job done" permeate the work environment. At such companies, ethically immoral people are certain to play down observance of ethical strategic actions and business conduct. Moreover, cultural pressures to utilize unethical means if circumstances become challenging can prompt otherwise honorable people to behave unethically. A perfect example of a company culture gone awry on ethics is Enron, a now-defunct but infamous company found guilty of one of the most sprawling business frauds in U.S. history.[19]

Enron's leaders pressured company personnel to be innovative and aggressive in figuring out how to grow current earnings—*regardless of the methods.* Enron's annual "rank and yank" performance evaluation process, in which the lowest-ranking 15 to 20 percent of employees were let go, made it abundantly clear that bottom-line results were what mattered most. The name of the game at Enron became devising clever ways to boost revenues and earnings, even if this sometimes meant operating outside established policies (and legal limits). In fact, outside-the-lines behavior was celebrated if it generated profitable new business.

A high-performance–high-rewards climate came to pervade the Enron culture, as the best workers (determined by who produced the best bottom-line results) received impressively large incentives and bonuses. On Car Day at Enron, an array of luxury sports cars arrived for presentation to the most successful employees. Understandably, employees wanted to be seen as part of Enron's star team and partake in the benefits granted to Enron's best and brightest employees. The high monetary rewards, the ambitious and hard-driving people whom the company hired and promoted, and the competitive, results-oriented culture combined to give Enron a reputation not only for trampling competitors but also for internal ruthlessness. The company's win-at-all-costs mindset nurtured a culture that gradually and then more rapidly fostered the erosion of ethical standards, eventually making a mockery of the company's stated values of integrity and respect. When it became evident in fall 2001 that Enron was a house of cards propped up by deceitful accounting and myriad unsavory practices, the company imploded in a matter of weeks—one of the biggest bankruptcies of all time, costing investors $64 billion in losses.

In contrast, when high ethical principles are deeply ingrained in the corporate culture of a company, culture can function as a powerful mechanism for communicating ethical behavioral norms and gaining employee buy-in to the company's moral standards, business principles, and corporate values. In such cases, the ethical principles embraced in the company's code of ethics and/or in its statement of corporate values are seen as integral to the company's identity, self-image, and ways of operating. The message that ethics matters—and matters a lot—resounds loudly and clearly throughout the organization and in its strategy and decisions. Illustration Capsule 9.2 discusses Novo Nordisk's approach to building an ethical culture and putting its ethical principles into practice.

WHY SHOULD COMPANY STRATEGIES BE ETHICAL?

There are two reasons why a company's strategy should be ethical: (1) because a strategy that is unethical is morally wrong and reflects badly on the character of the company and its personnel, and (2) because an ethical strategy can be good business and serve the self-interest of shareholders.

The Moral Case for an Ethical Strategy

LO 3

The costs of business ethics failures.

Managers do not dispassionately assess what strategic course to steer—how strongly committed they are to observing ethical principles and standards definitely comes into play in making strategic choices. Ethical strategy making is generally the product of managers who are of strong moral character (i.e., who are trustworthy, have integrity, and truly care about conducting the company's business honorably). Managers with high ethical principles are usually advocates of a corporate code of ethics and strong ethics compliance, and they are genuinely committed to upholding corporate values and ethical business principles. They demonstrate their commitment by displaying the company's stated values and living up to its business principles and ethical standards. They understand the difference between merely adopting value statements and codes of ethics and ensuring that they are followed strictly in a company's actual strategy and business conduct. As a consequence, ethically strong managers consciously opt for strategic actions that can pass the strictest moral scrutiny—they display no tolerance for strategies with ethically controversial components.

The Business Case for Ethical Strategies

In addition to the moral reasons for adopting ethical strategies, there may be solid business reasons. Pursuing unethical strategies and tolerating unethical conduct not only damages a company's reputation but also may result in a wide-ranging set of other costly consequences. Figure 9.1 shows the kinds of costs a company can incur when unethical behavior on its part is discovered, the wrongdoings of company personnel are headlined in the media, and it is forced to make amends for its behavior. The more egregious are a company's ethical violations, the higher the costs and the bigger the damage to its reputation (and to the reputations of the company personnel

ILLUSTRATION CAPSULE 9.2

How Novo Nordisk Puts Its Ethical Principles into Practice

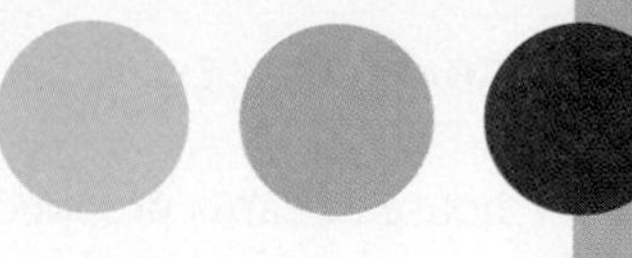

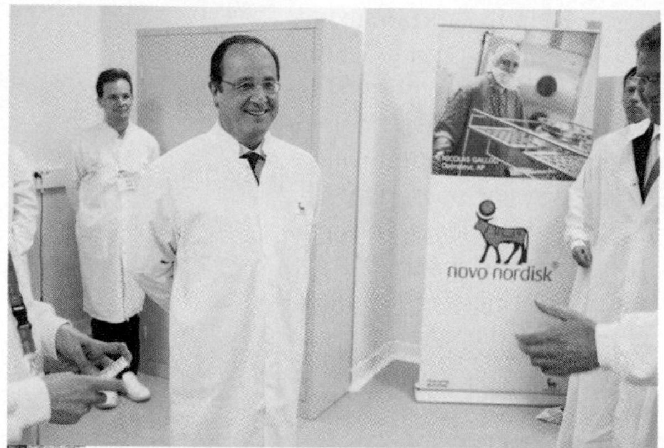

© Revelli-Beaumont/SIPA/Newscom

Novo Nordisk is a $15.2 billion global pharmaceutical company, known for its innovation and leadership in diabetes treatments. It is also known for its dedication to ethical business practices. In 2012, the company was listed as the global leader in business ethics by *Corporate Knights*, a corporate social responsibility advisory firm.

Novo Nordisk's company policies are explicit in their attention to both bioethics and business ethics. In the realm of bioethics, the company is committed to conducting its research involving people, animals, and gene technology in accordance with the highest global ethical standards. Moreover, the company requires that all of its suppliers and other external partners also adhere to Novo Nordisk's bioethical standards. In the realm of business ethics, the policies dictate (1) that high ethical standards be applied consistently across the company's value chain, (2) that all ethical dilemmas encountered be addressed transparently, and (3) that company officers and employees be held accountable for complying with all laws, regulations, and company rules.

Novo Nordisk's strong culture of responsibility helps translate the company's policies into practice. At Novo Nordisk, every employee pledges to conduct himself or herself according to the Novo Nordisk Way, a set of behavioral norms that has come to define the company's culture. It's a culture that promotes teamwork, cooperation, respect for others, and fairness. The commitment to business ethics grew out of those values, which are promoted throughout the company by hiring practices, management leadership, and employee mobility to foster a global one-company culture.

As part of this process, Novo Nordisk has set up a business ethics board, composed of senior management. The board identifies key ethical challenges for the company, drafting guidelines and developing training programs. The training programs are rigorous: All Novo Nordisk employees are trained annually in business ethics. The board is also responsible for ensuring compliance. It has set up an anonymous hotline and conducts an average of 40 to 50 audits each year. The goal of the audits is to maintain a culture that promotes the principles of the Novo Nordisk Way.

Implementing a code of ethics across an organization of 26,000 employees is very difficult and lapses do occur. But such incidents are exceptional and are swiftly addressed by the company. For example, when insider trading allegations came to light against a corporate executive, the company immediately suspended and subsequently fired the employee.

Note: Developed with Dennis L. Huggins.

Sources: J. Edwards, "Novo Nordisk Exec Charged with Insider Trading; Cash Stashed in Caribbean," *CBS News,* September 2008, www.cbsnews.com (accessed February 19, 2012); company filings and website (accessed April 1, 2014); Corporate Knights, "The 8th Annual Global 100," global100.org/ (accessed February 20, 2012).

---

involved). In high-profile instances, the costs of ethical misconduct can easily run into the hundreds of millions and even billions of dollars, especially if they provoke widespread public outrage and many people were harmed. The penalties levied on executives caught in wrongdoing can skyrocket as well, as the 150-year prison term sentence of infamous financier and Ponzi scheme perpetrator Bernie Madoff illustrates.

> Conducting business in an ethical fashion is not only morally right—it is in a company's enlightened self-interest.

The fallout of a company's ethical misconduct goes well beyond the costs of making amends for the misdeeds. Customers shun companies caught up in highly

FIGURE 9.1 The Costs Companies Incur When Ethical Wrongdoing Is Discovered

Visible Costs	Internal Administrative Costs	Intangible or Less Visible Costs
• Government fines and penalties • Civil penalties arising from class-action lawsuits and other litigation aimed at punishing the company for its offense and the harm done to others • The costs to shareholders in the form of a lower stock price (and possibly lower dividends)	• Legal and investigative costs incurred by the company • The costs of providing remedial education and ethics training to company personnel • The costs of taking corrective actions • Administrative costs associated with ensuring future compliance	• Customer defections • Loss of reputation • Lost employee morale and higher degrees of employee cynicism • Higher employee turnover • Higher recruiting costs and difficulty in attracting talented employees • Adverse effects on employee productivity • The costs of complying with often harsher government regulations

Source: Adapted from Terry Thomas, John R. Schermerhorn, and John W. Dienhart, "Strategic Leadership of Ethical Behavior," *Academy of Management Executive* 18, no. 2 (May 2004), p. 58.

publicized ethical scandals. Rehabilitating a company's shattered reputation is time-consuming and costly. Companies with tarnished reputations have difficulty in recruiting and retaining talented employees. Most ethically upstanding people are repulsed by a work environment where unethical behavior is condoned; they don't want to get entrapped in a compromising situation, nor do they want their personal reputations tarnished by the actions of an unsavory employer. Creditors are unnerved by the unethical actions of a borrower because of the potential business fallout and subsequent higher risk of default on loans.

Shareholders suffer major damage when a company's unethical behavior is discovered. Making amends for unethical business conduct is costly, and it takes years to rehabilitate a tarnished company reputation.

All told, a company's unethical behavior can do considerable damage to shareholders in the form of lost revenues, higher costs, lower profits, lower stock prices, and a diminished business reputation. To a significant degree, therefore, ethical strategies and ethical conduct are *good business.* Most companies understand the value of operating in a manner that wins the approval of suppliers, employees, investors, and society at large. Most businesspeople recognize the risks and adverse fallout attached to the discovery of unethical behavior. Hence, companies have an incentive to employ strategies that can pass the test of being ethical. Even if a company's managers are not personally committed to high ethical standards, they have good reason to operate within ethical bounds, if only to (1) avoid the risk of embarrassment, scandal, disciplinary action, fines, and possible jail time for unethical conduct on their part; and (2) escape being held accountable for lax enforcement of ethical standards and unethical behavior by personnel under their supervision.

STRATEGY, CORPORATE SOCIAL RESPONSIBILITY, AND ENVIRONMENTAL SUSTAINABILITY

LO 4

The concepts of corporate social responsibility and environmental sustainability and how companies balance these duties with economic responsibilities to shareholders.

The idea that businesses have an obligation to foster social betterment, a much-debated topic over the past 50 years, took root in the 19th century when progressive companies in the aftermath of the industrial revolution began to provide workers with housing and other amenities. The notion that corporate executives should balance the interests of all stakeholders—shareholders, employees, customers, suppliers, the communities in which they operate, and society at large—began to blossom in the 1960s. Some years later, a group of chief executives of America's 200 largest corporations, calling themselves the Business Roundtable, came out in strong support of the concept of **corporate social responsibility (CSR):**

> Balancing the shareholder's expectations of maximum return against other priorities is one of the fundamental problems confronting corporate management. The shareholder must receive a good return but the legitimate concerns of other constituencies (customers, employees, communities, suppliers and society at large) also must have the appropriate attention. . . . [Leading managers] believe that by giving enlightened consideration to balancing the legitimate claims of all its constituents, a corporation will best serve the interest of its shareholders.

Today, corporate social responsibility is a concept that resonates in western Europe, the United States, Canada, and such developing nations as Brazil and India.

CORE CONCEPT

Corporate social responsibility (CSR) refers to a company's *duty* to operate in an honorable manner, provide good working conditions for employees, encourage workforce diversity, be a good steward of the environment, and actively work to better the quality of life in the local communities where it operates and in society at large.

The Concepts of Corporate Social Responsibility and Good Corporate Citizenship

The essence of socially responsible business behavior is that a company should balance strategic actions to benefit shareholders against the *duty* to be a good corporate citizen. The underlying thesis is that company managers should display a *social conscience* in operating the business and specifically take into account how management decisions and company actions affect the well-being of employees, local communities, the environment, and society at large.[20] Acting in a socially responsible manner thus encompasses more than just participating in community service projects and donating money to charities and other worthy causes. Demonstrating social responsibility also entails undertaking actions that earn trust and respect from all stakeholders—operating in an honorable and ethical manner, striving to make the company a great place to work, demonstrating genuine respect for the environment, and trying to make a difference in bettering society. As depicted in Figure 9.2, corporate responsibility programs commonly include the following elements:

- *Striving to employ an ethical strategy and observe ethical principles in operating the business.* A sincere commitment to observing ethical principles is a necessary component of a CSR strategy simply because unethical conduct is incompatible with the concept of good corporate citizenship and socially responsible business behavior.
- *Making charitable contributions, supporting community service endeavors, engaging in broader philanthropic initiatives, and reaching out to make a difference in the lives of the disadvantaged.* Some companies fulfill their philanthropic obligations by spreading their efforts over a multitude of charitable and

FIGURE 9.2 The Five Components of a Corporate Social Responsibility Strategy

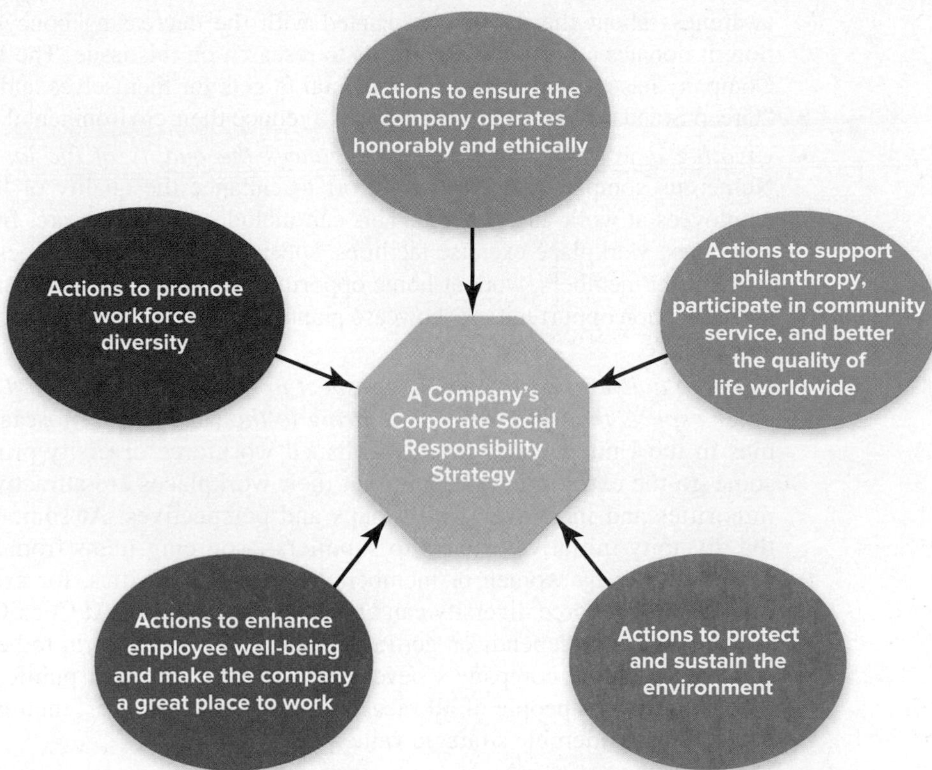

Source: Adapted from material in Ronald Paul Hill, Debra Stephens, and Iain Smith, "Corporate Social Responsibility: An Examination of Individual Firm Behavior," *Business and Society Review* 108, no. 3 (September 2003), p. 348.

community activities—for instance, Wells Fargo and Google support a broad variety of community, art, and social welfare programs. Others prefer to focus their energies more narrowly. McDonald's concentrates on sponsoring the Ronald McDonald House program (which provides a home away from home for the families of seriously ill children receiving treatment at nearby hospitals). Leading prescription drug maker GlaxoSmithKline and other pharmaceutical companies either donate or heavily discount medicines for distribution in the least developed nations. Companies frequently reinforce their philanthropic efforts by encouraging employees to support charitable causes and participate in community affairs, often through programs that match employee contributions.

- *Taking actions to protect the environment and, in particular, to minimize or eliminate any adverse impact on the environment stemming from the company's own business activities.* Corporate social responsibility as it applies to environmental protection entails actively striving to be a good steward of the environment. This means using the best available science and technology to reduce environmentally harmful aspects of the company's operations *below the levels required by prevailing environmental regulations.* It also means putting time and money into improving the environment in ways that extend beyond a company's own industry boundaries—such as participating in recycling projects, adopting energy conservation practices, and supporting efforts to clean up local water supplies. Häagen-Dazs, a maker of all-natural ice creams, started a social media campaign to raise awareness about the dangers associated with the decreasing honeybee population; it donates a portion of its profits to research on this issue. The Walt Disney Company has created strict environmental targets for themselves and created the "Green Standard" to inspire employees to reduce their environmental impact.

- *Creating a work environment that enhances the quality of life for employees.* Numerous companies exert extra effort to enhance the quality of life for their employees at work and at home. This can include onsite day care, flexible work schedules, workplace exercise facilities, special leaves for employees to care for sick family members, work-at-home opportunities, career development programs and education opportunities, showcase plants and offices, special safety programs, and the like.
- *Building a diverse workforce with respect to gender, race, national origin, and other aspects that different people bring to the workplace.* Most large companies in the United States have established workforce diversity programs, and some go the extra mile to ensure that their workplaces are attractive to ethnic minorities and inclusive of all groups and perspectives. At some companies, the diversity initiative extends to suppliers—sourcing items from small businesses owned by women or members of ethnic minorities, for example. The pursuit of workforce diversity can also be good business. At Coca-Cola, where strategic success depends on getting people all over the world to become loyal consumers of the company's beverages, efforts to build a public persona of inclusiveness for people of all races, religions, nationalities, interests, and talents have considerable strategic value.

CORE CONCEPT

A company's **CSR strategy** is defined by the specific combination of socially beneficial activities the company opts to support with its contributions of time, money, and other resources.

The particular combination of socially responsible endeavors a company elects to pursue defines its **corporate social responsibility strategy.** The specific components emphasized in a CSR strategy vary from company to company and are typically linked to a company's core values. Few companies have managed to integrate CSR as fully and seamlessly throughout their organization as Burt's Bees; there a special committee is dedicated to leading the organization to attain its CRS goals with respect to three primary areas: natural well-being, humanitarian responsibility, and environmental sustainability. General Mills also centers its CSR strategy around three themes: nourishing lives (via healthier and easier-to-prepare foods), nourishing communities (via charitable donations to community causes and volunteerism for community service projects), and nourishing the environment (via efforts to conserve natural resources, reduce energy and water usage, promote recycling, and otherwise support environmental sustainability).[21] Starbucks's CSR strategy includes four main elements (ethical sourcing, community service, environmental stewardship, and farmer support), all of which have touch points with the way that the company procures its coffee—a key aspect of its product differentiation strategy. Some companies use other terms, such as *corporate citizenship, corporate responsibility,* or *sustainable responsible business (SRB)* to characterize their CSR initiatives. Illustration Capsule 9.3 describes Warby Parker's approach to corporate social responsibility—an approach that ensures that social responsibility is reflected in all of the company's actions and endeavors.

Although there is wide variation in how companies devise and implement a CSR strategy, communities of companies concerned with corporate social responsibility

ILLUSTRATION CAPSULE 9.3

Warby Parker: Combining Corporate Social Responsibility with Affordable Fashion

Since its founding in 2010, Warby Parker has succeeded in selling over one million pairs of high-fashion glasses at a discounted price of $95—roughly 80 percent below the average $500 price tag on a comparable pair of eyeglasses from another producer. With more than 25 stores in the United States, the company has built a brand recognized universally as one of the strongest in the world; it consistently posts a net promoter score (a measure of how likely someone would be to recommend the product) of close to 90—higher than companies like Zappos and Apple.

Corporate responsibility is at Warby Parker's core. For each pair of glasses sold, the company provides international nonprofit partners like VisionSpring with a monthly donation of glasses; with Warby Parker's support, these partners provide basic eye exams and teach community members how to manufacture and sell glasses at very low prices to amplify beneficial effects in their communities. To date, VisionSpring alone has trained nearly 20,000 people across 35 countries with average impacts of 20 percent increase in income and 35 percent increase in productivity.

Efforts to be a responsible company expand beyond Warby Parker's international partnerships. The company voluntarily evaluates itself against benchmarks in the fields of "environment," "workers," "customers," "community," and "governance," demonstrating a nearly unparalleled dedication to outcomes outside of profit. The company is widely seen as an employer of choice and regularly attracts top talent for all roles across the organization. It holds to an extremely high environmental standard, running an entirely carbon neutral operation.

© Carolyn Cole/Los Angeles Times via Getty Images

While socially impactful actions matter at Warby Parker, the company is mindful of the critical role of its customers as well. Both founders spent countless hours coordinating partnerships with dedicated suppliers to ensure quality, invested deeply in building a lean manufacturing operation to minimize cost, and sought to build an organization that would keep buyers happy. The net effect is a very economically healthy company—they post around $3,000 in sales per square foot, in line with Tiffany & Co.—with financial stability to pursue responsibilities outside of customer satisfaction.

The strong fundamentals put in place by the firm's founders blend responsibility into its DNA and attach each piece of commercial success to positive outcomes in the world. The company was recently recognized as number one on *Fast Company*'s "Most Innovative Companies" list and continues to build loyal followers—both of its products and its CSR efforts—as it expands.

Note: Developed with Jeremy P. Reich.

Sources: Warby Parker and "B Corp" websites; Max Chafkin, "Warby Parker Sees the Future of Retail," *Fast Company,* February 17, 2015 (accessed February 22, 2016); Jenni Avins, "Warby Parker Proves Customers Don't Have to Care about Your Social Mission," *Quartz,* December 29, 2014 (accessed February 14, 2016).

(such as CSR Europe) have emerged to help companies share best CSR practices. Moreover, a number of reporting standards have been developed, including ISO 26000—a new internationally recognized standard for social responsibility set by the International Standards Organization (ISO).[22] Companies that exhibit a strong commitment to corporate social responsibility are often recognized by being included on lists such as *Corporate Responsibility* magazine's "100 Best Corporate Citizens" or *Corporate Knights* magazine's "Global 100 Most Sustainable Corporations."

Corporate Social Responsibility and the Triple Bottom Line

CSR initiatives undertaken by companies are frequently directed at improving the company's *triple bottom line (TBL)*—a reference to three types of performance metrics: *economic, social,* and *environmental.* The goal is for a company to succeed simultaneously in all three dimensions, as illustrated in Figure 9.3.[23] The three dimensions of performance are often referred to in terms of the "three pillars" of "people, planet, and profit." The term *people* refers to the various social initiatives that make up CSR strategies, such as corporate giving, community involvement, and company efforts to improve the lives of its internal and external stakeholders. *Planet* refers to a firm's ecological impact and environmental practices. The term *profit* has a broader meaning with respect to the triple bottom line than it does otherwise. It encompasses not only the profit a firm earns for its shareholders but also the economic impact that the company has on society more generally, in terms of the overall value that it creates and the overall costs that it imposes on society. For example, Procter & Gamble's Swiffer cleaning system, one of the company's best-selling products, not only offers an earth-friendly design but also outperforms less ecologically friendly alternatives in terms of its broader economic impact: It reduces demands on municipal water sources, saves electricity that would be needed to heat mop water, and doesn't add to the amount of detergent making its way into waterways and waste treatment facilities. Nike sees itself as bringing people, planet, and profits into balance by producing innovative new products in a more sustainable way, recognizing that sustainability is key to its future profitability. TOMS shoes, which donates a pair of shoes to a child in need in over 50 different countries for every pair purchased, has also built its strategy around maintaining a well-balanced triple bottom line.

Many companies now make a point of citing the beneficial outcomes of their CSR strategies in press releases and issue special reports for consumers and investors to review. Staples, the world's largest office products company, makes reporting

FIGURE 9.3 The Triple Bottom Line: Excelling on Three Measures of Company Performance

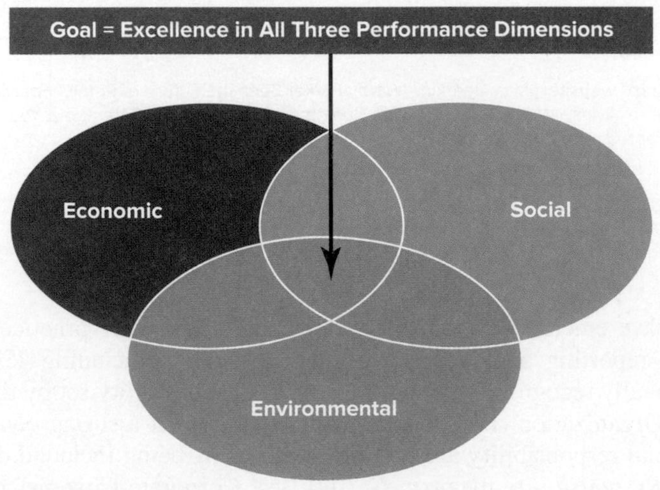

Source: Developed with help from Amy E. Florentino.

an important part of its commitment to corporate responsibility; the company posts a "Staples Soul Report" on its website that describes its initiatives and accomplishments in the areas of diversity, environment, community, and ethics. Triple-bottom-line reporting is emerging as an increasingly important way for companies to make the results of their CSR strategies apparent to stakeholders and for stakeholders to hold companies accountable for their impact on society. The use of standard reporting frameworks and metrics, such as those developed by the Global Reporting Initiative, promotes greater transparency and facilitates benchmarking CSR efforts across firms and industries.

Investment firms have created mutual funds consisting of companies that are excelling on the basis of the triple bottom line in order to attract funds from environmentally and socially aware investors. The Dow Jones Sustainability World Index is made up of the top 10 percent of the 2,500 companies listed in the Dow Jones World Index in terms of economic performance, environmental performance, and social performance. Companies are evaluated in these three performance areas, using indicators such as corporate governance, climate change mitigation, and labor practices. Table 9.1 shows a sampling of the companies selected for the Dow Jones Sustainability World Index in 2013.

TABLE 9.1 A Selection of Companies Recognized for Their Triple-Bottom-Line Performance in 2013

Name	Market Sector	Country
Volkswagen AG	Automobiles & Components	Germany
Australia & New Zealand Banking Group Ltd.	Banks	Australia
Siemens AG	Capital Goods	Germany
Adecco SA	Commercial & Professional Services	Switzerland
Panasonic Corp.	Consumer Durables & Apparel	Japan
Tabcorp Holdings Ltd.	Consumer Services	Australia
Citigroup Inc.	Diversified Financials	United States
BG Group PLC	Energy	United Kingdom
Woolworths Ltd.	Food & Staples Retailing	Australia
Nestlé SA	Food, Beverage, & Tobacco	Switzerland
Abbott Laboratories	Health Care Equipment & Services	United States
Henkel AG & Co. KGaA	Household & Personal Products	Germany
Allianz SE	Insurance	Germany
Akzo Nobel NV	Materials	Netherlands
Telenet Group Holding NV	Media	Belgium
Roche Holding AG	Pharmaceuticals, Biotechnology, & Life Sciences	Switzerland
Stockland	Real Estate	Australia

(continued)

TABLE 9.1 *(continued)*

Name	Market Sector	Country
Lotte Shopping Co. Ltd.	Retailing	Republic of Korea
Taiwan Semiconductor Manufacturing Co. Ltd.	Semiconductors & Semiconductor Equipment	Taiwan
SAP AG	Software & Services	Germany
Alcatel-Lucent	Technology Hardware & Equipment	France
KT Corp.	Telecommunication Services	Republic of Korea
Air France-KLM	Transportation	France
EDP–Energias de Portugal SA	Utilities	Portugal

Source: Adapted from RobecoSAM AG, **www.sustainability-indices.com/review/industry-group-leaders-2013.jsp** (accessed February 7, 2014).

What Do We Mean by *Sustainability* and *Sustainable Business Practices*?

The term *sustainability* is used in a variety of ways. In many firms, it is synonymous with corporate social responsibility; it is seen by some as a term that is gradually replacing *CSR* in the business lexicon. Indeed, sustainability reporting and TBL reporting are often one and the same, as illustrated by the Dow Jones Sustainability World Index, which tracks the same three types of performance measures that constitute the triple bottom line.

CORE CONCEPT

Sustainable business practices are those that meet the needs of the present without compromising the ability to meet the needs of the future.

More often, however, the term takes on a more focused meaning, concerned with the relationship of a company to its *environment* and its use of *natural resources*, including land, water, air, plants, animals, minerals, fossil fuels, and biodiversity. It is widely recognized that the world's natural resources are finite and are being consumed and degraded at rates that threaten their capacity for renewal. Since corporations are the biggest users of natural resources, managing and maintaining these resources is critical for the long-term economic interests of corporations.

CORE CONCEPT

A company's **environmental sustainability strategy** consists of its deliberate actions to protect the environment, provide for the longevity of natural resources, maintain ecological support systems for future generations, and guard against ultimate endangerment of the planet.

For some companies, this issue has direct and obvious implications for the continued viability of their business model and strategy. Pacific Gas and Electric has begun measuring the full carbon footprint of its supply chain to become not only a "greener" company but a more efficient energy producer.[24] Beverage companies such as Coca-Cola and PepsiCo are having to rethink their business models because of the prospect of future worldwide water shortages. For other companies, the connection is less direct, but all companies are part of a business ecosystem whose economic health depends on the availability of natural resources. In response, most major companies have begun to change *how* they do business, emphasizing the use of **sustainable business practices,** defined as those capable of meeting the needs of the present without compromising the ability to meet the needs of the future. Many have also begun to incorporate a consideration of environmental sustainability into their strategy-making activities.

Environmental sustainability strategies entail deliberate and concerted actions to operate businesses in a manner that protects natural resources and ecological support systems, guards against outcomes that will ultimately endanger the planet, and is therefore sustainable for centuries.[25] One aspect of environmental sustainability is keeping use of the Earth's natural resources within levels that can be replenished via the use of sustainable business practices. In the case of some resources (like crude oil, freshwater, and edible fish from the oceans), scientists say that use levels either are already unsustainable or will be soon, given the world's growing population and propensity to consume additional resources as incomes and living standards rise. Another aspect of sustainability concerns containing the adverse effects of greenhouse gases and other forms of air pollution to reduce their impact on undesirable climate and atmospheric changes. Other aspects of sustainability include greater reliance on sustainable energy sources; greater use of recyclable materials; the use of sustainable methods of growing foods (to reduce topsoil depletion and the use of pesticides, herbicides, fertilizers, and other chemicals that may be harmful to human health or ecological systems); habitat protection; environmentally sound waste management practices; and increased attempts to decouple environmental degradation and economic growth (according to scientists, economic growth has historically been accompanied by declines in the well-being of the environment).

Unilever, a diversified producer of processed foods, personal care, and home cleaning products, is among the many committed corporations pursuing sustainable business practices. The company tracks 11 sustainable agricultural indicators in its processed-foods business and has launched a variety of programs to improve the environmental performance of its suppliers. Examples of such programs include special low-rate financing for tomato suppliers choosing to switch to water-conserving irrigation systems and training programs in India that have allowed contract cucumber growers to reduce pesticide use by 90 percent while improving yields by 78 percent. Unilever has also reengineered many internal processes to improve the company's overall performance on sustainability measures. For example, the company's factories have reduced water usage by 63 percent and total waste by 67 percent since 1995 through the implementation of sustainability initiatives. Unilever has also redesigned packaging for many of its products to conserve natural resources and reduce the volume of consumer waste. The company's Suave shampoo bottles were reshaped to save almost 150 tons of plastic resin per year, which is the equivalent of 15 million fewer empty bottles making it to landfills annually. As the producer of Lipton Tea, Unilever is the world's largest purchaser of tea leaves; the company committed to sourcing all of its tea from Rainforest Alliance Certified farms, due to its comprehensive triple-bottom-line approach toward sustainable farm management. Illustration Capsule 9.4 sheds more light on Unilever's focus on sustainability.

Crafting Corporate Social Responsibility and Sustainability Strategies

While CSR and environmental sustainability strategies take many forms, those that both provide valuable social benefits *and* fulfill customer needs in a superior fashion may also contribute to a company's competitive advantage.[26] For example, while carbon emissions may be a generic social concern for financial institutions such as Wells Fargo, Ford's sustainability strategy for reducing carbon emissions has produced both competitive advantage and environmental benefits. Its Ford Fusion hybrid automobile not only is among the least polluting automobiles but also now ranks 1 out of 22 in hybrid cars, with exceptional fuel economy, a quiet powertrain, and a spacious cabin. It has gained the attention and loyalty of fuel-conscious buyers and given Ford a new green image. Green Mountain Coffee Roasters's commitment to protect the welfare of coffee growers and their families (in particular, making sure they receive a fair

ILLUSTRATION CAPSULE 9.4

Unilever's Focus on Sustainability

With over 53.3 billion euros in revenue in 2015, Unilever is one of the world's largest companies. The global consumer goods giant has products that are used by over 2 billion people on any given day. It manufactures iconic global brands like Dove, Axe, Hellman's, Heartbrand, and many others. What it is also known for, however, is its commitment to sustainability, leading GlobeScan's Global Sustainability Survey for sustainable companies with a score 2.5 times higher than its closest competitor.

Unilever implemented its sustainability plan in as transparent and explicit way as possible, evidenced by the Unilever Sustainable Living Plan (USLP). The USLP was released in 2010 by CEO Paul Polman, stating that the company's goal was to double the size of the business while halving its environmental footprint by 2020. Importantly, the USLP has remained a guiding force for the company, which dedicates significant resources and time to pursuing its sustainability goals. The plan is updated each year with targets and goals, as well as an annual progress report.

According to Polman, Unilever's focus on sustainability isn't just charity, but is really an act of self-interest. The company's most recent annual report states "growth and sustainability are not in conflict. In fact, in our experience, sustainability drives growth." Polman insists that this is the modern-day way to maximize profits, and that doing so is simply rational business thinking.

To help implement this plan, Unilever has instituted a corporate accountability plan. Each year, Unilever benchmarks its progress against three leading indices: the UN Global Compact, the Global Reporting Initiative's Index, and the UN Millennium Development Goals.

© McGraw-Hill Education/David A. Tietz, photographer

In its annual sustainability report, the company details its progress toward its many sustainability goals. Examples from 2014 include the 397 million people Unilever helped to improve their health and hygiene habits by 2014 as part of the company's goal of helping 1 billion people do so by 2020.

Unilever has also created new business practices to reach its ambitious targets. Unilever set up a central corporate team dedicated to spreading best sustainability practices from one factory or business unit to the rest of the company, a major change from how the siloed manner in which the company previously operated. Moreover, the company set up a "small actions, big differences" fund to invest in innovative ideas that help the company achieve its sustainability goal. To reduce emissions from the overall footprint of its products and extend its sustainability efforts to its entire supply chain, it has worked with its suppliers to source sustainable agricultural products, improving from 14 percent sustainable in 2010 to 48 percent in 2014.

Note: Developed with Byron G. Peyster.

Sources: **www.globescan.com/component/edocman/?view=document&id=179&Itemid=591; www.fastcocreate.com/3051498/behind-the-brand/why-unilever-is-betting-big-on-sustainability; www.economist.com/news/business/21611103-second-time-its-120-year-history-unilever-trying-redefine-what-it-means-be**; company website (accessed March 13, 2016).

price) also meets its customers' wants and needs. In its dealings with suppliers at small farmer cooperatives in Peru, Mexico, and Sumatra, Green Mountain pays fair trade prices for coffee beans. Green Mountain also purchases about 29 percent of its coffee directly from farmers to cut out intermediaries and see that farmers realize a higher price for their efforts—coffee is the world's second most heavily traded commodity after oil, requiring the labor of some 20 million people, most of whom live at the poverty level.[27] Its consumers are aware of these efforts and purchase Green Mountain coffee, in part, to encourage such practices.

CSR strategies and environmental sustainability strategies are more likely to contribute to a company's competitive advantage if they are linked to a company's competitively important resources and capabilities or value chain activities. Thus, it is common for companies engaged in natural resource extraction, electric power production, forestry and paper products manufacture, motor vehicles production, and chemical production to place more emphasis on addressing environmental concerns than, say, software and electronics firms or apparel manufacturers. Companies whose business success is heavily dependent on maintaining high employee morale or attracting and retaining the best and brightest employees are somewhat more prone to stress the well-being of their employees and foster a positive, high-energy workplace environment that elicits the dedication and enthusiastic commitment of employees, thus putting real meaning behind the claim "Our people are our greatest asset." Ernst & Young, one of the four largest global accounting firms, stresses its "People First" workforce diversity strategy that is all about respecting differences, fostering individuality, and promoting inclusiveness so that its more than 175,000 employees in over 150 countries can feel valued, engaged, and empowered in developing creative ways to serve the firm's clients. Costco Wholesale, the warehouse club, credits its success to its treatment of its employees, who are paid an average of $20.89 an hour, not including overtime—far above the industry average. Eighty-eight percent of Costco's employees have company-sponsored insurance; CEO Craig Jelinek is committed to ensuring that his people make a living wage and receive health benefits, an approach that he says "also puts more money back into the economy. It's really that simple." Between 2009 and 2014, Costco sales grew 39 percent and stock prices doubled—an anomaly in an industry plagued by turmoil and downsizing.

CSR strategies and environmental sustainability strategies that both provide valuable social benefits *and* fulfill customer needs in a superior fashion can lead to competitive advantage. Corporate social agendas that address only social issues may help boost a company's reputation for corporate citizenship but are unlikely to improve its competitive strength in the marketplace.

At Whole Foods Market, a $14.2 billion supermarket chain specializing in organic and natural foods, its environmental sustainability strategy is evident in almost every segment of its company value chain and is a big part of its differentiation strategy. The company's procurement policies encourage stores to purchase fresh fruits and vegetables from local farmers and screen processed-food items for more than 400 common ingredients that the company considers unhealthy or environmentally unsound. Spoiled food items are sent to regional composting centers rather than landfills, and all cleaning products used in its stores are biodegradable. The company also has created the Animal Compassion Foundation to develop natural and humane ways of raising farm animals and has converted all of its vehicles to run on biofuels.

Not all companies choose to link their corporate environmental or social agendas to their value chain, their business model, or their industry. For example, the Clorox Company Foundation supports programs that serve youth, focusing its giving on nonprofit civic organizations, schools, and colleges. However, unless a company's social responsibility initiatives become part of the way it operates its business every day, the initiatives are unlikely to catch fire and be fully effective. As an executive at Royal Dutch/Shell put it, corporate social responsibility "is not a cosmetic; it must be rooted in our values. It must make a difference to the way we do business."[28] The same is true for environmental sustainability initiatives.

The Moral Case for Corporate Social Responsibility and Environmentally Sustainable Business Practices

Every action a company takes can be interpreted as a statement of what it stands for.

The moral case for why businesses should act in a manner that benefits all of the company's stakeholders—not just shareholders—boils down to "It's the right thing to do." Ordinary decency, civic-mindedness, and contributions to society's well-being should be expected of any business.[29] In today's social and political climate, most business leaders can be expected to acknowledge that socially responsible actions are important and that businesses have a duty to be good corporate citizens. But there is a complementary school of thought that business operates on the basis of an implied social contract with the members of society. According to this contract, society grants a business the right to conduct its business affairs and agrees not to unreasonably restrain its pursuit of a fair profit for the goods or services it sells. In return for this "license to operate," a business is obligated to act as a responsible citizen, do its fair share to promote the general welfare, and avoid doing any harm. Such a view clearly puts a moral burden on a company to operate honorably, provide good working conditions to employees, be a good environmental steward, and display good corporate citizenship.

The Business Case for Corporate Social Responsibility and Environmentally Sustainable Business Practices

Whatever the moral arguments for socially responsible business behavior and environmentally sustainable business practices, there are definitely good business reasons why companies should be public-spirited and devote time and resources to social responsibility initiatives, environmental sustainability, and good corporate citizenship:

- *Such actions can lead to increased buyer patronage.* A strong visible social responsibility or environmental sustainability strategy gives a company an edge in appealing to consumers who prefer to do business with companies that are good corporate citizens. Ben & Jerry's, Whole Foods Market, Stonyfield Farm, TOMS, Green Mountain Coffee Roasters, and Patagonia have definitely expanded their customer bases because of their visible and well-publicized activities as socially conscious companies. More and more companies are also recognizing the cash register payoff of social responsibility strategies that reach out to people of all cultures and demographics (women, retirees, and ethnic groups).
- *A strong commitment to socially responsible behavior reduces the risk of reputation-damaging incidents.* Companies that place little importance on operating in a socially responsible manner are more prone to scandal and embarrassment. Consumer, environmental, and human rights activist groups are quick to criticize businesses whose behavior they consider to be out of line, and they are adept at getting their message into the media and onto the Internet. Pressure groups can generate widespread adverse publicity, promote boycotts, and influence like-minded or sympathetic buyers to avoid an offender's products.

The higher the public profile of a company or its brand, the greater the scrutiny of its activities and the higher the potential for it to become a target for pressure group action.

Research has shown that product boycott announcements are associated with a decline in a company's stock price.[30] When a major oil company suffered damage to its reputation on environmental and social grounds, the CEO repeatedly said that the most negative impact the company suffered—and the one that made him fear for the future of the company—was that bright young graduates were no longer attracted to working for the company. For many years, Nike received stinging criticism for not policing sweatshop conditions in the Asian factories that produced Nike footwear, a situation that caused Nike cofounder and chair Phil Knight to observe that "Nike has become synonymous with slave wages, forced overtime, and arbitrary abuse."[31] In response, Nike began an extensive effort to monitor conditions in the 800 factories of the contract manufacturers that produced Nike shoes. As Knight said, "Good shoes come from good factories and good factories have good labor relations." Nonetheless, Nike has continually been plagued by complaints from human rights activists that its monitoring procedures are flawed and that it is not doing enough to correct the plight of factory workers. As this suggests, a damaged reputation is not easily repaired.

- *Socially responsible actions and sustainable business practices can lower costs and enhance employee recruiting and workforce retention.* Companies with deservedly good reputations for social responsibility and sustainable business practices are better able to attract and retain employees, compared to companies with tarnished reputations. Some employees just feel better about working for a company committed to improving society. This can contribute to lower turnover and better worker productivity. Other direct and indirect economic benefits include lower costs for staff recruitment and training. For example, Starbucks is said to enjoy much lower rates of employee turnover because of its full-benefits package for both full-time and part-time employees, management efforts to make Starbucks a great place to work, and the company's socially responsible practices. Sustainable business practices are often concomitant with greater operational efficiencies. For example, when a U.S. manufacturer of recycled paper, taking eco-efficiency to heart, discovered how to increase its fiber recovery rate, it saved the equivalent of 20,000 tons of waste paper—a factor that helped the company become the industry's lowest-cost producer. By helping two-thirds of its employees to stop smoking and by investing in a number of wellness programs for employees, Johnson & Johnson saved $250 million on its health care costs over a 10-year period.[32]
- *Opportunities for revenue enhancement may also come from CSR and environmental sustainability strategies.* The drive for sustainability and social responsibility can spur innovative efforts that in turn lead to new products and opportunities for revenue enhancement. Electric cars such as the Chevy Volt and the Nissan Leaf are one example. In many cases, the revenue opportunities are tied to a company's core products. PepsiCo and Coca-Cola, for example, have expanded into the juice business to offer a healthier alternative to their carbonated beverages. General Electric has created a profitable new business in wind turbines. In other cases, revenue enhancement opportunities come from innovative ways to reduce waste and use the by-products of a company's production. Tyson Foods now produces jet fuel for B-52 bombers from the vast amount of animal waste resulting from its meat product business. Staples has become one of the largest nonutility corporate producers of renewable energy in the United States due to its installation of solar power panels in all of its outlets (and the sale of what it does not consume in renewable energy credit markets).
- *Well-conceived CSR strategies and sustainable business practices are in the best long-term interest of shareholders.* When CSR and sustainability strategies increase buyer patronage, offer revenue-enhancing opportunities, lower costs, increase productivity, and reduce the risk of reputation-damaging incidents, they contribute to the economic value created by a company and improve its profitability. A two-year study of leading companies found that improving environmental compliance and developing environmentally friendly products can enhance earnings per share, profitability, and the likelihood of winning contracts. The stock prices of companies that rate high on social and environmental performance

criteria have been found to perform 35 to 45 percent better than the average of the 2,500 companies that constitute the Dow Jones Global Index.[33] A review of 135 studies indicated there is a positive, but small, correlation between good corporate behavior and good financial performance; only 2 percent of the studies showed that dedicating corporate resources to social responsibility harmed the interests of shareholders.[34] Furthermore, socially responsible business behavior helps avoid or preempt legal and regulatory actions that could prove costly and otherwise burdensome. In some cases, it is possible to craft corporate social responsibility strategies that contribute to competitive advantage and, at the same time, deliver greater value to society. For instance, Walmart, by working with its suppliers to reduce the use of packaging materials and revamping the routes of its delivery trucks to cut out 100 million miles of travel, saved $200 million in costs (which enhanced its cost-competitiveness vis-à-vis rivals) and lowered carbon emissions.[35] Thus, a social responsibility strategy that packs some punch and is more than rhetorical flourish can produce outcomes that are in the best interest of shareholders.

Socially responsible strategies that create value for customers and lower costs can improve company profits and shareholder value at the same time that they address other stakeholder interests.

There's little hard evidence indicating shareholders are disadvantaged in any meaningful way by a company's actions to be socially responsible.

In sum, companies that take social responsibility and environmental sustainability seriously can improve their business reputations and operational efficiency while also reducing their risk exposure and encouraging loyalty and innovation. Overall, companies that take special pains to protect the environment (beyond what is required by law), are active in community affairs, and are generous supporters of charitable causes and projects that benefit society are more likely to be seen as good investments and as good companies to work for or do business with. Shareholders are likely to view the business case for social responsibility as a strong one, particularly when it results in the creation of more customer value, greater productivity, lower operating costs, and lower business risk—all of which should increase firm profitability and enhance shareholder value even as the company's actions address broader stakeholder interests.

Companies are, of course, sometimes rewarded for bad behavior—a company that is able to shift environmental and other social costs associated with its activities onto society as a whole can reap large short-term profits. The major cigarette producers for many years were able to earn greatly inflated profits by shifting the health-related costs of smoking onto others and escaping any responsibility for the harm their products caused to consumers and the general public. Only recently have they been facing the prospect of having to pay high punitive damages for their actions. Unfortunately, the cigarette makers are not alone in trying to evade paying for the social harms of their operations for as long as they can. Calling a halt to such actions usually hinges on (1) the effectiveness of activist social groups in publicizing the adverse consequences of a company's social irresponsibility and marshaling public opinion for something to be done, (2) the enactment of legislation or regulations to correct the inequity, and (3) decisions on the part of socially conscious buyers to take their business elsewhere.

KEY POINTS

1. Ethics concerns standards of right and wrong. Business ethics concerns the application of ethical principles to the actions and decisions of business organizations and the conduct of their personnel. Ethical principles in business are not materially different from ethical principles in general.
2. There are three schools of thought about ethical standards for companies with international operations:
   - According to the *school of ethical universalism,* common understandings across multiple cultures and countries about what constitutes right and wrong behaviors give rise to universal ethical standards that apply to members of all societies, all companies, and all businesspeople.
   - According to the *school of ethical relativism,* different societal cultures and customs have divergent values and standards of right and wrong. Thus, what is ethical or unethical must be judged in the light of local customs and social mores and can vary from one culture or nation to another.
   - According to the *integrated social contracts theory,* universal ethical principles based on the collective views of multiple cultures and societies combine to form a "social contract" that all individuals in all situations have a duty to observe. Within the boundaries of this social contract, local cultures or groups can specify what additional actions are not ethically permissible. However, universal norms always take precedence over local ethical norms.
3. Apart from the "business of business is business, not ethics" kind of thinking, three other factors contribute to unethical business behavior: (1) faulty oversight that enables the unscrupulous pursuit of personal gain, (2) heavy pressures on company managers to meet or beat short-term earnings targets, and (3) a company culture that puts profitability and good business performance ahead of ethical behavior. In contrast, culture can function as a powerful mechanism for promoting ethical business conduct when high ethical principles are deeply ingrained in the corporate culture of a company.
4. Business ethics failures can result in three types of costs: (1) visible costs, such as fines, penalties, and lower stock prices; (2) internal administrative costs, such as legal costs and costs of taking corrective action; and (3) intangible costs or less visible costs, such as customer defections and damage to the company's reputation.
5. The term *corporate social responsibility* concerns a company's *duty* to operate in an honorable manner, provide good working conditions for employees, encourage workforce diversity, be a good steward of the environment, and support philanthropic endeavors in local communities where it operates and in society at large. The particular combination of socially responsible endeavors a company elects to pursue defines its corporate social responsibility (CSR) strategy.
6. The triple bottom line refers to company performance in three realms: economic, social, and environmental. Increasingly, companies are reporting their performance with respect to all three performance dimensions.
7. *Sustainability* is a term that is used in various ways, but most often it concerns a firm's relationship to the environment and its use of natural resources. Sustainable business practices are those capable of meeting the needs of the present without

compromising the world's ability to meet future needs. A company's environmental sustainability strategy consists of its deliberate actions to protect the environment, provide for the longevity of natural resources, maintain ecological support systems for future generations, and guard against ultimate endangerment of the planet.

8. CSR strategies and environmental sustainability strategies that both provide valuable social benefits *and* fulfill customer needs in a superior fashion can lead to competitive advantage.
9. The moral case for corporate social responsibility and environmental sustainability boils down to a simple concept: It's the right thing to do. There are also solid reasons why CSR and environmental sustainability strategies may be good business—they can be conducive to greater buyer patronage, reduce the risk of reputation-damaging incidents, provide opportunities for revenue enhancement, and lower costs. Well-crafted CSR and environmental sustainability strategies are in the best long-term interest of shareholders, for the reasons just mentioned and because they can avoid or preempt costly legal or regulatory actions.

ASSURANCE OF LEARNING EXERCISES

LO 1, LO 4 1. Widely known as an ethical company, Dell recently committed itself to becoming a more environmentally sustainable business. After reviewing the About Dell section of its website (**www.dell.com/learn/us/en/uscorp1/about-dell**), prepare a list of 10 specific policies and programs that help the company achieve its vision of driving social and environmental change while still remaining innovative and profitable.

LO 2, LO 3 2. Prepare a one- to two-page analysis of a recent ethics scandal using your university library's access to LexisNexis or other Internet resources. Your report should (1) discuss the conditions that gave rise to unethical business strategies and behavior and (2) provide an overview of the costs resulting from the company's business ethics failure.

connect **LO 4** 3. Based on information provided in Illustration Capsule 9.3, explain how Warby Parker's CSR strategy has contributed to its success in the marketplace. How are the company's various stakeholder groups affected by its commitment to social responsibility? How would you evaluate its triple-bottom-line performance?

connect **LO 4** 4. Go to **www.google.com/green/** and read about the company's latest initiatives surrounding sustainability. What are Google's key policies and actions that help it reduce its environmental footprint? How does the company integrate the idea of creating a "better web that's better for the environment" with its strategies for creating profit and value. How do these initiatives help build competitive advantage for Google?

EXERCISE FOR SIMULATION PARTICIPANTS

1. Is your company's strategy ethical? Why or why not? Is there anything that your company has done or is now doing that could legitimately be considered "shady" by your competitors? **LO 1**
2. In what ways, if any, is your company exercising corporate social responsibility? What are the elements of your company's CSR strategy? Are there any changes to this strategy that you would suggest? **LO 4**
3. If some shareholders complained that you and your co-managers have been spending too little or too much on corporate social responsibility, what would you tell them? **LO 3, LO 4**
4. Is your company striving to conduct its business in an environmentally sustainable manner? What specific *additional* actions could your company take that would make an even greater contribution to environmental sustainability? **LO 4**
5. In what ways is your company's environmental sustainability strategy in the best long-term interest of shareholders? Does it contribute to your company's competitive advantage or profitability? **LO 4**

ENDNOTES

[1] James E. Post, Anne T. Lawrence, and James Weber, *Business and Society: Corporate Strategy, Public Policy, Ethics*, 10th ed. (New York: McGraw-Hill, 2002).

[2] Mark S. Schwartz, "Universal Moral Values for Corporate Codes of Ethics," *Journal of Business Ethics* 59, no. 1 (June 2005), pp. 27–44.

[3] Mark S. Schwartz, "A Code of Ethics for Corporate Codes of Ethics," *Journal of Business Ethics* 41, no. 1–2 (November–December 2002), pp. 27–43.

[4] T. L. Beauchamp and N. E. Bowie, *Ethical Theory and Business* (Upper Saddle River, NJ: Prentice-Hall, 2001).

[5] www.cnn.com/2013/10/15/world/child-labor-index-2014/ (accessed February 6, 2014).

[6] U.S. Department of Labor, "The Department of Labor's 2013 Findings on the Worst Forms of Child Labor," www.dol.gov/ilab/programs/ocft/PDF/2012OCFTreport.pdf.

[7] W. M. Greenfield, "In the Name of Corporate Social Responsibility," *Business Horizons* 47, no. 1 (January–February 2004), p. 22.

[8] Rajib Sanyal, "Determinants of Bribery in International Business: The Cultural and Economic Factors," *Journal of Business Ethics* 59, no. 1 (June 2005), pp. 139–145.

[9] Transparency International, *Global Corruption Report*, www.globalcorruptionreport.org.

[10] Roger Chen and Chia-Pei Chen, "Chinese Professional Managers and the Issue of Ethical Behavior," *Ivey Business Journal* 69, no. 5 (May–June 2005), p. 1.

[11] Antonio Argandoa, "Corruption and Companies: The Use of Facilitating Payments," *Journal of Business Ethics* 60, no. 3 (September 2005), pp. 251–264.

[12] Thomas Donaldson and Thomas W. Dunfee, "Towards a Unified Conception of Business Ethics: Integrative Social Contracts Theory," *Academy of Management Review* 19, no. 2 (April 1994), pp. 252–284; Andrew Spicer, Thomas W. Dunfee, and Wendy J. Bailey, "Does National Context Matter in Ethical Decision Making? An Empirical Test of Integrative Social Contracts Theory," *Academy of Management Journal* 47, no. 4 (August 2004), p. 610.

[13] Lynn Paine, Rohit Deshpandé, Joshua D. Margolis, and Kim Eric Bettcher, "Up to Code: Does Your Company's Conduct Meet World-Class Standards?" *Harvard Business Review* 83, no. 12 (December 2005), pp. 122–133.

[14] John F. Veiga, Timothy D. Golden, and Kathleen Dechant, "Why Managers Bend Company Rules," *Academy of Management Executive* 18, no. 2 (May 2004).

[15] www.reuters.com/article/2014/02/06/us-sac-martoma-idUSBREA131TL20140206.

[16] Lorin Berlin and Emily Peck, "National Mortgage Settlement: States, Big Banks Reach $25 Billion Deal," *Huff Post Business*, February 9, 2012, www.huffingtonpost.com/2012/02/09/-national-mortgage-settlement_n_1265292.html (accessed February 15, 2012).

[17] Ronald R. Sims and Johannes Brinkmann, "Enron Ethics (Or: Culture Matters More than Codes)," *Journal of Business Ethics* 45, no. 3 (July 2003), pp. 244–246.

[18] www.sfgate.com/business/bottomline/article/SEC-charges-Diamond-Foods-with-accounting-fraud-5129129.php (accessed February 7, 2014).

[19] Kurt Eichenwald, *Conspiracy of Fools: A True Story* (New York: Broadway Books, 2005).

[20] Timothy M. Devinney, "Is the Socially Responsible Corporation a Myth? The Good, the Bad, and the Ugly of Corporate Social Responsibility," *Academy of Management Perspectives* 23, no. 2 (May 2009), pp. 44–56.

[21] Information posted at www.generalmills.com (accessed March 13, 2013).

[22] Adrian Henriques, "ISO 26000: A New Standard for Human Rights?" *Institute for Human Rights and Business*, March 23, 2010, www.institutehrb.org/blogs/guest/iso_26000_a_new_standard_for_human_rights.html?gclid=CJih7NjN2alCFVs65QodrVOdyQ (accessed July 7, 2010).

[23] Gerald I. J. M. Zetsloot and Marcel N. A. van Marrewijk, "From Quality to Sustainability," *Journal of Business Ethics* 55 (2004), pp. 79–82.

[24] Tilde Herrera, "PG&E Claims Industry First with Supply Chain Footprint Project," GreenBiz.com, June 30, 2010, www.greenbiz.com/news/2010/06/30/-pge—claims-industry-first-supply-chain-carbon-footprint-project.

[25] J. G. Speth, *The Bridge at the End of the World: Capitalism, the Environment, and Crossing from Crisis to Sustainability* (New Haven, CT: Yale University Press, 2008).

[26] Michael E. Porter and Mark R. Kramer, "Strategy & Society: The Link between Competitive Advantage and Corporate Social

Responsibility," *Harvard Business Review* 84, no. 12 (December 2006), pp. 78–92.
[27] David Hess, Nikolai Rogovsky, and Thomas W. Dunfee, "The Next Wave of Corporate Community Involvement: Corporate Social Initiatives," *California Management Review* 44, no. 2 (Winter 2002), pp. 110–125; Susan Ariel Aaronson, "Corporate Responsibility in the Global Village: The British Role Model and the American Laggard," *Business and Society Review* 108, no. 3 (September 2003), p. 323.
[28] N. Craig Smith, "Corporate Responsibility: Whether and How," *California Management Review* 45, no. 4 (Summer 2003), p. 63.
[29] Jeb Brugmann and C. K. Prahalad, "Cocreating Business's New Social Compact," *Harvard Business Review* 85, no. 2 (February 2007), pp. 80–90.
[30] Wallace N. Davidson, Abuzar El-Jelly, and Dan L. Worrell, "Influencing Managers to Change Unpopular Corporate Behavior through Boycotts and Divestitures: A Stock Market Test," *Business and Society* 34, no. 2 (1995), pp. 171–196.
[31] Tom McCawley, "Racing to Improve Its Reputation: Nike Has Fought to Shed Its Image as an Exploiter of Third-World Labor Yet It Is Still a Target of Activists," *Financial Times,* December 2000, p. 14.
[32] Michael E. Porter and Mark Kramer, "Creating Shared Value," *Harvard Business Review* 89, no. 1–2 (January–February 2011).
[33] James C. Collins and Jerry I. Porras, *Built to Last: Successful Habits of Visionary Companies,* 3rd ed. (London: HarperBusiness, 2002).
[34] Joshua D. Margolis and Hillary A. Elfenbein, "Doing Well by Doing Good: Don't Count on It," *Harvard Business Review* 86, no. 1 (January 2008), pp. 19–20; Lee E. Preston, Douglas P. O'Bannon, Ronald M. Roman, Sefa Hayibor, and Bradley R. Agle, "The Relationship between Social and Financial Performance: Repainting a Portrait," *Business and Society* 38, no. 1 (March 1999), pp. 109–125.
[35] Leonard L. Berry, Ann M. Mirobito, and William B. Baun, "What's the Hard Return on Employee Wellness Programs?" *Harvard Business Review* 88, no. 12 (December 2010), p. 105.

CHAPTER 10

Building an Organization Capable of Good Strategy Execution

People, Capabilities, and Structure

© ImageZoo/Alamy Stock Photo

Learning Objectives

THIS CHAPTER WILL HELP YOU UNDERSTAND:

LO 1 What managers must do to execute strategy successfully.

LO 2 Why hiring, training, and retaining the right people constitute a key component of the strategy execution process.

LO 3 That good strategy execution requires continuously building and upgrading the organization's resources and capabilities.

LO 4 What issues to consider in establishing a strategy-supportive organizational structure and organizing the work effort.

LO 5 The pros and cons of centralized and decentralized decision making in implementing the chosen strategy.

In the end, a strategy is nothing but good intentions unless it's effectively implemented.

Clayton M. Christensen—*Professor and consultant*

I try to motivate people and align our individual incentives with organizational incentives. And then let people do their best.

John Liu—*Director, Whirlpool Corporation*

People are not your most important asset. The right people are.

Jim Collins—*Professor and author*

Once managers have decided on a strategy, the emphasis turns to converting it into actions and good results. Putting the strategy into place and getting the organization to execute it well call for different sets of managerial skills. Whereas crafting strategy is largely an analysis-driven activity focused on market conditions and the company's resources and capabilities, executing strategy is primarily operations-driven, revolving around the management of people, business processes, and organizational structure. Successful strategy execution depends on doing a good job of working with and through others; building and strengthening competitive capabilities; creating an appropriate organizational structure; allocating resources; instituting strategy-supportive policies, processes, and systems; and instilling a discipline of getting things done. Executing strategy is an action-oriented task that tests a manager's ability to direct organizational change, achieve improvements in day-to-day operations, create and nurture a culture that supports good strategy execution, and meet or beat performance targets.

Experienced managers are well aware that it is much easier to develop a sound strategic plan than it is to execute the plan and achieve targeted outcomes. A recent study of 400 CEOs in the United States, Europe, and Asia found that executional excellence was the number-one challenge facing their companies.[1] According to one executive, "It's been rather easy for us to decide where we wanted to go. The hard part is to get the organization to act on the new priorities."[2] It takes adept managerial leadership to convincingly communicate a new strategy and the reasons for it, overcome pockets of doubt, secure the commitment of key personnel, build consensus for how to implement the strategy, and move forward to get all the pieces into place and deliver results. *Just because senior managers announce a new strategy doesn't mean that organization members will embrace it and move forward enthusiastically to implement it.* Company personnel must understand—in their heads and hearts—why a new strategic direction is necessary and where the new strategy is taking them.[3] Instituting change is, of course, easier when the problems with the old strategy have become obvious and/or the company has spiraled into a financial crisis.

But the challenge of successfully implementing new strategic initiatives goes well beyond managerial adeptness in overcoming resistance to change. What really makes executing strategy a tougher, more time-consuming management challenge than crafting strategy are the wide array of managerial activities that must be attended to, the many ways to put new strategic initiatives in place and keep things moving, and the number of bedeviling issues that always crop up and have to be resolved. It takes first-rate "managerial smarts" to zero in on what exactly needs to be done and how to get good results in a timely manner. Excellent people-management skills and perseverance are needed to get a variety of initiatives underway and to integrate the efforts of many different work groups into a smoothly functioning whole. Depending on how much consensus building and organizational change is involved, the process of implementing strategy changes can take several months to several years. And executing the strategy with *real proficiency* takes even longer.

Like crafting strategy, *executing strategy is a job for a company's whole management team—not just a few senior managers.* While the chief executive officer and the heads of major units (business divisions, functional departments, and key operating units) are ultimately responsible for seeing that strategy is executed successfully, the process typically affects every part of the firm—all value chain activities and all work groups. Top-level managers must rely on the active support of middle and lower managers to institute whatever new operating practices are needed in the various operating units to achieve proficient strategy execution. Middle and lower-level managers must ensure that frontline employees perform strategy-critical value chain activities proficiently and produce operating results that allow companywide performance targets to be met. Consequently, *all company personnel are actively involved in the strategy execution process in one way or another.*

A FRAMEWORK FOR EXECUTING STRATEGY

CORE CONCEPT

Good strategy execution requires a *team effort*. All managers have strategy-executing responsibility in their areas of authority, and all employees are active participants in the strategy execution process.

LO 1

What managers must do to execute strategy successfully.

The managerial approach to implementing and executing a strategy always has to be customized to fit the particulars of a company's situation. Making minor changes in an existing strategy differs from implementing radical strategy changes. The techniques for successfully executing a low-cost provider strategy are different from those for executing a high-end differentiation strategy. Implementing a new strategy for a struggling company in the midst of a financial crisis is a different job from improving strategy execution in a company that is doing relatively well. Moreover, some managers are more adept than others at using particular approaches to achieving certain kinds of organizational changes. Hence, there's no definitive managerial recipe for successful strategy execution that cuts across all company situations and all strategies or that works for all managers. Rather, the specific actions required to execute a strategy—the "to-do list" that constitutes management's action agenda—always represent management's judgment about how best to proceed in light of prevailing circumstances.

The Principal Components of the Strategy Execution Process

Despite the need to tailor a company's strategy-executing approaches to the situation at hand, certain managerial bases must be covered no matter what the circumstances. These include 10 basic managerial tasks (see Figure 10.1):

1. Staffing the organization with managers and employees capable of executing the strategy well.
2. Developing the resources and organizational capabilities required for successful strategy execution.
3. Creating a strategy-supportive organizational structure.
4. Allocating sufficient resources (budgetary and otherwise) to the strategy execution effort.

5. Instituting policies and procedures that facilitate strategy execution.
6. Adopting best practices and business processes to drive continuous improvement in strategy execution activities.
7. Installing information and operating systems that enable company personnel to carry out their strategic roles proficiently.
8. Tying rewards and incentives directly to the achievement of strategic and financial targets.
9. Instilling a corporate culture that promotes good strategy execution.
10. Exercising strong leadership to drive the execution process forward and attain companywide operating excellence as rapidly as feasible.

When strategies fail, it is often because of poor execution. Strategy execution is therefore a critical managerial endeavor.

The two best signs of good strategy execution are whether a company is meeting or beating its performance targets and whether it is performing value chain activities in a manner that is conducive to companywide operating excellence.

How well managers perform these 10 tasks has a decisive impact on whether the outcome of the strategy execution effort is a spectacular success, a colossal failure, or something in between.

In devising an action agenda for executing strategy, managers should start by conducting *a probing assessment of what the organization must do differently to carry out the strategy successfully*. Each manager needs to ask the question "What needs to be done in my area of responsibility to implement our part of the company's strategy, and what should I do to get these things accomplished in a timely fashion?" It is then incumbent on every manager to determine *precisely how to make the necessary internal changes*. Successful strategy implementers have a knack for diagnosing what their organizations need to do to execute the chosen strategy well and figuring out how to get these things done efficiently. They are masters in promoting results-oriented behaviors on the part of company personnel and following through on making the right things happen to achieve the target outcomes.[4]

When strategies fail, it is often because of poor execution. Strategy execution is therefore a critical managerial endeavor. The two best signs of good strategy execution are whether a company is meeting or beating its performance targets and whether it is performing value chain activities in a manner that is conducive to companywide operating excellence. In big organizations with geographically scattered operating units, senior executives' action agenda mostly involves communicating the case for change, building consensus for how to proceed, installing strong managers to move the process forward in key organizational units, directing resources to the right places, establishing deadlines and measures of progress, rewarding those who achieve implementation milestones, and personally leading the strategic change process. Thus, the bigger the organization, the more that successful strategy execution depends on the cooperation and implementation skills of operating managers who can promote needed changes at the lowest organizational levels and deliver results. In small organizations, top managers can deal directly with frontline managers and employees, personally orchestrating the action steps and implementation sequence, observing firsthand how implementation is progressing, and deciding how hard and how fast to push the process along. Whether the organization is large or small and whether strategy implementation involves sweeping or minor changes, effective leadership requires a keen grasp of what to do and how to do it in light of the organization's circumstances. Then it remains for company personnel in strategy-critical areas to step up to the plate and produce the desired results.

FIGURE 10.1 The 10 Basic Tasks of the Strategy Execution Process

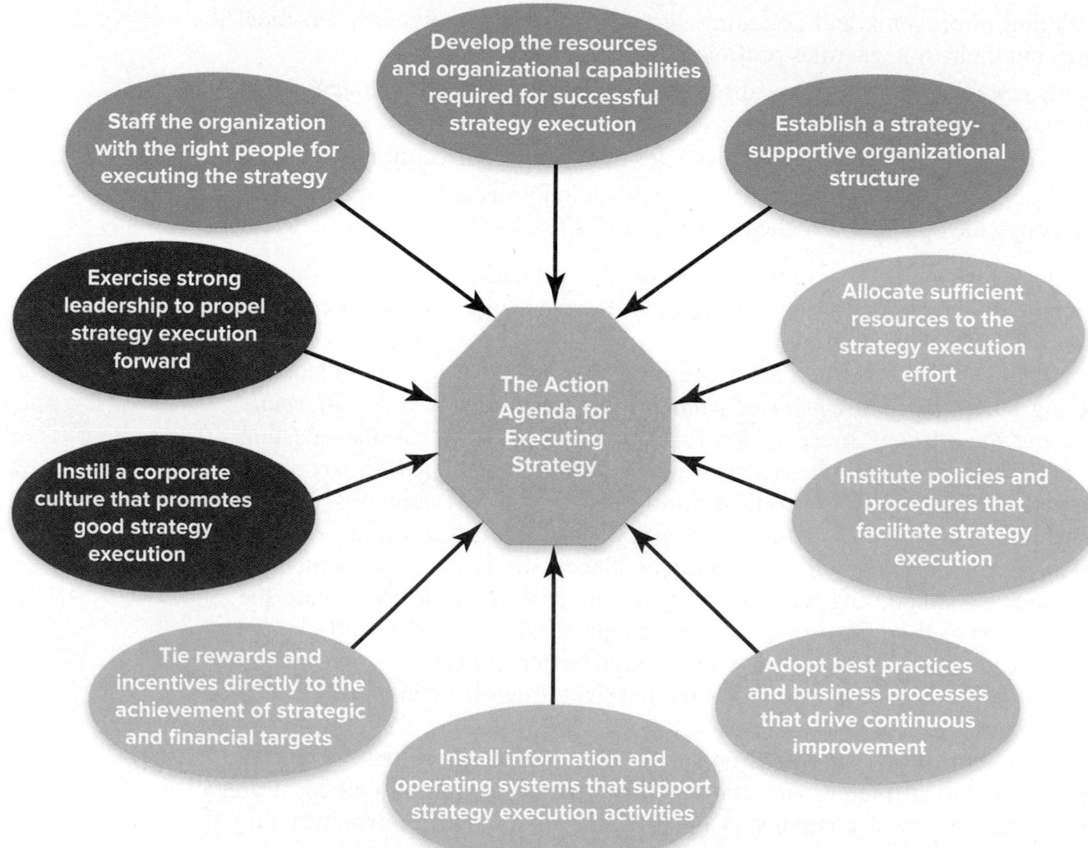

What's Covered in Chapters 10, 11, and 12 In the remainder of this chapter and in the next two chapters, we discuss what is involved in performing the 10 key managerial tasks that shape the process of executing strategy. This chapter explores the first three of these tasks (highlighted in blue in Figure 10.1): (1) staffing the organization with people capable of executing the strategy well, (2) developing the resources and building the organizational capabilities needed for successful strategy execution, and (3) creating an organizational structure supportive of the strategy execution process. Chapter 11 concerns the tasks of allocating resources (budgetary and otherwise), instituting strategy-facilitating policies and procedures, employing business process management tools and best practices, installing operating and information systems, and tying rewards to the achievement of good results (highlighted in green in Figure 10.1). Chapter 12 deals with the two remaining tasks: instilling a corporate culture conducive to good strategy execution, and exercising the leadership needed to drive the execution process forward (highlighted in purple).

BUILDING AN ORGANIZATION CAPABLE OF GOOD STRATEGY EXECUTION: THREE KEY ACTIONS

Proficient strategy execution depends foremost on having in place an organization capable of the tasks demanded of it. Building an execution-capable organization is thus always a top priority. As shown in Figure 10.2, three types of organization-building actions are paramount:

1. *Staffing the organization*—putting together a strong management team, and recruiting and retaining employees with the needed experience, technical skills, and intellectual capital.
2. *Acquiring, developing, and strengthening the resources and capabilities required for good strategy execution*—accumulating the required resources, developing

FIGURE 10.2 Building an Organization Capable of Proficient Strategy Execution: Three Key Actions

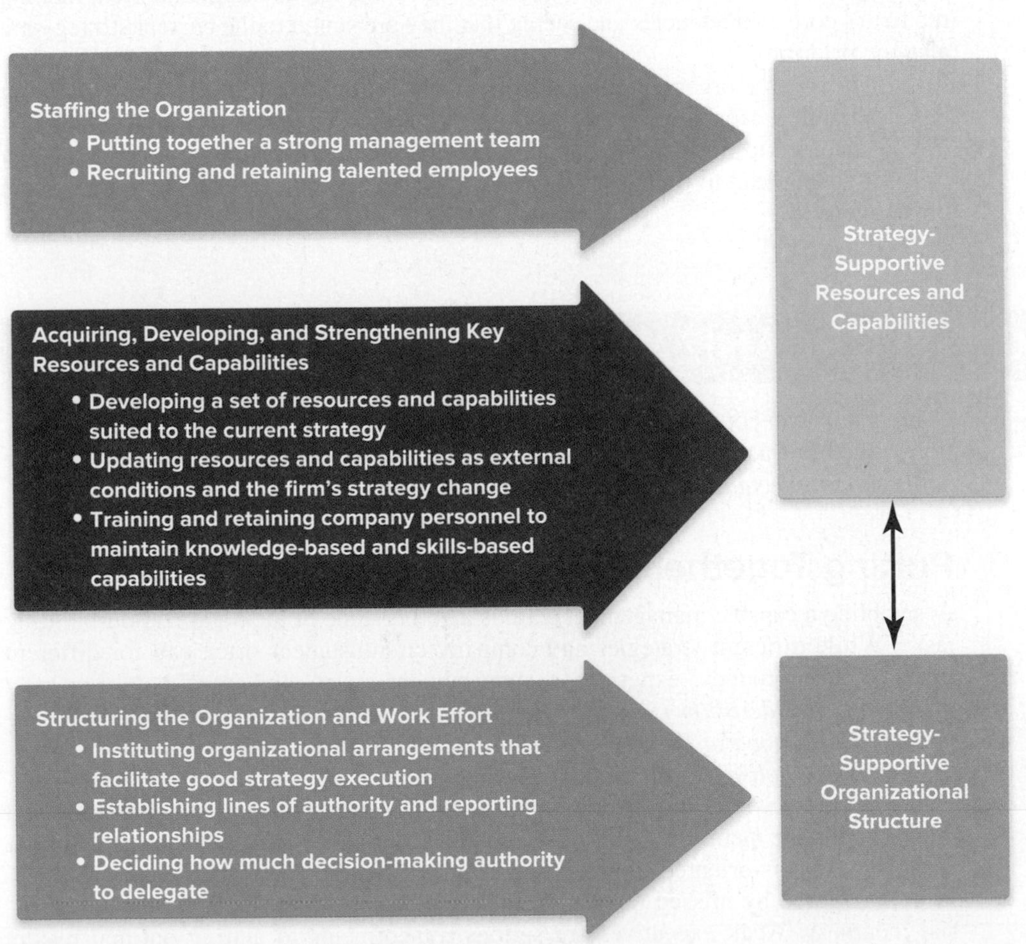

proficiencies in performing strategy-critical value chain activities, and updating the company's capabilities to match changing market conditions and customer expectations.

3. *Structuring the organization and work effort*—organizing value chain activities and business processes, establishing lines of authority and reporting relationships, and deciding how much decision-making authority to delegate to lower-level managers and frontline employees.

Implementing a strategy depends critically on ensuring that strategy-supportive resources and capabilities are in place, ready to be deployed. These include the skills, talents, experience, and knowledge of the company's human resources (managerial and otherwise)—see Figure 10.2. Proficient strategy execution depends heavily on competent personnel of all types, but because of the many managerial tasks involved and the role of leadership in strategy execution, assembling a strong management team is especially important.

If the strategy being implemented is a new strategy, the company may need to add to its resource and capability mix in other respects as well. But renewing, upgrading, and revising the organization's resources and capabilities is a part of the strategy execution process even if the strategy is fundamentally the same, since strategic assets depreciate and conditions are always changing. Thus, augmenting and strengthening the firm's core competencies and seeing that they are suited to the current strategy are also top priorities.

Structuring the organization and work effort is another critical aspect of building an organization capable of good strategy execution. An organization structure that is well matched to the strategy can help facilitate its implementation; one that is not well suited can lead to higher bureaucratic costs and communication or coordination breakdowns.

STAFFING THE ORGANIZATION

LO 2

Why hiring, training, and retaining the right people constitute a key component of the strategy execution process.

No company can hope to perform the activities required for successful strategy execution without attracting and retaining talented managers and employees with suitable skills and *intellectual capital.*

Putting Together a Strong Management Team

Assembling a capable management team is a cornerstone of the organization-building task.[5] While different strategies and company circumstances often call for different mixes of backgrounds, experiences, management styles, and know-how, *the most important consideration is to fill key managerial slots with smart people who are clear thinkers, good at figuring out what needs to be done, skilled in managing people, and accomplished in delivering good results.*[6] The task of implementing challenging strategic initiatives must be assigned to executives who have the skills and talents to handle them and who can be counted on to get the job done well. Without a capable, results-oriented management team, the implementation process is likely to be hampered by missed deadlines, misdirected or wasteful efforts, and managerial ineptness. Weak executives are serious impediments to getting optimal results because they are unable to differentiate between ideas that have merit and those that are misguided—the caliber of work done under their supervision suffers.[7] In contrast, managers with strong strategy implementation capabilities have a talent for asking tough, incisive questions. They know enough about the details of the business to be able to ensure the soundness of the decisions of the people around them, and they can discern whether the resources people are asking for to put the strategy in place make sense. They are good at getting things done through others, partly by making sure they have the right people under them, assigned to the right jobs. They consistently follow through on issues, monitor progress carefully, make adjustments when needed, and keep important details from slipping through the cracks. In short, they understand how to drive organizational change, and they know how to motivate and lead the company down the path for first-rate strategy execution.

Sometimes a company's existing management team is up to the task. At other times it may need to be strengthened by promoting qualified people from within or by bringing in outsiders whose experiences, talents, and leadership styles better suit the situation. In turnaround and rapid-growth situations, and in instances when a company doesn't have insiders with the requisite know-how, filling key management slots from the outside is a standard organization-building approach. In addition, it is important to identify and replace managers who are incapable, for whatever reason, of making the required changes in a timely and cost-effective manner. For a management team to be truly effective at strategy execution, it must be composed of managers who recognize that organizational changes are needed and who are ready to get on with the process.

Putting together a talented management team with the right mix of experiences, skills, and abilities to get things done is one of the first steps to take in launching the strategy-executing process.

The overriding aim in building a management team should be to assemble a *critical mass* of talented managers who can function as agents of change and further the cause of excellent strategy execution. Every manager's success is enhanced (or limited) by the quality of his or her managerial colleagues and the degree to which they freely exchange ideas, debate ways to make operating improvements, and join forces to tackle issues and solve problems. When a first-rate manager enjoys the help and support of other first-rate managers, it's possible to create a managerial whole that is greater than the sum of individual efforts—talented managers who work well together as a team can produce organizational results that are dramatically better than what one or two star managers acting individually can achieve.[8]

Illustration Capsule 10.1 describes Deloitte's highly effective approach to developing employee talent and a top-caliber management team.

Recruiting, Training, and Retaining Capable Employees

Assembling a capable management team is not enough. Staffing the organization with the right kinds of people must extend to all kinds of company personnel for value chain activities to be performed competently. *The quality of an organization's people is always an essential ingredient of successful strategy execution—knowledgeable, engaged employees are a company's best source of creative ideas for the nuts-and-bolts operating improvements that lead to operating excellence.* Companies like Mercedes-Benz, Alphabet, SAS, Boston Consulting Group, Edward Jones, Quicken Loans, Genentech, Intuit, Salesforce.com, and Goldman Sachs make a concerted effort to recruit the best and brightest people they can find and then retain them with excellent compensation packages, opportunities for rapid advancement and professional growth, and interesting assignments. Having a pool of "A players" with strong skill sets and lots of brainpower is essential to their business.

In many industries, adding to a company's talent base and building intellectual capital are more important to good strategy execution than are additional investments in capital projects.

ILLUSTRATION CAPSULE 10.1

Management Development at Deloitte Touche Tohmatsu Limited

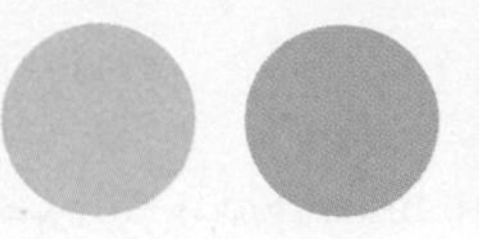

© Mathias Beinling/Alamy Stock Photo

Hiring, retaining, and cultivating talent are critical activities at Deloitte, the world's largest professional services firm. By offering robust learning and development programs, Deloitte has been able to create a strong talent pipeline to the firm's partnership. Deloitte's emphasis on learning and development, across all stages of the employee life cycle, has led to recognitions such as being ranked number-one on *Chief Executives*'s list of "Best Private Companies for Leaders" and being listed among *Fortune*'s "100 Best Companies to Work For." The following programs contribute to Deloitte's successful execution of its talent strategy:

- *Clear path to partnership.* During the initial recruiting phase and then throughout an employee's tenure at the firm, Deloitte lays out a clear career path. The path indicates the expected timeline for promotion to each of the firm's hierarchy levels, along with the competencies and experience required. Deloitte's transparency on career paths, coupled with its in-depth performance management process, helps employees clearly understand their performance. This serves as a motivational tool for top performers, often leading to career acceleration.
- *Formal training programs.* Like other leading organizations, Deloitte has a program to ensure that recent college graduates are equipped with the necessary training and tools for succeeding on the job. Yet Deloitte's commitment to formal training is evident at all levels within the organization. Each time an employee is promoted, he or she attends "milestone" school, a weeklong simulation that replicates true business situations employees would face as they transition to new stages of career development. In addition, Deloitte institutes mandatory training hours for all of its employees to ensure that individuals continue to further their professional development.
- *Special programs for high performers.* Deloitte also offers fellowships and programs to help employees acquire new skills and enhance their leadership development. For example, the Global Fellows program helps top performers work with senior leaders in the organization to focus on the realities of delivering client service across borders. Deloitte has also established the Emerging Leaders Development program, which utilizes skill building, 360-degree feedback, and one-on-one executive coaching to help top-performing managers and senior managers prepare for partnership.
- *Sponsorship, not mentorship.* To train the next generation of leaders, Deloitte has implemented formal mentorship programs to provide leadership development support. Deloitte, however, uses the term *sponsorship* to describe this initiative. A sponsor is tasked with taking a vested interest in an individual and advocating on his or her behalf. Sponsors help rising leaders navigate the firm, develop new competencies, expand their network, and hone the skills needed to accelerate their career.

Note: Developed with Heather Levy.

Sources: Company websites; www.accountingweb.com/article/leadership-development-community-service-integral-deloitte-university/220845 (accessed February 2014).

Facebook makes a point of hiring the very brightest and most talented programmers it can find and motivating them with both good monetary incentives and the challenge of working on cutting-edge technology projects. McKinsey & Company, one of the world's premier management consulting firms, recruits only cream-of-the-crop MBAs at the nation's top-10 business schools; such talent is essential to McKinsey's strategy of performing high-level consulting for the world's top corporations. The leading global accounting firms screen candidates not only on the basis of their accounting expertise but also on whether they possess the people skills needed to relate well with clients and colleagues. Zappos goes to considerable lengths to hire people who can have fun and be fun on the job; it has done away with traditional job postings and instead asks prospective hires to join a social network, called Zappos Insiders, where they will interact with current employees and have opportunities to demonstrate their passion for joining the company. Zappos is so selective about finding people who fit their culture that only about 1.5 percent of the people who apply are offered jobs.

In high-tech companies, the challenge is to staff work groups with gifted, imaginative, and energetic people who can bring life to new ideas quickly and inject into the organization what one Dell executive calls "hum."[9] The saying "People are our most important asset" may seem trite, but it fits high-technology companies precisely. Besides checking closely for functional and technical skills, Dell tests applicants for their tolerance of ambiguity and change, their capacity to work in teams, and their ability to learn on the fly. Companies like Zappos, Amazon.com, Google, and Cisco Systems have broken new ground in recruiting, hiring, cultivating, developing, and retaining talented employees—almost all of whom are in their 20s and 30s. Cisco goes after the top 10 percent, raiding other companies and endeavoring to retain key people at the companies it acquires. Cisco executives believe that a cadre of star engineers, programmers, managers, salespeople, and support personnel is the backbone of the company's efforts to execute its strategy and remain the world's leading provider of Internet infrastructure products and technology.

The best companies make a point of recruiting and retaining talented employees—the objective is to make the company's entire workforce (managers and rank-and-file employees) a genuine competitive asset.

In recognition of the importance of a talented and energetic workforce, companies have instituted a number of practices aimed at staffing jobs with the best people they can find:

1. Spending considerable effort on screening and evaluating job applicants—selecting only those with suitable skill sets, energy, initiative, judgment, aptitude for learning, and personality traits that mesh well with the company's work environment and culture.
2. Providing employees with training programs that continue throughout their careers.
3. Offering promising employees challenging, interesting, and skill-stretching assignments.
4. Rotating people through jobs that span functional and geographic boundaries. Providing people with opportunities to gain experience in a variety of international settings is increasingly considered an essential part of career development in multinational companies.
5. Making the work environment stimulating and engaging so that employees will consider the company a great place to work.
6. Encouraging employees to challenge existing ways of doing things, to be creative and innovative in proposing better ways of operating, and to push their ideas for new products or businesses. Progressive companies work hard at creating an environment in which employees are made to feel that their views and suggestions count.
7. Striving to retain talented, high-performing employees via promotions, salary increases, performance bonuses, stock options and equity ownership, benefit packages including health insurance and retirement packages, and other perks, such as flexible work hours and onsite day care.
8. Coaching average performers to improve their skills and capabilities, while weeding out underperformers.

DEVELOPING AND BUILDING CRITICAL RESOURCES AND CAPABILITIES

LO 3

That good strategy execution requires continuously building and upgrading the organization's resources and capabilities.

High among the organization-building priorities in the strategy execution process is the need to build and strengthen the company's portfolio of resources and capabilities with which to perform strategy-critical value chain activities. As explained in Chapter 4, a company's chances of gaining a sustainable advantage over its market rivals depends on the caliber of its resource portfolio. In the course of crafting strategy, managers may well have well have identified the strategy-critical resources and capabilities it needs. But getting the strategy execution process underway requires acquiring or developing these resources and capabilities, putting them into place, upgrading them as needed, and then modifying them as market conditions evolve.

If the strategy being implemented has important new elements, company managers may have to acquire new resources, significantly broaden or deepen certain capabilities, or even add entirely new competencies in order to put the strategic initiatives in place and execute them proficiently. But even when a company's strategy has not changed materially, good strategy execution still involves upgrading the firm's resources and capabilities to keep them in top form and perform value chain activities ever more proficiently.

Three Approaches to Building and Strengthening Capabilities

Building new competencies and capabilities is a multistage process that occurs over a period of months and years. It is not something that is accomplished overnight.

Building the right kinds of core competencies and competitive capabilities and keeping them finely honed is a time-consuming, managerially challenging exercise. While some assistance can be gotten from discovering how best-in-industry or best-in-world companies perform a particular activity, trying to replicate and then improve on the capabilities of others is easier said than done—for the same reasons that one is unlikely to ever become a world-class halfpipe snowboarder just by studying legendary Olympic gold medalist Shaun White.

With deliberate effort, well-orchestrated organizational actions and continued practice, however, it is possible for a firm to become proficient at capability building despite the difficulty. Indeed, by making capability-building activities a *routine* part of their strategy execution endeavors, some firms are able to develop *dynamic capabilities* that assist them in managing resource and capability change, as discussed in Chapter 4. The most common approaches to capability building include (1) developing and strengthening capabilities internally, (2) acquiring capabilities through mergers and acquisitions, and (3) developing new capabilities via collaborative partnerships.

Developing Capabilities Internally Internal efforts to create or upgrade capabilities is an evolutionary process that entails a series of deliberate and well-orchestrated steps as organizations search for solutions to their problems. The process is a complex one, since capabilities are the product of *bundles of skills and know-how that are integrated into organizational routines* and *deployed within activity systems* through the combined efforts of teams that are often cross-functional in nature, spanning a variety of departments and locations. For instance, the capability of speeding new products to market involves the *collaborative efforts* of personnel in R&D,

engineering and design, purchasing, production, marketing, and distribution. Similarly, the capability to provide superior customer service is a team effort among people in customer call centers (where orders are taken and inquiries are answered), shipping and delivery, billing and accounts receivable, and after-sale support. The process of building a capability begins when managers set an objective of developing a particular capability and organize activity around that objective.[10] Managers can ignite the process by having high aspirations and setting "stretch objectives" for the organization, as described in Chapter 2.[11]

Because the process is incremental, the first step is to develop the *ability* to do something, however imperfectly or inefficiently. This entails selecting people with the requisite skills and experience, upgrading or expanding individual abilities as needed, and then molding the efforts of individuals into a joint effort to create an organizational ability. At this stage, progress can be fitful since it depends on experimenting, actively searching for alternative solutions, and learning through trial and error.[12]

A company's capabilities must be continually refreshed and renewed to remain aligned with changing customer expectations, altered competitive conditions, and new strategic initiatives.

As experience grows and company personnel learn how to perform the activities consistently well and at an acceptable cost, the ability *evolves* into a tried-and-true competence. Getting to this point requires a *continual investment* of resources and *systematic efforts* to improve processes and solve problems creatively as they arise. Improvements in the functioning of a capability come from task repetition and the resulting *learning by doing* of individuals and teams. But the process can be accelerated by making learning a more deliberate endeavor and providing the incentives that will motivate company personnel to achieve the desired ends.[13] This can be critical to successful strategy execution when market conditions are changing rapidly.

It is generally much easier and less time-consuming to update and remodel a company's existing capabilities as external conditions and company strategy change than it is to create them from scratch. Maintaining capabilities in top form may simply require exercising them continually and fine-tuning them as necessary. Similarly, augmenting a capability may require less effort if it involves the recombination of well-established company capabilities and draws on existing company resources. For example, Williams-Sonoma first developed the capability to expand sales beyond its brick-and-mortar location in 1970, when it launched a catalog that was sent to customers throughout the United States. The company extended its mail-order business with the acquisitions of Hold Everything, a garden products catalog, and Pottery Barn, and entered online retailing in 2000 when it launched e-commerce sites for Pottery Barn and Williams-Sonoma. The ongoing renewal of these capabilities has allowed Williams-Sonoma to generate revenues of nearly $5 billion in 2014 and become the 21st largest online retailer in the United States. Toyota, en route to overtaking General Motors as the global leader in motor vehicles, aggressively upgraded its capabilities in fuel-efficient hybrid engine technology and constantly fine-tuned its famed Toyota Production System to enhance its already proficient capabilities in manufacturing top-quality vehicles at relatively low costs.

Managerial actions to develop core competencies and competitive capabilities generally take one of two forms: either strengthening the company's base of skills, knowledge, and experience or coordinating and integrating the efforts of the various work groups and departments. Actions of the first sort can be undertaken at all managerial levels, but actions of the second sort are best orchestrated by senior managers who not only appreciate the strategy-executing significance of strong capabilities but also have the clout to enforce the necessary cooperation and coordination among individuals, groups, and departments.[14]

Acquiring Capabilities through Mergers and Acquisitions Sometimes the best way for a company to upgrade its portfolio of capabilities is by acquiring (or merging with) another company with attractive resources and capabilities.[15] An acquisition aimed at building a stronger portfolio of resources and capabilities can be every bit as valuable as an acquisition aimed at adding new products or services to the company's lineup of offerings. The advantage of this mode of acquiring new capabilities is primarily one of speed, since developing new capabilities internally can, at best, take many years of effort and, at worst, come to naught. Capabilities-motivated acquisitions are essential (1) when the company does not have the ability to create the needed capability internally (perhaps because it is too far afield from its existing capabilities) and (2) when industry conditions, technology, or competitors are moving at such a rapid clip that time is of the essence.

At the same time, acquiring capabilities in this way is not without difficulty. Capabilities involve tacit knowledge and complex routines that cannot be transferred readily from one organizational unit to another. This may limit the extent to which the new capability can be utilized. For example, Facebook acquired Oculus VR, a company that makes virtual reality headsets, to add capabilities that might enhance the social media experience. Transferring and integrating these capabilities to other parts of the Facebook organization prove easier said than done, however, as many technology acquisitions fail to yield the hoped-for benefits. Integrating the capabilities of two companies is particularly problematic when there are underlying incompatibilities in their supporting systems or processes. Moreover, since internal fit is important, there is always the risk that under new management the acquired capabilities may not be as productive as they had been. In a worst-case scenario, the acquisition process may end up damaging or destroying the very capabilities that were the object of the acquisition in the first place.

Accessing Capabilities through Collaborative Partnerships A third way of obtaining valuable resources and capabilities is to form collaborative partnerships with suppliers, competitors, or other companies having the cutting-edge expertise. There are three basic ways to pursue this course of action:

1. *Outsource the function in which the company's capabilities are deficient to a key supplier or another provider.* Whether this is a wise move depends on what can be safely delegated to outside suppliers or allies and which internal capabilities are key to the company's long-term success. As discussed in Chapter 6, outsourcing has the advantage of conserving resources so that the firm can focus its energies on those activities most central to its strategy. It may be a good choice for firms that are too small and resource-constrained to execute all the parts of their strategy internally.
2. *Collaborate with a firm that has complementary resources and capabilities in a joint venture, strategic alliance, or other type of partnership established for the purpose of achieving a shared strategic objective.* This requires launching initiatives to identify the most attractive potential partners and to establish collaborative working relationships. Since the success of the venture will depend on how well the partners work together, potential partners should be selected as much for their management style, culture, and goals as for their resources and capabilities. In the past 15 years, close collaboration with suppliers to achieve mutually beneficial outcomes has become a common approach to building supply chain capabilities.

3. *Engage in a collaborative partnership for the purpose of learning how the partner does things, internalizing its methods and thereby acquiring its capabilities.* This may be a viable method when each partner has something to learn from the other and can achieve an outcome *beneficial to both partners.* For example, firms sometimes enter into collaborative marketing arrangements whereby each partner is granted access to the other's dealer network for the purpose of expanding sales in geographic areas where the firms lack dealers. But if the intended gains are only one-sided, the arrangement more likely involves an abuse of trust. In consequence, it not only puts the cooperative venture at risk but also encourages the firm's partner to treat the firm similarly or refuse further dealings with the firm.

The Strategic Role of Employee Training

Training and retraining are important when a company shifts to a strategy requiring different skills, competitive capabilities, and operating methods. Training is also strategically important in organizational efforts to build skill-based competencies. And it is a key activity in businesses where technical know-how is changing so rapidly that a company loses its ability to compete unless its employees have cutting-edge knowledge and expertise. Successful strategy implementers see to it that the training function is both adequately funded and effective. If better execution of the chosen strategy calls for new skills, deeper technological capability, or the building and using of new capabilities, training efforts need to be placed near the top of the action agenda.

The strategic importance of training has not gone unnoticed. Over 4,000 companies around the world have established internal "universities" to lead the training effort, facilitate continuous organizational learning, and upgrade their company's knowledge resources. Many companies conduct orientation sessions for new employees, fund an assortment of competence-building training programs, and reimburse employees for tuition and other expenses associated with obtaining additional college education, attending professional development courses, and earning professional certification of one kind or another. A number of companies offer online training courses that are available to employees around the clock. Increasingly, companies are expecting employees at all levels are expected to take an active role in their own professional development and assume responsibility for keeping their skills up to date and in sync with the company's needs.

Strategy Execution Capabilities and Competitive Advantage

As firms get better at executing their strategies, they develop capabilities in the domain of strategy execution much as they build other organizational capabilities. Superior strategy execution capabilities allow companies to get the most from their other organizational resources and competitive capabilities. In this way they contribute to the success of a firm's business model. But excellence in strategy execution can also be a more direct source of competitive advantage, since more efficient and effective strategy execution can lower costs and permit firms to deliver more value to customers. Superior strategy execution capabilities may also enable a company to react more quickly to market changes and beat other firms to the market with new products and services. This can allow a company to profit from a period of uncontested market dominance. See Illustration Capsule 10.2 for an example of Zara's route to competitive advantage.

ILLUSTRATION CAPSULE 10.2

Zara's Strategy Execution Capabilities

© Andrey Rudakov/Bloomberg via Getty Images

Zara, a major division of Inditex Group, is a leading "fast fashion" retailer. As soon as designs are seen in high-end fashion houses such as Prada, Zara's design team sets to work altering the clothing designs so that it can produce high fashion at mass-retailing prices. Zara's strategy is clever, but by no means unique. The company's competitive advantage is in strategy execution. Every step of Zara's value chain execution is geared toward putting fashionable clothes in stores quickly, realizing high turnover, and strategically driving traffic.

The first key lever is a quick production process. Zara's design team uses inspiration from high fashion and nearly real-time feedback from stores to create up-to-the-minute pieces. Manufacturing largely occurs in factories close to headquarters in Spain, northern Africa, and Turkey, all areas considered to have a high cost of labor. Placing the factories strategically close allows for more flexibility and greater responsiveness to market needs, thereby outweighing the additional labor costs. The entire production process, from design to arrival at stores, takes only two weeks, while other retailers take six months. Whereas traditional retailers commit up to 80 percent of their lines by the start of the season, Zara commits only 50 to 60 percent, meaning that up to half of the merchandise to hit stores is designed and manufactured during the season. Zara purposefully manufactures in small lot sizes to avoid discounting later on and also to encourage impulse shopping, as a particular item could be gone in a few days. From start to finish, Zara has engineered its production process to maximize turnover and turnaround time, creating a true advantage in this step of strategy execution.

Zara also excels at driving traffic to stores. First, the small lot sizes and frequent shipments (up to twice a week per store) drive customers to visit often and purchase quickly. Zara shoppers average 17 visits per year, versus 4 to 5 for The Gap. On average, items stay in a Zara store only 11 days. Second, Zara spends no money on advertising, but it occupies some of the most expensive retail space in town, always near the high-fashion houses it imitates. Proximity reinforces the high-fashion association, while the busy street drives significant foot traffic. Overall, Zara has managed to create competitive advantage in every level of strategy execution by tightly aligning design, production, advertising, and real estate with the overall strategy of fast fashion: extremely fast and extremely flexible.

Note: Developed with Sara Paccamonti.

Sources: Suzy Hansen, "How Zara Grew into the World's Largest Fashion Retailer," *The New York Times*, November 9, 2012, **www.nytimes.com/2012/11/11/magazine/how-zara-grew-into-the-worlds-largest-fashion-retailer.html?pagewanted=all** (accessed February 5, 2014); Seth Stevenson, "Polka Dots Are In? Polka Dots It Is!" *Slate*, June 21, 2012, **www.slate.com/articles/arts/operations/2012/06/zara_s_fast_fashion_how_the_company_gets_new_styles_to_stores_so_quickly.html** (accessed February 5, 2014).

Superior strategy execution capabilities are the only source of sustainable competitive advantage when strategies are easy for rivals to copy.

Because strategy execution capabilities are socially complex capabilities that develop with experience over long periods of time, they are hard to imitate. And there is no substitute for good strategy execution. (Recall the tests of resource advantage from Chapter 4.) As such, they may be as important a source of sustained competitive advantage as the core competencies that drive a firm's strategy. Indeed, they may be a far more important avenue for securing a competitive edge over rivals in situations where it is relatively easy for rivals to copy promising strategies. In such cases, the only way for firms to achieve lasting competitive advantage is to *out-execute* their competitors.

MATCHING ORGANIZATIONAL STRUCTURE TO THE STRATEGY

While there are few hard-and-fast rules for organizing the work effort to support good strategy execution, there is one: A firm's organizational structure should be *matched* to the particular requirements of implementing the firm's strategy. Every company's strategy is grounded in its own set of organizational capabilities and value chain activities. Moreover, every firm's organizational chart is partly a product of its particular situation, reflecting prior organizational patterns, varying internal circumstances, executive judgments about reporting relationships, and the politics of who gets which assignments. Thus, the determinants of the fine details of each firm's organizational structure are unique. But some considerations in organizing the work effort are common to all companies. These are summarized in Figure 10.3 and discussed in the following sections.

LO 4

What issues to consider in establishing a strategy-supportive organizational structure and organizing the work effort.

A company's organizational structure should be matched to the particular requirements of implementing the firm's strategy.

Deciding Which Value Chain Activities to Perform Internally and Which to Outsource

Aside from the fact that an outsider, because of its expertise and specialized know-how, may be able to perform certain value chain activities better or cheaper than a company can perform them internally (as discussed in Chapter 6), outsourcing can also sometimes contribute to better strategy execution. Outsourcing the performance

FIGURE 10.3 Structuring the Work Effort to Promote Successful Strategy Execution

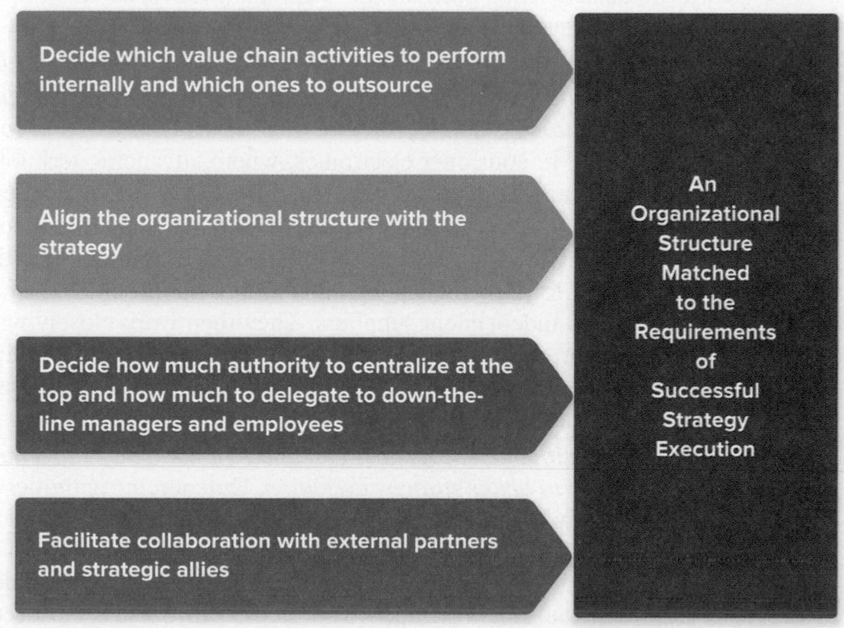

Wisely choosing which activities to perform internally and which to outsource can lead to several strategy-executing advantages—lower costs, heightened strategic focus, less internal bureaucracy, speedier decision making, and a better arsenal of organizational capabilities.

of selected activities to outside vendors enables a company to heighten its strategic focus and *concentrate its full energies on performing those value chain activities that are at the core of its strategy, where it can create unique value.* For example, E. & J. Gallo Winery outsources 95 percent of its grape production, letting farmers take on weather-related and other grape-growing risks while it concentrates its full energies on wine production and sales.[16] Broadcom, a global leader in chips for broadband communication systems, outsources the manufacture of its chips to Taiwan Semiconductor, thus freeing company personnel to focus their full energies on R&D, new chip design, and marketing. Nike concentrates on design, marketing, and distribution to retailers, while outsourcing virtually all production of its shoes and sporting apparel. Illustration Capsule 10.3 describes Apple's decisions about which activities to outsource and which to perform in-house.

Such heightened focus on performing strategy-critical activities can yield three important execution-related benefits:

- *The company improves its chances for outclassing rivals in the performance of strategy-critical activities and turning a competence into a distinctive competence.* At the very least, the heightened focus on performing a select few value chain activities should promote more effective performance of those activities. This could materially enhance competitive capabilities by either lowering costs or improving product or service quality. Whirlpool, ING Insurance, Hugo Boss, Japan Airlines, and Chevron have outsourced their data processing activities to computer service firms, believing that outside specialists can perform the needed services at lower costs and equal or better quality. A relatively large number of companies outsource the operation of their websites to web design and hosting enterprises. Many businesses that get a lot of inquiries from customers or that have to provide 24/7 technical support to users of their products around the world have found that it is considerably less expensive to outsource these functions to specialists (often located in foreign countries where skilled personnel are readily available and worker compensation costs are much lower) than to operate their own call centers. Dialogue Direct is a company that specializes in call center operation, with 14 such centers located in the United States.
- *The streamlining of internal operations that flows from outsourcing often acts to decrease internal bureaucracies, flatten the organizational structure, speed internal decision making, and shorten the time it takes to respond to changing market conditions.* In consumer electronics, where advancing technology drives new product innovation, organizing the work effort in a manner that expedites getting next-generation products to market ahead of rivals is a critical competitive capability. The world's motor vehicle manufacturers have found that they can shorten the cycle time for new models by outsourcing the production of many parts and components to independent suppliers. They then work closely with the suppliers to swiftly incorporate new technology and to better integrate individual parts and components to form engine cooling systems, transmission systems, electrical systems, and so on.
- *Partnerships with outside vendors can add to a company's arsenal of capabilities and contribute to better strategy execution.* Outsourcing activities to vendors with first-rate capabilities can enable a firm to concentrate on strengthening its own complementary capabilities internally; the result will be a more powerful package of organizational capabilities that the firm can draw upon to deliver more value to customers and attain competitive success. Soft-drink and beer manufacturers

ILLUSTRATION CAPSULE 10.3 Which Value Chain Activities Does Apple Outsource and Why?

© Qilai Shen/Bloomberg via Getty Images

Innovation and design are core competencies for Apple and the drivers behind the creation of winning products such as the iPod, iPhone, and iPad. In consequence, all activities directly related to new product development and product design are performed internally. For example, Apple's Industrial Design Group is responsible for creating the look and feel of all Apple products—from the MacBook Air to the iPhone, and beyond to future products.

Producing a continuing stream of great new products and product versions is key to the success of Apple's strategy. But executing this strategy takes more than innovation and design capabilities. Manufacturing flexibility and speed are imperative in the production of Apple products to ensure that the latest ideas are reflected in the products and that the company meets the high demand for its products—especially around launch.

For these capabilities, Apple turns to outsourcing, as do the majority of its competitors in the consumer electronics space. Apple outsources the manufacturing of products like its iPhone to Asia, where contract manufacturing organizations (CMOs) create value through their vast scale, high flexibility, and low cost. Perhaps no company better epitomizes the Asian CMO value proposition than Foxconn, a company that assembles not only for Apple but for Hewlett-Packard, Motorola, Amazon.com, and Samsung as well. Foxconn's scale is incredible, with its largest facility (Foxconn City in Shenzhen, China) employing over 450,000 workers. Such scale offers companies a significant degree of flexibility, as Foxconn has the ability to hire 3,000 employees on practically a moment's notice. Apple, more so than its competitors, is able to capture CMO value creation by leveraging its immense sales volume and strong cash position to receive preferred treatment.

Note: Developed with Margaret W. Macauley.

Sources: Company website; Charles Duhigg and Keith Bradsher, "How the U.S. Lost Out on iPhone Work," *The New York Times*, January 21, 2012, www.nytimes.com/2012/01/22/business/apple-america-and-a-squeezed-middle-class.html?pagewanted=all&_r=0 (accessed March 5, 2012).

cultivate their relationships with their bottlers and distributors to strengthen access to local markets and build loyalty, support, and commitment for corporate marketing programs, without which their own sales and growth would be weakened. Similarly, fast-food enterprises like Wendy's and Burger King find it essential to work hand in hand with franchisees on outlet cleanliness, consistency of product quality, in-store ambience, courtesy and friendliness of store personnel, and other aspects of store operations. Unless franchisees continuously deliver sufficient customer satisfaction to attract repeat business, a fast-food chain's sales and competitive standing will quickly suffer. Companies like Boeing, Aerospatiale, Verizon Communications, and Dell have learned that their central R&D groups cannot begin to match the innovative capabilities of a well-managed network of supply chain partners.

However, as emphasized in Chapter 6, a company must guard against going overboard on outsourcing and becoming overly dependent on outside suppliers. A company cannot be the master of its own destiny unless it maintains expertise and resource depth in performing those value chain activities that underpin its long-term competitive success.[17] Thus, with the exception of parts/components supply, the most frequently outsourced activities are those deemed to be strategically less important—like handling customer inquiries and requests for technical support, doing the payroll, administering employee benefit programs, providing corporate security, maintaining fleet vehicles, operating the company's website, conducting employee training, and performing an assortment of information and data processing functions.

Aligning the Firm's Organizational Structure with Its Strategy

CORE CONCEPT

A firm's **organizational structure** comprises the formal and informal arrangement of tasks, responsibilities, lines of authority, and reporting relationships by which the firm is administered.

The design of the firm's **organizational structure** is a critical aspect of the strategy execution process. The organizational structure comprises the formal and informal arrangement of tasks, responsibilities, and lines of authority and communication by which the firm is administered.[18] It specifies the linkages among parts of the organization, the reporting relationships, the direction of information flows, and the decision-making processes. It is a key factor in strategy implementation since it exerts a strong influence on how well managers can coordinate and control the complex set of activities involved.[19]

A well-designed organizational structure is one in which the various parts (e.g., decision-making rights, communication patterns) are aligned with one another and also matched to the requirements of the strategy. With the right structure in place, managers can orchestrate the various aspects of the implementation process with an even hand and a light touch. Without a supportive structure, strategy execution is more likely to become bogged down by administrative confusion, political maneuvering, and bureaucratic waste.

Good organizational design may even contribute to the firm's ability to create value for customers and realize a profit. By enabling lower bureaucratic costs and facilitating operational efficiency, it can lower a firm's operating costs. By facilitating the coordination of activities within the firm, it can improve the capability-building process, leading to greater differentiation and/or lower costs. Moreover, by improving the speed with which information is communicated and activities are coordinated, it can enable the firm to beat rivals to the market and profit from a period of unrivaled advantage.

Making Strategy-Critical Activities the Main Building Blocks of the Organizational Structure In any business, some activities in the value chain are always more critical to successful strategy execution than others. For instance, ski apparel companies like Sport Obermeyer, Arc'teryx, and Spyder must be good at styling and design, low-cost manufacturing, distribution (convincing an attractively large number of dealers to stock and promote the company's brand), and marketing and advertising (building a brand image that generates buzz among ski enthusiasts). For discount stockbrokers, like Scottrade and TD Ameritrade, the strategy-critical activities are fast access to information, accurate order execution, efficient record keeping and transaction processing, and full-featured customer service. With respect to such core value chain activities, it is important for management to build its organizational structure around proficient performance of these activities, making them the centerpieces or main building blocks in the enterprise's organizational structure.

The rationale is compelling: If activities crucial to strategic success are to have the resources, decision-making influence, and organizational impact they need, they must be centerpieces in the enterprise's organizational scheme. Making them the focus of structuring efforts will also facilitate their coordination and promote good internal fit—an essential attribute of a winning strategy, as summarized in Chapter 1 and elaborated in Chapter 4. To the extent that implementing a new strategy entails new or altered key activities or capabilities, different organizational arrangements may be required.

Matching Type of Organizational Structure to Strategy Execution Requirements Organizational structures can be classified into a limited number of standard types. Which type makes the most sense for a given firm depends largely on the firm's size and business makeup, but not so much on the specifics of its strategy. As firms grow and their needs for structure evolve, their structural form is likely to evolve from one type to another. The four basic types are the *simple structure,* the *functional structure,* the *multidivisional structure,* and the *matrix structure,* as described next.

1. Simple Structure A **simple structure** is one in which a central executive (often the owner-manager) handles all major decisions and oversees the operations of the organization with the help of a small staff.[20] Simple structures are also known as *line-and-staff structures,* since a central administrative staff supervises line employees who conduct the operations of the firm, or *flat structures,* since there are few levels of hierarchy. The simple structure is characterized by limited task specialization; few rules; informal relationships; minimal use of training, planning, and liaison devices; and a lack of sophisticated support systems. It has all the advantages of simplicity, including low administrative costs, ease of coordination, flexibility, quick decision making, adaptability, and responsiveness to change. Its informality and lack of rules may foster creativity and heightened individual responsibility.

CORE CONCEPT

A **simple structure** consists of a central executive (often the owner-manager) who handles all major decisions and oversees all operations with the help of a small staff. Simple structures are also called *line-and-staff structures* or *flat structures.*

Simple organizational structures are typically employed by small firms and entrepreneurial startups. The simple structure is the most common type of organizational structure since small firms are the most prevalent type of business. As an organization grows, however, this structural form becomes inadequate to the demands that come with size and complexity. In response, growing firms tend to alter their organizational structure from a simple structure to a *functional structure.*

2. Functional Structure A **functional structure** is one that is organized along functional lines, where a function represents a major component of the firm's value chain, such as R&D, engineering and design, manufacturing, sales and marketing, logistics, and customer service. Each functional unit is supervised by functional line managers who report to the chief executive officer and a corporate staff. This arrangement allows functional managers to focus on their area of responsibility, leaving it to the CEO and headquarters to provide direction and ensure that the activities of the functional managers are coordinated and integrated. Functional structures are also known as *departmental structures,* since the functional units are commonly called departments, and *unitary structures* or *U-forms,* since a single unit is responsible for each function.

CORE CONCEPT

A **functional structure** is organized into functional departments, with departmental managers who report to the CEO and small corporate staff. Functional structures are also called *departmental structures* and *unitary structures* or *U-forms.*

In large organizations, functional structures lighten the load on top management, in comparison to simple structures, and enable more efficient use of managerial resources. Their primary advantage, however, is greater *task specialization,* which promotes learning, enables the realization of scale economies, and offers productivity advantages not otherwise available. Their chief disadvantage is that the departmental boundaries can inhibit the flow of information and limit the opportunities for cross-functional cooperation and coordination.

The primary advantage of a functional structure is greater task specialization, which promotes learning, enables the realization of scale economies, and offers productivity advantages not otherwise available.

It is generally agreed that a functional structure is the best organizational arrangement when a company is in just one particular business (irrespective of which of the five generic competitive strategies it opts to pursue). For instance, a technical instruments manufacturer may be organized around research and development, engineering, supply chain management, assembly, quality control, marketing, and technical services. A discount retailer, such as Dollar General or Kmart, may organize around such functional units as purchasing, warehousing, distribution logistics, store operations, advertising, merchandising and promotion, and customer service. Functional structures can also be appropriate for firms with high-volume production, products that are closely related, and a limited degree of vertical integration. For example, General Motors now manages all of its brands (Cadillac, GMC, Chevrolet, Buick, etc.) under a common functional structure designed to promote technical transfer and capture economies of scale.

As firms continue to grow, they often become more diversified and complex, placing a greater burden on top management. At some point, the centralized control that characterizes the functional structure becomes a liability, and the advantages of functional specialization begin to break down. To resolve these problems and address a growing need for coordination across functions, firms generally turn to the *multidivisional structure*.

CORE CONCEPT

A **multidivisional structure** is a decentralized structure consisting of a set of operating divisions organized along business, product, customer group, or geographic lines and a central corporate headquarters that allocates resources, provides support functions, and monitors divisional activities. Multidivisional structures are also called *divisional structures* or *M-forms*.

3. Multidivisional Structure A **multidivisional structure** is a decentralized structure consisting of a set of operating divisions organized along market, customer, product, or geographic lines, along with a central corporate headquarters, which monitors divisional activities, allocates resources, performs assorted support functions, and exercises overall control. Since each division is essentially a business (often called a *single business unit* or *SBU),* the divisions typically operate as independent profit centers (i.e., with profit and loss responsibility) and are organized internally along functional lines. Division managers oversee day-to-day operations and the development of business-level strategy, while corporate executives attend to overall performance and corporate strategy, the elements of which were described in Chapter 8. Multidivisional structures are also called *divisional structures* or *M-forms,* in contrast with U-form (functional) structures.

Multidivisional structures are common among companies pursuing some form of diversification strategy or international strategy, with operations in a number of businesses or countries. When the strategy is one of unrelated diversification, as in a conglomerate, the divisions generally represent businesses in separate industries. When the strategy is based on related diversification, the divisions may be organized according to industries, customer groups, product lines, geographic regions, or technologies. In this arrangement, the decision about where to draw the divisional lines depends foremost on the nature of the relatedness and the strategy-critical building blocks, in terms of which businesses have key value chain activities in common. For example, a company selling closely related products to business customers as well as two types of end consumers—online buyers and in-store buyers—may organize its divisions according to customer groups since the value chains involved in serving the three groups differ. Another company may organize by product line due to commonalities in product development and production within each product line. Multidivisional structures are also common among vertically integrated firms. There the major building blocks are often divisional units performing one or more of the major processing steps along the value chain (e.g., raw-material production, components manufacture, assembly, wholesale distribution, retail store operations).

Multidivisional structures offer significant advantages over functional structures in terms of facilitating the management of a complex and diverse set of operations.[21] Putting business-level strategy in the hands of division managers while leaving corporate strategy to top executives reduces the potential for information overload and improves the quality of decision making in each domain. This also minimizes the costs of coordinating division-wide activities while enhancing top management's ability to control a diverse and complex operation. Moreover, multidivisional structures can help align individual incentives with the goals of the corporation and spur productivity by encouraging competition for resources among the different divisions.

But a multidivisional structure can also present some problems to a company pursuing related diversification, because having independent business units—each running its own business in its own way—inhibits cross-business collaboration and the capture of cross-business synergies, which are critical for the success of a related diversification strategy, as Chapter 8 explains. To solve this type of problem, firms turn to more complex structures, such as the matrix structure.

4. Matrix Structure A **matrix structure** is a combination structure in which the organization is organized along two or more dimensions at once (e.g., business, geographic area, value chain function) for the purpose of enhancing cross-unit communication, collaboration, and coordination. In essence, it overlays one type of structure onto another type. Matrix structures are managed through multiple reporting relationships, so a middle manager may report to several bosses. For instance, in a matrix structure based on product line, region, and function, a sales manager for plastic containers in Georgia might report to the manager of the plastics division, the head of the southeast sales region, and the head of marketing.

CORE CONCEPT

A **matrix structure** is a combination structure that overlays one type of structure onto another type, with multiple reporting relationships. It is used to foster cross-unit collaboration. Matrix structures are also called *composite structures* or *combination structures.*

Matrix organizational structures have evolved from the complex, overformalized structures that were popular in the 1960s, 70s, and 80s but often produced inefficient, unwieldy bureaucracies. The modern incarnation of the matrix structure is generally a more flexible arrangement, with a single primary reporting relationship that can be overlaid with a *temporary* secondary reporting relationship as need arises. For example, a software company that is organized into functional departments (software design, quality control, customer relations) may assign employees from those departments to different projects on a temporary basis, so an employee reports to a project manager as well as to his or her primary boss (the functional department head) for the duration of a project.

Matrix structures are also called *composite structures* or *combination structures.* They are often used for project-based, process-based, or team-based management. Such approaches are common in businesses involving projects of limited duration, such as consulting, architecture, and engineering services. The type of close cross-unit collaboration that a flexible matrix structure supports is also needed to build competitive capabilities in strategically important activities, such as speeding new products to market, that involve employees scattered across several organizational units.[22] Capabilities-based matrix structures that combine process departments (like new product development) with more traditional functional departments provide a solution.

An advantage of matrix structures is that they facilitate the sharing of plant and equipment, specialized knowledge, and other key resources. Thus, they lower costs by enabling the realization of economies of scope. They also have the advantage of flexibility in form and may allow for better oversight since supervision is provided from more than one perspective. A disadvantage is that they add another layer of management, thereby increasing bureaucratic costs and possibly decreasing response time to new situations.[23] In addition, there is a potential for confusion among employees due to dual reporting relationships and divided loyalties. While there is some controversy over the utility of matrix structures, the modern approach to matrix structures does much to minimize their disadvantages.[24]

LO 5

The pros and cons of centralized and decentralized decision making in implementing the chosen strategy.

Determining How Much Authority to Delegate

Under any organizational structure, there is room for considerable variation in how much authority top-level executives retain and how much is delegated to down-the-line managers and employees. In executing strategy and conducting daily operations, companies must decide how much authority to delegate to the managers of each organizational unit—especially the heads of divisions, functional departments, plants, and other operating units—and how much decision-making latitude to give individual employees in performing their jobs. The two extremes are to *centralize decision making* at the top or to *decentralize decision making* by giving managers and employees at all levels considerable decision-making latitude in their areas of responsibility. As shown in Table 10.1, the two approaches are based on sharply different underlying principles and beliefs, with each having its pros and cons.

Centralized Decision Making: Pros and Cons In a highly centralized organizational structure, *top executives retain authority for most strategic and*

TABLE 10.1 Advantages and Disadvantages of Centralized versus Decentralized Decision Making

Centralized Organizational Structures	Decentralized Organizational Structures
Basic tenets	**Basic tenets**
• Decisions on most matters of importance should be in the hands of top-level managers who have the experience, expertise, and judgment to decide what is the best course of action. • Lower-level personnel have neither the knowledge, time, nor inclination to properly manage the tasks they are performing. • Strong control from the top is a more effective means for coordinating company actions.	• Decision-making authority should be put in the hands of the people closest to, and most familiar with, the situation. • Those with decision-making authority should be trained to exercise good judgment. • A company that draws on the combined intellectual capital of all its employees can outperform a command-and-control company.
Chief advantages	**Chief advantages**
• Fixes accountability through tight control from the top. • Eliminates potential for conflicting goals and actions on the part of lower-level managers. • Facilitates quick decision making and strong leadership under crisis situations.	• Encourages company employees to exercise initiative and act responsibly. • Promotes greater motivation and involvement in the business on the part of more company personnel. • Spurs new ideas and creative thinking. • Allows for fast response to market change. • Entails fewer layers of management.
Primary disadvantages	**Primary disadvantages**
• Lengthens response times by those closest to the market conditions because they must seek approval for their actions. • Does not encourage responsibility among lower-level managers and rank-and-file employees. • Discourages lower-level managers and rank-and-file employees from exercising any initiative.	• May result in higher-level managers being unaware of actions taken by empowered personnel under their supervision. • Can lead to inconsistent or conflicting approaches by different managers and employees. • Can impair cross-unit collaboration.

operating decisions and keep a tight rein on business unit heads, department heads, and the managers of key operating units. Comparatively little discretionary authority is granted to frontline supervisors and rank-and-file employees. The command-and-control paradigm of centralized decision making is based on the underlying assumptions that frontline personnel have neither the time nor the inclination to direct and properly control the work they are performing and that they lack the knowledge and judgment to make wise decisions about how best to do it—hence the need for prescribed policies and procedures for a wide range of activities, close supervision, and tight control by top executives. The thesis underlying centralized structures is that strict enforcement of detailed procedures backed by rigorous managerial oversight is the most reliable way to keep the daily execution of strategy on track.

One advantage of a centralized structure, with tight control by the manager in charge, is that it is easy to know who is accountable when things do not go well. This structure can also reduce the potential for conflicting decisions and actions among lower-level managers who may have differing perspectives and ideas about how to tackle certain tasks or resolve particular issues. For example, a manager in charge of an engineering department may be more interested in pursuing a new technology than is a marketing manager who doubts that customers will value the technology as highly. Another advantage of a command-and-control structure is that it can facilitate strong leadership from the top in a crisis situation that affects the organization as a whole and can enable a more uniform and swift response.

But there are some serious disadvantages as well. Hierarchical command-and-control structures do not encourage responsibility and initiative on the part of lower-level managers and employees. They can make a large organization with a complex structure sluggish in responding to changing market conditions because of the time it takes for the review-and-approval process to run up all the layers of the management bureaucracy. Furthermore, to work well, centralized decision making requires top-level managers to gather and process whatever information is relevant to the decision. When the relevant knowledge resides at lower organizational levels (or is technical, detailed, or hard to express in words), it is difficult and time-consuming to get all the facts in front of a high-level executive located far from the scene of the action—full understanding of the situation cannot be readily copied from one mind to another. Hence, centralized decision making is often impractical—the larger the company and the more scattered its operations, the more that decision-making authority must be delegated to managers closer to the scene of the action.

Decentralized Decision Making: Pros and Cons In a highly decentralized organization, *decision-making authority is pushed down to the lowest organizational level capable of making timely, informed, competent decisions.* The objective is to put adequate decision-making authority in the hands of the people closest to and most familiar with the situation and train them to weigh all the factors and exercise good judgment. At Starbucks, for example, employees are encouraged to exercise initiative in promoting customer satisfaction—there's the oft-repeated story of a store employee who, when the computerized cash register system went offline, offered free coffee to waiting customers, thereby avoiding customer displeasure and damage to Starbucks's reputation.[25]

The ultimate goal of decentralized decision making is to put authority in the hands of those persons closest to and most knowledgeable about the situation.

The case for empowering down-the-line managers and employees to make decisions related to daily operations and strategy execution is based on the belief that a company that draws on the combined intellectual capital of all its employees can outperform a command-and-control company.[26] The challenge in a decentralized system is maintaining adequate control. With decentralized decision making, top management maintains control by placing limits on the authority granted to company personnel, installing companywide strategic control systems, holding people accountable for their decisions, instituting compensation incentives that reward people for doing their jobs well, and creating a corporate culture where there's strong peer pressure on individuals to act responsibly.[27]

Decentralized organizational structures have much to recommend them. Delegating authority to subordinate managers and rank-and-file employees encourages them to take responsibility and exercise initiative. It shortens organizational response times to market changes and spurs new ideas, creative thinking, innovation, and greater involvement on the part of all company personnel. At TJX Companies Inc., parent company of T.J.Maxx, Marshalls, and five other fashion and home decor retail store chains, buyers are encouraged to be intelligent risk takers in deciding what items to purchase for TJX stores—there's the story of a buyer for a seasonal product category who cut her own budget to have dollars allocated to other categories where sales were expected to be stronger. In worker-empowered structures, jobs can be defined more broadly, several tasks can be integrated into a single job, and people can direct their own work. Fewer managers are needed because deciding how to do things becomes part of each person's or team's job. Further, today's online communication systems and smartphones make it easy and relatively inexpensive for people at all organizational levels to have direct access to data, other employees, managers, suppliers, and customers. They can access information quickly (via the Internet or company network), readily check with superiors or whomever else as needed, and take responsible action. Typically, there are genuine gains in morale and productivity when people are provided with the tools and information they need to operate in a self-directed way.

But decentralization also has some disadvantages. Top managers lose an element of control over what goes on and may thus be unaware of actions being taken by personnel under their supervision. Such lack of control can be problematic in the event that empowered employees make decisions that conflict with those of others or that serve their unit's interests at the expense of other parts of the company. Moreover, because decentralization gives organizational units the authority to act independently, there is risk of too little collaboration and coordination between different units.

Many companies have concluded that the advantages of decentralization outweigh the disadvantages. Over the past several decades, there's been a decided shift from centralized, hierarchical structures to flatter, more decentralized structures that stress employee empowerment. This shift reflects a strong and growing consensus that authoritarian, hierarchical organizational structures are not well suited to implementing and executing strategies in an era when extensive information and instant communication are the norm and when a big fraction of the organization's most valuable assets consists of intellectual capital that resides in its employees' capabilities.

> Efforts to decentralize decision making and give company personnel some leeway in conducting operations must be tempered with the need to maintain adequate control and cross-unit coordination.

Capturing Cross-Business Strategic Fit in a Decentralized Structure Diversified companies striving to capture the benefits of synergy between separate businesses must beware of giving business unit heads full rein to operate independently. Cross-business strategic fit typically must be captured either by enforcing close cross-business collaboration or by centralizing the performance of functions requiring close coordination at the corporate level.[28] For example, if businesses with overlapping process and product technologies have their own independent R&D departments—each pursuing its own priorities, projects, and strategic agendas—it's hard for the corporate parent to prevent duplication of effort, capture either economies of scale or economies of scope, or encourage more collaborative R&D efforts. Where cross-business strategic fit with respect to R&D is important, one solution is to centralize the R&D function and have a coordinated corporate R&D effort that serves the interests of both the individual businesses and the company as a whole. Likewise, centralizing the related activities of separate businesses makes sense when there are opportunities to share a common sales force, use common distribution channels, rely on a common field service organization, use common e-commerce systems, and so on. Another structural solution to realizing the benefits of strategic fit is to create business groups consisting of those business units with common strategic-fit opportunities

Facilitating Collaboration with External Partners and Strategic Allies

Organizational mechanisms—whether formal or informal—are also required to ensure effective working relationships with each major outside constituency involved in strategy execution. Strategic alliances, outsourcing arrangements, joint ventures, and cooperative partnerships can contribute little of value without active management of the relationship. Unless top management sees that constructive organizational bridge building with external partners occurs and that productive working relationships emerge, the potential value of cooperative relationships is lost and the company's power to execute its strategy is weakened. For example, if close working relationships with suppliers are crucial, then supply chain management must enter into considerations of how to create an effective organizational structure. If distributor, dealer, or franchisee relationships are important, then someone must be assigned the task of nurturing the relationships with such forward-channel allies.

Building organizational bridges with external partners and strategic allies can be accomplished by appointing "relationship managers" with responsibility for making particular strategic partnerships generate the intended benefits. Relationship managers have many roles and functions: getting the right people together, promoting good rapport, facilitating the flow of information, nurturing interpersonal communication and cooperation, and ensuring effective coordination.[29] Multiple cross-organization ties have to be established and kept open to ensure proper communication and coordination. There has to be enough information sharing to make the relationship work and periodic frank discussions of conflicts, trouble spots, and changing situations.

Organizing and managing a network structure provides a mechanism for encouraging more effective collaboration and cooperation among external partners. A **network structure** is the arrangement linking a number of independent organizations involved in some common undertaking. A well-managed network structure typically includes one firm in a more central role, with the responsibility of ensuring that the right partners are included and the activities across the network are coordinated. The high-end Italian motorcycle company Ducati operates in this manner, assembling its motorcycles from parts obtained from a handpicked integrated network of parts suppliers.

> **CORE CONCEPT**
>
> A **network structure** is a configuration composed of a number of independent organizations engaged in some common undertaking, with one firm typically taking on a more central role.

Further Perspectives on Structuring the Work Effort

All organizational designs have their strategy-related strengths and weaknesses. To do a good job of matching structure to strategy, strategy implementers first have to pick a basic organizational design and modify it as needed to fit the company's particular business lineup. They must then (1) supplement the design with appropriate coordinating mechanisms (cross-functional task forces, special project teams, self-contained work teams, etc.) and (2) institute whatever networking and communications arrangements are necessary to support effective execution of the firm's strategy. Some companies may avoid setting up "ideal" organizational arrangements because they do not want to disturb existing reporting relationships or because they need to accommodate other situational idiosyncrasies, yet they must still work toward the goal of building a competitively capable organization.

What can be said unequivocally is that building a capable organization entails a process of consciously knitting together the efforts of individuals and groups. Organizational capabilities emerge from establishing and nurturing cooperative working relationships among people and groups to perform activities in a more efficient, value-creating fashion. While an appropriate organizational structure can facilitate this, organization building is a task in which senior management must be deeply involved. Indeed, effectively managing both internal organizational processes and external collaboration to create and develop competitively valuable organizational capabilities remains a top challenge for senior executives in today's companies.

KEY POINTS

1. Executing strategy is an action-oriented, operations-driven activity revolving around the management of people, business processes, and organizational structure. In devising an action agenda for executing strategy, managers should start by conducting a probing assessment of what the organization must do differently to carry out the strategy successfully. They should then consider precisely *how* to make the necessary internal changes.
2. Good strategy execution requires a *team effort.* All managers have strategy-executing responsibility in their areas of authority, and all employees are active participants in the strategy execution process.
3. Ten managerial tasks are part of every company effort to execute strategy: (1) staffing the organization with the right people, (2) developing the resources and building the necessary organizational capabilities, (3) creating a supportive organizational structure, (4) allocating sufficient resources (budgetary and otherwise), (5) instituting supportive policies and procedures, (6) adopting processes for continuous improvement, (7) installing systems that enable proficient company operations, (8) tying incentives to the achievement of desired targets, (9) instilling the right corporate culture, and (10) exercising internal leadership to propel strategy execution forward.
4. The two best signs of good strategy execution are that a company is meeting or beating its performance targets and is performing value chain activities in a manner that is conducive to companywide operating excellence. *Shortfalls in performance signal weak strategy, weak execution, or both.*
5. Building an organization capable of good strategy execution entails three types of actions: (1) *staffing the organization*—assembling a talented management team and recruiting and retaining employees with the needed experience, technical skills,

and intellectual capital; (2) *acquiring, developing, and strengthening strategy- supportive resources and capabilities*—accumulating the required resources, developing proficiencies in performing strategy-critical value chain activities, and updating the company's capabilities to match changing market conditions and customer expectations; and (3) *structuring the organization and work effort*—instituting organizational arrangements that facilitate good strategy execution, deciding how much decision-making authority to delegate, and managing external relationships.

6. Building core competencies and competitive capabilities is a time-consuming, managerially challenging exercise that can be approached in three ways: (1) developing capabilities internally, (2) acquiring capabilities through mergers and acquisitions, and (3) accessing capabilities via collaborative partnerships.
7. In building capabilities internally, the first step is to develop the *ability* to do something, through experimenting, actively searching for alternative solutions, and learning by trial and error. As experience grows and company personnel learn how to perform the activities consistently well and at an acceptable cost, the ability evolves into a tried-and-true capability. The process can be accelerated by making learning a more deliberate endeavor and providing the incentives that will motivate company personnel to achieve the desired ends.
8. As firms get better at executing their strategies, they develop capabilities in the domain of strategy execution. Superior strategy execution capabilities allow companies to get the most from their organizational resources and capabilities. But excellence in strategy execution can also be a more direct source of competitive advantage, since more efficient and effective strategy execution can lower costs and permit firms to deliver more value to customers. Because they are socially complex capabilities, superior strategy execution capabilities are hard to imitate and have no good substitutes. As such, they can be an important source of *sustainable* competitive advantage. Anytime rivals can readily duplicate successful strategies, making it impossible to *out-strategize* rivals, the chief way to achieve lasting competitive advantage is to *out-execute* them.
9. Structuring the organization and organizing the work effort in a strategy-supportive fashion has four aspects: (1) deciding which value chain activities to perform internally and which ones to outsource, (2) aligning the firm's organizational structure with its strategy, (3) deciding how much authority to centralize at the top and how much to delegate to down-the-line managers and employees, and (4) facilitating the necessary collaboration and coordination with external partners and strategic allies.
10. To align the firm's organizational structure with its strategy, it is important to make strategy-critical activities the main building blocks. There are four basic types of organizational structures: the simple structure, the functional structure, the multidivisional structure, and the matrix structure. Which is most appropriate depends on the firm's size, complexity, and strategy.

ASSURANCE OF LEARNING EXERCISES

connect

LO 1

1. The foundation of Nike's global sports apparel dominance lies in the company's continual ability to outcompete rivals by aligning its superior design, innovation, and marketing capabilities with outsourced manufacturing. Such a strategy necessitates a complex marriage of innovative product designs with fresh marketing techniques and a global chain of suppliers and manufacturers. Explore Nike's most recent strategic management changes (**news.nike.com/leadership**). How well do these changes reflect the company's focus on innovative design and marketing strategies? Has the company's relentless focus on apparel innovation affected its supply chain management? Do these changes—or Nike's strategy, more broadly—reflect the company's ubiquitous Swoosh logo and "Just Do It" slogan? Visit Nike's corporate website for more in-depth information: **nikeinc.com/pages/about-nike-inc**.

connect

LO 2

2. Search online to read about Jeff Bezos's management of his new executives. Specifically, explore Amazon.com's "S-Team" meetings (**management.fortune.cnn.com/2012/11/16/jeff-bezos-amazon/**). Why does Bezos begin meetings of senior executives with 30 minutes of silent reading? How does this focus the group? Why does Bezos insist new ideas must be written and presented in memo form? How does this reflect the founder's insistence on clear, concise, and innovative thinking in his company? And does this exercise work as a de facto crash course for new Amazon executives? Explain why this small but crucial management strategy reflects Bezos's overriding goal of cohesive and clear idea presentation.

LO 2, LO 3

3. Review Facebook's Careers page (**www.Facebook.com/careers/**). The page emphasizes Facebook's core values and explains how potential employees could fit that mold. Bold and decisive thinking and a commitment to transparency and social connectivity drive the page and the company as a whole. Then research Facebook's internal management training programs, called "employee boot camps," using a search engine like Google or Bing. How do these programs integrate the traits and stated goals on the Careers page into specific and tangible construction of employee capabilities? Boot camps are open to all Facebook employees, not just engineers. How does this internal training prepare Facebook employees of all types to "move fast and break things"?

LO 4

4. Review Valve Corporation's company handbook online: **www.valvesoftware.com/company/Valve_Handbook_LowRes.pdf**. Specifically, focus on Valve's corporate structure. Valve has hundreds of employees but no managers or bosses at all. Valve's gaming success hinges on innovative and completely original experiences like Portal and Half-Life. Does it seem that Valve's corporate structure uniquely promotes this type of gaming innovation? Why or why not? How would you characterize Valve's organizational structure? Is it completely unique, or could it be characterized as a multidivisional, matrix, or functional structure? Explain your answer.

LO 5

5. Johnson & Johnson, a multinational health care company responsible for manufacturing medical, pharmaceutical, and consumer goods, has been a leader in promoting a decentralized management structure. Perform an Internet search to gain some background information on the company's products, value chain activities, and leadership. How does Johnson & Johnson exemplify (or not exemplify) a decentralized management strategy? Describe the advantages and disadvantages of a decentralized system of management in the case of Johnson & Johnson. Why was it established in the first place? Has it been an effective means of decision making for the company?

EXERCISE FOR SIMULATION PARTICIPANTS

1. How would you describe the organization of your company's top-management team? Is some decision making decentralized and delegated to individual managers? If so, explain how the decentralization works. Or are decisions made more by consensus, with all co-managers having input? What do you see as the advantages and disadvantages of the decision-making approach your company is employing? **LO 5**
2. What specific actions have you and your co-managers taken to develop core competencies or competitive capabilities that can contribute to good strategy execution and potential competitive advantage? If no actions have been taken, explain your rationale for doing nothing. **LO 3**
3. What value chain activities are most crucial to good execution of your company's strategy? Does your company have the ability to outsource any value chain activities? If so, have you and your co-managers opted to engage in outsourcing? Why or why not? **LO 1, LO 4**

ENDNOTES

[1] Donald Sull, Rebecca Homkes, and Charles Sull, "Why Strategy Execution Unravels—and What to Do About It," *Harvard Business Review* 93, no. 3 (March 2015), p. 60.

[2] Steven W. Floyd and Bill Wooldridge, "Managing Strategic Consensus: The Foundation of Effective Implementation," *Academy of Management Executive* 6, no. 4 (November 1992), p. 27.

[3] Jack Welch with Suzy Welch, *Winning* (New York: HarperBusiness, 2005).

[4] Larry Bossidy and Ram Charan, *Execution: The Discipline of Getting Things Done* (New York: Crown Business, 2002).

[5] Christopher A. Bartlett and Sumantra Ghoshal, "Building Competitive Advantage through People," *MIT Sloan Management Review* 43, no. 2 (Winter 2002), pp. 34–41.

[6] Justin Menkes, "Hiring for Smarts," *Harvard Business Review* 83, no. 11 (November 2005), pp. 100–109; Justin Menkes, *Executive Intelligence* (New York: HarperCollins, 2005).

[7] Menkes, *Executive Intelligence*, pp. 68, 76.

[8] Jim Collins, *Good to Great* (New York: HarperBusiness, 2001).

[9] John Byrne, "The Search for the Young and Gifted," *Businessweek*, October 4, 1999, p. 108.

[10] C. Helfat and M. Peteraf, "The Dynamic Resource-Based View: Capability Lifecycles," *Strategic Management Journal* 24, no. 10 (October 2003), pp. 997–1010.

[11] G. Hamel and C. K. Prahalad, "Strategy as Stretch and Leverage," *Harvard Business Review* 71, no. 2 (March–April 1993), pp. 75–84.

[12] G. Dosi, R. Nelson, and S. Winter (eds.), *The Nature and Dynamics of Organizational Capabilities* (Oxford, England: Oxford University Press, 2001).

[13] S. Winter, "The Satisficing Principle in Capability Learning," *Strategic Management Journal* 21, no. 10–11 (October–November 2000), pp. 981–996; M. Zollo and S. Winter, "Deliberate Learning and the Evolution of Dynamic Capabilities," *Organization Science* 13, no. 3 (May–June 2002), pp. 339–351.

[14] Robert H. Hayes, Gary P. Pisano, and David M. Upton, *Strategic Operations: Competing through Capabilities* (New York: Free Press, 1996); Jonas Ridderstrale, "Cashing In on Corporate Competencies," *Business Strategy Review* 14, no. 1 (Spring 2003), pp. 27–38; Danny Miller, Russell Eisenstat, and Nathaniel Foote, "Strategy from the Inside Out: Building Capability-Creating Organizations," *California Management Review* 44, no. 3 (Spring 2002), pp. 37–55.

[15] S. Karim and W. Mitchell, "Path-Dependent and Path-Breaking Change: Reconfiguring Business Resources Following Acquisitions in the US Medical Sector, 1978–1995," *Strategic Management Journal* 21, no. 10–11 (October–November 2000), pp. 1061–1082; L. Capron, P. Dussauge, and W. Mitchell, "Resource Redeployment Following Horizontal Acquisitions in Europe and North America, 1988–1992," *Strategic Management Journal* 19, no. 7 (July 1998), pp. 631–662.

[16] J. B. Quinn, *Intelligent Enterprise* (New York: Free Press, 1992).

[17] Gary P. Pisano and Willy C. Shih, "Restoring American Competitiveness," *Harvard Business Review* 87, no. 7–8 (July–August 2009), pp. 114–125.

[18] A. Chandler, *Strategy and Structure* (Cambridge, MA: MIT Press, 1962).

[19] E. Olsen, S. Slater, and G. Hult, "The Importance of Structure and Process to Strategy Implementation," *Business Horizons* 48, no. 1 (2005), pp. 47–54; H. Barkema, J. Baum, and E. Mannix, "Management Challenges in a New Time," *Academy of Management Journal* 45, no. 5 (October 2002), pp. 916–930.

[21] H. Mintzberg, *The Structuring of Organizations* (Englewood Cliffs, NJ: Prentice Hall, 1979); C. Levicki, *The Interactive Strategy Workout*, 2nd ed. (London: Prentice Hall, 1999).

[22] O. Williamson, *Market and Hierarchies* (New York: Free Press, 1975); R. M. Burton and B. Obel, "A Computer Simulation Test of the M-Form Hypothesis," *Administrative Science Quarterly* 25 (1980), pp. 457–476.

[23] J. Baum and S. Wally, "Strategic Decision Speed and Firm Performance," *Strategic Management Journal* 24 (2003), pp. 1107–1129.

[24] C. Bartlett and S. Ghoshal, "Matrix Management: Not a Structure, a Frame of Mind," *Harvard Business Review*, July–August 1990, pp. 138–145.

[25] M. Goold and A. Campbell, "Structured Networks: Towards the Well Designed Matrix," *Long Range Planning* 36, no. 5 (2003), pp. 427–439.

[26] Iain Somerville and John Edward Mroz, "New Competencies for a New World," in Frances Hesselbein, Marshall Goldsmith, and Richard Beckard (eds.), *The Organization of the Future* (San Francisco: Jossey-Bass, 1997), p. 70.

[26] Stanley E. Fawcett, Gary K. Rhoads, and Phillip Burnah, "People as the Bridge to Competitiveness: Benchmarking the 'ABCs' of an Empowered Workforce," *Benchmarking: An International Journal* 11, no. 4 (2004), pp. 346–360.

[27] Robert Simons, "Control in an Age of Empowerment," *Harvard Business Review* 73 (March–April 1995), pp. 80–88.

[28] Jeanne M. Liedtka, "Collaboration across Lines of Business for Competitive Advantage," *Academy of Management Executive* 10, no. 2 (May 1996), pp. 20–34.

[29] Rosabeth Moss Kanter, "Collaborative Advantage: The Art of the Alliance," *Harvard Business Review* 72, no. 4 (July–August 1994), pp. 96–108.

CHAPTER 11

Managing Internal Operations

Actions That Promote Good Strategy Execution

© Jonathan McHugh/Alamy Stock Photo

Learning Objectives

THIS CHAPTER WILL HELP YOU UNDERSTAND:

LO 1 Why resource allocation should always be based on strategic priorities.

LO 2 How well-designed policies and procedures can facilitate good strategy execution.

LO 3 How best practices and process management tools drive continuous improvement in the performance of value chain activities and promote superior strategy execution.

LO 4 The role of information and operating systems in enabling company personnel to carry out their strategic roles proficiently.

LO 5 How and why the use of well-designed incentives and rewards can be management's single most powerful tool for promoting adept strategy execution.

Apple is a very disciplined company, and we have great processes. But that's not what it's about. Process makes you more efficient.

Steve Jobs—*Cofounder of Apple, Inc.*

Motivation is the art of getting people to do what you want them to do because they want to do it.

Dwight D. Eisenhower—*Thirty-fourth president of the United States*

I don't pay good wages because I have a lot of money; I have a lot of money because I pay good wages.

Robert Bosch—*Founder of engineering company Robert Bosch GmbH*

In Chapter 10, we emphasized that proficient strategy execution begins with three types of managerial actions: staffing the organization with the right people; acquiring, developing, and strengthening the firm's resources and capabilities; and structuring the organization in a manner supportive of the strategy execution effort.

In this chapter, we discuss five additional managerial actions that advance the cause of good strategy execution:

- Allocating ample resources to execution-critical value chain activities.
- Instituting policies and procedures that facilitate good strategy execution.
- Employing process management tools to drive continuous improvement in how value chain activities are performed.
- Installing information and operating systems that enable company personnel to carry out their strategic roles proficiently.
- Using rewards and incentives to promote better strategy execution and the achievement of strategic and financial targets.

ALLOCATING RESOURCES TO THE STRATEGY EXECUTION EFFORT

LO 1

Why resource allocation should always be based on strategic priorities.

Early in the strategy implementation process, managers must determine what resources (in terms of funding, people, and so on) will be required and how they should be distributed across the company's various organizational units. This includes carefully screening requests for more people and new facilities and equipment, approving those that will contribute to the strategy execution effort, and turning down those that don't. Should internal cash flows prove insufficient to fund the planned strategic initiatives, then management must raise additional funds through borrowing or selling additional shares of stock to investors.

A company's strategic priorities must drive how capital allocations are made and the size of each unit's operating budgets.

A company's ability to marshal the resources needed to support new strategic initiatives has a major impact on the strategy execution process. Too little funding and an insufficiency of other types of resources slow progress and impede the efforts of organizational units to execute their pieces of the strategic plan competently. Too much funding of particular organizational units and value chain activities wastes organizational resources and reduces financial performance. Both of these scenarios argue for managers to become deeply involved in reviewing budget proposals and directing the proper kinds and amounts of resources to strategy-critical organizational units.

A change in strategy nearly always calls for budget reallocations and resource shifting. Previously important units with a lesser role in the new strategy may need downsizing. Units that now have a bigger strategic role may need more people, new equipment, additional facilities, and above-average increases in their operating budgets. Implementing new strategy initiatives requires managers to take an active and sometimes forceful role in shifting resources, not only to better support activities now having a higher priority but also to capture opportunities to operate more cost-effectively. This requires putting enough resources behind new strategic initiatives to fuel their success and making the tough decisions to kill projects and activities that are no longer justified.

Google's strong support of R&D activities helped it grow to a $527 billion giant in just 18 years. In 2013, however, Google decided to kill its 20 percent time policy, which allowed its staff to work on side projects of their choice one day a week. While this side project program gave rise to many innovations, such as Gmail and AdSense (a big contributor to Google's revenues), it also meant that fewer resources were available for projects that were deemed closer to the core of Google's mission. In the years since Google killed the 20 percent policy, the company has consistently topped *Fortune, Forbes,* and *Fast Company* magazines' "most innovative companies" lists for ideas such as Google Glass, self-driving automobiles, and Chromebooks.

Visible actions to reallocate operating funds and move people into new organizational units signal a determined commitment to strategic change. Such actions can catalyze the implementation process and give it credibility. Microsoft has made a practice of regularly shifting hundreds of programmers to new high-priority programming initiatives within a matter of weeks or even days. Fast-moving developments in many markets are prompting companies to abandon traditional annual budgeting and resource allocation cycles in favor of resource allocation processes supportive of more rapid adjustments in strategy. In response to rapid technological change in the communications industry, AT&T has prioritized investments and acquisitions that have allowed it to offer its enterprise customers faster, more flexible networks and provide innovative new customer services, such as its Sponsored Data plan.

Merely fine-tuning the execution of a company's existing strategy seldom requires big shifts of resources from one area to another. In contrast, new strategic initiatives generally require not only big shifts in resources but a larger allocation of resources to the effort as well. However, there are times when strategy changes or new execution initiatives need to be made without adding to total company expenses. In such circumstances, managers have to work their way through the existing budget line by line and activity by activity, looking for ways to trim costs and shift resources to activities that are higher-priority in the strategy execution effort. In the event that a company needs to make significant cost cuts during the course of launching new strategic initiatives, managers must be especially creative in finding ways to do more with less. Indeed, it is common for strategy changes and the drive for good strategy execution to be aimed at achieving considerably higher levels of operating efficiency and, at the same time, making sure the most important value chain activities are performed as effectively as possible.

INSTITUTING POLICIES AND PROCEDURES THAT FACILITATE STRATEGY EXECUTION

LO 2

How well-designed policies and procedures can facilitate good strategy execution.

A company's policies and procedures can either support or hinder good strategy execution. Anytime a company moves to put new strategy elements in place or improve its strategy execution capabilities, some changes in work practices are usually needed. Managers are thus well advised to carefully consider whether existing policies and procedures fully support such changes and to revise or discard those that do not.

As shown in Figure 11.1, well-conceived policies and operating procedures facilitate strategy execution in three ways:

A company's policies and procedures provide a set of well-honed routines for running the company and executing the strategy.

1. *By providing top-down guidance regarding how things need to be done.* Policies and procedures provide company personnel with a set of guidelines for how to perform organizational activities, conduct various aspects of operations, solve problems as they arise, and accomplish particular tasks. In essence, they represent a store of organizational or managerial knowledge about efficient and effective ways of doing things—a set of well-honed *routines* for running the company. They clarify uncertainty about how to proceed in executing strategy and align the actions and behavior of company personnel with the

FIGURE 11.1 How Policies and Procedures Facilitate Good Strategy Execution

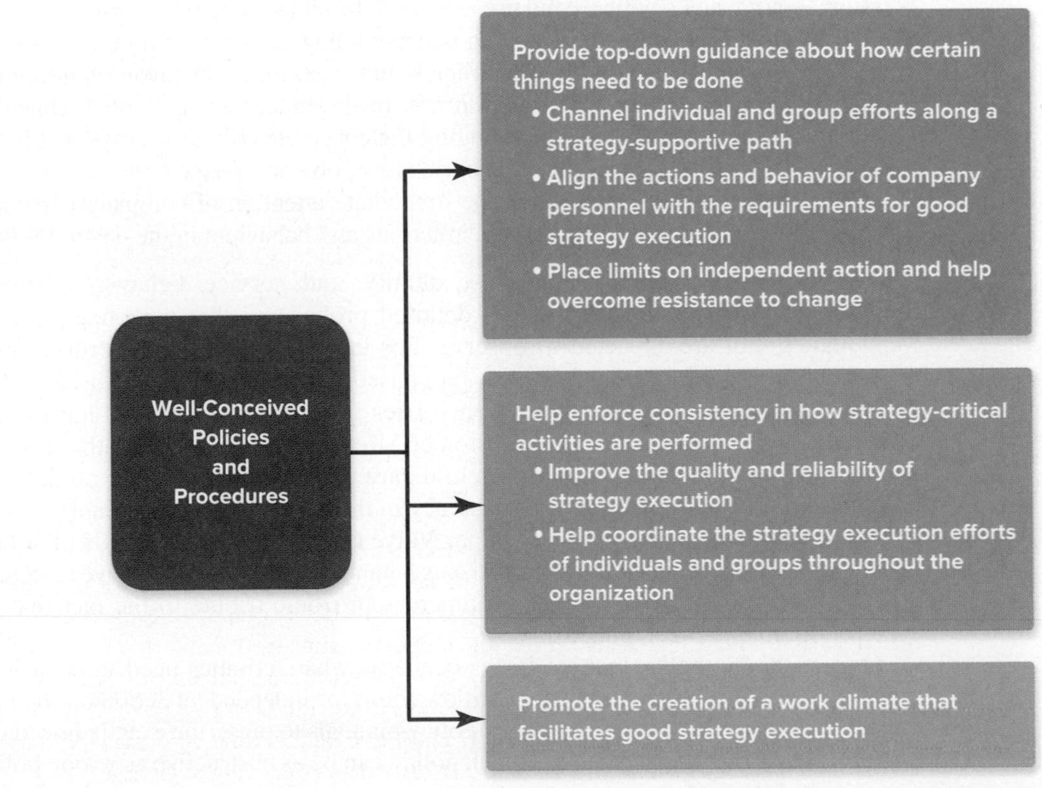

requirements for good strategy execution. Moreover, they place limits on ineffective independent action. When they are well matched with the requirements of the strategy implementation plan, they channel the efforts of individuals along a path that supports the plan. When existing ways of doing things pose a barrier to strategy execution initiatives, actions and behaviors have to be changed. Under these conditions, the managerial role is to establish and enforce new policies and operating practices that are more conducive to executing the strategy appropriately. Policies are a particularly useful way to counteract tendencies for some people to resist change. People generally refrain from violating company policy or going against recommended practices and procedures without gaining clearance or having strong justification.

2. *By helping ensure consistency in how execution-critical activities are performed.* Policies and procedures serve to standardize the way that activities are performed. This can be important for ensuring the quality and reliability of the strategy execution process. It helps align and coordinate the strategy execution efforts of individuals and groups throughout the organization—a feature that is particularly beneficial when there are geographically scattered operating units. For example, eliminating significant differences in the operating practices of different plants, sales regions, or customer service centers or in the individual outlets in a chain operation helps a company deliver consistent product quality and service to customers. Good strategy execution nearly always entails an ability to replicate product quality and the caliber of customer service at every location where the company does business—anything less blurs the company's image and lowers customer satisfaction.
3. *By promoting the creation of a work climate that facilitates good strategy execution.* A company's policies and procedures help set the tone of a company's work climate and contribute to a common understanding of "how we do things around here." Because abandoning old policies and procedures in favor of new ones invariably alters the internal work climate, managers can use the policy-changing process as a powerful lever for changing the corporate culture in ways that better support new strategic initiatives. The trick here, obviously, is to come up with new policies or procedures that catch the immediate attention of company personnel and prompt them to quickly shift their actions and behaviors in the desired ways.

To ensure consistency in product quality and service behavior patterns, McDonald's policy manual spells out detailed procedures that personnel in each McDonald's unit are expected to observe. For example, "Cooks must turn, never flip, hamburgers. If they haven't been purchased, Big Macs must be discarded in 10 minutes after being cooked and French fries in 7 minutes. Cashiers must make eye contact with and smile at every customer." Retail chain stores and other organizational chains (e.g., hotels, hospitals, child care centers) similarly rely on detailed policies and procedures to ensure consistency in their operations and reliable service to their customers. Video game developer Valve Corporation prides itself on a lack of rigid policies and procedures; its 37-page handbook for new employees details how things get done in such an environment—an ironic tribute to the fact that all types of companies need policies.

One of the big policy-making issues concerns what activities need to be strictly prescribed and what activities ought to allow room for independent action on the part of personnel. Few companies need thick policy manuals to prescribe exactly how daily operations are to be conducted. Too much policy can be as obstructive as wrong policy and as confusing as no policy. There is wisdom in a middle approach: *Prescribe enough policies to give organization members clear direction and to place reasonable boundaries on their actions; then empower them to act within these boundaries in pursuit of company goals.* Allowing company personnel to act with some degree of freedom is especially appropriate when individual creativity and initiative are more essential to good strategy execution than are standardization and strict conformity. Instituting policies that facilitate strategy execution can therefore mean policies more policies, fewer policies, or different policies. It can mean policies that require things be done according to a precisely defined standard or policies that give employees substantial leeway to do activities the way they think best.

There is wisdom in a middle-ground approach: Prescribe enough policies to give organization members clear direction and to place reasonable boundaries on their actions; then empower them to act within these boundaries in pursuit of company goals.

ADOPTING BEST PRACTICES AND EMPLOYING PROCESS MANAGEMENT TOOLS

Company managers can significantly advance the cause of competent strategy execution by adopting best practices and using process management tools to drive continuous improvement in how internal operations are conducted. One of the most widely used methods for gauging how well a company is executing its strategy entails benchmarking the company's performance of particular activities and business processes against "best-in-industry" and "best-in-world" performers.[1] It can also be useful to look at "best-in-company" performers of an activity if a company has a number of different organizational units performing much the same function at different locations. Identifying, analyzing, and understanding how top-performing companies or organizational units conduct particular value chain activities and business processes provide useful yardsticks for judging the effectiveness and efficiency of internal operations and setting performance standards for organizational units to meet or beat.

LO 3

How best practices and process management tools drive continuous improvement in the performance of value chain activities and promote superior strategy execution.

How the Process of Identifying and Incorporating Best Practices Works

As discussed in Chapter 4, *benchmarking* is the backbone of the process of identifying, studying, and implementing *best practices.* The role of benchmarking is to look outward to find best practices and then to develop the data for measuring how well a company's own performance of an activity stacks up against the best-practice standard. However, benchmarking is more complicated than simply identifying which companies are the best performers of an activity and then trying to imitate their approaches—especially if these companies are in other industries. Normally, the best practices of other organizations must be *adapted* to fit the specific circumstances of a company's own business, strategy, and operating requirements. Since each organization is unique, the telling part of any best-practice initiative is how well the company puts its own version of the best practice into place and makes it work. Indeed, a best practice remains little more than another company's interesting success story unless company personnel buy into the task of translating what can be learned from other companies into real action and results. The agents of change must be frontline employees who are convinced of the need to abandon the old ways of doing things and switch to a best-practice mindset.

Wide-scale use of best practices across a company's entire value chain promotes operating excellence and good strategy execution.

As shown in Figure 11.2, to the extent that a company is able to successfully adapt a best practice pioneered elsewhere to fit its circumstances, it is likely to improve its performance of the activity, perhaps dramatically—an outcome that promotes better strategy execution. It follows that a company can make giant strides toward excellent strategy execution by adopting a best-practice mindset and successfully *implementing the use of best practices across more of its value chain activities.* The more that organizational units use best practices in performing their work, the closer a company moves toward performing its value chain activities more effectively and efficiently. This is what operational excellence is all about. Employing best practices to improve internal operations and strategy execution has powerful appeal—legions of companies across the world are now making concerted efforts to employ best practices in performing many value chain activities, and they regularly benchmark their performance of these activities against best-in-industry or best-in-world performers.

Business Process Reengineering, Total Quality Management, and Six Sigma Quality Programs: Tools for Promoting Operating Excellence

Three other powerful management tools for promoting operating excellence and better strategy execution are business process reengineering, total quality management (TQM) programs, and Six Sigma quality control programs. Each of these merits discussion since many companies around the world use these tools to help execute strategies tied to cost reduction, defect-free manufacture, superior product quality, superior customer service, and total customer satisfaction.

Business Process Reengineering Companies searching for ways to improve their operations have sometimes discovered that the execution of strategy-critical activities is hampered by a disconnected organizational arrangement whereby pieces of an activity are performed in several different functional departments, with no one manager or group being accountable for optimal performance of the entire

FIGURE 11.2 From Benchmarking and Best-Practice Implementation to Operational Excellence in Strategy Execution

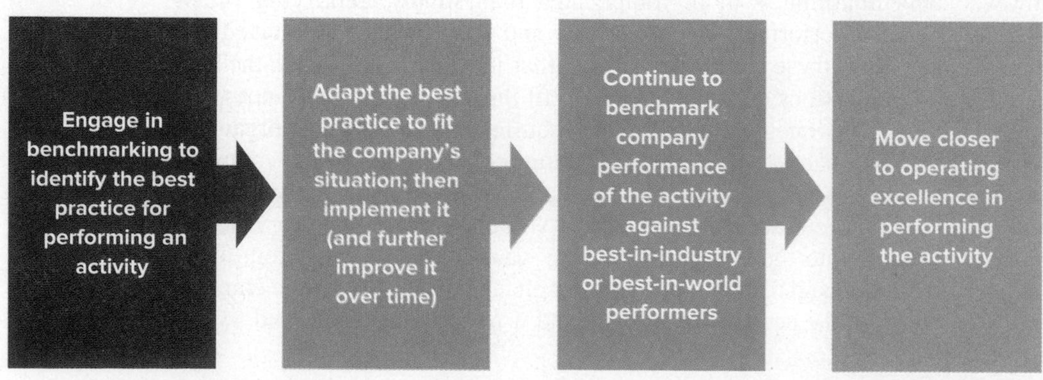

activity. This can easily occur in such inherently cross-functional activities as customer service (which can involve personnel in order filling, warehousing and shipping, invoicing, accounts receivable, after-sale repair, and technical support), particularly for companies with a functional organizational structure.

To address the suboptimal performance problems that can arise from this type of situation, a company can *reengineer the work effort,* pulling the pieces of an activity out of different departments and creating a cross-functional work group or single department (often called a *process department*) to take charge of the whole process. The use of cross-functional teams has been popularized by the practice of **business process reengineering,** which involves radically redesigning and streamlining the workflow (typically enabled by cutting-edge use of online technology and information systems), with the goal of achieving quantum gains in performance of the activity.[2]

CORE CONCEPT

Business process reengineering involves radically redesigning and streamlining how an activity is performed, with the intent of achieving quantum improvements in performance.

The reengineering of value chain activities has been undertaken at many companies in many industries all over the world, with excellent results being achieved at some firms.[3] Hallmark reengineered its process for developing new greeting cards, creating teams of mixed-occupation personnel (artists, writers, lithographers, merchandisers, and administrators) to work on a single holiday or greeting card theme. The reengineered process speeded development times for new lines of greeting cards by up to 24 months, was more cost-efficient, and increased customer satisfaction.[4] In the order-processing section of General Electric's circuit breaker division, elapsed time from order receipt to delivery was cut from three weeks to three days by consolidating six production units into one, reducing a variety of former inventory and handling steps, automating the design system to replace a human custom-design process, and cutting the organizational layers between managers and workers from three to one. Productivity rose 20 percent in one year, and unit manufacturing costs dropped 30 percent. Northwest Water, a British utility, used process reengineering to eliminate 45 work depots that served as home bases to crews who installed and repaired water and sewage lines and equipment. Under the reengineered arrangement, crews worked directly from their vehicles, receiving assignments and reporting work completion from computer terminals in their trucks. Crew members became contractors to Northwest Water rather than employees, a move that not only eliminated the need for the work depots but also allowed Northwest Water to eliminate a big percentage of the bureaucratic personnel and supervisory organization that managed the crews.[5]

While business process reengineering has been criticized as an excuse for downsizing, it has nonetheless proved itself a useful tool for streamlining a company's work effort and moving closer to operational excellence. It has also inspired more technologically based approaches to integrating and streamlining business processes, such as *enterprise resource planning,* a software-based system implemented with the help of consulting companies such as SAP (the leading provider of business software).

Total Quality Management Programs

Total quality management (TQM) is a management approach that emphasizes continuous improvement in all phases of operations, 100 percent accuracy in performing tasks, involvement and empowerment of employees at all levels, team-based work design, benchmarking, and total customer satisfaction.[6] While TQM concentrates on producing quality goods and fully satisfying customer expectations, it achieves its biggest successes when it is extended to employee efforts in *all departments*—human resources, billing, accounting, and information systems—that may lack pressing, customer-driven incentives to improve. It involves reforming the corporate culture and shifting to

CORE CONCEPT

Total quality management (TQM) entails creating a total quality culture, involving managers and employees at all levels, bent on continuously improving the performance of every value chain activity.

a continuous-improvement business philosophy that permeates every facet of the organization.[7] TQM aims at instilling enthusiasm and commitment to doing things right from the top to the bottom of the organization. Management's job is to kindle an organizationwide search for ways to improve that involves all company personnel exercising initiative and using their ingenuity. TQM doctrine preaches that there's no such thing as "good enough" and that everyone has a responsibility to participate in continuous improvement. TQM is thus a race without a finish. Success comes from making little steps forward each day, a process that the Japanese call *kaizen*.

TQM takes a fairly long time to show significant results—very little benefit emerges within the first six months. The long-term payoff of TQM, if it comes, depends heavily on management's success in implanting a culture within which the TQM philosophy and practices can thrive. But it is a management tool that has attracted numerous users and advocates over several decades, and it can deliver good results when used properly.

CORE CONCEPT

Six Sigma programs utilize advanced statistical methods to improve quality by reducing defects and variability in the performance of business processes.

Six Sigma Quality Control Programs **Six Sigma programs** offer another way to drive continuous improvement in quality and strategy execution. This approach entails the use of advanced statistical methods to identify and remove the causes of defects (errors) and undesirable variability in performing an activity or business process. When performance of an activity or process reaches "Six Sigma quality," there are *no more than 3.4 defects per million iterations* (equal to 99.9997 percent accuracy).[8]

There are two important types of Six Sigma programs. The Six Sigma process of define, measure, analyze, improve, and control (DMAIC, pronounced "de-may-ic") is an improvement system for existing processes falling below specification and needing incremental improvement. The Six Sigma process of define, measure, analyze, design, and verify (DMADV, pronounced "de-mad-vee") is used to develop *new* processes or products at Six Sigma quality levels. DMADV is sometimes referred to as Design for Six Sigma, or DFSS. Both Six Sigma programs are overseen by personnel who have completed Six Sigma "master black belt" training, and they are executed by personnel who have earned Six Sigma "green belts" and Six Sigma "black belts." According to the Six Sigma Academy, personnel with black belts can save companies approximately $230,000 per project and can complete four to six projects a year.[9]

The statistical thinking underlying Six Sigma is based on the following three principles: (1) All work is a process, (2) all processes have variability, and (3) all processes create data that explain variability.[10] Six Sigma's DMAIC process is a particularly good vehicle for improving performance when there are *wide variations* in how well an activity is performed. For instance, airlines striving to improve the on-time performance of their flights have more to gain from actions to curtail the number of flights that are late by more than 30 minutes than from actions to reduce the number of flights that are late by less than 5 minutes. Six Sigma quality control programs are of particular interest for large companies, which are better able to shoulder the cost of the large investment required in employee training, organizational infrastructure, and consulting services. For example, to realize a cost savings of $4.4 billion from rolling out its Six Sigma program, GE had to invest $1.6 billion and suffer losses from the program during its first year.[11]

Since the programs were first introduced, thousands of companies and nonprofit organizations around the world have used Six Sigma to promote operating excellence. For companies at the forefront of this movement, such as Motorola, General Electric (GE), Ford, and Honeywell (Allied Signal), the cost savings as a percentage of revenue varied from 1.2 to 4.5 percent, according to data analysis conducted by iSixSigma (an organization that provides free articles, tools, and resources concerning Six Sigma). More recently, there has been a resurgence of interest in Six Sigma practices, with companies such as Siemens, Coca-Cola, Ocean Spray, GEICO, and Merrill Lynch turning to Six Sigma as a vehicle to improve their bottom lines. In the first five years of its adoption, Six Sigma at Bank of America helped the bank reap about $2 billion in revenue gains and cost savings; the bank holds an annual "Best of Six Sigma Expo" to celebrate the teams and the projects with the greatest contribution to the company's bottom line. GE, one of the most successful companies implementing Six Sigma training and pursuing Six Sigma perfection across the company's entire operations, estimated benefits of some $10 billion during the first five years of implementation—its Lighting division, for example, cut invoice defects and disputes by 98 percent.[12]

Six Sigma has also been used to improve processes in health care. Froedtert Hospital in Milwaukee, Wisconsin, used Six Sigma to improve the accuracy of administering the proper drug doses to patients. DMAIC analysis of the three-stage process by which prescriptions were written by doctors, filled by the hospital pharmacy, and then administered to patients by nurses revealed that most mistakes came from misreading the doctors' handwriting. The hospital implemented a program requiring doctors to enter the prescription on the hospital's computers, which slashed the number of errors dramatically. In recent years, Pfizer embarked on 85 Six Sigma projects to streamline its R&D process and lower the cost of delivering medicines to patients in its pharmaceutical sciences division.

Illustration Capsule 11.1 describes Charleston Area Medical Center's use of Six Sigma as a health care provider coping with the current challenges facing this industry.

Despite its potential benefits, Six Sigma is not without its problems. There is evidence, for example, that Six Sigma techniques can stifle innovation and creativity. The essence of Six Sigma is to reduce variability in processes, but creative processes, by nature, include quite a bit of variability. In many instances, breakthrough innovations occur only after thousands of ideas have been abandoned and promising ideas have gone through multiple iterations and extensive prototyping. Google's chair, Eric Schmidt, has declared that applying Six Sigma measurement and control principles to creative activities at Google would choke off innovation altogether.[13]

A blended approach to Six Sigma implementation that is gaining in popularity pursues incremental improvements in operating efficiency, while R&D and other processes that allow the company to develop new ways of offering value to customers are given freer rein. Managers of these **ambidextrous organizations** are adept at employing continuous improvement in operating processes but allowing R&D to operate under a set of rules that allows for exploration and the development of breakthrough innovations. However, the two distinctly different approaches to managing employees must be carried out by tightly integrated senior managers to ensure that the separate and diversely oriented units operate with a common purpose. Ciba Vision, now part of eye care multinational Alcon, dramatically reduced operating expenses through the use of continuous-improvement programs, while simultaneously and harmoniously developing a new series of contact lens products that have allowed its revenues to increase by 300 percent over a 10-year period.[14] An enterprise that systematically and wisely applies Six Sigma methods to its value chain, activity by activity, can make major strides in improving the proficiency with which its strategy is executed without sacrificing innovation. As is the case with TQM, obtaining managerial commitment, establishing a quality culture, and fully involving employees are all of critical importance to the successful implementation of Six Sigma quality programs.[15]

Ambidextrous organizations are adept at employing continuous improvement in operating processes but allowing R&D to operate under a set of rules that allows for exploration and the development of breakthrough innovations.

ILLUSTRATION CAPSULE 11.1

Charleston Area Medical Center's Six Sigma Program

© ERproductions Ltd/Blend Images LLC

Established in 1972, Charleston Area Medical Center (CAMC) is West Virginia's largest health care provider in terms of beds, admissions, and revenues. In 2000, CAMC implemented a Six Sigma program to examine quality problems and standardize care processes. Performance improvement was important to CAMC's management for a variety of strategic reasons, including competitive positioning and cost control.

The United States has been evolving toward a pay-for-performance structure, which rewards hospitals for providing quality care. CAMC has utilized its Six Sigma program to take advantage of these changes in the health care environment. For example, to improve its performance in acute myocardial infarction (AMI), CAMC applied a Six Sigma DMAIC (define-measure-analyze-improve-control) approach. Nursing staff members were educated on AMI care processes, performance targets were posted in nursing units, and adherence to the eight Hospital Quality Alliance (HQA) indicators of quality care for AMI patients was tracked. As a result of the program, CAMC improved its compliance with HQA-recommended treatment for AMI from 50 to 95 percent. Harvard researchers identified CAMC as one of the top-performing hospitals reporting comparable data.

Controlling cost has also been an important aspect of CAMC's performance improvement initiatives due to local regulations. West Virginia is one of two states where medical services rates are set by state regulators. This forces CAMC to limit expenditures because the hospital cannot raise prices. CAMC first applied Six Sigma in an effort to control costs by managing the supply chain more effectively. The effort created a one-time $150,000 savings by working with vendors to remove outdated inventory. As a result of continuous improvement, a 2015 report stated that CAMC had achieved supply chain management savings of $12 million in the past four years.

Since CAMC introduced Six Sigma, over 100 quality improvement projects have been initiated. A key to CAMC's success has been instilling a continuous improvement mindset into the organization's culture. Dale Wood, chief quality officer at CAMC, stated: "If you have people at the top who completely support and want these changes to occur, you can still fall flat on your face. . . . You need a group of networkers who can carry change across an organization." Due to CAMC's performance improvement culture, the hospital ranks high nationally in ratings for quality of care and patient safety, as reported on the Centers for Medicare and Medicaid Services (CMS) website.

Note: Developed with Robin A. Daley

Sources: CAMC website; Martha Hostetter, "Case Study: Improving Performance at Charleston Area Medical Center," *The Commonwealth Fund,* November–December 2007, **www.commonwealthfund.org/publications/newsletters/quality-matters/2007/november-december/case-study-improving-performance-at-charleston-area-medical-center** (accessed January 2016); J. C. Simmons, "Using Six Sigma to Make a Difference in Health Care Quality," *The Quality Letter,* April 2002.

Business process reengineering aims at one-time quantum improvement, while continuous-improvement programs like TQM and Six Sigma aim at ongoing incremental improvements.

The Difference between Business Process Reengineering and Continuous-Improvement Programs Like Six Sigma and TQM

Whereas business process reengineering aims at *quantum gains* on the order of 30 to 50 percent or more, total quality programs like TQM and Six Sigma stress *ongoing incremental progress,* striving for inch-by-inch gains again and again in a never-ending stream. The two approaches to improved performance of value chain activities and operating excellence are not mutually exclusive; it makes sense to use them in tandem. Reengineering can be used first to produce a good basic design that yields quick, dramatic improvements in performing a business process. TQM or Six Sigma programs can then be used as a follow-on to reengineering and/or best-practice implementation to deliver incremental improvements over a longer period of time.

Capturing the Benefits of Initiatives to Improve Operations

The biggest beneficiaries of benchmarking and best-practice initiatives, reengineering, TQM, and Six Sigma are companies that view such programs not as ends in themselves but as tools for implementing company strategy more effectively. The least rewarding payoffs occur when company managers seize on the programs as novel ideas that might be worth a try. In most such instances, they result in strategy-blind efforts to simply manage better.

There's an important lesson here. Business process management tools all need to be linked to a company's strategic priorities to contribute effectively to improving the strategy's execution. Only strategy can point to which value chain activities matter and what performance targets make the most sense. Without a strategic framework, managers lack the context in which to fix things that really matter to business unit performance and competitive success.

To get the most from initiatives to execute strategy more proficiently, managers must have a clear idea of what specific outcomes really matter. Is it high on-time delivery, lower overall costs, fewer customer complaints, shorter cycle times, a higher percentage of revenues coming from recently introduced products, or something else? Benchmarking best-in-industry and best-in-world performance of targeted value chain activities provides a realistic basis for setting internal performance milestones and longer-range targets. Once initiatives to improve operations are linked to the company's strategic priorities, then comes the managerial task of building a total quality culture that is genuinely committed to achieving the performance outcomes that strategic success requires.[16]

Managers can take the following action steps to realize full value from TQM or Six Sigma initiatives and promote a culture of operating excellence:[17]

1. Demonstrating visible, unequivocal, and unyielding commitment to total quality and continuous improvement, including specifying measurable objectives for increasing quality and making continual progress.
2. Nudging people toward quality-supportive behaviors by:
   a. Screening job applicants rigorously and hiring only those with attitudes and aptitudes that are right for quality-based performance.
   b. Providing quality training for employees.
   c. Using teams and team-building exercises to reinforce and nurture individual effort. (The creation of a quality culture is facilitated when teams become more cross-functional, multitask-oriented, and increasingly self-managed.)
   d. Recognizing and rewarding individual and team efforts to improve quality regularly and systematically.
   e. Stressing prevention (doing it right the first time), not correction (instituting ways to undo or overcome mistakes).
3. Empowering employees so that authority for delivering great service or improving products is in the hands of the doers rather than the overseers—*improving quality has to be seen as part of everyone's job.*

4. Using online systems to provide all relevant parties with the latest best practices, thereby speeding the diffusion and adoption of best practices throughout the organization. Online systems can also allow company personnel to exchange data and opinions about how to upgrade the prevailing best-in-company practices.
5. Emphasizing that performance can and must be improved, because competitors are not resting on their laurels and customers are always looking for something better.

The purpose of using benchmarking, best practices, business process reengineering, TQM, and Six Sigma programs is to improve the performance of strategy-critical activities and thereby enhance strategy execution.

In sum, benchmarking, the adoption of best practices, business process reengineering, TQM, and Six Sigma techniques all need to be seen and used as part of a bigger-picture effort to execute strategy proficiently. Used properly, all of these tools are capable of improving the proficiency with which an organization performs its value chain activities. Not only do improvements from such initiatives add up over time and strengthen organizational capabilities, but they also help build a culture of operating excellence. All this lays the groundwork for gaining a competitive advantage.[18] While it is relatively easy for rivals to also implement process management tools, it is much more difficult and time-consuming for them to instill a deeply ingrained culture of operating excellence (as occurs when such techniques are religiously employed and top management exhibits lasting commitment to operational excellence throughout the organization).

INSTALLING INFORMATION AND OPERATING SYSTEMS

LO 4

The role of information and operating systems in enabling company personnel to carry out their strategic roles proficiently.

Company strategies can't be executed well without a number of internal systems for business operations. Qantas Airways, JetBlue, Ryanair, British Airways, and other successful airlines cannot hope to provide passenger-pleasing service without a user-friendly online reservation system, an accurate and speedy baggage-handling system, and a strict aircraft maintenance program that minimizes problems requiring at-the-gate service that delay departures. FedEx has internal communication systems that allow it to coordinate its over 100,000 vehicles in handling a daily average of 10.5 million shipments to more than 220 countries and territories. Its leading-edge flight operations systems allow a single controller to direct as many as 200 of FedEx's 650 aircraft simultaneously, overriding their flight plans should weather problems or other special circumstances arise. FedEx also has created a series of e-business tools for customers that allow them to ship and track packages online, create address books, review shipping history, generate custom reports, simplify customer billing, reduce internal warehousing and inventory management costs, purchase goods and services from suppliers, and respond to their own quickly changing customer demands. All of FedEx's systems support the company's strategy of providing businesses and individuals with a broad array of package delivery services and enhancing its competitiveness against United Parcel Service, DHL, and the U.S. Postal Service.

Amazon.com ships customer orders of books, CDs, and myriad other items from a global network of more than 120 warehouses in locations including the United States, China, and Germany. The warehouses are so technologically sophisticated that they require about as many lines of code to run as Amazon's website does. Using complex picking algorithms, computers initiate the order-picking process by sending signals to workers' wireless receivers, telling them which items to pick off the shelves in which order. Computers also generate data on mix-boxed items, chute backup times, line speed, worker productivity, and shipping weights on orders. Systems are upgraded regularly, and productivity improvements are aggressively pursued. Two new things that Amazon is trying out are drone delivery and a crowdsourcing app called On My

Way that would allow drivers to deliver part-time for Amazon in the same way that Uber drivers provide rides for people.

Otis Elevator, the world's largest manufacturer of elevators, with more than 2.5 million elevators and escalators installed worldwide, has a 24/7 remote electronic monitoring system that can detect when an elevator or escalator installed on a customer's site has any of 325 problems.[19] If the monitoring system detects a problem, it analyzes and diagnoses the cause and location, then makes the service call to an Otis mechanic at the nearest location, and helps the mechanic (who is equipped with a web-enabled cell phone) identify the component causing the problem. The company's maintenance system helps keep outage times under three hours—the elevators are often back in service before people even realize there was a problem. All trouble-call data are relayed to design and manufacturing personnel, allowing them to quickly alter design specifications or manufacturing procedures when needed to correct recurring problems. All customers have online access to performance data on each of their Otis elevators and escalators.

Well-conceived state-of-the-art operating systems not only enable better strategy execution but also strengthen organizational capabilities—enough at times to provide a competitive edge over rivals. For example, a company with a differentiation strategy based on superior quality has added capability if it has systems for training personnel in quality techniques, tracking product quality at each production step, and ensuring that all goods shipped meet quality standards. If these quality control systems are better than those employed by rivals, they provide the company with a competitive advantage. Similarly, a company striving to be a low-cost provider is competitively stronger if it has an unrivaled benchmarking system that identifies opportunities to implement best practices and drive costs out of the business faster than rivals. Fast-growing companies get an important assist from having capabilities in place to recruit and train new employees in large numbers and from investing in infrastructure that gives them the capability to handle rapid growth as it occurs, rather than having to scramble to catch up to customer demand.

Instituting Adequate Information Systems, Performance Tracking, and Controls

Accurate and timely information about daily operations is essential if managers are to gauge how well the strategy execution process is proceeding. Companies everywhere are capitalizing on today's technology to install real-time data-generating capability. Most retail companies now have automated online systems that generate daily sales reports for each store and maintain up-to-the-minute inventory and sales records on each item. Manufacturing plants typically generate daily production reports and track labor productivity on every shift. Transportation companies have elaborate information systems to provide real-time arrival information for buses and trains that is automatically sent to digital message signs and platform audio address systems.

Siemens Healthcare, one of the largest suppliers to the health care industry, uses a cloud-based business activity monitoring (BAM) system to continuously monitor and improve the company's processes across more than 190 countries. Customer satisfaction is one of Siemens's most important business objectives, so the reliability of its order management and services is crucial. Caesars Entertainment, owner of casinos and hotels, uses a sophisticated customer relationship database that records detailed information about its customers' gambling habits. When a member of Caesars's Total Rewards program calls to make a reservation, the representative can review previous spending, including average bet size, to offer an upgrade or complimentary stay at Caesars Palace or one of the company's other properties. At Uber, the popular ridesharing service, there are systems for locating vehicles near a customer and real-time demand monitoring to price fares during high-demand periods.

Information systems need to cover five broad areas: (1) customer data, (2) operations data, (3) employee data, (4) supplier and/or strategic partner data, and (5) financial performance data. All key strategic performance indicators must be tracked and reported in real time whenever possible. Real-time information systems permit company managers to stay on top of implementation initiatives and daily operations and to intervene if things seem to be drifting off course. Tracking key performance indicators, gathering information from operating personnel, quickly identifying and diagnosing problems, and taking corrective actions are all integral pieces of the process of managing strategy execution and overseeing operations.

Having state-of-the-art operating systems, information systems, and real-time data is integral to superior strategy execution and operating excellence.

Statistical information gives managers a feel for the numbers, briefings and meetings provide a feel for the latest developments and emerging issues, and personal contacts add a feel for the people dimension. All are good barometers of how well things are going and what operating aspects need management attention. Managers must identify problem areas and deviations from plans before they can take action to get the organization back on course, by either improving the approaches to strategy execution or fine-tuning the strategy. Jeff Bezos, Amazon.com's CEO, is an ardent proponent of managing by the numbers. As he puts it, "Math-based decisions always trump opinion and judgment. The trouble with most corporations is that they make judgment-based decisions when data-based decisions could be made."[20]

Monitoring Employee Performance Information systems also provide managers with a means for monitoring the performance of empowered workers to see that they are acting within the specified limits.[21] Leaving empowered employees to their own devices in meeting performance standards without appropriate checks and balances can expose an organization to excessive risk.[22] Instances abound of employees' decisions or behavior going awry, sometimes costing a company huge sums or producing lawsuits and reputation-damaging publicity.

Scrutinizing daily and weekly operating statistics is one of the ways in which managers can monitor the results that flow from the actions of subordinates without resorting to constant over-the-shoulder supervision; if the operating results look good, then it is reasonable to assume that empowerment is working. But close monitoring of operating performance is only one of the control tools at management's disposal. Another valuable lever of control in companies that rely on empowered employees, especially in those that use self-managed work groups or other such teams, is peer-based control. Because peer evaluation is such a powerful control device, companies organized into teams can remove some layers of the management hierarchy and rely on strong peer pressure to keep team members operating between the white lines. This is especially true when a company has the information systems capability to monitor team performance daily or in real time.

USING REWARDS AND INCENTIVES TO PROMOTE BETTER STRATEGY EXECUTION

It is essential that company personnel be enthusiastically committed to executing strategy successfully and achieving performance targets. Enlisting such commitment typically requires use of an assortment of motivational techniques and rewards. Indeed, *an effectively designed reward structure is the single most powerful tool management has for mobilizing employee commitment to successful strategy execution.* But incentives and rewards do more than just strengthen the resolve of company personnel to succeed—they also focus employees' attention on the accomplishment of specific strategy execution objectives. Not only do they spur the efforts of individuals to achieve those aims, but they also help coordinate the activities of individuals throughout the organization by aligning their personal motives with the goals of the organization. In this manner, reward systems serve as an indirect type of control mechanism that conserves on the more costly control mechanism of supervisory oversight.

LO 5

How and why the use of well-designed incentives and rewards can be management's single most powerful tool for promoting adept strategy execution.

To win employees' sustained, energetic commitment to the strategy execution process, management must be resourceful in designing and using motivational incentives—both monetary and nonmonetary. The more a manager understands what motivates subordinates and the more he or she relies on motivational incentives as a tool for achieving the targeted strategic and financial results, the greater will be employees' commitment to good day-in, day-out strategy execution and the achievement of performance targets.[23]

Incentives and Motivational Practices That Facilitate Good Strategy Execution

Financial incentives generally head the list of motivating tools for gaining wholehearted employee commitment to good strategy execution and focusing attention on strategic priorities. Generous financial rewards always catch employees' attention and produce *high-powered incentives* for individuals to exert their best efforts. A company's package of monetary rewards typically includes some combination of base-pay increases, performance bonuses, profit-sharing plans, stock awards, company contributions to employee 401(k) or retirement plans, and piecework incentives (in the case of production workers). But most successful companies and managers also make extensive use of nonmonetary incentives. Some of the most important nonmonetary approaches companies can use to enhance employee motivation include the following:[24]

A properly designed reward structure is management's single most powerful tool for mobilizing employee commitment to successful strategy execution and aligning efforts throughout the organization with strategic priorities.

CORE CONCEPT

Financial rewards provide **high-powered incentives** when rewards are tied to specific outcome objectives.

- *Providing attractive perks and fringe benefits.* The various options include coverage of health insurance premiums, wellness programs, college tuition reimbursement, generous paid vacation time, onsite child care, onsite fitness centers and massage services, opportunities for getaways at company-owned recreational facilities, personal concierge services, subsidized cafeterias and free lunches, casual dress every day, personal travel services, paid sabbaticals, maternity and paternity leaves, paid leaves to care for ill family members, telecommuting, compressed workweeks (four 10-hour days instead of five 8-hour days), flextime (variable work schedules that accommodate individual needs), college scholarships for children, and relocation services.
- *Giving awards and public recognition to high performers and showcasing company successes.* Many companies hold award ceremonies to honor top-performing individuals, teams, and organizational units and to celebrate important company milestones and achievements. Others make a special point of recognizing the outstanding accomplishments of individuals, teams, and organizational units at informal company gatherings or in the company newsletter. Such actions foster a positive *esprit de corps* within the organization and may also act to spur healthy competition among units and teams within the company.

- *Relying on promotion from within whenever possible.* This practice helps bind workers to their employer, and employers to their workers. Moreover, it provides strong incentives for good performance. Promoting from within also helps ensure that people in positions of responsibility have knowledge specific to the business, technology, and operations they are managing.
- *Inviting and acting on ideas and suggestions from employees.* Many companies find that their best ideas for nuts-and-bolts operating improvements come from the suggestions of employees. Moreover, research indicates that giving decision-making power to down-the-line employees increases their motivation and satisfaction as well as their productivity. The use of self-managed teams has much the same effect.
- *Creating a work atmosphere in which there is genuine caring and mutual respect among workers and between management and employees.* A "family" work environment where people are on a first-name basis and there is strong camaraderie promotes teamwork and cross-unit collaboration.
- *Stating the strategic vision in inspirational terms that make employees feel they are a part of something worthwhile in a larger social sense.* There's strong motivating power associated with giving people a chance to be part of something exciting and personally satisfying. Jobs with a noble purpose tend to inspire employees to give their all. As described in Chapter 9, this not only increases productivity but reduces turnover and lowers costs for staff recruitment and training as well.
- *Sharing information with employees about financial performance, strategy, operational measures, market conditions, and competitors' actions.* Broad disclosure and prompt communication send the message that managers trust their workers and regard them as valued partners in the enterprise. Keeping employees in the dark denies them information useful to performing their jobs, prevents them from being intellectually engaged, saps their motivation, and detracts from performance.
- *Providing an appealing working environment.* An appealing workplace environment can have decidedly positive effects on employee morale and productivity. Providing a comfortable work environment, designed with ergonomics in mind, is particularly important when workers are expected to spend long hours at work. But some companies go beyond the mundane to design exceptionally attractive work settings. Google management built the company's Googleplex headquarters campus to be "a dream workplace" and a showcase for environmentally correct building design and construction. Employees have access to dozens of cafés with healthy foods, break rooms with snacks and drinks, multiple fitness centers, heated swimming pools, ping-pong and pool tables, sand volleyball courts, and community bicycles and scooters to go from building to building. Apple and Facebook also have dramatic and futuristic headquarters projects underway.

For specific examples of the motivational tactics employed by several prominent companies (many of which appear on *Fortune*'s list of the 100 best companies to work for in America), see Illustration Capsule 11.2.

Striking the Right Balance between Rewards and Punishment

While most approaches to motivation, compensation, and people management accentuate the positive, companies also make it clear that lackadaisical or indifferent effort and subpar performance can result in negative consequences. At General

ILLUSTRATION CAPSULE 11.2

How the Best Companies to Work for Motivate and Reward Employees

Companies design a variety of motivational and reward practices to create a work environment that energizes employees and promotes better strategy execution. Other benefits of a successful recognition system include high job satisfaction, high retention rates, and increased output. Here's a sampling of what some of the best companies to work for in America are doing to motivate their employees:

© Ingvar Björk/Alamy Stock Photo

- Software developer SAS prioritizes work-life balance and mental health for its workforce of almost 7,000. The onsite health center it hosts for families of all employees maintains a staff of 53 medical and support personnel, including nurses, registered dietitians, lab technicians, and clinical psychologists. The sprawling headquarters also has a Frisbee golf course, indoor swimming pool, and walking and biking trails decorated with sculptures from the company's 4,000-item art collection. With such an environment, it should come as no surprise that 95 percent of employees report looking forward to heading to the office every day.
- Salesforce.com, a global cloud-computing company based in San Francisco, has been listed by *Forbes* magazine as the most innovative company in America. With its workforce more than tripling from 5,000 employees in 2012, Salesforce.com has worked hard to integrate new hires into existing teams. The company's recognition programs include rewards for achievement both in the office and in the larger community. For example, in 2013, top sellers were awarded two-week trips to Bhutan for their dedication and results.
- DPR Construction is one of the nation's top-50 general contractors, serving clients like Facebook, Pixar, and Genentech. The company fosters teamwork and equality across levels with features like open-office floor plans, business cards with no titles, and a bonus plan for employees. DPR also prioritizes safety for its employees. In 1999, a craftsperson who reached 30,000 consecutive safe work hours was rewarded with a new Ford F-150 truck. Management created a new safety award in his name that includes a plaque, a $2,000 trip, a 40-hour week off with pay, and a safety jacket with hours printed on it. In 2016, twenty-eight craftspeople received this generous award for their dedication to safety.
- Hilcorp, an oil and gas exploration company, made headlines in 2011 for its shocking generosity. After reaching its five-year goal to double in size, the company gave every employee a $50,000 dream car voucher (or $35,000 in cash). Building on this success, Hilcorp announced an incentive program that promised to award every employee $100,000 in 2015 if certain goals are met. Hilcorp met its targets in April 2015 and distributed checks to its employees in June of that same year.

Note: Developed with Meghan L. Cooney.

Sources: "100 Best Companies to Work For, 2014," *Fortune*, **money.cnn.com/magazines/fortune/best-companies/** (accessed February 15, 2014); company profiles, *GreatRated!*, **us.greatrated.com/sas** (accessed February 24, 2014).

Electric, McKinsey & Company, several global public accounting firms, and other companies that look for and expect top-notch individual performance, there's an "up-or-out" policy—managers and professionals whose performance is not good enough to warrant promotion are first denied bonuses and stock awards and eventually weeded out. At most companies, senior executives and key personnel in underperforming units are pressured to raise performance to acceptable levels and keep it there or risk being replaced.

As a general rule, it is unwise to take off the pressure for good performance or play down the adverse consequences of shortfalls in performance. There is scant evidence that a no-pressure, no-adverse-consequences work environment leads to superior strategy execution or operating excellence. As the CEO of a major bank put it, "There's a deliberate policy here to create a level of anxiety. Winners usually play like they're one touchdown behind."[25] A number of companies deliberately give employees heavy workloads and tight deadlines to test their mettle—personnel are pushed hard to achieve "stretch" objectives and are expected to put in long hours (nights and weekends if need be). High-performing organizations nearly always have a cadre of ambitious people who relish the opportunity to climb the ladder of success, love a challenge, thrive in a performance-oriented environment, and find some competition and pressure useful to satisfy their own drives for personal recognition, accomplishment, and self-satisfaction.

However, if an organization's motivational approaches and reward structure induce too much stress, internal competitiveness, job insecurity, and fear of unpleasant consequences, the impact on workforce morale and strategy execution can be counterproductive. Evidence shows that managerial initiatives to improve strategy execution should incorporate more positive than negative motivational elements because when cooperation is positively enlisted and rewarded, rather than coerced by orders and threats (implicit or explicit), people tend to respond with more enthusiasm, dedication, creativity, and initiative.[26]

Linking Rewards to Achieving the Right Outcomes

To create a strategy-supportive system of rewards and incentives, a company must reward people for accomplishing results, not for just dutifully performing assigned tasks. Showing up for work and performing assignments do not, by themselves, guarantee results. To make the work environment results-oriented, managers need to focus jobholders' attention and energy on what to *achieve* as opposed to what to *do*.[27] Employee productivity among employees at Best Buy's corporate headquarters rose by 35 percent after the company began to focus on the results of each employee's work rather than on employees' willingness to come to work early and stay late.

Incentives must be based on accomplishing the right results, not on dutifully performing assigned tasks.

The key to creating a reward system that promotes good strategy execution is to make measures of good business performance and good strategy execution the dominating basis for designing incentives, evaluating individual and group efforts, and handing out rewards.

Ideally, every organizational unit, every manager, every team or work group, and every employee should be held accountable for achieving outcomes that contribute to good strategy execution and business performance. If the company's strategy is to be a low-cost provider, the incentive system must reward actions and achievements that result in lower costs. If the company has a differentiation strategy focused on delivering superior quality and service, the incentive system must reward such outcomes as Six Sigma defect rates, infrequent customer complaints, speedy order processing and delivery, and high levels of customer satisfaction. If a company's growth is predicated on a strategy of new product innovation, incentives should be tied to such metrics as the percentages of revenues and profits coming from newly introduced products.

Incentive compensation for top executives is typically tied to such financial measures as revenue and earnings growth, stock price performance, return on investment, and creditworthiness or to strategic measures such as market share growth. However, incentives for department heads, teams, and individual workers tend to be tied to performance outcomes more closely related to their specific area of responsibility. For instance, in manufacturing, it makes sense to tie incentive compensation to such outcomes as unit manufacturing costs, on-time production and shipping, defect rates, the number and extent of work stoppages due to equipment breakdowns, and so on. In sales and marketing, incentives tend to be based on achieving dollar sales or unit volume targets, market share, sales penetration of each target customer group, the fate of newly introduced products, the frequency of customer complaints, the number of new accounts acquired, and measures of customer satisfaction. Which performance measures to base incentive compensation on depends on the situation—the priority placed on various financial and strategic objectives, the requirements for strategic and competitive success, and the specific results needed to keep strategy execution on track.

Illustration Capsule 11.3 provides a vivid example of how one company has designed incentives linked directly to outcomes reflecting good execution.

Additional Guidelines for Designing Incentive Compensation Systems It is not enough to link incentives to the right kinds of results—performance outcomes that signal that the company's strategy and its execution are on track. For a company's reward system to truly motivate organization members, inspire their best efforts, and sustain high levels of productivity, it is also important to observe the following additional guidelines in designing and administering the reward system:

The first principle in designing an effective incentive compensation system is to tie rewards to performance outcomes directly linked to good strategy execution and the achievement of financial and strategic objectives.

- *Make the performance payoff a major, not minor, piece of the total compensation package.* Performance bonuses must be at least 10 to 12 percent of base salary to have much impact. Incentives that amount to 20 percent or more of total compensation are big attention-getters, likely to really drive individual or team efforts. Incentives amounting to less than 5 percent of total compensation have a comparatively weak motivational impact. Moreover, the payoff for high-performing individuals and teams must be meaningfully greater than the payoff for average performers, and the payoff for average performers meaningfully bigger than that for below-average performers.
- *Have incentives that extend to all managers and all workers, not just top management.* It is a gross miscalculation to expect that lower-level managers and employees will work their hardest to hit performance targets if only a senior executives qualify for lucrative rewards.
- *Administer the reward system with scrupulous objectivity and fairness.* If performance standards are set unrealistically high or if individual and group performance evaluations are not accurate and well documented, dissatisfaction with the system will overcome any positive benefits.
- *Ensure that the performance targets set for each individual or team involve outcomes that the individual or team can personally affect.* The role of incentives is to enhance individual commitment and channel behavior in beneficial directions. This role is not well served when the performance measures by which company personnel are judged are outside their arena of influence.
- *Keep the time between achieving the performance target and receiving the reward as short as possible.* Nucor, a leading producer of steel products, has achieved high labor productivity by paying its workers weekly bonuses based on prior-week production levels. Annual bonus payouts work best for higher-level managers and for situations where the outcome target relates to overall company profitability.
- *Avoid rewarding effort rather than results.* While it is tempting to reward people who have tried hard, gone the extra mile, and yet fallen short of achieving performance targets because of circumstances beyond their control, it is ill advised to

ILLUSTRATION CAPSULE 11.3

Nucor Corporation: Tying Incentives Directly to Strategy Execution

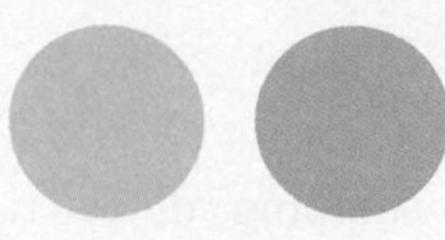

The strategy at Nucor Corporation, one of the three largest steel producers in the United States, is to be *the* low-cost producer of steel products. Because labor costs are a significant fraction of total cost in the steel business, successful implementation of Nucor's low-cost leadership strategy entails achieving lower labor costs per ton of steel than competitors' costs. Nucor management uses an incentive system to promote high worker productivity and drive labor costs per ton below those of rivals. Each plant's workforce is organized into production teams (each assigned to perform particular functions), and weekly production targets are established for each team. Base-pay scales are set at levels comparable to wages for similar manufacturing jobs in the local areas where Nucor has plants, but workers can earn a 1 percent bonus for each 1 percent that their output exceeds target levels. If a production team exceeds its weekly production target by 10 percent, team members receive a 10 percent bonus in their next paycheck; if a team exceeds its quota by 20 percent, team members earn a 20 percent bonus. Bonuses, paid every two weeks, are based on the prior two weeks' actual production levels measured against the targets.

Nucor's piece-rate incentive plan has produced impressive results. The production teams put forth exceptional effort; it is not uncommon for most teams to beat their weekly production targets by 20 to 50 percent. When added to employees' base pay, the bonuses earned by Nucor workers make Nucor's workforce among the highest paid in the U.S. steel industry. From a management perspective, the incentive system has resulted in Nucor having labor productivity levels 10 to 20 percent above the average of the unionized workforces at several of its largest rivals, which in turn has given Nucor a significant labor cost advantage over most rivals.

© *Buena Vista Images/Stone/Getty Images*

After years of record-setting profits, Nucor struggled in the economic downturn of 2008–2010, along with the manufacturers and builders who buy its steel. But while bonuses have dwindled, Nucor showed remarkable loyalty to its production workers, avoiding layoffs by having employees get ahead on maintenance, perform work formerly done by contractors, and search for cost savings. Morale at the company remained high, and Nucor's CEO at the time, Daniel DiMicco, was inducted into *IndustryWeek* magazine's Manufacturing Hall of Fame because of his no-layoff policies. As industry growth has resumed, Nucor has retained a well-trained workforce, more committed than ever to achieving the kind of productivity for which Nucor is justifiably famous. DiMicco had good reason to expect Nucor to be "first out of the box" following the crisis, and although he has since stepped aside, the company's culture of making its employees think like owners has not changed.

Sources: Company website (accessed March 2012); N. Byrnes, "Pain, but No Layoffs at Nucor," *BusinessWeek,* March 26, 2009; J. McGregor, "Nucor's CEO Is Stepping Aside, but Its Culture Likely Won't," *The Washington Post* Online, November 20, 2012 (accessed April 3, 2014).

do so. The problem with making exceptions for unknowable, uncontrollable, or unforeseeable circumstances is that once "good excuses" start to creep into justifying rewards for subpar results, the door opens to all kinds of reasons why actual performance has failed to match targeted performance. A "no excuses" standard is more evenhanded, easier to administer, and more conducive to creating a results-oriented work climate.

For an organization's incentive system to work well, the details of the reward structure must be communicated and explained. Everybody needs to understand how his or her incentive compensation is calculated and how individual and group performance targets contribute to organizational performance targets. The pressure to achieve the targeted financial and strategic performance objectives and continuously improve on strategy execution should be unrelenting. People at all levels must be held accountable for carrying out their assigned parts of the strategic plan, and they must understand that their rewards are based on the caliber of results achieved. But with the pressure to perform should come meaningful rewards. Without an attractive payoff, the system breaks down, and managers are left with the less workable options of issuing orders, trying to enforce compliance, and depending on the goodwill of employees.

The unwavering standard for judging whether individuals, teams, and organizational units have done a good job must be whether they meet or beat performance targets that reflect good strategy execution.

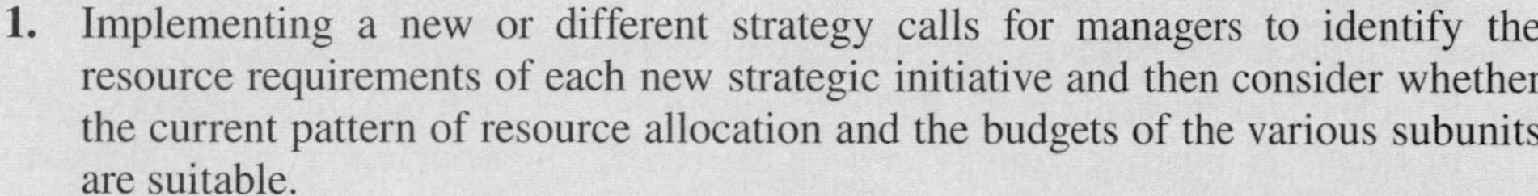

KEY POINTS

1. Implementing a new or different strategy calls for managers to identify the resource requirements of each new strategic initiative and then consider whether the current pattern of resource allocation and the budgets of the various subunits are suitable.
2. Company policies and procedures facilitate strategy execution when they are designed to fit the strategy and its objectives. Anytime a company alters its strategy, managers should review existing policies and operating procedures and replace those that are out of sync. Well-conceived policies and procedures aid the task of strategy execution by (1) providing top-down guidance to company personnel regarding how things need to be done and what the limits are on independent actions; (2) enforcing consistency in the performance of strategy-critical activities, thereby improving the quality of the strategy execution effort and coordinating the efforts of company personnel, however widely dispersed; and (3) promoting the creation of a work climate conducive to good strategy execution.
3. Competent strategy execution entails visible unyielding managerial commitment to best practices and continuous improvement. Benchmarking, best-practice adoption, business process reengineering, total quality management (TQM), and Six Sigma programs are important process management tools for promoting better strategy execution.
4. Company strategies can't be implemented or executed well without well-conceived internal systems to support daily operations. Real-time information systems and control systems further aid the cause of good strategy execution. In some cases, state-of-the-art operating and information systems strengthen a company's strategy execution capabilities enough to provide a competitive edge over rivals.
5. Strategy-supportive motivational practices and reward systems are powerful management tools for gaining employee commitment and focusing their attention on the strategy execution goals. The key to creating a reward system that promotes good strategy execution is to make measures of good business performance and good strategy execution the *dominating basis* for designing incentives, evaluating individual and group efforts, and handing out rewards. Positive motivational practices generally work better than negative ones, but there is a place for both. While financial rewards provide high-powered incentives, nonmonetary

incentives are also important. For an incentive compensation system to work well, (1) the performance payoff should be a major percentage of the compensation package, (2) the use of incentives should extend to all managers and workers, (3) the system should be administered with objectivity and fairness, (4) each individual's performance targets should involve outcomes the person can personally affect, (5) rewards should promptly follow the achievement of performance targets, and (6) rewards should be given for results and not just effort.

ASSURANCE OF LEARNING EXERCISES

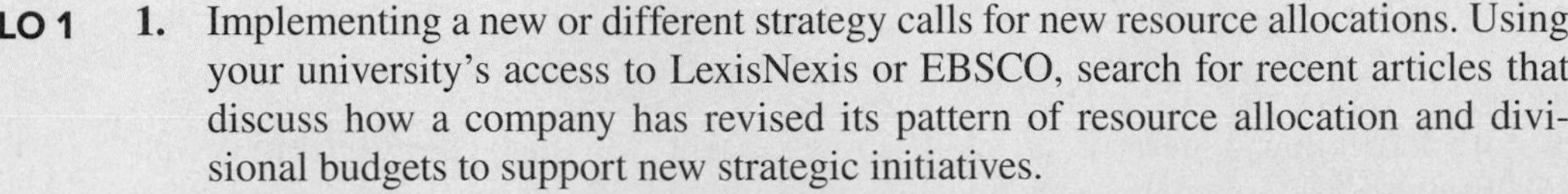

LO 1 1. Implementing a new or different strategy calls for new resource allocations. Using your university's access to LexisNexis or EBSCO, search for recent articles that discuss how a company has revised its pattern of resource allocation and divisional budgets to support new strategic initiatives.

LO 2 2. Policies and procedures facilitate strategy execution when they are designed to fit the company's strategy and objectives. Using your university's access to LexisNexis or EBSCO, search for recent articles that discuss how a company has revised its policies and procedures to provide better top-down guidance to company personnel on how to conduct their daily activities and responsibilities.

LO 3 3. Illustration Capsule 11.1 discusses Charleston Area Medical Center's use of Six Sigma practices. List three tangible benefits provided by the program. Explain why a commitment to quality control is particularly important in the hospital industry. How can the use of a Six Sigma program help medical providers survive and thrive in the current industry climate?

LO 3 4. Read some of the recent Six Sigma articles posted at **www.isixsigma.com**. Prepare a one-page report to your instructor detailing how Six Sigma is being used in two companies and what benefits the companies are reaping as a result. Further, discuss two to three criticisms of, or potential difficulties with, Six Sigma implementation.

LO 4 5. Company strategies can't be executed well without a number of support systems to carry on business operations. Using your university's access to LexisNexis or EBSCO, search for recent articles that discuss how a company has used real-time information systems and control systems to aid the cause of good strategy execution.

LO 5 6. Illustration Capsule 11.2 provides a sampling of motivational tactics employed by several prominent companies (many of which appear on *Fortune*'s list of the 100 best companies to work for in America). Discuss how rewards at SAS, **Salesforce.com**, DPR Construction, and Hilcorp aid in the strategy execution efforts of each company.

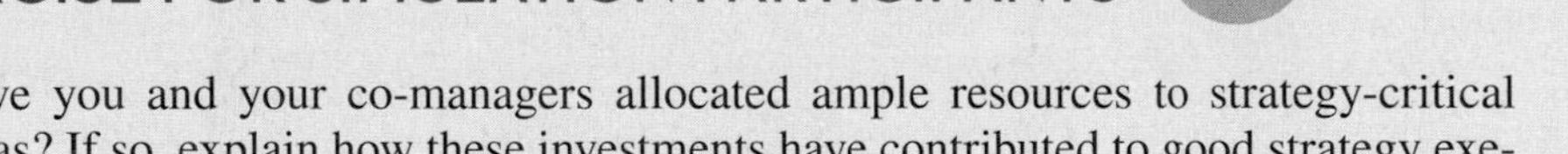

EXERCISE FOR SIMULATION PARTICIPANTS

1. Have you and your co-managers allocated ample resources to strategy-critical areas? If so, explain how these investments have contributed to good strategy execution and improved company performance. **LO 1**
2. What actions, if any, is your company taking to pursue continuous improvement in how it performs certain value chain activities? **LO 2, LO 3, LO 4**
3. Are benchmarking data available in the simulation exercise in which you are participating? If so, do you and your co-managers regularly study the benchmarking data to see how well your company is doing? Do you consider the benchmarking information provided to be valuable? Why or why not? Cite three recent instances in which your examination of the benchmarking statistics has caused you and your co-managers to take corrective actions to boost company performance. **LO 3**
4. What hard evidence can you cite that indicates your company's management team is doing a *better* or *worse* job of achieving operating excellence and executing strategy than are the management teams at rival companies? **LO 3**
5. Are you and your co-managers consciously trying to achieve operating excellence? Explain how you are doing this and how you will track the progress you are making. **LO 2, LO 3, LO 4**
6. Does your company have opportunities to use incentive compensation techniques? If so, explain your company's approach to incentive compensation. Is there any hard evidence you can cite that indicates your company's use of incentive compensation techniques has worked? For example, have your company's compensation incentives actually increased productivity? Can you cite evidence indicating that the productivity gains have resulted in lower labor costs? If the productivity gains have *not* translated into lower labor costs, is it fair to say that your company's use of incentive compensation is a failure? **LO 5**

ENDNOTES

[1] Christopher E. Bogan and Michael J. English, *Benchmarking for Best Practices: Winning through Innovative Adaptation* (New York: McGraw-Hill, 1994); Mustafa Ungan, "Factors Affecting the Adoption of Manufacturing Best Practices," *Benchmarking: An International Journal* 11, no. 5 (2004), pp. 504–520; Paul Hyland and Ron Beckett, "Learning to Compete: The Value of Internal Benchmarking," *Benchmarking: An International Journal* 9, no. 3 (2002), pp. 293–304; Yoshinobu Ohinata, "Benchmarking: The Japanese Experience," *Long-Range Planning* 27, no. 4 (August 1994), pp. 48–53.

[2] M. Hammer and J. Champy, *Reengineering the Corporation: A Manifesto for Business Revolution* (New York: HarperCollins, 1993).

[3] James Brian Quinn, *Intelligent Enterprise* (New York: Free Press, 1992); Ann Majchrzak and Qianwei Wang, "Breaking the Functional Mind-Set in Process Organizations," *Harvard Business Review* 74, no. 5 (September–October 1996), pp. 93–99; Stephen L. Walston, Lawton R. Burns, and John R. Kimberly, "Does Reengineering Really Work? An Examination of the Context and Outcomes of Hospital Reengineering Initiatives," *Health Services Research* 34, no. 6 (February 2000), pp. 1363–1388; Allessio Ascari, Melinda Rock, and Soumitra Dutta, "Reengineering and Organizational Change: Lessons from a Comparative Analysis of Company Experiences," *European Management Journal* 13, no. 1 (March 1995), pp. 1–13; Ronald J. Burke, "Process Reengineering: Who Embraces It and Why?" *The TQM Magazine* 16, no. 2 (2004), pp. 114–119.

[4] www.answers.com (accessed July 8, 2009); "Reengineering: Beyond the Buzzword," *Businessweek*, May 24, 1993, www.businessweek.com (accessed July 8, 2009).

[5] Gene Hall, Jim Rosenthal, and Judy Wade, "How to Make Reengineering Really Work," *Harvard Business Review* 71, no. 6 (November–December 1993), pp. 119–131.

[6] M. Walton, *The Deming Management Method* (New York: Pedigree, 1986); J. Juran, *Juran on Quality by Design* (New York: Free Press, 1992); Philip Crosby, *Quality Is Free: The Act of Making Quality Certain* (New York: McGraw-Hill, 1979); S. George, *The Baldrige Quality System* (New York: Wiley, 1992); Mark J. Zbaracki, "The Rhetoric and Reality of Total Quality Management," *Administrative Science Quarterly* 43, no. 3 (September 1998), pp. 602–636.

[7] Robert T. Amsden, Thomas W. Ferratt, and Davida M. Amsden, "TQM: Core Paradigm Changes," *Business Horizons* 39, no. 6 (November–December 1996), pp. 6–14.

[8] Peter S. Pande and Larry Holpp, *What Is Six Sigma?* (New York: McGraw-Hill, 2002); Jiju Antony, "Some Pros and Cons of Six Sigma: An Academic Perspective," *TQM Magazine* 16, no. 4 (2004), pp. 303–306; Peter S. Pande, Robert P. Neuman, and Roland R. Cavanagh, *The Six Sigma Way: How GE, Motorola and*

Other Top Companies Are Honing Their Performance (New York: McGraw-Hill, 2000); Joseph Gordon and M. Joseph Gordon, Jr., *Six Sigma Quality for Business and Manufacture* (New York: Elsevier, 2002); Godecke Wessel and Peter Burcher, "Six Sigma for Small and Medium-Sized Enterprises," *TQM Magazine* 16, no. 4 (2004), pp. 264–272.

[9] www.isixsigma.com (accessed November 4, 2002); www.villanovau.com/certificate-programs/six-sigma-training.aspx (accessed February 16, 2012).

[10] Kennedy Smith, "Six Sigma for the Service Sector," *Quality Digest Magazine,* May 2003; www.qualitydigest.com (accessed September 28, 2003).

[11] www.isixsigma.com/implementation/financial-analysis/six-sigma-costs-and-savings/ (accessed February 23, 2012).

[12] Pande, Neuman, and Cavanagh, *The Six Sigma Way,* pp. 5–6.

[13] "A Dark Art No More," *The Economist* 385, no. 8550 (October 13, 2007), p. 10; Brian Hindo, "At 3M, a Struggle between Efficiency and Creativity," *Businessweek,* June 11, 2007, pp. 8–16.

[14] Charles A. O'Reilly and Michael L. Tushman, "The Ambidextrous Organization," *Harvard Business Review* 82, no. 4 (April 2004), pp. 74–81.

[15] Terry Nels Lee, Stanley E. Fawcett, and Jason Briscoe, "Benchmarking the Challenge to Quality Program Implementation," *Benchmarking: An International Journal* 9, no. 4 (2002), pp. 374–387.

[16] Milan Ambroé, "Total Quality System as a Product of the Empowered Corporate Culture," *TQM Magazine* 16, no. 2 (2004), pp. 93–104; Nick A. Dayton, "The Demise of Total Quality Management," *TQM Magazine* 15, no. 6 (2003), pp. 391–396.

[17] Judy D. Olian and Sara L. Rynes, "Making Total Quality Work: Aligning Organizational Processes, Performance Measures, and Stakeholders," *Human Resource Management* 30, no. 3 (Fall 1991), pp. 310–311; Paul S. Goodman and Eric D. Darr, "Exchanging Best Practices Information through Computer-Aided Systems," *Academy of Management Executive* 10, no. 2 (May 1996), p. 7.

[18] Thomas C. Powell, "Total Quality Management as Competitive Advantage," *Strategic Management Journal* 16 (1995), pp. 15–37; Richard M. Hodgetts, "Quality Lessons from America's Baldrige Winners," *Business Horizons* 37, no. 4 (July–August 1994), pp. 74–79; Richard Reed, David J. Lemak, and Joseph C. Montgomery, "Beyond Process: TQM Content and Firm Performance," *Academy of Management Review* 21, no. 1 (January 1996), pp. 173–202.

[19] www.otiselevator.com (accessed February 16, 2012).

[20] Fred Vogelstein, "Winning the Amazon Way," *Fortune* 147, no. 10 (May 26, 2003), pp. 60–69.

[21] Robert Simons, "Control in an Age of Empowerment," *Harvard Business Review* 73 (March–April 1995), pp. 80–88.

[22] David C. Band and Gerald Scanlan, "Strategic Control through Core Competencies," *Long Range Planning* 28, no. 2 (April 1995), pp. 102–114.

[23] Stanley E. Fawcett, Gary K. Rhoads, and Phillip Burnah, "People as the Bridge to Competitiveness: Benchmarking the 'ABCs' of an Empowered Workforce," *Benchmarking: An International Journal* 11, no. 4 (2004), pp. 346–360.

[24] Jeffrey Pfeffer and John F. Veiga, "Putting People First for Organizational Success," *Academy of Management Executive* 13, no. 2 (May 1999), pp. 37–45; Linda K. Stroh and Paula M. Caligiuri, "Increasing Global Competitiveness through Effective People Management," *Journal of World Business* 33, no. 1 (Spring 1998), pp. 1–16; articles in *Fortune* on the 100 best companies to work for (various issues).

[25] As quoted in John P. Kotter and James L. Heskett, *Corporate Culture and Performance* (New York: Free Press, 1992), p. 91.

[26] Clayton M. Christensen, Matt Marx, and Howard Stevenson, "The Tools of Cooperation and Change," *Harvard Business Review* 84, no. 10 (October 2006), pp. 73–80.

[27] Steven Kerr, "On the Folly of Rewarding A While Hoping for B," *Academy of Management Executive* 9, no. 1 (February 1995), pp. 7–14; Doran Twer, "Linking Pay to Business Objectives," *Journal of Business Strategy* 15, no. 4 (July–August 1994), pp. 15–18.

CHAPTER 12

Corporate Culture and Leadership

Keys to Good Strategy Execution

© Andy Baker/Ikon Images/age fotostock

Learning Objectives

THIS CHAPTER WILL HELP YOU UNDERSTAND:

LO 1 The key features of a company's corporate culture and the role of a company's core values and ethical standards in building corporate culture.

LO 2 How and why a company's culture can aid the drive for proficient strategy execution.

LO 3 The kinds of actions management can take to change a problem corporate culture.

LO 4 What constitutes effective managerial leadership in achieving superior strategy execution.

Success goes to those with a corporate culture that assures the ability to anticipate and meet customer demand.

Tadashi Okamura—*Former president and CEO of Toshiba*

As we look ahead into the next century, leaders will be those who empower others.

Bill Gates—*Cofounder and former CEO and chair of Microsoft*

Leadership is practiced, not so much in words as in attitude and in actions.

Harold S. Geneen—*Former CEO and chair of ITT*

In the previous two chapters, we examined eight of the managerial tasks that drive good strategy execution: staffing the organization, acquiring the needed resources and capabilities, designing the organizational structure, allocating resources, establishing policies and procedures, employing process management tools, installing operating systems, and providing the right incentives. In this chapter, we explore the two remaining managerial tasks that contribute to good strategy execution: creating a corporate culture that supports good strategy execution and leading the strategy execution process.

INSTILLING A CORPORATE CULTURE CONDUCIVE TO GOOD STRATEGY EXECUTION

Every company has its own unique **corporate culture**—the shared values, ingrained attitudes, and company traditions that determine norms of behavior, accepted work practices, and styles of operating.[1] The character of a company's culture is a product of the core values and beliefs that executives espouse, the standards of what is ethically acceptable and what is not, the "chemistry" and the "personality" that permeate the work environment, the company's traditions, and the stories that get told over and over to illustrate and reinforce the company's shared values, business practices, and traditions. In a very real sense, the culture is the company's automatic, self-replicating "operating system" that defines "how we do things around here."[2] It can be thought of as the company's psyche or *organizational DNA*.[3] A company's culture is important because it influences the

CORE CONCEPT

Corporate culture refers to the shared values, ingrained attitudes, core beliefs, and company traditions that determine norms of behavior, accepted work practices, and styles of operating.

LO 1

The key features of a company's corporate culture and the role of a company's core values and ethical standards in building corporate culture.

organization's actions and approaches to conducting business. As such, it plays an important role in strategy execution and may have an appreciable effect on business performance as well.

Corporate cultures vary widely. For instance, the bedrock of Walmart's culture is zealous pursuit of low costs and frugal operating practices, a strong work ethic, ritualistic headquarters meetings to exchange ideas and review problems, and company executives' commitment to visiting stores, listening to customers, and soliciting suggestions from employees. The culture at Apple is customer-centered, secretive, and highly protective of company-developed technology. To spur innovation and creativity, the company fosters extensive collaboration and cross-pollination among different work groups. But it does so in a manner that demands secrecy—employees are expected not to reveal anything relevant about what new project they are working on, not to employees outside their immediate work group and especially not to family members or other outsiders; it is common for different employees working on the same project to be assigned different project code names. The different pieces of a new product launch often come together like a puzzle at the last minute.[4] W. L. Gore & Associates, best known for GORE-TEX, credits its unique culture for allowing the company to pursue multiple end-market applications simultaneously, enabling rapid growth from a niche business into a diversified multinational company. The company's culture is team-based and designed to foster personal initiative, with no traditional organizational charts, no chains of command, no predetermined channels of communication. The culture encourages multidiscipline teams to organize around opportunities and in the process leaders emerge. At Nordstrom, the corporate culture is centered on delivering exceptional service to customers, where the company's motto is "Respond to unreasonable customer requests," and each out-of-the-ordinary request is seen as an opportunity for a "heroic" act by an employee that can further the company's reputation for unparalleled customer service. Nordstrom makes a point of promoting employees noted for their heroic acts and dedication to outstanding service.

Illustration Capsule 12.1 describes the corporate culture of another exemplar company—Epic Systems, well known by health care providers.

Identifying the Key Features of a Company's Corporate Culture

A company's corporate culture is mirrored in the character or "personality" of its work environment—the features that describe how the company goes about its business and the workplace behaviors that are held in high esteem. Some of these features are readily apparent, and others operate quite subtly. The chief things to look for include:

- The values, business principles, and ethical standards that management preaches and *practices*—these are the key to a company's culture, but actions speak much louder than words here.
- The company's approach to people management and the official policies, procedures, and operating practices that provide guidelines for the behavior of company personnel.
- The atmosphere and spirit that pervades the work climate—whether the workplace is competitive or cooperative, innovative or resistant to change, collegial or politicized, all business or fun-loving, and the like.

ILLUSTRATION CAPSULE 12.1

Strong Guiding Principles Drive the High-Performance Culture at Epic

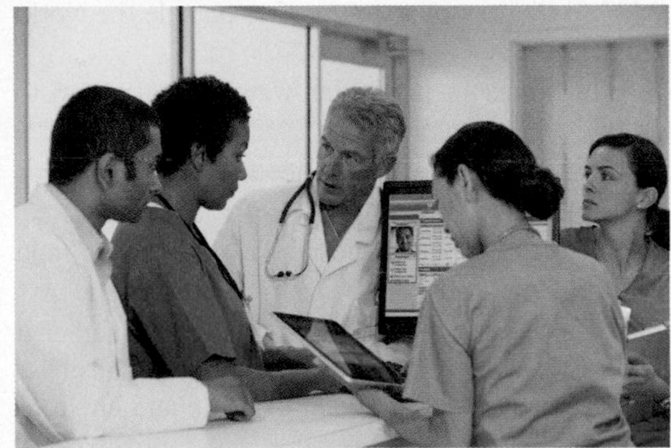

© Ariel Skelley/Blend Images/Getty Images

Epic Systems Corporation creates software to support record keeping for mid- to large-sized health care organizations, such as hospitals and managed care organizations. Founded in 1979 by CEO Judith Faulkner, the company claims that its software is "quick to implement, easy to use and highly interoperable through industry standards." Widely recognized for superior products and high levels of customer satisfaction, Epic won the Best Overall Software Suite award for the sixth consecutive year—a ranking determined by health care professionals and compiled by KLAS, a provider of company performance reviews. Part of this success has been attributed to Epic's strong corporate culture—one based on the slogan "Do good, have fun, make money." By remaining true to its 10 commandments and principles, its homegrown version of core values, Epic has nurtured a work climate where employees are on the same page and all have an overarching standard to guide their actions.

Epic's 10 Commandments:

1. Do not go public.
2. Do not be acquired.
3. Software must work.
4. Expectations = reality.
5. Keep commitments.
6. Focus on competency. Do not tolerate mediocrity.
7. Have standards. Be fair to all.
8. Have courage. What you put up with is what you stand for.
9. Teach philosophy and culture.
10. Be frugal. Do not take on debt for operations.

Epic's Principles:

1. Make our products a joy to use.
2. Have fun with customers.
3. Design in collaboration with users.
4. Make it easy for users to do the right thing.
5. Improve the patient's health and healthcare experience.
6. Generalize to benefit more.
7. Follow processes. Find root causes. Fix processes.
8. Dissent when you disagree; once decided, support.
9. Do what is difficult for us if it makes things easier for our users.
10. Escalate problems at the start, not when all hell breaks loose.

Epic fosters this high-performance culture from the get-go. It targets top-tier universities to hire entry-level talent, focusing on skills rather than personality. A rigorous training and orientation program indoctrinates each new employee. In 2002, Faulkner claimed that someone coming straight from college could become an "Epic person" in three years, whereas it takes six years for someone coming from another company. This culture positively affects Epic's strategy execution because employees are focused on the most important actions, there is peer pressure to contribute to Epic's success, and employees are genuinely excited to be involved. Epic's faith in its ability to acculturate new team members and stick true to its core values has allowed it to sustain its status as a premier provider of health care IT systems.

Note: Developed with Margo Cox.

Sources: Company website; communications with an Epic insider; "Epic Takes Back 'Best in KLAS' title," *Healthcare IT News*, January 29, 2015, **www.healthcareitnews.com/news/epic-takes-back-best-klas**; "Epic Systems' Headquarters Reflect Its Creativity, Growth," *Boston Globe*, July 28, 2015, **www.bostonglobe.com/business/2015/07/28/epic-systems-success-like-its-headquarters-blend-creativity-and-diligence/LpdQ5moDDS4UVilCVooRUJ/story.html** (accessed December 5, 2015).

- How managers and employees interact and relate to one another—whether people tend to work independently or collaboratively, whether communications among employees are free-flowing or infrequent, whether people are called by their first names, whether co-workers spend little or lots of time together outside the workplace, and so on.
- The strength of peer pressure to do things in particular ways and conform to expected norms.
- The actions and behaviors that management explicitly encourages and rewards and those that are frowned upon.
- The company's revered traditions and oft-repeated stories about "heroic acts" and "how we do things around here."
- The manner in which the company deals with external stakeholders—whether it treats suppliers as business partners or prefers hard-nosed, arm's-length business arrangements and whether its commitment to corporate citizenship and environmental sustainability is strong and genuine.

The values, beliefs, and practices that undergird a company's culture can come from anywhere in the organizational hierarchy. Typically, key elements of the culture originate with a founder or certain strong leaders who articulated them as a set of business principles, company policies, operating approaches, and ways of dealing with employees, customers, vendors, shareholders, and local communities where the company has operations. They also stem from exemplary actions on the part of company personnel and evolving consensus about "how we ought to do things around here."[5] Over time, these cultural underpinnings take root, come to be accepted by company managers and employees alike, and become ingrained in the way the company conducts its business.

The Role of Core Values and Ethics The foundation of a company's corporate culture nearly always resides in its dedication to certain core values and the bar it sets for ethical behavior. The culture-shaping significance of core values and ethical behaviors accounts for why so many companies have developed a formal value statement and a code of ethics. Of course, sometimes a company's stated core values and code of ethics are cosmetic, existing mainly to impress outsiders and help create a positive company image. But usually they have been developed to purposely mold the culture and communicate the kinds of actions and behavior that are expected of all company personnel. Many executives want the work climate at their companies to mirror certain values and ethical standards, partly because of personal convictions but mainly because they are convinced that adherence to such principles will promote better strategy execution, make the company a better performer, and positively impact its reputation.[6] Not incidentally, strongly ingrained values and ethical standards reduce the likelihood of lapses in ethical and socially approved behavior that mar a company's public image and put its financial performance and market standing at risk.

A company's culture is grounded in and shaped by its core values and ethical standards.

As depicted in Figure 12.1, a company's stated core values and ethical principles have two roles in the culture-building process. First, a company that works hard at putting its stated core values and ethical principles into practice fosters a work climate in which company personnel share strongly held convictions about how the company's business is to be conducted. Second, the stated values and ethical principles provide company personnel with guidance about the manner in which they are to do their jobs—which behaviors and ways of doing things are

A company's value statement and code of ethics communicate expectations of how employees should conduct themselves in the workplace.

FIGURE 12.1 The Two Culture-Building Roles of a Company's Core Values and Ethical Standards

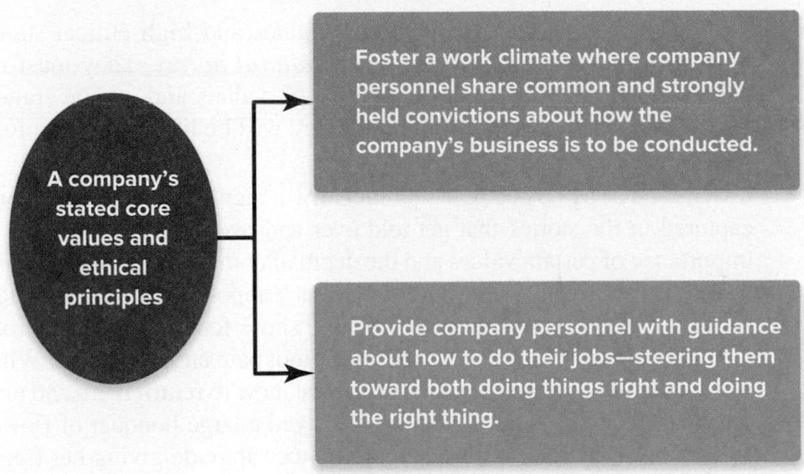

approved (and expected) and which are out-of-bounds. These value-based and ethics-based cultural norms serve as yardsticks for gauging the appropriateness of particular actions, decisions, and behaviors, thus helping steer company personnel toward both doing things right and doing the right thing.

Embedding Behavioral Norms in the Organization and Perpetuating the Culture Once values and ethical standards have been formally adopted, they must be institutionalized in the company's policies and practices and embedded in the conduct of company personnel. This can be done in a number of different ways.[7] Tradition-steeped companies with a rich folklore rely heavily on word-of-mouth indoctrination and the power of tradition to instill values and enforce ethical conduct. But most companies employ a variety of techniques, drawing on some or all of the following:

1. Screening applicants and hiring those who will mesh well with the culture.
2. Incorporating discussions of the company's culture and behavioral norms into orientation programs for new employees and training courses for managers and employees.
3. Having senior executives frequently reiterate the importance and role of company values and ethical principles at company events and in internal communications to employees.
4. Expecting managers at all levels to be cultural role models and exhibit the advocated cultural norms in their own behavior.
5. Making the display of cultural norms a factor in evaluating each person's job performance, granting compensation increases, and deciding who to promote.
6. Stressing that line managers all the way down to first-level supervisors give ongoing attention to explaining the desired cultural traits and behaviors in their areas and clarifying why they are important.

7. Encouraging company personnel to exert strong peer pressure on co-workers to conform to expected cultural norms.
8. Holding periodic ceremonies to honor people who excel in displaying the company values and ethical principles.

To deeply ingrain the stated core values and high ethical standards, companies must turn them into *strictly enforced cultural norms.* They must make it unequivocally clear that living up to the company's values and ethical standards has to be "a way of life" at the company and that there will be little toleration for errant behavior.

The Role of Stories Frequently, a significant part of a company's culture is captured in the stories that get told over and over again to illustrate to newcomers the importance of certain values and the depth of commitment that various company personnel have displayed. One of the folktales at Zappos, known for its outstanding customer service, is about a customer who ordered shoes for her ill mother from Zappos, hoping the company would remedy her mother's foot pain and numbness. When the shoes didn't work, the mother called the company to ask how to return them and explain why she was returning them. Two days later, she received a large bouquet of flowers from the company, along with well wishes and a customer upgrade giving her free expedited service on all future orders. Specialty food market Trader Joe's is similarly known for its culture of going beyond the call of duty for its customers. When a World War II veteran was snowed in without any food for meals, his daughter called several supermarkets to see if they offered grocery delivery. Although Trader Joe's technically doesn't offer delivery, it graciously helped the veteran, even recommending items for his low-sodium diet. When the store delivered the groceries, the veteran wasn't charged for either the groceries or the delivery. When Apple's iPad 2 was launched, one was returned to the company almost immediately, with a note attached that said "Wife said No!"[8] Apple sent the customer a refund, but it also sent back the device with a note reading "Apple says Yes!" Such stories serve the valuable purpose of illustrating the kinds of behavior the company reveres and inspiring company personnel to perform similarly. Moreover, each retelling of a legendary story puts a bit more peer pressure on company personnel to display core values and do their part in keeping the company's traditions alive.

Forces That Cause a Company's Culture to Evolve Despite the role of time-honored stories and long-standing traditions in perpetuating a company's culture, cultures are far from static—just like strategy and organizational structure, they evolve. New challenges in the marketplace, revolutionary technologies, and shifting internal conditions—especially an internal crisis, a change in company direction, or top-executive turnover—tend to breed new ways of doing things and, in turn, drive cultural evolution. An incoming CEO who decides to shake up the existing business and take it in new directions often triggers a cultural shift, perhaps one of major proportions. Likewise, diversification into new businesses, expansion into foreign countries, rapid growth that brings an influx of new employees, and the merger with or acquisition of another company can all precipitate significant cultural change.

Strong versus Weak Cultures

Company cultures vary widely in strength and influence. Some are strongly embedded and have a big influence on a company's operating practices and the behavior of company personnel. Others are weakly ingrained and have little effect on behaviors and how company activities are conducted.

Strong-Culture Companies The hallmark of a **strong-culture company** is the dominating presence of certain deeply rooted values, business principles, and behavioral norms that "regulate" the conduct of company personnel and determine the climate of the workplace.[9] In strong-culture companies, senior managers make a point of explaining and reiterating why these values, principles, norms, and operating approaches need to govern how the company conducts its business and how they ultimately lead to better business performance. Furthermore, they make a conscious effort to display these values, principles, and behavioral norms in their own actions—*they walk the talk.* An unequivocal expectation that company personnel will act and behave in accordance with the adopted values and ways of doing business leads to two important outcomes: (1) Over time, the professed values come to be widely shared by rank-and-file employees—people who dislike the culture tend to leave—and (2) individuals encounter strong peer pressure from co-workers to observe the culturally approved norms and behaviors. Hence, a strongly implanted corporate culture ends up having a powerful influence on behavior because so many company personnel are accepting of the company's culturally approved traditions and because this acceptance is reinforced by both management expectations and co-worker peer pressure to conform to cultural norms.

CORE CONCEPT

In a **strong-culture company,** deeply rooted values and norms of behavior are widely shared and regulate the conduct of the company's business.

Strong cultures emerge only after a period of deliberate and rather intensive culture building that generally takes years (sometimes decades). Two factors contribute to the development of strong cultures: (1) a founder or strong leader who established core values, principles, and practices that are viewed as having contributed to the success of the company; and (2) a sincere, long-standing company commitment to operating the business according to these established traditions and values. Continuity of leadership, low workforce turnover, geographic concentration, and considerable organizational success all contribute to the emergence and sustainability of a strong culture.[10]

In strong-culture companies, values and behavioral norms are so ingrained that they can endure leadership changes at the top—although their strength can erode over time if new CEOs cease to nurture them or move aggressively to institute cultural adjustments. The cultural norms in a strong-culture company typically do not change much as strategy evolves, either because the culture constrains the choice of new strategies or because the dominant traits of the culture are somewhat strategy-neutral and compatible with evolving versions of the company's strategy. As a consequence, *strongly implanted cultures provide a huge assist in executing strategy* because company managers can use the traditions, beliefs, values, common bonds, or behavioral norms as levers to mobilize commitment to executing the chosen strategy.

Weak-Culture Companies In direct contrast to strong-culture companies, weak-culture companies lack widely shared and strongly held values, principles, and behavioral norms. As a result, they also lack cultural mechanisms for aligning, constraining, and regulating the actions, decisions, and behaviors of company personnel. In the absence of any long-standing top management commitment to particular values, beliefs, operating practices, and behavioral norms, individuals encounter little pressure to do things in particular ways. Such a dearth of companywide cultural influences and revered traditions produces a work climate where there is no strong employee allegiance to what the company stands for or to operating the business in well-defined ways. While individual employees may well have some bonds of identification with and loyalty toward their department, their colleagues, their union, or their immediate boss, there's neither passion about the company nor emotional commitment to what it is trying to accomplish—a condition that often results in many employees' viewing their company as just a place to work and their job as just a way to make a living.

As a consequence, *weak cultures provide little or no assistance in executing strategy* because there are no traditions, beliefs, values, common bonds, or behavioral norms that management can use as levers to mobilize commitment to executing the chosen strategy. Without a work climate that channels organizational energy in the direction of good strategy execution, managers are left with the options of either using compensation incentives and other motivational devices to mobilize employee commitment, supervising and monitoring employee actions more closely, or trying to establish cultural roots that will in time start to nurture the strategy execution process.

Why Corporate Cultures Matter to the Strategy Execution Process

LO 2

How and why a company's culture can aid the drive for proficient strategy execution.

Even if a company has a strong culture, the culture and work climate may or may not be compatible with what is needed for effective implementation of the chosen strategy. When a company's present culture promotes attitudes, behaviors, and ways of doing things that are *in sync with the chosen strategy and conducive to first-rate strategy execution,* the culture functions as a valuable ally in the strategy execution process. For example, a corporate culture characterized by frugality and thrift prompts employee actions to identify cost-saving opportunities—the very behavior needed for successful execution of a low-cost leadership strategy. A culture that celebrates taking initiative, exhibiting creativity, taking risks, and embracing change is conducive to successful execution of product innovation and technological leadership strategies.[11]

A culture that is grounded in actions, behaviors, and work practices that are conducive to good strategy implementation supports the strategy execution effort in three ways:

1. *A culture that is well matched to the chosen strategy and the requirements of the strategy execution effort focuses the attention of employees on what is most important to this effort.* Moreover, it directs their behavior and serves as a guide to their decision making. In this manner, it can align the efforts and decisions of employees throughout the firm and minimize the need for direct supervision.
2. *Culture-induced peer pressure further induces company personnel to do things in a manner that aids the cause of good strategy execution.* The stronger the culture (the more widely shared and deeply held the values), the more effective peer pressure is in shaping and supporting the strategy execution effort. Research has shown that strong group norms can shape employee behavior even more powerfully than can financial incentives.
3. *A company culture that is consistent with the requirements for good strategy execution can energize employees, deepen their commitment to execute the strategy flawlessly, and enhance worker productivity in the process.* When a company's culture is grounded in many of the needed strategy-executing behaviors, employees feel genuinely better about their jobs, the company they work for, and the merits of what the company is trying to accomplish. Greater employee buy-in for what the company is trying to accomplish boosts motivation and marshals organizational energy behind the drive for good strategy execution. An energized workforce enhances the chances of achieving execution-critical performance targets and good strategy execution.

A strong culture that encourages actions, behaviors, and work practices that are in sync with the chosen strategy and conducive to good strategy execution is a valuable ally in the strategy execution process.

In sharp contrast, when a culture is in conflict with the chosen strategy or what is required to execute the company's strategy well, the culture becomes a stumbling block.[12] Some of the very behaviors needed to execute the strategy successfully run contrary to the attitudes, behaviors, and operating practices embedded in the prevailing culture. Such a clash poses a real dilemma for company personnel. Should they be loyal to the culture and company traditions (to which they are likely to be emotionally attached) and thus resist or be indifferent to actions that will promote better strategy execution—a choice that will certainly weaken the drive for good strategy execution? Alternatively, should they go along with management's strategy execution effort and engage in actions that run counter to the culture—a choice that will likely impair morale and lead to a less-than-enthusiastic commitment to good strategy execution? Neither choice leads to desirable outcomes. Culture-bred resistance to the actions and behaviors needed for good strategy execution, particularly if strong and widespread, poses a formidable hurdle that must be cleared for a strategy's execution to be successful.

The consequences of having—or not having—an execution-supportive corporate culture says something important about the task of managing the strategy execution process: *Closely aligning corporate culture with the requirements for proficient strategy execution merits the full attention of senior executives.* The culture-building objective is to create a work climate and style of operating that mobilize the energy of company personnel squarely behind efforts to execute strategy competently. The more deeply management can embed execution-supportive ways of doing things, the more management can rely on the culture to automatically steer company personnel toward behaviors and work practices that aid good strategy execution and veer from doing things that impede it. Moreover, culturally astute managers understand that nourishing the right cultural environment not only adds power to their push for proficient strategy execution but also promotes strong employee identification with, and commitment to, the company's vision, performance targets, and strategy.

It is in management's best interest to dedicate considerable effort to establishing a corporate culture that encourages behaviors and work practices conducive to good strategy execution.

Healthy Cultures That Aid Good Strategy Execution

A strong culture, provided it fits the chosen strategy and embraces execution-supportive attitudes, behaviors, and work practices, is definitely a healthy culture. Two other types of cultures exist that tend to be healthy and largely supportive of good strategy execution: high-performance cultures and adaptive cultures.

High-Performance Cultures Some companies have so-called high-performance cultures where the standout traits are a "can-do" spirit, pride in doing things right, no-excuses accountability, and a pervasive results-oriented work climate in which people go all out to meet or beat stretch objectives.[13] In high-performance cultures, there's a strong sense of involvement on the part of company personnel and emphasis on individual initiative and effort. Performance expectations are clearly delineated for the company as a whole, for each organizational unit, and for each individual. Issues and problems are promptly addressed; there's a razor-sharp focus on what needs to be done. The clear and unyielding expectation is that all company personnel, from senior executives to frontline employees, will display high-performance behaviors and a passion for making the company successful. Such a culture—permeated by a spirit of achievement and constructive pressure to achieve good results—is a valuable contributor to good strategy execution and operating excellence.[14]

The challenge in creating a high-performance culture is to inspire high loyalty and dedication on the part of employees, such that they are energized to put forth their very best efforts. Managers have to take pains to reinforce constructive behavior, reward top performers, and purge habits and behaviors that stand in the way of high productivity and good results. They must work at knowing the strengths and weaknesses of their subordinates to better match talent with task and enable people to make meaningful contributions by doing what they do best. They have to stress learning from mistakes and must put an unrelenting emphasis on moving forward and making good progress—in effect, there has to be a disciplined, performance-focused approach to managing the organization.

Adaptive Cultures The hallmark of adaptive corporate cultures is willingness on the part of organization members to accept change and take on the challenge of introducing and executing new strategies. Company personnel share a feeling of confidence that the organization can deal with whatever threats and opportunities arise; they are receptive to risk taking, experimentation, innovation, and changing strategies and practices. The work climate is supportive of managers and employees who propose or initiate useful change. Internal entrepreneurship (often called *intrapreneurship*) on the part of individuals and groups is encouraged and rewarded. Senior executives seek out, support, and promote individuals who exercise initiative, spot opportunities for improvement, and display the skills to implement them. Managers openly evaluate ideas and suggestions, fund initiatives to develop new or better products, and take prudent risks to pursue emerging market opportunities. As in high-performance cultures, the company exhibits a proactive approach to identifying issues, evaluating the implications and options, and moving ahead quickly with workable solutions. Strategies and traditional operating practices are modified as needed to adjust to, or take advantage of, changes in the business environment.

As a company's strategy evolves, an adaptive culture is a definite ally in the strategy-implementing, strategy-executing process as compared to cultures that are resistant to change.

But why is change so willingly embraced in an adaptive culture? Why are organization members not fearful of how change will affect them? Why does an adaptive culture not break down from the force of ongoing changes in strategy, operating practices, and behavioral norms? The answers lie in two distinctive and dominant traits of an adaptive culture: (1) Changes in operating practices and behaviors must *not* compromise core values and long-standing business principles (since they are at the root of the culture), and (2) changes that are instituted must satisfy the legitimate interests of key constituencies—customers, employees, shareholders, suppliers, and the communities where the company operates. In other words, what sustains an adaptive culture is that organization members perceive the changes that management is trying to institute as *legitimate,* in keeping with the core values, and in the overall best interests of stakeholders.[15] Not surprisingly, company personnel are usually more receptive to change when their employment security is not threatened and when they view new duties or job assignments as part of the process of adapting to new conditions. Should workforce downsizing be necessary, it is important that layoffs be handled humanely and employee departures be made as painless as possible.

Technology companies, software companies, and Internet-based companies are good illustrations of organizations with adaptive cultures. Such companies thrive on change—driving it, leading it, and capitalizing on it. Companies like Amazon, Google, Apple, Facebook, Adobe, Groupon, Intel, and Yelp cultivate the capability to act and react rapidly. They are avid practitioners of entrepreneurship and innovation, with a demonstrated willingness to take bold risks to create altogether new products, new businesses, and new industries. To create and nurture a culture that can adapt rapidly to shifting business conditions, they make a point of staffing their organizations with people who are flexible, who rise to the challenge of change, and who have an aptitude for adapting well to new circumstances.

In fast-changing business environments, a corporate culture that is receptive to altering organizational practices and behaviors is a virtual necessity. However, adaptive cultures work to the advantage of all companies, not just those in rapid-change environments. Every company operates in a market and business climate that is changing to one degree or another and that, in turn, requires internal operating responses and new behaviors on the part of organization members.

Unhealthy Cultures That Impede Good Strategy Execution

The distinctive characteristic of an unhealthy corporate culture is the presence of counterproductive cultural traits that adversely impact the work climate and company performance. Five particularly unhealthy cultural traits are hostility to change, heavily politicized decision making, insular thinking, unethical and greed-driven behaviors, and the presence of incompatible, clashing subcultures.

Change-Resistant Cultures Change-resistant cultures—where fear of change and skepticism about the importance of new developments are the norm—place a premium on not making mistakes, prompting managers to lean toward safe, conservative options intended to maintain the status quo, protect their power base, and guard their immediate interests. When such companies encounter business environments with accelerating change, going slow on altering traditional ways of doing things can be a serious liability. Under these conditions, change-resistant cultures encourage a number of unhealthy behaviors—avoiding risks, not capitalizing on emerging opportunities, taking a lax approach to both product innovation and continuous improvement in performing value chain activities, and responding more slowly than is warranted to market change. In change-resistant cultures, word quickly gets around that proposals to do things differently face an uphill battle and that people who champion them may be seen as something of a nuisance or a troublemaker. Executives who don't value managers or employees with initiative and new ideas put a damper on product innovation, experimentation, and efforts to improve.

Hostility to change is most often found in companies with stodgy bureaucracies that have enjoyed considerable market success in years past and that are wedded to the "We have done it this way for years" syndrome. General Motors, IBM, Sears, Borders, and Eastman Kodak are classic examples of companies whose change-resistant bureaucracies have damaged their market standings and financial performance; clinging to what made them successful, they were reluctant to alter operating practices and modify their business approaches when signals of market change first sounded. As strategies of gradual change won out over bold innovation, all four lost market share to rivals that quickly moved to institute changes more in tune with evolving market conditions and buyer preferences. While IBM and GM have made strides in building a culture needed for market success, Sears and Kodak are still struggling to recoup lost ground.

Politicized Cultures What makes a politicized internal environment so unhealthy is that political infighting consumes a great deal of organizational energy, often with the result that what's best for the company takes a backseat to political maneuvering. In companies where internal politics pervades the work climate, empire-building managers pursue their own agendas and operate the work units under their supervision as autonomous "fiefdoms." The positions they take on issues are usually aimed at protecting or expanding their own turf. Collaboration with other organizational units is viewed with suspicion, and cross-unit cooperation occurs grudgingly. The support or opposition of politically influential executives and/or coalitions among departments with vested interests in a particular outcome tends to shape what actions the company takes. All this political maneuvering takes away from efforts to execute strategy with real proficiency and frustrates company personnel who are less political and more inclined to do what is in the company's best interests.

Insular, Inwardly Focused Cultures Sometimes a company reigns as an industry leader or enjoys great market success for so long that its personnel start to believe they have all the answers or can develop them on their own. There is a strong tendency to neglect what customers are saying and how their needs and expectations are changing. Such confidence in the correctness of how the company does things and an unflinching belief in its competitive superiority breed arrogance, prompting company personnel to discount the merits of what outsiders are doing and to see little payoff from studying best-in-class performers. Insular thinking, internally driven solutions, and a must-be-invented-here mindset come to permeate the corporate culture. An inwardly focused corporate culture gives rise to managerial inbreeding and a failure to recruit people who can offer fresh thinking and outside perspectives. The big risk of insular cultural thinking is that the company can underestimate the capabilities of rival companies while overestimating its own—all of which diminishes a company's competitiveness over time.

Unethical and Greed-Driven Cultures Companies that have little regard for ethical standards or are run by executives driven by greed and ego gratification are scandals waiting to happen. Executives exude the negatives of arrogance, ego, greed, and an "ends-justify-the-means" mentality in pursuing overambitious revenue and profitability targets.[16] Senior managers wink at unethical behavior and may cross over the line to unethical (and sometimes criminal) behavior themselves. They are prone to adopt accounting principles that make financial performance look better than it really is. Legions of companies have fallen prey to unethical behavior and greed, most notably Turing Pharmaceuticals, Enron, Three Ocean Shipping, BP, AIG, Countrywide Financial, and JPMorgan Chase, with executives being indicted and/or convicted of criminal behavior.

Incompatible, Clashing Subcultures Although it is common to speak about corporate culture in the singular, it is not unusual for companies to have multiple cultures (or subcultures). Values, beliefs, and practices within a company sometimes vary significantly by department, geographic location, division, or business unit. As long as the subcultures are compatible with the overarching corporate culture and are supportive of the strategy execution efforts, this is not problematic. Multiple cultures pose an unhealthy situation when they are composed of incompatible subcultures that embrace conflicting business philosophies, support inconsistent approaches to strategy execution, and encourage incompatible methods of people management. Clashing subcultures can prevent a company from coordinating its efforts to craft and execute strategy and can distract company personnel from the business of business. Internal jockeying among the subcultures for cultural dominance impedes teamwork among the company's various organizational units and blocks the emergence of a collaborative approach to strategy execution. Such a lack of consensus about how to proceed is likely to result in fragmented or inconsistent approaches to implementing new strategic initiatives and in limited success in executing the company's overall strategy.

Changing a Problem Culture

LO 3

The kinds of actions management can take to change a problem corporate culture.

When a strong culture is unhealthy or otherwise out of sync with the actions and behaviors needed to execute the strategy successfully, the culture must be changed as rapidly as can be managed. This means eliminating any unhealthy or dysfunctional cultural traits as fast as possible and aggressively striving to ingrain new behaviors and work practices that will enable first-rate strategy execution. The more entrenched the unhealthy or mismatched aspects of a company culture, the more likely the culture will impede strategy execution and the greater the need for change.

Changing a problem culture is among the toughest management tasks because of the heavy anchor of ingrained behaviors and attitudes. It is natural for company personnel to cling to familiar practices and to be wary of change, if not hostile to new approaches concerning how things are to be done. Consequently, it takes concerted management action over a period of time to root out unwanted behaviors and replace an unsupportive culture with more effective ways of doing things. *The single most visible factor that distinguishes successful culture-change efforts from failed attempts is competent leadership at the top.* Great power is needed to force major cultural change and overcome the stubborn resistance of entrenched cultures—and great power is possessed only by the most senior executives, especially the CEO. However, while top management must lead the change effort, the tasks of marshaling support for a new culture and instilling the desired cultural behaviors must involve a company's whole management team. Middle managers and frontline supervisors play a key role in implementing the new work practices and operating approaches, helping win rank-and-file acceptance of and support for changes, and instilling the desired behavioral norms.

As shown in Figure 12.2, the first step in fixing a problem culture is for top management to identify those facets of the present culture that are dysfunctional and pose obstacles to executing strategic initiatives. Second, managers must clearly define the desired new behaviors and features of the culture they want to create. Third, they must convince company personnel of why the present culture poses problems and why and how new behaviors and operating approaches will improve company performance—the case for cultural reform has to be persuasive. Finally, and most important, all the talk about remodeling the present culture must be followed swiftly by visible, forceful actions to promote the desired new behaviors and work practices—actions that company personnel will interpret as a determined top-management commitment to bringing about a different work climate and new ways of operating. The actions to implant the new culture must be both substantive and symbolic.

Making a Compelling Case for Culture Change The way for management to begin a major remodeling of the corporate culture is by selling company personnel on the need for new-style behaviors and work practices. This means making a compelling case for why the culture-remodeling efforts are in the organization's best interests and why company personnel should wholeheartedly join the effort to do things somewhat differently. This can be done by:

- Explaining why and how certain behaviors and work practices in the current culture pose obstacles to good strategy execution.

FIGURE 12.2 Changing a Problem Culture

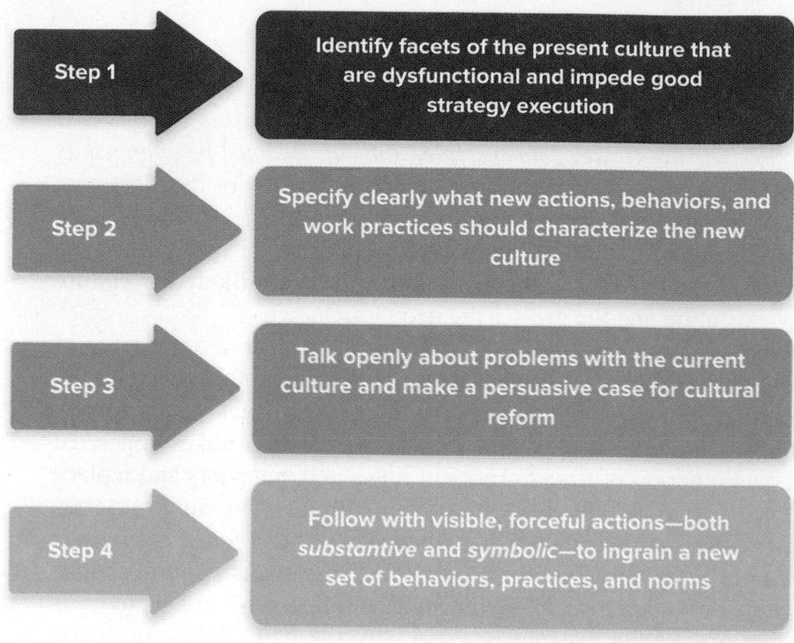

- Explaining how new behaviors and work practices will be more advantageous and produce better results. Effective culture-change leaders are good at telling stories to describe the new values and desired behaviors and connect them to everyday practices.
- Citing reasons why the current strategy has to be modified, if the need for cultural change is due to a change in strategy. This includes explaining why the new strategic initiatives will bolster the company's competitiveness and performance and how a change in culture can help in executing the new strategy.

It is essential for the CEO and other top executives to talk personally to personnel all across the company about the reasons for modifying work practices and culture-related behaviors. For the culture-change effort to be successful, frontline supervisors and employee opinion leaders must be won over to the cause, which means convincing them of the merits of *practicing* and *enforcing* cultural norms at every level of the organization, from the highest to the lowest. Arguments for new ways of doing things and new work practices tend to be embraced more readily if employees understand how they will benefit company stakeholders (particularly customers, employees, and shareholders). Until a large majority of employees accept the need for a new culture and agree that different work practices and behaviors are called for, there's more work to be done in selling company personnel on the whys and wherefores of culture change. Building widespread organizational support requires taking every opportunity to repeat the message of why the new work practices, operating approaches, and behaviors are good for company stakeholders and essential for the company's future success.

Substantive Culture-Changing Actions No culture-change effort can get very far when leaders merely talk about the need for different actions, behaviors, and work practices. Company executives must give the culture-change effort some teeth by initiating *a series of actions* that company personnel will see as unmistakably indicative of the seriousness of management's commitment to cultural change. The strongest signs that management is truly committed to instilling a new culture include:

- Replacing key executives who are resisting or obstructing needed organizational and cultural changes.
- Promoting individuals who have stepped forward to spearhead the shift to a different culture and who can serve as role models for the desired cultural behavior.
- Appointing outsiders with the desired cultural attributes to high-profile positions—bringing in new-breed managers sends an unambiguous message that a new era is dawning.
- Screening all candidates for new positions carefully, hiring only those who appear to fit in with the new culture.
- Mandating that all company personnel attend culture-training programs to better understand the new culture-related actions and behaviors that are expected.
- Designing compensation incentives that boost the pay of teams and individuals who display the desired cultural behaviors. Company personnel are much more inclined to exhibit the desired kinds of actions and behaviors when it is in their financial best interest to do so.
- Letting word leak out that generous pay raises have been awarded to individuals who have stepped out front, led the adoption of the desired work practices, displayed the new-style behaviors, and achieved pace-setting results.
- Revising policies and procedures in ways that will help drive cultural change.

Executives must launch enough companywide culture-change actions at the outset to leave no room for doubt that management is dead serious about changing the present culture and that a cultural transformation is inevitable. Management's commitment to cultural change in the company must be made credible. The series of actions initiated by top management must command attention, get the change process off to a fast start, and be followed by unrelenting efforts to firmly establish the new work practices, desired behaviors, and style of operating as "standard."

Symbolic Culture-Changing Actions There's also an important place for symbolic managerial actions to alter a problem culture and tighten the strategy–culture fit. The most important symbolic actions are those that top executives take to *lead by example.* For instance, if the organization's strategy involves a drive to become the industry's low-cost producer, senior managers must display frugality in their own actions and decisions. Examples include inexpensive decorations in the executive suite, conservative expense accounts and entertainment allowances, a lean staff in the corporate office, scrutiny of budget requests, few executive perks, and so on. At Walmart, all the executive offices are simply decorated; executives are habitually frugal in their own actions, and they are zealous in their efforts to control costs and promote greater efficiency. At Nucor, one of the world's low-cost producers of steel products, executives fly coach class and use taxis at airports rather than limousines. Top executives must be alert to the fact that company personnel will be watching their behavior to see if their actions match their rhetoric. Hence, they need to make sure their current decisions and actions will be construed as consistent with the new cultural values and norms.[17]

Another category of symbolic actions includes holding ceremonial events to single out and honor people whose actions and performance exemplify what is called for in the new culture. Such events also provide an opportunity to celebrate each culture-change success. Executives sensitive to their role in promoting strategy–culture fit make a habit of appearing at ceremonial functions to praise individuals and groups that exemplify the desired behaviors. They show up at employee training programs to stress strategic priorities, values, ethical principles, and cultural norms. Every group gathering is seen as an opportunity to repeat and ingrain values, praise good deeds, expound on the merits of the new culture, and cite instances of how the new work practices and operating approaches have produced good results.

The use of symbols in culture building is widespread. Numerous businesses have employee-of-the-month awards. The military has a long-standing custom of awarding ribbons and medals for exemplary actions. Mary Kay Cosmetics awards an array of prizes ceremoniously to its beauty consultants for reaching various sales plateaus, including the iconic pink Cadillac.

How Long Does It Take to Change a Problem Culture? Planting the seeds of a new culture and helping the culture grow strong roots require a determined, sustained effort by the chief executive and other senior managers. Changing a problem culture is never a short-term exercise; it takes time for a new culture to emerge and take root. And it takes even longer for a new culture to become deeply embedded. The bigger the organization and the greater the cultural shift needed to produce an execution-supportive fit, the longer it takes. In large companies, fixing a problem culture and instilling a new set of attitudes and behaviors can take two to five years. In fact, it is usually tougher to reform an entrenched problematic culture than it is to instill a strategy-supportive culture from scratch in a brand-new organization.

Illustration Capsule 12.2 discusses the approaches used at América Latina Logística (ALL) to change a culture that was grounded in antiquated practices and bureaucratic management.

LEADING THE STRATEGY EXECUTION PROCESS

LO 4

What constitutes effective managerial leadership in achieving superior strategy execution.

For an enterprise to execute its strategy in truly proficient fashion, top executives must take the lead in the strategy implementation process and personally drive the pace of progress. They have to be out in the field, seeing for themselves how well operations are going, gathering information firsthand, and gauging the progress being made. Proficient strategy execution requires company managers to be diligent and adept in spotting problems, learning what obstacles lay in the path of good execution, and then clearing the way for progress—the goal must be to produce better results speedily and productively. There must be constructive, but unrelenting, pressure on organizational units to (1) demonstrate excellence in all dimensions of strategy execution and (2) do so on a consistent basis—ultimately, that's what will enable a well-crafted strategy to achieve the desired performance results.

The specifics of how to implement a strategy and deliver the intended results must start with understanding the requirements for good strategy execution. Afterward comes a diagnosis of the organization's preparedness to execute the strategic initiatives and decisions on how to move forward and achieve the targeted results.[18]

ILLUSTRATION CAPSULE 12.2 Culture Transformation at América Latina Logística

© Pulsar Images/Alamy Stock Photo

For many, a steam-engine locomotive's stocky profile, billowing exhaust, and hiss evoke nostalgia for a bygone era. For the managers at América Latina Logística (ALL), which had just acquired the southern freight lines of the Brazilian Rail Network (RFFSA), such antiquated locomotives represented the difficulties they faced in fixing their ailing railroad system, of which RFFSA was just a piece.

At the time of this acquisition, ALL was losing money, struggling from decades of underinvestment, and encumbered by bureaucratic management. Half the network's bridges required repairs, over three-quarters of its rails were undersized for supporting standard-sized loads, and the system still relied on 20 steam-engine locomotives to move industrial customers' cargo.

CEO Alexandre Behring's priority was to transform ALL into a performance-oriented organization with the strong cost discipline necessary to support an overdue modernization program. He decided that this would require a complete cultural transformation for the company. His first step was to recruit a new management team and fire the dozens of political appointees previously administering the railroad. In his first 10 days, he and his COO interviewed the top-150 managers to evaluate their suitability. They selected 30 for additional responsibility and removed those who did not embrace the new direction. The company established a trainee program, and in four years hired 500 recent college graduates. In Behring's first year, he introduced a performance-based bonus program; in his second year, the company began comparing performance on operational indicators like car utilization and on-time delivery between divisions.

The top managers also took symbolic steps to demonstrate their commitment to the new culture and to reinforce the personnel and process changes they implemented. They sold cars previously reserved for officers' use and fired the chauffeurs retained to drive them. Behring became certified as a train conductor and spent a week each month working in the field, wearing the conductor uniform. For the first time, managers visited injured workers at home. The company created the "Diesel Cup" to recognize conductors who most effectively reduced fuel consumption.

Behring's new direction energized the company's middle managers and line employees, who had been demoralized after years of political interference and ineffectual leadership. In three years Behring transformed a company that hadn't made a hire in over a decade into one of the most desirable employers in Brazil, attracting 9,000 applications for 18 trainee positions. In 2000 ALL finally achieved profitability, enabled by the company's cultural transformation. ALL merged with Rumo Logistics in 2014 to create Latin America's largest railway and logistics company.

Note: Developed with Peter Jacobson.

Sources: Company website, **pt.all-logistica.com; www.strategy-business.com/article/ac00012?pg=1; blogs.hbr.org/2012/09/shape-strategy-with-simple-rul/**; Donald N. Sull, Fernando Martins, and Andre Delbin Silva, "America Latina Logistica," Harvard Business School case 9-804-139, January 14, 2004.

In general, leading the drive for good strategy execution and operating excellence calls for three actions on the part of the managers in charge:

- Staying on top of what is happening and closely monitoring progress.
- Putting constructive pressure on the organization to execute the strategy well and achieve operating excellence.
- Initiating corrective actions to improve strategy execution and achieve the targeted performance results.

Staying on Top of How Well Things Are Going

To stay on top of how well the strategy execution process is going, senior executives have to tap into information from a wide range of sources. In addition to communicating regularly with key subordinates and reviewing the latest operating results, watching the competitive reactions of rival firms, and visiting with key customers and suppliers to get their perspectives, they usually visit various company facilities and talk with many different company personnel at many different organizational levels—a technique often labeled **management by walking around (MBWA).** Most managers attach great importance to spending time with people at company facilities, asking questions, listening to their opinions and concerns, and gathering firsthand information about how well aspects of the strategy execution process are going. Facilities tours and face-to-face contacts with operating-level employees give executives a good grasp of what progress is being made, what problems are being encountered, and whether additional resources or different approaches may be needed. Just as important, MBWA provides opportunities to give encouragement, lift spirits, focus attention on key priorities, and create some excitement—all of which generate positive energy and help boost strategy execution efforts.

CORE CONCEPT

Management by walking around (MBWA) is one of the techniques that effective leaders use to stay informed about how well the strategy execution process is progressing.

The late Steve Jobs, famed cofounder of Apple, was noted for his practice of MBWA as CEO, spending a considerable amount of time on the floor with his employees every day. Walmart executives have had a long-standing practice of spending two to three days every week visiting Walmart's stores and talking with store managers and employees. Sam Walton, Walmart's founder, insisted, "The key is to get out into the store and listen to what the associates have to say." Jack Welch, the highly effective former CEO of General Electric, not only spent several days each month personally visiting GE operations and talking with major customers but also arranged his schedule so that he could spend time exchanging information and ideas with GE managers from all over the world who were attending classes at the company's leadership development center near GE's headquarters.

Many manufacturing executives make a point of strolling the factory floor to talk with workers and meeting regularly with union officials. Some managers operate out of open cubicles in big spaces filled with open cubicles for other personnel so that they can interact easily and frequently with co-workers. Managers at some companies host weekly get-togethers (often on Friday afternoons) to create a regular opportunity for information to flow freely between down-the-line employees and executives.

Mobilizing the Effort for Excellence in Strategy Execution

Part of the leadership task in mobilizing organizational energy behind the drive for good strategy execution entails nurturing a results-oriented work climate, where performance standards are high and a spirit of achievement is pervasive. Successfully leading the effort is typically characterized by such leadership actions and managerial practices as:

- *Treating employees as valued partners.* Some companies symbolize the value of individual employees and the importance of their contributions by referring to them as cast members (Disney), crew members (McDonald's), job owners (Graniterock), partners (Starbucks), or associates (Walmart, LensCrafters, W. L. Gore, Edward Jones, Publix Supermarkets, and Marriott International). Very often, there is a strong company commitment to training each employee thoroughly, offering attractive compensation and benefits, emphasizing promotion from within and promising career opportunities, providing a high degree of job security, and otherwise making employees feel well treated and valued.

- *Fostering an esprit de corps that energizes organization members.* The task here is to skillfully use people-management practices calculated to build morale, foster pride in working for the company, promote teamwork and collaborative group effort, win the emotional commitment of individuals and organizational units to what the company is trying to accomplish, and inspire company personnel to do their best in achieving good results.[19]
- *Using empowerment to help create a fully engaged workforce.* Top executives—and, to some degree, the enterprise's entire management team—must seek to engage the full organization in the strategy execution effort. A fully engaged workforce, where individuals bring their best to work every day, is necessary to produce great results.[20] So is having a group of dedicated managers committed to making a difference in their organization. The two best things top-level executives can do to create a fully engaged organization are (1) delegate authority to middle and lower-level managers to get the strategy execution process moving and (2) empower rank-and-file employees to act on their own initiative. Operating excellence requires that everybody contribute ideas, exercise initiative and creativity in performing his or her work, and have a desire to do things in the best possible manner.
- *Setting stretch objectives and clearly communicating an expectation that company personnel are to give their best in achieving performance targets.* Stretch objectives—those beyond an organization's current capacities—can sometimes spur organization members to increase their resolve and redouble their efforts to execute the strategy flawlessly and ultimately reach the stretch objectives. When stretch objectives are met, the resulting pride of accomplishment boosts employee morale and acts to spur continued drive to "overachieve" and perform at an exceptionally high level.
- *Using the tools of benchmarking, best practices, business process reengineering, TQM, and Six Sigma to focus attention on continuous improvement.* These are proven approaches to getting better operating results and facilitating better strategy execution.
- *Using the full range of motivational techniques and compensation incentives to inspire company personnel, nurture a results-oriented work climate, and reward high performance.* Managers cannot mandate innovative improvements by simply exhorting people to "be creative," nor can they make continuous progress toward operating excellence with directives to "try harder." Rather, they must foster a culture where innovative ideas and experimentation with new ways of doing things can blossom and thrive. Individuals and groups should be strongly encouraged to brainstorm, let their imaginations fly in all directions, and come up with proposals for improving the way that things are done. This means giving company personnel enough autonomy to stand out, excel, and contribute. And it means that the rewards for successful champions of new ideas and operating improvements should be large and visible. It is particularly important that people who champion an unsuccessful idea are not punished or sidelined but, rather, encouraged to try again. Finding great ideas requires taking risks and recognizing that many ideas won't pan out.

- *Celebrating individual, group, and company successes.* Top management should miss no opportunity to express respect for individual employees and appreciation of extraordinary individual and group effort.[21] Companies like Google, Mary Kay, Tupperware, and McDonald's actively seek out reasons and opportunities to give pins, ribbons, buttons, badges, and medals for good showings by average performers—the idea being to express appreciation and give a motivational boost to people who stand out in doing ordinary jobs. At Kimpton Hotels, employees who create special moments for guests are rewarded with "Kimpton Moment" tokens that can be redeemed for paid days off, gift certificates to restaurants, flat-screen TVs, and other prizes. Cisco Systems and 3M Corporation make a point of ceremoniously honoring individuals who believe so strongly in their ideas that they take it on themselves to hurdle the bureaucracy, maneuver their projects through the system, and turn them into improved services, new products, or even new businesses.

While leadership efforts to instill a results-oriented, high-performance culture usually accentuate the positive, negative consequences for poor performance must be in play as well. Managers whose units consistently perform poorly must be replaced. Low-performing employees must be weeded out or at least employed in ways better suited to their aptitudes. Average performers should be candidly counseled that they have limited career potential unless they show more progress in the form of additional effort, better skills, and improved ability to execute the strategy well and deliver good results.

Leading the Process of Making Corrective Adjustments

There comes a time at every company when managers have to fine-tune or overhaul the approaches to strategy execution since no action plan for executing strategy can foresee all the problems that will arise. Clearly, when a company's strategy execution effort is not delivering good results, it is the leader's responsibility to step forward and initiate corrective actions, although sometimes it must be recognized that unsatisfactory performance may be due as much or more to flawed strategy as to weak strategy execution.[22]

Success in making corrective actions hinges on (1) a thorough analysis of the situation, (2) the exercise of good business judgment in deciding what actions to take, and (3) good implementation of the corrective actions that are initiated. Successful managers are skilled in getting an organization back on track rather quickly. They (and their staffs) are good at discerning what actions to take and in bringing them to a successful conclusion. Managers who struggle to show measurable progress in implementing corrective actions in a timely fashion are candidates for being replaced.

The *process* of making corrective adjustments in strategy execution varies according to the situation. In a crisis, taking remedial action quickly is of the essence. But it still takes time to review the situation, examine the available data, identify and evaluate options (crunching whatever numbers may be appropriate to determine which options are likely to generate the best outcomes), and decide what to do. When the situation allows managers to proceed more deliberately in deciding when to make changes and what changes to make, most managers seem to prefer a process of incrementally solidifying commitment to a particular course of action.[23] The process that managers go through in deciding on corrective adjustments is essentially the same for both proactive and reactive changes: They sense needs, gather information, broaden and deepen their understanding of the situation, develop options and explore their pros and cons, put forth action proposals, strive for a consensus, and finally formally adopt an agreed-on course of action. The time frame for deciding what corrective changes to initiate can be a few hours, a few days, a few weeks, or even a few months if the situation is particularly complicated.

The challenges of making the right corrective adjustments and leading a successful strategy execution effort are, without question, substantial.[24] There's no generic, by-the-books procedure to follow. Because each instance of executing strategy occurs under different organizational circumstances, the managerial agenda for executing strategy always needs to be situation-specific. But the job is definitely doable. Although there is no prescriptive answer to the question of exactly what to do, any of several courses of action may produce good results. As we said at the beginning of Chapter 10, executing strategy is an action-oriented, make-the-right-things-happen task that challenges a manager's ability to lead and direct organizational change, create or reinvent business processes, manage and motivate people, and achieve performance targets. If you now better understand what the challenges are, what tasks are involved, what tools can be used to aid the managerial process of executing strategy, and why the action agenda for implementing and executing strategy sweeps across so many aspects of managerial work, then the discussions in Chapters 10, 11, and 12 have been a success.

A FINAL WORD ON LEADING THE PROCESS OF CRAFTING AND EXECUTING STRATEGY

In practice, it is hard to separate leading the process of executing strategy from leading the other pieces of the strategy process. As we emphasized in Chapter 2, the job of crafting and executing strategy consists of five interrelated and linked stages, with much looping and recycling to fine-tune and adjust the strategic vision, objectives, strategy, and implementation approaches to fit one another and to fit changing circumstances. The process is continuous, and the conceptually separate acts of crafting and executing strategy blur together in real-world situations. *The best tests of good strategic leadership are whether the company has a good strategy and business model, whether the strategy is being competently executed, and whether the enterprise is meeting or beating its performance targets.* If these three conditions exist, then there is every reason to conclude that the company has good strategic leadership and is a well-managed enterprise.

KEY POINTS

1. Corporate culture is the character of a company's internal work climate—the shared values, ingrained attitudes, core beliefs and company traditions that determine norms of behavior, accepted work practices, and styles of operating. A company's culture is important because it influences the organization's actions, its approaches to conducting business, and ultimately its performance in the marketplace. It can be thought of as the company's organizational DNA.
2. The key features of a company's culture include the company's values and ethical standards, its approach to people management, its work atmosphere and

company spirit, how its personnel interact, the strength of peer pressure to conform to norms, the behaviors awarded through incentives (both financial and symbolic), the traditions and oft-repeated "myths," and its manner of dealing with stakeholders.

3. A company's culture is grounded in and shaped by its core values and ethical standards. Core values and ethical principles serve two roles in the culture-building process: (1) They foster a work climate in which employees share common and strongly held convictions about how company business is to be conducted, and (2) they provide company personnel with guidance about the manner in which they are to do their jobs—which behaviors and ways of doing things are approved (and expected) and which are out-of-bounds. They serve as yardsticks for gauging the appropriateness of particular actions, decisions, and behaviors.
4. Company cultures vary widely in strength and influence. Some cultures are *strong* and have a big impact on a company's practices and behavioral norms. Others are *weak* and have comparatively little influence on company operations.
5. Strong company cultures can have either positive or negative effects on strategy execution. When they are in sync with the chosen strategy and well matched to the behavioral requirements of the company's strategy implementation plan, they can be a powerful aid to strategy execution. A culture that is grounded in the types of actions and behaviors that are conducive to good strategy execution assists the effort in three ways:
   - By focusing employee attention on the actions that are most important in the strategy execution effort.
   - By inducing peer pressure for employees to contribute to the success of the strategy execution effort.
   - By energizing employees, deepening their commitment to the strategy execution effort, and increasing the productivity of their efforts

   It is thus in management's best interest to dedicate considerable effort to establishing a strongly implanted corporate culture that encourages behaviors and work practices conducive to good strategy execution.
6. Strong corporate cultures that are conducive to good strategy execution are healthy cultures. So are high-performance cultures and adaptive cultures. The latter are particularly important in dynamic environments. Strong cultures can also be unhealthy. The five types of unhealthy cultures are those that are (1) change-resistant, (2) heavily politicized, (3) insular and inwardly focused, (4) ethically unprincipled and infused with greed, and (5) composed of incompatible, clashing subcultures. All five impede good strategy execution.
7. Changing a company's culture, especially a strong one with traits that don't fit a new strategy's requirements, is a tough and often time-consuming challenge. Changing a culture requires competent leadership at the top. It requires making a compelling case for cultural change and employing both symbolic actions and substantive actions that unmistakably indicate serious and credible commitment on the part of top management. The more that culture-driven actions and behaviors fit what's needed for good strategy execution, the less managers must depend on policies, rules, procedures, and supervision to enforce what people should and should not do.

8. Leading the drive for good strategy execution and operating excellence calls for three actions on the part of the manager in charge:
   - Staying on top of what is happening and closely monitoring progress. This is often accomplished through management by walking around (MBWA).
   - Mobilizing the effort for excellence in strategy execution by putting constructive pressure on the organization to execute the strategy well.
   - Initiating corrective actions to improve strategy execution and achieve the targeted performance results.

ASSURANCE OF LEARNING EXERCISES

1. Go to the company website for REI (**www.rei.com**). Click on Stewardship at the bottom of the page, and then click on some of the tabs below to learn more about the company's culture and values. What are the key features of its culture? Do features of REI's culture influence the company's ethical practices? If so, how? connect LO 1
2. Based on what you learned about REI from answering the previous question, how do you think the company's culture affects its ability to execute strategy and operate with excellence? LO 2
3. Illustration Capsule 12.1 discusses Epic's strategy-supportive corporate culture. What are the standout features of Epic's corporate culture? How does Epic's culture contribute to its winning best-in-class awards year after year? How does the company's culture make Epic a good place to work? connect LO 1, LO 2
4. If you were an executive at a company that had a pervasive yet problematic culture, what steps would you take to change it? Using Google Scholar or your university library's access to EBSCO, LexisNexis, or other databases, search for recent articles in business publications on "culture change." What role did the executives play in the culture change? How does this differ from what you would have done to change the culture? LO 3
5. Leading the strategy execution process involves staying on top of the situation and monitoring progress, putting constructive pressure on the organization to achieve operating excellence, and initiating corrective actions to improve the execution effort. Using your university's access to business periodicals, discuss a recent example of how a company's managers have demonstrated the kind of effective internal leadership needed for superior strategy execution. LO 4

EXERCISE FOR SIMULATION PARTICIPANTS

1. If you were making a speech to company personnel, what would you tell employees about the kind of corporate culture you would like to have at your company? What specific cultural traits would you like your company to exhibit? Explain. LO 1, LO 2
2. What core values would you want to ingrain in your company's culture? Why? LO 2

LO 3, LO 4 3. Following each decision round, do you and your co-managers make corrective adjustments in either your company's strategy or the way the strategy is being executed? List at least three such adjustments you made in the most recent decision round. What hard evidence (in the form of results relating to your company's performance in the most recent year) can you cite that indicates that the various corrective adjustments you made either succeeded at improving or failed to improve your company's performance?

LO 4 4. What would happen to your company's performance if you and your co-managers stick with the status quo and fail to make any corrective adjustments after each decision round?

ENDNOTES 

[1] Jennifer A. Chatham and Sandra E. Cha, "Leading by Leveraging Culture," *California Management Review* 45, no. 4 (Summer 2003), pp. 20–34; Edgar Shein, *Organizational Culture and Leadership: A Dynamic View* (San Francisco, CA: Jossey-Bass, 1992).
[2] T. E. Deal and A. A. Kennedy, *Corporate Cultures: The Rites and Rituals of Corporate Life* (Harmondsworth, UK: Penguin, 1982).
[3] Joanne Reid and Victoria Hubbell, "Creating a Performance Culture," *Ivey Business Journal* 69, no. 4 (March–April 2005), p. 1.
[4] Ibid.
[5] John P. Kotter and James L. Heskett, *Corporate Culture and Performance* (New York: Free Press, 1992), p. 7. See also Robert Goffee and Gareth Jones, *The Character of a Corporation* (New York: HarperCollins, 1998).
[6] Joseph L. Badaracco, *Defining Moments: When Managers Must Choose between Right and Wrong* (Boston: Harvard Business School Press, 1997); Joe Badaracco and Allen P. Webb, "Business Ethics: A View from the Trenches," *California Management Review* 37, no. 2 (Winter 1995), pp. 8–28; Patrick E. Murphy, "Corporate Ethics Statements: Current Status and Future Prospects," *Journal of Business Ethics* 14 (1995), pp. 727–740; Lynn Sharp Paine, "Managing for Organizational Integrity," *Harvard Business Review* 72, no. 2 (March–April 1994), pp. 106–117.
[7] Emily F. Carasco and Jang B. Singh, "The Content and Focus of the Codes of Ethics of the World's Largest Transnational Corporations," *Business and Society Review* 108, no. 1 (January 2003), pp. 71–94; Patrick E. Murphy, "Corporate Ethics Statements: Current Status and Future Prospects," *Journal of Business Ethics* 14 (1995), pp. 727–740; John Humble, David Jackson, and Alan Thomson, "The Strategic Power of Corporate Values," *Long Range Planning* 27, no. 6 (December 1994), pp. 28–42; Mark S. Schwartz, "A Code of Ethics for Corporate Codes of Ethics," *Journal of Business Ethics* 41, no. 1–2 (November–December 2002), pp. 27-43.
[8] mentalfloss.com/article/30198/11-best-customer-service-stories-ever (accessed February 22, 2014).
[9] Terrence E. Deal and Allen A. Kennedy, *Corporate Cultures* (Reading, MA: Addison-Wesley, 1982); Terrence E. Deal and Allen A. Kennedy, *The New Corporate Cultures: Revitalizing the Workplace after Downsizing, Mergers, and Reengineering* (Cambridge, MA: Perseus, 1999).
[10] Vijay Sathe, *Culture and Related Corporate Realities* (Homewood, IL: Irwin, 1985).
[11] Avan R. Jassawalla and Hemant C. Sashittal, "Cultures That Support Product-Innovation Processes," *Academy of Management Executive* 16, no. 3 (August 2002), pp. 42–54.
[12] Kotter and Heskett, *Corporate Culture and Performance*, p. 5.
[13] Reid and Hubbell, "Creating a Performance Culture," pp. 1–5.
[14] Jay B. Barney and Delwyn N. Clark, *Resource-Based Theory: Creating and Sustaining Competitive Advantage* (New York: Oxford University Press, 2007), chap. 4.
[15] Rosabeth Moss Kanter, "Transforming Giants," *Harvard Business Review* 86, no. 1 (January 2008), pp. 43–52.
[16] Kurt Eichenwald, *Conspiracy of Fools: A True Story* (New York: Broadway Books, 2005).
[17] Judy D. Olian and Sara L. Rynes, "Making Total Quality Work: Aligning Organizational Processes, Performance Measures, and Stakeholders," *Human Resource Management* 30, no. 3 (Fall 1991), p. 324.
[18] Larry Bossidy and Ram Charan, *Confronting Reality: Doing What Matters to Get Things Right* (New York: Crown Business, 2004); Larry Bossidy and Ram Charan, *Execution: The Discipline of Getting Things Done* (New York: Crown Business, 2002); John P. Kotter, "Leading Change: Why Transformation Efforts Fail," *Harvard Business Review* 73, no. 2 (March–April 1995), pp. 59–67; Thomas M. Hout and John C. Carter, "Getting It Done: New Roles for Senior Executives," *Harvard Business Review* 73, no. 6 (November–December 1995), pp. 133–145; Sumantra Ghoshal and Christopher A. Bartlett, "Changing the Role of Top Management: Beyond Structure to Processes," *Harvard Business Review* 73, no. 1 (January–February 1995), pp. 86–96.
[19] For a more in-depth discussion of the leader's role in creating a results-oriented culture that nurtures success, see Benjamin Schneider, Sarah K. Gunnarson, and Kathryn Niles-Jolly, "Creating the Climate and Culture of Success," *Organizational Dynamics*, Summer 1994, pp. 17–29.
[20] Michael T. Kanazawa and Robert H. Miles, *Big Ideas to Big Results* (Upper Saddle River, NJ: FT Press, 2008).
[21] Jeffrey Pfeffer, "Producing Sustainable Competitive Advantage through the Effective Management of People," *Academy of Management Executive* 9, no.1 (February 1995), pp. 55–69.
[22] Cynthia A. Montgomery, "Putting Leadership Back into Strategy," *Harvard Business Review* 86, no. 1 (January 2008), pp. 54–60.
[23] James Brian Quinn, *Strategies for Change: Logical Incrementalism* (Homewood, IL: Irwin, 1980).
[24] Daniel Goleman, "What Makes a Leader," *Harvard Business Review* 76, no. 6 (November–December 1998), pp. 92–102; Ronald A. Heifetz and Donald L. Laurie, "The Work of Leadership," *Harvard Business Review* 75, no. 1 (January–February 1997), pp. 124–134; Charles M. Farkas and Suzy Wetlaufer, "The Ways Chief Executive Officers Lead," *Harvard Business Review* 74, no. 3 (May–June 1996), pp. 110–122; Michael E. Porter, Jay W. Lorsch, and Nitin Nohria, "Seven Surprises for New CEOs," *Harvard Business Review* 82, no. 10 (October 2004), pp. 62–72.

PART 2

Cases in Crafting and Executing Strategy

CASE 01

Mystic Monk Coffee

connect

David L. Turnipseed
University of South Alabama

As Father Daniel Mary, the prior of the Carmelite Order of monks in Clark, Wyoming, walked to chapel to preside over Mass, he noticed the sun glistening across the four-inch snowfall from the previous evening. Snow in June was not unheard of in Wyoming, but the late snowfall and the bright glow of the rising sun made him consider the opposing forces accompanying change and how he might best prepare his monastery to achieve his vision of creating a new Mount Carmel in the Rocky Mountains. His vision of transforming the small brotherhood of 13 monks living in a small home used as makeshift rectory into a 500-acre monastery that would include accommodations for 30 monks, a Gothic church, a convent for Carmelite nuns, a retreat center for lay visitors, and a hermitage presented a formidable challenge. However, as a former high school football player, boxer, bull rider, and man of great faith, Father Prior Daniel Mary was unaccustomed to shrinking from a challenge.

Father Prior had identified a nearby ranch for sale that met the requirements of his vision perfectly, but its current listing price of $8.9 million presented a financial obstacle to creating a place of prayer, worship, and solitude in the Rockies. The Carmelites had received a $250,000 donation that could be used toward the purchase, and the monastery had earned nearly $75,000 during the first year of its Mystic Monk coffee-roasting operations, but more money would be needed. The coffee roaster used to produce packaged coffee sold to Catholic consumers at the Mystic Monk Coffee website was reaching its capacity, but a larger roaster could be purchased for $35,000. Also, local Cody, Wyoming, business owners had begun a foundation for those wishing to donate to the monks' cause. Father Prior Daniel Mary did not have a great deal of experience in business matters but considered to what extent the monastery could rely on its Mystic Monk Coffee operations to fund the purchase of the ranch. If Mystic Monk Coffee was capable of making the vision a reality, what were the next steps in turning the coffee into land?

THE CARMELITE MONKS OF WYOMING

Carmelites are a religious order of the Catholic Church that was formed by men who traveled to the Holy Land as pilgrims and crusaders and had chosen to remain near Jerusalem to seek God. The men established their hermitage at Mount Carmel because of its beauty, seclusion, and biblical importance as the site where Elijah stood against King Ahab and the false prophets of Jezebel to prove Jehovah to be the one true God. The Carmelites led a life of solitude, silence, and prayer at Mount Carmel before eventually returning to Europe and becoming a recognized order of the Catholic Church. The size of the Carmelite Order varied widely throughout the centuries with its peak in the 1600s and stood at approximately 2,200 friars living on all inhabited continents at the beginning of the 21st century.

The Wyoming Carmelite monastery was founded by Father Daniel Mary, who lived as a Carmelite hermit in Minnesota before moving to Clark, Wyoming, to establish the new monastery. The Wyoming Carmelites were a cloistered order and were allowed to leave the monastery only by permission of the bishop for medical needs or the death of a family member. The Wyoming monastery's abbey bore little resemblance to the great stone cathedrals and monasteries of Europe and was confined to a rectory that had once been a four-bedroom ranch-style home and an adjoining 42 acres of land that had been donated to the monastery.

There were 13 monks dedicated to a life of prayer and worship in the Wyoming Carmelite monastery. Since the founding of the monastery six years ago, there had been more than 500 inquiries from young men considering becoming a Wyoming Carmelite. Father Prior Daniel Mary wished to eventually have 30 monks who would join the brotherhood at ages 19 to 30 and live out their lives in the monastery. However, the selection criteria for acceptance into the monastery were rigorous, with the monks making certain that applicants understood the reality of the vows of obedience, chastity, and poverty and the sacrifices associated with living a cloistered religious life.

The Daily Activities of a Carmelite Monk

The Carmelite monks' day began at 4:10 a.m., when they arose and went to chapel for worship wearing traditional brown habits and handmade sandals. At about 6:00 a.m., the monks rested and contemplated in silence for one hour before Father Prior began morning Mass. After Mass, the monks went about their manual labors. In performing their labors, each brother had a special set of skills that enabled the monastery to independently maintain its operations. Brother Joseph Marie was an excellent mechanic, Brother Paul was a carpenter, Brother Peter Joseph (Brother Cook) worked in the kitchen, and five-foot, four-inch Brother Simon Mary (Little Monk) was the secretary to Father Daniel Mary. Brother Elias, affectionately known as Brother Java, was Mystic Monk Coffee's master roaster, although he was not a coffee drinker.

Each monk worked up to six hours per day; however, the monks' primary focus was spiritual, with eight hours of each day spent in prayer. At 11:40 a.m., the monks stopped work and went to Chapel. Afterward they had lunch, cleaned the dishes, and went back to work. At 3:00 p.m., the hour that Jesus was believed to have died on the cross, work stopped again for prayer and worship. The monks then returned to work until the bell was rung for Vespers (evening prayer). After Vespers, the monks had an hour of silent contemplation, an evening meal, and more prayers before bedtime.

The New Mount Carmel

Soon after arriving in Wyoming, Father Daniel Mary had formed the vision of acquiring a large parcel of land—a new Mount Carmel—and building a monastery with accommodations for 30 monks, a retreat center for lay visitors, a Gothic church, a convent for Carmelite nuns, and a hermitage. In a letter to supporters posted on the monastery's website, Father Daniel Mary succinctly stated his vision: "We beg your prayers, your friendship and your support that this vision, our vision may come to be that Mount Carmel may be refounded in Wyoming's Rockies for the glory of God."

The brothers located a 496-acre ranch for sale that would satisfy all of the requirements to create a new Mount Carmel. The Irma Lake Ranch was located about 21 miles outside Cody, Wyoming, and included a remodeled 17,800-square-foot residence, a 1,700-square-foot caretaker house, a 2,950-square-foot guesthouse, a hunting cabin, a dairy and horse barn, and forested land. The ranch was at the end of a seven-mile-long private gravel road and was bordered on one side by the private Hoodoo Ranch (100,000 acres) and on the other by the Shoshone National Park (2.4 million acres). Although the asking price was $8.9 million, the monks believed they would be able to acquire the property through donations and the profits generated by the monastery's Mystic Monk Coffee operations. The $250,000 donation they had received from an individual wishing to support the Carmelites could be applied toward whatever purpose the monks chose. Additionally, a group of Cody business owners had formed the New Mount Carmel Foundation to help the monks raise funds.

OVERVIEW OF THE COFFEE INDUSTRY

About 150 million consumers in the United States drank coffee, with 89 percent of U.S. coffee drinkers brewing their own coffee at home rather than purchasing ready-to-drink coffee at coffee shops and restaurants such as Starbucks, Dunkin' Donuts, or McDonald's. Packaged coffee for home brewing was easy to find in any grocery store and typically carried a retail price of $4 to $6 for a 12-ounce package. About 30 million coffee drinkers in the United States preferred premium-quality specialty coffees that sold for $7 to $10 per 12-ounce package. Specialty coffees were made from high-quality Arabica beans instead of the mix of low-quality Arabica beans and bitter, less flavorful Robusta beans that makers of value brands used. The wholesale price of Robusta coffee beans averaged $1.15 per pound, while mild Columbian Arabica wholesale prices averaged $1.43 per pound.

Prior to the 1990s, the market for premium-quality specialty coffees barely existed in the United States, but Howard Schultz's vision for Starbucks of bringing the Italian espresso bar experience to America helped specialty coffees become a large and thriving segment of the industry. The company's pursuit of its mission, "To inspire and nurture the human spirit—one person, one cup, and one neighborhood at a time," had allowed Starbucks to become an iconic brand in most parts of the world. The company's success had given rise to a number of competing specialty coffee shops and premium brands of packaged specialty coffee, including Seattle's Best, Millstone, Green Mountain Coffee Roasters, and First Colony Coffee and Tea. Some producers such as First Colony had difficulty gaining shelf space in supermarkets and concentrated on private-label roasting and packaging for fine department stores and other retailers wishing to have a proprietary brand of coffee.

Specialty coffees sold under premium brands might have been made from shade-grown or organically grown coffee beans, or have been purchased from a grower belonging to a World Fair Trade Organization (WFTO) cooperative. WFTO cooperative growers were paid above-market prices to better support the cost of operating their farms—for example, WFTO-certified organic wholesale prices averaged $1.55 per pound. Many consumers who purchased specialty coffees were willing to pay a higher price for organic, shade-grown, or fair trade coffee because of their personal health or social concerns—organic coffees were grown without the use of synthetic fertilizers or pesticides, shade-grown coffee plants were allowed to grow beneath the canopies of larger indigenous trees, and fair trade pricing made it easier for farmers in developing countries to pay workers a living wage. The specialty coffee segment of the retail coffee industry had grown dramatically in the United States, with retail sales increasing from $8.3 billion to $13.5 billion during the last seven years. The retail sales of organic coffee accounted for about $1 billion of industry sales and had grown at an annual rate of 32 percent for each of the last seven years.

MYSTIC MONK COFFEE

Mystic Monk Coffee was produced using high-quality fair trade Arabica and fair trade/organic Arabica beans. The monks produced whole-bean and ground caffeinated and decaffeinated varieties in dark, medium, and light roasts and in different flavors. The most popular Mystic Monk flavors were Mystical Chants of Carmel, Cowboy Blend, Royal Rum Pecan, and Mystic Monk Blend. With the exception of sample bags, which carried a retail price of $2.99, all varieties of Mystic Monk Coffee were sold via the monastery's website (**www.mysticmonkcoffee.com**) in 12-ounce bags at a price of $9.95. All purchases from the website were delivered by United Parcel Service (UPS) or the U.S. Postal Service. Frequent customers were given the option of joining a "coffee club," which offered monthly delivery of one to six bags of preselected coffee. Purchases of three or more bags qualified for free shipping. The Mystic Monk Coffee website also featured T-shirts, gift cards, CDs featuring the monastery's Gregorian chants, and coffee mugs.

Mystic Monk Coffee's target market was the segment of the U.S. Catholic population who drank coffee and wished to support the monastery's mission. More than 69 million Americans were members of the Catholic Church—making it four times larger than the second-largest Christian denomination in the United States. An appeal to Catholics to "use their Catholic coffee dollar for Christ and his Catholic church" was published on the Mystic Monk Coffee website.

Mystic Monk Coffee-Roasting Operations

After the morning religious services and breakfast, Brother Java roasted the green coffee beans delivered each week from a coffee broker in Seattle,

Washington. The monks paid the Seattle broker the prevailing wholesale price per pound, which fluctuated daily with global supply and demand. The capacity of Mystic Monk Coffee's roaster limited production to 540 pounds per day; production was also limited by time devoted to prayer, silent meditation, and worship. Demand for Mystic Monk Coffee had not yet exceeded the roaster's capacity, but the monastery planned to purchase a larger, 130-pound-per-hour roaster when demand further approached the current roaster's capacity. The monks had received a quote of $35,000 for the new larger roaster.

Marketing and Website Operations

Mystic Monk Coffee was promoted primarily by word of mouth among loyal customers in Catholic parishes across the United States. The majority of Mystic Monk's sales were made through its website, but on occasion telephone orders were placed with the monks' secretary, who worked outside the cloistered part of the monastery. Mystic Monk also offered secular website operators commissions on its sales through its Mystic Monk Coffee Affiliate Program, which placed banner ads and text ads on participating websites. Affiliate sites earned an 18 percent commission on sales made to customers who were directed to the Mystic Monk site from their site. The affiliate program's Share A Sale participation level allowed affiliates to refer new affiliates to Mystic Monk and earn 56 percent of the new affiliate's commission. The monks had also just recently expanded Mystic Monk's business model to include wholesale sales to churches and local coffee shops.

Mystic Monk's Financial Performance

At the conclusion of Mystic Monk Coffee's first year in operation, its sales of coffee and coffee accessories averaged about $56,500 per month. Its cost of sales averaged about 30 percent of revenues, inbound shipping costs accounted for 19 percent of revenues, and broker fees were 3 percent of revenues—for a total cost of goods sold of 52 percent. Operating expenses such as utilities, supplies, telephone, and website maintenance averaged 37 percent of revenues. Thus, Mystic Monk's net profit margin averaged 11 percent of revenues.

REALIZING THE VISION

During a welcome period of solitude before his evening meal, Father Prior Daniel Mary again contemplated the purchase of the Irma Lake Ranch. He realized that his vision of purchasing the ranch would require careful planning and execution. For the Wyoming Carmelites, coffee sales were a means of support from the outside world that might provide the financial resources to purchase the land. Father Prior understood that the cloistered monastic environment offered unique challenges to operating a business enterprise, but it also provided opportunities that were not available to secular businesses. He resolved to develop an execution plan that would enable Mystic Monk Coffee to minimize the effect of its cloistered monastic constraints, maximize the potential of monastic opportunities, and realize his vision of buying the Irma Lake Ranch.

CASE 02

Airbnb in 2016: A Business Model for the Sharing Economy

John D. Varlaro
Johnson & Wales University

John E. Gamble
Texas A&M University–Corpus Christi

"In the future, you will own what [assets] you want responsibility for," commented CEO and founder of Airbnb, Brian Chesky, concerning the sharing economy in an interview with Trevor Noah on *The Daily Show* in March 2016.[1] Airbnb was founded in 2008 when Chesky and a friend decided to rent their apartment to guests for a local convention. To accommodate the guests, they used air mattresses and referred to it as the "Air Bed & Breakfast." It was that weekend when the idea—and the potential viability—of a peer-to-peer room-sharing business model was born. While not yet a publicly traded company in 2016, Airbnb had seen immense growth and success in its eight-year existence. The room-sharing company had expanded to over 190 countries with more than 2 million listed properties, and had an estimated valuation of $30 billion. Airbnb seemed poised to revolutionize the hotel and tourism industry through its business model that allowed hosts to offer spare rooms or entire homes to potential guests, in a peer-reviewed digital marketplace.

This business model's success was leveraging what had become known as the sharing economy. Yet, with its growth and usage of a new business model, Airbnb was now faced with resistance, as owners and operators of hotels, motels, and bed and breakfasts were crying fowl. While these traditional brick-and-mortar establishments were subject to regulations and taxation, Airbnb hosts were able to circumvent and avoid such liabilities due to participation in Airbnb's digital marketplace. In other instances, Airbnb hosts had encountered legal issues due to city and state ordinances governing hotels and apartment leases. Stories of guests who would not leave and hosts needing to evict them because city regulations deemed the guests apartment leasees were beginning to make headlines.

As local city and government officials across the United States, and in countries like Japan, debated regulations concerning Airbnb, Brian Chesky needed to manage this new business model, which had led to phenomenal success within a new, sharing economy.

OVERVIEW OF ACCOMMODATION MARKET

Hotels, motels, and bed and breakfasts competed within the larger, tourist accommodation market. All businesses operating within this sector offered lodging, but were differentiated by their amenities. Hotels and motels were defined as larger facilities accommodating guests in single or multiple rooms. Motels specifically offered smaller rooms with direct parking lot access from the unit and amenities such as laundry facilities to travelers who were using their own transportation. Motels might also be located closer to roadways, providing guests quicker and more convenient access to highways. It was also not uncommon for motel guests to segment a longer road trip as they commuted to a vacation destination, thereby potentially staying at several motels during their travel. Hotels, however, invested heavily in additional amenities as they competed for all segments of travelers. Amenities, including on-premise spa facilities and fine dining, were often offered by the hotel. Further, properties offering spectacular views, bolstering a hotel

EXHIBIT 1 Major Market Segments for Hotels/Motels and Bed and Breakfast/Hostels Sectors, 2015

Market Segment	B&Bs	Hotels
Recreation	80%*	70%**
Business	12%	18%
Other, including meetings	8%	12%
Total	100%	100%

*The bed and breakfast market is primarily domestic.
**Includes both domestic and international travelers. Approximately 20 percent is associated with international travelers.

Source: www.ibisworld.com.

EXHIBIT 2 Hotel, Motel, and Bed and Breakfast Industry Costs as Percentage of Revenue, 2015

Costs	Hotels/ Motels	Bed and Breakfasts
Wages	26%	23%
Purchases	27%	21%
Depreciation	10%	9%
Marketing	2%	2%
Rent and Utilities	8%	11%
Other	12%	16%

Source: www.ibisworld.com, rounded to nearest percent.

as the vacation destination, may contribute to significant operating costs. In total, wages, property, and utilities, as well as purchases such as food, account for 61 percent of the industry's total costs (see Exhibit 1).[2]

Bed and breakfasts, however, were much smaller, usually where owner-operators offered a couple of rooms within their own home to accommodate guests. The environment of the bed and breakfast—one of a cozy, home-like ambience—was what the guest desired when booking a room. Contrasted with the hotel or motel, a bed and breakfast offered a more personalized, yet quieter atmosphere. Further, many bed and breakfast establishments were in rural areas where the investment to establish a larger hotel may have been cost prohibitive, yet the location itself could be an attraction to tourists. In these areas individuals invested in a home and property, possibly with a historical background, to offer a bed and breakfast with great allure and ambience for the guests' experiences. Thus, the bed and breakfast competed through offering an ambience associated with a more rural, slower pace through which travelers connected with their hosts and the surrounding community. A comparison of the primary market segments of bed and breakfasts and hotels in 2015 is presented in Exhibit 2.

While differing in size and target consumer, all hotels, motels, and bed and breakfasts were subject to city, state, and federal regulations. These regulations covered areas such as the physical property and food safety, access for persons with disabilities, and even alcohol distribution. Owners and operators were subject to paying fees for different licenses to operate. Due to operating as a business, these properties and the associated revenues were also subject to state and federal taxation.

A BUSINESS MODEL FOR THE SHARING ECONOMY

Startup companies have been functioning in a space commonly referred to as the "sharing economy" for several years. According to Chesky, the previous model for the economy was based on ownership.[3] Thus, operating a business first necessitated ownership of the assets required to do business. Any spare capacity the business faced—either within production or service—was a direct result of the purchase of hard assets in the daily activity of conducting business.

Airbnb and other similar companies, however, operated through offering a technological platform, where individuals with spare capacity could offer their services. By leveraging the ubiquitous usage of smartphones and the continual decrease in technology costs, these companies provided a platform for individuals to instantly share a number of resources. Thus, a homeowner with a spare room could offer it for rent. Or, the car owner with spare time could offer [his or her] services a couple of nights a week as a taxi service. The individual simply signed up through the platform and began to offer the service or resource. The company then charged a small transaction fee as the service between both users was facilitated.

Within its business model, Airbnb received a percentage of what the host received for the room. For Airbnb, its revenues were decoupled from the considerable operating expenses of traditional lodging establishments and provided it with significantly smaller operating costs than hotels, motels, and bed and breakfasts. Rather than expenses related to owning and operating real estate properties, Airbnb's expenses were that of a technology company. Airbnb's business model in 2016, therefore, was based on the revenue-cost-margin structure of an online marketplace, rather than a lodging establishment, with an estimated 11 percent fee per room stay.[4] The company's business model that generated fees from room bookings had allowed its revenues to increase from an estimated $6 million in 2010 to a projected $1.2 billion by 2017 (see Exhibit 3).

A Change in the Consumer Experience and Rate

Airbnb, however, was not just leveraging technology. It was also leveraging the change in how the current consumer interacted with businesses. In conjunction with this change seemed to be how the consumer had deemphasized ownership. Instead of focusing on ownership, consumers seemed to prefer sharing or renting. Other startup companies have been targeting these segments through subscription-based services and on-demand help. From luxury watches to clothing, experiencing—and not owning—assets seemed to be on the rise. Citing a more experiential-based economy, Chesky believed Airbnb guests desired a community and a closer relationship with the host—and there seemed to be support for this assertion.[5] A recent Goldman Sachs study showed that once someone used Airbnb, their preference for a traditional accommodation was greatly reduced.[6] The appeal of the company's value proposition with customers had allowed it to readily raise capital to support its growth, including an $850 million cash infusion in 2016 that raised its estimated valuation to $30 billion. A comparison of Airbnb's market capitalization to the world's largest hoteliers is presented in Exhibit 4.

Recognizing this shift in consumer preference, traditional brick-and-mortar operators were responding. Hilton was considering offering a hostel-like option to travelers.[7] Other entrepreneurs were constructing urban properties to specifically leverage Airbnb's platform and offer rooms only to Airbnb users, such as in Japan[8] where rent and hotel costs were extremely high.

To govern the community of hosts and guests, Airbnb had instituted a rating system. Popularized by companies such as Amazon, eBay, and Yelp, peer-to-peer ratings helped police quality. Both guests and hosts rated each other in Airbnb. This

EXHIBIT 4 Market Capitalization Comparison, August 2016 (in billion $)

Competitor	Market Capitalization
Airbnb	$30.0
Hilton Worldwide Holdings	22.8
Marriot International Inc.	$17.5
Intercontinental Hotels Group	9.9

Sources: "Airbnb Valued at $30 Billion in $850 Million Capital Raise," *Fortune,* August 6, 2016; **finance.yahoo.com**.

EXHIBIT 3 Airbnb Estimated Revenue and Bookings Growth, 2010–2017 (in millions)

Costs	2010	2011	2012	2013	2014	2015	2016	2017
Estimated Revenue	$6	$44	$132	$264	$436	$675	$945	$1,229
Estimated Bookings Growth	273%	666%	200%	100%	65%	55%	40%	30%

Source: Ali Rafat, "Airbnb's Revenues Will Cross Half Billion Mark in 2015," *Analysts Estimate,* March 25, 2015, **skift.com/2015/03/25/airbnbs-revenues-will-cross-half-billion-mark-in-2015-analysts-estimate/**.

approach incentivized hosts to provide quality service, while encouraging guests to leave a property as they found it. Further, the peer-to-peer rating system greatly minimized the otherwise significant task and expense of Airbnb employees assessing and rating each individual participant within Airbnb's platform.

Not Playing by the Same Rules

Local and global businesses criticized Airbnb for what they claimed were unfair business practices and lobbied lawmakers to force the company to comply with lodging regulations. These concerns illuminated how due to its business model, Airbnb and its users seemed to not need to abide by these same regulations. This could have been concerning on many levels. For the guest, regulations exist for protection from unsafe accommodations. Fire codes and occupation limits all exist to prevent injury and death. Laws also exist to prevent discrimination, as traditional brick-and-mortar accommodations are barred from not providing lodging to guests based on race and other protected classes. But, there seemed to be evidence that Airbnb guests had faced such discrimination from hosts.[9]

Hosts might also expose themselves to legal and financial problems from accommodating guests. There had been stories of hosts needing to evict guests who would not leave, and due to local ordinances the guests were actually protected as apartment leasees. Other stories highlighted rooms and homes being damaged by huge parties given by Airbnb guests. Hosts might also be exposed to liability issues in the instance of an injury or even a death of a guest.

Finally, there were accusations of businesses using Airbnb's marketplace to own and operate accommodations without obtaining the proper licenses. These locations appeared to be individuals on the surface, but were actually businesses. And, because of Airbnb's platform, these pseudo-businesses could operate and generate revenue without meeting regulations or claiming revenues for taxation.

"We Wish to Be Regulated, This Would Legitimize Us"

Recognizing that countries and local municipalities were responding to the local business owner and their constituents' concerns, Chesky and Airbnb have focused on mobilizing and advocating for consumers and business owners who utilize the app. Airbnb's website provided support for guests and hosts who wished to advocate for the site. A focal point of the advocacy emphasized how those particularly hit hard at the height of the recession relied on Airbnb to establish a revenue stream, and prevent the inevitable foreclosure and bankruptcy.

Yet, traditional brick-and-mortar establishments subject to taxation and regulations have continued to put pressure on government officials to level the playing field. "We wish to be regulated, this would legitimize us," Chesky remarked to Noah in the same interview on *The Daily Show.*[10] Proceeding forward and possibly preparing for a future public offering, Chesky would need to manage how their progressive business model—while fit for the new, global sharing economy—may not fit older, local regulations.

ENDNOTES

[1] Interview with Airbnb founder and CEO, Brian Chesky, *The Daily Show with Trevor Noah*, Comedy Central, February 24, 2016.

[2] *IBISWorld Industry Report 72111: Hotels & Motels in the US*, www.ibisworld.com.

[3] Interview with Airbnb founder and CEO, Brian Chesky, *The Daily Show with Trevor Noah*, Comedy Central, February 24, 2016.

[4] R. Ali, "Airbnb's Revenues Will Cross Half Billion Mark in 2015, Analysts Estimate," March 25, 2015, skift.com/2015/03/25/airbnbs-revenues-will-cross-half-billion-mark-in-2015-analysts-estimate/.

[5] Interview with Airbnb founder and CEO, Brian Chesky, *The Daily Show with Trevor Noah*, Comedy Central, February 24, 2016.

[6] Julie Verhage, "Goldman Sachs: More and More People Who Use Airbnb Don't Want to Go Back to Hotels," February 26, 2016, www.bloomberg.com/news/articles/2016-02-16/goldman-sachs-more-and-more-people-who-use-airbnb-don-t-want-to-go-back-to-hotels.

[7] D. Fahmy, "Millennials Spending Power Has Hilton Weighing a "Hostel-Like" Brand," March 8, 2016, www.bloomberg.com/businessweek.

[8] Y. Nakamura and M. Takahashi, "Airbnb Faces Major Threat in Japan, Its Fastest-Growing Market," February 18, 2016, www.bloomberg.com/news/articles/2016-02-18/fastest-growing-airbnb-market-under-threat-as-japan-cracks-down.

[9] R. Greenfield, "Study Finds Racial Discrimination by Airbnb Hosts," December 10, 2015, www.bloomberg.com/news/articles/2015-12-10/study-finds-racial-discrimination-by-airbnb-hosts.

[10] Interview with Airbnb founder and CEO, Brian Chesky, *The Daily Show with Trevor Noah*, Comedy Central, February 24, 2016.

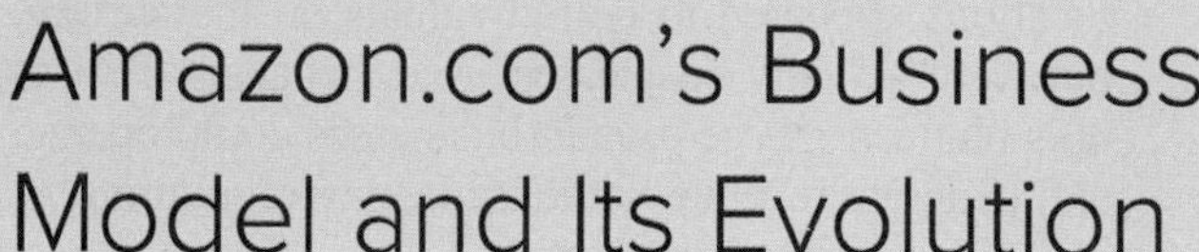

Amazon.com's Business Model and Its Evolution

Syeda Maseeha Qumer
IBS Hyderabad

Debapratim Purkayastha
IBS Hyderabad

In 2015, Seattle-based e-commerce giant **Amazon.com**, Inc. (Amazon) surprised investors by posting an unanticipated second quarterly profit in a row after struggling with profitability the previous year. In the third quarter ended September 30, 2015, Amazon's revenues increased by 20% to $23.2 billion, while net income was $79 million, compared with a net loss of $437 million in the corresponding quarter of the previous year. The revenue growth was attributed to the company's rapidly growing cloud-computing business, higher sales in North America, and initiatives to attract more customers. On the back of these unexpected quarterly results, Amazon shares surged, making it the most valuable retailer in the world surpassing Wal-Mart Stores Inc.[1] as of July 2015[2] (see Exhibits 1 and 2). *"They are showing investors that if they want to deliver profits, they can. Amazon is a dominant online retailer, well on its way to becoming one of the world's largest retailers,"*[3] said Michael Pachter, analyst at Wedbush Securities Inc.[4]

Launched as an online bookstore in 1995, Amazon quickly expanded beyond books to include all types of consumer goods. The company constantly innovated with its business model and moved from consumer electronics to cloud computing services and later into the technology business. Amazon's business model was built around low prices, a vast selection, fast and reliable delivery, and a convenient online customer experience. Besides offering customers a vast selection of products at low prices, Amazon also provided marketing and promotional services for third-party retailers and web services for developers. It was Amazon's relentless focus on value and selection along with innovations around shipping and handling cost reductions that had made it a leader in e-commerce, opined analysts.

EXHIBIT 1 Most Valuable Companies Included in the S&P 500, as of July 2015

Company	Industry	Market Value ($ billions)
Apple	Technology	$713.7
Google	Technology	462.5
Microsoft	Technology	370.1
Berkshire Hathaway	Financials	350.2
Exxon Mobil	Oil & Gas	339.3
Wells Fargo	Financials	299.5
Johnson & Johnson	Healthcare	277.9
Facebook	Technology	268
General Electric	Industrials	264.6
Amazon.com	**Retail**	**262.7**
JPMorgan Chase	Financials	258.4
Walmart	**Retail**	**233.5**

Source: http://www.usatoday.com/story/money/markets/2015/07/23/amazon-worth-more-walmart/30588783/.

Amazon reinvested much of its free cash flow in its growth. The company's strategy was to put long-term investment, market gains, and value creation ahead of short-term profits. Amazon constantly plowed cash back into the business and

EXHIBIT 2 Stock Price Performance of Amazon.com Relative to Walmart Stores, Inc.

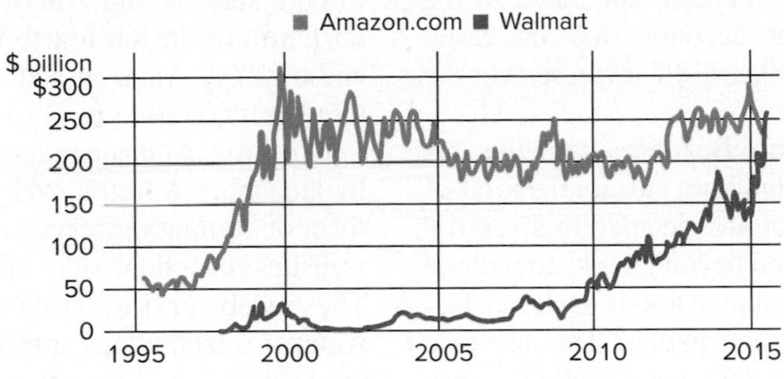

Source: **http://qz.com/462605/amazon-is-now-bigger-than-walmart/**.

continued building new businesses in the hope of getting greater returns in the future. Though the strategy helped the company in capturing a larger share of the e-commerce sector, it was consistently reporting losses. In the third quarter of 2014, Amazon spent about 12% of its revenues on technology and content including new-product development and licensing for music and video streaming. That led to the biggest quarterly loss the company had suffered in 14 years. Despite the lack of profits, Amazon's shareholders backed the strategy of the CEO, Jeff Bezos, of being indifferent to short-term earnings in anticipation of future profits.

According to some critics, if the huge investments made by Amazon did not work out, investors' patience would finally run out and the company would be in trouble. They felt that Amazon had boundless ambition, but going forward, the company would have to be selective about where it invested in order to turn profitable. Moreover, some analysts felt that between price-match guarantees, free shipping, and plans to go multi-channel, other competitors were finally catching up with Amazon in the online retail game. Amazon would need to work harder and meet the expectations of its customers to maintain its dominance in the highly competitive online retail sector, they added. Some analysts raised questions like: How can Amazon keep its prices low as it grows? Is it time for the company to adjust its "growth now profits later" formula? Should it stop entering new categories and markets and instead focus on making profits? Will Amazon shareholders continue to be patient?

BACKGROUND NOTE

Amazon was founded in June 1994 by Bezos. At that time, the internet was gaining popularity and was being considered as a potential business medium. To cash in on this trend, Bezos came up with the idea of selling books to a mass audience through the internet. In June 1995, Bezos launched his online bookstore, Amazon.com, named after the river Amazon. Amazon officially opened for business on July 6, 1995. At the beginning, Amazon's business model was based on the "sell all, carry few" strategy wherein Amazon offered more than a million books online, though it actually stocked only about 2000. The remaining titles were sourced predominantly through drop-shipping wherein Amazon forwarded customer orders to book publishers, who then shipped the products directly to the consumers. By the end of 1996, Amazon was offering about 2.5 million book titles. In 1996, the company's net sales were about $15.7 million and it reported a net loss of $5.7 million.

To attract customers, Amazon launched the Amazon Associates Program in July 1996. This was an affiliate marketing program which allowed smaller websites to sell books through a link to Amazon posted on their sites. These sites in turn received a commission of 15% for any referred purchase and 5% for any other purchase made by that consumer. The program was successful as was evident from the fact that about 800,000 associates had signed up with Amazon by September 2002. As the scale of Amazon's operations grew, its partners found it difficult to fulfill the company's quick shipment promise. As a result, Amazon began to build its own warehouses. In 1997, sales grew to $147.8 million, an 838% increase compared to the previous year. Customer accounts too increased from 180,000 to 1,510,000, a 738% increase over the preceding year.

Over a period of time, Bezos realised that his earlier business model would not sustain the kind of growth he was looking for and decided to diversify. In 1998, Amazon expanded beyond books to include all sorts of shippable consumer goods such as electronics, videos, and toys and games. This led to a reversal of its business model from a "sell all, carry few" strategy to a "sell all, carry more" model. The focus shifted to a business model built around excellent delivery and efficient logistics. Orders began to land quickly at the doorsteps of customers. To attract third party sellers, Amazon launched a feature called "Zshops" in September 1999, which enabled merchants and customers to set up online stores on Amazon for a monthly fee of $10 and a transaction cost of 1–5% of the value of the sale. Retailers and third party sellers registered on Zshop could sell their products on Amazon's site. Through Zshops, the company devised a new value proposition and by the end of 1999, Amazon's sales surpassed the billion dollar mark to reach $1.6 billion.

In early 2000, Amazon started offering technology services through its e-commerce platform called Amazon Enterprise Solutions. It entered into partnerships with traditional brick-and-mortar retailers such as Borders, Inc.[5] (Borders) and Target Corporation[6] (Target) and offered them its e-commerce and customer service infrastructure to sell their products. In 2000, Amazon's stock price dropped by more than two-thirds and analysts began to criticize the retailer for entering into too many product categories and spreading itself too thin. That year, the company posted a net loss of $1.4 billion and was on the verge of bankruptcy. To save his company from insolvency, Bezos decided to cut costs and restructure its business model. Amazon stopped selling products which were not profitable. As a cost-cutting measure, in January 2001, the company laid off 1,300 workers, closed down two warehouses, and shut down the customer-service center at Seattle. Bezos devised a strategy wherein Amazon decided not to expand its own warehouse inventory but to sell products through the warehouses of other companies. It allowed companies to sell their products online through Amazon and charged them a part of the sales. The strategy proved to be a success and Amazon posted a net profit of $5.1 million in the fourth quarter of 2002. By the end of 2002, Amazon had about 22.3 million registered users on its site.

In 2002, Amazon identified a new area of growth by launching Amazon Web Services (AWS), a platform of computing services offered online for other websites or client-side applications by Amazon. These web services provided developers access to Amazon's technology infrastructure that they could use to run virtually any type of business. Serving the needs of these developer customers required different processes, resources, and a new business model. Though at that point it was risky for Amazon to invest in new business models, Bezos went ahead and launched AWS. The move was largely successful as within five years of its launch, AWS had grown into one of the largest computing services platforms in the world.

In 2003, Amazon expanded its overseas business by launching international websites in Asia-Pacific and European countries. To deliver goods to end consumers at a reasonable price, Amazon employed a business model called the "Online Retailers of Physical Goods" wherein it obtained products directly from the distributors rather than stocking all the goods in its warehouse. In 2005, Amazon launched a free shipping program for its customers called Amazon Prime,[7] wherein customers received free two-day shipping on their purchases for a fee of $79 per year. According to industry observers, the program disrupted the retail industry by enveloping more customers into its fold and enhancing customer loyalty.

In 2006, Amazon developed a new business model aimed at serving an entirely different customer—third-party sellers. The company offered fulfillment services to sellers through the Fulfillment by Amazon (FBA) program where merchants sent cartons of their products to Amazon's warehouses while Amazon took the orders online, shipped the products, answered queries, and processed returns. Amazon gained a competitive advantage by publicly sharing its business model with small enterprises through the FBA program, said industry observers. By opening up its business to other retailers who were basically competitors, Amazon transformed its business from direct sales to a sales and service model, bringing many sellers under one roof and receiving commissions from their sales.

In late 2007, Amazon set up its research division Lab126 and launched the Kindle e-book reader. The e-book reader was a business model not only alien to Amazon but also potentially disruptive to the publishing industry. To launch Kindle, Amazon had to become an original equipment manufacturer (OEM) and partner with independent publishers to generate content for the Kindle. The Kindle was successful in the market and in the first year of its launch, Amazon sold an estimated 500,000 Kindles.

In July 2009, Amazon acquired US-based online shoe retailer Zappos for $847 million in stock and cash. In 2012, it forayed into the world of designer fashion, selling high end clothing, shoes, handbags, and accessories through its website Amazon Fashion. In April 2014, the company entered into the highly competitive video and games streaming market by releasing Fire TV.[8] Three months later, in an ambitious strategic move, Amazon debuted in the crowded smartphone market with the launch of Fire Phone. In order to bring the company closer to customers, Amazon opened its first physical store on the campus of Purdue University in West Lafayette, Indiana, in February 2015.

In 2014, Amazon's net sales increased 20% to $88.99 billion, compared to $74.45 billion in 2013. Net loss was $241 million, compared with net income of $274 million in 2013[9] (see Exhibit 3).

BUILDING AND EVOLVING THE BUSINESS MODEL

Over the years, Amazon had disrupted the online retail industry and transformed itself from an e-commerce player to a powerful digital media platform focused on growth and innovation. It constantly reinvented its business model and found new ways to create value for its customers. According to analysts, Amazon's business model was innovative

EXHIBIT 3 Amazon.com's Consolidated Income Statements, 2010–2014 (in millions of $)

	2014	2013	2012	2011	2010
Net product sales	$70,080	$60,903	$51,733	$42,000	$30,792
Net services sales	18,908	13,549	9,360	6,077	3,412
Net sales	88,988	74,452	61,093	48,077	34,204
Cost of sales	62,752	54,181	45,971	37,288	26,561
Gross profit	26,236	20,271	15,122	10,789	7,643
Fulfillment	10,766	8,585	6,419	4,576	2,898
Marketing	4,332	3,133	2,408	1,630	1,029
Technology and content	9,275	6,565	4,564	2,909	1,734
General and administrative	1,552	1,129	896	658	470
Other operating income (expense), net	133	114	159	154	106
Income from operations	178	745	676	862	1,406
Interest income	39	38	40	61	51
Interest expense	(210)	(141)	(92)	(65)	(39)
Other income (expense), net	(118)	(136)	(80)	(76)	(79)
Non-operating income (expense)	(289)	(239)	(132)	72	91
Income (loss) before income taxes	(111)	506	544	934	1,497
Provision for income taxes	(167)	(161)	(428)	(291)	(352)
Equity-method investment activity, net of tax	37	(71)	(155)	(12)	(7)
Net income (loss)	$ (241)	$ 274	$ (39)	$ 631	$ 1,152

Sources: Amazon.com Inc., Annual Reports.

EXHIBIT 4 Amazon's Business Model Evolution

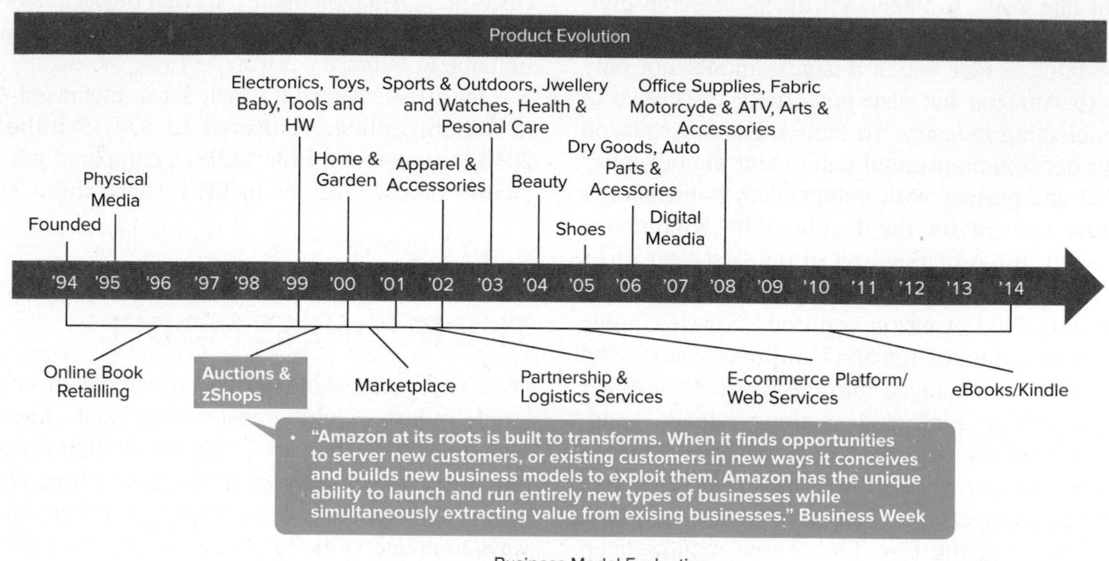

Source: **http://www.more-with-mobile.com/2014/02/google-nest-case-of-deja-vu.html.**

because it combined the company's online retail expertise with its ability to understand the needs of its customers. Amazon moved beyond books to foray into completely new product categories such as e-readers and enterprise cloud computing services (see Exhibit 4). When he founded the company, Bezos was aware that there would be a constant need to modify Amazon's business model to survive in the highly competitive online retail market. Since then, Amazon had been consistently evaluating and experimenting with its business model by developing expertise in e-commerce innovation and investing in multiple businesses to differentiate itself from brick-and-mortar retailers. According to industry experts, Amazon was successful largely because of its exceptional growth in new markets and adjoining markets. *"Amazon at its roots is built to transform. When it finds opportunities to serve new customers, or existing customers in new ways, it conceives and builds new business models to exploit them. Amazon has the unique ability to launch and run entirely new types of businesses while simultaneously extracting value from existing businesses,"*[10] said Mark W. Johnson co-founder of Innosight LLC.[11]

Amazon's business model was based on capturing growth through innovative disruption as the company believed that innovation was the key to sustainability. The four pillars of Amazon's business model were low prices, wide selection, convenience, and customer service. The attributes offered by Amazon, like low prices, vast selection, fast and reliable delivery, and a convenient online shopping experience, complemented each other. According to William C. Taylor, one of the founding editors of Fast Company, *"These value propositions are interrelated, and they all relate to the Web. We have the widest selection because we operate in the virtual world. We discount because we have a lower cost structure than physical stores do [. . .]. We also want to 'redecorate the store' for every customer. We can let people describe their preferences, analyze their past buying patterns, and create a home page specifically for them. These interactive features are going to be incredibly powerful. And you can't reproduce them in the physical world. Physical stores have to be designed for the lowest common denominator."*[12]

Low Prices

Amazon's value proposition of low prices ensured that customers got the best deal. Over the years, Amazon had proactively cut prices and offered free shipping in order to attract customers. Reportedly, the prices of goods sold by Amazon were up to 13%

lower than those prevailing in other online and brick-and-mortar stores.[13] According to industry observers, Amazon was able to offer the lowest prices possible to customers by improving its operating efficiencies, leveraging fixed costs, and allowing third party sellers to sell their products on the Amazon website and it passed on the savings to its customers in the form of lower prices. Moreover, Amazon had lower overhead costs as it did not have to maintain physical stores. The sales tax advantage it derived in some places where it did not have a physical presence also helped the company in keeping its prices low and gave it a cost advantage over brick-and-mortar stores. Also, "Frugality," one of the core values of Amazon, created significant savings for the company and allowed it to lower its prices (see Exhibit 5).

But some analysts felt that Amazon might not be as price competitive as it was perceived to be. According to them, Amazon gauged the most popular items in the online retail market and adjusted the prices of those items that shoppers were most likely to price compare. It offered huge discounts on its most popular products, while making profits on less popular ones. For instance, Amazon priced a best-selling router 20% below its competitor's price; at the same time, it priced a less popular model 29% more than its competitor. Offering consistently low prices on the best-selling items led to a perception among consumers that Amazon had the best prices overall, pointed out experts.

Wide Selection

Amazon offered customers the biggest selection of products. As of 2015, the Amazon website had about 20 product categories including Books; Movies; Music; Video Games; Electronics & Computers; Home & Garden; Tools; Toys; Kids & Baby; Grocery; Health & Beauty; Clothing; Shoes & Jewelry; Health & Beauty; Sports & Outdoors; and Automotive & Industrial. By purchasing large volumes of products directly from manufacturers, distributors, and publishers, Amazon received discounts from them. Amazon also expanded into new categories

EXHIBIT 5 Amazon Core Values

1. **Customer Obsession:** We start with the customer and work backward.

Invest in Customers First

"If you do build a great experience, customers tell each other about that. Word of mouth is very powerful."—**Jeff Bezos**

Customer Focus	Frugality	Innovation
"We start with the customer and work backward." Following a bottom-up approach, every decision at Amazon is driven by the customer's needs.	*"Amazon is spending money on things that matter to customers."* Frugality is part of the company's DNA. Amazon is continually looking for ways to do things cost-effectively.	*"I think frugality drives innovation, just like other constraints do."* Amazon is always looking for simple solutions in order to provide lower prices to its customer.

Amazon created a trusted, informative and loyal relationship with its customers.

2. **Innovation:** If you don't listen to your customers you will fail. But if you only listen to your customers you will also fail.
3. **Bias for Action:** We live in a time of unheralded revolution and insurmountable opportunity-provided we make every minute count.
4. **Ownership:** Ownership matters when you're building a great company. Owners think long-term, plead passionately for their projects and ideas, and are empowered to respectfully challenge decisions.
5. **High Hiring Bar:** When making a hiring decision we ask ourselves: "Will I admire this person? Will I learn from this person? Is this person a superstar?"
6. **Frugality:** We spend money on things that really matter and believe that frugality breeds resourcefulness, self-sufficiency, and invention!

Sources: **http://www.smartinsights.com; www.amazon.com/Values-Careers-Homepage.**

like film streaming and cloud computing. In order to expand the selection of new products available on its websites, Amazon launched programs such as the Merchants@ programs and the Syndicated Stores program wherein it enabled small businesses to offer their products for sale on its websites.

Amazon adopted a three-pronged strategy in order to widen its selection of products. It set up special teams' category-wise at its stores which focused on buying products, working with vendors, and expanding customers' selection. In its seller business where third parties were involved, Amazon appointed category managers who decided on the categories where they wanted sellers and subsequently invited them to do business. In certain categories like home décor where Amazon wanted to further augment the selection, it offered Product Ads, an advertising program that allowed sellers to promote their products on Amazon's website by uploading their catalogue. These Product Ads offered Amazon customers an unprecedented selection in a wide range of categories.

Convenience

The third pillar of the Amazon business model was convenience. Amazon offered customers hassle free anytime, anywhere ordering by using modern technology and ensuring that any product could be delivered cheaply and reliably through a simple order process accessible from customers' homes or offices. Amazon's website was browser friendly with easy-to-use functionality, fast and reliable delivery, timely customer service, feature rich content, and a trusted transaction environment. The website offered a selection of search tools to find books, music, videos, and other products based on keyword, title, subject, author, artist, publication date, etc. Amazon's website was designed to keep the download time to a minimum.

Customers could easily find products on the Amazon website through an easy to search format and also benefited from features such as user-generated reviews, product recommendations, browsing options, gift certificates, book excerpts, etc. According to analysts, the product ratings and reviews on the Amazon site made consumers informed, perceptive, and price sensitive. At Amazon, product availability was a priority and shipping was completed as close to the time of order as possible. The company ensured that a first time user became a habitual customer. For instance, if a book was unavailable, it would try to find a used copy. If the wrong product was shipped, the company made sure it accepted returns and provided the correct items as quickly as possible.

To conveniently ship items to customers, Amazon relied on an entirely automated order management system, closely linked to its suppliers and payment networks. The website offered customers up-to-date inventory availability information, estimated delivery date, and delivery shipment notifications. Customers could send products to multiple locations through different modes of payments such as credit card, wire transfer, or checks. They could check the shipping costs of each item before deciding on the mode of delivery. As soon as a customer placed an order, he/she received an e-mail confirming all the details. The customer's credit card was charged only when the order was actually shipped. Customers could track their orders in process and view the complete order history at any time using the "Your Account" feature on the company's website. Additionally, customers could cancel unshipped items, change delivery instructions and payment options, combine orders, edit gift options, and return items using the same feature. In case customers wanted to contact customer service representatives, they could do so by e-mail or phone.

Amazon operated customer service centers globally and fulfilled customer orders through the US and international fulfillment centers and warehouses. About 95% of the products were shipped on the day they were ordered. Products were packed in strong boxes with extra padding to ensure they reached customers in good condition. According to observers, the entire Amazon delivery system was so quick and convenient that it generated plenty of word-of-mouth recommendations. *"Consumers love Amazon because they can find whatever they want, order it with a click of a button, and get in within 24 hours, sometimes less. That presents an immense logistical challenge, which Amazon has solved with a vast, super-efficient, and super-expensive distribution system. These investments are driving Amazon forward and preventing rivals from catching up. More than that, they make up the essence of what the firm is,"*[14] said Adam Gale, Section editor at *Management Today.*

Customer Service

Customer service, loyalty, and customer retention were the three important aspects of Amazon's service culture. Offering compelling value to its customers had been the core strategy of Amazon since its inception. The company seduced customers through low prices, prompt delivery, a growing array of services and products, and exemplary customer attention. Amazon primarily focused on three primary customer groups—consumer customers, seller customers, and developer customers.

The company believed that a good customer experience would lead to repeat buyers. It worked relentlessly to develop and innovate ways by which customers could be served and satisfied. It provided easy-to-use functionality, fast and reliable fulfillment, and timely customer service. Amazon built a personal bond with customers by helping them make decisions through recommendations of items based on past purchases, user reviews and ratings, and suggestions on complementary purchases. Some of the customer-friendly features available on Amazon were a personalized shopping experience for each customer, book discovery through the "Search inside the Book" option, convenient checkout using "1-Click Shopping,"[15] and several community features such as Listmania,[16] Gold Box,[17] and Windowshop View.[18]

Amazon offered customers a variety of products and services, some of which it did not make any money on, but which made the customer much more valuable to it. The company invested heavily in building advanced technological infrastructure and spent huge sums of money on customer service and loyalty programs, even though it affected the operating margins of the company (see Exhibit 6). Some

EXHIBIT 6 Selected Features Offered to Consumer Customers by Amazon.com

Customer reviews	Reviews by registered users helped customers make informed purchase decisions.
Online reviews	Amazon let customers submit feedback on books and other products sold on the site. It was a popular online feature as consumers could share their thoughts with other readers.
Personalized recommendations	Amazon.com suggested books that registered users might like, based on their past purchases, customer ratings, and authors preferred.
Instant Order Update	It informed customers when they were about to purchase a product that they had already purchased.
Amazon Prime	This was a free two-day shipping for $79/year with no minimum purchase required. It could be upgraded to one-day/overnight shipping for $3.99.
FREE Super Saver Shipping	This feature provided all customers with free shipping on orders over $25 though some conditions applied.
1-Click Ordering	This allowed registered users to place an order by clicking just one button. It was not necessary for the customer to repeatedly fill in shipping and credit card information while buying products.
Where's My Stuff	This allowed customers to track the status of their shipment.
Wish List	Customers could make lists of products they would like to purchase or get as gifts. The list could be saved for online viewing by others.
Amazon.com Anywhere	This allowed customers to shop on Amazon using their wireless devices.
Purchase Circles	This showed lists of the most popular items purchased by customers in a given zip code.
Look Inside the Book	The shopper could browse through pages of books using this feature.
Search Inside the Book	Customers could search the text inside books for specific keywords.
Amazon Dash	A new device, this allowed customers to add groceries and household goods to their shopping lists using the AmazonFresh service.
May Day	The Mayday button enabled customers to connect to a live customer support professional for help with any type of product query within 15 seconds, 24/7, free of charge.

Note: The list is not exhaustive.

Sources: Compiled from various sources.

of the popular customer service initiatives launched by Amazon were Amazon Prime, Mayday,[19] One Day Delivery service,[20] Amazon Dash,[21] Amazon Lockers,[22] and Automatic refunds.[23] In December 2013, Amazon began working on a drone-based delivery system in the US called Amazon Prime Air to deliver packages at customers' doorsteps within 30 minutes in urban areas.

According to analysts, Amazon had built a deeply loyal customer base over the years. By the end of 2014, Amazon had a customer base of 270 million.[24] Experts attributed the increase in customer base mainly to the company's user-friendly website and excellent customer service. *"Amazon's customer service has always been recognized and applauded as world-class. This is remarkable, especially since it is a purely online retailer. Amazon has hardly any 'human' interactions—often considered crucial perception points for increasing customer satisfaction and loyalty—in the value delivery chain. Many companies try to emulate Amazon and cost-effectively provide higher levels of service through leveraging technology. But Amazon does not only 'deliver customer service'—they build powerful partnerships with their customers,"*[25] said Ron Kaufman, a leading customer service consultant.

AMAZON'S GROWTH WHEEL

In 2001, Bezos and his employees outlined a virtuous cycle called the "Amazon Flywheel," which they believed powered their business. Bezos once invited well-known author and business consultant Jim Collins (Collins) to participate in Amazon's executive retreat in 2001 to discuss the company's future. As part of the discussions, Collins told Bezos and his executives that they had to decide what they were best at. Drawing on Collins's concept of a flywheel, Bezos and his executives drew their own virtuous circle placing customer experience at the core of Amazon's flywheel. Internally, it was referred to as Bezos' napkin diagram as he drew it on a napkin.

Customer experience was at the core of Amazon's flywheel. According to the concept, growth would be faster when more customers visited the site. By offering low prices, a wide selection, and a great customer experience, Amazon was able to drive traffic (customers) and increase sales, which in turn attracted third party sellers and accelerated the wheel. By partnering with the best third party sellers, Amazon was able to offer a wide selection of products that added to economies of scale and allowed the company to benefit from a lower cost structure. This led to improvement in operating efficiencies and the savings were passed on to its customers in the form of lower prices and free shipping, which in turn attracted more customers (see Exhibit 7). When any part of this wheel was fed, it accelerated the loop and the cycle continued.

EXHIBIT 7 Amazon Flywheel

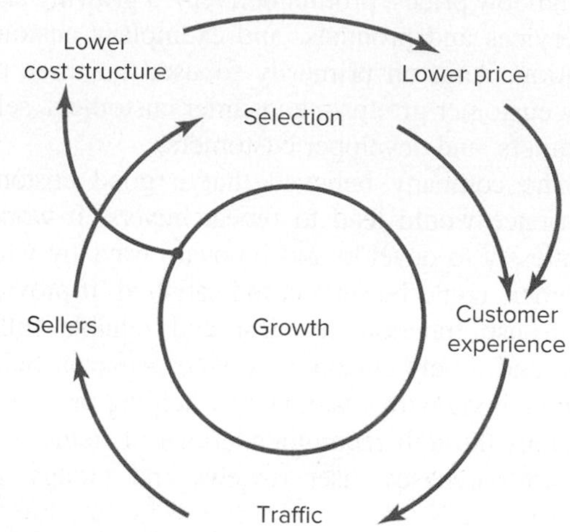

Source: www.amazon.com.

According to experts, Amazon focused on innovation, selection, price, and customer service that continuously improved the customer experience and resulted in market share gains. Commenting on the company's growth, Patrick O'Brien, a lead analyst at Verdict Retail,[26] said, *"They've managed to get top of mind on every category without doing anything creative—Amazon's 20 years isn't a marketing story, it's all about availability and scale."*[27]

GROWTH NOW, PROFITS LATER

Amazon generated revenues by selling millions of products to customers through its retail website and by charging third party sellers who sold products on Amazon's website. It also served as a platform for independent publishers to publish books on Kindle with a 35% or 70% royalty option. In addition, Amazon generated revenue from its cloud business by providing web technology infrastructure to developers and enterprises. It followed a high fixed costs and low marginal costs business model. According to Eugene Wei, a former Amazon employee, *"Amazon is a classic fixed cost business model, it uses the internet to get maximum leverage out of its fixed assets, and once it achieves enough volume of sales, the sum total of profits from all those sales exceed its fixed cost base, and it turns a profit."*[28]

Amazon's strategy was to put long-term investment and value creation ahead of short-term profits. The company constantly reinvested profits in its business and made investment decisions based on long-term market leadership considerations rather than short-term profitability. Amazon spent significantly on future expansion, and according to Bezos, the company was still in "Day One" of its growth. In a letter to shareholders in 1997, Bezos wrote, *"Long-term growth is what Amazon is about. Its focus is on years and decades, not quarters. It believes that if it has increased market leadership, it can get better deals on the goods it sells, and then increase its margins. That results in profits. This value will be a direct result of our ability to extend and solidify our current market leadership position. Market leadership can translate directly to higher revenue, higher profitability, greater capital velocity, and correspondingly stronger returns on invested capital."*[29]

Amazon adopted a profitless business model as it invested its free cash flow back into its business by expanding its operations and investing in new technology and customer service initiatives. Experts said that though Amazon generated profits on almost all transactions, it posted losses in some fiscal quarters due to significant investments in building new products, establishing warehouses, implementing and managing logistic systems, and offering free shipping. Amazon had spent about $14 billion on building 50 new warehouses since 2010. In 2012, Amazon acquired Kiva Systems Inc. (Kiva), a maker of robots that moved items around warehouses, for $775 million. In August 2014, it acquired Twitch Interactive, Inc. (Twitch), a video-game streaming company, for about $970 million. On the product front, in 2014, Amazon released its first smartphone, the Amazon Fire, and a video streaming box, Fire TV. It also spent $1.3 billion on its online streaming service Prime Instant Video. Critics alleged that Amazon sacrificed profit margins to undercut competition and gain customer loyalty. For instance, to gain a competitive advantage in the tablet market, Amazon sold the Kindle e-reader at cost, and lost about $11 per customer on its free shipping program, Amazon Prime, they said.

Despite growing sales, Amazon reported a loss in 2014. Apparently, a surge in spending on new product development and music and video licensing had resulted in a net loss of $437 million in the third quarter of 2014, the company's largest quarterly loss in 14 years.[30] In 2014, Amazon reported three losing quarters out of four and posted a yearly loss of $240 million against a net gain of $274 million in 2013.[31] When Matthew Yglesias, a blogger from Slate,[32] described the company as "a charitable organization being run by elements of the investment community for the benefit of consumers,"[33] Bezos took issue with this in a letter to shareholders and said that Amazon was a business whose strategy was to make its customers as happy as possible.

RESOURCES AND PROCESSES THAT SUPPORT THE STRATEGY

Technology

Amazon was one of the most innovative companies in the US. From the beginning, it had been at the forefront of innovation, adding and refining technology and changing the way customers shopped. On invention being a second nature at Amazon, Bezos said, *"Invention comes in many forms and at many scales. The most radical and transformative of inventions are often those that empower others to unleash their creativity—to pursue their dreams. That's a big part of what's going on with Amazon Web Services, Fulfillment by Amazon, and Kindle Direct Publishing. With AWS, FBA, and KDP, we are creating powerful self-service platforms that allow thousands of people to boldly experiment and accomplish things that would otherwise be impossible or impractical. These innovative, large-scale platforms are not zero-sum—they create win-win situations and create significant value for developers, entrepreneurs, customers, authors, and readers."*[34]

Some of the company's technological advances pioneered by Amazon included 1-Click, Recommendations, Reviews, Wish List, Autorip,[35] Kindle, Amazon Web Services, Amazon Cloud Drive,[36] Random Stow,[37] The SLAM (Scan, Label, Apply, Manifest),[38] Amazon Storyteller,[39] Amazon Studios,[40] KDP,[41] Fire TV, Fire Phone, and 3D printing.[42] Amazon had also come up with innovations that improved the customer experience such as May Day, Amazon Dash, and Amazon Echo.[43] Amazon also began working on a drone-based delivery system in the US called Amazon Prime Air that would deliver packages at customers' doorsteps within 30 minutes in urban areas.

Amazon Lab126, the research arm of the company, was responsible for innovation, research, and development of high-end consumer electronic devices like the Kindle family of products. Amazon also has a separate subsidiary, A9, that worked on innovations in search and advertising by creating mobile apps that allowed shoppers to shop conveniently on Amazon. Amazon also created its own internal experimentation platform called "Weblab" to evaluate improvements to its websites and products. In 2013, the company operated about 1,976 Weblabs worldwide. In 2014, Amazon spent about $8.72 billion on research and development.

Amazon achieved a competitive advantage by developing its own proprietary technologies, as well as technology licensed from third parties. The company's transaction-processing systems handled millions of items, multiple shipping addresses, and shipment methods. Amazon leveraged its big data resources to upgrade its customer recommendation system, which was integrated into nearly every part of the purchasing process right from product search to checkout. Explaining why Amazon continued to invest in technology, Bezos said, *"We use high-performance transactions systems, complex rendering and object caching, workflow and queuing systems, business intelligence and data analytics, machine learning and pattern recognition, neural networks and probabilistic decision making, and a wide variety of other techniques[. . .]. Many of the problems we face have no textbook solutions, and so we—happily—invent new approaches. [. . .] Technology infuses all of our teams, all of our processes, our decision-making, and our approach to innovation in each of our businesses. It is deeply integrated into everything we do. Invention is in our DNA and technology is the fundamental tool we wield to evolve and improve every aspect of the experience we provide our customers."*[44]

Product Development

The product development process at Amazon was customer-centric and focused on the value delivered to the customer. While developing new products, Amazon followed a unique philosophy called "working backward"—the company always thought from the customer's perspective back to the product, knowing at the front-end what the customer could expect, and working backwards allowing the team to build it. The goal of this approach was to drive clarity and simplicity through an explicit focus on customer. On the concept of "working backward" Bezos said, *"It is to say, rather than ask what are we good at and what else can we do with that skill, you ask, who are our customers? What do they need? And then you say we're going to give that to them regardless of whether we currently have the skills to do so, and we will learn those skills no matter how long it takes."*[45]

The "working backward" concept involved four steps—writing a press release, a Frequently Asked Questions document, a well-defined customer experience, and a User Manual.

The conceptualization of the product generally started with the product manager writing a press release for a prospective product outlining the value of the product to its potential customers. The press release outlined the features and benefits of the product and what kinds of problems it could solve. If the customers did not find the idea of the product interesting or exciting, the idea was shelved. The product manager then kept iterating on the press release until customers were satisfied with product's benefits. The feedback from the customers was then passed around internally at the company.

The next step involved preparing a Frequently Asked Questions document which included questions raised by the customers based on the press release. These questions were answered by the product team. The third step involved designing a well-defined customer experience to show the way a customer would use the product. For instance, for products with a user interface, the product development team built mock-ups of each screen that the customer used. The aim was to convey how a customer would fulfill his/her need using the product. The final step involved writing a user manual which offered details of the product and gave information to the customer on everything they needed to know to use the product.

Once the process was completed, it became clearer to the product development team what kind of product they would build. The concept of the new product was then explained to other teams within Amazon so that all the teams had a shared vision of the product. The "working backward" approach reduced the cycle time from concept-to-delivery with the customer at the forefront of every decision the company made. According to Ian McAllister, Director at Amazon, *"Once the project moves into development, the press release can be used as a touchstone; a guiding light. The product team can ask themselves, 'Are we building what is in the press release?' If they find they're spending time building things that aren't in the press release (overbuilding), they need to ask themselves why. This keeps product development focused on achieving the customer benefits and not building extraneous stuff that takes longer to build, takes resources to maintain, and doesn't provide real customer benefit."*[46]

Digitally Driven Supply Chain

Amazon had one of the most well developed supply chains in the world which included warehouse and transportation management, inbound and outbound shipping, demand forecasts, and inventory planning. Amazon's supply chain was fast paced and tightly integrated and minimized the need for human intervention by adopting advanced technology. For instance, whenever a customer ordered books online, the order-management system immediately communicated with the inventory and warehouse-management systems to find the optimal distribution center to fulfill the order and in less than a minute, the customer was informed about the delivery date of the items. The supply chain team at Amazon focused on customer experience and vendor management. This involved daily planning, analysis, metrics and communication, and managing operational relationships with vendors, fulfillment centers, and retail teams. In order to deliver products to customers quickly, Amazon installed robots in its warehouses. The robots cut out much of the hard picking work and brought items directly to workers, who then processed the orders. Though using robots was a costly investment, it resulted in cost advantages over time by streamlining operations and increasing the number of items being processed and shipped through Amazon warehouses. Amazon depended on shipping carriers such as UPS, FedEx, and USPS for delivering products to customers. The company also used drop shipping[47] wherein manufacturers shipped goods directly to consumers on its behalf.

Amazon boasted of one of the most advanced fulfillment networks in the world with large storage capacities. As of July 2015, Amazon managed about 149 active distribution centers the world over. In addition to warehouses, Amazon built sortation centers which took already packed orders from nearby Amazon fulfillment centers and sorted them according to the zip codes before sending them to shipping carriers for delivery to Amazon customers. Amazon had 19 sortation centers in the US as of November 2015.[48]

People

As of June 2015, Amazon had about 183,100 employees worldwide. These employees were empowered to make decisions quickly. Amazon was a decentralized company where independent ideas dominated over group thinking. Bezos instituted, as a company-wide rule, the concept of the "two-pizza team"—that is, any team should be small enough to be fed with two pizzas. Bezos used pizza as a metric for choosing the size of his teams. According to him, if a team could not be fed on two pizzas, then that team was too large. The concept limited the team to five to seven members. According to Bezos, the concept of the "two-pizza team" was not so much about the team size, as about autonomy and accountability and the team's fitness function.[49] Bezos felt that small teams tended to work better, communicate more effectively, move fast, and innovate and test their ideas independently. The teams were free to execute ideas, pursue creative strategies, and set their own internal priorities. According to analysts, the model helped Amazon to be innovative and attract and retain entrepreneurial talent. The "two pizza" teams conceived some of the popular features on Amazon's website such as the GoldBox deals, Bottom of the Page deals, and daily bargains on staples.

While hiring, the company looked for innovative and smart people who would increase the average level of productivity on whichever team they joined. Amazon had in place a "bar raiser" program, wherein a select group of Amazon employees volunteered to be part of interview committees. These full-time employees, called "bar raisers," in addition to their responsibilities, spent about 20 to 30 hours each week interviewing prospective hires. Bar raisers who evaluated a particular candidate got together to decide whether the candidate would be a good fit for company. If any of them had any objection to hiring the candidate, he/she was not be selected. According to Amazon, the basic premise behind this approach was to raise the bar for the next hire, so that the overall talent pool was always improving.

Marketing

To attract customers, Amazon focused on online marketing channels. Customers were directed to the company's websites primarily through a number of targeted online marketing channels such as the Associates program, sponsored search, portal advertising, e-mail marketing campaigns, and other initiatives like outdoor and TV advertising. Online advertising included paid search marketing, interactive ads on portals, e-mail campaigns, and search engine optimization.

The company also used free shipping offers such as Amazon Prime as effective marketing tools. The search feature on the Amazon site along with its product recommendation features allowed Amazon to connect its products with prospective customers.

Partnerships

Amazon partnered with or acquired a number of companies across different sectors such as Drugstore.com (pharmacy), Living.com (furniture), Pets.com (pet supplies), Wineshopper.com (wines), HomeGrocer.com (groceries), Sothebys.com (auctions), and Kozmo.com (urban home delivery). In most cases, Amazon purchased an equity stake in these partners and also charged them a fee for placement of their products on the Amazon site to promote and drive traffic to their sites. Amazon also facilitated formation of partnerships with smaller companies through its Associates programme.

Amazon also offered its e-commerce platform to other retailers and to individual sellers including technology services, merchandising, customer service, and order fulfillment. Programs such as "Merchants@" and "Syndicated Stores" enabled third party merchants to sell their products through Amazon. This arrangement provided customers a wider choice of products from numerous suppliers while helping Amazon to extend its reach into the customer base of other suppliers. In 2014, Amazon introduced the Amazon Seller App to help on-the-go sellers manage their businesses on Amazon directly from their mobile devices. Amazon's third-party sellers shipped 2 billion units in 2014, double the 2013 figure.[50] As of 2014, more than 40% of units were sold by more than two million third-party sellers worldwide.[51]

CHALLENGES

According to industry observers, Amazon over the years had disrupted other online retailers and brick-and-mortar stores and leveraged its e-commerce operations to become a retail Goliath. However, some critics felt that Amazon was too ambitious as it had been growing alarmingly and investing heavily. They felt that the strategy could backfire and that Amazon needed to be selective about the opportunities it pursued as it could not take customers and the competition for granted.

While Amazon was trying to dominate the online retail sector with its aggressive strategies, its competitors were not far behind. Between price-match guarantees, free shipping, and efforts to go multi-channel, other retailers were finally catching up with Amazon in the online retail game. Its biggest rival, Wal-Mart, was making online sales a high priority, moving forward. Other large online retailers too, like Google Shopping[52] and Alibaba.com,[53] were quickly gaining ground. Some experts felt that as the future favored multi-channel retail, Amazon would find it difficult to survive as a pure play retailer, going forward. In the technology business, Amazon was facing tough competition from tech giants such as Apple Inc.[54] and Google Inc.[55] In order to stay competitive, Amazon would have to develop some path breaking products, analysts said.

One of the biggest challenges for Amazon was to keep prices low as it grew. Reportedly, some consumers found that prices at Amazon were less compelling than they had once been. Analysts opined that Amazon needed to stay competitively priced as other retailers were finally price matching it. They said in the future, Amazon might have to raise prices to generate a profit for its shareholders, and this would threaten its reputation as a low cost leader. According to some observers, Amazon's key free shipping service Amazon Prime too had lost some appeal as rivals like Walmart and Target were challenging the Amazon shipping advantage by providing free shipping and offering instant pick up. Though Amazon admitted that it faced limitations in its quest to provide lower prices, the increase in Prime subscription fee by $20 in 2014 implied that it was facing problems from its low margin model. *"This is clearly a chink in the armor. Free shipping going from $25 to $35, a higher Prime membership rate, add-ons, slower Prime delivery, etc. seem to indicate that the business model is not as infallible as many believe. For me it all harks back to the dot-com bubble days, when huge losses for customer acquisition were acceptable, until, well—you know,"*[56] said Ken Lonyai, a digital innovative strategist.

Amazon's shipping carriers like the US Postal Service, UPS, and FedEx were considering increasing their shipping rates, a move that could affect the e-tailer's bottom line. In 2014, Amazon spent about $6.6 billion on delivery and received $3.1 billion in shipping fees,[57] which according to some analysts, was unsustainable. *"The company has been investing heavily in delivery, which gives it an edge over other retailers. The company is betting that by investing in shipping and perfecting the fulfillment process, it will create a huge barrier to competition. That has worked so far, but is it possible that Amazon could have bet wrong? Is it possible the company's greatest strength could also be the biggest threat to its business?"*[58] wondered Daniel B. Kline, editor of *The Boston Globe.*

For quite a considerable period of time, Amazon avoided paying local sales tax in states where it did not have a physical presence such as a warehouse. However, in October 2015, the US Senate passed the Bipartisan Marketplace Fairness Act, giving states the authority to collect sales taxes on online purchases even when the internet retailers were not based within their borders. If Amazon was forced to pay state sales taxes, which many analysts believed was inevitable, it would reduce its cost advantage and make it more vulnerable to competition.

Some observers criticized the fact that Amazon had a finger in every pie. According to them, the business was losing its shine as profits were dragged down by investments in fulfillment centers, updating products like the Kindle Fire tablet, and large acquisitions such as the takeover of Kiva and Twitch. Moreover, with the debacle of its Fire smartphone, Amazon took a $170 million charge related to the write-down of costs associated with unsold Fire phones.

For years, shareholders had backed Bezos's view that big investments were required to gain market share as Amazon's business opportunity was huge and would pay off in the long run. While the shareholders had been tolerant with the company's investment strategy, some analysts felt that they were increasingly showing signs of their patience wearing out as Amazon disappointed them with poor profits in 2014. Someday, investors would demand profits and that may cause Amazon to increase prices for almost everything, leading to a reduced pace of growth. *"Bezos seems driven by legacy, so it's unlikely he'll be content until Amazon is the last giant standing. Unfortunately for that dream, there is a little thing called competition and anti-trust legislation, which puts an inevitable cap on how big Amazon can be without being split apart. Nothing lasts forever, let alone grows forever. Eventually, Amazon's growth will stop, and then Bezos won't be able to hold off his investors any more. They will want their pay off, which means the firm will no longer be able to hold onto the lead over its rivals on price and innovation,"*[59] said Gale.

However, Bezos remained undaunted. He said Amazon's business model would continue to be to invest in its future. According to him, *"If you're going to take bold bets, they're going to be experiments. And if they're experiments you don't know ahead of time if they're going to work. Experiments are by their very nature prone to failure. But a few big successes compensate for dozens and dozens of things that didn't work. I've made billions of dollars of failures at Amazon.com. None of those things are fun, but they don't matter. What really matters is that companies that don't continue to experiment—companies that don't embrace failure—they eventually get in a desperate position, where the only thing they can do is make a 'Hail Mary' bet at the very end."*[60]

THE ROAD AHEAD

Going forward, the company planned to launch new digital products and service categories, build more fulfillment centers, power AWS, and expand the Kindle Fire Ecosystem. The company also planned to hire 100,000 people in North America for the holiday season.

In July 2015, Amazon surpassed Wal-Mart as the world's largest retailer by market value after a surprise second quarter profit that led to a surge in the company's stock value. Amazon shares rose 17%, giving the company a market value of $262.7 billion, compared to Wal-Mart's market capitalization of $233.5 billion. After it posted two consecutive quarterly profits in 2015, analysts noted that Amazon was a company capable of both investing in itself and sustaining long-term profits. Though, according to them, going forward, Amazon had a number of competitive weapons in its arsenal to drive customer loyalty and sustain market position, the battle would be tough as competitors were set to give the company a hard fight. The challenges that the company faced could severely threaten its business model, they added. About the challenges facing Amazon, Semil Shah, a columnist, had once questioned, *"Will their research arm at A9 Labs continue to provide the company with better science and experimentation? Will AWS continue to mint money for the company as enterprise shifts to hybrid cloud management models? Will the company be able to maintain its ability to execute across so many different types of business lines, let alone maintain focus? What types of acquisitions will it make? Will they stumble with respect to logistics as they bring their brand offline and local? Will they be able to carve out a sustainable piece of the mobile device ecosystem where Apple and Google have a headstart, and where Facebook most likely has to enter?"*[61]

ENDNOTES

[1] Wal-Mart was the largest retailer in the world with annual net sales of $482 billion in the fiscal year ended January 31, 2015. It operates a chain of retail stores in various formats worldwide.
[2] Shannon Pettypiece, "Amazon Passes Wal-Mart as Biggest Retailer by Market Value," www.bloomberg.com, July 24, 2015.
[3] Spencer Soper, "Amazon Posts Surprise Profit; Shares Soar," www.bloomberg.com, July 24, 2015.
[4] Wedbush Securities Inc. is a US-based financial services and investment firm.
[5] Borders, Inc. is an international bookseller based in Ann Arbor, Michigan, US.
[6] Target Corporation is one of the leading discount retailers in the US.
[7] In 2005, Bezos launched Amazon Prime, a membership program which offered customers a free two-day shipping on their purchases for a fee of $79 per year. In 2014, Amazon raised the annual fee for the Amazon Prime membership by $20 to $99, attributing the hike to an increase in fuel and shipping costs.
[8] Fire TV is a set-top box that plugs into HDTV for easy and instant access to Netflix, Prime Instant Video, Hulu Plus, and low-cost video rentals.
[9] "Amazon.com Announces Fourth Quarter Sales up 15% to $29.33 Billion," http://phx.corporate-ir.net, January 29, 2015.
[10] Mark W. Johnson, "Amazon's Smart Innovation Strategy," www.businessweek.com, April 12, 2010.
[11] Innosight LLC is a US-based strategic innovation consulting and investing company.
[12] William C. Taylor, "Who's Writing the Book on Web Business?" www.fastcompany.com, October 31, 1996.
[13] JP Mangalindan, "Amazon's Core? Frugality," http://fortune.com, March 26, 2012.
[14] Adam Gale, "Will Amazon Ever Be Profitable?" www.managementtoday.co.uk, July 15, 2015.
[15] This feature allows registered users to place an order by clicking just one button. It is not necessary for the customer to repeatedly fill in shipping and credit card information while buying products.
[16] The Listmania feature allows customers to share compiled lists of products with other consumers. These lists may be created using any product sold or offered on Amazon.
[17] Gold Box highlights special deals offered by Amazon by the day, hour, or availability.
[18] Windowshop View allows users on the website to browse products and view them in a 3D-simulated environment to get the feel of walking through an aisle.
[19] A new customer support feature called Mayday was launched on the company's new Kindle Fire HDX tablet in September 2013. The Mayday button enables customers to connect to a live customer support professional for help with any type of product query within 15 seconds, 24/7, free of charge.
[20] In November 2013, Amazon in collaboration with US Postal Service rolled out its One Day Delivery service to deliver packages to Amazon Prime members on Sunday. The service was initially started in Los Angeles and New York and later extended to Dallas, Houston, New Orleans, and Phoenix.
[21] In April 2014, Amazon launched a new device called named Amazon Dash that allowed customers to add groceries and household goods to their shopping lists using the AmazonFresh service. The Dash is a wand-like wireless device that includes a microphone and a barcode scanner, enabling customers to add items to an AmazonFresh shopping list by scanning a product's bar code or speaking its name.
[22] Amazon Locker is a self-service delivery location where customers can pick up and return their Amazon orders at their convenience with no additional costs. These lockers are available in a variety of locations throughout the US.
[23] In 2013, Amazon launched a new customer service tool called Automatic refunds where it proactively refunded customers if it felt that its customer experience was not up to the mark.
[24] www.statista.com/statistics/237810/number-of-active-amazon-customer-accounts-worldwide/
[25] Ron Kaufman, "Amazon Does Not 'Deliver Customer Service,' They Build Powerful Partnerships," http://ronkaufman.com, June 9, 2015.
[26] Verdict Retail is a UK-based retail consultancy.
[27] Thomas Hobbs, "Amazon at 20: The Brand, the Challenges and the Future," www.marketingweek.com, July 15, 2015.

[28] "Amazon and the 'Profitless Business Model' Fallacy," www.eugenewei.com, October 26, 2013.
[29] Jacob Donnelly, "Amazon: Its Business Model Explained," http://seekingalpha.com, October 27, 2014.
[30] Greg Bensinger, "Amazon's Spending Leads to Biggest Quarterly Loss in 14 Years," www.wsj.com, October 23, 2014.
[31] Megan Geuss, "Amazon Reports Modest Q4 Earnings and 2014 Loss, but Stock Soars," http://arstechnica.com, January 30, 2015.
[32] *Slate* is a daily online magazine.
[33] Matthew Yglesias, "Amazon Profits Fall 45 Percent, Still the Most Amazing Company in the World," www.slate.com, January 29, 2013.
[34] http://www.sec.gov/Archives/edgar/data/1018724/000119312512161812/d329990dex991.htm
[35] Amazon AutoRip gives customers free MP3 versions of CDs and vinyl music they purchase from Amazon. More than 350,000 albums are available for AutoRip.
[36] Amazon Cloud Drive lets customers securely store their digital files on the Amazon cloud and access them anywhere using the Cloud Drive desktop client or any web browser.
[37] Random stow assigns products across the warehouse based on prediction of order frequency. The items are stored in a random order at fulfillment centers so that items on the same order are nearer to each other and could be picked up easily.
[38] At the end of the packing process, packages move along conveyor belts to the SLAM where the package is weighed, the barcode on the package is scanned, and an address label is printed and added to the package. The whole process takes less than 1 second per package.
[39] Amazon Storyteller is a new application from Amazon Studios that turns a movie script into a storyboard. Users can choose the backgrounds, characters, and props to visually tell a story.
[40] Amazon Studios is the movie and series production arm of Amazon.
[41] Kindle Direct Publishing provides authors the opportunity to publish their books and earn revenue.
[42] In July 2014, Amazon launched a new store for 3D printed products, which has over 200 listings that can be customized by material, color, style, text, or size.
[43] Echo is a hands-free device designed around voice wherein a user asks for information and gets answers instantly.
[44] "Why I, Jeff Bezos, Keep Spending Billions on Amazon R&D," www.businessinsider.com, April 27, 2011.
[45] Daniel Lyons, "We Start with the Customer and We Work Backward," www.slate.com, December 24, 2009.
[46] "Amazon (company): What Is Amazon's Approach to Product Development and Product Management?" www.quora.com, May 18, 2012.
[47] Drop shipping is a supply chain management technique in which the retailer does not keep goods in stock, but instead transfers customer orders and shipment details to either the manufacturer or a wholesaler who then directly ships the goods to the customer.
[48] "Amazon Global Fulfillment Center Network," www.mwpvl.com, 2015.
[49] A fitness function is a single key business metric to provide the team with focus and accountability that the senior executive team agrees on with the team lead.
[50] Phil Wahba, "Amazon Gets Needed Boost in 2014 from Outside Sellers," http://fortune.com, January 5, 2015.
[51] Ryan Mac, "Jeff Bezos' Letter to Shareholders: 'Don't Just Swipe Right, Get Married (A Lot),'" www.forbes.com, April 24, 2015.
[52] Google Shopping is a shopping search engine from Google that allows users to find products for sale from online merchants and compare prices between different vendors.
[53] Alibaba.com is one of the leading Chinese e-commerce companies.
[54] Apple Inc. is a leading US-based technology company that designs, manufactures, and markets mobile communication and media devices, personal computers, and portable digital music players and sells a variety of related software, services, and third-party digital content and applications.
[55] Google Inc. is one of the biggest technology companies in the world involved in Internet-related services and products, computer software, and telecommunications equipment.
[56] George Anderson, "Is Amazon Prime Suffering from Its Own Success?" www.forbes.com, August 1, 2014.
[57] Steve Denning, "The Future of Amazon, Apple, Facebook and Google," www.forbes.com, April 9, 2015.
[58] "Is This the Biggest Threat to Amazon's Business Model?" www.fool.com, June 8, 2015.
[59] Adam Gale, "Will Amazon Ever Be Profitable?" www.managementtoday.co.uk, July 15, 2015.
[60] Jillian D'onfro, "Jeff Bezos: Here's Why It Wouldn't Matter If the Fire Phone Were a Flop," www.businessinsider.in, December 2, 2014.
[61] Semil Shah, "The Future of Amazon: Ambitious, Diverse, and Expansive," http://techcrunch.com, September 9, 2012.

CASE 04

Costco Wholesale in 2016: Mission, Business Model, and Strategy

connect

Arthur A. Thompson Jr.
The University of Alabama

Four years after being appointed as Costco Wholesale's president and chief executive officer, Craig Jelinek was proving fully capable of cementing the company's standing as one of the world's biggest and best consumer goods merchandisers. His predecessor, Jim Sinegal, cofounder and CEO of Costco Wholesale from 1983 until year-end 2011, had been the driving force behind Costco's 28-year evolution from a startup entrepreneurial venture into the third largest retailer in the United States, the seventh largest retailer in the world, and the undisputed leader of the discount warehouse and wholesale club segment of the North American retailing industry. Jelinek was handpicked by Sinegal to be his successor. Since January 2012, Jelinek had presided over Costco's growth from annual revenues of $89 billion and 598 membership warehouses at year-end fiscal 2011 to annual revenues of $116 billion and 686 membership warehouses at year-end fiscal 2015. Going into 2016, Costco ranked as the second largest retailer in both the United States and the world (behind Walmart).

COMPANY BACKGROUND

The membership warehouse concept was pioneered by discount merchandising sage Sol Price, who opened the first Price Club in a converted airplane hangar on Morena Boulevard in San Diego in 1976. Price Club lost $750,000 in its first year of operation, but by 1979 it had two stores, 900 employees, 200,000 members, and a $1 million profit. Years earlier, Sol Price had experimented with discount retailing at a San Diego store called Fed-Mart. Jim Sinegal got his start in retailing at the age of 18, loading mattresses for $1.25 an hour at Fed-Mart while attending San Diego Community College. When Sol Price sold Fed-Mart, Sinegal left with Price to help him start the San Diego Price Club store; within a few years, Sol Price's Price Club emerged as the unchallenged leader in member warehouse retailing, with stores operating primarily on the West Coast.

Although Price originally conceived Price Club as a place where small local businesses could obtain needed merchandise at economical prices, he soon concluded that his fledgling operation could achieve far greater sales volumes and gain buying clout with suppliers by also granting membership to individuals—a conclusion that launched the deep-discount warehouse club industry on a steep growth curve.

When Sinegal was 26, Sol Price made him the manager of the original San Diego store, which had become unprofitable. Price saw that Sinegal had a special knack for discount retailing and for spotting what a store was doing wrong (usually either not being in the right merchandise categories or not selling items at the right price points)—the very things that Sol Price was good at and that were at the root of Price Club's growing success in the marketplace. Sinegal soon got the San Diego store back into the black. Over the next several years, Sinegal continued to build his prowess and talents for discount merchandising. He mirrored Sol Price's attention to detail and absorbed all the nuances and subtleties of his mentor's style of operating—constantly improving store operations, keeping operating costs and overhead low, stocking items that moved quickly, and charging ultra-low prices that kept customers coming back to shop. Realizing that he had mastered the tricks of running a successful membership warehouse business from Sol Price, Sinegal decided to leave Price Club and form his own warehouse club operation.

Sinegal and Seattle entrepreneur Jeff Brotman (now chair of Costco's board of directors) founded Costco, and the first Costco store began operations in Seattle in 1983, the same year that Walmart launched its warehouse membership format, Sam's Club. By the end of 1984, there were nine Costco stores in five states serving over 200,000 members. In December 1985, Costco became a public company, selling shares to the public and raising additional capital for expansion. Costco became the first ever U.S. company to reach $1 billion in sales in less than six years. In October 1993, Costco merged with Price Club. Jim Sinegal became CEO of the merged company, presiding over 206 PriceCostco locations, with total annual sales of $16 billion. Jeff Brotman, who had functioned as Costco's chair since the company's founding, became vice chair of PriceCostco in 1993, and was elevated to chair of the company's board of directors in December 1994, a position he continued to hold in 2016.

In January 1997, after the spin-off of most of its non-warehouse assets to Price Enterprises Inc., PriceCostco changed its name to Costco Companies Inc. When the company reincorporated from Delaware to Washington in August 1999, the name was changed to Costco Wholesale Corporation. The company's headquarters was in Issaquah, Washington, not far from Seattle.

Jim Sinegal's Leadership Style

Sinegal was far from the stereotypical CEO. He dressed casually and unpretentiously, often going to the office or touring Costco stores wearing an open-collared cotton shirt that came from a Costco bargain rack and sporting a standard employee name tag that said, simply, "Jim." His informal dress and unimposing appearance made it easy for Costco shoppers to mistake him for a store clerk. He answered his own phone, once telling ABC News reporters, "If a customer's calling and they have a gripe, don't you think they kind of enjoy the fact that I picked up the phone and talked to them?"[1]

Sinegal spent considerable time touring Costco stores, using the company plane to fly from location to location and sometimes visiting 8 to 10 stores daily (the record for a single day was 12). Treated like a celebrity when he appeared at a store (the news "Jim's in the store" spread quickly), Sinegal made a point of greeting store employees. He observed, "The employees know that I want to say hello to them, because I like them. We have said from the very beginning: 'We're going to be a company that's on a first-name basis with everyone.'"[2] Employees genuinely seemed to like Sinegal. He talked quietly, in a commonsensical manner that suggested what he was saying was no big deal.[3] He came across as kind yet stern, but he was prone to display irritation when he disagreed sharply with what people were saying to him.

In touring a Costco store with the local store manager, Sinegal was very much the person-in-charge. He functioned as producer, director, and knowledgeable critic. He cut to the chase quickly, exhibiting intense attention to detail and pricing, wandering through store aisles firing a barrage of questions at store managers about sales volumes and stock levels of particular items, critiquing merchandising displays or the position of certain products in the stores, commenting on any aspect of store operations that caught his eye, and asking managers to do further research and get back to him with more information whenever he found their answers to his questions less than satisfying. Sinegal had tremendous merchandising savvy, demanded much of store managers and employees, and definitely set the tone for how the company operated its discounted retailing business. Knowledgeable observers regarded Jim Sinegal's merchandising expertise as being on a par with Walmart's legendary founder, Sam Walton.

In September 2011, at the age of 75, Jim Sinegal informed Costco's board of directors of his intention to step down as chief executive officer of the company effective January 2012. The board elected Craig Jelinek, president and chief operating officer since February 2010, to succeed Sinegal and hold the titles of both president and chief executive officer. Jelinek was a highly experienced retail executive with 37 years in the industry, 28 of them at Costco, where he started as one of the company's first warehouse managers in 1984. He had served in every major role related to Costco's business operations and merchandising activities during his tenure. When he stepped down as CEO, Sinegal retained his position on the company's board of directors and, at the age of 79, was reelected to another three-year term on Costco's board in December 2015.

COSTCO WHOLESALE IN 2016

In January 2016, Costco was operating 698 membership warehouses, including 488 in the United States and Puerto Rico, 90 in Canada, 36 in Mexico, 27 in the United Kingdom, 24 in Japan, 12 in South Korea, 11 in Taiwan, 8 in Australia, and 2 in Spain. Costco also sold merchandise to members at websites in the United States, Canada, the United Kingdom, Mexico, and South Korea. Over 81 million cardholders were entitled to shop at Costco, generating over $2.5 billion in membership fees for the company. Annual sales per store averaged about $166 million ($3.2 million per week), some 86 percent higher than the $89 million per year and $3.4 million per week averages for Sam's Club, Costco's chief competitor. In 2014, 165 of Costco's warehouses generated sales exceeding $200 million annually, up from 56 in 2010; and 60 warehouses had sales exceeding $250 million, including 2 that had more than $400 million in sales.[4] Costco was the only national retailer in the history of the United States that could boast of average annual revenue in excess of $160 million per location.

Exhibit 1 contains a financial and operating summary for Costco for fiscal years 2000, 2005, and 2011–2015.

COSTCO'S MISSION, BUSINESS MODEL, AND STRATEGY

Numerous company documents stated that Costco's mission in the membership warehouse business was "To continually provide our members with quality goods and services at the lowest possible prices."[5] However, in their "Letter to Shareholders" in the

EXHIBIT 1 Selected Financial and Operating Data for Costco Wholesale Corp., Fiscal Years 2000, 2005, and 2011–2015 ($ in millions, except for per share data)

	Fiscal Years Ending on Sunday Closest to August 31					
Selected Income Statement Data	**2015**	**2014**	**2013**	**2011**	**2005**	**2000**
Net sales	$113,666	$110,212	$102,870	$ 87,048	$ 51,862	$ 31,621
Membership fees	2,533	2,428	2,286	1,867	1,073	544
Total revenue	116,199	112,640	105,156	88,915	52,935	32,164
Operating expenses						
Merchandise costs	101,065	98,458	91,948	77,739	46,347	28,322
Selling, general, and administrative	11,445	10,899	10,104	8,682	5,044	2,755
Preopening expenses	65	63	51	46	53	42
Provision for impaired assets and store closing costs	–––	–––	–––	9	16	7
Operating income	3,624	3,220	3,053	2,439	1,474	1,037
Other income (expense)						
Interest expense	(124)	(113)	(99)	(116)	(34)	(39)
Interest income and other	104	90	97	60	109	54
Income before income taxes	3,604	3,197	3,051	2,383	1,549	1,052
Provision for income taxes	1,195	1,109	990	841	486	421

Selected Income Statement Data	2015	2014	2013	2011	2005	2000
Net income	$ 2,377	$ 2,058	$ 2,039	$ 1,462	$ 1,063	$ 631
Diluted net income per share	$ 5.37	$ 4.65	$ 4.63	$ 3.30	$ 2.18	$ 1.35
Dividends per share (not including special dividend of $5.00 in 2015 and $7.00 in 2013	$ 1.51	$ 1.33	$ 1.17	$ 0.89	0.43	0.00
Millions of shares used in per share calculations	442.7	442.5	440.5	443.1	492.0	475.7
Balance Sheet Data						
Cash and cash equivalents	$ 4,801	$ 5,738	$ 4,644	$ 4,009	$ 2,063	$ 525
Merchandise inventories	8,908	8,456	7,894	6,638	4,015	2,490
Current assets	17,299	17,588	15,840	13,706	8,238	3,470
Current liabilities	16,540	14,412	13,257	12,050	6,761	3,404
Net property and equipment	15,401	14,830	13,881	12,432	7,790	4,834
Total assets	33,440	33,024	30,283	26,761	16,514	8,634
Long-term debt	4,864	5,093	4,998	2,153	711	790
Stockholders' equity	10,843	12,515	11,012	12,573	8,881	4,240
Cash Flow Data						
Net cash provided by operating activities	$ 4,285	$ 3,984	$ 3,437	$ 3,198	$ 1,773	$ 1,070
Warehouse Operations						
Warehouses at beginning of year[a]	663	634	608	572	417	292
New warehouses opened (including relocations)	26	30	26	24	21	25
Existing warehouses closed (including relocations)	(3)	(1)	0	(4)	(5)	(4)
Warehouses at end of year	686	663	634	592	433	313
Net sales per warehouse open at year-end (in millions)[b]	$ 165.7	$ 164.0	$ 162.0	$ 147.1	$ 119.8	$ 101.0
Average annual growth at warehouses open more than a year	7%	6%	6%	10%	7%	11%
Members at Year-End						
Businesses (000s)	7,100	6,900	6,600	6,300	5,000	4,200
Gold Star members (000s)	34,000	31,600	28,900	25,000	16,200	10,500
Add-on cardholders (employees of business members, spouses of Gold Star members)	40,200	37,900	35,700	32,700	n.a.	n.a.
Total cardholders	81,300	76,400	71,200	64,000	—	—

a. Prior to 2011, the company's warehouses, 30 of which were opened in 2007 and two others in 2008-2009, were consolidated and reported as part of Costco's total operations at the beginning of fiscal 2011.
b. Sales for new warehouses opened during the year are annualized.

Note: Some totals may not add due to rounding and the fact that some line items in the company's statement of income were not included in this summary, for reasons of simplicity.

Sources: Company 10-K reports for fiscal years 2000, 2005, 2011, 2013, and 2015.

company's 2011 Annual Report, Costco's three top executives—Jeff Brotman, Jim Sinegal, and Craig Jelinek—provided a more expansive view of Costco's mission, stating:[6]

> The company will continue to pursue its mission of bringing the highest quality goods and services to market at the lowest possible prices while providing excellent customer service and adhering to a strict code of ethics that includes taking care of our employees and members, respecting our suppliers, rewarding our shareholders, and seeking to be responsible corporate citizens and environmental stewards in our operations around the world.

The centerpiece of Costco's business model entailed generating high sales volumes and rapid inventory turnover by offering fee-paying members attractively low prices on a limited selection of nationally branded and selected private-label products in a wide range of merchandise categories. Rapid inventory turnover—when combined with the low operating costs achieved by volume purchasing, efficient distribution, and reduced handling of merchandise in no-frills, self-service warehouse facilities—enabled Costco to operate profitably at significantly lower gross margins than traditional wholesalers, mass merchandisers, supermarkets, and supercenters. Membership fees were a critical element of Costco's business model because they provided sufficient supplemental revenues to boost the company's overall profitability to acceptable levels. Indeed, it was common for Costco's membership fees to exceed its entire net income, meaning that the rest of Costco's worldwide business operated on a slightly below breakeven basis (see Exhibit 1)—which translated into Costco's prices being exceptionally competitive when compared to the prices that Costco members paid when shopping elsewhere.

A second important business model element was that Costco's high sales volume and rapid inventory turnover generally allowed it to sell and receive cash for inventory before it had to pay many of its merchandise vendors, even when vendor payments were made in time to take advantage of early payment discounts. Thus, Costco was able to finance a big percentage of its merchandise inventory through the payment terms provided by vendors rather than by having to maintain sizable working capital (defined as current assets minus current liabilities) to facilitate timely payment of suppliers.

Costco's Strategy

The key elements of Costco's strategy were ultra-low prices, a limited selection of nationally branded and private-label products, a "treasure hunt" shopping environment, strong emphasis on low operating costs, and ongoing expansion of its geographic network of store locations.

Pricing Costco's philosophy was to keep customers coming in to shop by wowing them with low prices and thereby generating big sales volumes. Examples of Costco's 2015 sales volumes that contributed to low prices in particular product categories included 156,00 carats of diamonds, meat sales of $6.4 billion, seafood sales of $1.3 billion, television sales of $1.8 billion, fresh produce sales of $5.8 billion (sourced from 44 countries), 83 million rotisserie chickens, 7.9 million tires, 41 million prescriptions, 6 million pairs of glasses, and 128 million hot dog/soda pop combinations. Costco was the world's largest seller of fine wines ($965 million out of total 2015 wine sales of $1.7 billion).

For many years, a key element of Costco's pricing strategy had been to cap its markup on brand-name merchandise at 14 percent (compared to 20 to 50 percent markups at other discounters and many supermarkets). Markups on Costco's private-label Kirkland Signature items were a maximum of 15 percent, but the sometimes fractionally higher markups still resulted in Kirkland Signature items being priced about 20 percent below comparable name-brand items. Kirkland Signature products—which included vitamins, juice, bottled water, coffee, spices, olive oil, canned salmon and tuna, nuts, laundry detergent, baby products, dog food, luggage, cookware, trash bags, batteries, wines and spirits, paper towels and toilet paper, and clothing—were designed to be of *equal or better* quality than national brands.

As a result of these low markups, Costco's prices were just fractionally above breakeven levels, producing net sales revenues (not counting membership fees) that exceeded all operating expenses (merchandise costs + selling, general, and administrative expenses + preopening expenses and store relocation expenses) and contributed only several million dollars to operating profits. As can be verified from Exhibit 1, without the revenues from membership fees, Costco's net income after taxes would be miniscule because of its ultra-low pricing strategy and practice of capping the margins on branded goods at 14 percent and private-label goods at 15 percent).

Jim Sinegal explained the company's approach to pricing:

> We always look to see how much of a gulf we can create between ourselves and the competition. So that the competitors eventually say, "These guys are crazy. We'll compete somewhere else." Some years ago, we were selling a hot brand of jeans for $29.99. They were $50 in a department store. We got a great deal on them and could have sold them for a higher price but we went down to $29.99. Why? We knew it would create a riot.[7]

At another time, he said:

> We're very good merchants, and we offer value. The traditional retailer will say: "I'm selling this for $10. I wonder whether we can get $10.50 or $11." We say: "We're selling this for $9. How do we get it down to $8?" We understand that our members don't come and shop with us because of the window displays or the Santa Claus or the piano player. They come and shop with us because we offer great values.[8]

Indeed, Costco's markups and prices were so fractionally above the level needed to cover companywide operating costs and interest expenses that Wall Street analysts had criticized Costco management for going all out to please customers at the expense of increasing profits for shareholders. One retailing analyst said, "They could probably get more money for a lot of the items they sell."[9] During his tenure as CEO, Sinegal had never been impressed with Wall Street calls for Costco to abandon its ultra-low pricing strategy, commenting: "Those people are in the business of making money between now and next Tuesday. We're trying to build an organization that's going to be here 50 years from now."[10] He went on to explain why Costco's approach to pricing would remain unaltered during his tenure:

> When I started, Sears, Roebuck was the Costco of the country, but they allowed someone else to come in under them. We don't want to be one of the casualties. We don't want to turn around and say, "We got so fancy we've raised our prices, and all of a sudden a new competitor comes in and beats our prices."[11]

Product Selection Whereas typical supermarkets stocked about 40,000 items and a Walmart Supercenter or a SuperTarget might have 125,000 to 150,000 items for shoppers to choose from, Costco's merchandising strategy was to provide members with a selection of approximately 3,700 active items that could be priced at bargain levels and thus provide members with significant cost savings. Of these, about 85 percent were quality brand-name products and 15 percent carried the company's private-label Kirkland Signature brand, which were a growing percentage (over 20 percent) of merchandise sales. Management believed that there were opportunities to increase the number of Kirkland Signature selections and gradually build sales penetration of Kirkland-branded items to 30 percent of total sales.

Costco's product range covered a broad spectrum—rotisserie chicken, all types of fresh meats, seafood, fresh and canned fruits and vegetables, paper products, cereals, coffee, dairy products, cheeses, frozen foods, flat-screen televisions, iPods, digital cameras, fresh flowers, fine wines, caskets, baby strollers, toys and games, musical instruments, ceiling fans, vacuum cleaners, books, apparel, cleaning supplies, DVDs, light bulbs, batteries, cookware, electric toothbrushes, vitamins, and washers and dryers—but the selection in each product category was deliberately limited to fast-selling models, sizes, and colors. Many consumable products like detergents, canned goods, office supplies, and soft drinks were sold only in big-container, case, carton, or multiple-pack quantities. In a few instances, the selection within a product category was restricted to a single offering. For example, Costco stocked only a 325-count bottle of Advil—a size many shoppers might find too large for their needs. Sinegal explained the reasoning behind limited selections:

> If you had ten customers come in to buy Advil, how many are not going to buy any because you just have one size? Maybe one or two. We refer to that as the intelligent loss of sales. We are prepared to give up that one customer. But if we had four or five sizes of Advil, as most grocery stores do, it would make our business more difficult to manage. Our business can only succeed if we are efficient. You can't go on selling at these margins if you are not.[12]

The approximate percentage of net sales accounted for by each major category of items stocked by Costco is shown in Exhibit 2.

Costco had opened ancillary departments within or next to most Costco warehouses to give reasons to shop at Costco more frequently and make Costco

EXHIBIT 2 Costco's Sales by Major Product Category, 2005–2015

Merchandise Categories	2015	2010	2005
Food (fresh produce, meats and fish, bakery and deli products, and dry and institutionally packaged foods)	36%	33%	30%
Sundries (candy, snack foods, tobacco, alcoholic and nonalcoholic beverages, and cleaning and institutional supplies)	21%	23%	25%
Hardlines (major appliances, electronics, health and beauty aids, hardware, office supplies, garden and patio, sporting goods, furniture, cameras, and automotive supplies)	16%	18%	20%
Softlines (including apparel, domestics, jewelry, housewares, books, movie DVDs, video games and music, home furnishings, and small appliances)	11%	10%	12%
Ancillary and Other (gasoline, pharmacy, food court, optical, one-hour photo, hearing aids, and travel)	16%	16%	13%

Sources: Company 10-K reports, 2005, 2011 and 2015.

more of a one-stop shopping destination. Some locations had more ancillary offerings than others:

	2015	2010	2007
Total number of warehouses	686	540	488
Warehouses having stores with Food Court	680	534	482
One-Hour Photo Centers	656	530	480
Optical Dispensing Centers	662	523	472
Pharmacies	606	480	429
Gas Stations	472	343	279
Hearing Aid Centers	581	357	237

Sources: Company 10-K reports, 2007, 2011 and 2015.

Costco's pharmacies were highly regarded by members because of the low prices. The company's practice of selling gasoline at discounted prices at those store locations where there was sufficient space to install gas pumps had boosted the frequency with which nearby members shopped at Costco and made in-store purchases (only members were eligible to buy gasoline at Costco's stations). Almost all new Costco locations in the United States and Canada were opening with gas stations; globally, gas stations were being added at locations where local regulations and space permitted.

Treasure-Hunt Merchandising While Costco's product line consisted of approximately 3,700 active items, some 20 to 25 percent of its product offerings were constantly changing. Costco's merchandise buyers were continuously making one-time purchases of items that would appeal to the company's clientele and likely to sell out quickly. A sizable number of these items were high-end or name-brand products that carried big price tags—like $1,000 to $2,500 big-screen HDTVs, $800 espresso machines, expensive jewelry and diamond rings (priced from $50,000 to as high as $250,000), Movado watches, exotic cheeses, Coach bags, cashmere sports coats, $1,500 digital pianos, and Dom Perignon champagne. Dozens of featured specials came and went quickly, sometimes in several days or a week—like Italian-made Hathaway shirts priced at $29.99 and $800 leather sectional sofas. The strategy was to entice shoppers to spend more than they might by offering irresistible deals on big-ticket items or name-brand specials and, further, to keep the mix of featured and treasure-hunt items constantly changing so that bargain-hunting shoppers would go to Costco more frequently than for periodic "stock-up" trips.

Costco members quickly learned that they needed to go ahead and buy treasure-hunt specials that interested them because the items would very likely not be available on their next shopping trip. In many cases, Costco did not obtain its upscale treasure-hunt items directly from high-end manufacturers like Calvin Klein or Waterford (who were unlikely to want their merchandise marketed at deep discounts at places like Costco); rather, Costco buyers searched for opportunities to source such items legally on the gray market from other wholesalers or distressed retailers looking to get rid of excess or slow-selling inventory.

Management believed that these practices kept its marketing expenses low relative to those at typical retailers, discounters, and supermarkets.

Low-Cost Emphasis Keeping operating costs at a bare minimum was a major element of Costco's strategy and a key to its low pricing. As Jim Sinegal explained:[13]

> Costco is able to offer lower prices and better values by eliminating virtually all the frills and costs historically associated with conventional wholesalers and retailers, including salespeople, fancy buildings, delivery, billing, and accounts receivable. We run a tight operation with extremely low overhead which enables us to pass on dramatic savings to our members.

While Costco management made a point of locating warehouses on high-traffic routes in or near upscale suburbs that were easily accessible by small businesses and residents with above-average incomes, it avoided prime real estate sites in order to contain land costs.

Because shoppers were attracted principally by Costco's low prices and merchandise selection, most warehouses were of a metal pre-engineered design, with concrete floors and minimal interior décor. Floor plans were designed for economy and efficiency in use of selling space, the handling of merchandise, and the control of inventory. Merchandise was generally stored on racks above the sales floor and displayed on pallets containing large quantities of each item, thereby reducing labor required for handling and stocking. In-store signage was done mostly on laser printers; there were no shopping bags at the checkout counter—merchandise was put directly into the shopping cart or sometimes loaded into empty boxes. Costco warehouses ranged in size from 70,000 to 205,000 square feet; the average size was about 144,000 square feet. Newer units were usually in the 150,000- to 205,000-square-foot range. Images of Costco's warehouses are shown in Exhibit 3.

Warehouses generally operated on a seven-day, 70-hour week, typically being open between

EXHIBIT 3 Images of Costco's Warehouses

© Joe Raedle/Getty Images

© RJ Sangosti/The Denver Post via Getty Imagess

© Chris Kleponis/Bloomberg via Getty Images

© Alastair Wallace/Shutterstock

10:00 a.m. and 8:30 p.m. weekdays, with earlier closing hours on the weekend; the gasoline operations outside many stores usually had extended hours. The shorter hours of operation as compared to those of traditional retailers, discount retailers, and supermarkets resulted in lower labor costs relative to the volume of sales.

Growth Strategy Costco's growth strategy was to increase sales at existing stores by 5 percent or more annually and to open additional warehouses, both domestically and internationally. Average annual growth at stores open at least a year was 10 percent in fiscal 2011, 6 percent in both fiscal 2013 and 2014, and 7 percent in fiscal 2015. In fiscal 2011, sales at Costco's existing warehouses grew by an average of 10 percent, chiefly because members shopped Costco warehouses an average of 4 percent more often and spent about 5 percent more per visit than they did in fiscal 2010 (see Exhibit 1 for recent average annual sales increases at existing stores). Costco expected to open 32 new warehouses in its fiscal year beginning September 1, 2016: 22 in the United States, 3 in Canada, 2 each in Japan and Australia, and 1 each in the UK, Taiwan, and Spain. As of January 2016, 12 of these had already been opened.

Exhibit 4 shows a breakdown of Costco's geographic operations for fiscal years 2005, 2010, and 2015.

Marketing and Advertising

Costco's low prices and its reputation for making shopping at Costco something of a treasure-hunt made it unnecessary to engage in extensive advertising or sales campaigns. Marketing and promotional activities were generally limited to monthly coupon mailers to members, weekly e-mails to members from **Costco.com**, occasional direct mail to prospective new members, and regular direct marketing programs (such as *The Costco Connection,* a magazine published for members), in-store product sampling, and special campaigns for new warehouse openings.

EXHIBIT 4 Selected Geographic Operating Data, Costco Wholesale Corporation, Fiscal Years 2005–2015 ($ in millions)

	United States Operations	Canadian Operations	Other International Operations	Total
Year Ended August 30, 2015				
Total revenue (including membership fees)	$84,451	$17,341	$14,507	$116,199
Operating income	2,308	771	545	3,624
Capital expenditures	1,574	148	671	2,393
Number of warehouses	487	90	120	697
Year Ended August 29, 2010				
Total revenue (including membership fees)	$59,624	$12,501	$ 6,271	$ 77,946
Operating income	1,310	547	220	2,077
Capital expenditures	804	162	89	1,055
Number of warehouses	416	79	45	540
Year Ended August 28, 2005				
Total revenue (including membership fees)	$43,064	$ 6,732	$ 3,155	$ 52,952
Operating income	1,168	242	65	1,474
Capital expenditures	734	140	122	995
Number of warehouses	338	65	30	433

Note: The dollar numbers shown for "Other" countries represent only Costco's ownership share, since all foreign operations were joint ventures (although Costco was the majority owner of these ventures); the warehouses operated by Costco Mexico in which Costco was a 50 percent joint venture partner were not included in the data for the "Other" countries until fiscal year 2011.

Sources: Company 10-K reports, 2015, 2010, and 2007.

For new warehouse openings, marketing teams personally contacted businesses in the area that were potential wholesale members; these contacts were supplemented with direct mailings during the period immediately prior to opening. Potential Gold Star (individual) members were contacted by direct mail or by promotions at local employee associations and businesses with large numbers of employees. After a membership base was established in an area, most new memberships came from word of mouth (existing members telling friends and acquaintances about their shopping experiences at Costco), follow-up messages distributed through regular payroll or other organizational communications to employee groups, and ongoing direct solicitations to prospective business and Gold Star members.

Website Sales

Costco operated websites in the United States, Canada, Mexico, the United Kingdom, and Korea—both to enable members to shop for many in-store products online and to provide members with a means of obtaining a much wider variety of value-priced products and services that were not practical to stock at the company's warehouses. Examples of items that members could buy online at low Costco prices included sofas, beds, entertainment centers and TV lift cabinets, outdoor furniture, office furniture, kitchen appliances, billiard tables, and hot tubs. Members could also use the company's websites for such services as digital photo processing, prescription fulfillment, travel, the Costco auto program (for purchasing selected new vehicles with discount prices through participating dealerships), and other membership services. In 2015, Costco sold 465,000 vehicles through its 3,000 dealer partners; the big attraction to members of buying a new or used vehicle through Costco's auto program was being able to skip the hassle of bargaining with the dealer over price and, instead, paying an attractively low price prearranged by Costco. At Costco's online photo center, customers could upload images and pick up the prints at their local warehouse in little over an hour. Online sales had accounted for about 3 percent of total merchandise sales for the past three fiscal years ($3.4 billion in fiscal 2015).

Supply Chain and Distribution

Costco bought the majority of its merchandise directly from manufacturers, routing it either directly to its warehouse stores or to one of the company's cross-docking depots that served as distribution points for nearby stores and for shipping orders to members making online purchases. Depots received container-based shipments from manufacturers and reallocated these goods for combined shipment to individual warehouses, generally in less than 24 hours. This maximized freight volume and handling efficiencies. Going into 2016, Costco had 23 cross-docking depots with a combined space of 9.3 million square feet in the United States, Canada, and various other international locations. When merchandise arrived at a warehouse, it was moved straight to the sales floor; very little was stored in locations off the sales floor in order to minimize receiving and handling costs.

Costco had direct buying relationships with many producers of national brand-name merchandise and with manufacturers that supplied its Kirkland Signature products. Costco's merchandise buyers were always alert for opportunities to add products of top quality manufacturers and vendors on a one-time or ongoing basis. No one manufacturer supplied a significant percentage of the merchandise that Costco stocked. Costco had not experienced difficulty in obtaining sufficient quantities of merchandise, and management believed that if one or more of its current sources of supply became unavailable, the company could switch its purchases to alternative manufacturers without experiencing a substantial disruption of its business.

Costco's Membership Base and Member Demographics

Costco attracted the most affluent customers in discount retailing—the average income of individual members was about $75,000, with over 30 percent of members having annual incomes of $100,000 or more. Many members were affluent urbanites, living in nice neighborhoods not far from Costco warehouses. One loyal Executive member, a criminal defense lawyer, said, "I think I spend over $20,000–$25,000 a year buying all my products here from food to clothing—except my suits. I have to buy them at the Armani stores."[14] Another Costco loyalist said, "This is the best place in the world. It's like going to church on Sunday. You can't get anything better than this. This is a religious experience."[15]

Costco had two primary types of memberships: Business and Gold Star (individual). Business memberships were limited to businesses, but included individuals with a business license, retail sales license, or other evidence of business existence. A Business membership also included a free household card (a significant number of business members shopped at Costco for their personal needs). Business members also had the ability to purchase "add-on" membership cards for partners or associates in the business. Costco's current annual fee for Business and Gold Star memberships was $55 in the United States and Canada and varied by country in its other international operations. All paid memberships for Business members included a free household card. Individuals in the United States and Canada who did not qualify for a Business membership could purchase a Gold Star membership, which included a household card for another family member (additional add-on cards could not be purchased by Gold Star members).

Both Business and Gold Star members could upgrade to an Executive membership for an annual fee of $110. Executive members were entitled to an additional 2 percent savings on qualified purchases at Costco (redeemable at Costco warehouses), up to a maximum rebate of $750 per year. Executive members also were eligible for savings and benefits on various business and consumer services offered by Costco, including merchant credit card processing, small-business loans, auto and home insurance, long-distance telephone service, check printing, and real estate and mortgage services; these services were mostly offered by third-party providers and varied by state. In fiscal 2015, Executive members represented close to 40 percent of Costco's primary membership base and generally spent more than other members. Recent trends in membership are shown at the bottom of Exhibit 1. Members could shop at any Costco warehouse. Costco's member renewal rate was approximately 91 percent in the United States and Canada, and approximately 88 percent on a worldwide basis in 2015.

Costco warehouses accepted cash, checks, most debit cards, Visa, and a private-label Costco credit card. Costco accepted merchandise returns when members were dissatisfied with their purchases. Losses associated with dishonored checks were minimal because any member whose check had been dishonored was prevented from paying by check or cashing a check at the point of sale until restitution was made. The membership format facilitated strictly controlling the entrances and exits of warehouses, resulting in limited inventory losses of less than two-tenths of 1 percent of net sales—well below those of typical discount retail operations.

Warehouse Management

Costco warehouse managers were delegated considerable authority over store operations. In effect, warehouse managers functioned as entrepreneurs running their own retail operation. They were responsible for coming up with new ideas about what items would sell in their stores, effectively merchandising the ever-changing lineup of treasure-hunt products, and orchestrating in-store product locations and displays to maximize sales and quick turnover. In experimenting with what items to stock and what in-store merchandising techniques to employ, warehouse managers had to know the clientele who patronized their locations—for instance, big-ticket diamonds sold well at some warehouses but not at others. Costco's best managers kept their finger on the pulse of the members who shopped their warehouse location to stay in sync with what would sell well, and they had a flair for creating a certain element of excitement, hum, and buzz in their warehouses. Such managers spurred above-average sales volumes—sales at Costco's top-volume warehouses ran about $4 million to $7 million a week, with sales exceeding $1 million on many days. Successful managers also thrived on the rat race of running a high-traffic store and solving the inevitable crises of the moment.

Compensation and Workforce Practices

In September 2015, Costco had 117,000 full-time employees and 88,000 part-time employees. Approximately 14,000 hourly employees at locations in California, Maryland, New Jersey, and New York, as well as at one warehouse in Virginia, were represented by the International Brotherhood of Teamsters. All remaining employees were non-union.

Starting wages for new Costco employees were in the $10 to $12 range in 2015; hourly pay scales for warehouse jobs ranged from $12 to $23, depending on the type of job. Salaried employees in Costco warehouses could earn anywhere from $30,000 to $125,000 annually.[16] For example, salaries for merchandise managers were in the $60,000 to $70,000 range; salaries for supervisors ranged from $45,000 to $75,000; salaries for database, computer systems, and software applications developers/analysts/project managers were in the $85,000 to $105,000 range; and salaries for general managers of warehouses were in the $90,000 to $125,000 range. Employees enjoyed the full spectrum of benefits. Salaried employees were eligible for benefits on the first of the second month after the date of hire. Full-time hourly employees were eligible for benefits on the first day of the second month after completing 250 eligible paid hours; part-time hourly employees became benefit-eligible on the first day of the second month after completing 450 eligible paid hours. The benefit package included the following:

- Health care plans for full-time and part-time employees that included coverage for mental illness and substance abuse.
- A choice of a core dental plan or a premium dental plan.
- A pharmacy plan that entailed (1) co-payments of $3 for generic drugs and $10 to $50 for brand-name prescriptions filled at a Costco warehouse or online pharmacy and (2) co-payments of $15 to $50 for generic or brand-name prescriptions filled at all other pharmacies.
- A vision program that paid up to $60 for a refraction eye exam (the amount charged at Costco's Optical Centers) and had $175 annual allowances for the purchase of glasses and contact lenses at Costco Optical Centers. Employees located more than 25 miles from a Costco Optical Center could visit any provider of choice for annual eye exams and could purchase eyeglasses from any in-network source and submit claim forms for reimbursement.
- A hearing aid benefit of up to $1,750 every four years (available only to employees and their eligible dependents enrolled in a Costco medical plan, and the hearing aids had to be supplied at a Costco Hearing Aid Center).
- A 401(k) plan open to all employees who have completed 90 days of employment whereby Costco matched hourly employee contributions by 50 cents on the dollar for the first $1,000 annually to a maximum company match of $500 per year. The company's union employees on the West Coast qualified for matching contributions of 50 cents on the dollar to a maximum company match of $250 a year. In addition to the matching contribution, Costco also normally made a discretionary contribution to the accounts of eligible employees based on the number of years of service with the company (or in the case of union employees based on the straight-time hours worked). For other than union employees, this discretionary contribution was a percentage of the employee's compensation that ranged from a low of 3 percent (for employees with 1–3 years of service) to a high of 9 percent (for employees with 25 or more years of service). Company contributions to employee 410(k) plans were $408 million in fiscal 2013, $436 million in fiscal 2014, and $454 million in fiscal 2015.
- A dependent care reimbursement plan in which Costco employees whose families qualified could pay for day care for children under 13 or adult day care with pretax dollars and realize savings of anywhere from $750 to $2,000 per year.
- Confidential professional counseling services.
- Long-term and short-term disability coverage.
- Generous life insurance and accidental death and dismemberment coverage, with benefits based on years of service and whether the employee worked full-time or part-time. Employees could elect to purchase supplemental coverage for themselves, their spouses, or their children.
- An employee stock purchase plan allowing all employees to buy Costco stock via payroll deduction to avoid commissions and fees.

Although Costco's longstanding practice of paying good wages and good benefits was contrary to conventional wisdom in discount retailing, cofounder and former CEO Jim Sinegal, who originated the practice, firmly believed that having a well-compensated workforce was very important to executing Costco's strategy successfully. He said, "Imagine that you have 120,000 loyal ambassadors out there who are constantly saying good things about Costco. It has to be a significant advantage for you. . . . Paying good wages and keeping your people working with you is very good business."[17] When a reporter asked him about why Costco treated its workers so well compared to other retailers (particularly Walmart, which paid lower wages and had a skimpier benefits package), Sinegal replied: "Why shouldn't employees have the right to good wages and good careers. . . . It absolutely makes good business sense. Most people agree that we're the lowest-cost producer. Yet we pay the highest wages. So it must mean we get better productivity. Its axiomatic in our business—you get what you pay for."[18]

Good wages and benefits were said to be why employee turnover at Costco typically ran under 6 to 7 percent after the first year of employment. Some Costco employees had been with the company since its founding in 1983. Many others had started working part-time at Costco while in high school or college and opted to make a career at the company. One Costco employee told an ABC *20/20* reporter, "It's a good place to work; they take good care of us."[19] A Costco vice president and head baker said working for Costco was a family affair: "My whole family works for Costco, my husband does, my daughter does, my new son-in-law does."[20] Another employee, a receiving clerk who made about $40,000 a year, said, "I want to retire here. I love it here."[21] An employee with over two years of service could not be fired without the approval of a senior company officer.

Selecting People for Open Positions Costco's top management wanted employees to feel that they could have a long career at Costco. It was company policy to fill the vast majority of its higher-level openings by promotions from within; at one recent point, the percentage ran close to 98 percent, which meant that the majority of Costco's management team members (including warehouse, merchandise, administrative, membership, front end, and receiving managers) had come up through the ranks. Many of the company's vice presidents had started in entry-level jobs. According to Jim Sinegal, "We have guys who started pushing shopping carts out on the parking lot for us who are now vice presidents of our company."[22] Costco made a point of recruiting at local universities; Sinegal explained why: "These people are smarter than the average person, hardworking, and they haven't made a career choice."[23] On another occasion, he said, "If someone came to us and said he just got a master's in business at Harvard, we would say fine, would you like to start pushing carts."[24] Those employees who demonstrated smarts and strong people management skills moved up through the ranks.

But without an aptitude for the details of discount retailing, even up-and-coming employees stood no chance of being promoted to a position of warehouse manager. Top Costco executives who oversaw warehouse operations insisted that candidates for warehouse managers be top-flight merchandisers with a gift for the details of making items fly off the shelves. Based on his experience as CEO, Sinegal said, "People who have a feel for it just start to get it. Others, you look at them and it's like staring at a blank canvas. I'm not trying to be unduly harsh, but that's the way it works."[25] Most newly appointed warehouse managers at Costco came from the ranks of assistant warehouse managers who had a track record of being shrewd merchandisers and tuned into what new or different products might sell well given the clientele that patronized their particular warehouse. Just having the requisite skills in people management, crisis management, and cost-effective warehouse operations was not enough.

Executive Compensation Executives at Costco did not earn the outlandish salaries that had become customary over the past decade at most large corporations. In Jim Sinegal's last two years as Costco's CEO, he received a salary of $350,000 and a bonus of $190,400 in fiscal 2010 and a salary of $350,000 and a bonus of $198,400 in fiscal 2011. Cofounder and chair Jeff Brotman's compensation in 2010 and 2011 was the same as Sinegal's. Craig Jelinek's salary as president and CEO in fiscal 2015 was $699,810, and he received a bonus of $188,800; chair Jeff Brotman's salary was $650,000 and his bonus was also $188,800. Other high-paid officers at Costco received salaries in the $642,000–$712,000 range and bonuses of $75,000–$78,000 in 2015.

Asked why executive compensation at Costco was only a fraction of the amounts typically paid to top-level executives at other corporations with revenues and operating scale comparable to Costco's, Sinegal replied: "I figured that if I was making something like 12 times more than the typical person working on the floor, that that was a fair salary."[26] To another reporter, he said: "Listen, I'm one of the founders of this business. I've been very well rewarded. I don't require a salary that's 100 times more than the people who work on the sales floor."[27] During his tenure as CEO, Sinegal's employment contract was only a page long and provided that he could be terminated for cause.

However, while executive salaries and bonuses were modest in comparison with those at other companies Costco's size, Costco did close the gap via an equity compensation program that featured awarding restricted stock units (RSUs) to executives based on defined performance criteria. The philosophy at Costco was that equity compensation should be the largest component of compensation for all executive officers and be tied directly to achievement of pretax income targets. In November 2015, the Compensation Committee of the Board of Directors granted 41,716 RSUs to Craig Jelinek and Jeff Brotman (worth about $5.3 million on the date of the grant, but subject to time-vesting restrictions) and 21,900 shares (worth about $2.8 million on the date of grant, but also subject to various restrictions) to 3 other top-ranking executives. As of November 2015, Jim Sinegal was deemed to be the beneficial owner of 1.7 million shares of Costco stock, Jeff Brotman the beneficial owner of almost 480,000, and Craig Jelinek the beneficial owner of 270,000 shares. All directors and officers as a group (23 persons) were the beneficial owners of almost 3.48 million shares as of November 20, 2015.

Costco's Business Philosophy, Values, and Code of Ethics

Jim Sinegal, who was the son of a steelworker, had ingrained five simple and down-to-earth business principles into Costco's corporate culture and the manner in which the company operated. The following are excerpts of these principles and operating approaches:[28]

1. **Obey the law**—The law is irrefutable! Absent a moral imperative to challenge a law, we must conduct our business in total compliance with the laws of every community where we do business. We pledge to:
   - Comply with all laws and other legal requirements.
   - Respect all public officials and their positions.
   - Comply with safety and security standards for all products sold.
   - Exceed ecological standards required in every community where we do business.
   - Comply with all applicable wage and hour laws.
   - Comply with all applicable antitrust laws.
   - Conduct business in and with foreign countries in a manner that is legal and proper under United States and foreign laws.
   - Not offer, give, ask for, or receive any form of bribe or kickback to or from any person or pay to expedite government action or otherwise act in violation of the Foreign Corrupt Practices Act or the laws of other countries.
   - Promote fair, accurate, timely, and understandable disclosure in reports filed with the Securities and Exchange Commission and in other public communications by the Company.
2. **Take care of our members**—Costco membership is open to business owners, as well as individuals. Our members are our reason for being—the key to our success. If we don't keep our members happy, little else that we do will make a difference. There are plenty of shopping alternatives for our members, and if they fail to show up, we cannot survive. Our members have extended a trust to Costco by virtue of paying a fee to shop with us. We will succeed only if we do not violate the trust they have extended to us, and that trust extends to every area of our business. We pledge to:
   - Provide top-quality products at the best prices in the market.
   - Provide high-quality, safe, and wholesome food products by requiring that both vendors and employees be in compliance with the highest food safety standards in the industry.
   - Provide our members with a 100 percent satisfaction guaranteed warranty on every product and service we sell, including their membership fee.
   - Assure our members that every product we sell is authentic in make and in representation of performance.
   - Make our shopping environment a pleasant experience by making our members feel welcome as our guests.
   - Provide products to our members that will be ecologically sensitive.
   - Provide our members with the best customer service in the retail industry.
   - Give back to our communities through employee volunteerism and employee and corporate contributions to United Way and Children's Hospitals.
3. **Take care of our employees**—Our employees are our most important asset. We believe we have the very best employees in the warehouse club industry, and we are committed to providing them

with rewarding challenges and ample opportunities for personal and career growth. We pledge to provide our employees with:

- Competitive wages.
- Great benefits.
- A safe and healthy work environment.
- Challenging and fun work.
- Career opportunities.
- An atmosphere free from harassment or discrimination.
- An Open Door Policy that allows access to ascending levels of management to resolve issues.
- Opportunities to give back to their communities through volunteerism and fundraising.

4. **Respect our suppliers**—Our suppliers are our partners in business and for us to prosper as a company, they must prosper with us. To that end, we strive to:
   - Treat all suppliers and their representatives as we would expect to be treated if visiting their places of business.
   - Honor all commitments.
   - Protect all suppliers' property assigned to Costco as though it were our own.
   - Not accept gratuities of any kind from a supplier.
   - If in doubt as to what course of action to take on a business matter that is open to varying ethical interpretations, TAKE THE HIGH ROAD AND DO WHAT IS RIGHT.

   If we do these four things throughout our organization, then we will achieve our ultimate goal, which is to:

5. **Reward our shareholders**—As a company with stock that is traded publicly on the NASDAQ stock exchange, our shareholders are our business partners. We can only be successful so long as we are providing them with a good return on the money they invest in our company. . . . We pledge to operate our company in such a way that our present and future stockholders, as well as our employees, will be rewarded for our efforts.

Environmental Sustainability

In recent years, Costco management had undertaken a series of initiatives to invest in various environmental and energy saving systems. The stated objective was to ensure that the company's carbon footprint grew at a slower rate than the company's sales growth. Going into 2014, Costco had rooftop solar photovoltaic systems in operation at 77 of its facilities. All new facilities were being designed and constructed to be more energy efficient. Costco's metal warehouse design, which included use of recycled steel, was consistent with the requirements of the Silver Level LEED Standard—the certification standards of the organization Leadership in Energy and Environmental Design (LEED)—and nationally accepted as a benchmark green building design and construction. Costco's recently developed non-metal designs for warehouses had resulted in the ability to meet Gold Level LEED Standards.

Energy efficient lighting and energy efficient mechanical systems for heating, cooling, and refrigeration were being installed in all new facilities and at growing numbers of older facilities. Internet-based energy management systems had been installed, giving Costco the ability to regulate energy usage on an hourly basis at all of its warehouses in North America and at some international locations. These energy-saving initiatives had reduced the lighting loads on Costco's sales floors by 50 percent from 2001 to 2014.

Other initiatives included working with suppliers to make greater use of sales-floor-ready packaging, changing container shapes from round to square (to enable more units to be stacked on a single pallet on warehouse sales floors and to conserve on trucking freight costs), making greater use of recycled plastic packaging, reusing cardboard packaging (empty store cartons were given to members to carry their purchases home), and expanding the use of non-chemical water treatment systems used in warehouse cooling towers to reduce the amount of chemicals going into sewer systems. In addition, a bigger portion of the trash that warehouses generated each week, much of which was formerly sent to landfills, was being recycled into usable products or diverted to facilities that used waste as fuel for generating electricity. Grease recovery systems had been installed in increasing numbers of warehouses, resulting in the recovery of more than millions of pounds of grease from the waste stream.

Costco was committed to sourcing all of the seafood it sold from responsible and environmentally sustainable sources that were certified by the Marine Stewardship Council; in no instances did Costco sell seafood species that were classified as environmentally endangered and it monitored the aquaculture practices of its suppliers that farmed seafood. The company had long been committed to enhancing the welfare and proper handling of all animals used in food products sold at Costco. According to the company's official statement on animal welfare, "This is not only the right thing to do, it is an important moral and ethical obligation we owe to our members, suppliers, and most of all to the animals we depend on for products that are sold at Costco."[29] As part of the company's commitment, Costco had established an animal welfare audit program that utilized recognized audit standards and programs conducted by trained, certified auditors and that reviewed animal welfare both on the farm and at slaughter.

Costco had been an active member of the Environmental Protection Agency's Energy Star and Climate Protection Partnerships since 2002 and was a major retailer of Energy Star qualified compact fluorescent lamp (CFL) bulbs and LED light bulbs. Costco sold more than 35 million energy-saving CFL bulbs and 9 million LED light bulbs in the United States during 2011; since 2005, Costco had sold over 204 million energy-saving light bulbs.

COMPETITION

The wholesale club and warehouse segment of retailing in North America was a $172 billion business in 2015. There were three main competitors—Costco Wholesale, Sam's Club, and BJ's Wholesale Club. In early 2016, there were about 1,440 warehouse locations across the United States and Canada; most every major metropolitan area had one, if not several, warehouse clubs. Costco had about a 59 percent share of warehouse club sales across the United States and Canada, with Sam's Club (a division of Walmart) having roughly a 34 percent share and BJ's Wholesale Club and several small warehouse club competitors close to a 7 percent share.

Competition among the warehouse clubs was based on such factors as price, merchandise quality and selection, location, and member service. However, warehouse clubs also competed with a wide range of other types of retailers, including retail discounters like Walmart and Dollar General, supermarkets, general merchandise chains, specialty chains, gasoline stations, and Internet retailers. Not only did Walmart, the world's largest retailer, compete directly with Costco via its Sam's Club subsidiary, but its Walmart Supercenters sold many of the same types of merchandise at attractively low prices as well. Target, Kohl's, and **Amazon.com** had emerged as significant retail competitors in certain general merchandise categories. Low-cost operators selling a single category or narrow range of merchandise—such as Trader Joe's, Lowe's, Home Depot, Office Depot, Staples, Best Buy, PetSmart, and Barnes & Noble—had significant market share in their respective product categories. Notwithstanding the competition from other retailers and discounters, the low prices and merchandise selection found at Costco, Sam's Club, and BJ's Wholesale were attractive to small business owners, individual households (particularly bargain-hunters and those with large families), churches and nonprofit organizations, caterers, and small restaurants. The internationally located warehouses faced similar types of competitors.

Brief profiles of Costco's two primary competitors in North America are presented in the following sections.

Sam's Club

The first Sam's Club opened in 1984, and Walmart management in the ensuing years proceeded to grow the warehouse membership club concept into a significant business and major Walmart division. The concept of the Sam's Club format was to sell merchandise at very low profit margins, resulting in low prices to members. The mission of Sam's Club was "to make savings simple for members by providing them with exciting, quality merchandise and a superior shopping experience, all at a great value."[30]

In early 2016, there were 652 Sam's Club locations in the United States and Puerto Rico, many of which were adjacent to Walmart Supercenters, and an estimated 150 Sam's Club locations in Mexico, Brazil, and China. (Financial and operating data for the Sam's Club locations in Mexico, Brazil, and China were not separately available because Walmart grouped its reporting of all store operations in 26 countries outside the United States into a segment called Walmart International that did not break out different types of stores.) In fiscal year 2015, the Sam's Club locations in the United States and Puerto Rico had record revenues of $58 billion (including membership fees), making it the eighth largest retailer in the United States. Sam's Clubs

EXHIBIT 5 Selected Financial and Operating Data for Sam's Club, Fiscal Years 2001, 2010–2015

	Fiscal Years Ending January 31						
Sam's Club	2015	2014	2013	2012	2011	2010	2001
Sales in U.S.[a] (millions of $)	$58,020	$57,157	$56,423	$53,795	$49,459	$47,806	$26,798
Operating income in U.S. (millions of $)	1,976	1,843	1,859	1,865	1,695	1,515	942
Assets in U.S. (millions of $)	13,995	14,053	13,479	12,824	12,536	12,073	3,843
Number of U.S. and Puerto Rico locations at year-end	647	632	620	611	609	605	475
Average sales per year-end U.S. location, including membership fees (millions of $)	$ 89.6	$ 90.4	$ 91.0	$ 82.0	$ 81.2	$ 79.0	$ 56.4
Sales growth at existing U.S. warehouses open more than 12 months:							
Including gasoline sales	0.0%	0.3%	4.1%	8.4%	3.7%	−1.4%	n.a.
Not including gasoline sales	2.1%	1.6%	4.6%	5.2%	1.7%	0.7%	n.a.
Average warehouse size in U.S. (square feet)	134,000	133,800	133,500	133,200	133,000	133,000	122,100

a. The sales figure includes membership fees and is only for warehouses in the United States and Puerto Rico. For financial reporting purposes, Walmart consolidates the operations of all foreign-based stores into a single "international" segment figure. Thus, separate financial information for only the foreign-based Sam's Club locations in Mexico, China, and Brazil is not separately available.

Sources: Walmart's 10-K reports and annual reports, fiscal years 2015, 2012, 2010, and 2001.

ranged between 71,000 and 190,000 square feet, with the average being 134,000 square feet; many newer locations were larger than the current average. All Sam's Club warehouses had concrete floors, sparse décor, and goods displayed on pallets, simple wooden shelves, or racks in the case of apparel. In 2009–2010, Sam's Club began a long-term warehouse remodeling program for its older locations.

Exhibit 5 provides financial and operating highlights for selected years during 2001–2015.

Merchandise Offerings Sam's Club warehouses stocked about 4,000 items, a big fraction of which were standard and a small fraction of which represented special buys and one-time offerings. The treasure-hunt items at Sam's Club tended to be less upscale and less expensive than those at Costco. The merchandise selection included brand-name merchandise in a variety of categories and a selection of private-label items sold under the "Member's Mark," "Daily Chef," and "Sam's Club" brands. Most club locations had fresh-foods departments that included bakery, meat, produce, floral products, and a Sam's Café. A significant number of clubs had a one-hour photo processing department, a pharmacy that filled prescriptions, an optical department, and self-service gasoline pumps. Sam's Club guaranteed it would beat any price for branded prescriptions. Members could shop for a wider assortment of merchandise and services online at **www.samsclub.com**. The percentage composition of sales across major merchandise categories is shown in Exhibit 6.

Membership and Hours of Operation The annual fee for Sam's Club Business members was $45 for the primary membership card, with a spouse card available at no additional cost. Business members could add up to eight business associates for $45 each. Individuals could purchase a "Sam's Savings" membership card for $45. The membership cards for both individuals and businesses had an "Instant Savings" where limited-time promotional discounts were electronically loaded on a member's card and automatically applied at checkout. A Sam's Club Plus premium membership cost $100; in addition to eligibility for Instant Savings, Plus members had early shopping hour privileges, received discounts on select prescription drugs, and earned cash-back

EXHIBIT 6

Merchandise Categories	Fiscal Years Ending January 31		
	2015	2014	2013
Grocery and consumables (dairy, meat, bakery, deli, produce, dry, chilled or frozen packaged foods, alcoholic and nonalcoholic beverages, floral, snack foods, candy, other grocery items, health and beauty aids, paper goods, laundry and home care, baby care, pet supplies, and other consumable items and grocery items)	57%	56%	55%
Fuel and other categories (tobacco, snack foods, tools and power equipment, sales of gasoline, and tire and battery centers)	23%	23%	24%
Technology, office and entertainment (electronics, wireless, software, video games, movies, books, music, toys, office supplies, office furniture and photo processing)	7%	8%	8%
Home and apparel (home improvement, outdoor living, grills, gardening, furniture, apparel, jewelry, house wares, seasonal items, mattresses, and small appliances)	8%	8%	8%
Health and wellness (pharmacy and optical services, and over-the-counter drugs)	5%	5%	5%

rewards of $10 for every $500 they spent in qualifying pretax purchases.

Regular hours of operations were Monday through Friday from 10:00 a.m. to 8:30 p.m., Saturday from 9:00 a.m. to 8:30 p.m., and Sunday from 10:00 a.m. to 6:00 p.m,; Business and Plus cardholders had the ability to shop before the regular operating hours Monday through Saturday beginning at 7 a.m. All club members could use a variety of payment methods, including Visa credit and debit cards, American Express cards, and a Sam's Club 5-3-1 MasterCard. The pharmacy and optical departments accepted payments for products and services through members' health benefit plans.

Distribution Approximately 66 percent of the non-fuel merchandise at Sam's Club was shipped from some 24 distribution facilities dedicated to Sam's Club operations that were strategically located across the continental United States, and in the case of perishable items, from nearby Walmart grocery distribution centers; the balance was shipped by suppliers direct to Sam's Club locations. Of these 24 distribution facilities, 5 were owned/leased and operated by Sam's Club and 19 were owned/leased and operated by third parties. Like Costco, Sam's Club distribution centers employed cross-docking techniques whereby incoming shipments were transferred immediately to outgoing trailers destined for Sam's Club locations; shipments typically spent less than 24 hours at a cross-docking facility and in some instances were there only an hour. A combination of company-owned trucks and independent trucking companies were used to transport merchandise from distribution centers to club locations.

Employment In 2015, Sam's Club employed about 100,000 people across all aspects of its operations in the United States. While the people who worked at Sam's Club warehouses were in all stages of life, a sizable fraction had accepted job offers because they had minimal skill levels and were looking for their first job, or needed only a part-time job, or were wanting to start a second career. More than 60 percent of managers of Sam's Club warehouses had begun their careers at Sam's as hourly warehouse employees and had moved up through the ranks to their present positions.

BJ's Wholesale Club

BJ's Wholesale Club introduced the member warehouse concept to the northeastern United States in the mid-1980s and, as of 2016, had a total of 210 warehouses in 15 eastern states extending from Maine to Florida. A big percentage of these facilities were full-sized warehouse clubs that averaged about 114,000 square feet, but there were over 20 smaller format warehouse clubs that averaged approximately 73,000 square feet and were located in markets too small to support a full-sized warehouse. Approximately 85 percent of BJ's full-sized warehouse clubs had at least one Costco or Sam's Club warehouse operating in their trading areas (within a distance of 10 miles or less).

In late June 2011, BJ's Wholesale agreed to a buyout offer from two private equity firms and shortly thereafter became a privately held company.

Exhibit 7 shows selected financial and operating data for BJ's for fiscal years 2007 though 2011—the last years its financial and operating data were publicly available.

Product Offerings and Merchandising Like Costco and Sam's Club, BJ's Wholesale sold high-quality, brand-name merchandise at prices that were significantly lower than the prices found at supermarkets, discount retail chains, department stores, drugstores, and specialty retail stores like Best Buy. Its merchandise lineup of about 7,000 items included consumer electronics, prerecorded media, small appliances, tires, jewelry, health and beauty aids, household products, computer software, books, greeting cards, apparel, furniture, toys, seasonal items, frozen foods, fresh meat and dairy products, beverages, dry grocery items, fresh produce, flowers, canned goods, and household products. About

EXHIBIT 7 Selected Financial and Operating Data, BJ's Wholesale Club, Fiscal Years 2007 through 2011

	Jan. 29 2011	Jan. 30 2010	Jan. 31 2009	Feb. 2 2008	Feb. 3 2007 (53 weeks)
Selected Income Statement Data (in millions, except per share data)					
Net sales	$10,633	$ 9,954	$ 9,802	$ 8,792	$ 8,280
Membership fees	191	182	178	176	162
Other revenues	53	51	48	47	54
Total revenues	10,877	10,187	10,027	9,014	8,497
Cost of sales, including buying and occupancy costs	9,697	9,081	9,004	8,091	7,601
Selling, general and administrative expenses	934	875	799	724	740
Operating income	208	224	221	195	144
Net income	$ 95	$ 132	$ 135	$ 123	$ 72
Diluted earnings per share:	1.77	2.42	2.28	1.90	1.08
Balance Sheet and Cash Flow Data (in millions)					
Cash and cash equivalents	$ 101	$ 59	$ 51	$ 97	$ 56
Current assets	1,292	1,173	1,076	1,145	1,070
Current liabilities	987	1,006	909	946	867
Working capital	305	167	167	199	203
Merchandise inventories	981	930	860	877	851
Total assets	2,322	2,166	2,021	2,047	1,993
Long-term debt	—	1	1	2	2
Stockholders' equity	1,144	1,033	985	980	1,020
Cash flow from operations	229	298	224	305	173
Capital expenditures	188	176	138	90	191
Selected Operating Data					
Clubs open at end of year	189	187	180	177	172
Number of members (in thousands)	9,600	9,400	9,000	8,800	8,700
Average sales per club location (in millions)	$ 56.3	$ 53.2	$ 54.6	$ 49.7	$ 48.1
Sales growth at existing clubs open more than 12 months	4.4%	−1.9%	9.4%	3.7%	1.2%

Sources: Company 10-K reports for 2011, 2010, 2008, and 2007.

70 percent of BJ's product line could be found in supermarkets. Private-label goods accounted for approximately 10 percent of food and general merchandise sales. Members could purchase additional products at the company's website, **www.bjs.com**.

BJ's warehouses had a number of specialty services that were designed to enable members to complete more of their shopping at BJ's and to encourage more frequent trips to the clubs. Like Costco and Sam's Club, BJ's sold gasoline at a discounted price as a means of displaying a favorable price image to prospective members and providing added value to existing members; in 2012, there were gas station operations at 107 BJ's locations. Other specialty services included full-service optical centers (more than 150 locations), food courts, full-service Verizon Wireless centers, vacation and travel packages, garden and storage sheds, patios and sunrooms, a propane tank filling service, an automobile buying service, a car rental service, muffler and brake services operated in conjunction with Monro Muffler Brake, and electronics and jewelry protection plans. Most of these services were provided by outside operators in space leased from BJ's. In early 2007, BJ's abandoned prescription filling and closed all of its 46 in-club pharmacies.

Strategy Features That Differentiated BJ's

BJ's had developed a strategy and operating model that management believed differentiated the company from Costco and Sam's Club:

- Offering a wide range of choice—7,000 items versus 3,700 to 4,000 items at Costco and Sam's Club.
- Focusing on the individual consumer via merchandising strategies that emphasized a customer-friendly shopping experience.
- Clustering club locations to achieve the benefit of name recognition and maximize the efficiencies of management support, distribution, and marketing activities.
- Trying to establish and maintain the first or second industry leading position in each major market where it operated.
- Creating an exciting shopping experience for members with a constantly changing mix of food and general merchandise items and carrying a broader product assortment than competitors.
- Supplementing the warehouse format with aisle markers, express checkout lanes, self-checkout lanes, and low-cost video-based sales aids to make shopping more efficient for members.
- Being open longer hours than competitors; typical hours of operation were 9 a.m. to 7 p.m. Monday through Friday and 9 a.m. to 6 p.m. Saturday and Sunday.
- Offering smaller package sizes of many items.
- Accepting manufacturers' coupons.
- Accepting more credit card payment options.

Membership BJ's Wholesale Club had about 9.6 million members in 2011 (see Exhibit 6). In 2016, individuals and businesses could become members for a fee of $50 per year that included one free supplemental card. Both individual and business members could opt for a BJ's Perks Reward™ membership and earn 2 percent cash back on in-club and online purchases. Members paying the $50 membership fee could apply for a BJ's Perks Plus™ credit card (MasterCard) which had no annual credit card fee and earned 3 percent cash back on in-club and online purchases, 10-cents off per gallon at BJ's gas stations, and 1 percent cash back on all non-BJ's purchases everywhere MasterCard was accepted. Individuals and businesses with a BJ's Perks Reward™ membership could apply for a BJ's Perks Elite™ MasterCard which had no annual fee and earned 5 percent cash back on in-club and online purchases, 10 cents off per gallon at BJ's gas stations, and 1 percent cash back on all non-BJ's purchases everywhere MasterCard was accepted. BJ's accepted MasterCard, Visa, Discover, and American Express cards at all locations; members could also pay for purchases by cash or check. BJ's accepted returns of most merchandise within 30 days after purchase.

Marketing and Promotion BJ's increased customer awareness of its clubs primarily through direct mail, public relations efforts, marketing programs for newly opened clubs, and a publication called *BJ's Journal,* which was mailed to members throughout the year.

Warehouse Club Operations BJ's warehouses were located in both freestanding locations and shopping centers. As of 2011, construction and site development costs for a full-sized owned BJ's club were in the $6 to $10 million range; land acquisition costs ranged from $3 to $10 million but could be significantly higher in some locations. Each warehouse generally had an investment of $3 to $4 million for fixtures and equipment. Preopening expenses at a new club ran $1.0 to $2.0 million. Including space for parking, a typical full-sized BJ's club required 13 to 14 acres of land; smaller clubs typically required about 8 acres. Prior to being acquired in 2011, BJ's had financed all of its club expansions, as well as all other capital expenditures, with internally generated funds.

Merchandise purchased from manufacturers was routed either to a BJ's cross-docking facility or directly to clubs. Personnel at the cross-docking facilities broke down truckload quantity shipments from manufacturers and reallocated goods for shipment to individual clubs, generally within 24 hours. BJ's worked closely with manufacturers to minimize the amount of handling required once merchandise is received at a club. Merchandise was generally displayed on pallets containing large quantities of each item, thereby reducing labor required for handling, stocking, and restocking. Backup merchandise was generally stored in steel racks above the sales floor. Most merchandise was premarked by the manufacturer so it did not require ticketing at the club. Full-sized clubs had approximately $2 million in inventory. Management had been able to limit inventory shrinkage to no more than 0.2 percent of net sales in each of the last three fiscal years (a percentage well below those of other types of retailers) by strictly controlling the exits of clubs, by generally limiting customers to members, and by using state-of-the-art electronic article surveillance technology.

ENDNOTES

[1] As quoted in Alan B. Goldberg and Bill Ritter, "Costco CEO Finds Pro-Worker Means Profitability," an ABC News original report on *20/20*, August 2, 2006, abcnews.go.com/2020/Business/story?id=1362779 (accessed November 15, 2006).
[2] Ibid.
[3] As described in Nina Shapiro, "Company for the People," *Seattle Weekly*, December 15, 2004, www.seattleweekly.com (accessed November 14, 2006).
[4] Investopedia, "How Much Does a Costco Store Sell Each Year?" June 19, 2015, posted at www.investopedia.com/stock-analysis/061915/how-much-does-costco-store-sell-each-year-cost.aspx#ixzz3zF8H31dL (accessed February 4, 2016).
[5] See, for example, Costco's "Code of Ethics," posted in the investor relations section of Costco's website under a link titled "Corporate Governance and Citizenship" (accessed by the case author February 4, 2016).
[6] Costco Wholesale, 2011 Annual Report for the year ended August 28, 2011, p. 5.
[7] As quoted in ibid., pp. 128–29.
[8] Steven Greenhouse, "How Costco Became the Anti-Wal-Mart," *The New York Times*, July 17, 2005, www.wakeupwalmart.com/news (accessed November 28, 2006).
[9] As quoted in Greenhouse, "How Costco Became the Anti-Wal-Mart."
[10] As quoted in Shapiro, "Company for the People."
[11] As quoted in Greenhouse, "How Costco Became the Anti-Wal-Mart."
[12] Matthew Boyle, "Why Costco Is So Damn Addictive," *Fortune*, October 30, 2006, p. 132.
[13] Costco's 2005 Annual Report.
[14] As quoted in Goldberg and Ritter, "Costco CEO Finds Pro-Worker Means Profitability."
[15] Ibid.
[16] Based on information posted at www.glassdoor.com (accessed February 28, 2012).
[17] Ibid.
[18] Shapiro, "Company for the People."
[19] As quoted in Goldberg and Ritter, "Costco CEO Finds Pro-Worker Means Profitability."
[20] Ibid.
[21] As quoted in Greenhouse, "How Costco Became the Anti-Wal-Mart."
[22] As quoted in Goldberg and Ritter, "Costco CEO Finds Pro-Worker Means Profitability."
[23] Boyle, "Why Costco Is So Damn Addictive," p. 132.
[24] As quoted in Shapiro, "Company for the People."
[25] Ibid.
[26] As quoted in Goldberg and Ritter, "Costco CEO Finds Pro-Worker Means Profitability."
[27] As quoted in Shapiro, "Company for the People."
[28] Costco Code of Ethics, posted in the investor relations section of Costco's website (accessed February 8, 2016).
[29] "Mission Statement on Animal Welfare," posted at www.costco.com in the Investor relations section (accessed February 8, 2016).
[30] Walmart 2010 Annual Report, p. 8.

CASE 05

Competition in the Craft Beer Industry in 2016

John D. Varlaro
Johnson & Wales University

John E. Gamble
Texas A&M University–Corpus Christi

The appeal of locally produced or regional craft beers during the early 2010s gave a dramatic boost to the long-mature beer industry. Craft breweries, which by definition sold fewer than 6 million barrels (bbls) per year, expanded rapidly with the deregulation of intrastate alcohol distribution and retail laws and a change in consumer preferences toward unique and high-quality beers. The growing popularity of craft beers allowed the total beer industry in the United States to increase by 6.7 percent annually between 2011 and 2016 to reach $39.5 billion. The production of U.S. craft breweries more than doubled from 11.5 million bbls per year to about 24.5 million bbls per year during that time. In addition, production by microbreweries, which produced less than 15,000 bbls per year, almost tripled to 4 million bbls from 1.5 million bbls between 2011 and 2016.[1] Much of this impressive industry growth came at the expense of such well-known brands as Budweiser, Miller, Coors, and Bud Light, which experienced sluggish sales during the early 2010s because of a growing perception of mediocre taste.

Boston Beer Company, the second largest craft brewery in the United States and known for its Samuel Adams brand, reported a 4 percent increase over 2014 shipments of 4.2 million barrels in 2015.[2] By comparison, the annual revenues of Anheuser-Busch InBev SA, whose portfolio included global brands Budweiser, Corona, and Stella Artois and numerous international and local brands, declined during the same two-year period. However, the sales volume of Anheuser-Busch's flagship brands and its newly acquired and international brands such as Corona, Goose Island, Shock Top, Beck's, and St. Pauli Girl allowed it to control 45.8 percent of the U.S. market for beer in 2016.[3]

At the beginning of the second half of the 2010s, industry competition was increasing as grain price fluctuations affected cost structures and growing consolidation within the beer industry—led most notably by AB InBev's acquisition of several craft breweries, Grupo Modelo, and its pending $104 billion acquisition of SABMiller—created a battle for market share. The market for specialty beer was expected to gradually plateau by 2020 with annual industry growth slowing to 0.9 percent annually. Nevertheless, craft breweries and microbreweries were expected to expand in number and in terms of market share as consumers sought out new pale ales, stouts, wheat beers, pilsners, and lagers with regional or local flairs.

The Beer Market

The total economic impact of the beer market was estimated to be 1.5 percent of the total U.S. GDP in 2015 when variables such as jobs within beer production, sales, and distribution were included.[4] Exhibit 1 presents annual beer production statistics for the United States between 2006 and 2015.

Although U.S. production had declined since 2008, consumption was increasing elsewhere in the world, resulting in a forecasted global market of almost $700 billion in sales by 2020.[5] Global growth seemed to be fueled by the introduction of differing styles of beer to regions where consumers had not previously had access and the expansion of demographics not normally known for consuming beer. Thus, exported beer to both developed and developing

EXHIBIT 1 Barrels of Beer Produced in the United States, 2006–2015 (in millions)

Year	Barrels Produced (in millions)*
2006	198
2007	200
2008	200
2009	197
2010	195
2011	193
2012	196
2013	192
2014	193
2015	191

*Rounded to the nearest million.
Source: Alcohol and Tobacco Tax and Trade Bureau website.

EXHIBIT 2 Top 10 U.S. Breweries in 2014

Rank	Brewery
1	Anheuser-Busch, Inc.
2	MillerCoors
3	Pabst Brewing Co.
4	D.G. Yuengling and Son, Inc.
5	Boston Beer Co.
6	North American Breweries
7	Sierra Nevada Brewing Co.
8	New Belgium Brewing Co.
9	Craft Brewing Alliance
10	Lagunitas Brewing Co.

Source: Brewers Association.

EXHIBIT 3 Top 10 Global Beer Producers by Volume in 2014

Rank	Producer	Volume (millions of Barrels)*
1	AB InBev	351
2	SABMiller	249
3	Heineken	180
4	Carlsberg	110
5	Tsingtao (Group)	78
6	Molson Coors Brewing Company	54
7	Beijing Yanjing	45
8	Kirin	36
9	Castel BGI	26
10	Asahi	26

*Not in original report. Computed using 1 hL = .852 barrel for comparison; to nearest million bbl.
Source: AB InBev 2016 20-F SEC Document.

regions helped drive future growth. As an example, China recently saw a number of domestic craft breweries producing beer as well as experimenting with locally and regionally known flavors, enticing the domestic palette with flavors such as green tea.[6]

The Brewers Association, a trade association for brewers, suppliers, and others within the industry, designated a brewery as a craft brewer when output was less than 6 million barrels annually and the ownership was more than 75 percent independent of another non–craft beer producer or entity. The rapid increase in popularity for local beers allowed the number of U.S. brewers to increase from 3,000 in 2014 to 4,000 in 2015. Of these breweries, 99 percent were identified as craft breweries with distribution ranging from local to national. While large global breweries occupied the top four positions among the largest U.S. breweries, five craft breweries were ranked among the top-10 largest U.S. brewers in 2015—see Exhibit 2. Exhibit 3 presents the 10 largest beer producers worldwide in 2014. The number of craft breweries in each U.S. state are presented in Exhibit 4.

The Beer Production Process

The beer production process involves the fermentation of grains. The cereal grain barley is the most common grain used in the production of beer. Before fermentation, however, barley must be malted and milled. Malting allows the barley to germinate and produce the sugars that would be fermented by the yeast, yielding the sweetness of beer. By soaking the barley in water, the barley germinates, or grows, as it would when planted in the ground. This process is halted through the introduction of hot air and drying after germination began.

After malting, the barley is milled to break open the husk while also cracking the inner seed that

EXHIBIT 4 Number of Craft Brewers by State, 2015

State	Brewers	State	Brewers
Alabama	24	Montana	49
Alaska	27	Nebraska	33
Arizona	78	Nevada	34
Arkansas	26	New Hampshire	44
California	518	New Jersey	51
Colorado	284	New Mexico	45
Connecticut	35	New York	208
Delaware	15	North Carolina	161
Florida	151	North Dakota	9
Georgia	45	Ohio	143
Hawaii	13	Oklahoma	14
Idaho	50	Oregon	228
Illinois	157	Pennsylvania	178
Indiana	115	Rhode Island	14
Iowa	58	South Carolina	36
Kansas	26	South Dakota	14
Kentucky	24	Tennessee	52
Louisiana	20	Texas	189
Maine	59	Utah	22
Maryland	60	Vermont	44
Massachusetts	84	Virginia	124
Michigan	205	Washington	305
Minnesota	105	West Virginia	12
Mississippi	8	Wisconsin	121
Missouri	71	Wyoming	23

Source: Brewers Association.

has begun to germinate. Once milled, the barley is mashed, or added to hot water. The addition of the hot water produces sugar from the grain. This mixture is then filtered, resulting in the wort. The wort is then boiled, which sterilizes the beer. It is at this stage that hops are added. The taste and aroma of beer depends on the variety of hops and when the hops were added.

After boiling, the wort is cooled and then poured into the fermentor where yeast is added. The sugar created in the previous stages is broken down by the yeast through fermentation. The different styles of beer depend on the type of yeast used, typically either an ale or lager yeast. The time for this process could take a couple of weeks to a couple of months. After fermentation, the yeast is removed. The process is completed after carbon dioxide is added and the product is packaged.

Beer is a varied and differentiated product, with over 70 styles in 15 categories. Each style is dependent on a number of variables. These variables are controlled by the brewer through the process, and could include the origin of raw materials, approach to fermentation, and yeast used. For example, Guinness referenced on its website how barley purchased by the brewer was not only grown locally, but was also toasted specifically after malting, lending to its characteristic taste and color.[7] As another example of differentiation through raw materials, wheat beers, such as German-style *hefeweizen,* are brewed with a minimum of 50 percent wheat instead of barley grain.

Development of Microbreweries and Economies of Scale Although learning the art of brewing takes time, beer production lends itself to scalability and variety. For example, an amateur—or home brewer—could brew beer for home consumption. There had been a significant increase in the interest in home brewing, with over 1 million people pursuing the hobby in 2016.[8] It was also not uncommon for a home brewer to venture into entrepreneurship and begin brewing for commercial sales. However, the beer production was highly labor intensive with much of the work was done by hand. A certain level of production volume was necessary to achieve breakeven and make the microbrewery a successful commercial operation.

A small nanobrewery may brew a variety of flavor experiences and compete in niche markets, while the macrobrewery may focus on economies of scale and mass produce one style of beer. Both may attract consumers across segments, and were attributed to the easily scalable yet highly variable process of brewing beer. In contrast, a global producer such as AB InBev could produce beer for millions of consumers worldwide with factory-automated processes.

Legal Environment of Breweries As beer was an alcoholic beverage, the industry was subject to much regulation. Further, these regulations could vary by state and municipality. One such regulation was regarding sales and distribution.

Distribution could be distinguished through direct sales (or self-distribution), and two-tier and three-tier systems. Regulations permitting direct sales allow the brewery to sell directly to the consumer. Growlers, bottle sales, as well as tap rooms were all forms of direct, or retail, sales. There were usually requirements concerning direct sales, including limitations on volume sold to the consumer.

Even where self-distribution was legal, the legal volumes could be very small and limited. Very few brewers were exempt from distributing through wholesalers, referred to as a three-tier distribution system. And often to be operationally viable, brewers need access to this distribution system to generate revenue. In a three-tier system, the brewery must first sell to a wholesaler—the liquor or beer distributor. This distributor then sells to the retailer, who then ultimately sells to the consumer.

This distribution structure, however, had ramifications for the consumer, as much of what was available at retail outlets and restaurants was impacted by the distributor. This was further impacted by whether a brewery bottles or cans its beer, or distributes through kegs. While restaurants and bars could carry kegs, retail shelves at a local liquor store needed to have cans and bottles, as a relatively small number of consumers could accommodate kegs for home use. Thus, there may only be a few liquor stores or restaurants where a consumer may find a locally brewed beer. In states that do not allow self-distribution or on-premise sales, distribution and exposure to consumers could represent a barrier for breweries, especially those that were small or new.

The Alcohol and Tobacco Tax and Trade Bureau (TTB) was the main federal agency for regulating this industry. As another example of regulations, breweries were required to have labels for beers approved by the federal government, ensuring they meet advertising guidelines. In some instances, the TTB may need to approve the formula used for brewing the specific beer prior to the label receiving approval. Given the approval process, and the growth of craft breweries, the length of time this takes could reach several months. For a small microbrewery first starting, the delay in sales could potentially impact cash flow.

Employment law was another area impacting breweries. The Affordable Care Act (ACA) and changes to the Fair Labor Standards Act (FLSA) greatly affected labor cost in the industry. Where the ACA mandated health care coverage by employers, the FLSA changed overtime rules for employees previously classified as exempt or salaried. Finally, many states and municipalities passed or were considering passing increases to minimum wage. These changes in regulations could lead to significant increases in business costs, potentially impacting a brewery's ability to remain viable or competitive.

Lawsuits might also impact breweries' operations. Trademark infringement lawsuits regarding brewery and beer names were common. Further, food-related lawsuits could occur. In 2016, there were potential lawsuits against breweries distributing in California that did not meet the May 2016 requirement of providing an additional sign warning against pregnancy and BPA (Bisphenyl-A) consumption. BPA was commonly found in both cans and bottle caps, and thus breweries were potentially legally exposed, exemplifying the potential legal exposure to any brewery.

Suppliers to Breweries

One of the main suppliers to the industry were those who supply grain and hops. Growers might sell direct to breweries, or distribute through wholesalers. Brewers who wish to produce a grain-specific beer would be required to procure the specific grain. Further, recipes might call for a variety of grains, including rye, wheat, and corn. As previously mentioned, the definition of craft was changed not only to include a higher threshold for annual production, but it also was changed to not exclude producers who used other grains, such as corn, in their production. Finally, origin-specific beers, such as German- or Belgian-styles, might also require specific grains.

The more specialized the grain or hop, the more difficult it was to obtain. Those breweries, then, competing based on specialized brewing were required to identify such suppliers. Conversely, larger, global producers of single-style beers were able to utilize economies of scale and demand lower prices from suppliers. Organically grown grains and hops suppliers would also fall into this category of providing specialized ingredients, and specialty brewers tend to use such ingredients.

Exhibit 5 illustrates the amount of grain products used between 2010 and 2014 in the United States by breweries.

EXHIBIT 5 Total Grain Usage in the Production of Beer, 2010–2014 (in millions of pounds)

Grain*	2010	2011	2012	2013	2014
Corn	701	629	681	593	574
Rice	714	749	717	724	604
Barley	88	128	136	158	169
Wheat	22	24	26	30	33
Malt	4,147	4,028	4,117	3,916	3,689

*Includes products derived from the type of grain for brewing process.
Source: Alcohol and Tobacco Tax and Trade Bureau website.

It was estimated that hops acreage within the United States grew more than 16 percent from 2014 to 2015,[9] which seems to follow the growing demand due to the increased number of breweries. Hops were primarily grown in the Pacific Northwest states of Idaho, Washington, and Oregon. Washington's Yakima Valley was probably one of the more recognizable geographic-growing regions. There were numerous varieties of hops, however, and each contributes a different aroma and flavor profile. Hop growers have also trademarked names and varieties of hops. Further, as with grains, some beer styles require specific hops. Farmlands that were formerly known for hops have started to see a rejuvenation of this crop, such as in New England. In other areas, farmers were introducing hops as a new cash crop. Some hops farms were also dual purpose, combining the growing operations with brewing, thus serving as both a supplier of hops to breweries while also producing their own beer for retail. Recent news reports, however, were citing current and future shortages of hops due to the increased number of breweries. Rising temperatures in Europe led to a diminished yield in 2015, further impacting hops supplies. For breweries using recipes that require these specific hops, shortages could be detrimental to production.

Suppliers to the industry also include manufacturers and distributors of brewing equipment, such as fermentation tanks and refrigeration equipment. Purification equipment and testing tools were also necessary, given the brewing process and the need to ensure purity and safety of the product.

Depending on distribution and the distribution channel, breweries might need bottling or canning equipment. Thus breweries might invest heavily in automated bottling capabilities to expand capacity. Recently, however, there have been shortages in the 16-oz. size of aluminum cans.

How Breweries Compete: Innovation and Quality versus Price

The consumer might seek-out a specific beer or brewery's name, or purchase the lower-priced globally known brand. For some, beer drinking might also be seasonal, as tastes change with the seasons. Lighter beers were consumed in hotter months, while heavier beers were consumed in the colder months. Consumers might associate beer styles with the time of year or season. Oktoberfest and German-style beers were associated with fall, following the German-traditional celebration of Oktoberfest. Finally, any one consumer might enjoy several styles, or choose to be brewery or brand loyal.

The brewing process and the multiple varieties and styles of beer allow for breweries to compete across the strategy spectrum—low price and high volume, or higher price and low volume. Industry competitors, then, might target both price point and differentiation. The home brewer, who decides to invest a couple thousand dollars in a small space to produce very small quantities of beer and start a nanobrewery, might utilize a niche competitive strategy. The consumer might patronize the brewery on location, or seek it out on tap at a restaurant given the quality and the style of beer brewed. If allowed by law, the brewery might offer tastings or sell on-site to visitors. Further, the nanobrewer was free to explore and experiment with unusual flavors. To drive awareness, the brewer might enter competitions, attend beer festivals, or host tastings and "tap takeovers" at local restaurants. If successful, the brewer might invest in larger facilities and equipment to increase capacity with growing demand.

The larger, more established craft brewers, especially those considered regional breweries, might compete through marketing and distribution, while offering a higher value compared to the mass production of macrobreweries. However, the consumer might at times be sensitive to and desire the craft beer experience through smaller breweries—so much so that even craft breweries who by definition were craft might draw the ire of the consumer due to its size and scope. Boston Beer Company was one such company. Even though James Koch started it as a microbrewery, pioneering the craft beer movement in the 1980s, some craft beer consumers do not view it as authentically craft.

Larger macrobreweries mass produce and compete using economies of scale and established distribution systems. Thus, low cost preserves margins as lower price points drive volume sales. Many of these brands were sold en masse at sporting and entertainment venues, as well as larger restaurant chains, driving volume sales.

Companies like SABMiller and AB InBev possess brands within their portfolio that were sold under the perception of craft beer, in what Boston Beer Company deems the better beer category—beer with a higher price point, but also of higher quality. For example, Blue Moon—a Belgian-style wheat ale—was produced by MillerCoors. Blue Moon's market share had increased significantly since 2006 following the rise in craft beer popularity, competing against Boston Beer Company's Sam Adams in this better beer segment. AB InBev had also recently acquired the larger better-known craft breweries, including Goose Island, in 2011. With a product portfolio that includes both low-price and premium craft beer brands, macrobreweries were competing across the spectrum and putting pressure on breweries within the better and craft beer segments—segments demanding a higher price point due to production.

However, a recent lawsuit claimed the marketing of Blue Moon was misleading and its marketing obscured the ownership structure. Although the case was dismissed, it further illustrates consumer sentiment regarding what was perceived as craft beer. It also illustrates the power of marketing and how a macrobrewery might position a brand within these segments.

Consolidations and Acquisitions

In 2015 AB InBev offered to purchase SABMiller for $108 billion, which was recently approved by the European Union in May 2016. To allow for the acquisition, many of SABMiller's brands needed to be sold. Asahi Group Holdings Ltd. will be purchasing the European brands Peroni and Grolsch from SABMiller. Molson Coors will also be purchasing SABMiller's 58 percent ownership in MillerCoors LLC—originally a joint venture between Molson Coors and SABMiller. This will now leave Molson Coors with 100 percent ownership of MillerCoors. It should be noted that AB InBev and MillerCoors represent over 80 percent of the beer produced in the United States for domestic consumption.

Purchases of craft breweries by larger companies had also increased during the 2010s. AB InBev had purchased eight craft breweries since 2011, including Goose Island, Blue Point, and Devil's Backbone Brewing. MillerCoors—whose brands already include Killian's Irish Red, Leinenkugel's, and Foster's—just recently acquired Saint Archer Brewing Company. Ballast Point Brewing & Spirits was acquired by Constellations Brands. Finally, Heineken NV purchased a stake in Lagunitas Brewing Company. It would seem that craft beer and breweries had obtained the attention of not only the consumer, but also the larger multinational breweries and corporations.

PROFILES OF BEER PRODUCERS

Anheuser-Busch InBev

As the world's largest producer by volume, AB InBev employed over 150,000 people in 26 different countries. The product portfolio included the production, marketing, and distribution of over 200 beers, malt beverages, as well as soft drinks in 130 countries. These brands included Budweiser, Stella Artois, Leffe, and Hoegaarden.

AB InBev managed its product portfolio through three tiers. Global brands, such as Budweiser, Stella Artois, and Corona, were distributed throughout the world. International brands (Beck's, Hoegaarden, Leffe) were found in multiple countries. Local champions (i.e., local brands) represent regional or domestic brands acquired by AB InBev, such as Goose Island in the United States and Cass in South Korea. While some of the local brands were found in different countries, it was due to geographic proximity and the potential to grow the brand larger.

AB InBev estimated its market share in China as 19 percent, United States 46 percent, Brazil 68 percent, and Mexico 58 percent.[10] Its strength in brand recognition and focused marketing on what it deemed as core categories resulted in AB InBev as the top brewery in the United States, Brazil, and Mexico markets, and number three in China by volume. Significant growth had been recognized in the developing markets, including Mexico and the Asia Pacific region. Since 2013, volumes in Mexico have almost doubled, while volumes in Asia Pacific have increased by approximately 25 percent. This helped offset the approximate 3 percent decrease in volume in North America and the 2 percent decrease in Europe.

AB InBev invested heavily in marketing. Budweiser planned to sponsor the 2018 and 2022 FIFA World Cups™, as it had sponsored the 2014 competition. This marketing helped bolster the Budweiser brand, as it accounted for 11 percent of AB InBev's 2015 volume. It experienced a 7 percent growth in 2015, attributed to increased sales in China and Brazil. Bud Light—which held 47 percent of the premium light category as the best-selling beer in the United States—was official sponsor of the National Football League through 2022.

AB InBev had also actively acquired other brands and breweries since the 1990s, including Labatt in 1995, Beck's in 2002, Anheuser-Busch in 2008, and Grupo Modelo in 2013. All of these acquisitions proceeded the SABMiller purchase. These acquisitions provided AB InBev greater market share and penetration through combining marketing and operations to all brands. The reacquisition of the Oriental Brewery in 2014 was a good example of the potential synergies garnered. Cass was the leading beer in Korea and was produced by Oriental Brewery; however, while Cass represented the local brand for AB InBev in Korea, Hoegaarden was distributed in Korea, along with the global brands of Budweiser, Corona, and Stella Artois.

A summary of AB InBev's financial performance from 2013 to 2015 is presented in Exhibit 6.

Boston Beer Company

Approximately 1,400 people were employed at Boston Beer Company, one of the largest craft brewers by volume in the United States, having sold 4.1 million barrels in 2015. In 2015 it was ranked second largest craft brewing company, and fifth in size for overall brewing. Its primary brand was Samuel Adams, first introduced in 1984. The company history states the recipe for Sam Adams was actually company founder Jim Koch's great-great-grandfather's recipe. The story of Boston Beer Company and Jim Koch's success was referenced at times as the beginning of the craft beer movement, often citing how Koch originally sold his beer to bars with the beer and pitching on the spot.

This beginning seems to underpin much of Boston Beer Company's strategy as it competes in the higher value and higher price-point category it refers to as the *better beer segment.* Focusing on quality and taste, Boston Beer Company markets the Samuel Adams Boston Lager as the original beer

EXHIBIT 6 Financial Summary for AB InBev, 2013–2015 (in millions of $)

	2015	2014	2013
Revenue	$43,604	$47,063	$43,195
Cost of sales	(17,137)	(18,756)	(17,594)
Gross Profit	26,467	28,307	25,601
Distribution expenses	(4,259)	(4,558)	(4,061)
Sales and marketing expenses	(6,913)	(7,036)	(5,958)
Administrative expenses	(2,560)	(2,791)	(2,539)
Other operating income/expenses	1,032	1,386	1,160
Non-recurring items	136	(197)	6,240
Profit from operations (EBIT)	13,904	15,111	20,443
Depreciation, amortization and impairment	3,153	3,354	2,985
EBITDA	$17,057	$18,465	$23,428

Sources: AB InBev 2015 and 2014 Annual Reports to Shareholders.

Koch first discovered. Under the Sam Adams brand were several seasonal beers, including Sam Adams Summer Ale and Sam Adams Octoberfest. Other seasonal Sam Adams beers have limited release in seasonal variety packs, including Samuel Adams Harvest Pumpkin and Samuel Adams Holiday Porter. In addition, there was also the Samuel Adams Brewmaster's Collection, a much smaller, limited release set of beers at much higher points, including the Small Batch Collection and Barrel Room Collection. Utopia—its highest-priced beer—was branded as highly experimental and under very limited release.

In the spirit of craft beer and innovation, several years ago Boston Beer Company launched a craft brew incubator as a subsidiary, which had led to the successful development and sales of beers under the Traveler Beer Company brand. The incubator, Alchemy and Science, also built Concrete Beach Brewery and Coney Island Brewery. Accordingly, Alchemy and Science contributed to 7 percent of the total net sales in 2015.

Boston Beer Company had two non-beer brands. The Twisted Tea brand was launched 15 years ago, and the Angry Orchard brand 3 years ago. These other brands and products compete in the flavored malt beverage and the hard cider categories, respectively.

A summary of Boston Brewing Company's financial performance from 2013 to 2015 is presented in Exhibit 7.

Craft Brew Alliance

Craft Brew Alliance was the fifth largest craft brewing company in the United States, and was ranked ninth for overall brewing by volume. First founded in 2008, it represents the mergers between Redhook Brewery, Widmer Brothers Brewing, and Kona Brewing Company. Each brewery with substantial history, the decision to merge was to help assist with growth and meeting demand. Today Craft Brew Alliance includes Omission Brewery, Resignation Brewery, and Square Mile Cider Company. In addition to these five brands, Craft Brew Alliance operates five brewpubs. In total, there were 820 people employed at Craft Brew Alliance, producing just over 1 million barrels in 2015.

Craft Brew Alliance utilizes automated brewing equipment and distributes nationally through the Anheuser-Busch wholesaler network alliance, leveraging many of the logistics and thus cost advantages associated. Yet, it remains independent, leveraging both its craft brewery brands and the cost advantage associated with larger distribution networks. It was the only independent craft brewer to achieve

EXHIBIT 7 Financial Summary for Boston Brewing Company, 2013–2015 (in thousands of $)

	2015	2014	2013
Revenue	$1,024,040	$966,478	$793,705
Excise taxes	(64,106)	(63,471)	(54,652)
Cost of goods sold	(458,317)	(437,996)	(354,131)
Gross Profit	501,617	465,011	384,922
Advertising, promotional and selling expenses	273,629	250,696	207,930
General and administrative expenses	71,556	65,971	62,332
Impairment of assets	258	1,777	1,567
Operating Income	156,174	146,567	113,093
Interest income	56	21	31
Other expense, net	(1,220)	(994)	(583)
Provision for income taxes	56,596	54,851	42,149
Net Income	$ 98,414	$ 90,743	$ 70,392

Source: Boston Beer Company 2015 Annual Report.

this relationship. However, given the locations of the original founding breweries, sales were concentrated on the West Coast and Hawaii.

Craft Brew Alliance engages in contract brewing—a practice where space capacity in production was utilized to produce beer under contract for sale under a different label or brand. In addition, it had partnerships with retailers like Costco and Buffalo Wild Wings, garnering further consumer exposure as well as sales.

A summary of Craft Brew Alliance's financial performance from 2013 to 2015 is presented in Exhibit 8.

Strategic Issues Confronting Craft Breweries in 2016

The vast majority of the craft breweries might produce only enough beer for the local population in their area. Many of these breweries started the same way as the larger breweries: Home brewers or hobbyists decided to start to brew and sell their own beer. Many obtained startup capital through their own savings or soliciting investments from friends and family.

Given their entrepreneurial beginnings, these microbreweries and even smaller nanobreweries were usually located in industrial spaces. They were solely operated by the brewer-turned-entrepreneur, or a small staff of two or three. This staff would help with brewing and production, as well as potentially brewery tours and visits—probably the most common marketing and consumer relations tactic utilized by smaller breweries. While almost all breweries offered tours and tastings, these became ever more critical to the smaller brewery with limited capital for marketing and advertising. If on-site sales were available, the brewer was able to sell growlers to visitors.

Social media websites also offered significant exposure for free and had become a foundational element of these breweries' marketing. These websites helped the brewery reach the craft beer consumer, who tended to seek out and follow new and upcoming breweries. There were also mobile phone applications specific to the craft beer industry that could help a startup gain exposure. Participating in craft beer festivals, where local and regional breweries were able to offer samples to attendees, was another opportunity to gain exposure.

Some small microbreweries did not have enough employees for bottling and labeling, and had been known to solicit volunteers through social media. To gain exposure and boost sales, the brewery might host events at local restaurants, such as tap-takeovers, where several of its beers are featured on draft. If enough consumers were engaged, the local restaurant was enticed to purchase more beer from the distributor of the brewery. However, any number of variables—raw material shortages, tight retail competition, price-sensitive consumers—could dramatically impact future viability.

The number of beers available to the consumer throughout all segments and price points had

EXHIBIT 8 Financial Summary for Craft Brew Alliance, 2013–2015 (in thousands of $)

	2015	2014	2013
Revenue	$204,168	$200,022	$179,180
Cost of sales	(141,972)	(141,312)	(128,919)
Gross Profit	62,196	58,710	50,261
Selling, general and administrative expenses	57,932	53,000	46,461
Operating Income	4,264	5,710	3,800
Income before provision for income taxes	3,718	5,099	3,263
Provision for income taxes	1,500	2,022	1,304
Net Income	$ 2,218	$ 3,077	$ 1,959

Sources: Craft Brew Alliance 2014 Annual Report to Shareholders and 2016 10-K SEC Filing Report.

continued to steadily climb since the mid-2000s. It would seem that while the market for lower-price-point beer was stagnating in developing countries, sales of Budweiser and others were increasing overseas in developing markets. However, the significant growth seemed to be in the craft beer, or better beer, segments. Between 2013 and 2015 almost 1,500 new microbreweries opened across the United States. Compared to about 700 from 2010 to 2012,[11] it was clear that more individuals were viewing craft beer as a potential business.

Further, larger macrobreweries and regional craft breweries were seizing the opportunity to acquire other breweries as a method of obtaining distribution and branding synergies, while also mitigating the amount of direct competition. Complicating the competitive landscape were increasing availability and price fluctuations of raw materials. These sporadic shortages might impact the industry's growth and affect the production stability of breweries, especially those smaller operations that did not have capacity to purchase in bulk or outbid larger competitors. Overall, the growth in the consumers' desire for craft beer was likely to continue to attract more entrants, while encouraging larger breweries to seek additional acquisitions of successful craft beer brands.

ENDNOTES

1. Brewers Association.
2. Boston Beer Reports Fourth Quarter 2015 Results, Press Release, February 18, 2016.
3. Beer sales are commonly measured by barrels in America and hectoliters in Europe. The conversion is 1 hL = 0.852 barrel [U.S. beer]. AB InBev reported 233.7 million hL and 45.8 percent of the market in the 2016 20-K SEC filing. The Alcohol and Tobacco Tax and Trade Bureau Statistical Report for Beer in December 2015 shows production to be about 190.5 million barrels.
4. Beer Institute and National Beer Wholesalers Association, The Beer Industry Economic Contribution Study, 2015.
5. "World Beer Market—Opportunities and Forecasts, 2014–2020," www.alliedmarketresearch.com/beer-market (accessed May 24, 2016).
6. A. Ramzy, "China's Craft Breweries Find They May Have a 5,000-Year-Old Relative," *The New York Times*, May 25, 2016, www.nytimes.com/2016/05/26/world/asia/china-beer-history.html.
7. Guinness website.
8. American Homebrewers Association.
9. 2015 Hop Acreage Report Expanded, n.d., www.usahops.org/index.cfm?fuseaction=stat&pageID=8 (accessed May 26, 2016).
10. AB InBev March 2016 20-F Report. Rounded to nearest percent.
11. Brewers Association.

CASE 06

TOMS Shoes in 2016: An Ongoing Dedication to Social Responsibility

Margaret A. Peteraf
Tuck School of Business at Dartmouth

Sean Zhang and Meghan L. Cooney
Research Assistants, Dartmouth College

While traveling in Argentina in 2006, Blake Mycoskie witnessed the hardships that children without shoes experienced and became committed to making a difference. Rather than focusing on charity work, Mycoskie sought to build an organization capable of sustainable, repeated giving, where children would be guaranteed shoes throughout their childhood. He established Shoes for a Better Tomorrow, better known as TOMS, as a for-profit company based on the premise of the "One for One" Pledge. For every pair of shoes TOMS sold, TOMS would donate a pair to a child in need. By mid-2016, TOMS had given way over 50 million pairs of shoes in over 70 different countries.[1]

As a relatively new and privately held company, TOMS experienced consistent and rapid growth despite the global recession that began in 2009. By 2015, TOMS had matured into an organization with nearly 500 employees and almost $400 million in revenues. TOMS shoes could be found in several major retail stores such as Nordstrom, Bloomingdale's, and Urban Outfitters. In addition to providing shoes for underprivileged children, TOMS also expanded its mission to include restoring vision to those with curable sight-related illnesses by developing a new line of eyewear products. For an overview of how quickly TOMS expanded in its first seven years of business, see Exhibit 1.[2]

COMPANY BACKGROUND

While attending Southern Methodist University, Blake Mycoskie founded the first of his six startups, a laundry service company that encompassed seven colleges and staffed over 40 employees. Four startups and a short stint on *The Amazing Race* later, Mycoskie found himself vacationing in Argentina where he not only learned about the Alpargata shoe originally used by local peasants in the 14th century, but also witnessed the extreme poverty in rural Argentina.

Determined to make a difference, Mycoskie believed that providing shoes could more directly impact the children in these rural communities than delivering medicine or food. Aside from protecting children's feet from infections, parasites, and diseases, shoes were often required for a complete school uniform. In addition, research had shown that shoes were found to significantly increase children's

EXHIBIT 1 TOMS' Growth in Employees and Sales, 2006–2015

	2015	2014	2013	2012	2011	2010	2009	2008	2007	2006
Total Employees	470	450	400	320	250	72	46	33	19	4
Thousands of Pairs of Shoes Sold	25,000	10,000	7,250	2,700	1,300	1,000	230	110	50	10

Source: PrivCo, Private Company Financial Report, "TOM's Shoes, Inc.," created April 18, 2016.

self-confidence, help them develop into more active community members, and lead them to stay in school. Thus, by ensuring access to shoes, Mycoskie could effectively increase children's access to education and foster community activism, raising the overall standard of living for people living in poor Argentinian rural areas.

Dedicated to his mission, Mycoskie purchased 250 pairs of Alpargatas and returned home to Los Angeles, where he subsequently founded TOMS Shoes. He built the company on the promise of "One for One," donating a pair of shoes for every pair sold. With an initial investment of $300,000, Mycoskie's business concept of social entrepreneurship was simple: sell both the shoe and the story behind it. Building on a simple slogan that effectively communicated his goal, Mycoskie championed his personal experiences passionately and established deep and lasting relationships with customers.

Operating from his apartment with three interns he found on Craigslist, Mycoskie quickly sold out his initial inventory and expanded considerably, selling 10,000 pairs of shoes by the end of his first year. With family and friends, Mycoskie ventured back to Argentina, where they hand-delivered 10,000 pairs of shoes to children in need. Because he followed through on his mission statement, Mycoskie was able to subsequently attract investors to support his unique business model and expand his venture significantly.

When TOMS was initially founded, TOMS operated as the for-profit financial arm while a separate entity titled "Friends of TOMS" focused on charity work and giving. After 2011, operations at Friends of TOMS were absorbed into TOMS's own operations as TOMS itself matured. In Friends of TOMS's latest accessible 2011 501(c)(3) filing, assets were reported at less than $130,000.[3] Moreover, as of May 2013, the Friends of TOMS website was discontinued while TOMS also ceased advertising its partnership with Friends of TOMS in marketing campaigns and on its corporate website. The developments suggested that Friends of TOMS became a defunct entity as TOMS incorporated all of its operations under the overarching TOMS brand.

INDUSTRY BACKGROUND

Even though Mycoskie's vision for his company was a unique one, vying for a position in global footwear manufacturing was a risky and difficult venture. The industry was both stable and mature—one in which large and small companies competed on the basis of price, quality, and service. Competitive pressures came from foreign as well as domestic companies and new entrants needed to fight for access to downstream retailers.

Further, the cost of supplies was forecast to increase between 2013 and 2020. Materials and wages constituted over 70 percent of industry costs—clearly a sizable concern for competitors. Supply purchases included leather, rubber, plastic compounds, foam, nylon, canvas, laces, and so on. While the price of leather rose steadily each year, the price of rubber also began to climb at an average annual rate of 7.6 percent. Wages were expected to increase at a rate of 5.8 percent over a five-year period due to growing awareness of how manufacturers took advantage of cheap, outsourced labor.[4]

In order to thrive in the footwear manufacturing industry, firms needed to differentiate their products in a meaningful way. Selling good-quality products at a reasonable price was rarely enough; they needed to target a niche market that desired a certain image. Product innovation and advertising campaigns therefore became the most successful competitive weapons. For example, Clarks adopted a sophisticated design, appealing to a wealthier, more mature customer base. Nike, adidas, and Skechers developed athletic footwear and aggressively marketed their brands to reflect that image. Achieving economies of scale, increasing technical efficiency, and developing a cost-effective distribution system were also essential elements for success.

Despite the presence of established incumbents, global footwear manufacturing was an attractive industry to potential entrants based on the prediction of increased demand and therefore sales revenue. Moreover, the industry offered incumbents one of the highest profit margins in the fashion industry. But because competitors were likely to open new locations and expand their brands in order to discourage competition, new companies' only option was to attempt to undercut them on cost. Acquiring capital equipment and machinery to manufacture footwear on a large scale was expensive. Moreover, potential entrants also needed to launch costly large-scale marketing campaigns to promote brand awareness. Thus, successful incumbents were traditionally able to maintain an overwhelming portion of the market.

Building the TOMS Brand

Due to its humble beginnings, TOMS struggled to gain a foothold in the footwear industry. While companies like Nike had utilized high-profile athletes like Michael Jordan and Tiger Woods to establish brand recognition, TOMS had relatively limited financial resources and tried to appeal to a more socially conscious consumer. Luckily, potential buyers enjoyed a rise in disposable income over time as the economy recovered from the recession. As a result, demand for high-quality footwear increased for affluent shoppers, accompanied by a desire to act (and be *seen* acting) charitably and responsibly.

While walking through the airport one day, Mycoskie encountered a girl wearing TOMS shoes. Mycoskie recounts:

> I asked her about her shoes, and she went on to tell me this amazing story about TOMS and the model that it uses and my personal story. I realized the importance of having a story today is what really separates companies. People don't just wear our shoes, they tell our story. That's one of my favorite lessons that I learned early on.

Moving forward, TOMS focused more on selling the story behind the shoe rather than product features or celebrity endorsements. Moreover, rather than relying primarily on mainstream advertising, TOMS emphasized a grassroots approach using social media and word of mouth. With over 3.5 million Facebook "Likes" and over 2 million Twitter "Followers" in 2016, TOMS's social media presence eclipsed that of its much larger rivals, Skechers and Clarks. Based on 2016 data, TOMS had fewer "Followers" than Nike, and fewer "Likes" than both Nike and Adidas. However, TOMS had more "Followers" and "Likes" per dollar of revenue. So when taking company size into account, TOMS also had a greater media presence than the industry's leading competitors (see Exhibit 2 for more information).

TOMS's success with social media advertising can be attributed to the story crafted and championed by Mycoskie. Industry incumbents generally dedicated a substantial portion of revenue and effort to advertising since they were simply selling a product. TOMS, on the other hand, used its mission to ask customers to buy into a *cause,* limiting their need to devote resources to brand-building. TOMS lets its charitable work and social media presence generate interest for the company organically. This strategy also increased the likelihood that consumers would place repeat purchases and share the story behind their purchases with family and friends. TOMS's customers took pride in supporting a grassroots cause instead of a luxury footwear supplier and encouraged others to share in the rewarding act.

A BUSINESS MODEL DEDICATED TO SOCIALLY RESPONSIBLE BEHAVIOR

Traditionally, the content of advertisements for many large apparel companies focused on the attractive aspects of the featured products. TOMS's advertising, on the other hand, showcased its charitable contributions and the story of its founder Blake Mycoskie. While the CEOs of Nike, adidas, and Clarks rarely appeared in their companies' advertisements, TOMS ran as many ads with its founder as it did without him, emphasizing the inseparability of the TOMS's product from Mycoskie's story. In all of his appearances, Mycoskie was dressed in casual and friendly attire so that customers could easily relate to Blake and his mission. This advertising

EXHIBIT 2 TOMS' Use of Social Media Compared to Selected Footwear Competitors

	2015 Revenue (Mil. of $)	Facebook "Likes"	"Likes" per Mil. of $ in Revenue	Twitter "Followers"	"Followers" per Mil. of $ in Revenue
TOMS	$ 390	3,522,891	9,033	2,170,000	5,564
Clarks	2,123	1,634,803	770	42,300	20
Skechers	3,150	1,921,582	610	32,700	10
Adidas	16,920	23,362,006	1,380	2,650,000	157
Nike	30,700	24,020,024	782	4,070,000	133

Source: Author data from Facebook and Twitter, April 11, 2016; revenue numbers obtained from MarketWatch.

method conveyed a small-company feel and encouraged consumers to connect personally with the TOMS brand. It also worked to increase buyer patronage through differentiating the TOMS product from others. Consumers were convinced that every time they purchased a pair of TOMS, they became instruments of the company's charitable work. Representative advertisements for TOMS Shoes are presented in Exhibit 3.

As a result (although statistical measures of repeating-buying and total product satisfaction among TOMS's customers were not publicly available), the volume of repeat purchases and buyer enthusiasm likely fueled TOMS's success in a critical way. One reviewer commented, "This is my third pair of TOMS and I absolutely love them! . . . I can't wait to buy more"[5] Another wrote, "Just got my 25th pair! Love the color! They . . . are my all-time favorite shoe for comfort, looks & durability. AND they are for a great cause!! Gotta go pick out my next pair."[6]

Virtually all consumer reports on TOMS shoes shared similar themes. Though not cheap, TOMS footwear was priced lower than rivals' products, and customers overwhelmingly agreed that the value was worth the cost. Reviewers described TOMS as comfortable, true to size, lightweight, and versatile ("go with everything"). The shoes had "cute shapes and patterns" and were made of canvas and rubber that molded to customers' feet with wear. Because TOMS products were appealing and trendy yet also basic and comfortable, they were immune to changing fashion trends and consistently attracted a variety of consumers.

In addition to offering a high-quality product that people valued, TOMS was able to establish a positive repertoire with its customers through efficient distribution. Maintaining an online shop helped TOMS save money on retail locations but also allowed it to serve a wide geographic range. Further, the company negotiated with well-known retailers like Nordstrom and Neiman Marcus to assist in distribution. Through thoughtful planning and structured coordination, TOMS limited operation costs and provided prompt service for its customers.

Giving Partners

As it continued to grow, TOMS sought to improve its operational efficiency by teaming up with "Giving Partners," nonprofit organizations that helped distribute the shoes that TOMS donated. By teaming up with Giving Partners, TOMS streamlined its charity operations by shifting many of its distributional responsibilities to organizations that were often larger, more resourceful, and able to distribute TOMS shoes more efficiently. Moreover, these organizations possessed more familiarity and experience dealing with the communities that TOMS was interested in helping and could therefore better allocate shoes that suited the needs of children in the area. Giving Partners also provided feedback to help TOMS improve on its giving and distributional efforts.

EXHIBIT 3 Representative Advertisements for TOMS Shoes Company

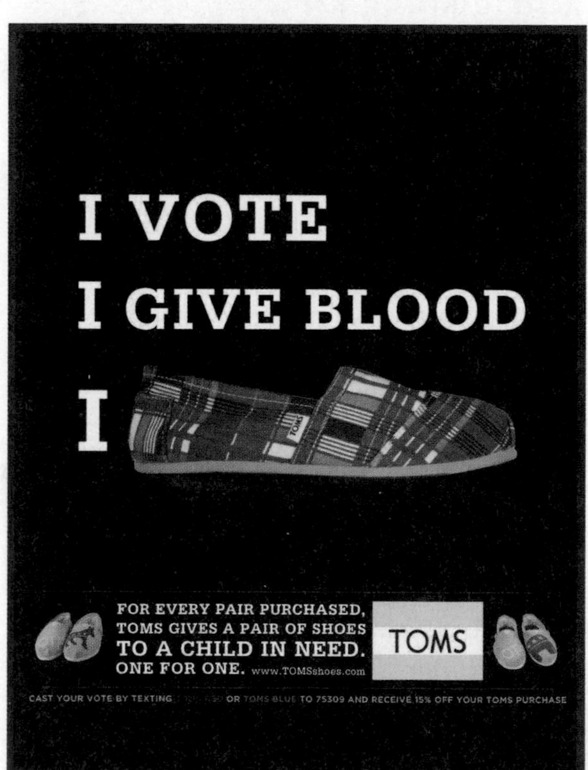

Instead of appealing to consumers desire for stylish footwear, Toms advertisements instead addresses the consumers sense of social consciousness by encouraging people to not only provide shoes to a child in need, but to also vote.

Source: Author data.

Each Giving Partner also magnified the impact of TOMS shoes by bundling its distribution with other charity work that the organization specialized in. For example, Partners in Health, a nonprofit organization that spent almost $100 million in 2012 on providing health care for the poor (more than TOMS's total revenue that year), dispersed thousands of shoes to schoolchildren in Rwanda and Malawi while also screening them for malnutrition. Cooperative giving further strengthened the TOMS brand by association with well-known and highly regarded Giving Partners. Complementary services expanded the scope of TOMS's mission, enhanced the impact that each pair of TOMS had on a child's life, and increased the number of goodwill and business opportunities available to TOMS.

In order to ensure quality of service and adherence to its fundamental mission, TOMS maintained five criteria for Giving Partners:[7]

- Repeat Giving: Giving partners must be able to work with the same communities in multiyear commitments, regularly providing shoes to the same children as they grow.
- High Impact: Shoes must aid Giving Partners with their existing goals in the areas of health and education, providing children with opportunities they would not have otherwise.
- Considerate of Local Economy: Providing shoes cannot have negative socioeconomic effects on the communities where shoes are given.
- Large Volume Shipments: Giving Partners must be able to accept large shipments of giving pairs.
- Health/Education Focused: Giving Partners must give shoes only in conjunction with health and education efforts.

As of 2016, TOMS had built relationships with over 100 Giving Partners including Save the Children, U.S. Fund for UNICEF, and IMA World Health. In order to remain accountable to its mission in these joint ventures, TOMS also performed unannounced audit reports that ensured shoes were distributed according to the One for One® model.

Building a Relationship with Giving Partners

Having Giving Partners offered TOMS the valuable opportunity to shift some of its philanthropic costs onto other parties. However, TOMS also proactively maintained strong relationships with its Giving Partners. Kelly Gibson, the program director of National Relief Charities (NRC), a Giving Partner and nonprofit organization dedicated to improving the lives of Native Americans, highlighted the respect with which TOMS treated its Giving Partners:

> TOMS treats their Giving Partners (like us) and the recipients of their giveaway shoes (the Native kids in this case) like customers. We had a terrific service experience with TOMS. They were meticulous about getting our shoe order just right. They also insist that the children who receive shoes have a customer-type experience at distributions.

From customizing Giving Partner orders to helping pick up the tab for transportation and distribution, TOMS treated its Giving Partners as valuable customers and generated a sense of goodwill that extended beyond its immediate One for One® mission. By ensuring that its Giving Partners and recipients of shoes were treated respectfully, TOMS developed a unique ability to sustain business relationships that other for-profit organizations more concerned with the financial bottom line did not.

MAINTAINING A DEDICATION TO CORPORATE SOCIAL RESPONSIBILITY

Although TOMS manufactured its products in Argentina, China, and Ethiopia (countries that have all been cited as areas with a high degree of child and forced labor by the Bureau of International Labor Affairs), regular third-party factory audits and a Supplier Code of Conduct helped ensure compliance with fair labor standards.[8] Audits were conducted on both an announced and unannounced basis while the Supplier Code of Conduct was publicly posted in the local language of every work site. The Supplier Code of Conduct enforced standards such as minimum work age, requirement of voluntary employment, nondiscrimination, maximum workweek hours, and right to unionize. It also protected workers from physical, sexual, verbal, or psychological harassment in accordance with a country's legally mandated standards. Workers were encouraged to report violations directly to TOMS, and suppliers found in violation of TOMS's Supplier Code of Conduct faced termination.

In addition to ensuring that suppliers met TOMS's ethical standards, TOMS also emphasized its own dedication to ethical behavior in a number of ways. TOMS was a member of the American Apparel and Footwear Association (AAFA) and was registered with the Fair Labor Association (FLA). Internally, TOMS educated its own employees on human trafficking and slavery prevention and partnered with several organizations dedicated to raising awareness about such issues, including Hand of Hope.[9]

Giving Trips

Aside from material shoe contributions, TOMS also held a series of "Giving Trips" that supported the broader notion of community service. Giving Trips were firsthand opportunities for employees of TOMS and selected TOMS customers to partake in the delivery of TOMS shoes. These trips increased the transparency of TOMS's philanthropic efforts, further engaging customers and employees. They generated greater social awareness as well, since participants on these trips often became more engaged in local community service efforts at home.

From a business standpoint, Giving Trips also represented a marketing success. First, a large number of participants were customers and journalists unassociated with TOMS who circulated their stories online through social media upon their return. Second, TOMS was able to motivate participants and candidates to become more involved in their mission by increasing public awareness. In 2013, instead of internally selecting customers to participate on the Giving Trips, TOMS opted to hold an open voting process that encouraged candidates to reach out to their known contacts and ask them to vote for their inclusion. This contest drew thousands of contestants and likely hundreds of thousands of voters, although the final vote tallies were not publicly released.

Environmental Sustainability

Dedicated to minimizing its environmental impact, TOMS pursued a number of sustainable practices that included offering vegan shoes, incorporating recycled bottles into its products, and printing with soy ink. TOMS also used a blend of organic canvas and postconsumer, recycled plastics to create shoes that were both comfortable and durable. By utilizing natural hemp and organic cotton, TOMS eliminated pesticide and insecticide use that adversely affected the environment.

In addition, TOMS supported several environmental organizations like Surfers Against Sewage, a movement that raised awareness about excess sewage discharge in the UK. Formally, TOMS was a member of the Textile Exchange, an organization dedicated to textile sustainability and protecting the environment. The company also participated actively in the AAFA's Environmental Responsibility Committee.

Creating the TOMS Workforce

When asked what makes a great employee, Mycoskie blogged,

> As TOMS has grown, we've continued to look for these same traits in the interns and employees that we hire. Are you passionate? Can you creatively solve problems? Can you be resourceful without resources? Do you have the compassion to serve others? You can teach a new hire just about any skill . . . but you absolutely cannot inspire creativity and passion in someone that doesn't have it.[10]

The company's emphasis on creativity and passion was part of the reason why TOMS relied so heavily on interns and new hires rather than experienced workers. By hiring younger, more inexperienced employees, TOMS was able to be more cost-effective in terms of personnel. The company could also recruit young and energetic individuals who were more likely to think innovatively and out the box. These employees were placed in specialized teams under the leadership of strong, experienced managerial talent. This human intellectual capital generated a competitive advantage for the TOMS brand.

Together with these passionate individuals, Mycoskie strove to create a family-like work atmosphere where openness and collaboration were celebrated. With his cubicle located in one of the most highly trafficked areas of the office (right next to customer service), Mycoskie made a point to interact with his employees on a daily basis, in all-staff meetings, and through weekly personal e-mails while traveling. Regarding his e-mails, Mycoskie reflected,

> I'm a very open person, so I really tell the staff what I'm struggling with and what I'm happy about. I tell them what I think the future of TOMS is. I want them to understand what I'm thinking. It's like I'm writing to a best friend.[11]

This notion of "family" was further solidified through company dinners, ski trips, and book clubs where TOMS employees were encouraged to socialize in informal settings. These casual opportunities to interact with colleagues created a "balanced" work atmosphere where employees celebrated not only their own successes, but the successes of their co-workers (see Exhibit 4).

Diversity and inclusion were also emphasized at TOMS. For example, cultural traditions like the Chinese Lunar New Year were celebrated publicly on the TOMS's company blog. Moreover, as TOMS began expanding and distributing globally, the company increasingly sought to recruit a more diverse workforce by hiring multilingual individuals who were familiar with TOMS's diverse customer base and could communicate with its giving communities.[12]

The emphasis that Mycoskie placed on each individual employee was one of the key reasons why employees at TOMS often felt "lucky" to be part of the movement.[13] Coupled with the fact that TOMS employees knew their efforts fostered social justice, these "Agents of Change," as they referred to themselves, were generally quite satisfied with their work, making TOMS *Forbes*'s 4th Most Inspiring Company in 2014. Overall, the culture allowed TOMS to recruit and retain high-quality employees invested in achieving its social mission.

EXHIBIT 4 TOMS Shoes Balanced Work Environment

Instead of appealing to consumers desire for stylish footwear, TOMS advertisements instead addresses the consumers sense of social consciousness by encouraging people to not only provide shoes to a child in need, but to also vote.

Source: TOMS

FINANCIAL SUCCESS AT TOMS

With a compound annual growth rate (CAGR) of 4.8 percent from 2010 to 2014, global footwear manufacturing developed into an industry worth over $289.7 billion.[14] While TOMS remained a privately held company with limited financial data, the estimated growth rate of TOMS's revenue was astounding. In the seven years after his company's inception, Mycoskie was able to turn his initial $300,000 investment into a company with over $200 million in yearly revenues. As shown in Exhibit 5, the average growth rate of TOMS on a yearly basis was 145 percent, even excluding its first major spike of 457 percent. During the same period, Nike experienced a growth rate of roughly 8.5 percent, with a *decline* in revenues from 2009 to 2010.

The fact that TOMS was able to experience consistent growth despite financial turmoil post-2008 illustrates the strength of the One for One movement to survive times of recession. Mycoskie attributed his success during the recession to two factors: (1) As consumers became more conscious of their spending during recessions, products like TOMS that gave to others actually became *more* appealing (according to Mycoskie); (2) the giving model that TOMS employed is not "priced in." Rather than commit a percentage of profits or revenues to charity, Mycoskie noted that TOMS simply gave away a pair for every pair it sold. This way, socially conscious consumers knew exactly where their money was going without having to worry that TOMS would cut back on its charity efforts in order to turn a profit.[15]

EXHIBIT 5 Revenue Comparison for TOMS Shoes and the Footwear Industry, 2006–2015

	2015	2014	2013	2012	2011	2010	2009	2008	2007	2006
TOMS (in Mils. of $s)										
Revenue	$ 390	$370.9	$ 285	$101.8	$ 46.9	$ 25.1	$ 8.4	$ 3.1	$ 1.2	$0.2
Growth (%)	5.1%	30.1%	180%	117%	86.9%	199%	171%	158.3%	500%	—
Industry (in Bils. of $s)										
Revenue	$191.6	$189.3	$175.3	$164.4	$169.4	$152.1	$148.6	$155.6	$131.3	N.A.
Growth (%)	1.2%	8.0%	6.6%	−3.0%	11.4%	2.4%	−4.5%	18.5%	19.9%	—

Note: N.A., Not available.

Source: "Global Footwear Manufacturing," *IBISWorld*, April 18, 2016, **http://clients1.ibisworld.com/reports/gl/industry/currentperformance.aspx?entid=500**.

Production at TOMS

Although TOMS manufactured shoes in Argentina, Ethiopia, and China, only shoes made in China were brought to the retail market. Shoes made in Argentina and Ethiopia were strictly used for donation purposes. TOMS retailed its basic Alpargata shoes in the $50 price range, even though the cost of producing each pair was estimated at around $9.[16] Estimates for the costs of producing TOMS's more expensive lines of shoes were unknown, but they retailed for upwards of $150.

In comparison, manufacturing the average pair of Nike shoes in Indonesia cost around $20, and they were priced at around $70.[17] Factoring in the giving aspect, TOMS seemed to have a slightly smaller markup than companies like Nike, yet it still maintained considerable profit margins. More detailed information on trends in TOMS's production costs and practices is limited due to the private nature of the company.

The Future

Because demand and revenues were predicted to increase in the global footwear manufacturing industry, incumbents like TOMS needed to find ways to defend their position in the market. One method was to continue to differentiate products based on quality, image, or price. Another strategy was to focus on research and development (R&D) and craft new brands and product lines that appealed to different audiences. It was also recommended that companies investigate how to mitigate the threat posed by an increase in supply costs.

In an effort to broaden its mission and product offerings, TOMS began to expand both its consumer base and charitable-giving product lines. For its customers, TOMS started offering stylish wedges, ballet flats, and even wedding apparel in an effort to reach more customers and satisfy the special needs of current ones. For the children it sought to help, TOMS expanded past its basic black canvas shoe offerings to winter boots to help keep children's feet dry and warm during the winter months in cold climate countries.

On another front, TOMS entered the eyewear market in hopes of restoring vision to the 285 million blind or visually impaired individuals around the world. For every pair of TOMS glasses sold, TOMS restored vision to one individual either through donating prescription glasses or offering medical treatment for those suffering from cataracts and eye infections. TOMS recently focused its vision-related efforts in Nepal, but also hoped to expand globally as the TOMS eyewear brand grew. As of 2016, TOMS had teamed up with 15 Giving Partners to help restore sight to 360,000 individuals in 13 countries.

ENDNOTES

[1] TOMS Shoes Company website, April 4, 2016, www.toms.com/what-we-give-shoes.

[2] Blake Mycoskie, web log post, *The Huffington Post,* May 26, 2013, www.huffingtonpost.com/blake-mycoskie/.

[3] *501c3Lookup,* June 2, 2013, 501c3lookup.org/FRIENDS_OF_TOMS/.

[4] "Global Footwear Manufacturing," *IBISWorld,* March 2014, clients1.ibisworld.com/reports/gl/industry/keystatistics.aspx?entid=500.

[5] Post by "Alexandria," TOMS website, June 2, 2013, www.toms.com/red-canvas-classics-shoes-1.

[6] Post by "Donna Brock," TOMS website, January 13, 2014, www.toms.com/women/bright-blue-womens-canvas-classics.

[7] TOMS website, June 2, 2013, www.toms.com/our-movement-giving-partners.

[8] Trafficking Victims Protection Reauthorization Act, United States Department of Labor, June 2, 2013, www.dol.gov/ilab/programs/ocft/tvpra.htm; TOMS website, June 2, 2013, www.toms.com/corporate-responsibility.

[9] Hand of Hope, "Teaming Up with TOMS Shoes," *Joyce Meyer Ministries,* June 2, 2013, www.studygs.net/citation/mla.htm.

[10] Blake Mycoskie, "Blake Mycoskie's Blog," *Blogspot,* June 2, 2013, blakemycoskie.blogspot.com/.

[11] Tamara Schweitzer, "The Way I Work: Blake Mycoskie of TOMS Shoes," *Inc.,* June 2, 2013, www.inc.com/magazine/20100601/the-way-i-work-blake-mycoskie-of-toms-shoes.html.

[12] TOMS Jobs website, June 2, 2013, www.toms.com/jobs/l.

[13] Daniela, "Together We Travel," TOMS Company Blog, June 3, 2013, blog.toms.com/post/36075725601/together-we-travel.

[14] "Global—Footwear," *Marketline: Advantage,* April 18, 2016.

[15] Mike Zimmerman, "The Business of Giving: TOMS Shoes," *Success,* June 2, 2013, www.success.com/articles/852-the-business-of-giving-toms-shoes.

[16] Brittney Fortune, "TOMS Shoes: Popular Model with Drawbacks," *The Falcon,* June 2, 2013, www.thefalcononline.com/article.php?id=159.

[17] *Behind the Swoosh* [Film]. Dir. Jim Keady, 1995.

CASE 07

Fitbit, Inc.: Has the Company Outgrown Its Strategy?

Rochelle R. Brunson
Baylor University

Marlene M. Reed
Baylor University

Fitbit revolutionized the personal fitness activity in 2009 with the introduction of its Tracker wearable activity monitor. By 2016 the company was a hit in the marketplace with Fitbit devices becoming nearly ubiquitous with fitness enthusiasts and health-conscious individuals wearing the devices and checking them throughout the day. The company's sales of activity monitors had increased from 5,000 units that year to 21.4 million connected health and fitness devices by year-end 2015. The company executed a successful IPO (initial public offering) in 2015 that boosted liquidity by $4.1 billion and recorded revenues of $1.86 billion by the conclusion of its first year as a public company. Fitbit's chief managers expected 2016 revenues in the range of $2.4 to $2.5 billion. However, on the last day of February 2016 the price of Fitbit stock plunged nearly 20 percent after the company announced that the sales and earnings in the first quarter would fall short of analysts' forecasts. The missed forecasted milestone created a dilemma for founders James Park and Eric Friedman, who were now faced with finding a strategy to turn things around at the now publicly traded company.

BACKGROUND ON FITBIT

Fitbit was founded in October 2007 by James Park (CEO) and Eric Friedman (CTO). The two men started the company after noticing the potential for using sensors in small wearable devices to track individuals' physical activities. Before they had a prototype, Park and Friedman took a circuit board in a wooden box around to venture capitalists to raise money. In 2008, Park and Friedman addressed the TechCrunch50 Conference drumming up preorders for their product. Neither man had any manufacturing experience, so they traveled to Asia and sought out suppliers and a company to produce the device for them.

Fitbit put its product named "Tracker" on the market at the end of 2009, and the company shipped approximately 5,000 units at that time. They had additional orders for 2,000 units on the books.

The product Park and Friedman developed was called an "activity monitor" which was a wireless-enabled wearable technology device (see Exhibit 1). The purpose of the Fitbit was to measure personal

EXHIBIT 1 Fitbit Ultra

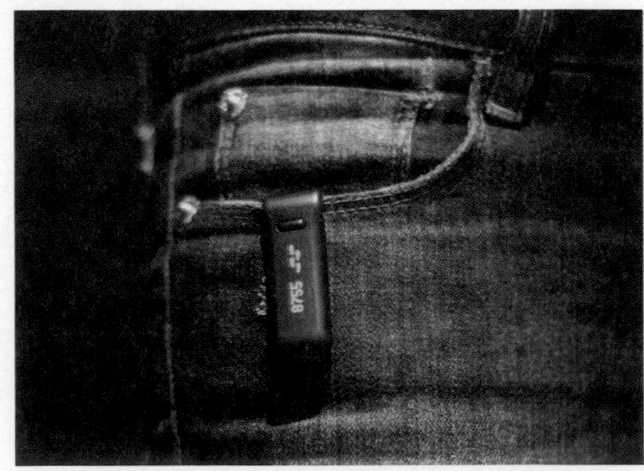

© Denis Kortunov

Source: Fitbit, Inc. website.

data such as number of steps walked, heart rate, quality of sleep, and steps climbed. The device could be clipped to one's clothing and worn all the time—even when the wearer was asleep. Included with the Tracker was a wireless base station that could receive data from the Tracker and charge its battery. The base station uploaded data to the Fitbit website when connected to a computer. This feature allowed the consumer to have an overview of physical activity, track goals, keep food logs, and interact with friends. The use of the website was free for the consumer.

Thereafter, the company developed a number of devices utilizing the Tracker technology. These devices are shown in Exhibit 2. Some of the later devices located the sensor technology in a watch that could be worn on the wrist (see Exhibit 3).

EXHIBIT 2 Activity Tracker Devices Developed by Fitbit

Name of Device	Capabilities and Options	Date First Unit Sold
Fitbit Tracker	Device with a clip to fit on clothing Sensed user movement Measured steps taken Distance walked, calories burned, floors climbed In black and teal only	2008
Fitbit Ultra	Digital clock Stopwatch Altimeter that measured slope of floors "Chatter" messages that occurred when Ultra moved New colors of plum and blue	2011
Fitbit Aria	Wi-Fi smart scale Recognized users wearing Fitbit trackers Measured weight, body mass index, and percentage of body fat	2012
Fitbit One	More vivid digital display Separate clip and charging cable Wireless sync dongle Used Bluetooth 4.0	September 2012
Fitbit Zip	Size of a quarter Tracked steps taken, distance traveled, and calories burned Included a disposable battery Lower price than other Fitbits	September 2012
Fitbit Flex	Worn on the wrist Tracked movement 24 hrs. a day including sleep patterns	May 2013
Fitbit Force	LED display showing time and daily activity Tracked activities in real time Vibrating alarm	October 2013
Fitbit Charge	Replacement for Fitbit Force Wristband displayed caller ID	October 2014
Fitbit Surge	Similar to a smart watch Monitored heart rate Tracked pace, distance, and elevation using GPS	October 2014
Fitbit Blaze	Similar to a smart watch Focused on fitness first Colored touchscreen Exchangeable strap and frame	2016

Source: Fitbit, Inc. website.

EXHIBIT 3 Fitbit Watch

© Tom Emrich

Source: Fitbit, Inc. website.

On May 17, 2015, Fitbit filed for an IPO with the Securities and Exchange Commission with an NYSE (New York Stock Exchange) listing. The IPO brought in $4.1 billion. The stock was initially priced at $20 but shortly thereafter the shares were trading for $35. By the end of February 2016 the shares had fallen to $14.

A study in 2015 by Diaz et al., published in the *International Journal of Cardiology,* investigated the Fitbit to see how reliable the device was, and whether it could be used to monitor patients' physical activity between clinic visits. The research indicated that the Fitbit One and Fitbit Flex reliably estimated step counts and energy expenditure during walking and running. These researchers also found that the hip-based Fitbit outperformed the Fitbit watch.[1]

Another study in 2015 by Cadmus-Bertram et al., published in the *American Journal of Preventative Medicine,* had essentially the same outcome as the Diaz study. Their study examined the Fitbit Tracker and website as a low-touch physical activity intervention. They were attempting to evaluate the feasibility of integrating the Fitbit Tracker and website into a physical activity intervention for postmenopausal women. Their conclusions were that the Fitbit was well accepted in their sample of women and was associated with increased physical activity at 16 weeks. In other words, merely wearing the Fitbit seemed to heighten the amount of physical exercise in which the women engaged.[2]

However, another study undertaken by Sasaki et al. in 2015 and reported in the *Journal of Physical Activity and Health* found that the Fitbit wireless activity tracker worn on the hip systematically underestimated the activity energy expended. These researchers suggested that the Fitbit management should consider refining the energy expenditure prediction algorithm to correct this consistent underestimation of activity in order to maximize the physical activity benefits for weight management and other health-related concerns.[3]

MISSION OF FITBIT

According to Fitbit, "The mission of Fitbit is to empower and inspire you to live a healthier, more active life. We design products and experiences that fit seamlessly into your life so that you can achieve your health and fitness goals, whatever they may be."[4]

THE ACTIVITY TRACKING INDUSTRY

There are a number of companies that would be considered competitors of Fitbit in the activity tracking—companies such as Garmin (originally producing GPS equipment for cars) and Under Armour (originally producing undergarments for men). There are also companies such as Apply who produce smart watches that perform many of the same tasks as Fitbit's devices.

Another company entering the market late was Jawbone. This company was formed in 1999, and its consumer devices were Bluetooth headphones and speakers initially and later fitness trackers. With the increased competition in the activity tracking industry in 2015, Jawbone dropped to seventh place in the second quarter from fifth place in the first quarter among makers of wearable tracking devices.

Xiaomi, a Chinese company, shipped 12 million wearable activity trackers in 2015. That gave the company a 15.5 percent global market share which was second to Fitbit with Apple, Garmin, and Samsung behind the two leaders. In 2014, Xiaomi had shipped 1.1 million units and garnered only 4 percent of the world market share.

The presence of Apple in the market had been almost as noteworthy as Xiaomi's. The Apple watch was first marketed in 2015, and in that year its market share went to 14.9 percent. This was in spite of the fact that Apple's product was priced much higher than either Fitbit or Xiaomi.

For many years, neuroscientists had only the electroencephalogram, or EEG, to detect signals that carried different stages of sleep or brain power surges brought about by seizures. This was a very cumbersome process. Then, in 2007, Dr. Philip Low in San Diego invented the Sleep Parametric EEG Automated Recognition System (SPEARS) algorithm. This invention allowed physicians the ability to create a cluster map of brain activity with information that was gleaned from one electrode. This advancement caught the attention of Tan Le, CEO of Emotiv (a company that manufactured EEG rigs for consumers). Le believes wearable activity devices may be the appropriate venue for this new medical breakthrough. This would open up far-reaching new uses for wearable activity tracking devices.[5]

As more devices enter the market, Fitbit's dominance in the present market diminishes. However, additional uses of the Fitbit tracker could boost its share again (see Exhibit 4).

PROBLEMS FOR FITBIT

Antenna

There were early problems with the design of Fitbit. For one thing, the antenna did not work properly. In regard to the antenna problems, CEO James Park said, "In my hotel room I was thinking this is it. We literally took a piece of foam and put it on the circuit board to fix an antenna problem."[6]

Design Flaw

The Fitbit Ultra had a permanently curved shape that allowed it to be clipped onto a piece of clothing. However, the plastic in the unit could not handle the strain at the looped end and would continually break. When this occurred, Fitbit offered the consumer replacement or repair of the unit.

Allergic Reactions

From the beginning of the company, Fitbit was plagued by problems. When Fitbit added Fitbit Flex and Fitbit Force to its list of products, the company began receiving complaints that the watchband was irritating the skin of consumers. The irritation was discovered to be caused by allergic reactions to nickel, and the products were recalled in early 2014. As many as 9,000 customers were reportedly affected, and the Force was replaced by a new model named Fitbit Charge which was believed to be allergen free. Unfortunately, customers continued to complain about allergic reactions to the new device as well.

Too Much Information

One of the greatest strengths of Fitbit from the very beginning was its website. By utilizing Bluetooth technology, information from the Fitbit could be uploaded to the web in order to track energy expended and compare one's performance with other Fitbit users. However, the company discovered in 2011 that users who recorded their sexual activity (time spent, not activity) were sharing their information with the world unknowingly. Therefore, Fitbit

EXHIBIT 4 Top Five Wearables Vendors by Shipments, Market Share, and Year-over-Year Growth 2014–2015 (units in millions)

Vendor	2014 Unit Shipments	2014 Market Share	2015 Unit Shipments	2015 Market Share	Year-over-Year Growth
Fitbit	10.9	37.9%	21.0	26.9%	93.2%
Xiaomi	1.1	4.0%	12.0	15.4%	951.8%
Apple	0.0	0.0%	11.6	14.9%	NA
Garmin	2.0	7.1%	3.3	4.2%	60.9%
Samsung	2.7	9.2%	3.1	4.0%	18.5%
Others	12.0	41.9%	27.0	34.5%	124.0%
Total	28.8	100.0%	78.1	100.0%	171.6%

Source: IDC Worldwide Quarterly Wearable Device Tracker, February 23, 2016.

realized that sharing all of a customer's information with the world was not a good idea, and the company changed the website so that information posted by the users was private by default.

Privacy Issues

U.S. Senator "Chuck" Schumer declared in August 2014 that Fitbit was a "privacy nightmare." He further stated that users' movements and health data were being tracked by the company and sold to third parties without their knowledge.[7] Schumer asked that the U.S. Federal Trade Commission undertake the regulation of fitness trackers. In response to this charge, Fitbit suggested that it did not sell data to third parties and would be glad to have the opportunity to work with Senator Schumer on this issue.

Cost of Launching New Products

In Fitbit's Form 8-K filing on February 22, 2016, the company warned that the costs that were related to two new products would negatively affect their first quarter earnings in 2016. They further stated that research and development would hurt operating margins in 2016. The two new products that Fitbit suggested it would launch in 2016 were Fitbit Blaze and Fitbit Alpha, and these two products would incur very large manufacturing costs. In addition, Fitbit's full-year research and development budget included the company's Digital Health strategy.[8]

FINANCIAL PERFORMANCE

On February 22, 2016, Fitbit reported revenue of $1.86 billion, diluted net income per share of $0.75, and adjusted EBITDA (earnings before interest, taxes, depreciation, and amortization) of $389.9 million—see Exhibit 5. The company's balance sheets for 2014 and 2015 are presented in Exhibit 6.[9]

Full-year 2015 Financial Highlights were shown in the filing as follows:

- Sold 21.4 million connected health and fitness devices.
- FY15 revenue increased 149 percent year-over-year, adjusted EBITDA increased 104 percent.
- U.S. comprised 74 percent of FY15 revenue; Europe, Middle East, and Africa, 11 percent; Asian Pacific, 10 percent; Americas, excluding the United States, 5 percent.
- Cash, cash equivalents, and marketable securities totaled $664.5 million at December 31, 2015, compared to $195.6 million at December 31, 2014, and $573.5 million at September 30, 2015.

EXHIBIT 5 Fitbit's Consolidated Statements of Operations, 2014–2015 (in thousands)

	2015	2014
Revenue	$1,857,998	$ 745,433
Cost of revenue	956,935	387,776
Gross profit	901,063	357,657
Operating expenses:		
Research and development	150,035	54,167
Sales and marketing	332,741	112,005
General and administrative	77,793	33,556
Change in contingent consideration	(7,704)	—
Total operating expenses	552,865	199,728
Operating income	348,198	157,929
Interest income (expense), net	(1,019)	(2,222)
Other expense, net	(59,230)	(15,934)
Income before income taxes	287,949	139,773
Income tax expense	112,272	7,996
Net income	$ 175,677	$ 131,777

Source: U.S. Securities and Exchange Commission, Form 8-K, Fitbit, Inc. for fiscal 2015.

EXHIBIT 6 Condensed Consolidated Balance Sheets, 2014–2015

	2015	2014
Assets		
Current assets		
Cash and cash equivalents	$ 535,846	$195,626
Marketable securities	128,632	—
Accounts receivable, net	469,200	238,859
Inventories	178,146	115,072
Prepaid expenses & other current assets	43,530	13,614
Total current assets	1,355,414	563,171
Property and equipment, net	44,501	26,435
Goodwill	22,157	—
Intangible assets, net	12,216	—
Deferred tax assets	83,020	42,001
Other assets	1,758	1,444
Total assets	$1,519,066	$633,051
Liabilities, Redeemable Convertible Preferred Stock and Stockholders' Equity		
Current liabilities		
Fitbit Force recall reserve	$ 5,122	$ 22,476
Accounts payable	260,842	195,666
Accrued liabilities	194,977	70,940
Deferred revenue	44,448	9,009
Income taxes payable	2,868	30,631
Long-term debt, current portion	—	132,589
Total current liabilities	508,257	461,311
Redeemable convertible preferred stock		
Warrant liability	—	15,797
Other liabilities	29,358	12,867
Total liabilities	537,615	489,975
Redeemable convertible preferred stock	—	67,814
Stockholders' equity		
Common stock & paid-in capital	737,841	7,983
Accumulated other comprehensive income	691	37
Retained earnings	242,919	67,242
Total stockholders' equity	981,451	75,262
Total liabilities and stockholders' equity	$1,519,066	$633,051

Source: U.S. Securities and Exchange Commission, Fitbit, Inc. 2015 Form 8-K.

Fitbit announced in the filing that it expected full-year 2016 revenue to be in the range of $2.4 to $2.5 billion which would be driven by the introduction of new products and expansion into new geographic territories. In addition, the company stated that it expected gross margins to range from 48.5 to 49.0 percent. Fitbit also expected adjusted EBITDA to range from $400 to $480 million.

ANALYSTS' ASSESSMENTS

After the 20 percent drop in the price of Fitbit stock late in February 2016, a number of Wall Street analysts gave their assessments of future movements of the company's stock. An analyst with Global Equities Research, Trip Chowdry, suggested that he believed the stock could fall another 50 percent. He speculated, "Gradually the market for single-purpose devices (fitness tracker) is heading toward zero, and there is nothing FIT can do to reverse the trend."[10] In addition, Chowdry commented that unlike Apple, Inc., Fitbit doesn't have a group of developers or a way of generating income as the App Store does. Even though the Fitbit tracker products were much cheaper than Apple's ($129 as compared to $349 for the cheapest Apple Watch Sport), Apple had an inventory of more products than Fitbit. Activity tracking is just a feature used by Fitbit, and this feature was being used in many other devices by a variety of companies.

Pacific Coast analysts downgraded the company's stock to sector weight from overweight because of expected weakness in sales in the coming year, and the limitation it has in differentiating its products. The Pacific Coast analysts suggested, "We do not expect any incrementally competitive product announcements from Apple in the next year, but we have to assume those will come at some point in 2017 or 2018."[11] Therefore, these analysts believe Apple remains a serious threat to Fitbit in the future.

Leerink analysts downgraded Fitbit's stock to market perform from outperform and also reduced the target price to buy the stock from $33 to $18. These analysts suggest that the company's new products are unproven, so they don't know how much they will add to sales.[12]

DECISION TIME

James Park and Eric Friedman were facing a decision about a strategy to improve the analysts' assessments of Fitbit. One comment that many people had made about Fitbit was that it needed to be more than a one-product company. Since the activity tracking feature was being used in many other devices by a variety of companies, Fitbit had to think of new uses of the tracker as well as new devices. As one journalist suggested, "Stand-alone fitness trackers are iPod in a world that's moving to iPhones."[13]

After all, Park had recently commented, "The next big leap will come when we tie into more detailed clinical research and create devices that can make lightweight medical diagnoses. You look at blood glucose meters today, I wouldn't necessarily say that those are the most attractive or consumer friendly devices. I would say consumer focused companies, whether it's us or Apple, probably have an inherent advantage in the future."[14] One possibility for the company was to become a platform—rather than just a product. That would entail moving into niche markets with devices that are designed for very specific and unique purposes. Some of the possibilities would be moving further into health care and corporate health care.[15]

ENDNOTES

[1] Keith M. Diaz, David J. Krupka, Melinda J. Chang, James Peacock, Yao Ma, Jeff Goldsmith, Joseph E. Schwartz, and Karina W. Davidson, "Fitbit: An Accurate and Reliable Device for Wireless Physical Activity Tracking," *International Journal of Cardiology*, no. 185 (2015), pp. 138–140.

[2] Lisa A. Cadmus-Bertram, Bess H. Marcus, Ruth E. Patterson, Barbara A. Parker, and Brittany L. Morey, "Randomized Trial of a Fitbit-Based Physical Activity Intervention for Women," *American Journal of Preventive Medicine* 49, no. 3 (2015), pp. 414–418.

[3] Jeffer Eidi Sasaki, Amanda Hickey, Marianna Mavilia, Jacquelynne Tedesco, Denish John, Sarah Kozey Keadle, and Patty S. Freedson, "Validation of the Fitbit Wireless Activity Tracker for Prediction of Energy Expenditure," *Journal of Physical Activity and Health* 12 (2015), pp. 149–154.

[4] Fitbit home page, www.fitbit.com/about (accessed March 3, 2016).

[5] Betsy Isaacson, "A Fitbit for Your Brain Is Around the Corner," *Newsweek.com*, April 13, 2016, www.newsweek.com/human-brain-eeg-technology-neuroscience-443368.

[6] Gary Marshall, "The Story of Fitbit: How a Wooden Box Became a $4 Billion Company," December 30, 2015, www.wareable.com/fitbit/youre-fitbit-and-you-know-it-how-a-wooden-box-became-a-dollar-4-billion-company (accessed March 2, 2016).

[7] Ibid., p. 5.

[8] U.S. Securities and Exchange Commission, Form 8-K Filing for fiscal year 2015 for Fitbit, Inc.

[9] Ibid., p. 5.

[10] Caitlin Huston, "Fitbit's Stock Is Tanking and It May Have More to Drop," *MarketWatch*, February 23, 2016, www.marketwatch.com/story/fitbits-stock-is-tanking-and-it-may-have-more-to-drop/ (accessed March 11, 2016).

[11] Ibid., p. 2.

[12] Ibid., p. 3.

[13] James Stables, "Fitbit Charge HR Review, *Fitbit Review*, December 15, 2015, www.wareable.com/fitbit/fitbit-charge-hr-review/ (accessed March 1, 2016).

[14] Ibid., p. 6.

[15] Ibid., p. 7.

CASE 08

Under Armour's Strategy in 2016—How Big a Factor Can the Company Become in the $250 Billion Global Market for Sports Apparel and Footwear?

Arthur A. Thompson
The University of Alabama

Founded in 1996 by former University of Maryland football player Kevin Plank, Under Armour was the originator of sports apparel made with performance-enhancing fabrics—gear engineered to wick moisture from the body, regulate body temperature, and enhance comfort regardless of weather conditions and activity levels. It started with a simple plan to make a T-shirt that provided compression and wicked perspiration off the wearer's skin, thereby avoiding the discomfort of sweat-absorbed apparel. Under Armour's innovative synthetic performance fabric T-shirts were an instant hit.

Nearly 20 years later, with 2015 revenues of $3.9 billion, Under Armour had a growing brand presence in the roughly $70 billion multisegment retail market for sports apparel, activewear, and athletic footwear in the United States. Its interlocking "U" and "A" logo was almost as familiar and well-known as industry-leader Nike's swoosh. Heading into 2016, Under Armour had an estimated 16 percent share of the United States market for sports apparel (up from 12.7 percent in 2012 and 11.1 percent in 2011).[1] In the synthetic performance apparel segment—a market niche with estimated U.S. sales close to $7 billion in 2015—Under Armour's market share was thought to exceed 35 percent.

However, across all segments (sports apparel, activewear, and athletic footwear) of the $250 billion global market in which the company competed, Under Armour still had a long way to go to overtake the two long-time industry leaders—Nike and The adidas Group. In fiscal 2015, Nike had U.S. sales of $11.3 billion and global sales of $30.6 billion, and it dominated both the U.S. and global markets for athletic footwear. In the United States, Nike's share of athletic footwear sales approached 60 percent (counting its Nike-branded footwear and sales of its Jordan and Converse brands) versus Under Armour's less than 3 percent share. Nike's 2015 global sales of athletic footwear were $18.3 billion (over 1 million pairs per day), dwarfing Under Armour's 2015 global footwear sales of $678 million. Germany-based The adidas Group—the industry's second-ranking company in terms of global revenues—had 2015 global sales of €16.9 billion (equivalent to about $18.8 billion), which included athletic footwear sales of €8.4 billion ($9.3 billion) and sports apparel sales of €7.0 billion ($7.7 billion).

Despite having global sales much smaller than its two global rivals, Under Armour was gaining ground and making its market presence felt. In North America, Under Armour had recently overtaken adidas to become the second largest seller of sports apparel, activewear, and athletic footwear.[2] Under Armour's 2015 North American sales of $3.56 billion were over 15 percent greater than The Adidas Group's 2015 North American sales of €2.75 billion (equivalent to about $3.03 billion). Moreover, Under Armour was growing at a faster percentage rate than both its bigger rivals. From 2010 through 2015, Under Armour's sales revenues grew at a compound annual rate of 30.1 percent. Nike's revenues from Nike Brand products during its most recent five fiscal years (June 1, 2010–May 31, 2015) grew at an 11.75 percent compound rate. Total revenues of The adidas Group grew at a compound rate of 7.1 percent during 2010–2015. But because Under Armour's revenues were much smaller than those of Nike and The adidas Group, its faster percentage rate of revenue growth did not translate into bigger revenue gains in absolute dollar terms. Under Armour's global revenues grew by just under $880 million in 2015. Nike's global revenues in 2015 were $2.8 billion above the 2014 level, more than three times greater than UA's dollar increase in revenues. The adidas Group's 2015 revenue gain of €2.4 billion (about $2.66 billion) was three times bigger than UA's dollar increase in revenues. So, in term of dollar revenues, Under Armour fell further behind Nike and The adidas Group in 2015. Consequently, it would take many years, if ever, for Under Armour's revenues to approach those of Nike, which touted itself as a growth company and was led by top executives intent on preserving Nike's standing as the global marker leader.

Nonetheless, founder and CEO Kevin Plank believed Under Armour's potential for long-term growth was exceptional for three reasons: (1) the company had built an incredibly powerful and authentic brand in a relatively short time, (2) there were significant opportunities to expand the company's narrow product lineup and brand-name appeal into product categories where it currently had little or no market presence, and (3) the company was only in the early stages of establishing its brand and penetrating markets outside North America. Plank's revenue objectives for Under Armour were global sales of $7.5 billion in 2018 and $10 billion in 2020. If these objectives were met and if Under Armour's strategy proved powerful enough to sustain a revenue growth rate of 20 percent or more for another 5 to 10 years thereafter, then Plank's vision of Under Armour becoming a major player on the global stage would be fulfilled.

COMPANY BACKGROUND

Kevin Plank honed his competitive instinct growing up with four older brothers and playing football. As a young teenager, he squirmed under the authority of his mother, who was the town mayor of Kensington, Maryland. When he was a high-school sophomore, he was tossed out of Georgetown Prep for poor academic performance and ended up at Fork Union Military Academy, where he learned to accept discipline and resumed playing high school football. After graduation, Plank became a walk-on special-teams football player for the University of Maryland in the early 1990s, ending his college career as the special-teams' captain in 1995. Throughout his football career, he regularly experienced the discomfort of practicing on hot days and the unpleasantness of peeling off sweat-soaked cotton T-shirts after practice.

During his later college years and in classic entrepreneurial fashion, Plank hit on the idea of using newly available moisture-wicking, polyester-blend fabrics to make next-generation, tighter-fitting shirts and undergarments that would make it cooler and more comfortable to engage in strenuous activities during high-temperature conditions.[3] While Plank had a job offer from Prudential Life Insurance at the end of his college days in 1995, he couldn't see himself being happy working in a corporate environment—he told the author of a 2011 *Fortune* article on Under Armour, "I would have killed myself."[4] Despite a lack of business training, Plank opted to try to make a living selling high-tech microfiber shirts. Plank's vision was to sell innovative, technically advanced apparel products engineered with a special fabric construction that provided supreme moisture management. A year of fabric and product testing produced a synthetic compression T-shirt that was suitable for wear beneath an athlete's uniform or equipment, provided a snug fit (like a second skin), and remained drier and lighter than a traditional cotton shirt. Plank formed KP Sports as a subchapter S corporation in Maryland in 1996 and commenced selling the shirt to athletes and sports teams.

The Company's Early Years

Plank's former teammates at high school, military school, and the University of Maryland included some 40 NFL players that he knew well enough to call and offer them the shirt he had come up with. He worked the phone and, with a trunk full of shirts in the back of his car, visited schools and training camps in person to show his products. Within a short time, Plank's sales successes were good enough that he convinced Kip Fulks, who played lacrosse at Maryland, to become a partner in his enterprise. Fulks's initial role was to leverage his connections to promote use of the company's shirts by lacrosse players. Their sales strategy was predicated on networking and referrals. But Fulks had another critical role—he had good credit and was able to obtain 17 credit cards that were used to make purchases from suppliers and charge expenses.[5] Operations were conducted on a shoestring budget out of the basement of Plank's grandmother's house in Georgetown, a Washington, DC, suburb. Plank and Fulks generated sufficient cash from their sales efforts that Fulks never missed a minimum payment on any of his credit cards. When cash flows became particularly tight, Plank's older brother Scott made loans to the company to help keep KP Sports afloat (in 2011 Scott owned 4 percent of the company's stock). It didn't take long for Plank and Fulks to learn that it was more productive to direct their sales efforts more toward equipment managers than to individual players. Getting a whole team to adopt use of the T-shirts that KP Sports was selling meant convincing equipment managers that it was more economical to provide players with a pricey $25 high-performance T-shirt that would hold up better in the long run than a cheap cotton T-shirt.

In 1998, the company's sales revenues and growth prospects were sufficient to secure a $250,000 small business loan from a tiny bank in Washington, DC; the loan enabled the company to move its basement operation to a facility on Sharp Street in nearby Baltimore.[6] As sales continued to gain momentum, the DC bank later granted KP Sports additional small loans from time to time to help fund its needs for more working capital. Then Ryan Wood, one of Plank's acquaintances from high school, joined the company in 1999 and became a partner. The company consisted of three jocks trying to gain a foothold in a growing, highly competitive industry against some 25+ brands, including those of Nike, adidas, Columbia, and Patagonia. Plank functioned as president and CEO; Kip Fulks was vice president of sourcing and quality assurance, and Ryan Wood was vice president of sales.

KP Sports's sales grew briskly as it expanded its product line to include high-tech undergarments tailored for athletes in different sports and for cold temperatures as well as hot temperatures, plus jerseys, team uniforms, socks, and other accessories. Increasingly, the company was able to secure deals not just to provide gear for a particular team but for most or all of a school's sports teams. However, the company's partners came to recognize the merits of tapping the retail market for high-performance apparel and began making sales calls on sports apparel retailers. In 2000, Galyan's, a large retail chain since acquired by Dick's Sporting Goods, signed on to carry KP Sports's expanding line of performance apparel for men, women, and youth. Sales to other sports apparel retailers began to explode, quickly making the retail segment of the sports apparel market the biggest component of the company's revenue stream. KP Sports had revenues totaling $5.3 million in 2000, with operating income of $0.7 million. The company's products were available in some 500 retail stores. Beginning in 2000, Scott Plank, Kevin's older brother, joined the company as vice president of finance, with operational and strategic responsibilities as well.

Rapid Growth Ensues

Over the next 15 years, the company's product line evolved to include a widening variety of shirts, shorts, underwear, outerwear, gloves, and other offerings. The strategic intent was to grow the business by replacing products made with cotton and other traditional fabrics with innovatively designed performance products that incorporated a variety of technologically advanced fabrics and specialized manufacturing techniques, all in an attempt to make the wearer feel "drier, lighter, and more comfortable." In 1999 the company began selling its products in Japan through a licensee. On January 1, 2002, prompted by growing operational complexity, increased financial requirements, and plans for further geographic expansion, KP Sports revoked its "S" corporation status and became a "C" corporation. The company opened a Canadian sales office in 2003 and began efforts to grow its market presence in Canada. In 2004, KP Sports became the outfitter of the University of Maryland football team and was a supplier to some 400 women's sports teams at NCAA Division 1-A colleges and universities. The company used independent sales agents to begin selling its products in the United Kingdom in 2005. SportsScanINFO estimated that as of 2004, KP Sports had a 73 percent share of the U.S. market for compression tops and bottoms, more than seven times that of its nearest competitor.[7]

As of 2005, about 90 percent of the company's revenues came from sales to some 6,000 retail stores in the United States and 2,000 stores in Canada, Japan, and the United Kingdom. In addition, sales were being made to high-profile athletes and teams, most notably in the National Football League, Major League Baseball, the National Hockey League, and major collegiate and Olympic sports. KP Sports had 574 employees at the end of September 2005.

KP Sports Is Renamed Under Armour

In late 2005, KP Sports changed its name to Under Armour and became a public company with an initial public offering (IPO) of 9.5 million shares of Class A common stock that generated net proceeds of approximately $114.9 million. Simultaneously, existing stockholders sold 2.6 million shares of Class A stock from their personal holdings. The shares were all sold at just above the offer price of $13 per share; on the first day of trading after the IPO, the shares closed at $25.30, after opening at $31 per share. Following these initial sales of Class A Under Armour stock to the general public, Under Armour's outstanding shares of common stock consisted of two classes: Class A common stock and Class B common stock. Holders of Class A common stock were entitled to one vote per share, and holders of Class B common stock were entitled to 10 votes per share, on all matters to be voted on by common stockholders. All of the Class B common stock was beneficially owned by Kevin Plank, giving him 83.0 percent of the combined voting power of all the outstanding common stock and the ability to control the outcome of substantially all matters submitted to a stockholder vote, including the election of directors, amendments to Under Armour's charter, and mergers or other business combinations.

At the time of Under Armour's IPO, Kevin Plank, Kip Fulks, and Ryan Wood were all 33 years old; Scott Plank was 39 years old. After the IPO, Kevin Plank owned 15.2 million shares of Under Armour's Class A shares (and all of the Class B shares), Fulks owned 2.125 million Class A shares, Wood owned 2.142 million Class A shares, and Scott Plank owned 3.95 million Class A shares. All four had opted to sell a small fraction of their common shares at the time of the IPO—these accounted for a combined 1.83 million of the 2.6 million shares sold from the holdings of various directors, officers, and other entities. Wood decided to leave his position as senior vice president of sales at Under Armour in 2007 to run a cattle farm. Fulks assumed the position of chief operating officer at Under Armour in September 2011, after moving up the executive ranks in several capacities, chiefly those related to sourcing, quality assurance, product development, and product innovation. In November 2015, following several changes in title and responsibility, Fulks was named chief marketing officer. In September 2012, Scott Plank, who was serving as the company's executive vice president of business development after holding several other positions in the company's executive ranks, retired from the company to start a real estate development company and pursue his passion for building sustainable urban environments.

Exhibit 1 summarizes Under Armour's financial performance during 2011–2015. Exhibit 2 shows the growth of Under Armour's quarterly revenues for 2010 through 2015. The company's strong financial performance propelled its stock price from $46 in early January 2013 to a high of $124 in March 2014; the stock split 2-for-1 in April 2014. The stock price was trading in the split-adjusted range of $80–$85 in March 2016, up over about 365 percent since March 2010.

In 2015, the company announced that a new C class of nonvoting stock would be created and that in 2016 the owner of each existing share of Class A and Class B stock would receive one share of nonvoting Class C stock that would be traded on the New York Stock Exchange under a different symbol (UA.C). This distribution was effectively a 2-for-1 stock split; after the distribution, Class B stock would cease to exist. The purpose of these changes was to preserve Kevin Plank's voting power—the dual Class A and Class B voting structure was set to end when Kevin Plank owned fewer than 15 percent of the total Class A and Class B shares outstanding (his ownership percentage was just under 16 percent in mid-2015). It was further announced that the nonvoting Class C shares would in the future be used for all equity-based employee compensation (stock bonuses and stock option grants) and for any stock-based acquisitions. Kevin Plank thus ended up with the same roughly 16 percent voting interest after the Class C stock distribution in April 2016 as before the distribution, a percentage he and the board of directors deemed big enough to protect the company's current governance structure from unwanted outside takeover.

EXHIBIT 1 Selected Financial Data for Under Armour, Inc., 2011–2015 (in 000s, except per share amounts)

Selected Income Statement Data	2015	2014	2013	2012	2011
Net revenues	$3,963,313	$3,084,370	$2,332,051	$1,834,921	$1,472,684
Cost of goods sold	2,057,766	1,152,164	1,195,381	955,624	759,848
Gross profit	1,905,547	1,512,206	1,136,670	879,297	712,836
Selling, general and administrative expenses	1,497,000	1,158,251	871,572	670,602	550,069
Income from operations	408,547	353,955	265,098	208,695	162,767
Interest expense, net	(14,628)	(5,335)	(2,933)	(5,183)	(3,841)
Other expense, net	(7,234)	(6,410)	(1,172)	(73)	(2,064)
Income before income taxes	386,685	342,210	260,993	203,439	156,862
Provision for income taxes	154,112	134,168	98,663	74,661	59,943
Net income	$ 232,573	$ 208,042	$ 162,330	$ 128,778	$ 96,919
Net income per common share					
Basic	$ 1.08	$ 0.98	$ 0.77	$ 0.62	$ 0.47
Diluted	1.05	0.95	0.75	0.61	0.46
Weighted average common shares outstanding					
Basic	215,498	213,227	210,696	208,686	206,280
Diluted	220,868	219,380	215,958	212,760	210,104
Selected Balance Sheet Data (in 000s)					
Cash and cash equivalents	$ 129,852	$ 593,175	$ 347,489	$ 341,841	$ 175,384
Working capital*	1,019,953	1,127,772	702,181	651,370	506,056
Inventories at year-end	783,031	536,714	469,006	319,286	324,409
Total assets	2,868,900	2,095,083	1,577,741	1,157,083	919,210
Total debt and capital lease obligations, including current maturities	669,000	284,201	152,923	61,889	77,724
Total stockholders' equity	1,668,222	1,350,300	1,053,354	816,922	636,432
Selected Cash Flow Data					
Net cash provided by operating activities	($ 44,104)	$ 219,033	$ 120,070	$ 199,761	$ 15,218

*Working capital is defined as current assets minus current liabilities.

Sources: Company 10-K reports for 2015, 2013, and 2012.

UNDER ARMOUR'S STRATEGY IN 2016

Under Armour's mission was "to make all athletes better through passion, design, and the relentless pursuit of innovation." The company's principal business activities in 2016 were the development, marketing, and distribution of branded performance apparel, footwear, and accessories for men, women, and youth. The brand's moisture-wicking apparel products were engineered in many designs and styles for wear in nearly every climate to provide a performance alternative to traditional products. Under Armour sport apparel was worn by athletes at all levels, from youth to professional, and by consumers with active lifestyles. In 2013, Under Armour acquired MapMyFitness, a provider of website services and mobile apps to fitness-minded consumers

EXHIBIT 2 Growth in Under Armour's Quarterly Revenues, 2010–2015 (in 000s)

	Quarter 1 (Jan.–March)		Quarter 2 (April–June)		Quarter 3 (July–Sept.)		Quarter 4 (Oct.–Dec.)	
	Revenues	Percent Change from Prior Year's Quarter 1	Revenues	Percent Change from Prior Year's Quarter 2	Revenues	Percent Change from Prior Year's Quarter 3	Revenues	Percent Change from Prior Year's Quarter 4
2010	$229,407	14.7%	$204,786	24.4%	$ 328,568	21.9%	$ 301,166	35.5%
2011	312,699	36.3%	291,336	42.3%	465,523	41.7%	403,126	33.9%
2012	384,389	23.0%	369,473	26.8%	575,196	23.6%	505,863	25.5%
2013	471,608	22.7%	454,541	23.0%	723,146	25.7%	682,756	35.0%
2014	641,607	36.0%	609,654	34.1%	937,908	29.7%	895,201	31.1%
2015	804,941	25.5%	783,577	28.5%	1,204,109	28.4%	1,170,686	30.8%

Sources: Company 10-K reports, 2015, 2013, 2012, and 2010.

across the world; Under Armour used this acquisition, along with several follow-on acquisitions in 2014–2015, to create what it termed a "connected fitness" business offering digital fitness subscriptions and licenses, mobile apps, and other fitness-tracking and nutritional tracking solutions to athletes and fitness-conscious individuals across the world. Kevin Plank expected the company's connected fitness strategic initiative to become a major revenue driver in the years to come—in 2015, UA's connected fitness revenues grew by 178 percent and generated 1.3 of total net revenues.

In 2015, 70.7 percent of Under Armour's total net sales were apparel items, with athletic footwear products, accessories, and connected fitness offerings accounting for the remainder—see Exhibit 3A. Just over 87 percent of Under Armour's 2015 sales were in North America; however, UA's top executives believed the company's international presence was still in the infant stage (Exhibit 3B) and that there was a huge opportunity for the company to grow sales to distributors and retailers outside North America by 30 to 50 percent annually for many years to come.

Growth Strategy

The company's growth strategy in 2016 consisted of seven strategic initiatives:

- Continuing to broaden the company's product offerings to men, women, and youth for wear in a widening variety of sports and recreational activities. In 2016, the special emphasis being placed on products for women was expected to result in women's sales of $1 billion.
- Targeting additional consumer segments for the company's ever-expanding lineup of performance products.
- Increasing its sales and market share in the athletic footwear segment.
- Securing additional distribution of Under Armour products in the retail marketplace in North America via not only store retailers and catalog retailers but also through Under Armour factory outlet and specialty stores and sales at the company's website.
- Expanding the sale of Under Armour products in foreign countries and becoming a global competitor in the world market for sports apparel, athletic footwear, and performance products.
- Growing global awareness of the Under Armour brand name and strengthening the appeal of Under Armour products worldwide.
- Growing the company's connected fitness business.

Product Line Strategy

For a number of years, expanding the company's product offerings and marketing them at multiple price points had been a key element of Under Armour's strategy. The goal for each new item added to the lineup of offerings was to provide consumers with a product that was a *superior*

EXHIBIT 3 Composition of Under Armour's Revenues, 2012-2015

A. Net Revenues by Product Category (in thousands of $)

	2015		2014		2013		2012	
	Dollars	Percent	Dollars	Percent	Dollars	Percent	Dollars	Percent
Apparel	$2,801,062	70.7%	$2,291,520	74.3%	$1,762,150	75.6%	$ 853,493	80.2%
Footwear	677,744	17.1	430,987	14.0	298,825	12.8	127,175	12.0
Accessories	346,885	8.8	275,409	8.9	216,098	9.3	43,882	4.1
Total net sales	$3,825,691	96.6%	$2,997,916	97.2%	$2,277,073	97.6%	$1,024,550	96.3%
License revenues	84,207	2.1	67,229	2.2	53,910	2.4	39,377	3.7
Connected fitness	53,415	1.3	19,225	0.6	1,068	0.0	—	—
Total net revenues	$3,963,313	100.0%	$3,084,370	100.0%	$2,332,051	100.0%	$1,063,927	100.0%

B. Net Revenues by Geographic Region (in thousands of $)

	2015		2014		2013		2012	
	Dollars	Percent	Dollars	Percent	Dollars	Percent	Dollars	Percent
North America	$3,455,737	87.2%	$2,796,374	90.7%	$2,193,739	94.1%	$ 997,816	93.7%
International	454,161	11.5	268,771	8.7	138,312	5.9	66,111	6.3
Connected fitness	53,415	1.3	19,225	0.6	1,068	0.0	—	—
Total net revenues	$3,963,313	100.0%	$3,084,370	100.0%	$2,332,051	100.0%	$1,063,927	100.0%

Sources: Company 10-K reports, 2015, 2013, 2012 and 2010.

alternative to the traditional products of rivals—striving to always introduce a superior product would, management believed, help foster and nourish a culture of innovation among all company personnel. According to Kevin Plank, "we focus on creating products you don't know you need yet, but once you have them, you won't remember how you lived without them."[8]

Apparel The company designed and merchandised three lines of apparel gear intended to regulate body temperature and enhance comfort, mobility, and performance regardless of weather conditions: HEATGEAR® for hot-weather conditions, COLDGEAR® for cold-weather conditions, and ALLSEASONGEAR® for temperature conditions between the extremes.

HeatGear HeatGear was designed to be worn in warm to hot temperatures under equipment or as a single layer. The company's first compression T-shirt was the original HeatGear product and was still one of the company's signature styles in 2015. In sharp contrast to a sweat-soaked cotton T-shirt that could weigh two to three pounds, HeatGear was engineered with a microfiber blend featuring what Under Armour termed a "Moisture Transport System" that ensured the body would stay cool, dry, and light. HeatGear was offered in a variety of tops and bottoms in a broad array of colors and styles for wear in the gym or outside in warm weather.

ColdGear Under Armour high-performance fabrics were appealing to people participating in cold-weather sports and vigorous recreational activities like snow skiing who needed both warmth and moisture-wicking protection from a sometimes overheated body. ColdGear was designed to wick moisture from the body while circulating body heat from hotspots to maintain core body temperature. All ColdGear apparel provided dryness and warmth in a single light layer that could be worn beneath a jersey, uniform, protective gear or ski-vest, or other cold-weather outerwear. ColdGear products generally were sold at higher price levels than other Under

Armour gear lines. A new ColdGear Infrared line, with a new fabric technology, was introduced in fall 2013 and in 2015 zip-up ColdGear items utilized the company's MagZip™ zippers, a magnetic quick zip closure that the company claimed "fixed zippers."

AllSeasonGear AllSeasonGear was designed to be worn in temperatures between the extremes of hot and cold and used technical fabrics to keep the wearer cool and dry in warmer temperatures while preventing a chill in cooler temperatures.

Each of the three apparel lines contained three fit types: compression (tight fit), fitted (athletic fit), and loose (relaxed). In 2016, Under Armour introduced apparel items containing MicroThread, a fabric technology that used elastomeric (stretchable) thread to create a cool moisture-wicking microclimate, prevented clinging and chafing, allowed garments to dry 30 percent faster and be 70 percent more breathable than similar Lycra construction, and were so lightweight as to "feel like nothing." It also began using a newly developed insulation called Reactor in selected ColdGear items and introduced a new apparel collection with an exclusive CoolSwitch coating on the inside of the fabric that pulled heat away from the skin, allowing the wearer to feel cooler and perform longer.

Footwear Under Armour began marketing footwear products for men, women, and youth in 2006 and has expanded its footwear line every year since. Its 2016 offerings included football, baseball, lacrosse, softball, and soccer cleats; slides; performance training footwear; running footwear; basketball footwear; golf shoes; and outdoor footwear. Under Armour's athletic footwear was light, breathable, and built with performance attributes for athletes. Innovative technologies (Charged Cushioning®, ClutchFit®, Micro G®, and SpeedForm®) were used to provide stabilization, directional cushioning, and moisture management, and all models and styles were engineered to maximize the wearer's comfort and control.

New footwear collections for men, women, and youth were introduced regularly, sometimes monthly and often seasonally. Most new models and styles incorporated fresh technological features of one kind or another. Since 2012, Under Armour had more than tripled the number of footwear styles/models priced above $100 per pair. Its best-selling offerings were in the basketball and running shoe categories. In early 2014, UA introduced a new premium running shoe, the SpeedForm Apollo, with a retail price of $100. Kevin Plank believed this new shoe model, which was a follow-on to the $120 SpeedForm RC introduced in 2013, had the potential to be one of the company's defining products and help take UA to the next level in the market for athletic footwear, particularly in the running shoe category where the company was striving to make major inroads. UA's marketing tagline for the SpeedForm Apollo was "this is what fast feels like."

To capitalize on a recently signed long-term endorsement contract with pro basketball superstar Stephen Curry, Under Armour began marketing a Stephen Curry Signature line of basketball shoes in 2014; the so-called Curry One models had a price point of $120. This was followed by a Curry Two collection in 2015 at a price point of $130, a Curry 2.5 collection (at a price point of $135) during the NBA playoffs in May–June 2016, and a Curry Three collection in fall 2016. Under Armour sought to leverage its signing of pro golfer Jordan Spieth to a 10-year endorsement contract in early 2015 by introducing an all-new golf shoe collection in April 2016—Spieth had a spectacular year on the Professional Golf Association (PGA) tour in 2015 and was named 2015 PGA Tour Player of the Year, an honor based on votes by his peers; the 2016 golf shoe collection had three styles, ranging in price from $160 to $220. Also in 2016, Under Armour debuted its first "smartshoe" (called the SpeedForm Gemini 2 Record Equipped) at a price point of $150; smartshoe models were equipped with the capability to connect automatically to UA's connected fitness website and record certain activities in the wearer's fitness tracking account. Another high-tech shoe introduced in Q1 2016, called the UA Architect and priced at $300, had a 3-D printed midsole; initial supplies sold out in 19 minutes at the company's website. New 3-D iterations were scheduled for launch later in 2016.

To support the company's attempt to rapidly grow its sales of athletic footwear, UA had doubled the size of its footwear team to 230 people in 2015 and planned to add more staff in time for the 2016 Summer Olympics and other important 2016 sporting events.

Accessories Under Armour's accessory line in 2016 included gloves, socks, headwear, bags, kneepads, custom-molded mouth guards, inflatable basketballs and footballs, and eyewear designed to be used and worn before, during, and after competition. All of these accessories featured performance advantages and functionality similar to other Under Armour products. For instance, the company's baseball batting, football, golf, and running gloves included HEATGEAR® and COLDGEAR® technologies and were designed with advanced fabrications to provide various high-performance attributes that differentiated Under Armour gloves from those of rival brands.

Connected Fitness In December 2013, Under Armour acquired MapMyFitness, which served one of the largest fitness communities in the world at its website, **www.mapmyfitness.com**, and offered a diverse suite of websites and mobile applications under its flagship brands MapMyRun and MapMyRide. Utilizing GPS and other advanced technologies, MapMyFitness provided users with the ability to map, record, and share their workouts. MapMyFitness had 22 million registered users as of March 2014, 30 percent of which were located outside the United States. Under Armour then acquired European fitness app Endomondo and food-logging app MyFitnessPal. As part of a larger effort to create the company's "next big thing," a multifaceted connected fitness dashboard that used four independently functioning apps (MapMyFitness, MyFitnessPal, Endomondo, and UA Record™) to enable subscribers to log workouts, runs, and foods eaten, and to see on a digital dashboard measures relating to their sleep, fitness, activity, and nutrition. Next, in late 2015, UA introduced a connected fitness system called Under Armour HealthBox™ that consisted of a multifunctional wrist band (that measured sleep, resting heart rate, steps taken, and workout intensity), heart rate strap, and a smart scale (that tracked body weight, body fat percentage, and progress toward a weight goal); the wrist band was water resistant, could be worn 24/7, and had Bluetooth connectivity with UA Record; the smart scale was also Wi-Fi-enabled and synced data to UA Record. Under Armour launched its first HealthBox commercial in April 2016.

As of April 2016, Under Armour had over 160 million users of its various connected fitness offerings.[9] New user registrations were growing at the rate of 100,000 per day. UA's launch of its $400 UA HealthBox bundle of connected fitness products was the second-best-selling item (behind Curry Two footwear models) on UA's e-commerce website in the first quarter of 2016. Kevin Plank was so enthusiastic about the long-term potential of Under Armour's connected fitness business that he had boosted the company's team of engineers and software developers from 20 to over 350 during 2014–2015.

Licensing Under Armour had licensing agreements with a number of firms to produce and market Under Armour apparel, accessories, and equipment. Under Armour product, marketing, and sales teams were actively involved in all steps of the design process for licensed products in order to maintain brand standards and consistency. During 2015, licensees sold UA-branded collegiate and Major League Baseball apparel and accessories, baby and kids' apparel, team uniforms, socks, water bottles, eyewear, inflatable footballs and basketballs, and certain other equipment items. Under Armour pre-approved all products manufactured and sold by licensees, and UA's quality assurance personnel were assigned the task of ensuring that licensed products met the same quality and compliance standards as the products Under Armour sold directly.

Marketing, Promotion, and Brand Management Strategies

Under Armour had an in-house marketing and promotions department that designed and produced most of its advertising campaigns to drive consumer demand for its products and build awareness of Under Armour as a leading performance athletic brand. The company's total marketing expenses were $417.8 million in 2015, $333.0 million in 2014, $246.5 million in 2013, $205.4 million in 2012, $167.9 million in 2011, $128.2 million in 2010, and $108.9 million in 2009. These totals included the costs of sponsoring events and various sports teams, the costs of athlete endorsements, and the costs of ads placed in a variety of television, print, radio, and social media outlets. All were included as part of selling, general, and administrative expenses shown in Exhibit 1.

Sports Marketing A key element of Under Armour's marketing and promotion strategy was to promote the sales and use of its products to high-performing athletes and teams on the high school, collegiate, and professional levels. This strategy included entering into outfitting agreements with a variety of collegiate and professional sports teams, sponsoring an assortment of collegiate and professional sports events, and selling Under Armour products directly to team equipment managers and to individual athletes.

Management believed that having audiences see Under Armour products (with the interlocking UA logo prominently displayed) being worn by athletes on the playing field helped the company establish on-field authenticity of the Under Armour brand with consumers. Considerable effort went into giving Under Armour products broad exposure at live sporting events, as well as on television, in magazines, and on a wide variety of Internet sites. Exhibit 3 shows the Under Armour logo and examples of its use on Under Armour products.

Going into 2016, Under Armour was the official outfitter of *all* the men's and women's athletic teams at Notre Dame, Boston College, Northwestern University, Texas Tech University, the University of Maryland, the University of South Carolina, the U.S. Naval Academy, the University of Wisconsin, the University of California, Auburn University, and the University of South Florida and *selected* sports teams at the University of Illinois, Northwestern University, the University of Minnesota, the University of Utah, the University of Indiana, the University of Missouri, Georgetown University, the University of Delaware, the University of Hawaii, Southern Illinois University, Temple University, Wichita State University, South Dakota State University, Wagner College, Whittier College, and La Salle University. All told, it was the official outfitter of over 100 Division I men's and women's collegiate athletic teams, growing numbers of high school athletic teams, and several Olympic sports teams; and it supplied sideline apparel and fan gear for many collegiate teams as well. In addition, Under Armour sold products to high-profile professional athletes and teams, most notably in the National Football League, Major League Baseball, the National Hockey League, and the National Basketball Association (NBA). Since 2006, Under Armour had been an official supplier of football cleats to the National Football League (NFL). Under Armour became the official supplier of gloves to the NFL beginning in 2011, and it began supplying the NFL with training apparel for athletes attending NFL tryout camps beginning in 2012. In 2011 Under Armour became the Official Performance Footwear Supplier of Major League Baseball. Starting with the 2011–2012 season, UA was granted rights by the NBA to show ads and promotional displays of players who were official endorsers of Under Armour products in their NBA game uniforms wearing UA-branded basketball footwear. Under Armour was the official supplier of competition suits, uniforms, and training resources for a number of U.S. teams in the 2014 Winter Olympics in Russia and the 2016 Summer Olympics in Brazil.

Internationally, Under Armour was also using sponsorships to broaden consumer awareness of its brand in Canada, Europe, and South America. In Canada, it was an official supplier of performance apparel to Hockey Canada, had advertising rights at many locations in the Air Canada Center during the Toronto Maple Leafs' home games, and was the Official Performance Product Sponsor of the Toronto Maple Leafs. In Europe, Under Armour was the official supplier of performance apparel to the Hannover 96 and Tottenham Hotspur soccer teams and the Welsh Rugby Union, among others. In 2014 and 2015, Under Armour became the official match-day and training wear supplier for the Colo-Colo soccer club in Chile, the Cruz Azul soccer team in Mexico, and the São Paulo soccer team in Brazil.

In addition to sponsoring teams and events, Under Armour's brand-building strategy was to secure the endorsement of individual athletes. One facet of this strategy was to sign endorsement contracts with newly emerging sports stars—examples included Milwaukee Bucks point guard Brandon Jennings, Golden State Warriors point guard Stephen Curry, Charlotte Bobcats point guard Kemba Walker, U.S. professional skier and Olympic gold medal winner Lindsey Vonn, 2012 National League (baseball) Most Valuable Player and World Series Champion Buster Posey, 2012 National League Rookie of the Year Bryce Harper of the Washington Nationals, Derrick Williams (the number two pick in the 2011 NBA draft), tennis phenom Sloane Stephens, WBC super-welterweight boxing champion Camelo Alvarez, and PGA golfer Jordan Spieth. But the company's growing roster of athletes also included established stars: NFL football players Tom Brady, Ray Lewis, Brandon Jacobs, Arian Foster, Miles Austin, Julio Jones, Devon Hester, Vernon Davis, Patrick Willis, Santana Moss, and Anquan Boldin; triathlon champion

Chris "Macca" McCormack; professional baseball players Ryan Zimmerman, Jose Reyes, and eight others; U.S. Women's National Soccer Team players Heather Mitts and Lauren Cheney; U.S. Olympic and professional volleyball player Nicole Branagh; Olympic snowboarder Lindsey Jacobellis; and U.S. Olympic swimmer Michael Phelps. In January 2014, Under Armour signed ballerina soloist Misty Copeland to a multiyear contract; later in 2014, Copeland was featured in Under Armour's largest advertising campaign to date for its women's apparel offerings. In 2016, Under Armour signed champion wrestler, actor, and producer Dwayne "The Rock" Johnson to play an integral role in promoting UA's connected fitness apparel, footwear, and accessory products.

Under Armour spent approximately $126.5 million in 2015 for athlete and superstar endorsements, various team and league sponsorships, athletic events, and other marketing commitments, compared to about $90.1 million in 2014, $57.8 million in 2013, $53.0 million in 2012, $43.5 million in 2011, and $29.4 million in 2010.[10] The company was contractually obligated to spend a minimum of $276.2 million for endorsements, sponsorships, events, and other marketing commitments during 2016–2018.[11] Under Armour did not know precisely what its future endorsement and sponsorship costs would be because its contractual agreements with most athletes were subject to certain performance-based variables and because it was actively engaged in efforts to sign additional endorsement contracts and sponsor additional sports teams and athletic events.

Retail Marketing and Product Presentation The primary thrust of Under Armour's retail marketing strategy was to increase the floor space *exclusively* dedicated to Under Armour products in the stores of its major retail accounts. The key initiative here was to design and fund Under Armour "concept shops"—including flooring, in-store fixtures, product displays, life-size athlete mannequins, and lighting—within the stores of its major retail customers. This shop-in-shop approach was seen as an effective way to gain the placement of Under Armour products in prime floor space, educate consumers about Under Armour products, and create a more engaging and sales-producing way for consumers to shop for Under Armour products.

In stores that did not have Under Armour concept shops, Under Armour worked with retailers to establish optimal placement of its products. In "big-box" sporting goods stores, it was important to be sure that Under Armour's growing variety of products gained visibility in all of the various departments (hunting apparel in the hunting goods department, footwear and socks in the footwear department, and so on). Except for the retail stores with Under Armour concept shops, company personnel worked with retailers to employ in-store fixtures and displays that highlighted the UA logo and conveyed a performance-oriented, athletic look (chiefly through the use of life-size athlete mannequins). The merchandising strategy was not only to enhance the visibility of Under Armour products but also reinforce the message that the company's brand was distinct from those of competitors.

Media and Promotion Under Armour advertised in a variety of national digital, broadcast, and print media outlets, as well as social and mobile media. Its advertising campaigns included a variety of lengths and formats and frequently included prominent athletes and personalities. Advertising and promotional campaigns in 2015–2016 featured Michael Phelps, Stephen Curry, Jordan Spieth, Tom Brady, Lindsey Vonn, Misty Copeland, and Dwayne Johnson.

Distribution Strategy

Under Armour products were available in roughly 17,000 retail store locations worldwide in 2016. Under Armour also sold its products directly to consumers through its own factory outlet and specialty stores, and website.

Wholesale Distribution In 2016, Under Armour had close to 11,000 points of distribution in North America. The company's biggest retail account was Dick's Sporting Goods, which in 2015 accounted for 11.5 percent of the company's net revenues. Other important retail accounts in the United States included The Sports Authority (which filed for bankruptcy in 2016 and was liquidating its stores at auction as of May 2016—prior to the bankruptcy, Sports Authority had been UA's second largest retail account), Academy Sports and Outdoors, Hibbett Sporting Goods, Modell's Sporting Goods, Bass Pro Shops, Cabela's, Footlocker, Finish Line, The Army and Air Force Exchange Service, and such well-known department store chains as Macy's, Nordstrom, Belk, Dillard's, and Lord & Taylor. In Canada, the company's biggest customers were Sportchek International and Sportman International. Roughly 75 percent of all sales made to retailers were to large-format national and regional retail chains. The remaining 25 percent of wholesale sales were to lesser-sized outdoor and other specialty retailers, institutional athletic departments, leagues, teams, and fitness specialists. Independent and specialty retailers were serviced by a combination of in-house sales personnel and third-party commissioned manufacturer's representatives. Under Armour's 2015 worldwide wholesale sales to all types of retailers were $2.7 billion.

Direct-to-Consumer Sales In 2015, 30.4 percent of Under Armour's net revenues were generated through direct-to-consumer sales, versus 23 percent in 2010 and 6 percent in 2005; the direct-to-consumer channel included sales of discounted merchandise at Under Armour's Factory House stores and full-price sales at company-owned retail stores (which the company called Brand Houses), and the company's global website (www.underarmour.com and in-country websites. The Factory House stores gave Under Armour added brand exposure and helped familiarize consumers with Under Armour's growing lineup of products while also functioning as an important channel for selling discontinued, out-of-season, and/or overstocked products at discount prices without undermining the prices of Under Armour merchandise being sold at the stores of retailers carrying Under Armour products, the company's Brand Houses, and the company's website. Going into 2016, Under Armour had 143 factory outlet stores in North America; these stores attracted some 50 million shoppers in 2015.

Under Armour opened its first company-owned Brand House store to showcase its branded apparel at a mall in Annapolis, Maryland. Over the next several years, Brand House stores were opened in high-traffic retail locations in the United States. At year-end 2015, the company was operating 10 Under Armour full-price Brand House stores in North America. Plans called for having some 200 Factory House and Brand House locations in North America by year-end 2018.[12]

UA management's e-commerce strategy called for sales at www.underarmour.com (and 26 other in-country websites as of 2016) to be one of the company's principal vehicles for sales growth in upcoming years. To help spur e-commerce sales, the company was endeavoring to establish a clearer connection between its website offerings and the brand initiatives being undertaken in retail stores. It was also enhancing the merchandising techniques and storytelling regarding the UA products being marketed at its websites. Management estimated that in 2016 some 90 million customers would shop at the company's websites and that e-commerce sales would be in the neighborhood of $1.25 billion.

Product Licensing In 2015, 2.1 percent of the company's net revenues ($84.2 million) came from licensing arrangements to manufacture and distribute Under Armour branded products. Under Armour preapproved all products manufactured and sold by its licensees, and the company's quality assurance team strived to ensure that licensed products met the same quality and compliance standards as company-sold products. Under Armour had relationships with several licensees for team uniforms, eyewear, and custom-molded mouth guards, as well as the distribution of Under Armour products to college bookstores and golf pro shops.

Distribution outside North America Under Armour's first strategic move to gain international distribution occurred in 2002 when it established a relationship with a Japanese licensee, Dome Corporation, to be the exclusive distributor of Under Armour products in Japan. The relationship evolved, with Under Armour making a minority equity investment in Dome Corporation in 2011 and Dome gaining distribution rights for South Korea. Dome sold Under Armour branded apparel, footwear, and accessories to professional sports teams, large sporting goods retailers, and several thousand independent retailers of sports apparel in Japan and South Korea. Under Armour worked closely with Dome to develop variations of Under Armour products to better accommodate the different sports interests and preferences of Japanese and Korean consumers.

A European headquarters was opened in 2006 in Amsterdam, the Netherlands, to conduct and oversee sales, marketing, and logistics activities across Europe. The strategy was to first sell Under Armour products directly to teams and athletes and then leverage visibility in the sports segment to access broader audiences of potential consumers. By 2011, Under Armour had succeeded in selling products to

Premier League Football clubs and multiple running, golf, and cricket clubs in the United Kingdom; soccer teams in France, Germany, Greece, Ireland, Italy, Spain, and Sweden; as well as First Division Rugby clubs in France, Ireland, Italy, and the United Kingdom. Sales to European retailers quickly followed on the heels of gains being made in the sports team segment. By year-end 2012, Under Armour had 4,000 retail customers in Austria, France, Germany, Ireland, and the United Kingdom and was generating revenues from sales to independent distributors who resold Under Armour products to retailers in Italy, Greece, Scandinavia, and Spain.

In 2010–2011, Under Armour began selling its products in parts of Latin America and Asia. In Latin America, Under Armour sold directly to retailers in some countries and in other countries sold its products to independent distributors who then were responsible for securing sales to retailers. In 2014, Under Armour launched efforts to Under Armour products available in over 70 of Brazil's premium points of sale and e-commerce hubs; expanded sales efforts were also initiated in Chile and Mexico.

In 2011, Under Armour opened a retail showroom in Shanghai, China, the first of a series of steps to begin the long-term process of introducing Chinese athletes and consumers to the Under Armour brand, showcase Under Armour products, and learn about Chinese consumers. Additional retail locations in Shanghai and Beijing soon followed, some operated by local partners. By April 2014, there were five company-owned and franchised retail locations in Mainland China that merchandised Under Armour products; additionally, the Under Armour brand had been recently introduced in Hong Kong through a partnership with leading retail chain GigaSports.

Under Armour began selling its branded apparel, footwear, and accessories to independent distributors in Australia, New Zealand, and Taiwan in 2014; these distributors were responsible for securing retail accounts to merchandise Under Armour products to consumers. The distribution of Under Armour products to retail accounts across Asia was handled by a third-party logistics provider based in Hong Kong.

In 2013, Under Armour organized its international activities into four geographic regions—North America (the United States and Canada), Latin America, Asia-Pacific, and Europe/Middle East/Africa (EMEA). In his Letter to Shareholders in the company's 2013 Annual Report, Kevin Plank said, "We are committed to being a global brand with global stories to tell, and we are on our way." Sales of Under Armour products outside North America accounted for 11.5 percent of the company's net revenues in 2015, up from 8.7 percent in 2014 and 6.3 percent in 2012 (see Exhibit 3B). Under Armour saw growth in foreign sales as the company's biggest market opportunity in upcoming years, chiefly because of the sheer number of people residing outside the United States who could be attracted to patronize the Under Armour brand. In 2013 Nike generated about 55 percent of its revenues outside the United States and adidas got about 60 percent of its sales outside its home market of Europe—these big international sales percentages for Nike and adidas were a big reason why Under Armour executives were confident that growing UA's international sales represented an enormous market opportunity for the company, despite the stiff competition it could expect from its two bigger global rivals. As a consequence, the company was entering foreign country markets at a brisk pace. The near-term target was to grow international revenues to 18 percent of total revenues by year-end 2018. Top management believed that the company could accelerate its growth in international sales by close to 50 percent annually during 2016–2018 (and perhaps a few years beyond).

Headed into 2016, Under Armour products were already being sold in China, Japan, Great Britain, Ireland, Germany, Austria, Belgium, the Netherlands, Greece, Italy, Spain, Sweden, Brazil, Chile, Bolivia, Ecuador, Peru, Mexico, Malaysia, Thailand, Australia, New Zealand, Philippines, South Korea, and Singapore—albeit in a relatively limited number of locations in many instances. In some of these countries, sales of Under Armour products were wholly or partly the result of efforts by licensees and local partners. But UA's internal efforts to secure international sales were accelerating. The company had 48 Factory Houses and Brand Houses in Brazil, China, Chile, and Mexico at year-end 2015. Plans called for having some 800 such stores in 40+ countries outside North America by year-end 2018. Exhibit 4 shows UA's geographic expansion plan.

Product Design and Development

Top executives believed that product innovation—as concerns both technical design and aesthetic design—was the key to driving Under Armour's sales growth and building a stronger brand name.

EXHIBIT 4 Under Armour's Schedule for Expanding Its Geographic Reach, 2016–2018

	2016	2017	2018
Europe, Middle East, Africa	France, Turkey, North Africa, South Africa	Bulgaria, Croatia, Romania, Czech Republic, Hungary, Ukraine, Poland, Slovakia, Russia, and most of the remaining countries of Africa	
Asia-Pacific	Indonesia, Vietnam, Brunei	India	
Latin America	Paraguay, Uruguay	Argentina	

UA products were manufactured with technically advanced specialty fabrics produced by third parties. The company's product development team collaborated closely with fabric suppliers to ensure that the fabrics and materials used in UA's products had the desired performance and fit attributes. Under Armour regularly upgraded its products as next-generation fabrics with better performance characteristics became available and as the needs of athletes changed. Product development efforts also aimed at broadening the company's product offerings in both new and existing product categories and market segments. An effort was made to design products with "visible technology," utilizing color, texture, and fabrication that would enhance customers' perception and understanding of the use and benefits of Under Armour products.

Under Armour's product development team had significant prior industry experience at leading fabric and other raw material suppliers and branded athletic apparel and footwear companies throughout the world. The team worked closely with Under Armour's sports marketing and sales teams as well as professional and collegiate athletes to identify product trends and determine market needs. Collaboration among the company's product development, sales, and sports marketing team had proved important in identifying the opportunity and market for four recently launched product lines and fabric technologies:

- CHARGED COTTON™ products, which were made from natural cotton but performed like the products made from technically advanced synthetic fabrics, drying faster and wicking moisture away from the body.
- STORM Fleece products, which had a unique, water-resistant finish that repelled water without stifling airflow.
- Products with a COLDBLACK® technology fabric that repelled heat from the sun and kept the wearer cooler outside.
- COLDGEAR® Infrared, a ceramic print technology applied to the inside of garments that provided wearers with lightweight warmth.

Under Armour executives projected that the innovative CHARGED COTTON and STORM product lines would generate combined revenues of $500 million in 2016.[13] In 2012, in partnership with Swiss Company, Schoeller, Under Armour introduced products with COLDBLACK technology which repelled heat from the sun and kept the wearer cooler outside.

Sourcing, Manufacturing, and Quality Assurance

Many of the high-tech specialty fabrics and other raw materials used in UA products were developed by third parties and sourced from a limited number of preapproved specialty fabric manufacturers; no fabrics were manufactured in-house. Under Armour executives believed outsourcing fabric production enabled the company to seek out and utilize whichever fabric suppliers were able to produce the latest and best performance-oriented fabrics to Under Armour's specifications, while also freeing more time for UA's product development staff to concentrate on upgrading the performance, styling, and overall appeal of existing products and expanding the company's overall lineup of product offerings.

In 2015, approximately 54 percent of the fabric used in UA products came from five suppliers, with primary locations in Malaysia, Taiwan, and Mexico. Because a big fraction of the materials used in UA products were petroleum-based synthetics, fabric costs were subject to crude oil price fluctuations. The cotton fabrics used in the CHARGED COTTON products were also subject to price fluctuations and varying availability based on cotton harvests.

In 2013, substantially all UA products were made by 44 primary manufacturers, operating in 16 countries; 10 manufacturers produced approximately 45 percent of UA's products. Approximately 63 percent of UA's products were manufactured in China, Jordan, Vietnam, and Indonesia. All manufacturers purchased the fabrics they needed from the 5 fabric suppliers preapproved by Under Armour. All of the makers of UA products were evaluated for quality systems, social compliance, and financial strength by Under Armour's quality assurance team, prior to being selected and also on an ongoing basis. The company strived to qualify multiple manufacturers for particular product types and fabrications and to seek out contractors that could perform multiple manufacturing stages, such as procuring raw materials and providing finished products, which helped UA control its cost of goods sold. All contract manufacturers were required to adhere to a code of conduct regarding quality of manufacturing, working conditions, and other social concerns. However, the company had no long-term agreements requiring it to continue to use the services of any manufacturer, and no manufacturer was obligated to make products for UA on a long-term basis. UA had subsidiaries in Hong Kong, Panama, Vietnam, Indonesia, and China to support its manufacturing, quality assurance, and sourcing efforts for its products.

Under Armour had a 17,000-square-foot Special Make-Up Shop located at one of its distribution facilities in Maryland where it had the capability to make and ship customized apparel products on tight deadlines for high-profile athletes and teams. While these apparel products represented a tiny fraction of Under Armour's revenues, management believed the facility helped provide superior service to select customers.

Inventory Management

Under Armour based the amount of inventory it needed to have on hand for each item in its product line on existing orders, anticipated sales, and the need to rapidly deliver orders to customers. Its inventory strategy was focused on (1) having sufficient inventory to fill incoming orders promptly and (2) putting strong systems and procedures in place to improve the efficiency with which it managed its inventories of individual products and total inventory. The amounts of seasonal products it ordered from manufacturers were based on current bookings, the need to ship seasonal items at the start of the shipping window in order to maximize the floor space productivity of retail customers, the need to adequately stock its Factory House and Brand House stores, and the need to fill customer orders. Excess inventories of particular products were either shipped to its Factory House stores or earmarked for sale to third-party liquidators.

However, the growing number of individual items in UA's product line and uncertainties surrounding upcoming consumer demand for individual items made it difficult to accurately forecast how many units to order from manufacturers and what the appropriate stocking requirements were for many items. New inventory management practices were instituted in 2012 to better cope with stocking requirements for individual items and avoid excessive inventory buildups. Year-end inventories of $783.0 million in 2015 equated to 138.9 days of inventory and inventory turnover of 2.63 turns per year.

COMPETITION

The $250 billion global market for sports apparel, athletic footwear, and related accessories was fragmented among some 25 brand-name competitors with diverse product lines and varying geographic coverage and numerous small competitors with specialized-use apparel lines that usually operated within a single country or geographic region. Industry participants included athletic and leisure shoe companies, athletic and leisure apparel companies, sports equipment companies, and large companies having diversified lines of athletic and leisure shoes, apparel, and equipment. In 2012, the global market for athletic footwear was about $75 billion and was forecasted to reach about $85 billion in 2018; growth was expected to be driven by rising population, increasing disposable incomes, rising health awareness, and the launching of innovative footwear designs and technology.[14] The global market for athletic and fitness apparel, estimated to be $135 billion in 2012, was forecast to grow about 4.3 percent annually and reach about $185 billion by 2020.[15] Exhibit 5 shows a representative sample of the best-known companies and brands in selected segments of the sports apparel, athletic footwear, and sports equipment industry.

EXHIBIT 5 Major Competitors and Brands in Selected Segments of the Sports Apparel, Athletic Footwear, and Accessory Industry, 2015

Performance Apparel for Sports (baseball, football, basketball, softball, volleyball, hockey, lacrosse, soccer, track & field, and other action sports)	Performance-Driven Athletic Footwear	Training/Fitness Clothing
• Nike • Under Armour • Eastbay • adidas • Russell	• Nike • Reebok • adidas • New Balance • Saucony • Puma • Rockport • Converse • Ryka • Asics • Li Ning	• Nike • Under Armour • Eastbay • adidas • Puma • Fila • lululemon athletica • Champion • Asics • SUGOI • Li Ning
Performance Activewear and Sports-Inspired Lifestyle Apparel	**Performance Skiwear**	**Performance Golf Apparel**
• Polo Ralph Lauren • Lacoste • Izod • Cutter & Buck • Timberland • Columbia • Puma • Li Ning • Many others	• Salomon • North Face • Descente • Columbia • Patagonia • Marmot • Helly Hansen • Bogner • Spyder • Many others	• Footjoy • Polo Golf • Nike • adidas • Puma • Under Armour • Ashworth • Cutter & Buck • Greg Norman • Many others

As Exhibit 5 indicates, the sporting goods industry consisted of many distinct product categories and market segments. Because the product mixes of different companies varied considerably, it was common for the product offerings of industry participants to be extensive in some segments, moderate in others, and limited to nonexistent in still others. Consequently, the leading competitors and the intensity of competition varied significantly from market segment to market segment. Nonetheless, competition tended to be intense in most every segment with substantial sales volume and typically revolved around performance and reliability, the breadth of product selection, new product development, price, brand-name strength and identity through marketing and promotion, the ability of companies to convince retailers to stock and effectively merchandise their brands, and capabilities of the various industry participants to sell directly to consumers through their own retail/factory outlet stores and/or at their company websites. It was common for the leading companies selling athletic footwear, sports uniforms, and sports equipment to actively sponsor sporting events and clinics and to contract with prominent and influential athletes, coaches, professional sports teams, colleges, and sports leagues to endorse their brands and use their products.

Nike was the clear global market leader in the sporting goods industry, with a global market share in athletic footwear of about 25 percent and a sports apparel share of 5 percent. The adidas Group, with businesses that produced athletic footwear, sports uniforms, fitness apparel, sportswear, and a variety of sports equipment and marketed them across the world, was the second largest global competitor. Profiles of these two major competitors of Under Armour follow.

Nike, Inc.

Incorporated in 1968, Nike was engaged in the design, development, and worldwide marketing and selling of footwear, sports apparel, sports equipment, and accessory products. Its principal businesses in fiscal years 2014–2015 are shown in the table below.

Nike had global sales of $30.6 billion and net income of $3.3 billion in fiscal 2015 ending May 31, 2015. Nike was the world's largest seller of athletic footwear, athletic apparel, and athletic equipment and accessories, with over 40,000 retail accounts worldwide, 931 company-owned stores, 52 distribution centers, and selling arrangements with independent distributors and licensees in over 190 countries—see Exhibit 6. About 54 percent of Nike's sales came from outside the United States in both 2014 and 2015. Nike had about 24,000 retail accounts in the United States that included footwear stores, sporting goods stores, athletic specialty stores, department stores, and skate, tennis, and golf shops. During fiscal 2015, Nike's three largest customers accounted for approximately 26 percent of sales in the United States; its three largest customers outside the United States accounted for about 12 percent of total non-U.S. sales. In fiscal 2015, Nike had sales of $6.6 billion at its company-owned stores and websites, up from $3.5 billion in fiscal 2012.

Nike expected to grow annual revenues to $50 billion in 2020 and had an ongoing target of annual earnings per share growth in the 14–16 percent range. To help reach its 2020 sales goal, Nike was planning to grow its website sales from about $1 billion in 2015 to over $7 billion in five years, to double sales of Jordan-branded footwear to $4.5 billion, and to grow sales of products for women from $5.7 billion to over $11 billion. For the first nine months of fiscal 2016, Nike reported sales of $30.3 billion and net income of $3.3 billion.

Principal Products Nike's athletic footwear models and styles were designed primarily for specific athletic use, although many were worn for casual or leisure purposes. Running, training, basketball, soccer, sport-inspired casual shoes, and kids' shoes were the company's top-selling footwear categories.

Businesses	Fiscal 2014 Revenues (in millions)	Fiscal 2015 Revenues (in millions)
Nike Brand footwear (over 800 models and styles)	$16,208	$18,318
Nike Brand apparel	8,109	8,636
Nike Brand equipment for a wide variety of sports	1,670	1,632
Converse (a designer and marketer of athletic footwear, apparel, and accessories)	1,684	1,982

Note: Revenues for Nike's wholly owned subsidiary, Hurley—a designer and marketer of action sports and youth lifestyle footwear and apparel, including shorts, tees, tanks, hoodies, and swimwear—were roughly $260 million annually and were allocated to the Nike Brand footwear and apparel business segments.

EXHIBIT 6 Nike's Worldwide Retail and Distribution Network, 2015

United States	Foreign Countries
• ~24,000 retail accounts	• ~20,000 retail accounts
• 185 Nike factory outlet stores	• 512 Nike factory outlet stores
• 33 Nike and NIKETOWN stores	• 73 Nike and NIKETOWN stores
• 92 Converse retail and factory outlet stores	• 7 Converse retail and factory outlet stores
• 29 Hurley stores	• —
• 7 Distribution centers	• 45 Distribution centers
• Company website (www.nike.com)	• Independent distributors and licensees in over 190 countries
	• Company website (www.nike.com)

It also marketed footwear designed for baseball, football, golf, lacrosse, cricket, outdoor activities, tennis, volleyball, walking, and wrestling. The company designed and marketed Nike-branded sports apparel and accessories for most all of these same sports categories, as well as sports-inspired lifestyle apparel, athletic bags, and accessory items. Footwear, apparel, and accessories were often marketed in "collections" of similar design or for specific purposes. It also marketed apparel with licensed college and professional team and league logos. Nike-brand offerings in sports equipment included bags, socks, sport balls, eyewear, timepieces, electronic devices, bats, gloves, protective equipment, and golf clubs. Nike was also the owner of the Converse brand of athletic footwear and the Hurley brand of swimwear, assorted other apparel items, and surfing gear.

Exhibit 7 shows a breakdown of Nike's sales of footwear, apparel, and equipment by geographic region for fiscal years 2013–2015.

EXHIBIT 7 Nike's Sales of Nike Brand Footwear, Apparel, and Equipment, by Geographic Region, Fiscal Years 2010-2015

	Fiscal Years Ending May 31		
Sales Revenues and Earnings (in millions)	2015	2014	2013
North America			
Revenues—Nike Brand footwear	$ 8,506	$ 7,495	$ 6,751
Nike Brand apparel	4,410	3,937	3,591
Nike Brand equipment	824	867	816
Total Nike Brand revenues	$ 13,740	$ 12,299	$ 11,158
Earnings before interest and taxes	$ 3,645	$ 3,077	$ 2,639
Profit margin	26.5%	25.0%	23.7%
Western Europe			
Revenues—Nike Brand footwear	$ 3,876	$ 3,299	$ 2,657
Nike Brand apparel	1,555	1,427	1,289
Nike Brand equipment	278	253	247
Total Nike Brand revenues	$ 5,709	$ 4,979	$ 4,193
Earnings before interest and taxes	$ 1,277	$ 855	$ 712
Profit margin	22.4%	17.2%	17.0%
Central & Eastern Europe			
Revenues—Nike Brand footwear	$ 827	$ 763	$ 672
Nike Brand apparel	495	532	468
Nike Brand equipment	95	92	89
Total Nike Brand revenues	$ 1,417	$ 1,387	$ 1,229
Earnings before interest and taxes	$ 247	$ 279	$ 234
Profit margin	17.4%	20.1%	19.0%
Greater China			
Revenues—Nike Brand footwear	$ 2,016	$ 1,600	$ 1,495
Nike Brand apparel	925	876	844
Nike Brand equipment	126	126	139
Total Nike Brand revenues	$ 3,067	$ 2,602	$ 2,478
Earnings before interest and taxes	$ 993	$ 816	$ 813
Profit margin	32.4%	31.4%	32.8%

EXHIBIT 7 (Continued)

Sales Revenues and Earnings (in millions)	Fiscal Years Ending May 31 2015	2014	2013
Japan			
Revenues—Nike Brand footwear	$ 452	$ 409	$ 439
Nike Brand apparel	230	276	337
Nike Brand equipment	73	86	100
Total Nike Brand revenues	$ 755	$ 771	$ 876
Earnings before interest and taxes	$ 100	$ 131	$ 139
Profit margin	13.2%	17.0%	15.9%
Emerging Markets			
Revenues—Nike Brand footwear	$ 2,641	$ 2,642	$ 2,621
Nike Brand apparel	1,021	1,061	962
Nike Brand equipment	236	246	249
Total Nike Brand revenues	$ 3,898	$ 3,949	$ 3,832
Earnings before interest and taxes	$ 818	$ 952	$ 985
Profit margin	21.0%	24.1%	25.7%
All Regions			
Revenues—Nike Brand footwear	$ 18,318	$ 16,208	$ 14,635
Nike Brand apparel	8,636	8,109	7,491
Nike Brand equipment	1,632	1,670	1,640
Total Nike Brand revenues	$ 28,586	$ 25,987	$ 23,766
Earnings before interest and taxes	$ 5,386	$ 4,738	$ 5,386
Profit margin	23.7%	22.6%	23.7%
Other Businesses			
Revenues—Converse	$ 1,982	$ 1,684	$ 1,449
Earnings before interest and taxes	$ 517	$ 496	$ 425
Profit margin	18.2%	16.8%	18.2%

Note: The revenue and earnings figures for all geographic regions include the effects of currency exchange fluctuations. The Nike Brand revenues for equipment include the Hurley brand, and the Nike Brand revenues for footwear include the Jordan brand. The earnings before interest and taxes figures associated with Total Nike Brand Revenues include those for the Hurley and Jordan brands.

Source: Nike's 10-K report for fiscal year 2015, pp. 26–31.

Marketing, Promotions, and Endorsements

Nike responded to trends and shifts in consumer preferences by (1) adjusting the mix of existing product offerings; (2) developing new products, styles, and categories; and (3) striving to influence sports and fitness preferences through aggressive marketing, promotional activities, sponsorships, and athlete endorsements. Nike spent $3.21 billion in fiscal 2015, $3.03 billion in 2014, and $2.75 billion in 2013 for what it termed "demand creation expense" that included the costs of advertising, promotional activities, and endorsement contracts. Well over 500 professional, collegiate, club, and Olympic sports teams in football, basketball, baseball, ice hockey, soccer, rugby, speed skating, tennis, swimming, and other sports wore Nike uniforms with the Nike swoosh prominently visible. There were over 1,000 prominent professional athletes with Nike endorsement contracts in 2011–2015, including former basketball great Michael Jordan, NFL players Drew Brees, Tony Romo, Marcus Mariota, Jameis Winston, Jason Witten, and Clay Mathews; Major

League Baseball players Albert Pujols, Derek Jeter, and Alex Rodriguez; NBA players LeBron James, Kobe Bryant, Kevin Durant, and Dwayne Wade; professional golfers Tiger Woods and Michelle Wie; soccer player Cristiano Ronaldo; and professional tennis players Victoria Azarenka, Maria Sharapova, Venus and Serena Williams, Roger Federer, and Rafael Nadal. When Tiger Woods turned pro, Nike signed him to a five-year $100 million endorsement contract and made him the centerpiece of its campaign to make Nike a factor in the golf equipment and golf apparel marketplace. Nike's long-standing endorsement relationship with Michael Jordan led to the introduction of the highly popular line of Air Jordan footwear and, more recently, to the launch of the Jordan brand of athletic shoes, clothing, and gear. In 2003 LeBron James signed an endorsement deal with Nike worth $90 million over 7 years. Golfer Rory McIlroy's 2013 deal with Nike was reportedly in the range of $150 million over 10 years. Because soccer was such a popular sport globally, Nike had more endorsement contracts with soccer athletes than with athletes in any other sport; track and field athletes had the second largest number of endorsement contracts.

Research and Development Nike management believed R&D efforts had been and would continue to be a key factor in the company's success. Technical innovation in the design of footwear, apparel, and athletic equipment received ongoing emphasis in an effort to provide products that helped reduce injury, enhance athletic performance, and maximize comfort.

In addition to Nike's own staff of specialists in the areas of biomechanics, chemistry, exercise physiology, engineering, industrial design, and related fields, the company utilized research committees and advisory boards made up of athletes, coaches, trainers, equipment managers, orthopedists, podiatrists, and other experts who reviewed designs, materials, concepts for product improvements, and compliance with product safety regulations around the world. Employee athletes, athletes engaged under sports marketing contracts, and other athletes wear-tested and evaluated products during the design and development process.

Manufacturing In fiscal 2015, Nike sourced its athletic footwear from 146 factories in 14 countries. About 95 percent of Nike's footwear was produced by independent contract manufacturers in Vietnam, China, and Indonesia but the company had manufacturing agreements with independent factories in Argentina, Brazil, India, and Mexico to manufacture footwear for sale primarily within those countries. Nike-branded apparel was manufactured outside the United States by 409 independent contract manufacturers located in 39 countries; most of the apparel production occurred in China, Vietnam, Thailand, Indonesia, Sri Lanka, Malaysia, and Cambodia.

The adidas Group

The mission of The adidas Group was to be the best sports brand in the world. Headquartered in Germany, its businesses and brands consisted of:

- adidas—a designer and marketer of active sportswear, uniforms, footwear, and sports products in football, basketball, soccer, running, training, outdoor, and six other categories (82.4 percent of Group sales in 2015).
- Reebok—a well-known global provider of athletic footwear for multiple uses, sports and fitness apparel, and accessories (10.3 percent of Group sales in 2013).
- TaylorMade-adidas Golf—a designer and marketer of TaylorMade golf equipment, Adams Golf equipment, adidas golf shoes and golf apparel, and Ashworth golf apparel (5.3 percent of Group sales in 2013).
- Reebok CCM Hockey—one of the world's largest designers, makers, and marketers of ice hockey equipment and apparel under the brand names Reebok Hockey and CCM Hockey (1.9 percent of Group sales in 2013).

Exhibit 8 shows the company's financial highlights for 2013–2015.

The company sold products in virtually every country of the world. In 2015, its extensive product offerings were marketed through thousands of third-party retailers (sporting goods chains, department stores, independent sporting goods retailer buying groups, lifestyle retailing chains, and Internet retailers), 1,850 company-owned and franchised adidas and Reebok branded "concept" stores, 872 company-owned adidas and Reebok factory outlet stores, 152 other adidas and Reebok stores with varying formats, and various company websites (such as **www.adidas.com**, **www.reebok.com**,

EXHIBIT 8 Financial Highlights for The adidas Group, 2013–2015 (in millions of €)

	2015	2014	2013
Income Statement Data			
Net sales	€16,915	€14,534	€14,203
Gross profit	8,168	6,924	7,001
Gross profit margin	48.3%	47.67%	49.3%
Operating profit	1,094	961	1,233
Operating profit margin	6.5%	6.6%	8.7%
Net income	668	568	839
Net profit margin	4.0%	3.9%	5.9%
Balance Sheet Data			
Inventories	€ 3,113	€ 2,486	€ 2,634
Working capital	2,133	2,970	2,125
Net sales by brand			
adidas	€13,939	€ 1,774	€11,059
Reebok	1,731	1,578	1,599
TaylorMade-adidas Golf	902	913	1,285
Reebok-CCM Hockey	317	269	260
Net sales by product			
Footwear	€ 8,360	€ 6,658	€ 6,587
Apparel	6,970	6,279	5,811
Equipment	1,585	1,597	1,806
Net sales by region			
Western Europe	€ 4,539	€ 3,793	€ 3,800
North America	2,753	2,217	3,362
Greater China	2,469	1,786	1,655
Latin America	1,783	1,612	1,575
Japan	776	744	*
Middle East, South Korea, and Southeast Asia/Pacific	2,388	1925	*
Russia and Commonwealth of Independent States	739	1,098	*

*Comparable data for 2013 were not available because the company redefined its geographic regions for reporting purposes beginning in 2015.

Sources: Company annual reports, 2015 and 2013.

and **www.taylormadegolf.com**). Wholesale sales to third-party retailers in 2015 were €12.7 billion (75.1 percent of the company's 2013 total net sales of €14.5 billion), while retail sales at the company's various stores and websites were €4.2 billion (24.9 percent of 2015 net sales).

Like Under Armour and Nike, both adidas and Reebok were actively engaged in sponsoring major sporting events, teams, and leagues and in using athlete endorsements to promote their products. Recent high-profile sponsorships and promotional partnerships included Official Sportswear Partner of the 2012 Olympic Games (adidas), outfitting all volunteers, technical staff, and officials as well as all the athletes in Team Great Britain; Official Sponsors and ball supplier of the 2010 FIFA World Cup, the

2011 FIFA Women's World Cup Germany, the 2014 FIFA World Cup in Brazil (adidas), and numerous other important soccer tournaments held by FIFA and the Union of European Football Associations or UEFA (adidas); Official Outfitters of NHL (Reebok), NFL (Reebok), NBA (adidas), WNBA (adidas) and NBA-Development League (adidas); Official Apparel and Footwear Outfitter for Boston Marathon and the London Marathon (adidas); Official Licensee of Major League Baseball fan and lifestyle apparel; (Reebok). Athletes that were under contract to endorse various of the company's brands included NBA players Derrick Rose, Tim Duncan, Damian Lillard, and John Wall; professional golfers Paula Creamer (LPGA), Jim Furyk, Sergio Garcia, Retief Goosen, Dustin Johnson, Kenny Perry, Justin Rose, and Mike Weir; soccer players David Beckham, Neymar Jr, and Lionel Messi; and various participants in the 2012 Summer Olympics, the 2014 Winter Olympics, and the 2016 Summer Olympics. In 2003, David Beckham, who had been wearing adidas products since the age of 12, signed a $160 million lifetime endorsement deal with adidas that called for an immediate payment of $80 million and subsequent payments said to be worth an average of $2 million annually for the next 40 years.[16] adidas was eager to sign Beckham to a lifetime deal not only to prevent Nike from trying to sign him but also because soccer was considered the world's most lucrative sport and adidas management believed that Beckham's endorsement of adidas products resulted in more sales than all of the company's other athlete endorsements combined. Companywide expenditures for advertising, event sponsorships, athlete endorsements, public relations, and other marketing activities were €1.89 million in 2015, €1.55 million in 2014, €1.46 billion in 2013, €1.50 billion in 2012, €1.36 billion in 2011, and €1.29 billion in 2010.

In 2015–2016, adidas launched a number of initiatives to become more North America–centric and regain its number two market position that was recently lost to Under Armour. This included a campaign to sign up to 250 National Football League players and 250 Major League Baseball players over the next three years; so far, it had signed NFL players Aaron Rodgers, C.J. Spiller, Robert Griffin III, Demarco Murray, Landon Collins, Von Miller, and 60 others, and MLB players Chase Utley, brothers B.J. and Justin Upton, Carlos Correa, Josh Harrison, and Chris Bryant. It had also signed Kanye West and Pharrell Williams. It had secured 1,100 new retail accounts that involved prominent displays of freshly styled adidas products and introduced a new running shoe with technological features that were expected to capture major attention in the athletic footwear marketplace. In 2015 and the first four months of 2016, these and related efforts had boosted sales of adidas products in North America by 31 percent. In 2016, adidas announced plans to sell its TaylorMade golf business to concentrate its resources more heavily on adidas products; sales of TaylorMade golf equipment were primarily in North America.

Research and development activities commanded considerable emphasis at The adidas Group. Management had long stressed the critical importance of innovation in improving the performance characteristics of its products. New apparel and footwear collections featuring new fabrics, colors, and the latest fashion were introduced on an ongoing basis to heighten consumer interest, as well as to provide performance enhancements—there were 39 "major product launches" in 2010, 48 in 2011, 36 in 2012, 43 in 2013, 46 in 2014, and 35 in 2015. About 1,000 people were employed in R&D activities at nine locations, of which four were devoted to adidas products, three to Reebok products, and one each for TaylorMade-adidas Golf and Reebok-CCM Hockey. In addition to its own internal activities, the company drew upon the services of well-regarded researchers at universities in Canada, the United States, England, and Germany. R&D expenditures in 2015 were €139 million, versus €126 million in 2014, €124 million in 2013, €128 million in 2012, €115 million in 2011, and €102 million in 2010.

Over 95 percent of production was outsourced to 320 independent contract manufacturers located in China and other Asian countries (79 percent), Europe (12 percent), and the Americas (9 percent). The Group operated 10 relatively small production and assembly sites of its own in Germany (1), Sweden (1), Finland (1), the United States (4), and Canada (3). Close to 96 percent of the Group's production of footwear was performed in Asia; annual volume sourced from footwear suppliers had ranged from a low of 239 million pairs to a high of 301 million pairs from 2011 to 2015. During the same time frame, apparel production ranged from 262 million to 364 million units and the production of hardware products ranged from 93 million to 113 million units.

Executives at The adidas Group expected that the Group's global sales would increase by 10 to 12 percent in 2016; management also wanted to achieve a 2016 operating margin of 6.5 to 7.0 percent and grow 2016 net income by 10 to 12 percent.

ENDNOTES

[1] "What's Driving Big Growth for Under Armour," www.trefis.com (accessed April 24, 2013); "Factors Underlying Our $74 Valuation of Under Armour," Part 1, February 28, 2014, www.trefis.com (accessed March 18, 2014); Andria Cheng, "Underdog Under Armour Still Has a Long Way to Go to Catch Up with Nike," *MarketWatch*, October 24, 2013, www.marketwatch.com (accessed March 18, 2014).

[2] Sara Germano, "Under Armour Overtakes adidas in the U.S. Sportswear Market," *The Wall Street Journal*, January 8, 2015, www.wsj.com (accessed April 19, 2016).

[3] Daniel Roberts, "Under Armour Gets Serious," *Fortune*, October 26, 2011, p. 156.

[4] Ibid.

[5] Ibid.

[6] Ibid.

[7] As stated on p. 53 of Under Armour's Prospectus for its initial public offering of common stock, dated November 17, 2005.

[8] Under Armour's Q4 2015 Earnings Call Transcript, January 26, 2016, www.seekingalpha.com, (accessed March 30, 2016).

[9] "Under Armour Kevin A. Plank on Q1 2016 Results—Earnings Call Transcript," April 21, 2016, www.seekingalpha.com (accessed April 21, 2016).

[10] Company 10-K reports, 2009, 2010, 2011, 2012, and 2013.

[11] Company 10-K report for 2015, p. 36.

[12] According to information in the company's slide presentation for Investors Day 2015, September 16, 2015.

[13] According to data in the company's slide presentation for Investors Day 2013, June 5, 2013.

[14] According to a report by Transparency Market Research, titled "Athletic Footwear Market—Global Industry Size, Market Share, Trends, Analysis and Forecast, 2012–2018" that was summarized in a September 26, 2012, press release by *PR Newswire*, www.prnewsire.com (accessed May 1, 2013).

[15] Allied Market Research, "World Sports Apparel Market—Opportunities and Forecasts, 2014–2020," October 2015, www.alliedmarketresearch.com (accessed April 25, 2016).

[16] Steve Seepersaud, "5 of the Biggest Athlete Endorsement Deals," www.askmen.com (accessed February 5, 2012).

lululemon athletica, inc. in 2016: Can the Company Get Back on Track? connect

Arthur A. Thompson
The University of Alabama

In May 2016, shareholders of lululemon athletica—a designer and retailer of high-tech athletic apparel sold under the lululemon athletica and ivivva athletica brand names—were concerned whether customers were losing enthusiasm for the company's stylish, premium-priced products. Revenue growth of 16.1 percent in fiscal 2013, 12.9 percent in 2014, and 14.6 percent in 2015 was well below the 36.9 percent increase in fiscal 2012. Average annual sales at lululemon's retail stores open at least 12 months had dropped from a record high of \$5.83 million per store in 2012 to \$5.44 million in 2013 to \$4.95 million in 2014 to \$4.57 million in 2015—a disturbingly big 21.6 percent decline.

Were these two disappointing performance metrics a reflection of lingering damage to the company's brand image stemming from design and product quality problems encountered in March 2013 when shipments of women's black Luon bottoms proved to be sheer and revealing of the garments being worn underneath. Or were other troublesome factors also at work? Was the market signaling that the "fad for lululemon apparel" was over? Might the heretofore "must have" appeal of lululemon's functional and stylish apparel among fitness-conscious women be a thing of the past, never to reappear? Would sales rejuvenation be impossible given that several important competitors (Under Armour, Nike, adidas, and The Gap's new Athleta brand retail stores) were broadening their product lines to include a bigger selection of fashionable, high-performance athletic and fitness apparel for women? Could the problem be due to a significant fraction of the company's customers switching to lower-priced brands and/or brands they considered to more cutting edge or more trend-setting or more appealingly designed? Were all of these factors in play and, if so, what strategic actions could lululemon management initiate to pump up the company's performance? And, given whatever actions top management might take to rejuvenate sales, how long would it be before stockholders could reasonably expect for the company's \$64 stock price (as of May 9, 2016) to climb above \$80 per share (where it was trading in March 2013 when the problems with the black Luon bottoms first surfaced and sales began to slack off)?

COMPANY BACKGROUND

A year after selling his eight-store surf-, skate- and snowboard-apparel chain called Westbeach Sports, Chip Wilson took the first commercial yoga class offered in Vancouver, British Columbia, and found the result exhilarating. But he found the cotton clothing used for sweaty, stretchy power yoga completely inappropriate. Wilson's passion was form-fitting performance fabrics and in 1998 he opened a design studio for yoga clothing that also served as a yoga studio at night to help pay the rent. He designed a number of yoga apparel items made of moisture-wicking fabrics that were light, form-fitting, and comfortable and asked local yoga instructors to wear the products and give him feedback. Gratified by the positive response, Wilson opened lululemon's first real store in the beach area of Vancouver in November 2000.

While the store featured yoga clothing designed by Chip Wilson and his wife Shannon,

Chip Wilson's vision was for the store to be a community hub where people could learn and discuss the physical aspects of healthy living—from yoga and diet to running and cycling, plus the yoga-related mental aspects of living a powerful life of possibilities. But the store's clothing proved so popular that dealing with customers crowded out the community-based discussions and training about the merits of living healthy lifestyles. Nonetheless, Chip Wilson and store personnel were firmly committed to healthy, active lifestyles, and Wilson soon came to the conclusion that for the store to provide staff members with the salaries and opportunities to experience fulfilling lives, the one-store company needed to expand into a multi-store enterprise. Wilson believed that the increasing number of women participating in sports, and specifically yoga, provided ample room for expansion, and he saw lululemon athletica's yoga-inspired performance apparel as a way to address a void in the women's athletic apparel market. Wilson also saw the company's mission as one of providing people with the components to live a longer, healthier, and more fun life.

Several new stores were opened in the Vancouver area, with operations conducted through a Canadian operating company, initially named Lululemon Athletica, Inc. and later renamed lululemon canada, inc. In 2002, the company expanded into the United States and formed a sibling operating company, Lululemon Athletica USA Inc. (later renamed lululemon usa, inc.), to conduct its U.S. operations. Both operating companies were wholly owned by affiliates of Chip Wilson. In 2004, the company contracted with a franchisee to open a store in Australia as a means of more quickly disseminating the lululemon athletica brand name, conserving on capital expenditures for store expansion (since the franchisee was responsible for the costs of operating and operating the store), and boosting revenues and profits. The company wound up its fiscal year ending January 31, 2005, with 14 company-owned stores, 1 franchised store, and net revenues of $40.7 million. A second franchised store was opened in Japan later in 2005. Franchisees paid lululemon a one-time franchise fee and an ongoing royalty based on a specified percentage of net revenues; lululemon supplied franchised stores with garments at a discount to the suggested retail price.

Five years after opening the first retail store, it was apparent that lululemon apparel was fast becoming something of a cult phenomenon and a status symbol among yoga fans in areas where lululemon stores had opened. Avid yoga exercisers were not hesitating to purchase $120 color-coordinated lululemon yoga outfits that felt comfortable and made them look good. Mall developers and mall operators quickly learned about lululemon's success and began actively recruiting lululemon to lease space for stores in their malls.

In December 2005, with 27 company-owned stores, 2 franchised stores, and record sales approaching $85 million annually, Chip Wilson sold 48 percent of his interest in the company's capital stock to two private equity investors: Advent International Corporation, which purchased 38.1 percent of the stock, and Highland Capital Partners, which purchased a 9.6 percent ownership interest. In connection with the transaction, the owners formed lululemon athletica inc. to serve as a holding company for all of the company's related entities, including the two operating subsidiaries, lululemon canada inc. and lululemon usa inc. Robert Meers, who had 15 years' experience at Reebok and was Reebok's CEO from 1996 to 1999, joined lululemon as CEO in December 2005. Chip Wilson headed the company's design team and played a central role in developing the company's strategy and nurturing the company's distinctive corporate culture; he was also chair of the company's board of directors, a position he had held since founding the company in 1998. Wilson and Meers assembled a management team with a mix of retail, design, operations, product sourcing, and marketing experience from such leading apparel and retail companies as Abercrombie & Fitch, Limited Brands, Nike, and Reebok.

Brisk expansion ensued. The company ended fiscal 2006 with 41 company-owned stores, 10 franchised stores, net revenues of $149 million, and net income of $7.7 million. In 2007, the company's owners elected to take the company public. The initial public offering took place on August 2, 2007, with the company selling 2,290,909 shares to the public and various stockholders selling 15,909,091 shares of their personal holdings. Shares began trading on the NASDAQ under the symbol LULU and on the Toronto Exchange under the symbol LLL.

In 2007, the company's announced growth strategy had five key elements:

1. ***Grow the company's store base in North America.*** The strategic objective was to add new stores to strengthen the company's presence in locations where it had existing stores and then selectively enter new geographic markets in the United States and Canada. Management believed that the company's strong sales in U.S. stores demonstrated the portability of the lululemon brand and retail concept.
2. ***Increase brand awareness.*** This initiative entailed leveraging the publicity surrounding the opening of new stores with grassroots marketing programs that included organizing events and partnering with local fitness practitioners.
3. ***Introduce new product technologies.*** Management intended to continue to focus on developing and offering products that incorporated technology-enhanced fabrics and performance features that differentiated lululemon apparel and helped broaden the company's customer base.
4. ***Broaden the appeal of lululemon products.*** This initiative entailed (1) adding a number of apparel items for men; (2) expanding product offerings for women and young females in such categories as athletic bags, undergarments, outerwear, and sandals; and (3) adding products suitable for additional sports and athletic activities.
5. ***Expand beyond North America.*** In the near term, the company planned to expand its presence in Australia and Japan and then, over time, pursue opportunities in other Asian and European markets that offered similar, attractive demographics.

The company grew rapidly. Fitness-conscious women began flocking to the company's stores not only because of the fashionable products but also because of the store ambience and attentive, knowledgeable store personnel. Dozens of new lululemon athletic retail stores were opened annually, and the company pursued a strategy of embellishing its product offerings to create a comprehensive line of apparel and accessories designed for athletic pursuits such as yoga, running, and general fitness; technical clothing for active female youths; and a selection of fitness and recreational items for men. Revenues topped $1 billion in fiscal 2011 and reached almost $1.6 billion in fiscal 2013.

Headed into fiscal year 2016, the company's products could be bought at its 320 retail stores in the United States and Canada, 31 stores in Australia and New Zealand, and 17 stores in 5 other foreign countries, plus the company's website, **www.lululemon.com**, and assorted other locations. In the company's most recent fiscal year ending January 31, 2016, retail store sales accounted for 73.6 percent of company revenues, website sales accounted for 19.5 percent, and sales in all other channels (showroom sales, sales at outlet centers, sales from temporary locations, licensing revenues, and wholesale sales to premium yoga studios, health clubs, fitness centers, and a few other retailers) accounted for 6.9 percent.

Exhibit 1 presents highlights of the company's performance for fiscal years 2011–2015. Exhibit 2 shows lululemon's revenues by business segment and geographic region for the same period.

lululemon's Evolving Senior Leadership Team

In January 2008, Christine M. Day joined the company as executive vice president, retail operations. Previously, she had worked at Starbucks, functioning in a variety of capacities and positions including president, Asia Pacific Group (July 2004–February 2007), co-president, Starbucks Coffee International (July 2003–October 2003), and senior vice president, North American Finance & Administration, and vice president, sales and operations for business alliances. In April 2008, Day was appointed as lululemon's president and chief operating officer, and was named chief executive officer and member of the board of directors in July 2008. During her tenure as CEO, Day expanded and strengthened the company's management team to support its expanding operating activities and geographic scope, favoring the addition of people with relevant backgrounds and experiences at such companies as Nike, Abercrombie & Fitch, The Gap, and Speedo International. She also spent a number of hours each week in the company's stores observing how customers shopped, listening to their comments and complaints, and using the information to tweak product offerings, merchandising, and store operations.

Company founder Chip Wilson stepped down from his executive role as lululemon's chief innovation and branding officer effective January 29, 2012, and moved his family to Australia; however,

EXHIBIT 1 Financial and Operating Highlights, lululemon athletica, Fiscal Years 2011–2015 (in millions of $)

Selected Income Statement Data	Fiscal Year 2015 (Ending Jan. 31, 2016)	Fiscal Year 2014 (Ending Feb. 1, 2015)	Fiscal Year 2013 (Ending Feb. 2, 2014)	Fiscal Year 2012 (Ending Feb. 3, 2013)	Fiscal Year 2011 (Ending Jan. 29, 2012)
Net revenues	$2,060.5	$1,797.2	$1,591.2	$1,370.4	$1,000.8
Cost of goods sold	1,063.4	833.0	751.1	607.5	431.6
Gross profit	997.2	914.2	840.1	762.8	569.3
Selling, general, and administrative expenses	628.1	538.1	448.7	386.4	282.3
Operating profit	369.1	376.0	391.4	376.4	287.0
Net profit (loss)	266.0	239.0	279.5	271.4	185.0
Earnings per share—basic	$ 1.90	$ 1.66	$ 1.93	$ 1.88	$ 1.29
Earnings per share—diluted	1.89	1.66	1.91	1.85	1.27
Balance Sheet Data					
Cash and cash equivalents	$ 501.5	$ 664.5	$ 698.6	$ 590.2	$ 409.4
Inventories	284.0	208.1	188.8	155.2	104.1
Total assets	1,314.1	1,296.2	1,252.3	1,051.1	734.6
Stockholders' equity	1,027.5	1,089.6	1,096.7	887.3	606.2
Cash Flow and Other Data					
Net cash provided by operating activities	$ 298.7	$ 314.4	$ 278.3	$ 280.1	$ 203.6
Capital expenditures	143.5	119.7	106.4	93.2	116.7
Store Data					
Number of corporate-owned stores open at end of period	363	302	254	211	174
Sales per gross square foot at corporate-owned stores open at least one full year	$ 1,541	$ 1,678	$ 1,894	$ 2,058	$ 2,004
Average sales at corporate-owned stores open at least one year (in millions)	$ 4.57	$ 4.95	$ 5.44	$ 5.83	$ 5.33

Sources: Company 10-K reports for fiscal years 2010, 2011, 2012, 2013, 2014, and 2015.

he continued on in his role as chair of the company's board of directors and focused on becoming a better board chair, even going so far as to take a four-day course on board governance at Northwestern University.[1] Christine Day promoted Sheree Waterson, who had joined the company in 2008 and had over 25 years of consumer and retail industry experience, as chief product officer to assume responsibility for product design, product development, and other executive tasks that Wilson had been performing. Shortly after the quality problems with the black Luon bottoms occurred, Waterson resigned her position and left the company. In October 2013, lululemon announced that Tara Poseley had been appointed to its Senior Leadership Team as chief product officer and would have responsibility for overseeing lululemon's design team, product design activities, merchandising, inventory activities, and strategic planning. Previously, Poseley held the position of interim president

EXHIBIT 2 lululemon athletica's Revenues and Income from Operations, by Business Segment and by Geographic Region, Fiscal Years 2011–2015 (dollars in millions)

Revenues by Business Segment	Fiscal Year 2015 (Ending Jan. 1 2016)	Fiscal Year 2014 (Ending Feb. 1, 2015)	Fiscal Year 2013 (Ending Feb. 2, 2014)	Fiscal Year 2012 (Ending Feb. 3, 2013)	Fiscal Year 2011 (Ending Jan. 29, 2012)
Corporate-owned stores	$1,516.3	$1,348.2	$1,229.0	$1,090.2	$ 816.9
Direct-to-consumer (e-commerce sales)	401.5	321.2	263.1	197.3	106.3
All other channels*	142.7	127.8	99.1	82.9	77.6
Total	$2,060.5	$1,797.2	$1,591.2	$1,370.4	$1,000.8
Percentage Distribution of Revenues by Business Segment					
Corporate owned stores	73.6%	75.0%	77.3%	79.6%	81.6%
Direct-to-consumer (e-commerce sales)	19.5%	17.9%	16.5%	14.4%	10.6%
All other channels*	6.9%	7.1%	6.2%	6.0%	7.8%
Total	100.0%	100.0%	100.0%	100.0%	100.0%
Income from Operations (before general corporate expenses), by Business Segment					
Corporate owned stores	$ 346.8	$ 356.6	$ 372.3	$ 375.5	$ 297.8
Direct-to-consumer (e-commerce sales)	166.4	132.9	110.0	84.7	44.2
All other channels*	5.8	9.5	14.0	19.9	21.1
Total Income from Operations (before general corporate expenses)	$ 498.3	$ 499.0	$ 496.3	$ 480.1	$ 363.1
Revenues by Geographic Region					
United States	$1,508.8	$1,257.4	$1,052.2	$ 839.9	$ 536.2
Canada	416.5	434.3	454.2	461.6	425.7
Outside of North America	135.2	105.5	84.8	68.9	38.9
Total	$2,060.5	$1,797.2	$1,591.2	$1,370.4	$1,000.8
Percentage Distribution of Revenues by Geographic Region					
United States	73.2%	70.0%	66.1%	61.3%	53.6%
Canada	20.2%	24.2%	28.5%	33.7%	42.5%
Outside of North America	6.6%	5.9%	5.3%	5.0%	3.9%
Total	100.0%	100.0%	99.9%	100.0%	100.0%

*The "All other channels" category included showroom sales, sales at lululemon outlet stores, sales from temporary store locations, licensing revenues, and wholesale sales to premium yoga studios, health clubs, fitness centers, and other wholesale accounts.

Sources: Company 10-K reports, fiscal years 2011, 2012, 2013, 2014, and 2015.

at Bebe Stores, Inc., president of Disney Stores North America (The Children's Place), CEO of Design Within Reach (DWR), and a range of senior merchandising and design management positions during her 15-year tenure at Gap Inc.

In the aftermath of the pants recall in March 2013, the working relationship between Christine Day and Chip Wilson deteriorated. Wilson made it clear that he would have handled the product recall incident differently and that he did not think there were problems with the design of the product or the quality of the fabric. But the differences between Day and Wilson went beyond the events of March 2013, especially when some consumers began to complain about the quality of the replacement pants. Wilson returned from Australia in May 2013, and weeks later Christine Day announced she would step down as CEO when her successor was named. A lengthy search for Day's replacement ensued.

In the meantime, Chip Wilson triggered a firestorm when, in an interview with Bloomberg TV in November 2013, he defended the company's design of the black Luon bottoms, saying, "Quite frankly, some women's bodies just actually don't work" with the pants. Although a few days later he publicly apologized for his remarks suggesting that the company's product quality issues back in March 2013 were actually the fault of overweight women, his apology was not well received. In December 2013, Wilson resigned his position as board chair and took on the lesser role of nonexecutive chair. A few months later, Wilson announced that he intended to give up his position as nonexecutive chair prior to the company's annual stockholders meeting in June 2014 but continue on as a member of the company's board of directors (in 2013–2014, Wilson was the company's largest stockholder and controlled 29.2 percent of the company's common stock).

In early December 2013, lululemon announced that its board of directors had appointed Laurent Potdevin as the company's chief executive officer and a member of its board of directors; Potdevin stepped into his role in January 2014 and, to help ensure a smooth transition, Christine Day remained with lululemon through the end of the company's fiscal year (February 2, 2014). Potdevin came to lululemon having most recently served as president of TOMS Shoes, a company founded on the mission that it would match every pair of shoes purchased with a pair of new shoes given to a child in need. Prior to TOMS, Potdevin held numerous positions at Burton Snowboards for more than 15 years, including president and CEO from 2005 to 2010; Burton Snowboards, headquartered in Burlington, Vermont, was considered to be the world's premier snowboard company, with a product line that included snowboards and accessories (bindings, boots, socks, gloves, mitts, and beanies); men's women's, and youth snowboarding apparel; and bags and luggage. Burton's grew significantly under Potdevin's leadership, expanding across product categories and opening additional retail stores.

Tension between Chip Wilson and lululemon's board of directors erupted at the company's annual shareholder's meeting in June 2014 when he voted his entire shares against reelection of the company's chair and another director. In February 2015, after continuing to disagree with lululemon executives and board members over the company's strategic direction and ongoing dissatisfaction with how certain lululemon activities were being managed, Wilson resigned his position on lululemon's board of directors. In August 2014, he sold half of his ownership stake to a private equity firm. In June 2015, lululemon filed documents with the Securities and Exchange Commission enabling Wilson to sell his remaining 20.1 million shares (equal to a 14.6 percent ownership stake worth about $1.3 billion) in the event he wished to do so. Meanwhile, Wilson, together with his wife and son, in 2014 had formed a new company, Kit and Ace, that specialized in high-end clothing for men and women made from a machine-washable, high-performance cashmere fabric; the innovative clothing line was designed for all-day wear and included a range of items suitable for running errands or attending an evening event. In 2016, there were some 60 Kit and Ace stores in the United States, Canada, Australia, Britain, and Japan.

THE YOGA MARKETPLACE

According to a "Yoga in America" study funded by the *Yoga Journal*, in 2015 there were 36.7 million people in the United States who had practiced yoga in the last six months in a group or private class setting, up from 20.4 million in 2012 and 15.8 million in 2008.[2] About 72 percent of the people who engaged in group or class yoga exercises were women, and close to 62 percent of all yoga practitioners were in the age range of 18–49.[3] About 74 percent of the people who practiced yoga in 2015 had done so for five years or less. The level of yoga expertise varied considerably: 56 percent of yoga practitioners considered themselves as beginners, 42 percent considered themselves as "intermediate," and 2 percent considered themselves to be in the expert/advanced category. Spending on yoga classes, yoga apparel, and related items was an estimated $16.8 billion, up from $10.3 billion in 2012 and $5.7 billion in 2008.[4]

The market for sports and fitness apparel was considerably larger, of course, than just the market for yoga apparel. The global market for all types of sportswear, activewear, and athletic apparel, estimated to be about $148 billion in 2015, was forecast to grow about 4.3 percent annually and reach about $185 billion by 2020.[5] In the United States, sales of activewear and all types of gym and fitness apparel, which included both items made with high-tech performance fabrics that wicked away moisture and items made mostly of cotton, polyester, stretch fabrics, and selected other synthetic fibers that lacked moisture-wicking and other high-performance features), was the fastest-growing segment of the apparel industry.[6]

lULULEMON'S STRATEGY AND BUSINESS IN 2016

lululemon athletica viewed its core mission as "creating components for people to live longer, healthier, fun lives."[7] The company's primary target customer was

> a sophisticated and educated woman who understands the importance of an active, healthy lifestyle. She is increasingly tasked with the dual responsibilities of career and family and is constantly challenged to balance her work, life and health. We believe she pursues exercise to achieve physical fitness and inner peace.[8]

In the company's early years, lululemon's strategy was predicated on management's belief that other athletic apparel companies were not effectively addressing the unique style, fit, and performance needs of women who were embracing yoga and a variety of other fitness and athletic activities. lululemon sought to address this void in the marketplace by incorporating style, feel-good comfort, and functionality into its yoga-inspired apparel products and by building a network of lululemon retail stores, along with an online store at the company's website, to market its apparel directly to these women. However, while the company was founded to address the unique needs and preferences of women, it did not take long for management to recognize the merits of broadening the company's market target to include fitness apparel for activities other than yoga and apparel for population segments other than adult women.

In 2009, lululemon opened its first ivviva-branded store in Vancouver, British Columbia, to sell high-quality, premium-priced dance-inspired apparel to female youth (*ivviva* was a word that lululemon made up). The Vancouver store was soon profitable, and 11 additional company-owned ivviva stores were opened in Canada and the United States during 2010–2013. In 2014–2015, the opening of new ivviva stores accelerated. As of January 31, 2016, there were 31 ivviva stores in the United States and 12 ivviva stores in Canada, plus an additional 28 ivviva showrooms (26 in the United States and 2 in Canada); showrooms displayed key styles and were open only part of the week so that ivviva personnel could be out in the community building relationships with local dance instructors and creating awareness of the ivviva brand of apparel, all in preparation for opening an ivivva retail store in upcoming months.

In 2013–2014, the company began designing and marketing products for men who appreciated the technical rigor and premium quality of athletic and fitness apparel. Management also believed that participation in athletic and fitness activities was destined to climb as people over 60 years of age became increasingly focused on living longer, healthier, active lives in their retirement years and engaged in regular exercise and recreational activities. Another demand-enhancing factor was that consumer decisions to purchase athletic, fitness, and recreational apparel were being driven not only by an actual need for functional products but also by a desire to create a particular lifestyle perception through the apparel they wore. Consequently, senior executives had transitioned lululemon's strategy from one of focusing exclusively on yoga apparel for women to one aimed at designing and marketing a wider range of healthy lifestyle–inspired apparel and accessories for women and men and dance-inspired apparel for girls.

As lululemon began fiscal year 2016, the company's business strategy had six core components:

- Broaden the lululemon product line to include both more items and items suitable for purposes other than just fitness-related activities.
- Grow the store base, both in North America and outside North America.
- Broaden awareness of the lululemon and ivivva brands and the nature and quality of the company's apparel offerings.
- Incorporate next-generation fabrics and technologies in the company's products to strengthen consumer association of the lululemon and ivivva brands with technically advanced fabrics and innovative features, thereby enabling lululemon to command higher prices for its products compared to the prices of traditional fitness and recreational apparel products made of cotton, rayon, polyester, and/or other synthetic fibers lacking the performance features of high-tech fabrics.
- Provide a distinctive in-store shopping experience, complemented with strong ties to fitness instructors and fitness establishments, local athletes and fitness-conscious people, and various community-based athletic and fitness events.
- Grow traffic and sales at the company's websites (**www.lululemon.com** and **www.ivviva.com**) to provide a distinctive and satisfying online shopping experience and to extend the company's reach into geographic markets where it did not have retail stores.

Product Line Strategy

In 2016, lululemon offered a diverse and growing selection of premium-priced performance apparel and accessories for women and men that were designed for healthy lifestyle activities such as yoga, swimming, running, cycling, and general fitness. Currently, the company's range of offerings included:

Women		Men
• Sports bras	• Swimwear	• Tops
• Tanks	• Socks and underwear	• Jackets and hoodies
• Sweaters and wraps	• Scarves	• Pants and shorts
• Jackets and hoodies	• Gear bags	• Gear bags and backpacks
• Long-sleeve and short-sleeve tops and tees	• Caps and headbands	• Caps and gloves
• Pants and crops	• Sweat cuffs and gloves	• Swimwear
• Shorts	• Water bottles	• Socks and underwear
• Skirts and dresses	• Yoga mats and props	• Run accessories
• Outerwear	• Instructional yoga DVDs	• Yoga mats, props, and instructional DVDs

Exhibit 3 shows a sampling of lululemon's products for men and women.

Most of the company's products for female youths were sold at ivivva stores and at the ivivva website, **www.ivivva.com**. The ivivva product line, while featuring dancing apparel, also included apparel for yoga and running; specific apparel items available under the ivivva label included leotards, shorts, dance pants, crop pants, tights, sports bras, tank tops, tees, jackets, hoodies, pullovers, caps, headbands, socks, bags, and other accessories.

lululemon's Strategy of Offering Only a Limited Range of Apparel Sizes In the months following the product recall of the too-sheer bottom pants in March 2013, lululemon officially revealed in a posting on its Facebook page that it did not offer clothing in plus sizes because focusing on sizes 12 and below was an integral part of its business strategy; according to the company's posting and to the postings of lululemon personnel who responded to comments

EXHIBIT 3 Examples of lululemon Apparel Items

(top left) © Dina Rudick/The Boston Globe via Getty Images; (top right) © Xaume Olleros/Bloomberg via Getty Images; (middle left) © Joe Raedle/Getty Images; (middle right and bottom) © Stuart C. Wilson/Getty Images for Lululemon Athletica

made by Facebook members who read the lululemon posting:[9]

> Our product and design strategy is built around creating products for our target guest in our size range of 2–12. While we know that doesn't work for everyone and recognize fitness and health come in all shapes and sizes, we've built our business, brand and relationship with our guests on this formula.
>
> We agree that a beautiful healthy life is not measured by the size you wear. We want to be excellent at what we do, so this means that we can't be everything to everybody and need to focus on specific areas. Our current focuses are in innovating our women's design, men's brand, and building our international market.
>
> At this time, we don't have plans to change our current sizing structure which is 2–12 for women.

Three years later, the largest size appearing in the size guide for women on lululemon's website was 12/XL, which was said to be suitable for a 40″ bust, 32.5″ waist, and 43" hips.

Retail Distribution and Store Expansion Strategy

After several years of experience in establishing and working with franchised stores in the United States, Australia, Japan, and Canada, top management in 2010 determined that having franchised stores was not in lululemon's best long-term strategic interests. A strategic initiative was begun to either acquire the current stores of franchisees and operate them as company stores or convert the franchised stores to a joint venture arrangement where lululemon owned the controlling interest in the store and the former franchisee owned a minority interest. By year-end 2011, all lululemon stores were company owned and operated.

As of May 2016, lululemon's retail footprint included:

- 48 stores in Canada scattered across seven provinces, but mainly located in British Columbia, Alberta, and Ontario.
- 229 stores in the United States (44 states and the District of Columbia), plus 33 showrooms.
- 26 stores and 1 showroom in Australia.
- 5 stores in New Zealand.
- 6 stores and 3 showrooms in the United Kingdom.
- 2 stores in Singapore, 2 stores in Hong Kong, 1 store and 4 showrooms in Germany, 1 store in Puerto Rico, 1 store in the United Arab Emirates, 2 showrooms each in France and China, and 1 showroom each in Sweden, Switzerland, the Netherlands, Japan, and Malaysia.
- 31 ivviva stores in the United States, plus 26 showrooms.
- 12 ivviva stores in Canada, plus 2 showrooms.

Management had announced that new store openings would be concentrated in the United States, Asia, and Europe, primarily in those locations where showrooms were already open or would be opening soon. In spite of lululemon's recent declines in sales-per-square-foot performance (see the bottom portion of Exhibit 1), management believed its sales revenues per square foot of retail space were close to the best in the retail apparel sector—for example, the stores of specialty fashion retailers like Old Navy, Banana Republic, The Gap, and Abercrombie & Fitch typically had 2015 annual sales averaging less than $500 per square foot of store space.

lululemon's Retail Stores: Locations, Layout, and Merchandising The company's retail stores were located primarily on street locations, in upscale strip shopping centers, in lifestyle centers, and in malls. Typically, stores were leased and were 2,500 to 3,000 square feet in size. Most all stores included space for product display and merchandising, checkout, fitting rooms, a restroom, and an office/storage area. While the leased nature of the store spaces meant that each store had its own customized layout and arrangement of fixtures and displays, each store was carefully decorated and laid out in a manner that projected the ambience and feel of a homespun local apparel boutique rather than the more impersonal, cookie-cutter atmosphere of many apparel chain stores.

The company's merchandising strategy was to sell all of the items in its retail stores at full price.[10] Special colors and seasonal items were in stores for only a limited time—such products were on 3-, 6-, or 12-week life cycles so that frequent shoppers could always find something new. Store inventories of short-cycle products were deliberately limited to help foster a sense of scarcity, condition customers to buy when they saw an item rather than wait, and avoid any need to discount unsold items. In one instance, a hot-pink color that launched in December was supposed to have a two-month shelf life, but supplies sold out in the first week. However, supplies of core products that did not change much from season to season were more ample to minimize the risk of lost sales due to items being out-of-stock. Approximately 95 percent of the merchandise in lululemon stores was sold at full price.[11]

One unique feature of lululemon's retail stores was that the floor space allocated to merchandising displays and customer shopping could be sufficiently cleared to enable the store to hold an in-store yoga class before or after regular shopping hours. Every store hosted a complimentary yoga class each week that was conducted by a professional yoga instructor from the local community who had been recruited to be a "store ambassador"; when the class concluded, the attendees were given a 15 percent off coupon to use in shopping for products in the store. From time to time, each store's yoga ambassadors demonstrated their moves in the store windows and on the sales floor. Exhibit 4 shows the exteriors of representative lululemon athletica stores.

EXHIBIT 4 Representative Exterior Scenes at lululemon Stores

© Stuart C. Wilson/Getty Images for Lululemon Athletica

lululemon's Showroom Strategy Over the years, lululemon had opened "showrooms" in numerous locations both inside and outside North America as a means of introducing the lululemon brand and culture to a community, developing relationships with local fitness instructors and fitness enthusiasts, and hosting community-related fitness events, all in preparation for the grand opening of a new lululemon athletica retail store in weeks ahead. Showroom personnel:

- Hosted get-acquainted parties for fitness instructors and fitness enthusiasts.
- Recruited a few well-regarded fitness instructors in the local area to be "store ambassadors" for lululemon products and periodically conduct in-store yoga classes when the local lululemon retail store opened.
- Advised people visiting the showroom on where to find great yoga or Pilates classes, fitness centers, and health and wellness information and events.
- Solicited a select number of local yoga studios, health clubs, and fitness centers to stock and retail a small assortment of lululemon's products.

Showrooms were open only part of the week so that showroom personnel could be out in the community meeting people, building relationships with yoga and fitness instructors, participating in local yoga and fitness classes and talking with attendees before and after class, promoting attendance at local fitness and wellness events, and stimulating interest in the soon-to-open retail store. lululemon used showrooms as a means of "pre-seeding" the opening of a lululemon retail store primarily in those locations where no other lululemon retail stores were nearby. Because the showroom strategy had worked so well in getting lululemon stores off to a good start, management had quickly adopted the use of showrooms to pre-seed the opening of ivivva stores.

Wholesale Sales Strategy

lululemon marketed its products to select premium yoga studios, health clubs, and fitness centers as a way to gain the implicit endorsement of local fitness personnel for lululemon branded apparel, familiarize their customers with the lululemon brand, and give them an opportunity to conveniently purchase lululemon apparel. Also, when certain styles, colors, and sizes of apparel items at luluemon retail stores were selling too slowly to clear out the inventories of items ordered from contract manufacturers, lululemon typically shipped the excess inventories to one or more of the 11 lululemon Factory Outlet stores in North America to be sold at discounted prices.

lululemon management did not want to grow wholesale sales to these types of establishments into a significant revenue contributor. Rather, the strategic objective of selling lululemon apparel to yoga studios, health clubs, and fitness centers was to build brand awareness, especially in new geographic markets both in North America and other international locations where the company intended to open new stores. Wholesale sales to outlet stores were made only to dispose of excess inventories and thereby avoid in-store markdowns on slow-selling items.

In January 2015, lululemon entered into a license and supply arrangement with a partner in the Middle East to operate lululemon athletica branded retail locations in the United Arab Emirates, Kuwait, Qatar, Oman, and Bahrain for an initial term of five years. lululemon retained the rights to sell lululemon products through its e-commerce websites in these countries. Under the arrangement, lululemon supplied the partner with lululemon products, training, and other support. As of January 31, 2016, there were two licensed stores in the United Arab Emirates, neither of which were included in the company-operated stores numbers in Exhibit 1.

The company's wholesale sales to all these channels accounted for net revenues of $142.7 million (6.9 percent of total net revenues) in fiscal 2015, versus net revenues of $77.6 million ((7.8 percent of the total) in fiscal 2011.

Direct-to-Consumer Sales Strategy

In 2009, lululemon launched its e-commerce website, **www.lululemon.com**, to enable customers to make online purchases, supplement its already-functioning phone sales activities, and greatly extend the company's geographic market reach. Management saw online sales as having three strategic benefits: (1) providing added convenience for core customers, (2) securing sales in geographic markets where there were no lululemon stores, and (3) helping build brand awareness, especially in new markets, including those outside North America. As of early 2016, the company operated country- and region-specific websites in Australia, Europe, the Middle East, and Asia, and brand-specific websites for both lululemon and ivivva (**www.ivivva.com**) products in North America. lululemon provided free shipping on all lululemon and ivivva orders to customers in North America; a shipping fee was charged to buyers in a number of international destinations.

The merchandise selection that lululemon offered to online buyers differed somewhat from what was available in the company's retail stores. A number of the items available in stores were not sold online; a few online selections were not available in the stores. Styles and colors available for sale online were updated weekly. On occasion, the company marked down the prices of some styles and colors sold online to help clear out the inventories of items soon to be out-of-season and make way for newly arriving merchandise—online customers could view the discounted merchandise by clicking on a "we made too much" link.

Direct-to-consumer sales at the company's websites had become an increasingly important part of the company's business, with e-commerce sales climbing from $106.3 million in fiscal 2011 (10.6 percent of total net revenues) to $401.5 million in fiscal 2015 (19.5 percent of total revenues)—equal to a compound annual growth rate of 39.4 percent.

In addition to making purchases, website visitors could browse information about what yoga was, what the various types of yoga were, and their benefits; learn about fabrics and technologies used in lululemon's products; read recent posts on lululemon's yoga blog; and stay abreast of lululemon activities in their communities. The company planned to continue to develop and enhance its e-commerce websites in ways that would provide a distinctive online shopping experience and strengthen its brand reputation.

Product Design and Development Strategy

lululemon's product design efforts were led by a team of designers based in Vancouver, British Columbia, partnering with various international designers. The design team included athletes and users of the company's products who embraced lululemon's design philosophy and dedication to premium quality. Design team members regularly visited retail stores in a proactive effort to solicit feedback on existing products from store customers and fitness ambassadors and to gather their ideas for product improvements and new products. In addition, the design team used various market intelligence sources to identify and track market trends. On occasion, the team hosted meetings in several geographic markets to discuss the company's products with local athletes, trainers, yogis, and members of the fitness industry. The design team incorporated all of this input to make fabric selections, develop new products, and make adjustments in the fit, style, and function of existing products.

The design team worked closely with its apparel manufacturers to incorporate innovative fabrics that gave lululemon garments such characteristics as stretch ability, moisture-wicking capability, color fastness, feel-good comfort, and durability. Fabric quality was evaluated via actual wear tests and by a leading testing facility. Before bringing out new products with new fabrics, lululemon used the services of leading independent inspection, verification, testing, and certification companies to conduct a battery of tests on fabrics for such performance characteristics as pilling, shrinkage, abrasion resistance, and colorfastness. Last, lululemon design personnel worked with leading fabric suppliers to identify opportunities to develop fabrics that lululemon could trademark and thereby gain added brand recognition and brand differentiation.

Where appropriate, product designs incorporated convenience features, such as pockets to hold credit cards, keys, digital audio players, and clips for heart rate monitors and long sleeves that covered the hands for cold-weather exercising. Product specifications called for the use of advanced sewing techniques, such as flat seaming, that increased comfort and functionality, reduced chafing and skin irritation, and strengthened important seams. All of these design elements and fabric technologies were factors that management believed enabled lululemon to price its high-quality technical athletic apparel at prices above those of traditional athletic apparel.

Typically, it took 8 to 10 months for lululemon products to move from the design stage to availability in its retail stores; however, the company had the capability to bring select new products to market in as little as two months. Management believed its lead times were shorter than those of most apparel brands due to the company's streamlined design and development process, the real-time input received from customers and ambassadors at its store locations, and the short times it took to receive and approve samples from manufacturing suppliers. Short lead times facilitated quick responses to emerging trends or shifting market conditions.

lululemon management believed that its design process enhanced the company's capabilities to develop top-quality products and was a competitive strength.

Sourcing and Manufacturing

Production was the only value chain activity that lululemon did not perform internally. lululemon did not own or operate any manufacturing facilities to produce fabrics or make garments. In 2015, fabrics were sourced from a group of approximately 60 fabrics manufacturers. Luon, which constituted about 30 percent of the fabric in lululemon's garments, was supplied by four fabric manufacturers. Garments were sourced from approximately 35 contract manufacturers, five of which produced approximately 65 percent of the company's products in fiscal 2015. However, the company deliberately refrained from entering into long-term contracts with any of its fabric suppliers or manufacturing sources, preferring instead to transact business on an order-by-order basis and rely on the close working relationships it had developed with its various suppliers over the years. During fiscal 2015, approximately 44 percent of the company's products were produced in Southeast Asia, approximately 28 percent in South Asia, approximately 20 percent in China, approximately 2 percent in North America, and the remainder in other regions. The company's North American manufacturers helped provide lululemon with the capability to speed select products to market and respond quickly to changing trends and unexpectedly high buyer demand for certain products.

lululemon took great care to ensure that its manufacturing suppliers shared lululemon's commitment to quality and ethical business conduct. All manufacturers were required to adhere to a vendor code of ethics regarding quality of manufacturing, working conditions, environmental responsibility, fair wage practices, and compliance with child labor laws, among others. lululemon utilized the services of a leading inspection and verification firm to closely monitor each supplier's compliance with applicable law, lululemon's vendor code of ethics, and other business practices that could reflect badly on lululemon's choice of suppliers.

Distribution Facilities

lululemon shipped products to its stores from owned or leased distribution facilities in the United States, Canada, and Australia. The company owned a 307,000-square-foot distribution center in Columbus, Ohio; and operated a leased 156,000-square-foot facility in Vancouver, British Columbia, and an 82,000-square-foot facility in Sumner, Washington. Both leased facilities were modern and cost-efficient. In 2011, the company began operations at a leased 54,000-square-foot distribution center in Melbourne, Australia, to supply its stores in Australia and New

Zealand. Management believed these four facilities would be sufficient to accommodate its expected store growth and expanded product offerings over the next several years. Merchandise was typically shipped to retail stores through third-party delivery services multiple times per week, thus providing stores with a steady flow of new inventory.

lululemon's Community-Based Marketing Approach and Brand-Building Strategy

One of lululemon's differentiating characteristics was its community-based approach to building brand awareness and customer loyalty. Local fitness practitioners chosen to be ambassadors introduced their fitness class attendees to the lululemon brand, thereby leading to interest in the brand, store visits, and word-of-mouth marketing. Each yoga-instructor ambassador was also called on to conduct a complimentary yoga class every four to six weeks at the local lululemon store they were affiliated with. In return for helping drive business to lululemon stores and conducting classes, ambassadors were periodically given bags of free products, and large portraits of each ambassador wearing lululemon products and engaging in physical activity at a local landmark were prominently displayed on the walls their local lululemon store as a means of helping ambassadors expand their clientele.

Every lululemon store had a dedicated community coordinator who developed a customized plan for organizing, sponsoring, and participating in local athletic, fitness, and philanthropic events. In addition, each store had a community events bulletin board for posting announcements of upcoming activities, providing fitness education information and brochures, and promoting the local yoga studios and fitness centers of ambassadors. There was also a chalkboard in each store's fitting room area where customers could scribble comments about lululemon products or their yoga class experiences or their appreciation of the assistance/service provided by certain store personnel; these comments were relayed to lululemon headquarters every two weeks. Customers could use a lululemon micro website to track their progress regarding fitness or progress toward life goals.

lululemon made little use of traditional advertising print or television advertisements, preferring instead to rely on its various grassroots, community-based marketing efforts and the use of social media (like Facebook and Twitter) to increase brand awareness, reinforce its premium brand image, and broaden the appeal of its products.

Store Personnel

As part of the company's commitment to providing customers with an inviting and educational store environment, lululemon's store sales associates, whom the company referred to as "educators," were coached to personally engage and connect with each guest who entered the store. Educators, many of whom had prior experience as a fitness practitioner or were avid runners or yoga enthusiasts, received approximately 30 hours of in-house training within the first three months of their employment. Training was focused on (1) teaching educators about leading a healthy and balanced life, exercising self-responsibility, and setting lifestyle goals, (2) preparing them to explain the technical and innovative design aspects of all lululemon products, and (3) providing the information needed for educators to serve as knowledgeable references for customers seeking information on fitness classes, instructors, and events in the community. New hires that lacked knowledge about the intricacies of yoga were given subsidies to attend yoga classes so they could understand the activity and better explain the benefits of lululemon's yoga apparel.

People who shopped at lululemon stores were called "guests," and store personnel were expected to "educate" guests about lululemon apparel, not sell to them. To provide a personalized, welcoming, and relaxed experience, store educators referred to their guests on a first name basis in the fitting and changing area, allowed them to use store restrooms, and offered them complimentary fresh-filtered water. Management believed that such a soft-sell, customer-centric environment encouraged product trial, purchases, and repeat visits.

Core Values and Culture

Consistent with the company's mission of "providing people with the components to live a longer, healthier and more fun life," lululemon executives sought to promote and ingrain a set of core values centered on developing the highest-quality products, operating with integrity, leading a healthy balanced life, and instilling in its employees a sense of self responsibility and the value of goal setting. The company sought to provide employees with a supportive and goal-oriented work environment; all employees were encouraged to set goals aimed at reaching their full professional, health, and personal potential. The company offered personal development workshops and goal-coaching to assist employees in achieving their goals. Many lululemon employees had a written set of professional, health and personal goals. All employees had access to a "learning library" of personal development books that included Steven Covey's *The Seven Habits of Highly Effective People,* Rhonda Byrne's *The Secret,* and Brian Tracy's *The Psychology of Achievement*.

Chip Wilson had been the principal architect of the company's culture and core values, and the company's work climate through 2013 reflected his business and lifestyle philosophy. Wilson had digested much of his philosophy about life in general and personal development into a set of statements and prescriptions that he called "the lululemon manifesto"—see **info.lululemon.com/about/our-story/manifesto**. The manifesto was considered to be a core element of lululemon's culture. Senior executives believed the company's work climate and core values helped it attract passionate and motivated employees who were driven to succeed and who would support the company's vision of "elevating the world from mediocrity to greatness"—a phrase coined by Chip Wilson in the company's early years.

Top management believed that its relationship with company employees was exceptional and a key contributor to the company's success.

COMPETITION

Competition in the market for athletic and fitness apparel was principally centered on product quality, performance features, innovation, fit and style, distribution capabilities, brand image and recognition, and price. Rivalry among competing brands was vigorous, involving both established companies who were expanding their production and marketing of performance products and recent entrants attracted by the growth opportunities.

lululemon competed with wholesalers and direct sellers of premium performance athletic apparel made of high-tech fabrics, most especially Nike, The adidas Group AG (which marketed athletic and sports apparel under its adidas, Reebok, and Ashworth brands), and Under Armour. Nike had a powerful and well-known global brand name, an extensive and diverse line of athletic and sports apparel, 2015 apparel sales of $8.6 billion ($4.4 billion in North America), and 2015 total revenues (footwear, apparel, and equipment) of $30.6 billion. Nike was the world's largest seller of athletic footwear and athletic apparel, with over 44,000 retail accounts worldwide, 931 company-owned stores, 52 distribution centers, and selling arrangements with independent distributors and licensees in over 190 countries; its retail account base for sports apparel in the U.S. included a mix of sporting goods stores, athletic specialty stores, department stores, and skate, tennis, and golf shops.

adidas and Reebok were both global brands that generated worldwide sports apparel revenues of approximately $7.7 billion in 2015; their product lines consisted of high-tech performance garments for a wide variety of sports and fitness activities, as well as recreational sportswear. The adidas Group sold products in virtually every country of the world. In 2015, its extensive product offerings were marketed through third-party retailers (sporting goods chains, department stores, independent sporting goods retailer buying groups, lifestyle retailing chains, and Internet retailers), 1,850 company-owned and franchised adidas and Reebok "concept" stores, 872 company-owned adidas and Reebok factory outlet stores, 152 other adidas and Reebok stores with varying formats, and various company websites (including **www.adidas.com** and **www.reebok.com**).

Under Armour, an up-and-coming designer and marketer of performance sports apparel, had total sales of $3.97 billion in 2015, of which $2.8 billion was in apparel. Like lululemon, Under Armour's apparel products were made entirely of technically advanced, high-performance fabrics and were designed to be aesthetically appealing, as well as highly functional and comfortable. Under Armour regularly upgraded its products as next-generation fabrics with better performance characteristics became available. Under Armour's product line included apparel for men, women, and children. Management was actively pursuing efforts to grow its sales to $7.5 billion by year-end 2018 and $10 billion by year-end 2010. Under Armour's business was currently concentrated in North America (87 percent of 2015 sales revenues), but it was accelerating efforts to expand globally. Under Armour products were available in over 17,000 retail stores worldwide in 2016, 11,000 of which were in North America. Under Armour also sold its products directly to consumers through 10 company-owned Brand House stores, 143 Under Armour factory outlet stores, and company websites. Plans called for having some 200 Factory House and Brand House locations in North America and 800 such stores in 40+ countries by year-end 2018.

Nike, The adidas Group, and Under Armour all aggressively marketed and promoted their high-performance apparel products and spent heavily to grow consumer awareness of their brands and build brand loyalty. All three sponsored numerous athletic events, provided uniforms and equipment with their logos to collegiate and professional sports teams, and paid millions of dollars annually to numerous high-profile male and female athletes to endorse their products. Like lululemon, they designed their own products but outsourced the production of their garments to contract manufacturers.

The Emergence of a New Formidable Competitor Specializing in Sports and Fitness Apparel for Women In 2011, fashion retailer Gap, with such brands as Gap, Banana Republic, and Old Navy, launched a new retailing chain named Athleta to compete head-on against lululemon in the market for comfortable, fashionable, high-performance women's apparel for workouts, sports, physically active recreational activities, and leisure wear. Athleta had grown from 1 retail store in 2011 to over 120 retail stores coast-to-coast as of early 2016; more Athleta stores were expected to open throughout 2016 and beyond. Athleta's expanding product line included swimwear, tops, bras, jackets, sweaters, pants, tights, shorts, tee shirt dresses, performance footwear, sneakers, sandals, bags, headwear, and gear. Items were colorful, stylish, and functional. In April 2016, the array of apparel items and color selections at Athleta's website exceeded those at lululemon's website; Athleta apparel items were typically available in sizes XXS, XS, S, M, L, XL, and plus sizes 1X and 2X. Athleta utilized well-known women athletes and local fitness instructors to serve as brand ambassadors by blogging for Athleta's website, teaching classes at local stores, and testing Athleta garments. In 2012, Athleta initiated its first national advertising campaign, "Power to the She," to promote the Athleta brand. In 2016, the tag line "The Power of She" was a prominent part of the home page on the Athleta website (**www.athleta.gap.com**). In addition, Athleta had a special social media website, **www.athleta.net/chi**, that connected women with interests in sports and fitness, nutrition and health, tutorials and training plans, and travel and adventure. In 2015, Gap, Inc. had 3,275 company-operated retail stores and 446 franchised stores worldwide that operated under such brand names as Gap, Old Navy, Banana Republic, Athleta, Piperlime, and Intermix. The product offerings at the 1,415 Gap-branded stores included a GapFit collection of fitness and lifestyle products for women.

A number of other national and regional retailers of women's apparel, seeking to capitalize on growing sales of activewear made of high-tech fabrics, were marketing one or more brands of fitness apparel suitable for yoga, running, gym exercise, and leisure activities. A few were selling these items under their own labels. For example, Nordstrom, a nationally respected department store retailer, was merchandising its own Zella line of attire for yoga, cross-training, workouts, swimming, and "beyond the workout"; many of the initial products in the Zella collection were designed by a former member of lululemon's design team. Zella-branded products were offered in regular sizes (XXS, XS, S, M, L, XL, and XXL) and plus sizes (1X, 2X, and 3X). Nordstrom was also marketing several other brands of activewear for women, men, and juniors, including Nike, Under Armour, Patagonia, Reebok, and adidas. In 2016, Nordstrom's activewear offerings could be purchased at 121 Nordstrom full-line department stores (typically 140,000 to 250,000 square feet in size) and 200 Nordstrom Rack stores (typically 30,000 to 50,000 square feet in size) in 39 states, at Nordstrom's website (**www.nordstrom.com**), and at the Nordstrom Rack website (**www.nordstromrack.com**).

Typically, the items in the GapFit, Athleta, and Zella collections were priced 10 percent to 25 percent below similar kinds of lululemon products. Likewise, Nike, Under Armour, adidas, and Reebok apparel items were usually less expensive than comparable lululemon-branded items.

ENDNOTES

[1] Beth Kowitt and Colleen Leahey, "LULULEMON: In an Uncomfortable Position," *Fortune*, September 16, 2013, p. 118.
[2] *2016 Yoga in America Study*, conducted by *Yoga Journal* and Yoga Alliance, January 2016, www.yogaalliance.org (accessed April 29, 2016); "Yoga in America," *Yoga Journal*, press release dated December 5, 2012, www.yogajournal.com (accessed April 7, 2014).
[3] *2016 Yoga in America Study*, conducted by *Yoga Journal* and Yoga Alliance, January 2016, www.yogaalliance.org (accessed April 29, 2016).
[4] *2016 Yoga in America Study*, conducted by *Yoga Journal* and Yoga Alliance, January 2016, www.yogaalliance.org (accessed April 29, 2016); "Yoga in America," *Yoga Journal*, press release dated December 5, 2012, www.yogajournal.com (accessed April 7, 2014).
[5] "World Sports Apparel Market Is Estimated to Garner $184.6 Billion by 2020—Allied Market Research," *PR Newswire*, October 8, 2015, www.prnewswire.com (accessed May 2, 2016).
[6] Renee Frojo, "Yoga Clothing Retailers Go to the Mat for Market Share," *San Francisco Business Times*, December 28, 2012, www.bizjournals.com/sanfrancisco (accessed April 10, 2014).
[7] www.lululemon.com (accessed May 2, 2016).
[8] Company 10-K report for the fiscal year ending January 31, 2016, p. 1.
[9] Kim Basin, "Lululemon Admits Plus-Size Clothing Is Not Part of Its 'Formula,'" August 2, 2013, www.huffingtonpost.com (accessed April 7, 2014).
[10] Dana Mattoili, "Lululemon's Secret Sauce," *The Wall Street Journal*, March 22, 2012, pp. B1–B2.
[11] Ibid.

CASE 10

Etsy, Inc.: Reimagining Innovation

Rochelle R. Brunson
Baylor University

Marlene M. Reed
Baylor University

Etsy was a market discovery of three New York entrepreneurs who saw that eBay had become too large and ineffective for craftspeople and artisans who wished to sell their one-of-a-kind products online. During a celebration of the company's 10th anniversary in 2015, Etsy CEO Chad Dickerson commented that "In 2005, you could sell on eBay, but it was a hostile environment."[1] While eBay's timed auction format made for an exciting marketplace for bargain-hunting consumers, Etsy promoted its ability to connect thoughtful consumers with artisans selling unique handcrafted items. More than 85 percent of Etsy sellers were women and 92 percent of Etsy buyers responded in a 2015 survey that Etsy offered products that could not be found elsewhere. Typical Etsy buyers valued craftsmanship and wanted to know how items were made and who made them. The ability to develop a direct relationship with the seller was important to many Etsy buyers who enjoyed a personalized shopping experience. Purchases made by Etsy buyers ranged from $5 ornaments to $50 handmade clothing items to $2,000 custom-made coffee tables. "Things on Etsy take longer [to sell], and we think that's an advantage. We encourage our sellers to keep their prices high," explained Dickerson.[2]

Approximately 25 million buyers had purchased merchandise totaling nearly $2.4 billion in 2015. And in mid-2016, 35 million items were listed for sale by 1.6 million sellers at **Etsy.com**. Etsy charged sellers a 3.5 percent transaction fee and a 20-cent listing fee and generated additional revenue from payment processing fees and the sales of shipping labels. The company's revenues had grown from $74.6 million in 2012 to $176.5 million in 2015. However, its losses during that time period had grown from $2.4 million to $54.0 million. Etsy's revenues for the six months ending June 30, 2016, had grown to $167.2 million from $119.9 million during the same period in the year prior and its net loss had declined to $6.1 million from $42.9 million during the six months ending June 30, 2015. The company's statement of operations for 2012 to 2015 is presented in Exhibit 1. Exhibit 2 presents Etsy's balance sheets for 2014 and 2015.

The company's improving performance had not gone unnoticed with Amazon announcing in May 2016 that it would launch a site featuring artisan goods named Handmade. Amazon believed that its free 2-day shipping to Prime members would give it an advantage over Etsy. Chad Dickerson and the company's chief lieutenants would need to refine the company's strategy to continue its path toward profitability and defend against the threat of powerful new entrants into its market. In June 2016, the company's stock continued to trade at about one-half of its IPO first-day closing price in April 2015. The strength of its strategy and the quality of its execution would determine if leery investors or its loyal sellers and buyers had a more accurate assessment of the company's long-term viability.

ETSY HISTORY AND BACKGROUND

Etsy was founded in an apartment in Brooklyn, New York, in June 2005 as an online marketplace for handmade goods and craft supplies. The initial version of the website took two and a half months

EXHIBIT 1 Statement of Operations for Etsy, Inc., 2012–2015 (in thousands except per share amounts)

	2015	2014	2013	2012
Revenue:				
Marketplace	$132,648	$108,732	$78,544	$55,330
Seller services	136,608	82,502	42,817	15,863
Other	4,243	4,357	3,661	3,409
Total revenue	273,499	195,591	125,022	74,602
Cost of revenue	96,979	73,633	47,779	24,493
Gross profit	176,520	121,958	77,243	50,109
Operating expenses:				
Marketing	66,771	39,655	17,850	10,902
Product development	42,694	36,634	27,548	18,653
General and administrative	68,939	51,920	31,112	21,909
Total operating expenses	178,404	128,209	76,510	51,464
(Loss) income from operations	(1,884)	(6,251)	733	(1,355)
Total other expense	(26,110)	(4,009)	(675)	(1,175)
(Loss) income before income taxes	(27,994)	(10,260)	58	(2,530)
Benefit (provision) for income taxes	(26,069)	(4,983)	(854)	145
Net loss	($ 54,063)	($15,243)	($796)	($2,385)
Net loss per share of common stock basic and diluted	($0.59)	($0.38)	($0.02)	($0.09)
Weighted average shares of common stock used in computing net loss per share basic and diluted	91,122,291	40,246,663	32,667,242	30,281,842

Source: Etsy, Inc. 2015 10-K.

to build. The original owners of Etsy were Robert Kalin, Chris Maguire, and Haim Schoppik. Robert Kalin suggested that he named the site Etsy because he wanted a nonsense word since they were building their brand from scratch. He had been watching Fellini's movie titled 8½ and writing down what he was hearing. He noticed that in the Italian language people often say "etsi" (which means "oh, yes"), and he believed he had found a unique name for the company.[3]

The originality of the company lay in the structure of the marketplace the organization offered. It was an online market for handcrafted products fashioned by such craftspeople as jewelers, candle makers, bag designers, and woodcutters. Although the company originally had offered only goods made in the United States, that changed in 2013 when the marketplace opened up to entrepreneurs around the world. Some of their bestsellers have been combat boots from Italy ($367), a snow goose necklace from North Carolina ($29), and a stainless-steel toilet roll holder from Oregon ($36).[4]

In 2008, Chad Dickerson joined Etsy as its first chief technology officer and created an engineering culture that treated "Code as Craft." Dickerson became CEO in 2011 and began championing the "re-imagination of commerce." In the beginning, Etsy added new tools and functionality to the site to gain greater exposure. In 2011, the company introduced a Facebook-like social networking system called People Search so that buyers and sellers could connect with one another and become friends.

EXHIBIT 2 Balance Sheets for Etsy, Inc., 2014–2015 (in thousands)

	2015	2014
ASSETS		
Current assets:		
Cash and cash equivalents	$271,244	$ 69,659
Short-term investments	21,620	19,184
Accounts receivable, net of allowancefor doubtful accounts of $1,841 and $2,071 as of December 31, 2014, and December 31,2015, respectively	20,275	15,404
Prepaid and other current assets	9,521	12,241
Deferred tax charge current	17,132	
Funds receivable and seller accounts	19,262	10,573
Total current assets	359,054	127,061
Restricted cash	5,341	5,341
Property and equipment, net	105,021	75,538
Goodwill	27,752	30,831
Intangible assets, net	2,871	5,410
Deferred tax charge net of current portion	51,396	—
Other assets	1,626	2,022
Total assets	$553,061	$246,203
LIABILITIES, CONVERTIBLE PREFERRED STOCK AND STOCKHOLDERS' EQUITY		
Current liabilities:		
Accounts payable	$ 14,382	$ 8,231
Accrued expenses	31,253	12,852
Capital lease obligations current	5,610	1,755
Funds payable and amounts due to sellers	19,262	10,573
Deferred revenue	4,712	3,452
Other current liabilities	4,903	4,590
Total current liabilities	80,122	41,453
Capital lease obligations net of current portion	7,571	3,148
Warrant liability		1,920
Deferred tax liabilities	61,420	149
Facility financing obligation	51,804	50,320
Other liabilities	21,646	1,913
Total liabilities	$222,563	$ 98,903

Source: Etsy, Inc. 2015 10-K.

From its beginning, Etsy has had many fans who applauded the online marketplace as "an antidote to global mass production and consumption and a stand against corporate branding."[5] The company's primary market was women, who made up 86 percent of Etsy sellers. While some women selling artisan products at Etsy were merely testing the market appeal of their craft, 76 percent of Etsy sellers considered their online stores a business. Sales through the Etsy marketplace was the sole occupation of 30 percent of Etsy sellers.

Some sellers like Julie Persons of Maine had begun as stay-at-home mothers interested in earning extra household income while pursuing their creative interests.[6] In 2015, 26 percent of Etsy sellers were homemakers with no paid employment prior to becoming an Etsy seller. Julie Persons's hobby had grown to provide a $40,000 to $45,000 annual income. After a corporate downsizing, Rebecca Plotnick opened an Etsy store featuring her photography and eventually matched her former corporate salary. After returning from one of her frequent photography trips to Europe, Plotnick explained, "Etsy has allowed me to live my dream. . . . I just came back from 6 weeks of traveling. What other job would let me do that?"[7]

Although 65 percent of Etsy's sellers made less than $100 a year on their shops, Alicia Shaffer's Three Bird Nest store had generated revenues of nearly $1 million in 2015. The store's unusual name was derived from a bird's nest tattoo Shaffer had which honored her three children. This entrepreneur lived in Livermore, California, and sold her assortment of 58 designs including socks, leg warmers, scarves, and lace headbands on Etsy's website. The prices of her goods ranged from $4 for a fabric cuff bracelet to $38 for a floral scarf. Due to the success of her business, by early 2016 Shaffer was employing 15 sewers, a photographer to shoot pictures of items for advertisements, and was even sourcing some items from India.[8]

Etsy proclaimed on its website that

> We are building a human, authentic and community-centric global and local marketplace. We are committed to using the power of business to create a better world through our platform, our members, our employees and the communities we serve. These guiding principles are core to our mission:
>
> - Make it easy to find and buy unique goods from real people every day, on any platform, online and offline, anywhere in the world.
> - Help creative entrepreneurs start, responsibly scale and enjoy their businesses with Etsy.
> - Communicate the power of human connection whenever anyone experiences Etsy.[9]

Etsy was also guided by five values:

- We are a mindful, transparent and humane business.
- We plan and build for the long term.
- We value craftsmanship in all we make.
- We believe fun should be part of everything we do.
- We keep it real, always.

The company's values were reflected in the way it managed its employees, with the company being ranked number six on *Fortune*'s list of Best Small and Medium Sized Company to Work For in 2015.

On March 3, 2015, Etsy announced that it had filed for a $100 million IPO. By the time the company went public on April 16, 2015, its stock closed at $30 giving it a market valuation of $1.8 billion. The successful IPO allowed Etsy to raise $237 million to fund its continued growth. However, by July 2015, the company's shares had fallen below $15. With the exception of a brief jump to the low-$20s in summer 2015, Etsy's stock traded in the $7 to $14 range from July 2015 to August 2016. Despite its poor stock market performance, its appeal with consumers continued to grow. By 2016, Etsy had become the fifth most visited marketplace site in the United States surpassed only by Amazon, eBay, Walmart, and Best Buy.

Etsy's Financial and Operating Performance

Etsy's revenues were generated from six primary sources in 2016:

1. Listing fee paid by Etsy craft artists ($0.20 for each item listed).
2. Fees paid by Etsy craft artists for each completed transaction (a 3.5 percent fee for sales completed on the website).
3. Fees for seller services that include services such as prominent placement in search results via Promoted Listings.
4. Payment processing via Direct Checkout.
5. Purchasing of shipping labels through Etsy's platform.
6. Fees received from a third-party payment processor.

The company's marketplace revenues included listing fees and transaction fees, while promoted listing fees, direct checkout, and shipping label fees were captured in its seller services revenue category. Third-party payment processing fees were included in the company's Other category of revenue. The contribution of each source of revenue is shown in Exhibit 3.

EXHIBIT 3 Etsy Inc. Revenues by Source, 2013–2015 (in thousands)

	2015	2014	2013
Marketplace	$132,648	$108,732	$ 78,544
Seller Services	136,608	82,502	42,817
Other	4,243	4,357	3,661
Revenue	$273,499	$195,591	$125,022

Source: Etsy, Inc. 2015 10-K.

The appeal of the company's business model had allowed revenues to grow at an exponential rate between 2005 and 2015. Its customer value proposition was compelling for both buyers and sellers and had resulted in an increase in active buyers from 14 million in 2013 to 24 million in 2015. Active sellers had increased from 1 million in 2013 to 1.6 million in 2015. The rapidly growing use of mobile devices was reflected in the company's key transaction statistics, with mobile visits accounting for 60 percent of page views in 2015 compared to 41 percent of customer traffic in 2013. In addition, gross merchandise sales (GMS) from a mobile device had increased from 30 percent of sales in 2013 to 43 percent of sales in 2016. The company had launched its "Buy on Etsy" mobile app in 2011, which was followed by its "Sell on Etsy" mobile app in 2014. There was some increase in sales outside the United States with international gross merchandise sales increasing from 28.4 percent of total GMS in 2013 to 29.8 percent of GMS in 2015. A summary of the other operational and financial data for Etsy, Inc. is presented in Exhibit 4.

Competitors

In 2016, the two largest online marketplaces in the United States were **Amazon.com** and **eBay.com**. The original goal of Amazon was to replicate a catalog business online. However, eBay had a different strategy. This company recognized the great potential in uniting buyers and sellers in an online auction. Amazon was launched in Seattle, Washington, as an online bookseller, but the company grew into the likeness of such big retailers as Walmart and Target. The products it sold ranged from cookware to hardware and everything in between. The rapid growth of Amazon occurred at the expense of profitability.

eBay had a much slower growth than Amazon. The focus of the company was always on hosting an auction site where buyers and sellers would meet and enter into mutually beneficial transactions. The initial public offerings of the two companies were strikingly parallel. Both initially offered shares of stocks at a price of $18. However, at the end of the first day of trading, Amazon's stock price was $30 and eBay stock ended at $47.37.

Since their initial IPOs, the stock prices went in opposite directions. The rise and fall of Amazon's share price since its IPO illustrated the rise and fall of the dot-com companies. Its stock price rose from $18 to over $100 in 2000 and then fell to the original

EXHIBIT 4 Other Operational and Financial Data for Etsy, Inc., 2012–2015 (in thousands except percent amounts)

	2015	2014	2013	2012
Gross merchandise sales (GMS)	$2,388,387	$1,931,981	$1,347,833	$895,152
Adjusted EBITDA	$31,007	$23,081	$16,947	$10,669
Active sellers	1,563	1,353	1,074	830
Active buyers	24,046	19,810	14,032	9,317
Percent mobile visits	60.00%	54.00%	41%	N/A
Percent mobile GMS	43.00%	37.00%	30%	N/A
Percent international GMS	29.80%	30.90%	28.40%	28.40%

Source: Etsy, Inc. 2015 10-K.

EXHIBIT 5 Etsy's Direct Competitors

Company Name	Country	Focus
DaWanda	Germany	Growth in European countries
ezebee.com	Switzerland	Global competitor catering to freelancers
Bonanza	United States	Clothing and fashion
Zibbet	Australia	Online craft marketplace
Hello Pretty	South Africa	Online craft marketplace
Tindie	Oregon	Technology and electronics

Source: **www.google.com/online-marketplaces/.**

price again. On the other hand, eBay's stock price showed a steady consistency in profitability.[10] In 2014, Amazon's sales amounted to $88.99 billion while eBay's total sales were $17.94 billion.

Smaller competitors that would be considered direct competitors to Etsy are shown in Exhibit 5.

Challenges for Etsy in 2016

Etsy was confronted with a number of strategic and operating issues in 2016 including complaints by buyers who found that items were difficult to find on Etsy, and the interface felt very slow. Other complaints concerning the company centered on the fact that some sellers felt they had little autonomy in the store's design and were subject to the site's rules and fees. Because of these constraints, many sellers moved to independent websites that gave them more flexibility and lower fees.

Grace Dobush, who shut down her Etsy store, suggested: "If you're working in high volume on high price points, using a customizable ecommerce platform such as Big Cartel or Shopify massively reduces your fee obligation."[11] Dobush also commented in an article in *The New York Times,* "Handmade businesses aren't infinitely scalable, just by the definition of the term. As Etsy has gotten bigger, it's gotten more like eBay."[12]

In 2011, Etsy added a feature that allowed users to search other users' buying histories and trace their purchases. The company thought this option would allow users to connect to others who had similar buying or selling habits. However, the users of this service complained that the feature violated their right to privacy. No response to their complaints was ever offered by company management.[13]

Also, when Dickerson announced in 2011 that Etsy would, in the future, allow sellers to outsource production to third parties and factories, many sellers became disenfranchised from the company. It was their feeling that management had betrayed the very nature of the marketplace that had initially been dedicated to handmade products.

Need for a Strategic Plan

By the spring of 2016, Etsy management was faced with the need for a new strategic plan that would address the challenges that it was facing. One of the questions was whether or not the move to outsourced and/or manufactured goods was appropriate for the company. If management deemed that it was not, was there any way of going back to the original mission of the company which was to be a marketplace for handmade goods?

Among its most important issues was its need to prove that its profit formula would allow for long-term viability. The company's results for the first six months of 2016 signaled that perhaps the company's business model was sound. Its revenues increased from $119.9 million in the first six months of 2015 to $167.2 million during the same period in 2016. But perhaps more importantly, the company's income from operations had swung from an $8.6 million loss for the six months ending June 30, 2015, to an $11.5 million operating profit in the first six months of 2016. The company continued to have a net loss for the six-month period ending June 30, 2016, but that loss had declined from $42.9 million for the six-month period ending June 30, 2015, to $6.1 million for the six-month period ending June 30, 2016.

The results were encouraging to the company's management, but investors had not yet responded positively to the company's latest financial report. The company's stock continued to trade under $15 in August 2016. With the entry of an aggressive and highly successful new rival in **Amazon.com**, the it could not be more urgent for Chad Dickerson and the company's chief managers to develop plans to improve the company's performance and operations.

ENDNOTES

[1] As quoted in "Etsy: The Little Marketplace That Could," *Fortune*, November 13, 2015.
[2] Ibid.
[3] Rob Lammie. "How Etsy, eBay, Reddit Got Their Names," *Mental Floss* (CNN), 2011.
[4] "The Art and Craft of Business," *The Economist*, July 4, 2014, **www.economist.com/news/business/21592656-etsy-starting-show-how-maker-movement-can-make-money-art-and-craft-business.**
[5] Hiroko Tabuchi, "Etsy's Success Gives Rise to Problems of Credibility and Scale," *The New York Times*, March 15, 2015.
[6] As discussed in "Meet the 86%: This Is Why Most Etsy Sellers Are Women," *Fortune*, August 2, 2015.
[7] Ibid.
[8] "How One Woman Makes Almost $1 million a Year on Etsy," *Fast Company*, **www.fastcodesign.com/3042352/**.
[9] Ibid.
[10] Sandeep Krishnamurthy, "A Comparative Analysis of eBay and Amazon," *Idea Group, Inc.*, 2004.
[11] Grace Dobush, "How Etsy Alienated Its Crafters and Lost Its Soul," *Wired*, February 19, 2015.
[12] Tabuchi, "Etsy's Success Gives Rise to Problems of Credibility and Scale."
[13] Jacqui Cheng, "Etsy Users Irked after Buyers' Purchases Exposed to the World," *Conde Nast*, March 15, 2011.

Gap Inc.: Can It Develop a Strategy to Connect with Consumers in 2016?

John D. Varlaro
Johnson & Wales University

John E. Gamble
Texas A&M University–Corpus Christi

"To not be considering Amazon and others would be—in my view—delusional," Art Peck, CEO of Gap Inc. remarked during a conversation with investors in May 2016. Faced with increased competition and a changing demographic amid a shifting shopping landscape, Peck needed to reverse Gap Inc.'s current trajectory and consider alternatives to improve sales and maintain its number two overall ranking.[1]

Complicating the turnaround, however, would be the increase in shopping mall vacancies, as well as the increased competition in retail. While higher-end malls continued to see improvements in foot traffic in 2015, consumers decreased shopping at lower-end malls, where empty storefronts were becoming common. Further, as shoppers became comfortable with online shopping, larger percentages of retail sales were occurring through e-commerce. Yet, companies such as the Indetix Group, known for its Zara brand, continually increased sales and expanded locations regardless of these environmental factors. Peck pondered how Gap could defend against unfavorable external factors and craft a strategy well-matched to the retail environment of the mid-2010s.

COMPANY HISTORY AND PERFORMANCE

Gap Inc. operated stores in 70 different countries in 2016 and was positioned as casual attire, with an emphasis on blue jeans and khakis. Offering apparel for the whole family, brands also included GapKids, babyGap, and GapMaternity. Banana Republic, in contrast, offered styles from business casual to formal, where attire could be both work and everyday. The Old Navy brand was positioned to compete at a lower price point in the casual, everyday apparel category.

The company was founded in 1969 by Doris and Don Fisher. The company first began selling Levi-branded jeans due to Don's experience in trying to find his own pair that fit. Initially meant to target a younger demographic, the name was derived from the phrase "generation gap." Gap started offering its own Gap-branded jeans in 1972, and went public in 1973. Gap acquired Banana Republic in the early 1980s, and launched the Old Navy brand in the 1990s. The company acquired the Athleta athletic apparel brand and launched its online fashion marketplace Piperlime in 2008 and acquired boutique retail chain Intermix in 2013. The company closed the Piperlime website and one retail location in 2015.

Gap became a household name in the 1990s through its clever advertising and merchandising strategy that made it largely responsible for making the jeans-and-t-shirt style ubiquitous during that decade. The company's strategy led to large and regular increases in net sales, which increased from \$1.9 billion in 1990 to \$11.6 billion in 1999.[2] Its net sales by the end of the decade were almost double the \$6.6 billion in 1997.

The company's sales growth declined dramatically in the 2000s as its merchandise became stale. The decline in sales growth had become a decline in total sales by 2015. Gap CEO Glen Murphy was replaced by Art Peck in February 2015 and charged with reversing the company's long-running lackluster performance and recent sales decline. Peck had joined GAP in 2005 and had held various executive positions with the company where he spearheaded the company's franchising initiative, executed its outlet store strategy, and led its digital and e-commerce division. Exhibit 1 presents a financial and operating summary for Gap, Inc. for 2011 through 2016.

The sales decline between 2014 and 2015 was reflected in every geographic region except Asia and every brand except Old Navy, which experienced a 1 percent increase in sales in 2015. When compared to 2011, net sales across brands had only increased from $14.5 billion to $15.8 billion in five years. Exhibit 2 shows Gap Inc. sales by brand and region for 2013 through 2015.

Comparable store sales declined 4 percent for the company between 2014 and 2015, with the greatest decline at 10 percent for Banana Republic. Comparable store sales for Gap stores declined by 6 percent and Old Navy store comparable store sales were unchanged between 2014 and 2015. Driving the decline in comparable store sales was the falloff in the company's sales per square foot, which had fallen from $365 in 2013 to $361 in 2014 to $337 in 2015. Exhibit 1 presents a financial and operating summary for Gap, Inc. for 2011 through 2016.

Amid the decline in store performance, leadership at Gap Inc. announced closures of underperforming stores in 2016 to improve operating costs. The closures affected primarily Gap stores in North America and Europe, while other regions saw net gains in numbers of stores by January 30, 2016—see Exhibit 3. The company's balance sheets for 2014 and 2015 are presented in Exhibit 4.

OVERVIEW OF THE FAMILY CLOTHING STORE INDUSTRY

With estimated revenues over $101.9 billion in 2016, competitors within this industry carried clothing lines and apparel for men, women, and children. Annual growth for the industry averaged 1.8 percent between 2011 and 2017 and is expected to grow by 1.6 percent annually between 2016 and 2021 to reach $110.4 billion. Key drivers of industry growth included per capita disposable income and demographic trends. Typically sales of clothing to women made up the majority of industry sales. Also, age demographics with gainful employment and disposable income were the largest purchasers of clothing in the United States. The percentage of revenue accounted for by demographic group is presented in Exhibit 5.

Brick-and-Mortar Retailers and E-commerce Sales

The first quarter of 2016 saw almost $93 billion in e-commerce sales in the United States.[3] While total retail sales had increased 2.2 percent from the first quarter of 2015, total e-commerce sales in the United States had increased by 15 percent for the same period in 2015 and accounted for almost 8 percent of total U.S. retail sales during the quarter.[4] The shift toward increasing consumer confidence in online shopping was evident in the sale of clothing and clothing accessories. Between 2010 and 2014, e-commerce sales of clothing and accessories experienced 200 percent growth, while traditional brick-and-mortar retail channel sales grew by 117 percent. Exhibit 6 compares the U.S. annual sales of clothing and clothing accessories by brick-and-mortar and e-commerce channels for 2010 through 2014 of family clothing industry within Clothing and Clothing Accessories.

The Hyperconnected Consumer and the Decline of Malls

A retailer selling through both brick-and-mortar stores and online marketplaces, while utilizing social media and e-mail for communications with consumers, is referred to as omnichannel. Combining both *omnipresence* (always there) and *distribution channel,* the practice considers that the consumer does not need to be physically present in a store to shop, purchase, or even think about shopping. Through a communication channel, such as an e-mail, a shopper may be brought to an online storefront. Browsing and shopping, then, can occur at anytime, anywhere.

EXHIBIT 1 Financial and Operating Summary for Gap, Inc., 2011–2015 (in millions except per share, store count, and employee data)

	2015	2014	2013	2012	2011
Operating Results ($ in millions)					
Net sales	$15,797	$16,435	$16,148	$15,651	$14,549
Gross margin	36.2%	38.3%	39.0%	39.4%	36.2%
Operating margin	9.6%	12.7%	13.3%	12.4%	9.9%
Net income	$ 920	$ 1,262	$ 1,280	$ 1,135	$ 833
Cash dividends paid	$ 377	$383	$321	$240	$ 236
Per Share Data (number of shares in millions)					
Basic earnings per share	$ 2.24	$ 2.90	$ 2.78	$ 2.35	$ 1.57
Diluted earnings per share	$ 2.23	$ 2.87	$ 2.74	$ 2.33	$ 1.56
Weighted-average number of shares—basic	411	435	461	482	529
Weighted-average number of shares—diluted	413	440	467	488	533
Cash dividends declared and paid per share	$ 0.92	$ 0.88	$ 0.70	$ 0.50	$ 0.45
Balance Sheet Information ($ in millions)					
Merchandise inventory	$ 1,873	$ 1,889	$ 1,928	$ 1,758	$ 1,615
Total assets	$ 7,473	$ 7,690	$ 7,849	$ 7,470	$ 7,422
Working capital	$ 1,450	$ 2,083	$ 1,985	$ 1,788	$ 2,181
Total long-term debt, less current maturities	$ 1,310	$ 1,332	$ 1,369	$ 1,246	$ 1,606
Stockholders' equity	$ 2,545	$ 2,983	$ 3,062	$ 2,894	$ 2,755
Other Data ($ and square footage in millions)					
Cash used for purchases of property and equipment	$ 726	$ 714	$ 670	$ 659	$ 548
Acquisition of business, net of cash acquired	$ —	$ —	$ —	$ 129	$ —
Percentage increase (decrease) in comparable sales	(4)%	—%	2%	5%	(4)%
Number of Company-operated store locations open at year-end	3,275	3,280	3,164	3,095	3,036
Number of franchise store locations open at year-end	446	429	375	312	227
Number of store locations open at year-end	3,721	3,709	3,539	3,407	3,263
Square footage of Company-operated store space at year-end	37.9	38.1	37.2	36.9	37.2
Percentage increase (decrease) in square footage of Company-operated store space at year-end	(0.5)%	2.4%	0.8%	(0.8)%	(2.6)%
Number of employees at year-end	141,000	141,000	137,000	136,000	132,000

Source: Gap, Inc. 2015 10-K.

EXHIBIT 2 Gap Inc.'s Net Sales by Brand and Region, 2013–2015

($ in millions) Fiscal 2015	Gap Global	Old Navy Global	Banana Republic Global	Other**	Total	Percentage of Net Sales
U.S.*	$3,303	$5,987	$2,211	$712	$12,213	77%
Canada	348	467	229	3	1,047	7
Europe	726	—	71	—	797	5
Asia	1,215	194	112	—	1,521	10
Other regions	159	27	33	—	219	1
Total	$5,751	$6,675	$2,656	$715	$15,797	100%
Sales growth (decline)	(7) %	1	(9)	(2)	(4)	

($ in millions) Fiscal 2015	Gap Global	Old Navy Global	Banana Republic Global	Other**	Total	Percentage of Net Sales
U.S.*	$3,575	$5,967	$2,405	$725	$12,672	77%
Canada	384	500	249	4	1,137	7
Europe	824	—	93	—	917	6
Asia	174	149	145	—	1,502	9
Other regions	2,545	3	30	—	207	1
Total	$6,165	$ 714	$2,922	$729	$16,435	100%
Sales growth (decline)	(3) %	6%	2%	8%	2%	

($ in millions) Fiscal 2015	Gap Global	Old Navy Global	Banana Republic Global	Other**	Total	Percentage of Net Sales
U.S.*	$3,575	$5,698	$2,365	$668	$12,531	77%
Canada	404	482	238	4	1,128	7
Europe	809	—	82	—	891	6
Asia	1,165	77	155	—	1,502	9
Other regions	173	—	28	—	201	1
Total	$6,351	$6,257	$2,868	$672	$16,148	100%
Sales growth (decline)	2%	2%	(1)%	70%	3%	

*U.S. includes the United States, Puerto Rico, and Guam.

**Includes Piperlime, Athleta, and Intermix.

Source: Gap Inc. 2015 10-K.

The buying habits of the consumer seem to have shifted since the growth of the Internet in the 1990s, as well as with smartphones in the mid-2000s. Most retailers were either online or brick and mortar. Further, in the early years of the online marketplace, there was often disbelief that a consumer would be willing to purchase a product online, either due to not seeing it or the sheer logistics of purchase and delivery. The tongue-in-cheek question of "Who would buy a 50-pound bag of dog food online?" may help illustrate this point. In other instances, experiments where a person would attempt to shop exclusively through online, and not visit any brick-and-mortar establishments, would make the newscast.

However, as technology and logistics improved, so did the ubiquitous nature of technology and its role in a consumer's life. Logistics and delivery systems improved. Further, the introduction of smartphones made Internet browsing—and shopping—easier. To this degree of adoption, demographics whose experiences with such technology had begun at earlier ages have now become a primary consumer.

EXHIBIT 3 Gap Inc. Number of Store Locations, Openings, Closings, and Total Square Footage by Brand and Location, 2015–2016

	January 31, 2015	Fiscal 2015		January 30, 2016	
	Number of Store Locations	Number of Stores Opened	Number of Stores Closed	Number of Store Locations	Square Footage (in millions)
Gap North America	960	34	128	866	9.1
Gap Asia	266	48	9	305	3.0
Gap Europe	189	4	18	175	1.5
Old Navy North America	1,013	36	19	1,030	17.3
Old Navy Asia	43	22	—	65	1.0
Banana Republic North America	610	24	22	612	5.1
Banana Republic Asia	44	7	—	51	0.2
Banana Republic Europe	11	1	2	10	0.1
Athleta North America	101	19	—	120	0.5
Piperlime North America	1	—	1	—	—
Intermix North America	42	2	3	41	0.1
Company-operated stores total	3,280	197	202	3,275	37.9
Franchise	429	52	35	446	N/A
Total	3,709	249	237	3,721	37.9
Increase (decrease) over prior year				0.3%	(0.5)%

Source: Gap Inc. 2015 10-K.

Thus, they did not experience as wide a divide between online and brick and mortar as previous demographics. The word *hyperconnected* recognizes then the consumer's relationship with a brand, and that the single act of purchasing had moved into this omnipresent, hyperconnected relationship through both online and brick and mortar.

These trends have contributed to both the increase in online sales as well as the decline in malls. Global online retail sales increased in 2014 by 20 percent to $840 billion. This figure was attributable to the increased sales by online retailers, but also the increased presence of brick-and-mortar retailers online.[5] Over the past 15 years, online purchases for some categories have increased from 30 cents to 70 cents per dollar spent.[6]

Second, the mall as destination declined. As the percentage of online sales increased dramatically, foot traffic in shopping malls decreased. While the loss in foot traffic mostly impacted the lower-productive malls, storefronts are now empty, once occupied by brands like Nordstrom and JCPenney. Due to these shifts, retailers are closing the non-performing anchor stores in lieu of their higher-performing locations. The list of retailers impacted by this is immense. Just recently, Macy's announced over 30 store closings and the restructuring of over 4,000 jobs[7] and Nordstrom announced in early 2016 its plan to restructure approximately 400 jobs.[8] As these anchor store locations are closed, foot traffic continues to fall, trickling down into the nonanchor retailers. For example, American Apparel, Aeropostale, and Pac Sun have all filed for bankruptcy protection.

The mall, as depicted in movies such as the 1990s movie *Mall Rats,* is no longer the place to hang out and be seen, either. Instead, the cultivation of an online presence through social media seems to help substitute. Thus, showing off a new outfit can be accomplished through photo-sharing apps and even video. A haul video—where the purchases from a shopping excursion are uploaded—can be

EXHIBIT 4 Gap Inc. Consolidated Balance Sheets, Fiscal 2014–Fiscal 2015 ($ and shares in millions except par value)

	January 30, 2016	January 31, 2015
ASSETS		
Current assets:		
Cash and cash equivalents	$1,370	$1,515
Merchandise inventory	1,873	1,889
Other current assets	742	913
Total current assets	3,985	4,317
Property and equipment, net	2,850	2,773
Other long-term assets	638	600
Total assets	$7,473	$7,690
LIABILITIES AND STOCKHOLDERS' EQUITY		
Current liabilities:		
Current maturities of debt	$ 421	$ 21
Accounts payable	1,112	1,173
Accrued expenses and other current liabilities	979	1,020
Income taxes payable	23	20
Total current liabilities	2,535	2,234
Long-term liabilities:		
Long-term debt	1,310	1,332
Lease incentives and other long-term liabilities	1,083	1,141
Total long-term liabilities	2,393	2,473
Commitments and contingencies		
Stockholders' equity:		
Common stock $0.05 par value		
Authorized 2,300 shares for all periods presented; Issued and Outstanding 397 and 421 shares	20	21
Retained earnings	2,440	2,797
Accumulated other comprehensive income	85	165
Total stockholders' equity	2,545	2,983
Total liabilities and stockholders' equity	$7,473	$7,690

Source: Gap Inc. 2015 10-K.

accomplished without the shopping mall. In addition, views and comments can be tracked and quantified in an online environment.

Competition through Fast Fashion

Fast fashion is the systematic shortening of the production-to-sales logistics within fashion retail. Traditionally, clothing was designed, manufactured, and then shipped to the retailer for sale, much of it occurring prior to the beginning of the season. These designs can be from within house designers, who use current trends, including fashion on display at fashion shows, to anticipate consumers' preferences. Retailers usually purchase inventory in bulk for the season to help improve costs. Buying an inventory of multiple designs for one season may also create a buffer when one style or design is not purchased, or is overpurchased, by the consumer. If a style does not sell in one location, it is usually internally transferred to another location. Or, eventually it is sold through a discount or staged-markdown sale.

EXHIBIT 5 Demographic Characteristics of Family Clothing Store Industry Customers, 2016

Percentage of Total Revenue by Segment within Family and Clothing Stores	
Segment	**Percentage**
Women's	60.1%
Men's	32.1%
Children's	7.8%
Percentage of Total Revenue by Generation within Family and Clothing Stores	
Market	**Percentage**
65 years and older	10.0%
Baby Boomers	24.5%
Generation X	35.5%
Generation Y	22.5%
Other	7.5%

Source: www.ibisworld.com.

These markdowns occur at the end of seasons, and help facilitate space for incoming stock while minimizing losses associated with designs that do not sell well for a season.

This approach, however, is not only costly but also can lead to missing consumer demands. In addition, it assumes the consumer wishes to purchase and maintain the clothing for a longer period of time. Fast fashion, however, conceives of clothing as consumable. Lower-priced clothing is moved faster through the retailer. Pushing these sales is a shortened production-to-retail cycle, where internal designers observe customer preferences and make orders and changes midseason. Thus, while most traditional retailers place their large production orders before a season, fast-fashion retailers place a majority of their orders midseason, allowing flexibility and overall lower costs and losses due to unsold or markdown apparel. The faster-fashion cycle also pushes the consumer to visit retailers more, as they continually monitor new clothing, while treating clothes as a disposable commodity.

PROFILES OF COMPETITORS

Inditex Group

No retailer seems to epitomize the fast-fashion approach more than Inditex Group. The company is able to quickly launch fresh, new apparel lines to meet rapidly evolving consumer preferences through its vertically integrated design and manufacturing strategy. The company's designers closely monitor new fashion and style trends to create new lines as often as every month for its Zara brand stores and other retail brands. The company is able to get its new items in stores quickly by use of a tightly managed global logistics network that includes 658 fabric manufacturers and 4,136 factories. The result is a stylish inventory of moderately priced apparel items that create a shopping frenzy in many of its stores across Europe and the rest of the world. In total, the company's supply chain was supported by 1,725 suppliers and 6,298 factories in 2015.

Inditex Group operated over 7,013 locations in 88 countries and 29 online markets in 2016. Its brands included Zara, Pull & Bear, Massimo

EXHIBIT 6 Clothing and Clothing Accessories Annual Sales by Channel, 2010–2014*

Channel	2014	2013	2012	2011	2010
Brick & Mortar**	$250,775	$246,313	$239,493	$228,438	$213,178
E-commerce***	46,833	40,262	33,579	28,309	23,550

**Estimated values, in millions of dollars.*

***Clothing and clothing accessories, stores NAICS code 448.*

****Itemized line "clothing and clothing accessories," under Total Electronic Shopping and Mail-Order Houses NAICS code 45411.*

Source: U.S. Census Bureau Website.

EXHIBIT 7 Financial Summary for Inditex Group, 2013–2015 (in millions of dollars*)

	2015	2014	2013
Revenue	$23,617	$20,472	$14,800
Cost of merchandise	(9,957)	(8,529)	(6,019)
Gross Profit	13,661	11,942	8,781
Operating expenses, including other losses/income	(8,353)	(7,297)	(5,307)
Amortization and Depreciation	(1,155)	(1,023)	(757)
Profit from operations (EBIT)	4,156	3,614	2,702
Net Earnings (after income taxes)	3,257	2,836	2,108

*Converted from euros with conversation rate of 1 euro = 1.13 U.S Dollars; rounded to nearest million dollar.

Sources: Inditex Group Annual Report, 2013, 2015.

Dutti, Bershka, Stradivarius, Oysho, Zara Home, and Uterqüe. In 2015, Inditex Group opened 330 new locations in 56 countries. In addition, Inditex Group started distributing its Zara brand through an official storefront on the largest online Chinese sales platform, Tmall.com.[9] The popularity of its Zara concept with consumers is reflected in its financial performance. Zara stores totaled to only 2,002 of the company's 7,000+ stores, but the brand accounted for 65 percent and 67 percent of the company's revenues and earnings before interest and taxes (EBIT), respectively, in 2016. Exhibit 7 presents a financial summary for the Inditex Group for 2013 through 2015.

Abercrombie & Fitch

Abercrombie & Fitch sells casual attire under its brands Abercrombie & Fitch, Hollister, and Gilly Hicks. Besides women's and men's clothing, it also sells children's clothing under its abercrombie kids brand. Abercrombie & Fitch is not a fast-fashion retailer and operates through a traditional logistics channel. It experienced a 13 percent decrease in net sales between 2011 and 2015, with its U.S. stores suffering the greatest. A casualty of the current competitive climate and the company's failing strategy is its discontinuation of its Gilly Hicks brand in 2014 and 2015. The company also closed a large number of its other branded stores in the United States between 2013 and 2015—see Exhibit 8. A summary of financial performance for 2013 through 2015 is presented in Exhibit 9.

EXHIBIT 8 Abercrombie & Fitch Global Locations by Brand, 2013–2015*

Brand	2015	2014	2013
Abercrombie & Fitch U.S.	250	253	266
Abercrombie & Fitch International	29	22	19
abercrombie U.S.	116	131	141
abercrombie International	6	5	6
Hollister U.S.	433	458	478
Hollister International	135	129	107
Gilly Hicks U.S.	0	1	17
Gilly Hicks International	0	7	7

*Numbers represent figures at beginning of year.

Source: Abercrombie & Fitch 2014 Annual Report.

EXHIBIT 9 Financial Summary for Abercrombie & Fitch Co., 2013–2015 (in thousands of dollars)

	2015	2014	2013
Revenue	$3,519	$3,744	$4,117
Gross Profit	2,157	2,314	2,575
Operating Income	73	114	81
Net Income	36	52	55

Source: Abercrombie & Fitch Co. Annual Report 2015.

In Search of a New Strategy for Gap Inc.

Art Peck and Gap Inc. were faced with stark changes in the retail industry. As the consumer's desire to shop and congregate at the mall decreased, steep declines in foot traffic created ghost malls in some suburban areas, with empty storefronts and missing anchor stores. Yet contradicting this trend was the continual growth in industry retail sales, bolstered by online sales. These online retail sales were not just staggering, but the tremendous success of some online retailers were significant. Most notably, Amazon alone may have accounted for 60 percent of the growth in 2015 online sales.[10]

Exacerbating the dilemma for Gap Inc. was the fast-fashion strategies of Inditex Group and others that had succeeded in meeting the consumer's desire for fresh styles of clothing and were rapidly expanding in North America and other countries markets quicker than other competitors. Moving forward, Peck and Gap's other key managers needed to identify a strategy to reverse its recent sales decline. However, such a plan would likely fail without a viable approach to reaching the hyperconnected consumer seeking superior customer value.

ENDNOTES

[1] www.ibusworld.com.
[2] Gap Inc. 1999 10-K.
[3] U.S. Census Bureau of the Department of Commerce. Figure reflects seasonality adjustment.
[4] Ibid.
[5] "Global Retail E-Commerce Keeps On Clicking: The 2015 Global Retail E-Commerce Index," www.atkearney.com/consumer-products-retail/e-commerce-index/full-report/-/asset_publisher/87xbENNHPZ3D/content/global-retail-e-commerce-keeps-on-clicking/10192 (accessed June 19, 2016).
[6] J. Boak and A. D'innocenzio, "As Online Shopping Intensifies, Outlook Dims for Mall Store," May 13, 2016, www.kansascity.com/latest-news/article77393162.html.
[7] H. Malcolm, "Macy's Announces Layoffs, Lists 36 Store Closures," January 7, 2016, www.usatoday.com/story/money/2016/01/06/macys-announces-layoffs-restructuring-after-disappointing-2015/78373358/ (accessed May 14, 2016).
[8] J. I. Tu, "Nordstrom Profit Plunges as Mall Stores Struggle," May 12, 2016, www.seattletimes.com/business/retail/nordstrom-comes-up-short-on-profit-joining-apparel-sectors-funk/ (accessed May 14, 2016).
[9] Ibid.
[10] T. Garcia, "Amazon Accounted for 60% of U.S. Online Sales Growth in 2015," May 3, 2016, www.marketwatch.com/story/amazon-accounted-for-60-of-online-sales-growth-in-2015-2016-05-03.

CASE 12

Uber in 2016: Can It Remain the Dominant Leader of the World's Fast-Emerging Ridesharing Industry?

Alex Edinger
The University of Alabama

Louis D. Marino
The University of Alabama

McKenna Marino
The University of Alabama

Molly Stepchuck
The University of Alabama

Standing in the streets of Paris on a cold winter's night in 2008, Garrett Camp and Trent Kalanick had trouble hailing a cab after attending the LeWeb Conference.[1] Instead of just complaining about the problem, in true entrepreneurial fashion the two developed an idea for a limo timeshare service that would be a mobile, fast, and upper-class option for travelers. Camp thought such an option would accomplish his goal of developing an iPhone app to help tackle the taxi issues in San Francisco. Camp began to work on the app in March 2009, and by mid-2009 Kalanick joined the firm as Uber's chief incubator. The first test run was conducted in New York in 2010 and the app was officially launched in San Francisco on May 31, 2010. Little did Garrett Camp know that his prototyping of an iPhone app would revolutionize the transportation business, and impact what is known today as the "sharing economy."[2]

As with many technologies that fundamentally challenge existing business models in an industry, termed *disruptive technologies,* as Uber and the sharing economy grew the company faced a number of challenges including increased competition from new entrants and educating the consumer base. However, in Uber's case the company also faced questions regarding the company's commitment to corporate social responsibility and ethics. Despite the potential social benefits associated with ridesharing, such as a reduction in crashes due to drunk and distracted driving, ethical issues plaguing the company included accusations of assaults involving customers and drivers, concerns regarding the background screening of its drivers, alleged hardball competitive tactics by Uber executives, concerns over the privacy of customers, and the classification of Uber drivers as independent contractors versus employees.

While some critics viewed Uber as a company with many faults, others saw the business as a game-changing boost to economies, especially to those individuals who faced unemployment. In recent years where economic hardships have hit America and countries abroad harder than any time in recent memory, Uber, and the extra income that could be generated through this service, was an important lifeline to many. While speaking at a conference in 2015, Travis Kalanick, Uber founder and chief executive officer, defended Uber arguing that the company provided larger paychecks and more flexibility for its drivers than they would otherwise have received, and touted several philanthropic activities the company supported including "Ride for a Cause," efforts to recruit veterans, and collecting donations for refugees in Europe.[3] Further research conducted by Mothers Against Drunk Driving (MADD) in 2014 demonstrated that crashes involving drunk drivers significantly declined in areas where drivers had more transportation options such as Uber. Indeed, the report credited Uber with reducing the number of drunk-driving-related crashes by an estimated 1,800 crashes in California between 2012 and 2014.[4]

While the company's commitment to ethics and corporate social responsibility may have been a topic open for debate, the company's success at growing both in the United States and internationally was unquestionable. In less than seven years since its founding, Uber had operations in over 400 cities that spanned more than 60 countries and the company was valued at close to $68 billion, higher than Honda, General Motors, or Ford. The question facing Uber's executives going forward was one that faced other firms that experienced explosive growth due to disruptive innovation. Specifically, could the company continue its impressive growth rate in the face of growing competition both domestically and abroad, lingering concerns regarding the company's commitment to ethical operations and corporate social responsibility, and increasing regulation?

COMPANY BACKGROUND

The Early Years

From its origin on the streets of Paris, by 2009 the then-titled Ubercab was officially founded, and by August of that year the company had raised $200,000. In January 2010, Kalanick went to Twitter to find tips on business developers and managers, to which a Foursquare business developer named Ryan Graves responded with "here's a tip. Email me." Graves became Uber's first employee and would eventually become a billionaire. Graves briefly became Ubercab's CEO, but was soon replaced by Kalanick again in 2010, with Graves staying on as the head of global operations for the company.[5]

In 2010, Ubercab started prelaunch testing on the streets of New York City. It had only three cars, but it believed if it could be successful on such a small scale in New York City, surely it would be able to take it to the masses. In positioning Uber, Kalanick was selling a lifestyle rather than just a cheaper taxi ride. "We just wanted to push a button and get a ride," he said. "And we wanted to get a classy ride. We wanted to be baller in San Francisco. That's all it was about."[6] Everyone Kalanick knew began asking to experience riding in style with Ubercab.[7]

Launch

It didn't take long for Ubercab to take its services to San Francisco. By July 2010, the company was established there and drivers could reserve rides through the mobile app or via text messaging. It was an instant success. In just 18 months after that cold night in Paris, the duo of Camp and Kalanick had instituted a service that would interrupt taxi services in the traditional sense and bring a new kind of transportation to the general public.

October 2010 turned out to be a rather eventful month in the young company's life. Uber had generated $1.25 million in funding as investors believed this app for an effortless ride would continue to grow.[8] Ubercab was on the fast track to building on its previous successes when the California Public Utilities Commission issued a cease and desist order to Uber. Many believed Uber was operating as an unlicensed cab company, even though Camp and Kalanick insisted on being a technology and lifestyle company. This prompted the company to officially change its name from "Ubercab" to simply "Uber."[9,10]

Continued Success

Uber's success continued to grow in 2011 as it raised another $11 million by February and expanded its market to New York, Seattle, Boston, Chicago, and Washington, DC. Then it launched its service in Paris in December 2011. The growing did not stop there, however, as it received another $37.5 million in funding.[11] At this point, Uber had raised a total of $49.95 million and the company was valued at a whopping $330 million.[12]

In December 2011, Uber started using surge pricing, which proved critical to its success. Surge pricing occurs when prices vary depending on the conditions in the market. According to Uber, surge pricing was simply supply and demand: When the number of drivers were low and demand was high, prices went up.[13]

Just two years later, Uber launched its app for BlackBerry devices.[14] This sign of true continued growth led California to regulate ridesharing programs such as Uber and Lyft. California began referring to these companies as "Transportation Network Companies."[15] However, Uber desired to be considered a technology communication platform that sold a certain lifestyle. It did not want to be considered a different kind of taxicab service.

In November 2013, Uber began helping drivers attain vehicles in order to maintain the quality of cars each driver used. Some of these drivers may have had varying levels of credit history, so Uber teamed up with car and financing companies to help them.[16] In 2014, Uber worked with AT&T to ensure every Android-based device would have a preinstalled Uber app.[17] Being in all of these pockets instantly made Uber grow into a larger market.

Uber's Growth

Uber benefited from a quick increase in popularity both with the number of drivers and the number of users. According to Uber's website, it saw an exponential increase in drivers within the United States. In July 2012 there were fewer than 25,000 drivers. This number had grown to over 160,000 drivers by January 2015 (see Exhibit 1).

While Uber did not publicly report its financial statements since it was not publicly traded, Bloomberg.com reported in June 2015 that the company had reported to prospective investors that Uber generated annual revenue of $415 million and an operating loss of $470 million. Despite the operating loss, Uber's valuation also demonstrated substantial growth increasing from approximately $18 billion to over $68 billion in 2016 (see Exhibit 2).[18]

UBER'S BUSINESS OPERATIONS

Uber operated through an app on mobile devices. The mobile device pinned the user's location and allowed the user to have a cab come to his or her exact location. The user could then track the car's location on the app's map as it approached. The rider also could track the car's location while en route, which was predetermined at the time the ride was requested. Before officially requesting a cab, Uber riders could estimate the cost of the ride. They could also choose to split the fare with other Uber users so that part of the cost was charged to another user's account. Payment for the ride was charged directly through the app to the user's credit card. The money did not pass through the hands of the driver at all and tips were not expected. The fare was determined by either distance or time, depending on the city and speed of the car. Uber had developed an algorithm to surge price levels during times of high demand. Users were notified when prices surged, and Uber applied for a patent for surge pricing.

Businesses could also set up accounts for employees to use. The business could restrict who was able to use its Uber account, where they could go, and at what times. This was geared toward meetings, events, travel, and late nights in the office.

EXHIBIT 1 Growth in the Number of Uber Drivers

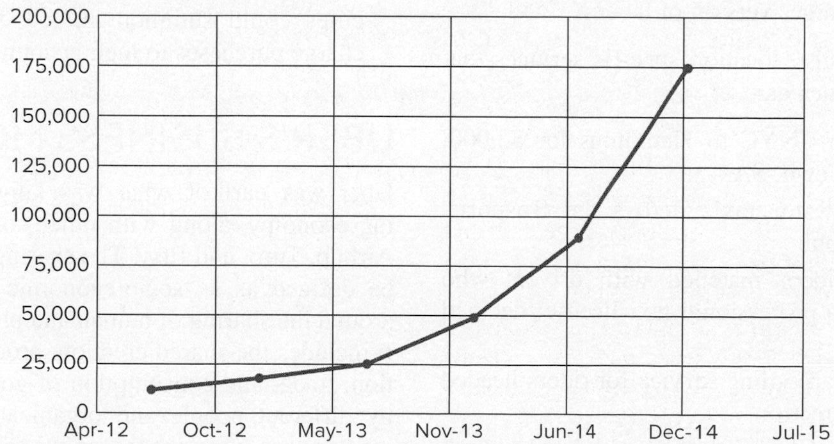

Source: Randy, "Chicago Taxi Driver Jobs Vs. Driving with Uber," Uber Newsroom, May 11, 2015, **newsroom.uber.com/us-illinois/tag/taxi-cab-jobs/** (accessed July 14, 2016).

EXHIBIT 2 Uber's Actual and Forecasted Revenue Growth

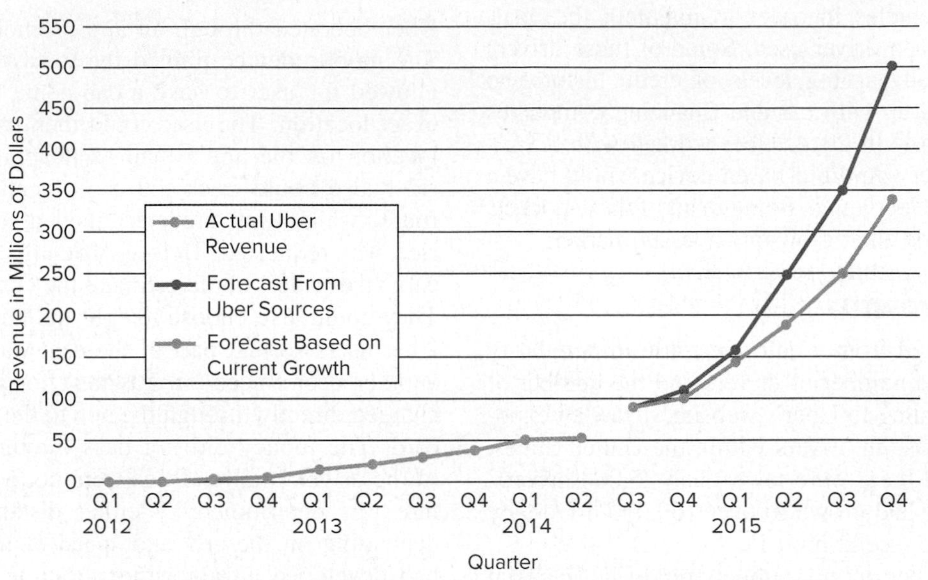

Source: Sam Biddle, "Here Are the Internal Documents That Prove Uber Is a Money Loser," Gawker, August 5, 2015.

When using Uber, riders had the option of a few different cars:

- Uber Taxi—normal licensed taxicabs.
- UberBlack—higher-end models (Mercedes, Cadillac) usually used for businesses.
- Uber X—2012; allowed drivers to drive users in their own nonluxury cars.
- Uber XL—a larger version of Uber X.

There were also location-specific services that Uber provided, such as:

- Uber Chopper—NYC to Hamptons for $3,000, also in Cape Town, SA.
- Uber Boat—water taxis across the Bosporus Strait in Istanbul.
- Uber Pop—riders matched with drivers who did not have a professional taxi license; deemed illegal.
- Uber Pool—carpooling service for riders headed in the same direction.
- Uber Garage—Uber partnered with local taxicab drivers.

Uber experimented with providing services as well:

- Uber Fresh—online food orders.
- Uber Rush—package delivery service.
- Uber Essentials—online ordering from a list of 100 items.
- Uber Ice Cream—July 2012; users in seven cities could summon an ice cream truck and charge purchases to their account.

UBER'S BUSINESS MODEL

Uber was part of what was known as the sharing economy, along with other companies such as Airbnb, Turo, and Etsy. The sharing economy could be defined as a "socio-economic ecosystem built around the sharing of human and physical resources. It includes the shared creation, production, distribution, trade, and consumption of goods and services by different people and organizations." Ridesharing services were not the only businesses that were part of the sharing economy. Airbnb was the world's fifth-largest lodging company, and it didn't own a single room.

The sharing economy was a system of collaborative consumption and could increase revenue for sellers while simultaneously minimizing costs for buyers. The rise of technology and entrepreneurship fostered the growth of the sharing economy. The sharing economy strengthened communities, decreased barriers of entry into business, and reduced environmental impact. However, the sharing economy also provided a way for people doing business to avoid paying taxes, obtaining proper insurance, or following all government regulations. Uber, just like other sharing economy members, thrived because of the benefits, but also came to many road blocks and lawsuits along the way.

In a broad sense, Uber classified itself as a technology company, rather than a transportation company, and asserted that it simply provided a platform for riders and drivers to connect, and therefore did not provide the actual transportation. Because of its self-classification into this category, it did not obtain the same licenses and registrations that a regular taxi company had to obtain. Uber's profits increased because it did not have to pay car registration fees to local governments in most cases. Lack of registration requirements also allowed Uber to enter markets more easily.

Another crucial and unique aspect of Uber's model was that its drivers were not considered employees of Uber. Instead, they were said to be independent contractors. This lessened Uber's liability for drivers' actions and obligations to pay certain taxes. Drivers were also then unable to unionize or receive benefits from Uber. Uber claimed that this was necessary to its business model and success. However, this was a blurry line that Uber walked. The IRS had a 20-point checklist that could be used to determine whether someone was an independent contractor.[19] Drivers could be considered contractors given the fact that they drove their own car, made their own schedule, and were not limited to just driving for Uber. However, drivers could lean more toward the side of employee as well, as Uber had claimed in other lawsuits that its services were not offered to the general public. Additionally, driver services were an integral part of Uber's business. Drivers in return could be too dependent on Uber's technology to be a contractor.

The interpretation of Uber drivers as independent contractors was challenged by a driver who brought suit against the company in California in 2015. The California Labor Commissioner ruled that in this specific case the Uber driver should be considered an employee rather than independent contractor. However, the ruling was not meant to be precedent setting and Uber settled a class action lawsuit in 2016 with drivers in California and Massachusetts for $84 million and an additional $16 million if Uber went public before the end of 2017. As a key element of this ruling, Uber was allowed to keep classifying drivers as independent contractors which allowed the company to maintain its labor based cost advantage. The drivers won the right to a formal grievance procedure with Uber and the ability to post signs in their cars saying that the drivers could accept tips. While Uber won this suit pertaining to the classification of its workers, concerns remained throughout the sharing economy regarding the employment classification status of its workers.[20]

COMPETITION IN THE RIDESHARING INDUSTRY

The taxi and limousine services industry in the United States was relatively fragmented with the largest companies generating less than 3 percent of the industry's overall projected $16.2 billion revenue in 2016.[21] The industry could be segmented into two basic types of companies including traditional taxi and limousine services and transportation network companies (TNC) or transportation network services (TNS) as they were sometimes called, such as Uber that used technology to facilitate ridesharing by connecting customers with drivers acting as independent contractors who owned their own businesses. Historically, Yellow Cab Company was the largest operator in the industry until 1960 when regulations established regions across the country and forced companies that wanted to operate across regions to have a headquarters including a repair center, an office and a lot in each region. Further complicating the establishment of national operations were the diverse rules and regulations that existed across regions. In 2016, the single largest operator was Yellow Cab Chicago which maintained 2,600 vehicles but accounted for less than 1 percent of industry revenues.[22] Industry experts estimated there were over 236,000 businesses operating in this industry, and projected that growth would slow from an average annual rate of 3.3 percent between 2011 and 2016 to an annual rate of 2.4 percent from 2016 to 2021.[23] Industry growth was attributed to a strong economy, GDP growth, and increase in tourism and business travel. Industry profitability was significantly influenced by oil prices, and traditional taxi and limousine services often faced regulations including mandated vehicle inspections, and rules that controlled the prices they could charge for standard fares, the price they charge per mile traveled, and any additional fees. Entry into the traditional sector of the industry could be very expensive, with potential entrants having to meet regulatory restrictions and purchase a license, also known as a medallion. These medallions could cost as little as $1,000 in a small market to as much as $1 million in large markets such as New York City. Access to these licenses was controlled in many markets making entry difficult. In some major markets drivers could lease a license from a corporate medallion owner, but these leases could cost each driver over $100 a day.[24] However, the entry of Uber into the transportation industry reduced the value of medallions in some major markets such as New York City with the average price of a medallion falling from $1 million in 2014 to $690,000 in 2015, leading to the loss of over $4 billion in value in New York City alone in one year (see Exhibits 3 and 4).[25]

Technology evolution had changed the way traditional companies interacted with their customers, causing some to develop their own ride-hailing apps, and had caused the rise of TNC companies that led to increasing competition from independent drivers entering the market. To combat Uber and other TNC services, traditional taxi companies tried to develop their own services such as Curb that they hoped would provide a similar service experience to Uber. While most of the apps from traditional taxicab companies met with failure, it was hoped that Curb could build on lessons learned and help improve the level of service provided by taxicabs. Curb was born out of a relaunch from the Taxi Magic app and was backed by Verifone Systems which provided entertainment and payment services in about half of New York City's green and yellow taxis.[26] The company was launched in 2016 and started small with only 16,000 cabs, but planned to expand its reach rapidly. Curb allowed users to hail and pay for metered taxis and to have the taxi waiting for a customer at a designated place and time. Curb charged a $1.95 service fee for each ride and the rider paid the normal taxi fee in addition to the service fee.

TNC companies such as Uber were not technically considered to be direct competitors in this market, but were considered to be complementary

EXHIBIT 3 Total Percentage of Rides: Uber vs. Taxi Services

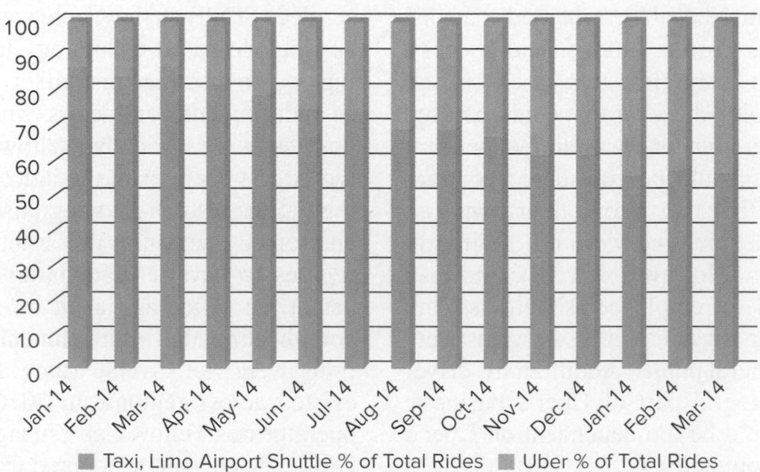

Source: Tangel, Andrew. "Uber Logs Major Gains in New York City, Figures Show." WSJ. Wall Street Journal, 25 Oct 2015. Web. 14 July 2016.

EXHIBIT 4 Percentage Change in New York City Since Jan. 2015 in Avg. Daily Trips

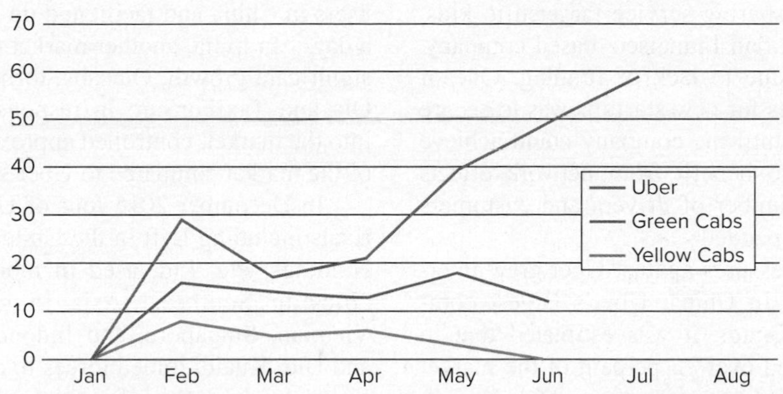

Source: Andrew Tangel, "Uber Logs Major Gains in New York City, Figures Show," *The Wall Street Journal*, October 25, 2015.

goods that helped facilitate transactions that could be considered substitutes to traditional taxi services. The extent to which these independent contractors had to adhere to the same regulations as traditional companies varied substantially and these conditions were set by each city independently. In some cities, drivers using the TNC services were not required to have a business license but were required only to pass a background check provided by the TNC. In other cities the TNC drivers were required to have their vehicles inspected, undergo more extensive background checks, provide proof of proper insurance (many personal policies will not cover accidents that occur while their clients are driving for a TNC), and have a business license but not a taxi license. By the end of 2015, 37 states had enacted laws or regulations relating to TNCs, especially having to do with insurance requirements.

Uber was the first TNC company, but its success gave rise to numerous competitors both in the United States and abroad. In the United States competition grew for Uber both at the local and regional level, but Uber's most significant competitor nationally was Lyft, which was founded in 2012. Lyft was based in San Francisco and worked similarly to Uber. Like Uber, Lyft offered multiple levels of service including Lyft Line (users shared rides to save money), Plain Lyft (single riders or small groups), Lyft Plus (SUVs and larger cars), and Lyft Premier (luxury vehicles). Lyft differentiated its vehicles by having drivers use pink mustaches on its vehicles. Similar to Uber, Lyft and its pink mustachioed cars also had prices well below taxis. However, Lyft's "Prime Time" pricing maxed out at three times the regular rate. Uber's surge pricing was known to go seven or eight times the normal cost. Lyft also conducted background checks, but drivers only needed to be 21 compared to Uber's minimum age of 23. The biggest difference between the two was the reported "feel" between the two cars. Uber strived to make the experience feel like a private driver. Lyft tried to make the experience feel more like a "buddy picking you up from a bar." Oftentimes Lyft riders were encouraged to sit in the front seat, focusing even more on the "buddy" aspect as opposed to the private driver feel of Uber.

Smaller rivals for Uber sprouted up regularly as well. These companies often did not have the funding to compete directly with Uber and so, instead, chose to target niches in either services Uber did not offer or in markets in which Uber did not compete. One such competitor was San Francisco–based Via which focused on drivers using smart cars. Another was Los Angeles–based HopSkipDrive which used rigorously screened CareDrivers to give rides to unaccompanied minors, and Zum which offered a similar service in San Mateo, California. In Boston, Fasten competed with Uber by paying drivers more, offering a minimum hourly guarantee to drivers, and passing the cost savings on to consumers. In markets such as Austin, Texas, where Uber chose not to compete due to regulatory concerns, ridesharing services such as Get Me developed to fill the need. However, success was not guaranteed for these niche services and a number, including Huddle, a San Francisco ridesharing service targeted to kids, and Sidecar, also a San Francisco–based company, ceased operations due to lack of funding. One of the major challenges for new startups was to secure sufficient funding until the company could achieve satisfactory scale to benefit from network effects that grew as the number of drivers and customers using the system expanded.

Competitive pressures against Uber grew internationally as well. In China, Uber's largest competitor was Didi Kuaidi; it was estimated that in 2015 Didi controlled over 75 percent of the market compared to Uber's 11 percent share. Didi Kuaidi, a strategic partner of Lyft, was founded in 2015 by a merger of China's two largest taxi-hailing companies and operated in more than 400 cities in China. By the end of 2015 the company had booked 1.43 billion rides and in May 2016 Apple invested $1 billion in Didi. Apple had planned to help Didi expand its ridesharing platform that served 300 million users in China and facilitated up to 11 million rides a day.[27] In India, another market that was poised for significant growth, Olacabs, formed by a merger of Ola and TaxiForSure in response to Uber's entry into the market, controlled approximately 14 percent of the market compared to Uber's 4.5 percent.

In December 2015 four of Uber's international rivals including Lyft in the United States; GrabTaxi Holdings, Pte. Ltd. used in more than two dozen cities in Southeast Asia in countries such as Vietnam, Singapore, and Indonesia; Ola in India; and Didi Kuaidi joined forces to allow users of each app to book and pay for rides in each competitor's respective country. For example, a GrabTaxi user traveling in the United States could book and pay for rides through Lyft using the GrabTaxi app already installed on the user's phone (see Exhibit 5).

EXHIBIT 5 Uber's Worldwide Presence and Competition

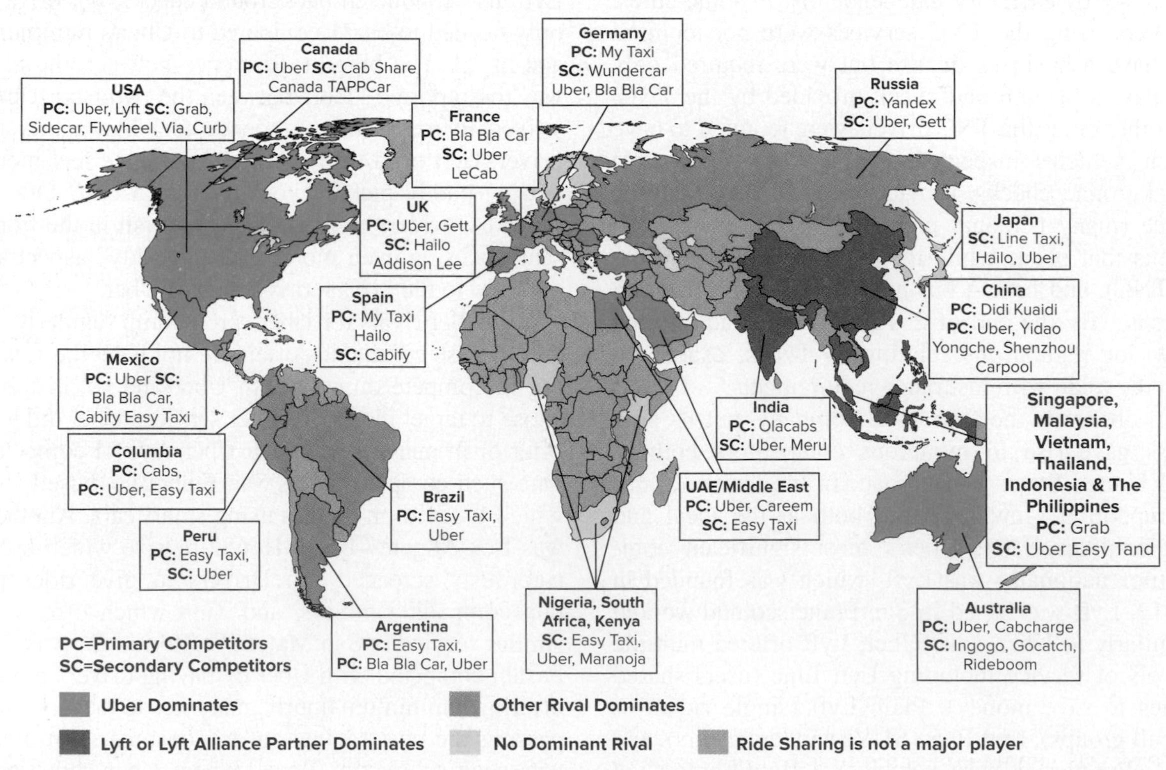

Source: Liyan Chen, "Uber Wants to Conquer the World, but These Companies Are Fighting Back (Map)," *Forbes*, September 28, 2015.

UBER AND ETHICS

In recent years, Uber came under fire for a variety of ethical issues. The company had been a target of scrutiny and criticism from not only taxi and other transportation companies, but also from government agencies and the public as a whole. Some of the primary ethical issues Uber faced included how they treated the drivers, recruitment tactics, a lack of background checks, aggressive engagement of competitors, and surge pricing. However, Uber had a response for each issue it faced and maintained that it employed strong and ethical business practices.

Driver Treatment

Despite Uber's 2016 settlement of the class action suits brought by its drivers, for the majority of Uber's existence it treated its drivers as contractors and not as employees. Uber argued that the drivers were basically in business for themselves and, therefore, they did not have to adhere to any sort of basic labor protections. That meant Uber didn't have to worry about minimum wage, overtime pay, unemployment insurance, or even protection from discrimination.

When off the clock, drivers tended to open up about their true feelings about Uber. One Uber driver reported that "Uber's like an exploiting pimp." The Los Angeles driver went on to say that "Uber takes 20 percent of my earnings, and they treat me like shit—they cut prices whenever they want. They can deactivate me whenever they feel like it, and if I complain, they tell me to fuck off." Tensions rose between the drivers and the management within the company as some of these drivers felt like "ants."[28]

In 2013, many drivers could make between $15 and $20 an hour when working full time. As many drivers signed up, Uber began changing the pricing per mile due to competition in the market. Since Uber drivers had no say in the pricing, and they needed to carry their own insurance, they were faced with "razor-thin margins." Some drivers who worked full time did not make minimum wage.

However, there were certainly some perks to being an Uber driver. These contractors had much more free time than taxi and public transportation drivers. Additionally, the ability to become an Uber driver was simple compared to cab drivers. Applying to become an Uber driver was as easy as visiting the website, filling out some forms, and passing a criminal background check. Uber was also known to offer a $100 sign-up bonus.[29]

Uber's Recruitment Tactics

Uber's recruitment tactics also came under fire. In 2014, Uber's competitor Lyft experienced Uber trying to poach many of its employees. Uber hired teams of independent contractors to use burner phones and multiple credit cards to hire rides from Lyft in a program called Operation SLOG.[30] These "Brand Ambassadors" got a ride from a Lyft driver and spent the trip trying to convince the driver to switch over to becoming a Uber driver. The Uber operatives used the burner phones and multiple credit cards because Lyft had a policy of banning riders it identified as recruiters.[31] Uber's approach to gaining employees contributed to Uber's win-at-all-costs reputation.[32]

However, Kalanick was quick to defend his company's approach by saying there was nothing wrong with giving the Lyft drivers information about a competing service as long as they paid the drivers the fare. Kalanick took to Twitter to state "the point is drivers deserve to have options [and] they are independent [and] shouldn't be restricted from other [opportunities]." Kalanick also argued that Uber paid the Lyft drivers, in the form of a fare, to listen to Uber's pitch and there was nothing illegal about the practice.[33]

Inadequate Background Checks

Another ethical issue Uber faced involved its recruiting tactics and background check procedures. These issues raised a public concern for safety and many Uber drivers were involved in a variety of crimes directed toward passengers. In fact, prosecutors in California claimed, "Uber's background checks had not flagged 25 drivers with criminal records across Los Angeles and San Francisco." One of these drivers had previously served 26 years in prison for second-degree murder, and others had various DUI and fraud convictions.

Most transportation companies used fingerprints and the background-check service called Live Scan to check drivers. This allowed the company to search through the FBI criminal record database. San Francisco District Attorney George Gascon said that a background check without fingerprints was "completely worthless." Uber, on the other hand, did not use fingerprints. Instead, it ran a social security trace to identify addresses associated with drivers and did criminal checks through national, state, and local databases for convictions in the past seven years.[34]

In 2016 both Uber and Lyft suspended operations in Austin, Texas, rather than comply with a regulation passed by Austin's city council in December 2015 that had several stipulations including required fingerprinting for drivers, restrictions on where passengers could be dropped off or picked up, a cumbersome data reporting system, and a requirement that cars had to be clearly marked with the company's logos.[35] The justifications for these regulations included rider safety and a need to create a fair playing field between ridesharing services and traditional taxis. The ordinance passed in a special election on May 7 by a vote of 48,673 for regulation and 38,539 against regulation in a city of 885,000 people. By June of the same year former customers of ridesharing turned to Facebook to arrange ridesharing and looked to other apps and services including Fare, Fasten, Wingz, zTrip, RideAustin, and InstaRyde.[36]

Driver Violence

Another significant safety issue cited by Uber critics was the number of assaults, rape, kidnappings, and even deaths associated with the drivers. Critics argued that Uber's delay in tightening its screening process resulted in multiple cases involving alleged sexual assaults of female passengers by male Uber drivers. In August 2015, a 39-year-old middle school teacher from Charleston, South Carolina, who moonlighted as an Uber driver, was accused of kidnapping a female passenger and demanding that she pay her fare in sexual favors.[37] In December 2014, a Boston driver pled guilty to multiple charges in the alleged rape of a passenger. In June 2014, Daveea Whitmire was charged with a misdemeanor of battery of a passenger. What was worse was that Whitmore had multiple drug-related felony convictions and yet somehow passed Uber's background checks. Uber stated that at the time of Uber's background check, the driver had passed and its process was top of the line. In October 2014, a woman was taken on a 20-mile ride in the middle of the night that ended in a dark, abandoned lot. The driver then locked the doors and trapped her inside and made the ordeal last for well over two hours. Uber later apologized saying it was an "inefficient route" and refunded her fare . . . partially. The most tragic of these Uber horror stories was in January 2014 when Uber driver Syed Muzaffer struck and killed a six-year-old girl in San Francisco. Uber claimed the driver was not technically logged onto the Uber app at the time of the accident, and took zero responsibility for the incident. To make matters worse, Muzaffer already had a reckless driving conviction, which Uber either did not uncover or deemed disqualifying during its background check.[38]

Passenger Refusal

Uber's success and actions did not go unnoticed or unquestioned. There were multiple instances of clashes with drivers and riders with disabilities. With 40 reported cases of drivers refusing to pick up blind passengers, the National Federation of the Blind brought a suit to Uber. The suit claimed "systemic civil rights violations" and told stories of drivers refusing due to their service animal, or abusing their service animal by shutting it in the trunk. Uber and the National Federation of the Blind were still in settlement negotiations.

Uber also ran into some issues with Americans with Disabilities Act (ADA) compliance. There were a number of alleged instances of drivers refusing to take a rider in a wheelchair. In some cases the drivers were reported to have claimed that the chair would not fit in their car in order to avoid the hassle. In one reported instance, the driver would not take the rider with disabilities because she "must not [have been] Christian." However, proponents of Uber argued that while these incidents were unfortunate, it was not clear whether Uber drivers had to comply with the ADA. Specifically, they argued that while ADA compliance was required for transportation companies, it was not required for technology companies and since Uber was not technically a public service, it did not have to comply.

Uber responded to individual passengers who encountered problems with their service by issuing them Uber gift cards. It also denied responsibility for the noncompliance claims due to the status of its drivers as contractors and not employees. The suit also called into question Uber's optional training program, during which drivers were told that they must pick up passengers with disabilities. Those working against Uber argued that the training program should be mandatory, not optional. This, among other problems, also led to a battle of whether Uber drivers could really be considered contractors, or if they needed to be classified as employees.[39]

Undermining Competitors

While Uber's success was impressive over the years, its tactics to undermine competition came into question. In August 2014 rival Lyft claimed that Uber employees ordered and then canceled thousands of Lyft rides in order to undermine their business. Uber shot back saying that Lyft employees also canceled some Uber rides, and Uber denied it ever intentionally canceled Lyft rides.[40] Critics of Uber argued that this was yet another example of the company's questionable ethics, but others argued that the company was simply playing competitive hardball and while the company may have had "sharp elbows," it did nothing that was illegal. In 2016 Uber filed a lawsuit against Olacabs, its main competitor in India, for disrupting Uber's service by allegedly creating fake user accounts and canceling rides. Uber accused Olacabs of creating over 90,000 fake accounts and making as many as 400,000 fraudulent ride requests in order to block Uber from gaining a competitive hold in India.[41]

Surge Pricing

While Uber stressed how surge pricing was simply supply and demand and provided increased incentives for drivers to operate during otherwise unattractive times, some critics stated that this tactic could result in absurdly high fares at peak times. A fine line was walked while Uber's surge pricing took effect. During three high-profile instances—New Year's Eve 2011, Hurricane Sandy in 2012, and a 2013 snowstorm—prices shot up to $35 per minute, or $175 minimum ride cost. Uber defended this by explaining supply and demand. It had to raise prices to incent more drivers to continue working and to deter some riders. If prices had stayed low, Uber argued that it would end up with unhappy customers who had to wait too long for a ride.[42]

There was debate as to whether these practices were really helpful for Uber's profits, and many angry riders may have strayed away from the service even after supply and demand levels returned to normal. Some riders also argued that when surge pricing was active and prices were rising dynamically, this provided drivers with an incentive to cancel a ride that had been accepted at a lower rate to book a ride at the higher rate, sometimes in as little as 30 minutes of having accepted the first ride. While Uber did not condone this practice there was no way for riders to rate their driver for a ride they never received.

Reactions to Uber

Uber's huge success demonstrated the popularity of the ridesharing service with the public at large. However, other businesses in various cities did not appear to be as happy when they saw Uber trying to drive into their towns. While Uber maintained it was a technology company to connect people, clearly one of its biggest competitors was traditional taxicab services, many of which voiced their distaste for Uber in various ways.

In Maryland, companies that historically were competitors came together to protest Uber. In fact, many rival taxi executives had begun to share notes and file complaints against Uber. Cabdrivers' main complaints were how Uber could offer services in many cases without needing to adhere to any rules or regulations. These protests became more and more common in America. However, many analysts simply said the taxi industry was behind the times technologically, and their business needed to change if they wanted to keep up in an ever-changing marketplace.[43]

In 2015 Uber suspended services in the entire state of Nevada. Uber did not obtain licenses for its cars because it again classified itself as a technology company rather than a transportation company. Uber claimed that the laws in the state of Nevada were outdated, and did not account for even the chance that someone could hail a cab over a handheld mobile device. It also claimed that its services were not for the entire public, but just available to the online community. The state did not agree, and decided that the online community was large enough to be considered the public. Nevada's attorney general saw Uber's lack of licenses only as a way for the company to minimize costs and maximize profits. All parties involved were fully aware of consumers' overwhelmingly positive response to the service Uber provides. Nevada believed that Uber figured it could launch and consumer support would ultimately make the law sway in their favor. After an almost yearlong suspension, Uber, as well as Lyft, received permits to operate in Nevada again in September 2015. As part of these permits Nevada implemented a new licensing category for ride-hailing companies and minor regulations. Both companies had again launched service by the end of 2015.

Situations similar to Nevada's were not uncommon on the local level as well. Uber left Auburn, Alabama, for what its general manager for region expansion referred to as "burdensome regulations that disregard our innovative business model." Auburn had requirements for commercial insurance, licensing fee payment, driver background checks, and identifying vehicle signage. In San Antonio, Texas, Uber exited after local regulations again were not changed enough in its favor. Services in Portland, Oregon, were also temporarily suspended in order for the city to have time to formulate the rules that would allow ridesharing. In each of these cases Uber was viewed as being willing to operate in a "gray area" of the law, or in some cases to operate in a manner contrary to local regulations.

Uber had a big impact not only in America, but internationally as well. Ironically, one of the biggest reactions to Uber occurred where the idea of Uber itself was born: France. In June 2015, thousands of cab drivers gathered to form blockades around airports and various train stations in protest of Uber (known as Uber Pop in France). Again, the protestors complained about how Uber drivers didn't need to buy taxi licenses, nor were they subject to regulations or inspections. An Uber Pop vehicle was overturned by the taxi drivers and many clashed with riot police.

In Toronto, Canada, cabbies held multiple protests in hopes of preventing Uber from entering their city. Many resorted to ripping off their shirts to symbolize how Uber would be taking the "shirts off [their] backs."

However, Uber thought it could have a positive impact on the taxi industry. David Plouffe of Uber said, "the market for people using for-hire vehicle transportation—whether it's taxi, limo, or ridesharing—is just going to grow. There's a big enough pie here for everybody to be successful." Plouffe also stated that cities should have welcomed Uber with open arms because of how little cash their drivers took during their services. Often, when taxi drivers collected cash, it could result in underreporting their incomes.

THE FUTURE

Uber tackled its share of issues, but its biggest problem may be yet to come. If more attacks against driver classification as contractors arose, it could become required to pay employees minimum wage. While a large and involved lawsuit could have the potential to take care of that, Uber's business model could become seriously disturbed.

A second area of concern had to do with increasing competition. Not only were traditional taxi companies fighting back with their own apps, a plethora of new entrants had entered the market at the local and regional levels. In 2016 the cab drivers in Austin, Texas, helped defeat an Uber- and Lyft-led ballot proposition that would have eased city regulations that held Uber and Lyft drivers to the same standard as taxicab drivers. One of the regulations that caused the most concern for Uber and Lyft was the requirement that all drivers had to have their fingerprints run through an FBI database for background checks.[44] Following the defeat of the proposition by Austin voters, Uber and Lyft withdrew from the market. This void in the market led to the entry of competitors such as Boston-based Fasten Inc. and InstaRyde, a Canadian-based company that was willing to comply with Austin's requirements. By June 2016 there were more than seven ridesharing services vying for the business Uber and Lyft had left behind. Competition for Uber was also growing internationally as startups sought to become the Uber of their country.

The question of how to regulate ridesharing apps was debated in cities worldwide. In 2015 the Chinese government proposed a draft of regulations that forced ridesharing apps to operate more like taxi fleets; India also considered a set of similar regulations. The Uber X service, known as Uber Pop in European markets, which allowed individuals to offer rides in private cars, was banned in most European markets by the end of 2015.[45] In June 2016 a consortium of mayors from 10 major cities including New York, Paris, Athens, Barcelona, Toronto, and Seoul joined forces to write a common set of rules for working with companies in the sharing economy such as Uber and Airbnb. The participants felt this move was necessary to counter Uber's procedure of targeting each city individually. The consortium of mayors planned to release the first draft of the new rules by fall 2016 and anticipated that as many as 30 cities would immediately adopt the rules, and forecasted that the new rules would eventually be adopted by hundreds of cities.

There was speculation that Uber planned to go public in 2017 or 2018.[46] Analysts believed this could be beneficial given the current overall weak status of the international stock market. However, there was also some concern that the regulatory and competitive pressures mounting against Uber could cause the company's valuation to drop.

The original intent of Uber was to create a new lifestyle for riders. "When you open up that app and you get that experience of like, 'I am living in the future. I pushed a button and a car rolled up and now I'm a frickin' pimp,' Garrett is the guy who invented that shit," Kalanick said.[47] The question that begged to be asked was, what were the true impacts on society from the creation of this lifestyle app?

ENDNOTES

1 newsroom.uber.com/ubers-founding/.

2 Ibid.

3 www.huffingtonpost.com/entry/travis-kalanrick-uber-dreamforce_us_55f9b649e4b0fde8b0cc932c.

4 "More Options. Shifting Mindsets. Better Choices," an ad sponsored by Uber and MADD, January 2015, 2q72xc49mze8bkcog2f01nlh-wpengine.netdna-ssl.com/wp-content/uploads/2015/01/UberMADD-Report.pdf.

5 www.businessinsider.com/how-a-tweet-turned-ryan-graves-into-a-billionaire-2015-3.

6 www.businessinsider.com/why-travis-kalanick-founded-uber-2013-11.

7 "Uber: Rising Valuation Amidst Ethical Woes," GBA 525 Fall Case Book, IBS Center for Management Research.

8 www.crunchbase.com/organization/uber/funding-rounds.

9 techcrunch.com/2010/10/25/ubercab-now-just-uber-shares-cease-and-desist-orders/.

10 "Uber: Rising Valuation Amidst Ethical Woes."

11 www.inc.com/business-insider/how-uber-became-the-most-valuable-startup-in-the-world.html.

12 fortune.com/2014/06/06/these-are-the-venture-firms-celebrating-ubers-massive-17b-valuation/.

13 qz.com/603600/ubers-former-head-of-growth-on-the-early-days-surge-pricing-and-on-demand-ice-cream/.

14 thenextweb.com/apps/2013/03/25/uber-redesigns-its-android-app-and-launches-on-blackberry-and-windows-phone/.

15 www.forbes.com/sites/tomiogeron/2013/09/19/california-becomes-first-state-to-regulate-ridesharing-services-lyft-sidecar-uberx/#1d5bb4fc67fe.

16 techcrunch.com/2013/11/24/uber-driver-car-financing/.

17 techcrunch.com/2014/05/28/uber-att/.

18 www.businessinsider.com/uber-leaked-financials-look-ugly-2015-6.

19 art.mt.gov/artists/IRS_20pt_Checklist_%20Independent_Contractor.pdf.

20 www.npr.org/sections/thetwo-way/2016/04/22/475210901/uber-settles-two-lawsuits-wont-have-to-treat-drivers-as-employees.

21 IbisWorld Taxi & Limousine Services Industry Report.

22 Ibid.

23 Ibid.

24 Ibid.

25 "Taxis v Uber Substitutes or Complements?" *The Economist,* August 10, 2015, www.economist.com/blogs/graphicdetail/2015/08/taxis-v-uber.

26 Andrew J. Hankins, "Taxi-Hailing App Curb to Relaunch with a New Attack Plan against Uber," March 23, 2016, www.theverge.com/2016/3/23/11294758/curb-app-taxi-hail-uber-nyc-verifone.

27 www.bloomberg.com/news/articles/2016-05-13/apple-invests-1-billion-in-uber-s-china-competitor-didi.

28 inthesetimes.com/working/entry/17201/uber_s_business_model_screwing_its_worker.

29 www.quora.com/What-are-the-pros-and-cons-of-becoming-a-Uber-versus-a-normal-taxi-driver-in-Singapore-for-jobless-PMETs.

30 voiceglance.com/is-ubers-audacious-recruiting-tactic-smart-business/.

31 www.pcworld.com/article/2599900/are-ubers-aggressive-recruitment-tactics-legal.html.

32 Ibid.

33 www.businessinsider.com/kalanick-defends-ubers-tactics-2014-8.

34 www.fastcompany.com/3050145/fast-feed/ubers-background-checks-missed-murder-and-dui-convictions-prosecutors-say.

35 thefederalist.com/2016/05/10/uber-lyft-were-driven-out-of-austin/.

36 www.businessinsider.com/what-happened-to-austin-texas-when-uber-and-lyft-left-town-2016-6.

37 www.huffingtonpost.com/entry/uber-driver-kidnap-raping-female-passenger_us_55cb354de4b0923c2beac92.

38 www.thedailybeast.com/articles/2014/11/19/the-ten-worst-uber-horror-stories.html.

39 mashable.com/2016/03/23/uber-ola-lawsuit/#4M3NB15yGmq3.

40 www.pcworld.com/article/2599900/are-ubers-aggressive-recruitment-tactics-legal.html.

41 www.theverge.com/2016/3/23/11292310/uber-ola-lawsuit-india-fake-rides-lyft.

42 www.theverge.com/2013/12/18/5221428/uber-surge-pricing-vs-price-gouging-law.

43 www.washingtonpost.com/local/trafficandcommuting/cab-companies-unite-against-uber-and-other-ride-share-services/2014/08/10/11b23d52-1e3f-11e4-82f9-2cd6fa8da5c4_story.html.

44 Curt Woodward, "In Austin, a Display of Ride-Hailing Wild West," May 26, 2016, www.bostonglobe.com/business/2016/05/25/uber-competitors-flock-austin-after-demand-giant-flees-regulation/VJlv0olHNa7lfS4pigTRpL/story.html.

45 "Legal Troubles—including 173 Lawsuits in the US—Threaten Uber's Global Push," October 5. 2015, www.businessinsider.com/r-legal-troubles-market-realities-threaten-ubers-global-push-2015-10.

46 techcrunch.com/2015/08/21/uber-plans-to-go-public-in-12-18-months-according-to-leaked-presentation/.

47 www.businessinsider.com/uber-travis-kalanick-bio-2014-1.

CASE 13

Panera Bread Company in 2016—Is the Company's Strategy to Rejuvenate Its Growth Working?

Mc Graw Hill Education connect

Arthur A. Thompson
The University of Alabama

In spring 2016, Panera Bread was widely regarded as the clear leader of the "fast-casual" segment of the restaurant industry—fast-casual restaurants were viewed as being a cut above traditional quick-service restaurants like McDonald's because of better food quality, limited table service, and, in many instances, often wider and more upscale menu selections. On average, 7.8 million customers patronized Panera Bread's 1,972 company-owned and franchised bakery-cafés each week, and Panera baked more specialty breads daily than any other bakery-café enterprise in North America. In 2015, Panera had corporate revenues of $2.7 billion, systemwide store revenues of $4.5 billion, and average sales of $2.5 million per store location.

In 2006, Panera Bread executives announced their strategic intent to grow the company from 1,027 locations to 2,000 locations by the end of 2010. But the advent of the Great Recession of 2008–2009 forced the company to drastically downscale the number of planned store openings; Panera ended 2009 with only 1,380 bakery-café locations. Then, in 2010 with a modest economic recovery seemingly underway, Panera's top executives decided that market conditions were favorable enough to permit the company, given customer enthusiasm for eating at Panera's bakery-cafés, to accelerate the number of new store openings and reinstitute their strategy to grow the company, albeit at a pace slower than what was envisioned back in 2006. The company proceeded to open a net of 76 new company-operated and franchised units in 2010, 88 new units in 2011, 111 new units in 2012, 125 units in 2013, 114 units in 2014, and 112 units in 2015. Going into 2016, Panera had 1,972 company-owned and franchised bakery-cafés in operation in 46 states, the District of Columbia, and Ontario, Canada. Plans called for opening 90 to 100 new company-operated and franchised units in 2016.

But despite the ongoing series of store openings, the company was struggling to grow revenues and earnings nearly as fast as top executives wanted. Revenue growth of 6.0 percent in 2014 and 6.1 percent in 2015 was well short of the robust 19.9 percent compound average growth achieved during 2009–2013. Moreover, sales at bakery-cafés open at least one year rose only 1.1 percent in 2014 and 1.9 percent in 2015, compared to 2.3 percent in 2013 and 6.5 percent in 2012. The slower-than-desired revenue growth, coupled with higher operating expenses, squeezed Panera's profitability, resulting in declines in net income from $196.2 million in 2013 to $179.3 million in 2014 and to $149.3 million in 2015 and drops in earnings per share from $6.85 in 2013 to $6.67 in 2014 to $5.81 in 2015.

Nonetheless, in February 2016, top management confidently expressed the belief that Panera had turned the corner and forecast that recently undertaken strategy initiatives would deliver positive earnings growth in 2016, accelerating further in 2017. In announcing the company's financial results for Q4 and full-year 2015 on February 9, 2016, Ron Shaich, Panera's chair and CEO, said:

> Our strategic plan is working. Our comps [company-owned store sales growth] of 3.6% in Q4 2015 and 6.4% in the first 41 days of Q1 2016 are leading indicators of the impact our initiatives are having. Further, we are confident that our results will continue to strengthen as the startup and transition costs associated with our initiatives begin to crest and our sales continue to grow. We now expect the EPS growth we saw in Q4 2015 will improve in 2016 and further accelerate in 2017. Today, we are confident we are on a path to return to sustained double-digit earnings growth.[1]

Panera indicated it was expecting EPS growth of 2–5 percent in 2016.

COMPANY BACKGROUND

In 1981, Louis Kane and Ron Shaich founded a bakery-café enterprise named Au Bon Pain Co., Inc. Units were opened in malls, shopping centers, and airports along the east coast of the United States and internationally throughout the 1980s and 1990s; the company prospered and became the dominant operator within the bakery-café category. In 1993, Au Bon Pain Co. purchased Saint Louis Bread Company, a chain of 20 bakery-cafés located in the St. Louis area. Ron Shaich and a team of Au Bon Pain managers then spent considerable time in 1994 and 1995 traveling the country and studying the market for fast food and quick-service meals. They concluded that many patrons of fast-food chains like McDonald's, Wendy's, Burger King, Subway, Taco Bell, Pizza Hut, and KFC could be attracted to a higher-quality quick dining experience. Top management at Au Bon Pain then instituted a comprehensive overhaul of the newly acquired Saint Louis Bread locations, altering the menu and the dining atmosphere. The vision was to create a specialty café anchored by an authentic, fresh dough, artisan bakery and upscale, quick-service menu selections. Between 1993 and 1997, average unit volumes at the revamped Saint Louis Bread units increased by 75 percent, and over 100 additional Saint Louis Bread units were opened. In 1997, the Saint Louis Bread bakery-cafés were renamed Panera Bread in all markets outside St. Louis.

By 1998, it was clear the re-concepted Panera Bread units had connected with consumers. Au Bon Pain management concluded the Panera Bread format had broad market appeal and could be rolled out nationwide. Ron Shaich believed Panera Bread had the potential to become one of the leading "fast-casual" restaurant chains in the nation. Shaich also believed that growing Panera Bread into a national chain required significantly more management attention and financial resources than the company could marshal if it continued to pursue expansion of both the Au Bon Pain and Panera Bread chains. He convinced the Au Bon Pain board of directors that the best course of action was for the company to go exclusively with the Panera Bread concept and divest the Au Bon Pain cafés. In August 1998, the company announced the sale of its Au Bon Pain bakery-café division for $73 million in cash to ABP Corp.; the transaction was completed in May 1999. With the sale of the Au Bon Pain division, the company changed its name to Panera Bread Company. The restructured company had 180 Saint Louis and Panera Bread bakery-cafés and a debt-free balance sheet.

Between January 1999 and December 2006, close to 850 additional Panera Bread bakery-cafés were opened, some company-owned and some franchised. In February 2007, Panera purchased a 51 percent interest in Arizona-based Paradise Bakery & Café, which operated 70 company-owned and franchised units in 10 states (primarily in the west and southwest) and had sales close to $100 million. At the time, Paradise Bakery units had average weekly sales of about $40,000 and an average check size of $8 to $9. Panera purchased the remaining 49 percent ownership of Paradise Bakery in June 2009. In 2008, Panera expanded into Canada, opening 2 locations in Ontario; since then, 10 additional units in Canada had been opened.

In May 2010, William W. Moreton, Panera's executive vice president and co-chief operating officer, was appointed president and chief executive officer and a member of the company's board. Ron Shaich, who had served as Panera's president and CEO since 1994 and as board chair or co-chair since 1988, transitioned to the role of executive board chair. In addition to the normal duties of board chair, Shaich maintained an active strategic role, with a particular focus on how Panera Bread could continue to be the best competitive alternative in the market segments the company served. However, on March 15, 2012, the company announced that Ron Shaich and Bill Moreton would become co-CEOs, effective immediately; Shaich's formal title was changed to board chair and co-CEO and Moreton's title became president and co-CEO. In August 2013, Shaich and Moreton took on new titles because of family-related issues that required more of Moreton's time—Shaich became board chair and CEO and Moreton was named executive vice chair, with a role of helping oversee Panera's business operations. In February 2015, Moreton also held the title of interim chief financial officer.

Over the years, Panera Bread had received a number of honors and awards. In 2015, *Fast Company* named Panera Bread as the Most Innovative Company in Food. In 2011, 2012, and 2013, Harris Poll EquiTrend® Rankings named Panera Bread as Casual Dining Restaurant Brand of the Year.[2] Zagat's 2012 Fast Food Survey of 10,500 diners ranked Panera as fourth for Top Food, second for Top Décor, and fifth for Top Service among national chains with fewer than 5,000 locations.[3] For nine of the past 12 years (2002–2013), customers had rated Panera Bread tops on overall satisfaction among large chain restaurants in Sandelman & Associates's Quick-Track study "Awards of Excellence" surveys; in Sandelman's 2012 Quick-Track study of more than 110,000 customers of quick-service restaurants, Panera ranked number one in the Attractive/Inviting restaurant category.[4]

A summary of Panera Bread's recent financial performance is shown in Exhibit 1. Exhibit 2 provides selected operating statistics for Panera's company-owned and franchised bakery-cafés.

PANERA BREAD'S CONCEPT AND STRATEGY

Panera Bread's identity was rooted in its fresh-baked artisan breads handcrafted with attention to quality and detail. The company's breads and baked products were a major basis for differentiating Panera from its competitors. According to Panera management, "bread is our passion, soul, and expertise, and serves as the platform that makes all of our other food special." The featured menu offerings at Panera locations included breads and pastries baked in-house, breakfast items and smoothies, made-to-order sandwiches, signature soups and salads, and café beverages. Recognizing that diners chose a dining establishment based on individual food preferences and mood, Panera strived to be the first choice for diners craving fresh-baked goods, a sandwich, soup, a salad, or a beverage served in a warm, friendly, comfortable dining environment. Its target market was urban workers and suburban dwellers looking for a quick-service meal or light snack and an aesthetically pleasing dining experience. Management's long-term objective and strategic intent was to make Panera Bread a nationally recognized brand name and to be the dominant restaurant operator in upscale, quick-service dining. Top management believed that success depended on "being better than the guys across the street" and making the experience of dining at Panera so attractive that customers would be willing to pass by the outlets of other fast-casual restaurant competitors to dine at a nearby Panera Bread bakery-café.[5]

Panera management's blueprint for attracting and retaining customers was called Concept Essence. Concept Essence underpinned Panera's strategy and embraced several themes that, taken together, acted to differentiate Panera from its competitors:

- Offering an appealing selection of artisan breads, bagels, and pastry products that are handcrafted and baked daily at each café location.
- Serving high-quality food at prices that represent a good value.
- Developing a menu with sufficiently diverse offerings to enable Panera to draw customers from breakfast through the dinner hours each day.
- Providing courteous, capable, and efficient customer service.
- Designing bakery cafés that are aesthetically pleasing and inviting.
- Offering patrons such a sufficiently satisfying dining experience that they are induced to return again and again.

Panera Bread's menu, store design and ambience, and unit location strategies enabled it to compete successfully in multiple segments of the restaurant business: breakfast, AM "chill" (when customers visited to take a break from morning-hour activities), lunch, PM "chill" (when customers visited to take a break from afternoon activities), dinner, and take-home, through both on-premise sales and off-premise catering. It competed with a wide

EXHIBIT 1 Selected Consolidated Financial Data for Panera Bread, 2011–2015 (in thousands, except for per-share amounts)

	2015	2014	2013	2012	2011
Income Statement Data					
Revenues:					
Bakery-café sales	$2,358,794	$2,230,370	$2,108,908	$1,879,280	$1,592,951
Franchise royalties and fees	138,563	123,686	112,641	102,076	92,793
Fresh dough and other product sales to franchisees	184,223	175,139	163,453	148,701	136,288
Total revenues	2,681,580	2,529,195	2,385,002	2,130,057	1,822,032
Bakery-café expenses:					
Food and paper products	715,502	669,860	625,622	552,580	470,398
Labor	754,646	685,576	625,457	559,446	484,014
Occupancy	169,998	159,794	148,816	130,793	115,290
Other operating expenses	334,635	314,879	295,539	256,029	216,237
Total bakery-café expenses	1,974,781	1,830,109	1,695,434	1,498,848	1,285,939
Fresh dough and other product cost of sales to franchisees	160,706	152,267	142,160	131,006	116,267
Depreciation and amortization	135,398	124,109	106,523	90,939	79,899
General and administrative expenses	142,904	138,060	123,335	117,932	113,083
Pre-opening expenses	9,089	8,707	7,794	8,462	6,585
Total costs and expenses	2,439,986	2,253,252	2,075,246	1,847,187	1,601,773
Operating profit	241,594	275,943	309,756	282,870	220,259
Interest expense	3,830	1,824	1,053	1,082	822
Other (income) expense, net	1,192	(3,175)	(4,017)	(1,208)	(466)
Income taxes	87,247	98,001	116,551	109,548	83,951
Less net income (loss) attributable to non-controlling interest	(17)	—	—	—	—
Net income to shareholders	$ 149,325	$ 179,293	$ 196,169	$ 173,448	$ 135,952
Earnings per share					
Basic	$5.81	$6.67	$6.85	$5.94	$4.59
Diluted	5.79	6.64	6.81	5.89	4.55
Weighted average shares outstanding					
Basic	25,685	26,881	28,629	29,217	29,601
Diluted	25,788	26,999	28,794	29,455	29,903
Balance Sheet Data					
Cash and cash equivalents	$ 241,886	$ 196,493	$ 125,245	$ 297,141	$ 222,640
Current assets	502,789	406,166	302,716	478,842	353,119
Total assets	1,475,318	1,390,686	1,180,862	1,268,163	1,027,322
Current liabilities	399,443	352,712	303,325	277,540	238,334
Total liabilities	654,718	654,718	177,645	168,704	372,246
Stockholders' equity	497,300	736,184	699,892	821,919	655,076
Cash Flow Data					
Net cash provided by operating activities	$ 318,045	$ 335,079	$ 348,417	$ 289,456	$ 236,889
Net cash used in investing activities	(165,415)	(211,317)	(188,307)	(195,741)	(152,194)
Net cash (used in) provided by financing activities	(107,237)	(52,514)	(332,006)	(19,214)	(91,354)
Net (decrease) increase in cash and cash equivalents	45,393	71,248	(171,896)	74,501	(6,659)

Sources: 2015 10-K report, pp. 43–46; 2014 10-K report, pp. 41–43; 2013 10-K report, pp. 41–43; 2011 10-K report, pp. 41–43.

EXHIBIT 2 Selected Operating Statistics, Panera Bread Company, 2010–2015

	2015	2014	2013	2012	2011	2010
Revenues at company-operated stores (in millions)	$2,358.8	$2,230.4	$2,108.9	$1,879.3	$1,593.0	$1,321.2
Revenues at franchised stores (in millions)	$2,478.0	$2,282.0	$2,175.2	$1,981.7	$1,828.2	$1,802.1
Systemwide store revenues (in millions)	$4,836.8	$4,512.4	$4,284.1	$3,861.0	$3,421.2	$3,123.3
Average annualized revenues per company-operated bakery-café (in millions)	$ 2.552	$12.502	$ 2.483	$ 2.435	$ 2.292	$ 2.179
Average annualized revenues per franchised bakery-café (in millions)	$ 2.479	$ 2.455	$ 2.448	$ 2.419	$ 2.315	$ 2,266
Average weekly sales, company-owned cafés	$49,090	$48,114	$47,741	$46,836	$44,071	$41,899
Average weekly sales, franchised cafés	$47,680	$47,215	$47,079	$46,526	$44,527	$43,578
Comparable bakery-café sales percentage increases*						
Company-owned outlets	3.0%	1.4%	2.6%	6.5%	4.9%	7.5%
Franchised outlets	1.0%	0.9%	2.0%	5.0%	3.4%	8.2%
System-wide	1.9%	1.1%	2.3%	5.7%	4.0%	7.9%
Company-owned bakery-cafés open at year-end	901	925	867	809	740	662
Franchised bakery-cafés open at year-end	1,071	955	910	843	801	791
Total bakery-cafés open	1,972	1,880	1,777	1,652	1,541	1,453

*The percentages for comparable store sales are based on annual changes at stores with an open date prior to the first day of the prior fiscal year (meaning that a store had to be open for all 12 months of the year to be included in this statistic).

Sources: Company 10-K reports for 2015, 2014, 2013, 2011, and 2010.

assortment of specialty food, casual dining, and quick-service establishments operating nationally, regionally, and locally. Its close competitors varied according to the menu item, meal, and time of day. For example, breakfast and AM "chill" competitors included Starbucks and McDonald's; close lunch and dinner competitors included such chains as Chili's, Applebee's, California Pizza Kitchen, Jason's Deli, Cracker Barrel, Ruby Tuesday, T.G.I. Friday's, Chipotle Mexican Grill, and Five Guys Burgers and Fries. In the bread and pastry segment, Panera competed with Corner Bakery Café, Atlanta Bread Company, Au Bon Pain, local bakeries, and supermarket bakeries.

Except for bread and pastry products, Panera's strongest competitors were dining establishments in the so-called fast-casual restaurant category. Fast-casual restaurants fill the gap between fast-food outlets and casual, full table service restaurants. A fast-casual restaurant provides quick-service dining (much like fast-food enterprises) but is distinguished by enticing menus, higher food quality, and more inviting dining environments; typical meal costs per guest are in the $7–$12 range. Some fast-casual restaurants have full table service, some have partial table service (with orders being delivered to the table after ordering and paying at the counter), and some are self-service (like fast-food establishments, with orders being taken and delivered at the counter). Exhibit 3 provides information on prominent national and regional dining chains that competed against Panera Bread in some or many geographic locations.

Panera Bread's growth strategy was to capitalize on Panera's market potential by opening both company-owned and franchised Panera Bread locations as fast as was prudent. So far, working closely with franchisees to open new locations had been a key component of the company's efforts to broaden its market penetration. Panera Bread had organized its

EXHIBIT 3 Representative Fast-Casual Restaurant Chains and Selected Full-Service Restaurant Chains in the United States, 2014–2015

Company	Number of Locations, 2013	Select 2014–2015 Financial Data	Key Menu Categories
Atlanta Bread Company	~100 company-owned and franchised bakery-cafés in 21 states	Not available (privately held company)	Fresh-baked breads, salads, sandwiches, soups, wood-fired pizza and pasta (select locations only), baked goods, desserts
Applebee's Neighborhood Grill and Bar* (a subsidiary of DineEquity)	2,000+ franchised locations in 49 states, two U.S. territories, and 16 countries outside the U.S.	2015 average annual sales of about $2.5 million per U.S. location	Beef, chicken, pork, seafood, and pasta entrees, plus appetizers, salads, sandwiches, a selection of under-500-calorie Weight Watchers–branded menu alternatives, desserts, and alcoholic beverages (about 12 percent of total sales)
Au Bon Pain	300+ company-owned and franchised bakery-cafés in 26 states and 5+ foreign countries	Not available (privately held company)	A focus on healthful, nutritious selections with superfood ingredients, including hot cereals, bagels, soups, salads, sandwiches and wraps, and coffee drinks
Buffalo Wild Wings*	1,170 locations in the U.S., Mexico, Canada, and Philippines	2015 revenues of $1.8 billion; average sales of $3.25 million per location	Chicken wings, chicken tenders, specialty hamburgers, sandwiches, flatbreads, salads, full bar
California Pizza Kitchen*(a subsidiary of Golden Gate Capital)	~300 locations in ~32 states, 16 countries, and 218 cities	Average annual sales of about $3.2 million per location	Signature California-style hearth-baked pizzas, plus salads, pastas, soups, sandwiches, appetizers, desserts, beer, wine, coffees, teas, and assorted beverages
Chili's Grill and Bar* (a subsidiary of Brinker International)	1,580 locations in 50 states and 307 locations in 30 foreign countries and territories	2015 average revenues of ~$2.9 million per location; 2015 average check size per customer of $14.52	Chicken, beef, and seafood entrees, steaks, appetizers, salads, sandwiches, desserts, and alcoholic beverages (14.1 percent of sales)
Chipotle Mexican Grill	2,000+ units	2015 revenues of $4.5 billion; average unit sales of ~$2.5 million; average check size $10.17	Gourmet burritos and tacos, salads, beverages (including margaritas and beers)
Corner Bakery Café	202 locations in 22 states and District of Columbia	2014 sales per location of $2.33 million; menu price range: $0.99 to $8.99	Specialty breads, hot breakfasts, signature sandwiches, grilled panini, pastas, seasonal soups and chili, made-to-order salads, sweets, coffees, and teas
Cracker Barrel*	637 combination retail stores and restaurants in 42 states	Restaurant-only sales of $2.27 billion in 2015; average sales per restaurant of $3.6 million; average guest check of $10.23; serves an average of ~1,000 customers per day per location	Two menus (all-day breakfast and lunch/dinner); named by *Technomics* in both 2013 and 2015 as the full restaurant category winner of its "Chain Restaurant Consumers' Choice Award"

(Continued)

Company	Number of Locations, 2013	Select 2014–2015 Financial Data	Key Menu Categories
Culver's	540+ locations in 22 states	2014 revenues of $1+ billion; average sales per location of $2.0 million	Signature hamburgers served on buttered buns, fried battered cheese curds, value dinners (chicken, shrimp, cod with potato and slaw), salads, frozen custard, milkshakes, sundaes, and fountain drinks
Einstein Noah Restaurant Group (Einstein Bros. Bagels, Noah's New York Bagels, Manhattan Bagel)	~850 company-owned, franchised, and licensed locations in 40 states	Annual revenue per company-owned unit of ~$850,000	Fresh-baked bagels, hot breakfast sandwiches, made-to-order lunch sandwiches, creamed cheeses and other spreads, salads, soups, and gourmet coffees and teas
Fazoli's (a subsidiary of Sun Capital Partners)	220+ locations in 26 states	2014 sales of ~$260 million	Spaghetti and meatballs, fettuccine alfredo, lasagna, ravioli, submarinos and panini sandwiches, pizza, entrée salads, garlic breadsticks, and desserts
Firehouse Subs	970+ locations in 42+ states (plans for 2,000 locations by 2020	Average unit sales of ~$800,000	Hot and cold subs, salads, sides, drinks, catering
Five Guys Burgers and Fries	1,500+ locations in 47 states and 6 Canadian provinces	2014 revenues of $1.2 billion	Hamburgers (with choice of 15 toppings), hot dogs, fries, and beverages
Jason's Deli	268+ locations in 29 states	2014 sales per unit of $2.66 million	Sandwiches, extensive salad bar, soups, loaded potatoes, desserts, catering services, party trays, and box lunches
Moe's Southwest Grill (a subsidiary of Focus Brands)	600+ locations in 37 states and the District of Columbia	Average annual sales per restaurant of ~$1.1 million	Burritos, quesadillas, fajitas, tacos, nachos, rice bowls (chicken, pork, or tofu), salads, a kid's menu, five side items, two desserts, soft drinks, iced tea, bottled water, and catering
McAlister's Deli (a subsidiary of Focus Brands)	350 locations in 26 states	Annual sales of $505 million; sales of $1.4 per location	Deli sandwiches, loaded baked potatoes, soups, salads, and desserts, plus sandwich trays, lunch boxes, and catering
Noodles & Company	~500 urban and suburban locations in 32 states and District of Columbia	2014 sales of $465 million; comparable store sales growth of 0.2% in 2014; average check size $8.00	Customizable Asian, Mediterranean, and American noodle/pasta entrees, soups, salads, sandwiches, alcoholic beverages
Olive Garden*	846 locations	2015 revenues of $3.8 billion; average sales per location of $4.5 million	Full Italian menu of appetizers (15), flatbreads (3), soups and salads (6), pastas (11), beef, chicken, and seafood entrees (20), desserts (8), kid's menu, wide beverage assortment
Panda Express	~1,500 locations across the U.S.	2014 revenues of $2.2 billion	A variety of Chinese entrées, including orange chicken, Kung Pao chicken, broccoli beef, eggplant tofu, angus steak (and 9 others), rice, steamed vegetables, beverages

Company	Number of Locations, 2013	Select 2014–2015 Financial Data	Key Menu Categories
Qdoba Mexican Grill (a subsidiary of Jack-in-the-Box, Inc.)	661 company-owned and franchised locations in 47 states, District of Columbia, and Canada	2015 average unit sales per location of $1.2 million; 2015 comparable store sales growth of 9.3%; 2015 average check size of $11.82	Signature burritos, tacos, taco salads, quesadillas, three-cheese nachos, Mexican gumbo, tortilla soup, five signature salsas, and breakfast selections at some locations
Ruby Tuesday*	692 company-owned and franchised locations in 44 states, plus 44 international locations in 13 foreign countries and Guam	Fiscal 2015 sales of $1.13 billion; average restaurant sales of $1.7 million; typical entrée price ranges of $8.99 to $20.99	Appetizers, handcrafted burgers, 35-item salad bar, steaks, chicken, crab cakes, lobster, salmon, tilapia, ribs, desserts, nonalcoholic and alcoholic beverages, and catering
Starbucks	~12,600 company-operated and licensed locations in the U.S. and 10,500+ international locations	2015 global revenues of $19.2 billion; sales of $1.38 million per company-operated location in the Americas	Italian-style espresso beverages, teas, sodas, juices, assorted pastries and confections; some locations offer sandwiches and salads
T.G.I. Friday's*	967 locations in 48 states and District of Columbia; 22 locations in 6 foreign countries	2014 annual revenues of ~$1.8 billion	Appetizers, salads, soups, burgers and other sandwiches, chicken, seafood, steaks, pasta, desserts, nonalcoholic and alcoholic beverages, party platters

**Denotes a full-service restaurant.*

Sources: Company websites, accessed February 16, 2016; *Nation's Restaurant News*, "Top 100 Restaurant Chains and Companies," June 15, 2015, www.nrn.com (accessed February 16, 2016).

business around company-owned bakery-café operations, franchise operations, and fresh dough operations; the fresh bread unit supplied dough and other products to all Panera Bread stores, both company-owned and franchised.

Panera Bread's Product Offerings and Menu

Panera Bread's artisan signature breads were made from four ingredients—water, natural yeast, flour, and salt; no preservatives or chemicals were used. Carefully trained bakers shaped every step of the process, from mixing the ingredients, to kneading the dough, to placing the loaves on hot stone slabs to bake in a traditional European-style stone deck bakery oven. Breads, as well as bagels, muffins, cookies, and other pastries, were baked fresh throughout the day at each café location. Exhibit 4 shows Panera's lineup of breads.

The Panera Bread menu was designed to provide target customers with products built on the company's bakery expertise, particularly its varieties of breads and bagels baked fresh throughout the day at each café location. The key menu groups were fresh-baked goods, hot breakfast selections, bagels and cream cheese spreads, hot Panini, made-to-order sandwiches and salads, soups, fruit smoothies, frozen drinks, beverages, and Espresso bar selections. Exhibit 5 summarizes the menu offerings at Panera Bread locations as of March 2015.

Menu offerings were regularly reviewed and revised to sustain the interest of regular customers, satisfy changing consumer preferences, and be responsive to various seasons of the year. Special soup offerings, for example, appeared seasonally. Product development was focused on providing food that customers would crave and trust to be tasty. New menu items were developed in test kitchens and then introduced in a limited number of the bakery-cafés to determine customer response and verify that preparation and operating procedures result in product consistency and high quality standards. If successful, they were then rolled out systemwide. New product introductions were integrated into periodic or seasonal menu rotations, referred to as "Celebrations." From 2013 through 2015, between 20 and 25 new and reintroduced menu items appeared on Panera's menu each year during the course of five Celebrations.

Over the past 10 years, Panera had responded to growing consumer interest in healthier, more nutritious menu offerings. In 2004, whole grain breads were introduced, and in 2005 Panera switched to the use of natural antibiotic chicken in all of Panera's chicken-related sandwiches and salads. Other recent health-related changes included using organic and all-natural ingredients in selected items, using unbleached flours in its breads, adding a yogurt-granola-fruit parfait and reduced-fat spreads for bagels to the menu, introducing fruit smoothies, increasing the use of fresh ingredients (like fresh-from-the-farm lettuces and tomatoes), and revising ingredients and preparation methods to yield 0 grams of artificial trans fat per serving. All of the menu boards and printed menus at company-owned Panera bakery-cafés included the calories for each food item. Also, Panera's website had a nutritional calculator showing detailed nutritional information for each individual menu item or combination of menu selections.

Off-Premises Catering In 2004–2005, Panera Bread introduced a catering program to extend its market reach into the workplace, schools, and parties and gatherings held in homes, and grow its breakfast-, lunch-, and dinner-hour sales without making capital investments in additional physical facilities. The first menu consisted of items appearing on the regular menu and was posted for viewing at the company's website. A catering coordinator was available to help customers make menu selections, choose between assortments or boxed meals, determine appropriate order quantities, and arrange

EXHIBIT 4 Panera's Line of Fresh-Baked Breads, February 2016

Artisan Breads	Specialty Breads
Country A crisp crust and nutty flavor. *Available in loaf.*	**Sourdough** Panera's signature sourdough bread with no fat, oil, sugar, or cholesterol. *Available in loaf.*
Whole Grain Moist and hearty, sweetened with honey. *Available in loaf.*	**Asiago Cheese** Standard sourdough recipe with Asiago cheese baked in and sprinkled on top. *Available in loaf.*
Rye With chopped rye kernels and caraway seeds. *Available in loaf.*	**Honey Wheat** Sweet and hearty with honey and molasses. *Available in loaf.*
French Slightly blistered crust, wine-like aroma. *Available in baguette; also served in portions as a side with many food selections.*	**All-Natural White Bread** Soft and tender white sandwich bread. *Available in loaf.*
Ciabatta A moist, chewy crumb with a thin crust and light olive oil flavor. *Available in loaf.*	**Tomato Basil** Sourdough bread made with tomatoes and basil, and sweet streusel topping. *Available in XL loaf.*
Focaccia Italian flatbread baked with olive oil and topped with either Asiago cheese or sea salt. *Available in loaf.*	**Cinnamon Raisin Swirl** Fresh dough made with flour, whole butter, and eggs, swirled with Vietnamese and Indonesian cinnamons, raisins, and brown sugar, topped with Panera's cinnamon crunch topping. *Available in loaf.*
Sprouted Whole Grain Roll *Available as single or pack of 6.*	
Soft Dinner Roll *Available as single or pack of 6.*	

Source: **www.panerabread.com** (accessed February 12, 2016).

EXHIBIT 5 Panera Bread's Menu Selections, March 2015

Bakery and Sweets

Artisan and Specialty Breads (14 varieties)
Bagels (11 varieties)
Scones (5 varieties)
Sweet Rolls (3 varieties)
Muffins and Muffies (6 varieties)
Artisan Pastries (7 varieties)
Brownie
Cookies (8 varieties)
Cinnamon Crumb Coffee Cake
Carrot Cake

Bagels & Cream Cheese Spreads
11 varieties of bagels, 7 varieties of spreads

Hot Breakfast
Breakfast Sandwiches (9 varieties)
Baked Egg Soufflés (3 varieties)
Spinach Mushroom and Sofrito

Strawberry Granola Parfait

Honey Almond Greek Yogurt Parfait

Steel Cut Oatmeal

Power Almond Quinoa Oatmeal

Fruit Smoothies (6 varieties)

Fresh Fruit Cup

Signature Hot Paninis
Frontega Chicken
Roast Turkey and Caramelized Kale
Steak and White Cheddar

Signature Sandwiches
Napa Almond Chicken Salad
Steak and Arugula
Italian Combo
Bacon Turkey Bravo

Soups (5 selections varying daily, plus seasonal specialties)

Options include:
Broccoli Cheddar
Bistro French Onion
Baked Potato
Low Fat All-Natural Chicken Noodle
Cream of Chicken and Wild Rice
New England Clam Chowder
Low Fat Vegetarian Garden Vegetable with Pesto
Low Fat Vegetarian Black Bean
Vegetarian Creamy Tomato
All-Natural Turkey Chili

Café Salads
Caesar: Classic, Greek

Signature Salads
Chicken Cobb
Chicken Cobb with Avocado
Chicken Caesar
Asian Sesame Chicken
Fuji Apple Chicken
Thai Chicken
BBQ Chicken
Mediterranean Quinoa with Almonds
Greek with Shrimp
Classic with Chicken
Greek with Chicken
Power Kale Caesar with Chicken
Chicken Soba Noodle

Broth Bowls
Thai Garden Chicken Wonton
Ricotta Sacchettini with Chicken
Lentil Quinoa with Chicken
Lentil Quinoa with Cage-Free Egg

Café Sandwiches
Smoked Ham and Swiss
Roasted Turkey and Avocado BLT
Tuna Salad
Mediterranean Veggie

(Continued)

EXHIBIT 5 Continued

Café Sandwiches *Continued*	**Beverages**
Italian Combo	Coffee (hot or iced)
Fontina Grilled Cheese	Hot Teas
Classic Grilled Cheese	Iced Tea
Sierra Turkey	Iced Green Tea
Smoked Turkey	Pepsi beverages
	Dr Pepper
Flatbread Sandwiches	Bottled Water
Turkey Cranberry	San Pellegrino
Mediterranean Chicken	Organic Milk or Chocolate Milk
Thai Chicken	Orange Juice
Tomato Mozzarella	Organic Apple Juice
Chicken Ham and Swiss	Lemonade
	Fruit Punch
Signature Pastas	Sierra Mist fountain soda
Chicken Sorrentina	Assorted other bottled beverages (5)
Chicken Tortellini Alfredo	
Mac & Cheese	**Frozen Drinks**
Pesto Sacchettini	Frozen Caramel
Tortellini Alfredo	Frozen Mocha
Pasta Primavera	
	Espresso Bar
Panera Kids	Espresso
Grilled Cheese Sandwich	Cappuccino
Peanut Butter and Jelly Sandwich	Caffe Latte
Smoked Ham Sandwich	Caffe Mocha
Smoked Turkey Sandwich	Vanilla Latte
Mac & Cheese	Caramel Latte
10 varieties of regular and seasonal soups	Skinny Caffe Mocha
3 salads	Chai Tea Latte (hot or iced)
2 squeezable varieties of yogurt	Signature Hot Chocolate

Source: Menu posted at **www.panerabread.com** (accessed February 12, 2016).

pickup or delivery times. Orders came complete with plates, napkins, and utensils, all packaged and presented in convenient, ready-to-serve-from packaging.

In 2010, Panera boosted the size of its catering sales staff and introduced sales training programs and other tools—factors that helped drive a 26 percent increase in catering sales in 2010. In 2011, Panera introduced an online catering system that catering customers could use to view the catering menu, place orders, specify whether the order was to be picked up or delivered to a specified location, and pay for purchases. The 65-item catering menu in 2015 included breakfast assortments, bagels and spreads, sandwiches and boxed lunches, salads, soups, pasta dishes, pastries and sweets, and a selection of beverages. In large geographic locations with multiple bakery-cafés, Panera operated catering-only "delivery hubs" to expedite deliveries of customer orders. Going forward, top executives at Panera believed that off-premise catering was an important revenue growth opportunity for both company-operated and franchised locations.

The MyPanera Loyalty Program

In 2010, Panera initiated a loyalty program to reward customers who dined frequently at Panera Bread locations. The introduction of the MyPanera program was completed systemwide in November and, by the end of December, some 4.5 million customers had signed up and become registered card members. Members presented their MyPanera card when ordering. When the card was swiped, the specific items being purchased were automatically recorded to learn what items a member liked. As Panera got an idea of a member's preferences over the course of several visits, a member's card was "loaded" with such "surprises" as complimentary bakery-café items, exclusive previews and tastings, cooking and baking tips, invitations to special events, ideas for entertaining, or recipe books. On a member's next visit, when an order was placed and the card swiped, order-taking personnel informed the member of the surprise award. Members could also go online at www.MyPanera.com and see if a reward was waiting on their next visit. At year-end 2015, the company's MyPanera program had over 22 million members, and in 2013, 2014, and 2015 approximately 50 percent of the transactions at Panera Bread bakery-cafés were attached to a MyPanera loyalty card.

Management believed that the loyalty program had two primary benefits. One was to entice members to dine at Panera more frequently and thereby deepen the bond between Panera Bread and its most loyal customers. The second was to provide Panera management with better marketing research data on the purchasing behavior of customers and enable Panera to refine its menu selections and market messages.

The Panera 2.0 Strategic Initiative

In 2012, Panera began testing a newly developed Panera 2.0 app that enabled digital ordering and payment by customers and that included capabilities store employees and managers could use to perform an assortment of internal operating activities. The app was adaptable to the differentiated needs of dine-in, to-go, and large-order delivery customers. The objectives of the Panera 2.0 technology were to enhance the guest experience, aid the introduction of marketing innovations, permit cost-efficient handling of a growing number of customer transactions volumes, and pave the way for greater operating efficiencies in its bakery-cafés. The tests in 14 bakery-cafés were such a huge success that Panera began rolling out the full Panera 2.0 experience to its entire network of company-operated and franchised bakery cafés in 2013, a process that management planned to complete in 2017. The company had converted 106 of its company-owned bakery-cafés to Panera 2.0 by year-end 2014 and another 304 were fully converted to Panera 2.0 by year-end 2015.

CEO Ron Shaich was pleased with the results in the bakery-cafés that had converted to Panera 2.0—sales growth was higher in the converted store locations than in the nonconverted locations and metrics relating to labor costs, operating improvements, and guest friction/complaints were also noticeably better in the converted locations. The data further indicated that it took three to four quarters for the effects of sales growth and operating efficiencies to gain full momentum in the converted Panera 2.0 cafés. Introduction of the "Rapid Pickup" component of Panera 2.0, which featured mobile ordering and payment for customers picking up orders at a particular bakery-café, was completed systemwide in early 2015. By year-end 2015, sales that were digitally placed and paid for were averaging 16 percent of total sales companywide but were averaging 22 percent of total sales at cafés that had converted to Panera 2.0 and approaching 25 percent of total sales at growing numbers of Panera bakery-cafés.

While Panera's rollout of Panera 2.0 was intended to speed service and checkout, as well as enable other operating efficiencies, some of Panera's biggest shareholders had expressed their concern to Ron Shaich that Panera 2.0 was being implemented too slowly and were also skeptical whether the new software would actually improve internal operating efficiency and boost customer traffic outside the lunch hour by as much as Panera executives hoped.

The "Panera at Home" Strategic Initiative

In 2013 Panera began selling Panera-branded soups (15 varieties), mac and cheese, salad dressings, packaged meats (roast pork, roast turkey, and roast beef), Panera coffee (7 varieties), and frozen breads through other retailers, primarily grocery chains. In 2015, Panera food products were available at select grocery locations in 48 states and its coffees could be purchased at Amazon.com. In 2015, sales of these products (roughly 49 items) totaled about $150 million and were growing about 50 percent annually. Panera's goal was to build Panera at Home into a business generating $1 billion in retail sales and over $300 million in wholesale revenues over time. In

2016 Panera expected to begin transitioning categories within its Panera at Home food portfolio from a licensed model to what it termed a "co-pack model" in which Panera managed the customer.

Panera's Latest Strategic Initiative: Delivering Orders to Customers

Panera management began working on prototyping and testing delivering orders to customers in 2012–2013. By year-end 2015, Panera had come up with a go-forward delivery model which it was testing at 25 cafés in two geographic markets. While the test was still in the early stages, Panera was generating delivery orders in the 25 test cafés averaging $5,000 per week, against a breakeven volume of $3,000 (exclusive of startup, training, and initial awareness costs).

In February 2016, Shaich explained why he was excited about the potential for order delivery to be a powerful new channel for sales and profit growth at Panera:[6]

> First, we believe we have the perfect product for Delivery. Salads and sandwiches are generally not heated and, therefore, travel well, especially at lunch. We also have brand credibility. Our foods are the preferred choice for many office meetings and gatherings. Delivery also uses our production capabilities without taxing lunchtime seats which are at or nearly at capacity.
>
> Second, our testing to date indicates delivery sales are highly incremental, which means we are reaching Panera users not already served through other channels. Third, our testing indicates delivery has the potential to [boost sales growth at existing stores] for multiple years at rates significantly higher than the rate of [growth without delivery]. Simply put, the trajectory of delivery sales growth is different than the trajectory of sales growth [without delivery].
>
> Fourth, steady state Delivery margins are particularly attractive since there's no order input cost associated with Delivery—all orders are indeed placed digitally—and no cost for heating and lighting the space in which the customer consumes the product. Indeed, customers consume the delivered product in their own space. The only relevant costs when we do delivery are production and the net cost of delivery, which in turn is very much a function of the level of sales per hour offset by the modest delivery fee we charge.
>
> Fifth, startup and transition costs are modest, very modest. We simply have to hire and train drivers and build awareness to reach our initial sales goals.
>
> And sixth, delivery leverages the tech capabilities we've already built. The digital ordering, payment, and production systems, integrated as they are, are already in place to enable [Panera] 2.0 and rapid pickup, and can be uniquely leveraged to support our Delivery business. Given our existing technology, Delivery appears to our cafe managers as just another to-go order. Orders come in over the same app, go through our existing kitchen display systems and are produced by the same staff for our drivers to bring to our customers. Thus, there's little material incremental capital investment beyond routing software required to support our Delivery business.

Panera had studied using third-party delivery services instead of building its own driver network. But management was not convinced outsourcing delivery drivers was the best way for Panera to go. Ron Shaich gave several reasons:[7]

> First, we don't want to be confined by the limited mass coverage presently offered by external delivery resources.
>
> And, second, we found that using our own drivers ensures a faster delivery time with more consistent quality of delivery for a better customer experience. We know this matters to our customer and we believe we can build a formidable competitive advantage on this.
>
> No third-party delivery operator offers the coverage to unlock the market potential we see out there and want to attack now. We've talked with every meaningful third-party provider out there and tested with many, and at best no single third-party delivery organization can support more than 15 percent of our markets.
>
> Further, in the markets they do operate within, their average coverage is below 50% of our cafés' delivery zones. That is to say, if you take an individual store, they only offer delivery to about 50% of the real estate we're trying to deliver to. So, as of today, using third-party drivers would allow us to serve less than 7% of what we perceive to be our potential delivery customers.
>
> We also are committed to offering a better delivery experience, one of consistent quality. Our goal is a 30- to 35-minute order-to-door time, which we have found possible, at least at this point—which we have not found possible, at least at this point, through third-party drivers.
>
> . . . given the size of the opportunity and our desire to move quickly, we cannot wait for third-party providers to expand their capabilities, nor are we willing to put up with present limitation of third-party services. Simply put, we will initially move forward with in-house drivers, believing this will lead to a more rapid rollout of delivery, making for a competitively more attractive experience for our customers, and lead to significantly more incremental profitability.

> All that said, let me state that we respect the third-party model and we'll continue to talk with any and all third-party providers relative to our markets. We are rigid in our commitment to build a real delivery business at Panera but flexible in execution, as we know the capabilities of independent delivery firms will continue to evolve rapidly.
>
> But, today, [using] in-house drivers allows us to move quickly to offer delivery at scale across the country with a better experience that serves as a competitive advantage for our guests.

Panera franchisees were as excited about delivering orders as was Panera management, chiefly because of the incremental sales and profit potential and the relatively small costs associated with adding delivery capability. As a consequence, the strategy was to roll out delivery simultaneously at both company-owned and franchised locations. In 2016, Panera expected to introduce order delivery at 200 to 300 company and franchised locations.

Panera's Nonprofit Pay-What-You-Want Bakery-Café Locations

In May 2010, Panera Bread converted one of its restaurants in a wealthy St. Louis suburb into a nonprofit "pay-what-you-want" Saint Louis Bread Cares bakery-café with the idea of helping to feed people in need and raising money for charitable work. A sign in the bakery-café said, "We encourage those with the means to leave the requested amount or more if you're able. And we encourage those with a real need to take a discount." The menu board listed "suggested funding levels," not prices. Payments went into a donation box, with the cashiers providing change and handling credit card payments. The hope was that enough generous customers would donate money above and beyond the menu's suggested funding levels to subsidize discounted meals for those who were experiencing economic hardship and needed help. The restaurant was operated by Panera's charitable Panera Bread Foundation; all profits from the store were donated to community programs.

After several months of operation, the Saint Louis Bread Cares store was judged to be successful enough that Ron Shaich, who headed the Panera Bread Foundation, opted to open two similar Panera Cares cafés—one in the Detroit suburb of Dearborn, Michigan, and one in Portland, Oregon. Two more locations were opened in 2012—one in Chicago and one in Boston. Panera expected to serve over 1 million people at the five pay-what-you-want locations in 2013.[8] Statistics showed that in 2013 about 60 percent of store patrons left the suggested amount, 20 percent left more, and 20 percent less, often significantly less.[9]

In March 2013, Panera introduced a special "Meal of Shared Responsibility"—turkey chili in a bread bowl—at a suggested retail price of $5.89 (tax included) at 48 locations in the St. Louis area. The idea was that those in need could get a nutritious 850-calorie meal for whatever they could afford to pay, while those who pay above the company's cost make up the difference.[10] The program was supported by heavy media coverage at launch, extensive in-store signage, and employees explaining how the meal worked. In July 2013, after serving about 15,000 of the turkey chili meals, Panera canceled the program, chiefly because few people in need were participating—an outcome attributed largely to most Panera locations in the St. Louis area being located in middle-class and affluent neighborhoods. Management indicated it would rethink its approach to social responsibility and possibly retool the program. Later in 2014, the Chicago location of Panera Cares was closed.

In 2016, the four locations in St. Louis, Dearborn, Boston, and Portland were still open, operating under the name Panera Cares Community Cafés. Since 2010, some 4 million guests had been served meals. In order to achieve the goal of feeding people with dignity and also sustain their operation, the Panera Bread Foundation had established four guidelines that guests at these Community Cafés were asked to observe:[11]

1. The suggested donation listed on the menu panel is the retail value of the meal and reflects the amount we need to cover our operating costs while also covering the cost of the meals for those who come in and are unable to contribute for their meal. We ask that those who are able contribute that amount do so.
2. For guests who cannot meet our suggested donation amount or donate your fair share, we ask that you limit yourself to one entreé and a beverage per week.
3. If you are unable to contribute for your meal, you may earn a meal voucher by volunteering for 1 hour per week in our community cafés. We are

not designed to be a permanent solution for those facing food insecurity, so if you are in need of additional services, please visit our resource area for more information.

4. We also ask that, as a general matter, meals provided to those who cannot contribute the full suggested donation amount are consumed in our community cafes as a means of building community.

Panera's Marketing Strategy

Panera management was committed to growing sales at existing and new unit locations, continuously improving the customer experience at its restaurants, and stimulating more frequent customer visits to its bakery-cafés. The core strategic initiatives to achieve these outcomes included periodically introducing new menu items during the Celebrations, increasing the enrollment of patrons in the MyPanera loyalty programs, and efforts to strengthen relationships with customers who, management believed, would then recommend dining at Panera to their friends and acquaintances. Panera hired a new chief marketing officer and a new vice president of marketing in 2010; both had considerable consumer marketing experience and were playing an important role in crafting the company's marketing strategy to increase awareness of the Panera brand, develop and promote appealing new menu selections, expand customer participation in the MyPanera loyalty program, and otherwise make dining at Panera bakery-cafés a pleasant and satisfying experience.

To promote the Panera brand and menu offerings to target customer groups, Panera employed a mix of radio, billboards, social networking, the Internet, and periodic cable television advertising campaigns. In recent years, Panera had put considerable effort into (a) improving its advertising messages to better capture the points of difference and the soul of the Panera concept and (b) doing a better job of optimizing the media mix in each geographic market.

Whereas it was the practice at many national restaurant chains to spend 3 to 5 percent of revenues on media advertising, Panera's advertising expenses had typically been substantially lower, running as low as 0.6 percent of systemwide sales at company-owned and franchised bakery-cafés in 2008. But in the past five years, Panera had started upping its advertising effort to help spur sales growth. Advertising expenses totaled $33.2 million in 2011 (1.00 percent of systemwide bakery-café sales), $44.5 million in 2012 (1.15 percent of systemwide bakery-café sales), $55.6 million in 2013 (1.30 percent of system-ide bakery-café sales), $65.5 million in 2014 (1.45 percent of systemwide bakery-café sales), and $68.5 million in 2015 (1.41 percent of systemwide bakery-café sales). The increased advertising expenses in 2014 were to support Panera's first-ever national television advertising campaign, an initiative that was financed by both Panera and its franchisees and that was continued in 2015.

Panera's franchise agreements required franchisees to contribute a specified percentage of their net sales to advertising. In 2014 and 2015, Panera's franchise-operated bakery-cafés were required to contribute 1.8 percent of their sales to a national advertising fund and to pay Panera a marketing administration fee equal to 0.4 percent of their sales—Panera contributed the same net sales percentages from company-owned bakery-cafés toward the national advertising fund and the marketing administration fee. Franchisees were also required in 2014 and 2015 to spend amounts equal to 0.8 percent of their net sales on advertising in their respective local markets.

FRANCHISE OPERATIONS

Opening additional franchised bakery-cafés was a core element of Panera Bread's strategy and management's initiatives to achieve the company's revenue growth and earnings targets. Panera Bread did not grant single-unit franchises, so a prospective franchisee could not open just one bakery-café. Rather, Panera Bread's franchising strategy was to enter into franchise agreements that required the franchise developer to open a number of units, typically 15 bakery-cafés in a period of six years. Franchisee candidates had to be well-capitalized, have a proven track record as excellent multiunit restaurant operators, and agree to meet an aggressive development schedule. Applicants had to meet eight stringent criteria to gain consideration for a Panera Bread franchise:

- Experience as a multiunit restaurant operator
- Recognition as a top restaurant operator
- Net worth of $7.5 million
- Liquid assets of $3 million
- Infrastructure and resources to meet Panera's development schedule for the market area the franchisee was applying to develop

- Real estate experience in the market to be developed
- Total commitment to the development of the Panera Bread brand
- Cultural fit and a passion for fresh bread

Exhibit 6 shows estimated costs of opening a new franchised Panera Bread bakery-café. The franchise agreement typically required the payment of a $5,000 development fee for each bakery-café contracted for in a franchisee's "area development agreement," a franchise fee of $30,000 per bakery-café (payable in a lump sum at least 30 days prior to the scheduled opening of a new bakery-café), and continuing royalties of 5 percent on gross sales at each franchised bakery-café. Franchise-operated bakery-cafés followed the same standards for in-store operating standards, product quality, menu, site selection, and bakery-café construction as did company-owned bakery-cafés. Franchisees were required to purchase all of their dough products from sources approved by Panera Bread. Panera's fresh dough facility system supplied fresh dough products to substantially all franchise-operated bakery-cafés. Panera did not finance franchisee construction or area development agreement payments or hold an equity interest in any of the franchisc-operated bakery-cafés. All area development agreemcnts executed after March 2003 included a clause allowing Panera Bread the right to purchase all bakery-cafés opened by the franchisee at a defined purchase price, at any time five years after the execution of the franchise agreement. During the 2010–2014 period, Panera purchased 84 bakery-cafés from the franchisees and had sold 5 company-owned stores to franchisees.

But in mid-April 2015, following a February announcement that Panera's expected earnings per share in 2015 would, at best, be flat in comparison to the $6.64 the company earned in 2014 and

EXHIBIT 6 Estimated Initial Investment for a Franchised Panera Bread Bakery-Café, 2012

Investment Category	Actual or Estimated Amount	To Whom Paid
Development fee	$5,000 per bakery-café contracted for in the franchisee's Area Development Agreement	Panera
Franchise fee	$35,000 ($5,000 of the development fee was applied to the $35,000 franchise fee when a new bakery-café was opened)	Panera
Real property	Varies according to site and local real estate market conditions	
Leasehold improvements	$334,000 to $ 938,500	Contractors
Equipment	$198,000 to $ 310,000	Equipment vendors, Panera
Fixtures	$ 32,000 to $ 54,000	Vendors
Furniture	$ 28,500 to $ 62,000	Vendors
Consultant fees and municipal impact fees (if any)	$ 51,500 to $ 200,250	Architect, engineer, expeditor, others
Supplies and inventory	$ 19,150 to $ 24,350	Panera, other suppliers
Smallwares	$ 24,000 to $ 29,000	Suppliers
Signage	$ 15,000 to $ 84,000	Suppliers
Additional funds (for working capital and general operating expenses for 3 months)	$175,000 to $ 245,000	Vendors, suppliers, employees, utilities, landlord, others
Total	**$917,150 to $1,984,100, plus real estate andrelated costs**	

Source: www.panerabread.com (accessed April 5, 2012).

shortly after Panera's executives had a "constructive dialogue" with activist shareholder Luxor Capital Group, Panera Bread announced that it would (a) expand its share-repurchase plan from $600 million to $750 million, (b) sell 73 of its 925 company-owned bakery-cafés to franchisees to raise money to help fund the added expenditures on repurchasing outstanding shares of the company's common stock, and (c) borrow $500 million to help fund the share-buyback plan. As things turned out, Panera ended up selling 75 company-owned bakery-cafés to franchisees by year-end 2015 and expected to sell about 35 additional company-owned stores to franchisees in 2016.

As of January 2016, Panera Bread had agreements with 33 franchise groups that operated 1,071 bakery-cafés. Panera's largest franchisee operated nearly 200 bakery-cafés in Ohio, Pennsylvania, West Virginia, Kentucky, and Florida. The company's franchise groups had committed to open an additional 128 bakery-cafés. If a franchisee failed to develop bakery-cafés on schedule, Panera had the right to terminate the franchise agreement and develop its own company-operated locations or develop locations through new franchisees in that market. However, Panera from time to time agreed to modify the commitments of franchisees to open new locations when unfavorable market conditions or other circumstances warranted the postponement or cancellation of new unit openings.

Panera provided its franchisees with support in a number of areas: market analysis and site selection assistance, lease review, design services and new store opening assistance, a comprehensive 10-week initial training program, a training program for hourly employees, manager and baker certification, bakery-café certification, continuing education classes, benchmarking data regarding costs and profit margins, access to company-developed marketing and advertising programs, neighborhood marketing assistance, and calendar planning assistance.

PANERA BREAD OPERATIONS

Site Selection and Café Environment

Bakery-cafés were typically located in suburban, strip mall, and regional mall locations. In evaluating a potential location, Panera studied the surrounding trade area, demographic information within that area, and information on nearby competitors. Based on analysis of this information, including utilization of predictive modeling using proprietary software, Panera developed projections of sales and return on investment for candidate sites. Cafés had proven successful as freestanding units and as both in-line and end-cap locations in strip malls and large regional malls. A number of the Panera Bread cafcafés that were free-standing or had suitable end-cap locations had installed drive-thru windows, a feature that tended to boost sales by about 20 percent.

The average Panera bakery-café size was approximately 4,500 square feet. Most all company-operated locations were leased. Lease terms were typically for 10 years, with one, two, or three 5-year renewal option periods. Leases typically entailed charges for minimum base occupancy, a proportionate share of building and common area operating expenses and real estate taxes, and a contingent percentage rent based on sales above a stipulated amount. Some lease agreements provided for scheduled rent increases during the lease term. The average construction, equipment, furniture and fixture, and signage cost for the 65 company-owned bakery-cafés opened in 2014 and the 57 bakery-cafés was $1,400,000 (excluding capitalized development overhead expenses), compared to average costs of $750,000 for 42 company-owned bakery-cafés opened in 2010 and $920,000 for 66 company-owned bakery-cafés opened in 2005.

Each bakery-café sought to provide a distinctive and engaging environment (what management referred to as "Panera Warmth"), in many cases using fixtures and materials complementary to the neighborhood location of the bakery-café. All Panera cafés used real china and stainless silverware, instead of paper plates and plastic utensils. Periodically, the company introduced new café designs aimed at further refining and enhancing the appeal of Panera bakery-cafés as a warm and appealing neighborhood gathering place. These designs tended to feature newly available furniture, cozier seating, and modernized décor. Some locations had fireplaces to further create an alluring and hospitable atmosphere. Many locations had outdoor seating, and all company-operated and most franchised locations had free wireless Internet to help make the bakery-cafés community gathering places where people could catch up on some work, hang out with friends, read the paper, or just relax (a strategy that Starbucks had used with great success).

Bakery-Café Operations

Panera's top executives believed that operating excellence was the most important element of Panera Warmth and that without strong execution and operational skills and energized café personnel who were motivated to provide pleasing service, it would be difficult to build and maintain a strong relationship with the customers patronizing its bakery-cafés. Additionally, top management believed high-quality restaurant management was critical to the company's long-term success. Bakery-café managers were provided with detailed operations manuals and all café personnel received hands-on training, both in small group and individual settings. The company had created systems to educate and prepare café personnel to respond to a customer's questions and do their part to create a better dining experience. Management strived to maintain adequate staffing at each café and had instituted competitive compensation for café managers and both full-time and part-time café personnel (who were called associates). Managers at cafés that had converted to Panera 2.0 were aggressively using the tool to improve a variety of operating metrics—and with demonstrated results.

Panera executives had established a "Joint Venture Program," whereby selected general managers and multiunit managers of company-operated bakery cafés could participate in a bonus program based upon a percentage of the store profit of the bakery-cafés they operated. The bonuses were based on store profit percentages generally covering a period of five years, and the percentages were subject to annual minimums and maximums. Panera management believed the program's multiyear approach (a) improved operator quality and management retention, (b) created team stability that generally resulted in a higher level of operating consistency and customer service for a particular bakery-café, (c) fostered a low rate of management turnover, and (d) helped drive operating improvements at the company's bakery-cafés. In 2013–2014, approximately 45 percent of the bakery-café operators Panera's company-owned locations participated in the Joint Venture Program.

Going into 2016, Panera Bread had approximately 47,200 employees. Approximately 44,400 were employed in Panera's bakery-cafe operations as bakers, managers, and associates, approximately 1,400 were employed in the fresh dough facility operations, and approximately 1,300 were employed in general or administrative functions, principally in the company's support centers. Roughly 23,800 employees worked, on average, at least 25 hours per week. Panera had no collective bargaining agreements with its associates and considered its employee relations to be good.

Panera's Bakery-Café Supply Chain

Panera operated a network of 24 facilities (22 company-owned and 2 franchise-operated) to supply fresh dough for breads and bagels on a daily basis to almost all of its company-owned and franchised bakery-cafés—one of the company's 22 facilities was a limited production operation co-located at a company-owned bakery-café in Ontario, Canada, that supplied dough to 17 Panera bakery-cafés in that market. All of the company's facilities were leased. Most of the 1,500 employees at these facilities were engaged in preparing dough for breads and bagels, a process that took about 48 hours. The dough-making process began with the preparation and mixing of starter dough, which then was given time to rise; other all-natural ingredients were then added to create the dough for each of the different bread and bagel varieties (no chemicals or preservatives were used). Another period of rising then took place. Next, the dough was cut into pieces, shaped into loaves or bagels, and readied for shipment in fresh dough form. There was no freezing of the dough, and no partial baking was done at the fresh dough facilities. Trained bakers at each bakery-café performed all of the baking activities, using the fresh doughs delivered daily.

Distribution of the fresh bread and bagel doughs (along with tuna, cream cheese spreads, and certain fresh fruits and vegetables) was accomplished through a leased fleet of about 225 temperature-controlled trucks operated by Panera personnel. The optimal maximum distribution route was approximately 300 miles; however, routes as long as 500 miles were sometimes necessary to supply cafés in outlying locations. In 2013–2014, the various distribution routes for regional facilities entailed making daily deliveries to 8–9 bakery-cafés.

Panera obtained ingredients for its doughs and other products manufactured at its regional facilities. While a few ingredients used at these facilities were sourced from a single supplier, there were numerous suppliers of each ingredient needed for fresh dough and cheese spreads. Panera contracted externally for the manufacture and distribution of sweet goods to its bakery-cafés. After delivery, sweet good products were finished with fresh toppings and other ingredients (based on Panera's own recipes) and baked to Panera's artisan standards by professionally trained bakers at each café location.

Panera had arrangements with several independent distributors to handle the delivery of sweet goods products and other items to its bakery-cafés, but the company had contracted with a single supplier to deliver the majority of ingredients and other products to its bakery-cafés two or three times weekly. Virtually all other food products and supplies for their bakery-cafés, including paper goods, coffee, and smallwares, were contracted for by Panera and delivered by the vendors to designated independent distributors for delivery to the bakery-cafés. Individual bakery-cafés placed orders for the needed supplies directly with a distributor; distributors made deliveries to bakery-cafés two or three times per week. Panera maintained a list of approved suppliers and distributors that all company-owned and franchised cafés could select from in obtaining food products and other supplies not sourced from the company's regional facilities or delivered directly by contract suppliers.

Although many of the ingredients and menu items sourced from outside vendors were prepared to Panera's specifications, the ingredients for a big majority of menu selections were generally available and could be obtained from alternative sources when necessary. In a number of instances, Panera had entered into annual and multiyear contracts for certain ingredients in order to decrease the risks of supply interruptions and cost fluctuation. However, Panera had only a limited number of suppliers of antibiotic-free chicken; because there were relatively few producers of meat products raised without antibiotics—as well as certain other organically grown items—it was difficult or more costly for Panera to find alternative suppliers.

Management believed the company's fresh dough-making capability provided a competitive advantage by ensuring consistent quality and dough-making efficiency (it was more economical to concentrate the dough-making operations in a few facilities dedicated to that function than it was to have each bakery-café equipped and staffed to do all of its baking from scratch). Management also believed that the company's growing size and scale of operations gave it increased bargaining power and leverage with suppliers to improve ingredient quality and cost and that its various supply-chain arrangements entailed little risk that its bakery-cafés would experience significant delivery interruptions from weather conditions or other factors that would adversely affect café operations.

The fresh dough made at the regional facilities was sold to both company-owned and franchised bakery-cafés at a delivered cost not to exceed 27 percent of the retail value of the product. Exhibit 7 provides financial data relating to each of Panera's three business segments: company-operated bakery-cafés, franchise operations, and the operations of the regional facilities that supplied fresh dough and other products. The sales and operating profits of the fresh dough and other products segment shown in Exhibit 7 represent only those transactions with franchised bakery-cafés. The company classified any operating profit of the regional facilities stemming from supplying fresh dough and other products to company-owned bakery-cafés as a reduction in the cost of food and paper products. The costs of food and paper products for company-operated bakery-cafés are shown in Exhibit 1.

Panera Bread's Management Information Systems

Each company-owned bakery-café had programmed point-of-sale registers that collected transaction data used to generate transaction counts, product mix, average check size, and other pertinent statistics. The prices of menu selections at all company-owned bakery-cafés were programmed into the point-of-sale registers from the company's data support centers. Franchisees were allowed access to certain parts of Panera's proprietary bakery-café systems and systems support; they were responsible for providing the appropriate menu prices, discount rates, and tax rates for system programming.

The company used in-store enterprise application tools and the capabilities of the Panera 2.0 app to (1) assist café managers in scheduling work hours for café personnel and controlling food costs, in order to provide corporate and retail operations management with quick access to retail data; (2) enable café managers to place online orders with distributors; and (3) to reduce the time café managers spent on administrative activities. The information collected electronically at café registers

EXHIBIT 7 Business Segment Information, Panera Bread Company, 2011–2015 (in thousands of dollars)

	2015	2014	2013	2012	2011
Segment revenues:					
Company bakery-café operations	$2,358,794	$2,230,370	$2,108,908	$1,879,280	$1,592,951
Franchise operations	138,563	123,686	112,641	102,076	92,793
Fresh dough and other product operations at regional facilities	382,110	370,004	347,922	312,308	275,096
Intercompany sales eliminations	(197,887)	(194,865)	(184,469)	(163,607)	(138,808)
Total revenues	$2,681,580	$2,529,195	$2,385,002	$2,130,057	$1,822,032
Segment operating profit:					
Company bakery-café operations	$ 366,905	$ 400,261	$ 413,474	$ 380,432	$ 307,012
Franchise operations	133,449	117,770	106,395	95,420	86,148
Fresh dough and other product operations at regional facilities	23,517	22,872	21,293	17,695	20,021
Total segment operating profit	$ 523,871	$ 540,903	$ 541,162	$ 493,547	$ 413,181
Depreciation and amortization:					
Company bakery-café operations	$ 105,535	$ 103,239	$ 90,872	$ 78,198	$ 68,651
Fresh dough and other product operations at regional facilities	9,367	8,613	8,239	6,793	6,777
Corporate administration	20,496	12,257	7,412	5,948	4,471
Total	$ 135,398	$ 124,109	$ 106,523	$ 90,939	$ 79,899
Capital expenditures:					
Company bakery-café operations	$ 174,633	$ 167,856	$ 153,584	$ 122,868	$ 94,873
Fresh dough and other product operations at regional facilities	12,175	12,178	11,461	13,434	6,483
Corporate administration	37,124	44,183	26,965	16,026	6,576
Total capital expenditures	$ 223,932	$ 224,217	$ 192,010	$ 152,328	$ 107,932
Segment assets					
Company bakery-café operations	$ 953,717	$ 953,896	$ 867,093	$ 807,681	$ 682,246
Franchise operations	13,049	13,145	10,156	10,285	7,502
Fresh dough and other product operations at regional facilities	75,634	65,219	62,854	60,069	47,710
Total segment assets	$1,475,318	$1,390,902	$ 940,103	$ 878,035	$ 737,458

Sources: Panera Bread's 2015 10-K report, p. 73; 2014 10-K report, p. 66; 2013 10-K report, p. 67; 2011 10-K report, p. 69.

was used to generate daily and weekly consolidated reports regarding sales, transaction counts, average check size, product mix, sales trends, and other operating metrics, as well as detailed profit-and-loss statements for company-owned bakery-cafés. These data were incorporated into the company's "exception-based reporting" tools.

Panera's regional facilities had software that accepted electronic orders from bakery-cafés and monitored delivery of the ordered products back to the bakery-cafés. Panera also had developed proprietary digital software to provide online training to employees at bakery-cafés, and online baking instructions for the baking personnel at each café.

THE RESTAURANT INDUSTRY IN THE UNITED STATES IN 2016

According to the National Restaurant Association, total food-and-drink sales at some 1.1 million foodservice locations of all types in the United States were projected to reach a record $783 billion in 2016, up from $587 billion in 2010.[12] Of the projected $783 billion in food-and-drink sales industry-wide in 2015, about $536 billion were expected to occur in commercial restaurants, with the remainder divided among bars and taverns, lodging place restaurants, managed food service locations, military restaurants, and other types of retail, vending, recreational, and mobile operations with foodservice capability. In 2013, unit sales averaged $966,000 at full-service restaurants and $834,000 at quick-service restaurants; however, very popular restaurant locations achieved annual sales volumes in the $2.5 million to $5 million range.

Restaurants were the nation's second-largest private employer in 2015 with about 14 million employees; employment in 2016 was expected to rise to 14.4 million people. Nearly half of all adults in the United States had worked in the restaurant industry at some point in their lives, and one out of three adults got their first job experience in a restaurant. More than 90 percent of all eating-and-drinking-place businesses had fewer than 50 employees, and more than 70 percent of these places were single-unit operations.

Even though the average U.S. consumer ate 76 percent of their meals at home, on a typical day, about 130 million U.S. consumers were foodservice patrons at an eating establishment—sales at commercial eating places were projected to average about $1.9 billion on a typical day in 2015. Average household expenditures for food away from home in 2014 were $2,787, equal to about 40 percent of total household expenditures for food.[13]

The restaurant business was labor-intensive, extremely competitive, and risky. Industry members pursued differentiation strategies of one variety of another, seeking to set themselves apart from rivals via pricing, food quality, menu theme, signature menu selections, dining ambiance and atmosphere, service, convenience, and location. To further enhance their appeal, some restaurants tried to promote greater customer traffic via happy hours, lunch and dinner specials, children's menus, innovative or trendy dishes, diet-conscious menu selections, and beverage/appetizer specials during televised sporting events (important at restaurants/bars with big-screen TVs). Most restaurants were quick to adapt their menu offerings to changing consumer tastes and eating preferences, frequently featuring heart-healthy, vegetarian, organic, low-calorie, and/or low-carb items on their menus. Research conducted by the National Restaurant Association indicated in 2015 that:[14]

- 68 percent of consumers were more likely to visit a restaurant that offered locally produced food items.
- 70 percent of consumers were more likely to visit a restaurant that offered healthy menu options.
- 72 percent of consumers believe restaurant technology increases convenience, while 42 percent said technology makes restaurant visits and ordering more complicated.

It was the norm at many restaurants to rotate some menu selections seasonally and to periodically introduce creative dishes in an effort to keep regular patrons coming back, attract more patrons, and remain competitive.

The profitability of a restaurant location ranged from exceptional to good to average to marginal to money-losing. Consumers (especially those that ate out often) were prone to give newly opened eating establishments a trial, and if they were pleased with their experience might return, sometimes frequently—loyalty to existing restaurants was low when consumers perceived there were better dining alternatives. It was also common for a once-hot restaurant to lose favor and confront the stark realities of a dwindling clientele, forcing it to either re-concept its menu and dining environment or go out of business. Many restaurants had fairly short lives. There were multiple causes for a restaurant's failure—a lack of enthusiasm for the menu or dining experience, inconsistent food quality, poor service, a poor location, meal prices that patrons deemed too high, and being outcompeted by rivals with more appealing menu offerings.

ENDNOTES

[1] Company press release, February 9, 2016.
[2] Harris Interactive press releases, March 16, 2011, and May 10, 2012, and information, **www.harrisinteractive.com** (accessed March 7, 2014).
[3] "Zagat Announces 2012 Fast-Food Survey Results," September 27, 2012, **www.prnewswire.com** (accessed March 7, 2014).
[4] Sandelman and Associates Quick-Track Surveys and Fast-Food Awards of Excellence Winners, and information included in "Press Kit," **www.panerabread.com** (accessed March 7, 2014).
[5] As stated in a presentation to securities analysts, May 5, 2006.
[6] Transcript of Panera Bread's conference call to discuss its 4th Quarter and full-year 2015 earning and performance, February 10, 2016, **www.seekingalpha.com** (accessed February 13, 2016).
[7] Ibid.
[8] Annie Gasparro, "A New Test for Panera's Pay-What-You-Can," *The Wall Street Journal*, June 4, 2013, **www.wsj.com** (accessed March 7, 2014).
[9] Ibid.
[10] Jim Salter, "Panera Suspends Latest Pay-What-You-Can Experiment in Stores," July 10, 2013, **www.huffingtonpost.com** (accessed March 7, 2014).
[11] Information posted at **www.paneracares.org** (accessed February 15, 2016).
[12] The statistical data in this section is based on information posted at **www.restaurant.org** (accessed February 21, 2016).
[13] Bureau of Labor Statistics, news release, September 3, 2015, **www.bls.gov** (accessed February 15, 2016).
[14] National Restaurant Industry, "2016 Restaurant Industry Pocket Factbook," **www.restaurant.org**, (accessed February 21, 2016).

CASE 14

Chipotle Mexican Grill in 2016: Can the Company Recover from Its *E. Coli* Disaster and Grow Customer Traffic Again?

connect

Arthur A. Thompson
The University of Alabama

Headed into August 2015, Chipotle (pronounced chi-POAT-lay) Mexican Grill's future looked rosy. Sales and profits in the first six months of 2015 were at record-setting levels, and expectations were that 2015 would be the company's best year ever, given the opening of over 200 new restaurants, ongoing enthusiasm for its menu offerings containing health-conscious and freshly prepared ingredients, and growing customer traffic at Chipotle's existing restaurant locations. But over the next five months, a series of events occurred that caught customers and Chipotle top executives by surprise.

- In August, a salmonella outbreak in Minnesota sickened 64 people who had eaten at a Chipotle Mexican Grill. The state's Department of Health later linked the illness to contaminated tomatoes served at the restaurant.
- In August, 80 customers and 18 employees at a Chipotle Mexican Grill in Southern California reported gastrointestinal symptoms of nausea, vomiting, and diarrhea that medical authorities and county health officials attributed to "norovirus." Norovirus is a highly contagious bug spread by contaminated food, improper hygiene, and contact with contaminated surfaces; the virus causes inflammation of the stomach or intestines, leading to stomach pain, nausea, diarrhea, and vomiting. After the reported food poisoning, the restaurant voluntarily closed, threw out all remaining food products, and sent home the affected employees. Employees who tested positive for norovirus remained off duty until they were cleared to return to work. County health officials also inspected the facility on two occasions and rendered passing grades, despite finding several minor violations. The restaurant reopened the following day, and no further food poisoning incidents occurred.
- In October, 55 people became ill from food poisoning after eating at 11 Chipotle locations in the Portland, Oregon, and Seattle, Washington, areas. Medical authorities attributed the illnesses to a strain of *E. coli* bacteria typically associated with contaminated food. Most ill people had eaten many of the same food items, but subsequent testing of the ingredients at the 11 Chipotle restaurants did not reveal any *E. coli* contamination. (When a restaurant serves foods with several ingredients that are mixed or cooked together and then used in multiple menu items, it is difficult for medical studies to pinpoint the specific ingredient or ingredients that might be contaminated.) A review of Chipotle's distribution records by state and federal regulatory officials was unable to identify a single food item or ingredient that could explain the outbreak. Nonetheless, out of an abundance of caution, Chipotle management

voluntarily closed all 43 Chipotle locations in the Portland and Seattle markets, pending a comprehensive review of the causes underlying the food contamination and a check of whether any of Chipotle's food suppliers were at fault. Chipotle management worked in close consultation and collaboration with state and federal health and food safety officials (including personnel from the Centers for Disease Control and Prevention (CDC), the U.S. Department of Agriculture's Food Safety and Inspection Service, and the U.S. Food and Drug Administration) throughout their investigation of the incident and also launched a massive internal effort review of the company's food preparation and food safety procedures. These internal actions included:

1. Confirming that more than 2,500 tests of Chipotle's food, restaurant surfaces, and equipment all showed no *E. coli.*
2. Confirming that no employees in the affected restaurants were sickened from the incident.
3. Expanding the testing of fresh produce, raw meat, and dairy items prior to restocking restaurants.
4. Implementing additional safety procedures, and audits, in all of its 2,000 restaurants to ensure that robust food safety standards were in place.
5. Working closely with federal, state, and local government agencies to further ensure that robust food safety standards were in place.
6. Replacing all ingredients in the closed restaurants.
7. Conducting additional deep cleaning and sanitization in all of its closed restaurants (and confirmed that the company would be conducting deep cleaning and sanitization additionally in all restaurants nationwide).

Meanwhile, the Federal Drug Administration sought to discover the sources of multiple widely distributed ingredients in an effort to identify a cause for the outbreak. The distribution path did not lead to an ingredient of interest. The FDA also conducted investigations of some suppliers, but did not find any evidence that those suppliers were the source of the outbreak. Ultimately, no food item was identified as causing the outbreak and no food item was ruled out as a cause, although fresh produce was suspected as the likely cause.

After health officials concluded it was safe to do so, all 43 restaurants in the Portland and Seattle markets reopened in late November 2015, roughly six weeks after the incident occurred.

- In early December 2015, five people in three states—Kansas (1), North Dakota (1), and Oklahoma (3)—became ill after eating at Chipotle Mexican Grill restaurants. Studies conducted by the CDC determined that all five people were infected with a rare strain of *E.coli* different from the infections in Oregon and Washington. However, investigators used sophisticated laboratory testing to determine that the DNA footprints of the illnesses in the Midwest were related to those in the Portland and Seattle areas.
- In mid-December 2015, about 120 Boston College students became ill after eating at a Chipotle Mexican Grill near the campus, an outbreak that local health officials attributed to a norovirus. Health officials also tested students for *E. coli* infections but the tests were negative.

Extensive reports of the last three incidents in the national media took a toll on customer traffic at most all Chipotle locations. Revenues at Chipotle restaurants dropped about 6.8 percent in the fourth quarter of 2015 compared to the fourth quarter of 2014; net income in the fourth quarter declined 44 percent compared to the same period a year earlier. The average decline in sales at Chipotle locations open at least twelve months was a stunning 14.6 percent in Q4 2015, after rising in the previous three quarters of 2015. The company's stock price crashed from an all-time high of $758 in early August 2015 to a low of $399 in early January 2016, although the stock price recovered to the $525 range in late February 2016 following a January announcement by the CDC that the prior food contamination and food safety issues at Chipotle were "over."

In announcing Chipotle's financial results for the fourth quarter of 2015 and full-year 2015 in February 2016, Steve Ells, founder, chair, and co-CEO of Chipotle Mexican Grill, laid out the measures Chipotle was taking to regain the confidence of customers and restore the appeal of dining at one of Chipotle's 2,000+ locations. Ells said:[1]

> The fourth quarter of 2015 was the most challenging period in Chipotle's history, but the Centers for Disease Control and Prevention has now concluded its investigation into the recent *E. coli* incidents associated with Chipotle. We are pleased to have this behind

> us and can place our full energies to implementing our enhanced food safety plan that will establish Chipotle as an industry leader in food safety. We are extremely focused on executing this program, which designs layers of redundancy and enhanced safety measures to reduce the food safety risk to a level as near to zero as is possible. By adding these programs to an already strong and proven food culture, we strongly believe that we can establish Chipotle as a leader in food safety just as we have become a leader in our quest for the very best ingredients we can find.

In the same announcement, Chipotle's co-CEO Monty Moran said:

> 2016 will be a very difficult year relative to our past performance. But, by staying true to our food culture and unique people culture, and layering on our rigorous food safety program, we are confident that we are now in a position to aggressively welcome customers into our restaurants and restore customer confidence in the things that make Chipotle great. With our full commitment to becoming an industry leader in food safety, and our continued focus on delivering an exceptional customer experience, we are confident that Chipotle will emerge as an even stronger company.

In February 2016, Chipotle shut all of its restaurants for a period of four hours to conduct food safety training for all store employees. That same day, in an effort to get customers back into its stores, Chipotle offered a free burrito to anyone who signed up on its website during certain hours. In mid-March 2016, Chipotle reported that January 2016 sales at Chipotle restaurants open at least 12 months fell by an average of 36.4 percent as compared to January 2015 and that February 2016 sales at these stores were 26.1 percent below the February 2015 level.[2] The company said it expected to report a $1 loss per share at best in the first quarter of 2016 (the company's first ever loss since becoming a public company in January 2006), compared to a net profit of $3.95 per share in the first quarter of 2015. To draw customers back into its stores, Chipotle further said it would be conducting mass mail-outs of coupons offering a free burrito, burrito, salad, or order of tacos as part of its marketing program for the first half of 2016.

Also in its mid-March 2016 announcement, Chipotle said it was considering stepping back from a couple of its earlier food safety changes.[3] One of these changes related to precooking beef before it arrived at restaurants in vacuum-sealed bags, where store employees would add spices to the bag without touching the meat, marinate it in refrigerators, and reheat it on a grill before putting it in containers for use on the serving line; furthermore, the spices were added to meat bags after stores closed to avoid any possible contamination with ingredients prepared in stores during the day. Previously, workers at Chipotle restaurants, wearing plastic gloves, transferred arriving raw beef and chicken to bowls, hand-rubbed the beef/chicken with adobo spices, and placed the bowls in refrigerators to let the meats marinate until they were cooked as needed for dishes being prepared on the serving line. The unspoken reason for abandoning the precooking of beef and reverting to the former procedures was thought to be complaints from customers that the precooked beef did not taste as good as when it came off the grill freshly cooked. Chipotle's principle points of differentiation from other restaurant chains had been its much-publicized use of fresh, natural ingredients and antibiotic-free, sustainably raised meats, coupled with in-store preparation and cooking of all dish ingredients—features that had spawned customer enthusiasm for eating at Chipotle restaurants. Management recognized that if customers were disappointed with the different taste of the beef dishes being prepared with the new techniques it would compound the problem of rejuvenating customer traffic to former levels.

Another procedural change being contemplated by Chipotle related to eliminating pathogen testing on certain ingredients, particularly beef sourced from Australia; such testing was costly and was thought by some Chipotle personnel to be an unnecessary food safety precaution. While Chipotle personnel investigating the fall 2015 food contamination problem suspected that the source of the *E. coli* was beef imported from Australia which somehow spread to other ingredients through cross-contamination.[4] Federal authorities had disagreed, saying that cross-contamination was unlikely because Chipotle's distribution records did not confirm Australian beef had been shipped to those restaurants where people reported becoming ill. Because Chipotle decided not to drop the Australian beef supplier, Chipotle had instituted pathogen testing for the imported beef as a precautionary measure.

Then in April 2016, Steve Ells's announcement of Chipotle's Q1 2016 performance contained some alarming numbers. Revenues of $834.5 million were 23.4 percent lower than the $1.09 billion reported in the first quarter of 2015. The company had a net loss of $26.4 million versus a net profit of $122.6 million in the prior year's first quarter. Sales at Chipotle restaurants open at least 12 months were down 29.7 percent; the average number of sales transactions at these restaurants was down 21.1 percent. He provided no guidance as to management's expectations what Chipotle's performance might be in the remaining three quarters of 2016.

CHIPOTLE MEXICAN GRILL'S EARLY YEARS

Steve Ells graduated from the Culinary Institute of America and then worked for two years at Stars Restaurant in San Francisco. Soon after moving to Denver, he began working on plans to open his own restaurant. Guided by a conviction that food served fast did not have to be low quality and that delicious food did not have to be expensive, he came up with the concept of Chipotle Mexican Grill. When the first Chipotle restaurant opened in Denver in 1993, it became an instant hit. Patrons were attracted by the experience of getting better-quality food served fast and dining in a restaurant setting that was more upscale and appealing than those of traditional fast-food enterprises. Over the next several years, Ells opened more Chipotle restaurants in Denver and other Colorado locations.

Ells's vision was "to change the way people think about and eat fast food." Taking his inspiration from features commonly found in many fine-dining restaurants, Ells's strategy for Chipotle Mexican Grill was predicated on six elements:

- Serving a focused menu of burritos, tacos, burrito bowls (a burrito without the tortilla) and salads.
- Using high-quality fresh ingredients and classic cooking methods to create great tasting, reasonably priced dishes prepared to order and ready to be served 1–2 minutes after they were ordered.
- Enabling customers to select the ingredients they wanted in each dish by speaking directly to the employees assembling the dish on the serving line.
- Creating an operationally efficient restaurant with an aesthetically pleasing interior.
- Building a special people culture comprised of friendly, high-performing people motivated to take good care of each customer and empowered to achieve high standards.
- Doing all of this with increasing awareness and respect for the environment and by using organically grown fresh produce and meats raised in a humane manner without hormones and antibiotics.

In 1998, intrigued by what it saw happening at Chipotle, McDonald's first acquired an initial ownership stake in the fledgling company, then acquired a controlling interest in early 2000. But McDonald's recognized the value of Ells's visionary leadership and kept him in the role of Chipotle's chief executive after it gained majority ownership. Drawing upon the investment capital provided by McDonald's and its decades of expertise in supply chain logistics, expanding a restaurant chain, and operating restaurants efficiently, Chipotle—under Ells's watchful and passionate guidance—embarked on a long-term strategy to open new restaurants and expand its market coverage. By year-end 2005, Chipotle had 489 locations in 24 states. As 2005 drew to a close, in somewhat of a surprise move, McDonald's top management determined that instead of continuing to parent Chipotle's growth, it would take the company public and give Chipotle management a free rein in charting the company's future growth and strategy. An initial public offering of shares was held in January 2006, and Steve Ells was designated as Chipotle's CEO and board chairman. During 2006, through the January IPO, a secondary offering in May 2006, and a tax-free exchange offer in October 2006, McDonald's disposed of its entire ownership interest in Chipotle Mexican Grill.

When Chipotle became an independent enterprise, Steve Ells and the company's other top executives kept the company squarely on a path of rapid expansion and continued to employ the same basic strategy elements that were the foundation of the company's success. Steve Ells functioned as the company's principal driving force for ongoing innovation and constant improvement. He pushed especially hard for new ways to boost "throughput"—the number of customers whose orders could be taken, prepared, and served per hour.[5] By 2012, Ells's mantra of "slow food, fast" had resulted in throughputs of 300 customers per hour at Chipotle's best restaurants.

During 2011–2015, Chipotle's revenues grew at a robust compound average rate of 18.7 percent. Net income grew at a compound rate of 19.4 percent, due not only to sales increases but also to improved operating efficiency that boosted profit margins. Growing customer visits and higher expenditures

EXHIBIT 1 Financial and Operating Highlights for Chipotle Mexican Grill, 2011–2015 (in 000s of dollars, except for per share items)

Income Statement Data	2015	2014	2013	2012	2011
Total revenue	$4,501,223	$4,108,269	$3,214,591	$2,731,224	$2,269,548
Food, beverage and packaging costs	1,503,835	1,420,994	1,073,514	891,003	738,720
As a % of total revenue	33.4%	34.6%	33.4%	32.6%	32.5%
Labor costs	1,045,726	904,407	739,800	641,836	543,119
As a % of total revenue	23.2%	22.2%	23.0%	23.5%	23.9%
Occupancy costs	262,412	230,868	199,107	171,435	147,274
As a % of total revenue	5.8%	5.6%	6.2%	6.3%	6.5%
Other operating costs	514,963	434,244	347,401	286,610	251,208
As a % of total revenue	11.4%	10.6%	10.8%	10.5%	11.1%
General and administrative expenses	250,214	273,897	203,733	183,409	149,426
As a % of total revenue	5.6%	6.7%	6.3%	6.7%	6.6%
Depreciation and amortization	130,368	110,474	96,054	84,130	74,938
Pre-opening costs	16,922	15,609	15,511	11,909	8,495
Loss on disposal of assets	13,194	6,976	6,751	5,027	5,806
Total operating expenses	3,737,634	3,397,469	2,681,871	2,275,359	1,918,986
Operating income	763,589	710,800	532,720	455,865	350,562
As a % of total revenue	17.0%	17.3%	16.6%	16.7%	15.5%
Interest and other income (expense) net	6,278	3,503	1,751	1,820	(857)
Income before income taxes	769,867	714,303	534,471	457,685	349,705
Provision for income taxes	(294,265)	(268,929)	(207,033)	(179,685)	(134,760)
Net income	$ 475,602	$ 445,374	$ 327,438	$ 278,000	$ 214,945
Earnings per share					
Basic	$15.30	$14.35	$ 10.58	$8.82	$6.89
Diluted	15.10	14.13	10.47	8.75	6.76
Weighted average common shares outstanding					
Basic	31,092	31,038	30,957	31,513	31,217
Diluted	31,494	31,512	31,281	31,783	31,775
Selected Balance Sheet Data					
Total current assets	$ 814,647	$ 859,511	$ 666,307	$ 546,607	$ 501,192
Total assets	2,725,066	2,527,317	2,009,280	1,668,667	1,425,308
Total current liabilities	279,942	245,710	199,228	186,852	157,453
Total liabilities	597,092	514,948	457,780	413,879	374,844
Total shareholders' equity	2,127,974	2,012,369	1,538,288	1,245,926	1,044,226
Other Financial Data					
Net cash provided by operating activities	$ 683,316	$ 682,067	$ 528,780	$ 419,963	$ 411,096
Capital expenditures	257,418	252,590	199,926	197,037	151,147
Restaurant Operations Data					
Restaurants open at year-end	2,010	1,783	1,595	1,410	1,230
Average annual sales for restaurants open at least 12 full calendar months	$2,424,000	$2,472,000	$2,169,000	$2,113,000	$2,013,000
Average annual sales increases at restaurants open at least 12 full calendar months	0.2%	16.8%	5.6%	7.1%	11.2%
Development and construction costs per newly-opened restaurant	$ 805,000	$ 843,000	$ 800,000	$ 800,000	$ 800,000

Source: Company 10-K report, 2015.

per customer visit drove average annual sales for Chipotle restaurants open at least 12 full calendar months from $1,085,000 in 2007 to $2,424,000 in 2015. The average check per customer ran $8 to $10 in 2011–2015. Exhibit 1 presents recent financial and operating data for Chipotle Mexican Grill.

CHIPOTLE MEXICAN GRILL IN 2016

Going into 2016, Chipotle operated 1,971 Chipotle restaurants in 46 states and the District of Columbia, as well as 11 in Canada, 7 in England, 4 in France, and 1 in Germany. Additionally, the company's restaurants included 13 ShopHouse Southeast Asian Kitchen restaurants, serving Asian-inspired cuisine, and Chipotle co-owned and operated 3 Pizzeria Locale restaurants, a fast-casual pizza concept, giving it a total of 2,010 restaurants. Chipotle management expected to open between 220 and 235 additional restaurants in 2016, including a small number of Chipotle restaurants outside the United States and ShopHouse and Pizzeria Locale restaurants within the United States.

Menu and Food Preparation

The menu at Chipotle Mexican Grill restaurants was quite limited—burritos, burrito bowls, tacos, and salads, plus soft drinks, fruit drinks, and milk. Except in restaurants where there were restrictions on serving alcoholic beverages, the drink options also included a selection of beers and margaritas. However, customers could customize their burritos, burrito bowls, tacos, and salads in hundreds of different ways. Options included four different meats or tofu, pinto beans or vegetarian black beans, brown or white rice tossed with lime juice and fresh-chopped cilantro, and a variety of such extras as sautéed peppers and onions, salsas, guacamole, sour cream, shredded cheese, lettuce, and tortilla chips seasoned with fresh lime and salt. In addition, it was restaurant policy to make special dishes for customers if the requested dish could be made from the ingredients on hand. Exhibit 2 shows some of the dishes served at Chipotle Mexican grill restaurants.

From the outset, Chipotle's menu strategy had been to keep it simple, do a few things exceptionally well, and not include menu selections (like coffee and desserts) that complicated store operations and impaired efficiency. While it was management's practice to consider menu additions, the menu offerings had remained fundamentally the same since the addition of burrito bowls in 2005 and tofu Sofritas (shredded organic tofu braised with chipotle chilis, roasted poblanos, and a blend of aromatic spices) as a meat alternative in 2013–2014. So far, Steve Ells had rejected the idea of adding a breakfast menu and opening earlier in the day.

The food preparation area of each restaurant was equipped with stoves and grills, pots and pans, and an assortment of cutting knives, wire whisks, and other kitchen utensils. There was a walk-in refrigerator stocked with ingredients, and supplies of herbs, spices, and dry goods such as rice. The work space more closely resembled the layout of the kitchen in a fine dining restaurant than the cooking area of typical fast food restaurant that made extensive use of automated cooking equipment and microwaves. Until the food contamination and food safety incidents in Q4 of 2015, all of the menu selections and optional extras were prepared from scratch in each Chipotle location—hours went into preparing food on-site, although some items were prepared from fresh ingredients in area commissaries. Kitchen crews used classic cooking methods: they marinated and grilled the chicken and steak, hand-cut produce and herbs, made fresh salsa and guacamole, and cooked rice in small batches throughout the day. While the food preparation methods were labor-intensive, the limited menu created efficiencies that helped keep costs down.

Food preparation methods at Chipotle's restaurants were overhauled in late 2015 in response to the food contamination incidents. The goal was to develop an industry-leading food safety program utilizing the assistance and recommendations of highly respected experts. Components of the new program included

- DNA-based testing of many ingredients to evaluate their quality and safety before they were shipped to Chipotle restaurants.
- Changes to food preparation and food handling practices, including washing and cutting some produce items (such as tomatoes and romaine lettuce) in central kitchens.
- Blanching of some produce items (including avocados, onions, jalapenos and citrus) in each restaurants before cutting them.
- New protocols for marinating meats.

EXHIBIT 2 Representative Dishes Served at Chipotle Mexican Grill Restaurants

© Chipotle Mexican Grill

- Utilizing the Food and Drug Administration's Hazard Analysis Critical Control Point (HACCP) management system to enhance internal controls relating to food safety.
- Instituting internal training programs to ensure that all employees thoroughly understand the company's newly imposed standards for food safety and food handling.
- Offering paid sick leave to employees to reduce incentives for employees to work while sick.
- Implementing stricter standards for food preparation, cleanliness, and food safety at all of the company's restaurants.
- Strengthening efforts to ensure that the company remained in full compliance with all applicable federal, state, and local food safety regulations.

Quality Assurance and Food Safety Chipotle's quality assurance department was charged with establishing and monitoring quality and food safety measures throughout the company's supply chain. There were quality and food safety standards for farms that grew ingredients used by company restaurants, approved suppliers, the regional distribution centers that purchased and delivered products to the restaurants, and frontline employees in the kitchen and on the serving lines at restaurants. The food safety programs for suppliers and restaurants were designed to ensure compliance with applicable federal, state, and local food safety regulations. Chipotle's training and risk management departments developed and implemented operating standards for food quality, preparation, cleanliness, and safety in company restaurants.

Chipotle's Commitment to "Food With Integrity"

In 2003–2004, Chipotle began a move to increase its use of organically grown local produce, organic beans, organic dairy products, and meats from animals that were raised in accordance with animal welfare standards and were never given feeds containing non-therapeutic antibiotics and growth hormones to speed weight gain. This shift in ingredient usage was part of a long-term management campaign to use top-quality, nutritious ingredients and improve "the Chipotle experience"—an effort that Chipotle designated as "Food With Integrity" and that top executives deemed critical to the company's vision of changing the way people think about and eat fast food. The thesis was that purchasing fresh ingredients and preparing them daily by hand in each restaurant were not enough.

To implement the Food With Integrity initiative, the company began working with experts in the areas of animal ethics to try to support more humane farming environments, and it started visiting the farms and ranches from which it obtained meats and fresh produce. It also began investigating using more produce supplied by farmers who respected the environment, avoided use of chemical fertilizers and pesticides, followed U.S. Department of Agriculture standards for growing organic products, and used agriculturally sustainable methods like conservation tillage methods that improved soil conditions and reduced erosion. Simultaneously, efforts were made to source a greater portion of products locally (within 350 miles of the restaurants where they were used) while in season. The transition to using organically grown local produce and naturally raised meats occurred gradually because it took time for Chipotle to develop sufficient sources of supply to accommodate the requirements of its growing number of restaurant locations. But substantial progress had been made. By year-end 2011, all of the sour cream and cheese Chipotle purchased was made from milk that came from cows that were not given rBGH (recombinant bovine growth hormone). The milk used to make much of the purchased cheese and a portion of the purchased sour cream was sourced from dairies that provided pasture access for their cows rather than housing them in confined spaces. Meats that were raised without the use of non-therapeutic antibiotics or added hormones and met other Chipotle standards were branded and promoted as "Responsibly Raised." In 2015, Chipotle completed a two-year initiative to stop using ingredients grown with genetically modified seeds in all of its dishes—to the extent that was possible. The naturally raised meats Chipotle used were still being raised on animal feeds containing grains that were genetically modified, and many of the branded beverages Chipotle served contained corn-based sweeteners typically made with genetically modified corn.

However, Chipotle faced ongoing challenges in *always* using organic products, locally grown produce, and naturally raised meats in *all* menu items at *all* of its restaurant locations. Despite the fact that growing numbers of farmers were entering into the production of these items and supplies were on the upswing, buyer demand was also rising rapidly. Consumer purchases of these items at their local farmers markets and supermarkets were growing swiftly, and mounting numbers of chefs at fine-dining establishments were incorporating organic and locally grown produce and natural meats into their dishes. Moreover, the costs incurred by organic farmers and the growers of naturally raised meats were typically higher. Organically grown crops often took longer to grow and crop yields were usually smaller. Growth rate and weight gain was typically lower for chickens, cattle, and pigs that were fed only vegetarian diets containing no antibiotics and for cattle that were not given growth hormones. Hence, the prices of organically grown produce and naturally raised meats were not only higher but also creeping upward because of supplier struggles to keep up with rising demand. Consequently, when periodic supply–demand imbalances for one ingredient or another produced market conditions where certain organic locally grown products and natural meats were either unavailable or prohibitively high-priced, some Chipotle restaurants temporarily reverted—*in the interest of preserving the company's reputation for providing great food* ***at reasonable prices*** *and protecting profit margins*—to the use of conventional products until supply conditions and prices improved. When certain Chipotle restaurants were forced to serve conventionally raised meat, it was company practice to disclose this temporary change on signage in each affected restaurant so that customers could avoid those meats if they choose to do so.

Despite the attendant price-cost challenges and supply chain complications, Chipotle executives were firmly committed to continuing the Food With Integrity initiative going forward. They felt it was very important for Chipotle to be a leader in responding to and acting on mounting consumer concerns about food nutrition, where their food came from, how fruits and vegetables were grown, and how animals used for meat were raised. And they definitely wanted customers to view Chipotle Mexican Grill as a place that used high-quality, "better for you" ingredients in its dishes. Given the record of growth in customer traffic at Chipotle restaurants, notwithstanding the recent food poisoning incidents, Chipotle executives believed the company could cope with the likelihood organic and natural meat ingredients would remain more expensive than conventionally raised, commodity-priced equivalents. Over the longer term, they anticipated the price volatility and shortages of organically grown ingredients and natural meats would gradually dissipate as growing demand for such products attracted more small farmers and larger agricultural enterprises to boost supplies.

Serving Orders Quickly

One of Chipotle's biggest innovations had been creating the ability to have a customer's order ready quickly. As customers moved along the serving line, they selected which ingredients they wanted in their burritos, burrito bowls, tacos, and salads by speaking directly to the employees that prepared the food and were assembling the order behind the counter. Much experimentation and fine-tuning had gone into creating a restaurant layout and serving line design that made the food-ordering and dish-creation process intuitive and time-efficient, thereby enabling a high rate of customer throughput. The throughput target was at least 200 and up to 300 customers per hour, in order to keep the numbers of customers waiting in line at peak hours to a tolerable minimum. Management was focused on further improving the speed at which customers moved through the service line in all restaurants, so that orders placed by fax, online, or via smartphone ordering apps could be accommodated without slowing service to in-store customers and compromising the interactions between customers and crew members on the service line. The attention to serving orders quickly was motivated by management's belief that while customers returned because of the great-tasting food they also liked their orders served fast without having a "fast-food" experience (even when they were not in a hurry). Delivery service was also offered in many areas through a number of third party services with whom the company had partnered.

Catering

In January 2013, Chipotle introduced an expanded catering program to help spur sales at its restaurants. The rollout began in the company's Colorado restaurants and was available at every Chipotle Mexican Grill, except those in New York City, in 2014. The program involved setting up a portable version of its service line for groups of 20 to 200 people; guests could create tacos and bowls with either two or three meat choices (including vegan Sofritas), fajita veggies, white and brown rice, black and pinto beans, four salsas, cheese, sour cream, guacamole, lettuce, chips, and soft flour and crispy corn tortillas. For customers wanting to accommodate a smaller group of 6 or more people, Chipotle offered a Burritos by the Box option with a choice of meat, Sofritas, or grilled veggies (or an assortment of these) plus white or brown rice, black beans, and cheese; with each two burritos, a bag of chips, tomatillo-green chili salsa, guacamole, and sour cream was included.

SUPPLY CHAIN MANAGEMENT PRACTICES

Top executives were acutely aware that m aintaining high levels of food quality in its restaurants depended in part on acquiring high-quality, fresh ingredients and other necessary supplies that met company specifications. Over the years, the company had developed long-term relationships with a number of reputable food industry suppliers that could meet Chipotle's quality standards and understood the importance of helping Chipotle live up to its Food With Integrity mission. It then worked with these suppliers on an ongoing basis to establish and implement a set of forward, fixed and formula pricing protocols for determining the prices that suppliers charged Chipotle for various items. Reliable suppliers that could meet Chipotle's quality specifications and were willing to comply with Chipotle's set of forward, fixed, and formula-pricing protocols and guidelines for certain products were put on Chipotle's list of approved suppliers. Chipotle was constantly working to increase the number of approved suppliers for ingredients subject to volatile prices and short supplies. In addition, Chipotle personnel diligently monitored industry news, trade issues, weather, exchange rates, foreign demand, crises and other world events so as to better anticipate potential impacts on ingredient prices.

Instead of making purchases directly from approved suppliers, Chipotle utilized the services of 24 independently owned and operated regional distribution centers to purchase and deliver ingredients and other supplies to Chipotle restaurants. These distribution centers were required to make all purchases from Chipotle's list of approved suppliers in accordance with the agreed-upon pricing guidelines and protocols.

RESTAURANT MANAGEMENT AND OPERATIONS

Chipotle's strategy for operating its restaurants was based on the principle that "the front line is key." The restaurant and kitchen designs intentionally placed most store personnel up front where they could speak to customers in a personal and hospitable manner, whether preparing food items or customizing the dish ordered by a customer moving along the service line. The open kitchen design allowed customers to see employees preparing and cooking ingredients, reinforcing that Chipotle's food was freshly made each day. Store personnel, especially those who prepared dishes on the serving line were expected to deliver a customer-pleasing experience "one burrito at a time," give each customer individual attention, and make every effort to respond positively to customer requests and suggestions. Special effort was made to hire and retain people who were personable and could help deliver a positive customer experience. Management believed that creating a positive and interactive experience helped build loyalty and enthusiasm for the Chipotle brand not only among customers but among the restaurant's entire staff.

Restaurant Staffing and Management

Each Chipotle Mexican Grill typically had a general manager (a position top management characterized as the most important in the company), an apprentice manager (in about 75 percent of the restaurants), 1 to 3 hourly service managers, 1 or 2 hourly kitchen managers, and an average of 23 full and part-time crew members. Busier restaurants had more crew members. Chipotle generally had two shifts at its restaurants, which simplified scheduling and facilitated assigning hourly employees with a regular number of work hours each week. Most employees were cross-trained to work at a variety of stations, both to provide people with a variety of skills and to boost labor efficiency during busy periods. Personnel were empowered to make decisions within their assigned areas of responsibility.

One of Chipotle's top priorities was to build and nurture a people-oriented, performance-based culture in each Chipotle restaurant; executive management believed that such a culture led to the best possible experience for both customers and employees. The foundation of that culture started with hiring good people to manage and staff the company's restaurants. One of the prime functions of a restaurant's general manger was to hire and retain crew members who had a strong work ethic, took pride in preparing food items correctly, enjoyed interacting with other people, exhibited enthusiasm in serving customers, and were team players in striving to operate the restaurant in accordance with the high standards expected by top management. A sizable number of Chipotle's crew members had been attracted to apply for a job at Chipotle because of either encouragement from an acquaintance who worked at Chipotle or their own favorable impressions of the work atmosphere while going through the serving line and dining at a Chipotle Mexican Grill. New crew members received hands-on, shoulder-to-shoulder training. In 2015, full-time crew members had average earnings of nearly $28,000 (regular compensation and bonuses, plus benefits for clothes, meals, insurance, and 401(k) contributions).[6] Total compensation averaged $33,000 for kitchen managers, $38,000 for service managers, $53,000 for apprentice managers, and $67,000 for general managers.

Top-performing store personnel could expect to be promoted because of the company's unusually heavy reliance on promotion from within—about

84 percent of salaried managers and about 97 percent of hourly managers had been promoted from positions as crew members. In several instances, a newly hired crew member had risen rapidly through the ranks and become the general manager of a restaurant in 9 to 12 months; many more high-performing crew members had been promoted to general managers within 2–4 years. The long-term career opportunities for Chipotle employees were quite attractive because of the company's rapid growth and the speed with which it was opening new stores in both new and existing markets.

The Position and Role of Restaurateur

The general managers who ran high-performing restaurants and succeeded in developing a strong, empowered team of hourly managers and crew members were promoted to restaurateur, a position that entailed greater leadership and culture-building responsibility. In addition to continuing to run their assigned restaurant, restaurateurs were typically given responsibility for mentoring one or more nearby restaurants and using their leadership skills to help develop the managers and building high-performing teams at the restaurants they mentored. At year-end 2013, Chipotle had over 400 restaurateurs overseeing nearly 40 percent of the company's Chipotle restaurants, including their home restaurant and others that they mentored. The average salary of Chipotle restaurateurs was $133,000 in 2015. Restaurateurs could earn bonuses up to $23,000 for their people development and team-building successes and for creating a culture of high standards, constant improvement, and empowerment in each of their restaurants. Restaurateurs whose mentoring efforts resulted in high-performing teams at four restaurants and the promotion of at least one of the four restaurant managers to restaurateur could be promoted to the position of apprentice team leader and become a full-time member of the company's field support staff.

Chipotle's field support system included apprentice team leaders, team leaders or area managers, team directors, executive team directors or regional directors, and restaurant support officers—over 100 of the people in these positions in 2014–2015 were former restaurateurs. In 2014, over two-thirds of Chipotle's restaurants were under the leadership and supervision of the company's 500 existing and former restaurateurs. The principal task of field support personnel was to foster a culture of employee empowerment, high standards, and constant improvement in each of Chipotle's restaurants. One of Chipotle's field support staff members had been hired as a crew member in 2003, promoted to general manager in 12 months, and—8 years after starting with Chipotle—was appointed as a team director (with responsibilities for 57 restaurants and 1400+ employees).[7]

A New Diagnostic and Planning Tool for Field Support Personnel

In 2013, Chipotle brought its entire field support team together for the purposes of (1) establishing clear expectations of what they were supposed to accomplish and (2) introducing a new restaurant diagnostic and planning tool developed by the company's co-CEO, Monty Moran. The tool was designed to help field leaders more effectively recognize what was keeping a restaurant general manager from achieving restaurateur status and to develop a clear plan of action to help general managers become a restaurateur more quickly. Use of the tool required field leaders to visit their restaurants, interview all crew members, determine the degree to which the restaurant had a team of empowered top performers, identify the root causes of weaker-than-desired financial and operating performance, create a corrective action plan, go over the plan with the restaurant's general manager, and indicate how they planned to help the general manager on an ongoing basis. Field leaders followed up each quarter to conduct more interviews, gauge progress, and create an updated plan, watching closely to see how the restaurant team was evolving and developing toward becoming a restaurateur-caliber team.

Monty Moran believed the new tool was producing tangible benefits:[8]

> In using the tool, our field leaders become aware of a great deal of information, including the strength of the team, the depth of the people pipeline to be sure the restaurant has the right people in place for continued development, the training systems that are in place, the scheduling, the financial metrics, and how well the restaurant is implementing the four pillars of great [customer] throughput [on the serving line].
>
> We're hearing over and over how excited managers are to have this tool in place. For nearly all of our restaurants, this tool is providing a new level of understanding as to our expectations and giving clear

direction to our GMs about how to become restaurateurs by taking some of the mystery out of what it takes to build this special culture. As of now, all of our non-restaurateur restaurants have plans in place to put them on the road to restaurateur, and our field teams will create new plans for each restaurant every quarter.

There was solid evidence that the new diagnostic and planning tool was delivering dividends: management reported that during the fourth quarter of 2013 customer throughput on the service line at Chipotle restaurants increased by an average of six transactions during the peak lunch hour and by an average of five transactions during the peak dinner hour.

MARKETING

Chipotle executives believed that word-of-mouth publicity from customers telling others about their favorable experiences at Chipotle restaurants was the most powerful marketing of all. But they also recognized the need to introduce the Chipotle brand to new customers and emphasize what made Chipotle different than other restaurants. Over the past 10 years, Chipotle had generated considerable media coverage from scores of publications that had largely favorable articles describing Chipotle's food, restaurant concept, and business; the company had also been featured in a number of television programs.

Marketing personnel paid close attention to presenting the Chipotle brand consistently and keeping advertising and promotional programs and in-store communications closely aligned with who Chipotle was, what the Chipotle experience was all about, and what differentiated Chipotle from other fast-food competitors. When Chipotle opened restaurants in new markets, it initiated a range of promotional activities to introduce Chipotle to the local community and to create interest in the restaurant. In markets where there were existing Chipotle restaurants, newly opened restaurants typically attracted customers in volumes at or near market averages without having to initiate special promotions or advertising to support a new opening.

Chipotle's advertising mix typically included print, outdoor, transit, theaters, radio, and online ads. In 2012, Chipotle Mexican Grill ran its first-ever national TV commercial during the broadcast of the Grammy Awards. The company had also run an ad campaign featuring its catering program. Over the past several years, the company had increased its use of digital, mobile, and social media in its overall marketing mix because it gave customers greater opportunity to access Chipotle in ways that were convenient for them and broadened Chipotle's ability to engage with its customers individually.

Chipotle management was well aware that such topics as the safety of ingredients grown with genetically modified seeds, the pros and cons of organically grown fruits and vegetables, why people ought to consider eating meats that come from animals raised humanely and without the use of antibiotics, the benefits of eating nutritious foods, and why Chipotle was deeply committed to its Food With Integrity mission were dimly understood by some customers and unfamiliar to or unappreciated by a big fraction of its customers. In 2013–2015, Chipotle created marketing programs to make people more curious about these food-related issues in the belief that the more they learned the more likely they would patronize Chipotle Mexican Grill locations. In 2013, Chipotle introduced its Scarecrow marketing program which included a three-minute animated short film and a game for iPads and iPhones aimed at sparking conversation about issues in industrial food production. *The Scarecrow* film had been viewed online nearly 12 million times as of early 2014, and the companion game has been downloaded nearly 600,000 times. Resulting discussions about these food issues had generated 500 million media impressions through news coverage of the program—a volume of coverage that Chipotle management believed would cost some $5 million to purchase as advertising.[9]

Continuing in the tradition of Scarecrow, Chipotle then launched "Farmed and Dangerous," an original scripted comedy series that consisted of four 30-minute episodes focusing on the introduction of a new petroleum-based animal feed created by Animoil, a fictional agribusiness company. The series used entertaining satire intended to make people more curious about their food and how it was produced. The success of the Scarecrow and Farmed and Dangerous initiatives prompted the company to step up the development of new video, music, and content programs, increasing its participation in local community events and conducting what the company called "Cultivate" festivals featuring food, music and information about healthy foods, organic agriculture, and the overuse of antibiotics in livestock farming. Cultivate festivals had been held in Chicago, San Francisco, Dallas, and Minneapolis, drawing total audiences exceeding 120,000 and reaching a much bigger audience with the attendant advertising and public relations activities. Executive management believed these newer marketing efforts allowed the company to forge stronger emotional connections with customers and communicate its story better and with more nuance than it could do through traditional advertising.

Chipotle's advertising and marketing costs totaled $69.3 million in 2015, versus $57.3 million in 2014, $44.4 million in 2013, $35.0 million in 2012, and $31.9 million in 2011 (these costs are included in "Other operating costs" in Exhibit 1).

In 2016, as Chipotle worked to reinvigorate the Chipotle Mexican Grill brand in the wake of the food safety-related incidents that occurred in the fourth quarter of 2015, management intended to place greater emphasis than usual on marketing campaigns that were specifically designed to drive traffic into its restaurants. An element of its 2016 marketing and communications efforts also focused on helping customers understand the changes Chipotle had recently made to establish the company as an industry leader in food safety.

RESTAURANT SITE SELECTION

Chipotle had an internal team of real estate mangers that devoted substantial time and effort to evaluating potential locations for new restaurants; from time to time, the internal team sought the assistance of external brokers with expertise in specific local markets. The site selection process entailed studying the surrounding trade area, demographic and business information within that area, and available information on competitors. In addition, advice and recommendations were solicited from external real estate brokers with expertise in specific markets. Locations proposed by the internal real estate team were visited by a team of operations and development management as part of a formal site ride; the team toured the surrounding trade area, reviewed demographic and business information on the areas, and evaluated the food establishment operations of competitors. Based on this analysis, along with the results of predictive modeling based on proprietary formulas, the company came up with projected sales and targeted returns on investment for a new location. Chipotle Mexican Grills had proved successful in a number of different types of locations, including in-line or end-cap locations in strip or power centers, regional malls, downtown business districts, freestanding buildings, food courts, outlet centers, airports, military bases, and train stations.

DEVELOPMENT AND CONSTRUCTION COSTS FOR NEW RESTAURANTS

The company's average development and construction costs per restaurant decreased from about $850,000 in 2009 to around $800,000 in 2011, 2012, and 2013 (see Exhibit 1), chiefly because of cost savings realized from building more lower-cost A Model restaurants and growing use of its new, simpler restaurant design. However, the costs of new openings jumped to an average of $843,000 in 2014, due to opening more freestanding restaurants (which were more expensive than end-caps and in-line sites in strip centers) and opening proportionately more sites in the northeastern United Sates where construction costs (and also sales volumes) were typically higher. Construction and development costs for new store openings in 2015 dropped to $805,000 and were expected to remain about the same in 2016. Exhibit 3 shows the interiors and exteriors of several Chipotle Mexican Grills.

Total capital expenditures were expected to be about $260 million in 2016, the big majority of which was for opening the planned 220–235 new stores. Capital expenditures in prior years are shown in Exhibit 1. Chipotle's chief financial officer expected that the company's annual cash flows from operations, together with current cash on hand, would be adequate to meet ongoing capital expenditures, working capital requirements, planned repurchases of common stock, and other cash needs for the foreseeable future.

THE SHOPHOUSE SOUTHEAST ASIA KITCHEN CONCEPT

Beginning in 2011, Ells launched a strategic initiative to begin testing and refining a second restaurant concept, ShopHouse Southeast Asian Kitchen. Ells believed that the fundamental principles on which Chipotle Mexican Grill restaurants were based—finding the very best sustainably raised ingredients, prepared and cooked using classical methods in front

EXHIBIT 3 Representative Interiors and Exteriors of Chipotle Mexican Grills

of the customer, and served in an interactive format by special people dedicated to providing a great dining experience—could be adapted to other cuisines. To test the Chipotle model with different ingredients and a different style of food, the company opened its first ShopHouse Southeast Asian Kitchen on DuPont Circle in Washington, D.C., in September 2011. In 2012–2015, Chipotle continued to refine the ShopHouse menu and restaurant designs and gauge customer response to the ShopHouse offering. By year-end 2015, there were 13 ShopHouse locations.

ShopHouse served a focused menu consisting of rice bowls, noodle bowls, or salad made with a choice of grilled steak, grilled chicken satay, pork and chicken meatballs, or organic tofu. In addition, rice bowls, noodle bowls, and salads included a choice of three vegetables (charred corn with garlic and sesame, green beans with roasted chili jam and crispy shallots, or squash with garlic, chilies, and Thai basil), a sauce (red or green curry, peanut sauce, or tamarind vinaigrette), garnishes (green papaya slaw, assorted pickled vegetables, and fresh cilantro and Thai basil), and toppings (toasted rice, crispy garlic, crushed peanuts, and fiery crushed chilies). Customers could have their dishes made anywhere from mega-spicy to mild. The flavors were a blend of Thai, Vietnamese, and Malaysian. As was the case at Chipotle, customers moved along a cafeteria-style line, with servers behind the counter customizing each order; there was room for seating or customers could have orders readied for take-out.

CHIPOTLE'S THIRD RESTAURANT CONCEPT—PIZZERIA LOCALE

In December 2013, Chipotle announced it was partnering with two Colorado restaurateurs to launch a fast-casual pizza restaurant concept called Pizzeria Locale that incorporated the Chipotle model. Seven months earlier, Chipotle and the two restaurateurs had partnered to open the first Pizzeria Locale in Denver; it featured a focused menu with a selection of classic pizzas and build-your-own pizzas using high-quality ingredients. The pizzas were then fired in a special Chipotle-designed, high-temperature pizza oven that baked the pizzas in less than 2 minutes and delivered results like an Italian wood-burning oven. The menu also included salads, meatballs, sliced-to-order prosciutto, a caramel chocolate pudding, beer, red and white wines on tap, and an assortment of nonalcoholic beverages. Three Pizzeria Locale locations were operating in Denver at year-end 2015.

Co-CEO Steve Ells said the following about the speed with which the company could open larger numbers of Shophouse and Pizzeria Locale restaurants, once he was satisfied that the Shophouse and Pizzeria Locale concepts had been "perfected":[10]

> When we are ready to expand at a faster rate, we certainly have the infrastructure in place. . . . [W]e have so much information on 1,600 specific sites now in the U.S. with Chipotles, and so we know exactly what regions, what markets, what intersections we would want to go to with these new concepts.

Part of Chipotle's stock price in early 2016 (while down from much higher levels, but still considered lofty by many investors) was predicated on investors' belief that the company had long-term potential not only to open hundreds more Chipotle restaurants but also to open 1,500 or more domestic locations of both ShopHouse and Pizzeria Locale restaurants—as well as hundreds of international restaurants for all three concepts, in which case Chipotle was likely to hit a second home run in fast-casual dining with ShopHouse and yet a third casual-dining home run with Pizzeria Locale, a rare and unusual feat for a relatively young company hopefully still rounding the bases on its first fast-casual dining home run concept.

In 2016, quick-fired, custom-order gourmet pizza restaurants were quickly spreading nationwide, with over 300 units in operation. At least two dozen enterprises—all very small compared to Chipotle—were opening multiple locations featuring build-your-own pizzas concept; the menus consisted of artisan and gourmet pizzas with a variety of crust options and premium toppings that were baked in high-temperature ovens and ready to serve in around 3 minutes. Restaurant industry analysts speculated that the custom-built, quick-fired gourmet pizza category was very likely to lead the restaurant industry in percentage sales growth and unit expansion in the next three to five years and quickly evolve into the next big, fast-growing fast-casual restaurant category.[11]

In late March 2016, Chipotle filed a trademark application for the term "Better Burgers." A company official commented, "It's a growth seed idea we are exploring."[12]

COMPETITION AND INDUSTRY TRENDS

Restaurant industry sales were forecast to be a record-high $783 billion in 2016 at over 1.1 million food establishments in the United States; the forecast represented a compound average growth rate of 4.9 percent since 2010.[13] According to survey data reported in the National Restaurant Association's *2016 Restaurant Industry Forecast,* 68 percent of consumers said they were more likely to visit a restaurant that offered locally produced food items; 70 percent said they were more likely to order more healthful options at restaurants than they were two years earlier; and 66 percent said they were more likely to eat a wider variety of ethnic cuisines than they did five years ago.

The restaurant industry was highly segmented by type of food served, number and variety of menu selections, price (ranging from moderate to very expensive), dining ambience (fast-food to casual dining to fine dining), level of service (place and pick up order at counter to full table service), and type of enterprise (locally owned, regional chain, or national chain). The number, size, and strength of competitors varied by region, local market area, and a particular restaurant's location within a given community. Competition among the various types of restaurants and foodservice establishments was based on such factors as type of food served, menu selection (including the availability of low-calorie and nutritional items), food quality and taste, speed and/or quality of service, price and value, dining ambience, name recognition and reputation, and convenience of location.

One category of restaurants was a hybrid called "fast-casual." Fast-casual restaurants—which included Chipotle Mexican Grill and its two closest competitors, Moe's Southwest Grill and Qdoba Mexican Grill—were perceived to have higher food quality, provide a slightly more upscale dining experience, and in some cases have enhanced service (like delivering orders to tables or even having full table service) as compared to "fast-food" or "quick-service" restaurants like McDonald's and Taco Bell. Fast-casual restaurant brands increased their collective annual sales by 12.8 percent to $30 billion in 2014. That growth was nearly twice that of any other restaurant segment, and fast-casual dining was expected to drive restaurant industry growth for years to come. Chipotle Mexican Grill was considered to be in the fast-casual category because of the fresh, high-quality ingredients in its dishes and because customers could customize their orders. Other chains considered to be in the fast-casual category included Panera Bread, Applebee's, Chili's, Cracker Barrel, Panda Express, Noodles & Company, Firehouse Subs, and Five Guys Burgers and Fries.

Like most enterprises in the away-from-home dining business, Chipotle had to compete for customers with national and regional quick-service, fast-casual, and casual dining restaurant chains, as well as locally owned restaurants and foodservice establishments. However, its closest competitors were the myriad of dining establishments that specialized in Mexican cuisine. The leading fast-food chain in the Mexican-style food category was Taco Bell. Chipotle's two biggest competitors in the fast-casual segment were Moe's Southwest Grill and Qdoba Mexican Grill. Other smaller chains, such as Baja Fresh (165 restaurants in 26 states) and California Tortilla (45 locations in 7 eastern states and District of Columbia), were also relevant competitors in those geographic locations where Chipotle also had restaurants. Below are brief profiles of Taco Bell, Moe's Southwest Grill, and Qdoba Mexican Grill.

Taco Bell

As of 2005, Taco Bell locations were struggling to attract customers. Throughout 2005–2011, the total number of Taco Bell restaurants, both domestically and internationally, declined as more underperforming locations were closed than new Taco Bell units were opened. In late 2011, Taco Bell's parent company, Yum! Brands, began a multiyear campaign to reduce company ownership of Taco Bell locations from 23 percent of total locations to about 16 percent; a total of 1,276 company-owned Taco Bell locations were sold to franchisees in 2010–2012. Yum! Brands also owned Pizza Hut and KFC (Kentucky Fried Chicken); the company sold its A&W All American and Long John Silver's brands in December 2011.

To counter stagnant sales and begin a strategy to rejuvenate Taco Bell, during 2010–2011 Taco Bell restaurants began rolling out a new taco with a Doritos-based shell called Doritos Locos Taco, which management termed a "breakthrough product designed to reinvent the taco." The launch was supported with an aggressive advertising campaign to inform the public about the new Doritos Locos Taco. The effort was considered a solid success, driving record sales of 375 million tacos in one year. In March 2012, Taco Bell began introducing a new Cantina Bell menu, a group of upgraded products conceptualized by celebrity Miami chef Lorena Garcia that included such ingredients and garnishes as black beans, cilantro rice, and corn salsa.[14] The new Cantina Bell menu items had undergone extensive testing in select geographic areas. In addition to the upscaled Cantina Bell selections, Taco Bell also introduced several new breakfast selections. According to Taco Bell president, Greg Creed, it was Taco Bell's biggest new product launch ever.

The upscaled menu at Taco Bell was a competitive response to growing consumer preferences for the higher-caliber, made-to-order dishes they could get at fast-casual Mexican-food chains like Chipotle, Moe's, and Qdoba. Taco Bell's new Cantina Bell items were priced below similar types of Chipotle products—the average ticket price for the new Cantina Bell selections was about $4.50 (compared to averages of $7.00 to $9.00 for meals at Chipotle, Moe's, and Qdoba). The rollout of the Cantina Bell menu was supported with a new slogan and brand campaign. Within a few months, it was clear that the new tacos and Cantina Bell menu selections were boosting customer traffic and sales at Taco Bell locations. In 2012–2013 expansion of Taco Bell locations resumed, with the vast majority of the new additions being franchised.

Going into 2016, Taco Bell had 6,400 company-owned, franchised, and licensed restaurant locations mostly in the United States, up from 6,200 at year-end 2014. About 86 percent of Taco Bell's locations were either franchised (80 percent) or licensed (6 percent) at year-end 2015. Management expected to grow Taco Bell to about 8,000 locations over the next five years or so. Systemwide sales at Taco Bell were $6.3 billion in 2015, equal to average sales per location of almost $1 million. Sales at Taco Bell restaurants systemwide open at least 12 months grew 8 percent in 2015, up from 4 percent in 2014. Taco Bell's mobile app had been downloaded over 3 million times. Taco Bell's 2016 menu contained 16 versions of tacos, 15 versions of burritos, 19 specialty items (including a newly introduced quesalupa, quesadillas, gorditas, chalupas, nachos, taco salads, Mexican pizza, and rollups), and 22 combos—all could be customized to order). In early 2016, Taco Bell launched a $1 morning value breakfast menu featuring 10 items.

Moe's Southwest Grill

Moe's Southwest Grill was founded in Atlanta, Georgia, in 2000 and acquired in 2007 by Atlanta-based FOCUS Brands, an affiliate of Roark Capital, a private equity firm. FOCUS Brands was a global franchisor and operator of over 4,500 ice cream shops, bakeries, restaurants and cafés under the brand names Carvel®, Cinnabon®, Schlotzsky's®, Moe's Southwest Grill®, Auntie Anne's, and McAlister's Deli®. Moe's currently serves the most awesome southwest fare at more than 500 locations in the United States and abroad. In 2015, there were more than 600 fast-casual Moe's Southwest Grill locations in 37 states and the District of Columbia. All Moe's locations were franchised. Average annual sales at Moe's locations were an estimated $1.1 million.

The menu at Moe's featured burritos, quesadillas, tacos, nachos, burrito bowls (with meat selections of chicken, pork, or tofu), and salads with a choice of two homemade dressings. Main dishes could be customized with a choice of 20 items that included a choice of protein (sirloin steak, chicken breast, pulled pork, ground beef, or organic tofu); grilled peppers, onions, and mushrooms; black olives; cucumbers; fresh chopped or pickled jalapenos; pico de gallo (handmade fresh daily); lettuce; and 6 salsas. There was a kids' menu and vegetarian, gluten-free, and low-calorie options, as well as a selection of five side items (including queso and guacamole), two desserts (cookie or brownie), soft drinks, iced tea, and bottled water. All meals were served with chips and salsa. Moe's used high quality ingredients, including all natural, cage-free, white breast meat chicken; steroid-free, grain-fed pulled pork; 100 percent grass-fed sirloin steak; and organic tofu. No dishes included trans fats or MSG (monosodium glutamate—a flavor enhancer), and no use was made of microwaves.

Moe's provided catering services; the catering menu included a fajitas bar, a taco bar, a salad bar, three sizes of burritos, a burrito box meal, and a selection of dips, cookies, and drinks. At some locations, customer orders could be taken online.

The company and its franchisees emphasized friendly hospitable service. When customers entered a Moe's location, it was the practice for employees to do a "Welcome to Moe's!" shout-out.

Qdoba Mexican Grill

The first Qdoba Mexican Grill opened in Denver in 1995. Rapid growth ensued and in 2003 the company was acquired by Jack in the Box, Inc., a large operator and franchisor of 2,250 Jack in the Box quick-service restaurants best known for its hamburgers. Jack in the Box had fiscal year 2015 revenues of $1.5 billion (the company's fiscal year was October 1 through September 30).[15]

In October 2015, there were 661 Qdoba restaurants in 47 states, the District of Columbia, and Canada, of which 322 were company-operated and 339 were franchise-operated; 19 underperforming company-owned Qdoba restaurants were closed during fiscal year 2015. However, management believed Qdoba had significant long-term growth potential—perhaps as many as 2,000 locations. A total of 17 new company-owned and 22 franchised Qdoba restaurants were opened in fiscal 2015 versus a net of 39 new Qdoba company owned and franchised locations in fiscal year 2014, 68 units in 2013, 44 units in 2012, and 129 units in fiscal 2009–2011. Plans for fiscal 2016 were to open 50 to 60 new company-owned and franchised restaurants.

In 2015, sales revenues at all company-operated and franchise-operated Qdoba restaurant locations averaged $1,169,000, compared to $1,017,000 in fiscal 2014, and $992,000 in fiscal 2011. Sales at all Qdoba restaurants open more than 12 months rose 9.3 percent in fiscal 2015, 6.0 percent in fiscal 2014, 0.8 percent in fiscal 2013, 2.4 percent in fiscal 2012, and 5.3 percent in fiscal 2011.

Menu Offerings and Food Preparation Qdoba Mexican Grill billed itself as an "artisanal Mexican kitchen" where dishes were handcrafted with fresh ingredients and innovative flavors by skilled cooks. The menu included burritos, tacos, taco salads, three-cheese nachos, grilled quesadillas, loaded tortilla soup, chips and dips, kids meals, and, at most locations, a variety of breakfast burritos and breakfast quesadillas. Burritos and tacos could be customized with choices of meats or just vegetarian ingredients and by adding three-cheese queso, guacamole, and a variety of sauces and salsas. Salads were served in a crunchy flour tortilla bowl with a choice of two meats, or vegetarian, and included black bean corn salsa and fat-free picante ranch dressing.

Orders were prepared in full view, with customers having multiple options to customize meals to their individual taste and nutritional preferences. Qdoba restaurants offered a variety of catering options that could be tailored to feed groups of five to several hundred. Most Qdoba restaurants operated from 10:30 AM to 10:00 PM and had seating capacity for 60 to 80 persons, including outdoor patio seating at many locations. The average check at company-operated restaurants in fiscal 2015 was $11.82.

Site Selection and New Restaurant Development Site selections for all new company-operated Qdoba restaurants were made after an economic analysis and a review of demographic data and other information relating to population density, traffic, competition, restaurant visibility and access, available parking, surrounding businesses, and opportunities for market penetration. Restaurants developed by franchisees were built to the parent company specifications on sites it had reviewed. Most Qdoba restaurants were located in leased spaces in conventional large-scale retail projects and food courts in malls, smaller neighborhood retail strip centers, on or near college campuses, and in airports. Development costs for new Qdoba restaurants typically ranged from $0.5 million to $1.5 million, depending on the geographic region and specific location.

Restaurant Management and Operations At Qdoba's company-owned restaurants, emphasis was placed on attracting, selecting, engaging and retaining people who were committed to creating long-lasting, positive impacts on operating results. The company's core development tool was a "Career Map" that provided employees with detailed education requirements, skill sets, and performance expectations by position, from entry level to area manager. High-performing general managers and hourly team members were certified to train and develop employees through a series of on-the-job and classroom training programs that focused on knowledge, skills, and behaviors. The Team Member Progression program within the Qdoba Career Map tool recognized and rewarded three levels of achievement for cooks and line servers who displayed excellence in their positions. Team members had to possess, or acquire, specific technical and behavioral skill sets to reach an achievement level. All restaurant personnel were expected to contribute to delivering a great guest experience in the company's restaurants.

There was a three-tier management structure for company-owned Qdoba restaurants. Restaurant managers were supervised by district managers, who were overseen by directors of operations, who reported to vice presidents of operations. Under Qdoba's performance system, vice presidents and directors were eligible for an annual incentive based on achievement of goals related to region level sales, profit, and companywide performance. District managers and restaurant managers were eligible for quarterly incentives based on growth in restaurant sales and profit and/or certain other operational performance standards.

Purchasing Distribution Beginning in March 2012, Qdoba and 90 percent of its franchisees entered into a five-year contract with an independent distributor to provide purchasing and distribution services for food ingredients and other supplies to Qdoba restaurants.

Advertising and Promotion The goals of Qdoba's advertising and marketing activities were to build brand awareness and generate customer traffic. Both company-owned and franchised restaurants contributed to a fund primarily used for producing and developing radio, print media, digital, and social media ads. Advertising was primarily done at the regional or local levels for both company and franchise owned and operated restaurants, and was determined by the local management.

ENDNOTES

[1] Company press release, February 2, 2016.
[2] Presentation to Bank of America Merrill Lynch Consumer Tech and Retail Conference, March 16 2016, **www.chipotle.com** (accessed March 25, 2016).
[3] Jesse Newman and Julie Jargon, "Chipotle Weighs Changing How It Handles Food," *The Wall Street Journal,* March 16, 2016, pp. B1–B2.
[4] Ibid., p. B2.
[5] David A. Kaplan, "Chipotle's Growth Machine," *Fortune,* September 26, 2011, p. 138.
[6] According to information posted in the careers section at **www.chipotle.com** (accessed February 18, 2012, May 13, 2013, and February 19, 2016).
[7] Ibid.
[8] *Chipotle Mexican Grill's CEO Discusses 2013 Results—Earnings Call Transcript,* January 30, 2014, **www.seekingalpha.com** (accessed February 8, 2014).
[9] Ibid.
[10] *Chipotle Mexican Grill's CEO Discusses 2013 Results—Earnings Call Transcript.*
[11] Alice Kelso, "Is Better Pizza the Next Fast Casual Category?" February 19, 2013, **www.fastcasual.com** (accessed February 12, 2014).
[12] Clark Schultz, "Chipotle Has Hamburger Plans," March 30, 2016, **www.seekingalpha.com** (accessed March 30, 2016).
[13] National Restaurant Association, *2014 Restaurant Industry Forecast* and "Fact at a Glance," **www.restaurant.org** (accessed February 12, 2014).
[14] Leslie Patton, "Taco Bell Sees Market Share Recouped with Chipotle Menu," *Bloomberg News,* January 11, 2012, **www.bloomberg.com** (accessed February 20, 2012).
[15] The statistics in this section are drawn from parent company Jack in the Box 2015 10-K report.

CASE 15

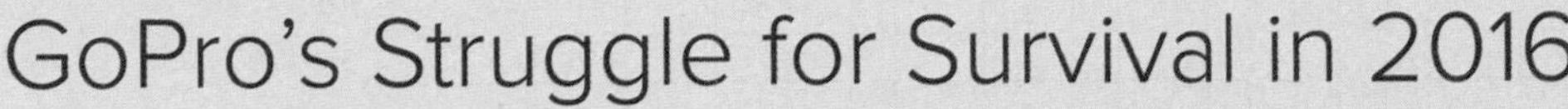

GoPro's Struggle for Survival in 2016

David L. Turnipseed
University of South Alabama

John E. Gamble
Texas A&M University–Corpus Christi

GoPro was among the best examples of how a company could create a new market based upon product innovations that customers understood and demanded. The company had grown from a humble beginning as a homemade camera tether and plastic case vendor in 2004 to an action camera vendor with $350,000 in sales in 2005 (its first full year of operation) to a global seller of consumer electronics with revenue of $1.6 billion in 2015. The company's shares had traded as high as $98 in October 2014, just months after its initial public offering (IPO) in June 2014. In 2014, GoPro was ranked number one most popular brand on YouTube with more than 640 million views, and an average of 845,000 views daily. In 2015, the average daily views were up to 1.01 million. Abruptly, in the third quarter of 2015, GoPro's magic disappeared and, by the fourth quarter of 2015, its revenues dropped by 31 percent from the prior year. In addition, its net income fell by 128 percent to a net loss of $34.5 million. By the end of December 2015, the stock traded at less than $20. A summary of the company's financial performance for 2011 through 2015 is presented in Exhibit 1.

GoPro's sales continued to slip in 2016. In mid-January, the company's stock was selling at less than the IPO price, and the company laid off 7 percent of its workforce. In early February, GoPro's stock traded below $10—see Exhibit 2. First quarter sales in 2016 were down 50 percent from the first quarter 2015 and 58 percent from the fourth quarter 2015. Net income had fallen from $16.8 million in the first quarter of

EXHIBIT 1 Financial Summary for GoPro, Inc., 2011–2015 (in thousands, except per share amounts)

Consolidated statements of operations data:	2015	2014	2013	2012	2011
Revenue	$1,619,971	$1,394,205	$985,737	$526,016	$234,238
Gross profit	673,214	627,235	361,784	227,486	122,555
Gross margin	41.8%	45.0%	36.7%	43.2%	52.3%
Operating income	54,748	187,035	98,703	53,617	38,779
Net income	36,131	128,088	60,578	32,262	24,612
Net income per share:					
Basic	$0.27	$1.07	$0.54	$0.07	$0.26
Diluted	$0.25	$0.92	$0.47	$0.07	$0.24

Source: GoPro, Inc. 2015 10-K.

EXHIBIT 2 GoPro's Stock Performance, June 2014–July 2016

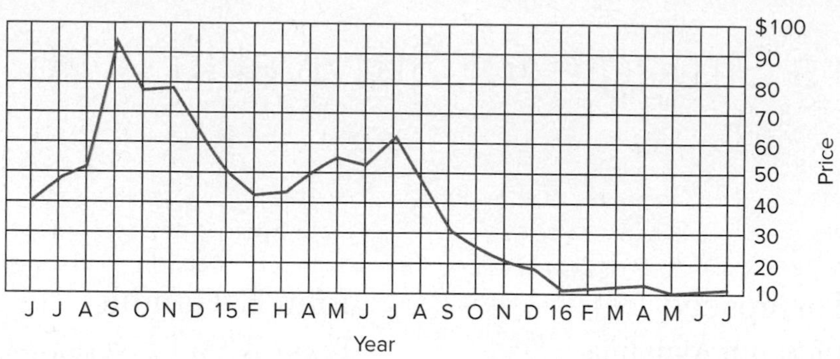

2015, to a loss of $107.5 million in the same period, 2016. The newly introduced HERO4 camera performed poorly and the company cut its price by half and reduced its product line to three cameras. The Karma camera drone, set for release in the first half of 2016, was inexplicably pushed back to winter, and there was no date for release of the HERO5 action camera. After the first quarter 2016 results were released, GoPro's stock dropped below $9. According to *Investor Place* (March 28, 2016), GoPro had essentially erased its once coveted title of Wall Street's darling and is now loathed by Wall Street.

Although continuing to be the market leader in action camera units sold, GoPro clearly had serious problems in mid-2016. Despite the problems, GoPro's management continued to be upbeat as it attempted to sell its action cameras in the stagnant niche. Its hopes were based on new acquisitions in mobile editing apps; a new sales, distribution, and equity partnership with Red Bull; and hopes for success of the Karma drone. Nick Woodman recognized that the action camera niche was just that—a niche—and it was saturated. The company that had begun as a hardware company began to focus on the Karma drone and software as a means of survival.

COMPANY HISTORY

GoPro began as the result of business failures. GoPro's founder, Nick Woodman, grew up in Silicon Valley, the son of wealthy parents (his father brokered the purchase of Taco Bell by Pepsi). Woodman started an online electronics store, **EmpowerAll.com**, which failed, and subsequently started an online gaming service, Funbug, that failed in the dot-com crash of 2001, costing investors $3.9 million. Woodman consoled himself after the failure of Funbug with an extended surfing vacation in Indonesia and Australia. While on vacation, he fashioned a wrist strap from a broken surfboard leash and rubber bands to attach a disposable Kodak camera to his wrist while on the water. Woodman's friend and current GoPro creative director, Brad Schmidt, joined the vacation, worked with the camera strap, and observed that Woodman needed a camera that could withstand the sea.

After his vacation, Woodman returned home and focused on developing a comprehensive camera, casing, and strap package for surfers. Originally incorporated as Woodman Labs, the company began doing business in 2004 as GoPro. Woodman found a 35-mm camera made in China that cost $3.05, and sent his homemade plastic case and $5,000 to an unknown company, "Hotax." A few months later, Woodman received his renderings and a 3-D model from the company, and sold his first GoPro camera in September 2004, at an action-sports trade show. Also that year, GoPro hired its first employee, Neil Dana, who was Woodman's college roommate.

The two-man company grossed $350,000 in 2005, the first full year of operation. Woodman wanted to keep the company private as long as possible: he invested $30,000 personally, his mother contributed $35,000, and his father added $200,000. In a fortunate coincidence for GoPro, in fall 2006

Google purchased a then-small company, YouTube, and in spring 2007 the GoPro HERO3 with VGA video was launched. According to Woodman, the competing name-brand cameras available at the time did not have good video quality. The combination of GoPro's HERO3 video quality and the increasing popularity of YouTube caused GoPro's sales to triple in 2007.

In 2007, although the company had revenues in the low seven figures, Woodman began to question his ability to take the firm further. He negotiated a deal to turn the company over to a group of outside investors, but before the deal was finalized (which was at the beginning of the 2008 financial crisis), the investors wanted to lower the valuation of the company. GoPro was profitable, and Woodman did not believe that the company was having any ill effects from the economy. He refused to negotiate the company's value down, and the company's sales were over $8 million that year. The company's growth continued and in 2010, Best Buy began carrying GoPro products, which was a clear indication that the company was accepted in the market.

In May 2011, GoPro received $88 million in investments from five venture capital firms (including Steamboat Ventures—Disney's venture capital company) which enabled Woodman, his family, and some GoPro executives to take cash from the company. Also in 2011, GoPro acquired CineForm, a small company that had developed a proprietary codex that quickly and easily converted digital video files among different formats. CineForm had used this codex in several movies including *Need for Speed* and *Slumdog Millionaire.* As part of GoPro, CineForm altered its 3-D footage tool into an editing program that became the company's first desktop application, GoPro Studio.

In December 2012 a Taiwanese manufacturing company, Foxconn (trading as Hone Hai Precision Industry Co.), bought 8.8 percent of GoPro for $200 million, which brought the value of the privately held company to about $2.25 billion, and *Forbes* reported Woodman's personal net worth to be about $1.73 billion. GoPro sold 2.3 million cameras and grossed $531 million in 2012; and in December of that year, GoPro replaced Sony as the highest-selling camera brand at Best Buy.

Sales of GoPro cameras at snow-sports retailers increased by 50 percent for the 2012–2013 ski season. GoPro almost doubled its revenues in each of three consecutive years, from $234.2 million in 2011, to $525 million in 2012, and $985 million in 2013, according to the U.S. Securities and Exchange Commission (SEC). Although revenues increased 87 percent in 2013 in that year, the decrease in revenue growth became obvious. According to its IPO filing, as of December 2013 the company had not derived any revenue from the distribution of its content on the GoPro Network; however, it announced plans to pursue new streams of revenue from the distribution of GoPro content. GoPro formed a new software division in 2013. Also in that year, the National Academy of Television Arts and Sciences recognized the company with a Technology and Engineering Emmy Award in the Inexpensive Small Rugged HD Camera category.

In June 2014, GoPro went public at an IPO price of $24.00 which valued the company at $2.7 billion. The IPO included a lockup agreement that prevented the Woodmans from selling any shares of GoPro stock for six months; four months later on October 2, 2014, the Woodmans made a donation of 5.8 million shares of GoPro stock into the Jill and Nick Woodman Foundation. A press release about the foundation stated that details about its mission would be announced at a later date, according to CNN. Share prices dropped 14 percent after the announcement and angered investors. Also, GoPro failed to meet investors' expectations when it released its first earnings report in August 2014.

GoPro increased emphasis on software and video sharing in 2015. In that year, GoPro tied with Apple on the Google Brand Leaderboard, which measures the most popular brands on YouTube. According to Google, more than 4.6 years of content was uploaded to YouTube in 2015 with GoPro in the title, an increase of 22 percent from 2014. Also in 2015, the company launched the GoPro Channel on Amazon Fire TV and Fire TV Stick with a custom-designed streaming channel that was a one-stop destination for delivering on-demand GoPro videos to Amazon customers.

Another 2015 development was the GoPro Channel on the PlayStation Network which allowed PlayStation owners to stream GoPro content on-demand, and browse GoPro cameras and accessories. PlayStation joined GoPro's growing roster of distribution partners including Amazon Fire TV,

Roku, Comcast Watchable, Sky, Vessel Entertainment, Xbox, LG, and Virgin America. The GoPro Mobile App was downloaded 2.75 million times in the fourth quarter, totaling almost 24 million cumulative downloads; Q4 installs of GoPro Studio totaled nearly 1.7 million, totaling over 15 million cumulative installs, with average daily video exports of over 49,000 in the fourth quarter.

GoPro purchased Kolor, a French company with experience making software for capturing and displaying virtual reality in 2016, and acquired Replay and Splice, two leading mobile video editing apps. Replay was video editing software that GoPro rebranded as Quik, and Splice was an app that promised desktop-level performance for editing video on an iPhone. The Kolor group assisted in the launch of a virtual reality social media platform that functioned both on the web and as an app. According to *The Verge* (June 2, 2016), Woodman understood that "the hardware-first chapter of GoPro" was coming to the end. He recognized that market saturation had created the problem, explaining it as "content guilt." According to Woodman, "Most people don't even watch their GoPro footage." He blamed the company for creating the problem by solving the capture side but leaving customers hanging in postproduction.

In April 2016, the investment bank Piper Jaffray reported that GoPro was gaining market share in a declining market, and that action camera ownership declined to 28 percent among teenage consumers, down from 31 percent a year previous, and 40 percent in 2013. This trend clearly indicated the need for GoPro to transform into something more than an action camera company. The GoPro brand and reputation had been made as a hardware company, and moving that reputation to a new market (i.e., software) would be difficult. Although GoPro created the market for wearable cameras, it found the content-creation software field crowded. Plus, *The Verge* (June 2, 2016) pointed out that the company had no clear way to monetize its software. According to Woodman, building the software team had been the most time-consuming project the company had undertaken. He believed that the benefits of success would be large because the amount of video being consumed was huge, and the market research company NPD Group reported that more than 80 percent of smartphone users stream video. Woodman also believed in the potential of Karma, GoPro's camera drone, scheduled for release in early 2016.

THE ACTION CAMERA INDUSTRY IN 2014–2016

Sales in the global action camera industry grew 44 percent in 2014, reaching 7.6 million units, and retail value of $3.2 billion. Action camera sales were projected to increase from the 5 million units sold in 2013 to 9 million units by 2018. Camera unit sales increased by 38 percent in North America in 2014; however, the largest growth came from the Asia Pacific region, which was up by 114 percent. Although the action camera market was expected to enjoy continued sales growth through at least 2019, several factors, including lengthening replacement cycles, were expected to slow the growth rate.

Consumer sales, primarily for extreme sports, had accounted for the largest part of global demand up to mid-2015, but professional sales, primarily driven by TV production, security, and law enforcement, were expected to increase. In 2014, consumers were responsible for 86 percent of action camera sales, with the remainder coming from professional uses. Although GoPro dominated the action camera industry in mid-2015, there was increased competition from other companies, including Garmin, TomTom, Canon, JVC, Ion America, Polaroid, and Sony. Other competitors were focusing on the adjacent market of wearable cameras for security and police officers.

A defining characteristic of the action camera industry in 2015 was the increase in the number of competitors. In early 2015, the market was experiencing rapid growth and attracted many new entrants, which had the expected effect on price (lower), quality (higher) and features (more). A list of producers of action cameras in February 2015 is presented in Exhibit 3.

Another 2015 industry trend was price polarization. Sales of low-end camera models priced under $200.00, and high-end models (including GoPro's $499.00 HERO4 Black) experienced increasing growth. The action camera industry experienced significant change in early 2015. A Futuresource analyst reported that the 360-degree capture that had recently become available would drive virtual reality applications over the coming months, especially for sports broadcasting. The company envisioned the percentage of 360-degree video action cameras growing from 1 percent in 2015 to 14 percent by 2019. In 2014, 95 percent of action cameras sold could take high-definition video with at least 720p

EXHIBIT 3 Action Camera Producers, February 2015

Key Brands		
Contour	iON Worldwide	
Drift Innovation	JVC Kenwood	
Garmin	PLR IP (Polaroid)	
GoPro	Rollei	
	Sony	
	Veho	
Other Prominent Brands		
Braun Photo Technik	HEDCAMz	Polaroid
Brinno	Hitachi	Pyle Audio
Chilli Technology	iSAW	RePlay XD
Delkin Devices	JVC	Shimono
EyeSee360	Liquid Image	Toshiba
Geonaute	Mobius Action Cam	Vievu
GoPole	Oregon Scientific	VIO POV
	Panasonic	Viofo
	PAPAGO	Xsories

Source: Wealth and Finance International, February 2016.

resolution; and approximately 85 percent of action cameras could take HD video in 1080p. About half of cameras sold could record video in ultra-high-definition 2160p, or 4K.

Going into 2016, the action camera industry experienced adjustments in usage: The demand for action cameras for professional applications had grown exponentially due to the focus on better viewing of sports events. Action cameras were increasingly being used for TV production and to record closer details of sports. The National Hockey League and Fishing League Worldwide had signed major contracts with iON, GoPro, and other vendors, and that professional segment of the industry was expected to have a high growth rate. Also, Global Market Insights pointed out increasing popularity of action cameras among all age groups and advanced product features as other factors providing massive growth potential.

The security industry was also finding increasing usage for action cameras going into 2016, which added additional fuel to the industry growth. Action cameras and especially drone-mounted action cameras were expected to be used increasingly in security applications globally. A leading vendor in the action camera–drones, Lifeline Response, had developed a smartphone app that could fly a drone to a needed location in emergencies. According to Technavio Research, professional use of action cameras would exceed casual usage by 2020.

In addition to increased demand for action cameras for professional applications, the industry was expanding also due to demand from developing countries, with the largest growth in the Asia Pacific region. Increasing disposable income, an increase in social networking, and rapid growth in adventure sport tourism were factors increasing sales in emerging countries. Several action camera vendors sponsored extreme sporting events in various emerging economies to promote their camera brands. European growth is predicted to be stable from 2016 to 2023.

The revenue growth rate in the action camera industry is expected to be lower than the growth rate in unit sales, due to a general price decline. The average action camera price is expected to decline to $226.00 by 2020, depressed primarily by a global increase in supply. In the first quarter, 2016, Technavio forecast that the value, by revenue, of the global action camera industry, which was $2.35 billion in 2015, would reach about $6 billion by 2020. However, young consumers were increasingly choosing smartphone cameras over traditional, which meant they were less likely to purchase an action camera.

The popularity of social networking sites was a major driver of the action camera industry in 2016 and price polarization continued as a crucial trend. Vendors began "bundling" their products (cameras and numerous accessories) to increase demand for cameras and accessories. Bundle packaging increased demand by offering cost-effectiveness to customers because the bundling reduced or eliminated the need to purchase additional equipment. Other industry trends in 2016 were increasing numbers of new entrants, which reduced prices, and increasing significance of the smartphone with enhanced quality and features which depressed demand.

THE DRONE INDUSTRY IN 2016

According to the NPD Group, in the 12 months ending April 2016, drone industry sales increased 224 percent year-over-year to nearly $200 million. Over the six months ending April 2016, drone sales growth accelerated to more than four times greater than the same time period last year. **Dronell.com** reported that in 2015, there was more than $30 million in seed funding raised (more than $20 million in the United States) for new drone startups and early stage financing. The majority of drones were purchased for video and photography, either for commercial or hobby reasons. The commercial and civilian drone market was expected to grow at a compound annual growth rate of 19 percent between 2015 and 2020 (versus 5 percent growth in military sales).

CNN reported in February 2016 that the two most promising tech industries in 2016 were drones and virtual reality. The drone industry is expected to grow to $6 billion in sales by 2020, and according to CNN, China was the clear leader, with the world's largest drone manufacturer, DJI. DJI's North American market share going into 2016 was 50 percent, and an estimated 70 percent worldwide. Although the commercial drone industry was still young, consolidation and major investments from large industrial conglomerates, defense contractors, and chip companies had begun.

Business Insider reported that several of the prominent early drone manufacturers were emerging from outside the U.S. market. Among the foreign manufacturers were the Canadian firm Aeryon, Switzerland-based senseFly (owned by France-based Parrot), publicly traded Swedish firm CybAero, Shenzhen, China-based DJI, and Korea-based Gryphon.

Drones with 4K cameras accounted for more than 33 percent of dollar sales in the 12 months ending April 2016, and those with GPS provided 64 percent of revenue. Those selling for more than $500.00 accounted for 56 percent of dollar sales during that period. The average sales price for a drone was more than $550.00 in April, which gave them one of the highest average retail prices of all technology categories. Exhibit 4 presents the drone industry's leading brands in dollar sales in April 2016.

The drone category continued to evolve as new products and features such as 4K cameras, Bluetooth, and built-in GPS revealed an expanding range of usage. The market was maturing and the NPD Group forecast continued interest in drones and increasing sales in 2016 and 2017.

Drones were a popular item in the 2015 holiday season. Sales (by unit) increased 445 percent from the 2014 holiday season. High consumer interest and competitive prices pushed sales for December 2015 up by 273 percent. Consumer research by the

EXHIBIT 4 Top-Selling Drone Brands Ranked by Percentage of U.S. Dollar Share, April 2016

Rank	Brand Name
1	DJI
2	Parrot
3	Protocol
4	Yuneec
5	3D Robotics

Source: The NPD Group/Retail Tracking Service, 12 months ending April 2016.

NPD Group revealed that even after the 2015 holiday season, drone purchase expectations, especially among younger consumers, remained high, which indicated continued growth and healthy demand. In October 2015, the Federal Aviation Administration (FAA) required registration of drones weighing between 0.55 and 55 pounds by December; however, during that period sales of drones (by dollars) at least doubled month over month.

Although there was growth potential for the drone industry, market leader DJI's scale enabled the company to reduce prices below those of competitors and offer a superior product. The global giant Apple entered into an exclusive contract with DJI to sell its DJI Phontom4 drone. This gave DJI immediate access to the Apple online store and over 400 brick-and-mortar stores. In May 2016 another Chinese company, Xiaomi, which had produced a GoPro HERO "knock-off," the Yi4k, launched a low-cost drone with an action camera selling for $380.00. The probability of success for a newcomer in the crowded drone industry appeared to be increasingly remote.

GOPRO'S BUSINESS MODEL AND STRATEGY

The action camera industry was a relatively young and evolving industry, and GoPro evolved within the industry. Although the company began as an action camera company, it had rapidly evolved into a diversified lifestyle company. The company's business focus, as set out in its 2015 annual report, was to develop product solutions that enabled consumers to capture, manage, share, and enjoy some of the most important moments in their lives. In addition to selling action cameras to capture live events, the company developed GoPro Entertainment, and planned to diversify into a number of related businesses, including software and drones.

GoPro's diversification and differentiation strategy was ambitious. The GoPro Annual Report, 2015, set out the strategy as follows:

> We intend to continue building our existing capture device business while also launching complementary new device categories including unmanned aircraft systems (drones) and devices to enable virtual reality content capturing. In addition, we expect to release new content management, editing and sharing solutions that will provide increased value to our consumers, introduce new revenue streams and further differentiate us from competitors.

The company focused on product leadership and innovation in its cameras, and also in mounts, accessories, and batteries. New products for 2016 included the company's next-generation capture device, the HERO5, the GoPro drone *Karma,* and devices to enable virtual reality content capture. The company increased its focus on solutions designed to simplify organizing, editing, and sharing content, and planned release of a content management platform for 2016—the GoPro for Desktop—which would facilitate offloading, accessing, and editing content.

GoPro's management envisioned the company as an entertainment brand. The distribution of content originally produced by GoPro was referred to as GoPro Entertainment, and the company attempted to leverage the sale of its cameras through GoPro Entertainment. The company continued to invest in GoPro Entertainment by developing, distributing and promoting GoPro Entertainment programming on its own and partner platforms.

Sales Channels

At the end of 2015, GoPro products were sold through direct sales channels in over 100 countries and over 40,000 retail outlets. The company also sold indirectly through its distribution channel. The direct sales channel was shrinking in 2015, providing 53 percent of revenue, compared to 59 percent in 2014. GoPro distributors accounted for the difference, with indirect sales increasing from 41 percent in 2014 to 48 percent in 2015. A small number of distributors and retailers accounted for a large portion of GoPro's revenue: the 10 largest customers (by revenue) contributed 52, 50, and 51 percent of revenues in fiscal 2015, 2014, and 2013, respectively.

Direct Sales GoPro sold directly to large and small retailers in the United States, Europe, the Middle East and Africa, and directly to consumers throughout the world through its e-commerce channels. The company believed that diverse direct sales channels were a key differentiator for the company and it segregated its products among those channels. GoPro used independent specialty retailers who generally carried higher-end products, and targeted its customers who were believed to be the early adopters of new technology. Big-box retailers with a national presence such as Amazon, Walmart, Target, and Best Buy were a second component of the direct sales channel. These retailers carried a variety of GoPro products and targeted its particular end user. GoPro felt that this allowed the company to maintain in-store product differentiation between its sales channels and protected its brand image in the specialty retail markets. Amazon accounted for 12 percent of GoPro's total revenues in 2015, and Best Buy accounted for 14 percent (down from 20 percent in 2014).

Mid-market retailers with a large regional or national presence were also part of GoPro's direct sales channel. Retailers focusing on sporting goods, consumer electronics, hunting, fishing, and motor sports carried a small subset of GoPro products targeted toward its end users. The full line of GoPro products were sold directly to consumers through the company's online store, gopro.com. The company marketed its e-commerce channel through online and offline advertising. GoPro felt that its e-commerce sales provided insight into its customers' shopping behavior and provided a platform from which the company could inform and educate its customers on the GoPro brand, products, and services.

Indirect Sales/Distributors GoPro sold to over 50 distributors who resold its products to retailers in international markets and to some mid-market vertical retailers in the United States. The company provided a sales support staff to help the distributors with planning product mix, marketing, in-store merchandising, development of marketing materials, order assistance, and education about the GoPro products. During 2015, GoPro converted part of its distributor sales into direct sales.

Merchandising, Marketing, and Advertising

GoPro's merchandising strategy focused on point-of-purchase displays that were provided to retailers at no cost. The POP displays showed GoPro content on a large video monitor, with GoPro's cameras and accessories arranged around the video monitor screen. At the end of 2015, the company had over 25,000 displays in retail outlets. The company's marketing and advertising efforts were focused on consumer engagement by exposing them to GoPro content, believing that this approach enhanced the brand while demonstrating the performance, versatility, and durability of its products. GoPro's marketing and advertising programs spanned a wide range of consumer interests and attempted to leverage traditional consumer and lifestyle marketing.

Social media were the core of GoPro's consumer marketing. The company's customers captured and shared personal GoPro content on social media platforms such as YouTube, Twitter, Facebook, Pinterest, and Instagram. User-generated content and GoPro originally produced content were integrated into advertising campaigns across billboards, print, television commercials, online, and other home advertising, and at consumer and trade shows. The shared GoPro content was also used to support the in-store marketing on the point-of-purchase displays.

GoPro's lifestyle marketing emphasized expansion of its brand awareness by engaging consumers through relationships with influential athletes, entertainers, brands, and celebrities who used GoPro products to create and share content with their consumers and fans. The company worked directly with its lifestyle partners to create content that was leveraged to their mutual benefit across the GoPro Network.

GoPro's Financial Performance

GoPro's 2015 revenues of $1.6 billion represented a 16 percent increase over 2014, primarily due to increased sales in Europe, Middle East, Africa, and the Asia Pacific region. Despite the uptrend in revenue, cost of revenue and operating expenses had increased in 2015 as well. Total operating expenses increased from 27 percent of revenue in 2013 to 38 percent of revenue in 2015, which contributed to the steep decline in net income from 2014 to 2015. In addition, GoPro's gross margin and operation margin in fiscal 2015 suffered from a sales volume decrease in the latter part of the year. This was primarily due to the reduction in the price of the HERO4 Session camera and the costs related to the retirement of the HERO entry-level camera. The global increase in hiring, which was an employee cost increase of $65.7 million or 60 percent, and an increase of $30.8 million in advertising and promotional costs were the primary drivers of the increase in operating expenses. During fiscal 2015, GoPro shipped 6.6 million capture devices, a 27 percent increase over fiscal 2014. GoPro's Consolidated Statements of Operations for 2013–2015 are presented in Exhibit 5. Its balance sheets for 2014 and 2015 are shown in Exhibit 6.

GoPro's sales were predominately from the Americas, with Europe, the Middle East, and Africa a distance second—see Exhibit 7. Revenue from outside the United States was 52 percent, 43 percent, and

EXHIBIT 5 GoPro, Inc. Consolidated Statements of Operations, 2013–2015 ($ in thousands)

	Year Ended December 31,					
	2015		2014		2013	
	Dollars	% of Revenue	Dollars	% of Revenue	Dollars	% of Revenue
Revenue	$1,619,971	100%	$1,394,205	100%	$985,737	100%
Cost of revenue	946,757	58	766,970	55	623,953	63
Gross profit	673,214	42	627,235	45	361,784	37
Operating expenses:						
Research and development	241,694	15	151,852	11	73,737	7
Sales and marketing	268,939	17	194,377	14	157,771	16
General and administrative	107,833	7	93,971	7	31,573	4
Total operating expenses	618,466	38	440,200	32	263,081	27
Operating income	54,748	3	187,035	13	98,703	10
Other expense, net	(2,163)	—	(6,060)	—	(7,374)	(1)
Income before income taxes	52,585	3	180,975	13	91,329	9
Income tax expense	16,454	1	52,887	4	30,751	3
Net income	$ 36,131	2%	$ 128,088	9%	$ 60,578	6%

Source: GoPro, Inc. 2015 10-K.

49 percent of the company's revenues for fiscal 2015, 2014, and 2013, respectively, and GoPro expected this portion to continue to be a significant part of revenues. Although there were no clear trends in the composition of sales revenue in the Americas, Europe, the Middle East, and Africa, there was an upward trend of revenue from outside the United States and from the Asia Pacific region. GoPro's supply chain partners had operations in Singapore, China, Czech Republic, the Netherlands, and Brazil. The company intended to expand operations in these, and perhaps other, countries as it increased its international presence.

According to NPD market research, in 2015, on a dollar sales basis, GoPro held 6 of the top 10 products, including the number one spot, in the digital camera/camcorder category, and was number one in accessory unit sales with 6 of the top 10 selling accessories. In the fourth quarter 2015, on a unit sales basis, GoPro had 6 of the top 10 action cameras in Europe, including all of the top 5 spots in December. Global sales were more than 50 percent of fiscal 2015 revenue, and combined Asian and European revenue increased 49 percent from 2014. China remained a top 10 market for GoPro in the fourth quarter.

GoPro Product Offerings in Mid-2016

In June 2016, GoPro's action camera offerings comprised three models: HERO4 Black, HERO4 Silver, and HERO Session. The HERO Session had one-button controls, was waterproof to 33 feet without a separate housing, and would automatically capture video and photos right-side-up even if mounted upside down. The HERO Session was small, the lightest of all GoPro cameras, and could record up to two hours on a charged battery. The Session sold for $199.99 in mid-2016.

The HERO4 Silver could capture HD video and photos, had a built-in touchscreen display to control the camera and play back shots, and enabled built-in video trimming. A characteristic of the HERO4 Silver was professional quality video and customizable settings for color, sharpness, exposure, white balance, and ISO (sensitivity to light). Other features included built-in Wi-Fi and Bluetooth, waterproof to 130 feet, time-lapse exposure for after-dark usage, a wide-angle lens, automatic adjustment to low-light conditions, and a new audio system with high-fidelity sound. The HERO4 Silver sold for $399.99.

EXHIBIT 6 GoPro, Inc. Consolidated Balance Sheets, 2014–2015

(in thousands, except par values)	December 31, 2015	December 31, 2014
Assets		
Current assets:		
Cash and cash equivalents	$ 279,672	$319,929
Marketable securities	194,386	102,327
Accounts receivable, net	145,692	183,992
Inventory	188,232	153,026
Prepaid expenses and other current assets	25,261	63,769
Total current assets	833,243	823,043
Property and equipment, net	70,050	41,556
Intangible assets, net	31,027	2,937
Goodwill	57,095	14,095
Other long-term assets	111,561	36,060
Total assets	$1,102,976	$917,691
Liabilities and Stockholders' Equity		
Current liabilities:		
Accounts payable	$ 89,989	$126,240
Accrued liabilities	192,446	118,507
Deferred revenue	12,742	14,022
Total current liabilities	295,177	258,769
Long-term taxes payable	21,770	13,266
Other long-term liabilities	13,996	4,452
Total liabilities	330,943	276,487
Stockholders' equity:		
Preferred stock, $0.0001 par value, 5,000 shares authorized; none issued	—	—
Common stock and additional paid-in capital, $0.0001 par value, 500,000 Class A shares authorized, 100,596 and 52,091 shares issued and outstanding, respectively; 150,000 Class B shares authorized, 36,005 and 77,023 shares issued and outstanding, respectively	663,311	533,000
Treasury stock, at cost, 1,545 shares and none, respectively	(35,613)	—
Retained earnings	144,335	108,204
Total stockholders' equity	772,033	641,204
Total liabilities and stockholders' equity	$1,102,976	$917,691

GoPro's HERO4 Black was advertised as professional quality and the company's most advanced camera. The HERO4 Black had a processor two times more powerful than its predecessor and shot video at twice the frame rate with better image quality. The camera had time-lapse capability, built-in Wi-Fi and Bluetooth, a smart remote that allowed multiple camera control up to 600 feet, enhanced low-light capability, and could capture high-fidelity sound. The HERO4 Black sold for $499.99.

GoPro advertised and offered "pre-orders" for its Omni virtual reality system, which operated with six cameras. Video footage from the cameras could be put together to create a 360-degree video. The Omni was priced at $4,999.00 (which included six HERO4 Black cameras): A purchaser's credit card

EXHIBIT 7 GoPro, Inc.'s Revenues by Geographic Region, 2013–2015

	Year Ended December 31,			2015 vs. 2014	2014 vs. 2013
(in thousands)	2015	2014	2013	% Change	% Change
Units shipped	6,584	5,180	3,849	27%	35%
Americas	$ 868,772	$ 890,352	$557,285	(2)%	60%
Percentage of revenue	54%	64%	56%		
Europe, Middle East, & Africa	535,260	371,197	322,226	44%	15%
Percentage of revenue	33%	27%	33%		
Asia Pacific region	215,939	132,656	106,226	63%	25%
Percentage of revenue	13%	9%	11%		
Total revenue	$1,619,971	$1,394,205	$985,737	16%	41%

Source: GoPro, Inc. 2015 10-K.

would be authorized upon order, but would not be charged until the Omni was shipped.

PROFILES OF GOPRO'S MAJOR COMPETITORS IN 2016

TomTom

TomTom, a Dutch company known for its GPS navigation systems, entered the action camera market in early 2015 with its Bandit camera. The Bandit had a wide-angle lens, a removable battery, and could operate up to three hours on a fully charged battery. Bandit users could wear a TomTom Multi-Sport Cardio GPS Watch and the Bandit camera could detect and tag exciting moments based on heart rate. Built-in motion and GPS sensors also enabled the Bandit to automatically find and tag exciting moments based on altitude, speed, G-forces, and acceleration. Footage could be processed on the camera without downloading, which made the editing process much faster and easier. The Bandit's battery and card reader were integrated into a USB stick, and the battery could be charged while video files were being downloaded. The Bandit sold for about $300.00.

ActiveOn

ActiveOn, founded in 2004, joined the field of action camera manufacturers with a small and inexpensive model—the ActiveOn CX, which sold for $119.99 in early 2016. This camera fit into the palm of the hand and could record high-definition video. The small camera offered several features not available in the lower line GoPros such as a 2-inch LCD viewfinder and an interchangeable battery that provided two hours of recording time per charge. The ActiveOn CX had an adjustable lens that could be set for sports, nighttime, and underwater photography. In September 2015, ActiveOn became the official camera of Cirque du Soleil.

ActiveOn brought a new dimension to action camera with its ActiveOn Solar X, released in early 2016. The emphasis on action camera development had been in connectivity and recording quality: battery life was maximized at 90 minutes to two hours. The Solar X offered two hours of operation with the built-in battery, and add-on solar panels that could provide an additional four hours of recording. ActiveOn developed a fast charging system, "Burst Speed Charging," that could charge the battery to 80 percent in 30 minutes or to 100 percent in an hour. The Solar X was priced at $450.00.

Ricoh Ricoh's latest action camera model, the WG-M2, offered a tough body that was freezeproof, shockproof, and did not need an extra case to go underwater. The camera had an ultra-wide viewing angle of 204 degrees (versus the average action camera angle of about 135 degrees), and a very high-speed recording rate which allows more data per frame and thus a more vivid picture. The WG-M2 had a stereo mic, a shake reduction feature, large controls that can be operated while wearing gloves, and could take time-lapse and slow-motion videos. The WG-M2 was priced at $299.95.

360fly

The 360fly was an action camera that took 360-degree video and enabled the operator to edit, enhance, and share the content from a smartphone to social media. A smartphone with the 360fly app controlled the camera. The app served as the camera's viewfinder, controller, and editor. A new-generation 4K 360fly camera was introduced in 2016, which was water resistant, with a single lens 360-degree video camera with live streaming and intuitive filming and editing advancements. 360fly was attempting to bring virtual reality to consumers.

360fly was also developing a 360-degree drone. Although the company had not announced the launch date for the drone, there was speculation that it could beat the GoPro Karma to the market. Priced at $399.99, the 360fly was carried at Best Buy and specialty retailers.

Sony

Sony entered the action camera market with a high-quality lineup. The Sony X1000V was a 4K camera with a 170 wide-angle lens and professional quality output. The camera recorded at a high rate to give better resolution and better low-light pictures. Sony's HDR-AS100V POV action camera produced high-definition video and still images, and included built-in GPS that could add speed, location, and trail information on the video. There was a built-in stereo mic, a high-speed data transfer to capture fast action, HDMI output for sharing video on TVs, steady-shot stabilization to digitally compensate for the motion of bicycles or motorcycles, and wireless uploading to smartphones or tablets. The HDR-AS100V POV camera was priced at $189.00 and was listed as top-rated model in *PC Magazine*'s Best Action Cameras of 2016.

Nikon

Camera giant Nikon announced in January that it was entering the action camera market. The company's first in its line of action cameras was the KeyMission 360, which recorded 360-degree video in 4K ultra-high-definition. The camera was dust, shock, and temperature resistant, waterproof to 100 feet, and included electronic vibration reduction to help produce sharp video. *Technowize* reported that the KeyMission 360 had the best audio quality of any action camera on the market. The KeyMission 360 was the "parent" camera in Nikon's family of action camera. The KeyMission 360 was expected to be released in late summer 2016 at a price of about $450.00.

Garmin International

Garmin International was far better known as a global leader in GPS navigation than for its action cameras; however, in September 2013 the company released its first action camera, the VIRB. The VIRB had a color display and was manufactured in a waterproof housing so an extra protective case was unnecessary. The success of the VIRB led to two new Garmin action cameras in 2015, the VIRB X and the VIRB XE. Both models had GPS, Wi-Fi, and full sensor support. The new models had support for Bluetooth data streams which allowed the use of a microphone to narrate action in real time, plus a Garmin app that enabled transfer of video and photos from the camera to a smartphone and then to social media. Gauges such as altitude and speed could be applied to the video. The VIRB X and VIRB XE were priced at $299.00 and $399.00, respectively. By early 2016 the VIRB Elite could be purchased for $237.00 at Best Buy.

Kodak

Kodak's PixPro SP1, priced at $162.99, was included in *PC Magazine*'s Best Action Cameras of 2016. The PixPro had a waterproof case, produced high-quality video, could withstand drops from 6 feet, had an integrated display for framing shots, stereo microphones, image stabilization, a zoom lens, and built-in Wi-Fi, and could be paired with iOS and Android smartphones. The PixPro sold for $299.00.

iONWorldwide iONWorldwide produced a range of cameras from automobile dash cameras to home monitors to action cameras. Its action camera, the iON Air Pro, was an HD video camera that was waterproof to 30 feet with no additional case. The Air Pro had a 170-degree field of view, low-light sensitivity, one-touch recording capability, and could connect to a smartphone or table through an iON app, which allowed the user to share content to social feeds in real time. Purchasers of the Air Pro camera received 10 GB of cloud storage free. The Air Pro had a long battery life of 2.5 continuous recording hours. The iON Air Pro 3 was available on Amazon for $135.00.

Polaroid

Polaroid entered the action camera market in September 2012 with a line of three low-priced cameras manufactured by C&A Marketing (a Polaroid license), but sold under the Polaroid name. The first Polaroid action cameras were the XS7, priced at $69.00; the XS20, priced at $99.00; and the XS100, priced at $199.00.

Polaroid then introduced three additional models in 2014. The Polaroid XS100i had a 170-degree wide-angle lens and integrated Wi-Fi for media capture with iOS and Android smartphones. The XS100i sold for $179.00. The XS1000i, which was intended to be a professional quality camera with Wi-Fi, high-definition video, anti-shake and gyro systems, and simultaneous still and video capability, sold for $179.99.

The Polaroid CUBE was added to the Polaroid action camera line in mid-2014. *PC Magazine*'s Best Action Cameras of 2016 included the Polaroid CUBE as a top-rated model. Polaroid's action camera line in the first quarter of 2016 included the CUBE XS100 Extreme Edition. The CUBE suggested retail price was $99.99, and *PC Magazine*'s Best Action Cameras of 2016 included the Polaroid CUBE as a top-rated model. Polaroid upgraded the CUBE to the CUBE+ which included Wi-Fi, image stabilization, and an 8 megapixel still capture feature. The CUBE+ was splash-resistant, shockproof, and included a microphone; numerous mountings were available for applications ranging from bikes to helmets to dogs. The CUBE+ could stream footage in real time and was compatible with both iOS and Android. A Wi-Fi enabled CUBE+ could pair with a smartphone for real-time view controls and shot framing. There was one control on the CUBE+ for on–off and to switch from video to still. The CUBE+ was priced at $149.99.

The Collapse of GoPro's Financial Performance

GoPro's expected sales for the fourth quarter of 2015 were $511 million. However, actual sales were $436 million, representing a 31 percent drop year-over-year. Fourth quarter sales were negatively affected by the poor market acceptance of the HERO4 camera. Retailers cut prices on the HERO4 and the company announced the end of the entry-level HERO. The results of the product realignment were charges of about $57 million to revenue, and the company expected sales revenue to drop by over 50 percent in the first quarter of 2016.

Compounding the company's financial problems was its increasing costs. Even though fourth quarter 2015 sales were down 31 percent from the same period the prior year, costs of revenue decreased only 7 percent. Consequently, gross profit dropped by 58 percent from the fourth quarter 2015, resulting in a fourth quarter 2015 operating loss of $41.3 million. Net loss for the fourth quarter of 2015 was $34.5 million. After the fourth quarter results were released, after-hours trading in GoPro stock was halted. When trading resumed, share prices fell 21 percent. GoPro's market value after release of the earnings report was about $1.25 billion, according to *Time* (February 4, 2016), which was about 10 percent of its peak value.

GoPro faced further problems in 2015 as the manufacturer of Polaroid's CUBE action camera, C&A Marketing, sued GoPro for patent violation. The suit alleges that GoPro infringed on C&A Marketing's patent for its Polaroid CUBE which was almost two years old when GoPro released its HERO4 Session. C&A Marketing asked for a halt on all GoPro HERO4 Session cameras, plus monetary damages, and all of GoPro's profit on the camera.

GoPro's management provided warning guidance for investors for the first quarter and full year of 2016, which indicated the seriousness of the sales and earnings downturn. First quarter sales were forecast to be less than first quarter 2015 sales and full year 2016 revenue was forecast to be less than 2015. The gross margin was expected to be down and EBITDA (earnings before interest, taxes, depreciation and amortization) was expected to be a $95 million loss.

GoPro's Performance in Mid-2016

During 2016, GoPro announced plans to reduce its product line back to three models, and introduce the company's Karma drone (which would record 4K video footage) and a new video editing system to enable users to make good video edits in minutes. The GoPro Channel launched SkyQ, a next-generation home entertainment system in early 2016. GoPro videos became available on two of the globe's largest TV platforms—Comcast in the United States and Sky, with 21 million customers in Austria, Italy, the UK, Germany, and Ireland. Despite these positive signs of market acceptance of GoPro video, there was no money directly produced.

January 2016 was particularly difficult for GoPro. Apple received a patent for a remote-controlled camera system, and Sony introduced a new high-resolution camera. Also in January, the company cut its workforce by 7 percent, which would cost the company $5–10 million in severance costs. GoPro announced that the company would stop offering any future quarterly guidance, and that its CFO, Jack Lazar, would leave the company in March 2016.

The company beat sales expectations slightly in the first quarter 2016; however, gross revenue was down 50 percent from the first quarter 2015 and gross margin of 32.5 percent was below expectations of 36 percent. The negative operating income ($121,435 million) for the first quarter of 2016 was 645 percent below the same period the prior year and the net loss ($107,459 million) was 742 percent below the prior year.

GoPro was faced with increasing competition from major competitors, including Samsung, Nikon, Canon, and Sony Corp. *InvestorPlace* reported on April 12, 2016, that Apple and Under Armour were rumored to be entering the increasingly crowded market, and Amazon was selling a GoPro alternative with a 4.4/5 rating for $91.00. A recent startup company, Sioeye, developed the first action camera that linked directly to the web and allowed real-time video sharing, without requiring a smartphone connection. Selling for $429.00, the Sioeye camera was Wi-Fi and 4G LTE connectivity enabled and the user could live-stream and narrate adventures to followers without the necessity of uploads.

Although GoPro had scheduled its Karma drone for a mid-2016 release, in May 2016 the company abruptly announced that Karma's introduction was pushed back to the holiday season. Postponing the drone release gave the established drone vendors such as Parrot, 3D Robotics, and DJI more time to solidify their positions as market leaders. The release of its new core product—the HERO5—was not expected to be released until October 2016, and the last new product, the HERO4 Session, was not a market success.

GoPro's first quarter 2016 financial results illustrated the continuation and exacerbation of the nose dive that had begun in the fourth quarter of 2015. Gross revenue was down by 50 percent, operating income was down by 645 percent, and net income decreased by 742 percent from the same period in 2015.

Despite the crash in sales, and profit, GoPro was the undisputed market leader in action cameras, with 85 percent market share according to the company's management. Although GoPro was still the market leader in action cameras, there was no obvious choice among the paths being considered for the company to reverse its decline and reestablish profitability. Rather than concentrate on new hardware to sell in the saturated action camera market, enter the crowded drone market, or develop software that does not provide profit, Woodman's options could be limited to thinking of GoPro as an attractive acquisition by a larger company.

EXHIBIT 8 GoPro, Inc. Statement of Operations, First Quarter 2015 versus First Quarter 2016 ($ in thousands, except per share amounts)

Three Months Ended March 31,	2016	2015	% Change
Revenue	$ 183,536	$363,109	(49.5)%
Gross margin			
GAAP	32.5%	45.1%	(1,260)bps
Non-GAAP	33.0%	45.2%	(1,220)bps
Operating income (loss)			
GAAP	(21,435)	22,268	(645.3)%
Non-GAAP	(96,798)	49,111	(297.1)%
Net income (loss)			
GAAP	(107,459)	16,752	(741.5)%
Non-GAAP	(86,740)	35,619	(343.5)%
Diluted net income (loss) per share			
GAAP	(0.78)	0.11	(809.1)%
Non-GAAP	(0.63)	0.24	(362.5)%
Adjusted EBITDA	(86,771)	56,507	(253.6)%

Source: GoPro 10-Q, May 5, 2016.

CASE 16

Tesla Motors in 2016: Will Its Strategy Be Defeated by Low Gasoline Prices and Mounting Competition?

connect

Arthur A. Thompson
The University of Alabama

Tesla Motors began shipping its trail-blazing Model S sedan in June 2012. The Model S was a fully electric, four door, five-passenger luxury sedan with an all-glass panoramic roof, high definition backup camera, a 17-inch touchscreen that controlled most of the car's functions, keyless entry, xenon headlights, dual USB ports, tire pressure monitoring, and numerous other features that were standard in most luxury vehicles. Fold-down second row seats were standard on the Model S; however, buyers had the option of ordering a third seating row with two rear-facing child seats, thus providing seating for five adults and two children. The Model S had a base price of $76,000–$106,000 (depending on which powertrain buyers selected) and, when equipped with options frequented selected by customers, carried a retail sticker price ranging from $95,000 to as much as $130,000.

Model S deliveries to customers in Europe began in August 2013, and deliveries to China began in spring 2014—the company's sales showroom in Beijing generated the heaviest traffic in early 2014 of any of Tesla's showrooms worldwide. In early 2014 Musk expressed confidence that sales of Tesla vehicles in Europe and China would exceed sales in the United States in two, no more than three, years. Sales to customers in Australia began in Q4 2014.

Customer purchases of Tesla's Model S climbed swiftly, from 2,653 vehicles in the July–December period of 2012 to 50,332 Model S vehicles in full-year 2015 (see Exhibit 1). In 2015 the Tesla Model S was the best-selling large luxury vehicle

EXHIBIT 1 Tesla's Deliveries of the Model S to Customers, by Quarter, 2012 through 2015

Period	Model S Deliveries	Period	Model S Deliveries	Period	Model S Deliveries	Period	Model S Deliveries
		Q1,2013	4,900	Q1,2014	6,457	Q1,2015	10,030
		Q2,2013	5,150	Q2,2014	7,579	Q2,2015	11,507
Q3, 2012	253	Q3,2013	5,500	Q3,2014	7,785	Q3,2015	11,603
Q4, 2012	2,400	Q4,2013	6,892	Q4,2014	9,834	Q4,2015	17,192
Totals	2,653		22,477		31,655		50,332

in the United States, with a unit volume of 25,202 vehicles. In second place was the Mercedes-Benz S-Class with sales of 21,394 vehicles; 2015 sales of the Model S were far above those of BMW's 700 series luxury sedan (9,292 vehicles), BMW's 600 series (8,146 vehicles), Audi's premium-priced A7 series (7,721 vehicles), the Lexus LS 460 luxury sedan (7,165 vehicles), Porsche's Panamera sedan (4,985 vehicles), and the Jaguar XJ (3,611 vehicles).[1]

The Model S was the most-awarded car of 2013, including *Motor Trend*'s 2013 Car of the Year award and *Automobile* magazine's 2013 Car of the Year award. The National Highway Traffic Safety Administration (NHTSA) in 2013, 2014, and 2015 awarded the Tesla Model S a 5-star safety rating, both overall and in every subcategory (a score achieved by approximately 1 percent of all cars tested by the NHTSA). *Consumer Reports* gave the Model S a score of 99 out of 100 points in 2013, 2014, and 2015, saying it was "better than anything we've ever tested." However, the Tesla Model S did not make the *Consumer Reports* list of the 10 Top Picks for 2016: Best Cars of the Year.

The sleek styling and politically correct power source of the Tesla Model S was thought to explain why thousands of wealthy individuals in countries where the Model S was being sold—eager to be a part of the migration from gasoline-powered vehicles to electric-powered vehicles and to publicly display support for a cleaner environment—had become early purchasers and advocates for the vehicle. Indeed, word-of-mouth praise for the Model S among current owners and glowing articles in the media were so pervasive that Tesla had not yet spent any money on advertising to boost customer traffic in its showrooms. In a presentation to investors, a Tesla officer said "Tesla owners are our best salespeople."[2] All the available evidence in 2013–2015 pointed to Tesla's Model S as being the best electric vehicle the world had ever seen.

According to Jessica Caldwell, senior analyst at **www.Edmunds.com** (a respected website for automotive industry data):[3]

> Influential people set trends while the mainstream aspires to follow. We've seen this countless times in many different retail sectors. Cars are no different, albeit more expensive than most other purchases. Additionally, with the proclivity of tech geek being chic, the Silicon Valley area will set trends faster than traditional high-income markets like New York that have roots in (highly vilified) banking.
>
> So, as Tesla increases the number of models on offer and price points, it could find itself in demand by more than just those in these wealthy enclaves. After all, most luxury car companies find the most volume in their entry-level vehicles.

Shipments of Tesla's Model X—a 7-passenger crossover SUV with "falcon-wing" rear doors that provided easy access to third-row seats and had a base price of $81,200 ($5,000 above the base price of the Model S) and a fully equipped price of as much as $140,000 for the high-end versions—began in the last quarter of 2015. The Model X was expected to reach a production rate of 1,000 vehicles per week in Q2 of 2016. Tesla management expected to sell or lease 80,000 to 90,000 new Model S and Model X vehicles in 2016, consisting of about 45,000 to 50,000 Model S vehicles and 36,000 to 40,000 Model X vehicles. Also, in early 2016, Tesla was in the final stages of completing its design of an entry-level electric vehicle (referred to as the Model 3) that was expected to have a retail sticker price of $35,000 to $40,000. Production of the Model 3 was scheduled to begin in late 2017, with deliveries to customers beginning in early 2018.

Elon Musk, Tesla's current chair and CEO, had a ground-breaking strategic vision for Tesla Motors that featured three major elements:

1. Bring a full-range of affordable electric-powered vehicles to market and become the world's foremost manufacturer of premium quality, high performance, electric vehicles.
2. Convince motor vehicle owners worldwide that electric-powered motor vehicles were an appealing alternative to gasoline-powered vehicles.
3. Accelerate the world's transition from carbon-producing, gasoline-powered motor vehicles to zero emission electric vehicles.

Musk's stated near-term strategic objective was for Tesla to achieve sales of about 500,000 electric vehicles annually by year-end 2020. Longer term, Musk's strategic intent was for Tesla to be the world's biggest and most highly regarded producer of electric-powered motor vehicles, dramatically increasing the share of electric vehicles on roads across the world and causing global use of gasoline-powered motor vehicles to fall into permanent long-term decline.

At its core, therefore, Tesla's strategy was aimed squarely at utilizing the company's battery and electric drivetrain technology to disrupt the world automotive industry in ways that were sweeping and transformative. If Tesla's strategy proved to be as successful as Elon Musk believed it would be, industry observers expected that the Tesla's competitive position and market standing vis-à-vis the world's best-known automotive manufacturers would be vastly stronger in 2025 than it was in 2016.

But in 2016 there were three mounting challenges with the potential to imperil Musk's vision for Tesla Motors:

1. Gasoline prices across much of the world had dropped significantly in 2015 and early 2016—in the United States to levels below $2 per gallon—and were widely expected to remain low for two or more years because of a worldwide oil glut that was likely to be long-term. Low gasoline prices made the purchase of electric vehicles far less attractive, given that electric vehicles were higher priced than vehicles with gasoline engines and given that electric vehicles were limited to range of 50 to 300 miles on a single battery charge.
2. Tesla was facing the prospect of much more formidable competition from growing numbers of vehicle manufacturers (like BMW, Audi, Mercedes, Porsche, and Lexus) across the world that were developing high-end electric vehicles with features and engine configurations that would enable them to compete head-on with the Model S and Model X. Other auto manufacturers (Ford, Chevrolet, Toyota, and BMW) had already introduced low-end twin engine (one battery-powered, the other gasoline-powered) that would compete against the Model 3, and they were working to improve these models substantially to make them even more attractive to buyers than the Model 3.
3. Tesla was struggling to prove it could lower costs enough to be both price competitive and profitable. In 2015, Tesla reported a net loss of $888.7 million on its sales of 50,332 Model S vehicles—equal to a loss of $17,650 per car. This exceeded Tesla's 2014 loss of $294.5 million on sales of 31,655 Model S vehicles (a loss of $9,290 per car) and its 2013 net loss of $74.0 million on sales of 22,442 Model S vehicles (a loss of $3,300 per car). While the mounting losses per car sold were partly, perhaps largely, due to the sizable new product development costs associated with the Model X and Model 3 and to the required accounting treatments for both leased vehicles and Tesla's generous stock compensation plan, it was nonetheless alarming that the more vehicles Tesla sold the more money it lost per vehicle, an outcome that had to be reversed soon.

COMPANY BACKGROUND

Tesla Motors was incorporated in July 2003 by Martin Eberhard and Marc Tarpenning, two Silicon Valley engineers who believed it was feasible to produce an "awesome" electric vehicle. The namesake of Tesla Motors was the genius Nikola Tesla (1856–1943), an electrical engineer and scientist known for his impressive inventions (of which more than 700 were patented) and his contributions to the design of modern alternating-current (AC) power transmission systems and electric motors. Tesla Motors's first vehicle, the Tesla Roadster (an all-electric sports car) introduced in early 2008, was powered by an AC motor that descended directly from Nikola Tesla's original 1882 design.

Financing Early Operations

Eberhard and Tarpenning financed the company until Telsa Motors's first round of investor funding in February 2004. Elon Musk contributed $6.35 million of the $6.5 million in initial funding and, as the company's majority investor, assumed the position of chair of the company's board of directors. Martin Eberhard put up $75,000 of the initial $6.5 million, with two private equity investment groups and a number of private investors contributing the remainder.[4] Shortly thereafter, the company had a second round of investor funding amounting to $13 million, with Musk and a third private equity investment group being the principal capital contributors.

A third round of investor funding in May 2006 raised $40 million in additional capital for the young company, the majority of which was contributed by Elon Musk and an investment group called Technology Partners. This third round included capital contributions from Google cofounders Sergey Brin and Larry Page, former eBay president Jeff Skoll, Hyatt heir Nick Pritzker, and three other venture capital firms. A fourth round of private financing in May 2007 brought in an additional $45 million in new investment capital. Heavy product R&D expenditures and several product design changes forced yet a fifth financing round of $40 million in February 2008. Of the $145 million in equity capital raised in these first five financing rounds, Elon Musk contributed about $74 million, making him the company's largest shareholder.[5]

In May 2009, when the company was struggling to cope with still another cash crunch and also overcome a series of glitches in getting the Model S into production, Germany's Daimler AG, the maker of Mercedes vehicles, announced it was acquiring an equity stake of almost 10 percent in Tesla for a reported $50 million and that a Daimler executive would become a member of Tesla's board of directors.[6] Daimler's investment signaled a strategic partnership with Tesla to accelerate the development of Tesla's lithium-ion battery technology and electric drivetrain technology and to collaborate on electric cars being developed at Mercedes. In July 2009, Daimler announced that it had sold 40 percent of its ownership interest in Tesla to Aabar Investments in Abu Dhbai.[7]

In June 2009, following two years of lobbying effort by Tesla in behalf of its loan applications, the company received approval for about $465 million in low-interest loans from the U.S. Department of Energy to accelerate the production of affordable, fuel-efficient electric vehicles; the loans were part of DOE's $25 billion Advanced Technology Vehicle Manufacturing Program created in 2007 during the George Bush administration and funded in September 2008, which provided incentives to new and established automakers to build more fuel-efficient vehicles and reduce the country's dependence on foreign oil. Tesla intended to use $365 million for production engineering and assembly of its forthcoming Model S and $100 million for a powertrain manufacturing plant employing about 650 people that would supply all-electric powertrain solutions to other automakers and help accelerate the availability of relatively low-cost, mass-market electric vehicles.

In September 2009, Tesla Motors raised $82.5 million from Daimler, Fjord Capital Partners, Aabar Investments, and other undisclosed investors; Elon Musk did not contribute to this funding round. Tesla indicated the funds raised would be used primarily to open additional sales and service centers for its vehicles.

In June 2010, Tesla Motors became a public company, raising $226 million with an initial public offering of 13,300,000 shares of common stock sold at a price of $17.00 per share; of the shares sold to the public, 11,880,600 shares were offered by the company and 1,419,400 shares were offered by selling stockholders. In addition, the selling stockholders granted the underwriters a 30-day option to purchase up to an additional aggregate of 1,995,000 shares of common stock to cover over-allotments, if any. Tesla's shares began trading on Tuesday, June 29, 2010, on the NASDAQ under the ticker symbol TSLA. Tesla Motors was the first American car company to go public since Ford Motor Company's IPO in 1956. In October 2012, Tesla completed a follow-on offering of 7.97 million shares from which it received net proceeds of $222.1 million.

Management Changes at Tesla

In August 2007, with the company plagued by production delays, cofounder Martin Eberhard was ousted as Tesla's CEO and replaced with an interim CEO who headed the company until Ze'ev Drori, an Israeli-born American technology entrepreneur and avid car enthusiast, was named the company's president and CEO in November 2007. Drori was specifically tasked by the company's board of directors to get company's delayed Tesla Roadster into production and start deliveries to customers as fast as possible. To combat continuing production delays (the latest of which involved problems in designing and developing a reliable, tested transmission that would last many miles) and "out-of-control" costs that were burning through the company's investment capital at a rate that disturbed investors, Drori conducted a performance review of the company's 250+ employees and contractors and proceeded to fire or lay off roughly 10 percent of the company's workforce, including several executives, high-ranking members of the company's automotive engineering team, and other heretofore key employees.[8]

Although Drori succeeded in getting the Tesla Roadster into production in March and initiating deliveries to customers, in October 2008, Musk decided it made more sense for him to take on the role as Tesla's chief executive—while continuing to serve as board chair—because he was making all the major decisions anyway. Drori was named vice chair but then opted to leave the company in December

2008. By January 2009, Tesla had raised $187 million and delivered 147 of its first-generation Roadster vehicle. Musk declared that the company would be cash-flow positive by mid-2009.

Elon Musk

Elon Musk was born in South Africa, taught himself computer programming and, at age 12, made $500 by selling the computer code for a video game he invented.[9] In 1992, after spending two years at Queen's University in Ontario, Canada, Musk transferred to the University of Pennsylvania where he earned an undergraduate degree in business and a second degree in physics. During his college days, Musk spent some time thinking about two important matters that he thought merited his time and attention later in his career: one was that the world needed an environmentally clean method of transportation; the other was that it would be good if humans could colonize another planet.[10] After graduating from the University of Pennsylvania, he decided to move to California and pursue a PhD in applied physics at Stanford but with the specific intent of working on energy storage capacitors that could be used in electric cars. However, he promptly decided to leave the program after two days to pursue his entrepreneurial aspirations instead.

Musk's first entrepreneurial venture was to join up with his brother, Kimbal, and establish Zip2, an Internet software company that developed, hosted, and maintained some 200 websites involving "city guides" for media companies, including the *New York Times,* the *Chicago Tribune,* and other newspapers in the Hearst, Times Mirror, and Pulitzer Publishing chains. In 1999 Zip2 was sold to a wholly owned subsidiary of Compaq Computer for $307 million in cash and $34 million in stock options—Musk received a reported $22 million from the sale.[11]

In March 1999, Musk cofounded X.com, a Silicon Valley online financial services and e-mail payment company. One year later, X.com acquired Confinity, which operated a subsidiary called PayPal. Musk was instrumental in the development of the person-to-person payment platform and, seeing big market opportunity for such an online payment platform, decided to rename X.com as PayPal. Musk pocketed about $150 million in eBay shares when PayPal was acquired by eBay for $1.5 billion in eBay stock in October 2002.

In June 2002, Elon Musk with an investment of $100 million of his own money founded his third company, Space Exploration Technologies (SpaceX), to develop and manufacture space launch vehicles, with a goal of revolutionizing the state of rocket technology and ultimately enabling people to live on other planets. He vowed to revolutionize the space industry with a low-cost, reliable satellite launcher that charged $6 million a flight—less than half the going rate for small payloads. Upon hearing of Musk's new venture into the space flight business, David Sacks, one of Musk's former colleagues at PayPal, said: "Elon thinks bigger than just about anyone else I've ever met. He sets lofty goals and sets out to achieve them with great speed."[12] In 2011, Musk vowed to put a man on Mars in 10 years.[13] In May 2012, a SpaceX Dragon cargo capsule powered by a SpaceX Falcon Rocket completed a near flawless test flight to and from the International Space Station; the successful test flight prompted Musk to say that the mission, in his view, marked a turning point toward rapid advancement in space transportation technology, one that would pave the way for routine cargo deliveries and commercial space flights.[14] Since May 2012, under a $1.6 billion contract with NASA, the SpaceX Dragon had delivered cargo to and from the Space Station multiple times, in the first of at least 12 cargo resupply missions. On December 21, 2015, the SpaceX's Falcon 9 rocket delivered 11 communications satellites to orbit, and the first-stage of the rocket returned and landed at Landing Zone 1—the first-ever orbital class rocket landing. The company currently had under development the Falcon Heavy, which would be the world's most powerful rocket and it also was working on developing reusable rockets. SpaceX was both profitable and cash-flow positive in 2013–2015. As of 2016, it had completed over 70 launches, representing some $10 billion in contracts, and had over 3,000 employees. Headquartered in Hawthorne, California, SpaceX was owned by management, employees, and private equity firms; Elon Musk was the company's CEO and chief designer.

Elon Musk's other active business venture was SolarCity Inc., a full-service provider of solar system design, financing, solar panel installation, and ongoing system monitoring for homeowners, municipalities, businesses (including Intel, Walmart, Walgreens, and eBay), over 400 schools (including Stanford University), nonprofit organizations, and military bases. Going into 2016, SolarCity managed more solar systems for homes than any other solar company in the United States. SolarCity had revenues of $399 million in 2015, but the company's net losses had grown in size every year since 2009, reaching $768.8 million in 2015 (about 80 percent greater than its revenues from operating leases and sales of solar energy systems and components). Investors were generally bullish on SolarCity's future prospects; the company's stock price rose from about $10.50 in late December 2012 to an all-time high of $85 in March 2013. But then, with the company's losses growing, investor sentiment cooled and SolarCity's stock price dropped off, trading mainly in the $40 to $60 range until mid-December 2015, when investor concerns about the size of SolarCity's mounting losses drove the stock down to the $16–$20 range in February 2016. Elon Musk was the chair of SolarCity's board of directors and owned 21.4 percent of the outstanding shares of the company as of March 31, 2015.

On August 12, 2013, Musk published a blog post detailing his design for a solar-powered, city-to-city elevated transit system called the Hyperloop that could take passengers and cars from Los Angeles to San Francisco (a distance of 380 miles) in 30 minutes. He then held a press call to go over the details. In Musk's vision, the Hyperloop would transport people via aluminum pods enclosed inside steel tubes. He described the design as looking like a shotgun with the tubes running side by side for most of the route and closing the loop at either end.[15] The tubes would be mounted on columns 50 to 100 yards apart, and the pods inside would travel up to 800 miles per hour. The pods could be small to carry just people or enlarged to allow people to drive a car into a pod and depart. Musk estimated that a Los Angeles–to–San Francisco Hyperloop could be built for $6 billion with people-only pods, or $10 billion for the larger pods capable of holding cars with people inside. Musk claimed his Hyperloop alternative would be four times as fast as California's proposed $70 billion high-speed train, with ticket costs being "much cheaper" than a plane ride. While pods would be equipped with an emergency brake for safety reasons, Musk said the safe distance between the pods would be about 5 miles, so you could have about 70 pods between Los Angeles and San Francisco that departed every 30 seconds. Musk stated that riding on the Hyperloop would be pleasant and super-smooth, with less lateral acceleration—which is what tends to make people feel motion sick—than a subway ride and no sudden movements due to turbulence (as is the case with airplanes). Musk said travel via a Hyperloop system between cities less than 1,000 miles apart would be quicker than flying because of the time it took to board and deplane airline passengers and the time it took for planes to take off and land at busy airports. Musk announced that he would not form a company to build Hyperloop systems; rather he was releasing his design in hopes that others would take on such projects.

Since 2008, many business articles had been written about Musk's brilliant entrepreneurship in creating companies with revolutionary products that either spawned new industries or disruptively transformed existing industries. In a 2012 *Success* magazine article, Musk indicated that his commitments to his spacecraft, electric car, and solar panel businesses were long term and deeply felt.[16] The author quoted Musk as saying, "I never expect to sort of sell them off and do something else. I expect to be with those companies as far into the future as I can imagine." Musk indicated he was involved in SolarCity and Tesla Motors "because I'm concerned about the environment," while "SpaceX is about trying to help us work toward extending life beyond Earth on a permanent basis and becoming a multiplanetary species." The same writer described Musk's approach to a business as one of rallying employees and investors without creating false hope.[17] The article quoted Musk as saying:

> You've got to communicate, particularly within the company, the true state of the company. When people really understand it's do or die but if we work hard and pull through, there's going to be a great outcome, people will give it everything they've got.

Asked if he relied more on information or instinct in making key decisions, Musk said he made no bright-line distinction between the two.[18]

> Data informs the instinct. Generally, I wait until the data and my instincts are in alignment. And if either the data or my instincts are out of alignment, then I sort of keep working the issue until they are in alignment, either positive or negative.

Musk was widely regarded as being an inspiring and visionary entrepreneur with astronomical ambition and willingness to invest his own money in risky and highly problematic business ventures—on several occasions, Musk's ventures had approached the brink of failure in 2008–2009, and then unexpectedly emerged with seemingly bright prospects. He set stretch performance targets and high product quality standards, and he pushed hard for their achievement. He exhibited perseverance, dedication, and an exceptionally strong work ethic—he typically worked 85 to 90 hours a week. Most weeks, Musk split his time between SpaceX and Tesla. He was at SpaceX's Los Angeles–based headquarters on Monday and Thursday and at various Tesla facilities in the San Francisco Bay Area on Tuesday and Wednesday.[19] On Friday he split his time between both companies—Tesla Design had offices in the same office park in a southern Los Angeles suburb as SpaceX; Musk's personal residence was about 18 miles away in a northern Los Angeles suburb.

However, Musk got mixed marks on his management style. He was praised for his grand vision of what his companies could become and his ability to shape the culture of his startup companies, but criticized for being hard to work with, partly because of his impatience for action and results, his intensity and sometimes hands-on micro-management of certain operational and product design issues, and the frequency with which overruled others and imposed his wishes when big decisions had to be made. But virtually no one had disparaged his brilliant intellect, inventive aptitude, and exceptional entrepreneurial abilities. In 2016, it was hard to dispute that Musk—at the age of 45—had already made a name for himself in two ways:[20]

- He had envisioned the transformative possibilities of the Internet, a migration from fossil fuels to sustainable energy, and expanding life beyond Earth.
- His companies (Tesla, SpaceX, and SolarCity) had put him in position to personally affect the path the world would take in migrating from fossil fuels to sustainable energy and to expanding life beyond Earth. Musk won the 2010 Automotive Executive of the Year Innovator Award for expediting the development of electric vehicles throughout the global automotive industry. *Fortune* magazine named Elon Musk its 2013 Businessperson of the Year.

In 2015 Musk's base salary as Tesla's CEO was $37,584, an amount required by California's minimum wage law; however, he was accepting only $1 in salary. Musk controlled 37.2 million shares of common stock in Tesla Motors (worth some $9.47 billion in April 2016) and had been granted options for about additional 80 million shares, subject to Tesla Motors achieving specified increases in market capitalization and 10 designated performance milestones by 2023.[21]

Recent Financial Performance and Financing Activities

Exhibits 2 and 3 present recent financial statement data for Tesla Motors.

In May 2013, Tesla raised over $1 billion by issuing new shares of common stock totaling $360 million

EXHIBIT 2 Consolidated Statement of Operations, Tesla Motors, 2011–2015 (in thousands, except share and per share data)

	Fiscal Years Ending December 31				
	2015	2014	2013	2012	2011
Income Statement Data:					
Revenues:					
Automotive	$3,740,973	$3,007,012	$1,921,877	$354,344	$101,748
Services and other	305,052	191,344	91,619	31,355	46,860
Total revenues	4,046,025	3,198,356	2,013,496	413,256	204,242
Cost of revenues:					
Automotive	2,823,302	2,145,749	1,483,321	371,658	115,482
Services and other	299,220	170,936	73,913	11,531	27,165

(*Continued*)

	2015	2014	2013	2012	2011
Total cost of revenues	3,122,522	2,316,615	1,557,234	383,189	142,647
Gross profit (loss)	923,503	881,671	456,262	30,067	61,595
Operating expenses:					
Research and development	717,900	464,700	231,976	273,978	208,981
Selling, general, and administrative	922,232	603,660	285,569	150,372	104,102
Total operating expenses	1,640,132	1,068,360	517,545	424,350	313,083
Loss from operations	(716,629)	(186,689)	(61,283)	(394,283)	(251,488)
Interest income	1,508	1,126	189	288	255
Interest expense	(18,851)	(100,886)	(32,934)	(254)	(43)
Other income (expense), net	(41,652)	1,813	22,602	(1,828)	(2,646)
Loss before income taxes	(875,624)	(284,636)	(71,426)	(396,077)	(253,922)
Provision for income taxes	13,039	9,404	2,588	136	489
Net loss	$ (888,663)	$ (294,040)	$ (74,014)	$ (396,213)	$ (254,411)
Net loss per share of common stock, basic and diluted	$(6.93)	$(2.36)	$(0.62)	$(3.69)	$(2.53)
Weighted average shares usedin computing net loss pershare of common stock, basic and diluted	128,202,000	124,539,343	119,421,414	107,349,188	100,388,815
Balance Sheet Data:					
Cash and cash equivalents	$ 1,196,908	$ 1,905,713	$ 845,889	$ 201,890	$ 255,266
Inventory	1,277,838	953,675	340,355	268,504	50,082
Total current assets	2,791,403	3,198,657	1,265,939	524,768	372,838
Property, plant, and equipment, net	3,403,334	1,829,267	738,494	552,229	298,414
Total assets	8,092,460	5,830,460	2,411,816	1,114,190	713,448
Total current liabilities	2,816,274	2,107,166	675,160	539,108	191,339
Long-term debt and capital leases	2,040,375	1,818,785	598,974	401,495	268,335
Total stockholders' equity	1,088,944	911,710	667,120	124,700	224,045
Cash Flow Data:					
Cash flows from operating activities	$ (524,499)	$(57,337)	$264,804	$(266,081)	$(128,034)
Proceeds from issuance of common stock in public offerings	730,000	—	360,000	221,496	172,410
Purchases of property and equipment excluding capital leases	(1,634,850)	(969,885)	(264,224)	(239,228)	(184,226)
Net cash used in investing activities	(1,673,551)	(990,444)	(249,417)	(206,930)	(162,258)
Net cash provided by financing activities	1,523,523	2,143,130	635,422	419,635	446,000

Sources: Company 10-K reports for 2014 and 2015.

EXHIBIT 3 Tesla's Financial Performance for 2015 versus 2014, GAAP versus Non-GAAP

	2015	2014
Revenues (GAAP)	$4,046,025	$3,198,356
Model S revenues deferred due to lease accounting	1,245,517	400,185
Revenues (Non-GAAP)	5,291,542	3,598,541
Gross profit (loss) (GAAP)	923,502	881,671
Model S gross profit deferred due to lease accounting	309,515	82,626
Stock-based compensation expense	19,244	17,455
Gross profit (loss) (Non-GAAP)	1,252,261	981,752
Research and development expenses (GAAP)	717,900	464,700
Stock-based compensation expense	(89,309)	(62,601)
Research and development expenses (Non-GAAP)	628,591	402,099
Selling, general, and administrative expenses (GAAP)	922,232	603,660
Stock-based compensation expense	(89,466)	(76,411)
Selling, general and administrative expenses (Non-GAAP)	832,786	527,219
Net loss (GAAP)	$ (888,663)	$ (294,040)
Stock-based compensation expense	197,999	156,496
Non-cash interest expense related to convertible notes and other borrowing	86,247	75,019
Model S gross profit deferred due to lease accounting	309,515	82,616
Net income (loss) (Non-GAAP)	$ (294,902)	$20,101
Net income (loss) per common share, basic (GAAP)	$(6.93)	$(2.36)
Net income (loss) per common share, basic (Non-GAAP)	(2.30)	0.16
Shares (in 000s) used in per share calculation, basic (GAAP and Non-GAAP)	128,202	124,573

Special Note on GAAP vs. Non-GAAP Treatments: Under generally accepted accounting principles (GAAP), revenues and costs of leased vehicles must be recorded and apportioned across the life of the lease; with non-GAAP lease accounting, all revenues and costs of a leased vehicle are recorded at the time the lease is finalized. Under GAAP, stock compensation must be expensed and allocated to the associated cost category; non-GAAP accounting excludes stock compensation as a cost because it is a non-cash item. Many companies, including Tesla Motors, believe non-GAAP treatments are useful in understanding company operations and actual cash flows. In Tesla's case, the non-GAAP treatments exclude such non-cash items as stock-based compensation, and non-cash interest expense related to Tesla's 1.5 percent convertible senior notes.

Sources: Tesla Motors's Shareholder Letter, Q4 2015, February 10, 2016, www.ir.teslamotors.com (accessed February 25, 2016).

and selling $660 million of 1.50 percent convertible senior notes. Elon Musk personally purchased 1.08 million of the newly issued shares of common stock at the public offering price, boosting his investment in Tesla by another $100 million. Tesla used about $450 million of the debt and equity proceeds to fully pay off its 2009 loan from the U.S. Department of Energy, including an $11 million fee for early payment. Additional borrowing in the form of convertible and other debt totaling $2.6 billion in 2014-15, along with another $730 million stock issue in 2015, was used to help fund capital expenditures of $970 million in 2014 and $1.6 billion in capital expenditures in 2015. Management expected that $618 million of previously issued convertible debt due in 2018 would likely be converted into shares of common stock in 2016.

Tesla ended 2015 with $1.2 billion in cash and cash equivalents. Executive management expected that the company's current level of liquidity, coupled with projected future cash flows from operating activities, was likely to provide adequate liquidity in 2016 based on current plans. However, if market conditions proved favorable, management said it would evaluate the merits of opportunistically pursuing actions to further boost the company's cash balances and overall liquidity. Top management expected that the company's capital expenditures in 2016 would total about $1.5 billion to further expand production capacity for the Model S and Model X, begin installation of Model 3 vehicle production machinery, fund ongoing construction work for the company's large-scale factory to build batteries and battery packs for its vehicles, and expand Tesla's geographic network of sales galleries, service centers, and Supercharger stations.

TESLA'S STRATEGY TO BECOME THE WORLD'S BIGGEST AND MOST HIGHLY REGARDED PRODUCER OF ELECTRIC VEHICLES

In 2016, Tesla's strategy was focused on broadening the company's model lineup, expanding the company's production capacity, stepping up the pace of constructing a new $5 billion plant to produce batteries and battery packs for Tesla's vehicles, and adding sales galleries, service centers, and Supercharger stations in the United States, much of Europe, China, and Australia.

Product Line Strategy

So far, Tesla had introduced three models—the Tesla Roadster, the Model S, and the Model X—with a fourth, the Model 3, approaching production startup. But the Model 3 posed a much different challenge than the three previous models, all of which had prices in the $80,000 to $130,000 range. The Model 3 was Tesla's first low-priced, entry-level model that management badly wanted to market at a base price of $35,000. The problem was that the lithium-ion battery pack was the single biggest cost component in the Model S and Model X—a cost reputedly in the neighborhood of $25,000 as of 2014. Hence, whether Tesla could profitably introduce the Model 3 at a base price of $35,000 hinged on how fast and how far the company could drive down the costs of a battery pack for Model 3 via greater scale economies in battery production and cost-saving advances in battery technology—just equipping the Model 3 with less powerful electric motors would not, by itself, be sufficient.

Tesla's First Vehicle—the Tesla Roadster

Following Tesla's initial funding in 2004, Musk took an active role within the company. Although he was not involved in day-to-day business operations, he nonetheless exerted strong influence in the design of the Tesla Roadster, a two-seat convertible that could accelerate from 0 to 60 miles per hour in as little as 3.7 seconds, had a maximum speed of about 120 miles per hour, could travel about 245 miles on a single charge, and had a base price of $109,000. Musk insisted from the beginning that the Roadster have a lightweight, high-strength carbon fiber body, and he influenced the design of components of the Roadster ranging from the power electronics module to the headlamps and other styling features.[22] Prototypes of the Roadster were introduced to the public in July 2006. The first "Signature One Hundred" set of fully equipped Roadsters sold out in less than three weeks; the second hundred sold out by October 2007. General production began in March 2008.New models of the Roadster were introduced in July 2009 (including the Roadster Sport with a base price of $128,500) and in July 2010. Sales of Roadster models to countries in Europe and Asia began in 2010. From 2008 through 2012, Tesla sold more than 2,450 Roadsters in 31 countries.[23] Sales of Roadster models ended in December 2012 so that the company could concentrate exclusively on producing and marketing the Model S. However, Tesla announced that in early 2015 Roadster owners would be able to obtain a Roadster 3.0 package that enabled a 40–50 percent improvement in driving range to as much as 400 miles on a single charge;

EXHIBIT 4 Tesla's Model S Sedan

(top left) © Wang Zhao/AFP/Getty Images; (top right) © Spencer Platt/Getty Images; (bottom) © Tribune Content Agency LLC/ Alamy Stock Photo

management expected to introduce additional Roadster updates in future years.

Tesla's Second Vehicle—the Model S Customer deliveries of Tesla's second vehicle, the sleek, eye-catching Model S sedan (see Exhibit 4), began in July 2012. Tesla introduced several new options for the Model S in 2013, including a subzero weather package, parking sensors, upgraded leather interior, several new wheel options, and a yacht-style center console. Xenon headlights and a high definition backup camera were made standard equipment on all Model S cars. In 2014 an all-wheel-drive powertrain was introduced to provide buyers with four powertrain options. The Model S powertrain options were further modified in April 2015 and then modified yet again later on in 2015 to that shown in Exhibit 5. The Tesla Model S provided best-in-class storage space of 63.4 cubic feet, including storage in the trunk and inside the cabin (58.1 cubic feet) and under the hood (5.3 cubic feet); this compared quite favorably with the 14.0 cubic-foot trunk capacity of BMW's large 7-series sedan, the 16.3 cubic-foot capacity of a Mercedes S-class sedan, and the 18.0 cubic-foot trunk capacity of the large Lexus 460 sedan.

In April 2015, Tesla sent software updates to all Model S vehicles previously delivered to customers that included a new "Range Assurance" feature, an always-running application within the car's navigation system that kept tabs on the vehicle's battery charge level and the locations of Tesla Supercharging stations and parking-spot chargers in the vicinity; when the vehicle's battery began running low, an

EXHIBIT 5 Features, Performance, and Pricing of Tesla's Three Model S Versions, 2015–2016

	70D All-Wheel Drive	90D All-Wheel Drive	P90D All-Wheel Drive
EPA certified range	240 miles	288 miles	270 miles
0 to 60 mph	5.2 seconds	4.2 seconds	3.1 seconds
Top speed	140 mph	155 mph	155 mph
Powertrain	Dual motors (front axle and rear axle)	Dual motors (front axle and rear axle)	High performance, dual motors (front axle and rear axle), smart-air suspension
Motor power	259 horsepower, front and rear	259 horsepower, front and rear	259 horsepower front, 503 horsepower rear
Battery	70 kWh microprocessor controlled lithium-ion battery	90 kWh microprocessor controlled lithium-ion battery	90 kWh microprocessor controlled lithium-ion battery
Base price (including destination charge)	$76,200	$86,200	$106,200
Price, with typical options	$95,450	$115,000	$125,000
New vehicle limited warranty	4 years or 50,000 miles, whichever comes first	4 years or 50,000 miles, whichever comes first	4 years or 50,000 miles, whichever comes first
Battery and drive unit warranty	8 years, infinite miles	8 years, infinite miles	8 years, infinite miles
Tesla Supercharger	Standard	Standard	Standard
Tech package with autopilot features	$4,250 (optional)	$4,250 (optional)	$4,250 (optional)
Premium interior and lighting	$3,000 (optional)	$3,000 (optional)	$3,000 (optional)
Supercharging capability			
Standard 110-volt wall outlets	Complete recharge overnight	Complete recharge overnight	Complete recharge overnight
240-volt outlet, with a single onboard charger	29 miles of range per hour	29 miles of range per hour	29 miles of range per hour
240-volt outlet, with twin onboard chargers	58 miles of range per hour	58 miles of range per hour	58 miles of range per hour
Tesla Supercharger enabled	50% in 20 minutes 80% in 40 minutes 100% in 75 minutes	50% in 20 minutes 80% in 40 minutes 100% in 75 minutes	50% in 20 minutes 80% in 40 minutes 100% in 75 minutes
Airbags	8	8	8
Total cargo volume	31.6 cubic feet	31.6 cubic feet	31.6 cubic feet

Sources: www.teslamotors.com and www.edmunds.com (accessed April 9, 2015, and February 26, 2016, respectively).

alert appeared on the navigation screen, along with a list of nearby Tesla Supercharger stations and public charging facilities. A second warning appeared when the vehicle was about to go beyond the radius of nearby chargers without enough juice to get to the next facility, at which point drivers were directed to the nearest charge point.

A few weeks later, another software update with a Trip Planner feature was sent out. Trip Planner consisted of a GPS navigation tweak that enabled drivers to plan long-distance trips based on the best charging options both en route and at the destination. The software displayed the fastest, most convenient route to the destination on the console screen, indicating where drivers needed to stop and how long they would need to plug in along the way to maintain sufficient battery power. The software was programmed to pull in new data about every 30 seconds, updating to show which charging facilities were vacant so the vehicle would not end up waiting in line for a plug.

In 2015, Tesla also announced the availability of an autopilot feature on new orders of the Model S. The autopilot option included a forward-looking camera, radar, and 360-degree sonar sensors with real-time traffic updates. An autopilot-equipped Model S could be automatically driven on the open road and in dense stop and go traffic. Changing lanes was as simple as a tap of the turn signal. Upon arriving at the destination, the autopilot control could detect a parking spot and automatically park the vehicle. Standard equipment safety features constantly monitored stop signs, traffic signals, and pedestrians, as well as unintentional lane changes. The autopilot features of the Model S were launched in Q4 of 2015 for 40,000 Model S vehicles previously delivered globally; the initial autopilot features were then rapidly enhanced and expanded with several "over-the-air" software updates in late 2015 and early 2016. The latest autopilot software version (February 2016) enabled variable speed cruise control (to match the flow of traffic), automatic lane centering (including around curves), camera-enabled automatic high/low beam headlights, self-parking, automatic self-braking, and blind spot warning; future autopilot software updates were expected to enable forward collision warning and other capabilities (potentially including self-driving). The autopilot parking features allowed vehicles to be parked or unparked with the driver inside or outside the vehicle and included locating a vacant parallel parking spot and smoothing backing into it, automatically parking in an open stall when pulling into a Tesla Supercharger station, automatically parking in an owner's garage at home, and—when calendar syncing was engaged—checking current traffic conditions to determine how much time was needed to make the driver's first appointment, starting the motor and turning on the climate control, opening the garage door, pulling out of the garage, and meeting the driver at the curb.

In the United States, customers who purchased a Model S (or any other Tesla model) were eligible for a federal tax credit of up to $7,500; a number of states also offered rebates on electric vehicle purchases, with states like California and New York offering rebates as high as $7,500. Customers who leased a Model S were not entitled to rebates.

Tesla's Third Vehicle—the Model X Crossover SUV To reduce the development costs of the Model X, Tesla had designed the Model X so that it could share about 60 percent of the Model S platform. The Model X had seating for seven adults, dual electric motors that powered an all-wheel-drive system, and a driving range of about 260 miles per charge. The Model X's distinctive "falcon-wing doors" provided easy access to the second and third seating rows, resulting in a profile that resembled a sedan more than an SUV (see Exhibit 6). All Model Xs featured two electric motors, one powering the front wheels and one powering the back wheels to create a standard all-wheel-drive system; the three drivetrain options for the Model X in 2016 were the same as for the Model S (see Exhibit 5). The driver-side door could auto-open as the driver approached, and auto-close once the driver was inside with a foot on the brake. Driver safety and convenience features include forward collision warning and automatic emergency braking, blind spot monitoring and parking assist, and a near hospital-grade cabin air filtration system.

As of March 2016, the first runs of Model Xs were sold out through the first half of 2016. Tesla executives forecast that that the company would deliver 36,000 to 40,000 Model Xs to customers in 2016. However, shipments on the Model X in the first eight weeks of 2016 were said to numbers only in the low hundreds each week, principally because of nagging problems with the falcon-wing doors (which, almost from the outset, had posed numerous design challenges, unexpectedly high engineering costs, and frequent delays in obtaining parts that functionally satisfactorily). Production has risen to 750 Model X vehicles per week by the end of March 2016.

EXHIBIT 6 Tesla's Model X Crossover

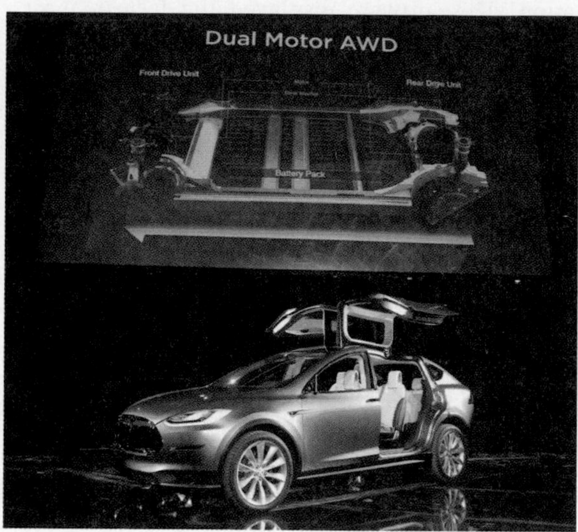

© Tim Rue/Bloomberg via Getty Images

Tesla's Fourth Vehicle—the Model 3 Buyer reaction to the Model 3 was overwhelmingly positive (see Exhibit 7). Over the next two weeks, some 350,000 individuals paid a $1,000 deposit to reserve a place in line to obtain a Model 3. Because of the tremendous amount of interest in the Model 3, Elon Musk announced in early May 2016 that Tesla was advancing its schedule to begin producing the Model 3 from late 2017 to mid-2017 and further that it was going to accelerate its efforts to expand production capacity, with a goal of getting to a production run rate of 500,000 units annually by year-end 2018 instead of year-end 2020. He added that Tesla would begin a major effort to produce somewhere between 100,000 to 200,000 Model 3 vehicles in the second half of 2017, depending on the ability of suppliers to provide the planned volumes of the different components that would be outsourced. He also said that there was a high probability that all of the people who had placed reservations would actually receive their vehicle in 2018. Analysts viewed these targets as extremely ambitious, but Musk countered that the Model 3 had been designed to enable efficient, high-volume production. But there was no disagreement that Tesla would have to raise $2–3 billion of new capital to fund the newly planned increases in production capacity, to add the necessary management expertise, and to hire and train so many new production workers—all within a relatively short time frame (14 months).

EXHIBIT 7 Tesla's Model 3

© dpa picture alliance/Alamy Stock Photo

One factor that might prove problematic for many prospective Model 3 buyers in the United States was a provision stating that once the *cumulative* sales volume of a manufacturer's zero emission vehicles in the United States reached 200,000 vehicles, the size of the $7,500 federal tax credit entered a 1-year phase-out period whereby buyers of qualifying vehicles were "eligible for 50 percent of the credit if acquired in the first two quarters of the phase-out period and 25 percent of the credit if acquired in the third or fourth quarter of the phase-out period." Purchasers of that manufacturer's vehicles were not eligible for any federal tax credit after the phase-out period. Given Musk's announcement of producing 100,000 or more Model 3 vehicles by year-end 2017, sales of Tesla vehicles in the United States would likely surpass the 200,000 level sometime in 2018. Analysts speculated that many customers in the United States placing reservations for the Model 3 might be unaware of this expiration provision (although, of course, legislation might subsequently be enacted to revive the tax credit provision for additional buyers of Tesla vehicles). Tax credits for European buyers of zero-emission Tesla vehicles in 2016 could run as high as $20,000 in some countries, but in countries where the tax incentives were highest, moves were underway to lower them (in Norway in 2013, the tax incentive to buy a Model S could run as high as $134,000).[24]

Distribution Strategy: A Company-Owned and Operated Network of Retail Stores and Service Centers

Tesla sold its vehicles directly to buyers and also provided them with after-sale service through a network of company-owned sales galleries and service centers. This contrasted sharply with the strategy of rival motor vehicle manufacturers, all of whom sold vehicles and replacement parts at wholesale prices to their networks of franchised dealerships that in turn handled retail sales, maintenance and service, and warranty repairs. Management believed that integrating forward into the business of traditional automobile dealers and operating its own retail sales and service network had three important advantages:

1. *The ability to create and control its own version of a compelling buying customer experience,* one that was differentiated from the buying experience consumers had with sales and service locations of franchised automobile dealers. Having customers deal directly with Tesla-employed sales and service personnel enabled Tesla to (a) engage and inform potential customers about electric vehicles in general and the advantages of owning a Tesla in particular and (b) build a more personal relationship with customers and, hopefully, instill a lasting and favorable impression of Tesla Motors, its mission, and the caliber and performance of its vehicles.
2. *The ability to achieve greater operating economies in performing sales and service activities.* Management believed that a company-operated sales and service network offered substantial opportunities to better control inventory costs of both vehicles and replacement parts, manage warranty service and pricing, maintain and strengthen the Tesla brand, and obtain rapid customer feedback.
3. *The opportunity to capture the sales and service revenues of traditional automobile dealerships.* Rival motor vehicle manufacturers sold vehicles and replacement parts at wholesale prices to their networks of franchised dealerships that in turn handled retail sales, maintenance and service, and warranty repairs. But when Tesla buyers purchased a vehicle at a Tesla-owned sales gallery, Tesla captured the full retail sales price, roughly 10 percent greater than the wholesale price realized by vehicle manufacturers selling through franchised dealers. And, by operating its own service centers, it captured service revenues not available to vehicle manufacturers who relied upon their franchised dealers to provide need maintenance and repairs. Furthermore, Tesla management believed that company-owned service centers avoided the conflict of interest between vehicle manufacturers and their franchised dealers where the sale of warranty parts and repairs by a dealer were a key source of revenue and profit for the dealer but where warranty-related costs were typically a substantial expense for the vehicle manufacturer.

Tesla Sales Galleries and Showrooms Currently, all of Tesla's sales galleries and showrooms were in or near major metropolitan areas; some were in prominent regional shopping malls and others were on highly visible sites along busy thoroughfares. Most sales locations had only several vehicles in stock. While some customers purchased their vehicles from the available inventory, most preferred to order a custom-equipped car in their preferred color.

Tesla was aggressively expanding its network of sales galleries and service centers to broaden its geographic presence and to provide better maintenance and repair service in areas with a high concentration of Model S customers. In 2013, Tesla began combining its sales and service activities at a single location (rather than having separate locations, as earlier had been the case); experience indicated that combination sales and service locations were more cost-efficient and facilitated faster expansion of the company's retail footprint. At the end of 2015, Tesla had 208 sales and service locations around the world, and planned to open 80 more sales galleries and service centers in 2016. Tesla's strategy was to have sufficient service locations to ensure that after-sale services were available to owners when and where needed.

However, in the United States there was a lurking problem with Tesla's strategy to bypass distributing through franchised Tesla dealers and sell directly to consumers. Going back many years, franchised automobile dealers in the United States had feared that automotive manufacturers might one day decide to integrate forward into selling and servicing the vehicles they produced. To foreclose any attempts by manufacturers to compete directly against their franchised dealers, automobile dealers in every state in the United States had formed statewide franchised dealer associations to lobby for legislation blocking motor vehicle manufacturers from becoming retailers of new and used cars and providing maintenance and repair services to vehicle owners. Legislation either forbidding or severely restricting the ability of automakers to sell vehicles directly to the public had been passed in 48 states; these laws had been in effect for many years, and franchised dealer associations were diligent in pushing for strict enforcement of these laws.

As sales of the Model S rose briskly in 2013–2015 and Tesla continued opening more sales galleries and service centers, both franchised dealers and statewide dealer associations became increasingly anxious about "the Tesla problem" and what actions might need to be taken. Dealers and dealer trade association in a number of states were openly vocal about their concerns and actively began lobbying state legislatures to consider either enforcement actions against Tesla or amendments to existing legislation that would bring a halt to Tesla's efforts to sell vehicles at company-owned showrooms. A host of skirmishes ensued in states like Ohio, New Jersey, New York, Texas, Arizona, Maryland, Georgia, Indiana, West Virginia, Virginia, Pennsylvania, and Michigan. In several cases, settlements were reached that allowed Tesla to open a select few sales locations, but the numbers were capped. In states where manufacturer direct sales to consumers were expressly prohibited in 2015–2016 (Texas, Arizona, Connecticut), Tesla could still have sales galleries, service centers, and Supercharger locations—what it could not do at its limited number of sales galleries was take orders, conduct test drives, deliver cars, or discuss pricing with potential buyers. Buyers in these states could place an order for a Tesla online (but not in a Tesla sales gallery) at **www.teslamotors.com**, specify when they wanted the car to arrive, and then either have it delivered to a nearby Tesla service center for pickup or have it delivered directly to their home or business location. As of March 2016, only Michigan, Utah, and West Virginia prevented Tesla from opening sales galleries in their states.

Tesla Service Centers Tesla's strategy was to have sufficient service locations to ensure that after-sale services were available to owners when and where needed. The company had over 118 service locations as of year-end 2015.

Tesla Roadster owners could upload data from their vehicle and send it to a service center on a memory card; Model S owners had an on-board system that could communicate directly with a service center, allowing service technicians to diagnose and remedy many problems before ever looking at the vehicle. When maintenance or service was required, a customer could schedule service by contacting a Tesla service center. Some service locations offered valet service, where the owner's car was picked up, replaced with a very well-equipped Model S loaner car, and then returned when the service was completed—there was no additional charge for valet service. In some locations, owners could opt to have service performed at their home, office, or other remote location by a Tesla Ranger mobile technician who had the capability to perform a variety of services that did not require a vehicle lift. Tesla Rangers could perform most warranty repairs, but the cost of their visit was not covered under the New Vehicle Limited Warranty. Ranger service pricing was based on a per visit, per vehicle basis; there was a $100 minimum charge per Ranger visit.

Prepaid Maintenance Program Tesla offered a comprehensive maintenance program for every new vehicle, which included plans covering prepaid maintenance for up to eight years or up to 100,000 miles and an Extended Service plan. The maintenance plans covered annual inspections and the replacement of wear and tear parts, excluding tires and the battery. The Extended Service plan covered the repair or replacement of vehicle parts for up to an additional four years or up to an additional 50,000 miles after the expiration of the four-year or 50,000-mile new vehicle limited warranty.

Tesla's Supercharger Network: Providing Recharging Services to Owners on Long-Distance Trips A major component of Tesla's strategy to build rapidly growing long-term demand for its vehicles was to make battery-recharging while driving long distances convenient and worry-free for all Tesla vehicle owners. Tesla's solution to providing owners with ample and convenient recharging opportunities was to establish an extensive geographic network of recharging stations. Tesla's Supercharger stations were strategically placed along major highways connecting city centers, usually at locations with such nearby amenities as roadside diners, cafés, and shopping centers that enabled owners to have a brief rest stop or get a quick meal during the recharging process—about 90 percent of Model S buyers opted to have their vehicle equipped with supercharging capability when they ordered their vehicle. All Model S owners were entitled to use the free supercharging service at any of Tesla's Supercharging stations to get a 50 percent recharge in 20 minutes, an 80 percent recent recharge in 40 minutes, or a 100 percent recharge in 75 minutes. As of year-end 2015, Tesla had 584 Supercharger stations open worldwide; each station had 4 to 10 charging spaces. About 300 new Supercharger locations were planned in North America, Europe, and Asia for 2016.

Exhibit 8 shows a Tesla Supercharger station and selected Tesla sales galleries and service centers.

Tesla executives expected that the company's planned Supercharger network would relieve much of the "range anxiety" associated with driving on a long distance trip. However, even with many Supercharger locations strategically positioned along major travel routes, it was likely that Tesla owners in China, Canada, and parts of Europe would still be inconvenienced by having to deviate from the shortest direct route and detour to the closest Supercharger station for needed recharging. The degree to which range anxiety and "detour frustration" might prompt future vehicle shoppers to steer away from buying a Tesla was a risk that Tesla still had to prove it could hurdle.

Technology and Product Development Strategy

Headed into 2016, Tesla had spent over $2.0 billion on research and development (R&D) activities to design, develop, test, and refine the components

EXHIBIT 8 A Tesla Supercharger Station and Selected Tesla Sales Galleries and Service Centers

(left) © Zhang Peng/LightRocket via Getty Images; (right) © Kiyoshi Ota/Bloomberg via Getty Images

and systems needed to produce top-quality electric vehicles and, further, to design and develop prototypes of the Tesla Roadster, Model S, Model X, and Model 3 vehicles (see Exhibit 1 for R&D spending during 2011–2015). Tesla executives believed the company had developed core competencies in powertrain and vehicle engineering and innovative manufacturing techniques. The company's core intellectual property was contained in its electric powertrain technology—the battery pack, power electronics, induction motor, gearbox, and control software which enabled these key components to operate as a system. Tesla personnel had designed each of these major elements for the Tesla Roadster and Model S; much of this technology was being used in the powertrain components that Tesla built for other manufacturers and was scheduled for use in the Model X, Model 3, and future Tesla vehicles.

Tesla's powertrain was a compact, modular system with far fewer moving parts than the powertrains of traditional gasoline-powered vehicles, a feature that enabled Tesla to implement powertrain enhancements and improvements as fast as they could be identified, designed, and tested. Tesla had incorporated its latest powertrain technology into the Model S and also into the powertrain components that it built and sold to other makers of electric vehicles; plus, it was planning to use much of this technology in its forthcoming electric vehicles.

Although Tesla had more than 500 patents and pending patent applications domestically and internationally in a broad range of areas, in 2014, Tesla announced a patent policy whereby it irrevocably pledged the company would not initiate a lawsuit against any party for infringing Tesla's patents through activity relating to electric vehicles or related equipment so long as the party was acting in good faith. Elon Musk said the company made this pledge in order to encourage the advancement of a common, rapidly evolving platform for electric vehicles, thereby benefiting itself, other companies making electric vehicles, and the world. Investor reaction to this announcement was largely negative on grounds that it would negate any technology-based competitive advantage over rival manufacturers of electric vehicles—which, many investors viewed as being considerable.

Battery Pack Over the years, Tesla had tested hundreds of battery cells of different chemistries and performance features. It had an internal battery cell testing lab and had assembled an extensive performance database of the many available lithium-ion cell vendors and chemistry types. Based on this evaluation, it had elected to use "18650 form factor" lithium-ion battery cells, chiefly because a battery pack containing 18650 cells offered two to three times the driving range of the lithium-ion cells used by other makers of electric vehicles. Moreover, Tesla had been able to obtain large quantities of the 18650 lithium-ion cells for its battery pack (each pack had about 7,000 of the 18650 cells) at attractive prices because global lithium-ion battery manufacturers were suffering from a huge capacity glut, having overbuilt production capacity in anticipation of a fast-growing buyer demand for electric vehicles that so far had failed to materialize.

Management believed that the company's accumulated experience and expertise had produced a core competence in battery pack design and safety, putting Tesla in position to capitalize on the substantial battery cell investments and advancements being made globally by battery cell manufacturers and by its own battery technology personnel as concerned energy storage capacity, longevity, power delivery, and costs per kilowatt-hour of the battery packs used in current and forthcoming models. Tesla's battery pack design in 2013–2015 gave it the ability to change battery cell chemistries and vendors, while retaining the company's existing investments in software, electronics, testing, and other powertrain components. Going forward, Tesla intended to maintain the flexibility to quickly incorporate the latest advancements in battery technology, change battery cell chemistries if needed, and continue to optimize battery pack system performance and cost for its future vehicles.

Power Electronics The power electronics in Tesla's powertrain system had two primary functions, the control of torque generation in the motor while driving and the control of energy delivery back into the battery pack while charging. The first function was accomplished through the drive inverter, which was directly responsible for the performance, energy-use efficiency, and overall driving experience of the vehicle. The second function, charging the battery pack, was accomplished by the vehicle's charger, which converted alternating current (usually from a wall outlet or other electricity source) into direct current which could be accepted by the battery. Most Model S owners ordered vehicles equipped with twin chargers in order to cut the charging time in half.

Owners could use any available source of power to charge their vehicle. A standard 12-amp/110-volt wall outlet could charge the battery pack to full capacity in about 42 hours for vehicles equipped with a single charger, or 21 hours with a twin charger. Tesla recommended that owners install *at least* a 24-amp/240-volt outlet in their garage or carport (the same voltage used by many electric ovens and clothes dryers), which permitted charging at the rate of 34 miles of range per hour of charging time on vehicles equipped with a twin charger. But Tesla strongly recommended the installation of a more powerful 40-amp/240-volt outlet that charged at the rate of 58 miles of range per hour of charge when a Model S was equipped with twin chargers. Model S vehicles came standard with three adapters: a 12-amp/110-volt adapter, a 40-amp/240-volt adapter, and a J1772 public charging station adapter; other adapters could be purchased online.

Control Software The battery pack and the performance and safety systems of Tesla vehicles required the use of numerous microprocessors and sophisticated software. For example, computer-driven software monitored the charge state of each of the cells of the battery pack and managed all of the safety systems. The flow of electricity between the battery pack and the motor had to be tightly controlled in order to deliver the performance and behavior expected in the vehicle. There were software algorithms that enabled the vehicle to mimic the "creep" feeling which drivers expected from an internal combustion engine vehicle without having to apply pressure on the accelerator. Other algorithms controlled traction, vehicle stability, and the sustained acceleration and regenerative braking of the vehicle. Drivers used the vehicle's information systems to optimize performance and charging modes and times. In addition to the vehicle control software, Tesla had developed software for the infotainment system of the Model S and Model X. Almost all of the software programs had been developed and written by Tesla personnel. In 2014–2016, Tesla utilized the bulk of its expertise to develop and enhance its software for vehicle autopilot functionality, including such features as road tracking, lane changing, automated parking, driver warning systems, automated braking, and self-driving.

Tesla's strategy was to routinely enhance the performance of its models by sending wireless software updates to the microprocessors on board each vehicle it had sold.

Vehicle Design and Engineering

Tesla had devoted considerable effort to creating significant in-house capabilities related to designing and engineering portions of its vehicles, and it had become knowledgeable about the design and engineering of those parts, components, and systems that it purchased from suppliers. Tesla personnel had designed and engineered the body, chassis, and interior of the Model S and Model X and were working on the designs and engineering of these same components for the Model 3. As a matter of necessity, Tesla was forced to redesign the heating, cooling, and ventilation system for its vehicles to operate without the energy generated from an internal combustion engine and to integrate with its own battery-powered thermal management system. In addition, the low voltage electric system which powered the radio, power windows, and heated seats had to be designed specifically for use in an electric vehicle. Tesla had developed expertise in integrating these components with the high-voltage power source in the Model S and in designing components that significantly reduced their load on the vehicle's battery pack, so as to maximize the available driving range.

Tesla personnel had accumulated considerable expertise in lightweight materials, since an electric vehicle's driving range was heavily impacted by the vehicle's weight and mass. The Tesla Roadster had been built with an in-house designed carbon fiber body to provide a good balance of strength and mass. The Model S and Model X had a lightweight aluminum body and a chassis that incorporated a variety of materials and production methods to help optimize vehicle weight, strength, safety, and performance. In addition, top management believed that the company's design and engineering team had core competencies in computer aided design and crash test simulations; this expertise was expected to reduce the product development time of new models.

Manufacturing Strategy

Tesla contracted with Lotus Cars, Ltd. to produce Tesla Roadster "gliders" (a complete vehicle minus the electric powertrain) at a Lotus factory in Hethel, England. The Tesla gliders were then shipped to a Tesla facility in Menlo Park, California, where the battery pack, induction motors, and other powertrain components were installed as part of the final assembly process. The production of Roadster gliders ceased in January 2012.

In May 2010, Tesla purchased the major portion of a recently closed automobile plant in Fremont, California, for $42 million; months later, Tesla purchased some of the plant's equipment for $17 million. The facility—formerly a General Motors manufacturing plant (1960–1982), then operated as joint venture between General Motors and Toyota (1984–2010) to showcase Toyota's famed production system and produce Toyota Corolla and Tacoma vehicles—was closed in 2010 when GM pulled out of the joint venture and Toyota elected to cease its production of several thousand vehicles per week and permanently lay off about 4,700 workers. Tesla executives viewed the facility as one of the largest, most advanced, and cleanest automotive production plants in the world, and the space inside the 5.5-million-square-foot main building was deemed sufficient for Tesla to produce about 500,000 vehicles annually (approximately 1 percent of the total worldwide car production), thus giving Tesla plenty of room to grow its output of electric vehicles. The Fremont plant's location in the northern section of Silicon Valley facilitated hiring talented engineers already residing nearby and because the short distance between Fremont and Tesla's Palo Alto headquarters ensured "a tight feedback loop between vehicle engineering, manufacturing, and other divisions within the company."[25] Tesla officially took possession of the 350-acre site in October 2010, renamed it the Tesla Factory, and immediately launched efforts to get a portion of the massive facility ready to begin manufacturing components and assembling the Model S in 2012.

In December 2012, Tesla opened a new 60,000-square-foot facility in Tilburg, Netherlands, about 50 miles from the port of Rotterdam, to serve as the final assembly and distribution point for all Model S vehicles sold in Europe and Scandinavia. The facility, called the Tilburg Assembly Plant, received nearly complete vehicles shipped from the Tesla Factory, performed certain final assembly activities, conducted final vehicle testing, and handled the delivery to customers across. It also functioned as Tesla's European service and parts headquarters. Tilburg's central location and its excellent rail and highway network to all major markets on the European continent allowed Tesla to distribute to anywhere across the continent in about 12 hours. The Tilburg operation had been expanded to over 200,000 square feet in order to accommodate a parts distribution warehouse for service centers throughout Europe, a center for remanufacturing work, and a customer service center. A nearby facility in Amsterdam provided corporate oversight for European sales, service, and administrative functions.

Tesla's manufacturing strategy was to source a number of parts and components from outside suppliers but to design, develop, and manufacture in-house those key components where it had considerable intellectual property and core competencies (namely lithium-ion battery packs, electric motors, gearboxes, and other powertrain components) and to perform all assembly-related activities itself. In 2016, the Tesla Factory contained several production-related activities, including stamping, machining, casting, plastics molding, robotics-assisted body assembly, paint operations, final vehicle assembly, and end-of-line quality testing—see Exhibit 9. In addition, the Tesla Factory manufactured lithium-ion battery packs, electric motors, gearboxes, and certain other components for its vehicles. During 2014 and 2015, installations of new equipment boosted the annual production capacity of the Tesla Factory from about 21,500 vehicles in 2013 to nearly 60,000 vehicles at year-end 2015. In 2014, Tesla began producing and machining various aluminum components at a facility in Lathrop, California; in 2016, Tesla was nearing completion of an expansion at the Lathrop facility to include an aluminum castings operation. In late 2015, Tesla completed construction of a new high-volume paint shop and a new bodyshop line capable of turning out 3,500 Model S and Model X bodies per week (enough for 175,000 vehicles annually). Over the course of 2016, management planned to make significant additional investments at the Tesla Factory, including a new bodyshop with space and equipment for Model 3 final assembly.

Initially, production costs for the Model S were adversely impacted by an assortment of startup costs at the Tesla Factory, manufacturing inefficiencies associated with inexperience and low-volume production, higher prices for component parts during the first several months of production runs, and higher logistics costs associated with the immaturity

EXHIBIT 9 Scenes of Assembly Operations at the Tesla Factory

(top left) © Steve Proehl/Getty Images; (top right) © Jasper Juinen/Bloomberg via Getty Images; (bottom left) © Winni Wintermeyer/For Manager Magazin; (bottom right) © Jasper Juinen/Bloomberg via Getty Images

of Tesla's supply chain. However, as Tesla engineers redesigned various elements of the Model S for greater ease of manufacturing, supply chain improvements were instituted, and production volumes approached 1,000 vehicles per week in 2014, manufacturing efficiency rose, the costs of some parts decreased, and overall production costs per vehicle trended downward. Further manufacturing efficiency gains were made in 2015, and more were expected in 2016 as production of the Model X ramped up.

Tesla had encountered a number of unexpected quality problems in the first two to three months of manufacturing the Model X. Getting the complicated hinges on the falcon-wing doors to function properly proved to be particularly troublesome. Customers who received the first wave of Model X deliveries also reported problems with the front doors and windows and with the 17-inch dashboard touchscreen freezing (a major problem because so many functions were controlled from this screen). However, these problems had been largely resolved by early March 2016, and weekly production volumes of the Model X rose steadily in over the next three months.

Tesla's "Gigafactory" to Produce Battery Packs In February 2014, Tesla announced that it and unnamed partners would invest $4–5 billion through 2020 in a "gigafactory" capable of producing enough lithium-ion batteries to make battery packs for 500,000 vehicles (plus Tesla's recently developed energy storage products for both businesses and homeowners)—the planned output of the battery factory in 2020 exceeded the *total global production of lithium batteries in 2013*. Tesla said its direct investment in the project would be $2 billion. Tesla indicated the new plant (named the Tesla Gigafactory) would reduce the company's battery pack cost by more than 30 percent—to around $200 per kWh by some estimates (from the current estimated level of about $300 per kWh). The schedule called for facility construction in 2014–2015, equipment installation in 2016, and initial production in 2016–2017. Plans called for the plant to be built on a 500- to 1,000-acre site, employ about 6,500 workers, have about 10 million square feet of space on two levels, and be powered by wind and solar generating facilities located nearby.

Evaluation of finalist plant sites in five states (Nevada, Arizona, New Mexico, Texas, and California) began immediately; competition among the five states to win the plant was fierce but in September 2014, Tesla announced that a site in an industrial park east of Reno, Nevada, would be the location of the Tesla Gigafactory. It was speculated that the Nevada site was chosen partly because the state offered Tesla a lucrative incentive package said to be worth $1.25 billion over 20 years and partly because the only commercially active lithium mining operation in the United States was in a nearby Nevada county (this county was reputed to have the fifth-largest deposits of lithium in the world). In early 2016, construction of the Tesla Gigafactory was proceeding at a rapid clip, with completed space already available for production of Tesla's energy storage products (which began in the last quarter of 2015).

Less than a month after announcing its intent to build the Gigafactory, Tesla sold $920 million of convertible senior notes due 2019 carrying an interest rate of 0.25 percent and $1.38 billion in convertible senior notes due 2021 carrying an interest rate of 1.25 percent. The senior notes due 2019 were convertible into cash, shares of Tesla's common stock, or a combination thereof, at Tesla's election. The convertible senior notes due 2021 were convertible into cash and, if applicable, shares of Tesla's common stock (subject to Tesla's right to deliver cash in lieu of shares of common stock). To protect existing shareholders against ownership dilution that might result from the senior notes being converted into additional shares of Tesla stock, Tesla immediately entered into convertible note hedge transactions and warrant transactions at an approximate cost of $186 million that management expected would reduce potential dilution of existing shareholder interests and/or offset cash payments that Tesla was required to make in excess of the principal amounts of the 2019 notes and 2021 notes.

In 2016, Tesla announced that it was on track to achieve a 30 percent cost reduction in the battery pack for the Model 3, plus ongoing annual cost reductions of 5–8 percent and ongoing improvements in battery performance of 5–8 percent annually. In addition, the company had discovered ways to build an improved lithium-ion battery that would be larger, safer, and require fewer individual batteries per battery pack. Furthermore, all these cost and performance improvements would affect the battery packs used in the Model S and Model X. These technological advances materially enhanced the ability of the Gigafactory to supply Tesla's need for battery packs as the sales volumes of Tesla models grew.

Supply Chain Strategy Tesla's Model S and Model X used over 3,000 purchased parts and components sourced globally from over 350 suppliers, the majority of whom were currently single-source suppliers. It was the company's practice to obtain the needed parts and components from multiple sources whenever feasible, and Tesla management expected able to secure alternate sources of supply for many single sourced components within a year or two. However, qualifying alternate suppliers for certain highly customized components—or producing them internally—was thought to be both time-consuming and costly, perhaps even requiring modifications to a vehicle's design.

While Tesla had developed close relationships with the suppliers of lithium-ion battery cells and certain other key system parts, it typically did not have long-term agreements with them. The one big exception was the relationship Tesla had with Panasonic to supply Tesla with lithium-ion batteries. Tesla began collaborating with Panasonic in 2010 to develop battery cells based on the 18650 form factor and nickel-based lithium-ion chemistry. In October 2011, Tesla and Panasonic finalized an agreement whereby Panasonic would supply Tesla with sufficient battery cells to build more than 80,000 vehicles over the next four years. In October 2013, Tesla and Panasonic agreed to extend the supply agreement though the end of 2017, with Tesla agreeing to purchase a minimum of 1.8 billion lithium-ion battery cells and Panasonic agreeing to provide Tesla with preferential prices. Panasonic had a major role in producing batteries at the Gigafactory.

Marketing Strategy

In 2014–2015, Tesla's principal marketing goals and functions were to:

- Generate demand for the company's vehicles and drive sales leads to personnel in the Tesla's showrooms and sales galleries.
- Build long-term brand awareness and manage the company's image and reputation.
- Manage the existing customer base to create brand loyalty and generate customer referrals.
- Obtain feedback from the owners of Tesla vehicles and make sure their experiences and suggestions for improvement were communicated to Tesla personnel engaged in designing, developing, and/or improving the company's current and future vehicles.

As the first company to commercially produce a federally compliant, fully electric vehicle that achieved market-leading range on a single charge, Tesla had been able to generate significant media coverage of the company and its vehicles. Management expected this would continue to be the case for some time to come. So far, the extensive media coverage, glowing praise from both new Model S owners and admiring car enthusiasts (which effectively enlarged Tesla's sales force at zero cost), and the decisions of many green-minded affluent individuals to help lead the movement away from gasoline-powered vehicles had combined to drive good traffic flows at Tesla's sales galleries and create a backlog of orders for the Model S. As a consequence, going into 2016 the company had achieved a growing volume of sales without traditional advertising and at relatively low marketing costs. Nonetheless, Tesla did make use of pay-per-click advertisements on websites and mobile applications relevant to its target clientele. It also displayed and demonstrated its vehicles at such widely attended public events as the Detroit, Los Angeles, and Frankfurt auto shows and at a few small private events attended by people who were likely to be intrigued by its vehicles.

Tesla's Innovative Resale Guarantee Program for New Vehicle Purchases During the second quarter of 2013, Tesla instituted its first big internal marketing and sales promotion campaign to spur demand for its Model S vehicles and give owners complete peace of mind about the long-term value of the product. Model S buyers in the United States were given the option of selling their vehicle back to Tesla within a window of 36 to 39 months after delivery for a guaranteed percentage of the purchase price, thus enabling them to enjoy the benefits of Model S ownership without concern for the vehicle's resale value. The buyback option was extended to buyers in selected European and Asia-Pacific countries in 2014 and 2015. In certain markets, Tesla had extended the guaranteed buyback price option to partner financial institutions who made 3-year auto financing loans to Model S buyers.

Tesla, in partnership with various financial institutions, began leasing vehicles to customers in 2014; the number and percentage of customers opting to lease Model S vehicles increased substantially in 2015. By year-end 2015, Tesla was not only offering loans and leases in North America, Europe and Asia through its various partner financial institutions, but it was also offering loans and leases directly through its own captive finance subsidiaries in certain areas of the United States, Germany, Canada, and Great Britain. Tesla management intended to broaden its financial services offerings during the next several years.

Tesla's offer to buy back Model S cars from customers using its lease-buyback financing option had the potential to provide Tesla with another profitable revenue stream—selling used Tesla vehicles at prices above the buyback price. According to one analyst, "Buying back three-year-old cars at a set price means Tesla to a great extent can control the secondary market for Model S and other cars it brings out. The company's going to be the main buyer and get a chance to earn a second gross profit on the same car."[26] The analyst estimated that sales of used Model S vehicles in 2016 could mean an added $350–370 million in revenues for Tesla in 2016 and perhaps an added $40 million in annual gross profit.

Even though Tesla received full upfront payment for the vehicles sold under the resale guarantee financing program, generally accepted accounting principles (GAAP) required Tesla to treat transactions under the resale guarantee program as leased vehicles and to spread the recognition of revenue and cost over the contractual term of the resale value guarantee (36 to 39 months). If a Model S owner decided not to sell their vehicle back to Tesla by the end of the resale value guarantee term, any deferred revenue and the vehicle's undepreciated book value were then recognized as revenues from automotive sales and as a cost of automotive sales, respectively. The impact of lease accounting on Tesla's revenues can be seen in Exhibit 3.

The resale guarantee program exposed Tesla to the risk that the vehicles' resale value could be lower than its estimates and also to the risk that the volume of vehicles sold back to Tesla at the guaranteed resale price might be higher than the company's estimates. GAAP required such risks to be accounted for on Tesla's financial statements by establishing a reserves account (a contingent liability in the current liabilities section of the balance sheet) deemed sufficient to cover these risks.

Sales of Regulatory Credits to Other Automotive Manufacturers

Because Tesla's electric vehicles had no tailpipe emissions of greenhouse gases or other pollutants, Tesla earned zero emission vehicle (ZEV) and greenhouse gas (GHG) credits on each vehicle sold in the United States. Moreover, it also earned corporate average fuel economy (CAFE) credits on its sales of vehicles because of their high equivalent miles per gallon ratings. All three of these types of regulatory credits had significant market value because the manufacturers of traditional gasoline-powered vehicles were subject to assorted emission and mileage requirements set by the U.S. Environmental Protection Agency (EPA) and by certain state agencies charged with protecting the environment within their borders; automotive manufacturers whose vehicle sales did not meet prevailing emission and mileage requirements were allowed to achieve compliance by purchasing credits earned by other automotive manufacturers. Tesla had entered into contracts for the sale of ZEV and GHG credits with several automotive manufacturers, and it also routinely sold its CAFE credits. Tesla's sales of ZEV, GHG, and CAFE credits produced revenues of $2.8 million in 2010, $2.7 million in 2011, $40.5 million in 2012, $194.4 million in 2013, $216.3 million in 2014, and $168.7 million in 2015. In Exhibit 2, these amounts were included on Tesla's income statement in the revenue category labeled "Automotive."

Wall Street analysts frequently noted that the revenues Tesla earned from the sales of regulatory credits were a material factor in preventing Tesla's bottom line from looking significantly worse in 2013, 2014, and 2015. However, while the company intended to sell regulatory credits earned from future sales of its vehicles for as long as such opportunities were available, Tesla executives maintained that the long-term viability and profitability of Tesla's business model was not predicated on revenues from the sale of regulatory credits.

The May 2015 Launch of Tesla Energy

In spring 2015, Tesla announced the formation and launch of Tesla Energy, a new subsidiary that would begin producing and selling two energy storage products in the second half of 2015— Powerwall for homeowners and Powerpack for industrial and commercial customers. Powerwall was a lithium-ion battery charged either by electricity generated from a home's solar panels or from power company sources when electric rates were low; Powerwall came in two models—a 10-kWh model for $3,500 and a 7-kWh model for $3,000. Tesla saw Powerwall as principally a product that energy-conscious homeowners with a rooftop solar system could use to lower their monthly electric bills by programming Powerwall to power their homes during certain hours when the rates of some power companies were high and then recharging the battery during the late-night hours when rates were low. However, Powerwall home batteries could also be used as a backup power source in case of unexpected power company outages. Homeowners with energy needs greater than 7 kWh or 10 kWh or for periods longer than the life of a single battery charge (about two hours) could install multiple models. Both Powerwall models were guaranteed for ten years.

Powerpack models were 100kw lithium-ion batteries that industrial and commercial enterprises could use for a variety of purposes, with most installations using a minimum of 10 Powerpack batteries and perhaps as many as 20 to 30 batteries. Elon Musk saw Powerpack also being used by utilities for energy storage.

In the first week after the announcement introducing Powerwall and Powerpack, Tesla received 38,000 reservations for Powerwall (although residential buyers could place a reservation with no money down) and requests from 2,500 companies indicating interest in installing or distributing Powerpack batteries. In the remaining months of 2015, Tesla moved swiftly to prepare its supply chain and production teams to begin volume builds on both new products. Production began at the Tesla Factory in Fremont and then shifted to the Gigafactory in the last part of 2015. In early 2016, both Powerwall and Powerpack production was operating smoothly and expanding at the Gigafactory. The first Powerwalls built had been installed at buyer locations in the United States, Australia, and Germany; sales leads for Powerwalls in Germany and Australia had quickly outstripped those for Tesla's vehicles. Musk said Tesla was on track to steadily boost its gross margins on sales of Powerwalls and Powerpacks during 2016, allowing Tesla to realize positive cash contributions despite rapid growth in production and sales. Musk said that buyer demand for Powerwalls and Powerpacks might prove strong enough in 2016 for the company to consider expanding the battery-making capacity of the Gigafactory beyond the amount currently planned.

Panasonic agreed to partner with Tesla in building and operating the Tesla Gigafactory in mid-2014. According to the agreement, Tesla had responsibility for preparing, providing, and managing the land, buildings, and utilities, with Panasonic having responsibility for investing in the equipment and manufacturing the batteries. About 50 percent of the floor space in the Gigafactory was expected to be devoted to Panasonic's battery-making activities, with the activities of battery-related materials and components suppliers and Tesla's Powerwall and Powerpack battery pack operations taking up the other half.

The Electric Vehicle Segment of the Global Automotive Industry

Global sales of passenger cars and SUVs in 2014 and 2015 were roughly 65.0 million. Sales of other types of vehicles (light or pickup trucks, heavy or cargo-carrying trucks, recreational vehicles, buses, and minibuses) totaled just over 23 million. In 2015, global sales of plug-in electric vehicles totaled 550,300 units, about 0.6 percent of global vehicle sales—plug-in vehicles included both battery-only vehicles and so-called plug-in hybrid electric vehicles equipped with a gasoline or diesel engine for use when the vehicle's battery pack (rechargeable only from an external plug-in source) was depleted, usually after a distance of 20 to 50 miles.[27] Global sales of hybrid electric vehicles in 2015 were approximately 2.0 million units (about 2.3 percent of global vehicle sales). Hybrid vehicles were jointly powered by an internal combustion engine and an electric motor that ran on batteries charged by "regenerative braking" [28] and the internal combustion engine; the batteries in a hybrid vehicle could not be restored to a full charge by connecting a plug to an external power source.

Total light vehicle sales in the United States in 2015 were a record 17.5 million units, of which 7.55 million were passenger cars (43 percent) and close to 10 million (57 percent) were SUVs and light trucks; the forecast for 2016 was for sales of 17.7 million vehicles. Sales of plug-in electric vehicles in the United States in 2015 were 116,100 units, down from 122,400 in 2014 (Exhibit 10). The three best-selling electric vehicles in the United States in 2013, 2014, and 2015 were the Tesla Model S, Nissan LEAF, and Chevrolet Volt. Sales of hybrid vehicles in the United States totaled 495,529 units in 2013, 443,824 units in 2014, and 384,400 units in 2015; the three best-selling models in all three years were the Toyota Prius, Toyota Camry, and Ford Fusion.[29] Toyota Motor Corp. was the global leader in sales of hybrid vehicles, with cumulative sales exceeding 8.5 million units at the end of 2015 and projected sales of 1.3 million units annually in 2015 and 2016.[30]

Worldwide production of battery-powered electric vehicles in 2015–2016 was projected to be 800,000 to 900,000 vehicles (roughly 1 percent of total motor vehicle production). But with gasoline prices dropping under $2 per gallon in late 2015 and early 2016 in the United States, the vehicle models posting the biggest sales gains in the United States were pricey pickup trucks, SUVs, and luxury passenger cars. Sales of electric plug-in and hybrid vehicles in the United States eroded in 2015 and fell off even further in early 2016. Sales of such vehicles were much stronger in those countries where gasoline prices were highest. Despite the near-term likelihood of relatively low gasoline prices across much of the world, virtually all motor vehicle manufacturers were expected to have more battery-powered and hybrid models on the market in upcoming years. In mid-2013 Volkswagen announced its intentions to become the world's largest seller of electric vehicles

EXHIBIT 10 Sales of Plug-in Electric Vehicles in the United States, 2013–2015

Best-Selling Models	2013	2014	2015
Tesla Model S	17,650	17,300	25,202
Nissan LEAF	22,610	30,200	17,269
Chevrolet Volt	23,094	18,805	15,393
BMW i3	—	6,092	11,024
Ford Fusion Energi	6,089	11,550	9,750
Ford C-Max Energi	7,154	8,433	7,591
Toyota Prius Plug-in Hybrid	12,088	13,264	4,191
Fiat 500e	2,310	5,132	6,194
All Others	4,260	12,243	19,532
US Total	95,642	123,049	116,099
Worldwide	Not available	320,713	550,297

Source: Inside EVs, "Monthly Plug-in Sales Scorecard," **www.insideevs.com** (accessed May 19, 2015, and March 3, 2016).

by 2018. Toyota executives expected that it would cease producing gasoline-powered vehicles by 2050. Some motor vehicle industry analysts and researchers had boldly projected that worldwide sales of hybrid and plug-in vehicles would reach 6.6 million annual units by 2020 and 35 percent of global vehicles sales by 2040.[31]

But despite the comparatively low sales volumes and market shares for plug-in electric vehicles and hybrids in the United States and other countries, executives at automotive companies across the world were closely watching the strategic moves that Elon Musk was making and the waves that Tesla was making in the marketplace with its new Model X and forthcoming Model 3. There was no question in 2016 and beyond that Tesla was faced with intensifying competition in the global marketplace for electric-powered vehicles:

- In late 2013, BMW began selling its all-new i3 series electric car models that had a lightweight, carbon fiber reinforced plastic body, lithium-ion batteries with a driving range of 80–100 miles on a single charge, a 170-horsepower electric motor, and a base price of $41,350; customers could also get the BMW i3 with a range extender package (base price of $45,200) that included a 34-horsepower motor used only to maintain the charge of the of the lithium-ion battery at an approximate 5 percent charge and extend the driving range to 160–180 miles per charge. BMW sold more than 16,000 i3s in 2014 and 25,000 i3s in 2015. In mid-2014, BMW began selling a super-premium sporty, high-tech electric vehicle called the i8 that had a three-cylinder electric motor, a supplemental gasoline engine for higher speeds, scissor doors, flamboyant aerodynamic flourishes, and an electric-only driving range of about 22 miles. Global sales of the i8 were 1,741 units in 2014 and close to 5,000 units in 2015; the 2015 base price of BMW's i8 was $137,450.
- Mercedes-Benz launched sales of its premium compact B-Class electric vehicle in the United States in mid-2014; the four-door, five-passenger vehicle (base price of $41,450) was built on an entirely new platform compared to other B-Class models with traditional gasoline engines, had an estimated driving range of 115 miles on a single charge, accelerated from 0 to 60 miles per hour in less than 10 seconds, delivered 174 horsepower, had a top speed of 100 miles per hour, utilized an electric powertrain system custom-designed and produced by Tesla, and was loaded with safety features. Mercedes B-Class electric vehicles with a range extender package were also available. The new electric B-Class models competed directly with BMW's i3 series electric car.
- While a number of automakers had a near-term focus on hybrids with a very short battery-only

range, media reports indicated that Mercedes, BMW, Porsche, and Audi were working on producing fully electric vehicles with a 300+ mile driving range on a single charge by 2018.

- In late 2015, both Cadillac and Audi introduced new plug-in hybrid luxury sedans (the Cadillac CT6 and the Audi A6L eTron) with an electric-only range of just over 60 miles on a single charge. Initially, both models were being produced and sold only in China. However, Cadillac was expected to begin selling the hybrid plug-in version of the CT6 in North America and elsewhere in late 2016 or early 2017.
- Executives at GM were acutely aware that cures were needed for the disappointingly small sales volume of the much ballyhooed Chevrolet Volt. GM was rumored to be nearing production of a next-generation compact electric car that could go 200 miles on a single charge, be equipped with a generator for battery charging, and have a base price close to $30,000. The new version of the Volt would likely be introduced in Fall 2016.
- At the 2016 Geneva International Motor Show, automakers pushing new electric models and/or plans for forthcoming models included Opel (a subsidiary of General Motors), PSA Peugeot Citroen, BMW, Mercedes-Benz, Hyundai, Honda, and Volkswagen.

Hydrogen Fuel Cells: An Alternative to Electric Batteries

Many of the world's major automotive manufacturers, while actively working on next-generation battery-powered electric vehicles, were nonetheless hedging their bets by also pursuing the development of hydrogen fuel cells as an alternative means of powering future vehicles. Toyota was considered the leader in developing hydrogen fuel cells and, in 2015, was sharing some of its fuel cell technology patents for free with other automotive companies in an effort to spur whether there was merit in installing fuel cells and building out a hydrogen charging network. Audi, Honda, Toyota, Mercedes-Benz, and Hyundai had recently introduced first-generation models powered by hydrogen fuel cells.[32]

Hydrogen fuel cells could be refueled with hydrogen in three to five minutes. California and several states in the northeastern United States already had a number of hydrogen refueling stations. Existing gasoline stations could add hydrogen refueling capability at a cost of about $1.5 million. A full tank of hydrogen provided vehicles with a driving range of about 310 miles. While battery-powered vehicles were currently cheaper than fuel-cell-powered vehicles, experts expected that cheaper materials, more efficient fuel cells, and scale economies would in upcoming years enable producers of fuel cell vehicles to match the prices of battery-powered electric vehicles.

ENDNOTES

[1] "Tesla Fourth Quarter 2015 Shareholder Letter," February 10, 2016.

[2] Jeff Evanson, Tesla Motors Investor Presentation, September 14, 2013, www.teslamotors.com (accessed November 29, 2013).

[3] Ibid.

[4] John Reed, "Elon Musk's Groundbreaking Electric Car," *FT Magazine*, July 24, 2009, www.ft.com (accessed September 26, 2013).

[5] Ibid.

[6] Tesla press release, May 19, 2009; Michael Arrington, "Tesla Worth More Than Half a Billion after Daimler Investment," May 19, 2009, www.techcrunch.com (accessed September 30, 2013).

[7] "Abu Dhabi Takes Part of Daimler's Investment Stake," July 13, 2009, www.marketwatch.com.

[8] Chris Morrison, "Tesla's Layoffs: Bad Blood, a Bloodbath, or Business as Usual?" January 11, 2008, www.venturebeat.com (accessed September 24, 2013).

[9] Josh Friedman, "Entrepreneur Tries His Midas Touch in Space," *Los Angeles Times*, April 23, 2003, www.latimes.com (accessed September 16, 2013).

[10] David Kestenbaum, "Making a Mark with Rockets and Roadsters," National Public Radio, August 9, 2007, www.npr.org (accessed September 17, 2013).

[11] Ibid.

[12] Ibid.

[13] Video interview with Alan Murray, "Elon Musk: I'll Put a Man on Mars in 10 Years," *The Wall Street Journal*, December 1, 2011, www.wsj.com/video/elon-musk-ill-put-a-man-on-mars-in-10-years/CCF1FC62-BB0D-4561-938C-DF0DEFAD15BA.html (accessed September 16, 2013).

[14] William Harwood, "SpaceX Dragon Returns to Earth, Ends Historic Trip," CNET, May 31, 2012, www.cbsnews.com (accessed September 16, 2013).

[15] Ashlee Vance, "Revealed: Elon Musk Explains the Hyperloop, the Solar-Powered High-Speed Future of Inter-City Transportation," *Bloomberg*

Businessweek, August 12, 2013, www.businessweek.com (accessed September 25, 2013).
[16] Mike Seemuth, "From the Corner Office—Elon Musk," *Success,* April 10, 2011, www.success.com (accessed September 25, 2013).
[17] Ibid.
[18] Ibid.
[19] Jay Yarow, "A Day in the Life of Elon Musk, the Most Inspiring Entrepreneur in the World," *BusinessInsider,* July 24, 2012, www.businessinsider.com (accessed September 25, 2013).
[20] Terry Dawes, "Why Critics Love to Hate Elon Musk," June 10, 2013, www.cantechletter.com (accessed September 26, 2016).
[21] Tesla's Proxy Statement, April 17, 2013, pp. 28–30.
[22] Martin Eberhard, "Lotus Position" [Blog], July 25, 2006, www.teslamotors.com/blog/lotus-position (accessed September 17, 2013).
[23] 2013 10-K report, p. 4.
[24] Angelo Young, "Tesla Owners in Norway Get $134,000 Tax Break, Which Is More Than the Base Price of the Model S," *International Business Times,* December 13, 2013, www.ibtimes.com (accessed April 6, 2016).
[25] Company press release, May 20, 2010.
[26] As quoted in Alan Ohnsman, "Tesla Model S Buyback Offer May Generate More Revenue," September 10, 2013, www.bloomberg.com (accessed December 10, 2013).
[27] Inside EVs, "Monthly Plug-in Sales Scorecard," www.insideevs.com (accessed March 3, 2016).
[28] Regenerative braking involved capturing the energy lost during braking by using the electric motor as a generator and storing the captured energy in the battery. Hybrids could not use off-board sources of electricity to charge the batteries—hybrids could use only regenerative braking and the internal combustion engine to charge. The extra power provided by the electric motor in a hybrid vehicle enabled faster acceleration and also allowed for use of a smaller internal combustion engine.
[29] U.S. Department of Energy, "U.S. Hybrid Electric Vehicle Sales, by Model," www.afdc.energy.gov (accessed March 4, 2016).
[30] Toyota press release, October 24, 2014, www.corporatenews.pressroom.toyota.com (accessed April 6, 2015).
[31] Silvio Marcacci, "Electric Vehicles Speeding toward 7% of All Global Sales by 2020," September 30, 2013, www.cleantechnica.com (accessed March 3, 2016); "Electric Cars to Be 35 Percent of Global Sales by 2040: Energy Analyst," February 25, 2016, www.greencarreports.com (accessed March 3, 2016).
[32] George Ghanem, "Avoid Tesla Because Hydrogen Is the New Electric," March 6, 2016, www.seekingalpha.com (accessed March 7, 2016).

CASE 17

The South African Wine Industry in 2016: Where Does It Go from Here?

A. J. Strickland
The University of Alabama

Jarryd Botha
The University of Alabama, MBA 2017

Going into 2016, South Africa, the African continent's most developed economy, was being battered by the global weakness in demand for commodities. The country's unemployment rate was rising and a recession appeared almost certain, but there was a bright spot in the economic picture: the South African wine industry. South Africa was the world's eighth-largest wine producer, accounting for about 4 percent of global wine production. The fertile vineyards of South Africa had produced wine volume that increased 20 percent from 2012 to 2016, to approximately 420 million liters annually. Local profit margins for domestic wine were 2 percent in South Africa, but exported wines were sold for an average of 400 percent more than sold domestically. Consequently, over half of South African wine was exported. Europe, the UK, and Africa were major consumers. Exports to China had increased by 40 percent and to Texas by 60 percent in 2015.

Despite the positive trends for the South African vintners, there were troubling signs on the horizon. The South African economy and infrastructure were having difficulties. The rand was weakening against major currencies and the effect of the exchange rate was unknown. South African wine production dropped by 2 percent in 2015. Potential global competitors were emerging rapidly: China had tripled its vineyard acreage since 2000 and in 2015 and 2016, it had the second-largest vineyard acreage in the world. Chile, Argentina, New Zealand, and Australia had begun to produce quality wine and had cheaper land and labor than many traditional wine-producing countries. According to Jean-Marie Aurand, director general of the International Organization of Vine and Wine, 2015 was a year of stability and consolidation.

For South African vintners, 2016 would be a year of assessment as they attempted to make sense of the conflicting signals and set a course that would enable the industry to reverse its slide and reestablish an upward trajectory as a significant international competitor, both in quantity and quality of wine.

THE SOUTH AFRICAN WINE INDUSTRY

South Africa was a relative newcomer to the global wine industry, yet its winemaking heritage dated back to February 1659, when the first grapes were pressed. The Dutch East India Company established a refreshment station at the Cape of South Africa in 1652 to provide fresh food to the company's merchant ships en route to India. Jan van Riebeeck, the first governor of the Cape (later Cape Town), planted a vineyard in 1655, and South African winemaking began four years later, leading to more grapevines being planted.

In 1679, Simon van der Stel succeeded van Riebeeck as commander of Cape Town and planted a vineyard on his farm which he named Constantia. Van der Stel was knowledgeable about winemaking and viticulture, a passionate vintner, and his Constantia wines were very good. Constantia wines are now among the most highly rated sweet wines in the world.

Cape Town's climate, soil, and slopes provided the perfect environment for grapes to grow; however, infestation and the First Boer War in 1880 briefly halted wine production; but by 1882, the Cape's wine industry was thriving. Due to war with France, British import duties favored exports from the region, which resulted in a surge of business coming to the Cape wine lands. By 1825, the industry began a steady decline, and as a result of increasing British tariffs and the Second Boer War (1889– 1902), the Cape wine industry productivity slowed.

In 1918, a cooperative of winegrowers, KWV (Ko-operative Wijnbouwers Vereniging), was established to stabilize, support, and structure the young industry. The KWV Act was passed in the South African parliament in 1924 giving the cooperative certain administrative responsibilities and established it as the sole importer and exporter of "surplus alcohol." Within a short time period, KWV imposed a minimum price on wine which resulted in a large excess supply. Due to the KWV's policies, quantity of wine was more important than quality, which impacted the overall market. These regulations, combined with anti-apartheid trade regulations, pushed the industry into decline.

In 1990, State President F. W. deKlerk disbanded the African National Congress two years early, and the ban on anti-apartheid political parties (e.g., African National Congress) was lifted, which resulted in world markets being reopened to exports from South Africa. In April 1992, the first South African wines since 1986 arrived in Savannah, Georgia, after the United States lifted sanctions in July 1991. Nelson Mandela's rise to presidency brought changes, and the KWV was stripped of most of its regulatory power. The Cape wine industry reaped the benefits of a free market, and exports increased, leading to more wineries opening, clustering in regions just outside Cape Town known as Stellenbosch and Paarl. South Africa had become an international competitor in the global wine industry and a producer of award-winning wines that were gaining recognition in crucial international markets. Exhibit 1 shows the winegrowing areas in South Africa.

There were over 100,000 hectares (247,000 acres) of vineyard in South Africa in 2016. White wine cultivation was the most popular plant variety, with 18 percent Chenin Blanc grapes. Red wine varieties comprised 45.4 percent of vineyards nationally, and 11.5 percent was Cabernet Sauvignon. In years prior to 2016, approximately 40 percent

EXHIBIT 1 Winegrowing Areas in South Africa

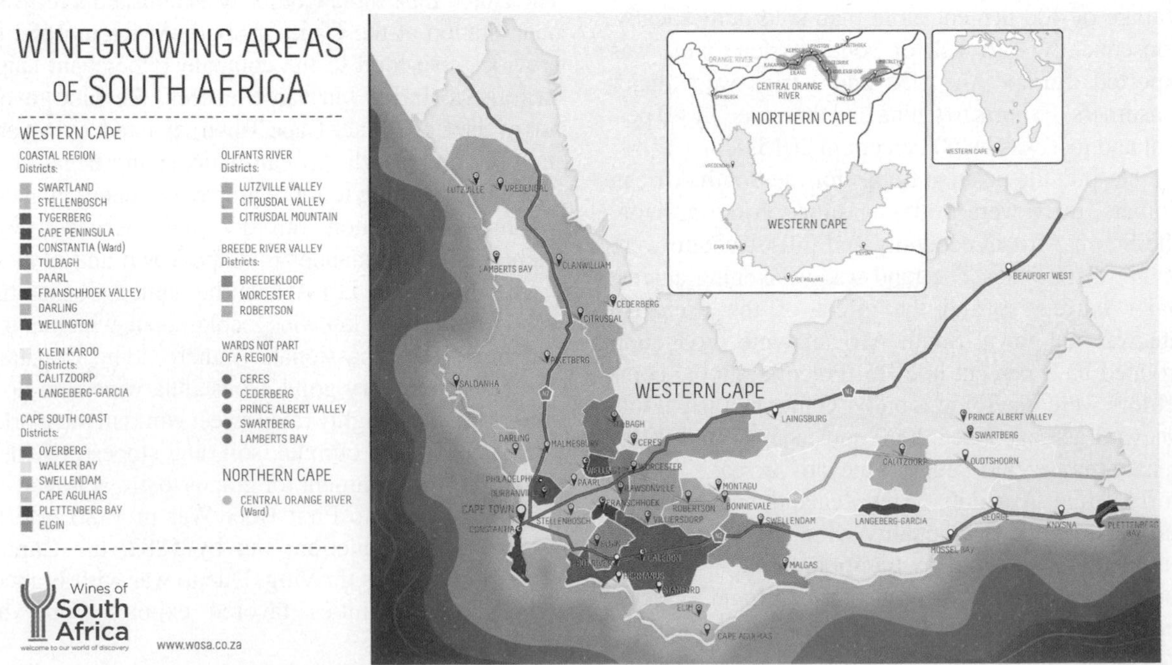

Used by permission of Wines of South Africa.

of the vineyards were replanted to keep up with industry trends. One of the biggest shifts was moving from the historical norm of mass producing wine to more refined techniques of producing quality wine. Higher-quality varieties included Sauvignon Blanc and Chardonnay, which produced the top-class white wines, Shiraz, and Pinot Noir.

Although almost all vine varieties grown in the Cape region were originally imported, there were over five different local blends. The most renowned was the red Pinotage. Pinotage, indigenous to South Africa, was a blend of Pinot Noir and Hermitage (Cinsaut), which prior to 2016 was grown in a larger scale than its counterparts. As the wine industry changed, so did the winemakers. Experimentation among blends became popular and winemakers were constantly trying to innovate new varieties as they struggled to keep pace with industry trends.

The majority of wine producers in South Africa during 2011 delivered and marketed their grapes to 50 producer cellars (a winery where grapes are processed and marketed on behalf of a group of grape producers). An article in 2011 illustrates how wine production was distributed in South Africa:

> These cellars produce or receive between 70–80% of the total wine crop. Most of the wine produced by these cellars is sold in bulk to one or several of the 60 wholesalers who in turn are represented by a few large role players and a considerable number of smaller role players. The balance of the total crop is produced by 493 private wine cellars and 26 producing wholesalers. Primary wine producers are very fragmented, their bargaining power is very low, they are price takers and too fragmented to integrate lower in the value chain in order to obtain representation or improve their bargaining power.[1]

Exhibits 2 and 3 show the growth of wineries and wine production from 2005 to 2014.

South Africa progressively aligned its wine production to trends in international wine demand. According to a 2015 study, approximately $25 billion (R36.1 billion) in wine production contributed to South Africa's overall gross domestic product (GDP), and about $13 billion (R19.3 billion) of that was from the Cape region. The wine industry's total contribution to GDP was 1.2 percent. The growth of wine's GDP contribution had been at least 10 percent per annum since 2003. Employment within the wine industry topped 300,000, which made it the largest permanent employer in the agriculture sector. A typical winemaker earned between $18,000 (R260 000) to $28,000 (R415 000) per year. A season's earnings were directly attributed to the yield of the vineyard and the skills and ability to craft good wines that could be sold at a profit.

Global Driving Forces in the South African Wine Industry

Although the South African wine industry in 2016 was robust and the driving forces of the industry appeared to be ushering in a period of increased growth and profitability, it was also a period of climatic challenge. South Africa's largest wine export market was China, and according to PricewaterhouseCooper's 2015 wine industry survey, China

EXHIBIT 2 Number of Wine Producers, Wine Cellars, Producer Cellars, and Producing Wholesalers in South Africa, 2005–2014

	2005	2006	2007	2008	2009	2010	2011	2012	2013	2014
Number of primary wine producers	4,360	4,183	3,999	3,839	3,667	3,596	3,527	3,440	3,323	3,314
Number of wine cellars which crush grapes	581	572	560	585	604	573	582	582	564	559
Producers cellars	65	65	59	58	57	54	52	50	50	49
Producing wholesalers	21	17	20	23	23	26	25	23	21	25

Source: Data taken from http://www.wosa.co.za/The-Industry/Statistics/SA-Wine-Industry-Statistics/

EXHIBIT 3 South African Wine Production, 2005–2014 (in millions of liters)

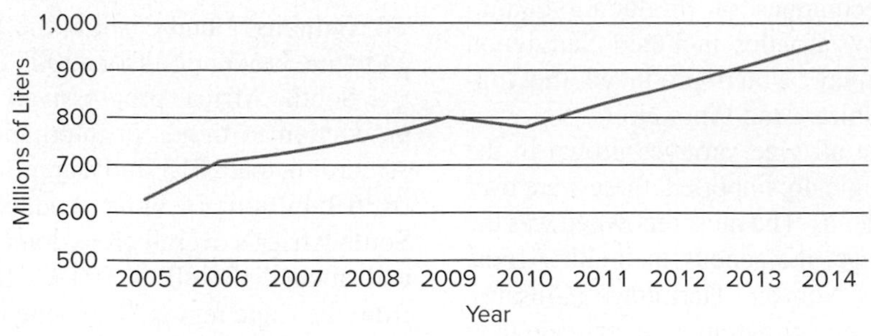

Source: Data taken from **http://www.wosa.co.za/The-Industry/Statistics/SA-Wine-Industry-Statistics/**

was likely to replace the United States as the world's largest economy by 2030 (measured by market exchange rate). The developing countries overtook the developed world in terms of contribution to GNP in 2008 and were forecast to provide 57 percent of global GDP by 2030. South Africa's largest growth opportunities for wine exports were China and Africa, but in order to realize the market potential, wine exporters in South Africa needed to think creatively and carefully prepare to take advantage of these economic power shifts.

Increasing urbanization was expected to have a strong positive impact on the South African wine industry. The urbanization trend showed the urban population increase from 35 percent in 1960 to 54 percent in 2015, and by 2050, two-thirds of the world's population is expected to live in urban areas, according to PwC's industry survey. China and Nigeria were two of the three top urbanizing countries, and South Africa's two largest export markets. The South Africa's wine industry should benefit from the trend because urban consumers were more likely to embrace the culture of drinking wine as their choice beverage.

Climate change and resource scarcity were significant global "game changers" that had the potential to affect the South African wine industry. The average global temperature was expected to rise by over 2 degrees Centigrade in the 21st century, and the potential for drought was pervasive in South Africa. In fact, *Science Daily* (February 24, 2016) reported that South Africa was struggling with the worst drought in 30 years, resulting in reduced yield for crops (including grapes) and livestock deaths. South Africa's wine industry would need to evaluate the effect of drought and climate change, and plan accordingly to preempt the deleterious effects.

Demographic shifts would require that the South African wine industry understand the implications of these changes and consumer segmentation to take full advantage of this opportunity. One of three children born worldwide by 2050 would be born in sub-Saharan Africa, and 62 percent of sub-Saharan Africans living today are younger than 25 years. Worldwide, there would be 1 billion more people by 2025, 300 million of whom were predicted to be 65 years of age or older. *The Economist* (August 4, 2015) reported that by 2050, Nigeria's population would be 413 million, overtaking the United States as the world's third most populous nation, and the Congo and Ethiopia would grow to more than 195 million and 188 million, respectively, which was over double their present size.

Domestic Wine Consumption

South Africa's domestic wine sales amounted to about \$27 million (R394.6 million) in 2014, up approximately 6.8 percent from the previous year. Nationwide beer consumption was almost 10 times that of wine (see Exhibit 4).

Local demand suffered because margins on wine were a dismal 2 percent; however, global consumers were willing to pay up to four times the domestic price. The Cape wine lands were a hotspot for tourists who wanted to embrace the beauty and serenity of the region.

EXHIBIT 4 Alcoholic Beverage Consumption in South Africa, 2011–2015 (millions of liters)

	2011	2012	2013	2014 (estimate)	2015 (estimate)
Beer	2,969	3,016	3,061	3,100	3,120
Wine	353	361	369	379	385
Spirits (excl. brandy)	76	82	84	90	90
Brandy	39	36	33	31	30
Ready to drink	391	432	466	470	480
Total	3,827	3,927	4,013	4,070	4,105

Source: SA Wine Industry Statistics (SAWIS).

Constantia, Stellenbosch, Paarl, and others provided tourists the opportunity to try local wines and food and experience the culture of those areas. Thus, many vineyards incorporated wine tasting and tours in order to spur growth. In the summer, tourists flocked to popular wine farms and towns to escape the cold winter months of the Northern Hemisphere. This provided tourists with an opportunity to experience the historical nuance of these wineries while increasing the income of wine farms catering to tourist demands.

Global Wine Consumption

Global wine consumption in 2015 was approximately 240 million hectoliters (hectoliter = 100 liters), unchanged from 2014, and a decrease of 12 million hectoliters from 2007 (see Exhibit 5). Traditional markets played a large role in global consumption. According to the *Wall Street Journal,* the United States dominated the world in wine consumption. In 2013, it accounted for 12 percent of global wine consumption. An average bottle of wine contained 0.75 liter, which meant that almost four billion bottles were consumed by the United States. France was the second-highest consumer, followed closely by Italy, Germany, and China. Italy and France had the highest consumption per capita.

The top three countries in spending on wine were the United States, France, and the UK. The leading market research firm for alcoholic beverages, IWSR, predicted in 2016 that the combined still-wine markets of the UK and United States would exceed $50 billion. However, growth prospects in Asia, especially China, would provide great opportunities for

EXHIBIT 5 Global Wine Production versus Consumption, 2001–2013 (millions of cases)

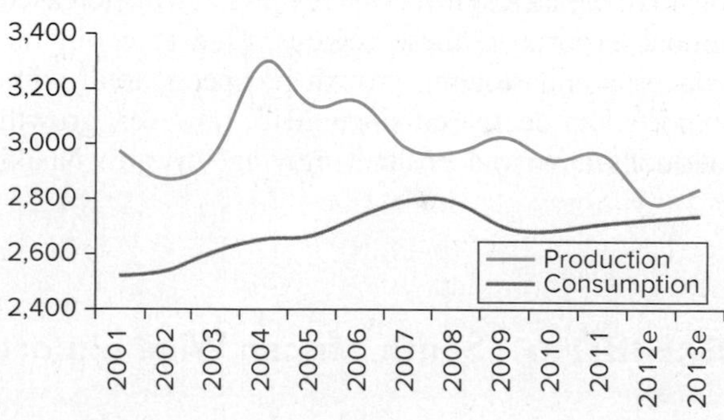

Source: Reuters.

wine exporters in the future. China grew 69 percent in terms of wine consumption from 2009 to 2013 and was forecast to grow another 25 percent leading up to 2018.

Global Demand and Exports

The wine trade was becoming increasingly international: In 2015, 43 percent of wine was consumed in a country other than where it was produced. The growth in demand for South African wines arose primarily from international demand. Exports played a key role in industry profitability and sustained production. South Africa was the eighth-largest wine producer in the world in 2015, and accounted for approximately 4.0 percent of global wine volume. Total wine exports were 422.7 million liters in 2014, down from the previous year. In 2015, exports decreased by 0.6 percent to 420.0 million liters. Total red and white wine exports also dropped in 2014 (see Exhibit 6).

The decreased exports were blamed partially on new wine producers with the ability to produce at lower costs than the South Africans, as set out in an article on global wine demand:

> Upstart wine regions such as Argentina, Australia, Chile, New Zealand and South Africa rely on cheaper land, lower-cost labor, lax environmental laws, or labor saving devices and commodity taxes to compete in the global marketplace. They have won market share by challenging vintners in the U.S. with high quality, low priced wine.[2]

Due to shortfalls in the European harvest in 2013 and 2014, wine demand from countries such as Russia and Germany increased dramatically for South African wines. This demand, coupled with positive media and favorable reviews, drove increased global exports to these regions. Due to economic concerns and slowing growth prospects, total wine exports had decreased since 2013, however, growth outlooks appeared positive moving forward. Ntsiki Biyela, a local winemaker, stated, "Texas will buy every last grape we have," and that her wineries sales volume to the Lone Star state were up by more than 60 percent in 2015. A report from 2014 stated:

> According to GTA data, the 2014 South Africa's wine exports to the United States decreased by 25 percent to 25 million liters, from the record high exports to the United States of 32 million liters. South Africa industry contacts indicated that they are still looking into the reasons for the decrease in exports to the United States. However, in general, wines priced under US$9.00/bottle underperformed in the United States and the total United States wine imports decreased by 4 percent in 2014. A long term comparison shows that South Africa wine exports to the United States have grown from 12,971,841 liters in 2011 to 24,460,215 liters in 2014. Wine exports to the United States are mainly in bulk and represent 68 percent of total exports. Red wine exports to the United States increased by 240 percent in 2013, and represents now 43 percent of total exports. In 2012, red wine exports to the United States only represented 17 percent of total exports.[3]

A 2016 CNN news article, "This Beer Nation's Wine Industry Is Booming," explored the increases in the global demand for South African wine and the prospects for further growth. The United Kingdom, Europe, and other African countries were all major

EXHIBIT 6 South African Wine Exports, 2003–2015

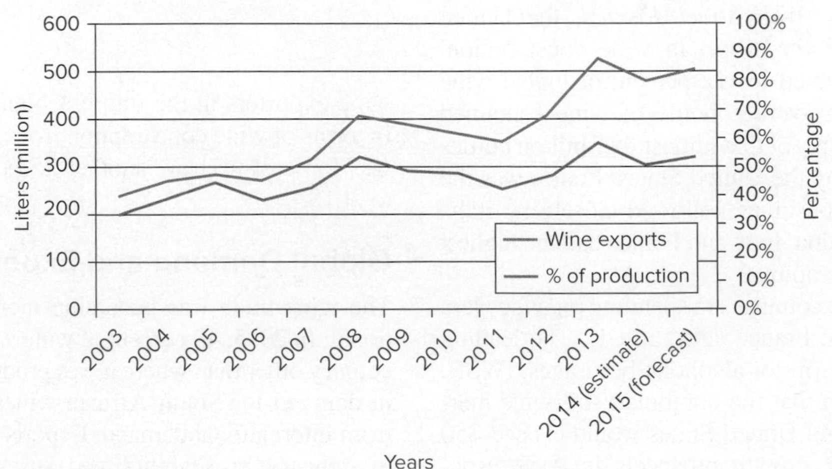

Source: SAWIS.

EXHIBIT 7 Major Markets of South African Wine in 2014

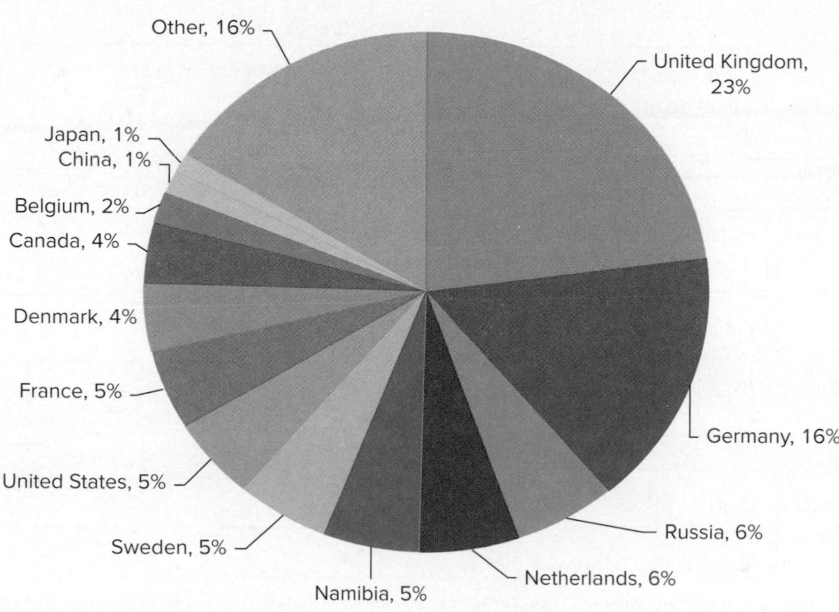

Source: Global Trade Atlas.

consumers of South African wine. Despite the economic slowdown in China, wine imports from South Africa were up 40 percent in 2015. Production in South Africa during 2016 slowed due to wildfires and the worst drought in the last century, but winemakers were still confident they could meet global demand. Exhibit 7 presents a pie chart comparison of major markets for South African wine in 2014.

Australian wine consultant James Herrick provided insight into vital concepts that South African winemakers should be aware of:

> From the sheer logistics and cost exercise of meeting the world demand for wine, and with a lot of low cost producers in the world, there is a limit to the extent to which South Africa could continue to be efficient enough to meet that demand for low cost wine.
>
> The countries that end up occupying that market for low cost wines will be the most efficient. South Africa—because of distance, because of its farms, because of its cost of money, and because of its geography and topography—will have a hard time competing.
>
> For the SA wine industry to survive it would help if it could move its production slowly towards the more premium end, because that's where the margin is, and that's where the value for the consumer is.[4]

A bottle of midrange wine sold for approximately $3.39 in South Africa, and that same bottle of wine sold for approximately $12 in the United States, a 72 percent difference in price. The typical cost to export a container of wine (13,824 750-ml bottles) from South Africa to the United States was $1,830 in 2014, up from $1,531 in 2011.

The South African Wine Supply Chain

According to a study released in 2013, a more efficient supply chain could help the wine industry and enable South Africa to better handle global competitiveness. The study also revealed how a lack of supply chain awareness was restricting wine producers from making the gains they were capable of. "Many cellars are still thinking like fruit farmers who merely sell their produce to exporters. It's a mindset that can, and must urgently change, if the South Africa wine industry is to be competitive," said Joubert van Eeden, study author and senior lecturer at Stellenbosch University's Department of Logistics.[5] He also mentioned that the majority of research done by wine connoisseurs was related to growing grapes and crafting wine; however, there was little focus on the ability to get

EXHIBIT 8 The Complexity of the Supply Chain

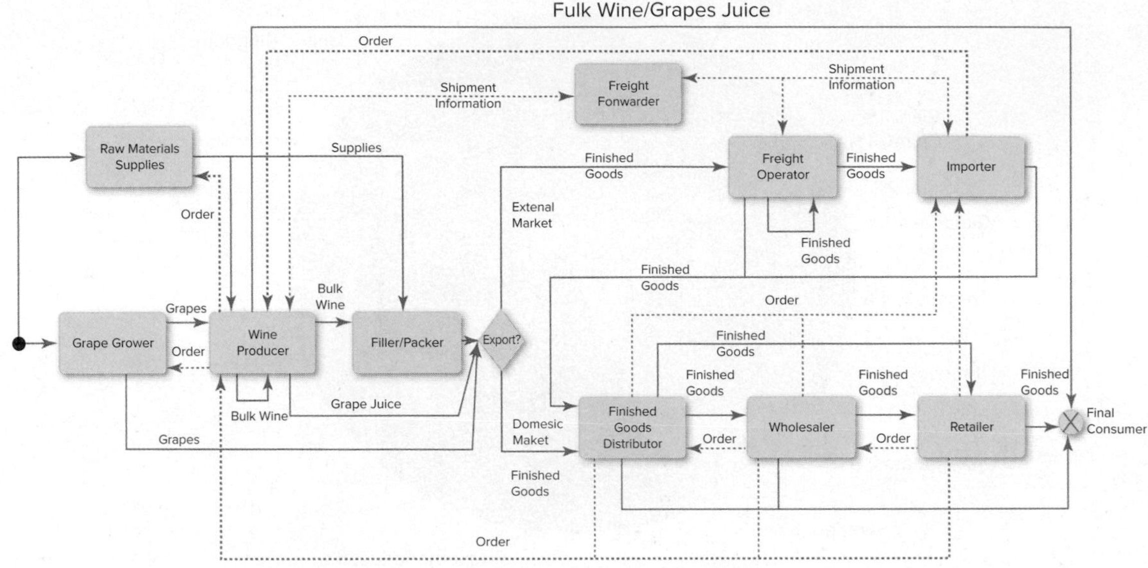

Source: www.embassyconferences.co.za/media/file_icons/Wine%20Supply%20Chain%20Survey.pdf (original source F. A. Garcia et al., *International Journal of Production Economics* 135 (2012), pp. 284–298.

wine into the hands of consumers. Van Eeden stated that "Many cellars don't recognize the existence of several supply chains and most that are engaged in supply chain management are in the very early stages of supply chain maturity,"[6] revealing the inexperience in supply chain awareness (see Exhibit 8).

Income and Production Costs

Although wine production regulations had eased since the end of apartheid, the industry was still subject to taxes and levies:

> Tax on Domestic wine South African Revenue Service (SARS) taxes domestic wine through the excise tax. On February, 25, 2015, the Minister of Finance, Mr. Nhlanhla Nene, announce excise tax of 7% on natural wine, 7% on sparkling wine and 4.8% on fortified wine. . . . In addition, there is also a 14 percent VAT (Value Added Tax) charged on all wines sold in South Africa.[7]

These taxes resulted in thinner margins for wine producers. Due to the complexity of the wine-producing process, when the economic outlook was weak the wine industry could be volatile. The *New York Times* explained, "In Italy, France and parts of the United States, 8 to 10 acres of premium grape-growing land can yield long-term investment returns of as much as 20 percent a year, depending on market demand for contract grape purchases. In Australia and South Africa, brokers say 40 to 60 acres is the minimum."[8] Land cost was only taxes, and insurance also had to be included. Exhibit 9 shows the breakdown of income and expenditures of grape production, and Exhibit 10 shows the cost of individual bottles of wine in 2009.

SOUTH AFRICA'S WINE INDUSTRY MOVES INTO 2016

South Africa had a dynamic wine industry in 2014, but like the economy, it showed signs of slowing down. South African economic growth slowed to 1.5 percent in 2014, with unemployment at over 25 percent, substantially more for black youth, and increasing. Thirty-six percent of the population was below the poverty line. South Africa's unemployment, poverty,

EXHIBIT 9 Breakdown of Income and Expenditures of Grape Production, 2004–2014

INCOME & EXPENDITURE STATEMENT	2004	2005	2006	2007	2008	2009	2010	2011	2012	2013	2014
Average price per ton (rand)	2,383	1,916	1,763	1,766	1,807	2,113	2,192	2,383	2,416	2,524	2,682
Average yield per hectare (tons)	13.11	13.79	15.34	15.58	16.31	15.55	14.73	15.08	16.98	17.50	17.69
TOTAL INCOME (R/ha)	31,236	26,424	27,043	27,513	29,479	32,857	32,281	35,943	41,023	44,171	47,456
Direct costs (R/ha)	2,459	2,426	2,391	2,482	2,855	3,463	3,920	3,992	4,150	4,670	5,382
Labour (R/ha)	6,317	6,590	6,878	6,949	6,956	7,905	8,477	9,111	9,630	10,639	12,001
Mechanisation (R/ha)	2,667	2,852	3,004	3,219	3,533	4,022	4,142	4,633	4,868	5,501	5,952
Other overheads (R/ha)	2,778	3,142	3,326	3,367	3,357	3,649	4,108	4,706	5,186	5,849	4,914
ANNUAL CASH EXPENDITURES	14,221	15,010	15,599	16,017	16,702	19,039	20,648	22,443	23,834	26,659	29,235
GROSS MARGIN (R/ha)	17,015	11,414	11,444	11,496	12,777	13,818	11,633	13,500	17,189	17,512	18,221
Provision for replacement (R/ha)	4,779	5,633	5,733	6,108	6,876	7,541	7,937	8,140	8,606	9,080	9,439
NET FARMING INCOME (R/ha)	12,236	5,781	5,711	5,388	5,901	6,277	3,696	5,360	8,583	8,432	8,781

Source: **http://www.wineland.co.za/technical/the-cost-of-wine-grape-cultivation-and-top-achievers-in-difficult-times-part-1**. *Note: These amounts are in rands per hectare. Exchange rate as per 4/11/2016: 1 US Dollar = R14.77 [14]*

EXHIBIT 10 Breakdown of the Cost of Individual Bottles of Wine in 2009

- Bottle price is R2.74
- Labels could run from R0.5R0 at low end to R1.50 for high-quality label
- Bottling costs (including filters) R0.65 per bottle
- Labeling costs R0.50
- Box and inserts to protect bottles R0.75 per bottle
- Subtotal of R6.00 to R7.00 for the packaging depending on quality—say R6.50
- R1.46 to SARS (Tax Collector) for customs and excise

Source: www.vnl.co.za/2009/07/09/retailing-wines-for-under-r30-in-south-africa-is-only-possible-for-factories%E2%80%A6/.

Note: These amounts are in rands per hectare. Exchange rate as per April 11, 2016: 1 US Dollar = R14.77.

and inequality were among the highest in the world. The economic picture for South Africa was generally negative (Exhibit 11).

The availability of dependable electricity was a problem and the rolling blackouts in 2014–2015 were the worst since 2008. According to the CIA *World Factbook,* South African economic growth could not exceed 3 percent until the electrical supply problem was resolved. Other factors limiting economic growth were skills shortages, declining global competitiveness, and frequent work stoppages due to strikes. The state-run power company ESKOM was building three new generating plants but had encountered construction delays at two, which meant the country would continue to have problems with economic growth. The rand showed continued weakness against the U.S. dollar and major currencies (Exhibit 12) .

Roland Peens, director of Winecellar.co.za, writing in *MoneyWeb* (January 6, 2016), pointed out several trends for the South African wine industry in 2016. Although winery costs had risen, the weaker rand made South African wines a better value in the export markets, which saved many struggling wineries. Peens expected South African wine to become increasingly expensive. Demand pull for the better wines increased prices for the best exported wines, and producers increased prices for the lesser, local wines to reach toward parity with the export markets.

EXHIBIT 11 Key Economic Indicators for South Africa, 2011–2015

South Africa Economy Data	2011	2012	2013	2014	2015
Population (million)	51.6	52.3	53.2	54.0	54.9
GDP per capita (USD)	8,656	7,621	6,698	6,608	5,994
GDP (USD bn)	446	399	356	357	329
Economic Growth (GDP, annual variation in %)	3.2	2.2	2.2	1.6	1.3
Consumption (annual variation in %)	4.9	3.4	2.9	1.4	1.6
Investment (annual variation in %)	5.7	3.6	7.6	−0.4	1.4
Industrial Production (annual variation in %)	2.8	2.2	1.4	0.1	0.0
Unemployment Rate	24.8	24.9	24.7	25.1	25.4
Public Debt (% of GDP)	38.2	40.9	44.2	47.1	50.1
Exchange Rate (vs USD)	8.07	8.48	10.47	11.57	15.50
Trade Balance (USD billion)	6.4	−4.6	−7.0	−7.7	−4.2
Exports (annual variation in %)	34.1	−14.3	−6.3	0.6	−9.2
Imports (annual variation in %)	39.2	−5.0	−3.8	1.3	−12.0
External Debt (% of GDP)	26.5	35.5	38.3	40.7	—

Source: FocusEconomics, 2016.

EXHIBIT 12 Value of the Rand versus the U.S. Dollar, 2000–2016

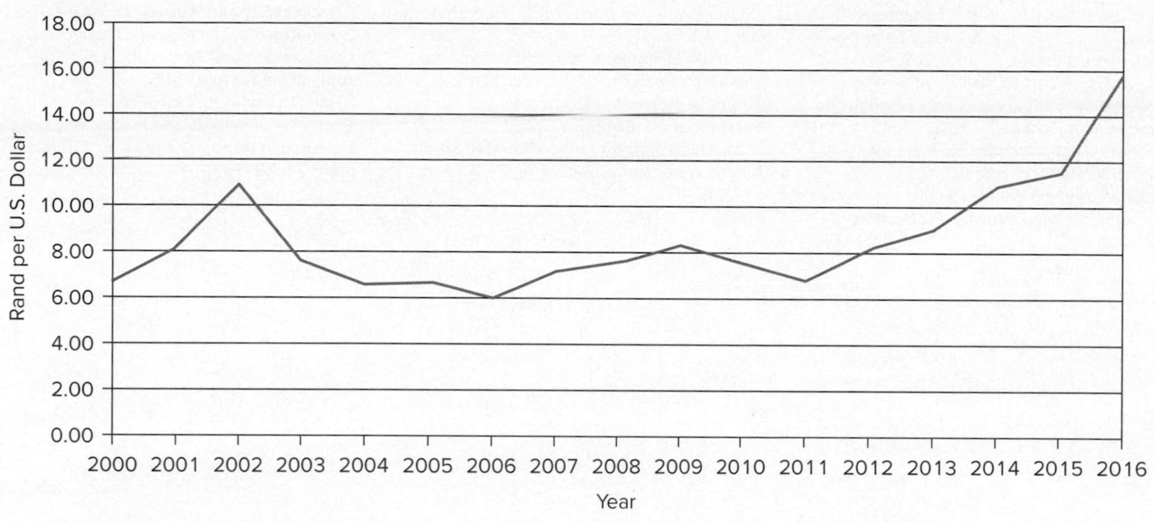

Source: BusinessTech, January 2016.

The gap between luxury and lesser wines widened: the most expensive South African wines were about 100 times more expensive than the least expensive. With the French multiple at 10,000, there was a big gap for South African wines. Another opportunity for the wine industry was the e-commerce boom, with more fine wines being sold online as logistics and service levels improved.

South Africa expected its greatest vintage to come to market in 2015 and 2016, and the investment potential of vintage South African wines to increase. Peens pointed out that the trend in early 2016 was for lighter reds and wines with less alcohol and more character and freshness, and that producers unwilling to adapt to these changes could lose market share. Also, new varieties of grapes were being developed that were expected to be accepted by the market.

Despite some positive trends for the South African wine industry, there was a significant negative climatic trend: the drought that had plagued the country for several years. According to *Africa News* (July 26, 2016), South Africa was experiencing the driest summer and the lowest rainfall in over 110 years. The driest year on record was 2015, and the country's food security was threatened. Vineyards without irrigation were expected to have significantly lower yields and the management of water was becoming increasingly important.

As South African vintners contemplated the future of their industry in the coming years, their fate was unclear. Several external environmental trends suggested an industry upturn and a coming period of prosperity, while others indicated a flat or possibly negative future. Making sense of the conflicting signals was a difficult but necessary task for South Africa's vintners, and one that had important implications for the individual farms and wine producers, the industry, and the country.

ENDNOTES 

[1] Dana Buys, "Retailing Wines for under R30 in South Africa Is Only Possible for Factories," Vrede En Lust Estate, July 9, 2009, www.vnl.co.za/2009/07/09/retailing-wines-for-under-r30-in-south-africa-is-only-possible-for-factories%E2%80%A6/ (accessed April 21, 2016).
[2] Thomas Ulrich, "Probing the Research Gap," *Wines & Vines*, December 2007.
[3] Justina Torry and Wellington Sikuka, *The South African Wine Industry: Production, Consumption and Trade*, USDA Foreign Agricultural Service, 2015.
[4] Norman McFarlane, "Bulk Wine Exports: The Elephant in the SA Wine Industry Room," *A Man in the Kitchen*, September 26, 2012.
[5] "Improved Supply Chain to Promote South African Wine: Study," *Global Times*, August 27, 2013.
[6] Ibid.
[7] Justina Torry and Wellington Sikuka, *The South African Wine Industry: Production, Consumption and Trade*, USDA Foreign Agricultural Service, 2015.
[8] Holly Hubbard Preston,"Personal Business; Vineyards and Profits May Not Go Hand in Hand," *The New York Times*, June 24, 2001.

CASE 18

Ford Motor Company: New Strategies for International Growth

Nicole Daniel
Tuck School of Business at Dartmouth

Thomas Lawton
Tuck School of Business at Dartmouth

INTRODUCTION

John Casesa, group vice president of Ford Motor Company's Global Strategy team, gazed out from his office window at Ford's corporate headquarters in Dearborn, Michigan, on a cold January day in 2016. The warm and tropical climate of Mumbai seemed worlds away from snowy Dearborn but Casesa's attention had been on India for some time now. Hired the year previously after nearly 25 years as an investment banker in the automotive industry, Casesa had been charged with the implementation of new initiatives under the *One Ford Plan.* Originally designed to help Ford return to global profitability in its core automotive business after the Great Recession, the One Ford Plan had been further refined to help Ford aggressively pursue emerging opportunities that were an extension of the Ford brand.

A key facet of this plan was the introduction of *Smart Mobility,* which reflected Ford's intent to branch out from its core automotive market. Smart Mobility sought to position Ford as a company that embraced technological innovation and a leader in connectivity and mobility, while leveraging its existing strength as a global automotive powerhouse. Casesa's team had devised an idea called *Dynamic Shuttle,* a taxi-like service at prices similar to mass transit and enabled by smartphone access. While other application-based ride-service companies typically moved 1 or 2 people per ride, Dynamic Shuttle had the aspirations of utilizing shuttles to transport up to 12 people per ride, and was thought to be an ideal solution for emerging economies with large urban populations who cannot afford personal transportation.

After analysis of population demographics and profitability estimates, Casesa's team had decided to create a Dynamic Shuttle pilot in India. The large urban population, including a subset of aspirational workers that Casesa believed would be ideal Dynamic Shuttle customers, as well as the overcrowded metropolitan transport systems and growing smartphone adoption, made India an ideal environment to test the pilot. If successful, it could serve as a model for creating Dynamic Shuttle programs in other countries. Ford, however, could not develop the program alone. It would need a partner that had the right business model and similar aspirations for growth potential and scalability, along with the willingness to expand into the Indian market. The team had found five potential candidates to partner with but had yet to determine the most appropriate one.

Casesa reviewed the agenda for his team's meeting that afternoon. What criteria were most important in determining who Ford should partner with, and did any of the identified prospects best fit Ford's needs? What characteristics would ensure a successful launch of Dynamic Shuttle in India?

FORD MOTOR COMPANY

Founded in 1903 by Henry Ford and a group of 11 investors, the Ford Motor Company had modest origins, launching in a converted factory on Mack Avenue in Detroit that produced only a few cars per day. Ford quickly differentiated itself, however, through a variety of unique production and employment practices that transformed the automobile industry and positioned Ford at the forefront of technological innovation. The 1908 launch of the Model T, later voted as the Car of the Century by a panel of industry experts, revolutionized manufacturing production globally.[1] Produced on the world's first assembly-line production model, the Model T was assembled by individual workers who remained in one place on the line and performed the same task every shift as vehicle parts passed before them on a conveyor belt. The implementation of the assembly line and conveyor belt, and the scale opportunities it afforded, allowed Ford to quickly surpass its competitors. Then in 1914, Ford began offering a standardized wage of $5/day to its factory employees, vaulting many of its low-skilled workers into the middle class and enabling them to afford the products they helped produce for the first time.

In the 1920s Ford purchased the Lincoln Motor Company, a competitor, and moved most of the combined company's production operations to the Ford Rouge Complex in nearby Dearborn, Michigan. By the end of the decade the company was producing 1.5 million cars annually, a huge ramp-up in production from the Mack Avenue facility's original output. Ford also played a vital role in assisting the Allied forces during the Second World War. Suspending automobile production for the duration of the war, the company converted its assembly lines to churn out B-24 Liberators at the rate of 1 per hour, or nearly 600 every month, utilizing the same mass-production techniques first piloted by the Model T 30 years earlier.

The 1950s and 1960s witnessed the introduction of some of Ford's most iconic vehicles and family lines, including the Mustang and the Thunderbird, which quickly became international symbols of American consumerism in the postwar era. Throughout the next several decades, Ford continued its global expansion. By the 1990s, the company refocused its attention on automotive concerns and financial services. Organic growth, in the form of newly opened Asian operations and the establishment of the Ford Motor Credit Company, the firm's financial arm, was complemented by a series of high-profile acquisitions. In 1989–1990, Ford purchased Jaguar, a British manufacturer of luxury cars, and in 1993 added Aston Martin. Later acquisitions in the 1990s included rental car company Hertz Corporation in 1994, Volvo's automotive division in 1999, and Britain's Land Rover brand of sport-utility vehicles in 2000. All four brands were placed in the newly created Premier Automotive Group. Ford also made a significant investment in the more economically priced Japanese automobile producer Mazda, rounding out its profile of global brands and automobiles that appealed across the spectrum to all types of drivers.

Despite these investments in global growth, Ford struggled as it entered the 21st century, and sought to shrink its portfolio. By 2007, the company had divested the majority of Aston Martin to a consortium of investors and car enthusiasts for nearly $850 million, and the following year sold Jaguar and Land Rover to Tata Motors Ltd., an Indian conglomerate. When the Great Recession crippled markets in 2008–2009, the American automobile industry centered in Detroit was hit especially hard. Through the Troubled Assets Relief Program (TARP), the U.S. government made over $13 billion in government loans available to struggling automobile makers. Although Ford had secured a $23.6 billion lending facility a year earlier and thus did not require government relief, it was not completely exempt from needing to downsize through the recession. The company closed 13 plants and laid off more than 50,000 of its nearly 200,000 employees to decrease capacity. In 2010 the automaker announced an agreement to sell Volvo to the Chinese automotive conglomerate Zhejiang Geely Holding, and later announced it would discontinue its Mercury line, a brand first conceptualized in the 1930s to bridge the price gap between the Ford and Lincoln brands. By the end of fiscal year 2015, Ford's total revenues were $149.6 billion. The 6.7million cars sold globally in that year comprised nearly 94 percent of that revenue.[2]

Ford Motor Company's income statements for 2013 through the second quarter of 2016 are presented in Exhibit 1. The company's balance sheets for 2013 through 2015 are presented in Exhibit 2.

The Modern Automobile Industry

The modern automotive industry was one of the largest in the world; in 2015, industry experts anticipated that nearly 90 million vehicles were sold globally.[3] The U.S. auto market was approximately 10 percent of that worldwide total, with 7.7 million passenger cars sold in 2014, and the industry in the United States comprised the largest single manufacturing

EXHIBIT 1 Ford Motor Company Quarterly and Annual Income Statements, 2013 - Second Quarter 2016 (in millions except per share amounts)

	2nd Quarter	1st Quarter	2015	2014	2013
	06/30/2016	03/31/2016			
Automotive revenues	$ 36,932	$ 35,257	$ 140,566	$ 135,782	$ 139,369
Financial services revenues	2,553	2,461	8,992	8,295	7,548
Total revenues	39,485	37,718	149,558	144,077	146,917
Automotive cost of sales	-	30,281	124,041	123,516	125,234
Selling, administrative & other expenses	2,661	3,823	14,999	14,117	13,176
Financial services interest expense	-	658	2,454	2,699	2,860
Financial services provision for credit & insurance losses	-	141	417	305	208
Total costs & expenses	37,267	34,903	141,911	140,637	141,478
Automotive interest expense	212	200	773	797	829
Automotive interest income & other income (loss), net	389	404	1,188	76	974
Financial services other income (expense), net	82	91	372	348	(348)
Equity in net income (loss) of affiliated companies	398	541	1,818	1,275	1,069
Income (loss) before income taxes	2,875	3,651	10,252	4,342	7,001
Provision for (benefit from) income taxes	903	1,196	666	559	577
Net income (loss)	1,972	2,455	7,371	3,186	7,148
Less: loss (income) attributable to noncontrolling interests	(2)	(3)	200	154	-
Net income (loss) attributable to Ford Motor Company	$ 1,970	$ 2,452	$ 7,373	$ 3,187	$ 7,155
Weighted average shares outstanding - basic	3,973	3,970	3,969	3,912	3,935
Weighted average shares outstanding - diluted	3,997	3,996	4,002	4,045	4,087
Year end shares outstanding	3,902	3,973	3,970	3,956	3,944
Net income (loss) per share - basic	$0.50	$0.62	$1.86	$0.81	$1.82
Net income (loss) per share - diluted	$0.49	$0.61	$1.84	$0.80	$1.76
Cash dividends declared	$0.15	$0.40	$0.60	$0.50	$0.40

Source: Ford Motor Company 10-K and 10-Q reports, various years.

enterprise in terms of total product value, value added by manufacturer, and the total of wage earners employed throughout the industry.[4,5] For other industrialized nations with strong automobile industries, including countries in the European Union, Japan, and South Korea, the dominance of the automobile industry on gross domestic product (GDP), and especially on exports, had grown exponentially over the latter half of the 20th century.

Ford Motor Company was one of the leading car manufacturers on both a profitability and production basis, but other major competitors included

EXHIBIT 2 Ford Motor Company Balance Sheet Data, 2013–2016 ($ in millions)

	12/31/2015	12/31/2014	12/31/2013
Cash & cash equivalents	$ 14,272	$ 10,757	$ 14,468
Marketable securities	20,904	20,393	22,100
Receivables, net	101,975	101,975	101,975
Inventories	8,319	7,866	7,708
Other current assets	59,480	48,496	37,477
Fixed assets, net	19,975	19,040	18,298
Total assets	$ 224,925	$ 208,527	$ 202,026
Total current liabilities	$ 188,591	$ 195,645	$ 179,373
Total long-term liabilities	7,677	(11,950)	(3,763)
Total equity (deficit)	28,657	24,832	26,416
Total liabilities and shareholders' equity	$ 224,925	$ 208,527	$ 202,026

Source: Ford Motor Company 2015 10-K.

General Motors (also U.S. based, in Detroit), Toyota (a Japanese automaker, whose portfolio also included the Lexus luxury car brand), and Volkswagen (a German manufacturer that also owned Audi). While Ford primarily operated in the mid- to lower-priced end of the pricing spectrum, it had also owned stakes in more luxury brands such as Land Rover and Jaguar, as noted. Major competitors of these brands included producers like BMW and Daimler-Benz (also German manufacturers), Acura (the luxury arm of Honda in Japan), and at an even higher price point, boutique manufacturers like Porsche, Ferrari, and Maserati.

Consolidation and decentralization were two of the major trends of the industry. Part of this was due to the overall capital intensity of the industry; heavy investments in equipment and large production facilities have traditionally been required in order to achieve economies of scale. As attitudes on environmental impact have evolved, so too have more stringent regulations been placed on the industry that require greater costs on the part of the manufacturer. Ford, as noted, was a pioneer in the industry in the United States due to its innovative production facilities and creation of the assembly-line process, aimed at lowering overall production costs. These savings, however, were being offset by higher transportation costs as the industry globalized. Asian automakers such as Honda and Toyota in Japan had pioneered a "just-in-time" inventory method whereby noncritical component parts were outsourced to independent suppliers producing close to assembly plants and then sent back to the production facility at the time needed. Toyota had also pioneered a production method known as kaizen, now adopted by many industries ex-automobiles globally, that emphasized continuous process improvement throughout the organization.

Ford was not alone in adopting an international acquisition strategy at the end of the 20th century. Major domestic competitors like Chrysler infamously merged in 1998 with Daimler-Benz, the producer of luxury brand Mercedes, and then later took controlling interest in Japanese manufacturer Mitsubishi in 2000. GM, which had purchased controlling interests in Saab (Sweden) and Subaru (Japan), began to look toward overseas consolidation as a method for keeping production costs lower and diversifying into new markets outside the United States. While traditionally the most profitable markets have been developed countries with significant middle-class purchasing power, developing nations, with larger populations overall and growing percentage of middle-class workers, have become greater consumers. In 2015, Chinese consumers purchased more vehicles than in the United States (21.1 million passenger cars), although at lower margins.[6]

FORD MOTOR COMPANY'S STRATEGY IN THE 21ST CENTURY

Following the Great Recession, Ford's global strategy had largely been focused on returning the company to profitability in each of the markets it operates in. Under then-CEO Alan Mulally, the company developed the One Ford Plan, as noted earlier. The four elements of the One Ford Plan included:

- Aggressively restructure Ford to operate profitably at the current demand and changing model mix
- Accelerate development of new products Ford's customers want and value
- Finance out the plan and improve Ford's balance sheet
- Work together effectively as one team

Under the One Ford Plan, Ford shifted from having many regional platforms to a focus on fewer, more global production platforms to better capitalize on economies of scale. The company began to launch more products off fewer platforms, and revamped older vehicle families with technological improvements designed to win over new buyers. The Fiesta, originally a supermini car first sold in Europe and Latin America in the 1970s, launched in the United States in 2010, followed by the launch of the Brazil-based mini-utility vehicle the EcoSport in India and Europe. Ford transformed its global bestseller, the F-series, a line of pickup trucks produced since the postwar era and the bestselling vehicle in the United States for 34 years running (1981–2015), switching from steel to aluminum, a feat unprecedented in manufacturing at such high volume.[7,8]

Much of Ford's strategy shifts had been in response to the rapidly evolving external environment for automotive companies in the 2010s. The emergence of ride-share companies like Uber and Lyft in the United States, Didi in China, and Ola in India, and participation by technological giants such as Google and Apple in the development of autonomous (otherwise known as driverless) cars had caused automakers to reconsider how to compete in what had developed into a completely different world from the Detroit of Henry Ford. Mark Fields, Mulally's successor to the CEO position in 2014, recognized the need to adapt in an increasingly competitive automobile landscape. In 2015, Fields hired John Casesa, a long-time automobile industry analyst and former investment banker, to lead the newly created Global Strategy team. Casesa had been tasked with accelerating the implementation of the One Ford Plan, and revamping the Global Strategy team's mandate.

In early 2016, CEO Fields championed updating the One Ford Plan to better reflect Ford's business needs. These refined initiatives included:

- Strengthening and investing in Ford's core business, including design, development, manufacturing, and marketing of great cars, trucks, SUVs, and electrified vehicles
- Aggressively pursuing emerging opportunities through *Ford Smart Mobility,* Ford's plan to be a leader in connectivity, mobility, autonomous vehicles, the customer experience, and data and analytics
- Transforming the customer experience to combine Ford's great products with great experiences customers want and value[9]

Fields's vision for Ford as it entered the third decade of the 21st century was to transform Ford into both a strong automotive *and* mobility company. The company had rededicated itself to "delivering smart mobility solutions at the right place and the right time, and transforming the way that people move, as Henry Ford did when he started the company back in 1903."

The Smart Mobility Platform and Dynamic Shuttle Concept

A key component of Ford's Smart Mobility platform was assessing the strategic markets and locations where the program could be implemented. Ford began to pilot a concept known as the Dynamic Shuttle program in Dearborn and one other city in the United States, with the aim of expanding the program on a global scale.

The concept of the Dynamic Shuttle was an on-demand shuttle that could be accessed via a user's mobile phone, and be dispatched either directly to the requesting customer (usually in developed markets), or to a pickup location within a short walk that aggregated multiple customers for pickup (potentially in more rural areas or areas with poor infrastructure). The pricing of the shuttle was usually at a premium to mass transit in the market but a cost save compared to a taxi service or a ride-hailing service (such as Uber, Lyft, and Ola). Additionally, unlike a traditional bus service, dynamic shuttling's algorithms and "learning capability" offered much greater flexibility in pickup and departure times and locations.

The program had multiple goals. It aimed to exist as a new transport ride-sharing platform in the space between scheduled (mass-transit) and private transport, enabled by smartphone development and penetration. Less expensive than a taxi, it expected to offer a more comfortable and convenient experience than mass transit. Typically, the shuttle anticipated serving between 4 and 6 people in developed countries and up to 12 passengers in developing countries per ride. In developing countries, Dynamic Shuttle could also be used to connect riders from their home communities to mass-transit routes, if passengers lived long distances from a major transit line.

Some startups had started dynamic shuttles in cities like New York, Chicago, and Helsinki. Competitors like Uber and Lyft, through their analogous UberPOOL and Lyft Line services, had also begun to experiment with their own conceptualization of shared, or pooled, rides, and by mid-2015 over 50 percent of Uber's fares and 60 percent of Lyft's in the San Francisco market were based on carpooling services.[10] Yet for the most part, no ride-hailing smartphone-based app service was at the carrying capacity of a full shuttle, as Ford intended, and most pilots in developed countries were too small in size and scale compared to the possibilities already offered in many developing nations. Ford's hope was to experiment with the shuttle to learn as much as possible from both a technological and operational perspective, but eventually the company hoped to quickly scale and enter into markets where mobility and movement of people are true problems.

THE INDIAN MASS-TRANSIT MARKET

Emerging economies, with large populations, densely populated urban areas, overcrowded streets, and clogged transport and infrastructure systems, presented a unique challenge for a shuttle concept. In considering which developing economy to launch Dynamic Shuttle, Ford considered two options. One obvious choice was China, but for many reasons, including the need for unique joint venture agreements mandated by the Chinese government, Casesa's Global Strategy Team decided to investigate the feasibility of a Dynamic Shuttle launch in India. Should Dynamic Shuttle launch successfully there, Casesa's team was confident it could act as a test case for other densely populated countries coping with mobility issues that had a need for a program like Dynamic Shuttle.

India was anticipated to have a population of nearly 1.5 billion residents by 2020.[11] As one of the most populous and densest countries in the world, India faced the challenge of needing to facilitate transport for millions of people daily. The Indian transport system consisted of multiple modes, including walking, bicycling, various forms of rickshaws, bus and metro systems, and regional railways.

In densely populated urban areas of India, demand for public transport often exceeded capacity. Trains in Mumbai, the most populous city in India, carried over 7.5 million riders per day, a sixfold increase over the last 40 years, while daily capacity on its trains had only doubled.[12] Yet for a city as densely populated as Mumbai, with its 20 million residents, continuing to build new infrastructure and extending the woefully inadequate means of public transportation was often limited, if not impossible. Besides the overcrowded public transportation, India's tropical climate could lead to uncomfortable traveling experiences. Research in cities like Mumbai found that some customers would pay at least a 25 percent premium to ride in air-conditioned cabs versus ones without air-conditioning.[13]

RIDE-HAILING APPLICATIONS IN THE 21ST CENTURY

One of the most prevalent competitors to traditional taxi cabs in the ride-hailing industry was Uber. Founded in California in 2009, Uber primarily functioned as a car-hailing mobile application, via which users could request car services from their smartphones. Revenue was generated by charging users a fare for accessing and using the service, and then split between Uber and the driver, who was often viewed by the company as an independent contractor. Fares were calculated through a proprietary algorithm that takes into account time (both for the driver to arrive and the total estimated ride), distance, and demand. Uber's pricing structure could either be less expensive or at a premium to the local taxi market. The company had experienced explosive growth in its first six years, raising over $10 billion in capital, completing 1 billion rides, and spreading to nearly 70 countries and 360 cities.[14,15] Major competitors with similar business models included Lyft in the United States, BlablaCar in France (a ride-sharing app), Didi Kuaidi in China, and Ola in India. Statistics related to smartphone and ride-hailing services usage in India are presented in Exhibits 5-7.

As mentioned, despite its dominance over competitors in major metropolitan cities throughout the world, Uber was not the only ride-hailing app in India, nor did it even occupy the dominant position in the Indian domestic market. In mid-2015, the company injected over $1 billion in investments in its Indian operations, with the goal of handling over 1 million rides on a daily basis, similar to its current capacity in both China and the United States.[16] Yet while Uber could be found in over 22 Indian metropolitan areas by the end of 2015, its ridership statistics were much less impressive, with the company citing on average only 250,000 rides per day.[17] Instead, the dominant ride-hailing app-based company in India, Ola, was speculated to actually achieve Uber's goal of over 1 million rides on a daily basis spread across the 350,000 vehicles in its platform, and could be found in over 102 Indian cities. Through aggressive tactics more suited to the Indian market, including acceptance of cash instead of credit-card smartphone-based payments, better utilization of rickshaws and cheaper modes of transportation, and diffusion of the business to second- and third-tier Indian cities, Ola was able to outpace Uber in the Indian ride-hailing market. As of December 2015, Ola, Lyft, Didi Kuaidi, and GrabTaxi (a Southeast Asian app) had also pledged to allow customers of each company to use their local apps in different markets, in an attempt to continue to block Uber's growth.[18]

Smartphone usage in India, projected to grow to nearly 317.1 million users by 2019, combined with the population statistics and competitive environment described above, indicated India would be a ripe market for a smartphone-based ride applications.[19,20] As noted, however, neither Uber nor Ola had successfully piloted the concept of a mass-scale ride-hailing *shuttle* in their Indian business model. For this reason, Ford's Global Strategy Team ultimately selected India as the pilot country for the launch of its Dynamic Shuttle pilot program.

FORD'S INDIAN MARKET ASSESSMENT

The Ford team assessed a number of key variables, including population statistics, income levels, and daily mileage traveled to calculate a potential market share for Dynamic Shuttle. Total available mileage, rather than number of potential customers or conversion rates, was used as a baseline for calculations, as basic profitability for most ride-hailing and ride-sharing programs are calculated on a mileage basis (i.e., not per customer). It was essential, however, to determine an appropriate customer base for the pilot. Casesa's team first analyzed total population statistics of Indians living in urban areas (nearly 500 million), and then specifically drilled down by income segmentation into those who made between approximately INR 90,000–200,000 per annum (roughly defined as "seekers"), and those who made between INR 200,000–500,000, (roughly defined as "aspirational workers"). Seekers and aspirational workers could not afford personal transportation and were in most instances still likely to use mass transit for their professional commutes, yet had the disposable income available to potentially pay a premium for an easier ride. This population yielded approximately 280 million potential shuttle riders.

The team then considered the different modes of transportation available to riders in major cities. Approximately 70 percent of the miles traveled by Indian commuters in cities on a daily basis were through mass transit, an obvious target, but the team also considered the miles traveled by commuters on motorcycles as a possible customer segment that could be converted to Dynamic Shuttle. On the high end of estimates, approximately 73 percent of the miles traveled by Indian commuters on a daily basis were thought to be within Dynamic Shuttle's target market. The team next deliberated the transport alternatives already available to commuters, including two-wheelers, trains, buses, and shared modes like rickshaws and taxis, and broke out the percentage usage rate by a variety of income levels. With these factors in mind, and the assumption of an 8 percent conversion or take rate, the estimates for annual mileage traveled by seekers and aspirational workers in a given year using Dynamic Shuttle was thought to be in the range of 65–90 billion miles. With an average rider cost of $0.30 per mile, Ford calculated a potential annual revenue of $19–26 billion. (See Exhibit 3 for further details on the team's analysis.)

Dynamic Shuttle Business Model and Partner Selection

Business Model Once the market potential for Dynamic Shuttle in India was estimated, Casesa's team deliberated on the best path for market entry. Ford had established plants in India in the late 1920s, and Ford India had operated as a wholly owned subsidiary of Ford Motor Company since 1995, with manufacturing facilities in Chennai and Gujarat.[21]

The team assessed three different options for the Dynamic Shuttle rollout. In the first model, Ford Motor Company and Ford Motor Credit Corporation (Ford's financial and lending arm) would provide the vehicles, financing, and parts and servicing. This solution was more complete and enabled more in-house control, but operating its own fleet on the ground would incur heavy capital requirements, as Ford would have to own the overall assets (the vehicles themselves), a strain on the company's overall capital. The second option identified was to organically develop the technology in-house and sell it to companies already in operation to help them create this business. This option was ultimately rejected due to the slower speed of development, especially in light of the necessity of starting operations and scaling the business model quickly. The model ultimately selected was for Ford Smart Mobility to choose a partner that would establish operations on the ground in India. With this partner, Ford would establish a franchise model, which would facilitate the platform, payment system, and create a joint business model.

Strategic Imperatives for Partner Selection Ford's vision for Dynamic Shuttle was to choose a partner whose current business model most closely aligned with their view of the offering. The team considered key questions and solutions that each partner would need to satisfy, provided below. After thinking through these key imperatives, the team identified five potential partners. A matrix is provided in Exhibit 4 with details on how each partner aligned with the goals and competencies needed to successfully execute on the project. Key considerations for the team included:

- **Business Model:** Would the shuttle have defined stops (B2C) or offer on-demand services? Are rides shared (usually with 1 other person) or a true shuttle (up to 12 passengers)?
- **Customer Strategy:** Who is the primary competitor, and where does demand come from?
- **Scalability of Algorithms:** What is the number of cities the partner currently operates in?
- **City Relationship:** Has the partner cultivated relationships with cities to operate the business?
- **Physical Products:** Who actually owns the vehicles in operation?
- **Operating Franchise Model:** Can the partner quickly develop a franchise model?
- **Willingness to Accept Investment:** To what degree could Ford be a controlling stakeholder?
- **User Experience:** Is customer feedback and/or research on the partner's ability to deliver on promised experience positive?
- **Growth Potential:** What are the partner's plans for growth?
- **Applicability and Flexibility of Algorithm:** Can the partner's technology (mapping and algorithms) adapt to different needs and new locations? How easily is it replicated?

Partner Selection Casesa and his team had answered the basics: identified the market for Dynamic Shuttle's first international pilot (India); defined the business model necessary to execute on the pilot; deliberated on specific strategic initiatives and imperatives needed for a hypothetical partner. Their focus now shifted to evaluating the five potential partners Ford could align with to bring Dynamic Shuttle to India. As he sat down to review the agenda for his next meeting with the Global Strategy Team, the key discussion item remained:

> *Which partner would be the best match for Ford in terms of business model, growth, technology, and operational efficiency to successfully launch a Dynamic Shuttle pilot in India?*

EXHIBIT 3 Market Sizing Analysis and Revenue Projections for Dynamic Shuttle in India

Step 1: Indian Population Segmentation			
Total Indian Population	1,311,051		
Number living in urban araas	419,939		
Income Segmentation		**%**	**INR Income**
Rich		3%	> INR 1,000,000
Strivers		6%	INR 500,000 to 1,000,000
Seekers		***25%***	***INR 200,000 to 500,000***
Aspirational Workers		***40%***	***INR 90,000 to 200,000***
Deprived		26%	< INR 90,000
Total # Seekers and Aspirational	272,960		

Step 2 - Travel Methodology	***What kind of travel would Dynamic Shuttle replace?***	
Mode of Transit	**Total Miles/Yr**	**%**
Personal Vehicle	593	25.79%
Taxi/Uber	17	0.74%
Motorcycle	123	5.35%
Mass Transit	1,565	68.07%
Total	2,299	100.00
% of total miles for customer segment	**73.42%**	**(High End Estimate)**

Alternative - Mumbai-Metro Area Specific	**Income**					
Vehicle Type	**90,000,000**	**180,000**	**300,000**	**420,000**	**540,000**	**660,000**
Car	1.00%	2.00%	6.00%	13.00%	21.00%	24.00%
Two-Wheeler	***5.00%***	***8.00%***	***9.00%***	***9.00%***	10.00%	12.00%
Train	***22.00%***	***28.00%***	***30.00%***	***29.00%***	21.00%	23.00%
Bus	***12.00%***	***13.00%***	***15.00%***	***15.00%***	15.00%	15.00%
Shared Mode (Rickshaw, Taxi)	***4.00%***	***4.00%***	***5.00%***	***6.00%***	8.00%	9.00%
Walk/Bike	56.00%	45.00%	35.00%	28.00%	28.00%	17.00%
Total Highlighted Modes of Travel	43.00%	53.00%	59.00%	59.00%		
% of total miles for customer segment	**53.50%**	**(Low End Estimate)**				

Step 3 - Mileage & Revenue Calculations		
Total Transit Miles/Year in Urban Areas		2,299 *billion*
Miles/Urban Dweller		0.0055 *billion*
# Seekers & Aspirational		272,960 *billion*
Total mileage Seekers & Aspirational		1,494 *billion*
% total miles of customer segment		
Low end estimate (53.5%)		799 *billion*
High end estimate (73.42%)		1,097 *billion*
8% Uptake rate assumption		
Low end estimate		64 *billion*
High end estimate		88 *billion*
Assumed cost/mile	$ 0.30	
Revenue calculation		
High end estimate	$ 19.19	*billion USD*
Low end estimate	$ 26.33	*billion USD*

EXHIBIT 4 Competency Matrix for Dynamic Shuttle Prospective Partners

	DYNAMIC SHUTTLE Competency Matrix				
	Vrigg	Ryderz	Car-Go	Shuttlex	Qquark
Partner Business Model	Shuttle (Defined Stops)	On Demand Shuttle	On Demand Shuttle	Shared Ride Services	Shared Ride Services
Partner Customer Strategy	**Increase/augment access to mass transit.**	**Competing with existing mass transit - replace, value prop = more upscale**	**Taxi-like business; replace taxi hailling**	**Taxi-like business; replace taxi hailling**	**Taxi- like business; replace taxi hailling**
How Scalable Are Partner Algorithms	3 Cities currently	2 Cities currently	1 City	Very scalable	Very scalable
City Relationships (# cities type of relationship, ride sharing v. dynamic shuttle)	3 US major cities Understand regulations but also developed relationship with the city	2 US major cities Understand regulations but also developed relationship with the city	1 US major city due to number of cities, more ridesharing, haven't had to develop relationships with cities	50+ Cities. ride-sharing. haven't had to develop relationships with cities.	8 Cities. Ride-sharing haven't had to develop relationships with cities
Physical Products (Who Own the Vehicles)	City and small fleets Purpose built vehicles (Vans)	Drivers or Small fleets	Indvidual Drivers. Large SUVs.	Indvidual Drivers. Large SUVs.	Indvidual Drivers. Large SUVs.
Operating Franchise Model	Expressed interest to franchise	Expressed interest to franchise	Expressed interest to franchise	Very mature, expansion plans may not include franchise model	Faling Business
Willingness to Accept Investment	None since seed funding 54 mil	Series B closed $ 37 million total	Wholly owned by transportation company	Over $ 1 Billion	$ 50 million
User Experience (App and Service)	Strong app, people interested in the purpose-built vehicles. Benchmark experience showed service not consistent	Strong UX, strong focus on customer acquisition and customer data	App is not as polished, unclear the goals of service	Mature and strong app - drivers incentivized to provide good user experience	App design is good, but business model is failing service TBD
Growth Potential (# employess, growth curve, #customers)	25 employees, aim for 100 by end of 2015, Adapting to different cities. 5% wk/wk growth. Constrained by ability to grow	Very customercentric in data presentation. 30 employees, 50/50 in operation and tech. 1 million riders per year, 250 drivers, up to 1200 mid 2016	Higher maintenance, high growth potential 50% month over month growth	Mature, ability to impact the business is difficult. Low maintenance	Take over failing business Resource intensive to get involved with.
Applicability of Algorithm/Flexibility	Complex algorithm aggregates people to go to set destinations. Operates during rush hour. Limited dynamic functioning. Usually within 5 min walk On-demand and pre-book	On-demand Can flex in real-time. Operate 6:30 to 9. Closest to Ford model of dynamic shuttle	Similar to on-demand model by Ryderz, but with a less 1 fleible algorithm	Dynamic but only from one rider to another	Has true dynamic capability as demonstrated by package pick up/drop off

OTHER COMPETENCIES					
Fleet Management	Y	R	Y	R	R
Customer Support / Help Desk / CRM	Y	Y	Y	G	G
Customer Scale & Insights (incl. Analytics)	Y	Y	Y	G	Y

EXHIBIT 5 Smartphone Usage in India (millions) from 2013 to 2019

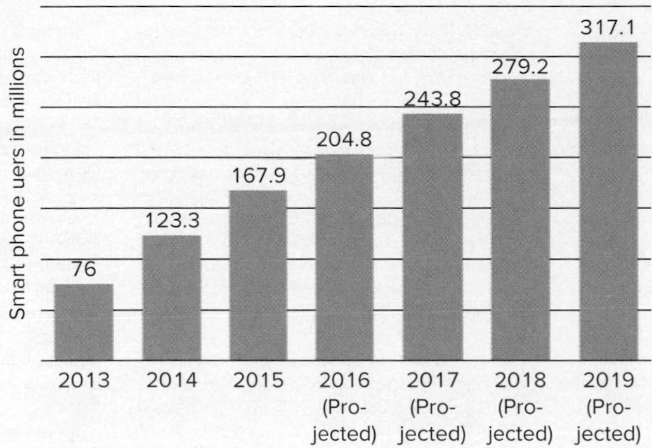

EXHIBIT 6 Daily Completed Rides by Uber and Ola in India as of December 2015

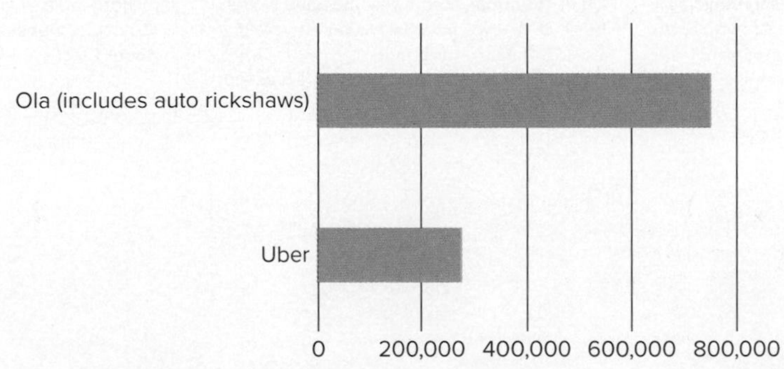

Source: Uber, Ola, atlas.qz.com/charts/NJ3EKY2R.

EXHIBIT 7 Uber's Reach versus the Competition as of September 2015

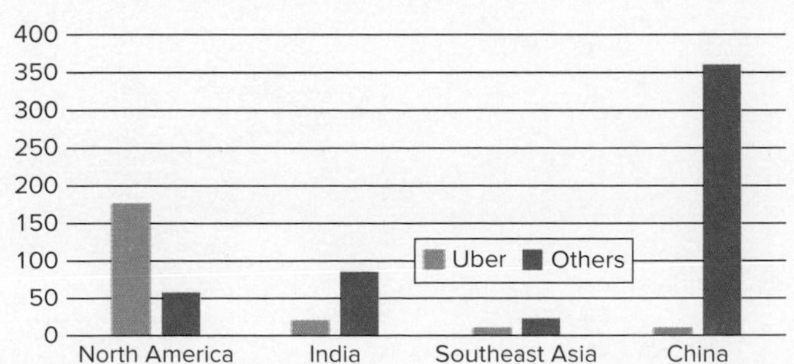

Source: atlas.qz.com/charts/NJdXd64C.

ENDNOTES

[1] James G. Cobb, "This Just In: Model T Gets Award," *The New York Times,* December 24, 1999, www.nytimes.com/1999/12/24/automobiles/this-just-in-model-t-gets-award.html.

[2] "Ford 4Q and Full Year Earnings Review and 2016 Outlook," Ford Motor Co., last modified January 28, 2016 (preliminary results)," corporate.ford.com/content/dam/corporate/en/investors/investor-events/Quarterly%20Earnings/2015/2015-4Q-earnings-slides-20160127.pdf.

[3] OICA, "Worldwide Vehicle Sales from 2005 to 2015 (in Units)," www.statista/statistics/265859/vehicle-sales-worldwide/.

[4] kfz-betrieb, "Revenue of the Leading Automotive Manufacturers Worldwide in 2014 (in Billion Euros)," www.statista.com/statistics/232958/revenue-of-the-leading-car-manufacturers-worldwide/.

[5] *Encyclopædia Britannica,* s.v. "automotive industry," www.britannica.com/topic/automotive-industry/The-modern-industry (accessed March 11, 2016).

[6] CAAM, "Automobile Sales in China from January 2015 to January 2016 (in 1,000 Units)."

[7] Kelly Pleskot, "The 15 Best-Selling Vehicles of 2015: Ford F-Series Keeps Its Crown," *Motor Trend,* January 5, 2016, www.motortrend.com/news/the-15-best-selling-vehicles-of-2015-ford-f-series-keeps-its-crown/.

[8] Eve P., "Ford F-Series Trucks Number One for 35 Years Running," social.ford.com/content/fordsocial/en/articles/quality/fo/22086-ford-f-series-trucks-number-one-for-35-years-running.html (accessed March 18, 2016).

[9] "One Ford Card," www.at.ford.com/news/cn/Pages/One%20Ford%20Card.aspx (accessed March 18, 2016).

[10] Ellen Huet, "The Case for Carpooling: Inside Lyft and Uber's Quest to Squeeze More People in The Backseat," *Forbes,* August 18, 2015, www.forbes.com/sites/ellenhuet/2015/08/18/inside-lyfts-and-ubers-carpooling-quest-uberpool-lyft-line/#4b1b7d5c11a5.

[11] United Nations, Population Division, "World Population Prospects 2015," esa.un.org/unpd/wpp/Graphs/Probabilistic/POP/TOT/ (accessed March 18, 2016).

[12] Julien Bouissou, "Mumbai's Rail Commuters Pay a High Human Price for Public Transport," *The Guardian,*October 29, 2013, www.theguardian.com/world/2013/oct/29/india-mumbai-population-rail-accidents.

[13] Deven Jadav, "Various AC and NON Air-conditioned Taxi Fares in Mumbai—Fare Rate Chart," Mumbai 77.com, last modified November 1, 2011, www.mumbai77.com/city/1918/travel/taxi-fare-rates/.

[14] Uber Technologies Inc., PrivCo. (accessed March 18, 2016).

[15] Sriram Sharma, "Uber vs. Ola in India: How Do They Stack Up?," *Gadgets 360,* last modified February 5, 2016, gadgets.ndtv.com/apps/features/uber-vs-ola-in-india-how-do-they-stack-up-798608.

[16] Jon Russell, "Uber Is Investing $1B to Grow Its Business in India to 1M Rides Per Day," *Tech Crunch,*July 31, 2015, techcrunch.com/2015/07/31/one-billllllllllllion/#.fb5p9ub:mWyk.

[17] Jon Russell, "Ola, the Company Beating Uber in India, Raises $500M at a $5B Valuation," *Tech Crunch,*November 17, 2015, techcrunch.com/2015/11/17/ola-the-company-beating-uber-in-india-lands-500m-in-fresh-investment/.

[18] Ibid.

[19] Ingrid Lunden, "Lift, Didi, Ola and GrabTaxi Partner in Global Tech, Service Alliance to Rival Uber," *Tech Crunch,* December 3, 2015, techcrunch.com/2015/12/03/lyft-didi-ola-and-grabtaxi-partner-in-global-tech-service-alliance-to-rival-uber/.

[20] Cindy Liu, "Worldwide Internet and Mobile Users," *eMarketer,* August 17, 2015.

[21] "Ford India—Corporate Profile," Ford Motor Co. website, www.india.ford.com/about (accessed March 18, 2016).

CASE 19

The Green Music Center at Sonoma State University

Katie Robinson
Sonoma State University

Seconds ticked by in silence. . . . Eyes darted around the room. . . . Bodies shifted in seats in the meeting room at the Green Music Center. . . . There was an air of trepidation in the April 2016 meeting of the GMC Board of Advisors Finance Committee as they processed what Sonoma State University Vice President for Administration & Finance and CFO Larry Furukawa-Schlereth had just presented. While the GMC's presenting series had thus far maintained a balanced budget all four years of operation, it needed to prepare for the expiration of its $1.25 million annual MasterCard sponsorship in three years' time, which had heavily subsidized operations up until that point. In response to this new information, committee members casually bandied about suggestions with little consideration for their practicality, each of which was addressed accordingly by GMC executive management. "Is there any room for efficiencies in expenses?" A fine idea, but one that didn't take into consideration the already lean operations that had been extensively examined the prior year. "Can development raise more in sponsorships?" There was most certainly room for growth, but 200 percent over three years seemed unlikely. "Can we increase revenue in ticket sales?" A possibility, but one that would require an overhaul in the type of programming offered by the center, as well as additional marketing expenses.

Once the sponsorship ended, either external fundraising would need to take its place or the university would need to subsidize operations. This decision was to be made in July as a new president, Dr. Judy Sakaki, came into the university with new ideas and priorities relative to her predecessor. This was not the first time (nor would it be the last) that the university needed to consider the importance of the music center in its mission to provide its students with a broad cultural perspective within the liberal arts framework. Both the Green Music Center and Sonoma State had mission statements that reflected the importance of education and community engagement. If Dr. Sakaki were to choose to not financially support the music center, alternative fundraising might ultimately cause both organizations to lose sight of their established missions.

SONOMA STATE UNIVERSITY

The Green Music Center (GMC) was located on the manicured grounds of Sonoma State University (SSU), 1 of the 23 campuses of the public California State University System. While each of the campuses had radically different cultures from one another, they were all ultimately governed under the same directives from the state of California. The mission of SSU specifically was

> to prepare students to be learned persons who: have a foundation for life-long learning; have a broad cultural perspective; have a keen appreciation of intellectual and aesthetic achievements; will be active citizens and leaders in society; are capable of pursuing fulfilling careers in a changing world; and are concerned with contributing to the health and well-being of the world at large.[1]

This case was prepared by Katie Robinson, Sonoma State University MBA 2016, under the supervision of Dr. Armand Gilinsky, Sonoma State University.

SSU hoped to produce well-rounded and intelligent graduates, but also took consideration of the community immediately around it. Following the stated mission statement was the addition of "The University also recognizes its obligation to serve as an educational and cultural resource for people in the surrounding communities." Both education and community interests were also reflected in the GMC's mission:

> To create transformative experiences in the arts and education that promotes active learning by all and contributes to the cultural and economic betterment of our community.[2]

The mission of the GMC was set in the early days of planning, long before the center coalesced into its current form. While the wordsmithing had developed since its founding in the early 90s, the core inclusive mission had remained unchanged: to serve an expansive segment of the campus and community, and address broad tastes and perspectives in its programming. In addition to being a hub of cultural activity, the Green Music Center would also offer an opportunity to bring Sonoma State University and the larger Sonoma County community together. Sitting on a university campus, there had always been an element of educational involvement with the greater GMC vision, but the level of prominence in the mission statement had fluctuated throughout the years.

SSU (and by extension the GMC) benefited from extensive economies of scale provided by the state of California; however, as a state-funded entity the university was also limited in certain of its actions. The use of taxpayer dollars created obstacles for any entity operating within a public university setting. For example, by law the university was limited in the activities it could conduct to generate additional revenue. SSU, and therefore the GMC, could not sell alcohol, accept stock gifts, or invest revenue earnings, which were fairly commonplace practices in private performing arts centers.

Working within the context of a large state bureaucracy also added a level of complexity and expense not typically experienced by similar private institutions. New processes were created and implemented at the university to accommodate the shortened timelines required in the performing arts business. The conflict between obligations of SSU and the best practices in the private performing arts world became most apparent in the area of tax compliance—see Exhibit 1. A state-funded entity must follow IRS guidelines to the letter, while smaller private centers attempted a more loose interpretation, especially relating to ticket sales. Artist would often "buy out" performances to avoid tax implications associated with ticket sale revenue.

Heavy reliance on state funding led to volatile state university campus budgets from 2008 to 2012, due to the drastic economic shifts of the Great Recession. The overall California State University (CSU) budget was decreased, significantly increasing the importance of every dollar spent. A series of budget cuts also saw the elimination of the General Obligation Bond program, which had been used to fund construction of academic spaces. Many of the campuses in the system were already at maximum student capacity resulting in stagnant systemwide enrollment growth. Pre-recession enrollment growth had been crucial for building programs and bolstering the self-support (housing, parking, campus life) activities on campus. SSU was in a unique position in this regard, since the Academic Wing of the Green Music Center added an additional 1,281 full-time equivalent (FTE) students' (approximate headcount of 1,340 students overall) worth of enrollment capacity. With this new classroom space came an allocation from the CSU to cover all maintenance and operation costs of the new space. While not all 1,281 FTEs had been yet added to the enrollment target of the university by 2016, the additional capacity allowed the university to enroll every additional student the CSU system would allocate. As each FTE brought approximately $10,000 of tuition revenue per year into the university, the full 1,281 would ultimately yield over $12M in revenue to the university operating fund. Approximately half of the additional revenue would be used to fund 61 new faculty positions, and the remainder would be used for other university priorities, such as academic advising, or campus life initiatives.

Sonoma County

The Green Music Center at Sonoma State University was encompassed by the rolling hills of the wine country of Sonoma County. Tourism in the area was ever increasing since dipping during the recession, and there was consequently an increase in jobs in the

EXHIBIT 1 Sonoma State University Performing Arts Contracts and Reporting Policies

TYPE OF AGREEMENT/LANGUAGE TO USE WHEN ENTERED INTO WITH:				
	Named Individual	Named Multiple Individuals	Company Name f/s/o Named Individual(s)	Company Name Only, or Company f/s/o "Group's Name"
Standard Agreement Language (w/Agent)	Between SSU and "Named Individual" acting through "Agent"	Between SSU and "Named Individuals" acting through "Agent"	Between SSU and "Company's Name" fso "Individual's Name" acting through "Agent"	Between SSU and "Company's Name" fso "Group Name" acting through "Agent"
Standard Agreement Language (No Agent)	Between SSU and "Named Individual"	Between SSU and "Named Individuals"	Between SSU and "Company's Name" fso "Individual's Name"	Between SSU and "Company's Name" fso "Group Name"
Producer's Agreement Language	Between SSU and Producer f/s/o "Artist's Name/Group." Language throughout the contract confirms the producer is liable for all contract provisions, not the artist.			

NOTE: This is not a common occurrence. Use when an artist's agent, speaker's bureau, or entertainment agency produces the performance, i.e., the producer bears the costs of obtaining artist and pays for all costs associated with the tour including travel, lodging, and other business expenses. The producer assumes customary business and financial risk for the performance. The Producer's Beneficial Owner of Income form must be completed.

PAYEE IS ARTIST'S AGENT, SPEAKER'S BUREAU, TALENT AGENCY, ENTERTAINMENT AGENCY, ETC. Artist/Performer (*as identified in contract*) is (are):				
	Named Individual	Named Multiple Individuals	Company Name f/s/o Named Individual(s)	Company Name Only, or Company f/s/o "Group's Name"
Required Form(s)*	204 or W-8/W-9 for artist	204 or W-8/W-9 for each artist	204 or W-8/W-9 for company or individual	204 or W-8/W-9 for company
Federal W/H & Reporting				
US Citizen or Company	n/a**	n/a**	n/a**	n/a**
US Nonresident	(30%) 1042-S***	(30%) 1042-S***	(30%) 1042-S***	(30%) 1042-S***
CA State W/H & Reporting				
CA Resident	n/a	n/a	n/a	n/a
Non-CA Resident	(7%) 592-B	(7%) 592-B	(7%) 592-B	(7%) 592-B
Immigration Docs	Passport, visa, I-94, I-797, Foreign National Data Collection Form		n/a	n/a
Treaty (U.S. TIN or Foreign Tax Identification Req'd)	Form 8233. However, reduced W/H due to tax treaties for artists are generally not allowed by the IRS			W-8BEN-E, Business Profits Article[1]

Note: If agreement is a Producer's Agreement, the forms noted above are required for the Producer, i.e., the forms are not required to be collected for the performer.

(*Continued*)

PAYEE IS ARTIST OR ARTIST'S LLC, CORPORATION, OR DBA Artist/Performer (as identified in contract) is (are):				
	Named Individual	Named Multiple Individuals	Company Name f/s/o Named Individual(s)	Company f/s/o "Group's Name"
Required Form(s)*	204 or W-8/W-9 for artist	204 or W-8/W-9 for each artist	204 or W-8/W-9 for company or individual	204 or W-8/W-9 for company
Federal Reporting				
US Citizen or Company	1099-MISC	1099-MISC	1099-MISC (except corps)	1099-MISC (except corps)
US Nonresident	(30%) 1042-S***	(30%) 1042-S***	(30%) 1042-S***	(30%) 1042-S***
CA State W/H & Reporting				
CA Resident	n/a	n/a	n/a	n/a
Non-CA Resident	(7%) 592-B	(7%) 592-B	(7%) 592-B	(7%) 592-B
Immigration Docs	Passport, visa, I-94, I-797, Foreign National Data Collection Form		n/a	n/a
Treaty (U.S. TIN or Foreign Tax Identification Req'd)	Form 8233. However, reduced W/H due to tax treaties for artists are generally not allowed by the IRS			W-8BEN-E, Business Profits Article

(1)Entity must certify performers do not share in profits. Must complete "Company's Beneficial Owner of Income Certification Statement."

Note: If 204 Form or W-8/W-9 is not obtained as noted above, up to 30 percent federal withholding and 7 percent state withholding is required.

Source: Sonoma State University, 2016.

*Performer or company name on 204 form or W-8/W-9 must match performer/company name identified in the contract.

**1099-MISC issued to performer by agent, per contract.

***30 percent W/H required if determined to be a NRA for tax purposes, unless tax treaty and applicable docs submitted.

service and hospitality sectors. While these industries were on the rise, the largest composition of jobs in the county was still those in government services and the public sector. There was also a heavy concentration of jobs in the health sector, which would likely increase as the baby boomer population aged. As can be seen in Exhibit 2, Sonoma County had a significantly larger percentage of the population over the age of 65, compared to the entire Bay Area, state of California, and United States. Unemployment rose considerably in 2010 due to the recession, but had been steadily declining since and the county maintained lower unemployment rates than the state as a whole. Per capita income decreased significantly in 2009, but had steadily risen since, bypassing the previous high water mark by 2015. Median household income, however, had not yet recovered to its previous high by 2016. Considering the small size of the county, the GMC provided a fairly substantial economic impact. According to the Economic Outlook Calculator, the GMC generated $328k in local government tax revenue, and $425k in state tax revenue annually—see Exhibit 3.

Sonoma County boasted beautiful weather[4] and excellent air quality. The generally pleasant weather meant that most of the recreation and leisure activities in the county took place outdoors. Whether it was wine tasting, hiking, or floating down the Russian River, Sonoma County residents generally enjoyed being outside. This was beneficial for the lawn seating at the GMC as it allowed the organization to differentiate itself from the Wells Fargo Center for the Arts, its primary competitor in the county, while

EXHIBIT 2 Demographics of Sonoma County versus Bay Area, California, and United States[3]

	Sonoma (2014)	Bay Area (2010)	California (2014)	United States (2014)
Total Population	502,146	7,150,000	39,144,000	321,419,000
Age: Under 18	20.60%	22.30%	23.60%	23.10%
Age: Over 65	16.70%	12.30%	12.90%	14.50%
White	64.60%	52.50%	38.50%	62.10%
Hispanic	26.10%	23.50%	38.60%	17.40%
Black	1.90%	6.70%	6.50%	13.20%
Other	7.40%	17.30%	16.40%	7.30%
Bachelor's Degree or Higher	32.60%	25.20%	31%	29.30%
Median Household Income	$ 63,800	$ 76,000	$ 61,500	$ 53,500
Median Home Value	$414,500	$637,000	$371,400	$175,700
Income to Home Value Ratio	15.39%	11.93%	16.56%	30.45%

EXHIBIT 3 Economic Impact of the Green Music Center in Sonoma County

	Total Expenditures	FTE Jobs	Household Income	Local Government Revenue	State Government Revenue
Nonprofit Arts and Culture Organizations:	$6,226,000	207.3	$5,277,905	$253,087	$335,021
Nonprofit Arts and Culture Audiences:	$1,561,300	39.3	$ 812,095	$ 75,692	$ 90,040
Total Industry Impact: (The Sum of Organizations and Audiences)	$7,787,300	246.7	$6,090,000	$328,779	$425,061

Source: *The Nonprofit Sector in Brief 2015*. Washington, DC: Urban Institute, 2015.

also embracing the culture of the county. Most other direct music and entertainment competition was located 40 miles south in San Francisco. The largest indirect competitors for entertainment and leisure activities were dining out, going to the movies, and hiking and outdoor activities.[5]

Performing Arts Industry

The U.S. nonprofit industry was a behemoth encompassing fields such as health care, public affairs, religion, education, environment, and many more. There were nearly 1.1 million registered public charities in the United States, 836 of which were registered in Sonoma County.[6] In 2014 individual giving amounted to $258 billion in the United States; arts and culture made up only 4.8 percent of this charitable giving.[7] Once considered a cultural necessity, the arts had since been largely considered a luxury. As such, organizations had to work increasingly harder to find supplemental funding in addition to individual donations. The first national public sector support for the arts was the creation of the National Endowment of the Arts (NEA) in 1965 under President Johnson. The same organization found itself under attack 20 years later during the Reagan administration, and had been a conservative target ever since. Around that same time corporations started donating to the arts, in part to increase corporate visibility,[8] and ultimately would make up a substantial portion of funding. The nonprofit arts industry had modernized slowly, and typically adopted new processes on the business side, leaving its core mission of entertainment and cultural expansion largely untouched. However, as society's interpretation of the industry evolved so too would the mission itself.

According to the nationwide NEA 2015 study, approximately 45 percent of adults attended music performing arts events. This included jazz, classical music, opera, Latin music, and outdoor festivals. On average, patrons attended two to three performances per year. Attendance had seen an increase in older adults, and while still predominantly attended by white patrons, there had been a relative increase of African American and Hispanic patronage over the last decade or so. The NEA study showed that of the attendees 83.2 percent were White, 5.5 percent were Hispanic, 5.1 percent were African American, and 6.2 percent were Other. 25.7 percent of attendees were over 65; however, approximately 46 percent were over 55. The NEA survey read:

> In 2012 . . . women were slightly more likely to attend a classical music concert than men, non-Hispanic white adults had a higher rate of attendance than other racial or ethnic subgroups, and better-educated adults had a higher rate of attendance than less-educated adults. (p. 10)

Due to the fact that music performances were a luxury service, there was room for growth as the overall income of the Sonoma area increased. Per the Nonprofit Nation: "Increases in the income, educational attainment, and discretionary time of Americans are other likely factors in the growth of arts and culture activity" (p. 161). Increasingly, classical music performances were becoming available exclusively to high income earners. Between 2007 and 2014 the average ticket price at a not-for-profit theater rose by 23 percent.[9] As the national wage disparity widened and ticket prices increased, nonprofit performing arts centers needed to reconsider their mission and how best to implement it, and do it sooner rather than later.

The Early Years

The idea for what would become the Green Music Center was first articulated concurrently by three parties in the 1990s with modest but radically different intentions. The first was Sonoma State University President Ruben Armiñana and his wife Marne Olsen who had frequented Seiji Ozawa Hall at Tanglewood in The Berkshires (shown in Exhibit 4), and envisioned a similar outdoor musical experience for Sonoma County. At the time Sonoma State University was struggling financially and Armiñana had been tasked with reinventing the campus to better meet community and student needs. Unknowingly, telecommunications tycoon and Bach Choir fanatic Donald Green and his wife Maureen proposed a $1 million gift to the university to build a choral facility. As the idea for a choral space grew, it eventually merged with Armiñana's vision for a concert hall, prompting the Greens to increase their gift to $5 million. The third and final partner to join the project was the Santa Rosa Symphony, which was dissatisfied with the acoustical limitations at their current

EXHIBIT 4 Ozawa Hall at Tanglewood

© Jeff Greenberg/Alamy Stock Photo

facility. An agreement was struck that the symphony would help raise funds for the project in exchange for a 25-year residency. The project quickly expanded to include a 1,400-seat concert hall, 250-seat recital hall, practice classrooms, faculty offices, and a hospitality space, with a projected budget of $22 million in 1997.

Ground on the facility was broken in October 2000. At this point the project had increased in scope to a cost of $43 million, $25 million of which had already been committed. Scope creep became the theme over the next decade of construction. Each new donation brought with it new demands, ultimately increasing the cost of the center to over $120 million. As the building's price tag increased, the president faced steep opposition from many of the faculty who claimed the music center was diverting resources from the academic purpose of the university, and they were not being appropriately consulted in regards to the evolving project. The Academic Senate passed a resolution in March 2006 declaring that they never requested construction of a music center, and as such no future growth funds should be diverted from Academic Affairs to support the operation of the Green Music Center. In 2007 this tension reached a boiling point, and 450 professors and lecturers took a vote of no confidence in President Armiñana. Between the vote of no confidence, a few bad budget years, and the bust of the telecom industry (a significant source of donations), construction of the Green Music Center went on hiatus from 2002 to 2005.

While the original intention was to build the entire Center with individual donor funds, new institutional partners arrived to help shoulder the burden and reinvigorate the project. The California State University System issued $13 million in bond funding to pay for the Academic Wing, which included faculty offices and classroom space. Sonoma State Enterprises, a university auxiliary, financed almost $7 million to fund the hospitality wing—a natural fit as it managed all catering on campus. Finally in 2011, the remaining fundraising was provided by a $12 million gift from Joan and Sanford I. Weill, allowing completion of the Green Music Center, and an opening date of September 29, 2012.

The Operational Years

As with any new venture, the first few years of operations were tumultuous and filled with learning experiences. The lean and "green" staff faced a steep curve in determining which kind of performances to program, where and to whom to market them, what kind of production equipment was required, and other logistical issues such as the different security staff needed for a classical versus a country concert. A board of advisors was established to offer both financial support, and operational guidance. The center produced the MasterCard Performance Series, which comprised approximately 30 concerts at Weill Hall that ran every year from October to May. In July through September the summer series at Weill Hall and Lawn showcased 15–20 more popular artists, and the annual summer chamber music festival, ChamberFest, offered patrons sustained exposure to highly skilled classical musicians in an intimate festival setting in the Schroeder Recital Hall. The Sundays at Schroeder series also made use of the hall with an affordably priced series that combined accessible classical programming, with an afternoon curtain time that was particularly appealing to both local audiences and weekend visitors.

In 2016 the GMC supported student activities in several ways: The On-Campus Presents (OCP) series produced a series of 7–10 shows programmed specifically to the SSU students. The various spaces were also utilized by student clubs for events and fundraisers. Finally, the largest user of the concert hall was far and away the music department. Music reserved the concert hall for approximately 110 performances, as well as all associated rehearsals.

Over time, members of the faculty at SSU came to see the opportunities the Green Music Center brought to the campus, but there remained some factions that had not disassociated the center from the turmoil of budget cuts and vote of no confidence in the prior years. For this reason, any decisions made about the Green Music Center, especially those related to financial support, existed within a micro political maelstrom. In September 2015 the chair of the Academic Senate, Richard Senghas, recommended the body discuss and publish a position statement on Green Music Center, as the 2006 resolution was no longer an accurate representation of the faculty's relationship with the center. As Senghas stated, "The position statement is being drafted in the spirit of utilizing the world-class facility that is available to us, and taking advantage of the teaching environment it provides." He expanded, "there are many opportunities to more closely integrate the

GMC with the students, especially in the areas of internships and direct experiences."

Financials

The Green Music Center operated in the 2015–2016 year on an approximately $6.23 million budget, and was positioned with revenues exceeding expenses—see Exhibit 5. This was primarily due to the MasterCard sponsorship of $1.25 million annually for operations, which was higher in 2015–2016 due to a cash-flow correction from the prior year. The sponsorship was scheduled to expire in 2019, at which point if operations and fundraising activities continued at the status quo, the GMC would be facing an annual *deficit*. The projected deficit was based on the existing organizational structure and

EXHIBIT 5 2015–2016 Green Music Center Budget

Revenue	
Ticket Sales and Earned Revenue	$ 3,000,000
Board Contributions	800,000
Annual Giving	330,000
MasterCard Sponsorship	1,837,000
Other Sponsorships	350,000
Net Gala Revenue	107,489
Other Fundraising	105,133
University Support	50,000
Foundation Grants	100,000
TOTAL	$ 6,679,622
Expenses	
Artist Expenses	$ 2,580,000
Production and Related Support	744,000
Marketing, Advertising, Communications	853,000
Salaries and Consultants	1,772,000
Development Operating Expense	100,000
General Operating Expense	177,000
TOTAL	6,226,000
NET INCOME (LOSS)	$ 453,622
Plus Prior Year Net Income (Loss)	-
CLOSING BALANCE	$ 453,622

Source: Green Music Center, 2016.

programming level. Exhibit 6 shows a multiyear projection based on several scenarios, including 100 percent external, 100 percent internal, and joint funding models. Many variable expenses that fluctuated with the number of programs included artist expense, production, and marketing and communications. As the number of performances decreased, so did these amounts; however, associated revenue from those shows were lost as well. Typically only a third of a performing arts venue's revenue should be expected from ticket sales[10]—these revenues should offset any artist and production costs, creating a net zero for the direct costs. All other fixed operating expenses would therefore be funded from alternative sources, primarily fundraising.

If the university were to commit to financially supporting the center at a minimal level for campus use only, expenses could be considerable scaled back: the marketing department could be downsized as there would not be a need to market shows outside the campus community; there would be no need for a development department, as there would be no need for outside funding; the artistic planning staff could be shrunk, as there would not be full seasons to produce. Per the GMC fiscal officer, for a scaled-back student-centered version of the center the university could plan on a base investment of $1.6 million to cover all salaries and operations. This figure was based on the assumption that students would be charged enough for tickets to offset the cost of the artist fees and related production. If discounted tickets were offered, the university's level of support would have to increase proportionately. The question of whether Sonoma State University should be offering this level of support has arisen due to the extensive use of the hall for the Music Department, student club events, and the OCP performance series. Exhibit 7 shows the 2015–2016 SSU budget including self-supports and auxiliaries, with the GMC making up 3.5 percent of the entire university budget.

Fundraising and Development

There was a delicate balance of science and art to be struck in fundraising. On one hand, there were industry best practice guidelines and suggestions for campaigns to raise funds. On the other hand, it took a talented and creative department to paint the ideal picture of the organization to stand apart from the million other nonprofits in the country.

EXHIBIT 6 Financial Projections for Green Music Center Utilizing Four Revenue Scenarios

Scenario #1: Revenues Remain at Current Levels

Assumptions:
1. The university does not contribute any additional funding.
2. External fundraising isn't increased.
3. 2015–2016 MasterCard Sponsorship higher due to cash-flow inconsistency.

	2015–2016	2016–2017	2017–2018	2018–2019	2019–2020	2020–2021	2021–2022	2022–2023
Revenue								
Ticket Sales and Earned Revenue	$ 3,000,000	$ 3,000,000	$ 3,000,000	$ 3,000,000	$ 3,000,000	$ 3,000,000	$ 3,000,000	$ 3,000,000
Board Contributions	800,000	800,000	800,000	800,000	800,000	800,000	800,000	800,000
Annual Giving	330,000	330,000	330,000	330,000	330,000	330,000	330,000	330,000
MasterCard Sponsorship	1,837,000	1,250,000	1,250,000	1,250,000	0	0	0	0
Other Sponsorships	350,000	350,000	350,000	350,000	350,000	350,000	350,000	350,000
Net Gala Revenue	107,489	107,489	107,489	107,489	107,489	107,489	107,489	107,489
Other Fundraising	105,133	105,133	105,133	105,133	105,133	105,133	105,133	105,133
University Support	50,000	50,000	50,000	50,000	50,000	50,000	50,000	50,000
Foundation Grants	100,000	100,000	100,000	100,000	100,000	100,000	100,000	100,000
TOTAL REVENUE	6,679,622	6,092,622	6,092,622	6,092,622	4,842,622	4,842,622	4,842,622	4,842,622
Less Expenses	6,226,000	6,226,000	6,226,000	6,226,000	6,226,000	6,226,000	6,226,000	6,226,000
Plus Prior Year Net Income (Loss)	0	453,622	320,244	186,866	53,488	(1,329,890)	(2,713,268)	(4,096,646)
NET INCOME (LOSS)	$ 453,622	$ 320,244	$ 186,866	$ 53,488	($ 1,329,890)	($ 2,713,268)	($ 4,096,646)	($ 5,480,024)

(*Continued*)

Scenario #2: Externally Funded

Assumptions:
1. The university does not contribute any additional funding.
2. Annual giving and sponsorships increase by 20 percent annually.
3. Foundations and grants increase 10 percent annually.
4. Creation of a $2 million endowment that will grow by 2 percent, and distribute 4 percent of market value annually.

	2015–2016	2016–2017	2017–2018	2018–2019	2019–2020	2020–2021	2021–2022	2022–2023
Revenue								
Ticket Sales and Earned Revenue	$ 3,000,000	$ 3,000,000	$ 3,000,000	$ 3,000,000	$ 3,000,000	$ 3,000,000	$ 3,000,000	$ 3,000,000
Board Contributions	800,000	800,000	800,000	800,000	800,000	800,000	800,000	800,000
Annual Giving	330,000	396,000	475,200	570,240	684,288	821,146	862,203	862,203
MasterCard Sponsorship	1,837,000	1,250,000	1,250,000	1,250,000	0	0	0	0
Other Sponsorships	350,000	420,000	504,000	604,800	725,760	870,912	958,003	958,003
Net Gala Revenue	107,489	107,489	107,489	107,489	107,489	107,489	107,489	107,489
Other Fundraising	105,133	105,133	105,133	105,133	105,133	105,133	105,133	105,133
University Support	50,000	50,000	50,000	50,000	50,000	50,000	50,000	50,000
Foundation Grants	100,000	110,000	121,000	133,100	146,410	161,051	177,156	194,872
Endowment Revenue	0	0	0	0	80,000	81,600	83,232	84,897
TOTAL REVENUE	6,679,622	6,238,622	6,412,822	6,620,762	5,699,080	5,997,331	6,143,216	6,162,596
Less Expenses	6,226,000	6,226,000	6,226,000	6,226,000	6,226,000	6,226,000	6,226,000	6,226,000
Plus Prior Year Net Income (Loss)	0	453,622	466,244	653,066	1,047,828	520,908	292,239	209,455
NET INCOME (LOSS)	$ 453,622	$ 466,244	$ 653,066	$ 1,047,828	$ 520,908	$ 292,239	$ 209,455	$ 146,051

(Continued)

Scenario #3: University Funded

Assumptions:
1. Expenses are reduced to $602,000 to support only student performances.
2. The university pays entire cost of presenting series and support.

	2015–2016	2016–2017	2017–2018	2018–2019	2019–2020	2020–2021	2021–2022	2022–2023
Revenue								
Ticket Sales and Earned Revenue	$ 3,000,000	$ 0	$ 0	$ 0	$ 0	$ 0	$ 0	$ 0
Board Contributions	800,000	0	0	0	0	0	0	0
Annual Giving	330,000	0	0	0	0	0	0	0
MasterCard Sponsorship	1,837,000	1,250,000	1,250,000	1,250,000	0	0	0	0
Other Sponsorships	350,000	0	0	0	0	0	0	0
Net Gala Revenue	107,489	0	0	0	0	0	0	0
Other Fundraising	105,133	0	0	0	0	0	0	0
University Support	50,000	101,622	148,756	352,000	1,602,000	1,602,000	1,602,000	1,602,000
Foundation Grants	100,000	0	0	0	0	0	0	0
TOTAL REVENUE	6,679,622	1,351,622	1,398,756	1,602,000	1,602,000	1,602,000	1,602,000	1,602,000
Less Expenses	6,226,000	1,602,000	1,602,000	1,602,000	1,602,000	1,602,000	1,602,000	1,602,000
Plus Prior Year Net Income (Loss)	0	453,622	203,244	0	0	0	0	0
NET INCOME (LOSS)	$ 453,622	$ 203,244	$ 0	$ 0	$ 0	$ 0	$ 0	$ 0

(Continued)

Scenario #4: Joint Model

Assumptions:

1. Annual giving, sponsorships, foundations, and grants increase by 5 percent annually.
2. Creation of a $2 million endowment that will grow by 2 percent, and distribute 4 percent of market value annually.
3. The university will fund the remaining need within the organization.

	2015–2016	2016–2017	2017–2018	2018–2019	2019–2020	2020–2021	2021–2022	2022–2023
Revenue								
Ticket Sales and Earned Revenue	$ 3,000,000	$ 3,000,000	$ 3,000,000	$ 3,000,000	$ 3,000,000	$ 3,000,000	$ 3,000,000	$ 3,000,000
Board Contributions	800,000	800,000	800,000	800,000	800,000	800,000	800,000	800,000
Annual Giving	330,000	346,500	363,825	382,016	401,117	421,173	442,232	464,343
MasterCard Sponsorship	1,837,000	1,250,000	1,250,000	1,250,000	0	0	0	0
Other Sponsorships	350,000	367,500	385,875	405,169	425,427	446,699	469,033	492,485
Net Gala Revenue	107,489	107,489	107,489	107,489	107,489	107,489	107,489	107,489
Other Fundraising	105,133	105,133	105,133	105,133	105,133	105,133	105,133	105,133
University Support	50,000	50,000	50,000	50,000	889,898	1,136,279	1,084,870	1,030,941
Foundation Grants	100,000	105,000	110,250	115,763	121,551	127,628	134,010	140,710
Endowment Revenue	0	0	0	0	80,000	81,600	83,232	84,897
TOTAL REVENUE	6,679,622	6,131,622	6,172,572	6,215,570	5,930,615	6,226,000	6,226,000	6,226,000
Less Expenses	6,226,000	6,226,000	6,226,000	6,226,000	6,226,000	6,226,000	6,226,000	6,226,000
Plus Prior Year Net Income (Loss)	0	453,622	359,244	305,816	295,386	0	0	0
NET INCOME (LOSS)	$ 453,622	$ 359,244	$ 305,816	$ 295,386	$ 0	$ 0	$ 0	$ 0

EXHIBIT 7 The Green Music Center as a Percentage of the Sonoma State University Budget*[11]

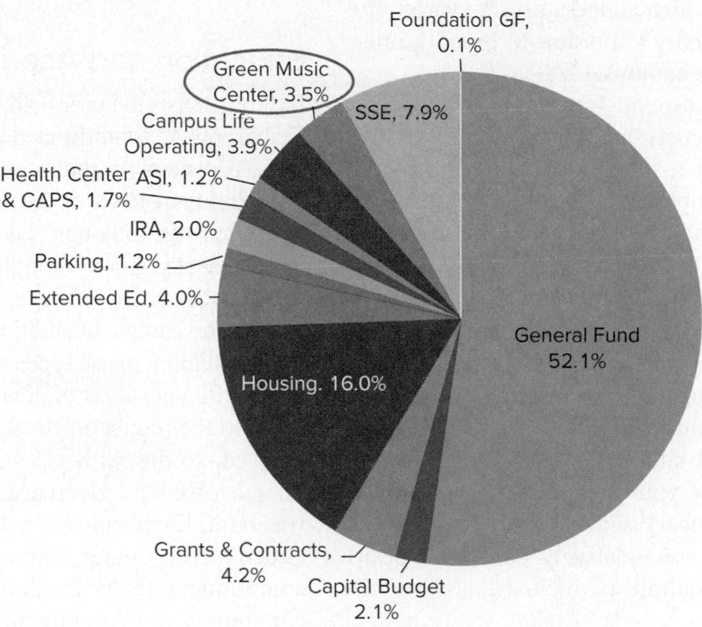

*Only General Fund is state-funded; all other areas generate own revenue.

The underlying consensus was that a potential donor would not give unless he or she felt a personal connection to the cause. By this understanding the largest pool of potential donors would be the patrons who engaged with the Green Music Center by attending performances.

There were challenges to fundraising that were present at all similar institutions, and some that were specific to the Green Music Center. Performing arts centers on college campuses tended to face an identity crisis since they were set amongst a younger demographic, but that was not necessarily the demographic that was most likely to contribute to either earned revenue or philanthropy. Additionally, there were many competing priorities across a university campus, particularly those that were state-funded. Finally, when there was student programming in the same space, patrons had difficulty differentiating between student performances, and those associated with a presenting season. These challenges would persist as the organization worked to figure out what type of programming it would offer in the face of looming budget obstacles and funding challenges. Broader programming could expand the audience, but might also dilute the connection regular patrons felt with the center.

Programming and Engagement

The most efficient way to engage a potential donor or a member of the community was through programming. Per Senior Director for Development Steven Berry, the more performances patrons attended, the closer they felt to the venue and to the service it provided. The diverging needs, resources, and mission of the Green Music Center created a problem when deciding which types of shows should be programmed. In 2015–2016 there were three types of programming targeted by the GMC.

There were approximately 30 winter shows geared toward the wider Sonoma County community, which tended to be classical, jazz, vocal, and world music, and averaged $55 per ticket. These shows at a higher price point attracted the demographic that was most likely to donate to support operations. It was absolutely imperative to keep offering these types of performances in order to forge a connection with patrons, and ultimately create a pipeline of donors. These shows also added a diverse variety to help fulfil the university's mission to broadly integrate culture onto the campus.

There were also around 15 summer shows that were more popular artists, and that allowed the selling of lawn seats at a lower price point—around $15–20 each. Although the lawn seats were more affordable, the shows were not necessarily programmed toward children or families. This was one area where programming failed to meet the mission of the GMC—to be accessible to the community. As Berry put it, "It is important to serve the community as a whole, and not just act as a center for culture." This meant shows must not only be affordable so entire families could attend, but also needed to be fun and engaging for younger audiences. A movie night or matinee concert with a children's themed activity beforehand was relatively easy to coordinate, and created a culture of inclusiveness for all age and income levels.

The third and final subset of programming was acts that would appeal to the on-campus population. It was important to connect with the nearly 9,000 students on campus and ensure that they were able to enjoy all the GMC had to offer. Of course student programming tended to be radically different than classical, world, jazz, or family-focused, as it was often louder music or less than family-friendly comedy sets. Among its peer institutions, the GMC was unique in that it had an arm specifically designed to book performances aimed at the students (On-Campus Presents). The other peer organizations were fairly consistent in that they programmed almost exclusively to community members with only the occasional show for students, usually organized by the student body government.

There was an expectation that if a popular artist was booked, he or she would attract many patrons, and ultimately provide additional revenue. As Exhibit 8 shows, there was not a direct correlation between the GMC shows that sold the most tickets and the shows that produced the highest net income. In the top 20 shows by ticket sales, many of the shows took a loss because they had exorbitant artist fees, but these performances attracted a broad audience and had a high correlation to donor attendance. This conflict exhibits that the shows with the most patrons do not necessarily maximize revenue. As the GMC worked to establish a balance of programming to best fit its patrons, it experienced drastic swings in ticket prices, number of attendees and net income per show—see Exhibit 9.

Education and Academic Integration

Exhibit 10 lists the peer institutions of the Green Music Center: public, state-funded universities with performing arts centers on their campus similar in scope and programming. Each of the institutions partnered with K–12 schools, although the level of involvement varied drastically. Some brought the younger students in to watch an artist rehearse, while others coordinated classes and camps. In addition to providing arts education to children, these types of programs attracted gifts and a different subset of donors.

As the concept of the Green Music Center evolved, so did its K–12 initiatives. Oddly enough, this involvement decreased once the concert hall was built. Each summer between 2001 and 2006 the Green Music Center (under construction) proved its commitment to establishing arts education in the community through Greenfarm. Partnering with the Santa Rosa Symphony, Greenfarm provided conservatory-level training down to beginning music lessons for budding musicians over a five-week program, ultimately culminating in a final youth festival. When the GMC completed construction, and began offering concerts, it invited K–12 students to several of the performances free of charge. Since that time the GMC had continued to act as a home for the Santa Rosa Symphony's youth programs, but had not continued the Greenfarm program, nor fully fleshed out any of its own in association with the university.

As demonstrated by the active participation in the Osher Lifelong Learning Institute, an adult education program at Sonoma State University, there was extensive interest in continued learning after the age of 50 in Sonoma County. This was a prime population for engagement considering 17 percent of the county's population is over 65 and the NEA study posited that almost half of performing arts attendees to be over 50. As this population was generally retired, they might have time to act as volunteers for some of the events at the GMC or possibly K–12 programming. A partnership with OLLI would allow the GMC to fully live out its mission by reaching the broader community and integrating

EXHIBIT 8 Top 20 Green Music Center Shows by Tickets Sold and Net Income

Top 20 Shows, by Number of Tickets Sold			Top 20 Shows, by Net Income (ticket sales less artist fee)		
	Tickets	Net Income		Tickets	Net Income
Violinist	2,093	$ 18,108	Cellist*	1,392	$66,375
Jazz Musician	1,876	$ 20,193	Bach*	1,278	$49,812
Opera Singer	1,509	($ 29,450)	Singer-Pianist	1,085	$45,694
Cellist*	1,392	$ 66,375	Broadway Singer*	1,242	$44,584
Cellist*	1,377	$ 33,785	Singer-Songwriter*	1,333	$44,469
Broadway Singer*	1,348	$ 31,248	World Music*	1,343	$40,046
Baroque Orchestra	1,347	$ 7,290	Violinist	772	$36,867
Jazz	1,345	($ 15,388)	Cellist*	1,377	$33,785
World Music*	1,343	$ 40,046	Broadway Singer*	1,348	$31,248
Vocalist*	1,338	$ 31,006	Vocalist*	1,338	$31,006
Singer-Songwriter*	1,333	$ 44,469	World Music	961	$30,765
Philharmonic Orchestra	1,305	($149,614)	Pianist	831	$30,534
World Music*	1,282	$ 22,457	Violinist*	1,165	$30,439
Bach*	1,278	$ 49,812	Jaz Singer	1,090	$25,429
Opera	1,256	($ 48,851)	World Music	1,029	$25,291
Pianists	1,251	$ 6,370	Saxophonist	1,069	$22,651
Broadway Singer*	1,242	$ 44,584	World Music*	1,282	$22,457
Violinist	1,222	($ 23,783)	Flutist	804	$21,737
Violinist*	1,165	$ 30,439	Dance	980	$21,711
World Music	1,151	$ 15,962	String Quartet	819	$20,568

*Denotes artist is on both lists.

Source: Green Music Center, 2016.

EXHIBIT 9 Green Music Center Ticket Sales and Performance

WINTER				
	2012–2013	2013–2014	2014–2015	2015–2016
Avg # Tickets Sold/Show	941	939	760	596
Avg Ticket Price	$ 3.09	$ 57.23	$ 62.10	$ 53.03
Avg Net Income/Show	$(147.00)	$(13,565.00)	$10,227.00	$3,234.00
SUMMER				
		2013–2014	2014–2015	2015–2016
Avg # Tickets Sold/Show		2,469	2,305	2,270
Avg Ticket Price		$ 50.76	$ 46.08	$ 42.29
Avg Net Income/Show		$27,189.00	$15,019.00	$9,625.00

EXHIBIT 10 Peer Group Comparison for the Green Music Center

	Sonoma State	Michigan State	UNLV	George Mason	University of Georgia
Are staff paid as University employees?	No	No*	Yes	Yes	Yes
Is there a designated position to coordinate community and educational programs?	No	Yes	No	Yes	No
Is there K–12 Educational Programming?	Yes	Yes	Yes	Yes	Yes
Does the organization integrate into University Academics?	Yes	Yes	No	No	Yes
Are there any continuing education programs?	No	Yes	No	Yes	No
Does the organization program to families?	No	Yes	No	Yes	No
Does the performing arts center program primarily to the community?	Yes	Yes	Yes	Yes	Yes
Does the performing arts center program to students?	Yes	No	No	No	No

Source: Green Music Center, 2016.

*While the staff is funded independently, the performing arts center at Michigan State receives approximately $1M in student fees to produce shows for the students.

academics, albeit not with traditional university students. Additionally, it would echo the university's mission of fostering lifelong learning.

The final component to education was the integration of the Green Music Center within the academic landscape of Sonoma State University. As it stood in 2016, academic involvement within the University was limited, but full of potential. The GMC supported the academic mission by providing free tickets to any performance that a professor would like to bring their class to through the Academic Integration program. The onus was then on the professor to create a curriculum that integrated the performance.

There were a myriad of options to further integrate the arts into academics, but they required far more hours of planning and coordination than the GMC staff could manage at its capacity. For example, many artists were willing to write into their rider that they would teach a master class or allocate some of their rehearsal time to working with SSU students, but this required negotiating with the artist and professors designing the content of the class. These collaborations were not just limited to music students, or those in the School of Performing Arts, but every department which boasted a creative side. In fact, this cross-discipline was the foundation of a liberal arts education which Sonoma State prided itself on.

There remains room for growth within SSU's integration of the arts, but not without some additional investment. According to SSU's Arts Dramaturg (a permanent faculty on a course release) Scott Horstein:

> Given the current initial success of using arts integration to involve students from all subjects in the life of the GMC, the Arts Dramaturg is currently studying models at other institutions to assess the capacity for expansion. The program as currently funded, through the course release for the Arts Dramaturg faculty, will continue to build on its success. However, there is clearly potential to engage many, many faculty and students deeply and widely. Expansion is partly a matter of human resources, but may partly be a matter of finding additional faculty (or hiring outside staff) with the skill set and relationships necessary for managing arts integration.

Moving Forward

The board of advisors' Finance Committee called the meeting to an end and began to pack up their papers. The room was filled with furrowed brows and an air of consternation, as the group reflected on the decisions awaiting Dr. Sakaki, the new Sonoma State University president. Her impending directives would dictate the future of the Music Center soon to meet a fiscal impasse. As Vice President Furukawa-Schlereth had informed the committee, she would determine the university's financial support, and ultimately the mission of the Green Music Center. Several difficult questions and decisions lay before her:

- Is the music center positioned well to maintain earned revenue and increase donations to remain externally funded?
- Does the programming and related activities at GMC reflect the stated mission?
- Could the GMC be reimagined to further integrate with the university and the community?
- Do the missions of the Green Music Center and Sonoma State University align closely enough to justify financial support?

The day drew to a close with many questions and few answers, as the sun began to set over the rolling Sonoma hills. But a single glimmer of sunshine, a single ray of hope, still danced through the west window at the Green Music Center.

ENDNOTES

1 Sonoma State University website, www.sonoma.edu/about/mission.html (accessed April 3, 2016).

2 Green Music Center internal document.

3 Population estimates, July 1, 2015 (V2015), www.census.gov/quickfacts/table/PST045215/06097 (accessed March 10, 2016).

4 "Temperature–Precipitation–Sunshine–Snowfall," www.usclimatedata.com/climate/sonoma/california/united-states/usca1076 (accessed March 10, 2016).

5 Prescott & Associates, comp., *Green Music Center Audience & Brand Development Research*, 2014.

6 "All Registered Nonprofit Organizations in Sonoma County," nccsweb.urban.org/PubApps/geoShowOrgs.php?id=c06097 (accessed March 10, 2016).

7 B. S.(2015). *The Nonprofit Sector in Brief, (Rep.).* Washington D.C.: Urban Institute.

8 N. Craig Smith, "The New Corporate Philanthropy," 1994, hbr.org/1994/05/the-new-corporate-philanthropy (accessed March 22, 2016).

9 Theatre Communications Group, "Average Single Ticket Price at Not-for-Profit Theatres in the United States from 2007 to 2014 (in U.S. Dollars)," in *Statista—The Statistics Portal*, 0-www.statista.com.iii.sonoma.edu/statistics/197188/us-not-for-profit-theatres-average-single-ticket-price-since-2005/ (accessed April 16, 2016).

10 M. O'Neill, *Nonprofit Nation: A New Look at the Third America* (San Francisco: Jossey-Bass, 2002).

11 "Sonoma State University," *Reporting Transparency*, May 4, 2016.

CASE 20

Ricoh Canada Inc.

Jonathan Fast
Queen's University

Prescott C. Ensign
Wilfrid Laurier University

In January 2016, Glenn Laverty, president and CEO of Ricoh Canada Inc., was going to meet with his executive management team to develop the company's strategy for the next three years (see Exhibit 1). Ricoh Canada Inc. (RCI), a wholly owned subsidiary of Ricoh Americas Corporation, had its head office in Toronto, Ontario, and employed over 2,100 people in Canada. Its parent, Ricoh Company Ltd., headquartered in Japan, was an international leader in the digital imaging and document management industry. It operated in more than 200 countries and regions, and employed 108,000 people worldwide. Ricoh Company Ltd. had worldwide sales of $20 billion in 2015.

RCI was facing saturation in the market segment that was its primary source of revenue—delivery and maintenance of printing/copying devices to customers. Canon and Xerox were both strong competitors in this segment, and Laverty was concerned: "We will see an increasingly rapid shrinkage in our traditional market during the next five years." Areas of opportunity included document management systems and IT services. RCI defined services as a combination of onsite and offsite resources that supported business operations infrastructure. These resources included cloud computing, remote monitoring, and other innovations. RCI could have used this technology to make customer information more secure, mobile, and personal.

Laverty openly admitted his dilemma with services by saying, "What services to develop further and how aggressively to market them is still an unknown." He knew providing more services would require additional investment, but the questions of how much and to what area were the real issues. Given RCI's current financial position, how realistic was it for RCI to transition to a services company?

BACKGROUND

Ricoh Canada Inc. adopted its current name in 1997, but had been operating in Canada under various names since 1924. RCI was a sales organization that used a lease and service model with its office imaging equipment. All the equipment was manufactured in Ricoh's high-quality and efficient facilities in Japan. A transfer pricing system was used when product was shipped from the parent corporation to its subsidiaries. To summarize, RCI's focus was on using its direct channel and dealer network to sell and service the inventory coming from Japan. RCI moved into digital printing in the 1990s and became a dominant player in the Canadian market. It accounted for 20 percent of Canadian market sales in the high-end multifunction product segment in 2015.

In August 2008, the parent company, Ricoh Company Ltd., acquired IKON Office Solutions (IKON) for $1.6 billion. IKON was the world's largest independent provider of document management systems and services. It used copiers, printers, and multifunction printer technologies from leading manufacturers, and document management software and systems from companies like Captaris Inc., Kofax Ltd., and Electronics for Imaging Inc. The acquisition strengthened Ricoh's North American direct sales network and gave it control of the dealer

Note: The quotes in this case were based on interviews. We thank the executives at Ricoh Canada Inc. for graciously meeting with us.
Used by permission of Thunderbird School of Global Management.

EXHIBIT 1 Organizational Chart for Ricoh Canada Inc.

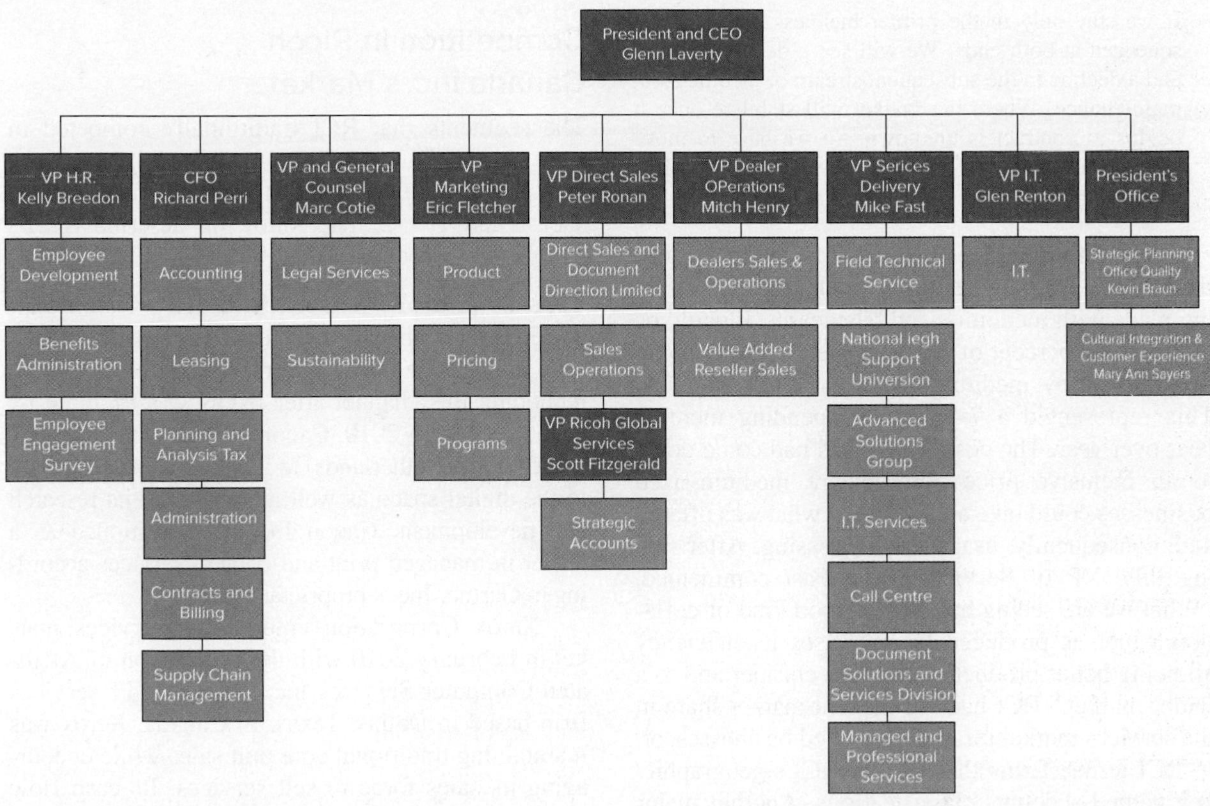

Source: Internal company documents.

network on which its largest competitor, Canon Inc., relied heavily. Following the acquisition, workforce integration did not take place as rapidly as Ricoh Company Ltd. management had anticipated.

State of the Market

In 2015, Laverty had asked his management team to look at the state of the services market. The way he saw it, three trends were pushing RCI toward services: shifts in technology, user behavior, and corporate behavior. The advent of digital storage and document management technologies meant that customers were printing fewer documents. Using digital documents allowed for faster and more effective workflows as well as greater accessibility. Digital documents were available to anyone over the Internet. Laverty mentioned, "Modern businesses were striving to become paperless offices, which is a very scary thing for anyone at Ricoh to say out loud."

The team found that the Canadian services market was worth $24 billion in 2015. By comparison, the size of the hardware/break and fix market—RCI's primary revenue source—was $4.5–$5 billion with growth in 2015 of 2 percent. It was clear that technological advancements in tablet and mobile device networks were disrupting RCI's legacy business. By 2019, the printer/copier market was estimated to shrink by 3 percent annually, and this downward trend would accelerate after that point. Laverty pointed out, "It has never been easier not to print something, and that means trouble for everyone in the industry. We have to adapt or face extinction." Early signs of this were already present; mergers and acquisitions activity had been rampant in the traditional market as big competitors sought to protect profits by buying competitors. As Laverty told his management team:

> If we stay only in the printer business, RCI will be squeezed at both ends. We will see a decline in sales and a decline in the subsequent stream of income from maintenance. Where the market will stabilize once it begins to contract is unknown. So we have to move beyond this segment. Planning for negative growth is not acceptable.

When the services market was broken down further, it became clear that big changes were taking place with medium-sized businesses. It could be seen that 42 percent of services spending was going to be made by medium-sized businesses in 2016. This represented a 7.4 percent spending increase year over year. The cost of services had come down to an inclusive price point where medium-sized businesses could take advantage of what was offered and, consequently, usage was increasing. After seeing this, VP of Services Mike Fast commented, "What we are seeing here is the good kind of deflation which is produced by increases in efficiency allowing better products to be sold cheaper and to a wider market." RCI had a 2 percent market share in the services market for medium-sized businesses, or, in RCI terms, firms that fit into RCI's geographic/key named accounts classifications. Another major trend was small to medium-sized businesses shifting toward cloud services where IT infrastructure was handled for them. As volume on the cloud increased, cloud services were able to achieve economies of scale and flexibility. From a consumer perspective, using the cloud was much more cost-effective than upgrading an in-house server network and corresponding support resources. Finally, companies were demanding software to better share information across an organization whether it be document management, process management, or communication management.

Consumer studies of the services market indicated that consumers considered a long list of factors when assessing a provider. These included cost-effectiveness; environmental sustainability; information security and compliance; business process streamlining; change management; worker productivity; information optimization; and strategic infrastructure. VP of Marketing Eric Fletcher advised Laverty that all of his team's research had been pointing to one factor: "The primary interest of consumers was a provider who could unify services in the company at a reasonable cost."

Competition in Ricoh Canada Inc.'s Market

The segments that RCI traditionally competed in were extremely competitive (see Exhibits 2 and 3). Competitors could be broken down into two groups: Tier 1 and Tier 2. The following describes RCI's competitors' recent strategic moves.

Tier 1—Canon, Xerox, and HP Canon Canada Inc. had relied heavily on IKON for both unit sales and service infrastructure, so it was focusing on rebuilding this channel after IKON was acquired by Ricoh. In March 2010, Canon Inc. acquired Océ NV (based in the Netherlands) to increase its market share in the digital space as well as to expand its research and development. Canon Inc. was positioned as a leader in managed print and content services according to Gartner Inc.'s proprietary research.

Xerox Corporation entered the services market in February 2010 with the acquisition of Affiliated Computer Services Inc. (ACS), an IT services firm based in Dallas, Texas. In Canada, Xerox was maintaining traditional core unit sales while encouraging its sales force to sell services. Its cash flow from the traditional product lines was expected to fund the expansion into services. Xerox Canada had performed well with its major accounts in health care and government. Recently, Xerox had launched cloud services.

Hewlett-Packard Company (HP), in Canada and worldwide, had a very strong brand and customer network for its IT hardware. It was using this reputation to move into services. HP acquired EDS (Electronic Data Systems) on August 28, 2008, to give it the ability to combine hardware and services to create holistic offerings to customers. The integration of services with hardware was ongoing.

Tier 2—Konica Minolta and Others Konica Minolta Business Solutions Canada Ltd. was strong in the A3 (standard European format) printer segment. Its pricing on a cost per page basis was low, almost to the point of disrupting the market. Also, it was introducing a new A3 color lineup, making it hard for others to compete within the A3 color segment. Konica Minolta products had good image quality and performance.

EXHIBIT 2 Laser Printer Market Share for A4, A3, Dealer, and Direct Segments, 2012–2015

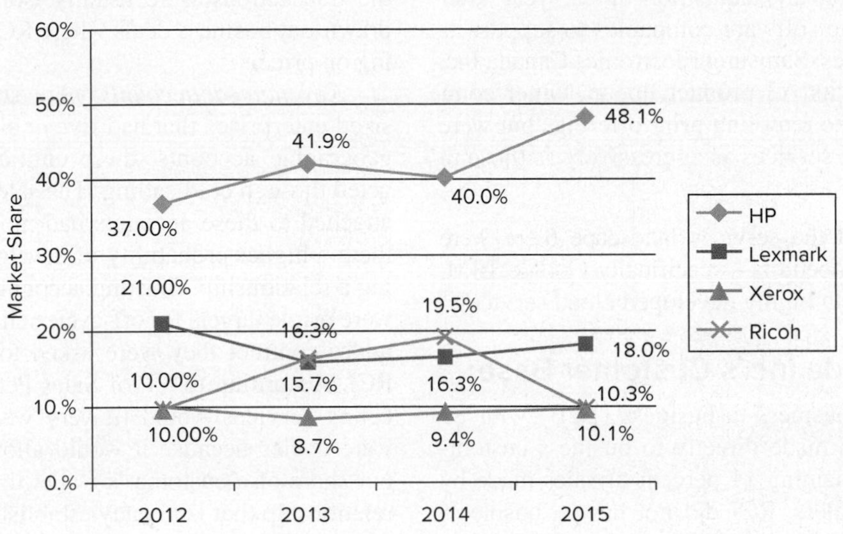

Source: Internal company documents.

EXHIBIT 3 Market Share for Multifunction Products (Printer, Scanner, Fax) over $1,000, 2012–2015

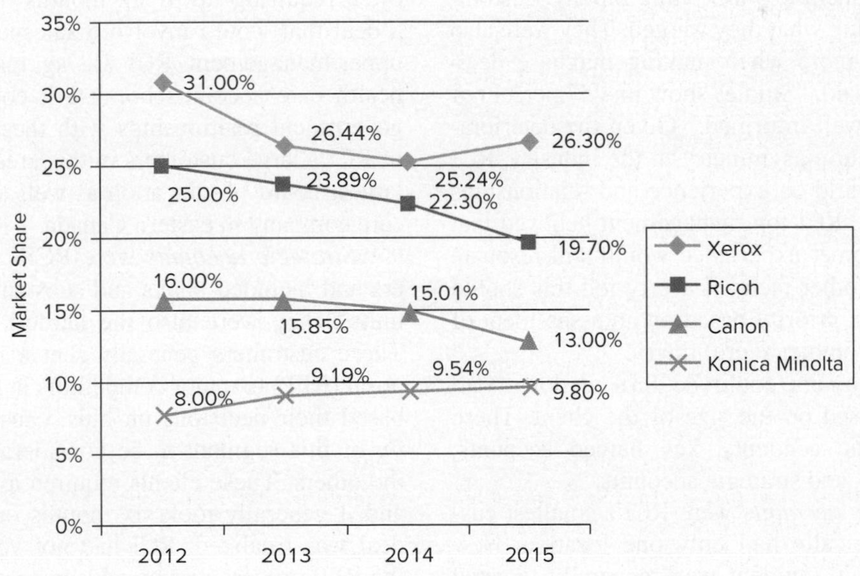

Source: Internal company documents.

Lexmark had left the inkjet printing business and turned its attention to improving its A4 (standard North American format) laser printer lineup. Lexmark was on an acquisition spree, year after year gobbling up software companies to support its growth objectives. Samsung Electronics Canada Inc. was expanding its A3 product lineup. Other competitors were also retooling print offerings but were not moving into services as aggressively as those in Tier 1.

Other Within the services landscape there were several large competitors—specifically, Google, IBM, and Amazon with highly developed cloud services.

Ricoh Canada Inc.'s Customer Base

RCI had sold business-to-business (B2B) with 89 percent of sales made directly to business customers, and the remaining 11 percent of sales made by independent dealers. RCI did not have a business-to-consumer (B2C) line, although most of RCI's primary competitors (Canon, Xerox, and HP) did. Laverty did not see the B2C market providing long-term growth because it was so competitive. However, he was open to anything should sufficient evidence be presented.

Part of RCI's strategic dilemma was that the profile of its customers was morphing rapidly; customers were changing what they wanted. They were also discriminating more when making purchase decisions. Laverty said, "Studies show that 57 percent of customers are well informed." Given the deterioration of information asymmetry in the industry, RCI was trying to build on experience and relationships with customers. RCI top management believed that a positive customer experience would still resonate more than any other factor. Laverty felt this should continue to be a priority based on an assessment of the NPS (net promoter score) metric.

RCI's customers could be broken down into four classes based on the size of the client. These were geographic accounts, key named accounts, major accounts, and strategic accounts.

Geographic accounts were RCI's smallest customers and typically had only one location. New customers in this segment were generally targeted through cold calling by RCI's sales force. The way this worked was that a salesperson was given a postal code and then pitched products to all small businesses within it. The estimated success rate of cold calling was 1 in 10. Most new business based on client count was generated in this manner. These customers offered the highest margins because the transactions were usually isolated, rather than drawn-out business deals where RCI would be fighting on price.

Key named accounts were small to medium-sized enterprises that had five or six locations. Like geographic accounts, these entities were also targeted through cold calling. The sales representatives attached to these accounts had more tenure, giving them a higher probability of developing and nurturing a relationship. Existing accounts in this segment were prime targets for off-cycle selling. That is, once under contract they were asked to buy more from RCI. According to VP of Sales Peter Ronan, "Marketing services would fit very well between hardware cycles because it would allow us to increase our share of a customer's wallet through a business relationship that is already established."

Major accounts included large customers like hospitals and colleges/universities. The complexity of these clients required more customization in product and service offerings. Together with strategic accounts, this defined the key GEM market (government, education, and medical market). Transactions with these entities required more internal resources, often requiring up to six months or more to close a deal that would involve a salesperson as well as upper management. RCI was aggressively targeting health care accounts because it could leverage its government relationships with these clients. Some of RCI's large customers in this area were Canada's largest board of education as well as a large health care company in eastern Canada.

Strategic accounts were RCI's largest customers and included banks and substantial government units. They were also the hardest deals to close. These customers generally sent a request for proposal (RFP) to major competitors in the industry and based their decisions on bids, causing the formality of this segment to be considerably higher than the others. These clients required a lot of attention, and it generally took six months or more before a deal was finalized. RCI had not yet determined if the RFP process was an advantage or disadvantage. RCI's track record in this realm was mixed, but it had managed to win contracts with a large life insurance company, two of Canada's big five banks, and Canada's largest food retailer. Government units

EXHIBIT 4 Projected Spending Growth for Major Accounts and Strategic Accounts, 2015–2019

Who	2015	2016	2017	2018	2019	Trends
Health care	7%	6%	7%	6%	6%	• Paper intensive to electronically automated • Cloud-based storage and sharing • Mobile workflow
Legal	4%	4%	4%	5%	5%	• Huge growth in electronically stored information • Legal process outsourcing • Working remotely and information security
Government	−1%	−1%	2%	2%	3%	• Shared cloud hubs in 65% of provinces by 2015 • Need for more cross-government collaboration
College/university	3%	3%	3%	4%	4%	• More e-learning on smaller budgets • Looking for cost reductions and ongoing support
Public school K–12	0%	2%	3%	4%	3%	• More e-learning on smaller budgets • Looking for cost reductions and ongoing support
Private school K–12	5%	4%	4%	4%	4%	• More e-learning on smaller budgets • Looking for cost reductions and ongoing support

Source: Internal company documents.

were an area where RCI would have liked to have focused more resources because they offered exposure into the broader public sector. For example, under Canada's government-run health care system, hospitals could buy products using the same prices set in government contracts without having to send out a separate tender. See Exhibit 4 for a review of projected growth in spending for major and strategic accounts.

Service Offerings in 2016

RCI's services could be broken into three segments: Technical Services (traditional break and fix), Professional Services, and Managed Services. Technical Services was the largest in terms of revenue, producing $193 million, or 39 percent of revenue in 2015, but the growth potential was limited (see Exhibit 5). RCI's total revenue from Professional Services and Managed Services was $52 million in 2015. With regard to Professional Services and Managed Services, Laverty stated, "Currently, we don't have a lot of volume in these areas, but we have some cool technology. We are just not completely sure how to use all of it. Also, given our relative inexperience in the services market, we need to figure out where RCI should operate relative to competitors."

Technical Services was based on the legacy business and involved servicing machines in the field. From the standpoint of a service-level agreement, customers had become more demanding, and RCI had been able to grow its market share in this area by meeting or exceeding customer expectations. The field technical team was the backbone of the service agreements. RCI had a very strong ERP system (Baan) and 550 well-trained personnel. VP of Services Mike Fast said, "These guys aren't your traditional copier technicians; they are highly trained, and have competencies, like networking skills, that extend beyond the machine."

EXHIBIT 5 Revenue, Market Share, and Margin for Ricoh Canada Services, 2015

Services Revenue Breakdown	2015	Percentage of Total Revenue	Market Share	Margin	Annual Market Growth
Break/Fix—Hardware maintenance and support	$193M	39%	23%	36%	2%
Total Technical	$193M				
Managed Document Services (MDS)—Business process consulting	$ 4M	<1%	1%	21%	3%
Legal Document Services (LDS)—Litigation support services	$ 5M	$<1%	30%	60%	2%
Ricoh Document Management (RDM)—Print, fulfillment, and imaging	$ 5M	1%	1%	20%	-5%
Ricoh Management Services (RMS)—Onsite/offsite resources	$ 25M	5%	25%	13%	1%
Total Managed Services	$ 40M				
IT/Professional Services—Solution consulting, IT hardware, remote monitoring, deployment services	$ 12M	2%	0%	46%	Consulting—18% IT Services —5% ($900B global market)
Cloud—Software as a service (SaaS), backup as a service (BaaS)	$ 0	0%	0%	N.A.	SaaS—17.9% ($14.5B global market) BaaS— 40% ($5.6B global market)
Total Professional Services	$ 12M				

Source: Author created.

Note: N.A. = Not applicable.

Professional Services helped customers streamline and better integrate their workflow processes. The solutions currently offered included: Managed Document Services (MDS), IT hardware, and remote monitoring and deployment services. MDS was designed to increase the efficiency of information transfer within an organization. For example, the software could read scanned images and automatically route documents to those who approved and/or used them. This concept could extend point-to-point across an organization using programmed rules that fit the business's structure. MDS helped a small or large company increase its workflow efficiency, manage its network, enhance its security, and troubleshoot when problems arose. Revenue for MDS was reported under Managed Services due to corporate restructuring, but was controlled as a part of Professional Services.

Professional Services helped a prospective company build the IT components, including both hardware and software, necessary to run company workflows. Although not yet released, IT services included cloud services and disaster recovery support. RCI's cloud services were intended to be a gateway to critical information. Corporate planning was under way in Japan and margins for this segment of the business were expected to be 56 percent at launch in the first quarter of 2016. The profile of Professional Services as RCI described it is found in Exhibit 6.

Managed Services encompassed three areas: (1) imaging print and fulfillment (Ricoh Document Management or RDM); (2) onsite managed services (Ricoh Management Services or RMS); and (3) litigation support services (Legal Document Services or LDS). Image print and fulfillment was just as the

EXHIBIT 6 Profile of Ricoh Canada Inc.'s IT and Professional Services (IT/PS)

RCI's IT and Professional Services division is dedicated to creating a tailored suite of IT Services and software solutions designed to assist clients in meeting their business objectives. The IT/PS team delivers expert technical and business solution expertise to support any size organization, in any industry in a consistent, reliable and cost-effective manner.

RCI's IT/PS department is well equipped to address customer business challenges such as helping maintain competitive advantage while mitigating risk, fulfilling compliance & industry governance measures, ensuring predictable cost and operating expense support & accountability—all standardized around customer business needs. RCI's role is to assist customers in meeting their organizational objectives & goals while maximizing business potential and minimizing infrastructure support costs and security exposure.

RCI's services team works directly with industry leading IT vendors to deliver world-class end-to-end technology solutions to customers that result in reduced IT project costs and greater ROI on technology investments. RCI offers a single source for business solutions designed to deliver tangible business outcomes for customers that are services-centric, technology-enabled and people-driven.

Source: Internal company documents.

name suggests. RCI had two centers: one located in Aurora, Ontario, and the other in Vancouver, British Columbia. The items (e.g., books or posters) were printed for customers and then held in inventory. Onsite managed services were customer-specific services such as conference management, internal print room management, and reception services. Legal Document Services was a niche service to support law firms during litigation through a process called electronic document discovery. RCI scanned legal documents and recorded them digitally so that law firms could search and retrieve them.

Services support teams (consultants and solution engineers) operated as an overlay structure to the sales channel, with sales owning the customer relationship. Support teams educated the sales channel and identified opportunities within the market. The sales team engaged the support team as subject matter experts when pursuing opportunities with potential customers. Furthermore, support teams also engaged in more traditional consulting activities focused on enterprise software and hardware needs. Teams from this group went into businesses, studied operations, and then made recommendations. This gave RCI the ability to design the most efficient workflow for the business, providing comprehensive solutions. In general, the consulting service was free for customers who subsequently bought RCI products. Independent dealers were able to use these support teams to supplement operations, improve knowledge, and integrate with RCI.

RCI Sales Team

RCI's direct sales force of 380 people was focused on maintaining existing customer relationships while hunting for *net* new opportunities. For a breakdown of the sales force by customer segment, see Exhibit 7. The difference between a new customer and a net new customer was that a net new customer had never purchased an RCI product before. For the sales force, the time spent on repeat business versus new business was approximately at a 4 to 1 ratio. Over half of new business in any given year, based on the number of clients, came from geographic accounts that

EXHIBIT 7 Ricoh Canada's Sales Force Breakdown by Customer Segment, 2015

Dealer Operations	2
Sales—Corporate	21
Sales—Major Accounts	84
Sales—Geographic/Key Named Accounts	175
Sales—Strategic Accounts	23
Sales—DDLP (Document Direction Limited Partnership)	51
Selling Dealer	15
Selling Software	9
Total	380

Source: Author created.

were acquired through cold calling. Senior salespeople managed major and strategic accounts, while new hires targeted geographic customers primarily through cold calling. Overall, RCI had a reputation for treating its salespeople well.

RCI's sales force would need additional training if RCI was to continue to expand its services offerings. The current estimate was $6,095 per person (this included rep costs, instructor costs, material, training sessions, a technology show, and revenue lost from not selling during training). Kevin Braun, director of quality and strategic planning, believed this cost might even be too low, saying:

> My belief is that we do not spend enough on training our sales team. This is a new area for most of them and we are heavily relying on support staff to assist them in these early stages. This issue is of high priority for the EMT [executive management team], but it is my personal opinion this number should be close to doubled. Finally, the recruitment process for salespeople also needs to change—to candidates that have more content/specific knowledge in services.

RCI's independent dealer network would have to undergo significant change to address a large-scale shift to services. First, salespersons at the dealers would have to learn about services and how to sell them. In the past, they had only sold hardware. Second, dealers would have to be interested in selling services. At many dealers, salespeople were vested in their positions or near retirement so were not motivated. Glenn Laverty and Peter Ronan recognized the problem: "We must find a way to encourage the sale of our services or find new dealers that specialize in selling our services. Although hardware is still a very important part of RCI's business, we must figure out a way to balance the legacy business while creating growth in services."

The Financial Quagmire

RCI's investment capital came from income generated by its legacy business. The current CFO, Richard Perri, said, "The issue RCI presently faces from a financial perspective is how to allocate these funds to generate the best returns." Laverty and Perri wondered how realistic it was for RCI to invest in services growth given RCI's current financial position. Laverty said, "We have to make sure we have the internal resources to make a dent in the services market. A lot of these things take scale, and at the very least we need to know how much growth to plan for." See Exhibit 8 for a summary of revenue, expenses, and total gross profit for 2015, and Exhibit 9 for the 2015 balance sheet.

RCI's revenue was affected by exchange rate fluctuations because the products it sold were manufactured in Japan and inventoried in the United States on their way to Canada. CFO Richard Perri told Laverty, "We need to consider hedging these currencies to provide stability in business planning. The greenback, in particular, has been the subject of much speculation given proposed interest rate increases."

Management

In the prior five years, RCI had experienced 110 percent turnover in its executive management team; some had left voluntarily, while others had been forced out. This turnover reflected the need for creative thinking in the executive suite. The replacements were tech savvy, had fresh ideas, and could think outside the box, but the high turnover had created a leadership crisis. According to Laverty, "Recruiting new people and getting them up to speed as a team has not been as fast as we had hoped. It takes time for everyone to settle in. This makes it even more crucial for us to have a strategy for RCI that we can unify around."

Performance Management

Because RCI was part of a Japanese corporation, it followed the practices of its parent. RCI was heavily involved in planning, assessing past performance, and revising goals. Every month, each member of the RCI executive management team had a one-on-one meeting with the head of Ricoh Americas Corporation in Caldwell, New Jersey. At that meeting, they reviewed past performance and future initiatives. RCI executives also traveled to Japan biannually for weeklong meetings with their counterparts from other regions to discuss the future of the company on a global scale. Laverty often told his management team, "As an organization, we must always be actively looking for criticism from our customers that will help us refine and improve our operations." To this end, everyone took the concept of kaizen (continuous improvement) seriously.

EXHIBIT 8 Financial Summary for Ricoh Canada, 2015

Income Statement	2013	2014	2015
Revenue			
Sales (Hardware)	$ 82,370	$192,116	$192,790
Key (incl. DDLP)	84,771	89,232	91,701
Major Accounts	65,085	69,239	68,338
Strategic Accounts	14,628	14,202	14,551
Dealer Sales	17,887	19,442	18,200
Rental & Other	6,307	7,008	10,059
Affiliate	1,201	1,452	2,824
Parts, Supplies, & Paper	43,111	44,512	45,728
Service	185,475	187,013	192,546
IT/PS Services	6,622	8,209	12,402
IT Services	478	784	1,477
Cloud	0	0	0
Professional Services	6,144	7,425	10,925
Managed Services	36,411	37,004	40,667
Total Revenue	461,497	477,313	497,016
Total Gross Profit	154,538	158,386	159,467
Sales GP%	33.24%	33.99%	29.10%
Key (incl. DDLP) GP%	41.44%	42.34%	36.10%
Major Accounts GP%	29.75%	29.86%	26.80%
Strategic Accounts GP%	11.93%	13.06%	8.10%
Dealer Sales GP%	24.55%	25.19%	19.20%
Expenses			
Sales	53,541	54,634	56,094
IT/PS Services	3,242	3,308	3,647
Managed Services	2,966	3,026	3,303
Dealer	2,739	2,795	2,780
Marketing	8,642	8,818	9,226
Operations	29,261	29,858	30,348
G&A	23,843	24,330	23,283
Amortization	2,431	2,481	2,739
Total Expenses	126,665	129,250	131,420
Operating Profit	$ 27,873	$ 29,136	$ 28,047

Source: Internal company documents.

RCI placed emphasis on what it called a Net Promoter Score (NPS). This score was based on customers' responses to the question: "Would you recommend RCI to another company?" RCI's NPS scores were consistently high (see the Customer Satisfaction Survey 2009–2015 in Exhibit 10), while scores from other companies that utilized an NPS assessment were often negative, indicating that more customers would not recommend that company than would. This metric measured the emotional connection a customer felt during interactions with RCI; it was particularly valuable for providing input on a

EXHIBIT 9 Ricoh Canada's Balance Sheet, 2013–2015

Balance Sheet	2013	2014	2015
Assets			
Current Assets			
Cash and cash equivalents	$ 26,363	$ 33,358	$ 59,228
Trade Accounts receivable, net	97,631	102,786	97,565
Inventories	38,056	42,562	34,070
Other Current Assets	10,255	9,941	10,786
	172,305	188,647	201,649
Lease receivable	5,427	8,102	5,957
Property, plant and equipment, net	6,063	11,620	12,039
Goodwill	20,306	44,863	44,863
Intangibles, net	15,618	15,601	15,601
Other assets	10,388	5,705	9,119
	57,802	85,892	87,579
Total Assets	$230,107	$274,539	$289,228
Liabilities			
Current Liabilities			
Accounts payable and accrued liabilities	$ 40,986	$ 48,900	$ 56,217
Due to affiliates	20,609	24,588	28,657
Current portion of lease Payable	3,610	4,307	4,406
Other Current Liabilities	6,446	7,691	8,075
	71,650	85,485	97,356
Lease payable	4,720	5,631	5,722
Promissory note	11,916	14,217	13,146
Other long-term liabilities	1,324	1,580	1,800
	17,960	21,428	20,668
Shareholders' Equity			
Share Capital	72,634	86,659	74,868
Contributed Surplus	11,615	13,857	15,670
Retained Earnings	56,248	67,108	80,666
	140,496	167,625	171,204
Total Liabilities & Shareholders' Equity	$230,107	$274,539	$289,228

Source: Internal company documents

customer's satisfaction with an employee (e.g., when a machine was being fixed or when dealing with a local sales representative). RCI was dedicated to the success of its customers, which gave it a reputation as one of the most trusted brands in the market.

RCI's focus on NPS began because of its lease and service business model—where interactions with the customer were frequent, particularly for machine maintenance. RCI believed that a positive social experience helped promote a long-term relationship, and with 80 percent of RCI's sales effort focused on repeat customers, it was easy to see why a long-term focus on customers was important. Employees were trained in interpersonal skills so that they handled interactions positively. Laverty often reminded everyone, "It is amazing just how far a smile can go."

EXHIBIT 10 Results for Ricoh Canada Customer Satisfaction Survey, 2009–2015

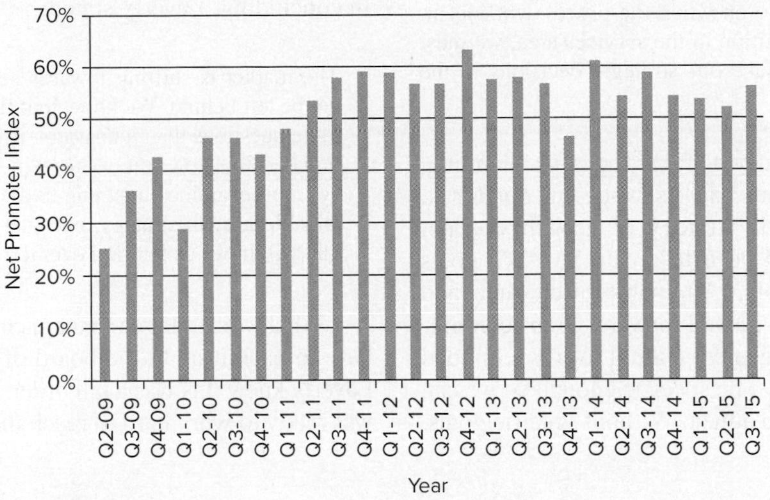

Source: Internal company documents.

Services Growth Strategies

RCI's management team was considering a number of growth strategies for Professional Services and Managed Services. These included growth by acquisitions, partnerships, alliances, and/or organic growth.

Any domestic acquisition would have to be funded by RCI. Even in terms of global acquisitions, such as in the case of IKON, RCI was responsible for financing the Canadian arm of that business. But, were partnerships and alliances more critical for the transition to services than outright acquisitions? Could a partnership or alliance be used for knowledge transfer to Ricoh? How feasible was it to think that another company could provide a foundation for how RCI would compete in the services market?

Could Ricoh Canada Inc. rely solely on organic growth? If history were a guide, RCI would have to rely on the head office in Japan to develop innovations in services. By itself, RCI did not have the engineering personnel to develop products because almost all research and development efforts were done in Japan and the United States. In this situation, RCI would have focused on cost-cutting initiatives in the legacy business and sales of existing services technology, while waiting for Japan to introduce new offerings. In addition, because services developed in Japan or the United States were designed for launch on a global scale, RCI was limited in its ability to tailor products to the Canadian marketplace. But as Laverty told his team, "Perhaps this isn't impossible. How different can the services in Canada be from those of businesses globally?"

The Final Decision

As president and CEO, Laverty wrote to his management team:

> With a corporate shift to Managed and Professional Services, RCI will have to ensure that the Ricoh brand does not erode. We will have to get past the hurdle of being known as the printer guys if we intend to become more than that. Customers will need to be assured that RCI is a serious player in the Managed Services and Professional Services industries, especially when continued support in key functionalities such as cloud services is a priority for a prospective customer. RCI must also figure out a way to handle failures when delivering new services. Any failures could give a signal to the market that we are not competent in those services or are not ready to handle large-scale projects.

> Since this is new territory for RCI, there is no doubt that unexpected challenges will occur. We must work closely with Eric Fletcher, VP of Marketing, who may be the deciding vote on when the process will occur. With all the competition in the services area, we must move ahead and make our strategic decisions in the very near future.

Given Ricoh Canada Inc.'s focus on planning, the management team had its work cut out for it. Having just a generic strategy of growth was not enough. They would need to create SMART goals (Specific, Measurable, Attainable, Relevant, and Time-bound) as they moved forward. In his communication to the management team, Laverty reminded them, "Our goals must be specific enough so we can measure progress and adjust. Without specific goals, we will lose sight of what is important and end up stuck between two markets."

In concluding, Laverty stated:

> The market is shifting towards services, and we must not be left behind. We know that figuring this out raises more questions than it answers. But the important question is still: "How can we grow in the area of services?" We must examine our strengths and come up with a sustainable growth strategy, one that we can put in place that will move us forward over the next three years.

Whatever strategy the team chose, Laverty would have to back it up to the board of directors in Japan. Laverty knew this was a tall order, but he felt his team was ready to work hard to reach this stretch goal.

CASE 21

Mondelēz International: Has Corporate Restructuring Produced Shareholder Value?

connect

John E. Gamble
Texas A&M University–Corpus Christi

Mondelēz International was among the world's largest snack foods makers with $7 billion brands including Cadbury, LU, Milka, Cadbury Dairy Milk, Trident, Nabisco, and Oreo. The company's brand portfolio in 2016 included another 44 well-known brands such as Triscuit, Toblerone, Wheat Thins, Ritz, Philadelphia, Nilla, BelVita, Chips Ahoy!, and Tang. Even though some of its brands had histories dating beyond 100 years, the company had come into existence only in 2012 after a corporate restructuring at Kraft Foods. Kraft Foods Inc. was the world's second-largest processed foods company in 2012 with annual revenues of more than $54 billion in 2011. The company's global lineup of brands included Maxwell House, Oreo, Cadbury, Chips Ahoy!, Honey Maid, Dentyne, Velveeta, Cheez Whiz, Oscar Mayer, and Kraft. In all, the company had 12 brands with annual revenues exceeding $1 billion each and approximately 80 brands that generated annual revenues of more than $100 million each. The majority of Kraft Foods's brands held number one market shares in their product categories, which created strong business units in North America, Europe, and developing markets.

Even though Kraft Foods's business units produced strong profits, slow growth in the processed foods industry in North America and parts of Europe had restricted the company's ability to deliver increases in shareholder value. In fact, the trading range of the company's shares in 2011 was relatively unchanged from that in 2007 when it became an independent company after a spinoff by the Altria Group (formerly Philip Morris). Some of the lackluster growth in its share price could be attributed to the economic slowdown that began in 2007, but the company's upper management and its board believed the underlying cause of its poor market performance was a corporate strategy that was not sufficiently focused on growth.

The company implemented a corporate restructuring in 2012 to create a high-growth global snacks business and a high-margin North American grocery business. The new snacks-oriented company would include all of Kraft Foods's business units and brands in Europe and developing markets, plus its U.S. snacks business and would be named Mondelēz International. Mondelēz (pronounced mohn-dah-Leez) was a newly coined word that drew on "mundus," the Latin root for the word world, and "delez," which was meant to express "delicious." The creators of the name added "International" to capture the global nature of the business. The remainder of the company's Kraft Foods North American business unit would become known as Kraft Foods Group upon completion of the spinoff.

By 2016, Mondelēz International had successfully achieved its internationalization goals, with 79 percent of its revenues generated outside the United States in 2015. But the United States remained the company's largest market, making up 17 percent, 18 percent, and 21 percent of its sales in 2013, 2014, and 2015, respectively. No other country accounted for 10 percent of Mondelēz's sales.

However, the overall effectiveness of the corporate restructuring was questionable with the company's stock performance largely tracking the S&P 500 and its revenues in decline. The company's income from continuing operations grew from 2014 to 2015, but only because of a $6.8 billion pretax gain from the spinoff of its coffee business in France. Drawing focus on the need for improved performance, activist investor William Ackman took a $5.5 billion stake in the company in July 2015. Ackman believed that management should dramatically improve the company's performance or that the company should be a candidate for acquisition by a better-performing industry rival. A summary of Mondelēz International's financial performance from 2011 to 2015 is presented in Exhibit 1. The performance of the company's stock performance between April 2011 and August 2016 is presented in Exhibit 2.

COMPANY HISTORY

Mondelēz International's marquee brands all had rich histories that began with the efforts of entrepreneurs who were inspired to launch new businesses that could provide consumers with value and support for their families. But Mondelēz International, as a corporate entity, resulted from the 2012 spinoff of Kraft Foods's North American grocery business to shareholders. Under the terms of the proposal, each Kraft Foods Inc. shareholder received one share of the newly created Kraft Foods Group for every three shares of Kraft Foods Inc. owned by the shareholder. At the conclusion of the spinoff, Kraft Foods Inc. changed its name to Mondelēz International, Inc. and its ticker symbol became MDLZ. The KFT ticker symbol was retired after the transaction. Shares of the newly formed Kraft Foods Group would trade under the ticker symbol KRFT.

Kraft Foods's broad portfolio of brands resulted from a series of mergers and acquisitions dating to 1928 when Kraft Cheese Company merged with Phenix Cheese Corporation, which was the maker of Philadelphia cream cheese. The proliferation of brands owned by Kraft in 2012 accelerated in 1988 when Philip Morris Companies purchased Kraft for

EXHIBIT 1 Financial Summary for Mondelēz International, Inc., 2011–2015 (in millions, except per share amounts)

	2015	2014	2013	2012	2011
Continuing Operations					
Net revenues	$29,636	$34,244	$35,299	$35,015	$35,810
Earnings from continuing operations, net of taxes	7,291	2,201	2,332	1,606	1,764
Net earnings attributable to Mondelēz International:					
Per share, basic	$4.49	$1.29	$1.30	$0.90	$0.99
Per share, diluted	$4.44	$1.28	$1.29	$0.88	$0.99
Cash Flow and Financial Position					
Net cash provided by operating activities	3,728	3,562	6,410	3,923	4,520
Capital expenditures	1,514	1,642	1,622	1,610	1,771
Property, plant and equipment, net	8,362	9,827	10,247	10,010	13,813
Total assets	62,843	66,771	72,464	75,421	93,701
Long-term debt	14,557	13,821	14,431	15,519	23,013
Total Mondelēz International shareholders' equity	28,012	27,750	32,373	32,276	35,271
Shares outstanding at year end	1,580	1,664	1,705	1,778	1,768
Per Share and Other Data					
Book value per shares outstanding	17.73	16.68	18.99	18.15	19.95
Dividends declared per share	0.64	0.58	0.54	1.00	1.16
Common Stock closing price at year end	44.84	36.33	35.30	25.45	37.36
Number of employees	99,000	104,000	107,000	110,000	126,000

Source: Mondelēz International, Inc. 2015 10-K.

EXHIBIT 2 Performance of Mondelēz International, Inc.'s Common Shares, April 2011–August 2016

(a) Trend in Mondelēz International's Common Stock Price

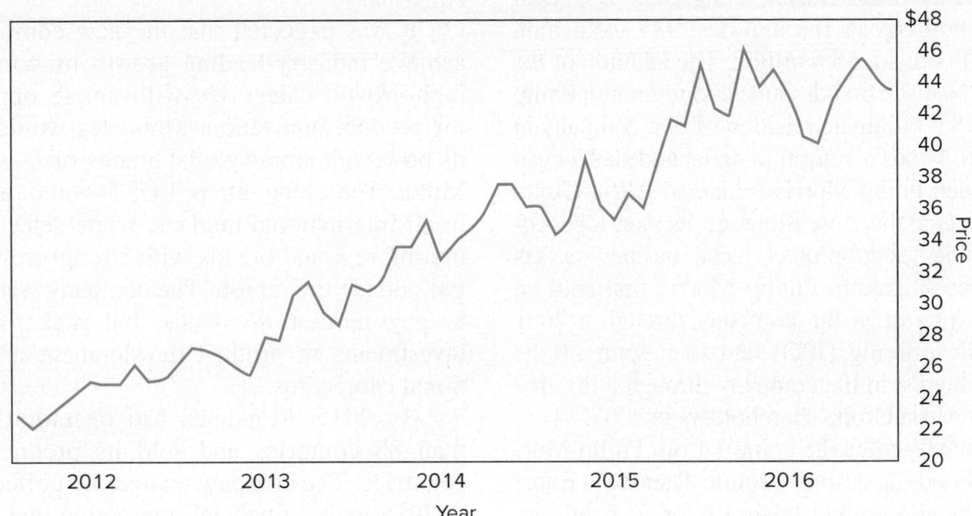

(b) Performance of Mondelēz International's Stock Price versus the S&P 500 Index

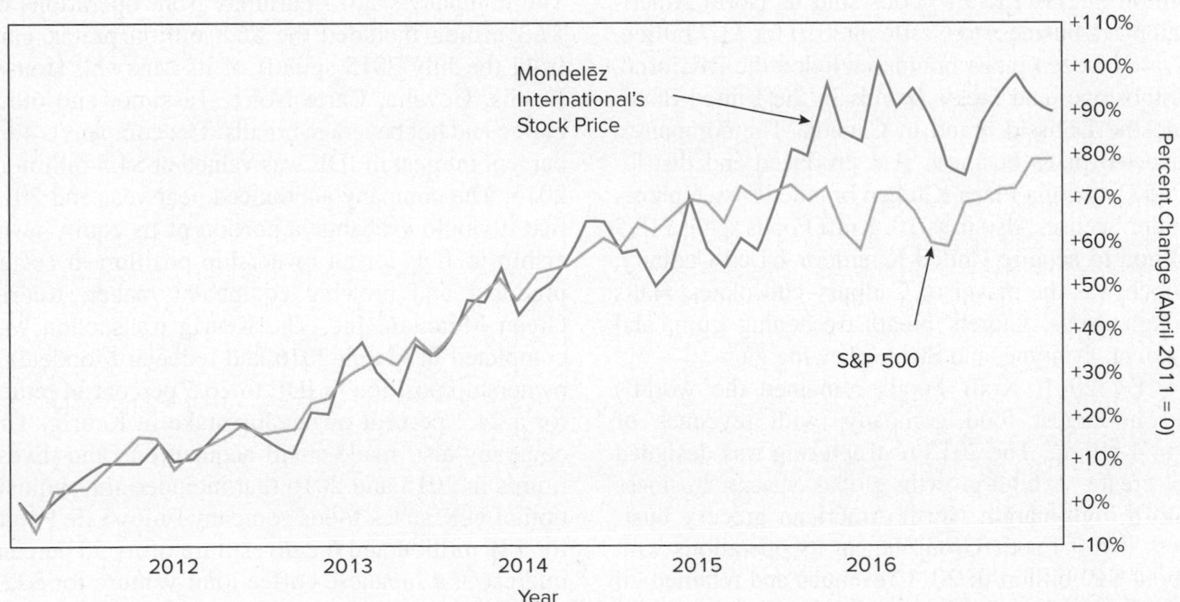

$12.9 billion. Philip Morris's acquisition of Kraft was part of a corporate strategy focused on diversifying the company beyond its well-known cigarette business that included the Marlboro, Virginia Slims, Parliament, and Basic brands. At the time of the acquisition of Kraft, Philip Morris had already acquired brands such as Oscar Mayer, Tang, Jell-O, Crystal Light, and Post cereals through the 1985 acquisition of General Foods for $5.6 billion. The addition of the company's Nabisco brands came about through Philip Morris's $18.9 billion acquisition of that company in 2000. Kraft Foods's return to independence began in 2001, when Philip Morris (renamed Altria Group in 2003) began the divestiture of its non-tobacco-related businesses to protect those business assets from tobacco litigation. Phillip Morris first sold an 11 percent interest in the company through a 2001 initial public offering (IPO) and then spun off its remaining interest in the company through a tax-free dividend to Altria Group shareholders in 2007.

Immediately after the spinoff from Philip Morris, Kraft Foods acquired Groupe Danone's European cracker and cookie business for $7.6 billion. In 2008, Kraft Foods spun off its Post cereals business as a tax-free distribution to shareholders. Post cereals included brands such as Honey Bunches of Oats, Pebbles, Shredded Wheat, Selects, Grape Nuts, and Honeycomb and recorded sales of $1.1 billion in 2007. Kraft Foods sold its North American pizza business to Nestlé in 2010 for $3.7 billion. Kraft's frozen pizza brands included the DiGiorno, Tombstone, and Jack's brands in the United States and the Delissio brand in Canada. The company's divested pizza business also produced and distributed California Pizza Kitchen branded frozen pizzas under license. Also in 2010, Kraft Foods spent $18.5 billion to acquire United Kingdom–based Cadbury, which was the maker of Cadbury chocolates, Halls cough drops, Clorets breath-freshening gum, and Trident, Dentyne, and Stride chewing gum.

By 2011, Kraft Foods remained the world's second-largest food company, with revenues of $54.4 billion. The 2012 restructuring was designed to create a high-growth global snacks business and a high-margin North American grocery business. Kraft Foods Group began its operations with about $19 billion in 2011 revenues and retained all of the company's business operations and brands in North America such as Kraft macaroni and cheese dinner, Capri Sun, and Miracle Whip salad dressing. Mondelēz International began its operations with about $35.8 billion in 2011 revenues and included the U.S. Snacks divisions and all Kraft Foods businesses in Europe and developing markets in Eastern Europe, Asia/Pacific, Middle East/Africa, and South America.

It was expected that the new company could achieve industry-leading growth by competing in high-growth categories with ample opportunities for product innovation. Mondelēz would focus on its powerful, iconic global brands such as Cadbury, Milka, Toblerone, Oreo, LU, Tassimo, and Jacobs in all international markets, while selectively promoting regional brands with strong growth potential outside the region. The company was expected to pay modest dividends, but make substantial investments in product development and promotional campaigns.

By 2016, Mondelēz had operations in more than 80 countries and sold its products in 165 countries. The company exited the coffee business in 2015 with a financial transaction that combined its coffee brands with those of Netherlands-based D.E. Master Blenders to create a new company, Jacobs Douwe Egberts (JDE). Mondelēz recorded a pretax gain of $6.8 billion in 2015 and retained a 43.5 percent equity interest in the new company. The company's 2015 earnings from operations of $7.3 billion included the $6.8 billion pretax gain from the July 2015 spinoff of its Maxwell House, Jacobs, Gevalia, Carte Noire, Tassimo, and other coffee and hot beverage brands. The company's 43.5 percent interest in JDE was valued at $4.5 billion in 2015. The company announced near year-end 2015 that it would exchange a portion of its equity ownership in JDE for an ownership position in coffee producer and brewing equipment maker, Keurig Green Mountain Inc. The Keurig transaction was completed in March 2016 and reduced Mondelēz's ownership position in JDE to 26.5 percent in return for a 24.2 percent ownership stake in Keurig. The company also made small acquisitions and divestitures in 2015 and 2016 that included the acquisition of U.S. snack foods company Enjoy Life Foods for $81 million and the divestiture of its 50 percent interest in a Japanese coffee joint venture for $225 million and the sale of local Finnish biscuit brands for $16 million.

MONDELĒZ INTERNATIONAL'S CORPORATE STRATEGY AND BUSINESS SEGMENT PERFORMANCE IN 2016

Mondelēz International's strategy was directed at exploiting its powerful brands of snack foods across the 165 country markets where its products were sold. Brands such as Oreo, Milka, Cadbury, Nabisco, Honey Maid, Trident, and Tang were popular in almost all markets where the company competed and provided for a range of products that cut across most all consumer snacking desires. For example, the company's product line included biscuits or cookies, chocolate, candy, gum, and beverages. The company's acquisitions were directed at expanding its brand portfolio into rapidly growing snack categories. The company's 2015 acquisition of Enjoy Life Foods added allergen-free and gluten-free chips and nut-free chocolate and seed and fruit products to its lineup of snacks.

The company's strategy sought to expand margins through programs to boost cost-efficiency in its manufacturing and supply chain activities. However, the company was committed to providing additional resources needed to expand marketing and sales capabilities in key markets, especially in emerging markets. The company announced its Sustainability 2020 goals in 2015 for reducing carbon emissions, reducing deforestation within its agricultural supply chain, focusing on water reduction efforts, and reducing packaging and manufacturing waste. The promotion of moderation in snacking was also an important element of the company's social responsibility and sustainability strategy.

The company was organized into five reportable segments based on geographic markets: North America; Latin America; Asia Pacific; Europe; and Eastern Europe, Middle East, and Africa (EEMEA). Within each geographic reporting division were five product categories—biscuits (including cookies, crackers, and salted snacks), chocolate, gum and candy, beverages, and cheese and grocery. Exhibit 3 presents a financial summary for its geographic segments for 2013 through 2015. The revenue contributions of each product category in each geographic region are presented in Exhibit 4.

All of the five business segments competed in product markets that were characterized by strong competitive rivalry that required strong distribution and marketing skills to attract consumer demand and

EXHIBIT 3 Financial Summary for Mondelēz International's Geographic Segments, 2013–2015 (in millions)

Net revenues	2015	2014	2013
Latin America	$ 4,988	$ 5,153	$ 5,382
Asia Pacific	4,360	4,605	4,952
EEMEA	2,786	3,638	3,915
Europe	10,528	13,912	14,059
North America	6,974	6,936	6,991
Net revenues	$29,636	$34,244	$35,299
Earnings from continuing operations before income taxes	**2015**	**2014**	**2013**
Operating income:			
Latin America	$ 485	$ 475	$ 570
Asia Pacific	268	385	512

(Continued)

EEMEA	194	327	379
Europe	1,277	1,770	1,699
North America	1,105	922	889
Unrealized gains/(losses) on hedging activities	96	(112)	62
General corporate expenses	(383)	(317)	(287)
Amortization of intangibles	(181)	(206)	(217)
Benefit from indemnification resolution	—	—	336
Gains on coffee business transactions and divestitures	6,822	—	30
Loss on deconsolidation of Venezuela	(778)	—	—
Acquisition-related costs	(8)	(2)	(2)
Operating income	8,897	3,242	3,971
Interest and other expense, net	(1,013)	(688)	(1,579)
Earnings from continuing operations before income taxes	$ 7,884	$ 2,554	$ 2,392

Total assets

	2015	2014	2013
Latin America	$ 4,673	$ 6,470	$ 6,860
Asia Pacific	7,936	8,068	8,487
EEMEA	3,867	5,153	6,951
Europe	19,683	24,568	27,599
North America	21,175	21,287	21,705
Equity method investments	5,387	662	659
Unallocated assets	122	563	203
Total assets	$62,843	$66,771	$72,464

Depreciation expense

	2015	2014	2013
Latin America	$ 94	$ 118	$ 107
Asia Pacific	114	112	107
EEMEA	66	90	88
Europe	274	359	359
North America	165	174	199
Total depreciation expense	$ 713	$ 853	$ 860

Capital expenditures

	2015	2014	2013
Latin America	$ 354	$ 460	$ 412
Asia Pacific	311	356	268
EEMEA	197	219	254
Europe	390	429	478
North America	262	178	210
Total capital expenditures	$ 1,514	$ 1,642	$ 1,622

Source: Mondelēz International, Inc. 2015 10-K.

EXHIBIT 4 Mondelēz International's Net Revenues by Product Category and Geographic Region, 2013–2015 (in millions)

For the Year Ended December 31, 2015						
	Latin America	Asia Pacific	EEMEA	Europe	North America	Total
Biscuits	$1,605	$1,264	$ 535	$ 2,420	$5,569	$11,393
Chocolate	840	1,444	896	4,638	256	8,074
Gum & Candy	1,091	717	544	757	1,149	4,258
Beverages	767	401	543	1,549	—	3,260
Cheese & Grocery	685	534	268	1,164	—	2,651
Total net revenues	$4,988	$4,360	$2,786	$10,528	$6,974	$29,636
For the Year Ended December 31, 2014						
	Latin America	Asia Pacific	EEMEA	Europe	North America	Total
Biscuits	$1,322	$1,177	$ 642	$ 2,882	$5,486	$11,509
Chocolate	1,054	1,555	1,082	5,394	296	9,381
Gum & Candy	1,176	776	646	908	1,154	4,660
Beverages	940	465	981	3,292	—	5,678
Cheese & Grocery	661	632	287	1,436	—	3,016
Total net revenues	$5,153	$4,605	$3,638	$13,912	$6,936	$34,244
For the Year Ended December 31, 2013						
	Latin America	Asia Pacific	EEMEA	Europe	North America	Total
Biscuits	$1,288	$1,311	$ 677	$ 2,940	$5,480	$11,696
Chocolate	1,143	1,632	1,181	5,385	326	9,667
Gum & Candy	1,380	849	673	968	1,185	5,055
Beverages	907	470	1,113	3,340	—	5,830
Cheese & Grocery	664	690	271	1,426	—	3,051
Total net revenues	$5,382	$4,952	$3,915	$14,059	$6,991	$35,299

Source: Mondelēz International, Inc. 2015 10-K.

ensure product availability in supermarkets, discount clubs, mass merchandisers, convenience stores, drug stores, and retail food locations serviced by its food distribution operations. Brand building, consumer health and wellness, and advertising and promotions were all critical to success in the industry. In fact, Mondelēz's ability to compete against lower-priced branded and store-brand products was a function of its ability to successfully differentiate its products from lower-priced alternatives. Also, differentiation was essential to retaining shelf space as the retail grocery industry consolidated and provided retailers with greater leverage in negotiations with food manufacturers. The company's successful differentiation of its products had also allowed it to achieve organic revenue growth of 3.7 percent in 2015 and 2.5 percent in 2014 through net price increases.

The company's processed foods divisions had experienced cost increases as inflationary forces had led to higher prices for commodities used in the manufacture of its products such as coffee, cocoa, oils, nuts, and sugar. However, Mondelēz utilized commodity hedging to protect against spikes in ingredient costs. In addition, price increases made possible by its strong product differentiation had more than offset the increased cost of commodity inputs in 2015. Also, the production of Mondelēz International's products was regulated by the U.S. Food and Drug Administration in the United States, and similar organizations in the 165 countries where its products were sold. The company's packaging practices were also regulated by governmental agencies in the United States and the European Union.

Latin America

In 2015, Modelēz International's Latin American division experienced a 3.2 percent decline in revenue, primarily because of unfavorable exchange rates and declining sales. The strong U.S. dollar relative to the Brazilian real, Mexican peso, Venezuelan bolivar, and Argentinean peso accounted for the majority of exchange rate losses. The sales decline was brought about by the elimination of selected low-margin products from its product mix and consumer resistance to price increases. The spinoff of the company's coffee brands also affected sales in Latin America in 2015. Mondelēz's operating income increased by 2.1 percent in 2015 as a result of price increases and lower operating costs.

Asia Pacific

Mondelēz International's revenues in Asia Pacific declined by $245 million during 2015—primarily for the same reasons that caused the decline in net revenues in Latin America. Exchange rate losses related to the value of the U.S. dollar relative to the Australian dollar, Indian rupee, and Japanese yen; consumer resistance to price increases; the elimination of low-margin products; and spinoff of coffee brands all contributed to the decline. Operating income for the segment declined by 30.4 percent between 2014 and 2015 because of restructuring costs, higher ingredient costs, and higher advertising and promotion expense. However, price increases and lower manufacturing costs helped prevent a larger operating loss in the region during 2015.

Eastern Europe, Middle East, and Africa

The mix of exchange rate losses, the negative impact of price increases on consumer demand, and the elimination of the coffee business contributed to a 23.4 percent decline in net revenues between 2014 and 2015 for the company's Eastern Europe, Middle East, and Africa segment. The division's operating income declined by 40.7 percent in 2015 because of higher commodity costs, the deconsolidation of its coffee business, and higher advertising and promotion expense.

Europe

Segment revenues declined by 24.3 percent in Europe between 2014 and 2015 after the spinoff of the company's coffee brands and the effect of exchange rate adjustments and volume declines associated with price increases. The segment's operating income declined by 27.9 percent in 2015 because of coffee deconsolidation costs, higher ingredient costs, and higher advertising and promotion expense. Earlier in the decade, the segment had been among the company's most successful divisions, with traditionally strong revenue and operating income growth. The company held a number one position in the snack foods industry in Europe, which was growing 1.4 times faster than the overall European processed foods industry. While growth in the snack foods industry in Europe was attractive, developing markets in Latin America and Asia offered the most attractive growth opportunities for Mondelēz, Nestlé, and other food companies in 2016.

North America

Net revenues increased by $38 million or one-half of 1 percent because of an accounting calendar change, the acquisition of Enjoy Life Foods, and added revenues from slight price cuts on Mondelēz's best-selling cookie and candy brands. The volume increases in biscuits and candy were partially offset by volume declines in gum and chocolate which saw price increases during the year. Operating income in North America increased by 19.8 percent between 2014 and 2015 because of lower manufacturing costs; lower selling, general and administrative expenses; the absence of restructuring costs; and lower commodity prices.

MONDELĒZ INTERNATIONAL'S PERFORMANCE IN LATE 2016

Mondelēz International's results since its spinoff from Kraft Foods had been mixed with little sustained growth in revenues or profit measures excluding the effects of one-time extraordinary

EXHIBIT 5 Mondelēz International, Inc. Income Statements, 2013–2015 (in millions, except per share amounts)

	2015	2014	2013
Net revenues	$29,636	$34,244	$35,299
Cost of sales	18,124	21,647	22,189
Gross profit	11,512	12,597	13,110
Selling, general and administrative expenses	7,577	8,457	8,679
Asset impairment and exit costs	901	692	273
Gains on coffee business transactions and divestitures	(6,822)	—	(30)
Loss on deconsolidation of Venezuela	778	—	—
Amortization of intangibles	181	206	217
Operating income	8,897	3,242	3,971
Interest and other expense, net	1,013	688	1,579
Earnings from continuing operations before income taxes	7,884	2,554	2,392
Provision for income taxes	593	353	60
Earnings from continuing operations	7,291	2,201	2,332
Earnings from discontinued operations, net of income taxes	—	—	1,603
Net earnings	7,291	2,201	3,935
Noncontrolling interest	24	17	20
Net earnings attributable to Mondelēz International	$ 7,267	$ 2,184	$ 3,915
Per share data:			
Basic earnings per share attributable to Mondelēz International:			
Continuing operations	$4.49	$1.29	$1.30
Discontinued operations	—	—	0.91
Net earnings attributable to Mondelēz International	$4.49	$1.29	$2.21
Diluted earnings per share attributable to Mondelēz International:			
Continuing operations	$4.44	$1.28	$1.29
Discontinued operations	—	—	0.90
Net earnings attributable to Mondelēz International	$4.44	$1.28	$2.19
Dividends declared	$0.64	$0.58	$0.54

Source: Mondelēz International, Inc. 2015 10-K.

items. Both revenues and net earnings before divestiture gains had been in decline since 2013—see Exhibit 5. While trends in its revenues and operating income had been mostly negative, its stock had performed well since the divestiture of its coffee brands. The divestiture and subsequent equity interest in the coffee business had resulted in some changes to its balance sheets. The company's balance sheets for 2014 and 2015 are presented in Exhibit 6.

The company's results for the first half of 2016 continued to be disappointing, with revenues for the first half of the year declining by 17 percent from $15.4 billion to $12.8 billion. The company's operating income declined by 18 percent from $1.65 billion to $1.36 billion. The company's net earnings for the six-month period ending June 30, 2016, improved to $1.0 billion from $739 million after a gain from an equity investment exchange related to

EXHIBIT 6 Mondelēz International, Inc. Balance Sheets, 2010–2011 (in millions)

ASSETS		
Cash and cash equivalents	$ 1,870	$ 1,631
Trade receivables (net of allowances of $54 at December 31, 2015, and $66 at December 31, 2014)	2,634	3,802
Other receivables (net of allowances of $109 at December 31, 2015, and $91 at December 31, 2014)	1,212	949
Inventories, net	2,609	3,480
Deferred income taxes	—	480
Other current assets	633	1,408
Total current assets	8,958	11,750
Property, plant and equipment, net	8,362	9,827
Goodwill	20,664	23,389
Intangible assets, net	18,768	20,335
Prepaid pension assets	69	53
Equity method investments	5,387	662
Other assets	635	755
TOTAL ASSETS	$62,843	$66,771
LIABILITIES		
Short-term borrowings	$ 236	$ 1,305
Current portion of long-term debt	605	1,530
Accounts payable	4,890	5,299
Accrued marketing	1,634	2,047
Accrued employment costs	844	946
Other current liabilities	2,713	2,880
Total current liabilities	10,922	14,007
Long-term debt	14,557	13,821
Deferred income taxes	4,750	5,512
Accrued pension costs	2,183	2,912
Accrued postretirement health care costs	499	526
Other liabilities	1,832	2,140
TOTAL LIABILITIES	34,743	38,918
EQUITY		
Common Stock, no par value (5,000,000,000 shares authorized and 1,996,537,778 shares issued at December 31, 2015, and December 31, 2014)	—	—
Additional paid-in capital	31,760	31,651
Retained earnings	20,700	14,529
Accumulated other comprehensive losses	(9,986)	(7,318)
Treasury stock, at cost (416,504,624 shares at December 31, 2015, and 332,896,779 shares at December 31, 2014)	(14,462)	(11,112)
Total Mondelēz International Shareholders' Equity	28,012	27,750
Noncontrolling interest	88	103
TOTAL EQUITY	28,100	27,853
TOTAL LIABILITIES AND EQUITY	$62,843	$66,771

Source: Mondelēz International, Inc. 2015 10-K.

its exchange of ownership in the JDE coffee investment for a 24.2 percent ownership in Keurig.

Mondelēz International's chair and CEO Irene Rosenfeld saw positive signs in the results of the first six months of 2016. "Despite a challenging macro environment, our strong execution and first-half performance give us confidence in delivering our 2016 outlook and 2018 margin targets. Our ongoing focus on operational efficiency enables us to invest for sustainable, profitable growth in our Power Brands, white-space expansion and sales capabilities. This is evidenced by our upcoming launch of Milka chocolate in China, a $2.8 billion market with significant growth potential, and our substantial investment in e-commerce."[1] Activist investor William Ackman, who was the company's third-largest shareholder with a 5.6 percent stake in the company, continued to suggest in mid-2016 that the company must lower costs and improve sales significantly or find a buyer for the company. Going into the last half of 2016, Mondelēz management was confident in its corporate strategy and projected that the company would achieve 2 percent organic revenue growth and a 15–16 percent operating income margin to deliver double-digit growth in EPS by year-end.

ENDNOTE

[1] As quoted in "Mondelez International Reports Q2 Results," Globe Newswire, July 27, 2016.

CASE 22

LVMH in 2016: Its Diversification into Luxury Goods

connect

John E. Gamble
Texas A&M University–Corpus Christi

In 2016, LVMH Moët Hennessy Louis Vuitton was the world's largest luxury products company with annual sales of €35.7 billion and a business portfolio that included some of the most prestigious brand names in wines, spirits, and champagnes, fashion, watches and jewelry, and perfumes and cosmetics. The French conglomerate's business portfolio also included a luxury yacht producer, a 19th-century-styled French amusement park, two prestigious Parisian department stores, duty-free stores, a retail cosmetics chain, high-end luxury hotels, and a variety of French media properties. Even though no one needed LVMH's products—certain vintages of its Dom Pérignon champagne could retail for well over $1,000, its Givenchy dresses frequently sold for $5,000 or more, and popular Zenith chronograph watches carried retail prices of more than $10,000—the company's products were desired by millions across the world. LVMH CEO Bernard Arnault suggested desire for the company's products "in some way, fulfills a fantasy. You feel as if you must buy it, in fact, or else you won't be in the moment. You will be left behind."[1]

The company's business portfolio began to take shape in 1987 when Louis Vuitton, known worldwide for its purses and luggage, merged with the maker of Moët & Chandon champagne and Hennessy cognac. LVMH's current lineup of star luxury brands was forged by Bernard Arnault, who became CEO of the company in 1989 and promptly set about acquiring such names as Fendi, Donna Karan, Givenchy, Celine, Marc Jacobs, and Nicholas Kirkwood in fashion and leather goods; TAG Heuer, Bulgari, and Zenith in watches and jewelry; and Le Bon Marche and Sephora in retailing. By 2016 Arnault had assembled a portfolio of 70 luxury brands, which he categorized as a collection of star brands and rising stars. When asked about the managerial challenges of developing star brands, Arnault stated, "Mastering the paradox of star brands is very difficult and rare—fortunately. In my opinion, there are fewer than ten star brands in the luxury world."[2]

Arnault believed LVMH's collection of star brands such as Moët & Chandon, Krug, Louis Vuitton, Givenchy, and Parfums Christian Dior and its rising stars like Edun, Nicholas Kirkwood, and Marc Jacobs would lead to long-term corporate advantage since star brands had staying power. "The brand is built, if you wish, for eternity. It has been around for a long time; it has become an institution. Dom Pérignon is a perfect example. I can guarantee that people will be drinking it in the next century. It was created 250 years ago, but it will be relevant and desired for another century and beyond that."[3]

Arnault's rapidly growing portfolio had allowed LVMH to grow from approximately €2.5 billion in 1990 to €35.7 billion in 2015. The company set revenue and operating profit records in 2015, with both growing by 16 percent since 2014. The company's stellar performance was driven by the appeal of its iconic brands and a mix of its newer aspirational brands. However, the company's overall performance was negatively impacted by acquisitions thought to be rising stars that did not materialize. Arnault had select divestitures of underperforming businesses, the most recent of which was the announced sale of Donna Karan International in July 2016. The planned $650 million divestiture was to be completed by early 2017. Also, several LVMH businesses competed in glamorous industries, but had failed to make meaningful contributions to the company's performance. There was a concern among certain analysts that Arnault, as the company's majority shareholder and CEO, was able to utilize the company's ample cash flows to make acquisitions based on his personal interests rather than based on potential to boost shareholder value. A summary of LVMH's financial performance between 2011 and 2015 is presented in Exhibit 1.

COMPANY HISTORY

LVMH's history as an enterprise is traced to 1743 when Moët & Chandon was established in the Champagne Province in northeastern France. Moët & Chandon not only became among France's premier brands of champagne, but was also sought after outside of France with exports accounting for a large percentage of its sales by the 20th century. The company first diversified in 1968 when it acquired Parfums Christian Dior and a 1971 merger between Moët & Chandon and Champagne Mercier combined's two best-selling brands of champagne. The company changed its name to Moët-Hennessy when it again merged in 1971, this time with Jas Hennessy & Co., the world's second-largest producer of cognac.

The company diversified further in 1987 as the French government launched into an era of privatization to promote economic growth and reduce the country's excessively high unemployment rate. The families who controlled Moët-Hennessy and leather goods designer Louis Vuitton saw a merger between their two companies as their best strategy to prevent the companies from becoming takeover targets of large international corporations that were making investments in France. The $4 billion merger that created LVMH Moët-Hennessy Louis Vuitton allowed the heirs of the two companies' founders to retain

EXHIBIT 1 LVMH Income Statements, 2011–2015 (in millions of euros, except per share amounts)

	2015	2014	2013	2012	2011
Revenue	€35,664	€30,638	€29,016	€28,103	€23,569
Cost of sales	12,553	10,801	9,997	9,917	8,092
Gross margin	23,111	19,837	19,019	18,186	15,567
Marketing and selling expenses	13,830	11,744	10,767	10,101	8,360
General and administrative expenses	2,663	2,373	2,212	2,164	1,944
Income (loss) from joint ventures and associates	13	5	23	—	—
Profit from recurring operations	6,605	5,715	6,017	5,921	5,263
Other operating income (expenses)	(221)	(284)	(119)	(182)	(109)
Operating profit	6,384	5,431	5,898	5,739	5,154
Cost of net financial debt	78	115	101	140	151
Other financial income (expenses)	(336)	3,062	(97)	126	–91
Net financial income (expense)	(413)	2,947	(198)	(10)	(236)
Income taxes	1,969	2,273	1,753	1,820	1,453
Net profit before minority interests	4,001	6,105	3,947	3,909	3,465
Minority interests	428	457	511	485	400
Net profit	€3,573	€5,648	€3,436	€3,424	€3,065
Earnings per share, basic	€7.11	€11.27	€6.87	€6.86	€6.27
Earnings per share, diluted	€7.08	€11.21	€6.83	€6.82	€6.23

Source: LVMH annual reports.

control of LVMH with a combined ownership of 50 percent of outstanding shares. The new ownership structure also placed Hennessy heir and chair Alain Chevalier in the position of chair of LVMH while Vuitton family member and company president, Henry Racamier, became LVMH's director general.

The new company became France's 40th-largest company with total revenues in 1987 of FF 13.1 billion ($2.1 billion) and a portfolio of such well-known luxury brands as Veuve Clicquot, Moët & Chandon and Dom Pérignon champagnes, Hennessy cognac, Christian Dior and Givenchy perfumes and cosmetics, and Louis Vuitton leather handbags and luggage. On the day the merger was consummated, LVMH chair Alain Chevalier also signed an international distribution agreement with British brewer Guinness PLC to improve the distribution of the company's champagne and cognac brands in and the United States. The joint venture with Guinness called for both firms to acquire interlocking interests of about 10 percent of each company's shares and accounted for nearly one-fourth of LVMH and Guinness profits within the joint venture's first year.

The success of the LVMH–Guinness joint venture led Alain Chevalier to propose that Guinness purchase an additional 10 percent interest in LVMH to further protect the company from possible foreign raiders. The growing relative importance of the company's wine and champagne businesses and the proposal for increased ownership of LVMH shares by Guinness became worrisome to Racamier and other Vuitton family members who believed the company's core business should center on fashion and leather goods. To fortify the company's focus on haute couture, Racamier asked Bernard Arnault (the owner of Christian Dior, Celine, and Christian Lacroix brands) in mid-1988 to purchase shares of LVMH and join forces with Vuitton heirs in their disagreement with Chevalier.

Thirty-nine-year-old Bernard Arnault had only recently become known among France's business elite, since only four years before he was building condominiums in Florida for his family's modest real estate and construction firm. Arnault returned to France in 1984 and purchased nearly bankrupt Agache-Willot-Boussac—a state-owned conglomerate of retailing, fashion, and manufacturing. Arnault sold the assets of Agache-Willot-Boussac's poor performing businesses and retained its profitable businesses, of which Christian Dior was the most notable. Within three years the company had earned $112 million on revenues of $1.9 billion. In 1987, Arnault leveraged Christian Dior's cash flow to purchase Celine, a fashion and leather goods company and the launch of a new fashion brand headed by France's hottest young designer, Christian Lacroix.

Upon the invitation of LVMH Director General Racamier to become an LVMH shareholder, Arnault also met with LVMH chair Chevalier before forming a joint venture with Guinness PLC to purchase 37 percent of LVMH shares. Guinness was receptive to Arnault's proposal to form the joint venture since it assured the British company's management that its highly profitable distribution agreement with LVMH would remain intact, despite the feud between Hennessy and Vuitton clans. The joint venture provided Arnault with a 60 percent interest in the joint venture while Guinness held 40 percent and made Bernard Arnault the largest shareholder of LVMH by November 1988. After becoming LVMH's largest shareholder and asked of his intentions to bring about management changes at the company, Bernard Arnault commented that he approved of chair Chevalier's strategies, but "his problem is that he is not a major shareholder. In the businesses I manage, I'm the principal shareholder; and that helps me control the situation."[4]

Bernard Arnault became LVMH's president in January 1989 and chair in mid-1990 after prevailing in an 18-month legal battle with Henry Racamier, who had petitioned the court to invalidate a portion of Arnault's stake in LVMH. Upon becoming chair, Arnault launched an aggressive plan to transform LVMH into France's largest company. Arnault dismissed LVMH's top management; folded Dior, Celine, and Christian Lacroix into LVMH; and began making rapid acquisitions to expand the company's portfolio of luxury brands. Many French executives resented Arnault's business tactics and questioned his motives in becoming the head of LVMH, with an ex-LVMH officer calling Arnault "an asset shuffler, a raider, a French Donald Trump."[5]

LVMH UNDER BERNARD ARNAULT

When Bernard Arnault became president of LVMH in January 1989, the company was the world's leading luxury products group with revenues of FF 16.4 billion (approximately 2.5 billion euros) and net income of FF 2.0 billion (approximately

300 million euros) in 1988. The company's business portfolio included champagnes and wines; cognac and spirits; luggage, leather goods, and accessories; and perfumes and beauty products. LVMH's champagnes and wines business unit was the global leader in premium champagnes with some of the oldest and most prestigious brands in the world. Dom Pérignon was arguably the best-known brand of champagne, Ruinart was the world's oldest champagne company, and Mercier was France's best-selling brand of champagne. Moët & Chandon, Canard-Duchêne, Veuve Clicquot Ponsardin, and Henriot rounded out LVMH's portfolio of centuries-old champagne brands. LVMH's champagne and wine division also included the respected Napa Valley sparkling wine producer Domaine Chandon. LVMH's cognac and spirits business, like its champagnes and wines business unit, possessed two of the most prestigious brands worldwide with Hennessy and Hine—both founded in the mid-1700s and consistently recognized by connoisseurs for quality.

Louis Vuitton accounted for the largest share of LVMH's luggage, leather goods, and accessories division's sales with market-leading positions in luggage and travel accessories worldwide. Louis Vuitton's luggage had been popular since the mid-1800s when Vuitton's monogrammed products first became available to affluent travelers who visited his store. Loewe was a prestigious Spanish brand that earned the distinction of Supplier to the Royal Household in 1905 and had since become noted for fine ready-to-wear leather and textile apparel, handbags, and travel accessories. Loewe also marketed a fragrance line.

LVMH's perfumes and beauty products division was composed of three different houses: Parfums Christian Dior was internationally renowned for its quality, innovation, and prestige and was the leading prestige brand of fragrance in France. The brand was also among the fastest growing in the United States and held the number one position in Western Europe. Parfums Givenchy was among the most successful prestige brands in the United States and had extended its product line to include cosmetics in 1988.

LVMH's Rapid Growth under Bernard Arnault

LVMH's rapid portfolio diversification began shortly after Arnault gained a controlling percentage of company shares when it acquired Givenchy Couture in November 1988. LVMH's management had been working to unite its Parfums Givenchy with Givenchy Couture since 1987 and agreed on terms with Hubert de Givenchy just prior to Arnault becoming president of LVMH in January 1989. In 1990 Arnault purchased an additional interest in Loewe and purchased all assets of Pommery—the largest vineyard in the Champagne Province and producer of champagnes since 1860. Arnault's most ambitious target during 1990 was Guinness PLC. Arnault increased LVMH's share in Guinness from about 12 to 24 percent in what was suggested by outsiders as an attempt to make LVMH the world's largest alcoholic beverage seller with more $5.5 billion in sales and a vast international distribution network.

Arnault abandoned his quest to gain a controlling stake in Guinness in 1994 when Guinness management agreed to a stock swap between LVMH and the British brewer that netted LVMH $1.9 billion in cash. Arnault had initiated a few small acquisitions of fashion and spirits businesses between 1990 and 1994, but LVMH's $1.9 billion cash infusion that resulted from the Guinness stock swap allowed Arnault to pursue his pledge to shareholders that "We're going to buy more luxury companies" in cosmetics, perfume, fashion, and retailing.[6] Arnault initially focused on L'Oréal, a leading manufacturer and marketer of cosmetics with 1993 sales of $6 billion, and French drug manufacturer Sanofi, who bought Yves Saint-Laurent in 1993. However, neither company was acquired by LVMH, and Arnault brought additional fashion and fragrance brands to the company's portfolio and diversified outside of luxury goods with the purchase of three of France's leading financial and business publications—*Investir, La Tribune Desfosses,* and *L'Agefi.* Arnault also utilized the company's cash reserves to expand the number of company-owned retail stores where its Louis Vuitton and Loewe leather goods and Celine, Christian Dior, and Givenchy could be found.

Bernard Arnault believed that LVMH control of the retail channels where its products were sold was critical to the success of luxury brands. The use of company-owned retail locations allowed LVMH to not only make certain its products were of the highest quality and most elegant, but also allowed the company to ensure its products were sold by retailers offering the highest level of customer service. Arnault believed that ultimately the finer points of retailing impacted the overall image of luxury products as much as the products' attributes. This belief drove the company's moves into vertical integration into the operation of Louis Vuitton, Christian Dior, and other designer-label stores in Paris, New York, Beverly Hills, and other locations and also led to the $2.5 billion acquisition of DFS (Duty Free Shoppers) in 1996. San Francisco–based DFS operated a chain of 180 duty-free boutiques in

Asia and various international airports. Arnault saw DFS as an ideal acquisition candidate since the chain specialized in the sale of luxury goods to affluent international travelers and since its stores were concentrated in Asia. Asia was among LVMH's best geographic markets, accounting for as much as two-thirds of the sales of such products as Louis Vuitton luggage.

Arnault expanded further into retailing in 1997 with the acquisition of French cosmetics retailer Sephora and the purchase of a 30 percent interest in Douglas International, a German beauty-goods retailer with 190 stores in Europe and the United States. LVMH also expanded its line of fine champagnes in a 1997 acquisition of Château d'Yquem—a brand produced under such care and exacting standards that each vine yielded just one glass of champagne. Arnault again made an attempt to have LVMH become the world's largest wine and spirits producer and distributor when he spent $2.3 billion in 1997 to purchase 11 percent of Grand Metropolitan PLC—a British food conglomerate with $1.5 billion in annual wine and spirits sales. Arnault used the ownership position in Grand Met to insert himself into merger negotiations that were underway between Guinness and Grand Met. Arnault proposed an alternate merger scenario that would combine Guinness, Grand Met, and LVMH and make LVMH the controlling entity with a 35 percent stake in the three-way merger. Guinness and Grand Met shareholders rejected the proposal, but provided Arnault with a $400 million payoff to allow the two-way merger to proceed, an 11 percent interest in the new company, and a seat on its board of directors.

Arnault expanded LVMH's retailing operations beyond specialty retailing in 1998 with the acquisition of famous Parisian department stores La Belle Jardiniere and Le Bon Marché, but his boldest acquisition spree occurred during 1999 and 2000. During the two-year period, Arnault created a new watch and jewelry division with the purchase of TAG Heuer, Chaumet, and Zenith, and pushed the company into makeup artist quality cosmetics with the purchase of Bliss, Benefit, Make Up For Ever, and Fresh.

Arnault's buying binge also expanded the company's media operations with the addition of a French radio network and magazines targeted to music aficionados and art connoisseurs; added New World wine producers located in the United States and Australia; obtained new retail outlets for its products with the acquisition of an Italian cosmetics retailing chain and Starboard Cruise Services, which offered duty-free shopping aboard 100 cruise ships sailing in the Caribbean and elsewhere; and enhanced its line of champagnes with Krug—the producer of some of the world's most expensive champagnes. Arnault also added the fashion houses of Emilio Pucci, Thomas Pink, and Fendi.

Arnault had attempted to add Gucci to the company's impressive lineup of designer brands by purchasing more than 34 percent of the Italian fashion label's shares, but was thwarted by rival French conglomerate Pinault-Printemps-Redout (PPR) when it acquired 42 percent of Gucci shares. The battle for control of Gucci pitted France's two wealthiest men, LVMH's Arnault and PPR's Francois Pinault, against each other in a battle that would eventually be won by Pinault in 2001 but would provide Arnault with more than $1.8 billion for his stake in Gucci.

In 2002, Arnault launched a takeover run at Hermès with a series of secret cash-settled equity swaps that totaled 23.2 percent of Hermès shares by 2014. The equity swaps went unnoticed by Hermès family shareholders for eight years at which time Hermès heirs pursued Arnault and LVMH with criminal insider trading charges and also began purchasing shares to prevent a takeover of the company. Hermès heirs accumulated 50.2 percent of company shares by 2014, which ended the possibility of a voting majority by Arnault. Hermès CEO Axel Dumas, a sixth-generation Hermès family member, called it "the battle of my generation. . . . Hermès is not for sale, and we are going to fight to stay independent."[7] Arnault agreed to spin off the 23.2 percent interest in Hermès to LVMH shareholders in 2014 after LVMH had been fined $10 million by French regulators for violating securities disclosure regulations. Even though the settlement brokered in French civil courts ended Arnault's attempt to acquire Hermès, it provided LVMH with a $5 billion gain on its purchases of Hermès shares. The company's most noteworthy acquisitions after Arnault's takeover attempt of Hermès included Fendi in 2003; Glenmorangie in 2005; Belvedere in 2007; Hublot, Royal Van Lent, and Dior in 2009; and Bulgari in 2011.

In 2016, Bernard Arnault was ranked 14th on *Forbes*'s list of billionaires with a net worth of $36.7 billion. His wealth was primarily related to the Arnault family group's 46.6 percent ownership stake in LVMH. The ownership was structured through his 70 percent interest in Christian Dior, which owned a 40+ percent share of LVMH. Bernard Arnault also held a separate stake in LVMH of approximate 6 percent in LVMH. The Arnault family group controlled 62.9 percent of voting rights exercised at shareholders' meetings. The company had a market capitalization of €73.6 billion at year-end 2015 and had consistently outperformed the CAC 40 index of the largest public French companies since 2009.

A list of major LVMH's acquisitions between 1987 and 2016 is presented in Exhibit 2. The company's stock performance from 2006 through August 2016 is presented in Exhibit 3.

EXHIBIT 2 LVMH Acquisitions, 1987–2015

Year	Company Acquired	Principal Business
1987	Hine	Cognac production
1988	Givenchy	Haute couture, ready-to-wear fashions
1990	11.4% of Guinness Plc (United Kingdom)	Brewing and spirits production and distribution
	10.75% of Loewe SA (Spain)	Leather goods, fashion
	Pommery	Champagne production
1993	Christian Lacroix	Haute couture, ready-to-wear fashions
	Kenzo	Haute couture, ready-to-wear fashions/fragrances
	55% of Desfosses International	Media production, magazines, radio
1994	Outstanding 50% of *Investir*	Financial magazine
	49.99% of Djedi Holding (Guerlain)	Fragrances
1995	Further 41% of Fred Joillier	Haute couture, ready-to-wear fashions
	44% of Desfosses International	Media production, magazines, radio
1996	Further 76% of Loewe SA (Spain)	Leather goods, fashion
	Outstanding interest in Djedi Holding (Guerlain)	Fragrances
	54% of Celine SA	Haute couture, ready-to-wear fashions
	Remaining interest in Fred Joaillier	Haute couture, ready-to-wear fashions
	58.75% of DFS (USA)	Duty-free retail shops in Asia/Pacific, airports
	Remaining 46% of Celine	Haute couture, ready-to-wear fashions
1997	51% of Chateau d'Yquem	Champagne production
	Sephora	Cosmetics retailing
1998	Further 37% of Chateau d'Yquem	Champagne production
	Marie-Jeanne Godard	Fragrances
	Le Bon Marché	Parisian department store
	99% of La Belle Jardiniere	Parisian retailer
1999	Krug	Champagne production
	Bliss	Cosmetics production, health spas
	Benefit	Cosmetics production
	Increased interest to 64% in Chateau d'Yquem	Champagne production
	TAG Heuer	Watch design and assembly
	Thomas Pink	Haute couture, ready-to-wear fashions
	Ebel	Watch design and assembly
	Chaumet	Watch design and assembly
	Make Up For Ever	Cosmetics producer

(*Continued*)

Year	Company Acquired	Principal Business
	Zenith	Watch design and assembly, mechanism production
	Radio Classique & SID Editions	French radio stations, media
	72.5% interest in Phillips, de Pury & Luxembourg	Fine art auctioning
2000	Starboard Cruise Services	Duty-free cruiseline retailing
	67% of Emilio Pucci (Italy)	Haute couture, ready-to-wear fashions
	Omas (Italy)	Writing Instrument production
	Fresh	Cosmetics production
	60% of Newton Vineyards	Winery and vineyards
	Mountadam Vineyards	Winery and vineyards
	Art & Auction, Connaissance des Arts	Art magazines
2001	Majority interest in La Samaritaine	Parisian department store
	Donna Karan International	Apparel
	Acqua di Parma	Fragrances
2003	Rossimoda	Footwear
	Fendi	Fashion, leather
2005	Glenmorangie	Spirits
2007	*Les Echos*	Newspaper, media
	Belvedere	Spirits
	Wen Jun	Spirits (China)
2008	Numanthia Termes	Wines
	Hublot	Watches
	Royal Van Lent	Yacht production
	Dior	Apparel, fragrances
2009	Chateau Cheval Blanc	Wines
2011	Bulgari	Jewelry, watches, fragrances
	Investir	Magazine, media
2013	Cova Montenapoleone	Milan, Italy café
	Loro Piana	Fashion
	Nicholas Kirkwood	Fashion
2014	Domaine du Clos des Lambrays	Wines
2015	Luxola	Cosmetics

Sources: LVMH Annual Reports; various years; Extel Financial Limited Annual Card, April 24, 2002.

LVMH'S APPROACH TO BUILDING SHAREHOLDER VALUE IN LUXURY PRODUCTS BUSINESSES

LVMH's corporate strategy under Bernard Arnault included diversification into the sale of luxury products of varying types. The company's wines, champagnes, haute couture and ready-to-wear fashions, cosmetics, fragrances, watches, and jewelry were among the most innovative, prestigious, elegant, and expensive produced. The company's retailing division focused on the sale of luxury items—whether LVMH products or brands offered by rival producers. The company's other businesses included periodicals of interest to the financial and art communities, custom luxury yacht production, and fine hotels. LVMH's broad collection of businesses was grouped into six business units. Exhibit 4 presents LVMH's

EXHIBIT 3 Market Performance of LVMH's Common Stock, 2006–August 2016

(a) Trend in LVMH's Common Stock Price

(b) Performance of LVMH's Stock Price versus the Euronext Paris Exchange

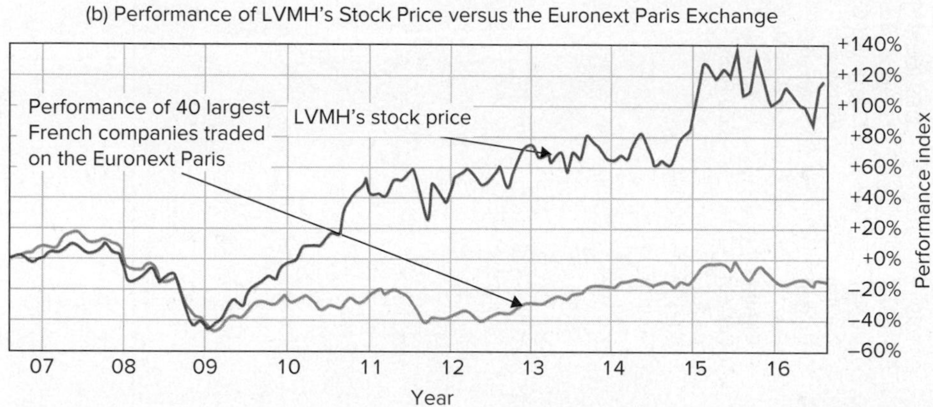

business portfolio in 2016. LVMH's performance by business group for 2014 and 2015 is presented in Exhibit 5. The company's balance sheets for 2014 and 2015 are presented in Exhibit 6. Exhibit 7 illustrates the company's free cash flows from operations for 2014 and 2015.

Wine and Spirits

The production of extraordinary class wine and champagne required considerable attention to detail and decades-long commitment to quality. For example, Château d'Yquem's vineyards were cultivated over generations and were made up of vines grown from individually selected seeds. Also, on nine occasions during the 20th century the winery rejected an entire harvest, viewing all grapes from the season as unworthy of the brand. Wine production also required technical expertise to develop techniques to improve the immune systems of vines to prevent grape diseases and the skills of master blenders, who selected combinations of grapes that would result in exceptional vintages. Not any less important was the time required to produce fine wines and champagnes, some of which were aged for several years prior to distribution. Distribution from production facilities to retail outlets was typically handled by either a subsidiary, joint venture, or third party.

In 2016 LVMH was the world's leading champagne producer with a 20.1 percent market share and sales volume of 61.4 million bottles in 2015. The company was also number one in the global cognac market with a 46.5 percent market share and sales

EXHIBIT 4 LVMH'S Business Portfolio in 2016

Wines and Spirits	Fashion and Leather Goods	Perfumes and Cosmetics	Watches and Jewelry	Selective Retailing	Other Activities
Moët & Chandon	Louis Vuitton	Parfums	TAG	DFS (Duty Free	Royal Van Lent luxury yachts
Dom Pérignon	Loewe	Christian Dior	Heuer	Shoppers)	Jardin d'Acclimation amusement
Veuve Clicquot	Celine	Guerlain	Hublot	Starboard Cruise	and leisure park
Krug	Berluti	Parfums	Zenith	Services	La Samaritaine department store
Mercier	Loro Piana	Givenchy	Bulgari	Sephora	renovation
Ruinart	Kenzo	Perfumes	Fred	Le Bon Marché	*Investir* financial publication
Château d'Yquem	Givenchy	Loewe	Chaumet	La Grande Epicerie	*Les Echos* daily newspaper
Domaine Chandon	Christian	Kenzo Parfums	LVMH/De	de Paris	*Connaissance des Arts* art
California	Dior	Fresh	Beers		magazine
Domine Chandon	Marc Jacobs	Benefit	joint		Cheval Blanc luxury hotels
Australia	Nicholas	Cosmetics	venture		Nowness art and culture video
Chandon Argentina	Kirkwood	Make Up For			channel
Cloudy Bay	Edun	Ever			
Cape Mentelle	Fendi	Acqua di			
Chandon do Brasil	Emilio Pucci	Parma			
Chandon China	Thomas Pink				
Hennessy	Donna Karan				
Newton					
Ardbeg					
Château Cheval					
Blanc					
Glenmorangie					
Wen Jun					
Bodegas Chandon					
Belvedere					
Numanthia					
Terrazas de los Andes					
Cheval des Andes					
10 Cane Rum					

Source: LVMH website.

EXHIBIT 5 LVMH's Performance by Business Group, 2014–2015 (in millions of euros)

Revenues	2015	2014
Wine & Spirits	€ 4,603	€ 3,973
Fashion & Leather Goods	12,369	10,828
Perfumes & Cosmetics	4,517	3,916
Watches & Jewelry	3,308	2,782
Selective Retailing	11,233	9,534
Other activities and eliminations	(366)	(395)
Total	€35,664	€30,638
Profit from Recurring Operations	**2015**	**2014**
Wine & Spirits	€ 1,363	€ 1,147
Fashion & Leather Goods	3,505	3,189
Perfumes & Cosmetics	525	415
Watches & Jewelry	432	283
Selective Retailing	934	882
Other activities and eliminations	(154)	(201)
Total	€ 6,605	€ 5,715
Operating Investments	**2015**	**2014**
Wine & Spirits	€ 233	€ 152
Fashion & Leather Goods	553	585
Perfumes & Cosmetics	229	221
Watches & Jewelry	204	191
Selective Retailing	399	389
Other activities and eliminations	337	237
Total	€ 1,955	€ 1,775
Depreciation and Amortization	**2015**	**2014**
Wine & Spirits	€ 132	€ 119
Fashion & Leather Goods	641	555
Perfumes & Cosmetics	183	149
Watches & Jewelry	199	171
Selective Retailing	366	296
Other activities and eliminations	42	41
Total	€ 1,563	€ 1,331

Source: LVMH 2015 Annual Report.

EXHIBIT 6 LVMH's Balance Sheets, 2014–2015 (in millions of euros)

Assets	2015	2014
Brands and other intangible assets	€13,572	€13,031
Goodwill	10,122	8,810
Property, plant and equipment	11,157	10,387
Investments in joint ventures and associates	729	519
Non-current available for sale financial assets	574	580
Other non-current assets	552	489
Deferred tax	1,945	1,436
Non-current assets	38,651	35,252
Inventories and work in progress	10,096	9,475
Trade accounts receivable	2,521	2,274
Income taxes	384	354
Other current assets	2,355	1,916
Cash and cash equivalents	3,594	4,091
Current assets	18,950	18,110
Total assets	€57,601	€53,362
Liabilities and Equity		
Share capital	€ 152	€ 152
Share premium account	2,579	2,655
Treasury shares and LVMH share-settled derivatives	(240)	(374)
Cumulative translation adjustment	1,137	492
Revaluation reserves	349	1,019
Other reserves	16,189	12,171
Net profit, Group share	3,573	5,648
Equity, Group share	24,339	21,763
Minority interests	1,460	1,240
Total equity	25,799	23,003
Long-term borrowings	4,511	5,054
Non-current provisions	1,950	2,291
Deferred tax	4,685	4,392
Other non-current liabilities	7,957	6,447
Non-current liabilities	19,103	18,184
Short-term borrowings	3,769	4,189
Trade accounts payable	3,960	3,606
Income taxes	640	549
Current provisions	421	332
Other current liabilities	3,909	3,499
Current liabilities	12,699	12,175
Total liabilities and equity	€57,601	€53,362

Source: LVMH 2015 Annual Report.

EXHIBIT 7 LVMH's Statements of Cash Flows, 2014–2015 (in millions of euros)

	2015	2014
Cash from operations before changes in working capital	€ 7,945	€ 7,080
Net interest paid	75	116
Income taxes paid	1,807	1,639
Working capital requirements	429	718
Operating investments	1,955	1,775
Free cash flow*	€ 3,679	€ 2,832

**Before available for sale financial assets and investments, transactions relating to equity and financing activities.*

Source: LVMH 2015 Annual Report.

volume of 76 million bottles in 2015. Ninety-four percent of LVMH's wine and spirits were sold outside of France. LVMH's still wine sales benefited from Moët-Hennessy's international distribution network and began to gain praise from connoisseurs beyond their domestic markets. The company's recent expansion into luxury spirits would also generate distribution synergies with wines and champagnes. Revenues for the division increased by nearly 18 percent between 2014 and 2015 as the result of favorable currency translation benefits; solid performance of its champagne and cognac brands in the United States, Europe, and Japan; and the efficiency of the company's international distribution network. In addition, the success of the company's recently acquired spirits brands—Genmorangie, Ardbeg, and Belvedere—contributed to the division's growth.

Fashion and Leather Goods

The fashion and leather industry entailed the recruitment of highly talented and creative designers who were able to create a line of apparel or accessories that appealed to some segment of consumers. Designers had considerable leeway with the direction of their designs since individual tastes and preferences varied considerably among consumers. Other important elements of creating high-end apparel and leather goods included the selection of fabrics or leather and the quality of construction. LVMH's Louis Vuitton products were all hand assembled by craftspeople who had trained for years perfecting their talents. Apparel and leather goods were distributed to either third-party retailers or company-owned retail locations.

LVMH's Louis Vuitton was the world's leading luxury brand and the foundation of LVMH's Fashion and Leather Goods division that had increased sales by 23 percent and operating income by nearly 12 percent between 2013 and 2015. LVMH's Fashion and Leather Goods division also included such prestigious brands as Kezno, Marc Jacobs, Berlucci, Thomas Pink, Pucci, Givenchy, Celine, Loro Biana, Kenzo, and Fendi. The group outpaced its key rivals as the Prada Group's sales declined by 1 percent during 2015, Hermès's sales grew by 18 percent, and Groupe Gucci's sales increased by 15 percent. France accounted for 9 percent of the division's sales.

Perfumes and Cosmetics

Success in the global cosmetics, fragrance, and skin care industry was largely attributable to the ability of producers to develop new combinations of chemicals and natural ingredients to create innovative and unique fragrances and develop cosmetics that boasted product benefits beyond cleansing and moisturizing to anti-aging, anti-pollution, and tissue regeneration. LVMH's fragrances, cosmetics, and skin care brands were among the world's most prestigious and innovative in their formulations. In addition to product innovation, LVMH's strategy for the division focused on heavy advertising and media investments, connection with its couture brands, and global expansion of its brands. The sales and operating profit of LVMH's perfumes and cosmetics division had grown by 22 and 27 percent, respectively, between 2013 and 2015.

The division's growth was attributed to its iconic French fragrances such as *Miss Dior* and *J'adore* by Christian Dior and because of its hit new fragrances such as its men's fragrance *Sauvage* and its recently acquired brands such as Acqua di Parma. The division also benefited from the popularity of its Dior and Guerlain skin care products and cosmetics and relatively new American cosmetics brands such as Benefit, Fresh, and Make Up For Ever, and the success of its Sephora retail cosmetics operations. Sephora's network of stores located in Europe, the United States, and Japan carried LVMH's perfumes and cosmetics brands, which were also sold by prestigious retailers around the world. Even though LVHM's perfumes and cosmetics division had recorded impressive growth rates, its sales were only about one-sixth that of industry leader L'Oréal. Approximately 88 percent of the division's sales were outside of France.

Watches and Jewelry

The watch and jewelry industry was much like the fashion and cosmetics and fragrances industries in that it was highly fragmented with multiple product categories and wide-ranging price points. The upscale segment of the industry also reflected the fashion industry's demand for quality and creative or distinctive designs. The producers of many exquisite timepieces such as Rolex, Cartier, and Patek Phillipe maintained long-established lines not only known for style, but also craftsmanship and accuracy. Most manufacturers of upmarket watches also added new models from time to time that were consistent with the company's tradition, history, and style. Watch production involved the development and production of the movement (although many watch manufacturers purchased movements from third-party suppliers), case design and fabrication, and assembly. Watches were rarely sold by manufacturers directly to consumers, but were usually distributed to independent jewelers or large upscale department stores for retail sale to consumers.

LVMH's watch and jewelry division was established in 1999 with the acquisitions of TAG Heuer, Chaumet, and Zenith. LVMH launched a joint venture with De Beers to market solitaire diamonds in 2001 and the Hublot and Bulgari brands were added in 2008 and 2011, respectively. The Bulgari brand to set sales records in 2015 with extensions of its classic *Serpenti* collection and the development of new *Diva* and *Lucea* collections. The division's strategy focused on creativity and product innovation along with expert craftsmanship. The company retrenched its TAG Heuer brand to its core lines like *Formula 1, Aquaracer,* and *Carrera* after several new watch styles had failed to succeed in the marketplace. The company's Zenith *El Primero* automatic chronograph had been an icon since its introduction in 1962 and was considered by many watch aficionados to be the best automatic chronograph in its price range. In fact, the automatic chronograph movement utilized in its *El Primero* also equipped the Rolex *Daytona* and other fine Swiss chronographs.

The division recorded a sales increase of nearly 23 percent between 2013 and 2015. However, its operating profits had fluctuated from €367 million in 2013 to €283 million in 2014, to €432 million in 2015. Only 7 percent of LVMH's sales of watches and jewelry originated from France.

Selective Retailing

LVMH's selective retailing division was made up of DFS and Starboard Cruise Services duty-free stores, the Le Bon Marché department store, and Sephora cosmetics stores. The division also operated upscale Galleria shopping malls located in downtown areas of major air destinations primarily in the Asia-Pacific region. LVMH's Gallerias featured DFS stores, Sephora, and designer boutiques such as Louis Vuitton, Hermès, CHANEL, Prada, Fendi, Celine, Bulgari, and Tiffany. Le Bon Marché was Paris's most exclusive department store and Sephora was among the leading retail beauty chains in Europe and North America. The company was rapidly expanding the Sephora retail chain across the developed world with nearly 100 new stores opened in 2015 in Australia, Southeast Asia, and the Middle East. Sephora carried LVMH's products and other prestigious brands of cosmetics, fragrances, and skin care products including CHANEL, Dolce and Gabbana, Elizabeth Arden, Hugo Boss, Naomi Campbell, Gianni Versace, and Burberry.

The division's 2001 sales grew by nearly 18 percent during 2015 and 7 percent in 2014. The division's operating profits had fluctuated from €908 million in 2013, to €882 in 2014, to €934 in 2015. In addition, the division was relatively capital intensive with annual operating investments accounting for 40 percent or more of its annual operating profits.

Other Activities

LVMH also maintained a business unit made up of media, luxury yacht production, a leisure park, and a luxury hotel chain. LVMH believed the businesses were important elements of its business portfolio because of the company's obligation to be an ambassador for culture and because of the natural linkage between its luxury brands and *l'art de vivre* (translated as "the art of living.") The newest member of LVMH's media lineup was *Nowness*—a video channel dedicated to art, culture, fashion, music, food, and travel. Other media properties included *Investir,* France's leading online and print daily investment publication; Radio Classique's network of radio stations across France that attracted 600,000 listeners per day; *Connaissance des Arts* that was a benchmark art publication; and *Les Echos,* a leading French daily newspaper.

Jardin D'Acclimation was France's first leisure and amusement park that opened in 1860 and included historic amusement rides, a miniature steam-powered train, walking trails, and sitting areas. LVMH began the Cheval Blanc hotel chain in 2006, which offered guests the most luxurious accommodations along with world-class services tailored to the individual requests of each guest. In 2016, LVMH operated Cheval Blanc hotels in Courchevel, Maldives, and Saint Barthelemy in the Caribbean. The fourth Cheval Blanc was scheduled to open in late 2016 and would be attached to La Samaritaine in Paris. La Samaritaine was a former iconic department store dating to 1870 that had fallen into disrepair and was owned by LVMH. The company was engaged in a massive renovation of the 860,000-square-foot facility that would again make it among the finest department stores in Paris's historic city center. In addition to shopping space, the renovation would include the adjoining Cheval Blanc hotel, a DFS emporium, a flagship Louis Vuitton store, office space, 96 residential apartments, a day-care center, and a restaurant. The grand reopening was scheduled for late 2016.

The remaining business included in LVMH's Other Activities was Royal Van Lent. The Dutch yacht maker dated to 1849 and built only custom-designed yachts larger than 50 meters. The massive luxury yachts were sold under the Feadship brand name and were among the most elegant in the Mediterranean and the Caribbean. *Ocean Victory,* a private yacht built by Royal Van Lent, was the third most expensive yacht sold in the world in 2014 with a sales price of $120 million. Feadship considered its $125 million Ecstasea built in 2004 as one of its most distinguishable yachts and its hybrid-powered 274-foot Savannah yacht among its most innovative. The Savannah was delivered to a Swedish billionaire in 2015 who paid an estimated $100 million for the vessel. Despite the high sales prices of Feadship yachts, LVMH's Other Activities recorded operating losses in 2014 and 2015 and had never earned a profit in the company's history.

LVMH'S CORPORATE STRATEGY

Although much of LVMH's growth was attributable to the acquisition of new businesses, Arnault placed an emphasis on internal growth by exploiting common strategies and capturing synergies across the portfolio. While the company organizational structure and operating principles ensured that each business was autonomous, Arnault demanded that each of the corporation's businesses demonstrate commitment to creativity and innovation and product excellence. The long-term success of LVMH's brands, in Arnault's view, was largely a function of artistic creativity, technological innovation, and the closest attention to every detail of the production process.

The image and reputation of the company's products were seen as equal to the creativity and craftsmanship employed during the development and production of LVMH luxury goods since image was a product dimension that defied logic, but caused consumers to have strong desires for a particular brand. Arnault believed that image was priceless and irreplaceable and required stringent management control over every element of a brand's image, including advertisements, corporate announcements, and speeches by management and designers.

Control over the distribution and sale of its products was the final element of LVMH's corporate strategy and allowed its divisions to listen to customer needs, better understand their tastes, and anticipate their desires. LVMH's ownership of more than 1,500 retail locations in developed countries throughout the world also allowed the company to refine its brand's images with controlled store aesthetics, a consistent retailing approach, and irreproachable customer service.

Bernard Arnault discussed LVMH's strategic approach to managing its portfolio of star and rising star brands in an interview with *Harvard Business Review:*[8]

> ***Product Quality***
>
> Quality also comes from hiring very dedicated people and then keeping them for a long time. We try to keep the people at the brands, especially the artisans—the seamstresses and other people who make the products—because they have the brand in their bones.
>
> ***Innovation***
>
> Fashion comes from innovation—the creativity of the designers. That is sometimes harder to guarantee than quality, but just as important.
>
> If you think and act like a typical manager around creative people—with rules, policies, data on customer preferences, and so forth—you will quickly kill their talent. Our whole business is based on giving our artists and designers complete freedom to invent without limits.
>
> ***Image***
>
> Without growth, it is not a star brand, as far as I am concerned. Growth is [mainly] a function of high desire. Customers must want the product. That sounds simple, I am sure, but to get advertising right is very, very difficult.
>
> ***Craftsmanship and the Production Process***
>
> If you walk into a Vuitton factory, you will see very few machines. Almost every piece is made by hand. . . . We give our craftsmen and women fantastic training . . . and that allows us to offer a very high quality product at a cost that makes our business very profitable.

LVMH's Performance in 2016

Going into the last half of 2016, LVMH's performance had slowed from 2015 with revenue and operating profit achieving 3 and 4 percent year-over-year increases, respectively. The strongest contributors to the sales and operating profit gains included its wine and spirits division, with a revenue increase of 7 percent and operating profit increase of 17 during the first six months of 2016. The division's cognacs performed especially well with volume gains of 13 percent. The sales of its perfumes and cosmetics increased by 5 percent during the first six months of 2016 as Parfums Christian Dior products *J'Adore, Miss Dior,* and *Sauvage* continued as top-sellers and the new foundation *Forever* and *Dior Addict* lipstick achieved good international performance. In addition, the company's newer cosmetics lines, Fresh, Benefit, and Make Up For Ever all achieved good starts to 2016. Operating profit for the division increased by 9 percent during the first six months of 2016.

The revenues of LVMH's fashion and leather goods products declined by 1 percent during the first half of 2016 as terrorism across Europe greatly affected tourism in the region. In addition, the company had entered into an agreement to divest is long-struggling Donna Karan business by early 2017 for $650 million. Donna Karan became known worldwide during the late 1980s as her sophisticated business suits became a hit with executive women and her DKNY casual wear obtained a dedicated following among urban women for after-business attire. But as early as 1996, Donna Karan International began to lose favor with upscale consumers and began to lose prestigious retail accounts like Neiman Marcus when DKNY liquidated its growing inventories to discounter T.J.Maxx. The brand was never able to recover and achieve the rising star status envisioned by Bernard Arnault.

The company's watches and jewelry division experienced a 4 percent revenue increase and no change in operating profit during the first six months of 2016 as the TAG Heuer refocusing strategy began to produce results and Bulgari sales exceeded management's expectations. Even though Selective Retailing sales grew by 4 percent during the first six months of 2016, division operating profit declined by 5 percent. The company planned to expand its Galleria in Macao, open a Galleria in Cambodia, and open new Sephora flagship stores in Boston and Paris by year-end 2016. The company's Other Activities recorded a €123 million loss during the first six months of 2016 compared to a €75 million loss during the first half of 2015.

LVMH's revenues, operating profits, and free cash flows had produced attractive returns for shareholders and had made Bernard Arnault the world's 14th wealthiest person. However, some investors questioned the impact of LVMH's businesses outside its core on shareholder value. The mix of businesses included in the Other Activities division shared the purpose of "bringing together people who share a passion for lifestyle, culture, and the arts,"[9] but it was unclear how the businesses benefited LVMH shareholders. The Other Actvities division had never earned an operating profit and required substantial annual operating investments.

Investors and analysts had called for the divestiture of nonperforming LVMH brands almost since the early 2000s, but with the exception of the divestiture of Omas pens and the sale of the company's art auctioning houses, Arnault had not been sympathetic to such opinions. He had long dismissed suggestions that the company should consider the sale of DFS, Star Cruise Services, Le Bon Marché, La Samaritaine, and Sephora. A Merrill Lynch luxury goods analyst likened Arnault's penchant for acquisitions to that of a collector of fine art (which Arnault was) by observing, "Arnault has rarely sold anything."[10] An ABN Ambro analyst characterized Arnault as "not a man who likes to admit he has been wrong on a number of occasions . . . so the disposal process may be slow."[11]

ENDNOTES

[1] As quoted in "The Perfect Paradox of Star Brands: An Interview with Bernard Arnault of LVMH," *Harvard Business Review* 79, no. 9 (October 2001), p. 116.

[2] Ibid.

[3] Ibid.

[4] As quoted in "Pivotal Figure Emerges in Moet-Vuitton Feud," *The New York Times,* September 19, 1988, p. D1.

[5] Both quotes from "Bernard Arnault Is Building a Huge Empire—But Can He Manage It?" *BusinessWeek,* July 30, 1990, p. 48.

[6] As quoted in "Arnault Is Shopping," *BusinessWeek,* February 7, 1994, p. 44.

[7] Susan Adams, "Hermès and LVMH Make Peace," *Forbes,* September 11, 2014.

[8] As quoted in Suzy Welaufer, "The Perfect Paradox of Star Brands: An Interview with Bernard Arnault of LVMH," *Harvard Business Review,* October 2001.

[9] As quoted at **www.lvmh.com/houses/other-activities.**

[10] As quoted in "Retailing Is 'Non-core' for LVMH, Says Arnault," *Financial Times,* November 21, 2001, Section: Companies and Finance Europe, p. 30.

[11] As quoted in "LVMH's Auction House Sale Reflects Troubles," *The Daily Deal,* February 21, 2001.

CASE 23

Robin Hood

connect

Joseph Lampel
Alliance Manchester Business School

It was in the spring of the second year of his insurrection against the High Sheriff of Nottingham that Robin Hood took a walk in Sherwood Forest. As he walked, he pondered the progress of the campaign, the disposition of his forces, the Sheriff's recent moves, and the options that confronted him.

The revolt against the Sheriff had begun as a personal crusade. It erupted out of Robin's conflict with the Sheriff and his administration. However, alone Robin Hood could do little. He therefore sought allies, men with grievances and a deep sense of justice. Later he welcomed all who came, asking few questions and demanding only a willingness to serve. Strength, he believed, lay in numbers.

He spent the first year forging the group into a disciplined band, united in enmity against the Sheriff and willing to live outside the law. The band's organization was simple. Robin ruled supreme, making all important decisions. He delegated specific tasks to his lieutenants. Will Scarlett was in charge of intelligence and scouting. His main job was to shadow the Sheriff and his men, always alert to their next move. He also collected information on the travel plans of rich merchants and tax collectors. Little John kept discipline among the men and saw to it that their archery was at the high peak that their profession demanded. Scarlett took care of the finances, converting loot to cash, paying shares of the take, and finding suitable hiding places for the surplus. Finally, Much the Miller's son had the difficult task of provisioning the ever-increasing band of Merry Men.

The increasing size of the band was a source of satisfaction for Robin, but also a source of concern. The fame of his Merry Men was spreading, and new recruits were pouring in from every corner of England. As the band grew larger, their small bivouac became a major encampment. Between raids the men milled about, talking and playing games. Vigilance was in decline, and discipline was becoming harder to enforce. "Why," Robin reflected, "I don't know half the men I run into these days."

The growing band was also beginning to exceed the food capacity of the forest. Game was becoming scarce, and supplies had to be obtained from outlying villages. The cost of buying food was beginning to drain the band's financial reserves at the very moment when revenues were in decline. Travelers, especially those with the most to lose, were now giving the forest a wide berth. This was costly and inconvenient to them, but it was preferable to having all their goods confiscated.

Robin believed that the time had come for the Merry Men to change their policy of outright confiscation of goods to one of a fixed transit tax. His lieutenants strongly resisted this idea. They were proud of the Merry Men's famous motto: "Rob the rich and give to the poor." "The farmers and the townspeople," they argued, "are our most important allies. How can we tax them, and still hope for their help in our fight against the Sheriff?"

Robin wondered how long the Merry Men could keep to the ways and methods of their early days. The Sheriff was growing stronger and becoming better organized. He now had the money and the men and was beginning to harass the band, probing for its weaknesses. The tide of events was beginning to turn against the Merry Men. Robin felt that the campaign must be decisively concluded before the Sheriff had a chance to deliver a mortal blow. "But how," he wondered, "could this be done?"

Robin had often entertained the possibility of killing the Sheriff, but the chances for this seemed increasingly remote. Besides, killing the Sheriff might satisfy his personal thirst for revenge, but it would not improve the situation. Robin had hoped that the perpetual state of unrest and the Sheriff's failure to collect taxes would lead to his removal from office. Instead, the Sheriff used his political connections to obtain reinforcement. He had powerful friends at court and was well regarded by the regent, Prince John.

Prince John was vicious and volatile. He was consumed by his unpopularity among the people, who wanted the imprisoned King Richard back. He also lived in constant fear of the barons, who had first given him the regency but were now beginning to dispute his claim to the throne. Several of these barons had set out to collect the ransom that would release King Richard the Lionheart from his jail in Austria. Robin was invited to join the conspiracy in return for future amnesty. It was a dangerous proposition. Provincial banditry was one thing, court intrigue another. Prince John had spies everywhere, and he was known for his vindictiveness. If the conspirators' plan failed, the pursuit would be relentless and retributions swift.

The sound of the supper horn startled Robin from his thoughts. There was the smell of roasting venison in the air. Nothing was resolved or settled. Robin headed for camp promising himself that he would give these problems his utmost attention after tomorrow's raid.

CASE 24

Dilemma at Devil's Den

Allan R. Cohen
Babson College

Kim Johnson
Babson College

My name is Susan, and I'm a business student at Mt. Eagle College. Let me tell you about one of my worst experiences. I had a part-time job in the campus snack bar, The Devil's Den. At the time, I was 21 years old and a junior with a concentration in finance. I originally started working at the Den in order to earn some extra spending money. I had been working there for one semester and became upset with some of the happenings. The Den was managed by contract with an external company, College Food Services (CFS). What bothered me was that many employees were allowing their friends to take free food, and the employees themselves were also taking food in large quantities when leaving their shifts. The policy was that employees could eat whatever they liked free of charge while they were working, but it had become common for employees to leave with food and not to be charged for their snacks while off duty as well.

I felt these problems were occurring for several reasons. For example, employee wages were low, there was easy access to the unlocked storage room door, and inventory was poorly controlled. Also, there was weak supervision by the student managers and no written rules or strict guidelines. It seemed that most of the employees were enjoying freebies, and it had been going on for so long that it was taken for granted. The problem got so far out of hand that customers who had seen others do it felt free to do it whether they knew the workers or not. The employees who witnessed this never challenged anyone because, in my opinion, they did not care and they feared the loss of friendship or being frowned upon by others. Apparently, speaking up was more costly to the employees than the loss of money to CFS for the unpaid food items. It seemed obvious to me that the employees felt too secure in their jobs and did not feel that their jobs were in jeopardy.

The employees involved were those who worked the night shifts and on the weekends. They were students at the college and were under the supervision of another student, who held the position of manager. There were approximately 30 student employees and 6 student managers on the staff. During the day there were no student managers; instead, a full-time manager was employed by CFS to supervise the Den. The employees and student managers were mostly freshmen and sophomores, probably because of the low wages, inconvenient hours (late weeknights and weekends), and the duties of the job itself. Employees were hard to come by; the high rate of employee turnover indicated that the job qualifications and the selection process were minimal.

The student managers were previous employees chosen by other student managers and the full-time CFS day manager on the basis of their ability to work and on their length of employment. They received no further formal training or written rules beyond what they had already learned by working there. The student managers were briefed on how to close the snack bar at night but still did not get the job done properly. They received authority and responsibility over events occurring during their

shifts as manager, although they were never actually taught how and when to enforce it! Their increase in pay was small, from a starting pay of just over minimum wage to an additional 15 percent for student managers. Regular employees received an additional nickel for each semester of employment.

Although I only worked seven hours per week, I was in the Den often as a customer and saw the problem frequently. I felt the problem was on a large enough scale that action should have been taken, not only to correct any financial loss that the Den might have experienced but also to help give the student employees a true sense of their responsibilities, the limits of their freedom, respect for rules, and pride in their jobs. The issues at hand bothered my conscience, although I was not directly involved. I felt that the employees and customers were taking advantage of the situation whereby they could "steal" food almost whenever they wanted. I believed that I had been brought up correctly and knew right from wrong, and I felt that the happenings in the Den were wrong. It wasn't fair that CFS paid for others' greediness or urges to show what they could get away with in front of their friends.

I was also bothered by the lack of responsibility of the managers to get the employees to do their work. I had seen the morning employees work very hard trying to do their jobs, in addition to the jobs the closing shift should have done. I assumed the night managers did not care or think about who worked the next day. It bothered me to think that the morning employees were suffering because of careless employees and student managers from the night before.

I had never heard of CFS mentioning any problems or taking any corrective action; therefore, I wasn't sure whether they knew what was going on, or if they were ignoring it. I was speaking to a close friend, Mack, a student manager at the Den, and I mentioned the fact that the frequently unlocked door to the storage room was an easy exit through which I had seen different quantities of unpaid goods taken out. I told him about some specific instances and said that I believed that it happened rather frequently. Nothing was ever said to other employees about this, and the only corrective action was that the door was locked more often, yet the key to the lock was still available upon request to all employees during their shifts.

Another lack of strong corrective action I remembered was when an employee was caught pocketing cash from the register. The student was neither suspended nor threatened with losing his job (nor was the event even mentioned). Instead, he was just told to stay away from the register. I felt that this weak punishment happened not because he was a good worker but because he worked so many hours and it would be difficult to find someone who would work all those hours and remain working for more than a few months. Although a customer reported the incident, I still felt that management should have taken more corrective action.

The attitudes of the student managers seemed to vary. I had noticed that one in particular, Bill, always got the job done. He made a list of each small duty that needed to be done, such as restocking, and he made sure the jobs were divided among the employees and finished before his shift was over. Bill also stared down employees who allowed thefts by their friends or who took freebies themselves; yet I had never heard of an employee being challenged verbally, nor had anyone ever been fired for these actions. My friend Mack was concerned about theft, or so I assumed, because he had taken some action about locking the doors, but he didn't really get after employees to work if they were slacking off.

I didn't think the rest of the student managers were good motivators. I noticed that they did little work themselves and did not show much control over the employees. The student managers allowed their friends to take food for free, thereby setting bad examples for the other workers, and allowed the employees to take what they wanted even when they were not working. I thought their attitudes were shared by most of the other employees: not caring about their jobs or working hard, as long as they got paid and their jobs were not threatened.

I had let the "thefts" continue without mention because I felt that no one else really cared and may even have frowned on me for trying to take action. Management thus far had not reported significant losses to the employees so as to encourage them to watch for theft and prevent it. Management did not threaten employees with job loss, nor did they provide employees with supervision. I felt it was not my place to report the theft to management, because I was just an employee and I would be overstepping the student managers. Also, I was unsure whether management would do anything about it anyway—maybe they did not care. I felt that talking to the student managers or other employees would be useless, because they were either abusing the rules themselves or clearly aware of what was going on and just ignored it. I felt that others may have frowned on me and made it uncomfortable for me to continue working there. This would be very difficult for me, because I wanted to become a student manager the next semester and did not want to create any waves that might have prevented me from doing so. I recognized the student manager position as a chance to gain some managerial and leadership skills, while at the same time adding a great plus to my résumé when I graduated. Besides, as a student manager, I would be in a better position to do something about all the problems at the Den that bothered me so much.

What could I do in the meantime to clear my conscience of the freebies, favors to friends, and employee snacks? What could I do without ruining my chances of becoming a student manager myself someday? I hated just keeping quiet, but I didn't want to make a fool of myself. I was really stuck.

CASE 25

Southwest Airlines in 2016: Culture, Values, and Operating Practices

connect

Arthur A. Thompson
The University of Alabama

John E. Gamble
Texas A&M University–Corpus Christi

In 2016, Southwest Airlines was the world's second-largest airline in terms of total passengers boarded (144.6 million in 2015), trailing only Delta Air Lines, which boarded just over 180 million passengers in 2015 (counting those on flights operated by Delta's regional and international joint venture partners). However, based on the most recent data available from the U.S. Department of Transportation, the number of originating domestic passengers boarding Southwest flights exceeded those of Delta and its other two biggest rivals—American Airlines and United Airlines (see Exhibit 1). Southwest also had the enviable distinction of being the only major air carrier in the world that had been profitable for 43 consecutive years (1973–2015). In 2015, Southwest was named to *Fortune*'s list of the World's Most Admired Companies for the 22nd consecutive year, coming in at number seven.

From humble beginnings in 1971 as a scrappy underdog with quirky practices that once flew mainly to "secondary" airports (rather than high-traffic airports like Chicago O'Hare, Los Angeles International, Dallas–Fort Worth International, and Hartsfield–Jackson International Airport in Atlanta), Southwest had climbed up through the industry ranks to become a major competitive force in the domestic segment of the U.S. airline industry. It had weathered industry downturns, dramatic increases in the price of jet fuel, cataclysmic falloffs in airline traffic due to terrorist attacks and economy-wide recessions, and fare wars and other attempts by rivals to undercut its business, all the while adding more and more flights to more and more airports. The number of passengers flying Southwest had increased from 72.6 million in 2000 to 144.6 million in 2015. At year-end 2015, Southwest had a fleet of 704 Boeing 737 aircraft serving 97 destinations in 40 states, the District of Columbia, Puerto Rico, Mexico, Costa Rica, Belize, Jamaica, the Bahamas, Aruba, and the Dominican Republic. Southwest planned to begin flights to Cuba in 2016, if approved by the U.S. Department of Transportation.

In 2015, Southwest earned record after-tax profits of $2.2 billion on revenues of $19.8 billion, easily surpassing the 2014 record after-tax profits of $1.2 billion on revenues of $18.6 billion. In May 2016, Southwest's board of directors authorized a $2.0 billion share repurchase program (on top of a recently completed $1.5 billion share repurchase program announced in May 2015) and increased the quarterly dividend to $0.10 per share starting June 2016, up from $0.075 per share (starting in June 2015) and $0.06 per share in 2014. The June 2016 dividend payment marked the 159th consecutive quarter Southwest had paid a dividend to shareholders.

COMPANY BACKGROUND

In late 1966, Rollin King, a San Antonio entrepreneur who owned a small commuter air service, marched into Herb Kelleher's law office with a plan to start a low-cost/low-fare airline that would shuttle passengers between San Antonio, Dallas, and Houston.[1] Over the years, King had heard many Texas business executives complain about the length of time that it took to drive between the three cities and the

EXHIBIT 1 Total Number of Domestic and International Passengers Traveling on Selected U.S. Airlines, 2000, 2005, 2010, 2013–2015 (in thousands)

Carrier	Total Number of Enplaned Passengers (including both passengers paying for tickets and passengers traveling on frequent flyer awards)					
	2000	2005	2010	2013	2014	2015
American Airlines (see Note 1)						
Domestic	68,319	77,297	65,774	65,070	66,384	93,280
International	17,951	20,710	20,424	19,962	24,444	25,010
Total	86,270	98,007	86,198	85,032	87,828	118,290
Delta Air Lines (see Note 2)						
Domestic	97,965	77,581	90,141	98,590	106,220	114,904
International	7,596	8,359	19,390	18,925	21,798	22,828
Total	105,561	85,940	109,531	117,515	128,018	137,732
Southwest Airlines (see Note 3)						
Domestic	**72,568**	**88,436**	**106,270**	**115,323**	**126,695**	**142,408**
International	**—**	**—**	**—**	**—**	**500**	**2,167**
Total	**72,568**	**88,436**	**106,270**	**115,323**	**127,195**	**144,575**
United Airlines (see Note 4)						
Domestic	72,450	55,173	43,323	65,221	64,668	69,179
International	10,625	10,356	9,727	22,209	25,203	25,713
Total	83,075	65,529	53,050	87,430	89,871	94,892

Note 1: American Airlines and US Airways merged in December 2013, but continued to operate under their separate names through 2014. Previously, US Airways had merged with America West in September 2005.
Note 2: Delta Air Lines and Northwest Airlines merged in October 2008; however, combined reporting did not begin until 2010.
Note 3: Southwest Airlines acquired AirTran in late 2010; starting in 2013 and continuing into 2014, AirTran flights were rebranded as Southwest Airlines flights. Southwest's first international flights began when some of AirTran's international flights were rebranded as Southwest flights in 2013.
Note 4: United Airlines acquired Continental Airlines in 2010, and the two companies began joint reporting of passenger traffic in 2012. Prior to 2012, traffic count data are only for United flights.

Source: U.S. Department of Transportation, Bureau of Transportation Statistics, Air Carrier Statistics, Form T-100.

expense of flying the airlines currently serving these cities. His business concept for the airline was simple: Attract passengers by flying convenient schedules, get passengers to their destination on time, make sure they have a good experience, and charge fares competitive with travel by automobile. Kelleher, skeptical that King's business idea was viable, dug into the possibilities during the next few weeks and concluded a new airline was feasible; he agreed to handle the necessary legal work and also to invest $10,000 of his own funds in the venture.

In 1967, Kelleher filed papers to incorporate the new airline and submitted an application to the Texas Aeronautics Commission for the new company to begin serving Dallas, Houston, and San Antonio.[2] But rival airlines in Texas pulled every string they could to block the new airline from commencing operations, precipitating a contentious four-year parade of legal and regulatory proceedings. Kelleher led the fight on the company's behalf, eventually prevailing in June 1971 after winning two appeals to the Texas Supreme Court and a favorable ruling from

U.S. Supreme Court. Kelleher recalled, "The constant proceedings had gradually come to enrage me. There was no merit to our competitors' legal assertions. They were simply trying to use their superior economic power to squeeze us dry so we would collapse before we ever got into business. I was bound and determined to show that Southwest Airlines was going to survive and was going into operation."[3]

In January 1971, Lamar Muse was brought in as the CEO to get operations underway. Muse was an aggressive and self-confident airline veteran who knew the business well and who had the entrepreneurial skills to tackle the challenges of building the airline from scratch and then competing head-on with the major carriers. Through private investors and an initial public offering of stock in June 1971, Muse raised $7 million in new capital to purchase planes and equipment and provide cash for startup. Boeing agreed to supply three new 737s from its inventory, discounting its price from $5 million to $4 million and financing 90 percent of the $12 million deal. Muse was able to recruit a talented senior staff that included a number of veteran executives from other carriers. He particularly sought out people who were innovative, wouldn't shirk from doing things differently or unconventionally, and were motivated by the challenge of building an airline from scratch. Muse wanted his executive team to be willing to think like mavericks and not be lulled into instituting practices at Southwest that imitated what was done at other airlines.

Southwest's Struggle to Gain a Market Foothold

In June 1971, Southwest initiated its first flights with a schedule that soon included 6 roundtrips between Dallas and San Antonio and 12 roundtrips between Houston and Dallas. But the introductory $20 one-way fares to fly the Golden Triangle, well below the $27 and $28 fares charged by rivals, attracted disappointingly small numbers of passengers. To try to gain market visibility and drum up more passengers, Southwest undertook some creative actions to supplement its ad campaigns publicizing its low fares:

- Southwest decided to have its flight attendants dress in colorful hot pants and white knee-high boots with high heels. Recruiting ads for Southwest's first group of attendants headlined "Attention, Raquel Welch: You can have a job if you measure up." Two thousand applicants responded and those selected for interviews were asked to come dressed in hot pants to show off their legs—the company wanted to hire long-legged beauties with sparkling personalities. Over 30 of Southwest's first graduating class of 40 flight attendants consisted of young ladies who were cheerleaders and majorettes in high school and thus had experience performing skimpily dressed in front of people.
- A second attention-getting action was to give passengers free alcoholic beverages during daytime flights. Most passengers on these flights were business travelers. Management's thinking was that many passengers did not drink during the daytime and that with most flights being less than an hour's duration it would be cheaper to simply give the drinks away rather than collect the money
- Taking a cue from being based at Dallas Love Field, Southwest began using the tagline "Now There's Somebody Else Up There Who Loves You." The routes between Houston, Dallas, and San Antonio became known as the Love Triangle. Southwest's planes were referred to as Love Birds, drinks became Love Potions, peanuts were called Love Bites, drink coupons were Love Stamps, and tickets were printed on Love Machines. The "love" campaign set the tone for Southwest's approach to its customers and company efforts to make flying Southwest Airlines an enjoyable, fun, and differentiating experience. (Later, when the company went public, it chose LUV as its stock-trading symbol.)
- In order to add more flights without buying more planes, the head of Southwest's ground operations came up with a plan for ground crews to off-load passengers and baggage, refuel the plane, clean the cabin and restock the galley, on-load passengers and baggage, do the necessary pre-flight checks and paperwork, and push away from the gate in 10 minutes. The 10-minute turnaround became one of Southwest's signatures during the 1970s and 1980s. (In later years, as passenger volume grew and many flights were filled to capacity, the turnaround time gradually expanded to 25 minutes—because it took more time to unload and load 125 passengers, as compared to a half-full plane with just 60 to 65 passengers. Even so, the 25-minute average turnaround times

at Southwest during the 2000–2009 period were shorter than the 30–50 minute turnarounds typical at other major airlines.)

- In late November 1971, Lamar Muse came up with the idea of offering a $10 fare to passengers on the Friday night Houston–Dallas flight. With no advertising, the 112-seat flight sold out. This led Muse to realize that Southwest was serving two quite distinct types of travelers in the Golden Triangle market: (1) business travelers who were more time sensitive than price sensitive and wanted weekday flights at times suitable for conducting business, and (2) price-sensitive leisure travelers who wanted lower fares and had more flexibility about when to fly.[4] He came up with a two-tier on-peak and off-peak pricing structure in which all seats on weekday flights departing before 7 PM were priced at $26 and all seats on other flights were priced at $13. Passenger traffic increased significantly—and systemwide on-peak and off-peak pricing soon became standard across the whole airline industry.
- In 1972, the company decided to move its flights in Houston from the newly opened Houston Intercontinental Airport (where it was losing money and where it took 45 minutes to get to downtown) to the abandoned Houston Hobby Airport located much closer to downtown Houston. Despite being the only carrier to fly into Houston Hobby, the results were spectacular—business travelers who flew to Houston frequently from Dallas and San Antonio found the Houston Hobby location far more convenient and passenger traffic doubled almost immediately.
- In early 1973, in an attempt to fill empty seats on its San Antonio–Dallas flights, Southwest cut its regular $26 fare to $13 for all seats, all days, and all times. When Braniff International, at that time one of Southwest's major rivals, announced $13 fares of its own, Southwest retaliated with a two-page ad run in the Dallas newspapers headlining "Nobody is going to shoot Southwest Airlines out of the sky for a lousy $13," and containing copy saying Braniff was trying to run Southwest out of business. The ad announced that Southwest would not only match Braniff's $13 fare but that it would also give passengers the choice of buying a regular-priced ticket for $26 and receiving a complimentary fifth of Chivas Regal scotch, Crown Royal Canadian whiskey, or Smirnoff vodka (or, for nondrinkers, a leather ice bucket). Over 75 percent of Southwest's Dallas–Houston passengers opted for the $26 fare, although the percentage dropped as the two-month promotion wore on and corporate controllers began insisting that company employees use the $13 fare. The local and national media picked up the story of Southwest's offer, proclaiming the battle as a David versus Goliath struggle in which the upstart Southwest did not stand much of a chance against the much larger and well-established Braniff; grassroots sentiment in Texas swung to Southwest's side.

All these moves paid off. The resulting gains in passenger traffic allowed Southwest to report its first-ever annual profit in 1973.

More Legal and Regulatory Hurdles

During the rest of the 1970s, Southwest found itself embroiled in another round of legal and regulatory battles. One battle involved Southwest's refusal to move its flights from Dallas Love Field, located 10 minutes from downtown, to the newly opened Dallas–Fort Worth Regional Airport, which was 30 minutes from downtown Dallas. Local officials were furious because they were counting on fees from Southwest's flights in and out of DFW to help service the debt on the bonds issued to finance the construction of DFW. Southwest's position was that it was not required to move because it had not agreed to do so or been ordered to do so by the Texas Aeronautics Commission—moreover, the company's headquarters were located at Love Field. The courts eventually ruled Southwest's operations could remain at Love Field.

A second battle ensued when rival airlines protested Southwest's application to begin serving several smaller cities in Texas; their protest was based on arguments that these markets were already well served and that Southwest's entry would result in costly overcapacity. Southwest countered that its low fares would allow more people to fly and grow the market. Again, Southwest prevailed and its views about low fares expanding the market proved accurate. In the year before Southwest initiated service, 123,000 passengers flew from Harlingen Airport in the Rio Grande Valley to Houston, Dallas, or San Antonio; in the 11 months following Southwest's initial flights, 325,000 passengers flew to the same three cities.

Believing that Braniff and Texas International were deliberately engaging in tactics to harass Southwest's operations, Southwest convinced the U.S. government to investigate what it considered predatory tactics by its chief rivals. In February 1975, Braniff and Texas International were indicted by a federal grand jury for conspiring to put Southwest out of business—a violation of the Sherman Antitrust Act. The two airlines pleaded "no contest" to the charges, signed cease-and-desist agreements, and were fined a modest $100,000 each.

When Congress passed the Airline Deregulation Act in 1978, Southwest applied to the Civil Aeronautics Board (now the Federal Aviation Administration) to fly between Houston and New Orleans. The application was vehemently opposed by local government officials and airlines operating out of DFW because of the potential for passenger traffic to be siphoned away from DFW. The opponents solicited the aid of Fort Worth congressman Jim Wright, then the majority leader of the U.S. House of Representatives, who took the matter to the floor of the House of Representatives; a rash of lobbying and maneuvering ensued. What emerged came to be known as the Wright Amendment of 1979: no airline may provide nonstop or through-plane service from Dallas Love Field to any city in any state except for locations in Texas, Louisiana, Arkansas, Oklahoma, and New Mexico. Southwest was prohibited from advertising, publishing schedules or fares, or checking baggage for travel from Dallas Love Field to any city it served outside the five-state "Wright Zone." The Wright Amendment continued in effect until 1997 when Alabama, Mississippi, and Kansas were added to the five-state Wright Zone; in 2005, Missouri was added to the zone. In 2006, after a heated battle in Congress, legislation was passed and signed into law that repealed the Wright Amendment beginning in October 2014. With the repeal of the Wright Amendment, Southwest Airlines increased flight activity from Dallas Love Field by 50 percent to add 20 new nonstop destinations with 180 daily departures to a total of 50 nonstop destinations.

The Emergence of a Combative Can-Do Culture at Southwest

The legal, regulatory, and competitive battles that Southwest fought in these early years produced a strong esprit de corps among Southwest personnel and a drive to survive and prosper despite the odds. With newspaper and TV stories reporting Southwest's difficulties regularly, employees were fully aware that the airline's existence was constantly on the line. Had the company been forced to move from Love Field, it would most likely have gone under, an outcome that employees, Southwest's rivals, and local government officials understood well. According to Southwest's former president, Colleen Barrett, the obstacles thrown in Southwest's path by competitors and local officials were instrumental in building Herb Kelleher's passion for Southwest Airlines and ingraining a combative, can-do spirit into the corporate culture:[5]

> They would put twelve to fifteen lawyers on a case and on our side there was Herb. They almost wore him to the ground. But the more arrogant they were, the more determined Herb got that this airline was going to go into the air—and stay there.
>
> The warrior mentality, the very fight to survive, is truly what created our culture.

When Lamar Muse resigned in 1978, Southwest's board wanted Herb Kelleher to take over as chair and CEO. But Kelleher enjoyed practicing law and, while he agreed to become board chair, he insisted that someone else be CEO. Southwest's board appointed Howard Putnam, a group vice president of marketing services at United Airlines, as Southwest's president and CEO in July 1978. Putnam asked Kelleher to become more involved in Southwest's day-to-day operations, and over the next three years Kelleher got to know many of the company's personnel and observe them in action. Putnam announced his resignation in fall 1981 to become president and COO at Braniff International. This time, Southwest's board succeeded in persuading Kelleher to take on the additional duties of CEO and president.

Sustained Growth Transforms Southwest into the Domestic Market Share Leader, 1981–2015

When Herb Kelleher took over in 1981, Southwest was flying 27 planes to 14 destination cities and had $270 million in revenues and 2,100 employees. Over the next 20 years, Southwest Airlines prospered under Kelleher's leadership. When Kelleher stepped down as CEO in mid-2001, the company had 350 planes flying to 58 U.S. airports, annual revenues of $5.6 billion, over 30,000 employees, and 64 million fare-paying passengers annually.

Under the two CEOs who succeeded Kelleher, Southwest continued its march to becoming the market share leader in domestic air travel, growing to 2015 revenues of $19.8 billion and 49,600 employees, flying 704 planes to 97 airports in 40 states and 7 destinations outside the United States, and transporting some 118 million-plus fare-paying passengers and some 144 million-plus passengers (including those traveling on frequent flyer awards) in 2015. In the process, the company won more industry Triple Crown awards for best on-time record, best baggage handling, and fewest customer complaints than any other U.S. airline. While Southwest fell short of its on-time performance and baggage handling goals in some years, it still led the domestic airline industry in customer satisfaction and received other awards and recognitions, including Best Domestic Airline for Customer Service by *Executive Travel* magazine's Leading Edge Awards, Brand of the Year in the Value Airline Category by the Harris Poll, and the top ranking by *InsideFlyer* magazine for Best Customer Service and Best Loyalty Credit Card.

Exhibit 2 provides a five-year summary of Southwest's financial and operating performance. Exhibit 3 provides selected financial and operating data for major U.S. air carriers during 1995–2015.

HERB KELLEHER: THE CEO WHO TRANSFORMED SOUTHWEST INTO A MAJOR AIRLINE

Herb Kelleher majored in philosophy at Wesleyan University in Middletown, Connecticut, graduating with honors. He earned his law degree at New York University, again graduating with honors and also serving as a member of the law review. After graduation, he clerked for a New Jersey Supreme Court justice for two years and then joined a law firm in Newark. Upon marrying a woman from Texas and becoming enamored with Texas, he moved to San Antonio where he became a successful lawyer and came to represent Rollin King's small aviation company.

When Herb Kelleher took on the role of Southwest's CEO in 1981, he made a point of visiting with maintenance personnel to check on how well the planes were running and talking with the flight attendants. Kelleher did not do much managing from his office, preferring instead to be out among the troops as much as he could. His style was to listen and observe and to offer encouragement. Kelleher attended most graduation ceremonies of flight attendant classes, and he often appeared to help load bags on "Black Wednesday," the busy travel day before Thanksgiving. He knew the names of thousands of Southwest employees and was held in the highest regard by Southwest employees. When he attended a Southwest employee function, he was swarmed like a celebrity.

Kelleher had an affinity for bold-print Hawaiian shirts, owned a tricked-out motorcycle, and made no secret of his love for smoking and Wild Turkey whiskey. He loved to make jokes and engage in pranks and corporate antics, prompting some people to refer to him as the "clown prince" of the airline industry. He once appeared at a company gathering dressed in an Elvis costume and had arm-wrestled a South Carolina company executive at a public event in Dallas for rights to use "Just Plane Smart" as an advertising slogan.[6] Kelleher was well known inside and outside the company for his combativeness, particularly when it came to beating back competitors. On one occasion, he reportedly told a group of veteran employees, "If someone says they're going to smack us in the face—knock them out, stomp them out, boot them in the ditch, cover them over, and move on to the next thing. That's the Southwest spirit at work."[7] On another occasion, he said, "I love battles. I think it's part of the Irish in me. It's like what Patton said, 'War is hell and I love it so.' That's how I feel. I've never gotten tired of fighting."[8]

While Southwest was deliberately combative and flamboyant in some aspects of its operations, when it came to the financial side of the business Kelleher insisted on fiscal conservatism, a strong balance sheet, comparatively low levels of debt, and zealous attention to bottom-line profitability. While believing strongly in being prepared for adversity, Kelleher had an aversion to Southwest personnel spending time drawing up all kinds of formal strategic plans, saying "Reality is chaotic; planning is ordered and logical. The meticulous nit-picking that goes on in most strategic planning processes creates a mental straightjacket that becomes disabling in an industry where things change radically from one day

EXHIBIT 2 Summary of Southwest Airlines's Financial and Operating Performance, 2011–2015

	Year Ended December 31				
	2015	2014	2013	2012	2011
Financial Data (in millions, except per share amounts):					
Operating revenues	$19,820	$18,605	$17,699	$17,088	$15,658
Operating expenses	15,704	16,380	16,421	16,465	14,965
Operating income	4,116	2,225	1,278	623	693
Other expenses (income) net	637	409	69	(62)	370
Income before taxes	3,479	1,816	1,209	685	323
Provision for income taxes		680	455	264	145
Net income	1,298	$1,136	$754	$421	$178
Net income per share, basic	$3.30	$1.65	$1.06	$0.56	$0.23
Net income per share, diluted	$3.27	$1.64	$1.05	$0.56	$0.23
Cash dividends per common share	$0.2850	$0.2200	$0.1300	$ .0345	$0.0180
Total assets at period-end	$21,312	$19,723	$19,345	$18,596	$18,068
Long-term obligations at period-end	2,541	2,434	2,191	2,883	3,107
Stockholders' equity at period-end	7,358	6,775	7,336	6,992	6,877
Operating Data:					
Revenue passengers carried	118,171,211	110,496,912	108,075,976	109,346,509	103,973,759
Enplaned passengers	144,574,882	135,767,188	133,155,030	133,978,100	127,551,012
Revenue passenger miles (RPMs) (000s)[1]	117,499,879	108,035,133	104,348,216	102,874,979	97,582,530
Available seat miles (ASMs) (000s)[2]	140,501,409	131,003,957	130,344,072	128,137,110	120,578,736
Load factor[3]	83.6%	82.5%	80.1%	80.3%	80.9%
Average length of passenger haul (miles)	994	978	966	941	939
Average length of each flight (miles)	750	721	703	693	679
Trips flown	1,267,358	1,255,502	1,312,785	1,361,558	1,317,977
Average passenger fare	$154.85	$159.80	$154.72	$147.17	$141.90
Passenger revenue yield per RPM (cents)[4]	15.57¢	16.34¢	16.02¢	15.64¢	15.12¢
Operating revenue per ASM (cents)[5]	13.98¢	14.20¢	13.58¢	13.34¢	12.99¢

(Continued)

	Year Ended December 31				
	2015	2014	2013	2012	2011
Passenger revenue per ASM (cents)[(6)]	13.02¢	13.48¢	12.83¢	12.56¢	12.24¢
Operating expenses per ASM (cents)[(7)]	11.18¢	12.50¢	12.60¢	12.85¢	12.41¢
Operating expenses per ASM, excluding fuel (cents)	8.61¢	8.46¢	8.18¢	8.07¢	7.73¢
Operating expenses per ASM, excluding fuel and profit sharing (cents)	8.17¢	8.19¢	8.01¢	7.98¢	7.65¢
Fuel costs per gallon, including fuel tax	$1.90	$2.93	$3.16	$3.30	$3.19
Fuel consumed, in gallons (millions)	1,901	1,801	1,818	1,847	1,764
Active full time equivalent employees	49,583	46,278	44,381	45,861	45,392
Aircraft in service at period-end[(8)]	704	665	681	694	698

(1)A revenue passenger mile is one paying passenger flown one mile.
(2)An available seat mile (ASM) is one seat (empty or full) flown one mile. Also referred to as "capacity," which is a measure of the space available to carry passengers in a given period.
(3)Revenue passenger miles divided by available seat miles.
(4)Calculated as passenger revenue divided by revenue passenger miles. It represents the average cost paid by a paying passenger to fly one mile.
(5)Calculated as operating revenue divided by available seat miles. It is a measure of operating revenue production based on the total available seat miles flown during a particular period.
(6)Calculated as passenger revenue divided by available seat miles. It is a measure of passenger revenue production based on the total available seat miles flown during a particular period.
(7)Calculated as operating expenses divided by available seat miles. Also referred to as "unit costs" or "cost per available seat mile," this is the average cost to fly an aircraft seat (empty or full) one mile.
(8)Includes leased aircraft and excludes aircraft that were not available for service, in storage, held for sale, or held for return to the lessor.

Sources: Southwest Airlines 10-K report, 2013, 2015.

to the next." Kelleher wanted Southwest managers to think ahead, have contingency plans, and be ready to act when it appeared that the future held significant risks or when new conditions suddenly appeared and demanded prompt responses.

Kelleher was a strong believer in the principle that employees—not customers—came first:[9]

> You have to treat your employees like your customers. When you treat them right, then they will treat your outside customers right. That has been a very powerful competitive weapon for us. You've got to take the time to listen to people's ideas. If you just tell somebody no, that's an act of power and, in my opinion, an abuse of power. You don't want to constrain people in their thinking.

Another indication of the importance that Kelleher placed on employees was the message he had penned in 1990 that was prominently displayed in the lobby of Southwest's headquarters in Dallas:

> The people of Southwest Airlines are "the creators" of what we have become—and of what we will be.
>
> Our people transformed an idea into a legend. That legend will continue to grow only so long as it is

EXHIBIT 3 Selected Operating and Financial Data for Major U.S. Airline Carriers, 1995, 2000, 2005, 2010, 2013–2015

	1995	2000	2005	2010	2013	2014	2015
Passengers (in millions)	559.0	666.2	738.3	720.5	740.9	761.0	796.9
Flights (in thousands)	8,062	9,035	11,564	9,521	9,152	8,954	8,895
Revenue Passenger Miles (in billions)	603.4	692.8	778.6	798.0	834.8	858.0	899.0
Available Seat Miles (in billions)	807.1	987.9	1,002.7	972.6	1,004.1	1,028.5	1,073.1
Load Factor	67.0	72.4	77.7	82.0	83.1	83.4	83.8
Passenger Revenues (in millions)	$69,470	$93,622	$93,500	$103,978	$120,641	$128,705	$126,170
Operating Profit (Loss) (in millions)	$ 5,852	$ 7,014	$ 447	$ 10,517	$ 12,519	$ 16,674	$ 30,777
Net Profit (Loss) excluding one-time charges and gains (in millions)	$ 2,283	$ 2,486	($ 5,782)	$ 3,665	$ 12,711	$ 8,502	$ 26,398
Total Employees	546,987	679,967	562,467	531,224	552,581	558,368	576,139

Sources: Air Transport Association, *2005 Economic Report*, p. 7; U.S. Department of Transportation, Bureau of Transportation Statistics, Airline Traffic Data Press Releases, various years.

nourished—by our people's indomitable spirit, boundless energy, immense goodwill, and burning desire to excel.

Our thanks—and our love—to the people of Southwest Airlines for creating a marvelous family and a wondrous airline.

In June 2001, Herb Kelleher stepped down as CEO but continued on in his role as chair of Southwest's board of directors and the head of the board's executive committee; as chair, he played a lead role in Southwest's strategy, expansion to new cities and aircraft scheduling, and governmental and industry affairs. In May 2008, after more than 40 years of leadership at Southwest, Kelleher retired as chair (but he remained a full-time Southwest employee until July 2013 and carried the title of Chairman Emeritus in 2016).

EXECUTIVE LEADERSHIP AT SOUTHWEST: 2001–2016

In June 2001 Southwest Airlines, responding to anxious investor concerns about the company's leadership succession plans, began an orderly transfer of power and responsibilities from Herb Kelleher, age 70, to two of his most trusted protégés. James F. Parker, 54, Southwest's general counsel and one of Kelleher's most trusted protégés, succeeded Kelleher as Southwest's CEO. Another of Kelleher's trusted protégés, Colleen Barrett, 56, Southwest's executive vice president–customers and self-described keeper of Southwest's pep rally corporate culture, became president and chief operating officer.

James Parker, CEO, 2001–2004

James Parker's association with Herb Kelleher went back 23 years to the time when they were colleagues at Kelleher's old law firm. Parker moved over to Southwest from the law firm in February 1986. Parker's profile inside the company as Southwest's vice president and general counsel had been relatively low, but he was Southwest's chief labor negotiator and much of the credit for Southwest's good relations with employee unions belonged to Parker. Parker and Kelleher were said to think much alike, and Parker was regarded as having a good sense of humor, although he did not have as colorful and flamboyant a personality as Kelleher. Parker was seen as an honest, straight-arrow kind of person who had a strong grasp of Southwest's culture and market niche and who could be nice or tough, depending on the situation. When his appointment was announced, Parker said:[10]

> There is going to be no change of course insofar as Southwest is concerned. We have a very experienced leadership team. We've all worked together for a long time. There will be evolutionary changes in Southwest, just as there have always been in our history. We're going to stay true to our business model of being a low-cost, low-fare airline.

Parker retired unexpectedly, for personal reasons, in July 2004, stepping down as CEO and vice chair of the board and also resigning from the company's board of directors. He was succeeded by Gary C. Kelly.

Colleen Barrett, Southwest's President, 2001–2008

Barrett began working with Kelleher as his legal secretary in 1967 and had been with Southwest since 1978. As executive vice president–customers, Barrett had a high profile among Southwest employees and spent most of her time on culture-building, morale-building, and customer service; her goal was to ensure that employees felt good about what they were doing and felt empowered to serve the cause of Southwest Airlines.[11] She and Kelleher were regarded as Southwest's guiding lights, and some analysts said she was essentially functioning as the company's chief operating officer prior to her formal appointment as president. Much of the credit for the company's strong record of customer service and its strong-culture work climate belonged to Barrett.

Barrett had been the driving force behind lining the hallways at Southwest's headquarters with photos of company events and trying to create a family atmosphere at the company. Believing it was important to make employees feel cared about and important, Barrett had put together a network of contacts across the company to help her stay in touch with what was happening with employees and their families. When network members learned about events that were worthy of acknowledgment, the word quickly got to Barrett—the information went into a database and an appropriate greeting card or gift was sent. Barrett had a remarkable ability to give gifts that were individualized and connected her to the recipient.[12]

Barrett was the first woman appointed as president and COO of a major U.S. airline. In October 2001, *Fortune* included Colleen Barrett on its list of the 50 most powerful women in American business (she was ranked number 20). Barrett retired as president in July 2008.

Gary C. Kelly, Southwest's CEO, 2004–Present

Gary Kelly was appointed vice chair of the board of directors and chief executive officer of Southwest effective July 15, 2004. Prior to that time, Kelly was executive vice president and chief financial officer from 2001 to 2004, and vice president–finance and chief financial officer from 1989 to 2001. He joined Southwest in 1986 as its controller. In 2008, effective with the retirement of Kelleher and Barrett, Kelly assumed the titles of board chair, CEO, and president.

When Kelly was named CEO in 2004, Herb Kelleher said:[13]

> Gary Kelly is one of our brightest stars, well respected throughout the industry and well known, over more than a decade, to the media, analyst, and investor communities for his excellence. As part of our Board's succession planning, we had already focused on Gary as Jim Parker's successor, and that process has simply been accelerated by Jim's personal decision to retire. Under Gary's leadership, Southwest has achieved the strongest balance sheet in the American airline industry; the best fuel hedging position in our industry; and tremendous progress in technology.

In his first two years as CEO, Kelly and other top-level Southwest executives sharpened and fine-tuned Southwest's strategy in a number of areas, continued to expand operations (adding both more flights and initiating service to new airports), and worked to maintain the company's low-cost advantage over its domestic rivals.

Kelly saw four factors as keys to Southwest's recipe for success:[14]

- Hire great people, treat 'em like family.
- Care for our Customers warmly and personally, like they're guests in our home.
- Keep fares and operating costs lower than anybody else by being safe, efficient, and operationally excellent.
- Stay prepared for bad times with a strong balance sheet, lots of cash, and a stout fuel hedge.

To guide Southwest's efforts to be a standout performer on these four key success factors, Kelly had established five strategic objectives for the company:[15]

- Be the best place to work.
- Be the safest, most efficient, and most reliable airline in the world.
- Offer customers a convenient flight schedule with lots of flights to lots of places they want to go.
- Offer customers the best overall travel experience.
- Do all of these things in a way that maintains a low cost structure and the ability to offer low fares.

In 2008–2009, Kelly initiated a slight revision of Southwest's mission statement and also spearheaded a vision statement that called for a steadfast focus on a triple bottom line of Performance, People, and Planet—see Exhibit 4.

In 2010, Kelly initiated one of the biggest strategic moves in the company's history: the acquisition of AirTran Airways, a low-fare, low-cost airline that served 70 airports in the United States, Mexico, and the Caribbean (19 of the airports AirTran served coincided with airports served by Southwest). In 2011, Kelly initiated a five-year strategic plan that featured five strategic initiatives:

- Integrating AirTran into Southwest.
- Modernizing Southwest Airlines's existing aircraft fleet.
- Adding over 100 new Boeing 737-800 aircraft to the Southwest fleet.
- Launching international service and a new reservation system.
- Growing membership in the company's Rapid Rewards® frequent flyer program.

EXHIBIT 4 Southwest Airlines's Mission, Vision, and Triple-Bottom-Line Commitment to Performance, People, and Planet

THE MISSION OF SOUTHWEST AIRLINES The mission of Southwest Airlines is dedication to the highest quality of Customer Service delivered with a sense of warmth, friendliness, individual pride, and Company Spirit.

OUR VISION Become the world's most loved, most flown, and most profitable airline.

TO OUR EMPLOYEES We are committed to provide our Employees a stable work environment with equal opportunity for learning and personal growth. Creativity and innovation are encouraged for improving the effectiveness of Southwest Airlines. Above all, Employees will be provided the same concern, respect, and caring attitude within the organization that they are expected to share externally with every Southwest Customer.

TO OUR COMMUNITIES Our goal is to be the hometown airline of every community we serve, and because those communities sustain and nurture us with their support and loyalty, it is vital that we, as individuals and in groups, embrace each community with the SOUTHWEST SPIRIT of involvement, service, and caring to make those communities better places to live and work.

TO OUR PLANET We strive to be a good environmental steward across our system in all of our hometowns, and one component of our stewardship is efficiency, which by its very nature, translates to eliminating waste and conserving resources. Using cost-effective and environmentally beneficial operating procedures (including facilities and equipment), allows us to reduce the amount of materials we use and, when combined with our ability to reuse and recycle material, preserves these environmental resources.

TO OUR STAKEHOLDERS Southwest's vision for a sustainable future is one where there will be a balance in our business model between Employees and Community, the Environment, and our Financial Viability. In order to protect our world for future generations, while meeting our commitments to our Employees, Customers, and Stakeholders, we will strive to lead our industry in innovative efficiency that conserves natural resources, maintains a creative and innovative workforce, and gives back to the Communities in which we live and work.

Source: 2014 Southwest Airlines One Report, **www.southwest.com** (accessed May 20, 2016).

SOUTHWEST AIRLINES'S STRATEGY IN 2016

From day one, Southwest had pursued a low-cost/low-price/no-frills strategy to make air travel affordable to a wide segment of the population. While specific aspects of the strategy had evolved over the years, three strategic themes had characterized the company's strategy throughout its existence and still had high profiles in 2016:

- Charge fares that were very price competitive and, in some cases, appealingly lower than what rival airlines were charging.
- Create and sustain a low-cost operating structure.
- Make it fun to fly on Southwest and provide customers with a top-notch travel experience.

Fare Structure Strategy

Southwest employed a relatively simple fare structure displayed in ways that made it easy for customers to choose the fare they preferred. In 2016, Southwest's fares were bundled into four major categories: "Wanna Get Away®," "Anytime," and "Business Select®," and fares for seniors (people 65 and older):

1. Wanna Get Away fares were always the lowest fares and were subject to advance purchase requirements. No fee was charged for changing to a previously purchased ticket to a different time or day of travel (rival airlines charged a change fee of $100 to $175), but applicable fare differences were applied. The purchase price was nonrefundable but the funds could be applied to future travel on Southwest, provided the tickets were not canceled or changed within 10 minutes of a flight's scheduled departure.
2. Anytime fares were refundable and changeable, and funds could also be applied toward future travel on Southwest. Anytime fares also included a higher frequent flyer point multiplier under Southwest's Rapid Rewards® frequent flyer program than do Wanna Get Away fares.
3. Business Select fares were refundable and changeable, and funds could be applied toward future travel on Southwest. Business Select fares also included additional perks such as priority boarding, a higher frequent flyer point multiplier than other Southwest fares (including twice as many points per dollar spent as compared to Wanna Get Away fares), priority security and ticket counter access in select airports, and one complimentary adult beverage coupon for the day of travel (for customers of legal drinking age). The Business Select fare had been introduced in 2007 to help attract economy-minded business travelers; Business Select customers had early boarding privileges, received extra Rapid Rewards (frequent flyer) credit, and a free cocktail.
4. Fares for seniors were typically priced between the Wanna Get Away and Anytime fares. No fee was charged for changing a previously purchased ticket to a different time or day of travel, but applicable fare differences were applied. The purchase price was nonrefundable, but funds could be applied to future travel on Southwest, provided the tickets were not canceled or changed within ten minutes of a flight's scheduled departure. Fares for seniors were not displayed on the list of fare options at the company's website unless customers checked a box indicating that one or more passengers were 65 years of age or older.

In 2008, rival airlines instituted a series of add-on fees—including a fuel surcharge for each flight, fees for checking bags, fees for processing frequent flyer travel awards, fees for buying a ticket in person at the airport or calling a toll-free number to speak with a ticket agent to make a reservation, fees for changing a previously purchased ticket to a different flight, and fees certain for in-flight snacks and beverages—to help defray sky-rocketing costs for jet fuel (which had climbed from about 15 percent of operating expenses in 2000 to 40 percent of operating expenses in mid-2008) and try to bolster their operating performance. Southwest, however, choose to forego "à la carte" pricing and stuck with an all-inclusive fare price. During 2009 and periodically thereafter, Southwest ran "Bags Fly Free™" ad campaigns to publicize the cost-savings of flying Southwest rather than paying the $20 to $50 fees that rival airlines charged for a first or second checked bag. Southwest also had run ads promoting its policy of not charging a fee for changing a previously purchased ticket to a different flight.

When advance reservations were weak for particular weeks or times of the day or on certain routes, Southwest made a regular practice of initiating special fare promotions to stimulate ticket sales to stimulate ticket sales on flights that otherwise would have had numerous empty seats. The company's use of special fare sales and Bags Fly Free ads to combat slack air travel during much of the Great Recession in 2008–2009 resulted in company-record load factors (the percentage of all available seats on all flights that were occupied by fare-paying passengers) for every month from July through December 2009.

Southwest was a shrewd practitioner of the concept of price elasticity, proving in one market after another that the revenue gains from increased ticket sales and the volume of passenger traffic would more than compensate for the revenue erosion associated with low fares. When Southwest entered the Florida market with an introductory $17 fare from Tampa to Fort Lauderdale, the number of annual passengers flying the Tampa–Fort Lauderdale route jumped 50 percent to more than 330,000. In Manchester, New Hampshire, passenger counts went from 1.1 million in 1997, the year prior to Southwest's entry, to 3.5 million in 2000 and average one-way fares dropped from just over $300 to $129. Southwest's success in stimulating higher passenger traffic at airports across the United States via low fares and frequent flights had been coined the "Southwest Effect" by personnel at the U.S. Department of Transportation. Exhibit 5 shows the cities and airports Southwest Airlines served in July 2016.

Southwest's Strategy to Create and Sustain Low-Cost Operations

Southwest management fully understood that earning attractive profits by charging low fares necessitated the use of strategy elements that would enable the company to become a low-cost provider of commercial air service. There were three main components of Southwest's strategic actions to achieve a low-cost operating structure: using a single aircraft type for all flights, creating an operationally efficient point-to-point route structure, and striving to perform all value chain activities in a cost-efficient manner.

Use of a Single Aircraft Type For many years, Southwest's aircraft fleets had consisted only of

EXHIBIT 5 Southwest's Aircraft Fleet as of December 31, 2015

Type of Aircraft	Number	Seats	Average Age	Comments
Boeing 737-300	118	137/143	22 years	Southwest was Boeing's launch customer for this model.
Boeing 737-500	11	122	24 years	Southwest was Boeing's launch customer for this model.
Boeing 737-700	471	143	11 years	Southwest was Boeing's launch customer for this model in 1997. All were equipped with satellite-delivered broadband Internet reception capability.
Boeing 737-800	104	175	2 years	All were equipped with satellite-delivered broadband Internet reception capability.
Total	704			

Other Fleet-Related Facts

Average age of aircraft fleet—approximately 12 years
Average aircraft trip length—750 miles, with an average duration of 2 hours and 2 minutes
Average aircraft utilization—nearly 6 flights per day and 11 hours and 10 minutes of flight time
Fleet size—1990: 106; 1995: 224; 2000: 344; 2009: 537
Firm orders for new aircraft—2016: 36; 2017–2027: 289

Sources: Company 10-K report, 2015; information posted at **www.southwest.com** (accessed May 18, 2016).

Boeing 737 aircraft. Operating only one type of aircraft produced many cost-saving benefits: minimizing the size of spare parts inventories, simplifying the training of maintenance and repair personnel, improving the proficiency and speed with which maintenance routines could be done, and simplifying the task of scheduling planes for particular flights. In 2013, Southwest operated the biggest fleet of Boeing 737 aircraft in the world. Exhibit 5 provides information about Southwest's aircraft fleet.

Southwest's Point-to-Point Route Structure Strategy Southwest's point-to-point scheduling of flights was more cost-efficient than the hub-and-spoke systems used by most all rival airlines. Hub-and-spoke systems involved passengers on many different flights coming in from spoke locations (and sometimes another hub) to a central airport or hub within a short span of time and then connecting to an outgoing flight to their destination—a spoke location or another hub). Most flights arrived and departed a hub across a two-hour window, creating big peak–valley swings in airport personnel workloads and gate utilization—airport personnel and gate areas were very busy when hub operations were in full swing and then were underutilized in the interval awaiting the next round of inbound–outbound flights. In contrast, Southwest's point-to-point routes permitted scheduling aircraft to minimize the time aircraft were at the gate, currently approximately 25 minutes, thereby reducing the number of aircraft and gate facilities that would otherwise be required. Furthermore, with a relatively even flow of incoming–outgoing flights and gate traffic, Southwest could staff its terminal operations to handle a fairly steady workload across a day whereas hub-and-spoke operators had to staff their operations to serve three or four daily peak periods.

Exhibit 6 shows the cities and airports served by Southwest in mid-2016. Going into 2016, Southwest had nonstop service between 637 airports. In 2015, Southwest's average passenger airfare was $154.85 one way, and the average passenger trip length was approximately 994 miles.

Striving to Perform All Value Chain Activities Cost-Effectively Southwest made a point of scrutinizing every aspect of its operations to find ways to trim costs. The company's strategic actions to reduce or at least contain costs were extensive and ongoing.

- Sharply rising prices for jet fuel over the past from the mid-2000s through 2014 that caused fuel expenses to rise from 16.5 percent of total operating expenses in 2003 to between 28 and 38 percent of total operating expenses between 2006 and 2014 had prompted a number of projects to increase fuel efficiency, including:
  - The installation of "blended winglets" on all of its planes beginning in 2007 and then, in 2014, starting to upgrade its aircraft fleet with newly designed split scimitar winglets—see Exhibit 7. These winglets reduced lift drag, allowed aircraft to climb more steeply and reach higher flight levels quicker, improved cruising performance, helped extend engine life and reduce maintenance costs, and reduced fuel burn.
  - The use of auto-throttle and vertical navigation procedures to maintain optimum cruising speeds.
  - The introduction of new engine start procedures to support using a single engine for runway taxiing.
  - Reductions in engine aircraft idle speed while on the ground.
- Southwest was the first major airline to introduce ticketless travel (eliminating the need to print and process paper tickets); by 2007 ticketless travel accounted for more than 95 percent of all ticket sales.
- Southwest was also the first airline to allow customers to make reservations and purchase tickets at the company's website (thus bypassing the need to pay commissions to travel agents for handling the ticketing process and reducing staffing requirements at Southwest's reservation centers). Selling a ticket on its website cost Southwest roughly $1, versus $3–4 for a ticket booked through its own internal reservation system and as much as $15 for tickets purchased through travel agents and professional business travel partners. Online ticket sales at Southwest's website grew swiftly, accounting for 74 percent of Southwest's revenues in 2009 and 80 percent of all company bookings in 2015.
- For most of its history, Southwest stressed flights into and out of airports in medium-sized cities and less-congested airports in major metropolitan areas (Chicago Midway, Detroit Metro, Houston Hobby, Dallas Love Field, Baltimore–Washington International, Burbank, Manchester, Oakland,

EXHIBIT 6 Airports and Cities Served by Southwest Airlines, December 2015

Southwest's Top 10 Airports by Departures	Daily Departures	Number of Gates	Nonstop Cities Served
Chicago Midway	233	34	64
Las Vegas	214	24	59
Baltimore/Washington	208	29	61
Denver	184	22	57
Dallas (Love Field)	180	18	51
Phoenix	167	24	48
Houston (Hobby)	161	19	51
Atlanta	126	18	37
Los Angeles	124	15	26
Orlando	113	16	40

Other Airports Served by Southwest Airlines			
Akron-Canton OH	Grand Rapids MI	Oklahoma City	Seattle/Tacoma
Albany	Greenville/Spartanburg SC	Omaha	Spokane
Albuquerque	Harlingen/South Padre Island TX	Ontario CA	Tampa
Amarillo	Hartford/Springfield	Orange County CA	Tucson
Austin	Indianapolis	Panama City FL	Tulsa
Birmingham	Jacksonville	Pensacola FL	Washington, DC (Dulles)
Boise	Kansas City	Philadelphia	Washington, DC (Reagan National)
Boston Logan	Little Rock	Pittsburgh	West Palm Beach
Buffalo	Long Island	Portland OR	Wichita KS
Burbank CA	Louisville	Portland ME	
Charleston	Lubbock	Providence	**International**
Charlotte	Manchester NH	Raleigh-Durham	Aruba
Cleveland	Memphis	Reno/Tahoe	Belize City
Columbus OH	Midland/Odessa TX	Richmond	Cabo San Lucas
Corpus Christi TX	Milwaukee	Rochester	Cancun
Dayton OH	Minneapolis/St. Paul	Sacramento	Liberia, Costa Rica
Des Moines	Nashville	St. Louis	Mexico City
Detroit Metro	Newark	Salt Lake City	Montego Bay
El Paso	New Orleans	San Antonio	Nassau
Flint MI	New York (LaGuardia)	San Diego	Punta Cana DOM
Fort Lauderdale	Norfolk/Virginia Beach	San Francisco	Puerto Vallarta
Fort Myers/Naples	Oakland	San Jose	San Juan

Sources: Company 10-K report, 2015; information posted at **www.southwest.com** (accessed May 18, 2016).

EXHIBIT 7 Southwest's Fuel-Saving Blended Winglets and Split Scimitar Winglets

Blended Winglets (first installations began in 2007); fuel savings of about 3.5 percent per aircraft.

© Southwest Airlines

New Split Scimitar Winglets (first installations began in 2014); fuel savings of about 5.0 to 5.5 percent per aircraft.

© Southwest Airlines

Source: Southwest Airlines.

San Jose, Providence, and Fort Lauderdale–Hollywood). This strategy helped produce better-than-average on-time performance and reduce the fuel costs associated with planes sitting in line on crowded taxiways or circling airports waiting for clearance to land. It further allowed the company to avoid paying the higher landing fees and terminal gate costs at such high-traffic airports like Atlanta's Hartsfield–Jackson International, Chicago's O'Hare, and Dallas–Fort Worth (DFW) where landing slots were controlled and rationed to those airlines willing to pay the high fees. More recently, however, having already initiated service to almost all of the medium-sized cities and less-congested airports where there were good opportunities for sustained growth in passenger traffic and revenues, Southwest had begun initiating service to airports in large metropolitan cities where air traffic congestion was a frequent problem—such as Los Angeles LAX, Boston Logan International, New York LaGuardia, Denver, San Francisco, Philadelphia, and Atlanta (when it acquired AirTran).

- To economize on the amount of time it took terminal personnel to check in passengers and to simplify the whole task of making reservations, Southwest dispensed with the practice of assigning each passenger a reserved seat. Initially, passengers were given color-coded plastic cards with the letters A, B, or C when they checked in at the boarding gate. Passengers then boarded in groups, according to the color/letter on their card, sitting in whatever seat was open when they got on the plane. In 2002, Southwest abandoned the use of plastic cards and began printing a big, bold A, B, or C on the boarding pass when the passenger checked in at the ticket counter; passengers then boarded in groups according to the letter on their boarding pass. In 2007–2008, Southwest introduced an enhanced boarding method that automatically assigned each passenger a specific number within the passenger's boarding group at the time of check-in; passengers then boarded the aircraft in that numerical order. All passengers could check in online up to 24 hours before departure time and print out a boarding pass, thus bypassing counter check-in (unless they wished to check baggage).
- Southwest flight attendants were responsible for cleaning up trash left by deplaning passengers and otherwise getting the plane presentable for passengers to board for the next flight. Rival carriers had cleaning crews come on board to perform this function until they incurred heavy losses in

2001–2005 and were forced to institute stringent cost-cutting measures that included abandoning use of cleaning crews and copying Southwest's practice.

- Southwest did not have a first-class section in any of its planes and had no fancy clubs for its frequent flyers to relax in at terminals.
- Southwest did not provide passengers with baggage transfer services to other carriers—passengers with checked baggage who were connecting to other carriers to reach their destination were responsible for picking up their luggage at Southwest's baggage claim and then getting it to the check-in facilities of the connecting carrier. (Southwest booked tickets involving only its own flights; customers connecting to flights on other carriers had to book such tickets either through travel agents or the connecting airline).
- Starting in 2001, Southwest began converting from cloth to leather seats; the team of Southwest employees that investigated the economics of the conversion concluded that an all-leather interior would be more durable and easier to maintain, more than justifying the higher initial costs.
- Southwest was a first-mover among major U.S. airlines in employing fuel hedging and derivative contracts to counteract rising prices for crude oil and jet fuel. From 1998 through 2008, the company's fuel hedging activities produced fuel savings of about $4.0 billion over what it would have spent had it paid the industry's average price for jet fuel. But unexpectedly large declines in jet fuel prices in late 2008 and 2009 resulted in reported losses of $408 million on the fuel hedging contracts that the company had in place during 2009. Since then, the company's fuel hedging activities had continued to be ineffective in reducing fuel expenses; the company recognized losses on its fuel hedging activities of $324 million in 2010, $259 million in 2011, $157 million in 2012, and $118 million in 2013. Southwest's fuel hedging strategy involved modifying the amount of its future fuel requirements that were hedged based on management's judgments about the forward market prices of crude oil and jet fuel. As of January 2016, the company had fuel derivative contracts in place for ~20 percent of its expected fuel consumption in 2016, ~65 percent of expected fuel consumption in 2017, and ~35 percent of expected fuel consumption in 2018.
- Southwest regularly upgraded and enhanced its management information systems to speed data flows, improve operating efficiency, lower costs, and upgrade its customer service capabilities. In 2001, Southwest implemented use of new software that significantly decreased the time required to generate optimal crew schedules and help improve on-time performance. In 2007–2008, Southwest invested in next-generation technology and software to improve its ticketless system and its back office accounting, payroll, and human resource information systems. During 2009, the company replaced or enhanced its point-of-sale, electronic ticketing and boarding, and revenue accounting systems. During 2010, it completed an initiative to convert to a new SAP Enterprise Resource Planning application that would replace its general ledger, accounts payable, accounts receivable, payroll, benefits, cash management, and fixed asset systems; the conversion was designed to increase data accuracy and consistency and lower administrative support costs.

For many decades, Southwest's operating costs had been lower than those of rival U.S. airline carriers—see Exhibit 8 for comparative *costs per revenue passenger mile* among the five major U.S. airlines during the 1995–2015 period. Exhibit 9 shows trends in Southwest's operating costs *per available seat mile* rather than per passenger-occupied seat.

Making It Fun to Fly Southwest: The Strategy to Provide a Top-Notch Travel Experience

Southwest's approach to delivering good customer service and building a loyal customer clientele was predicated on presenting a happy face to passengers, displaying a fun-loving attitude, and doing things in a manner calculated to provide passengers with a positive flying experience. The company made a special effort to employ gate personnel who enjoyed interacting with customers, had good interpersonal skills, and displayed cheery, outgoing personalities. A number of Southwest's gate personnel let their wit and sense of humor show by sometimes entertaining those in the gate area with trivia questions or contests such as "who has the biggest hole in their sock." Apart from greeting passengers coming onto planes and assisting them in finding open seats and stowing

EXHIBIT 8 Comparative Operating Cost Statistics per Revenue Passenger Mile, Major U.S. Airlines, 1995, 2000, 2005, 2010–2015

	Total Salaries and Fringe Benefits		Costs incurred per revenue passenger mile (in cents)							
	Pilots and Copilots	All Employees	Fuel and Oil	Maintenance	Rentals	Landing Fees	Advertising	General and Administrative	Other Operating Expenses	Total Operating Expenses
American Airlines										
1995	0.94¢	5.59¢	1.53¢	1.34¢	0.59¢	0.22¢	0.19¢	1.14¢	3.65¢	14.25¢
2000	1.16	5.77	2.04	1.90	0.48	0.23	0.18	0.58	3.30	14.48
2005	0.90	4.65	3.67	1.42	0.41	0.32	0.10	0.95	3.66	15.18
2010	0.88	5.18	4.57	1.92	0.47	0.35	0.13	1.23	3.68	17.53
2011	0.89	5.27	5.82	1.91	0.51	0.31	0.15	1.82	4.07	19.87
2012	0.86	5.17	6.10	1.87	0.43	0.30	0.12	1.91	3.70	19.61
2013	0.91	4.39	5.94	1.82	0.57	0.31	0.14	1.35	4.38	18.90
2014	1.01	4.63	5.56	1.92	0.66	0.31	0.07	1.56	4.46	19.18
2015	1.27	5.01	3.08	1.77	0.67	0.30	0.07	2.26	3.93	17.09
Delta Air Lines										
1995	1.27¢	4.97¢	1.70¢	1.16¢	0.71¢	0.30¢	0.18¢	0.43¢	4.07¢	13.53¢
2000	1.27	5.08	1.73	1.41	0.54	0.22	0.12	0.74	3.03	12.85
2005	0.93	4.31	3.68	1.10	0.38	0.22	0.16	0.84	6.01	16.69
2010	0.91	4.15	4.51	1.33	0.14	0.28	0.10	0.64	6.26	17.41
2011	0.95	4.27	5.77	1.41	0.15	0.28	0.13	0.54	7.09	19.65
2012	0.99	4.57	5.97	1.53	0.15	0.28	0.14	0.71	6.85	20.21
2013	1.11	4.82	5.42	1.58	0.13	0.28	0.13	0.68	6.61	19.65
2014	1.15	5.17	6.43	1.56	0.16	0.28	0.12	1.03	5.95	20.70
2015	1.19	5.55	3.45	1.47	0.18	0.27	0.12	1.38	5.08	17.50
Southwest Airlines										
1995	0.92¢	3.94¢	1.56¢	1.21¢	0.79¢	0.35¢	0.41¢	1.09¢	1.56¢	10.91¢
2000	0.86	4.22	1.95	1.22	0.48	0.31	0.35	1.42	0.96	10.91
2005	1.18	4.70	2.44	1.17	0.31	0.34	0.29	0.73	1.23	11.21
2010	1.37	4.97	4.63	1.47	0.28	0.46	0.26	0.83	1.32	14.23
2011	1.37	4.99	5.76	1.47	0.23	0.45	0.26	0.98	1.35	15.50
2012	1.57	5.66	6.70	1.86	0.42	0.51	0.26	1.29	1.72	18.43

(Continued)

	Total Salaries and Fringe Benefits		Costs incurred per revenue passenger mile (in cents)							
	Pilots and Copilots	All Employees	Fuel and Oil	Maintenance	Rentals	Landing Fees	Advertising	General and Administrative	Other Operating Expenses	Total Operating Expenses
2013	1.59	5.87	6.38	1.85	0.46	0.52	0.23	1.21	1.68	18.19
2014	1.46	5.64	5.23	1.58	0.35	0.47	0.20	1.22	1.49	16.17
2015	1.46	5.69	3.07	1.44	0.25	0.42	0.18	1.02	1.28	13.35
United Airlines										
1995	0.86¢	4.73¢	1.51¢	1.51¢	0.90¢	0.29¢	0.17¢	0.53¢	2.92¢	12.58¢
2000	1.15	5.75	1.98	1.84	0.73	0.28	0.21	0.76	3.09	14.65
2005	0.62	3.72	3.53	1.60	0.35	0.30	0.16	0.60	5.09	15.35
2010	0.67	4.34	4.46	1.86	0.32	0.38	0.06	1.31	5.24	17.96
2011	0.69	4.38	5.60	2.14	0.32	0.36	0.08	1.38	6.07	20.34
2012	0.74	4.71	5.97	1.72	0.44	0.35	0.09	1.57	5.84	20.69
2013	0.95	5.01	5.59	1.70	0.41	0.35	0.10	1.38	6.19	20.74
2014	1.09	5.11	5.31	1.68	0.38	0.38	0.10	1.37	6.07	20.41
2015	1.12	5.45	3.44	1.50	0.32	0.36	0.11	1.58	5.04	17.81

Note 1: Cost per revenue passenger mile for each of the cost categories in this exhibit is calculated by dividing the total costs for each cost category by the total number of revenue passenger miles flown, where a revenue passenger mile is equal to one paying passenger flown one mile. Costs incurred per revenue passenger mile thus represent the costs incurred per ticketed passenger per mile flown

Note 2: US Airways and America West started merging operations in September 2005, and joint reporting of their operating costs began in late 2007. Effective January 2010, data for Delta Air Lines include the combined operating costs of Delta and Northwest Airlines; the merger of these two companies became official in October 2008. United Airlines acquired Continental Airlines in 2010, and the two companies began joint reporting of operating expenses in 2012.

Note 3: America Airlines and US Airways merged in December 2013, but continued to operate under their separate names through 2014. Previously, US Airways had merged with America West in September 2005.

Note 4: Delta Air Lines and Northwest Airlines merged in October 2008; however, combined reporting did not begin until 2010.

Note 5: Southwest Airlines acquired AirTran in late 2010; starting in 2013 and continuing into 2014, AirTran flights were rebranded as Southwest Airlines flights. Southwest's first international flights began when some of AirTran's international flights were rebranded as Southwest flights in 2013.

Note 6: United Airlines acquired Continental Airlines in 2010, and the two companies began joint reporting of passenger traffic in 2012. Prior to 2012, traffic count data are only for United flights.

EXHIBIT 9 Southwest Airlines's Operating Expenses per Available Seat Mile, Various Years 1995–2015

	Costs (in cents) per available seat mile						
Expense Category	2015	2014	2013	2010	2005	2000	1995
Salaries, wages, bonuses, and benefits	4.54¢	4.14¢	3.86¢	3.76¢	3.27¢	2.81¢	2.40¢
Fuel and oil	2.57	4.04	4.42	3.68	1.58	1.34	1.01
Maintenance materials and repairs	0.72	0.75	0.83	0.76	0.52	0.63	0.60
Aircraft rentals	0.17	0.22	0.28	0.18	0.19	0.33	0.47
Landing fees and other rentals	0.83	0.85	0.85	0.82	0.53	0.44	0.44
Depreciation	0.72	0.72	0.66	0.64	0.55	0.47	0.43
Acquisition and integration	0.03	0.10	0.07	—	—	—	—
Other operating expenses	1.60	1.68	1.63	1.45	1.41	1.71	1.72
Total	**11.18¢**	**12.50¢**	**12.60¢**	**11.29¢**	**8.05¢**	**7.73¢**	**7.07¢**

Note: Figures in this exhibit differ from those for Southwest in Exhibit 8 because the cost figures in Exhibit 8 are based on *cost per passenger revenue mile,* whereas the cost figures in this exhibit are based on *cost per available seat mile.* Costs per revenue passenger mile represent the costs per ticketed passenger per mile flown, whereas costs per available seat mile are the *costs per seat per mile flown (irrespective of whether the seat was occupied or not).*

Sources: Company 10-K reports and annual reports, various years.

baggage, flight attendants were encouraged to be engaging, converse and joke with passengers, and go about their tasks in ways that made passengers smile. On some flights, attendants sang announcements to passengers on takeoff and landing. On one flight while passengers were boarding, an attendant with bunny ears popped out of an overhead bin exclaiming "Surprise!" The repertoires to amuse passengers varied from flight crew to flight crew.

During their tenure, both Herb Kelleher and Colleen Barrett had made a point of sending congratulatory notes to employees when the company received letters from customers complimenting particular Southwest employees; complaint letters were seen as learning opportunities for employees and reasons to consider making adjustments. Employees were provided the following policy guidance regarding how far to go in trying to please customers:

> No Employee will ever be punished for using good judgment and good old common sense when trying to accommodate a Customer—no matter what our rules are.[16]
>
> When you empower People to make a positive difference everyday, you allow them to decide. Most guidelines are written to be broken as long as the Employee is leaning toward the Customer. We follow the Golden Rule and try to do the right thing and think about our Customer.[17]

Southwest executives believed that conveying a friendly, fun-loving spirit to customers was the key to competitive advantage. As one Southwest manager put it, "Our fares can be matched; our airplanes and routes can be copied. But we pride ourselves on our customer service."[18]

Southwest's emphasis on point-to-point flights enabled many passengers to fly nonstop to their destinations, thereby cutting total trip time and avoiding not only the added built-in travel time to make connections but also the oft-encountered delays associated with connecting flights (late incoming flights, potential equipment failures requiring repairs at the gate, and late departures). In recent years, about 72 percent of Southwest's passengers flew nonstop to their destination—nonstop travel was a major contributor to providing customers with a top-notch travel experience.

In 2007, Southwest invested in an "extreme gate makeover" to improve the airport experience of customers. The makeover included adding (1) a business-focused area with padded seats, tables with power outlets, power stations with stools, and a large screen TV with news programming; and (2) a family-focused area with smaller tables and chairs, power stations for charging electrical devices, and kid-friendly TV programming. Later, Southwest added free wireless Internet service for passengers waiting in its gate areas.

In 2013–2014, Southwest began offering in-flight satellite-based Internet service on all of its 737-700 and 737-800 aircraft, representing over 75 percent of Southwest's fleet. Southwest's arrangement with its Internet service provider enabled the company to control the pricing of in-flight Internet service (which in 2014 was $8 a day per device, including stops and connections). The addition of in-flight Internet service, coupled with the free wireless service available in all of Southwest's gate areas, meant that passengers traveling on a Southwest airplane equipped with satellite Internet service had gate-to-gate connectivity for small portable electronic devices—in early 2016, Southwest was the only carrier currently offering gate-to-gate connectivity on 80 percent of its total aircraft fleet.

In 2013, Southwest joined with DISH Network to give customers free access to 17 live channels and 75 on-demand recorded episodes from various TV series at no additional charge. This promotion was later extended through the end of 2014. Shortly thereafter, Southwest added a selection of movies-on-demand (currently priced at $5 per movie) to its entertainment offerings and, in December 2013, became the first airline to offer a messaging-only option for $2 a day per device, including all stops and connections. Passengers did not have to purchase in-flight Internet service to access television offerings, movies-on-demand, or the messaging-only service.

In 2013, Southwest introduced a completely redesigned Southwest mobile website and app for iPhone and Android that had more features and functionality. The app enabled passengers to begin using mobile boarding passes.

Strategic Plan Initiatives, 2013–2016

Integrating Southwest's and AirTran's Operations The process of integrating AirTran into Southwest's operation began in 2013 and was completed by year-end 2014, with the last AirTran flight operating on December 28, 2014. Important integration accomplishments included:

- Transitioning of AirTran's Atlanta hub into a point-to-point operation to capture the efficiencies related to the scheduling of aircraft, flight crews, and ground staff.
- In addition to converting AirTran's flight schedules into a point-to-point operation, Southwest had merged and optimized the combined Southwest–AirTran flight schedules.
- Southwest had established a Southwest presence in all AirTran cities not currently served by Southwest and rebranded all AirTran operations and activities as Southwest.
- Conversion of AirTran's Boeing 737-700 aircraft to the Southwest fleet.
- AirTran's flight attendants had transitioned from the Association of Flight Attendants–CWA ("AFA") to the Transportation Workers of America union representing Southwest's flight attendants.

Southwest's Fleet Modernization Initiative

Southwest had multiple efforts underway to modernize its aircraft fleet. One effort, referred to by Southwest as *Evolve—The New Southwest Experience,* entailed retrofitting and refreshing the cabin interior of its fleet of 471 Boeing 737-700 planes. The goal of the Evolve program was to enhance customer comfort, personal space, and the overall travel experience while improving fleet efficiency and being environmentally responsible. The cabin refresh featured recyclable carpet, a brighter color scheme, and more durable, eco-friendly, and comfortable seats that weighed less than the prior seats. By maximizing the space inside the plane, Evolve allowed for six additional seats on each retrofitted aircraft, along with more climate-friendly and cost-effective materials. Southwest retrofitted 78 of its 737-300 aircraft with Evolve in 2013. In addition, the new 737-800 aircraft entering the company's fleet had the Evolve interior. The 17 AirTran 737-700 aircraft that were transferred to Southwest's fleet at year-end-2013 were refreshed with the new Evolve interior, and the remaining 35 AirTran 737-700 aircraft were refreshed with the Evolve interior when they became part of the Southwest fleet in the second half of 2014.

Furthermore, Southwest had divested AirTran's fleet of Boeing 717-200 aircraft. It had negotiated an agreement with Delta Air Lines, Inc. and Boeing Capital Corp. to lease or sublease AirTran's 88 Boeing 717-200 aircraft to Delta. Deliveries to

Delta began in September 2013. The company did not want to keep Boeing 717-200 planes in its aircraft fleet because of the added maintenance and repair costs associated with having a second type of plane in its fleet. Moreover, replacing the Boeing 717 aircraft capacity with Boeing 737 capacity provided incremental revenue opportunities with more seats per aircraft, while costing approximately the same amount to fly on a per-trip basis as the smaller Boeing 717 aircraft.

Incorporating Larger Boeing Aircraft into Southwest's Fleet Starting in 2012, Southwest began a long-term initiative to replace older Southwest aircraft with a new generation of Boeing aircraft that had greater seating capacity, a quieter interior, LED reading and ceiling lighting, improved security features, reduced maintenance requirements, increased fuel efficiency, and the capability to fly longer distances without refueling. Of the 704 active aircraft in Southwest's fleet at year-end 2015, the company had plans to remove 122 Boeing 737-300 aircraft (with 143 seats and an average age of 20 years) and 15 Boeing 737-500 aircraft (with 122 seats and an average age of 22 years) from its fleet over the next five years and replace them with new Boeing 737-700s (143 seats), 737-800s (175 seats), and 737-MAX aircraft (up to 189 seats). While Southwest had added 54 new Boeing 737-700 and 737-800 planes to its fleet in 2012–2013 and 52 Boeing 737-800 aircraft delivered in 2014–2015, 56 Boeing 737-700 aircraft were scheduled to be delivered in 2016–2018 (with options to take delivery on an additional 36 planes) and 200 737-MAX aircraft to be delivered during 2017–2024 (with options to take delivery on an additional 83 planes—Southwest was Boeing's launch customer for the 737-MAX. Plans called for some of the new aircraft to be leased from third parties rather than being purchased—of the company's current fleet of 704 aircraft, 581 were owned and 123 were leased.

Southwest expected that the new Boeing 737-800 and 737-MAX aircraft would significantly enhance the company's capabilities to (1) more economically fly long-haul routes (the number of short-haul flights throughout the domestic airline industry had been declining since 2000); (2) improve scheduling flexibility and more economically serve high-demand, gate-restricted, slot-controlled airports by adding seats to such destinations without increasing the number of flights; and (3) boost overall fuel efficiency to reduce overall costs. Additionally, the aircraft would enable Southwest to profitably expand its operations to new, more distant destinations (including extended routes over water) such as Hawaii, Alaska, Canada, Mexico, and the Caribbean. Southwest management expected that the new Boeing 737-MAX planes would have the lowest operating costs of any single-aisle commercial airplane on the market.

Launching International Service and a New Reservation System In January 2014, Southwest launched an international reservation system separate from its domestic reservation system (but linked to and accessible from www.southwest.com) and began selling tickets for its inaugural international daily nonstop service on Southwest aircraft beginning July 1, 2014, to Jamaica (Montego Bay), the Bahamas (Nassau), and Aruba (Oranjestad). The company added service to new Latin American destinations in 2015, including San Jose, Costa Rica; Puerto Vallarta, Mexico; Belize City, Belize; and Liberia, Costa Rica. The company expected to add flights to additional near-international locations in 2016 after the opening of a five-gate international terminal and customs facility and Hobby Airport in October 2015. Southwest also operated international flights from Fort Lauderdale, Florida.

Growing Southwest's Rapid Rewards Frequent Flyer Program Southwest's current Rapid Rewards frequent flyer program, launched in March 2011, linked free travel awards to the number of points members earned purchasing tickets to fly Southwest (the previous version of the Rapid Rewards program had tied free travel awards to the number of flight segments flown during a 24-month period). The amount of points earned was based on the fare and fare class purchased, with higher fare products (like Business Select) earning more points than lower fare products (like Wanna Get Away). Likewise, the amount of points required to be redeemed for a flight was based on the fare and fare class purchased. Rapid Rewards members could also earn points through qualifying purchases with Southwest's Rapid Rewards Partners (which included car rental agencies, hotels, restaurants, and retail locations), and they could purchase points. Members who opted to obtain a Southwest co-branded Chase® Visa credit card, which had an annual fee of $99, earned 2 points for every dollar spent on purchases of Southwest tickets and on purchases with Southwest's car rental and hotel partners, and they earned 1 point on every dollar spent everywhere else. Holders of Southwest's co-branded Chase Visa credit card could redeem credit card points for items other than travel on Southwest, including international flights on other airlines, cruises, hotel stays, rental cars, gift cards, event tickets, and more. The most active members of Southwest's Rapid Rewards program qualified for priority check-in and security lane access (where available), standby priority, free in-flight Wi-Fi, and—provided they flew 100 qualifying flights or earned 110,000 qualifying points in a calendar year—automatically received a Companion Pass, which provided for unlimited free roundtrip travel for one year to any destination available on Southwest for a designated companion of the qualifying Rapid Rewards Member.

Rapid Rewards members could redeem their points for every available seat, every day, on every flight, with no blackout dates. Points did not expire so long as the Rapid Rewards Member had points-earning activity during the most recent 24 months.

In 2016, the current Rapid Rewards program had exceeded management's expectations with respect to the number of frequent flyer members added, the amount spent per member on airfare, the number of flights taken by members, the number of Southwest's co-branded Chase Visa credit card holders added, the number of points sold to business partners, and the number of frequent flyer points purchased by program members.

Southwest had enabled the members of AirTran's A+ Rewards frequent flyer program to transfer their loyalty rewards to Southwest Rapid Rewards. In 2015, the members of the Southwest Rapid Rewards frequent flyer program redeemed approximately 7.3 million flight awards, accounting for approximately 12.0 percent of revenue passenger miles flown. This was significantly higher than the 2012 redemptions of approximately 4.5 million flight awards (accounting for approximately 9.0 percent of revenue passenger miles flown) and the 2011 redemptions of approximately 3.7 million flight awards (accounting for approximately 8.6 percent of revenue passenger miles flown).

Southwest's Growth Strategy

Southwest's strategy to grow its business consisted of (1) adding more daily flights to the cities/airports it currently served and (2) adding new cities/airports to its route schedule.

It was normal for customer traffic to grow at the airports Southwest served. Hence, opportunities were always emerging for Southwest to capture additional revenues by adding more flights at the airports already being served. Sometimes these opportunities entailed adding more flights to one or more of the same destinations and sometimes the opportunities entailed adding flights to a broader selection of Southwest destinations, depending on the mix of final destinations the customers departing from a particular airport were flying to.

To spur growth beyond that afforded by adding more daily flights to cities/airports currently being served, it had long been Southwest's practice to add one or more new cities/airports to its route schedule annually. In selecting new cities, Southwest looked for city pairs that could generate substantial amounts of both business and leisure traffic. Management believed that having numerous flights flying the same routes appealed to business travelers looking for convenient flight times and the ability to catch a later flight if they unexpectedly ran late. As a general rule, Southwest did not initiate service to a city/airport unless it envisioned the potential for originating at least 8 flights a day there and saw opportunities to add more flights over time—in Denver, for example, Southwest had boosted the number of daily departures from 13 in January 2006 (the month in which service to and from Denver was initiated) to 79 daily departures in 2008, 129 daily departures in May 2010, and 184 daily departures in 2016.

On a number of occasions, when rival airlines had cut back flights to cities that Southwest served, Southwest had quickly moved in with more flights of its own, believing its lower fares would attract more passengers. When Midway Airlines ceased operations in November 1990, Southwest moved in overnight and quickly instituted flights to Chicago's Midway Airport. Southwest was a first-mover in adding flights on routes where rivals cut their offerings following 9/11. When American Airlines closed its hubs in Nashville and San Jose, Southwest immediately increased the number of its flights into and out of both locations. When US Airways trimmed its flight schedule for Philadelphia and Pittsburgh, Southwest promptly boosted its flights into and out of those airports. Southwest initiated service to Denver when United, beset with financial difficulties, cut back operations at its big Denver hub. In 2016, it was clear that Southwest intended to pick up the pace in adding service to more locations, particularly larger metropolitan airports, places like Hawaii and Alaska, and international destinations.

Marketing, Advertising, and Promotion Strategies

Southwest was continually on the lookout for novel ways to tell its story, make its distinctive persona come alive, and strike a chord in the minds of air travelers. Many of its print ads and billboards were deliberately unconventional and attention-getting so as to create and reinforce the company's maverick, fun-loving, and combative image. The company launched its TransFAREncy campaign in 2015 that focused on its easy-to-understand pricing that did not include hidden fees for checked bags, preferred seating, or flight changes. The other three largest U.S.-based airlines typically included upcharges for baggage or seat selection either immediately prior to online fare payment or upon airport check-in. In addition, American, Delta, and United all issued either nonrefundable tickets or tickets that included hefty change fees that could exceed the cost of a new ticket.

Previous campaigns had promoted the company's performance as "The Low-Fare Airline" and "The All-Time On-Time Airline," and its Triple Crown awards. One of the company's billboard campaigns touted the frequency of the company's flights with such phrases as "Austin Auften," "Phoenix Phrequently," and "L.A. A.S.A.P." Each holiday season since 1985 Southwest had run a "Christmas card" ad on TV featuring children and their families from the Ronald McDonald Houses and Southwest employees. Fresh advertising campaigns were launched periodically—Exhibit 10 shows four representative ads.

Southwest tended to advertise far more heavily than any other U.S. carrier. Passenger traffic at Southwest subsequently rose while passenger volumes went in the opposite direction at Southwest's largest competitors—all of which had recently introduced or increased fees for checked baggage.

The company periodically launched national and local advertising and promotional campaigns to highlight what management believed were important points of differentiation between Southwest and rival airlines. These differentiating features included:

- Being the only major U.S. airline not to charge additional fees for first and second checked bags—moreover, Southwest allowed each ticketed customer to check one stroller and one car seat free of charge, in addition to the two free checked bags.
- Being the only major U.S. airline not to impose a fee for customers to change their travel schedules. Nor did Southwest impose additional fees for items such as seat selection, fuel surcharges, snacks, curb-side check-in, and telephone reservations.
- Offering a wide range of in-flight entertainment options and conveniences for passengers (in-flight Internet service, access to 17 live channels and episodes of 75 different television series, movies-on-demand, and messaging).

Southwest management believed these differentiating features—along with its low fares, network size, numerous nonstop flights, friendly customer service, and Rapid Rewards program—had been instrumental in helping grow passenger traffic on Southwest flights, build market share, and increase revenues. The company's advertising and promotional expenditures totaled $218 million in 2015, $207 million in 2014, and $208 million in 2015; these expenditures were included in "other operating expenses" in Exhibit 9.

SOUTHWEST'S PEOPLE MANAGEMENT PRACTICES AND CULTURE

Whereas the litany at many companies was that customers come first, at Southwest the operative principle was that "employees come first and customers come second." The high strategic priority placed on employees reflected management's belief that delivering superior service required employees who not only were passionate about their jobs but who also knew the company was genuinely concerned for their well-being and committed to providing them with job security. Southwest's thesis was simple: Keep employees happy—then they will keep customers happy.

EXHIBIT 10 Four Samples of Southwest's Ads

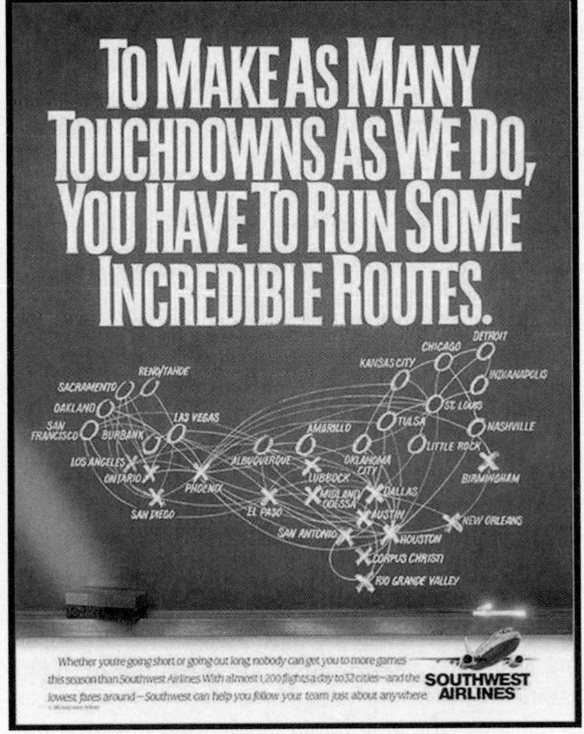

© Southwest Airlines

Since becoming the company's CEO, Gary Kelly had continuously echoed the views of his predecessors: "Our People are our single greatest strength and our most enduring long term competitive advantage."[19]

The company changed the personnel department's name to the People Department in 1989. Later, it was renamed the People and Leadership Development Department.

Recruiting, Screening, and Hiring

Southwest hired employees for attitude and trained for skills. Herb Kelleher explained:[20]

> We can train people to do things where skills are concerned. But there is one capability we do not have and that is to change a person's attitude. So we prefer an unskilled person with a good attitude . . . [to] a highly skilled person with a bad attitude.

Management believed that delivering superior service came from having employees who genuinely believed that customers were important and that treating them warmly and courteously was the right thing to do, not from training employees to *act* like customers are important. The belief at Southwest was that superior, hospitable service and a fun-loving spirit flowed from the heart and soul of employees who themselves were fun-loving and spirited, who liked their jobs and the company they worked for, and who were also confident and empowered to do their jobs as they saw fit (rather than being governed by strict rules and procedures).

Southwest recruited employees by means of newspaper ads, career fairs and Internet job listings; a number of candidates applied because of Southwest's reputation as one of the best companies to work for in America and because they were impressed by their experiences as a customer on Southwest flights. Recruitment ads were designed to capture the attention of people thought to possess Southwest's "personality profile." For instance, one ad showed Herb Kelleher impersonating Elvis Presley and had the message:[21]

> Work In A Place Where Elvis Has Been Spotted. The qualifications? It helps to be outgoing. Maybe even a bit off center. And be prepared to stay for a while. After all, we have the lowest employee turnover rate in the industry. If this sounds good to you, just phone our jobline or send your resume. Attention Elvis.

Colleen Barrett elaborated on what the company looked for (see Exhibit 11) in screening candidates for job openings:[22]

> We hire People to live the Southwest Way. They must possess a Warrior Spirit, lead with a Servant's Heart, and have a Fun-LUVing attitude. We hire People who fight to win, work hard, are dedicated, and have a passion for Customer Service. We won't hire People if something about their behavior won't be a Cultural fit. We hire the best. When our new hires walk through the door, our message to them is you are starting the flight of your life.

All job applications were processed through the People and Leadership Development Department.

EXHIBIT 11 Personal Traits, Attitudes, and Behaviors That Southwest Wanted Employees to Possess and Display

Living the Southwest Way		
Warrior Spirit	**Servant's Heart**	**Fun-LUVing Attitude**
• Work hard	• Follow The Golden Rule	• Have FUN
• Desire to be the best	• Adhere to the Basic Principles	• Don't take yourself too seriously
• Be courageous	• Treat others with respect	• Maintain perspective (balance)
• Display a sense of urgency	• Put others first	• Celebrate successes
• Persevere	• Be egalitarian	• Enjoy your work
• Innovate	• Demonstrate proactive Customer Service	• Be a passionate team player
	• Embrace the SWA Family	

Source: **www.southwest.com** (accessed August 18, 2010).

Screening Candidates In hiring for jobs that involved personal contact with passengers, the company looked for people-oriented applicants who were extroverted and had a good sense of humor. It tried to identify candidates with a knack for reading people's emotions and responding in a genuinely caring, empathetic manner. Southwest wanted employees to deliver the kind of service that showed they truly enjoyed meeting people, being around passengers, and doing their job, as opposed to delivering the kind of service that came across as being forced or taught. Kelleher elaborated: "We are interested in people who externalize, who focus on other people, who are motivated to help other people. We are not interested in navel gazers."[23] In addition to a "whistle while you work" attitude, Southwest was drawn to candidates who it thought would be likely to exercise initiative, work harmoniously with fellow employees, and be community-spirited.

Southwest did not use personality tests to screen job applicants nor did it ask them what they would or should do in certain hypothetical situations. Rather, the hiring staff at Southwest analyzed each job category to determine the specific behaviors, knowledge, and motivations that job holders needed and then tried to find candidates with the desired traits—a process called targeted selection. A trait common to all job categories was teamwork; a trait deemed critical for pilots and flight attendants was judgment. In exploring an applicant's aptitude for teamwork, interviewers often asked applicants to tell them about a time in a prior job when they went out of their way to help a co-worker or to explain how they had handled conflict with a co-worker. Another frequent question was: "What was your most embarrassing moment?" The thesis here was that having applicants talk about their past behaviors provided good clues about their future behaviors.

To test for unselfishness, Southwest interviewing teams typically gave a group of potential employees ample time to prepare five-minute presentations about themselves; during the presentations in an informal conversational setting, interviewers watched the audience to see who was absorbed in polishing their presentations and who was listening attentively, enjoying the stories being told, and applauding the efforts of the presenters. Those who were emotionally engaged in hearing the presenters and giving encouragement were deemed more apt to be team players than those who were focused on looking good themselves. All applicants for flight attendant positions were put through such a presentation exercise before an interview panel consisting of customers, experienced flight attendants, and members of the People and Leadership Department. Flight attendant candidates who got through the group presentation interviews then had to complete a three-on-one interview conducted by a recruiter, a supervisor from the hiring section of the People and Leadership Department, and a Southwest flight attendant; following this interview, the three-person panel tried to reach a consensus on whether to recommend or drop the candidate.

Training

Apart from the FAA-mandated training for certain employees, training activities at Southwest were designed and conducted by Southwest Airlines University (formerly the University for People). The curriculum included courses for new recruits, employees, and managers. Learning was viewed as a never-ending process for all company personnel; the expectation was that each employee should be an "intentional learner," looking to grow and develop not just from occasional classes taken at Southwest Airlines University but also from their everyday on-the-job experiences.

Southwest Airlines University conducted a variety of courses offered to maintenance personnel and other employees to meet the safety and security training requirements of the Federal Aviation Administration, the U.S. Department of Transportation, the Occupational Safety and Health Administration, and other government agencies. And there were courses on written communications, public speaking, stress management, career development, performance appraisal, decision making, leadership, customer service, corporate culture, environmental stewardship and sustainability, and employee relations to help employees advance their careers.

Leadership development courses that focused on developing people, team-building, strategic thinking, and being a change leader were keystone offerings. New supervisors attended a four-week course "Leadership Southwest Style" that emphasized coaching, empowering, and encouraging, rather than supervising or enforcing rules and regulations. New managers attended a two-and-a-half-day course on "Next-Level leadership." There were courses for employees wanting to explore whether a management career was for them and courses for high-potential employees wanting to pursue a long-term career at Southwest. From time to time, supervisors and executives attended courses on corporate culture, intended to help instill, ingrain, and nurture such cultural themes as teamwork, trust, harmony, and diversity. All employees who came into contact with customers, including pilots, received customer care training. Altogether, Southwest employees spent over 1.7 million hours in training sessions of one kind or another in 2015:[24]

Job Category	Amount of Training
Maintenance and support personnel	148,300 hours
Customer support and services personnel	214,700 hours
Flight attendants	241,700 hours
Pilots	476,300 hours
Ground operations personnel	656,400 hours

The OnBoarding Program for Newly Hired Employees Southwest had a program called OnBoarding "to welcome New Hires into the Southwest Family" and provide information and assistance from the time they were selected until the end of their first year. All new hires attended a full-day orientation course that covered the company's history, an overview of the airline industry and the competitive challenges that Southwest faced, an introduction to Southwest's culture and management practices, the expectations of employees, and demonstrations on "Living the Southwest Way." The culture introduction included a video called the *Southwest Shuffle* that featured hundreds of Southwest employees rapping about the fun they had on their jobs (at many Southwest gatherings, it was common for a group of employees to do the Southwest Shuffle, with the remaining attendees cheering and clapping). All new hires also received safety training. Anytime during their first 30 days, new employees were expected to access an interactive online tool—OnBoarding Online Orientation—to learn more about the company. During their first year of employment, new hires were invited to attend a "LUV@First Bite Luncheon" in the city where they worked; these luncheons were held on the same day as Leadership's Messages to the Field; at these luncheons, there were opportunities to network with other new hires and talk with senior leaders.

An additional element of the OnBoarding program involved assigning each new employee to an existing Southwest employee who had volunteered to sponsor a new hire and be of assistance in acclimating the new employee to the job and Living the Southwest Way; each volunteer sponsor received training from Southwest's OnBoarding Team in what was expected of a sponsor. Much of the indoctrination of new employees into the company's culture was done by the volunteer sponsor, co-workers, and the new employee's supervisor. Southwest made active use of a one-year probationary employment period to help ensure that new employees fit in with its culture and adequately embraced the company's cultural values.

Promotion

Approximately 80 to 90 percent of Southwest's supervisory positions were filled internally, reflecting management's belief that people who had "been there and done that" would be more likely to appreciate and understand the demands that people under them were experiencing and, also, more likely to enjoy the respect of their peers and higher-level managers. Employees could either apply for supervisory positions or be recommended by their present supervisor.

Employees being considered for managerial positions of large operations (Up and Coming Leaders) received training in every department of the company over a six-month period in which they continued to perform their current job. At the end of the six-month period, candidates were provided with 360-degree feedback from department heads, peers, and subordinates; personnel in the People and Leadership Department analyzed the feedback in deciding on the specific assignment of each candidate.[25]

Compensation and Benefits

Southwest's pay scales and fringe benefits were quite attractive compared to other major U.S. airlines (see Exhibit 12). Southwest's average pay for pilots in 2013 was anywhere from 31 to 92 percent higher than the average pay for pilots at American Airlines, Delta Air Lines, and United Airlines; the average pay for Southwest's flight attendants ranged from as little as 12 percent higher to as much as 38 percent higher than these same rivals. Its benefit package was the best of any domestic airline in 2013.

In 2016, in addition to vacation, paid holidays, and sick leave, Southwest offered full-time and

EXHIBIT 12 Employee Compensation and Benefits at Selected U.S. Airlines, 2005, 2009, and 2013

	Southwest Airlines	American Airlines	Delta Air Lines	United Airlines
Average pilot wage/salary				
2005	**$157,420**	$137,734	$155,532	$114,789
2009	**176,225**	137,482	137,948	125,465
2013	**229,290**	144,266	174,196	153,786
Averageflightattendantwage/salary				
2005	**$ 42,045**	$ 46,191	$ 40,037	$ 35,450
2009	**46,839**	50,933	39,161	40,559
2013	**61,277**	52,000	45,945	47,588
All-employeeaveragewage/salary				
2005	**$ 62,122**	$ 57,889	$ 57,460	$ 49,863
2009	**75,624**	62,961	56,030	58,239
2013	**81,675**	68,269	72,960	68,056
Averagebenefitsperemployee				
2005	**$ 26,075**	$ 24,460	$ 39,379	$ 20,980
2009	**23,820**	30,516	28,279	22,749
2013	**34,573**	27,028	32,638	32,222

Note: Data after 2013 was not available.

Sources: **www.airlinepilotcentral.com**; **www.airlinefinancials.com** (both accessed May 22, 2013).

part-time Southwest and AirTran employees a benefits package that included:

- A 401(k) retirement savings plan
- A profit-sharing plan
- Medical and prescription coverage
- Mental health chemical dependency coverage
- Vision coverage
- Dental coverage
- Adoption assistance
- Mental health assistance
- Life insurance
- Accidental death and dismemberment insurance
- Long-term disability insurance
- Dependent life insurance
- Dependent care flexible spending account
- Health care flexible spending account
- Employee stock purchase plan
- Wellness program
- Flight privileges
- Health care for committed partners
- Early retiree health care

Company contributions to employee 410(k) and profit-sharing plans totaled $1.74 billion during 2009–2013. In 2013, Southwest's contribution to the profit-sharing plan represented about 6 percent of each eligible employee's compensation. Employees participating in stock purchases via payroll deduction bought 1.7 million shares in 2011, 2.2 million shares in 2012, and 1.5 million shares in 2013 at prices equal to 90 percent of the market value at the end of each monthly purchase period.

Employee Relations

About 83 percent of Southwest's 45,000 employees belonged to a union. An in-house union—the

Southwest Airline Pilots Association (SWAPA)—represented the company's pilots. The Teamsters Union represented Southwest's stock clerks and flight simulator technicians; a local of the Transportation Workers of America represented flight attendants; another local of the Transportation Workers of America represented baggage handlers, ground crews, and provisioning employees; the International Association of Machinists and Aerospace Workers represented customer service and reservation employees, and the Aircraft Mechanics Fraternal Association represented the company's mechanics.

Management encouraged union members and negotiators to research their pressing issues and to conduct employee surveys before each contract negotiation. Southwest's contracts with the unions representing its employees were relatively free of restrictive work rules and narrow job classifications that might impede worker productivity. All of the contracts allowed any qualified employee to perform any function—thus pilots, ticket agents, and gate personnel could help load and unload baggage when needed and flight attendants could pick up trash and make flight cabins more presentable for passengers boarding the next flight.

Except for one brief strike by machinists in the early 1980s and some unusually difficult negotiations in 2000–2001, Southwest's relationships with the unions representing its employee groups had been harmonious and nonadversarial for the most part. However, the company was engaged in difficult contract negotiations with its pilots in 2016.

Contract Negotiations with the Southwest Airlines Pilots' Association

Contract negotiations between Southwest Airlines management and SWAPA involved a number of issues, including pay. In 2015, the contracted hourly rate of pay for a Boeing 737 captain at Southwest Airlines was $216 with 78 guaranteed hours per month. The hourly rate of pay for an American 737 captain was $235 with 73 guaranteed hours, while Delta 737 captains were paid $217 per hour for 65 guaranteed hours and captains of United Airlines Boeing 737s were paid $236 per hour for 70 guaranteed hours per month.

In mid-2016, SWAPA and its member pilots were concerned with an hourly rate of pay that was the lowest among major carriers and had been unchanged since 2011. Pilots were also seeking improvements to work rules and flying schedules and a separate wage rate for larger 737-MAX aircraft. It was typical in the airline industry for pilot hourly rates of pay to increase with the size of the aircraft. Southwest's pilots were concerned that the company had made a firm order for 200 Boeing 737-MAX aircraft and had options on an additional 191 planes for delivery between 2017 and 2027, but had not negotiated a wage rate with pilots who would fly the larger planes. The SWAPA and management had sent a tentative agreement to membership for a vote in September 2015, but the terms were rejected by Southwest's pilots in November 2015. The SWAPA filed suit against Southwest Airlines in May 2016 concerning the lack of a contract with pilots to fly the 737-MAX planes scheduled for delivery in 2017.

The No-Layoff Policy

Southwest Airlines had never laid off or furloughed any of its employees since the company began operations in 1971. The company's no-layoff policy was seen as integral to how the company treated its employees and management efforts to sustain and nurture the culture. According to Kelleher,[26]

> Nothing kills your company's culture like layoffs. Nobody has ever been furloughed here, and that is unprecedented in the airline industry. It's been a huge strength of ours. It's certainly helped negotiate our union contracts. . . . We could have furloughed at various times and been more profitable, but I always thought that was shortsighted. You want to show your people you value them and you're not going to hurt them just to get a little more money in the short term. Not furloughing people breeds loyalty. It breeds a sense of security. It breeds a sense of trust.

Southwest had built up considerable goodwill with its employees and unions over the years by avoiding layoffs. Both senior management and Southwest employees regarded the three recent buyout offers as a better approach to workforce reduction than involuntary layoffs.

Operation Kick Tail

In 2007, Southwest management launched an internal initiative called Operation Kick Tail, a multiyear call to action for employees to focus even more attention on providing high-quality customer service, maintaining low costs, and nurturing the Southwest culture. One component of this initiative involved giving a Kick Tail Award to employees when they did something exemplary to make a positive difference in a customer's travel experience or in the life of a co-worker or otherwise stood out in exhibiting the values in Living the Southwest Way (Exhibit 11).

Gary Kelly saw this aspect of Operation Kick Tail as a way to foster the employee attitudes and commitment needed to provide "Positively Outrageous Customer Service;" he explained:

> One of Southwest's rituals is finding and developing People who are "built to serve." That allows us to provide a personal, warm level of service that is unmatched in the airline industry.

Southwest management viewed the Operation Kick Tail initiative as a means to better engage and incentivize employees to strengthen their display of the traits in Living the Southwest Way (and achieve a competitive edge keyed to superior customer service).

Management Style

At Southwest, management strived to do things in a manner that would make Southwest employees proud of the company they worked for and its workforce practices. Managers were expected to spend at least one-third of their time out of the office, walking around the facilities under their supervision, observing firsthand what was going on, listening to employees and being responsive to their concerns. A former director of people development at Southwest told of a conversation he had with one of Southwest's terminal managers:[27]

> While I was out in the field visiting one of our stations, one of our managers mentioned to me that he wanted to put up a suggestion box. I responded by saying that, Sure—why don't you put up a suggestion box right here on this wall and then admit you are a failure as a manager?" Our theory is, if you have to put up a box so people can write down their ideas and toss them in, it means you are not doing what you are supposed to be doing. You are supposed to be setting your people up to be winners. To do that, you should be there listening to them and available to them in person, not via a suggestion box. For the most part, I think we have a very good sense of this at Southwest. I think that most people employed here know that they can call any one of our vice presidents on the telephone and get heard, almost immediately.
>
> The suggestion box gives managers an out; it relinquishes their responsibility to be accessible to their people, and that's when we have gotten in trouble at Southwest—when we can no longer be responsive to our flight attendants or customer service agents, when they can't gain access to somebody who can give them resources and answers.

Company executives were very approachable, insisting on being called by their first names. At new employee orientations, people were told, "We do not call the company chairman and CEO Mr. Kelly, we call him Gary." Managers and executives had an open door policy, actively listening to employee concerns, opinions, and suggestions for reducing costs and improving efficiency.

Employee-led initiatives were common. Southwest's pilots had been instrumental in developing new protocols for takeoffs and landings that conserved fuel. Another frontline employee had suggested not putting the company logos on trash bags, saving an estimated $250,000 annually. Rather than buy 800 computers for a new reservations center in Albuquerque, company employees determined that they could buy the parts and assemble the PCs themselves for half the price of a new PC, saving the company $1 million. It was Southwest clerks that came up with the idea of doing away with paper tickets and shifting to e-tickets.

There were only four layers of management between a frontline supervisor and the CEO. Southwest's employees enjoyed substantial authority and decision-making power. According to Kelleher:[28]

> We've tried to create an environment where people are able to, in effect, bypass even the fairly lean structures that we have so that they don't have to convene a meeting of the sages in order to get something done. In many cases, they can just go ahead and do it on their own. They can take individual responsibility for it and know they will not be crucified if it doesn't work out. Our leanness requires people to be comfortable in making their own decisions and undertaking their own efforts.

From time to time, there were candid meetings of frontline employees and managers where operating problems and issues between and among workers and departments were acknowledged, openly discussed, and resolved.[29] Informal problem avoidance and rapid problem resolution were seen as managerial virtues.

Southwest's Two Big Core Values—LUV and Fun

Two core values—LUV and fun—permeated the work environment at Southwest. LUV was much more than the company's ticker symbol and a recurring theme in Southwest's advertising campaigns.

Over the years, LUV grew into Southwest's codeword for treating individuals—fellow employees and customers—with dignity and respect and demonstrating a caring, loving attitude. LUV and red hearts commonly appeared on banners and posters at company facilities, as reminders of the compassion that was expected toward customers and other employees. Practicing the Golden Rule, internally and externally, was expected of all employees. Employees who struggled to live up to these expectations were subjected to considerable peer pressure and usually were asked to seek employment elsewhere if they did not soon leave on their own volition.

Fun at Southwest was exactly what the word implies and it occurred throughout the company in the form of the generally entertaining behavior of employees in performing their jobs, the ongoing pranks and jokes, and frequent company-sponsored parties and celebrations (which typically included the Southwest Shuffle). On holidays, employees were encouraged to dress in costumes. There were charity benefit games, chili cook-offs, Halloween parties, new Ronald McDonald House dedications, and other special events of one kind or another at one location or another almost every week. According to one manager, "We're kind of a big family here, and family members have fun together."

Culture-Building Efforts

Southwest executives believed that the company's growth was primarily a function of the rate at which it could hire and train people to fit into its culture and consistently display the traits and behaviors set forth in Living the Southwest Way. Kelly said, "some things at Southwest won't change. We will continue to expect our people to live what we describe as the 'Southwest Way,' which is to have a Warrior Spirit, Servant's Heart, and Fun-Loving Attitude. Those three things have defined our culture for 36 years."[30]

The Corporate Culture Committee Southwest formed a Corporate Culture Committee in 1990 to promote "Positively Outrageous Service" and devise tributes, contests, and celebrations intended to nurture and perpetuate the Southwest Spirit and Living the Southwest Way. The committee was composed of 100 employees who had demonstrated their commitment to Southwest's mission and values and zeal in exhibiting the Southwest Spirit and Living the Southwest Way. Members came from a cross-section of departments and locations and functioned as cultural ambassadors, missionaries, and storytellers during their two-year term.

The Corporate Culture Committee had four all-day meetings annually; ad hoc subcommittees formed throughout the year met more frequently. Over the years, the committee had sponsored and supported hundreds of ways to promote and ingrain the traits and behaviors embedded in Living the Southwest Way—examples included promoting the use of red hearts and LUV to embody the spirit of Southwest employees caring about each other and Southwest's customers, showing up at a facility to serve pizza or ice cream to employees or to remodel and decorate an employee break room. Kelleher indicated, "We're not big on Committees at Southwest, but of the committees we do have, the Culture Committee is the most important."[31]

In addition, there was a Culture Services Team in Southwest's executive office dedicated solely to ensuring that the culture of Southwest Airlines remained alive and well; the team's duties included coordinating the yearly Messages to the Field, planning Spirit Parties at various locations, writing commendations and congratulatory notes to employees exhibiting outstanding performances, organizing the company's Annual Awards Banquet, and supporting the Corporate Culture Committee. Each major department and geographic operating unit had a Local Culture Committee charged with organizing culture-building activities and nurturing the Southwest Spirit within their unit. More recently, the company had created a new position in each of its major operating departments and largest geographic locations called Culture Ambassador; the primary function of cultural ambassadors was to nurture the Southwest Spirit by helping ensure that the Local Culture Committee had the resources needed to foster the culture at each of their locations, planning and coordinating departmental celebrations and employee appreciation events, and acting as a liaison between the local office and the corporate office on culture-related matters.

Efforts to Nurture and Sustain the Southwest Culture Apart from the efforts of the Corporate Culture Committee, the Local Culture Committees, and the cultural ambassadors, Southwest management sought to reinforce the company's core values and culture via a series of employee recognition programs to single out and praise employees for their outstanding contributions to customer service, operational excellence, cost-efficiency, and display of the Southwest Spirit. In addition to Kick Tail awards, there were "Heroes of the Heart" awards, *Spirit* magazine Star of the Month awards, President's Awards, and LUV Reports whereby one or more employees could recognize other employees for an outstanding performance or contribution.

Other culture-supportive activities included a CoHearts mentoring program, a Day in the Field program where employees spent time working in another area of the company's operations, a Helping Hands program where volunteers from around the system traveled to work two weekend shifts at other Southwest facilities that were temporarily shorthanded or experiencing heavy workloads, and periodic Culture Exchange meetings to celebrate the Southwest Spirit and company milestones. Almost every event at Southwest was videotaped, which provided footage for creating such multipurpose videos as *Keepin' the Spirit Alive* that could be shown at company events all over the system and used in training courses. The concepts of LUV and fun were spotlighted in all of the company's training manuals and videos.

Southwest's monthly employee newsletter often spotlighted the experiences and deeds of particular employees, reprinted letters of praise from customers, and reported company celebrations of milestones. A quarterly news video, *As the Plane Turns,* was sent to all facilities to keep employees up to date on company happenings, provide clips of special events, and share messages from customers, employees, and executives. The company had published a book for employees describing "outrageous" acts of service.

In 2012, Southwest launched the SWAG (Southwest Airlines Gratitude) initiative, which included a software tool that enabled each employee to set up a profile that listed all the recognitions and awards he or she received. This tool also allowed the employee to send commendations to other employees recognizing their hardworking efforts and/or exemplary performance. Employees who won Kick Tail, Heroes of the Heart, Star of the Month, and President's Awards were credited with SWAG points that could be redeemed in the company's SWAG Shop, which contained thousands of items and enabled employees to reward themselves however they found most meaningful.

Employee Productivity

Management was convinced the company's strategy, culture, esprit de corps, and people management practices fostered high labor productivity and contributed to Southwest having low labor costs in comparison to the labor costs at its principal domestic rivals (Exhibit 9). When a Southwest flight pulled up to the gate, ground crews, gate personnel, and flight attendants hustled to perform all the tasks requisite to turn the plane quickly—employees took pride in doing their part to achieve good on-time performance. Southwest's turnaround times were in the 25- to 30-minute range, versus an industry average of around 45 minutes. In 2015, just as had been the case for many years, Southwest's labor productivity compared quite favorably with its chief domestic competitors:

	Productivity Measure	
	Passengers Enplaned per Employee, 2015	Employees per Plane, 2015
Southwest Airlines	**2,869**	**72**
American Airlines	1,147	109
Delta Air Lines	1,633	104
United Airlines	1,129	116

Source: Bureau of Transportation Statistics, various data tables.

Southwest Airlines's Competitive Standing in 2016

Under Herb Kelleher, instituting practices, procedures, and support systems that promoted operating excellence had become a tradition and a source of company pride. Much time and effort over the years had gone into finding the most effective ways to do aircraft maintenance, to operate safely, to make baggage handling more efficient and baggage transfers more accurate, and to improve the percentage of on-time arrivals and departures. Believing that air travelers were more likely to fly Southwest if its flights were reliable and on-time, Southwest's managers constantly monitored on-time arrivals and departures, making inquiries when many flights ran behind and searching for ways to improve on-time performance. One initiative to help minimize weather and operational delays involved the development of a state-of-the-art flight dispatch system.

Southwest's current CEO, Gary Kelly, had followed Kelleher's lead in pushing for operating excellence. One of Kelly's strategic objectives for Southwest was "to be the safest, most efficient, and most reliable airline in the world." Southwest managers and employees in all positions and ranks were proactive in offering suggestions for improving Southwest's practices and procedures; those with merit were quickly implemented. Southwest was considered to have one of the most competent and thorough aircraft maintenance programs in the commercial airline industry and, in 2016 was widely regarded as the best operator among U.S. airlines. Exhibit 13 presents data comparing Southwest against its four domestic rivals on four measures of operating performance.

EXHIBIT 13 Comparative Statistics on On-Time Flights, Mishandled Baggage, Boarding Denials Due to Oversold Flights, and Passenger Complaints for Major U.S. Airlines, 2000, 2005, 2010, 2013, 2015–2016

Percentage of Scheduled Flights Arriving within 15 Minutes of the Scheduled Time (during the previous 12 months ending in May of each year)						
Airline	2000	2005	2010	2013	2015	2016
American Airlines	75.8%	78.0%	79.6%	77.6%	76.3%	81.7%
Delta Air Lines	78.3	76.4	77.4	84.5	85.2	87.2
Southwest Airlines	**78.7**	**79.9**	**79.5**	**76.7**	**76.8**	**81.1**
United Airlines	71.6	79.8	85.2	79.3	76.3	80.9

Mishandled Baggage Reports per 1,000 Passengers (in May of each year)						
Airline	2000	2005	2010	2013	2015	2016
American Airlines	5.44	4.58	4.36	3.02	4.38	3.08
Delta Air Lines	3.64	6.21	4.90	2.15	1.82	1.56
Southwest Airlines	**4.14**	**3.46**	**4.97**	**3.72**	**3.20**	**2.77**
United Airlines	6.71	4.00	4.13	3.47	2.85	2.29

Involuntary Denied Boardings per 10,000 Passengers Due to Oversold Flights (January through March of each year)						
Airline	2000	2005	2010	2013	2015	2016
American Airlines	0.59	0.72	0.75	0.36	0.79	0.84
Delta Air Lines	0.44	1.06	0.29	0.52	0.22	0.10
Southwest Airlines	**1.70**	**0.74**	**0.76**	**0.66**	**1.04**	**0.91**
United Airlines	1.61	0.42	1.00	1.37	1.00	0.49

Complaints per 100,000 Passengers Boarded (in May of each year)						
Airline	2000	2005	2010	2013	2015	2016
American Airlines	2.77	1.01	1.08	1.99	3.32	1.99
Delta Air Lines	1.60	0.91	1.21	0.53	0.56	0.45
Southwest Airlines	**0.41**	**0.17**	**0.29**	**0.36**	**0.40**	**0.29**
United Airlines	5.07	0.87	1.47	1.89	2.32	1.99

Sources: Office of Aviation Enforcement and Proceedings, Air Travel Consumer Report, various years.

ENDNOTES

[1] Kevin and Jackie Freiberg, *NUTS! Southwest Airlines' Crazy Recipe for Business and Personal Success* (New York: Broadway Books, 1998), p. 15.
[2] Ibid., pp. 16–18.
[3] Katrina Brooker, "The Chairman of the Board Looks Back," *Fortune,* May 28, 2001, p. 66.
[4] Feiberg and Freiberg, *NUTS!*, p. 31.
[5] Ibid., pp. 26–27.
[6] Ibid., pp. 246–247.
[7] As quoted in the *Dallas Morning News,* March 20, 2001.
[8] Quoted in Brooker, "The Chairman of the Board Looks Back," p. 64.
[9] Ibid., p. 72.
[10] As quoted in *The Seattle Times,* March 20, 2001, p. C3.
[11] Speech at Texas Christian University, September 13, 2007, www.southwest.com (accessed September 8, 2008).
[12] Freiberg and Freiberg, *NUTS!*, p. 163.
[13] Company press release, July 15, 2004.
[14] Speech to Greater Boston Chamber of Commerce, April 23, 2008, www.southwest.com (accessed September 5, 2008).
[15] Speech to Business Today International Conference, November 20, 2007, www.southwest.com (accessed September 8, 2008).
[16] As cited in Freiberg and Freiberg, *NUTS!*, p. 288.
[17] Speech by Colleen Barrett on January 22, 2007, www.southwest.com (accessed September 5, 2008).
[18] Brenda Paik Sunoo, "How Fun Flies at Southwest Airlines," *Personnel Journal* 74, no. 6 (June 1995), p. 70.
[19] Statement posted in the Careers section at www.southwest.com (accessed August 18, 2010, and May 16, 2016). Kelly's statement had been continuously posted at www.southwest.com since 2009.
[20] As quoted in James Campbell Quick, "Crafting an Organizational Structure: Herb's Hand at Southwest Airlines," *Organizational Dynamics* 21, no. 2 (Autumn 1992), p. 51.
[21] Southwest's ad titled "Work in a Place Where Elvis Has Been Spotted"; Sunoo, "How Fun Flies at Southwest Airlines," pp. 64–65.
[22] Speech to the Paso Del Norte Group in El Paso, Texas, January 22, 2007, www.southwest.com (accessed September 5, 2008).
[23] Quick, "Crafting an Organizational Structure," p. 52.
[24] Southwest's "2015 One Report," www.southwest.com (accessed May 16, 2014).
[25] Sunoo, "How Fun Flies at Southwest Airlines," p. 72.
[26] Brooker, "The Chairman of the Board Looks Back," p. 72.
[27] Freiberg and Freiberg, *NUTS!*, p. 273.
[28] Ibid., p. 76.
[29] Hallowell, "Southwest Airlines: A Case Study Linking Employee Needs Satisfaction and Organizational Capabilities to Competitive Advantage," p. 524.
[30] Speech to Business Today International Conference, November 20, 2007, www.southwest.com (accessed September 8, 2008).
[31] Freiberg and Freiberg, *NUTS!*, p. 165.

CASE 26

Rosen Hotels & Resorts: Delivering Superior Customer Service

Randall D. Harris
Texas A&M University–Corpus Christi

"That's really what it's all about, isn't it?" said Harris Rosen, president of Rosen Hotels & Resorts. "Exemplary service. What we've discovered, and I'm sure that others have identified as well, is that there is a distinct relationship between enthusiastic, happy associates and the company that they work for." Rosen, 76, was the founder, president, and chief operating officer of Rosen Hotels & Resorts. Founded in 1974 in Orlando, Florida, Rosen began with the purchase of one hotel in June of 1974 during the 1970's OPEC oil embargo and a slumping tourist market. In 2016, he presided over a chain of seven hotels and two wholly owned subsidiaries in the greater Orlando, Florida, metropolis.

A special attitude and an infectious warmth seemed to exude from all of the Rosen Hotels & Resorts associates. "We have excellent leadership," said Sarah Sherwin, conference center sales manager at Rosen Shingle Creek, one of the seven hotels in the Rosen Hotels portfolio. "Having Mr. Rosen locally, he's just someone who's great to look up to. He takes care of his associates and he gives back to the community. It's nice to know I'm working for an organization such as ours," she said. Exhibit 1 presents an overview of Rosen Hotels & Resorts. Exhibit 2 presents a photo of Rosen Shingle Creek, the company's premier 1,501 guestroom conference facility.

The Golden Rule really described the culture of the Rosen Hotels organization, according to Jonni Kimberly, director of human resources. "It's one thing for a manager in an organization to put their hand on your shoulder and say 'I understand what you're going through' but it's another thing to say 'I understand what you're going through and we're going to help you go through it,'" said Kimberly. This level of caring was reflected in real services for Rosen associates. There was an on-site health care clinic that associates could visit while on the clock and an outreach center to assist associates and their dependents with real-life situations, like the loss of a family member or a medical emergency.

Guests at Rosen Hotels & Resorts said they enjoyed a tremendous hotel experience. "I had the experience of my life at this hotel," one guest said, talking about Rosen Shingle Creek. "The staff were really friendly and professional. The hotel was very clean, beautiful and peaceful. I love it!" Customers often spoke about the friendly staff, competitive room rates, and the spacious, clean, and comfortable rooms. Many Rosen Hotels guests were long-time repeat customers. Some, in fact, had been returning for 25 to 30 years.

The Rosen ethos was also reflected in the company's commitment to corporate social responsibility. In 1993, as it became clear that financial success for the Rosen organization was ensured, Harris Rosen had an epiphany and began to give back. The Tangelo Park Program, which was created out of that decision, ensured that every child living in the Tangelo Park neighborhood would have not only a free preschool education, but that each of them would be able to go to college, technical school, or a Florida public university, free of charge. This made Rosen Hotels & Resorts not only a terrific place to visit but also an active and caring member of the greater Orlando, Florida, community.

EXHIBIT 1 Rosen Hotels & Resorts—Locations and Subsidiaries

Hotel/Subsidiary Name	Address	Target Market/ Subsidiary Focus	Website
Rosen Inn	6327 International Drive Orlando, FL 32819	Leisure Traveler	www.roseninn6327.com/
Rosen Inn International	7600 International Drive Orlando, FL 32819	Leisure Traveler	roseninn7600.com/
Rosen Inn Pointe Orlando	9000 International Drive Orlando, FL 32819	Leisure Traveler	www.roseninn9000.com/
Rosen Plaza Hotel	9700 International Drive Orlando, FL 32819	Convention Traveler	www.rosenplaza.com/
Rosen Centre Hotel	9840 International Drive Orlando, FL 32819	Convention Traveler	www.rosencentre.com/
Rosen Shingle Creek	9939 Universal Blvd. Orlando, FL 32819	Convention Traveler	www.rosenshinglecreek.com/
Clarion Inn Lake Buena Vista	8442 Palm ParkwayLake Buena Vista, FL 32836	Leisure Traveler	www.clarionlbv.com/
ProvInsure	9700 International Drive Orlando, FL 32819-8114	Health Care, Risk Management, Benefits	www.provinsure.com/
Millennium Technology Group	7657 Golf Channel Drive Orlando FL, 32819	Information Technology	mtg-fl.com/

Source: Rosen Hotels & Resorts.

EXHIBIT 2 Rosen Shingle Creek

Source: Rosen Hotels & Resorts

U.S. HOTEL AND MOTEL INDUSTRY

Companies in the U.S. hotel and motel industry provided short-term accommodations in hotels, motels, motor hotels, and resort hotels and motels. Many establishments also offered other services such as food and beverages, recreation, conference facilities, laundry, and on-site parking. The industry was highly concentrated, with the top five companies earning approximately 42 percent of industry revenue. Exhibit 3 shows selected financial and operating statistics for the top five lodging chains in 2015.

Recent Performance

Following the global financial crisis of 2007–2008, growth recovered in the U.S. hotel and motel industry and had been strong from 2011 to 2015. Overall, the hotel industry had outperformed the broader U.S. economy and was driven by robust demand growth from both leisure and business travelers, as well as international business and leisure travelers visiting the United States. Over the five years to 2015, the industry was expected to grow at an annualized rate of 3.7 percent to reach $166.5 billion in revenues.

Approximately 50 percent of industry revenue came from domestic leisure travelers. According to the U.S. Travel Association, about three out of every four trips were taken for leisure purposes. Business travelers accounted for about 30.5 percent of industry revenue. In the business segment, general business travel accounted for about 18.2 percent of industry revenue while meetings, conferences, and events accounted for 12.3 percent of industry spending. In general, business travelers spent more than leisure travelers, making them an attractive segment of the market for hotel and motel chains to pursue.

EXHIBIT 3 Selected Financial and Operating Statistics for the Five Major U.S. Hotel Chains, 2015

Company Name	U.S. Market Share	Number of Properties	Number of Employees, 2015	Revenues, 2015	Net Income, 2015	Key Brands
Hilton Worldwide Holdings Inc.	13.7%	4,000	157,000	$22.9 billion	$748 million	Hilton, Hilton Garden Inn, Doubletree, Embassy Suites, Hampton, Homewood Suites
Marriott International, Inc.	13.5%	4,175	127,500	$22.5 billion	$859 million	Marriott, Ritz-Carlton, SpringHill Suites, Fairfield Inn, Residence Inn, Courtyard, Townplace Suites
Intercontinental Hotels Group PLC	7.5%	4,900	7,797	$12.5 billion	$391 million	Intercontinental, Crowne Plaza, Holiday Inn, Holiday Inn Express, Staybridge Suites, Candlewood Suites
Starwood Hotels & Resorts Worldwide Inc.	3.7%	1,207	188,000	$5.8 billion	$489 million	Sheraton, Westin, W, Four Points by Sheraton, St. Regis, Le Meridien, Element
Wyndham Worldwide Corporation	3.7%	5,700	37,700	$5.5 billion	$612 million	Ramada, Super 8 Motels, Travelodge, Days Inn, Howard Johnson, Amerihost Inn, Knights Inn, Villager, Wingate Inns

Sources: IBISWorld; Mergent Online.

International visitors to the United States accounted for about 19.5 percent of industry revenue. Major countries of origin for international visitors included Canada, Mexico, the UK, Japan, and Germany.

Hotel development had been sluggish following the global economic recession. Development of new hotels hit a low in 2011. As the economy began to accelerate from 2011 to 2015, demand for hotel rooms began to move ahead of room inventory, causing room rates to rise. In the hotel industry, the metric used to track this was called RevPAR, or revenue per available room. RevPAR was typically calculated as the average daily room rate times the occupancy rate. In 2015, industry RevPAR had continued to rise, and hotel chains were planning for increased hotel expansions and new hotel and motel openings.

Online Hotel Reservations

The widespread adoption and increasing usage of the Internet had greatly benefited the U.S. hotel and motel industry. Hotel operators were increasingly using the Internet to gather information about prospective and future clients, target and focus their marketing campaigns, manage customer reservations, and purchase supplies for their properties, all while lowering costs. Guest rewards programs frequently used targeted e-mails to communicate with their members to drive repeat hotel business, particularly for frequent travelers.

Travelers were also increasingly using the Internet to connect to lodging providers. In 2015, the number one channel by which hotel guests booked their reservation was the websites of the major hotel/motel chains. Fully 27.9 percent of all bookings in 2014 were via the hotel website. Hotel website bookings were up 6.9 percent in fiscal 2014, almost double the growth rate of the industry. Online travel agents, such as Expedia and Priceline.com, were 14.9 percent of all hotel/motel bookings. Increasingly, hotel operators were selling a portion of their unsold rooms via these online travel agents, thereby increasingly their revenues and occupancy rates. Exhibit 4 presents the channels for hotel room reservations in 2014.

The platform by which customers were purchasing online was also beginning to be increasingly conducted via mobile applications. Mobile technologies, including smartphones, tablets, and wearable devices, were an increasingly important technological gateway for room bookings. Adara Global estimated that two in three hotel guests had a smartphone, with 78 percent smartphone ownership for frequent travelers between the ages of 18 to 48. Hotel chain La Quinta Inn & Suites estimated that mobile devices drove 23 percent of its digital traffic in 2012. Hotel Marketing.com was forecasting that mobile was poised to become the dominant method for online booking in the very near future, particularly for last-minute hotel reservations.

Orlando, Florida: The Number One Tourist Destination

The number one tourist destination in the United States was Orlando, Florida. In 2015, the greater

EXHIBIT 4 Share of Hotel and Motel Reservations by Booking Method, 2014

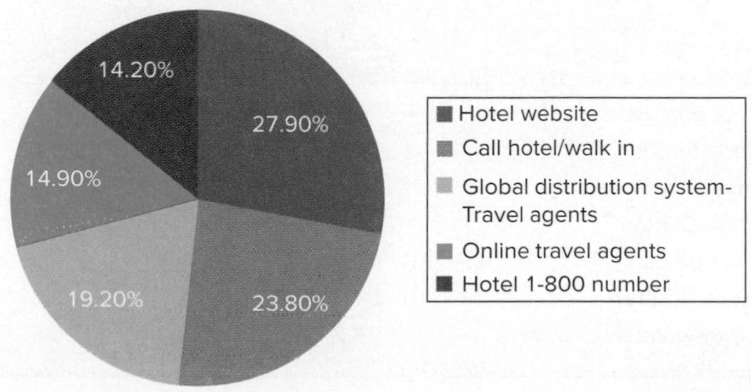

Sources: TravelClick; IBISWorld.

Orlando metropolitan area hosted 66 million visitors, according to Visit Orlando. Many visitors to Orlando, particular from outside the United States, arrived via the Orlando International Airport (Airport Code: MCO). Orlando International Airport handled 35 million passengers in 2014, up almost 3 percent for the year, according to the Orlando Economic Development Commission. The primary driver for hotel occupancy in Orlando was tourist attractions: Orlando boasted four major theme parks (including Walt Disney World, Universal Studios, and SeaWorld Orlando), as well as two water parks. Travel to Orlando was also heavily driven by trade shows and conventions hosted at the Orange County Convention Center. In 2014, the convention center hosted 1.1 million attendees, an all-time high.

The 2015 demand in the Orlando market for hotel and motel rooms was very strong. Tracking national trends, hotel operators had been slow to expand or build new hotels following the 2007–2008 recession. As a result, room inventory in Orlando increased only 1.7 percent in the first half of 2015, while demand for rooms increased 5.7 percent. As a result, room occupancy rates, average daily rates, and revenue per available room (RevPAR) had all shown strong growth in 2015. Exhibit 5 shows metro Orlando hospitality statistics for 2012–2014.

Orlando Tourism and Lodging Patterns

The Orlando hotel market was divided into seven submarkets. Two of these markets, the Lake Buena Vista district and the International Drive district, accounted for approximately 64 percent of total hotel inventory. The Lake Buena Vista district represented hotels and motels that were adjacent or nearby to the Walt Disney World Resort, located to the southwest of Orlando along the Interstate 4 corridor. The International Drive district, located in the central or west central part of Orlando, was the area closest to the Universal Studios theme parks, Sea World, and the Orange County Convention Center.

EXHIBIT 5 Metro Orlando Hospitality Statistics, 2012–2014

Average Daily Room Rate ($)				
Rank	Submarket	2012	2013	2014
1	Lake Buena Vista	$103.65	$114.98	$120.62
2	International Drive	$109.03	$111.84	$119.02
3	Orlando South	$ 98.00	$ 99.13	$104.76
4	Orlando Central	$ 76.00	$ 77.50	$ 84.43
5	Kissimmee East	$ 74.96	$ 77.29	$ 82.06
6	Orlando North	$ 70.72	$ 71.76	$ 76.01
7	Kissimmee West	$ 65.44	$ 62.25	$ 62.97

Hotel Occupancy Rate (%)				
Rank	Submarket	2012	2013	2014
1	Lake Buena Vista	76.1%	77.1%	81.3%
2	Orlando South	70.0%	73.4%	76.2%
3	International Drive	70.6%	71.5%	74.5%
4	Orlando Central	63.0%	66.5%	70.1%
5	Kissimmee East	62.0%	62.9%	64.3%
6	Orlando North	57.3%	61.9%	63.9%
7	Kissimmee West	54.2%	55.0%	59.4%

Source: HVS Miami.

EXHIBIT 6 Metro Orlando Hotel Inventory Distribution, 2015

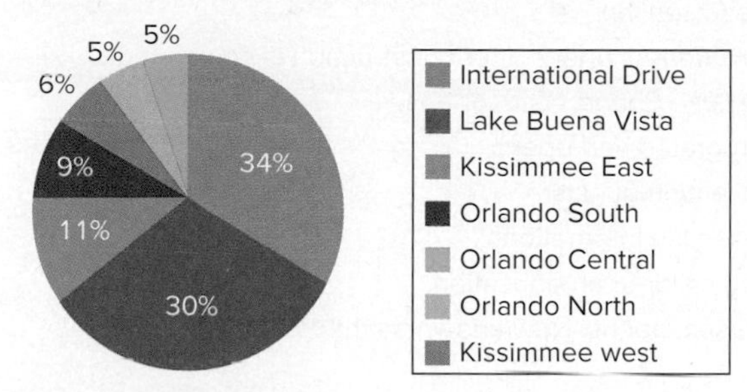

Source: HVS Miami.

International Drive ran north–south along Interstate 4, north of the Disney complex. Hotel development and demand growth had been particularly heavy in both of these areas. In addition, International Drive was increasingly becoming a tourist destination of its own accord, with restaurants, nightclubs a brand-new 400-foot observation wheel. Exhibit 6 presents Metro Orlando Inventory Distribution in 2015.

Orlando was the second-largest hotel market in the United States, with 489 properties and 127,420 rooms. The largest hotel owner and operator in the market, with 19 properties and 24,432 rooms, was the Walt Disney World Resort. Disney alone accounted for approximately 20 percent of the Orlando hotel market. Most of the Disney properties were located in the Lake Buena Vista district near the Walt Disney World Resort. All of the major hotel and motel chains had a presence in the Orlando market. Rosen Hotels & Resorts, with 7 properties and approximately 6,300 rooms, held about 5 percent of the Orlando market. The majority of the Rosen properties were located on International Drive, near Universal Studios and the Orange County Convention Center, with one property in the Lake Buena Vista district near Walt Disney World.

ROSEN HOTELS & RESORTS

"He came from a very humble family on the lower East Side of New York City," said Dr. Abraham Pizam, dean of the Rosen College of Hospitality at the University of Central Florida. "Whatever he achieved throughout the years, he achieved by his own sweat, tears and brains." Harris Rosen traveled a long road to reach the current success of Rosen Hotels & Resorts. Rosen recalled when he did all of the gardening, and many of the other roles, by himself at his first hotel. "One has to sacrifice, I think," Rosen said, "Although living where you work for sixteen years is a bit crazy. But it required that kind of attention." Exhibit 7 presents a timeline of key events in the Rosen Hotels & Resorts history.

Company History

At the age of 10, Harris Rosen worked weekends for his dad at the Waldorf Astoria hotel in New York City. His father was a security engineer and poster painter and earned extra money creating place cards for the hotel's fancy banquets. Harris's job (for which he was paid one penny per card) was to erase any pencil marks on the card and place them in a shoebox in alphabetical sequence. Then Harris and his dad would take the cards to the Waldorf ballroom. There they would meet with the banquet manager, who would have the cards placed around the appropriate table. To get to the ballroom, Harris and his dad would often have to take an elevator. One day as they were entering the elevator, Harris noticed a beautiful young blonde woman standing next to a tall, distinguished gentleman. Harris quietly asked his dad to introduce him to the young lady. His dad said, "First I will introduce you to the gentleman." Harris met Ambassador Joseph Kennedy (U.S. ambassador to Great Britain), who then introduced Harris to the young lady—Marilyn Monroe. Meeting Marilyn Monroe helped determined Harris's destiny because he thought if he could meet someone like Marilyn Monroe in the elevator of a hotel, then the hotel industry was really a business that he wanted to consider.

Upon completing high school, Harris was admitted to Cornell University's School of Hotel Administration, where he majored in hotel management. A member of the ROTC program, he graduated from Cornell after four years and immediately went into the military. After basic training at Fort Bragg, North Carolina, he served as a first lieutenant for three years, including overseas assignments in Asia and Europe. Harris still returns to Fort Bragg, home of the 82nd airborne, to do an annual 15,000-foot jump with the Golden Knights. After Rosen was discharged from the military he returned to New York City and went to work at the Waldorf Astoria.

EXHIBIT 7 Key Milestones in the Rosen Hotels & Resorts History

1974: Harris Rosen purchases a Quality Inn, now known as the *Rosen Inn International*.

1975: Rosen purchases the International Inn, now known as the *Rosen Inn*.

1984: The Quality Inn Plaza, now known as *Rosen Inn at Pointe Orlando*, opens after construction is completed.

1987: Comfort Inn Lake Buena Vista, now known as *Clarion Inn Lake Buena Vista*, opens.

1989: GRSC Insurance Agency, now named *ProvInsure*, is incorporated and opens.

1991: Clarion Plaza, now known as *Rosen Plaza*, opens for convention guests.

1991: The first Rosen Medical Center opens adjacent to the Rosen Inn International.

1993: The Tangelo Park Pilot Program is launched, guaranteeing children an education.

1995: Rosen's second full-service convention property, Omni Rosen, opens. Now known as the *Rosen Centre Hotel*.

1997: *Millennium Technology Group* opens for business.

2004: The University of Central Florida Rosen College of Hospitality Management opens.

2006: *Rosen Shingle Creek* opens for convention business with 1,501 guest rooms and 462,000 square feet of meeting space.

2012: Brand-new 12,000-square-foot Rosen Medical Center opens.

Source: Rosen Hotels & Resorts.

The only job available at the Waldorf at the time was a file clerk in the Personnel Department. In a relatively short time, Rosen worked his way up to sales manager in the Convention Sales department and then was promoted to the Hilton Hotels Management Training Program. During the next several years, Harris worked in six Hilton Hotels throughout the United States. In Dallas, Texas, he was hired by an insurance company owner who had just acquired a hotel in Acapulco, Mexico. Harris moved to Acapulco to manage the hotel. After about a year there, the presidency in Mexico changed. The new government passed a law that prevented non-Mexican citizens from owning more than 49 percent of any real estate property. As a result, Harris's boss sold 51 percent of his equity in the Acapulco hotel. A Mexican group took over the hotel, and Harris was terminated.

Disheartened, he drove to California and quickly learned that the Walt Disney Company was planning a huge new development, Walt Disney World, in Orlando, Florida. Rosen applied for a job and was hired as an administrator of hotel planning for Walt Disney World. He spent about a year in California and then moved to Orlando, working as a planning and hotel management supervisor for several years. Walt Disney World opened in October 1971. In 1973, he was called in for a meeting with his boss. Harris hoped that the meeting was about a promotion and a raise. Instead, he was told that even though he did a great job for the company, he was not a good fit for the Disney organization. Harris was again terminated.

In October 1973, the Organization of the Petroleum Exporting Countries (OPEC) had declared an oil embargo. In the United States, gas prices spiked and supplies were being rationed. As a result, in Orlando, the tourism industry was in complete disarray. Many hotels were in serious financial trouble; some had declared bankruptcy and others were being foreclosed. Despite these circumstances, Harris believed that he could succeed. He started looking for a hotel to purchase. After months of searching, he found a small motel in Orlando on International Drive with frontage onto Interstate 4. He approached the owner of the hotel about a meeting.

The owner, desperate to get out of the hotel business, hugged Rosen tightly after hearing of Rosen's interest in buying the hotel. "He actually cracked one of my ribs," said Rosen. The financial condition of the hotel was stressed as well. The property was operating at 15 percent occupancy and was hemorrhaging cash. The owner also told Rosen that he had not had a chance to spend any time with his wife and three children and was a mess both psychologically and physically. The owner regarded Rosen as a lifesaver.

After a series of meetings, Harris Rosen found himself in a room with the hotel owner and a representative from the hotel's mortgage company. The banker asked Rosen, "Harris, how much money do you have in the bank?" Rosen paused for a moment and then said, "Sir, I have about $20,000 in the bank." The banker extended his hand and said, "We have a deal. $20,000 down, and you assume the $2.5 million mortgage."

The deal was struck right then and there on June 24, 1974. "Wow," thought Rosen, "I just purchased a hotel running at 15 percent occupancy. I must be crazy!" He walked into his office, sat down behind his desk, and cried. He thought that he had just done the dumbest thing in the world. However, Harris Rosen also had a plan. He began to aggressively market his property to the many motor coach companies along the East Coast, traveling (often hitchhiking) to court their business, and offering them dramatically discounted room rates to secure their business. "Motor coaches were still able to get gas," said Rosen. Eventually, the OPEC oil embargo ended and business began to slowly pick up. Rosen bought a second hotel a year later, and from there his business began to grow. "And that," said Rosen, "was just the beginning."

Organization and Leadership

In 2016, Rosen Hotels & Resorts consisted of seven hotels: Rosen Inn International, Rosen Inn, Rosen Inn Pointe Orlando, Rosen Plaza, Rosen Centre, Rosen Shingle Creek, and the Clarion Inn Lake Buena Vista. Each hotel had its own management team and staff. There were also two subsidiaries, the ProvInsure Insurance Company and the Millennium Technology Group. ProvInsure handled health care, onsite clinics, benefits, risk management and consulting both for Rosen Hotels and for outside clients. The Millennium Technology Group was involved with technology solutions including network security, technology compliance issues, IT staffing, videoconferencing, phone systems, and technology consulting.

In addition to the leadership of the seven hotels and the two subsidiaries, there were a number of centralized functions. Human resources was centralized, as well as health services, reservations, and convention marketing. Harris Rosen's office was onsite at the Rosen Inn International, where he had been for 42 years. "We are not a stereotypical company," said Rosen, "For example, we have never had an organization chart. I don't like them. I don't believe they serve any real purpose and instead they can inhibit a free flow of ideas and suggestions crucial to the success of any company."

Sarah Sherwin at Rosen Shingle Creek agreed. "Everyone shares ideas with each other. It's a true open door policy. We do follow some form of organizational structure, I report to my director, associate director, and so forth, but if I do have an idea, I can go straight to Mr. Rosen, I can go straight to whomever the respective department heads is, it's no problem at all. It's welcomed." Jonni Kimberly thought that this open approach to communication was a big part of what made Rosen Hotels not only an excellent place to visit, but a great place to work. "So, you can have an idea," she said, "and you can share the idea and see your idea implemented, and you can see all of that happen pretty quickly."

The company promoted heavily from within, and turnover was arguably the lowest in the hospitality industry. "We only recruit externally if we have to," said Kimberly, "When we opened what is now Rosen Plaza, it was our first convention facility and we recruited externally because we had to. That was 26 years ago and a lot of those folks are still with us."

Summarizing his leadership philosophy, Rosen said, "To be a leader, you must always set an example. Leading from the front is essential."

Strategy

The hotels within Rosen Hotels & Resorts competed in two sectors of the Orlando hotel market: leisure and convention. Rosen Inn, Rosen Inn International, Rosen Inn Pointe Orlando, and Clarion Inn Lake Buena Vista all competed in the leisure segment, with the location of three of these hotels on International Drive, putting them in close proximity to Universal Studios. International Drive had also become a destination itself, with dozens of restaurants, tourist sites, and attractions all along International Drive as well. The Clarion Inn Lake Buena Vista, the remaining leisure hotel, competed with hotels near Walt Disney World. The International Drive hotels competed mostly in the economy price range, while the Clarion Inn hotel competed at a slightly higher rate.

In addition, Rosen had three convention hotels: Rosen Plaza, Rosen Centre, and the Rosen Shingle Creek. Both the Rosen Plaza and the Rosen Centre were located next to the Orange County Convention Center, and competed in the meeting convention and trade show markets. Rosen Shingle Creek, in addition to catering to the convention market, was a convention and meeting facility in its own right, with close to 500,000 square feet of meeting space. The Shingle Creek facility featured the second-largest column-free ballroom in America, with over 95,000 square feet of space. The convention hotels competed in the upper midscale to upscale price range.

The Rosen Hotels competed in the leisure and convention markets on a number of competitive factors, including location, facilities, amenities, food and beverages, price, and customer service. "The hospitality industry," said Rosen, "is an industry driven primarily by just one thing, great service!!!"

Yield Management and Pricing Strategy

Harris Rosen was generally credited with being a pioneer in yield management. "Most of us think that the airlines invented the process of yield management, but he was one of the first to adopt it officially in his hotels, more than 40 years ago," said Abraham Pizam, dean of the Rosen College of Hospitality. Simply put, yield management was hotel room pricing that reflected supply and demand, and that kept the hotel as full as possible. When times got tough, Rosen hotels would drop their prices. "You cannot generate revenue from an empty room," said Rosen. "We call it heads in beds," said Sarah Sherwin, "You know, as long as you have heads in beds, you're creating jobs for everyone; it's important to make sure that our hotels are occupied, so that our housekeepers have jobs, and they can feed their families." Other hotels, including Disney, had also begun to practice some type of yield management. However, very few hotels could compete with Rosen Hotels on price because all of the hotels had been paid for in cash, leaving Rosen Hotels completely debt free.

Employee Benefits

"The benefits package, featuring our own on-site medical clinic, is probably among the best in the industry," said Harris Rosen. Rosen Hotels was self-insured, meaning that much of the company's health care was actually funded and run by the Rosen organization. And—it was affordable. "It's very affordable," said Sarah Sherwin, "Very affordable monthly and our co-pay at the clinic is $5. Annual physicals are complimentary, bloodwork is free, co-pays for offsite visits are $35, and hospital visits do not exceed $750 per hospital visit for a maximum of 2 visits per year. After the second hospital stay, there is no charge. Hospital visits won't break the bank," she said, "We're really well taken care of." "Our health care plan 'RosenCare' has been analyzed by health care experts who have determined if America replicated the Rosen Healthcare program as a nation we could save a minimum of $1 trillion a year," said Rosen. (The Affordable Care Act was health care legislation signed into law in 2010 by President Obama.) Other associate benefits included generic prescription coverage provided by Walmart. "About 93 percent of our associates do not pay anything for their prescriptions," said Rosen.

Rosen Hotels also assisted with retirement planning, and had a family outreach center. "Our outreach center has a social worker and a psychologist, where we deal with helping people through the loss of a family member, emergency situations, housing, and child care," said Jonni Kimberly, "Whatever a person needs, there's a place at work for them to go to get help." Another notable benefit for associates was education scholarships. Dependents of Rosen associates were eligible for free tuition scholarships after the associate had been with the company for three years of service. Rosen associates received free tuition scholarships for themselves to attend college after five years of service. Exhibit 8 presents highlights of the Rosen Hotels benefits package. "If your associates are happy, and if they really love working for you, they will treat guests with the kindness and benevolence you've never, ever imagined," said Rosen.

Rosen Goes Green

Rosen Hotels & Resorts prided themselves on their green initiatives. "As a company, we've always been dedicated to environmentally sound practices and keenly focused on evaluating and improving green standards wherever possible," said DeeDee Baggitt, Rosen Hotel's director of engineering and facilities. Six of the Rosen Hotels carried the Two Palm Green Lodge designation under the Florida Department

EXHIBIT 8 Rosen Hotels & Resorts—Associate Benefits

Medical Coverage and Insurance

Rosen Hotels & Resorts provides accessible and affordable health care for Rosen associates and their dependents. Primary Care physicians are located in the Rosen Medical Center, located steps away from most Rosen properties. Associates can visit the Medical Center "on the clock." The Medical Center includes a fitness facility and an on-site physical therapy wing.

Prescription Coverage

Prescription coverage is included as part of associate medical benefits. Co-pays are inexpensive and in some cases free of charge.

Family Outreach Center

The mission of the Family Outreach Center is to help people help themselves. The Center provides social service information, referrals and emergency support to Rosen associates and their dependents.

Daycare Supplement

The Rosen organization provides a supplement to daycare costs for dependent children of associates under the age of four.

Retirement Planning

Rosen associates are encouraged to begin retirement savings by deferring a portion of their income to a 401K retirement account. Rosen Hotels & Resorts matches a portion of weekly retirement deferrals.

Career Training and Advancement

All new employees receive a full day orientation session. Ongoing training includes certification courses, language classes and professional development workshops.

Education

After five years of employment, associates receive a scholarship to attend a public or private college or attend a vocational school of their choice. Dependents of Rosen associates are eligible for educational scholarships after the associate has reached three years of employment.

Source: Rosen Hotels & Resorts.

of Environmental Protection's Green Lodging Program. Rosen Shingle Creek carried a Three Palm designation, and engaged in a number of leading green initiatives, including converting used cooking oil from the hotel into biofuel to operate their golf course equipment. All three of the Rosen convention hotels also carried an APEX designation for meeting or exceeding sustainable meeting standards. The Rosen Medical Center, built in 2012, was a LEED Certified building. "We don't claim to be experts, but we can say that we have been practicing conservation efforts for many years and continue to look for ways to reduce, reuse and recycle wherever possible," said Rosen.

Corporate Social Responsibility

In 1993, Harris Rosen was sitting in his office. "It was kind of like an epiphany," said Rosen. "I stopped what I was doing, and I heard my inner voice say it was time to say 'Thank you, God.'" Out of that moment was born Rosen Hotels's commitment to corporate social responsibility.

> Within a very short period of time we put together a program for the Tangelo Park Program (an underserved community), providing every 2, 3 and 4 year old in the Tangelo Park neighborhood with a free preschool education. After high school every youngster who is accepted to a community college, 4 year public college or technical school will have everything paid for–room, board, tuition, books etc. In the 23 years we have been engaged with the Tangelo Park program we have sent 350 youngsters to College from a neighborhood that was graduating 55% from high school. During the past 8 years our high school graduation rate has soared to 100% and about 70% of our kids go on to college; and 77% of them graduate either from the two year program or the four year program. Everything of course is paid for.

"This has been so good for the children of Tangelo Park," said Diondra Newton, principal at Tangelo Park Elementary, "You see a huge difference between kids who did the program and those who come from elsewhere." One of Tangelo Park's recent high school graduates, going on to college, agreed. "He has taken the burden off me and my entire family," said Arian Plaza. Exhibit 9 shows a picture of Harris Rosen. He was currently replicating the Tangelo Park program in an even more challenging downtown Orlando neighborhood, the Parramore district, which was five times the size of Tangelo Park.

For the past 20 years the Harris Rosen Foundation had been involved in relief efforts in Haiti, providing school supplies, health care supplies, and more than 250 water filtration systems capable of providing clean drinking water for approximately 200,000 people. A school was also under construction near Port Au Prince.

Approximately 15 years ago, Rosen had donated the land and funds for what was now the largest hospitality college in the nation. The Rosen College of Hospitality at the University of Central Florida had more than 3,500 students and was ranked the fifth best hospitality college in the world. Harris Rosen had created a $5 million scholarship endowment at the college that provided more than 160 scholarships annually. The Harris Rosen Foundation had also recently assisted in the completion of a new auditorium at the Jack & Lee Rosen Southwest Orlando Jewish Community Center. The preschool at the center was considered among the very best in Central Florida.

"I realize that some people are a bit leery when I talk to them about my concept of 'responsible capitalism' but I absolutely believe that we have an obligation to offer a helping hand to those in need," said Rosen. "For me, an individual who has been blessed beyond anything I could ever have imagined, it is essential to demonstrate my gratitude."

Financial Performance

Rosen Hotels & Resorts was a private company. It considered itself a rather unusual private-sector company because the company was completely debt free. "If we are planning any refurbishing, renovation, or other capital initiatives or perhaps considering constructing new properties, we do not start until we have sufficient funds in the bank," said Rosen. "Recently, we had a rather extensive refurbishing program that lasted over five years and we spent

EXHIBIT 9 Harris Rosen

Source: Rosen Hotels & Resorts.

close to $200 million. We believe it is a significant advantage to be a debt free company."

Rosen Shingle Creek was Rosen Hotels & Resorts's signature property. Rosen, discussing this property, provided insights on the financial management of the company:

> In 2006, on my birthday, September 9, we completed the construction of Rosen Shingle Creek, a 1,501-room property with a beautiful golf course and about a half million square feet of meeting space. The construction was completed in about 18 months at a cost of approximately $200,000 per room or $300 million. We believe our cost was significantly less than what major hotels might spend per room primarily because we are so intimately involved with planning the architectural work, and of course the construction, enabling us to save a tremendous amount of money.

Another recent event offered a look at financial decision making. The company has recently opened Zayde's kosher catering at the Rosen Plaza Hotel, offering kosher catering at both on-site and off-site venues. "One of our catering managers came to me and demonstrated rather clearly that he believed there was a great market for kosher foods," said Rosen. "We studied it, asked lots of questions, and without much fanfare made the decision to proceed. The cost? About $3.5 million. The return on that investment if we are fortunate could be less than 5 years."

STR Analytics published comparative financial results for the hotel industry. Comparative hotel financial results for independent Orlando hotels in the economy class are presented in Exhibit 10. These financial results were comparable to the leisure hotels in the Rosen Hotel chain, such as Rosen

EXHIBIT 10 Orlando Comparative Hotel Financial Results for Independent Hotels—Economy Class, 2013–2014

	2013	2013	2014	2014
	Amount per Available Room	Amount per Occupied Room Night	Amount per Available Room	Amount per Occupied Room Night
REVENUE				
Rooms	$10,926	$52.60	$12,862	$54.04
Food	1,316	6.34	1,615	6.79
Beverage	347	1.67	488	2.05
Other Food & Bev	10	0.05	23	0.10
Other Operated Departments	1,440	6.93	1,420	5.97
Miscellaneous Income	407	2.00	1,110	4.70
TOTAL REVENUE	14,446	69.55	17,519	73.60
DEPARTMENTAL EXPENSES				
Rooms	4,159	20.02	5,114	21.49
Food & Beverage	1,528	7.35	1,759	7.39
Other	617	2.97	644	2.70
TOTAL DEPARTMENTAL EXPENSES	6,304	30.35	7,517	31.58
TOTAL DEPARTMENTAL PROFITS	8,142	39.20	10,002	42.02
OPERATING EXPENSES	5,058	24.35	5,750	24.16
GROSS OPERATING PROFIT	$ 3,084	$14.85	$ 4,252	$17.87
EBITDA	$ 1,949	$ 9.38	$ 2,931	$12.31

Source: STR Analytics.

Inn (which was Rosen's property closest to Universal Studios), Rosen Inn International, and Rosen Inn Pointe Orlando.

FUTURE OUTLOOK

"So here we are," said Harris Rosen, "42 years later, debt free, approximately 6,300 rooms, about 4,500 associates who work with us. Close to 6,000 covered lives, including dependents." Rosen believed that his hotel group would continue to grow. "I suspect that before I leave we'll add perhaps another 1,000 rooms," he said. Several hotels had recently gone through renovations, and plans were underway to add rooms at the three convention properties. "But we don't do any refurbishing or construction until we have enough money in the bank," said Rosen, "That in many instances is hundreds of millions of dollars."

Analysts are generally positive on growth in the hotel industry through 2020. Orlando also continues to lead the United States in tourism and in growth, particularly in leisure travel. Rosen, however, sounded a cautionary note. "Generally speaking, there is a lot of uncertainty in the world today," he said, "That is impacting every aspect of our business." Rosen was concerned about a number of markets that Orlando had relied on for many years, including Brazil and Puerto Rico. Rosen said that the strategy was to keep the hotels in top shape. "There's always something to do," he said. "If we're not building something, we are renovating or refurbishing, which we believe are critical for our success."

Guests at Rosen Hotels & Resorts continued to be amazed at the quality, customer service, and value at the company's Orlando hotels. "I would definitely stay here again," said one satisfied customer, "We felt safe, and there was lots to see and enjoy." When asked about what made the Rosen organization unique, Rosen replied, "I think we care just a little bit more. We are driven to always try to do the right thing."

CASE 27

Nucor Corporation in 2016: Contending with the Challenges of Low-Cost Foreign Imports and Weak Demand for Steel Products

connect

Arthur A. Thompson
The University of Alabama

In 2016, Nucor Corp., with a production capacity of 29 million tons, was the largest manufacturer of steel and steel products in North America and ranked as the 13th largest steel company in the world based on tons shipped in 2014. It was regarded as a low-cost producer, and it had a sterling reputation for being a global first-mover in implementing cost-effective steel-making production methods and practices throughout its operations.

Heading into 2016, Nucor had 24 steel mills with the capability to produce a diverse assortment of steel shapes (steel bars, sheet steel, steel plate, and structural steel) and additional finished steel manufacturing facilities that made steel joists, steel decking, cold finish bars, steel buildings, steel mesh, steel grating, steel fasteners, and fabricated steel reinforcing products. The company's lineup of product offerings was the broadest of any steel producer serving steel users in North America. Nucor had 2015 revenues of $16.4 billion and net profits of $357.7 million, far below its 2008 pre-recession peak of $23.7 billion in revenues and $1.8 billion in net profits and also substantially worse than its 2014 revenues of $21.1 billion and net profits of $714 million. Nucor's sharp declines in sales and net profits in 2015 resulted from eroding market prices for many steel products and a sharp falloff in customer orders in several major product categories, both largely due to a surge in ultra-cheap imported steel products coming from a variety of foreign sources (but mainly China). The outlook for 2016 was not encouraging.

COMPANY BACKGROUND

Nucor began its journey from obscurity to a steel industry leader in the 1960s. Operating under the name of Nuclear Corporation of America in the 1950s and early 1960s, the company was a maker of nuclear instruments and electronics products. After suffering through several money-losing years and facing bankruptcy in 1964, Nuclear Corporation of America's board of directors opted for new leadership and appointed F. Kenneth Iverson as president and CEO. Shortly thereafter, Iverson concluded that the best way to put the company on sound footing was to exit the nuclear instrument and electronics business and rebuild the company around its profitable South Carolina–based Vulcraft subsidiary that was in the steel joist business—Iverson had been the head of Vulcraft prior to being named president. Iverson moved the company's headquarters from Phoenix, Arizona, to Charlotte, North Carolina, in 1966, and proceeded to expand the joist business with new operations in Texas and Alabama. Then, in 1968, top management decided to integrate backward into steelmaking, partly because of the benefits of supplying its own steel requirements for producing steel joists and partly because Iverson saw opportunities to capitalize on newly emerging technologies to produce steel more cheaply. In 1972 the company adopted the name Nucor Corporation, and Iverson initiated a long-term strategy to grow Nucor into a major player in the U.S. steel industry.

By 1985 Nucor had become the seventh largest steel company in North America, with revenues of $758 million, six joist plants, and four state-of-the-art steel mills that used electric arc furnaces to produce new steel products from recycled scrap steel. Moreover, Nucor had gained a reputation as an excellently managed company, an accomplished low-cost producer, and one of the most competitively successful manufacturing companies in the country.[1] A series of articles in *The New Yorker* related how Nucor, a relatively small American steel company, had built an enterprise that led the whole world into a new era of making steel with recycled scrap steel. Network broadcaster NBC did a business documentary that used Nucor to make the point that American manufacturers could be successful in competing against low-cost foreign manufacturers.

Under Iverson's leadership, Nucor came to be known for its aggressive pursuit of innovation and technical excellence in producing steel, rigorous quality systems, strong emphasis on workforce productivity and job security for employees, cost-conscious corporate culture, and skills in achieving low costs per ton produced. The company had a very streamlined organizational structure, incentive-based compensation systems, and steel mills that were among the most modern and efficient in the United States. Iverson proved himself as a master in crafting and executing a low-cost provider strategy, and he made a point of practicing what he preached when it came to holding down costs throughout the company. The offices of executives and division general managers were simply furnished. There were no company planes and no company cars, and executives were not provided with company-paid country club memberships, reserved parking spaces, executive dining facilities, or other perks. To save money on his own business expenses and set an example for other Nucor managers, Iverson flew coach class and took the subway when he was in New York City.

When Iverson left the company in 1998 following disagreements with the board of directors, he was succeeded briefly by John Correnti and then Dave Aycock, both of whom had worked in various roles under Iverson for a number of years. In 2000, Daniel R. DiMicco, who had joined Nucor in 1982 and risen up through the ranks to executive vice president, was named president and CEO. DiMicco was Nucor's chair and CEO through 2012. Like his predecessors, DiMicco continued to pursue Nucor's longstanding strategy to aggressively grow the company's production capacity and product offerings via both acquisition and new plant construction; tons sold rose from 11.2 million in 2000 to 25.2 million in 2008. Then the unexpected financial crisis in the fourth quarter of 2008 and the subsequent economic fallout caused tons sold in 2009 to plunge to 17.6 million tons and revenues to nosedive from $23.7 billion in 2008 to $11.2 billion in 2009.

Even though the steel industry remained in the doldrums until he retired in 2012, DiMicco was undeterred by the depressed market demand for steel and proceeded to expand Nucor's production capabilities and range of product offerings. It was his strong belief that Nucor should be opportunistic in initiating actions to strengthen its competitive position despite slack market demand for steel because doing so put the company in even better position to significantly boost its financial performance when market demand for steel products grew stronger. DiMicco expressed his thinking thusly:[2]

> Nucor uses each economic downturn as an opportunity to grow stronger. We use the good times to prepare for the bad, and we use the bad times to prepare for the good. Emerging from downturns stronger than we enter them is how we build long-term value for our stockholders. We get stronger because our team is focused on continual improvement and because our financial strength allows us to invest in attractive growth opportunities throughout the economic cycle.

During DiMicco's 12-year tenure, Nucor completed more than 50 acquisitions, expanding Nucor's operations from 18 locations to more than 200, boosting revenues from $4.8 billion in 2000 to $19.4 billion at the end of 2012, and transforming Nucor into the undisputed leader in providing steel products to North American buyers. When DiMicco retired at the end of 2012, he was succeeded by John J. Ferriola, who had served as Nucor's president and COO since 2011. Ferriola immediately embraced Nucor's strategy of investing in down markets to better position Nucor for success when the economy strengthened and market demand for steel products became more robust.

Going into 2016, Nucor was the biggest, most cost-efficient, and most diversified steel producer in North America. It had the capacity to produce 29 million tons of steel annually at its 24 steel mills. All of its steel mills were among the most modern and efficient mills in the United States. The breadth of Nucor's product line in steel mill products and finished steel products was unmatched; it competed in 11 distinct product categories. No other producer of steel products in North America competed in more than 5 of the 11 product categories in which Nucor competed.[3] Moreover, Nucor was the North American market leader in 9 of the 11 product categories in which it had a market presence—steel bars, structural steel, steel reinforcing bars, steel joists, steel deck, cold-finished bar steel, metal buildings, steel pilings distribution, and rebar fabrication, distribution, and place.[4] In the other two categories in North America where Nucor competed, it ranked number two in sales of plate steel and number three in sales of sheet steel.

With the exception of 3 quarters in 2009, 1 quarter in 2010, and the 4th quarter of 2015, Nucor earned a profit in every quarter of every year since 1966—a truly remarkable accomplishment in a mature and cyclical business where it was common for industry members to post losses when demand for steel sagged. As of February 2016, Nucor had paid a dividend for 171 consecutive quarters and had raised the base dividend it paid to stockholders for 43 consecutive years (every year since 1973 when the company first began paying cash dividends). In years when earnings and cash flows permitted, Nucor had paid a supplemental year-end dividend in addition to the base quarterly dividend. Exhibit 1 provides highlights of Nucor's growth and performance since 1970. Exhibit 2 shows Nucor's sales by product category for 1990–2015. Exhibit 3 contains a summary of Nucor's financial and operating performance during 2011–2015.

EXHIBIT 1 Nucor's Growing Presence in the Market for Steel, 1970–2015

Year	Total Tons Sold to Outside Customers	Average Price per Ton	Net Sales (in millions)	Earnings before Taxes (in millions)	Pretax Earnings per Ton	Net Earnings (in millions)
1970	207,000	$245	$ 50.8	$ 2.2	$ 10	$ 1.1
1975	387,000	314	121.5	11.7	30	7.6
1980	1,159,000	416	482.4	76.1	66	45.1
1985	1,902,000	399	758.5	106.2	56	58.5
1990	3,648,000	406	1,481.6	111.2	35	75.1
1995	7,943,000	436	3,462.0	432.3	62	274.5
2000	11,189,000	425	4,756.5	478.3	48	310.9
2001	12,237,000	354	4,333.7	179.4	16	113.0
2002	13,442,000	357	4,801.7	227.0	19	162.1
2003	17,473,000	359	6,265.8	70.0	4	62.8
2004	19,109,000	595	11,376.8	1,725.9	96	1,121.5
2005	20,465,000	621	12,701.0	2,027.1	104	1,310.3
2006	22,118,000	667	14,751.3	2,692.4	129	1,757.7
2007	22,940,000	723	16,593.0	2,253.3	104	1,471.9
2008	25,187,000	940	23,663.3	2,790.5	116	1,831.0
2009	17,576,000	637	11,190.3	(470.4)	(28)	(293.6)
2010	22,019,000	720	15,844.6	194.9	9	134.1
2011	23,044,000	869	20,023.6	1,169.9	53	778.2
2012	23,092,000	841	19,429.3	764.4	34	504.6
2013	23,730,000	803	19,052.0	693.6	30	488.0
2014	25,413,000	830	21,105.1	1,102.7	44	713.9
2015	22,680,000	725	16,439.3	570.8	26	357.7

Source: Company records posted at www.nucor.com (accessed February 10, 2016).

EXHIBIT 2 Nucor's Sales of Steel Mill and Finished Steel Products to Outside Customers, by Product Category, 1990–2015

	Tons Sold to Outside Customers (in thousands)									
	Steel Mill Products					Finished Steel Products				
Year	Sheet Steel (2015 capacity of ~13.1 million tons)	Steel Bars (2015 capacity of ~9.1 million tons)	Structural Steel (2015 capacity of ~3.7 million tons)	Steel Plate (2015 capacity of ~2.9 million tons)	Total (2015 capacity of ~29 million tons)	Steel Joists (2015 capacity of ~715,000 tons)	Steel Deck (2015 capacity of ~530,000 tons)	Cold Finished Steel (2015 capacity of ~920,000 tons)	Rebar Fabrication (2015 capacity of ~1.7 million tons) and Other Products*	Total Tons Sold
2015	8,080	4,790	2,231	1,905	17,006	427	401	449	4,397	22,680
2014	8,153	5,526	2,560	2,442	18,681	421	396	504	5,411	25,413
2013	7,491	5,184	2,695	2,363	17,733	342	334	474	4,847	23,730
2012	7,622	5,078	2,505	2,268	17,473	291	308	492	4,528	23,092
2011	7,500	4,680	2,338	2,278	16,796	288	312	494	5,154	23,044
2010	7,434	4,019	2,139	2,229	15,821	276	306	462	5,154	22,019
2009	5,212	3,629	1,626	1,608	12,075	264	310	330	4,596	17,576
2008	7,505	5,266	2,934	2,480	18,185	485	498	485	4,534	25,187
2007	8,266	6,287	3,154	2,528	20,235	542	478	449	1,236	22,940
2006	8,495	6,513	3,209	2,432	20,649	570	398	327	174	22,118
2005	8,026	5,983	2,866	2,145	19,020	554	380	342	169	20,465
2004	8,078	5,244	2,760	1,705	17,787	522	364	271	165	19,109
2003	6,954	5,530	2,780	999	16,263	503	353	237	117	17,473
2002	5,806	2,947	2,689	872	12,314	462	330	226	110	13,442
2001	5,074	2,687	2,749	522	11,032	532	344	203	126	12,237
2000	4,456	2,209	3,094	20	9,779	613	353	250	194	11,189
1995	2,994	1,799	1,952	—	6,745	552	234	234	178	7,943
1990	420	1,382	1,002	—	2,804	443	—	134	163	104	3,648

*Other products include steel fasteners (steel screws, nuts, bolts, washers, and bolt assemblies), steel mesh, steel grates, metal building systems, light gauge steel framing, and scrap metal.

Source: Company records posted at **www.nucor.com** (accessed February 11, 2016).

EXHIBIT 3 Five-Year Financial and Operating Summary, Nucor Corporation, 2011–2015 ($ in millions, except per share data and sales per employee)

	2015	2014	2013	2012	2011
FOR THE YEAR					
Net sales	$ 16,439.3	$ 21,105.1	$ 19,052.0	$ 19,429.3	$ 20,023.6
Costs, expenses and other:					
Cost of products sold	14,858.0	19,198.6	17,641.4	17,915.7	18,142.1
Marketing, administrative and other expenses	459.0	520.8	481.9	454.9	439.5

	2015	2014	2013	2012	2011
Equity in (earnings) losses of minority-owned enterprises	(5.3)	(13.5)	(9.3)	13.3	10.0
Impairment and losses on assets	244.8	25.4	—	30.0	13.9
Interest expense, net	173.5	169.3	146.9	162.4	166.1
Total	15,730.0	19,900.6	18,260.9	18,576.3	18,771.8
Earnings before income taxes and non-controlling interests	709.2	1,204.6	791.1	852.9	1,251.8
Provision for income taxes	213.2	388.8	205.6	259.8	390.8
Net earnings (loss)	496.1	815.8	585.5	593.1	861.0
Less earnings attributable to the minority interest partners of Nucor's joint ventures*	138.4	101.8	97.5	88.5	82.8
Net earnings (loss) attributable to Nucor stockholders	$ 357.7	$ 713.9	$ 488.0	$ 504.6	$ 778.2
Net earnings (loss) per share:					
Basic	$1.11	$2.22	$1.52	$1.58	$2.45
Diluted	1.11	2.22	1.52	1.58	2.45
Dividends declared per share	$1.49	$1.48	$1.4725	$1.4625	$1.4525
Percentage of net earnings to net sales	2.2%	3.4%	2.6%	2.6%	3.9%
Return on average stockholders' equity	4.8%	9.3%	6.4%	6.7%	10.7%
Capital expenditures	$ 374.1	$ 668.0	$ 1,230.4	$ 1,019.3	$ 450.6
Acquisitions (net of cash acquired)	19.1	768.6	—	760.8	4.0
Depreciation	625.8	652.0	535.9	534.0	522.6
Sales per employee (000s)	690	921	859	906	974
AT YEAR END					
Cash, cash equivalents, and short-term investments	$ 2,039.5	$ 1,124.1	$ 1,511.5	$ 1,157.1	$ 2,563.3
Current assets	5,754.4	6,441.9	6,410.0	5,661.4	6,708.1
Current liabilities	1,385.2	2,097.8	1,960.2	2,029.6	2,396.1
Working capital	4,369.2	4,344.1	4,449.8	3,631.8	4,312.0
Cash provided by operating activities	2,157.0	1,342.8	1,077.9	1,200.4	1,032.6
Current ratio	4.2	3.1	3.3	2.8	2.8
Property, plant and equipment	$ 4,891.2	$ 5,287.6	$ 4,917.0	$ 4,283.1	$ 3,755.6
Total assets	14,250.4	15,615.9	15,203.3	14,152.1	14,570.4
Long-term debt (including current maturities)	4,360.6	4,376.9	4,380.2	3,630.2	4,280.2
Percentage of long-term debt to total capital**	37.0%	36.0%	35.6%	31.5%	35.7%
Stockholders' equity	7,416.9	7,772.5	7,645.8	7,641.6	7,474.9
Shares outstanding (000s)	317,962	319,033	318,328	317,663	316,749
Employees	23,700	23,600	22,300	22,200	20,800

*The principal joint venture responsible for these earnings is the Nucor-Yamato Steel Company, of which Nucor owns 51 percent. This joint venture operates a structural steel mill in Blytheville, Arkansas, and is the largest producer of structural steel beams in the Western Hemisphere.

**Total capital is defined as stockholders' equity plus long-term debt.

Sources: Nucor's 2013 Annual Report, p. 43; Nucor's 2015 10-K, p. 32.

NUCOR'S STRATEGY TO BECOME THE BIGGEST AND MOST DIVERSIFIED STEEL PRODUCER IN NORTH AMERICA, 1967–2016

In its nearly 50-year march to become North America's biggest and most diversified steel producer, Nucor relentlessly expanded its production capabilities to include a wider range of steel shapes and more categories of finished steel products. However, most every steel product that Nucor produced was viewed by buyers as a "commodity." Indeed, the most competitively relevant feature of the various steel shapes and finished steel products made by the world's different producers was that, for any given steel item, there were very few, if any, differences in the products of rival steel producers. While some steelmakers had plants where production quality was sometimes inconsistent or on occasions failed to meet customer-specified metallurgical characteristics, most steel plants turned out products of comparable metallurgical quality—one producer's reinforcing bar was essentially the same as another producer's reinforcing bar, a particular type and grade of sheet steel made at one plant was essentially identical to the same type and grade of sheet steel made at another plant.

The commodity nature of steel products meant that steel buyers typically shopped the market for the best price, awarding their business to whichever seller offered the best deal. The ease with which buyers could switch their orders from one supplier to another forced steel producers to be very price competitive. In virtually all instances, the going market price of each particular steel product was in constant flux, rising or falling in response to shifting market circumstances (or shifts in the terms that particular buyers or sellers were willing to accept). As a consequence, spot market prices for commodity steel products bounced around on a weekly or even daily basis. Because competition among rival steel producers was so strongly focused on price, it was incumbent on all industry participants to be cost-competitive and operate their production facilities as efficiently as they could.

Nucor's success over the years stemmed largely from its across-the-board prowess in cost-efficient operations for all the product categories in which it elected to compete. Nucor's top executives were very disciplined in executing Nucor's strategy to broaden the company's product offerings; no moves to enter new steel product categories were made unless management was confident that the company had the resources and capabilities needed to operate the accompanying production facilities efficiently enough to be cost-competitive.

Finished Steel Products

Nucor's first venture into steel in the late 1960s, via its Vulcraft division, was principally one of fabricating steel joists and joist girders from steel that was purchased from various steelmakers. Vulcraft expanded into the fabrication of steel decking in 1977. The division expanded its operations over the years and, as of 2016, Nucor's Vulcraft division was the largest producer and leading innovator of open-web steel joists, joist girders, and steel deck in the United States. It had seven plants with annual capacity of 715,000 tons that made steel joists and joist girders and nine plants with 530,000 tons of capacity that made steel deck; typically, about 85 percent of the steel needed to make these products was supplied by various Nucor steelmaking plants. Vulcraft's joist, girder, and decking products were used mainly for roof and floor support systems in retail stores, shopping centers, warehouses, manufacturing facilities, schools, churches, hospitals, and, to a lesser extent, multistory buildings and apartments. Customers for these products were principally nonresidential construction contractors.

In 1979, Nucor began fabricating cold finished steel products. These consisted mainly of cold drawn and turned, ground, and polished steel bars or rods of various shapes—rounds, hexagons, flats, channels, and squares—made from carbon, alloy, and leaded steels based on customer specifications or end-use requirements. Cold finished steel products were used in tens of thousands of products, including anchor bolts, hydraulic cylinders, farm machinery, air conditioner compressors, electric motors, motor vehicles, appliances, and lawn mowers. Nucor sold cold finish steel directly to large-quantity users in the automotive, farm machinery, hydraulic, appliance, and electric motor industries and to steel service centers that in turn supplied manufacturers needing only relatively small quantities. In 2015, Nucor Cold Finish was the largest producer of cold finished bar products in North

America and had facilities in Missouri, Nebraska, South Carolina, Utah, Wisconsin, Ohio, Georgia, and Ontario, Canada, with a capacity of about 920,000 tons per year. It obtained most of its steel from Nucor's mills that made steel bar. This factor, along with the fact that all of Nucor's cold finished facilities employed the latest technology and were among the most modern in the world, resulted in Nucor Cold Finish having a highly competitive cost structure. It maintained sufficient inventories of cold finish products to fulfill anticipated orders. Sales of cold finished steel products were 449,000 tons in 2015, down 11 percent from 504,000 tons in 2014.

Nucor produced metal buildings and components throughout the United States under several brands: Nucor Building Systems, American Buildings Company, Kirby Building Systems, Gulf States Manufacturers, and CBC Steel Buildings. In 2016, the Nucor Buildings Group had 11 metal buildings plants with an annual capacity of approximately 465,000 tons. Nucor's Buildings Group began operations in 1987 and currently had the capability to supply customers with buildings ranging from less than 1,000 square feet to more than 1,000,000 square feet. Complete metal building packages could be customized and combined with other materials such as glass, wood, and masonry to produce a cost-effective, aesthetically pleasing building built to a customer's particular requirements. The buildings were sold primarily through an independent builder distribution network. The primary markets served were commercial, industrial, and institutional buildings, including distribution centers, automobile dealerships, retail centers, schools, warehouses, and manufacturing facilities. Nucor's Buildings Group obtained a significant portion of its steel requirements from the Nucor bar and sheet mills. Sales were 307,000 tons in 2015, an increase of 5 percent over 292,000 tons in 2014.

Another Nucor division produced steel mesh, grates, and fasteners. Various steel mesh products were made at two facilities in the United States and one in Canada that had combined annual production capacity of about 128,000 tons. Steel and aluminum bar grating, safety grating, and expanded metal products were produced at several North American locations that had combined annual production capacity of 103,000 tons. Nucor Fastener, located in Indiana, began operations in 1986 with the construction of a $25 million plant. At the time, imported steel fasteners accounted for 90 percent of the U.S. market because U.S. manufacturers were not competitive on cost and price. Iverson said, "We're going to bring that business back; we can make bolts as cheaply as foreign producers." Nucor built a second fastener plant in 1995, giving it the capacity to supply about 20 percent of the U.S. market for steel fasteners. Currently, these two facilities had annual capacity of over 75,000 tons and produced carbon and alloy steel hex head cap screws, hex bolts, structural bolts, nuts and washers, finished hex nuts, and custom-engineered fasteners that were used for automotive, machine tool, farm implement, construction, military, and various other applications. Nucor Fastener obtained much of the steel it needed from Nucor's mills that made steel bar.

Beginning in 2007, Nucor—through its newly acquired Harris Steel subsidiary—began fabricating, installing, and distributing steel reinforcing bars (rebar) for highways, bridges, schools, hospitals, airports, stadiums, office buildings, high-rise residential complexes, and other structures where steel reinforcing was essential to concrete construction. Harris Steel had over 70 fabrication facilities in the United States and Canada, with each facility serving the surrounding local market. Since acquiring Harris Steel, Nucor had more than doubled its rebar fabrication capacity to over 1,700,000 tons annually. Total fabricated rebar sales in 2015 were 1,190,000 tons, up from 1,185,000 tons in 2014. Much of the steel used in making fabricated rebar products was obtained from Nucor steel plants that made steel bar. Fabricated reinforcing products were sold only on a contract bid basis.

Steel Mill Products

Nucor entered the market for steel mill products in 1968, when the decision was made to build a facility in Darlington, South Carolina, to manufacture steel bars. The Darlington mill was one of the first steelmaking plants of major size in the United States to use electric arc furnace technology to melt scrap steel and cast molten metal into various shapes. Electric arc furnace technology was particularly appealing to Nucor because the labor and capital requirements to melt steel scrap and produce crude steel were far lower than those at conventional integrated steel mills where raw steel was produced using coke ovens, basic oxygen blast furnaces, ingot casters, and multiple types of finishing facilities to make crude steel from iron ore, coke, limestone, oxygen, scrap steel, and other ingredients. By 1981, Nucor had four steel mills making carbon and alloy steels in bars, angles, and light structural shapes; since then, Nucor had undertaken extensive capital projects to keep these facilities modernized and globally competitive. During 2000–2011, Nucor aggressively expanded its market presence in steel bars and by 2012 had 13 bar mills located across the United States that produced concrete reinforcing bars, hot-rolled bars, rods, light shapes, structural angles, channels, and guard rail in carbon and alloy steels; in 2015, these 13 plants had total annual capacity of approximately 9.1 million tons. Four of the 13 mills made hot-rolled special quality bar manufactured to exacting specifications. The products of the 13 bar mills had wide usage and were sold primarily to customers in the agricultural, automotive, construction, energy, furniture, machinery, metal building, railroad, recreational equipment, shipbuilding, heavy truck, and trailer industries.

Recently, Nucor had completed a $290 million project to expand its wire rod and special quality steel bar production capabilities at three existing bar mills by 1 million tons annually. The expansion enabled Nucor to produce engineered bar for the most demanding applications (and realize a significantly higher price) while maintaining its market share in commodity bar products by shifting production to its other bar mills that were operating below capacity. Incremental investments were underway in 2016 to expand Nucor's special quality steel bar production capabilities. In addition, an existing wire rod and bar mill in Kingman, Arizona, was renovated to boost production capacity from 200,000 tons annually to 500,000 tons annually and put Nucor in a strong position to serve wire rod and rebar customers in the southwestern U.S. market.

Expansion into Sheet Steel In the late 1980s, Nucor entered into the production of sheet steel at a newly constructed plant in Crawfordsville, Indiana. Flat-rolled sheet steel was used in the production of motor vehicles, appliances, steel pipe and tubes, and other durable goods. The Crawfordsville plant was the first in the world to employ a revolutionary thin slab casting process that substantially reduced the capital investment and costs to produce flat-rolled sheet steel. Thin-slab casting machines had a funnel-shaped mold to squeeze molten steel down to a thickness of 1.5–2.0 inches, compared to the typically 8- to 10-inch-thick slabs produced by conventional casters. It was much cheaper to then build and operate facilities to roll thin-gauge sheet steel from 1.5- to 2-inch-thick slabs than from 8- to 10-inch-thick slabs. When the Crawfordsville plant first opened in 1989, it was said to have costs $50 to $75 per ton below the costs of traditional sheet steel plants, a highly significant cost advantage in a commodity market where the going price at the time was $400 per ton. *Forbes* magazine described Nucor's pioneering use of thin-slab casting as the most substantial, technological, industrial innovation in the past 50 years.[5] By 1996 two additional sheet steel mills that employed thin-slab casting technology were constructed and a fourth mill was acquired in 2002, giving Nucor the capacity to produce 11.3 million tons of sheet steel products annually. Nucor also operated two Castrip sheet production facilities, one built in 2002 at the Crawfordsville plant and a second built in Arkansas in 2009; these facilities used the breakthrough strip casting technology that involved the direct casting of molten steel into final shape and thickness without further hot or cold rolling. The process allowed for lower capital investment, reduced energy consumption, and smaller scale plants, and improved environmental impact (because of significantly lower emissions). A fifth sheet mill with annual capacity of 1.8 million tons, strategically located on the Ohio River in Kentucky, was acquired in 2014, giving Nucor a total flat-rolled capacity of 13.1 million tons.

Entry into Structural Steel Products Also in the late 1980s, Nucor added wide-flange steel beams, pilings, and heavy structural steel products to its lineup of product offerings. Structural steel products were used in buildings, bridges, overpasses, and similar such projects where strong weight-bearing support was needed. Customers included construction companies, steel fabricators, manufacturers, and steel service centers. To gain entry to the structural steel segment, in 1988 Nucor entered into a joint venture with Yamato-Kogyo, one of Japan's major producers of wide-flange beams, to build a new structural steel mill in Arkansas; a second mill was built on the same site in the 1990s that made the Nucor–Yamato venture in Arkansas the largest structural beam facility in the Western Hemisphere. In 1999, Nucor started operations at a third structural steel mill in South Carolina. The mills in Arkansas and South Carolina both used a special continuous casting method that was quite cost-effective. In 2014, the Nucor–Yamato mill completed a $115 million project to add several new sheet piling sections, increase production of single sheet widths by 22 percent, and provide customers with a lighter stronger sheet covering more area at a lower installed cost. Going into 2016, Nucor had the capacity to make 3.7 million tons of structural steel products annually.

Entry into the Market for Steel Plate Starting in 2000, Nucor began producing steel plate of various thicknesses and lengths that was sold to manufacturers of heavy equipment, ships, barges, bridges, rail cars, refinery tanks, pressure vessels, pipe and tube, wind towers, and similar products. Steel plate was made at two mills in Alabama and North Carolina that had combined capacity of about 2.9 million tons. In 2011–2013, Nucor greatly expanded its plate product capabilities by constructing a 125,000-ton heat treating facility and a 120,000-ton normalizing line at its North Carolina plate mill. These investments yielded two big strategic benefits: (1) enabling the North Carolina mill to produce higher-margin plate products sold to companies making pressure vessels, tank cars, tubular structures for offshore oil rigs, and naval and commercial ships; and (2) reducing the mill's exposure to competition from foreign producers of steel plate who lacked the capability to match the features of the steel plate Nucor produced for these end-use customers.

The Cost-Efficiency of Nucor's Steel Mills All of Nucor's 24 steel mills used electric arc furnaces, whereby scrap steel and other metals were melted and the molten metal then poured into continuous casting systems. Sophisticated rolling mills converted the billets, blooms, and slabs produced by various casting equipment into rebar, angles, rounds, channels, flats, sheet, beams, plate, and other finished steel products. Nucor's steel mill operations were highly automated, typically requiring fewer operating employees per ton produced than the mills of rival companies. High worker productivity at all Nucor steel mills resulted in labor costs roughly 50 percent lower than the labor costs at the integrated mills of companies using union labor and conventional blast furnace technology. Nucor's value chain (anchored in using electric arc furnace technology to recycle scrap steel) involved far fewer production steps, far less capital investment, and considerably less labor than the value chains of companies with integrated steel mills that made crude steel from iron ore.

However, despite Nucor's demonstrated skills in operating steel mills at low costs per ton, it had been stymied throughout the 2010–2015 period in its quest to operate its 24 steel mills as cost-efficiently as they were capable of being operated. Ever since the Great Recession of 2008–2009, the combination of an anemic economic recovery, depressed market demand for steel products, industrywide overcapacity, and fierce competition from foreign imports in certain product categories had forced Nucor to operate its steel mills well below full capacity. Whereas in the first three quarters of 2008, Nucor's steel mills operated at an average of 91 percent of full capacity, the average capacity utilization rates at Nucor's steel mills were 54 percent in 2009, 70 percent in 2010, 74 percent in 2011, 75 percent in 2012, 76 percent in 2013, 78 percent in 2014, and 68 percent in 2015 (including tons shipped to outside customers and tons shipped to Nucor facilities making finished steel products). Likewise, subpar average capacity utilization rates at Nucor's facilities for producing finished steel products—54 percent in 2010, 57 percent in 2011, 58 percent in 2012, 61 percent in 2013, 66 percent in 2014, and 61 percent in 2015—had impaired Nucor's ability to keep overall production costs for finished steel products as low as they would otherwise have been at higher levels of capacity utilization. Nucor's unused capacity for producing so many types of steel mill and finished steel products during 2009–2015 represented one of the longest and deepest periods of overcapacity in Nucor's history.

Pricing and Sales

Since 2012, approximately 86 percent of the steel shipped from Nucor's steel mills had gone to external customers. The balance of the company's steel mill shipments went to supply the steel needs of the company's joist, deck, rebar fabrication, fastener, metal buildings, and cold finish operations. The big majority of Nucor's steel sales were to customers who placed orders monthly based on their immediate upcoming needs; Nucor's pricing strategy was to charge customers the going spot price on the day an order was placed. Shifting market demand–supply conditions and spot market prices caused Nucor's average sales prices per ton to fluctuate from quarter to quarter, sometimes by considerable amounts—see Exhibit 4. It was Nucor's practice to quote the same payment terms to all customers and for customers to pay all shipping charges.

EXHIBIT 4 Nucor's Average Quarterly Sales Prices for Steel Products, by Product Category, 2011–2015

	Average Sales Prices per Ton Sold					
Period	Sheet Steel	Steel Bars	Structural Steel	Steel Plate	All Steel Mill Products	All Finished Steel Products*
2011						
Qtr 1	$755	$779	$831	$ 880	$789	$1,274
Qtr 2	894	803	923	1,029	891	1,361
Qtr 3	800	811	901	1,021	847	1,381
Qtr 4	744	796	891	946	806	1,395
2012						
Qtr 1	$780	$823	$866	$ 929	$824	$1,387
Qtr 2	759	795	905	922	812	1,395
Qtr 3	707	745	973	837	775	1,371
Qtr 4	690	723	956	778	751	1,420
2013						
Qtr 1	$699	$732	$949	$ 769	$756	$1,380
Qtr 2	676	731	959	765	746	1,374
Qtr 3	693	708	923	753	741	1,369
Qtr 4	724	709	969	767	763	1,378
2014						
Qtr 1	$744	$737	$941	$ 816	$783	$1,348
Qtr 2	737	732	1,039	837	789	1,367
Qtr 3	750	738	1,011	838	793	1,369
Qtr 4	712	724	1,063	875	776	1,432
2015						
Qtr 1	$663	$698	$996	$ 805	$732	$1,404
Qtr 2	560	623	991	691	646	1,380
Qtr 3	552	625	926	648	635	1,351
Qtr 4	508	558	923	588	588	1,367

*An average of the steel prices for steel deck, steel joists and girders, steel buildings, cold finished steel products, steel mesh, fasteners, fabricated rebar, and other finished steel products.

Source: Company records posted at **www.nucor.com** (accessed February 21, 2016).

Nucor marketed the output of its steel mills and steel products facilities mainly through an in-house sales force; there were salespeople located at most every Nucor production facility. Going into 2016, approximately 50 percent of Nucor's sheet steel sales were to contract customers (versus 65 percent in 2012–2013 and 30 percent in 2009); these contracts for sheet steel were usually for periods of 6 to 12 months, were noncancelable, and permitted price adjustments to reflect changes in the market pricing for steel and/or raw material costs at the time of shipment. The other 50 percent of Nucor's sheet steel shipments and virtually all of the company's shipments of plate, structural, and bar steel were at the prevailing spot market price—customers not purchasing sheet steel rarely ever wanted to enter into a contract sales agreement. Nucor's steel mills maintained inventory levels deemed adequate to fill the expected incoming orders from customers. The average prices Nucor received for its various steel mill products are shown in the first four columns of Exhibit 4; the average prices received for sheet steel, steel bars, and steel plate in the last quarter of 2015 were 20 to 27 percent lower than in the first quarter of 2015 and the lowest of any quarter since 2010.

Nucor sold steel joists and joist girders, and steel deck on the basis of firm, fixed-price contracts that, in most cases, were won in competitive bidding against rival suppliers. Longer-term supply contracts for these items that were sometimes negotiated with customers contained clauses permitting price adjustments to reflect changes in prevailing raw materials costs. Steel joists, girders, and deck were manufactured to customers' specifications and shipped immediately; Nucor's plants did not maintain inventories of steel joists, girders, or steel deck. Nucor also sold fabricated reinforcing products only on a construction contract bid basis. However, cold finished steel, steel fasteners, steel grating, wire, and wire mesh were all manufactured in standard sizes, with each facility maintaining sufficient inventories of its products to fill anticipated orders; most all sales of these items were made at the prevailing spot price. The average prices Nucor received for its various finished steel products are shown in the last column of Exhibit 4.

NUCOR'S STRATEGY TO GROW AND STRENGTHEN ITS BUSINESS AND COMPETITIVE CAPABILITIES

Starting in 2000, Nucor embarked on a five-part growth strategy that involved new acquisitions, new plant construction, continued plant upgrades and cost reduction efforts, international growth through joint ventures, and greater control over raw materials costs.

Strategic Acquisitions

Beginning in the late 1990s, Nucor management concluded that growth-minded companies like Nucor might well be better off purchasing existing plant capacity rather than building new capacity, provided the acquired plants could be bought at bargain prices, economically retrofitted with new equipment if need be, and then operated at costs comparable to (or even below) those of newly constructed state-of-the-art plants. At the time, the steel industry worldwide had far more production capacity than was needed to meet market demand, forcing many companies to operate in the red. Nucor had not made any acquisitions since about 1990, and a team of five people was assembled in 1998 to explore acquisition possibilities that would strengthen Nucor's customer base, geographic coverage, and lineup of product offerings.

For almost three years, no acquisitions were made. But then the economic recession that hit Asia and Europe in the late 1990s reached the United States in full force in 2000–2001. The September 11, 2001, terrorist attacks further weakened steel purchases by such major steel-consuming industries as construction, automobiles, and farm equipment. Many steel companies in the United States and other parts of the world were operating in the red. Market conditions in the U.S. were particularly grim. Between October 2000 and October 2001, 29 steel companies in the United States, including Bethlehem Steel Corp. and LTV Corp., the nation's third and fourth largest steel producers, respectively, filed for bankruptcy protection. Bankrupt steel companies accounted for about 25 percent of U.S. capacity. *The Economist* noted that of the 14 steel companies tracked by Standard & Poor's, only Nucor was indisputably healthy. Some experts believed that close to half of the U.S. steel industry's production capacity might be forced to close before conditions improved; about 47,000 jobs in the U.S. steel industry had vanished since 1997.

One of the principal reasons for the distressed market conditions in the United States was a surge in imports of low-priced steel from foreign countries. Outside the United States, weak demand and a glut of capacity had driven commodity steel prices to 20-year lows in 1998. Globally, the industry had about 1 billion tons of annual capacity, but puny demand had kept production levels in the 750 to 800 million tons per year range during 1998–2000. A number of foreign steel producers, anxious to keep their mills running and finding few good market opportunities elsewhere, began selling steel in the U.S. market at cut-rate prices in 1997–1999. Nucor and other U.S. companies reduced prices to better compete and several filed unfair trade complaints against foreign steelmakers. The U.S. Department of Commerce concluded in March 1999 that steel companies in six countries (Canada, South Korea, Taiwan, Italy, Belgium, and South Africa) had illegally dumped stainless steel in the United States, and the governments of Belgium, Italy, and South Africa further facilitated the dumping by giving their steel producers unfair subsidies that at least partially made up for the revenues losses of selling at below-market prices. Congress and the Clinton administration opted to not impose tariffs or quotas on imported steel, which helped precipitate the number of bankruptcy filings. However, the Bush administration was more receptive to protecting the U.S. steel industry from the dumping practices of foreign steel companies. In October 2001, the U.S. International Trade Commission (ITC) ruled that increased steel imports of semi-finished steel, plate, hot-rolled sheet, strip and coils, cold-rolled sheet and strip, and corrosion-resistant and coated sheet and strip were a substantial cause of serious injury, or threat of serious injury, to the U.S. industry. In March 2002, the Bush administration imposed tariffs of up to 30 percent on imports of selected steel products to help provide relief from Asian and European companies dumping steel in the United States at ultra-low prices.

Even though market conditions were tough for Nucor, management concluded that oversupplied steel industry conditions and the number of beleaguered U.S. companies made it attractive to expand Nucor's production capacity via acquisition. Starting in 2001 and continuing through 2015, the company proceeded to make a series of strategic acquisitions to strengthen Nucor's competitiveness, selectively expand its product offerings improve its ability to serve customers in particular geographic locations, and boost the company's financial performance in times when market demand for steel was strong enough to boost prices to more profitable levels:

- In 2001, Nucor paid $115 million to acquire substantially all of the assets of Auburn Steel Company's 400,000-ton steel bar facility in Auburn, New York. This acquisition gave Nucor expanded market presence in the Northeast and was seen as a good source of supply for a new Vulcraft joist plant being constructed in Chemung, New York.
- In November 2001, Nucor announced the acquisition of ITEC Steel Inc. for a purchase price of $9 million. ITEC Steel had annual revenues of $10 million and produced load bearing light gauge steel framing for the residential and commercial market at facilities in Texas and Georgia. Nucor was impressed with ITEC's dedication to continuous improvement and intended to grow ITEC's business via geographic and product line expansion.
- In July 2002, Nucor paid $120 million to purchase Trico Steel Company, which had a 2.2 million ton sheet steel mill in Decatur, Alabama. Trico Steel was a joint venture of LTV (which owned a 50 percent interest) and two leading international steel companies—Sumitomo Metal Industries and British Steel. The joint venture partners had built the mill in 1997 at a cost of $465 million, but Trico was in Chapter 11 bankruptcy proceedings at the time of the acquisition and the mill was shut down. The Trico mill's capability to make thin sheet steel with a superior surface quality added competitive strength to Nucor's strategy to gain sales and market share in the flat-rolled sheet segment. By October 2002, two months ahead of schedule, Nucor had restarted operations at the Decatur mill and was shipping products to customers.
- In December 2002, Nucor paid $615 million to purchase substantially all of the assets of Birmingham Steel Corporation, which included four bar mills in Alabama, Illinois, Washington, and Mississippi. The four plants had capacity of approximately 2 million tons annually. Top executives believed the Birmingham Steel acquisition

would broaden Nucor's customer base and build profitable market share in bar steel products.

- In August 2004, Nucor acquired a cold rolling mill in Decatur, Alabama, from Worthington Industries for $80 million. This 1-million-ton mill, which opened in 1998, was located adjacent to the previously acquired Trico mill and gave Nucor added ability to service the needs of sheet steel buyers located in the southeastern United States.
- In June 2004, Nucor paid a cash price of $80 million to acquire a plate mill owned by Britain-based Corus Steel that was located in Tuscaloosa, Alabama. The Tuscaloosa mill, which currently had capacity of 700,000 tons that Nucor management believed was expandable to 1 million tons, was the first U.S. mill to employ a special technology that enabled high-quality wide steel plate to be produced from coiled steel plate. The mill produced coiled steel plate and plate products that were cut to customer-specified lengths. Nucor intended to offer these niche products to its commodity plate and coiled sheet customers.
- In February 2005, Nucor completed the purchase of Fort Howard Steel's operations in Oak Creek, Wisconsin; the Oak Creek facility produced cold finished bars in size ranges up to 6-inch rounds and had approximately 140,000 tons of annual capacity.
- In June 2005, Nucor purchased Marion Steel Company located in Marion, Ohio, for a cash price of $110 million. Marion operated a bar mill with annual capacity of about 400,000 tons; the Marion location was within close proximity to 60 percent of the steel consumption in the United States.
- In May 2006, Nucor acquired Connecticut Steel Corporation for $43 million in cash. Connecticut Steel's bar products mill in Wallingford had annual capacity to make 300,000 tons of wire rod and rebar and approximately 85,000 tons of wire mesh fabrication and structural mesh fabrication, products that complemented Nucor's present lineup of steel bar products provided to construction customers.
- In late 2006, Nucor purchased Verco Manufacturing Co. for approximately $180 million; Verco produced steel floor and roof decking at one location in Arizona and two locations in California. The Verco acquisition further solidified Vulcraft's market leading position in steel decking, giving it total annual capacity of over 500,000 tons.
- In January 2007, Nucor acquired Canada-based Harris Steel for about $1.07 billion. Harris Steel had 2005 sales of Cdn$1.0 billion and earnings of Cdn$64 million. The company's operations consisted of (1) Harris Rebar which was involved in the fabrication and placing of concrete reinforcing steel and the design and installation of concrete post-tensioning systems; (2) Laurel Steel which manufactured and distributed wire and wire products, welded wire mesh, and cold finished bar; and (3) Fisher & Ludlow which manufactured and distributed heavy industrial steel grating, aluminum grating, and expanded metal. In Canada, Harris Steel had 24 reinforcing steel fabricating plants, 2 steel grating distribution centers, and 1 cold finished bar and wire processing plant; in the United States it had 10 reinforcing steel fabricating plants, 2 steel grating manufacturing plants, and 3 steel grating manufacturing plants. Harris had customers throughout Canada and the United States and employed about 3,000 people. For the past three years, Harris had purchased a big percentage of its steel requirements from Nucor. Nucor management opted to operate Harris Steel as an independent subsidiary.
- Over several months in 2007 following the Harris Steel acquisition, Nucor through its new Harris Steel subsidiary acquired rebar fabricator South Pacific Steel Corporation, Consolidated Rebar, Inc., a 90 percent equity interest in rebar fabricator Barker Steel Company, and several smaller transactions—all aimed at growing its presence in the rebar fabrication marketplace.
- In August 2007, Nucor acquired LMP Steel & Wire Company for a cash purchase price of approximately $27.2 million, adding 100,000 tons of cold drawn steel capacity.
- In October 2007, Nucor completed the acquisition of Nelson Steel, Inc. for a cash purchase price of approximately $53.2 million, adding 120,000 tons of steel mesh capacity.
- In the third quarter of 2007, Nucor completed the acquisition of Magnatrax Corporation, a leading provider of custom-engineered metal buildings, for a cash purchase price of approximately $275.2 million. The Magnatrax acquisition enabled Nucor's Building System Group to become the second largest metal building producer in the United States.
- In August 2008, Nucor's Harris Steel subsidiary acquired Ambassador Steel Corporation for

a cash purchase price of about $185.1 million. Ambassador Steel was one of the largest independent fabricators and distributors of concrete reinforcing steel—in 2007, Ambassador shipped 422,000 tons of fabricated rebar and distributed another 228,000 tons of reinforcing steel. Its business complemented that of Harris Steel and represented another in a series of moves to greatly strengthen Nucor's competitive position in the rebar fabrication marketplace.

- Another small rebar fabrication company, Free State Steel, was acquired in late 2009, adding to Nucor's footprint in rebar fabrication.
- In June 2012, Nucor acquired Skyline Steel, LLC and its subsidiaries for a cash price of approximately $675.4 million. Skyline was a market-leading distributor of steel pilings, and it also processed and fabricated spiral weld pipe piling, rolled and welded pipe piling, cold-formed sheet piling, and threaded bar. The Skyline acquisition paired Skyline's leadership position in the steel piling distribution market with Nucor's own Nucor–Yamato plant in Arkansas that was the market leader in steel piling manufacturing. To capitalize on the strategic fits between Skyline's business and Nucor's business, Nucor launched a $155 million capital project at the Nucor–Yamato mill to (1) add several new sheet piling sections, (2) increase the production of single sheet widths by 22 percent, and (3) produce a lighter, stronger sheet covering more area at a lower installed cost—outcomes that would broaden the range of hot-rolled steel piling products Nucor could market through Skyline's distribution network in the United States, Canada, Mexico, and the Caribbean.
- In 2014, Nucor acquired Gallatin Steel Company for approximately $779 million. Gallatin produced a range of flat-rolled steel products (principally steel pipe and tube) at a mill with annual production capacity of 1.8 million tons that was located on the Ohio River in Kentucky. The Gallatin mill strengthened Nucor's position as the North American market leader in hot-rolled steel products by boosting its capacity to supply customers in the Midwest region, the largest flat-rolled consuming market region in the United States.
- In 2015, Nucor acquired Gerdau Long Steel's two facilities in Ohio and Georgia that produced cold-drawn steel bars and had combined capacity of 75,000 tons per year. These facilities, purchased for about $75 million, strengthened Nucor's already strong competitive position in cold-finished steel bars by expanding Nucor's geographic coverage and range of cold-finished product offerings.

Aggressively Investing to Expand the Company's Internal Production Capabilities

Complementing Nucor's ongoing strategic efforts to grow its business via acquisitions was a strategy element to invest aggressively in (1) the construction of new plant capacity and (2) enhanced production capabilities at existing plants whenever management spotted opportunities to boost sales with an expanded range of product offerings and/or strengthen its competitive position vis-à-vis rivals by lowering costs per ton or expanding its geographic coverage. The purpose of making ongoing capital investments was to improve efficiency and lower production costs at each and every facility it operated.

This strategy element had been in place since Nucor's earliest days in the steel business. Nucor always built state-of-the-art facilities in the most economical fashion possible and then made it standard company practice to invest in plant modernization and efficiency improvements whenever cost-saving opportunities emerged.

Examples of Nucor's efforts included the following:

- In 2006, Nucor announced that it would construct a new $27 million facility to produce metal buildings systems in Brigham City, Utah. The new plant, Nucor's fourth building systems plant, had capacity of 45,000 tons and gave Nucor national market reach in building systems products.
- In 2006, Nucor initiated construction of a $230 million state-of-the-art steel mill in Memphis, Tennessee, with annual capacity to produce 850,000 tons of special quality steel bars. Management believed this mill, together with the company's other special bar quality mills in Nebraska and South Carolina, would give Nucor the broadest, highest-quality, and lowest-cost offering of special quality steel bar in North America.
- In 2009, Nucor opened an idle and newly renovated $50 million wire rod and bar mill in Kingman, Arizona, that had been acquired in 2003.

Production of straight-length rebar, coiled rebar, and wire rod began in mid-2010; the plant had initial capacity of 100,000 tons, with the ability to increase annual production to 500,000 tons.

- The construction of a $150 million galvanizing facility located at the company's sheet steel mill in Decatur, Alabama, gave Nucor the ability to make 500,000 tons of 72-inch-wide galvanized sheet steel, a product used by motor vehicle and appliance producers and in various steel frame and steel stud buildings. The galvanizing process entailed dipping steel in melted zinc at extremely high temperatures; the zinc coating protected the steel surface from corrosion.
- In 2013 Nucor installed caster and hot mill upgrades at its Berkeley, South Carolina, sheet mill that enabled it to roll light-gauge sheet steel to a finished width of 74 inches. This new capability (which most foreign competitors did not have) opened opportunities to sell large quantities of wide-width, flat-rolled products to customers in a variety of industries while at the same time providing the mill with less exposure to competition from imports of less wide, flat-rolled products.
- A 2016 project to install a $75 million cooling process at the Nucor–Yamato mill in Arkansas was expected to generate savings on alloy costs of $12 million annually.

Nucor's Strategy to Be a First-Mover in Adopting the Best, Most Cost-Efficient Production Methods

The third element of Nucor's competitive strategy was to be a technology leader and first-rate operator of all its production facilities—outcomes that senior executives had pursued since the company's earliest days. Two approaches to improving and expanding Nucor's steelmaking capabilities and achieving low costs per ton were utilized:

- Being quick to implement disruptive technological innovations that would give Nucor a sustainable competitive advantage because of the formidable barriers rivals would have to hurdle to match Nucor's cost-competitiveness and/or product quality and/or range of products offered.
- Being quick to implement ongoing advances in production methods and install the latest and best steelmaking equipment, thus providing Nucor with a path to driving down costs per ton and/or leapfrogging competitors in terms of product quality, range of product offerings, and/or market share.

Nucor's biggest success in pioneering trailblazing technology had been at its Crawfordsville, Indiana, facilities where Nucor installed the world's first facility for direct strip casting of carbon sheet steel—a process called Castrip®. The Castrip process, which Nucor tested and refined for several years before implementing it in 2005, was a major technological breakthrough for producing flat-rolled, carbon, and stainless steels in very thin gauges because (1) it involved far fewer process steps to cast metal at or very near customer-desired thicknesses and shapes and (2) the process drastically reduced capital outlays for equipment and produced sizable savings on operating expenses (by enabling the use of cheaper grades of scrap metal and requiring 90 percent less energy to process liquid metal into hot-rolled steel sheets). An important environmental benefit of the Castrip process was cutting greenhouse gas emissions by up to 80 percent. Seeing these advantages earlier than rivals, Nucor management had the foresight to acquire exclusive rights to Castrip technology in the United States and Brazil. Once it was clear that the expected benefits of the Castrip facility at Crawfordsville were indeed going to become a reality, Nucor in 2006 launched construction of a second Castrip facility on the site of its structural steel mill in Arkansas.

Since technological breakthroughs (like the Castrip process) were relatively rare, Nucor management made a point of scouring locations across the world for reports of possible cost-effective technologies, ways to improve production methods and efficiency, and new and better equipment that could be used to improve operations and/or lower costs in Nucor's facilities. All such reports were checked out thoroughly, including making trips to inspect promising new developments firsthand if circumstances warranted. Projects to improve production methods or install more efficient equipment were promptly undertaken when the investment payback was attractive.

The Drive for Improved Efficiency and Lower Production Costs When Nucor acquired plants, it drew upon its ample financial strength and cash flows from operations to immediately fund efforts to get them up to Nucor standards—a process that employees called "Nucorizing." This included not only revising production methods and installing better equipment but also striving to increase operational efficiency by reducing the amount of time, space, energy, and manpower it took to produce steel products and paying close attention to worker safety and environmental protection practices.

Simultaneously, Nucor's top-level executives insisted upon continual improvement in product quality and cost at every company facility. Most all of Nucor's production locations were ISO 9000 and ISO 14000 certified. The company had a "BEST-marking" program aimed at being the industrywide best performer on a variety of production and efficiency measures. Managers at all Nucor plants were accountable for demonstrating that their operations were competitive on both product quality and cost vis-à-vis the plants of rival companies. A deeply embedded trait of Nucor's corporate culture was the expectation that plant-level managers would be persistent in initiating actions to improve product quality and keep costs per ton low relative to rival plants.

Nucor management viewed the task of pursuing operating excellence in its manufacturing operations as a continuous process. According to former CEO Dan DiMicco:[6]. We talk about 'climbing a mountain without a peak' to describe our constant improvements. We can take pride in what we have accomplished, but we are never satisfied.

The strength of top management's commitment to funding projects to improve plant efficiency, keep costs as low as possible, and achieve overall operating excellence was reflected in the company's capital expenditures for new technology, plant improvements, and equipment upgrades (see Exhibit 5). The beneficial outcomes of these expenditures, coupled with companywide vigilance and dedication to discovering and implementing ways to operate most cost-efficiently, were major contributors to Nucor's standing as North America's lowest-cost, most diversified provider of steel products.

EXHIBIT 5 Nucor's Capital Expenditures for New Plants, Plant Expansions, New Technology, Equipment Upgrades, and Other Operating Improvements, 2000–2015

Year	Capital Expenditures (in millions)	Year	Capital Expenditures (in millions)
2000	$415.0	2008	$1,019.0
2001	261.0	2009	390.5
2002	244.0	2010	345.2
2003	215.4	2011	450.6
2004	285.9	2012	1,019.3
2005	331.5	2013	1,230.4
2006	338.4	2014	568.9
2007	520.4	2015	364.8

Sources: Company records, accessed at **www.nucor.com**, various dates; data for 2009–2015 are from the 2013 10-K report, p. 43, and the 2015 10-K report, p. 45.

Shifting Production from Lower-End Steel Products to Value-Added Products

During 2010–2015, Nucor undertook a number of actions to shift more of the production tonnage at its steel mills and steel products facilities to "value-added products" that could command higher prices and yield better profit margins than could be had by producing lower-end or commodity steel products. Examples included:

- Adding new galvanizing capability at the Decatur, Alabama, mill that enabled Nucor to sell 500,000 tons of corrosion-resistant, galvanized sheet steel for high-end applications.
- Expanding the cut-to-length capabilities at the Tuscaloosa, Alabama, mill that put the mill in position to sell as many as 200,000 additional tons per year of cut-to-length and tempered steel plate.
- Shipping 250,000 tons of new steel plate and structural steel products in 2010 that were not offered in 2009, and further increasing shipments of these same new products to 500,000 tons in 2011.
- Completing installation of a heat-treating facility at the Hertford County, North Carolina, plate mill in 2011 that gave Nucor the capability to produce as much as 125,000 tons annually of heat-treated steel plate ranging from 3/16 of an inch through 2 inches thick.

- Installing new vacuum degassers at the Hickman, Arkansas, sheet mill and Hertford County, North Carolina, mill to enable production of increased volumes of higher-value sheet steel, steel plate, steel piping, and tubular products.
- Investing $290 million at its three steel bar mills to enable the production of steel bars and wire rod for the most demanding engineered bar applications and also put in place state-of-the-art quality inspection capabilities. The project enabled Nucor to offer higher-value steel bars and wire rod to customers in the energy, automotive, and heavy truck and equipment markets (where the demand for steel products had been relatively strong in recent years).
- Completing installation of a new 120,000-ton "normalizing" process for making steel plate at the Hertford County mill in June 2013; the new normalizing process allowed the mill to produce a higher grade of steel plate that was less brittle and had a more uniform fine-grained structure (which permitted the plate to be machined to more precise dimensions). Steel plate with these qualities was more suitable for armor plate applications and for certain uses in the energy, transportation, and shipbuilding industries. Going into 2014, the normalizing process, coupled with the company's recent investments in a vacuum tank degasser and a heat-treating facility at this same plant, doubled the Hertford mill's capacity to produce higher-quality steel plate products that commanded a higher market price.
- Modernizing the casting, hot-rolling, and downstream operations at the Berkeley, South Carolina, mill in 2013 to enable the production of 72-inch-wide sheet steel and lighter gauge hot-rolled and cold-rolled steel products with a finished width of 74 inches, thereby opening opportunities for Nucor to sell higher-value sheet steel products to customers in the agricultural, pipe and tube, industrial equipment, automotive, and heavy-equipment industries. In 2015, the Berkeley mill shipped 150,000 tons of wider-width products and was pursuing a goal of increasing shipments to 400,000 tons.
- Instituting a $155 million project at the Nucor–Yamato mill in 2014 to produce lighter, wider, and stronger steel pilings and a second $75 million project in 2016 to produce structural steel sections with high-strength, low-alloy grade chemistry; both projects helped Nucor grow sales of value-added structural steel products that had above-average profitability.
- Acquiring two Gerdau Long Steel facilities in 2015 that produced higher-margin, value-added cold-finished bars sold to steel service centers and other customers across the United States.

Product upgrades had also been undertaken at several Nucor facilities making cold-finished and fastener products. Senior management believed that all of these upgrades to higher-value product offerings would boost revenues and earnings in the years ahead.

Global Growth via Joint Ventures

In 2007, Nucor management decided it was time to begin building an international growth platform. The company's strategy to grow its international revenues had two elements:

- Establishing foreign sales offices and exporting U.S.-made steel products to foreign markets. Because about 60 percent of Nucor's steelmaking capacity was located on rivers with deep water transportation access, management believed that the company could be competitive in shipping U.S.-made steel products to customers in a number of foreign locations.
- Entering into joint ventures with foreign partners to invest in steelmaking projects outside North America. Nucor executives believed that the success of this strategy element was finding the right partners to grow with internationally.

Nucor opened a Trading Office in Switzerland and proceeded to establish international sales offices in Mexico, Brazil, Colombia, the Middle East, and Asia. The company's Trading Office bought and sold steel and steel products that Nucor and other steel producers had manufactured. In 2010, approximately 11 percent of the shipments from Nucor's steel mills were exported. Customers in South and Central America presented the most consistent opportunities for export sales, but there was growing interest from customers in Europe and other locations.

In January 2008, Nucor entered in a 50–50 joint venture with the European-based Duferco Group to establish the production of beams and other long products in Italy, with distribution in Europe and

North Africa. A few months later, Nucor acquired 50 percent of the stock of Duferdofin–Nucor S.r.l. for approximately $667 million (Duferdofin was Duferco's Italy-based steelmaking subsidiary). In 2013, Duferdofin–Nucor operated at various locations a steel melt shop and bloom/billet caster with an annual capacity of 1.1 million tons, two beam rolling mills with combined capacity of 1.1 million tons, a 495,000-ton merchant bar mill, and a 60,000-ton trackshoes/cutting edges mill. The customers for the products produced by Duferdofin–Nucor were primarily steel service centers and distributors located both in Italy and throughout Europe. So far, the joint venture project had not lived up to the partners' financial expectations because all of the plants made construction-related products. The European construction industry had been hard hit by the economic events of 2008–2009 and the construction-related demand for steel products in Europe was very slowly creeping back toward pre-crisis levels. Ongoing losses at Duferdofin–Nucor and revaluation of the joint venture's assets had resulted in Nucor's investment in Duferdofin–Nucor being valued at $412.9 million at December 31, 2014, and $258.2 million at December 31, 2015.

In early 2010, Nucor invested $221.3 million to become a 50–50 joint venture partner with Mitsui USA to form NuMit LLC—Mitsui USA was the largest wholly owned subsidiary of Mitsui & Co., Ltd., a diversified global trading, investment, and service enterprise headquartered in Tokyo, Japan. NuMit LLC owned 100 percent of the equity interest in Steel Technologies LLC, an operator of 25 sheet steel processing facilities throughout the United States, Canada, and Mexico. The NuMit joint venture was profitable in both 2012 and 2013. At the end of 2015, Nucor's investment in NuMit was $314.5 million, which consisted of the initial investment plus additional capital contributions and equity method earnings less distributions to Nucor; Nucor received distributions from NuMit of $6.7 million in 2013, $52.7 million in 2014, and $13.1 million in 2015.

Nucor's Raw Materials Strategy

Scrap metal and scrap substitutes were Nucor's single biggest cost—all of Nucor's steel mills used electric arc furnaces to make steel products from recycled scrap steel, scrap iron, pig iron, hot briquetted iron (HBI), and direct reduced iron (DRI). On average, it took approximately 1.1 tons of scrap and scrap substitutes to produce a ton of steel—the proportions averaged about 70 percent scrap steel and 30 percent scrap substitutes. Nucor was the biggest user of scrap metal in North America, and it also purchased millions of tons of pig iron, HBI, DRI, and other iron products annually—top-quality scrap substitutes were especially critical in making premium grades of sheet steel, steel plate, and special bar quality steel at various Nucor mills. Scrap prices were driven by market demand-supply conditions and could fluctuate significantly—see Exhibit 6. Rising scrap prices adversely impacted the company's costs and ability to compete against steelmakers that made steel from scratch using iron ore, coke, and traditional blast furnace technology.

Nucor's raw materials strategy was aimed at achieving greater control over the costs of all types of metallic inputs (both scrap metal and iron-related substitutes) used at its steel plants. A key element of this strategy was to backward integrate into the production of 6 to 7 million tons per year of high-quality scrap substitutes (chiefly pig iron and direct reduced iron) at either its own wholly owned and operated plants or at plants jointly owned by Nucor and other partners—integrating backward into supplying a big fraction of its own iron requirements held promise of raw material savings and less reliance on outside iron suppliers. The costs of producing pig iron and direct reduced iron (DRI) were not as subject to steep swings as was the price of scrap steel.

Nucor's first move to execute its long-term raw materials strategy came in 2002 when it partnered with the Rio Tinto Group, Mitsubishi Corporation, and Chinese steelmaker Shougang Corporation to pioneer Rio Tinto's HIsmelt® technology at a new plant to be constructed in Kwinana, Western Australia. The HIsmelt technology entailed converting iron ore to liquid metal or pig iron and was both a replacement for traditional blast furnace technology and a hot metal source for electric arc furnaces. Rio Tinto had been developing the HIsmelt technology for 10 years and believed the technology had the potential to revolutionize ironmaking and provide low-cost, high-quality iron for making steel. Nucor had a 25 percent ownership in the venture and had a joint global marketing agreement with Rio Tinto to license the technology to other interested steel companies. The Australian plant represented the world's first commercial application of the HIsmelt technology; it had a capacity of over 880,000 tons and was expandable to 1.65 million tons at an attractive capital cost per incremental ton. Production started in January 2006. However, the joint venture partners opted to permanently close the HIsmelt plant in December 2010 because the project, while technologically acclaimed, proved to be financially unviable. Nucor's loss in the joint venture partnership amounted to $94.8 million.

In April 2003, Nucor entered a joint venture with Companhia Vale do Rio Doce (CVRD) to construct and operate an environmentally friendly $80 million pig iron project in northern Brazil. The project, named Ferro Gusa Carajás, utilized two conventional mini-blast furnaces to produce about 418,000 tons of pig iron per year, using iron ore from CVRD's Carajás mine in northern Brazil. The charcoal fuel for the plant came exclusively from fast-growing eucalyptus trees in a cultivated forest in northern Brazil owned by a CVRD subsidiary. The cultivated forest removed more carbon dioxide from the atmosphere than the blast furnace emitted, thus counteracting global warming—an outcome that appealed to Nucor management. Nucor invested $10 million in the project and was a 22 percent owner. Production of pig iron began in the fourth quarter of 2005; the joint venture agreement called for Nucor to purchase all of the plant's production. However, Nucor sold its interest in the project to CVRD in April 2007.

Nucor's third raw-material sourcing initiative came in 2004 when it acquired an idled direct reduced iron (DRI) plant in Louisiana, relocated all of the plant assets to Trinidad and Tobago (a dual-island nation off the coast of South America near Venezuela), and expanded the project (named Nu-Iron Unlimited) to a capacity of 2 million tons. The plant used a proven technology that converted iron ore pellets into direct reduced iron. The Trinidad site was chosen because it had a long-term and very cost-attractive supply of natural gas (large volumes of natural gas were consumed in the plant's production process), along with favorable logistics for receiving iron ore and shipping direct reduced iron to Nucor's steel mills in the United States. Nucor entered into contracts with natural gas suppliers to purchase natural gas in amounts needed to operate the Trinidad through 2028. Production began in January 2007. Nu-Iron personnel at the Trinidad plant had recently achieved world-class product quality levels in making DRI; this achievement allowed Nucor to use an even larger percentage of DRI in producing the most demanding steel products.

In September 2010, Nucor announced plans to build a $750 million DRI facility with annual capacity of 2.5 million tons on a 4,000-acre site in St. James Parish, Louisiana. This investment moved Nucor two-thirds of the way to its long-term objective of being able to supply 6 to 7 million tons of its requirements for high-quality scrap substitutes. However, the new DRI facility was the first phase of a multiphase plan that included a second 2.5-million-ton DRI facility, a coke plant, a blast furnace, an iron ore pellet plant, and a steel mill. Permits for both DRI plants were received from the Louisiana Department of Environmental

EXHIBIT 6 Nucor's Costs for Scrap Steel and Scrap Substitute, 2000–2015

Period	Average Cost of Scrap and Scrap Substitute per Ton Used	Period	Average Cost of Scrap and Scrap Substitute per Ton Used
		2014	
2000	$120	Quarter 1	$398
2001	101	Quarter 2	384
2002	110	Quarter 3	379
2003	137	Quarter 4	363
2004	238	**Average**	381
2005	244		
		2015	
2006	246	Quarter 1	$324
2007	278	Quarter 2	271
2008	438	Quarter 3	262
2009	303	Quarter 4	219
2010	351	**Average**	270
2011	439		
2012	407		
2013	376		

Source: Nucor's Annual Reports for 2011, 2009, 2007 and information posted in the investor relations section at www.nucor.com (accessed April 12, 2012, April 15, 2014, and February 11, 2016).

Quality in January 2011. Construction of the first DRI unit at the St. James site began in 2011, and production began in late 2013 and was rapidly ramped up toward capacity in 2014. However, the plant experienced significant operating losses in the first three quarters of 2014 due to low yields in converting iron ore pellets into direct reduced iron. In the fourth quarter of 2014 there was an equipment failure that shut down operations until early 2015. But the Louisiana DRI facility's performance in 2015 was impaired by (1) higher-cost iron ore purchased in 2014 at the fourth quarter of 2014 that could not be used until 2015 when the facility resumed operations after equipment repairs were made, and (2) a planned maintenance outage in Q4 of 2015. Due to adverse market conditions that forced Nucor's steel mills to operate well below capacity in 2015, the Louisiana DRI plant did not resume operation until early 2016. While in 2014 a Nucor official had indicated that Nucor's use of DRI in its steel mills was expected to give the company an approximate $75 per ton cost advantage in producing a ton of steel over traditional integrated steel mills using conventional blast furnace technology, so far the Louisiana DRI plant's problems had prevented Nucor from realizing any cost-saving benefits from its $750 million investment in the plant, and all activities relating to a second 2.5-million-ton DRI facility, a coke plant, a blast furnace, an iron ore pellet plant, and a steel mill at the St. James Parish site in Louisiana had been put on hold.[7] Nonetheless, Nucor management believed that the recent investments in its two DRI plants (in Trinidad and Tobago and Louisiana) had put the company in better position going forward to manage its overall costs of metallic materials and the associated supply-related risks.

Because producing DRI was a natural gas intensive process, Nucor entered into a long-term, onshore natural gas working interest drilling program with Encana Oil & Gas, one of North America's largest producers of natural gas, to help offset the company's exposure to future increases in the price of natural gas consumed by the DRI facility in St. James Parish. Nucor entered into a second and more significant drilling program with Encana in 2012. All natural gas from Nucor's working interest drilling program with Encana was being sold to outside parties. In December 2013, Nucor and Encana agreed to temporarily suspend drilling new gas wells because of expectations that the natural gas pricing environment would be weak in 2014. By the middle of 2014, when all of the in-process wells were completed, Nucor management believed the over 300 producing wells would provide a full hedge against the Louisiana DRI plant's expected consumption of natural gas into 2015. However, discoveries of abundant natural gas supplies in late 2014 and throughout 2015 (via the highly successful exploration efforts of companies employing fracking technology in areas close to Louisiana where there were big shale deposits containing both oil and natural gas) kept the Nucor–Encana drilling program shut down. Nucor did not expect the program to resume operations until the market price of natural gas climbed to levels that made it economic to produce gas at the wells already drilled. Nucor's investment in the drilling program and related activities was $135.9 million at December 31, 2015.

The Acquisition of the David J. Joseph Company In February 2008, Nucor acquired the David J. Joseph Company (DJJ) and related affiliates for a cash purchase price of approximately $1.44 billion, the largest acquisition in Nucor's history. DJJ was one of the leading scrap metal companies in the United States, with 2007 revenues of $6.4 billion. It processed about 3.5 million tons of scrap iron and steel annually at some 35 scrap yards and brokered over 20 million tons of iron and steel scrap and over 500 million pounds of nonferrous materials in 2007. DJJ obtained scrap from industrial plants, the manufacturers of products that contained steel, independent scrap dealers, peddlers, auto junkyards, demolition firms, and other sources. The DJJ Mill and Industrial Services business provided logistics and metallurgical blending operations and offered on-site handling and trading of industrial scrap. The DJJ Rail Services business owned over 2,000 railcars dedicated to the movement of scrap metals and offered complete railcar fleet management and leasing services. Nucor was familiar with DJJ and its various operations because it had obtained scrap from DJJ since 1969. Most importantly, though, all of DJJ's businesses had strategic value to Nucor in helping gain control over its scrap metal costs. Within months of completing the DJJ acquisition (which was operated as a separate subsidiary), the DJJ management team acquired four other scrap processing companies. Additional scrap processors were acquired during 2010–2014, and several new scrap yards were opened. As of year-end 2015, DJJ had 72 operating facilities in 16 states (along with multiple brokerages offices in the United

States and certain foreign countries) and total annual scrap processing capacity of 5.2 million tons. And, because of DJJ's railcar fleet, Nucor could quickly and cost-efficiently deliver scrap to its steel mills.

Nucor's Commitment to Being a Global Leader in Environmental Performance

Every Nucor facility was evaluated for actions that could be taken to promote greater environmental sustainability. Measurable objectives and targets relating to such outcomes as reduced use of oil and grease, more efficient use of electricity, and sitewide recycling were in place at each plant. Computerized controls on large electric motors and pumps and energy-recovery equipment to capture and reuse energy that otherwise would be wasted had been installed throughout Nucor's facilities to lower energy usage—Nucor considered itself to be among the most energy-efficient steel companies in the world. All of Nucor's facilities had water-recycling systems. Nucor even recycled the dust from its electric arc furnaces because scrap metal contained enough zinc, lead, chrome, and other valuable metals to recycle into usable products; the dust was captured in each plant's state-of-the-art bag house air pollution control devices and then sent to a recycler that converted the dust into zinc oxide, steel slag, and pig iron. The first Nucor mill received ISO 14001 Environmental Management System certification in 2001; as of year-end 2015, all of Nucor's facilities were ISO 14001 certified.

Nucor's sheet mill in Decatur, Alabama, used a measuring device called an opacity monitor, which gave precise, minute-by-minute readings of the air quality that passed through the bag house and out of the mill's exhaust system. While rival steel producers had resisted using opacity monitors (because they documented anytime a mill's exhaust was out of compliance with its environmental permits, even momentarily), Nucor's personnel at the Decatur mill viewed the opacity monitor as a tool for improving environmental performance. They developed the expertise to read the monitor so well that they could pinpoint in just a few minutes the first signs of a problem in any of the nearly 7,000 bags in the bag house—before those problems resulted in increased emissions. Their early-warning system worked so well that the division applied for a patent on the process, with an eye toward licensing it to other companies.

Organization and Management Philosophy

Nucor had a simple, streamlined organizational structure to allow employees to innovate and make quick decisions. The company was highly decentralized, with most day-to-day operating decisions made by group or plant-level general managers and their staff. Each group or plant operated independently as a profit center and was headed by a general manager, who in most cases also had the title of vice president. The group manager or plant general manager had control of the day-to-day decisions that affected the group or plant's profitability.

The organizational structure at a typical plant had four layers:

- General manager
- Department manager
- Supervisor/professional
- Hourly employee

Group managers and plant managers reported to one of five executive vice presidents at corporate headquarters. Nucor's corporate staff was exceptionally small, consisting of about 100 people in 2013, the philosophy being that corporate headquarters should consist of a small cadre of executives who would guide a decentralized operation where liberal authority was delegated to managers in the field. Each plant had a sales manager who was responsible for selling the products made at that particular plant; such staff functions as engineering, accounting, and personnel management were performed at the group/plant level. There was a minimum of paperwork and bureaucratic systems. Each group/plant was expected to earn about a 25 percent return on total assets before corporate expenses, taxes, interest, or profit sharing. As long as plant managers met their profit targets, they were allowed to operate with minimal restrictions and interference from corporate headquarters. There was a very friendly spirit of competition from one plant to the next to see which facility could be the best performer, but since all of the vice presidents and general managers shared the same bonus systems they functioned pretty much as a team despite operating their facilities individually. Top executives did not hesitate to replace group or plant managers who consistently struggled to achieve profitability and operating targets.

Workforce Compensation Practices

Nucor was a largely nonunion "pay for performance" company with an incentive compensation system that rewarded goal-oriented individuals and did not put a maximum on what they could earn. All employees, except those in the recently acquired Harris Steel and DJJ subsidiaries that operated independently from the rest of Nucor, worked under one of four basic compensation plans, each featuring incentives related to meeting specific goals and targets:

1. *Production Incentive Plan*—Production line jobs were rated on degree of responsibility required and assigned a base wage comparable to the wages paid by other manufacturing plants in the area where a Nucor plant was located. But in addition to their base wage, operating and maintenance employees were paid weekly bonuses based on the number of tons by which the output of their production team or work group exceeded the "standard" number of tons. All operating and maintenance employees were members of a production team that included the team's production supervisor, and the tonnage produced by each work team was measured for each work shift and then totaled for all shifts during a given week. If a production team's weekly output beat the weekly standard, team members (including the team's production supervisor) earned a specified percentage bonus for each ton produced above the standard—production bonuses were paid weekly (rather than quarterly or annually) so that workers and supervisors would be rewarded immediately for their efforts. The standard rate was calculated based on the capabilities of the equipment employed (typically at the time plant operations began), and no bonus was paid if the equipment was not operating (which gave maintenance workers a big incentive to keep a plant's equipment in good working condition)—Nucor's philosophy was that when equipment was not operating everybody suffered and the bonus for downtime ought to be zero. Production standards at Nucor plants were seldom raised unless a plant underwent significant modernization or important new pieces of equipment were installed that greatly boosted labor productivity. It was common for production incentive bonuses to run from 50 to 150 percent of an employee's base pay, thereby pushing compensation levels up well above those at other nearby manufacturing plants. Worker efforts to exceed the standard and get a bonus did not so much involve working harder as it involved good teamwork and close collaboration in resolving problems and figuring out how best to exceed the production standards.
2. *Department Manager Incentive Plan*—Department managers earned annual incentive bonuses based primarily on the percentage of net income to dollars of assets employed for their division. These bonuses could be as much as 80 percent of a department manager's base pay.
3. *Professional and Clerical Bonus Plan*—A bonus based on a division's net income return on assets was paid to employees that were not on the production worker or department manager plan.
4. *Senior Officers Annual Incentive Plan*—Nucor's senior officers did not have employment contracts and did not participate in any pension or retirement plans. Their base salaries were set at approximately 90 percent of the median base salary for comparable positions in other manufacturing companies with comparable assets, sales, and capital. The remainder of their compensation was based on Nucor's annual overall percentage of net income to stockholder's equity (ROE) and was paid out in cash and stock. Once Nucor's ROE reached a threshold of than 3 percent, senior officers earned a bonus equal to 20 percent of their base salary. If Nucor's annual ROE was 20 percent or higher, senior officers earned a bonus equal to 225 percent of their base salary. Officers could earn an additional bonus up to 75 percent of their base salary based on a comparison of Nucor's net sales growth with the net sales growth of members of a steel industry peer group. There was also a long-term incentive plan that provided for stock awards and stock options. The structure of these officer incentives was such that bonus compensation for Nucor officers fluctuated widely—from close to zero (in years when industry conditions were bad and Nucor's performance was subpar) to 400 percent (or more) of base salary (when Nucor's performance was excellent).
5. *Senior Officers Long-Term Incentive Plan*—The long-term incentive was intended to balance the short-term focus of the annual incentive plan by rewarding performance over multiyear periods. These incentives were received in the form of

cash (50 percent) and restricted stock (50 percent) and covered a performance period of three years; 50 percent of the long-term award was based on how Nucor's three-year ROAIC (return on average invested capital) compared against the three-year ROAIC of the steel industry peer group and 50 percent was based on how Nucor's three-year ROAIC compared against a multi-industry group of well-respected companies in capital-intensive businesses similar to that of steel.

Nucor management had designed the company's incentive plans for employees so that bonus calculations involved no discretion on the part of a plant/division manager or top executives. This was done to eliminate any concerns on the part of workers that managers or executives might show favoritism or otherwise be unfair in calculating or awarding incentive awards.

There were two other types of extra compensation:

- *Profit Sharing*—Each year, Nucor allocated at least 10 percent of its operating profits to profit-sharing bonuses for all employees (except senior officers). Depending on company performance, the bonuses could run anywhere from 1 percent to over 20 percent of pay. Twenty percent of the bonus amount was paid to employees in the following March as a cash bonus and the remaining 80 percent was put into a trust for each employee, with each employee's share being proportional to their earnings as a percentage of total earnings by all workers covered by the plan. An employee's share of profit sharing became vested after one full year of employment. Employees received a quarterly statement of their balance in profit sharing.
- *401(k) Plan*—Both officers and employees participated in a 401(k) plan where the company matched from 5 to 25 percent of each employee's first 7 percent of contributions; the amount of the match was based on how well the company was doing.

In 2015, entry-level, hourly workers at a Nucor plant could expect to earn $40,000 to $50,000 annually (including bonuses). Earnings for more experienced production workers were often in the $70,000 to $95,000 range. Total compensation for salaried managers varied from $60,000 to $200,000, depending on level of management, type of job (accounting, engineering, sales, information technology), years of experience, and geographic location. It was common for worker compensation at Nucor plants to be double or more the average earned by workers at other manufacturing companies in the states where Nucor's plants were located. Nucor employees earned three times the local average manufacturing wage. Nucor management philosophy was that workers ought to be excellently compensated because the production jobs were strenuous and the work environment in a steel mill was relatively dangerous.

Employee turnover in Nucor mills was extremely low; absenteeism and tardiness were minimal. Each employee was allowed four days of absences and could also miss work for jury duty, military leave, or the death of close relatives. After this, a day's absence cost a worker the entire performance bonus pay for that week and being more than a half-hour late to work on a given day resulted in no bonus payment for the day. When job vacancies did occur, Nucor was flooded with applications from people wanting to get a job at Nucor; plant personnel screened job candidates very carefully, seeking people with initiative and a strong work ethic.

Employee Relations and Human Resources

Employee relations at Nucor were based on four clear-cut principles:

1. Management is obligated to manage Nucor in such a way that employees will have the opportunity to earn according to their productivity.
2. Employees should feel confident that if they do their jobs properly, they will have a job tomorrow.
3. Employees have the right to be treated fairly and must believe that they will be.
4. Employees must have an avenue of appeal when they believe they are being treated unfairly.

The hallmarks of Nucor's human resource strategy were its incentive pay plan for production exceeding the standard and the job security provided to production workers—despite being in an industry with strong down cycles, Nucor had made it a practice not to lay off workers. Instead, when market conditions were tough and production had to be cut back, workers were assigned to plant maintenance projects, cross-training programs, and other activities calculated to boost the plant's performance when market conditions improved.

Nucor took an egalitarian approach to providing fringe benefits to its employees; employees had the same insurance programs, vacation schedules, and holidays as upper-level management. However, certain benefits were not available to Nucor's officers. The fringe benefit package at Nucor included:

- *Medical and Dental Plans*—The company had a flexible and comprehensive health benefit program for officers and employees that included wellness and health care spending accounts.
- *Tuition Reimbursement*—Nucor reimbursed up to $3,000 of an employee's approved educational expenses each year and up to $1,500 of a spouse's educational expenses for two years.
- *Service Awards*—After each five years of service with the company, Nucor employees received a service award consisting of five shares of Nucor stock.
- *Scholarships and Educational Disbursements*—Nucor provided the children of every employee (except senior officers) with college funding of $3,000 per year for four years to be used at accredited academic institutions.
- *Other Benefits*—Long-term disability, life insurance, vacation.

Most of the changes Nucor made in work procedures came from employees. The prevailing view at Nucor was that the employees knew the problems of their jobs better than anyone else and were thus in the best position to identify ways to improve how things were done. Most plant-level managers spent considerable time in the plant, talking and meeting with frontline employees and listening carefully to suggestions. Promising ideas and suggestions were typically acted upon quickly and implemented—management was willing to take risks to try worker suggestions for doing things better and to accept the occasional failure when the results were disappointing. Teamwork, a vibrant team spirit, and a close worker–management partnership were much in evidence at Nucor plants.

Nucor plants did not utilize job descriptions. Management believed job descriptions caused more problems than they solved, given the teamwork atmosphere and the close collaboration among work group members. The company saw formal performance appraisal systems as a waste of time and added paperwork. If a Nucor employee was not performing well, the problem was dealt with directly by supervisory personnel and the peer pressure of work group members (whose bonuses were adversely affected).

Employees were kept informed about company and division performance. Charts showing the division's results in return-on-assets and bonus payoff were posted in prominent places in the plant. Most all employees were quite aware of the level of profits in their plant or division. Nucor had a formal grievance procedure, but grievances were few and far between. The corporate office sent all news releases to each division where they were posted on bulletin boards. Each employee received a copy of Nucor's annual report; it was company practice for the cover of the annual report to consist of the names of all Nucor employees.

All of these practices had created an egalitarian culture and a highly motivated workforce that grew out of former CEO Ken Iverson's radical insight: employees, even hourly clock punchers, would put forth extraordinary effort and be exceptionally productive if they were richly rewarded, treated with respect, and given real power to do their jobs as best they saw fit.[8] There were countless stories of occasions when managers and workers had gone beyond the call of duty to expedite equipment repairs (in many instances even using their weekends to go help personnel at other Nucor plants solve a crisis); the company's workforce was known for displaying unusual passion and company loyalty even when no personal financial stake was involved. As one Nucor worker put it, "At Nucor, we're not 'you guys' and 'us guys.' It's all of us guys. Wherever the bottleneck is, we go there, and everyone works on it."[9]

It was standard procedure for a team of Nucor veterans, including people who worked on the plant floor, to visit with their counterparts as part of the process of screening candidates for acquisition.[10] One of the purposes of such visits was to explain the Nucor compensation system and culture face-to-face, gauge reactions, and judge whether the plant would fit into "the Nucor way of doing things" if it was acquired. Shortly after making an acquisition, Nucor management moved swiftly to institute its pay-for-performance incentive system and to begin instilling the egalitarian Nucor culture and idea-sharing. Top priority was given to looking for ways to boost plant production using fewer people and without making substantial capital investments; the take-home pay of workers at newly acquired plants typically went up rather dramatically. At the Auburn Steel plant, acquired in 2001, it took Nucor about six months to convince workers that they would be better off under Nucor's pay system; during that time Nucor paid people under the old Auburn Steel system but posted what they would have earned under Nucor's system. Pretty soon, workers were convinced to make the changeover—one worker's pay climbed from $53,000 in the year prior to the acquisition to $67,000 in 2001 and to $92,000 in 2005.[11]

New Employees Each plant/division had a "consul" responsible for providing new employees with general advice about becoming a Nucor teammate and serving as a resource for inquiries about how things were done at Nucor, how to navigate the division and company, and how to resolve issues that might come up. Nucor provided new employees with a personalized plan that set forth who would give them feedback about how well they were doing and when and how this feedback would be given; from time to time, new employees met with the plant manager for feedback and coaching. In addition, there was a new employee orientation session that provided a hands-on look at the plant/division operations; new employees also participated in product group meetings to provide exposure to broader business and technical issues. Each year, Nucor brought all recent college hires to the Charlotte headquarters for a forum intended to give the new hires a chance to network and provide senior management with guidance on how best to leverage their talent.

THE WORLD STEEL INDUSTRY

After global production of crude steel hit a record high of 1,670 million tons in 2014, production dropped off in 2015 to 1,599 million tons—see Exhibit 7. Steelmaking capacity worldwide was approximately 2,300 million tons in 2015, resulting in global excess capacity of 700 million tons and a 2015 capacity utilization rate of 69.5 percent (up from a historically unprecedented low of 52 percent in 2009, but down from 74.2 percent in 2014). Worldwide demand for steel mill products grew an average of about 3.8 percent annually during 2008–2014, but the annual growth rate was quite volatile, ranging from a decline of 6.1 percent (2008–2009) to a high of 7.9 percent (2010–2011).[12] Worldwide steel demand fell an estimated 1.7 percent in 2015, but was forecast to grow a scant 0.7 percent in 2016.

The six biggest steel-producing countries in 2015 were:[13]

Country	Total Production of Crude Steel	Percent of Worldwide Production
China	804 million tons	50.3%
Japan	105 million tons	6.6%
India	89 million tons	5.6%
United States	79 million tons	4.9%
Russia	71 million tons	4.4%
South Korea	69 million tons	4.3%

The global marketplace for steel was considered to be relatively mature and highly cyclical as a result of ongoing ups and downs in the world economy or the economies of particular countries. It was also intensely price competitive and expected to remain so until the 700 million tons of excess steelmaking capacity across the world shrunk substantially and global demand for steel products more closely matched global supplies.

In general, competition within the global steel industry was intense and expected to remain so. Companies with excess production capacity were active in seeking to increase their exports of steel to foreign markets. During 2005–2015, the biggest steel-exporting countries were China, Japan, South Korea, Russia, the Ukraine, and Germany; the biggest steel-importing countries during this same period were the United States, Germany, South Korea, Thailand, China, Italy, France, and Turkey. China, Germany, and South Korea were both big exporters and big importers because domestic steel makers had more capacity to make certain types and grades of steel than was needed locally (and thus strived to export such products to other countries) but lacked sufficient domestic capability to produce certain types and grades of finished steel products needed by domestic customers (which consequently had to be imported).

The overhang of excess steelmaking capacity worldwide put mounting pressure on the prices of many steel products in 2013–2015, a condition that

EXHIBIT 7 Worldwide Production of Crude Steel, with Compound Average Growth Rates, 1975–2015

Year	World Crude Steel Production (millions of tons)	Compound Average Growth Rates in World Crude Steel Production	
		Period	Percentage Rate
1975	709	1975–1980	2.2%
1980	789	1980–1985	0.1%
1985	793	1985–1990	1.4%
1990	849	1990–1995	–0.5%
1995	827	1995–2000	0.5%
2000	849	2000–2005	6.2%
2005	1,148	2005–2010	4.5%
2010	1,433	2010–2015	2.2%
2011	1,538		
2012	1,560		
2013	1,650		
2014	1,670		
2015	1,599		

Sources: World Steel Association, *Steel Statistical Yearbook,* various years; "Crude Steel Production 2015," www.worldsteel.org, (accessed March 9, 2016).

was widely expected to continue in 2016 and beyond. Much of the world's excess steelmaking capacity was in China, but there were pockets of excess capacity in many other countries. Chinese steelmakers had responded to slumping domestic demand for steel products in 2015 by exporting record amounts of steel to other countries and securing buyers with artificially low prices (that were partly enabled by Chinese currency devaluations which made Chinese exports cheaper in foreign markets and partly enabled by subsidies and other financial assistance the Chinese government provided to domestic steelmakers, a number of which were wholly or partly government-owned).

Total Chinese exports of steel rose from 94 million tons in 2014 to almost 123 million tons in 2015—an amount that was bigger than the total amount produced by steelmakers in the United States and Canada.[14] A big fraction of China's exported steel was sold to customers at prices that significantly undercut the prices of local steelmakers and allowed the Chinese sellers to steal away market share. The price of hot-rolled steel coil in the United States dropped about 40 percent to under $400 per ton in 2015, with domestic mills idling as much as 38 percent of capacity after imports climbed by 38 percent in 2014; the price drop contributed to a loss of $1.5 billion at U.S. Steel Corp. and an almost $8 billion loss at ArcelorMittal.[15] According to ArcelorMittal's CEO, the Chinese steel industry lost $10 billion in 2015, which "proves they are dumping."[16] A number of countries, at the urging of domestic steelmakers suffering from lost sales and falling domestic steel prices in 2014–2015, began investigating whether their markets were a dumping ground for unfairly traded, low-priced steel produced in China and certain other countries.

Exhibit 8 shows the world's 15 largest producers of steel in 2014.

Steelmaking Technologies

Steel was produced either by integrated steel facilities or "mini-mills" that employed electric arc furnaces. Integrated mills used blast furnaces to produce hot metal typically from iron ore pellets, limestone, scrap steel, oxygen, assorted other metals, and coke (coke was produced by firing coal in large coke ovens and was the major fuel used in blast furnaces to produce molten iron). Melted iron from the blast furnace

EXHIBIT 8 Top 15 Producers of Crude Steel Worldwide, 2005, 2010, and 2014

		Crude Steel Production (in millions of tons)		
2014 Rank	Company (Headquarters)	2005	2010	2014
1.	ArcelorMittal (Luxembourg)	120.9	98.2	98.1
2.	Nippon Steel (Japan)	35.3	35.0	49.3
3.	Hebei Group (China)	—	52.9	47.1
4.	Baosteel (China)	25.0	37.0	43.3
5.	POSCO (South Korea)	33.6	35.4	41.4
6.	Shagang Group (China)	—	23.2	35.3
7.	Ansteel (China)	13.1	22.1	34.3
8.	Wuhan Group (China)	14.3	16.6	33.1
9.	JFE (Japan)	32.9	31.1	31.4
10.	Shougang Group (China)	—	25.8	30.8
11.	Tata Steel (India)	—	23.2	26.2
12.	Shandong Steel Group (China)	—	23.2	23.3
13.	Nucor (USA)	20.3	18.3	21.4
14.	HYUNDAI Steel Company (South Korea)	—	12.9	20.6
15.	United States Steel (USA)	21.3	22.3	19.7

Sources: World Steel Association, "Top Steel Producers 2014," **www.worldsteel.org** (accessed March 9, 2016); Wikipedia, "List of Steel Producers" (accessed March 9, 2016).

EXHIBIT 9 U.S. Exports and Imports of Steel Mill Products, 2005–2014 (in millions of tons)

Year	U.S. Exports of Steel Mill Products	U.S. Exports of Steel Mill Products
2005	9.4 million tons	30.2 million tons
2006	9.6	42.2
2007	9.8	27.7
2008	12.0	24.6
2009	9.2	15.3
2010	11.8	22.5
2011	13.3	26.6
2012	13.6	30.9
2013	12.5	29.8
2014	12.0	41.4

Source: World Steel Association, *Steel Statistical Yearbook, 2015*, **www.worldsteel.org** (accessed March 11, 2016).

process was then run through the basic oxygen process to produce liquid steel. To make flat-rolled steel products, liquid steel was either fed into a continuous caster machine and cast into slabs or else cooled in slab form for later processing. Slabs were further shaped or rolled at a plate mill or hot strip mill. In making certain sheet steel products, the hot strip mill process was followed by various finishing processes, including pickling, cold-rolling, annealing, tempering, galvanizing, or other coating procedures. These various processes for converting raw steel into finished steel products were often distinct steps undertaken at different times and in different on-site or off-site facilities rather than being done in a continuous process in a single plant facility—an integrated mill was thus one that had multiple facilities at a single plant site and could therefore not only produce crude (or raw) steel but also run the crude steel through various facilities and finishing processes to make hot-rolled and cold-rolled sheet steel products, steel bars and beams, stainless steel, steel wire and nails, steel pipes and tubes, and other finished steel products. The steel produced by integrated mills tended to be purer than steel produced by electric arc furnaces since less scrap was used in the production process (scrap steel often contained nonferrous elements that could adversely affect metallurgical properties). Some steel customers required purer steel products for their applications.

Mini-mills used an electric arc furnace to melt steel scrap or scrap substitutes into molten metal which was then cast into crude steel slabs, billets, or blooms in a continuous casting process. As was the case at integrated mills, the crude steel was then run through various facilities and finishing processes to make hot-rolled and cold-rolled sheet steel products, steel bars and beams, stainless steel, steel wire and nails, steel pipes and tubes, and other finished steel products. Mini-mills could accommodate short production runs and had relatively fast product changeover time. The electric arc technology employed by mini-mills offered two primary competitive advantages: capital investment requirements that were 75 percent lower than those of integrated mills and a smaller workforce (which translated into lower labor costs per ton shipped).

Initially, companies that used electric arc furnace technology were able to make only low-end steel products (such as reinforcing rods and steel bars). But when thin-slab casting technology came on the scene in the 1980s, mini-mills were able to compete in the market for flat-rolled carbon sheet and strip products; these products sold at substantially higher prices per ton and thus were attractive market segments for mini-mill companies. Carbon sheet and strip steel products accounted for about 50–60 percent of total steel production and represented the last big market category controlled by the producers employing basic oxygen furnace and blast furnace technologies. Thin-slab casting technology, developed in Germany, was pioneered in the United States by Nucor at its plants in Indiana and elsewhere. Other mini-mill companies in the United States and across the world were quick to adopt thin-slab casting technology because the low capital costs of thin-slab casting facilities, often coupled with lower labor costs per ton, gave mini-mill companies a cost and pricing advantage over integrated steel producers, enabling them to grab a growing share of the global market for flat-rolled sheet steel and other carbon steel products. Many integrated producers also switched to thin-slab casting as a defensive measure to protect their profit margins and market shares.

In 2014, about 74 percent of the world's steel mill production was made at large integrated mills and about 26 percent was made at mills that used electric arc furnaces. In the United States, however, 62.6 percent of the steel was produced at mills employing electric arc furnaces and 37.4 percent at mills using blast furnaces and basic oxygen processes.[18] Large integrated steel mills using blast furnaces, basic oxygen furnaces, and assorted casting and rolling equipment typically had the ability to manufacture a wide variety of steel mill products but faced significantly higher energy costs and were often burdened with higher capital and fixed operating costs. Electric-arc furnace mill producers were challenged by increases in scrap prices but tended to have lower capital and fixed operating costs compared with the integrated steel producers. However, the quality of the steel produced using blast furnace technologies tended to be superior to that of electric arc furnaces unless, like at many of Nucor's facilities, the user of electric arc furnaces invested in additional facilities and processing equipment to enable the production of upgraded steel products.

Industry Consolidation In both the United States and across the world, industry downturns and the overhang of excess production capacity had over the years precipitated numerous mergers and acquisitions. Some of the mergers/acquisitions were the result of a financially and managerially strong company seeking to acquire a high-cost or struggling steel company at a bargain price and then pursue cost reduction initiatives to make newly acquired steel mill operations more cost-competitive. Other mergers/acquisitions, particularly in China where very significant mergers and acquisitions occurred in the 2005–2012 period, reflected the strategies of growth-minded steel companies looking to expand their production capacity and/or geographic market presence.

NUCOR AND COMPETITION IN THE U.S. MARKET FOR STEEL

Nucor's broad product lineup meant that it was an active participant in the U.S. markets for a wide variety of finished steel products and unfinished steel products, plus the markets for scrap steel and scrap substitutes. Nucor executives considered all the market segments and product categories in which it competed to be intensely competitive, many of which were populated with both domestic and foreign rivals. For the most part, competition for steel mill products and finished steel products was centered on price and the ability to meet customer delivery requirements. And, due to global overcapacity, many of the world's steelmakers were actively seeking new business in whatever geographic markets they could find willing buyers.

But with steel imports capturing roughly 34 percent of the market for finished and semi-finished steel products in the United States in 2014–2015, Nucor found itself trapped in a fierce competitive battle with rival global and domestic steel producers to win orders from the buyers of steel bar, structural steel, steel plate, cold-finished steel, and certain other steel products (see Nucor's 2015 sales decline for these products in Exhibit 3). Nucor's shipments of sheet steel held up well in 2015 (see Exhibit 3) because of near-record sales of motor vehicles in North America (motor vehicle manufacturers were major purchasers of sheet steel). Headed into 2016, Nucor management did not foresee any signs of a meaningful and sustained upswing in domestic demand for steel products that would relieve the stiff competitive pressures on its sales and profits.

In Nucor's 2013 10-K report, CEO John Ferriola said:[19]

> Imported steel and steel products continue to present unique challenges for us because foreign producers often benefit from government subsidies, either directly through government-owned enterprises or indirectly through government-owned or controlled financial institutions. Foreign imports of finished and semi-finished steel accounted for approximately 30% of the U.S. steel market in 2013 despite significant unused domestic capacity. Rebar and hot-rolled bar were impacted especially hard by imports in 2013 as imports of these products increased by 23% and 15%, respectively, over 2012 levels. Increased imports of bar have translated into even lower domestic utilization rates for that product—utilization in the mid-60% range—and significant decreases in domestic bar pricing in 2013. Competition from China, the world's largest producer and exporter of steel, which produces more than 45% of the steel produced globally, is a major challenge in particular. We believe that Chinese producers, many of which are government-owned in whole or in part, benefit from their government's manipulation of foreign currency exchange rates and from the receipt of government subsidies, which allow them to sell steel into our markets at artificially low prices.
>
> China is not only selling steel at artificially low prices into our domestic market but also across the globe. When they do so, steel products which would otherwise have been consumed by the local steel customers in other countries are displaced into global markets, which compounds the issue. In a more indirect manner, but still significant, is the import of fabricated steel products, such as oil country tubular goods, wind towers and other construction components that were produced in China.

In Nucor's 2015 Annual Report, Ferriola told shareholders:[20]

> [W]e are not sitting idly by as unfairly traded imports continue to come into the U.S. market. We are aggressively fighting back. Last year, Nucor and the entire steel industry scored a significant victory when Congress passed legislation strengthening our nation's trade laws. These important changes to trade law enforcement will help us fight back more effectively against the surge of illegally dumped and subsidized imports. These changes were long overdue. Our trade laws had not been updated in more than 20 years. While these new trade laws alone will not solve the serious issues facing the U.S. steel industry due to systemic steel overcapacity overseas, they do put us in a much stronger position to hold foreign governments and steel producers accountable for violating trade laws.
>
> Nucor has also joined other U.S. steel companies in filing trade cases for several flat-rolled products, including corrosion-resistant, hot-rolled and cold-rolled steel. The International Trade Commission has made preliminary determinations of injury in all three cases, allowing the investigations to proceed. Nucor will continue to assess market conditions in other product areas and pursue cases when appropriate.

Many foreign steel producers had costs on a par with or even below those of Nucor, although their competitiveness in the U.S. market varied significantly according to the prevailing strength of their local currencies versus the U.S. dollar and the extent to which they received government subsidies.

Nucor's Two Largest Domestic Competitors

Consolidation of the industry into a smaller number of larger and more efficient steel producers had heightened competitive pressures for Nucor and most other steelmakers. Nucor had two major rivals in the United States—the USA division of ArcelorMittal and United States Steel.

ArcelorMittal USA In 2016, ArcelorMittal USA operated 27 facilities, including 4 large integrated steel mills, 6 electric arc furnace plants, and 4 rolling and finishing plants. Its facilities were considered to be modern and efficient. Its product lineup included hot-rolled and cold-rolled sheet steel, steel plate, steel bars, railroad rails, high-quality wire rods, rebar, grinding balls, structural steel, tubular steel, and tin mill products. Much of its production was sold to customers in the automotive, trucking, off-highway, agricultural equipment, and railway industries, with the balance being sold to steel service centers and companies in the appliance, office furniture, electrical motor, packaging, and industrial machinery sectors.

Globally, ArcelorMittal was the world's largest steel producer, with steelmaking operations in 19 countries on four continents, annual production capacity of about 120 million tons of crude steel, and steel shipments of 84.6 million tons in 2015. It had worldwide sales revenues of $79.3 billion and a net loss of $1.1 billion in 2014 and worldwide sales revenues of $63.6 billion and a net loss of $7.9 billion in 2015.[21] ArcelorMittal also lost money on its worldwide operations in 2012 and 2013; its most recent profitable year was 2011. One important cause of ArcelorMittal's poor financial performance was the industry's massive amount of excess capacity, which had spurred steel producers in China, Japan, India, Russia, and other locations to dump steel products at artificially low prices in many of the geographic markets where ArcelorMittal had operations (and thereby push down the market prices of many steel products to unprofitable levels).

U.S. Steel U.S. Steel was an integrated steel producer of flat-rolled and tubular steel products with major production operations in the United States and Europe. It had 2015 crude steel production capacity of 17 million tons in the United States and 5 million tons in Europe. U.S. Steel's production of crude steel in the United States was 11.3 million tons in 2015. Prior to the permanent shutdown of a major U.S. facility in 2015 and two major facilities in Canada in 2013 and 2014 that produced crude steel, the company's production of crude steel in North America had been substantially higher—17.0 million tons in 2014 and 17.9 million tons in 2013.

U.S. Steel's operations were organized into three business segments: flat-rolled products (which included all of its integrated steel mills that produced steel slabs, rounds, steel plate, sheet steel, and tin mill products), U.S. Steel Europe, and tubular products. The flat-rolled segment primarily served North American customers in the transportation (including automotive), construction, container, appliance, and electrical industries, plus steel service centers and manufacturers that bought steel mill products for conversion into a variety of finished steel products. U.S. Steel's flat-rolled business segment had 2015 sales of $8.3 billion and an operating loss of $237 million, 2014 sales of $11.7 billion and operating income of $709 million, and 2013 sales of $11.6 billion and operating income of $105 million. Its tubular products segment had 2015 sales of $898 million and an operating loss of $179 million, 2014 sales of $2.8 billion and operating income of $261 million, and 2013 sales of $2.8 billion and operating income of $190 million.

U.S. Steel's exports of steel products from the United States totaled 234,000 tons in 2015, 263,000 tons in 2014, and 365,000 tons in 2013. U.S. Steel had a labor cost disadvantage versus Nucor and ArcelorMittal USA, partly due to the lower productivity of its unionized workforce and partly due to its retiree pension costs. In 2013, U.S. Steel launched a series of internal initiatives to "get leaner faster, right-size, and improve our performance."[22] In early 2016, however, these initiatives had not yet borne much fruit, although the benefits of closing the two Canadian facilities in 2014 and the U.S. facility in 2015 might help return the company to profitability in the years ahead.

ENDNOTES

[1] Tom Peters and Nancy Austin, *A Passion for Excellence: The Leadership Difference* (New York: Random House, 1985); "Other Low-Cost Champions," *Fortune*, June 24, 1985.
[2] Nucor's 2011 annual report, p. 4.
[3] February 2016 Investor Presentation, **www.nucor.com** (accessed March 21, 2016).
[4] March 2014 Investor Presentation, **www.nucor.com** (accessed April 22, 2014).
[5] According to information posted at **www.nucor.com** (accessed October 11, 2006).
[6] Nucor's 2008 annual report, p. 5.
[7] March 2014 Investor Presentation.
[8] Nanette Byrnes, "The Art of Motivation," *BusinessWeek*, May 1, 2006, p. 57.
[9] Ibid., p. 60.
[10] Ibid.
[11] Ibid.
[12] World Steel Association, "World Steel in Figures 2015," p. 16, **www.worldsteel.org** (accessed March 10, 2016).
[13] World Steel Association, "Crude Steel Production Data, January–December 2016 versus 2015," statistics section, **www.worldsteel.org** (accessed March 10, 2016).
[14] Zacks Equity Research, "China's Steel Exports Shoot Up 20% to Record High," January 15, 2016, **www.zacks.com** (accessed March 10, 2016); Nucor's 2015 Annual Report, p.4.
[15] John W. Miller and William Mauldin, "U.S. Imposes 266% Duty on Some Chinese Imports," *Wall Street Journal*, March 1, 2016, **www.wsj.com** (accessed March 14, 2016).
[16] Ibid.
[17] As quoted in Sonja Elmquist, "U.S. Calls for 256% Tariff on Imports of Steel from China," December 22, 2015, **www.bloombergbusiness.com** (accessed March 14, 2016).
[18] World Steel Association, "World Steel in Figures 2015," p. 10, **www.worldsteel.org** (accessed March 10, 2016).
[19] Company 10-K report, 2011, p. 6.
[20] Company annual report, p. 6.
[21] Company annual report, 2015.
[22] Company 10-K report 2013, p. 12.

CASE 28

Tim Cook's Leadership and Management Style: Building His Own Legacy at Apple

Debapratim Purkayastha
IBS Hyderabad

Barnali Chakroborty
Author and Research Associate

"We want diversity of thought. . . . We want diversity of style. We want people to be themselves. It's this great thing about Apple. You don't have to be somebody else. You don't have to put on a face when you go to work and be something different. But the thing that ties us all is we're brought together by values. We want to do the right thing. We want to be honest and straightforward. We admit when we're wrong and have the courage to change."[1]
—Tim Cook, CEO of Apple Inc., in 2012.

"While the market may worry, those who have stuck by Apple through it all know there's only more excellence ahead."[2]
—Edward Marczak, an author and executive editor of *MacTech* magazine, in August 2011.

"Jobs would figure out how to put the pieces together. Everything just filtered through his eyes. I think it's going to be very difficult for them to come up with the next big thing. They've lost their heart and soul."[3]
—Michael A. Cusumano, a professor in the Sloan School of Management at M.I.T., in June 2014.

In March 2015, Tim Cook (Cook), the CEO of technology giant, Apple Inc. (Apple), was named as the "world's greatest leader" by *Fortune* magazine.[4] Apple, a US-based company, designed, manufactured, and marketed mobile communication and media devices, personal computers, and portable digital music players, and sold a variety of related software, services, peripherals, networking solutions, and third-party digital content and applications.

Despite being regularly compared with the legendary founder CEO, Steve Jobs (Jobs), Cook had his own strengths. Since becoming the CEO, Cook had transformed himself from a soft-spoken operations manager to a high-profile leader at Apple. After replacing Jobs, he not only led the company to even greater financial success, but also changed the culture of the company along the way. Apple grew to become the world's most valuable company after Cook took the helm. His emphasis on the existing strengths of the organization, his belief in consensus building among leading executives, and his lack of interest in micromanagement indicated a democratic management style. Moreover, his leadership qualities including focus on core products, long-term orientation, transparency, advocacy of human rights, and sustainable development made him an example for future business leaders.

Cook also took an interest in philanthropy and had plans to give away all his wealth, after providing for the college education of his 10-year-old nephew. As of March 2015, Cook's net worth was about $120 million along with restricted stock worth $665 million if it were to be fully vested.[5] While he had already started donating money, he wanted to

This case was written by Barnali Chakroborty, under the direction of Debapratim Purkayastha, IBS Hyderabad. It was compiled from published sources, and is intended to be used as a basis for class discussion rather than to illustrate either effective or ineffective handling of a management situation.

develop a systematic approach toward philanthropy. Under him, Apple was also gradually shedding its image of a sustainability laggard.

Nevertheless, Cook also faced a number of management challenges including the disappointment with some of new products like Apple Maps, the fallout with GT Advanced Technologies, and the hiring fiasco of John Browett (Browett) as Apple's retail chief. Analysts opined that Apple was indeed different under Cook, but it was yet to be seen whether he would be able to turn Apple into a tech powerhouse. Commenting on the criticisms he faced, Cook said he had learnt to ignore his critics. "I'm not running for office. I don't need your vote. I have to feel myself doing what's right. If I'm the arbiter of that instead of letting the guy on TV be that or someone who doesn't know me at all, then I think that's a much better way to live."[6] Analysts felt Cook was finally stepping out of the shadow of Jobs; that he was no longer just the custodian of a legacy, but was actively building his own.

BACKGROUND NOTE

The history of Apple can be traced back to the mid-1970s, when three friends—Steve Jobs (Jobs), Ronald Wayne (Wayne), and Steve Wozniak (Wozniak) decided to start a business of making personal computers (PC). At that time, Jobs and Wayne worked for Atari[7] and Wozniak was working at HP.[8] On April 1, 1976, Apple Computers was founded. Initially they assembled fifty personal computers (PC) in the garage of Jobs' father. The PCs were custom-built for a local computer store, and were sold at $666.66 per system. They named the system Apple I, and built another 200 PCs before working on the next version. On January 03, 1977, Apple was incorporated.

In April 1977, Apple II, a much improved version of the first with differences in the display, was launched. However, to market this product, Apple needed a lot of financing. At that time, Mike Markkula, a venture capitalist, invested $92,000 in the company. In May 1980, Apple III was launched to compete with IBM's first PC named the IBM-PC. Apple III was priced at $1,395. However, due to a design fault, Apple was forced to recall thousands of the Apple III computers. Apple made losses of over $60 million due to this recall.

In December 1980, Apple came out with its initial public offering (IPO), in which around 4.6 million shares were sold for $ 22 each. Throughout the 1980s and 1990s, Apple introduced several new products. In January 1983, Apple launched LISA, its first Graphical User Interface (GUI) computer, which introduced the words "mouse," "icon," and "desktop" to the world. LISA was priced at $10,000. The very next year, Apple introduced the Apple Macintosh which was built inside a beige case and had a black and white monitor, a mouse, and a keyboard, and was the first personal computer with a floppy drive.

However, Jobs was ousted in a boardroom struggle in 1985. He returned in 1996 to save the company, which was in a mess. Upon his return as CEO, Jobs began rebuilding Apple, which was on the verge of a collapse and transformed it into one of the most successful and profitable companies in the world. His vision of building "insanely great" products made Apple a market leader in the technology industry. Apple transformed the music industry with products like the iPod music player and the iTunes store, and created new product categories with the iPhone smartphone and the iPad tablet.

According to industry experts, Apple had achieved unparalleled success with its products not just because of its technological competence, but because of its culture that encouraged innovation. Apple was considered the most innovative company and also topped the list of "Most admired companies" in 2008 and 2009.

Over the years, Apple expanded its product portfolio which included the iPhone, iPad, Mac, iPod, Apple TV, consumer and professional software applications, iOS and OS X operating systems, iCloud, and a variety of accessory, service, and support offerings. The company also provided digital content and applications through the iTunes Store, App Store, iBooks Store, and Mac App Store. Exhibit 1 presents an overview of Apple's Product Portfolio in 2016.

Apple reported net sales of $182,795 million in fiscal[9] 2014, an increase of 7% compared to the previous fiscal. During 2014, the company's domestic and international net sales accounted for 38% and 62%, respectively of total net sales. A financial summary for Apple Inc. from 2010 through 2014 is presented in Exhibit 2.

TIM COOK: THE JOURNEY AT APPLE

Cook was born in 1960 in Mobile, Alabama. His father was a shipyard worker and his mother worked

EXHIBIT 1 Apple Inc.'s Product Portfolio in 2016

iPhone
The iPhone is Apple's line of smartphones that combines a phone, music player, and internet device in one product, and is based on Apple's iOS Multi-Touch operating system. The iPhone has an integrated photo and video camera and photo library app, and on qualifying devices, also includes Siri, a voice activated intelligent assistant. The iPhone works with the iTunes Store, the App Store, and iBooks Store for purchasing, organizing, and playing music, movies, TV shows, podcasts, books, and apps. It is compatible with both Mac and Windows personal computers and Apple's iCloud services which provide synchronization of mail, contacts, calendars, apps, music, photos, documents, and more across users' devices.
iPad
The iPad and iPad mini are Apple's line of multi-purpose tablets based on Apple's iOS Multi-Touch operating system. The iPad has an integrated photo and video camera and photo library app, and on qualifying devices, also includes Siri. The iPad works with the iTunes Store, the iBooks Store, and the App Store for purchasing and playing music, movies, TV shows, podcasts, books, and apps. It is compatible with both Mac and Windows personal computers and Apple's iCloud services.
Mac
Mac is Apple's line of desktop and portable personal computers. It features Intel microprocessors and the OS X operating system and includes Mail, the Safari web browser, Messages, Calendars, Reminders, Contacts, and the iLifesuite of software apps. The company's desktop computers include iMac, Mac Pro, and Mac mini. The Company's portable computers include MacBook Pro and MacBook Air.
iPod
Apple's iPod line of portable digital music and media players includes the iPod touch, iPod nano, iPod shuffle, and iPod classic. All the iPods work with iTunes for purchase and synchronization of content. The iPod touch, based on the company's iOS Multi-Touch operating system, is a flash-memory-based iPod with an integrated photo and video camera and photo library app, and also includes Siri. The iPod touch works with the iTunes Store, the App Store, and the iBooks Store for the purchase and playing of music, movies, TV shows, podcasts, books, and apps. The iPod touch is compatible with both Mac and Windows personal computers and Apple's iCloud services.
iTunes and the iTunes Store
The Apple's iTunes app, available for both Mac and Windows personal computers, keeps users' music, movies, and TV shows organized in one place. iTunes is integrated with the iTunes Store, the App Store, and the iBooks Store. The iTunes Store allows users to purchase and download music and TV shows and to rent or purchase movies. The iBooks Store features e-books from major and independent publishers. iTunes U® allows users to download free lectures, videos, and more from top universities, museums, and other institutions. iTunes also features Genius mixes to find songs that go together and organize them into genre-based mixes and Home Sharing to allow users to stream content from one computer to another computer as well as to iOS devices and newer versions of the Company's Apple TV.
Mac App Store
The Mac App Store allows customers to discover, download, and install Mac apps. It offers applications in education, games, graphics and design, lifestyle, productivity, utilities, and other categories. The Company's OS X operating system software and its iLife, iWork, and other application software titles are also available on the Mac App Store.
iCloud
iCloud is the Company's cloud service, which stores music, photos, applications, contacts, calendars, documents and more, keeping them up-to-date and available on multiple iOS devices and Mac and Windows personal computers.

Operating System Software iOS
iOS is the company's Multi-Touch operating system that serves as the foundation for iOS devices. Apps delivered with iOS for qualifying devices include the Safari web browser, FaceTime video calling, Maps with turn-by-turn directions, Mail, Contacts, Calendar, Clock, Weather, Calculator, Notes, Reminders, Stocks, Compass, and Messages. Devices running the iOS are compatible with both Mac and Windows personal computers and Apple's iCloud services.
OS X
OS X, the Company's Mac operating system, is built on an open-source UNIX-based foundation and provides an intuitive and integrated computer experience. In addition to Mail, the Safari web browser, Messages, Calendars, Reminders, Contacts, and the iLifesuite of software apps, Mavericks also includes a new Maps app and a new iBooks app that both work with their iOS counterparts.
Application Software iLife
iLife for Mac is the company's consumer-oriented digital lifestyle software application suite included with all Mac computers. iLife features iPhoto, a digital photo application for storing, viewing, editing, and sharing photos; iMovie, a digital video editing application; and GarageBand, a music creation application that allows customers to play, record, and create music. The company also has Multi-Touch versions of these iLife applications designed specifically for use on the iPhone and iPad. Beginning in September 2013, both iPhoto and iMovie for iOS became available as free downloads with all new iOS devices.
iWork
iWork for Mac is the company's integrated productivity suite designed to help users create, present, and publish documents, presentations, and spreadsheets. iWork includes Pages for word processing and page layout, Keynote for presentations, and Numbers for spreadsheets.
Other Application Software
The company also sells various other application software, including its professional line of applications, Final Cut Pro, LogicPro X, and its FileMakerPro database software.
Displays & Peripheral Products
Apple manufactures the Apple LED Cinema Display and Thunderbolt Display. The Company also sells a variety of Apple-branded and third-party Mac-compatible and iOS-compatible peripheral products, including printers, storage devices, computer memory, digital video and still cameras, pointing devices, and various other computing products and supplies.
Apple TV
Apple TV connects to consumers' high definition TVs and enables them to access iTunes content directly for streaming HD video, playing music, and viewing photos. Content from Netflix, YouTube, Flickr, MLB, Hulu Plus, iTunes Radio, and other media services is also available. Apple TV allows streaming iTunes content from Macs and Windows personal computers through Home Share and through AirPlay from compatible Mac and iOS devices. Compatible Mac and iOS devices can also mirror their device screens as well as stream and play games on Apple TV.
Apple Watch
In September 2014, Apple announced Apple Watch, a personal electronic device that combines new precision watch technology with an iOS-based user interface created specifically for a smaller device. Apple Watch features Digital Crown, a unique navigation tool that allows users to seamlessly scroll, zoom and navigate. It also enables customers to communicate in new ways from their wrist and features Force Touch, a technology that senses the difference between a tap and a press and allows users to access controls within apps.

(Continued)

EXHIBIT 1 Continued

iOS and Mac Developer Programs
The Company's iOS and Mac Developer Programs support app developers with the development, testing, and distribution of iOS and Mac apps through the App Store and the Mac App Store.
Product Support and Services
AppleCare offers a range of support options for the company's customers. These include assistance that is built into software products, printed and electronic product manuals, online support including comprehensive product information as well as technical assistance, the AppleCare Protection Plan ("APP"), and the AppleCare+ Protection Plan ("AC+").

Source: Adapted from Company Website.

EXHIBIT 2 Financial Summary for Apple Inc., 2010–2014

Fiscal year ended September 30	2014	2013	2012	2011	2010
Net Sales	$182,795	$170,910	$156,508	$108,249	$ 65,225
Net Income	39,510	37,037	41,733	25,992	14,013
Earnings per Share					
Basic	$ 6.49	$ 5.72	$ 6.38	$ 4.01	$ 2.20
Diluted	$ 6.45	$ 5.68	$ 6.31	$ 3.95	$ 2.16
Cash Dividends declared per share	$ 1.82	$ 1.64	$ 0.38	$ 0.00	$ 0.00
Total cash, cash equivalents and marketable securities	$155,239	$146,761	$121,251	$ 81,570	$ 51,011
Total Assets	231,839	207,000	176,064	116,371	75,183
Total Shareholders' Equity	111,547	123,549	118,210	76,615	47,791

Source: Adapted from Company Annual Reports.

in a drug store. He had two siblings. Tim Cook graduated from Auburn University in 1982 with a bachelor's degree in industrial engineering. He went on to earn an M.B.A. from Duke University's Fuqua School of Business in 1988. Talking about his childhood days, Cook reminisced, "Growing up in Alabama in the 1960s I saw the devastating impact of discrimination. Remarkable people were denied opportunity and were treated without basic human dignity solely because of the color of their skin."[10]

Cook spent the early years of his career at IBM.[11] For 12 years, he worked for IBM and went on to become the Director of North American Fulfillment at the company before leaving in 1994. His next job was as Chief Operating Officer (COO) of the Reseller Division of Intelligent Electronics, a position he held for three years before joining Compaq Computer[12] in 1997. In 1998, when he was 37 and the Vice President of Corporate Materials at Compaq, he was brought into Apple by Jobs. Cook was responsible for procurement and inventory operations at Compaq and had no intention of leaving the company. However, Jobs managed to convince him to join Apple. At that time, Apple's supply chain was in an absolute mess and Job wanted to implement the just-in-time system that Michael Dell had done at Dell. Cook also shared Jobs' vision and decided to join Apple. "I knew what I wanted, and I met Tim, and he wanted the same thing. So we started to work together, and before long I trusted him to know exactly what to do. He had the same vision I did, and we could interact at a high strategic level, and I could just forget about a lot of things unless he came and pinged me," said Jobs.[13]

Upon joining Apple, Cook realized that the company's supply chain was too cumbersome to handle. Consequently, he reduced the number of key suppliers from 100 to 24 and the number of warehouses from 19 to 9. By September of 1998, Cook managed to decrease inventory level to 6 days and reduce the manufacturing cycle time from 4 months to 2 months.[14] In his biography of Jobs, Walter Isaacson wrote, "Cook reduced the number of Apple's key suppliers from a hundred to twenty-four, forced them to cut better deals to keep the business, convinced many to locate next to Apple's plants, and closed ten of the company's nineteen warehouses. By reducing the places where inventory could pile up, he reduced inventory. Jobs had cut inventory from two months' worth of product down to one by early 1998. By September of that year, Cook had gotten it to six days. By the following September, it was down to an amazing two days' worth. In addition, he cut the production process for making an Apple computer from four months to two. All of this not only saved money, it also allowed each new computer to have the very latest components available."[15]

Cook's tenure at Apple was marked by huge successes in terms of products including launching the Apple OS X operating system, the iPod, the iPhone, and the iPad. In 2002, Cook became executive vice president for worldwide sales and operations. Appreciating Cook's efforts in the procurement and supply chain practices at Apple, Jobs made him the Chief Operations Officer (COO) in 2005.

In 2011, Jobs recommended Cook's name as his successor. "I strongly recommend that we execute our succession plan and name Tim Cook as CEO of Apple. Tim Cook came out of procurement which is just the right background for what we needed,"[16] said Jobs. Cook replaced Jobs three times during his medical leave of absence.[17] He eventually became the company's CEO six weeks before Jobs died, in October 2011.

As CEO, Cook continued with his emphasis on slashing inventories. In 2012, Apple was said to turn inventory every 5 days and its supply chain network was considered the best in the world by Gartner.[18] Cook maintained that technology manufacturers should not keep a large inventory as any new innovation could depreciate the value of inventory very quickly. By 2013, Apple had 154 key suppliers and one central warehouse with approximately 250 owned stores.[19] "Inventory is fundamentally evil. You kind of want to manage it like you're in the dairy business. If it gets past its freshness date, you have a problem,"[20] said Cook.

In 2014, Apple introduced several new products and services including the iPad Air, its fifth generation iPad, and iPad mini with Retina display, the iPhone 6 and 6 Plus, Apple Pay, Apple Watch, the iPad Air 2, iPad mini 3, iMac with Retina 5K Display, and an updated Mac mini, among others. During 2014, the company under Cook's direction, completed various business acquisitions, including those of Beats Music, LLC, which offered a subscription streaming music service, and Beats Electronics, LLC, which made Beats headphones, speakers, and audio software.

Steve Jobs' Shadow

Analysts felt that Cook's challenges as a CEO were compounded by the fact that he was succeeding Jobs, whose name was inextricably associated with Apple. Alan Deutschman, in his book *The Second Coming of Steve Jobs,* wrote, "No one denied that Apple's rise was aided immeasurably by his [Steve Jobs'] astonishing energy and persuasiveness and charisma and chutzpah (a word that he loved). And it was his personality that created the company's culture and mystique."[21]

Since its inception, Apple had focused on innovation and ventured into those markets where it could make a significant contribution. According to analysts, one of the main goals of the company was to make technology seamless for the customer. Moreover, the employees at Apple were looked upon as a bunch of mutinous, arrogant kids who were seen as rebelling against the old order. Yet, according to Jobs, they came out with products that were "insanely great." At least in the initial years, the employees shared a deep distaste for IBM, according to some analysts. While IBM focused on building huge machines, Apple worked toward developing inexpensive computers for "every man, woman, child, and chimpanzee on earth."[22] The company manufactured those products which were meaningful and profitable. For creating such products, it employed people who were hard working and committed. It fostered a culture of dedication and hard work in the company. Fun was an integral part of the culture and the company engaged in many rituals that were designed to be fun. For instance, it organized after hour parties, promoted playfulness at work, and even organized magic shows at training programs.[23] Apple was one of the pioneers of the "work hard, play hard" ethic. Analysts said Apple adopted a style that was not too formal or hierarchical and an approach that was more results-driven. According to some employees, the work culture at Apple was driven by a passion for products and attention to the minutest details.

In the late 1990s, when Jobs returned as CEO of Apple, he realized that the company's culture had changed under four successive CEOs. He felt that it lacked innovation and the company's entrepreneurial drive had given way to a culture marked by complacency. Jobs emphasized that the company should move back to the culture that had existed at the company when he was at the helm and that the energy and flair of Apple's past should be recreated. "How did he achieve his ends? By resurrecting an existing means: the company's past culture that incited employees to create something "insanely great." "The result was the iMac, an affordable computer with a unique, colorful look that harkened back to the early days of Apple and its innovative Apple II and Macintosh computers,"[24] wrote Eric Abrahamson, Professor at the Columbia Business School. More innovative products such as the path-breaking iPod, iPhone, and iPad followed.

In addition to emphasizing that the employees should go back to the old way of doing things, Jobs too acted just as he had done when he had founded Apple. In the Cupertino facility, he usually wore shorts and a T-shirt and when he announced new product launches at the MacWorld conference, he wore a black mock turtleneck and blue jeans.[25] Analysts felt that Jobs had a strong influence on the culture at Apple. They felt that he inspired the employees at Apple to come out with unconventional products by thinking differently. According to Richard Shim, a research manager for International Data Corporation's[26] Personal Computing program, "Apple tends to defy convention. . . . More often than not, it works out for them."[27] This was in part due to the quirky style adopted by Jobs from an early date. For instance, in 1983, when the team working on the Mac asked Jobs for a standard for which they should aim, Jobs' answer was "the Beatles."[28] He would often inspire the employees working at Apple to "change the world." Experts felt that the company had achieved unprecedented success with its product launches not only because of its technology, but because of its culture that fostered innovation. Commenting on the values imbibed by employees at Apple, Daniel Ernst, an analyst at Hudson Square Research,[29] said, "Jobs has driven into the DNA of Apple that they want to make products that are very well-built and very easy to use. Everyone I've met at Apple, from the clerk to the chief financial officer, gets that. . . . If Jobs were to disappear permanently tomorrow, it wouldn't change this company one iota."[30]

However, some analysts felt that a key concern facing the company and Jobs' successor was that Apple was much too strongly associated with its charismatic leader. It was a common perception that the fortunes of the company were tied to that of Jobs. According to Charles R. Wolf, an analyst at Needham & Company, LLC,[31] "Apple is Steve Jobs and Steve Jobs is Apple."[32] Jobs was widely credited with having saved the company during the 1990s and with having played a key role in the development of innovative products like the iPod, the iPhone, and the iPad.[33] Rob Enderle (Enderle), Enderle Group's[34] principal analyst, said, "Once you remove him [Jobs], there's a danger it [Apple] could become more like a traditional company. . . . Without Steve Jobs, can they still create magic?"[35] In the months leading up to Jobs' death, analysts pointed out that any adverse news about Jobs' health made the Apple stock fall and led to a fall of the company's market cap by a couple of billion dollars in a single trading session.[36]

Analysts felt that with Apple being so strongly associated with Jobs, how the company would perform in his absence would be a key concern for all stakeholders. Jobs was seen as the source of Apple's innovation as it was he who was credited with inspiring Apple employees to come out with path-breaking products. "I think Apple would be more of an ordinary company without him—it would be much less audacious, daring, and artistic,"[37] said Andy Hertzfeld, a former employee. Some analysts too echoed this view and said that it was difficult to imagine Apple without Jobs.

Analysts felt that Jobs would be missed for his vision as he was very good at figuring out what the next big thing would be. Elmer-DeWitt said, "Once you get a bunch of people in a room, none of whom is more powerful than the other, you start to get products that are literally designed by committee and that's what Apple products never were. . . . They were always designed by very smart people that Steve chose. But ultimately there was one guy who had final say on them. It remains to be seen whether there's someone at Apple who can step up and take over that role."

Experts also pointed out that while Jobs' leadership style had largely worked for him, it could lead to disastrous consequences if others tried to follow the same approach. Critics also pointed to the dark side of Jobs' personality. Some people who had worked with him considered him to be a megalomaniac and a person with whom 'the highs were unbelievable but the lows were unimaginable.'[38] Jobs drew criticism for subjecting his employees to tyrannical outbursts and fostering a culture of secrecy at the company.[39] His leadership style also attracted criticism. Jobs was known for berating employees when he did not get his way, and of even firing people just to prove a point. He played a vital role in engineering a regime of secrecy at Apple and was successful in refining the secretive culture at Apple. The company always maintained tight control over information. Apple was extremely guarded about new product developments and it was widely believed that Jobs personally approved every piece of official communication coming out of Apple.[40] According to writer, speaker, and entrepreneur, William C Taylor, "In terms of the impact his products have had on the world, Steve Jobs represents the face of business at its best. And yet, in terms of his approach to leadership, Jobs represents the face of business—well, if not at its worst, then certainly not as something worth emulating. . . . Jobs, for all of his virtues, clings to the Great Man Theory of Leadership—a CEO-centric model of executive power that is outmoded, unsustainable, and, for most of us mere mortals, ineffective in a world of non-stop change."[41]

However, Cook, who had shared a great friendship with Jobs and had even unsuccessfully tried to offer him a portion of his liver when Jobs was struggling to find a donor, felt that Jobs' personality was largely misunderstood. According to him, "Steve cared. . . . He cared deeply about things. Yes, he was very passionate about things, and he wanted things to be perfect. And that was what was great about him. A lot of people mistook that passion for arrogance."[42]

Cook's Leadership and Management Style

As the CEO of the technology giant Apple, Cook chose a democratic management approach. Instead of being a complete contrast to Jobs, Cook adopted some of the legendary founder's existing practices and created a unique leadership style. Industry experts observed that the fact that Cook had filled in for Jobs thrice during his medical leave of absence proved that Jobs had a lot of faith in him. Jobs had told Cook that while leading Apple, he should never ask himself "What would Steve Jobs do?" Instead, he should take decisions thinking of Apple as his own company. In an internal email, Cook declared that he would stay true to the unique culture of Apple. "I want you to be confident that Apple is not going to change. I cherish and celebrate Apple's unique principles and values. Steve built a company and culture that is unlike any other in the world and we are going to stay true to that—it is in our DNA,"[43] said Cook. Cook not only managed to protect Apple's unique culture but also added value wherever he could. While Jobs had created a distinct corporate culture for Apple and guarded it for decades, Cook was credited with gradually modifying it with his unique perspectives, and ingeniously redefining Apple's image.

Analysts also applauded Cook for not trying to fix everything in the company after taking over as the CEO. Apple already had a distinctive brand image, innovative products, a unique culture, and a flat management structure. Instead of changing things in the company that were right, Cook realized that whatever Apple had achieved was because of its products and its focus on customers.

Cook followed Jobs' style while launching new products. For instance, his keynote presentation had a number of videos to inspire the public to buy Apple's products. However, his leadership style and management approach were totally different from that of Jobs. His way of running the leading innovative company set an example for business executives and leaders.

According to his former colleagues at both Compaq and Apple, Cook was a complete workaholic. He would get up at 4:30am, spend an hour or so in the gym, and be ready for work by six. According to Yukari Iwatani Kane's book *Haunted Empire,* "[Cook] will fly to Asia, spend three days there, fly back, land at 7am at the airport and be in the office by 8.30am, interrogating someone about some numbers."[44]

Cook always stressed on team work. His aim to work as a team often led to slower decision-making, but it also reduced a certain disorder that came from managing Apple vigorously like Jobs did. While commenting on Cook's style of running the company, Eddy Cue, senior vice president for Internet software and services, said, "He never tried to be Steve. He tried to always be himself. He has been very good at letting us do our thing. He's aware and involved at the high end, and he gets involved as needed. Steve got involved at the pixel level."[45]

When Cook took over as the CEO in October 2011, he was known as a shy, hard worker, and a cool technocrat. However, his public appearances over the next three and half years showed that he was stepping out of the shadow of his predecessor. Jobs believed in total secrecy about the company and never made public speeches apart from the presentations he made while rolling out Apple's new products. In contrast, Cook preferred more public exposure of Apple's key executives. In February 2015, when the *New Yorker*[46] published a 16,000-word profile of Jony Ive, Apple's chief designer, it was applauded by industry experts. While this ensured that the company got exposure in the media, it also played an important role in employee retention. According to Cook, "My objective is to raise the public profile of several of the folks on the executive team, and others as well. Because I think that's good for Apple at the end of the day."[47]

Cook also emphasized on core products and had a long-term orientation. According to him, "I mean, if you really look at it, we have four iPods. We have two main iPhones. We have two iPads, and we have a few Macs. That's it."[48] Analysts opined that while Apple Pay or Apple Watch may not be huge profit drivers, they could push up sale of the core products, as iTunes had increased the sales of the iPod and ultimately the Mac. According to Jean-Louis Gassée, an Apple executive in the 1980s and writer of a widely read weekly column on Apple in the email newsletter, *The Monday Note,* "I have a simplified view of Apple. They have and always have had one business, personal computers. Now they make them in three sizes, small, medium, and large—the iPhone, the iPad, and notebook and desktop computers. Everything else, including Apple Watch in the case of the iPhone, exists to push up the margins of those products. Tim is playing the long game in his own way."[49]

Cook also took ownership of his decisions be it the occasional hiring blunder or coming out into the open about his sexual preference. In early 2013, when Cook faced a senior management challenge regarding his high profile hire from outside the company, he chose to take it as a lesson. Cook hired John Browett (Browett), the former head of the UK-based discount electronics chain Dixon's, as the head of Apple's high-touch retail operation. However, Browett was a complete misfit at Apple, and was asked to resign in March 2013. Cook took the issue as an example. "That was a reminder to me of the critical as importance of cultural fit, and that it takes some time to learn that. [As CEO] you're engaged in so many things that each particular thing gets a little less attention. You need to be able to operate on shorter cycles, less data points, less knowledge, less facts. When you're an engineer, you want to analyze things a lot. But if you believe that the most important data points are people, then you have to make conclusions in relatively short order. Because you want to push the people who are doing great. And you want to either develop the people who are not or, in a worst case, they need to be somewhere else,"[50] said Cook.

In June 2013, Cook decided to surrender up to one-third of his stock based compensation if Apple's stock underperformed compared to other S&P 500 components over the next eight years.[51] Cook was given one million shares of Apple when he was appointed CEO of the company. Besides, all of Cook's compensation was equity based. By doing so, he not only held himself accountable but also set a powerful example for others.

Cook was also appreciated for his straightforwardness and the company made some buzz on the sustainability front. In particular, it shed its tag of being an environmental laggard. In February 2014, at an annual shareholder meeting, Cook was asked to disclose the costs of Apple's energy sustainability programs and to make a commitment to doing only those things that were profitable. The usually calm and composed Cook burst out saying that he did not consider "bloody ROI" in all the activities that Apple engaged in. "If you want me to do things only for ROI reasons, you should get out of this stock,"[52] he thundered. In September 2014, Cook said he did not believe that there was a trade-off between the economy and the environment. "If you innovate and you set the bar high, you will find a way to do both. You must do both."[53]

In October 2014, Cook announced publicly that he was gay. The announcement made the once low-profile and extremely private executive a global role model and the only openly gay CEO in the Fortune 500. Cook also used the platform as Apple's CEO to opine on subjects as diverse as human rights, access to education, female representation on Wall Street, immigration reform, privacy rights, and racial inequality in his home state of Alabama. "The company I am so fortunate to lead has long advocated for human rights and equality for all. We'll continue to fight for our values, and I believe that any CEO of this incredible company, regardless of race, gender, or sexual orientation, would do the same. And I will personally continue to advocate for equality for all people until my toes point up,"[54] commented Cook.

Industry experts observed that under Cook's leadership, Apple had become a much more socially aware company and was working to improve conditions in its overseas factories. When Apple received criticism about standards of Apple's global operations, Cook decided to be transparent and set new industry standards. "You want to be the pebble in the pond that creates the ripple for change,"[55] said Cook.

Challenges

Cook had to face his share of criticism too. He was criticized for not preparing himself to face the media glare and the analysis that came with succeeding a legend. He himself agreed with that criticism. While commenting on the criticisms, he said, "I have thick skin, but it got thicker. What I learned after Steve passed away, what I had known only at a theoretical level; an academic level maybe, was that he was an incredible heat shield for us, his executive team. None of us probably appreciated that enough because it's not something we were fixated on. We were fixated on our products and running the business. But he really took any kind of spears that were thrown. He took the praise as well. But to be honest, the intensity was more than I would ever have expected."[56]

Cook was ridiculed for what critics called blunder with Apple Maps and previously with Apple's voice recognition software, Siri. In 2012, since the iPhone 5 release, and the Maps fiasco, Apple has lost $30 billion in stock market value.[57] Analysts blamed Cook for not being aware of the problems with Apple Maps, and said it showed that he did not care about the quality of Apple products. "This is just simply an area where companies like Google and Nokia have had a tremendous head start. Clearly Apple did not prepare from day one to build its own mapping application,"[58] said Ross Rubin, a principal analyst with Reticle Research.

While comparing Cook with the legendary founder of Apple, it was often said that "He's no Steve Jobs." Some analysts also had doubts whether Apple could remain innovative under Cook and whether he would be able to replicate the Jobs magic. Analysts opined that companies lost their way after they lost their legendary founders and cited the examples of Microsoft's[59] Bill Gates and Intel's[60] Andy Grove. Cook was ridiculed for launching Apple Maps and for introducing a cheaper version of the iPhone to challenge the progress of Google's Android. Analysts were worried that the company was running out of ideas in the post-Jobs era. They opined that without industry-leading innovations, Apple would become the next Sony which, though it remained a large conglomerate, no longer defined the landscape without leading innovation. "It's fair to say that Apple is going through a transition period. They have to organize product development in a different way, the way they think about strategic positions. Things are becoming much more systematic under Tim Cook and in many ways that's a good thing. There was certainly a lot of chaos under Jobs. But it was a creative chaos. It was the type of atmosphere where Steve pushed people to outperform even their highest expectations,"[61] said Michael Cusumano, a Sloan School of Management professor at MIT.

Since Cook came from an operations background, he was criticized for not being a "subject-matter expert" on critical areas such as product development, design, and marketing. Analysts also questioned his ability to ensure that the spirit of innovation continued at Apple. "Cook is very talented. But he doesn't have Jobs' innovative spirit—it's just not in the DNA. Visionaries are easy to find, but great visionaries who can go from concept to reality to execution to mass marketing are rare indeed,"[62] said James Post, professor at the Boston University School of Management.

Analysts were worried whether Apple could continue its growth momentum which had helped it to increase sales from $65 billion in sales in the 2010 fiscal year to $171 billion in 2013.[63] In 2013, Apple generated $171 billion in revenue and $37 billion in profit,[64] but sales grew by only 9 percent.[65] While analysts praised Cook for his move to split the stock, increase dividend, and engineer a $90 billion buyback—steps which helped the shares to bounce back—they contended that he did not have the vision to lead Apple into the next league. They said that during 2012 and 2013, Apple's sales growth had declined to low single digits—see Exhibit 3. The analysts pointed out that during this period of low sales growth, Cook did not diversify Apple's product line; rather, he kept the same line of products at the same price in place.

These criticisms did not, however, bother Cook. According to him, "I thought I was reasonable at that before, but I've had to become great at it. You pick up certain skills when the truck is running across your back. Maybe this will be something great that I'll use in other aspects of my life over time."[66]

Cook also had support from his colleagues at Apple. They praised him for his approachability and intellect and insisted that Apple still had innovation as its central mission. "Honestly, I don't think anything's changed. People felt exactly the same way when we were working on the iPhone. It is hard for all of us to be patient. It was hard for Steve. It is hard for Tim,"[67] said Jonathan Ive, head of design at Apple.

LOOKING AHEAD

In 2014, Apple launched the large-screen iPhone 6 and the even bigger iPhone 6 Plus. The company also introduced a new payment system, Apple Pay, and Apple Watch. The new iPhones' sales were impressive with 74.5 million of them being sold in the last quarter of 2014, and the company generating $18 billion in profits. Between September 2009 and September 2014, the stock price of Apple increased from approximately $100 to $400 per share and the market capitalization touched $700 billion—see Exhibit 4. Moreover, since 2010, under Cook's leadership, Apple's cash hoarding had tripled to more than $150 billion despite the fact that the company had spent a total of $92.6 billion in dividends and buybacks, something which was not encouraged during Jobs' era.[68]

Nonetheless, industry experts were of the view that Apple would need to remain a step ahead of its competitors and would need to replicate the success Jobs had with creating products with interoperability. They opined that while products like the iPad, iPhone, and Apple TV were sold as stand-alone devices, they should work together. For example, users could

EXHIBIT 3 Apple's Year-Over-Year Revenue Growth, Q1 2012–Q4 2013

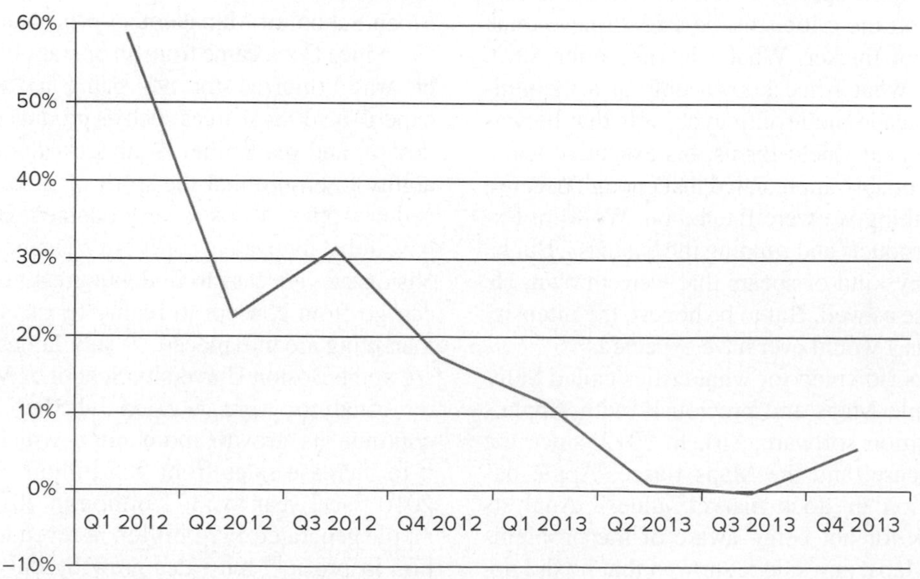

Source: Jay Yarow, "It's Time to Seriously Consider Whether Tim Cook Has Mismanaged Apple," **www.businessinsider.in**, April 23, 2014.

EXHIBIT 4 Apple's Stock Performance Relative to the S&P 500 Index, the Dow Jones US Technology Supersector Index, September 2009–September 2014

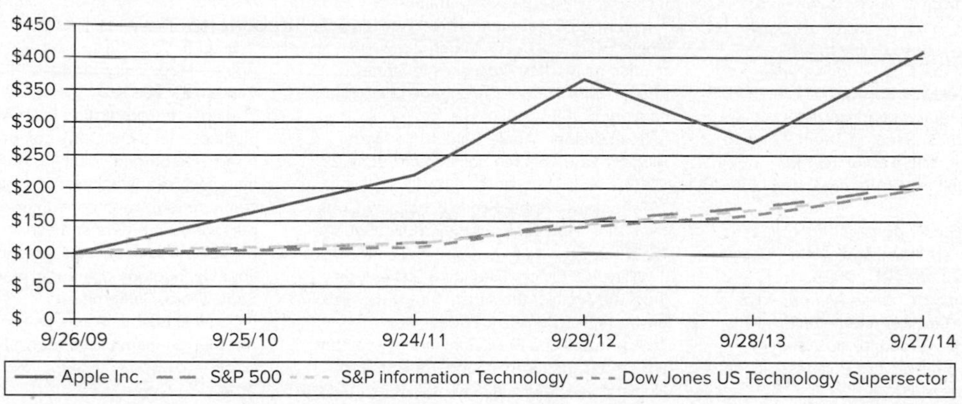

Source: Adapted from Company Annual Reports.

stream movies from the iPad or iPhone to TV sets connected to the Apple TV device. "Longer term, who knows? Things happen so rapidly in this industry, and new competitors and technologies can appear out of the blue, that it's hard to predict what will happen to any firm, much less a company that's been as innovative as Apple,"[69] said Owen Linzmayer, author of *Apple Confidential 2.0.*

While it was yet to be seen whether the Apple Watch or new services like Apple Pay or Apple's acquisition of Beats would be financially successful or not, analysts were hopeful that under Cook's leadership, Apple would remain at the helm of tech innovation. According to Michael Useem, the prominent Wharton management professor and director of the school's Center for Leadership and Change Management, "In my own small world the question of whether Cook can sustain Apple's momentum comes up more often than just about any other question on top management these days."[70]

ENDNOTES

[1] Eric Markowitz, "5 Essential Leadership Lessons from Tim Cook," www.inc.com, December 6, 2012.
[2] Agam Shah, "What Challenges Does Tim Cook's Apple Face?" www.macworld.com, August 25, 2011.
[3] Matt Richtel and Brian X. Chen, "Tim Cook, Making Apple His Own," www.nytimes.com, June 15, 2014.
[4] Joe Rossignol, "Tim Cook Named 'World's Greatest Leader,' Reflects on Leading Post-Jobs Era at Apple," www.macrumors.com, March 26, 2015.
[5] Adam Lashinsky, "Apple's Tim Cook Leads Different," www.fortune.com, March 26, 2015.
[6] Ibid.
[7] Atari, Inc. was an American video game and home computer company founded in 1972.
[8] Hewlett-Packard Company or HP is an American multinational information technology company headquartered in Palo Alto, California, US.
[9] Apple's fiscal year is the 52- or 53-week period that ends on the last Saturday of September.
[10] Dominic Rushe, "Apple Doesn't Need another Charismatic Leader, It Needs Tim Cook," www.theguardian.com, September 7, 2014.
[11] The International Business Machines Corporation (commonly referred to as IBM) is an American multinational technology and consulting corporation, with headquarters in Armonk, New York.
[12] Compaq Computer Corporation was a company founded in 1982 that developed, sold, and supported computers and related products and services. It became the largest supplier of PC systems during the 1990s before being overtaken by HP in 2001.
[13] Dominic Rushe, "Apple Doesn't Need another Charismatic Leader, It Needs Tim Cook."
[14] "7 Traits of Great Supply Chain Leader: A Case of Tim Cook," www.supplychainopz.com.
[15] "Tim Cook: From Supply Chain Management to CEO," www.procurious.com, January 22, 2015.
[16] Ibid.
[17] In October 2003, Jobs was diagnosed with an islet cell neuroendocrine tumor, a form of pancreatic cancer. Jobs' health remained an ongoing concern for the company and its investors since 2009. In January 2011, Jobs, then 56, took unexpected leave for the third time.

[18] Gartner, Inc. is an American information technology research and advisory firm headquartered in Stamford, Connecticut, US.
[19] "Apple Had the Best Supply Chain in the World for the Last Four Years, Here Is What You Can Learn from It," www.tradegecko.com, April 3, 2014.
[20] Ibid.
[21] Alan Deutschman, *The Second Coming of Steve Jobs* (Broadway Books, 2001).
[22] Jean Lipman-Blumen and Harold J. Leavitt, *Hot Groups: Seeding Them, Feeding Them, and Using Them to Ignite Your Organization* (Oxford University Press, USA, May 20, 1999).
[23] Edgar H. Schein, *Organizational Culture and Leadership* (Third edition, Jossey-Bass Publishers, September 21, 2004).
[24] Eric Abrahamson, *Change Without Pain: How Managers Can Overcome Initiative Overload, Organizational Chaos, and Employee Burnout* (Harvard Business School Press, December 4, 2003).
[25] William Belgard and Steven R. Rayner, *Shaping the Future: A Dynamic Process for Creating and Achieving Your Company's Strategic Vision* (First edition, AMACOM, May 17, 2004).
[26] International Data Corporation (IDC) is a market research and analysis firm specializing in information technology, telecommunications, and consumer technology markets. It is headquartered in Framingham, Massachusetts.
[27] Alex Pham, "Steve Jobs Set to Return to Apple," www.latimes.com, June 29, 2009.
[28] Brian Caulfield, "The Apple Mafia," www.forbes.com, February 18, 2009.
[29] Founded in 2004, Hudson Square Research is a New York-based institutional equity research firm focused on the technology, media, telecommunications, and consumer segments.
[30] Alex Pham, "Steve Jobs Set to Return to Apple," www.latimes.com, June 29, 2009.
[31] Founded in 1985, Needham & Company, LLC, is an investment banking and asset management firm focused primarily on serving emerging growth companies and their investors.
[32] Joe Nocera, "Apple's Culture of Secrecy," www.nytimes.com, July 26, 2008.
[33] James Rogers, "Apple Investors Seek Jobs Succession Plan," money.msn.com, February 23, 2011.
[34] The Enderle Group is a US-based technology consulting and information services firm.
[35] Alex Pham, "Steve Jobs Set to Return to Apple," www.latimes.com, June 29, 2009.
[36] www.mydigitalfc.com/stock-market/infosys-likely-surge-high-volume-558
[37] Ina Fried, "Celebrating Three Decades of Apple," www.cnet.com, March 28, 2006.
[38] Brian Leavy, *Key Processes in Strategy: Themes and Theories* (Cengage Learning, January 1996).
[39] Scott Kirsner, "Apple Chief Is No Model, Blogger Says," search.boston.com, June 29, 2009.
[40] Tom Krazit, "Apple Faces Credibility Crisis over Jobs' Health," news.cnet.com, January 15, 2009.
[41] William C. Taylor, "Decoding Steve Jobs: Trust the Art, Not the Artist," blogs.harvard-business.org, June 23, 2009.
[42] Rick Tetzeli and Brent Schlender, "The Steve Jobs You Didn't Know: Kind, Patient, and Human," www.fastcompany.com, March 17, 2015.
[43] Steve Tobak, "Leadership Lessons from Apple CEO Tim Cook," www.entrepreneur.com, September 10, 2014.
[44] Dominic Rushe, "Apple Doesn't Need Another Charismatic Leader, It Needs Tim Cook," www.theguardian.com, September 7, 2014.
[45] Adam Lashinsky, "Apple's Tim Cook Leads Different," www.fortune.com, March 26, 2015.
[46] *The New Yorker* is an American magazine published by Condé Nast.
[47] Adam Lashinsky, "Apple's Tim Cook Leads Different."
[48] Paul Morello, "11 Leadership Lessons We Can Learn from Tim Cook," www.lifehack.org
[49] Adam Lashinsky, "Apple's Tim Cook Leads Different," www.fortune.com, March 26, 2015.
[50] Ibid.
[51] Steve Tobak, "One CEO Puts His Money Where His Mouth Is," www.foxbusiness.com, June 25, 2013.
[52] Steve Denning, "Why Tim Cook Doesn't Care About 'The Bloody ROI,'" www.forbes.com, March 7, 2014.
[53] Marc Gunther, "Apple CEO Tim Cook at Climate Week: 'The time for inaction has passed,'" www.theguardian.com, September 23, 2014.
[54] Andrew Gumbel, "Tim Cook: Out, Proud, Apple's New Leader Steps into the Limelight," www.theguardian.com, November 2, 2014.
[55] Adam Lashinsky, "Apple's Tim Cook Leads Different," www.fortune.com, March 26, 2015.
[56] Ibid.
[57] Jean Louis Gassee, "Apple's $30bn Maps Mistake," www.theguardian.com October 1, 2012.
[58] Brian X. Chen, "Tim Cook Apologizes for Apple's Maps," bits.blogs.nytimes.com, September 28, 2012.
[59] Microsoft Corporation is an American multinational technology company headquartered in Redmond, Washington, that develops, manufactures, licenses, supports, and sells computer software, consumer electronics, and personal computers and services.
[60] Intel Corporation is an American multinational technology company headquartered in Santa Clara, California.
[61] Dominic Rushe, "Apple Doesn't Need Another Charismatic Leader, It Needs Tim Cook," www.theguardian.com, September 7, 2014.
[62] Agam Shah, "What Challenges Does Tim Cook's Apple Face?" www.macworld.com, August 25, 2011.
[63] Matt Richtel and Brian X. Chen, "Tim Cook, Making Apple His Own," www.nytimes.com, June 15, 2014.
[64] Dominic Rushe, "Apple Doesn't Need Another Charismatic Leader, It Needs Tim Cook," www.theguardian.com, September 7, 2014.
[65] Matt Richtel and Brian X. Chen, "Tim Cook, Making Apple His Own," www.nytimes.com, June 15, 2014.
[66] Adam Lashinsky, "Apple's Tim Cook Leads Different," www.fortune.com, March 26, 2015.
[67] Matt Richtel and Brian X. Chen, "Tim Cook, Making Apple His Own," www.nytimes.com, June 15, 2014.
[68] Adam Lashinsky, "Apple's Tim Cook Leads Different," www.fortune.com, March 26, 2015.
[69] Agam Shah, "What Challenges Does Tim Cook's Apple Face?" www.macworld.com, August 25, 2011.
[70] Adam Lashinsky, "Apple's Tim Cook Leads Different," www.fortune.com, March 26, 2015.

CASE 29

NCAA Football: Is It Worth It?

A. J. Strickland
The University of Alabama

J. D. Gilbert
The University of Alabama, MBA/JD 2017

Jacoby Jackson was a highly touted, senior 4-star football recruit from Celina, Texas, finishing high school in the spring of this school year. Throughout Jacoby's life, he wanted to play college football at the Division I university in his home state of Texas. Being a highly skilled 6-foot 6-inch, 240-pound tight end, Jacoby was receiving scholarship offers from many major college football programs throughout the country. Jacoby was also an outstanding student inside the classroom, which led to academic opportunities at Ivy League schools. A few weeks ago, Jacoby watched the *Concussion*[1] film with his parents and began to question if playing football in college would be beneficial in the long run, given all the health risks associated with playing the sport. Many college recruiters were informing Jacoby that helmets and the school's concussion protocol were highly effective in preventing concussions. With National Signing Day for high school football recruits approaching in a few weeks, Jacoby was still undecided about his football and/or academic future.

COLLEGIATE ATHLETICS OVERVIEW

For every high school athlete, the dream of playing at the collegiate level slowly turns into a reality for a chosen few like Jacoby Jackson. Over 8 million high school athletes dwindled into the 460,000 student-athletes that competed at the National Collegiate Athletic Association (NCAA) level as of 2015. The primary goal of these high school athletes was to be awarded a financial scholarship to assist the rising costs of furthering his or her education. NCAA Divisions I and II schools provided over $2.7 billion in athletic scholarships annually. Depending on the school and the sport, athletes could receive either a full award, a partial award, or no reward. These scholarships could be used to complete a bachelor's degree, as well as a master's degree. One of the most competitive scholarships awarded was the full-ride collegiate football scholarship. These full-ride football scholarships typically covered tuition and fees, room, board, books, and most recently cost of attendance. Collegiate football provided more full-ride scholarships than any other sport.

The possibility of receiving a full-ride scholarship to a university was a motivating force for any aspiring football player. Besides furthering one's education, this was the most common route for football standouts to reach an even bigger goal of playing in the National Football League. The NFL's rules stated that a player must be removed from high school for three years to be eligible for the NFL draft. This did not force a player to compete at the college level, but collegiate football was where virtually all NFL careers began. With lucrative television exposure and the prestige that came with being a collegiate football player, these athletes were able to showcase their skills at the highest level possible before the NFL. With over 850 college football programs and more than 80,000 college football players, college football scholarships were becoming a highly sought-after item during the recruiting process. Recruiting typically began at the high school level; however, with advancements in technology and social media, names began circulating at the Pee-Wee football level as to who would be the next highly sought-after recruit.

Collegiate Football Scholarship Breakdown[2]

There were many different routes a high school football player could take to achieve the goal of playing at the college level. The NCAA Division I Football Bowl Series was the premier level of college football. As of 2015 each program had 85 full-ride scholarships; they could award up to 25 new scholarships annually to incoming recruits. This level of football made up only about 20 percent of the opportunities to play college football, although this was the level of football that was mostly seen played. The average person primarily thinks of the Football Bowl Series level as college football, although there were numerous other opportunities.

The NCAA Division I Football Championship Series level of college football was the second opportunity recruits had to acquire financial scholarships. These programs had 63 scholarships per team, but the scholarships could be divided up into partial scholarships allocated to field a team. Typically full-ride scholarships were given to the more skilled players. At the NCAA Division II level, programs had 36 scholarships available to field a roster. The majority of these scholarships were partial scholarships in order to field a competitive team at this level. The National Association of Intercollegiate Athletics football programs were able to award 24 scholarships partially allocated as well. The National Junior College Athletic Association offered two-year football programs with 85 full-ride scholarships available. This level of football was highly utilized by players who may not be ruled academically eligible to compete at the higher levels. Division III schools, along with Ivy League programs, did not offer athletic scholarships but offered financial assistance and academic scholarships to players who qualified.

College Football Scholarship Value: The Cost of Attendance

College football scholarships varied in amounts, depending on the school and the state in which the recruit was a resident. As is the case at most public universities, a resident within the state paid less than an out-of-state student. These scholarships covered the full cost of attendance, which was broadly defined as the average cost to attend college for one academic year. The cost of attendance was determined annually considering survey and consumer price data, which included tuition and estimated average costs for books and supplies, room and board, transportation, and personal expenses. These cost-of-attendance scholarships provided substantial aid to college football players who faced strict guidelines from the NCAA regarding pay-to-play allegations and accepting money from boosters.

These scholarships had not always covered the entire cost of attendance. The decision to cover the full cost of attendance was approved in January 2015, and took effect in August 2015. This allowed many universities time to budget for the estimated costs of higher monetary scholarships. With the new rule adoptions, an athlete's cost of attendance could be adjusted for his individual circumstances, ranging from child care to medical expenses. These cost-of-attendance scholarships had become a major role in the recruiting process of high school athletes. Student-athletes could take advantage of these cost-of-attendance scholarships by pocketing the excess cash. For example, a student could receive money to cover the costs of residential housing on campus. If the athlete opted to live in off-campus housing that was relatively cheaper than on-campus living, the athlete got to keep the excess cash.

Jacoby understood that the money gained from the cost of attendance would be very beneficial in supporting him throughout college and reducing his student loans to pay after college. For Jacoby's in-state university where he was offered a football scholarship, the cost of attendance was around $26,000 per year. This entire cost would be covered in his athletic college scholarship. Furthermore, Jacoby had only been accepted to the Ivy League university and had not been awarded a financial scholarship. The cost of attendance at this well-known out-of-state university would be almost double the cost of attendance with the football scholarship. Exhibit 1 shows the costs at the two schools for the 2015–2016 year. Jacoby could continue his football career at this university, but no athletic scholarships were awarded at this level of competition unless financial assistance was awarded.

Academic Route

As Jacoby weighed the costs and benefits of receiving a college football scholarship versus attending the prestigious academic college, Jacoby wanted to know

EXHIBIT 1 Cost Comparisons of Football versus School for 2015–2016 Year

	Football Scholarship	Ivy League
Tuition/fees	$ 9,830	$45,278
Room and board	$11,456	$15,381
Books/other	$ 5,160	$ 3,741

Note: These are yearly costs of attendance for 2015–2016.
Sources: **www.collegedata.com/cs/data/college/college_pg03_tmpl.jhtml?schoolId=788**; college.harvard.edu/financial-aid/how-aid-works/cost-attendance.

the graduating salaries of each university. Because Jacoby understood that the chance to play in the NFL was very slim, he wanted to ensure that he would have a career long after his football-playing days ended. Based on his findings, going the academic school route tended to produce almost double the starting salaries of students 10 years after graduation.[3] Jacoby needed to weigh these options against his dream of playing tight end in the NFL (see Exhibit 2).

Jacoby considered this scenario: After college, assuming the NFL was not in his future, Jacoby took a job with a sports marketing firm working in Dallas, Texas, earning the salaries shown in Exhibit 2. The annual salary growth rate increased by 3 percent given every year Jacoby remained at the company past his initial 10 years. His employer matched his 401(k) up to 5 percent, earning interest of 5 percent yearly. Jacoby would be able to retire from the company in 25 years.

Probability of Making the National Football League

Besides playing football for his favorite university in his home state of Texas, Jacoby had a lifelong goal of playing in the NFL. Because the rules stated that a professional football player must be at least three years removed from high school, Jacoby understood that attending college was the most profitable way to improve his skills as a player while earning an education. However, the probability to continue his career in the NFL was less than 2 percent. Because Jacoby was not beginning his collegiate football career until the next fall, he belonged to a statistic of about 8 in 10,000 high school senior football players who would eventually be drafted by an NFL team.[4] Although Jacoby was very confident in his ability to turn pro, these numbers were very low to safely assume Jacoby would develop into an NFL-caliber player.

In Exhibit 3, the percentage of NCAA to Major Pro column represents the number of NCAA football players selected in the NFL draft divided by the number of draft-eligible players. Although players did not have to be drafted to make the NFL, this was

EXHIBIT 2 Estimated Salaries after 10 Years

College Choice	Starting Median Salary	Mid-Career (10-yr) Median Salary	Mid-Career (10-yr) 25th Percentile Salary	Mid-Career (10-yr) 75th Percentile Salary
Football Scholarship	$49,700	$ 93,900	$67,400	$129,000
Prestigious Academia	$59,100	$126,000	$91,200	$137,000

Source: **online.wsj.com/public/resources/documents/info-Salaries_for_Colleges_by_Type-sort.html**.

EXHIBIT 3 Estimated Probability of Competing in the NFL

NCAA Participants	Approximate # Draft Eligible	# Draft Slots	# NCAA Drafted	% NCAA to Major Pro
71,291	15,842	256	255	1.6%

Source: **www.ncaa.org/about/resources/research/football**.

EXHIBIT 4 Division I and Power Five Conference NFL Comparison

NCAA Level	% NCAA to NFL
Division I	4.0%
Power Five Conference	10.1%

Source: www.ncaa.org/about/resources/research/football.

EXHIBIT 5 Minimum Base Salary Projection for 2014 Lower Draft Picks (3rd through 7th Round)

	Year 1	Year 2	Year 3	Year 4
Base Salaries	$420,000	$510,000	$600,000	$690,000

Source: mmqb.si.com/2014/05/22/nfl-rookie-contract-negotiations

the common route to competing in the NFL. Because Jacoby's scholarship offer from the university in his home state was an FBS Division I scholarship within the Power Five Conferences (ACC, Big Ten, Big 12, Pac-12 and SEC), his percentages would increase to play professional football at the next level when he became draft eligible in three years (see Exhibit 4).

Salaries at the Professional Football Level

Before the NFL and the National Football League Players Association (NFLPA) reworked the collective bargaining agreement (CBA) in 2011, rookies drafted out of college had more leverage in signing more luxurious first contracts. No longer could players like Sam Bradford, in 2010, sign a six-year, $76 million contract without touching the field in the NFL. Before 2011, NFL teams were given a salary cap that could be allocated to incoming rookies that could reach as high as 60 percent for some first-round draft picks. In 2016, each pick had a predetermined monetary amount and contract length of four years. However, only the top 16 picks in the draft were able to sign a contract for guaranteed money for four years. The vast majority of picks after the first two rounds signed contracts for four years of nonguaranteed money with bonuses predetermined by the new CBA (see Exhibit 5).[5]

Jacoby planned to play tight end for the remainder of his collegiate and possibly professional career. Statistically, tight ends are not known for being drafted as highly as other positions such as quarterbacks, wide receivers, and offensive linemen. This provided another uphill battle Jacoby would face when attempting to be drafted highly in his future draft year. Based on statistical data from the previous 10 years, 2005–2014, tight ends made up only 5.7 percent (145 of 2,560) of all draft picks in these years with an average first-round selection pick of 21. Only 9 tight ends of the 145 tight ends drafted in the last 10 years were drafted in the first round, with only 2 of those 9 first-round picks drafted within the top 16, which allowed them to receive a guaranteed money contract for their first four years under the new collective bargaining agreement.[6]

The Dangers of NFL Money Unlike the National Basketball Association, Major League Baseball, and National Hockey League, the NFL did not have to guarantee money in contracts besides the signing bonus. A large majority of players lived on the league minimum, estimating that three-quarters of an NFL team likely did not make a million dollars in their careers. NFL players were paid throughout the 17 weeks of the regular season that made up the most of their salary. This was an issue because the players may not have saved enough money to live on for the remaining 35 weeks of the year, especially with the spending habits that could occur during a rookie's first season earning six or seven figures trying to keep up with NFL superstars.

In ESPN Films's 30 for 30 documentary *Broke,* former NFL coach Herman Edwards explained this monetary issue with a creative analogy: "There's a problem when you have beer money and champagne taste." The players would get so caught up in the lifestyle they were then able to afford, they forgot it could be taken away in the NFL at any time. Besides the top players with guaranteed contracts, most players could have their paycheck taken away at any time due to off-the-field issues or injuries. A 2015 study from the National Bureau of Economic Research (NBER) showed that 15.7 percent of NFL players drafted between 1996 and 2003 filed for bankruptcy within

12 years of retirement. Although only about 2 percent filed for bankruptcy two years after retirement, a substantial growth rate in bankruptcy filing of these players continued throughout the first 12 years. These players could have taken advantage of the NFL retirement plan to ensure they had a steady flow of income for years to come (see Exhibits 6 and 7).

The average career of a first-round draft pick was nearly three times longer than the career length of the average player. Of the nine tight ends selected in the first round, Dustin Keller was the only player not on an NFL roster at the beginning of the 2014 season. These first-round tight ends had sustained long careers in the league, which led to more overall career earnings. The average NFL salary experienced an increase as player age increased for those who were able to sustain longevity in the league. However, 70 percent of the NFL's players fell between the ages of 22 and 27, before the large increase in salary could occur. Also, the decrease in the number of players still playing at those older ages was greatly alarming. This number was expected to continue to fall as concussion awareness continued to rise among players (see Exhibit 8).

Concussion Issues

A reason more players were retiring early was due to the new information surrounding concussion statistics and brain damage resulting to football players later in life. Jacoby's parents were greatly concerned that if Jacoby continued to play football at the collegiate level, and possibly pro level, he could gravely injure himself. As Jacoby's signing day was less than

EXHIBIT 6 NFL Retirement Plans

Retirement Plan	Pension Plan	401 (k) Program	Annuity Plan
Credited Seasons Needed	3 seasons	2 seasons	4 seasons
Age Before Collection	55 years	N/A	35
Payments per Season			
2015–2017	$660 monthly	Match up to $26,000 annually	$80,000 annually
2018–2020	$720 monthly	Match up to $28,000 annually	$95,000 annually

Source: nfllabor.files.wordpress.com/2010/01/collective-bargaining-agreement-2011-2020.pdf.

EXHIBIT 7 NFL Career Length

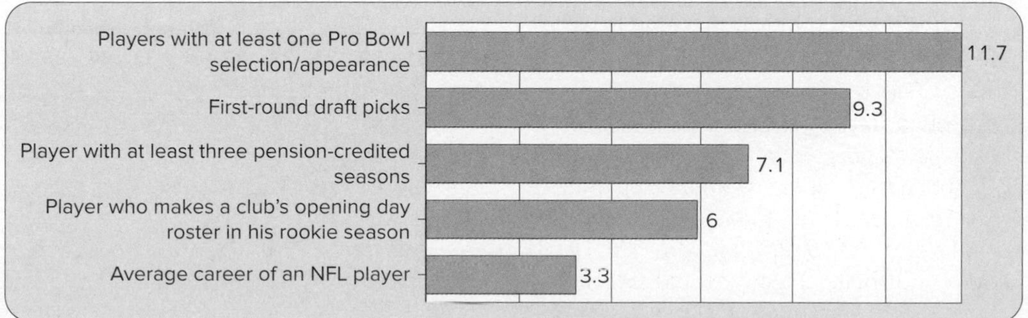

Source: Statista and NFL.com.[7]

EXHIBIT 8 NFL Salary and Age Distribution Comparison

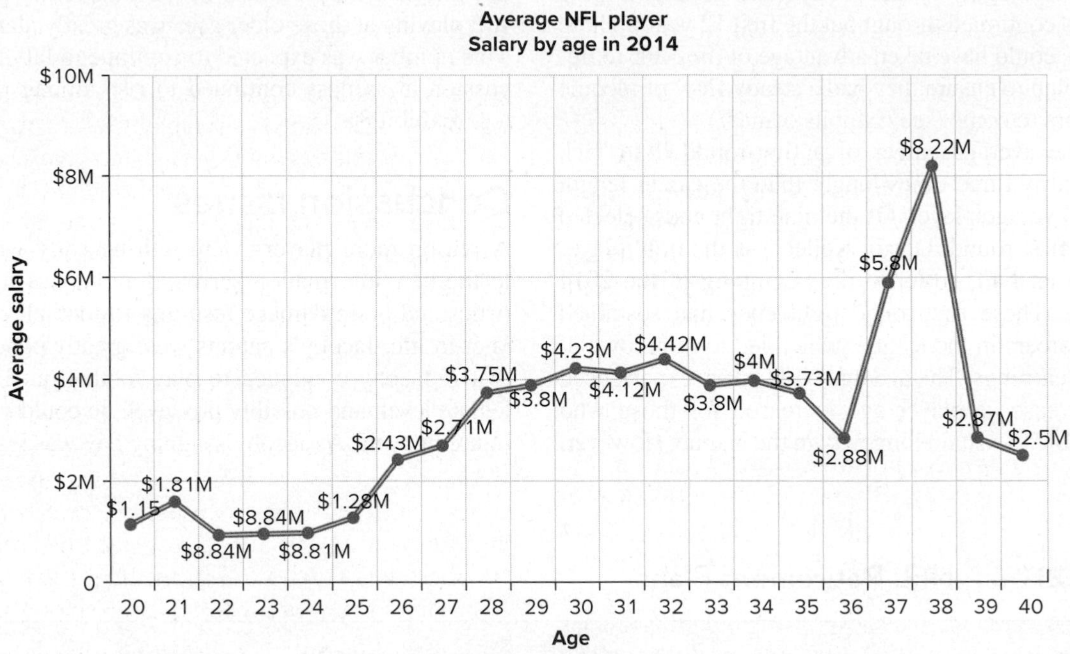

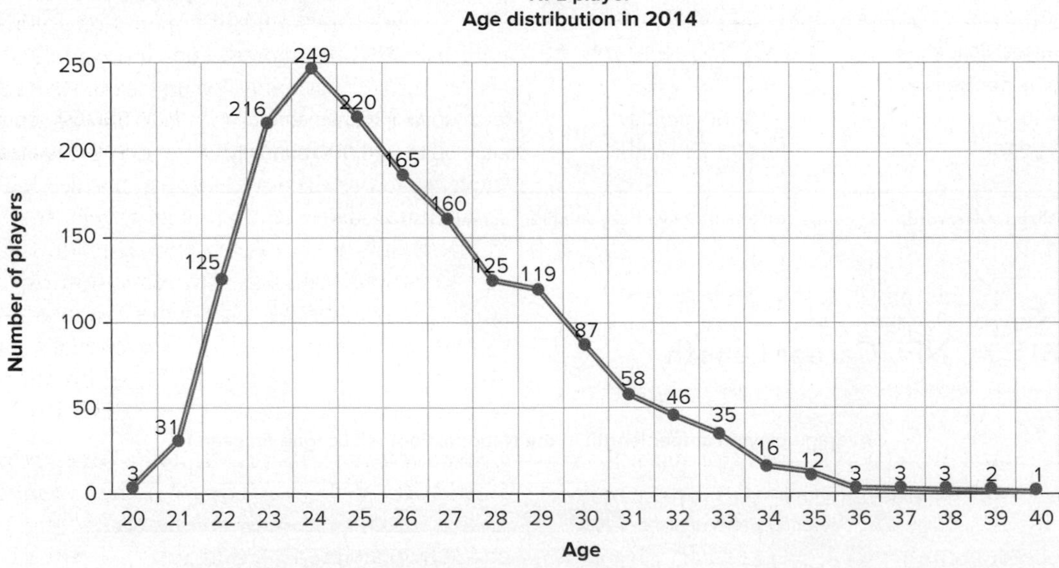

Source: www.besttickets.com/blog/nfl-player-census-2014/.

a month away, he and his parents went to see the film *Concussion.* The film solidified Jacoby's parents' concern about the health and safety of their only child. *Concussion* follows Dr. Bennet Omalu throughout some of his experiences researching chronic traumatic encephalopathy, more commonly known as CTE. Jacoby had never fully considered the damage his brain took whenever he took hits to the head as a high school football player. He also knew that giving up his college football scholarship would cost him a lot of money in student loans whether he still attended his in-state university or attended the prestigious academic school in the New England area.

CTE: What Is It? CTE is a progressive degenerative disease of the brain found in athletes and others with historical repetitive brain trauma. It can result from concussions as well as repetitive hits to the head causing brain trauma. This results in degeneration of brain tissue and causes a buildup of an abnormal protein known as tau. These symptoms can begin anywhere from months to decades after the last suffered brain trauma took place. Resulting effects of CTE include memory loss, confusion, impaired judgment, impulse control problems, aggression, depression, and progressive dementia.[8] This disease has been linked to the suicide of multiple NFL players as well.

Concussions: The Beginning[9] In 1994, NFL commissioner Paul Tagliabue created the Mild Traumatic Brain Injury (MTBI) committee. At the time concussions were still seen as a minor issue compared to other areas and injuries within the game. In 1997, new return-to-play guidelines were installed when the American Academy of Neurology announced that repetitive concussions could cause brain damage to the players. In 1999, the NFL Retirement Board ruled in favor of Mike Webster, claiming that the head injuries he suffered in the NFL led to his diagnosis of dementia. This was the first case of its kind in NFL history. In 2002, Dr. Omalu examined Webster's brain, eventually discovering the first case of CTE identified in football players.

Between the finding of CTE in 2002 and the beginning of 2005, the NFL's MTBI committee continued to dispute evidence that playing football led to a higher risk of brain injuries. In 2005, Dr. Omalu published the CTE findings in the journal *Neurosurgery.* Over the next few years, Dr. Omalu would find CTE in the brains of multiple former NFL players who committed suicide. In 2007, the NFL hosted its first NFL Concussion summit in efforts to combat the issue, only 13 years after the MTBI was created. The first time the NFL acknowledged that concussions had long-term effects on the brain was in December 2009. New return-to-play guidelines were issued and any player that exhibited symptoms of a concussion was not allowed to return to play that same day.

In fall 2010, the first reported case of CTE at the collegiate level was found in a 21-year-old college football player. The player had never been treated for a concussion, which raised concerns that the number of hits sustained throughout a football career could lead to CTE. In March 2011, the NFL made its first rule change to combat concussions by moving kickoffs to the 35-yard line to reduce collisions. In 2013, the NFL announced that an independent neurologist would be on the sidelines of every team to perform a systematic checklist when a head, neck, or spine injury occurred. That same year, the NFL settled a $765 million lawsuit with retired NFL players without admitting any wrongdoing (see Exhibit 9).

Concussions: NFL In 2015, concussions rose 58 percent in the NFL with a reported 182 concussions. This changed the trend in concussions, which had decreased to 114 reported concussions in 2014. Jeff Miller, the NFL's senior vice president, stated that the increased concussion number in 2015 was likely possible due to the enhanced screening processes being implemented to diagnose concussions, as well as the trainers and independent neurologists being more active in attempting to spot concussion symptoms. Reports of concussions resulting from helmet-to-helmet collisions also rose from 58 in 2014 to 92 helmet-to-helmet concussions reported in 2015. Concussions made up almost 11 percent (182 of 1,672) of overall injuries reported in the NFL in 2015 (see Exhibit 10).

Concussions: High School and College Football Concussions were an issue facing players not only in the NFL but also at the high school and collegiate levels. A study in 2013 by the Institute of Medicine, funded by the NFL, estimated that high school football players suffered 11.2 concussions for every 10,000 games and practices, whereas the collegiate rate was only 6.3.[10] In 2014, the NCAA announced its $30 million alliance with the U.S. Department of Defense to conduct research into concussion and head impact related injuries. This research would be conducted on over 37,000 male

EXHIBIT 9 NFL Concussion Yearly Injury Reports, 2009–2013

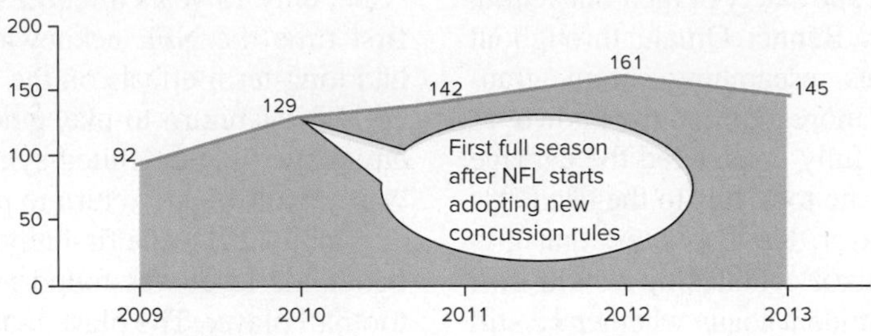

Source: www-tc.pbs.org/wgbh/pages/frontline/art/cats/concussions/summary-charts/CW-roundup-chart4a.png.

EXHIBIT 10 NFL Concussion Statistics, 2012–2015

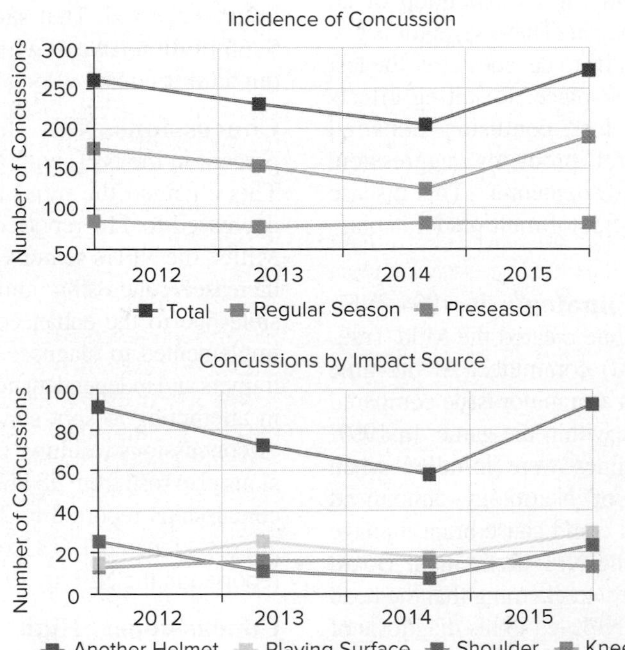

Source: www.forbes.com/sites/abigailtracy/2016/02/04/nfl-cte-football-concussions-injuries-helmet-vicis-zero1-super-bowl/#4b34ab7059c5.

and female collegiate athletes over the next three years. A preseason concussion evaluation would be conducted and followed up by further evaluations when related injuries occurred. This was intended to provide more concussion information for the NCAA, which was not accessible before this initiative.

This new research would be used to combat concussion issues within all college sports, but was expected to bring about major changes with concussion reporting in college football. The NCAA's concussion policy required only that schools receive written acknowledgments from athletes that they had received education on concussions and were required to report symptoms to the staff. A study in 2014 at the FCS level (Division I lower level) estimated that only one concussion was diagnosed in college football for every six suspected concussions. The study calculated that for every one diagnosed concussion, there were 21 other head-related injuries that went unreported, but necessarily a concussion each time. Coach's perception of concussions and how the players viewed the coach's perception seemed to play a large role in whether the concussion symptoms were reported by the players. It was also found that players, such as offensive linemen or running backs, who take the most hits throughout the game may think these symptoms are just part of their normal routine.[11] If these symptoms became a normality to players at the collegiate level, it would likely spill over into their professional careers in the NFL.

Preventing Concussions

No Full-Contact Practices One level of collegiate football combatted the concussion issue with full force. Beginning in 2016, Ivy League schools would no longer have full-contact practices during the regular season in hopes to reduce head injuries. The Ivy League already had the strictest rules preventing excessive contact at practice, but had now revolutionized the way schools could reduce practice-related concussions by eliminating full-contact drills within practice. Dartmouth was the first Ivy League school to implement these no-full-contact practices in 2010. When full-contact practices were completely eliminated, the school used a virtual mobile player to tackle and chase around the field, as if it were any other player. Until 2015, the NFL had also seen concussions decrease after the amount of full-contact practice days were decreased in 2012 by league officials.

Helmet Technology Helmets are the safety pad that prevent players from receiving even worse head injuries in football than are already sustained. A revolutionizing helmet that could decrease the number of concussions would benefit football players greatly. The VICIS Zero1 football helmet attempted to help lower concussions with its innovative technology to reduce the impact forces of helmets. Unlike regular helmets, the Zero1 helmet used a soft outer shell that embraced the impact and spread the force omnidirectionally. The Zero1 helmet cost around $1,500 per helmet, which was at least $1,000 more than other helmets on the market. VICIS hoped to attract NFL and collegiate teams first, then spread to the high school markets to help reduce concussion numbers nationally.

In order to reduce the number of concussions, what if the NFL completely banned the use of all helmets? Hines Ward, a former Pittsburgh Steelers wideout, was among those advocating that football helmets do more harm than good. Ward told the *Dan Patrick Show,* "If you want to prevent concussions, take the helmet off." Although this idea seemed very far-fetched, Ward's rationale for his reasoning was not. He believes players use their helmet like a weapon, giving them more ability to deliver a big hit, rather than protecting players from receiving a big hit. If players did not wear these protective helmets, the players would play less recklessly, and therefore prevent fewer head shots from opposing players. However, skull fractures would likely increase (even if concussions decreased) from the removal of helmets off football players, which would not increase the overall safety of the game.[12]

CTE Results

As of September 2015, the Department of Veterans Affairs and Boston University had discovered CTE in 96 percent of NFL players examined and 79 percent of those examined who played football at some point in their life. Forty percent of those testing positive for CTE played either offensive or defensive line in their playing time, assisting the theory that repetitive hits increase likelihood for this disease. CTE can still not be positively discovered in living players who believe they are suffering from the disease. Researchers are still trying to find cures in order to saves lives in the future. The resulting trend still shows a distinctive link between football and long-term brain disease based on results of football players who have donated their brains to CTE research.[13]

Players' Reactions to CTE Issues

Patton Robbinette Patton Robinette, the starting redshirt junior quarterback at the University of Vanderbilt, decided in the spring of 2015 to quit playing college football to focus on medical school.

He cited a concussion that occurred during the previous football season as being one of the reasons he had decided to give up the sport. Robinette stated, "This team means the world to me and I love playing football more than anything. It's been tough coming to a decision that is right for my family and I, and protects my health and future." Robinnette started at the Vanderbilt School of Medicine the following summer to study orthopedics.[14]

Chris Borland In the spring of 2015, Chris Borland became the most highly profiled NFL player to retire due to the risk of head injury. Borland retired at age 24 after playing one season with the San Francisco 49ers, and played collegiate football at the University of Wisconsin. Borland never suffered a concussion in his one season in the NFL, but did state he had two previous concussions in his life. Borland was a third-round pick in the draft the previous year and scheduled to make $540,000 in his upcoming second season. Borland felt that to be the successful NFL player he envisioned himself being, he would have to take risks that could lead to CTE. Borland claimed, "I just honestly want to do what is best for my health. From what I've researched and what I've experienced, I don't think it's worth the risk."[15]

Wes Welker Wes Welker, a wide receiver picked up by the St. Louis Rams in the middle of the 2015 NFL season, is one of many NFL players not affected by the concussion statistics. Welker's concussion history of six overall concussions included three within nine months and two within three weeks. Welker was cleared by doctors to return to the football field while making this decision to return to the game for another season. Welker stated, "I already played a full season without a concussion, so I'm not really worried about it. I know I'm the poster child right now and everything else. I'm good, and I'm ready to play some ball."[16]

Jacoby's Decision

National Signing was approaching within a few weeks and Jacoby was still undecided whether he was going to look past the health risk associated with playing football at the collegiate level or focus solely on his education. He was pressured from all of his friends at school to accept the collegiate scholarship at the in-state university and continue his dream of playing in the NFL. His close family and relatives kept reminding Jacoby of all the health risks associated with continuing his football career. This college decision coming in two weeks also placed a financial burden on Jacoby. If he chose not to accept the football scholarship, he was turning down a free college education in return to pay for it on his own at possibly a more expensive university. This decision that 18-year-old Jacoby had to make in the upcoming weeks would affect him the remainder of his life. Was the risk of his mental and physical health, for which there was no cure for CTE at the time, worth the possibility of the fame and fortune of an NFL career and a free college education?

ENDNOTES

1 www.sonypictures.com/movies/concussion/.
2 www.athleticscholarships.net/football scholarships.htm.
3 online.wsj.com/public/resources/documents/info-Salaries_for_Colleges_by_Type-sort.html.
4 www.ncaa.org/about/resources/research/football.
5 mmqb.si.com/2014/05/22/nfl-rookie-contract-negotiations.
6 www.drafthistory.com/index.php/positions/te.
7 www.statista.com/statistics/240102/average-player-career-length-in-the-national-football-league/.
8 www.bu.edu/cte/about/what-is-cte/.
9 www.pbs.org/wgbh/frontline/article/timeline-the-nfls-concussion-crisis/.
10 www.pbs.org/wgbh/frontline/article/high-school-football-players-face-bigger-concussion-risk/.
11 www.cbssports.com/collegefootball/writer/jon-solomon/24734520/studies-show-magnitude-of-college-footballs-concussion-problem.
12 profootballtalk.nbcsports.com/2012/12/04/hines-ward-if-you-want-to-prevent-concussions-take-the-helmet-off/.
13 www.pbs.org/wgbh/frontline/article/new-87-deceased-nfl-players-test-positive-for-brain-disease/.
14 espn.go.com/college-football/story/_/id/12568585/patton-robinette-vanderbilt-commodores-ends-playing-career-citing-health-concerns.
15 espn.go.com/espn/otl/story/_/id/12496480/san-francisco-49ers-linebacker-chris-borland-retires-head-injury-concerns.
16 www.cbssports.com/nfl/eye-on-football/25370064/wes-welker-im-really-not-worried-about-concussion-history.

CASE 30

Rhino Poaching in South Africa: Do National Parks Have Sufficient Resources to Fight Wildlife Crime?

A. J. Strickland
The University of Alabama

Markus Hofmeyr
South African National Parks (SANParks)

Mike Fulmer
The University of Alabama, MBA 2016

Dr. Markus Hofmeyr, the head of Veterinary Wildlife Services (VWS) for South African National Parks (SANParks), and his team were by default involved with a persistent crime problem that was harming the rhinoceros population within South Africa's largest park, Kruger National. The onslaught for wildlife poaching across Africa had not slowed down since 2007, with more than 1,200 rhino slain in 2015 alone.[1] Although Hofmeyr and his team had allocated time toward solving wildlife crime on the veterinary and translocation side of things, it was not a primary resource requirement before poaching started (see Exhibit 1). The department used significant resources to implement the biological management plan to help offset some of the poaching losses.

Hofmeyr's team was significantly involved with the biological management of rhino. From 2008 until to 2015 over 5,940 African rhino had been poached leaving only approximately 26,000 rhino still alive in Africa.[2] The average annual growth rate of rhino poached from 2008 to 2015 was 28.8 percent (see

EXHIBIT 1 Mission and Responsibility of Veterinary Wildlife Services Department of SANParks

- Planning and implementing the wildlife management program for SANParks involving translocation, handling, and holding of wildlife (including reintroduction and removal of wildlife into and from national parks, respectively)
- Disease monitoring and management where populations are involved
- Facilitating and implementing the wildlife sales program for SANParks (including rhino sales)
- Facilitating and implementing the wildlife economy transformation donation program of SANParks
- Assisting SANParks research when wildlife are handled and samples required
- Researching to improve core functions
- Training of operations and veterinary skills for the wildlife industry
- Managing the biobank for SANParks

Source: www.sanparks.org/conservation/veterinary/about/default.php.

EXHIBIT 2 The Growth of the Number of Rhinos Poached within South Africa

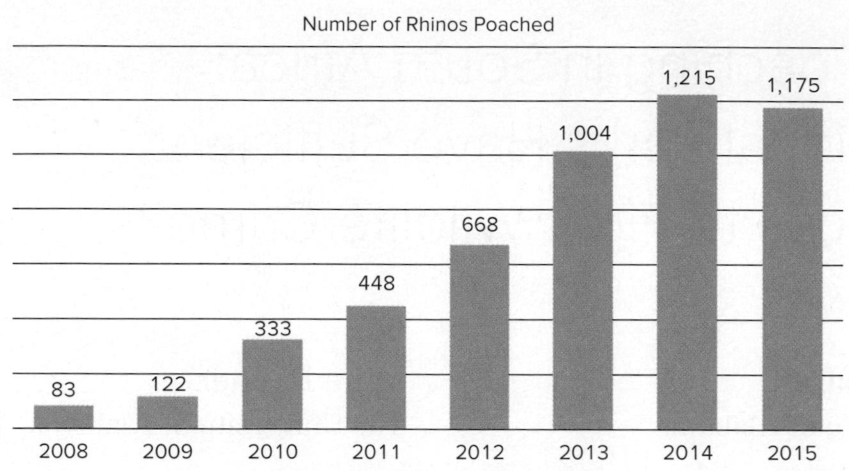

Source: **www.environment.gov.za/mediarelease/rhinopoaching_wildlifetrade.**

Exhibit 2). The SANParks rhino steering committee had identified that the major issue underlying the ever-increasing poaching onslaught was linked to the country's inability to deal with organized crime syndicates and massive inequality and limited economic opportunities for communities surrounding the KNP (both in Mozambique and in SA). The organized crime syndicates were in the business of illegal wildlife trade to Asia. SANParks was faced with the disheartening challenge of how to stop the illegal trade of rhino horns, which continued to fuel relentless deaths of an increasing number of rhino.

The crime syndicates within Asia and southern Africa would continue at all costs as long as there were substantial profits to be made through the illegal trade of rhino horns. As time passed, the stronger and more organized these syndicates became in this highly profitable area.

The driver was simply the value of the rhino horn, which was valued at ~U.S.$80,000/kg at the end-user market. To make matters worse, the demand for the horn was increasing as opposed to decreasing, primarily from Vietnam and China (see Exhibit 3).[3]

KRUGER NATIONAL PARK

Kruger National Park was established in South Africa in 1898, first as a game reserve. In 1926 it was proclaimed as a national park to protect the fast-dwindling wildlife areas. By the turn of the century, it was estimated that white rhino were extinct in Kruger. The first translocation of white rhino back to Kruger National Park occurred in 1961; 345 white rhino had been relocated from the parks in Kwa Zulu Natal by the mid-1970s. In 2015, the Scientific Services for SANParks estimated that approximately 8,000 white rhino and 350 black rhino existed in Kruger National Park. Even though poaching took a toll on the rhino population, Kruger National Park still had the largest rhino population in the world[4] (see Exhibits 4 and 5).

Kruger National Park covered 7,722 square miles (20,000 square kilometers), roughly the size of Massachusetts in conservation area, with eight gates that controlled the flow of traffic into the park (see Exhibit 6). Since its establishment, it had become known for its unrivaled wildlife diversity and easy viewing. It was also known for its world leadership in advanced environmental management techniques, research, and policies. Many viewed Kruger as the best national park in Africa in all aspects—management, infrastructure, and, of course, biodiversity. Kruger was the flagship of South Africa's 19 national parks and contained a variety of species: 336 trees, 49 fish, 34 amphibians, 114 reptiles, 507 birds, and 147 mammals. Over time, the park developed into a tourist attraction because of the wildlife and beautiful

EXHIBIT 3 Map of South Africa with Bordering Countries (top-right KNP green area)

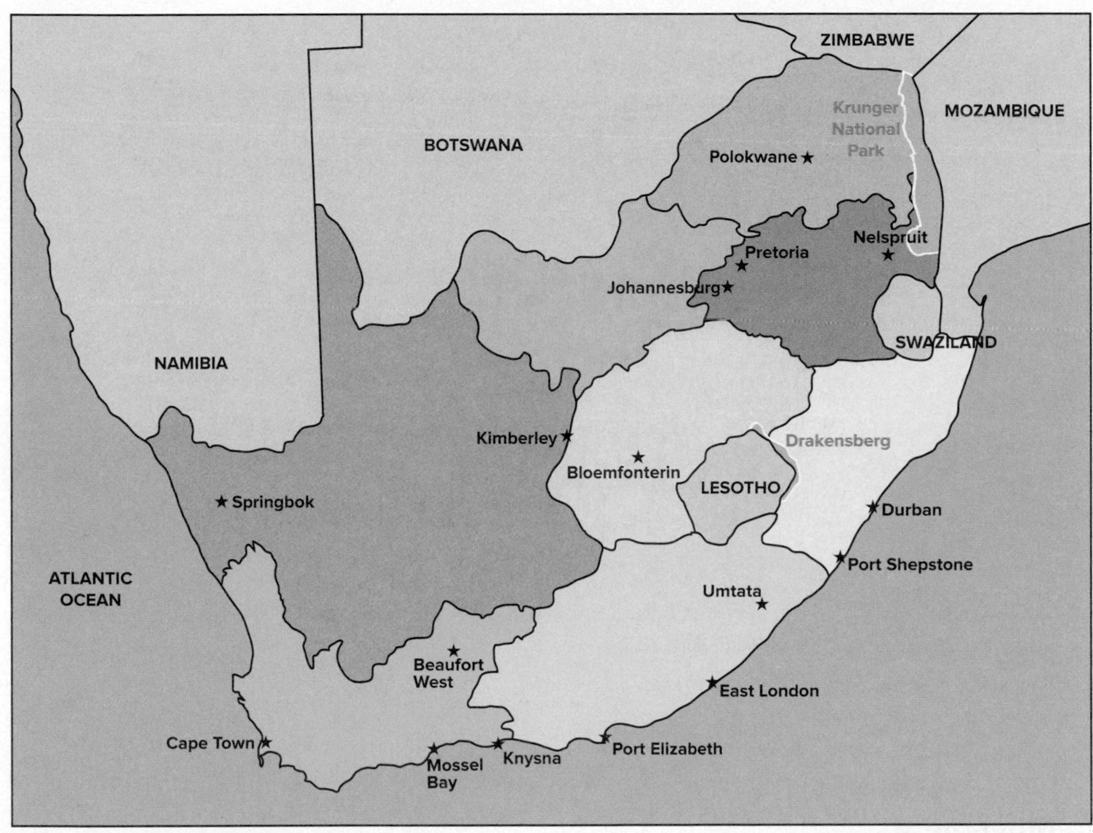

Source: www.panoramainfo.co.za/maps.htm.

EXHIBIT 4 Black and White Rhino Population within KNP (2015)

	Black and White Rhino Population	
	Africa	KNP
White Rhino	19,682–21,077	7,500–8,500
Black Rhino	5,042–5,455	350–450

Sources: Data provided by the International Union for Conservation of Nature (IUCM) and Special Survival Commission's African Rhino Specialist Group (AfRSG), www.iucn.org/content/iucn-reports-deepening-rhino-poaching-crisis-africa.

scenery representative of South Africa's Lowveld region. Tourist operations were quite large, with the park offering 21 rest camps, 7 private lodge concessions, and 11 private safari lodges. Some lodges operated in partnership between communities and private companies, which provided concessions for parcels of land (Mukuleke contractual park area). The concessions were placed on tender, and areas were allocated for 25- to 30-year leases, during which operational activities linked with tourism were allowed. At the end of the period, the fixed assets became the property of Kruger, which could decide to extend the lease or retender the concession. An integral part of Kruger National Park's conservation effort was wildlife capture. Traditionally, capturing wildlife allowed Kruger National Park to translocate certain wildlife species to the other national parks in South Africa and neighboring countries as well as to private reserves in South Africa. The experienced wildlife capture ability allowed for extensive research to take place on disease and wildlife biology in KNP.

EXHIBIT 5 Population of Rhino across the World

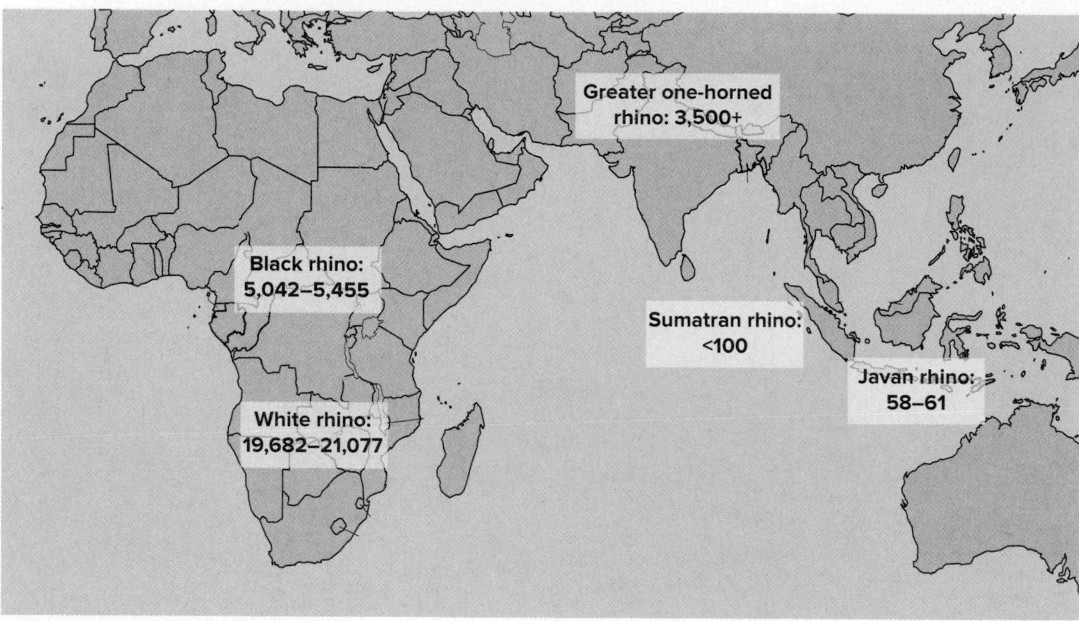

Source: www.savetherhino.org/rhino_info/rhino_population_figures.

Rhino Movement

When the demand for rhino horns increased in the late 2000s, much of the poaching took place outside the park on private and provincial game reserves. These rhino were much easier to target due to less protection from rangers and conservation departments. Individual property owners had a hard time policing their own land due to lack of resources and government protection. Over time the trend reversed and now was more effectively policed on private reserves as private owners were more flexible to implement innovative protection strategies. Most rhino were now poached in Kruger National Park and provincial reserves which, due to government procurement rules, were less flexible to adapt quickly to the changing environment. Organized crime had increased efforts to poach rhino and pushed for more sophisticated means of killing. The situation had resulted in all aspects of management, including on SANParks Veterinary Wildlife Services, to try to reverse the trend. The majority of rhino were within certain areas of South Africa, specifically Kruger National Park. Kruger had rangers in the conservation department, but due to the scale and complexity of the problem it had required an ever-increasing allocation of resources toward the protection of rhino at the expense of other conservation activities and hence was a totally unsustainable solution (see Exhibit 7).

The war to protect the rhino against poachers was a continually evolving arms race between the crime syndicates and the Kruger National Park ranger services. The major problem was that crime syndicates have more money to spend on advances in the development of weapons, technology, and corruption in order to be one step ahead of the park rangers. Crime syndicates also have more free cash flow to pay top dollar for informants. Therefore, rhino poaching had resulted in a completely unsustainable requirement by park management to try and resolve a problem, which arises outside the boundaries of the park, and where they have no mandate to operate. Without dealing a significant blow to organized crime and providing real economic opportunities to communities living next to the park the onslaught was unlikely to decrease.

EXHIBIT 6 Map of Kruger National Park

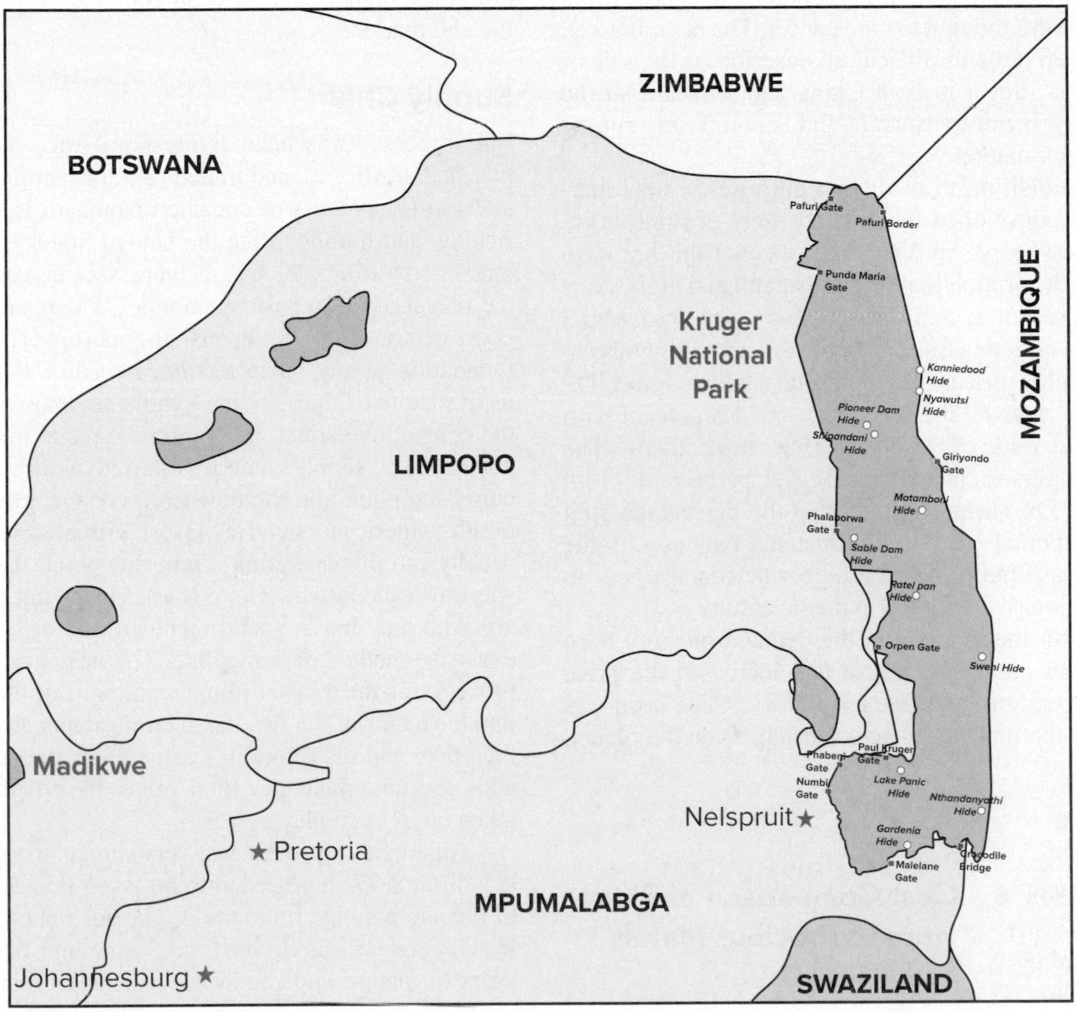

ZIMBABWE
BOTSWANA
Kruger National Park
MOZAMBIQUE
LIMPOPO
Madikwe
Pretoria
Nelspruit
MPUMALABGA
Johannesburg
SWAZILAND
Pafuri Gate
Pafuri Border
Punda Maria Gate
Kanniedood Hide
Nyawutsi Hide
Pioneer Dam Hide
Shipandani Hide
Giriyondo Gate
Matambeni Hide
Phalaborwa Gate
Sable Dam Hide
Ratel pan Hide
Orpen Gate
Sweni Hide
Paul Kruger Gate
Phabeni Gate
Numbi Gate
Lake Panic Hide
Nthandanyathi Hide
Gardenia Hide
Malelane Gate
Crocodile Bridge

Source: © SANParks.org 2004–2011.

EXHIBIT 7 Rhino within Kruger National Park

Major Uses of the Horn

The major use of rhino horns from the end user's perspective was for carvings, recreational purposes, and traditional medicinal purposes. Although it has not been proven to have actual benefit, the horn is ground into a powder and used in a number of traditional medicinal mixes to cure all kinds of diseases.

The irony is that the horn consisted of keratin, which is the same structural protein found in human hair and nails. The demand in the past few years had increased in Asian countries. The most significant areas of use were in China and Vietnam. China's medicinal use of horns dates back centuries for curing ailments including fever, headache, delusions, and nausea. In Vietnam, the powder is inhaled through the nostrils to relieve pain from overconsumption of alcohol the night before. Recently, rhino horns were thought to cure cancer. The main market, however, remains difficult to describe, as the sale of horns is illegal in both China and Vietnam so the industry is not transparent and is completely run by the black market.

In addition to medicinal purposes, a new market had developed for the end users of rhino horn. Businesspeople in Vietnam collected the horns to use as decoration to represent wealth and high status or to present as a gift. These end users bring about a more serious issue with wealth and willingness to pay higher prices. Vietnam and China's real GDP growth rates in 2015 were 6.5 and 6.8 percent with a world rank of 23rd and 19th, respectively. The United States ranked a mere 2.4 percent in 114th place.[5] Dr. Hofmeyr suggested the percentage split of medicinal versus wealth/status end use of the horn was unknown, but a bigger percentage goes to recreational rather than to medicinal use.

With the increase in the demand of rhino horn in Asian countries, it also had increased the price for the end product (see Exhibit 8). Rhino horn was one of the most expensive substances on the planet.

EXHIBIT 8 Cost Comparison of Rhino Horn to Precious Metals and Illegal Drugs

Precious Metal or Drug	Price per Kilogram
Gold Spot*	$41,438.78
Silver Spot*	556.84
Platinum Spot*	31,023.14
Heroin Wholesale	33,689.00
Cocaine Wholesale	48,885.00
Rhino Horn	~80,000

*Represents the spot rate for the precious metals on June 17, 2016, from Bloomberg Markets.

Note: 1 Kg = 2.2 lb.

Sources: www.bloomberg.com/markets/commodities/futures/metals; US Office of National Drug Control Policy, 2010, www.unodc.org/unodc/secured/wdr/Cocaine_Heroin_Prices.pdf.

The declining rhino population had left only a limited supply that will continue to drive the price per horn even higher than ~U.S.$80,000 per kilogram at the end market.

Supply Chain

The process in which rhino horn was illegally poached, trafficked, and traded can draw similar parallels to the process of cocaine manufacturing, trafficking, and trading. Take the United States cocaine market, for example, where there was demand for the illegal drug. In basic economics, a demand for a good without a supply opens an opportunity for the foundation of any business. Since cocaine is illegal in the United States, crime syndicates must run in the competitive arena with high margins to meet the demand. The supply chain was started by turning the cultivated plant into the powdered cocaine grown in South American countries. Host crime syndicates usually run this operation. From this point, the drug was trafficked into the United States by an intermediary who may pay a government official or have an exclusive method of smuggling. The next step in the process was the transfer of mass amounts of the drug into the hands of the American crime syndicates who then take and distribute it. Each step in the process adds a premium to the final price due to the risk taken on by each player.

Although the process was very similar, there were key differences that needed to be taken into account in the international rhino trade. The coca plant, from which cocaine was derived, takes one and one half years to mature and produce, whereas reproduction for rhino was much longer and slower; rhino cows have calves every 2–3 years. The time for the calf to mature depends on the sex; males take 8–10 years and females 4–5 years.[6] Rhino rarely become ill except when they are very stressed or injured. Rhino remain at the bottom of the large mammal list in carrying diseases. They have very few natural enemies (except when they are calves when predators do kill a small percentage). This is also the reason they were so easily poached as they have not evolved fast enough to be frightened of humans, who had little impact on them until rifles and bullets became available.

A Day in the Life of a Villager

The country to the east of South Africa also had land bordering Kruger National Park: Mozambique.

The borders of Mozambique along the park boundary were major hot spots for crime syndicates to recruit villagers to kill rhino and retrieve the horns. These villagers survive on a very small annual income. Around 52 percent of the Mozambique population was below the poverty line. Mozambique's gross national income per capita was U.S.$600.[7] The majority of the labor force, approximately 81 percent, was in the agriculture industry (subsistence farming). The crime syndicates went into these villages to hire teams to find and kill the rhino. The syndicates paid the person who shot the rhino U.S.$25,000 and the person who carried the horn U.S.$8,000 (see Exhibit 9). The villagers' choice was already made when it came to the deciding factors in their standard of living. They were extremely poor and needed to provide for their family. When the horn was delivered to the crime syndicates, the teams were paid in full with cash. It would be difficult to do otherwise when faced with no other real economic prospects to improve their livelihoods. The risks were high as poachers were killed during contacts with rangers, but the rewards were so enticing and large that even the fear of death was not enough to keep them out of the park.

Organization of the Crime Syndicates

Crime syndicates were a highly complex structure with multiple levels of a centralized management. Criminals whose sole business operation was in the illegal market of drug trafficking, arms trafficking, and human trafficking ran these enterprises. The issue of rhino poaching had now reached such criminal proportions that the South African government had classified it a serious economic crime due to the loss of natural heritage and the large amount of illicit cash involved with the poaching syndicates. There were, unfortunately, insufficient resources (funds and human capital) to effectively combat all the crime issues in South Africa and often rhino poaching cases were handled by a few dedicated but overworked investigators and prosecutors.

EXHIBIT 9 Rhino after Horn Had Been Removed by Poachers

© A. J. Strickland

Potential Options Available

The issue was how to slow down or stop the illegal trade of rhino horn from taking place. Recent researchers have concluded there were potential options available but not limited to the following:

Farming Rhino Farming rhino were easy to protect because they were in a small area that can be well managed, similar to cattle feedlots. They were easier to secure far away from international borders due to the distance poachers had to travel from other countries. It was, however, very costly and could only be managed by wealthy farmers. It also does not add major value to the conservation of free-range wild rhino. Farmers who were engaged in the effort hoped that rhino horns will one day be legally traded as the income generated (a horn can be harvested every three to five years) will offset the security costs of protecting, feeding and managing the rhino. Rhino horn trade, however, was regulated by the CITES convention and was currently not allowed. The latest CITES convention where this issue was debated was in September 2016 in South Africa. There were significant interest groups who do not believe that it will be possible to trade horn and protect them so the chances of it being approved were very slim (M. Hofmeyr per opinion).

Demand Reduction The regions of Asia where rhino horns were most heavily used were China and Vietnam. There was increased pressure to inform the populations of these areas that the purchase of rhino horn and powder had a direct effect on the declining rhino population. This was easier said than done. Cigarettes are a good example. The use of cigarettes was widely linked to health issues and still people continue to smoke tobacco. In China, the use of rhino horn was mainly medicinal to cure fever, headaches, delusions, nausea, and even cancer. Reversing a culture's opinions on a specific issue takes time. Regretfully, attempting to put pressure on the Chinese and Vietnamese governments has not proven successful so far. There were, however, a great number of NGOs who were taking up the challenge and in the long-term this will decrease the value and make it unprofitable to poach rhino.

Developing Fake Horn Increasing the supply of synthetic horn in Asia, in theory, would reduce the demand of wild rhino horn illegally traded from Africa. In turn, having a sufficient share of the market with synthetic horn could drive the price of the real horn to all-time highs. One problem with a fake horn was how to differentiate between the two. Several companies have been able to replicate rhino horn in a lab. The synthetic horns have the same chemical breakdown.

Dehorning If you were able to remove the horn, the demand to kill rhino would reduce. However, removing all the rhino horns would be costly and would take at least four years to complete. The horn that remains had a certain weight and with current prices was still incentive enough to poach the rhino.

Collaring

Capture event: U.S.$300–$500 depending on the helicopter flight time

Satellite unit: U.S.$2,500–$3,000 lasting only 18 months

RFID chip: Would work well with a base station in small areas

The investment of U.S.$100,000 was too risky because of yearly maintenance.

Technology placed on rhino had a risky outcome as it often only detected or alerted when the rhino was already dead. It is critical to use technology to prevent the poacher from getting to the rhino—the ultimate goal must be to reduce rhino killed.

Investing in Intelligence The crime syndicates were always one-step ahead of the park rangers. It was believed that the syndicates have compromised rangers to get information. This information may be the specific location of the rhino or what area the rangers were watching. The information does not stop there; it goes higher up to government officials. The information could also contain the strategies the park and government have in order to stop the trade and poaching of the rhino. Stopping the outflow of information would be a great help in capturing the boss/head of the operations, although identifying the workers/sellers will provide an easier start. Actionable intelligence to prevent poachers getting to rhino and preemptively arresting them will be a worthwhile return on investment.

Investing in the People Promoting the long-term care of the park makes local stakeholders proud of their homeland and park. Civil society needs to be behind the park to ensure public support. Investing in stakeholder engagement, community development, and leveraging opportunities to improve livelihoods and service delivery in neighboring areas will assist with community attitude and support for the park, making it more difficult for criminal syndicates to establish themselves in surrounding communities. Without local community support, no long-term solution will be found for the poaching problem.

Attaining the Help of Developed Countries The ability to leverage developed countries' resources to stop the trafficking is essential. These abilities include tracing the cash flow through the United States and international banks. Banks can get involved by freezing withdrawals of large amounts of cash before it reaches the hands of crime syndicates which would slow down their operations. Rhino killing was more than a poaching issue—it was a serious economic and crime issue. Developed countries have the possibility to play a pivotal role in stopping the poaching of rhinos.

Dr. Hofmeyr's Decision

As head of Veterinary Wildlife Services for SANParks, Dr. Hofmeyr's primary responsibility was to support SANParks management through the delivery of a professional service related to capture, translocation, and veterinary care in support of conservation of all the species that live in the 19 parks in South Africa. Rhino poaching, while a huge concern due to the loss of the rhino, will not be stopped inside the parks without government assistance to combat the economic and criminal syndicate crime outside the parks.

As Dr. Hofmeyr was preparing his next year's budget, the question was how much more of his budget could be diverted from conversation to anti-poaching activities. The issue was how to combat rhino poaching when he was spending a large percentage of his time and budget on rhino management related activities, knowing that the percentage of his budget would continue to increase, which meant less attention to other key wildlife management requirements. Or, should he utilize one of the other options for dealing with the rhino management and crime activities? The neglect of other conservation management actions within the park would result in a never-ending spiral of problems for SANParks into the future. Action must be taken swiftly and efficiently before it was too late.

If this issue was not dealt with quickly, looking at solutions that are different from the current ones applied, it would threaten the entire rhino population, which would affect the core business of SANParks and impact on stakeholders across the world.

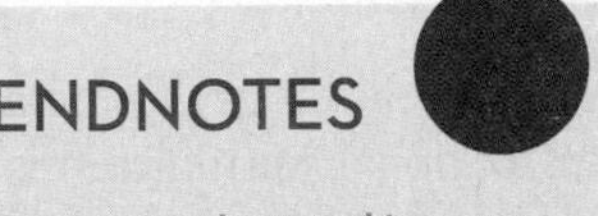

ENDNOTES

[1] news.nationalgeographic.com/2016/01/160121-rhino-poaching-statistics-South-Africa-trade-lawsuit/.
[2] www.savetherhino.org/rhino_info/poaching_statistics.
[3] www.iucn.org/content/iucn-reports-deepening-rhino-poaching-crisis-africa.
[4] S. M. Ferreira, C. Greaver, G. A. Knight, M. H. Knight, I. P. J. Smit, and D. Pienaar, "Disruption of Rhino Demography by Poachers May Lead to Population Declines in Kruger National Park, South Africa," PLoS ONE 10, no. 6 (2015), p. e0127783. doi:10.1371/journal.pone.012778.
[5] www.cia.gov/library/publications/the-world-factbook/rankorder/2003rank.html#ch.
[6] rhinos.org/state-of-the-rhino/.
[7] www.cia.gov/library/publications/resources/the-world-factbook/geos/mz.html.

CASE 31

Conflict Palm Oil and PepsiCo's Ethical Dilemma

Syeda Maseeha Qumer
IBS Hyderabad

Debapratim Purkayastha
IBS Hyderabad

In September 2015, US-based consumer food giant, PepsiCo Inc. (PepsiCo), was dropped from the annual Dow Jones Sustainability Indices (DJSI)[1] as, according to some reports, the company's sustainability performance had failed to make the grade. PepsiCo was singled out by a number of environmental groups for its continued use of large quantities of Conflict Palm Oil,[2] the production of which was responsible for large-scale destruction of rainforests, human rights violations, and climate pollution in tropical countries like Indonesia where palm oil was produced. The groups criticized PepsiCo for not having a robust sustainable palm oil policy and for not acknowledging the damage its supply chain had caused in countries such as Indonesia and Malaysia. According to an international environmental and human rights organization, the Rainforest Action Network (RAN), *"What Pepsi does has a huge impact on the climate, the rainforests of Southeast Asia, and the people and animals that rely on these forests for their lives and livelihoods. The company is a major Conflict Palm Oil laggard. It is dragging its feet and is refusing to admit it even has a problem. It could rise above its competitors and do the right thing, but, instead, it has relied on half measures and a commitment with gaps big enough to drive a bulldozer through."*[3]

Palm oil obtained from the fruit of the oil palm tree and the most widely used vegetable oil in the world, went into the processing of a wide array of food and non-food products. Over the years, the demand for palm oil had increased sharply as it was one of the cheapest vegetable oils on the global market with no trans fats. The rising demand led to large-scale deforestation across South East Asia with rainforests being cleared to make way for palm oil plantations. This added to global warming emissions and resulted in a shrinking of the habitat of many already threatened species.

On the heels of a wave of zero deforestation commitments from other consumer products companies, PepsiCo committed through the Roundtable for Sustainable Palm Oil[4] (RSPO) in 2010 to source exclusively 100% RSPO certified sustainable palm oil by 2015.

Conflict Palm Oil posed an ethical dilemma for PepsiCo which bought approximately 470,045 metric tonnes of palm oil annually, making the company the biggest purchaser of palm oil worldwide.[5] Several environmental groups criticized PepsiCo for selling its popular products like Doritos and Lays, which were not covered by the commitment to use responsible palm oil, at the expense of the environment. PepsiCo was one of the "Snack Food 20"[6] group of companies targeted by RAN's Conflict Palm Oil campaign for its inadequate palm oil policy. The group repeatedly called on PepsiCo's CEO Indra Nooyi (Nooyi) to go on record about her company's continued use of palm oil. According to RAN, PepsiCo's commitment to sourcing sustainable palm oil was weak and it should adopt and implement a responsible palm oil procurement policy. With mounting pressure, PepsiCo announced a new Forest Stewardship Policy and Palm Oil Commitment in May 2014. Though in the new policy PepsiCo included measures which it claimed went beyond RSPO standards, it failed to guarantee that its entire supply chain would be free from deforestation and social conflict. Meanwhile, several campaigns were launched by environmental activists that targeted specific brands of PepsiCo over the palm oil issue making it a PR nightmare for the company.

Following months of protests from several environmental groups, PepsiCo came out with a revamped palm oil commitment in September 2015. Though the new commitment identified the company's sources of palm all the way back to the plantation and addressed workers' rights, it did not cover any joint venture in which PepsiCo had a minority stake. Environmental groups were disappointed with the changes in the new commitment and said PepsiCo continued to fail to take responsibility for the impact of its products sold globally. Given the size and impact of its business, PepsiCo was expected to play a huge role in the problematic global production of Conflict Palm Oil. PepsiCo, however, insisted that its policy was strong enough. But criticism of the company grew more strident and PepsiCo was projected as a "Conflict Palm Oil laggard." This put the brands and corporate reputation of PepsiCo at serious risk. According to Ginger Cassady, Forest Program Director at RAN, *"Reforming the palm oil sector is not an easy task. Real change will only be achieved if PepsiCo invests the time and resources to implement innovative solutions that address the depth, scope, and urgency of the problems currently caused by palm oil production in its supply chain. My question for you Ms. Nooyi is will PepsiCo commit to necessary revisions to its policies, and invest the resources needed to eliminate Conflict Palm Oil from the global palm oil supply chain?"*[7]

ABOUT PEPSICO

PepsiCo, headquartered in Purchase, New York, USA, was a global food and beverage company. Its products are sold in more than 200 countries and territories around the world. Its portfolio included 22 brands that each generated more than $1 billion in estimated annual retail sales. For the year 2014, PepsiCo had total revenues of $66.68 billion and net profit of $6.51 billion (see Exhibit 1).

The origins of PepsiCo date back to the late 19th century when a young pharmacist Caleb Bradham (Bradham) started selling a refreshing drink called "Brad's Drink" in his pharmacy. The drink was later renamed Pepsi-Cola, and went on to become a key challenger to rival brand Coca-Cola. In 1965, Pepsi-Cola merged with Frito-Lay[8] to form PepsiCo Inc. In the subsequent years, the company reshaped its portfolio, built new capabilities, invested in new geographies, and went on to become a key player in the global beverage market along with the Coca-Cola Company (Coca-Cola).

In the new millennium, PepsiCo decided to focus on its packaged foods business to effectively compete with Coca-Cola. It also acquired Tropicana, the world's biggest producer of branded juices, in July 1998. Other steps taken by PepsiCo included hiving-off its bottling operations into a separate new company called the Pepsi Bottling Group (PBG). The company's restructuring efforts paid off and its operating profits rose from $ 2.58 billion for the year 1998 to $ 3.23 billion in 2000. In December 2005, PepsiCo overtook Coca-Cola in market capitalization for the first time as its market value reached $98.4 billion, compared with $97.9 billion for Coca-Cola. Analysts attributed the company's growth to a diversified product portfolio and a strong marketing strategy.

EXHIBIT 1 Financial Summary for PepsiCo, Inc. 2011–2014 (in billions of $)

	2014	2013	2012	2011
Total Revenue	$66.68	$66.42	$65.49	$66.50
Gross Profit	35.80	35.17	34.20	34.91
Operating Income	9.58	9.71	9.11	9.63
Net Income	6.51	6.74	6.18	6.44

Source: www.nasdaq.com/symbol/pep/financials?query=income-statement#ixzz3syQYQ7ED.

As of 2014, PepsiCo was one of the world's leading food and beverage companies that marketed, distributed, and sold a wide variety of beverages, foods, and snacks to customers in more than 200 countries. The company owned a global portfolio of diverse brands, and of them, 22, including Pepsi, Lays, Quaker, Tropicana, Aquafina, and Gatorade, generated more than $1 billion each in annual retail sales. The company operated through six segments—Frito-Lay North America (FLNA), Quaker Foods North America (QFNA), Latin America Foods (LAF), PepsiCo Americas Beverages (PAB), PepsiCo Europe (Europe), and PepsiCo Asia, Middle East and Africa (AMEA). In 2014, the company generated more than $66 billion in revenues.

However, the growth in the company's business led to more controversies dogging its operations. The company faced criticism from environmentalists regarding the effect of its operations on the environment. Its beverage products were packed in plastic bottles and tin cans, which the environmental activists alleged, could cause environmental pollution. The company was also criticized for the contents in its snack and beverage products, which were blamed for leading to an increase in health problems like obesity and diabetes.

In the face of growing criticism, PepsiCo started to focus more on sustainable development practices worldwide. It started a new sustainable development program in 2009 with a five-year mission "Performance with Purpose."

"Performance with Purpose"

Faced with environmental and social criticism, in 2009, PepsiCo started an ambitious new sustainable development program called "Performance with Purpose" under the leadership of Nooyi, who took charge as CEO in 2006. India-born Nooyi was a graduate of Madras Christian College in Chemistry, Physics, and Mathematics, a management graduate from the Indian Institute of Management, Calcutta, and Master's in Public and Private Management from Yale. After stints with companies such as ABB, Johnson and Johnson, and Management consulting firm, Boston Consulting Group, she joined PepsiCo as the chief strategist in 1994. She served as the Senior Vice-President of Strategic Planning and Development and Chief Financial Officer of PepsiCo before becoming the CEO.

The "Performance with Purpose" mission was based on the belief that the financial performance of the organization must go hand-in-hand with its responsibilities toward society and the environment. The declaration by PepsiCo called the "The Promise of PepsiCo" had 47 commitments which were to guide the organization over the following decade. The "Performance with Purpose" contained both promises made to its shareholders for providing good financial returns and the promises made toward the society and environment. In its promise to shareholders viz. "Performance," PepsiCo vowed to deliver superior and sustainable financial performance, to maximize their wealth. PepsiCo's responsibilities toward the society and the environment were broadly categorized into three areas viz. Human Sustainability, Environmental Sustainability, and Talent Sustainability.

Human sustainability referred to the efforts put in by PepsiCo to meet the different nutritional needs of the people. Environmental sustainability focused on protecting the environment and reducing PepsiCo's reliance on natural resources and conserving them for future generations. It also focused on mitigating the impact of its operations on the environment. Talent sustainability focused on developing its employees by building the skills required to meet its growth needs and making PepsiCo an attractive target for the world's best brains. Commenting on PepsiCo's initiatives in sustainable development, Nooyi said, *"The talents and skills of our global workforce, coupled with our operational capabilities, provide PepsiCo with a unique opportunity to have a positive impact on society. The goal of our sustainable development journey is to operate as a force for bringing greater good to the world."*[9]

Under its environmental sustainability initiatives, PepsiCo promised to be a good citizen of the world committed to protecting natural resources by proper use of land, energy, and packaging in its operations. For the company, a large part of its sustainability efforts involved reducing the negative effects resulting from the production and consumption of its products. This included "going green" through water conservation and the reduction of waste products and reducing its carbon footprint. PepsiCo committed to increasing its water use efficiency by 20% by 2015. In view of the protests that it was facing in countries like India regarding its water use practices, it promised to strive for a positive water balance in its operations where water was scarce. It also promised to use more recycled material in its packaging operations to reduce environmental damage. PepsiCo committed to counter climate change by improving electricity use efficiency by 20% by 2015, reducing the fuel used by 25% by 2015, reducing the greenhouse gas (GHG) emissions from its operations, and applying on its farmed lands agricultural practices that had proved to be sustainable.

PepsiCo's focus and the progress it had made on sustainable development gave it good results, according to analysts. In recognition of the progress it had made till then on sustainable development, PepsiCo was named as the top food and beverage company in the DJSI Food and Beverage Super sector and included in the Dow Jones Sustainability Indexes for the year 2011.[10] PepsiCo was the only company based in the US to earn the top ranking in the 19 super sectors assessed. It was the third consecutive year that PepsiCo had been named as the leader in the beverage sector. However, PepsiCo's successes on sustainable development didn't make it impervious to controversy. Some environmental activist groups continued to criticize its practices.

PALM OIL AND RAINFORESTS

Palm oil, obtained from the fruit of the oil palm tree (Botanical name *Elaeis guineensis*), was the most widely used vegetable oil in the world and went into the processing of a wide array of food products including cookies, chocolates, peanut butter, crackers, breakfast bars, potato chips, instant noodles, baby formula, margarine, and dry and canned soups. Its non-food uses were in detergents, soaps, personal care products, and as a feedstock for biofuels. The palm tree, native to Western Africa, was grown mostly in the tropics. About 85% of palm oil was sourced from the tropical countries of Indonesia, Malaysia, and Papua New Guinea (PNG) where rainforests mostly occurred (see Exhibit 2).

Over the years, the demand for palm oil had increased sharply as it was one of the cheapest vegetable oils available on the global market with no trans fats. By 2013 the production of palm oil reached nearly 55 million metric tons and surpassed Soya oil to become the world's most widely traded and used edible vegetable oil. In the US, the consumption of palm oil grew rapidly, increasing nearly sixfold since 2000 to reach 1.25 million metric tons in 2012.[11]

However, the rising demand for palm oil led to large-scale deforestation across Southeast Asia (see Exhibit 3). Rainforests were cleared to make way for palm oil plantations in nations with large tropical forests such as Indonesia and Malaysia. This severely impacted the environment and the local communities and led to the destruction of carbon-rich forests and peatlands.[12] The large-scale oil palm expansion between 1990 and 2010 resulted in direct forest loss of about 3.5 million hectares in total in Indonesia, Malaysia, and PNG. In 2009, the Indonesian government announced plans to allocate approximately 18 million more hectares of rainforests for palm oil cultivation.[13]

EXHIBIT 2 Global Demand for Vegetable Oil, 2002–2016

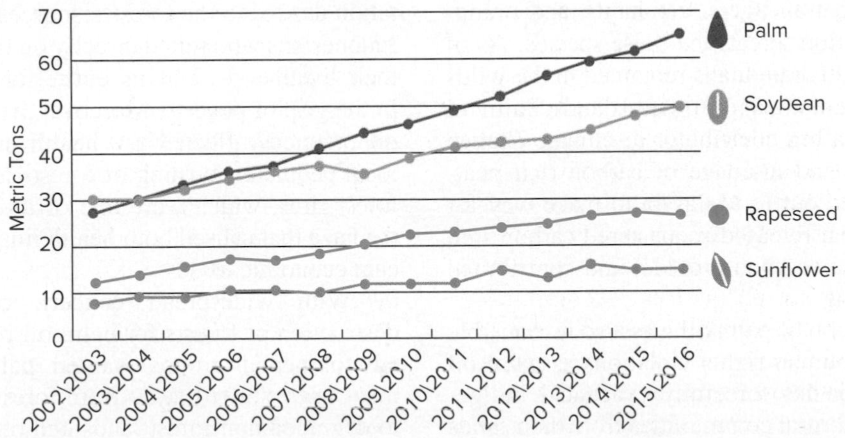

Source: *Oilseeds—World Markets and Trade*, USDA, June 2015.

EXHIBIT 3 Palm Oil Supply Chain

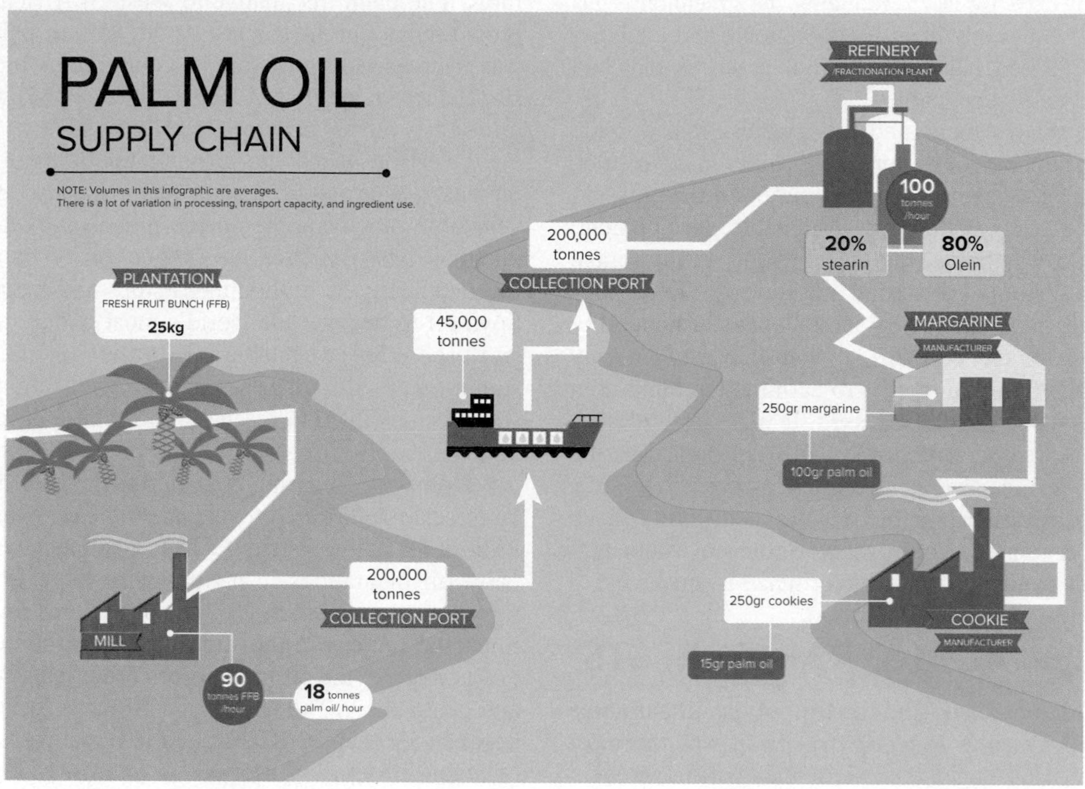

Source: **www.rspo.org/certification/how-rspo-certification-works.**

Tropical rainforests covered about 7% of the earth's surface and were vital to the ecosystem as they nurtured about 50% of the world's plants and animals. Indonesia's tropical rainforests provided a critical habitat to species including the highly endangered Sumatran tigers, elephants, and orangutans. Deforestation threatened these species. As of 2014, only 60,600 orangutans remained in the wilds of Indonesia's Sumatra and Borneo islands. Palm oil production was a big contributor to climate change as deforestation and drainage of carbon rich peatlands was carried out in Malaysia to make way for palm oil trees that released sequestered carbon into the atmosphere as carbon dioxide, and contributed to global warming.

The production of palm oil was also responsible for widespread human rights violations as palm oil producing companies forcefully evacuated indigenous peoples and rural communities from their lands and pushed them into forced and child labor. Rural communities in Indonesia, Malaysia, PNG, Liberia, Cameroon, Latin America, and other rainforest regions often faced threats to their security and derived marginal economic benefits by the expansion of palm oil production. A single palm oil plantation destroyed the forest resources of thousands of Indonesians who relied directly on the rainforests for their livelihoods, leaving entire forest communities in the grip of poverty. Moreover, irresponsible palm oil practices affected the health and wellbeing of local people as burning of forests led to large-scale forest fires, which were one of the main causes of the haze that caused both health impacts and significant economic losses.

With widespread concern over large-scale destruction of forests for palm oil production, some environmental groups wanted palm oil development to be shifted away from forests and peatlands to degraded non-forest lands and other areas. These groups put pressure on major palm oil companies to move new plantations away from forest lands and adopt better labor standards.

Round Table on Sustainable Palm Oil (RSPO)

In an effort to stop the tide of criticism against rainforest destruction and to get the sector to move toward sustainable palm oil, the global palm oil industry created the Round Table on Sustainable Palm Oil (RSPO) in 2004. The aim of RSPO was to promote the growth and use of sustainable palm oil. It was a not-for-profit group that united stakeholders from seven sectors of the palm oil industry comprising palm oil producers, processors or traders, consumer goods manufacturers, retailers, banks/investors, and environmental and social non-governmental organizations (NGOs), committed to produce, source, or use sustainable palm oil certified by the RSPO. As of 2015, RSPO had more than 1,700 members worldwide.

RSPO developed a set of environmental and social criteria which companies had to comply with in order to produce Certified Sustainable Palm Oil (CSPO). Palm oil producers were certified after accredited certifying bodies carried out a strict verification of the production process in accordance with RSPO principles and criteria for sustainable palm oil production. All companies in the supply chain that used RSPO certified sustainable oil products were audited to prevent overselling and mixing palm oil with non-sustainable palm oil products. In case of infringement of the rules and standards, their certificates could be withdrawn at any time.

With mounting pressure from green groups, many companies began to make public commitments of their own to use deforestation-free palm oil in their products. Nestlé S.A and Unilever were two of the first consumer packaged food companies to make deforestation free palm oil commitments. Following this, PepsiCo too committed, through the RSPO, to source exclusively 100% RSPO certified sustainable palm oil for its products by 2015. In 2013, it further strengthened this commitment to purchase 100% Physical RSPO certified palm oil by 2020, giving additional visibility to its palm oil supply chain. However, PepsiCo which used huge amounts of palm oil annually in its products was accused of lagging behind in its efforts to source sustainable palm oil. In 2014, the company purchased approximately 470,045 metric tons of palm oil, which represented approximately 0.7% of the total global supply, for its snack foods.[14] It was alleged that PepsiCo's products were made using palm oil grown in Indonesia by some of the companies associated with the destruction of rainforests.

Rainforest Action Network (RAN)

RAN, a prominent environmental NGO based in San Francisco, California, had been working to protect rainforests and the human rights of those living in and around those forests. Established in 1985, the organization's mission was to *"campaign for the forests, their inhabitants, and the natural systems that sustain life by transforming the global marketplace through education, grassroots organizing, and non-violent direct action."*[15] RAN played a key role in strengthening the rainforest conservation movement globally by supporting activists in rainforest countries as well as mobilizing consumers and community action groups through media campaigns, conferences, and publications.

With Conflict Palm Oil being one of the world's leading causes of rainforest destruction and a major driver of human induced climate change, RAN put pressure on some well-known food companies in the world to get Conflict Palm Oil off the shelves. In September 2013, RAN launched a campaign called "Conflict Palm Oil" to eliminate deforestation, human rights violations, and carbon pollution from the palm oil supply chains of US snack food companies. As part of the campaign, RAN identified 20 major global food manufacturing companies using Conflict Palm Oil. These included PepsiCo, Heinz, Hershey's, Kraft, and Smuckers. RAN felt that these companies, which it dubbed as the "Snack Food 20," had the power to get involved with their global supply chains to transform the way palm oil was traded and produced if they each adopted strong policies with clear public commitments and time-bound implementation plans. According to RAN, the implementation of responsible palm oil policies by the "Snack Food 20" companies would increase the demand for sustainable palm oil and drive a transition to transparent and traceable palm oil supply chains.

To make these major food companies commit to using only traceable palm oil, RAN launched another national campaign called *"The Last Stand of the Orangutan: The Power Is in Your Palm."* As part of the campaign, several RAN supporters wore orangutan masks and held signs displaying the logos of the Snack Food 20 companies and banners reading, *"Cut Conflict Palm Oil, Not Rainforests."* Lindsey Allen, executive director of RAN, said, *"In the 21st century, customers don't want to buy crackers and cookies that are responsible for pushing the world's last wild orangutans to extinction and for horrifying child labor violations. That's why Rainforest Action Network is putting these top 20 snack food companies using 'conflict palm oil' on notice."*[16]

RAN singled out PepsiCo as a major Conflict Palm Oil laggard on the "Snack Food 20" list as it had failed to put adequate policies and procurement practices in place, and was almost unquestionably using Conflict Palm Oil. Despite being the world's largest globally distributed snack food company and using a whopping 457,200 metric tons of palm oil annually in snacks like Quaker Chewy Granola Bars, Cheetos, and Lay's potato chips, PepsiCo was dragging its feet, refusing to even admit to the problem, said RAN. According to Gemma Tillack (Tillack), Senior Agribusiness Campaigner of RAN, *"The only thing standing in the way of PepsiCo doing the right thing and taking a leadership position on this urgent issue is the company's refusal to act. PepsiCo's continued unwillingness to take responsibility for the consequences of the palm oil in its supply chain is shocking. While more and more of its peers have acknowledged the crisis created by Conflict Palm Oil production and engaged with experts like us to adopt binding policies to root out the problem, PepsiCo continues to fry its chips and fill its products with palm oil sourced from unknown plantations."*[17]

According to RAN, PepsiCo had a weak palm commitment that lacked a time-bound implementation plan to cut out Conflict Palm Oil. RAN felt that the RSPO certified palm oil certificates that were awarded to companies for sustainable palm oil production by no means guaranteed that all of their palm oil was being procured from sustainable sources. Though the RSPO provided criteria for CSPO and offered certification, its standard did not adequately address the risks of purchasing palm oil associated with deforestation and human rights violations, the group added. As a result, palm oil certified by the RSPO while being more sustainable than conventional palm oil, was not deforestation free. RAN urged PepsiCo to go beyond RSPO-certified palm oil and adopt a new global responsible palm oil procurement policy and implementation plan to ensure that the palm oil in its supply chain was fully traceable, legally grown, and sourced from verified responsible palm oil producers.

RAN pointed out to the reputational risk PepsiCo ran by sourcing Conflict Palm Oil. As more consumers become aware of the dangers of palm oil production, PepsiCo had to break its ties to the drastic deforestation and shocking human rights violations in its supply chain, especially in Indonesia and Malaysia, where the risks of destroying critical rainforest and continued human rights abuses were extremely high, it said (see Exhibit 4). RAN even offered to work with the company to find solutions and draft a comprehensive, time bound responsible palm oil policy. *"Palm oil is found in nearly 50 percent of the packaged foods on our grocery store shelves, and tragically it is also the leading cause of orangutan extinction and rainforest destruction in Indonesia and Malaysia. PepsiCo and the Snack Food 20 can and must solve their problem with Conflict Palm Oil before it's too late for the great red ape,"*[18] said Tillack.

However, PepsiCo refuted the allegations saying that it was a member of the RSPO, and had committed to purchase exclusively 100% certified sustainable palm oil for PepsiCo products by 2015. The company said it had integrated responsible palm oil procurement guidelines with its sourcing strategies. *"While we are working in a number of regions to convert to oils that are low in saturated fat, in some parts of the world, palm oil is often our only option. When we do purchase palm oil, we look for suppliers that operate responsibly and in a sustainable manner,"*[19] said Aurora Gonzalez, spokesperson of PepsiCo.

PEPSICO'S PALM OIL POLICY

In March 2014, the Union of Concerned Scientists[20] (UCS) released a scorecard grading the palm oil sourcing commitments of 30 top companies in the packaged food, fast food, and personal care sectors including PepsiCo. According to the report, PepsiCo, with a score of 33.7 points out of 100, had demonstrated "little commitment" to procuring palm oil from deforestation-free sources. Environmentalists demanded that PepsiCo should look into its palm oil policies and solve the Conflict Palm Oil problem.

Following this, PepsiCo adopted a new Forestry Stewardship Policy and Palm Oil Specific Commitment in May 2014, saying that it was an improvement over its 2010 and 2013 pledges which were limited to using palm oil certified under the RSPO

EXHIBIT 4 Link between Consumers and Rainforest Destruction

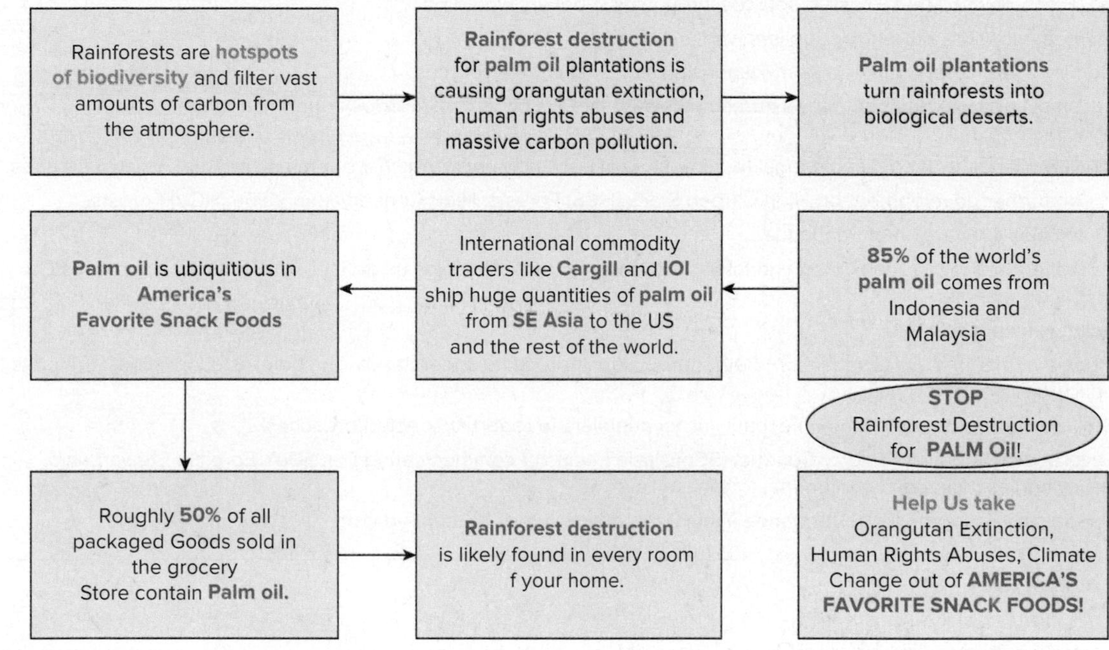

Source: www.ran.org.

(see Exhibit 5). In its new policy, PepsiCo committed to contributing to the promotion of responsible and sustainable sources of palm oil and realizing zero deforestation in company-owned and operated activities and supply chain by 2020. As per the new policy, the tons of palm oil sourced annually by PepsiCo would largely be free of deforestation and peatlands conversion by 2016. Through its new commitment, the company planned to partner with the RSPO and other trade associations, government agencies, non-governmental organizations, and other critical external stakeholders to usher in positive changes and improvements in the palm oil supply chain and industry. Analysts felt that the adoption of these commitments was a vital first step as it validated PepsiCo's commitment to set a higher standard than required by the RSPO. The new policy stated: *"As outlined in PepsiCo's Forestry Stewardship Policy, PepsiCo is committed to doing business the right way and to realizing zero deforestation in our company-owned and -operated activities and supply chain. We recognize that PepsiCo has a responsibility to ensure that we and our suppliers operate in accordance with applicable legal requirements and practice responsible forestry stewardship. PepsiCo is opposed to illegal or irresponsible deforestation practices. While we are committed to the RSPO and its process and standards, we recognize that in some regions of the world, additional measures may be necessary."*[21]

Following through on its 2010 commitment, the company planned to source palm oil only through direct suppliers who were also members of RSPO. It planned to collaborate with governments and NGOs to monitor its suppliers for compliance with its Forestry Stewardship and Land Use Policies, in order to reach 100% traceability and accountability to the mill level by 2016 and to the farm/plantation level by 2020. Moreover, PepsiCo planned to support sustainable agriculture practices through the PepsiCo Sustainable Farming Initiative. Workers would be encouraged to report grievances, violations, and policy breaches through PepsiCo's SpeakUp! hotline and website. The commitment also included specific provisions on no conversion of high carbon stock forests and high conservation value areas or peatlands. It wanted suppliers to adhere to free, prior, and informed consent (FPIC) in interacting with local communities around new plantation development.

EXHIBIT 5 PepsiCo Palm Oil Commitment (May 2014)

By 2016, the palm oil that PepsiCo sources through its suppliers would be:

- Sourced exclusively through suppliers who are members of the RSPO.
- Confirmed to have originated from responsible and sustainable sources.
- In compliance with the company's Forestry Stewardship Policy, which includes adherence to the following principles:
  - ✓ Compliance with applicable legal requirements of each country in which it operates and from which it sources.
  - ✓ No further development on High Carbon Stock (HCS) Forests, High Conservation Value (HCV) Forests.
  - ✓ No new conversion of Peatlands.
  - ✓ Adherence to the Free, Prior, and Informed Consent (FPIC) principles as defined and outlined in the PepsiCo Land Use Policy.

In addition, PepsiCo would:

- Engage with appropriate industry and other groups to improve its understanding of deforestation issues, adapt its policy, and achieve goals.
- Provide appropriate grievance mechanisms for suppliers to report suspected breaches.
- Leverage its Supplier Code of Conduct (SCoC) as a means of communicating PepsiCo's Forestry Stewardship Policy and associated commitments to its suppliers.
- Periodically report on its performance against this policy and its associated commitments.

Source: Adapted from **www.pepsico.com**.

PepsiCo: Not Doing Enough?

Some environmental groups such as Greenpeace International[22] (Greenpeace), RAN, SumOfUs.org[23] (SumOfUs), and the UCS expressed concerns over PepsiCo's new commitment. They felt that while PepsiCo had acknowledged the problem related to Conflict Palm Oil, its commitments fell short in several key areas as the sustainability measures adopted in the new action plan were weaker than the ones adopted by its peers in the consumer packaged food industry. According to them, the commitment was at odds with the company's publicly stated values as had not taken any explicit efforts to trace palm oil back to the source, to ensure that it was deforestation-free. In July 2014, the groups sent a joint communication to Nooyi pointing out the gaps in the revised palm oil commitment and the need to fill those gaps in order to drive the needed changes in PepsiCo's global supply chains. *"Palm oil is in many of its products, from Quaker Oats to Grandma's Homestyle cookies, PepsiCo's announcement that it's joining so many other companies in improving how it sources palm oil is excellent news, but it could do more to ensure that it is delivering on its promise,"*[24] said Calen May-Tobin, an analyst with UCS.

According to experts, the new policy lacked a time-bound implementation plan and failed to commit to tracing the company's palm oil to the plantations where the oil palm fruit grew. They said the new commitments lacked independent third party verification of its suppliers' compliance and a strong commitment to full traceability and a prohibition of the use of fire. Moreover, the policy did not lend clear support to small and local producers and failed to outline strong human rights protections for local communities and workers, they added. According to Joao Talocchi, a campaigner at Greenpeace, *"While PepsiCo's announcement includes measures that go beyond the RSPO, such as the protection of high carbon stock forests and all peatlands, it still lacks a strong commitment to full traceability, a demand for similar commitments from its suppliers, and most importantly, an implementation plan. Consumer companies such as P&G, Unilever, and Nestle have already committed to policies that—if fully implemented—will guarantee their products will become free from deforestation. There's no reason PepsiCo can't follow suit."*[25]

Some experts were skeptical about PepsiCo's ability to source responsible palm oil within the aggressive timeframe set by the company in its commitment. According to the new commitment, it would source 100% of its oil from deforestation free sources by 2016. In 2013, PepsiCo had expanded its palm oil commitment to cover 100% physically sourced oil by 2020. Reportedly in 2012–2013, PepsiCo sourced 20% of its oil from RSPO certified sources and in the following year (2013–2014) the number increased to 21%. Experts questioned whether the company would be able to get the remaining 79% of its oil from RSPO certified sources as there was only a year remaining for the company to fulfil its commitment. They said the critical gaps in the commitment must be addressed first before the company set a new global benchmark for responsible palm oil procurement. *"Commitments are just the first step. Pepsi Perfect might look great on a label, but it's what's inside the bottle that counts. When it comes to palm oil, what counts is how commitments translate into action. And that is where some major concerns about PepsiCo's commitment crop up,"*[26] said Calen May-Tobin, a lead analyst with the Tropical Forest and Climate Initiative. Hanna Thomas, senior campaigner at SumofUs, added, *"We hope that PepsiCo will take a look over their policies and the current gaps, and make the decision to be a leader in their industry. It's no good to just do the bare minimum. PepsiCo is such a large company with such a huge amount of purchasing power, they should be out in front and taking the impacts of the snack food industry seriously."*[27]

However, PepsiCo felt it had done enough and said its new palm oil policy was part of a broader 2020 zero deforestation commitment across various commodities.

Consumer Campaigns

On May 20, 2014, a Global Day of Action to Cut Conflict Palm Oil was organized by Palm Oil activists wherein a series of events were held across the world to call on PepsiCo and other companies in the consumer food sector to cut down Conflict Palm Oil from their global product lines. Thousands of people took part in demonstrations around the world as they gathered on college campuses, beaches, public squares, and multiple PepsiCo factories to send a common message: *"PepsiCo, the Power is #InYourPalm to eliminate Conflict Palm Oil."* Also a petition was launched by SumofUs calling on PepsiCo to commit to a zero deforestation policy for palm oil. More than 223,000 people from around the world signed the petition.

In November 2014, PepsiCo pulled out its newly launched drink Pepsi True[28] from online retail site **Amazon.com** after environmental activists and consumers left thousands of negative reviews on the product's page urging the company to adopt better palm oil policies. The product was later reinstated. However, PepsiCo said the outcry was a planned effort to mislead consumers and insisted that its palm policy was strong enough. *"Pepsi True was subject to an orchestrated effort to post inaccurate information about our product and PepsiCo's palm oil policy. A few critics have repeatedly been both inaccurate and misleading about our commitments to traceable, sustainable palm oil. PepsiCo has committed to zero deforestation in our activities and sourcing and to 100% sustainable palm oil by 2015. Our critics would be hard pressed to find many companies who have taken PepsiCo's holistic approach to land policy, forest stewardship. and responsible sourcing,"*[29] said a spokesperson from PepsiCo.

However, environmental activists continued to press PepsiCo to cut Conflict Palm Oil from its supply chain saying that the company could not hide the destruction that it refused to eliminate from its supply chain (refer to Exhibit 6). *"Clearly, any of us who have earned a one-star review would react with consternation, so imagine the teeth grating at PepsiCo headquarters with 3,900 negative reviews rolling in over the weekend. But with companies including Nestlé, Mars, and P&G among the other global firms committing to sustainable palm oil, PepsiCo's tepid policy is making it stand out for the wrong reasons. Its competitors are committing to plans that include transparency, tractability, and full safeguards for human rights. PepsiCo's reputation, especially as consumers become more aware of the dangers of palm oil, would be quickly repaired with a more watertight policy instead of continuing its war of words,"*[30] remarked Leon Kaye, a strategic communications specialist.

On December 9, 2014, RAN and Orangutan Outreach[31] together organized a Global Call-In Day wherein consumers ranged against PepsiCo and pointed out the consequences of its using Conflict Palm Oil. Through this initiative, the environmental groups wanted to expose the threat to the Leuser Ecosystem.[32] A month later, in January 2015, SumOfUs targeted PepsiCo's Doritos snacks by releasing an online ad to coincide with the Doritos "Crash the Super Bowl" competition that invited customers to submit ads for the popular crisps with the winning ad being aired during the Super Bowl. The ad titled *"A Cheesy Love Story—The Ad Doritos Don't Want You to See"* featured a couple falling in love over their common

EXHIBIT 6 Palm Oil Reduction Consumer Campaigns

Source: SumOfUs

Source: Rainforest Action Network

© Sonny Tumbelaka/AFP/Getty Images

Sources: **action.sumofus.org/a/doritos-palm-oil/; redapes.org/orangutan-outreach-ran-join-forces-to-challenge-pepsi/; www.ran.org/the_power_is_in_your_palm; thegreendivas.com/2014/09/05/dear-pepsico-conflict-palm-oil/.**

love for Doritos, getting married, then going off to a honeymoon to a tropical rainforest. But on arrival there, they find the forest had been cut down to plant palm oil trees. Then the tagline appears *"Doritos, May contain traces of rainforest."* The organization felt that the Super Bowl platform could be used to educate consumers the world over about PepsiCo's inadequate palm oil sourcing policy. The ad received more than 1.5 million views on YouTube.

Defending its palm oil policy, PepsiCo said, *"It is no surprise that SumofUs' continual mischaracterizations of our palm oil commitments are patently false and run counter to the positive reception our policies have received from expert organizations in this arena. PepsiCo has repeatedly stated that we are absolutely committed to 100 percent sustainable palm oil in 2015 and to zero deforestation in our activities and sourcing. This latest public relations stunt, focused on fiction rather than facts, does nothing to foster positive dialogue or affect positive change. We find our policies effective and stand by them."*[33]

A day after the launch of the Doritos ad, RAN came up with another ad targeting PepsiCo's popular snack Quaker Oats Chewy Bars. The ad featured the photo of a little boy with his arms crossed in anger, with a box of chewy bars in the background. The tagline of the ad was *"Pepsico, you need a time out!"* The ad conveyed that PepsiCo was acting like a stubborn child—one who wanted all the toys (profits in PepsiCo's case) but no responsibility. Some activists also criticized PepsiCo's #LiveForNow[34] marketing campaign and wondered whether by "living for now," PepsiCo meant it could not care less about tomorrow. They were referring to PepsiCo's weak commitment to using sustainable palm oil.

A Revised Commitment

Following months of protests from several environmental groups over its use of Conflict Palm Oil, PepsiCo released a new palm oil commitment on September 21, 2015 (see Exhibit 7). Through its revamped policy, PepsiCo strengthened its commitment to upholding the rights of local communities and workers and identified the plantations where the palm oil used in its products grew. However, according to experts, the biggest loophole in the commitment was that it did not cover any joint venture in which PepsiCo had a minority stake. The policy did not apply to PepsiCo products made by its Joint Venture Partner (JVP), Indofood Sukses Makmur Tbk (Indofood),[35] in Indonesia.[36] This implied that PepsiCo's products sold in Indonesia were not covered by any zero deforestation commitment.

Indofood Agri Resources Ltd., the palm oil arm of Indofood, was the third largest private palm oil company in Indonesia with an annual revenue of USD 1.2 billion in 2014.[37] The company was involved in

EXHIBIT 7 PepsiCo Palm Oil Commitment (September 2015)

PepsiCo's palm oil sources globally would:

- Be sourced exclusively through direct suppliers who are members of the RSPO.
- Comply with the company's Forestry Stewardship Policy, which includes adherence to the following principles:
  - ✓ Compliance with applicable legal requirements of each country in which it operates and from which it sources.
  - ✓ No further development on High Carbon Stock (HCS) Forests1 or High Conservation Value (HCV) Areas.
  - ✓ No new conversion of any Peatlands and the use of best management practices for existing plantations on Peatlands.
- Adhere to the principle of Free, Prior, and Informed Consent (FPIC)—as defined and outlined in the company's Land Use Policy.
- Adhere to the Universal Declaration of Human Rights, be in basic compliance with applicable laws, prohibit forced, compulsory or child labor, follow ethical recruitment practices, respect freedom of association, recognize the rights of all workers including temporary, migrant, and contract workers; and cooperate with reasonable assessment processes requested by PepsiCo.
- In conjunction with the company's support of RSPO's standards, PepsiCo is committed to working with governments, NGOs, suppliers, and other companies to ensure RSPO's no burning policy is realized through better monitoring and new technology

In addition, PepsiCo would:

- Achieve 100% traceability to the mill level for all its palm oil and palm kernel oil, and assess suppliers' operations and landholdings on PepsiCo's Forestry Stewardship and Land Use Policies and the principles of this commitment by 2016.
- Achieve traceability to the Farm/Plantation level of its palm oil and palm kernel oil by 2020.
- Request its palm oil suppliers to report on greenhouse gas emissions through the CDP Supply Chain or similar program.
- Work with its suppliers to ensure that these policies are implemented in such a way that supports the inclusion of smallholders
- Engage with appropriate industry and other groups to improve company's understanding of deforestation, forest conservation, indigenous and customary land tenure rights, human rights, and labor rights issues in the palm oil industry, adapt our policy, and achieve its goals.
- Use an appropriate means of communicating PepsiCo's palm oil commitments and associated policies to its suppliers, such as the PepsiCo Supplier Code of Conduct (SCoC).
- Leverage the PepsiCo Sustainable Farming Initiative to support implementation of sustainable agriculture practices that enable farmers to increase production on currently farmed land and minimize impacts on the surrounding area.
- Support a confidential and safe process for investigating grievances raised by affected parties by making the PepsiCo SpeakUp! hotline available, along with any supplier provided grievance mechanisms, for the reporting of suspected breaches of this policy to PepsiCo. In instances where outstanding land rights disputes exist in its supply chain, the company encourages its suppliers to utilize the principles of FPIC to reach a resolution.

Source: Adapted from **www.pepsico.com**.

large scale production and processing of palm oil with its plantations covering a total area of 246,000 hectares in Sumatra and Kalimantan (Borneo).[38] Indofood was the only maker of PepsiCo products in Indonesia. The company did not have a responsible palm oil policy. It was reportedly involved in some questionable business practices, including deforestation through clearing and burning rainforests, labor rights violations, and social conflicts with local communities. According to RAN, in 2013 and 2014, Indofood cleared 1,000 hectares of untouched tropical rainforest in East Kalimantan. Apparently the company had used fire to prepare land for new plantations, as satellite images revealed a burned area of nearly 200 hectares inside Indofood's palm oil plantation in East Kalimantan. Moreover going forward Indofood intended to develop 5,000 to 10,000 hectares of new palm oil plantations annually.

With Indofood being exempted from the new palm oil policy, environmentalists said every drop of palm oil used to make PepsiCo products in Indonesia was at risk of having a negative impact on people and the environment. Experts pointed out that PepsiCo's palm oil commitment should apply to all suppliers selling palm oil that was used to make PepsiCo branded products sold globally, not just the products made in PepsiCo's own facilities. *"Rainforest Action Network is disappointed that PepsiCo continues to fail to take responsibility for the impact of its products sold globally. PepsiCo has a huge role to play in the highly problematic global production of Conflict Palm Oil, but will continue to accept 'business as usual' operations from its suppliers, including Indofood. With this action plan, PepsiCo has failed to set a deadline for breaking the links between its products and companies that are destroying rainforests and peatlands, and abusing human and labor rights. Instead, its action plan reconfirms to only source physically certified palm oil by 2020—a deadline out of step with what is needed,"*[39] said Tillack.

According to RAN, PepsiCo's new palm oil commitment had a loophole the size of Indonesia and failed to address the fundamental problems of rainforest destruction. In order to earn the trust of customers, PepsiCo must close this loophole and take action to clean up its supply chain, including the operations of Indofood, the group added. *"A company earns trust from its consumers not only by making quality products, but by being honest and transparent in its actions [. . .]. If it (PepsiCo) is not forthright about the bounds of its palm oil commitment it risks serious damage to its credibility. After all, trust is like a mirror, difficult to build, easy to break,"*[40] said Calen May-Tobin, a lead analyst with the Tropical Forest and Climate Initiative.

With palm oil being Indonesia's most valuable agricultural export, the Indonesian government opposed zero-deforestation pledge by some palm oil firms. Though the Indonesian government acknowledged the problem of widespread deforestation, it was reported to have asked major palm oil companies to go back on their deforestation pledges they had made in 2014 as it was concerned that the pledges made by the companies were causing big problems for smaller palm oil firms in their supply chain. Moreover, the government had asked palm oil firms which had signed the Indonesian Palm Oil Pledge (IPOP)[41] to exempt small holders because it felt that they were not yet ready to achieve the same level of sustainable forest practices as the big players. Some environmental groups reported that Indonesian government was advising some big palm oil companies to water down their stance by urging them to continue to buy palm oil from their suppliers, even if that company was involved in cutting down forests for new plantations. Allegedly the pressure from the national government came after local governments in Indonesia began taking away concessions from palm oil companies which tried to convert palm oil plantations into conservation forests.

THE ROAD AHEAD

In April 2015, UCS came out with a revised scorecard, ranking companies based on their commitment to deforestation free palm oil. The score of each company was recalculated to account for their progress compared to the previous year. As per the scorecard, in 2015, PepsiCo made remarkable progress on its commitment to source deforestation free palm oil compared to the previous year, by scoring 80.7 points out of 100 (see Exhibit 8). Environmentalists attributed the growth to the new Forestry Policy and the palm oil commitment made by the company in 2014 that improved transparency and traceability in its supply chains. They pointed out, however, that though PepsiCo had been successful to some extent in sourcing sustainable palm oil as was evident from the scorecard, it did not guarantee that its supply chain was completely free of Conflict Palm Oil (see Exhibit 9). According to UCS, *"PepsiCo talks a good game, but the Union of Concerned Scientists (UCS) is skeptical about PepsiCo's ability to follow through on its commitment. The UCS scorecard is based on commitments to buying only deforestation-free palm oil, which is just one issue associated with palm oil production. Just because we gave the company a passing grade does not give PepsiCo a free pass on human rights, health, or other environmental issues. This is akin to getting a B- in English, but failing math, science and geography. One passing grade does not make a star student."*[42]

As the global demand for palm oil continued to grow, tropical forests across Southeast Asia, Africa, and Latin America were at risk of being converted into large-scale palm oil plantations. In 2012, Indonesia reportedly lost 840,000 hectares (3,250 square miles) of forest while Brazil lost a still more massive 460,000 hectares[43] to palm oil plantations. In 2015, Indonesia continued to lead the growth in global palm oil supply, contributing about 32.7 million tonnes from its palm areas.[44] According to observers, with

EXHIBIT 8 UCS Scorecard for Commitment to Sustainable Palm Oil Sourcing by Packaged Food Companies, 2014–2015

Company	Score 2014	Score 2015
Nestlé S.A.	85.5	90.5 (Green)
Danone	51.5	89.2 (Green)
Kellogg's Co.	52.8	88.5 (Green)
ConAgra Foods, Inc.	35.5	84.1 (Green)
Unilever	83.5	83.4 (Green)
PepsiCo, Inc.	**33.7**	**80.7** (Green)
General Mills	42.6	77.8 (Green)
Heinz Company	37.1	42.9 (Yellow)
Mondelēz International, Inc.	68.6	36.8 (Yellow)
Kraft Foods Group Inc.	0	10 (Pink)

Green–Strong commitment

Yellow–Some commitment

Pink–Little commitment

Orange–No commitment

*The list is not exhaustive.

Source: www.ucsusa.org/global-warming/stop-deforestation/palm-oil-scorecard-2015#.Vkl7KHYrLIU.

EXHIBIT 9 UCS Scorecard for Actual Sourcing of Sustainable Palm Oil by Packaged Food Companies, 2014–2015

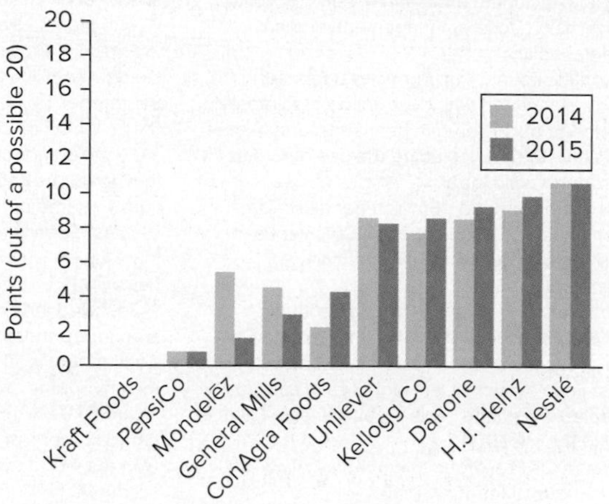

Source: www.ucsusa.org/sites/default/files/attach/2015/04/ucs-palm-oil-scorecard-2015.pdf.

palm oil demand set to double by 2030, the sourcing of sustainable palm oil would become a critical issue.

Going forward, PepsiCo planned to step up its efforts to source responsible palm oil by understanding its supply chain, confirming the location of the plantations from which it sourced its palm oil, and independently verifying that the suppliers were not involved in deforestation or violation of human rights in any of their operations. The company planned to map the supply chains of its suppliers to ensure that the palm oil it received came from responsible and sustainable sources and was also in compliance with the company's Forestry Stewardship Policy and Land Use Policy.

Industry observers felt that PepsiCo had a crucial role to play in eliminating Conflict Palm Oil from food supply and that the company should strengthen its palm oil policies and practices and commit to sourcing exclusively from suppliers with traceable, transparent, verified, and accountable supply chains across all operations. Some analysts said the company should step up and break the link between its products and the factors responsible for the destruction of rainforests in order to dismiss customer concerns. It should start taking the palm oil issue seriously and use its buying power to drive real change on the ground, they added. They also pointed out that the Conflict Palm Oil problem was not an easy one to solve. According to Sasha Orman, Editor of FDF World,[45] *"But with palm oil such a critical issue right now, does PepsiCo's commitment go far enough to enact change? Not everyone is 100 percent convinced yet. The Union of Concerned Scientists (UCS) published a critique raising questions about the wording of PepsiCo's plan, noting that—while much of it is solid and promising—it only appears to apply to fully PepsiCo-owned lands and operations. Will the company's joint venture projects covered by the Forestry Stewardship Policy? With that said, it is not certain one way or another yet whether PepsiCo will hold its joint ventures to the same sustainability standards as its fully-owned projects. But in a case like this, PepsiCo's actions down the line will speak for themselves and reveal the full extent of the company's commitment."*[46]

ENDNOTES

[1] The DJSI is the first global index to track the leading sustainability-driven companies worldwide based on a range of social, environmental, and governance-based criteria, including assessments on corporate governance, crisis management, and environmental policy.

[2] Conflict Palm Oil is produced under conditions associated with destruction of rainforests, drainage of carbon-rich peatlands, and human rights violations, including the use of forced labor and child labor.

[3] Annette Gartland, "Environmentalists Urge Consumers to Pressure PepsiCo Over Palm Oil," time2transcend.wordpress.com, December 9, 2014.

[4] In an effort to raise awareness about the adverse consequences of palm oil plantations on peatlands and to transform the sector toward sustainable palm oil, the global palm oil industry created the Round Table on Sustainable Palm Oil (RSPO) in 2004.

[5] "Palm Oil Free Year," palmoilfreeyear.wordpress.com, January 7, 2015.

[6] The "Snack Food 20" group comprised Campbell Soup Co.; ConAgra Foods Inc.; Dunkin' Brands Group Inc.; General Mills Inc.; Grupo Bimbo; Hillshire Brands Co.; H.J. Heinz Co.; Hormel Foods Corp.; Kellogg Co.; Kraft Food Group Inc.; Krispy Kreme Doughnuts Corp.; Mars Inc.; Mondelēz International Inc.; Nestlé S.A.; Nissin Foods Holdings Co.; PepsiCo Inc.; Hershey Co.; J.M. Smucker Co.; Toyo Suisan Kaisha Ltd.; and Unilever.

[7] "Pepsi AGM RAN Statement," d3n8a8pro7vhmx.cloudfront.net, 2015.

[8] Frito-Lay, the world's largest maker of snack chips in the world.

[9] "PepsiCo Releases Sustainable Development Report," www.bevnet.com, January 6, 2009.

[10] "PepsiCo Named Top Food and Beverage Company in 2011 Dow Jones Sustainability Index," www.csrwire.com, September 9, 2011.

[11] Jason Mark, "What's Fueling the Demand for the Palm Oil Destroying the Rainforests of Indonesia?" www.earthisland.org, October 9, 2013.

[12] Peatlands are carbon-rich swampy areas.

[13] "Indonesia Allocates 18 Million Hectares of Land for Palm Oil," www.thejakartapost.com, December 2, 2009.

[14] www.rspo.org/file/acop2014b/submissions/pepsico-ACOP2014b.pdf.

[15] www.ran.org/our-mission.

[16] Jenn Harris, "Rainforest Action Network to PepsiCo, General Mills: Stop Killing Orangutans," www.latimes.com, September 13, 2013.

[17] Gemma Tillack, "All Eyes on PepsiCo: Will It Come Clean or Keep Trafficking Conflict Palm Oil?" www.ran.org, November 10, 2014.

[18] "Campaign Targets 'Conflict Palm Oil' in US Snack Foods'" oneworld.org, September 12, 2013.

[19] Jenn Harris, "Rainforest Action Network to PepsiCo, General Mills: Stop Killing Orangutans," www.latimes.com, September 13, 2013.

[20] The Union of Concerned Scientists (UCS) is a US-based nonprofit science advocacy group that develops and implements practical solutions to some of the earth's pressing problems such as global warming.

[21] www.pepsico.com/Assets/Download/PepsiCo_Palm_Oil_Commitments.pdf.

[22] Founded in 1971, Greenpeace International is an independent global environmental organization that works to protect and conserve the environment and to promote peace.

[23] SumOfUs.org is a non-profit online activism group comprising consumers, investors, and workers world over who hold corporations accountable for their actions and forge a new, sustainable, and just path for the global economy.

[24] "PepsiCo's New Palm Oil Commitment Marks Major Improvement, but Other Companies Are Going Further, Science Group Says," www.ucsusa.org, May 20, 2014.

[25] "PepsiCo Announces Zero Deforestation Commitment for Palm Oil," news.mongabay.com, May 21, 2014.

[26] "When It Comes to Palm Oil, PepsiCo Is Less Than Perfect," blog.ucsusa.org, March 26, 2015.

[27] Kacey Culliney, "PepsiCo: SumOfUs Doritos Palm Oil Attack Is 'Patently False,'" www.bakeryandsnacks.com, January 19, 2015.

[28] In October 2015, PepsiCo launched a mid-calorie soda called Pepsi True. The soda was rolled out for sale exclusively online through Amazon.com.

[29] Rhett A. Butler, "Activists Hijack Pepsi's New Product Launch on Amazon over Deforestation," news.mongabay.com, November 20, 2014.

[30] Leon Kaye, "Pepsi True Savaged on Amazon over Palm Oil Controversy," www.triplepundit.com, November 24, 2014.

[31] Orangutan Outreach is a New York–based non-profit organization whose mission is to save the critically endangered orangutans and protect their rainforest habitat.

[32] Leuser Ecosystem, located in the Aceh district of northern Sumatra, is an area of more than 1.8 million hectares and the only place on earth where tigers, elephants, rhinos, and orangutans can be found living together in the wild.

[33] "PepsiCo Defends Doritos' Palm Oil Policy," www.edie.net, January 14, 2015.

[34] Launched in April 2012, the "Live for Now" campaign invited Pepsi fans to live each moment to the fullest through global pop-culture platforms including relationships with music and entertainment brand evangelists, digital innovation, epic events, and unique partnerships.

[35] Indofood Sukses Makmur Tbk is one of the largest food processing companies in Southeast Asia. The company forms part of the Salim Group, Indonesia's biggest conglomerate. The company manufactures PepsiCo's products in Indonesia.

[36] Producing more than 33 million tonnes of palm oil annually, Indonesia has the highest rates of deforestation in the world, and is the fifth largest emitter of greenhouse gases, largely due to the expansion of plantations on peatland forests.

[37] "A Loophole the Size of Indonesia," d3n8a8pro7vhmx.cloudfront.net, September 2015.

[38] Sumatra and Kalimantan are the largest islands in Indonesia and are home to some of the world's most diverse rainforests.

[39] Emma Lierley, "PepsiCo Misses Mark with New Action Plan as Indonesia Burns for Palm Oil," www.ran.org, November 2, 2015.

[40] Calen May-Tobin, "PepsiCo's New Palm Oil Commitment: Transparency, Trust, and the Company You Keep," blog.ucsusa.org, September 24, 2015.

[41] Signed in September 2014, the Indonesia Palm Oil Pledge (IPOP) is an agreement among leading palm oil producers that commits them to industry-leading sustainability practices. The pledge was signed by the CEOs of palm oil companies like Asian Agri, Cargill, Golden Agri Resources and Wilmar.

[42] Dan Ashley, "Popular Snack Foods May Cause Rainforest Destruction," abc7news.com, July 10, 2015.

[43] Samuel Oakford, "Indonesia Is Killing the Planet for Palm Oil," news.vice.com, July 4, 2014.

[44] "Growth in Global Palm Oil Supply, Demand Expected," www.dailyexpress.com.my, February 2, 2015.

[45] *FDF World* is an online food and drink magazine featuring news, information, and trends from across the food, drink, and franchising industries.

[46] Sasha Orman, "PepsiCo Commits to a New Zero Deforestation Palm Oil Policy," www.fdfworld.com, September 29, 2015.

Guide to Case Analysis

I keep six honest serving men
(They taught me all I knew);
Their names are What and Why and When;
And How and Where and Who.

Rudyard Kipling

In most courses in strategic management, students use cases about actual companies to practice strategic analysis and to gain some experience in the tasks of crafting and implementing strategy. A case sets forth, in a factual manner, the events and organizational circumstances surrounding a particular managerial situation. It puts readers at the scene of the action and familiarizes them with all the relevant circumstances. A case on strategic management can concern a whole industry, a single organization, or some part of an organization; the organization involved can be either profit seeking or not-for-profit. The essence of the student's role in case analysis is to diagnose and size up the situation described in the case and then to recommend appropriate action steps.

WHY USE CASES TO PRACTICE STRATEGIC MANAGEMENT?

> A student of business with tact
> Absorbed many answers he lacked.
> But acquiring a job,
> He said with a sob,
> "How does one fit answer to fact?"

The foregoing limerick was used some years ago by Professor Charles Gragg to characterize the plight of business students who had no exposure to cases.[1] The facts are that the mere act of listening to lectures and sound advice about managing does little for anyone's management skills and that the accumulated managerial wisdom cannot effectively be passed on by lectures and assigned readings alone. If anything had been learned about the practice of management, it is that a storehouse of ready-made textbook answers does not exist. Each managerial situation has unique aspects, requiring its own diagnosis, judgment, and tailor-made actions. Cases provide would-be managers with a valuable way to practice wrestling with the actual problems of actual managers in actual companies.

The case approach to strategic analysis is, first and foremost, an exercise in learning by doing. Because cases provide you with detailed information about conditions and problems of different industries and companies, your task of analyzing company after company and situation after situation has the twin benefit of boosting your analytical skills and exposing you to the ways companies and managers actually do things. Most college students have limited managerial backgrounds and only fragmented knowledge about companies and real-life strategic situations. Cases help substitute for on-the-job experience by (1) giving you broader exposure to a variety of industries, organizations, and strategic problems; (2) forcing you to assume a managerial role (as opposed to that of just an onlooker); (3) providing a test of how to apply the tools and techniques of strategic management; and (4) asking you to come up with pragmatic managerial action plans to deal with the issues at hand.

Objectives of Case Analysis

Using cases to learn about the practice of strategic management is a powerful way for you to accomplish five things:[2]

1. Increase your understanding of what managers should and should not do in guiding a business to success.
2. Build your skills in sizing up company resource strengths and weaknesses and in conducting strategic analysis in a variety of industries and competitive situations.
3. Get valuable practice in identifying strategic issues that need to be addressed, evaluating strategic alternatives, and formulating workable plans of action.
4. Enhance your sense of business judgment, as opposed to uncritically accepting the authoritative crutch of the professor or "back-of-the-book" answers.
5. Gain in-depth exposure to different industries and companies, thereby acquiring something close to actual business experience.

If you understand that these are the objectives of case analysis, you are less likely to be consumed with curiosity about "the answer to the case." Students who have grown comfortable with and accustomed to textbook statements of fact and definitive lecture notes are often frustrated when discussions about a case do not produce concrete answers. Usually, case discussions produce good arguments for more than one course of action. Differences of opinion nearly always exist. Thus, should a class discussion conclude without a strong, unambiguous consensus on what to do, don't grumble too much when you are not told what the answer is or what the company actually did. Just remember that in the business world answers don't come in conclusive black-and-white terms. There are nearly always several feasible courses of action and approaches, each of which may work out satisfactorily. Moreover, in the business world, when one elects a particular course of action, there is no peeking at the back of a book to see if you have chosen the best thing to do and no one to turn to for a provably correct answer. The best test of whether management action is "right" or "wrong" is results. If the results of an action turn out to be "good," the decision to take it may be presumed "right." If not, then the action chosen was "wrong" in the sense that it didn't work out.

Hence, the important thing for you to understand about analyzing cases is that the managerial exercise of identifying, diagnosing, and recommending is aimed at building your skills of business judgment. Discovering what the company actually did is no more than frosting on the cake—the actions that company managers actually took may or may not be "right" or best (unless there is accompanying evidence that the results of their actions were highly positive).

The point is this: The purpose of giving you a case assignment is not to cause you to run to the library or surf the Internet to discover what the company actually did but, rather, to enhance your skills in sizing up situations and developing your managerial judgment about what needs to be done and how to do it. The aim of case analysis is for you to become actively engaged in diagnosing the business issues and managerial problems posed in the case, to propose workable solutions, and to explain and defend your assessments—this is how cases provide you with meaningful practice at being a manager.

Preparing a Case for Class Discussion

If this is your first experience with the case method, you may have to reorient your study habits. Unlike lecture courses where you can get by without preparing intensively for each class and where you have latitude to work assigned readings and reviews of lecture notes into your schedule, a case assignment requires conscientious preparation before class. You will not get much out of hearing the class discuss a case you haven't read, and you certainly won't be able to contribute anything yourself to the discussion. What you have got to do to get ready for class discussion of a case is to study the case, reflect carefully on the situation presented, and develop some reasoned thoughts. Your goal in preparing the case should be to end up with what you think is a sound, well-supported analysis of the situation and a sound, defensible set of recommendations about which managerial actions need to be taken.

To prepare a case for class discussion, we suggest the following approach:

1. ***Skim the case rather quickly to get an overview of the situation it presents.*** This quick overview should give you the general flavor of the situation and indicate the kinds of issues and problems that you will need to wrestle with. If your instructor has provided you with study questions for the case, now is the time to read them carefully.
2. ***Read the case thoroughly to digest the facts and circumstances.*** On this reading, try to gain full command of the situation presented in the case. Begin to develop some tentative answers to the study questions your instructor has provided. If your instructor has elected not to give you assignment questions, then start forming your own picture of the overall situation being described.
3. ***Carefully review all the information presented in the exhibits.*** Often, there is an important story in the numbers contained in the exhibits. Expect the information in the case exhibits to be crucial enough to materially affect your diagnosis of the situation.
4. ***Decide what the strategic issues are.*** Until you have identified the strategic issues and problems in the case, you don't know what to analyze, which tools and analytical techniques are called for, or otherwise how to proceed. At times the strategic issues are clear—either being stated in the case or else obvious from reading the case. At other times you will have to dig them out from all the information given; if so, the study questions will guide you.
5. ***Start your analysis of the issues with some number crunching.*** A big majority of strategy cases call for some kind of number crunching—calculating assorted financial ratios to check out the company's financial condition and recent performance, calculating growth rates of sales or profits or unit volume, checking out profit margins and the makeup of the cost structure, and understanding whatever revenue-cost-profit relationships are present. See Table 1 for a summary of key financial ratios, how they are calculated, and what they show.

6. ***Apply the concepts and techniques of strategic analysis you have been studying.*** Strategic analysis is not just a collection of opinions; rather, it entails applying the concepts and analytical tools described in Chapters 1 through 12 to cut beneath the surface and produce sharp insight and understanding. Every case assigned is strategy related and presents you with an opportunity to usefully apply what you have learned. Your instructor is looking for you to demonstrate that you know how and when to use the material presented in the text chapters.
7. ***Check out conflicting opinions and make some judgments about the validity of all the data and information provided.*** Many times cases report views and contradictory opinions (after all, people don't always agree on things, and different people see the same things in different ways). Forcing you to evaluate the data and information presented in the case helps you develop your powers of inference and judgment. Asking you to resolve conflicting information "comes with the territory" because a great many managerial situations entail opposing points of view, conflicting trends, and sketchy information.
8. ***Support your diagnosis and opinions with reasons and evidence.*** The most important things to prepare for are your answers to the question "Why?" For instance, if after studying the case you are of the opinion that the company's managers are doing a poor job, then it is your answer to "Why?" that establishes just how good your analysis of the situation is. If your instructor has provided you with specific study questions for the case, by all means prepare answers that include all the reasons and number-crunching evidence you can muster to support your diagnosis. If you are using study questions provided by the instructor, generate at least two pages of notes!
9. ***Develop an appropriate action plan and set of recommendations.*** Diagnosis divorced from corrective action is sterile. The test of a manager is always to convert sound analysis into sound actions—actions that will produce the desired results. Hence, the final and most telling step in preparing a case is to develop an action agenda for management that lays out a set of specific recommendations on what to do. Bear in mind that proposing realistic, workable solutions is far preferable to casually tossing out off-the-top-of-your-head suggestions. Be prepared to argue why your recommendations are more attractive than other courses of action that are open.

As long as you are conscientious in preparing your analysis and recommendations, and have ample reasons, evidence, and arguments to support your views, you shouldn't fret unduly about whether what you've prepared is "the right answer" to the case. In case analysis, there is rarely just one right approach or set of recommendations. Managing companies and crafting and executing strategies are not such exact sciences that there exists a single provably correct analysis and action plan for each strategic situation. Of course, some analyses and action plans are better than others; but, in truth, there's nearly always more than one good way to analyze a situation and more than one good plan of action.

Participating in Class Discussion of a Case

Classroom discussions of cases are sharply different from attending a lecture class. In a case class, students do most of the talking. The instructor's role is to solicit student participation, keep the discussion on track, ask "Why?" often, offer alternative views, play the devil's advocate (if no students jump in to offer opposing views), and otherwise lead the discussion. The students in the class carry the burden for analyzing the situation and for being prepared to present and defend their diagnoses and recommendations. Expect a classroom environment, therefore, that calls for your size-up of the situation, your analysis, what actions you would take, and why you would take them. Do not be dismayed if, as the class discussion unfolds, some insightful things are said by your fellow classmates that you did not think of. It is normal for views and analyses to differ and for the comments of others in the class to expand your own thinking about the case. As the old adage goes, "Two heads are better than one." So it is to be expected that the class as a whole will do a more penetrating and searching job of case analysis than will any one person working alone. This is the power of group effort, and its virtues are that it will help you see more analytical applications, let you test your analyses and judgments against those of your peers, and force you to wrestle with differences of opinion and approaches.

TABLE 1 Key Financial Ratios: How to Calculate Them and What They Mean

Ratio	How Calculated	What It Shows
Profitability ratios		
1. Gross profit margin	$\frac{\text{Sales} - \text{Cost of goods sold}}{\text{Sales}}$	Shows the percentage of revenues available to cover operating expenses and yield a profit. Higher is better and the trend should be upward.
2. Operating profit margin (or return on sales)	$\frac{\text{Sales} - \text{Operating expenses}}{\text{Sales}}$ or $\frac{\text{Operating income}}{\text{Sales}}$	Shows the profitability of current operations without regard to interest charges and income taxes. Higher is better and the trend should be upward.
3. Net profit margin (or net return on sales)	$\frac{\text{Profits after taxes}}{\text{Sales}}$	Shows after-tax profits per dollar of sales. Higher is better and the trend should be upward.
4. Total return on assets	$\frac{\text{Profits after taxes} + \text{Interest}}{\text{Total assets}}$	A measure of the return on total monetary investment in the enterprise. Interest is added to after-tax profits to form the numerator since total assets are financed by creditors as well as by stockholders. Higher is better and the trend should be upward.
5. Net return on total assets (ROA)	$\frac{\text{Profits after taxes}}{\text{Total assets}}$	A measure of the return earned by stockholders on the firm's total assets. Higher is better, and the trend should be upward.
6. Return on stockholder's equity (ROE)	$\frac{\text{Profits after taxes}}{\text{Total stockholders' equity}}$	Shows the return stockholders are earning on their capital investment in the enterprise. A return in the 12–15% range is "average," and the trend should be upward.
7. Return on invested capital (ROIC)—sometimes referred to as return on capital employed (ROCE)	$\frac{\text{Profits after taxes}}{\text{Long-term debt} + \text{Total stockholders' equity}}$	A measure of the return shareholders are earning on the long-term monetary capital invested in the enterprise. A higher return reflects greater bottom-line effectiveness in the use of long-term capital, and the trend should be upward.
8. Earnings per share (EPS)	$\frac{\text{Profits after taxes}}{\text{Number of shares of common stock outstanding}}$	Shows the earnings for each share of common stock outstanding. The trend should be upward, and the bigger the annual percentage gains, the better.
Liquidity ratios		
1. Current ratio	$\frac{\text{Current assets}}{\text{Current liabilities}}$	Shows a firm's ability to pay current liabilities using assets that can be converted into cash in the near term. Ratio should definitely be higher than 1.0; ratios of 2 or higher are better still.
2. Working capital	Current assets – Current liabilities	Bigger amounts are better because the company has more internal funds available to (1) pay its current liabilities on a timely basis and (2) finance inventory expansion, additional accounts receivable, and a larger base of operations without resorting to borrowing or raising more equity capital.
Leverage ratios		
1. Total debt-to-assets ratio	$\frac{\text{Total debt}}{\text{Total assets}}$	Measures the extent to which borrowed funds have been used to finance the firm's operations. Low fractions or ratios are better—high fractions indicate overuse of debt and greater risk of bankruptcy.
2. Long-term debt-to-capital ratio	$\frac{\text{Long-term debt}}{\text{Long-term debt} + \text{Total stockholders' equity}}$	An important measure of creditworthiness and balance sheet strength. Indicates the percentage of capital investment that has been financed by creditors and bondholders. Fractions or ratios below .25 or 25% are usually quite satisfactory since monies invested

(*Continued*)

TABLE 1 *(Continued)*

Ratio	How Calculated	What It Shows
Leverage ratios (Continued)		
		by stockholders account for 75% or more of the company's total capital. The lower the ratio, the greater the capacity to borrow additional funds. Debt-to-capital ratios above 50% and certainly above 75% indicate a heavy and perhaps excessive reliance on debt, lower creditworthiness, and weak balance sheet strength.
3. Debt-to-equity ratio	Total debt / Total stockholders' equity	Should usually be less than 1.0. High ratios (especially above 1.0) signal excessive debt, lower creditworthiness, and weaker balance sheet strength.
4. Long-term debt-to-equity ratio	Long-term debt / Total stockholders' equity	Shows the balance between debt and equity in the firm's *long-term* capital structure. Low ratios indicate greater capacity to borrow additional funds if needed.
5. Times-interest-earned (or coverage) ratio	Operating income / Interest expenses	Measures the ability to pay annual interest charges. Lenders usually insist on a minimum ratio of 2.0, but ratios above 3.0 signal better creditworthiness.
Activity ratios		
1. Days of inventory	Inventory / Cost of goods sold ÷ 365	Measures inventory management efficiency. Fewer days of inventory are usually better.
2. Inventory turnover	Cost of goods sold / Inventory	Measures the number of inventory turns per year. Higher is better.
3. Average collection period	Accounts receivable / Total sales revenues ÷ 365 or Accounts receivable / Average daily sales	Indicates the average length of time the firm must wait after making a sale to receive cash payment. A shorter collection time is better.
Other important measures of financial performance		
1. Dividend yield on common stock	Annual dividends per share / Current market price per share	A measure of the return that shareholders receive in the form of dividends. A "typical" dividend yield is 2–3%. The dividend yield for fast-growth companies is often below 1% (maybe even 0); the dividend yield for slow-growth companies can run 4–5%.
2. Price-earnings ratio	Current market price per share / Earnings per share	P-E ratios above 20 indicate strong investor confidence in a firm's outlook and earnings growth; firms whose future earnings are at risk or likely to grow slowly typically have ratios below 12.
3. Dividend payout ratio	Annual dividends per share / Earnings per share	Indicates the percentage of after-tax profits paid out as dividends.
4. Internal cash flow	After-tax profits + Depreciation	A quick and rough estimate of the cash the business is generating after payment of operating expenses, interest, and taxes. Such amounts can be used for dividend payments or funding capital expenditures.
5. Free cash flow	After-tax profits + Depreciation – Capital expenditures – Dividends	A quick and rough estimate of the cash a company's business is generating after payment of operating expenses, interest, taxes, dividends, and desirable reinvestments in the business. The larger a company's free cash flow, the greater is its ability to internally fund new strategic initiatives, repay debt, make new acquisitions, repurchase shares of stock, or increase dividend payments.

To orient you to the classroom environment on the days a case discussion is scheduled, we compiled the following list of things to expect:

1. Expect the instructor to assume the role of extensive questioner and listener.
2. Expect students to do most of the talking. The case method enlists a maximum of individual participation in class discussion. It is not enough to be present as a silent observer; if every student took this approach, there would be no discussion. (Thus, expect a portion of your grade to be based on your participation in case discussions.)
3. Be prepared for the instructor to probe for reasons and supporting analysis.
4. Expect and tolerate challenges to the views expressed. All students have to be willing to submit their conclusions for scrutiny and rebuttal. Each student needs to learn to state his or her views without fear of disapproval and to overcome the hesitation of speaking out. Learning respect for the views and approaches of others is an integral part of case analysis exercises. But there are times when it is OK to swim against the tide of majority opinion. In the practice of management, there is always room for originality and unorthodox approaches. So while discussion of a case is a group process, there is no compulsion for you or anyone else to cave in and conform to group opinions and group consensus.
5. Don't be surprised if you change your mind about some things as the discussion unfolds. Be alert to how these changes affect your analysis and recommendations (in the event you get called on).
6. Expect to learn a lot in class as the discussion of a case progresses; furthermore, you will find that the cases build on one another—what you learn in one case helps prepare you for the next case discussion.

There are several things you can do on your own to be good and look good as a participant in class discussions:

- Although you should do your own independent work and independent thinking, don't hesitate before (and after) class to discuss the case with other students. In real life, managers often discuss the company's problems and situation with other people to refine their own thinking.
- In participating in the discussion, make a conscious effort to contribute, rather than just talk. There is a big difference between saying something that builds the discussion and offering a long-winded, off-the-cuff remark that leaves the class wondering what the point was.
- Avoid the use of "I think," "I believe," and "I feel"; instead, say, "My analysis shows _____" and "The company should do _____ because _____." Always give supporting reasons and evidence for your views; then your instructor won't have to ask you "Why?" every time you make a comment.
- In making your points, assume that everyone has read the case and knows what it says. Avoid reciting and rehashing information in the case—instead, use the data and information to explain your assessment of the situation and to support your position.
- Bring the printouts of the work you've done on Case-Tutor or the notes you've prepared (usually two or three pages' worth) to class and rely on them extensively when you speak. There's no way you can remember everything off the top of your head—especially the results of your number crunching. To reel off the numbers or to present all five reasons why, instead of one, you will need good notes. When you have prepared thoughtful answers to the study questions and use them as the basis for your comments, everybody in the room will know you are well prepared, and your contribution to the case discussion will stand out.

Preparing a Written Case Analysis

Preparing a written case analysis is much like preparing a case for class discussion, except that your analysis must be more complete and put in report form. Unfortunately, though, there is no ironclad procedure for doing a written case analysis. All we can offer are some general guidelines and words of wisdom—this is because company situations and management problems are so diverse that no one mechanical way to approach a written case assignment always works.

Your instructor may assign you a specific topic around which to prepare your written report. Or, alternatively, you may be asked to do a comprehensive written case analysis, where the expectation is that you will (1) identify all the pertinent issues that management needs to address, (2) perform whatever analysis and evaluation is appropriate, and (3) propose an action plan and set of recommendations addressing the issues you have identified. In going through the exercise of identify, evaluate, and recommend, keep the following pointers in mind.[3]

Identification It is essential early on in your written report that you provide a sharply focused diagnosis of strategic issues and key problems and that you demonstrate a good grasp of the company's present situation. Make sure you can identify the firm's strategy (use the concepts and tools in Chapters 1–8 as diagnostic aids) and that you can pinpoint whatever strategy implementation issues may exist (again, consult the material in Chapters 10–12 for diagnostic help). Consult the key points we have provided at the end of each chapter for further diagnostic suggestions. Consider beginning your report with an overview of the company's situation, its strategy, and the significant problems and issues that confront management. State problems/issues as clearly and precisely as you can. Unless it is necessary to do so for emphasis, avoid recounting facts and history about the company (assume your professor has read the case and is familiar with the organization).

Analysis and Evaluation This is usually the hardest part of the report. Analysis is hard work! Check out the firm's financial ratios, its profit margins and rates of return, and its capital structure, and decide how strong the firm is financially. Table 1 contains a summary of various financial ratios and how they are calculated. Use it to assist in your financial diagnosis. Similarly, look at marketing, production, managerial competence, and other factors underlying the organization's strategic successes and failures. Decide whether the firm has valuable resource strengths and competencies and, if so, whether it is capitalizing on them.

Check to see if the firm's strategy is producing satisfactory results and determine the reasons why or why not. Probe the nature and strength of the competitive forces confronting the company. Decide whether and why the firm's competitive position is getting stronger or weaker. Use the tools and concepts you have learned about to perform whatever analysis and evaluation is appropriate. Work through the case preparation exercise on Case-TUTOR if one is available for the case you've been assigned.

In writing your analysis and evaluation, bear in mind four things:

1. You are obliged to offer analysis and evidence to back up your conclusions. Do not rely on unsupported opinions, over-generalizations, and platitudes as a substitute for tight, logical argument backed up with facts and figures.
2. If your analysis involves some important quantitative calculations, use tables and charts to present the calculations clearly and efficiently. Don't just tack the exhibits on at the end of your report and let the reader figure out what they mean and why they were included. Instead, in the body of your report cite some of the key numbers, highlight the conclusions to be drawn from the exhibits, and refer the reader to your charts and exhibits for more details.
3. Demonstrate that you have command of the strategic concepts and analytical tools to which you have been exposed. Use them in your report.
4. Your interpretation of the evidence should be reasonable and objective. Be wary of preparing a one-sided argument that omits all aspects not favorable to your conclusions. Likewise, try not to exaggerate or overdramatize. Endeavor to inject balance into your analysis and to avoid emotional rhetoric. Strike phrases such as "I think," "I feel," and "I believe" when you edit your first draft and write in "My analysis shows" instead.

Recommendations The final section of the written case analysis should consist of a set of definite recommendations and a plan of action. Your set of recommendations should address all of the problems/issues you identified and analyzed. If the recommendations come as a surprise or do not follow logically from the analysis, the effect is to weaken greatly your suggestions of what to do. Obviously, your recommendations for actions should offer a reasonable prospect of success. High-risk, bet-the-company recommendations should be made with caution. State how your recommendations will solve the problems you identified. Be sure the company is financially able to carry out what you recommend; also check to see if your recommendations are workable in terms of acceptance by the persons involved, the organization's competence to implement them, and prevailing market and environmental constraints. Try not to hedge or weasel on the actions you believe should be taken.

By all means state your recommendations in sufficient detail to be meaningful—get down to some definite nitty-gritty specifics. Avoid such unhelpful statements as "the organization should do more planning" or "the company should be more aggressive in marketing its product." For instance, if you determine that "the firm should improve its market position," then you need to set forth exactly how you think this should be done. Offer a definite agenda for action, stipulating a timetable and sequence for initiating actions, indicating priorities, and suggesting who should be responsible for doing what.

In proposing an action plan, remember there is a great deal of difference between, on the one hand, being responsible for a decision that may be costly if it proves in error and, on the other hand, casually suggesting courses of action that might be taken when you do not have to bear the responsibility for any of the consequences.

A good rule to follow in making your recommendations is: Avoid recommending anything you would not yourself be willing to do if you were in management's shoes. The importance of learning to develop good managerial judgment is indicated by the fact that, even though the same information and operating data may be available to every manager or executive in an organization, the quality of the judgments about what the information means and which actions need to be taken does vary from person to person.[4]

It goes without saying that your report should be well organized and well written. Great ideas amount to little unless others can be convinced of their merit—this takes tight logic, the presentation of convincing evidence, and persuasively written arguments.

Preparing an Oral Presentation

During the course of your business career it is very likely that you will be called upon to prepare and give a number of oral presentations. For this reason, it is common in courses of this nature to assign cases for oral presentation to the whole class. Such assignments give you an opportunity to hone your presentation skills.

The preparation of an oral presentation has much in common with that of a written case analysis. Both require identification of the strategic issues and problems confronting the company, analysis of industry conditions and the company's situation, and the development of a thorough, well-thought-out action plan. The substance of your analysis and quality of your recommendations in an oral presentation should be no different than in a written report. As with a written assignment, you'll need to demonstrate command of the relevant strategic concepts and tools of analysis and your recommendations should contain sufficient detail to provide clear direction for management. The main difference between an oral presentation and a written case is in the delivery format. Oral presentations rely principally on verbalizing your diagnosis, analysis, and recommendations and visually enhancing and supporting your oral discussion with colorful, snappy slides (usually created on Microsoft's PowerPoint software).

Typically, oral presentations involve group assignments. Your instructor will provide the details of the assignment—how work should be delegated among the group members and how the presentation should be conducted. Some instructors prefer that presentations begin with issue identification, followed by analysis of the industry and company situation analysis, and conclude with a recommended action plan to improve company performance. Other instructors prefer that the presenters assume that the class has a good understanding of the external industry environment and the company's competitive position and expect the presentation to be strongly focused on the group's recommended action plan and supporting analysis and arguments. The latter approach requires cutting straight to the heart of the case and supporting each recommendation with detailed analysis and persuasive reasoning. Still other instructors may give you the latitude to structure your presentation however you and your group members see fit.

Regardless of the style preferred by your instructor, you should take great care in preparing for the presentation. A good set of slides with good content and good visual appeal is essential to a first-rate presentation. Take some care to choose a nice slide design, font size and style, and color scheme. We suggest including slides covering each of the following areas:

- An opening slide covering the "title" of the presentation and names of the presenters.
- A slide showing an outline of the presentation (perhaps with presenters' names by each topic).
- One or more slides showing the key problems and strategic issues that management needs to address.
- A series of slides covering your analysis of the company's situation.
- A series of slides containing your recommendations and the supporting arguments and reasoning for each recommendation—one slide for each recommendation and the associated reasoning will give it a lot of merit.

You and your team members should carefully plan and rehearse your slide show to maximize impact and minimize distractions. The slide show should include all of the pizzazz necessary to garner the attention of the audience, but not so much that it distracts from the content of what group members are saying to the class. You should remember that the role of slides is to help you communicate your points to the audience. Too many graphics, images, colors, and transitions may divert the audience's attention from what is being said or disrupt the flow of the presentation. Keep in mind that visually dazzling slides rarely hide a shallow or superficial or otherwise flawed case analysis from a perceptive audience. Most instructors will tell you that first-rate slides will definitely enhance a well-delivered presentation, but that impressive visual aids, if accompanied by weak analysis and poor oral delivery, still add up to a substandard presentation.

Researching Companies and Industries via the Internet and Online Data Services

Very likely, there will be occasions when you need to get additional information about some of the assignee cases, perhaps because your instructor has asked you to do further research on the industry or company or because you are simply curious about what has happened to the company since the case was written. These days, it is relatively easy to run down recent industry developments and to find out whether a company's strategic and financial situation has improved, deteriorated, or changed little since the conclusion of the case. The amount of information about companies and industries available on the Internet and through online data services is formidable and expanding rapidly.

It is a fairly simple matter to go to company websites, click on the investor information offerings and press release files, and get quickly to useful information. Most company websites allow you to view or print the company's quarterly and annual reports, its 10-K and 10-Q filings with the Securities and Exchange Commission, and various company press releases of interest. Frequently, a company's website will also provide information about its mission and vision statements, values statements, codes of ethics, and strategy information, as well as charts of the company's stock price. The company's recent press releases typically contain reliable information about what of interest has been going on—new product introductions, recent alliances and partnership agreements, recent acquisitions, summaries of the latest financial results, tidbits about the company's strategy, guidance about future revenues and earnings, and other late-breaking company developments. Some company web pages also include links to the home pages of industry trade associations where you can find information about industry size, growth, recent industry news, statistical trends, and future outlook. Thus, an early step in researching a company on the Internet is always to go to its website and see what's available.

Online Data Services LexisNexis, Bloomberg Financial News Services, and other online subscription services available in many university libraries provide access to a wide array of business reference material. For example, the web-based LexisNexis Academic Universe contains business news articles from general news sources, business publications, and industry trade publications. Broadcast transcripts from financial news programs are also available through LexisNexis, as are full-text 10-Ks, 10-Qs, annual reports, and company profiles for more than 11,000 U.S. and international companies. Your business librarian should be able to direct you to the resources available through your library that will aid you in your research.

Public and Subscription Websites with Good Information Plainly, you can use a search engine such as Google or Yahoo! or MSN to find the latest news on a company or articles written by reporters that have appeared in the business media. These can be very valuable in running down information about recent company developments. However, keep in mind that the information retrieved by a search engine is "unfiltered" and may include sources that are not reliable or that contain inaccurate or misleading information. Be wary of information provided by authors who are unaffiliated with reputable organizations or publications and articles that were published in off-beat sources or on websites with an agenda. Be especially careful in relying on the accuracy of information you find posted on various bulletin boards. Articles covering a company or issue should be copyrighted or published by a reputable source. If you are turning in a paper containing information gathered from the Internet, you should cite your sources (providing the Internet address and date visited); it is also wise to print web pages for your research file (some web pages are updated frequently).

The Wall Street Journal, *Bloomberg Businessweek, Forbes, Barron's*, and *Fortune* are all good sources of articles on companies. The online edition of *The Wall Street Journal* contains the same information that is available daily in its print version of the paper, but the *WSJ* website also maintains a searchable database of all *The Wall Street Journal* articles published during the past few years. *Fortune* and *Bloomberg Businessweek* also make the content of the most current issue available online to subscribers as well as provide archives sections that allow you to search for articles published during the past few years that may be related to a particular keyword.

The following publications and websites are particularly good sources of company and industry information:

Securities and Exchange Commission EDGAR database (contains company 10-Ks, 10-Qs, etc.)
http://www.sec.gov/edgar/searchedgar/companysearch
Google Finance
http://finance.google.com
CNN Money
http://money.cnn.com
Hoover's Online
http://hoovers.com
The Wall Street Journal Interactive Edition
www.wsj.com
Bloomberg Businessweek
www.businessweek.com and www.bloomberg.com
Fortune
www.fortune.com
MSN Money Central
http://moneycentral.msn.com
Yahoo! Finance

Some of these Internet sources require subscriptions in order to access their entire databases.

You should always explore the investor relations section of every public company's website. In today's world, these websites typically have a wealth of information concerning a company's mission, core values, performance targets, strategy, recent financial performance, and latest developments (as described in company press releases).

Learning Comes Quickly With a modest investment of time, you will learn how to use Internet sources and search engines to run down information on companies and industries quickly and efficiently. And it is a skill that will serve you well into the future. Once you become familiar with the data available at the different websites mentioned above and learn how to use a search engine, you will know where to go to look for the particular information that you want. Search engines nearly always turn up too many information sources that match your request rather than too few. The trick is to learn to zero in on those most relevant to what you are looking for. Like most things, once you get a little experience under your belt on how to do company and industry research on the Internet, you will be able to readily find the information you need.

The Ten Commandments of Case Analysis

As a way of summarizing our suggestions about how to approach the task of case analysis, we have put together what we like to call "The Ten Commandments of Case Analysis." They are shown in Table 2. If you observe all or even most of these commandments faithfully as you prepare a case either for class discussion or for a written report, your chances of doing a good job on the assigned cases will be much improved. Hang in there, give it your best shot, and have some fun exploring what the real world of strategic management is all about.

TABLE 2 The Ten Commandments of Case Analysis

To be observed in written reports and oral presentations, and while participating in class discussions:

1. Go through the case twice, once for a quick overview and once to gain full command of the facts. Then take care to explore the information in every one of the case exhibits.
2. Make a complete list of the problems and issues that the company's management needs to address.
3. Be thorough in your analysis of the company's situation (make a minimum of one to two pages of notes detailing your diagnosis).

(*Continued*)

TABLE 2 *(Continued)*

4. Look for opportunities to apply the concepts and analytical tools in the text chapters—all of the cases in the book have very definite ties to the material in one or more of the text chapters!!!!
5. Do enough number crunching to discover the story told by the data presented in the case. (To help you comply with this commandment, consult Table 1 in this section to guide your probing of a company's financial condition and financial performance.)
6. Support any and all off-the-cuff opinions with well-reasoned arguments and numerical evidence. Don't stop until you can purge "I think" and "I feel" from your assessment and, instead, are able to rely completely on "My analysis shows."
7. Prioritize your recommendations and make sure they can be carried out in an acceptable time frame with the available resources.
8. Support each recommendation with persuasive argument and reasons as to why it makes sense and should result in improved company performance.
9. Review your recommended action plan to see if it addresses all of the problems and issues you identified. Any set of recommendations that does not address all of the issues and problems you identified is incomplete and insufficient.
10. Avoid recommending any course of action that could have disastrous consequences if it doesn't work out as planned. Therefore, be as alert to the downside risks of your recommendations as you are to their upside potential and appeal.

ENDNOTES

[1] Charles I. Gragg, "Because Wisdom Can't Be Told," in *The Case Method at the Harvard Business School,* ed. M. P. McNair (New York: McGraw-Hill, 1954), p. 11.

[2] Ibid., pp. 12–14; and D. R. Schoen and Philip A. Sprague, "What Is the Case Method?" in *The Case Method at the Harvard Business School,* ed. M. P. McNair, pp. 78–79.

[3] For some additional ideas and viewpoints, you may wish to consult Thomas J. Raymond, "Written Analysis of Cases," in *The Case Method at the Harvard Business School,* ed. M. P. McNair, pp. 139–63. Raymond's article includes an actual case, a sample analysis of the case, and a sample of a student's written report on the case.

[4] Gragg, "Because Wisdom Can't Be Told,"p. 10.

COMPANY INDEX

B

C

D

E

F

G

H

I

J

K

L

M

N

O

P

Q

R

S

T

U

V

W

Y

Z

NAME INDEX

A

B

C

D

E

F

G

H

I

J

N

O

P

T

U

V

W

Y

Z

SUBJECT INDEX

A

B

C

D

Chadron State College

1. 4 Mindset by Dweck
2. 2 Self-Awareness:
3. 3 Know yourself, replace
4. 2 failure with learning
5. 4
6. 5
7. 5

Growth Midset

You need to work for things (opportunities)

"What can you learn" "Not yet"

3 Way to Change Brain

1. Physically grow your brain
2. Speed up your brain
   focus intesly on 1 thing
3. Re-wire your brain
   practice

"Failure is an opportunity to grow"

Resilient leader are able to cope/adapt and bounce back from setbacks.

Failure of ~~at~~ getting a C in Math.
6th grade
First every bad grade I ever got.

Failure was missing an exam in Geology class in college which broke the goal I had to get all As.

It prepared me to be kinder on myself. It's more important to learn than to measure myself to a letter grade.

E

F

G

H

I

J

K

L

M

P

Q

R

S

T

W

Z